THE MODERN CROSSWORD DICTIONARY

Compilers of crosswords are a law unto themselves. When filling in designs, preparatory to clueing, they are unrestricted in their choice of words, phrases, etc. A number of 15-letter examples, chosen at random, follow to illustrate the vast fields open to the compilers – fields that have never before been covered by a single reference book –

AIR MINISTRY ROOF, BULLDOG DRUMMOND, DANCE OF THE HOURS, ERNEST HEMINGWAY, FISH AND CHIP SHOP, GET ON WITH THE JOB, HANSEL AND GRETEL, ITALIAN VERMOUTH, KITTEN ON THE KEYS, LOOK BACK IN ANGER, MOLOTOV COCKTAIL, NUREMBERG TRIALS, ON THE BRADEN BEAT, PRESIDENT NASSER, QUICK OFF THE MARK, ROOM TO SWING A CAT, SUNDAY NEWSPAPER, TWO AND FOURPENCE, UNDER LOCK AND KEY, VENGEANCE IS MINE, WISDOM OF SOLOMON, YOURS FAITHFULLY

The Modern Crossword Dictionary covers all these 'phrases' and nearly 50,000 others. Together with the word section at the end of the book, it will prove to be of inestimable value to solvers and compilers alike.

D1268893

THE MODERN CROSSWORD DICTIONARY

Compiled by

NORMAN G. PULSFORD

A PAN ORIGINAL

PAN BOOKS LTD : LONDON

First published 1967 by

PAN BOOKS LTD.,

33 Tothill Street, London, S.W.1

ISBN 0 330 63128 4

2nd Printing 1968
3rd Printing 1972
4th Printing 1973

PRINTED AND BOUND IN ENGLAND BY
HAZELL WATSON AND VINEY LTD
AYLESBURY, BUCKS

FOREWORD

The 'Phrase' section of this book is unique in its method of presentation. Within its pages you will find: Films, Novels, Plays, Fictional and Historical Characters, Musical Works, Song Titles, Pop Groups, Animals, Birds, Insects, Fish, Television and Radio Programmes, Buildings, Streets, Locations, Geographical Names, Celebrities, Games, Hobbies, Foreign Terms, Things to Eat, Drink and Wear, and tens of thousands of everyday terms, phrases and expressions.

All the items are tabulated according to the number of letters which they contain, and are set out in strictly alphabetical order for quick and easy reference.

The section has been especially compiled as an aid to solvers of the more difficult 'Cryptic' Crosswords published in *The Times*, *The Daily Telegraph*, the *Daily Express*, the *Evening News*, the *Evening Standard*, the *Sunday Times*, the *Sunday Telegraph*, the *Sunday Express*, and so on.

It frequently happens that a solver is held up by one particular clue, the answer to which is a phrase with one or two interlocking letters already inserted. Let us assume that the clue is: 'He might play one a single piece (8, 2, 5)', and that you have 'B' as the first letter. The second phrase under the heading 'B-15' at once gives you your answer: 'Bachelor of Music'. Naturally, when the first letter has not already been inserted, further research will be necessary.

In order to save space, most plurals and past participles have been omitted. Thus, when the 15-letter answer to a clue is obviously in the plural, it must, in most cases, be looked for under the '14' heading. A similar adjustment must be made when the answer is obviously a past participle. 'Backing down' and 'Holding over', for example, must be looked for under 'Back down' and 'Hold over'.

The 'Word' section will be extremely useful to solvers of the easier 'straightforward' crosswords as published in the *Evening News*, the *Evening Standard* and the *Daily Mirror*.

The compilation of this book has taken a little under five years. Here are some of the sources from which we culled our information: three standard dictionaries; one American dictionary; one 20-volume encyclopaedia; *Roget's Thesaurus*; *Brewer's Dictionary of Phrase and Fable*; *Who's Who In The Theatre*; *Pears Cyclopaedia*; *Whitaker's Almanack*; *Philip's Gazetteer*, and more than 20,000 published crosswords.

NORMAN G. PULSFORD

CONTENTS

PHRASES

A—8

A BAD TIME	ALL ALIKE	ARMY CAMP
A BIT MUCH	ALL ALONE	ARMY LIFE
ABOVE ALL	ALL ALONG	ARMY LIST
ABOVE PAR	ALL ASKEW	ARMY RANK
ACCEPT IT	ALL AT SEA	ARMY TYPE
ACES HIGH	ALL BLACK	ART CLASS
ACES WILD	ALL CLEAR	ART PAPER
ACID BATH	ALLEY CAT	ARTS CLUB
ACID DROP	ALL FARES	ARTY TYPE
ACID TEST	ALL FOUND	ARUM LILY
ACT A PART	ALL FOURS	AS A WHOLE
ACT BADLY	ALL HANDS	ASCOT HAT
ACT OF GOD	ALL HOURS	AS GOOD AS
ACT OF WAR	ALL IN ALL	ASH GROVE
ACT THREE	ALL IN ONE	ASH TREES
ACUTE EAR	ALL KINDS	AS IT WERE
ADAM BEDE	ALL MY EYE	ASK FOR IT
ADAM'S ALE	ALL NIGHT	ASK LEAVE
ADAM'S RIB	ALL QUIET	ASK MERCY
ADDING UP	ALL READY	AS STATED
ADD WATER	ALL RIGHT	ASWAN DAM
ADMIT ONE	ALL ROADS	AS WELL AS
ADMIT TWO	ALL ROUND	AT A GUESS
A FAIR COP	ALL'S FAIR	AT ANCHOR
A FAST ONE	ALL SIDES	AT A PARTY
AFTER ALL	ALL SORTS	AT A PINCH
AFTER TEA	ALL SOULS	AT A PRICE
AFTER YOU	ALL'S WELL	AT BOTTOM
AGE GROUP	ALL THE GO	AT DINNER
A GOOD BUY	ALL THERE	AT HARROW
A GOOD FEW	ALL WRONG	AT LENGTH
A GOOD RUN	ALPHA RAY	AT LOW EBB
AIM A BLOW	ALTER EGO	AT NO TIME
AIR COVER	ANDY CAPP	ATOM BOMB
AIR FORCE	A NEW LEAF	AT OXFORD
AIR LINER	ANTS' NEST	AT RANDOM
AIR POWER	ANZAC DAY	AT SCHOOL
AIR RAIDS	APPLE PIE	AT SUNSET
AIR ROUTE	APPLE PIP	AT THE BAR
AIR SENSE	APTLY PUT	AT THE END
AIR SPACE	ARC LAMPS	AT THE OFF
A LA CARTE	ARC LIGHT	AT THE TOP
ALAN LADD	ARK ROYAL	AT THE ZOO
AL CAPONE	ARMED MAN	ATTIC WIT
AL FRESCO	ARM IN ARM	AUDIT ALE
AL JOLSON	ARMS BEND	AU GRATIN
	ARMS RACE	AU REVOIR

AUTO DA FE
AVE MARIA
AWAY GAME
AWAY TEAM
AWAY WINS

B—8
BABE RUTH
BABY CARE
BABY CARS
BABY DOLL
BABY FACE
BABY FOOD
BABY GIRL
BABY LOVE
BABY MINE
BABY SHOW
BABY TALK
BABY WOOL
BACK AWAY
BACK AXLE
BACK DOOR
BACK DOWN
BACKED UP
BACK HAIR
BACK KICK
BACK PAGE
BACK RENT
BACK ROOM
BACK SEAT
BACKS OUT
BACK SPIN
BACK STUD
BACK VIEW
BACK YARD
BACON FAT
BAD ACTOR
BAD BLOOD
BAD BOOKS
BAD CAUSE
BAD COUGH
BAD DEBTS
BAD DREAM
BAD FAIRY
BAD FAITH
BAD GRACE
BAD HABIT
BAD HEART
BAD IMAGE
BAD LANDS
BAD LAYER

BAD LIGHT
BAD LIVER
BAD LOGIC
BAD LOSER
BADLY OFF
BAD MARKS
BAD MIXER
BAD MONEY
BAD NIGHT
BAD ODOUR
BAD PATCH
BAD PENNY
BAD POINT
BAD PRESS
BAD SCORE
BAD SHAPE
BAD SHOTS
BAD SIGHT
BAD SMELL
BAD SPORT
BAD START
BAD STATE
BAD STORY
BAD TASTE
BAD TERMS
BAD THING
BAD TIMES
BAD TOOTH
BAD TRADE
BALD HEAD
BALD PATE
BALES OUT
BALL BOYS
BALL GAME
BALL GOWN
BANK DOWN
BANK LOAN
BANK NOTE
BANK ON IT
BANK RATE
BARE FEET
BARE HEAD
BARE IDEA
BARE LEGS
BARE NECK
BARE WORD
BASE COIN
BASS CLEF
BASS DRUM
BASS HORN
BASS NOTE

BATH BUNS
BATH CHAP
BATH CUBE
BATH ROBE
BATH SOAP
BATTLE ON
BAY HORSE
BAY TREES
BEACH HUT
BEADY EYE
BEAR ARMS
BEAR DOWN
BEAR LEFT
BEAR PAIN
BEARS OUT
BEAR WITH
BE A SPORT
BEAT BACK
BEAT DOWN
BEATEN UP
BEAT IT UP
BEATS OFF
BEAT TIME
BEAU NASH
BED LINEN
BEEF STEW
BEER HALL
BEE STING
BEG LEAVE
BE IN DEBT
BE IN LOVE
BELL TENT
BELOW PAR
BE MY LOVE
BEND DOWN
BEND OVER
BEN NEVIS
BENNY LEE
BE NO MORE
BENT BACK
BE ON CALL
BE ON EDGE
BE POLITE
BE SEATED
BE SILENT
BEST CUTS
BEST DAYS
BEST EVER
BEST FORM
BEST GIRL
BEST LOVE

BEST PART	BLACK BOX	BODY BLOW
BEST SUIT	BLACK CAP	BODY HEAT
BEST TEAM	BLACK CAT	BOIL AWAY
BEST TIME	BLACK DOG	BOIL DOWN
BEST TOGS	BLACK EYE	BOIL OVER
BEST WINE	BLACK INK	BOLD DEED
BETEL NUT	BLACK KEY	BOLD FACE
BE UNKIND	BLACK MAN	BOLD MOVE
BEVIN BOY	BLACK OUT	BOLD TYPE
BIG APPLE	BLACK RAT	BOMB SITE
BIG BREAK	BLACK ROD	BONA FIDE
BIG BUILD	BLACK SEA	BONAR LAW
BIG BULLY	BLACK TEA	BONE IDLE
BIG CHIEF	BLACK TIE	BOOK CLUB
BIG CROWD	BLESS YOU	BOOKED UP
BIG DEALS	BLIND EYE	BOOK ENDS
BIG DRINK	BLIND MAN	BOOK SHOP
BIG FIGHT	BLOCK OUT	BOOM TOWN
BIG FILMS	BLOOD RED	BORN DEAD
BIG GIRLS	BLOOD TIE	BORN FOOL
BIG HOUSE	BLOTS OUT	BORN RICH
BIG IDEAS	BLOW AWAY	BOTH ENDS
BIG MATCH	BLOW COLD	BOTH WAYS
BIG MONEY	BLOW DOWN	BOTTLE UP
BIG MOUTH	BLOW HARD	BOTTOM UP
BIG NOISE	BLOWN OUT	BOUGHT IN
BIG PIECE	BLOW OVER	BOUGHT UP
BIG RACES	BLUE BABY	BOUNCE IN
BIG SCORE	BLUE BIRD	BOUNCE UP
BIG SHOTS	BLUE BOOK	BOW BELLS
BIG STAND	BLUE EYES	BOWL OVER
BIG STICK	BLUE FUNK	BOXER DOG
BIG STIFF	BLUE LAMP	BOYS' CLUB
BIG STORM	BLUE MOON	BOY SCOUT
BIG STUFF	BLUE NILE	BRAIN BOX
BIG WHEEL	BLUE ROOM	BRAIN FAG
BILLY BOY	BLUE RUIN	BRAND NEW
BILLY CAN	BLUE STAR	BRASS HAT
BIND OVER	BLUE SUIT	BRAVE MAN
BIRD CALL	BLUNT END	BREAD BIN
BIRD LIFE	BLURT OUT	BREAK OFF
BIRD LORE	BOARD OUT	BREAK OUT
BIRD SEED	BOAT CLUB	BREAKS IN
BIRD SONG	BOAT RACE	BREAKS UP
BIT BY BIT	BOBBY PIN	BREN GUNS
BITE INTO	BOBBY VEE	BRET HART
BITER BIT	BOB DYLAN	BRIAN RIX
BIT OF FUN	BOB MAJOR	BRICK RED
BLACK ART	BOB MINOR	BRIM OVER
BLACK BAG	BOB ROYAL	BRING OFF
BLACK BAT	BODE EVIL	BRING OUT

BRINGS IN	BY INCHES	CART AWAY
BRINGS ON	BY ITSELF	CARVE OUT
BRINGS TO	BY LETTER	CASE BOOK
BRINGS UP	BY MYSELF	CASH BOOK
BROKEN IN	BY MY WILL	CASH DESK
BROKEN UP	BY NATURE	CASH DOWN
BROWN ALE	BY RETURN	CASHED IN
BROWN COW	BY RIGHTS	CASH SALE
BROWN EGG	BY STAGES	CAST A FLY
BROWN OWL	BY THE ARM	CAST A NET
BROWN RAT	BY THE SEA	CAST AWAY
BRUSH OFF	BY THE WAY	CAST DICE
BUBBLE UP		CAST DOWN
BUCKLE ON	**C—8**	CAST IRON
BUCKLE TO	CABIN BOY	CAST LOTS
BUCKLE UP	CAB RANKS	CASTS OFF
BULL NECK	CAFE NOIR	CASTS OUT
BULL'S EYE	CALF LOVE	CATCH OUT
BULLY OFF	CALL A CAB	CAT LOVER
BUMP INTO	CALL AWAY	CATS' EYES
BUMPS OFF	CALL BACK	CATS' HOME
BUN FIGHT	CALL DOWN	CAT SHOWS
BUNGED UP	CALLED IN	CAT'S MEAT
BUNNY HUG	CALLED UP	CAUGHT ON
BUN PENNY	CALL GIRL	CAUGHT UP
BUOYED UP	CALL OVER	CELL MATE
BURN AWAY	CALLS FOR	CHALK OUT
BURN DOWN	CALLS OFF	CHANCE IT
BURNT OAK	CALLS OUT	CHECK OFF
BURNT OUT	CALL TIME	CHECK OUT
BURST OUT	CALL UPON	CHECKS IN
BUS DEPOT	CALM DOWN	CHECKS UP
BUS FARES	CAME BACK	CHEERS UP
BUSH FIRE	CAME DOWN	CHEESE IT
BUS QUEUE	CAMP FIRE	CHESS SET
BUS STOPS	CAMP SITE	CHEW OVER
BUSY BEES	CANON LAW	CHEZ NOUS
BUSY LIFE	CAPE HORN	CHINA CUP
BUSY TIME	CAPE TOWN	CHINA EGG
BUSY TOWN	CAP IT ALL	CHINA SEA
BUTTED IN	CAR CRASH	CHINA TEA
BUTTER UP	CARD GAME	CHIN CHIN
BUTTON UP	CARD VOTE	CHIP SHOT
BUY BLIND	CARE A LOT	CHOIR BOY
BUY CHEAP	CAR FERRY	CHOKE OFF
BUZZ BOMB	CAR PARKS	CHOP DOWN
BY A FLUKE	CAR RALLY	CHOP SUEY
BY CHANCE	CARRY OFF	CHUCK OUT
BY CHEQUE	CARRY OUT	CHURN OUT
BY GEORGE	CAR SMASH	CIDER CUP
BY HALVES		CIGAR ASH

CIGAR BOX	COLD MEAL	CREAM TEA
CISCO KID	COLD MEAT	CREEP OFF
CITY DESK	COLD MILK	CREEP OUT
CITY GENT	COLD PACK	CREW CUTS
CITY HALL	COLD PORK	CRIED OUT
CITY LIFE	COLD ROOM	CRIES OFF
CITY WALL	COLD SNAP	CROCKS UP
CIVIL LAW	COLD WAVE	CROSS NOW
CIVIL WAR	COLD WIND	CROSS OFF
CLASS WAR	COLOUR UP	CROSS OUT
CLAY PIPE	COME AWAY	CROWN HIM
CLEAN CUT	COME BACK	CROW OVER
CLEAN OUT	COME DOWN	CRUDE OIL
CLEANS UP	COME HERE	CRUEL ACT
CLEAR DAY	COME HOME	CRUEL SEA
CLEAR OFF	COME INTO	CRY ALOUD
CLEAR OUT	COME LAST	CRY "HAVOC"
CLEAR SKY	COME NEAR	CRY OF JOY
CLEARS UP	COME NEXT	CRY QUITS
CLEAR WIN	COME OVER	CRY "SHAME"
CLOCK OUT	COMES OFF	CUBE ROOT
CLOCKS IN	COMES OUT	CUP FINAL
CLOSED IN	COME TRUE	CUP OF TEA
CLOSE FIT	COME UPON	CURLED UP
CLOSE RUN	COME UP TO	CUSHY JOB
CLOSE SET	COMING IN	CUT A DASH
CLOSES UP	COMING ON	CUT GLASS
CLOSE TIE	COMING TO	CUT GRASS
CLOTH CAP	CON AMORE	CUT IN TWO
CLUB BORE	COOL CARD	CUT IT OFF
CLUB FEES	COOL DOWN	CUT IT OUT
CLUB LIFE	COOL FISH	CUT LOOSE
COAL CART	COOL HAND	CUT NO ICE
COAL DUST	COOL HEAD	CUT PRICE
COAL FIRE	COOPED UP	CUT RATES
COAL MINE	COPE WITH	CUT ROUND
COAL SEAM	COPY DOWN	CUTS BACK
COCA COLA	CORK TIPS	CUTS DEAD
CODE NAME	CORN CURE	CUTS DOWN
CODE WORD	CORN LAWS	CUTS FINE
CODS' ROES	COSY CAFE	CUT SHORT
COKE FIRE	COSY CHAT	
COLD BATH	COTTON ON	**D—8**
COLD BEEF	COUGHS UP	DAILY USE
COLD CURE	COUNT OUT	DAIRY COW
COLD DISH	COUNT TEN	DAME TROT
COLD DUCK	COUPLE UP	DAMP DOWN
COLD FEET	COVERS UP	DANNY BOY
COLD FISH	COW'S MILK	DARK AGES
COLD FOOD	CRACKS UP	DARK BLUE
COLD LAMB	CREAM BUN	DARK DAYS

DARK DEED	DEATH RAY	DO HOMAGE
DARK GREY	DEED POLL	DOLLED UP
DARK HAIR	DEEP BLUE	DONE DOWN
DARK LADY	DEEP COMA	DO NO GOOD
DARK ROOM	DEEP DOWN	DO NO HARM
DARK SIDE	DEEP NOTE	DORIS DAY
DARK SKIN	DEEP SIGH	DO SCALES
DARK SUIT	DEEP SNOW	DO THE LOT
DART PAST	DEEP TONE	DOUBLE UP
DASH AWAY	DEER PARK	DOVE GREY
DASH DOWN	DEFY TIME	DO WISELY
DASH INTO	DE GAULLE	DOWN BEAT
DATE PALM	DE LA MARE	DOWN LINE
DAVE KING	DENSE FOG	DOWN TOWN
DAVID LOW	DERBY DAY	DOWN WIND
DAVIS CUP	DEREK ROY	DRAG DOWN
DAVY LAMP	DESK WORK	DRAG HUNT
DAY BOOKS	DE VALERA	DRAGS OUT
DAY BY DAY	DEVON MAN	DRAIN DRY
DAY DREAM	DICE GAME	DRAW AWAY
DAY NURSE	DID RIGHT	DRAW BACK
DAY OR TWO	DID WRONG	DRAW LOTS
DAY SHIFT	DIED AWAY	DRAW NEAR
DAY'S WORK	DIED DOWN	DRAW NIGH
DEAD BALL	DIED HARD	DRAW NIGH
DEAD BEAT	DIE HAPPY	DRAWN OFF
DEAD BODY	DIG A HOLE	DRAWN OUT
DEAD CALM	DIG A MINE	DRAW REIN
DEAD CERT	DIGS DEEP	DRAW WELL
DEAD DUCK	DIM LIGHT	DREAM MAN
DEAD EASY	DINED OUT	DRIED EGG
DEAD FLAT	DINE LATE	DRIED OUT
DEAD HAND	DIRTY DOG	DRINKS UP
DEAD HEAT	DIRTY SKY	DRIVE MAD
DEAD KEEN	DISHED UP	DRIVE OFF
DEAD LEAF	DIVAN BED	DRIVE OUT
DEAD LOSS	DO A TRICK	DROP AWAY
DEAD NUTS	DO BATTLE	DROP DEAD
DEAD SHOT	DO BETTER	DROP DOWN
DEAD SLOW	DOCTOR NO	DROPS OFF
DEAD SPIT	DOG FIGHT	DROPS OUT
DEAD SURE	DOG LATIN	DRY BONES
DEAD WOOD	DOG LOVER	DRY BREAD
DEAF EARS	DOGS' HOME	DRY CELLS
DEAF MUTE	DOG SHOWS	DRY COUGH
DEAL WITH	DOG'S LIFE	DRY FACTS
DEAN INGE	DOG'S NOSE	DRY FRUIT
DEAR DEAR!	DOG'S TAIL	DRY GOODS
DEAR LIFE	DOG TEAMS	DRYING UP
DEAR SIRS	DOG TRACK	DRY PLATE
DEATH BED	DOG WATCH	DRY TOAST
		DR. WATSON

DUCK DOWN	EASY TIME	EXCUSE ME
DUCK POND	EASY WORD	EXTRA MAN
DUCK'S EGG	EAT A MEAL	EXTRA PAY
DUCK SOUP	EATS AWAY	EXTRA RUN
DUE NORTH	EATS DIRT	EYES LEFT
DUE SOUTH	EAU DE VIE	EYE TO EYE
DULL ACHE	ECCE HOMO	
DULL PAIN	EDEN KANE	
DULL THUD	EDGE AWAY	F—8
DULL WORK	EGG FLIPS	FACE CARD
DUMB SHOW	EGG PLANT	FACE DOWN
DUMMY RUN	EGG SALAD	FACE LIFT
DUST BOWL	EGG SAUCE	FACE ODDS
DUST TRAP	EGG SPOON	FACE PACK
DUTCH GIN	EGG TIMER	FACE RUIN
DUTCH HOE	EIGHT MEN	FACE UP TO
DUTY CALL	ELDER SON	FADE AWAY
DUTY FREE	EL DORADO	FADED OUT
DUTY LIST	ELM TREES	FAIR COPY
DUTY PAID	EMIT RAYS	FAIR DEAL
DYED HAIR	EMPTY BOX	FAIR GAME
DYING BED	EMPTY CAN	FAIR HAIR
DYING DAY	EMPTY TIN	FAIR HAND
DYING MAN	END HOUSE	FAIR ISLE
DYING OUT	END IT ALL	FAIR LADY
	END SEATS	FAIR MAID
	END TO END	FAIR NAME
E—8	ENEMY SPY	FAIR PLAY
EAGLE EYE	ENTRY FEE	FAIR SKIN
EARL HAIG	EPIC FILM	FAIR SWOP
EARLY AGE	EPIC POEM	FAIR WAGE
EARLY MAN	EPIC POET	FAIR WIND
EARN FAME	EQUAL PAY	FALL AWAY
EARN LESS	ET CETERA	FALL BACK
EARN MORE	ETON CROP	FALL DOWN
EAR PLUGS	ETON SUIT	FALL FLAT
EASED OFF	EVEN BEAT	FALL FOUL
EASED OUT	EVEN DATE	FALL OPEN
EASE OVER	EVEN KEEL	FALL OVER
EAST SIDE	EVEN PACE	FALL SICK
EAST WIND	EVEN TIME	FALLS ILL
EAST WING	EVERY BIT	FALLS OFF
EASY BEAT	EVERY DAY	FALLS OUT
EASY COME	EVERY ONE	FALL UPON
EASY DROP	EVERY WAY	FALSE GOD
EASY GAME	EVIL DAYS	FALSE RIB
EASY LIFE	EVIL DEED	FAN CLUBS
EASY MIND	EVIL HOUR	FANCY BOX
EASY PACE	EVIL LIFE	FAN DANCE
EASY PREY	EVIL OMEN	FAR ABOVE
EASY ROAD	EVIL STAR	FAR AHEAD
EASY TASK		FAR APART

FAR BELOW	FIFTH SET	FIRST LAP
FARM EGGS	FIFTH TEE	FIRST MAN
FARM HAND	FIGHT FOR	FIRST OUT
FARM LAND	FIGHT OFF	FIRST ROW
FAR NORTH	FIGHT SHY	FIRST SET
FAR SIGHT	FILE AWAY	FIRST TEE
FAR SOUTH	FILE DOWN	FIR TREES
FAST AWAY	FILE PAST	FISH CAKE
FAST CARS	FILL A GAP	FISH DISH
FAST DAYS	FILLED IN	FISH FORK
FAST LIFE	FILM FANS	FISH POND
FAST RACE	FILM PLAY	FISH SHOP
FAST TIME	FILM SHOW	FISH TANK
FAST WORK	FILM STAR	FISH TEAS
FATAL DAY	FINAL BID	FIT STATE
FAT STOCK	FINAL DAY	FITS WELL
FATTEN UP	FIND A JOB	FITTED IN
FAT WOMAN	FIND A WAY	FITTED UP
FAWN UPON	FIND BAIL	FIVE DAYS
FEAST DAY	FIND ROOM	FIVE DEEP
FEED WELL	FINDS OUT	FIVE FEET
FEEL BLUE	FIND TIME	FIVE QUID
FEEL COLD	FINE AIRS	FIVE SETS
FEEL EASY	FINE ARTS	FIX A DATE
FEEL FINE	FINE BIRD	FIX A TIME
FEEL GOOD	FINE CHAP	FLAG DAYS
FEEL HURT	FINE DAYS	FLAG DOWN
FEEL LAZY	FINE DOWN	FLARED UP
FEEL LIKE	FINE EDGE	FLAT BEER
FEEL PAIN	FINE FARE	FLAT FACE
FEEL SAFE	FINE GOLD	FLAT FEET
FEEL SICK	FINE LADY	FLAT FISH
FEELS ILL	FINE RAIN	FLAT NOSE
FEEL SORE	FINE SHOW	FLAT RACE
FEEL SURE	FINE VIEW	FLAT RATE
FEEL WARM	FINISH UP	FLAT ROOF
FEEL WELL	FIR CONES	FLAT SPIN
FELL AN OX	FIRE AWAY	FLAT TYRE
FELL BACK	FIRE DAMP	FLAT WASH
FELL DOWN	FIRE RISK	FLEA PITS
FELL FLAT	FIRE UPON	FLEE FROM
FELO DE SE	FIRM DATE	FLEET ARM
FELT HATS	FIRM GRIP	FLEW AWAY
FEME SOLE	FIRM HAND	FLEW HIGH
FENCED IN	FIRM HOLD	FLEW HOME
FETCH OUT	FIRM HOPE	FLEW SOLO
FEW WORDS	FIRST ACT	FLICK OFF
FIELD DAY	FIRST AID	FLIES OFF
FIERY RED	FIRST BID	FLING OFF
FIFTH DAY	FIRST BUS	FLING OUT
FIFTH ROW	FIRST DAY	FLIP SIDE

FLIT PAST
FLOP DOWN
FLOUR BIN
FLOW BACK
FLOW OVER
FLUFF OUT
FLUSH OUT
FLY ABOUT
FLY A KITE
FLY APART
FOAM BATH
FOG BOUND
FOGGY DAY
FOIST OFF
FOLD ARMS
FOLD BACK
FOLD DOWN
FOLDED UP
FOLD OVER
FOLK LORE
FOLK SONG
FOLK TALE
FOLLOW ON
FOLLOW UP
FOND HOPE
FOOD FISH
FOOL AWAY
FOR A JOKE
FOR A LARK
FOR A SONG
FOR A TERM
FOR A TIME
FORCE OUT
FORGET IT
FOR KEEPS
FOR KICKS
FORKS OUT
FOR SHAME
FORT KNOX
FORTY ALL
FOUL BLOW
FOUL DEED
FOUL PLAY
FOUND OUT
FOUR ACES
FOUR DAYS
FOUR DEEP
FOUR FEET
FOUR LAPS
FOUR ONES
FOUR QUID

FOUR TENS
FOUR TWOS
FOWL PEST
FREE BEER
FREE CITY
FREE COPY
FREE FLOW
FREE GIFT
FREE HAND
FREE KICK
FREE LIFT
FREE LIST
FREE LOVE
FREE MEAL
FREE MILK
FREE PASS
FREE PLAY
FREE PORT
FREE RIDE
FREE SEAT
FREE TIME
FREE TO GO
FREE VOTE
FREE WILL
FRESH AIR
FRESH EGG
FRESH TEA
FRET AWAY
FRIED EGG
FROM AFAR
FRONT MAN
FRONT ROW
FROZEN UP
FRUIT PIE
FUEL BILL
FUEL TANK
FULL BLUE
FULL CREW
FULL FACE
FULL LIFE
FULL LOAD
FULL MEAL
FULL MOON
FULL OF GO
FULL PLAY
FULL SAIL
FULL SIZE
FULL STOP
FULL TIDE
FULL TILT
FULL TIME

FULL TOSS
FULL WELL
FUMED OAK
FUN FAIRS
FUNNY HAT
FUNNY MAN
FUR COATS
FUR STOLE
FUR TRADE
FUR WRAPS
FUSE WIRE
FUSS OVER

G—8
GAD ABOUT
GAG BOOKS
GAIN TIME
GAIN UPON
GAME BIRD
GAME LAWS
GAME PIES
GAMMA RAY
GAMMY LEG
GANG SHOW
GAOL BIRD
GAS BOARD
GAS FIRES
GAS METER
GAS PLANT
GAS STOVE
GATHER IN
GATHER UP
GAVE A TUG
GAVE AWAY
GAVE BACK
GAY PARTY
GAY SMILE
GAY SPARK
GET ABOUT
GET A GOAL
GET AHEAD
GET A LIFT
GET ALONG
GET ANGRY
GET A RISE
GET BELOW
GET CLEAR
GET CROSS
GET DRUNK
GET FRESH
GET GOING

GET IDEAS	GO ABOARD	GOLD RING
GET LEAVE	GO ABROAD	GOLD RUSH
GET LOOSE	GO ABSENT	GOLD VASE
GET OLDER	GO ACROSS	GOLD VEIN
GET RATTY	GO ADRIFT	GOLD WIRE
GET READY	GO ALL OUT	GOLF BALL
GET RID OF	GO AND SEE	GOLF CLUB
GET RIGHT	GO AROUND	GO MODERN
GET ROUGH	GO ASHORE	GO NATIVE
GET ROUND	GO ASTERN	GONE AWAY
GETS AWAY	GO ASTRAY	GONE DOWN
GETS BACK	GOBBLE UP	GONE WEST
GETS EVEN	GO BEHIND	GOOD BALL
GETS OVER	GO BEYOND	GOOD BOOK
GETS RICH	GO BY BOAT	GOOD CASE
GETS WELL	GO BY RAIL	GOOD CAST
GET THERE	GO BY ROAD	GOOD CHAP
GET TIRED	GO BY SHIP	GOOD COOK
GET TOUGH	GO BY TAXI	GOOD COPY
GET UPSET	GO BY TRAM	GOOD CROP
GET WORSE	GO BY TUBE	GOOD DEAL
GIFT GOAL	GOD BLESS	GOOD DEBT
GIFT SHOP	GO DIRECT	GOOD DEED
GIN AND IT	GOD OF WAR	GOOD DRAW
GINGER UP	GOD'S ACRE	GOOD FACE
GINNED UP	GOD SPEED	GOOD FARE
GIN RUMMY	GOD'S WILL	GOOD FEED
GIN SLING	GOES AWAY	GOOD FIRE
GIVE AWAY	GOES BACK	GOOD FOLK
GIVE BACK	GOES DOWN	GOOD FOOD
GIVE HEED	GOES OVER	GOOD FORM
GIVE HOPE	GOES SLOW	GOOD GAME
GIVE IN TO	GOES WEST	GOOD GATE
GIVE IT UP	GOES WITH	GOOD GIRL
GIVEN OUT	GO FOR HIM	GOOD HAND
GIVE ODDS	GO HALVES	GOOD HAUL
GIVE OVER	GO HUNGRY	GOOD HOPE
GIVE PAIN	GO IN FEAR	GOOD HOST
GIVES EAR	GOING MAD	GOOD IDEA
GIVES WAY	GOING OFF	GOOD KING
GIVE VENT	GOING OUT	GOOD LADY
GIVING UP	GOINGS ON	GOOD LAND
GLAD HAND	GO IN RAGS	GOOD LIFE
GLAD NEWS	GO INSIDE	GOOD LUCK
GLAD RAGS	GOLD COIN	GOOD MEAL
GLASS EYE	GOLD DUST	GOOD MOOD
GLASS JAW	GOLD FOIL	GOOD MOVE
GLEE CLUB	GOLD LACE	GOOD NAME
GLUM FACE	GOLD LEAF	GOOD NEWS
GNAT BITE	GOLD MINE	GOOD OMEN
GNAW AWAY	GOLD REEF	GOOD PACE

GOOD PALS	GREAT JOY	H—8
GOOD PART	GREAT MAN	HAD WORDS
GOOD PLAN	GREAT TOM	HAIL A BUS
GOOD SEAT	GREAT WAR	HAIL A CAB
GOOD SHOT	GREAT WIT	HAIL MARY
GOOD SHOW	GREEK ART	HAIRY APE
GOOD SIGN	GREEK GOD	HALF A CUP
GOOD SOIL	GREEK URN	HALF A MAN
GOOD SORT	GREEN EYE	HALF A TON
GOOD SOUL	GREEN FEE	HALF DEAD
GOOD TIME	GREEN FLY	HALF EACH
GOOD TIPS	GREEN HAT	HALF FARE
GOOD TRIM	GREEN INK	HALF FULL
GOOD TURN	GREEN MAN	HALF MILE
GOOD TYPE	GREEN TEA	HALF MOON
GOOD VIEW	GREY COAT	HALF OVER
GOOD WASH	GREY DAWN	HALF TIME
GOOD WIFE	GREY EYES	HALL MARK
GOOD WILL	GREY HAIR	HALT SIGN
GOOD WINE	GREY MARE	HAM ACTOR
GOOD WORD	GREY SUIT	HAM HOUSE
GOOD WORK	GRIM FACE	HAMMER IN
GOOD YEAR	GRIM JOKE	HAM ROLLS
GO ON DECK	GRIM LOOK	HAM SALAD
GO ON FOOT	GRIM TASK	HAND BACK
GOON SHOW	GRIM VIEW	HAND DOWN
GO PLACES	GRIP HARD	HAND IT IN
GO PURPLE	GROPE FOR	HAND OVER
GO RACING	GROW COLD	HAND PUMP
GO SHARES	GROW COOL	HANDS OFF
GO STEADY	GROW DARK	HANDS OUT
GO SURETY	GROW LESS	HANG BACK
GO TO GAOL	GROWN MAN	HANG DOWN
GO TO HELL	GROW PALE	HANG FIRE
GO TOO FAR	GROW PEAS	HANG ON TO
GO TO SEED	GROW RICH	HANG OVER
GO TO TOWN	GROWS OLD	HANGS OUT
GO TO WORK	GROW UPON	HAPPY BOY
GOUGE OUT	GROW WEAK	HAPPY MAN
GRADE ONE	GROW WILD	HARD AT IT
GRADE TWO	GUARD DOG	HARD BALL
GRAF SPEE	GUESS HOW	HARD BLOW
GRAND AIR	GUESS WHO	HARD CASE
GRAND SUM	GUIDE DOG	HARD CASH
GRAY'S INN	GULP DOWN	HARD COAL
GREAT AGE	GUN FIGHT	HARD CORE
GREAT AUK	GUNGA DIN	HARD FACT
GREAT DAY	GUN METAL	HARD FATE
GREAT FUN	GYM DRESS	HARD GAME
GREAT GUY	GYM SHOES	HARD HEAD
GREAT HIT	GYM SLIPS	HARD KICK

HARD LIFE	HELP OVER	HIRED OUT
HARD LOOK	HELPS OUT	HIRED VAN
HARD LUCK	HEMMED IN	HIS GRACE
HARD ROES	HEN PARTY	HIT IT OFF
HARD SEAT	HENS' EGGS	HITS BACK
HARD TACK	HERB BEER	HITS HARD
HARD TASK	HERE GOES	HIT TO LEG
HARD TIME	HERE WE GO	HOCK SHOP
HARD TONE	HER GRACE	HOG'S BACK
HARD UPON	HERNE BAY	HOLD BACK
HARD WEAR	HIDE AWAY	HOLD DEAR
HARD WORD	HIGH AIMS	HOLD DOWN
HARD WORK	HIGH BALL	HOLD FAST
HARK BACK	HIGH CARD	HOLD GOOD
HARM'S WAY	HIGH COST	HOLD HARD
HARP UPON	HIGH DIVE	HOLD ON TO
HAT TRICK	HIGHER UP	HOLD OVER
HAUL BACK	HIGH FEES	HOLDS OFF
HAUL DOWN	HIGH GEAR	HOLDS OUT
HAULED IN	HIGH HAND	HOLD SWAY
HAVE A BET	HIGH HATS	HOLD WITH
HAVE A FAG	HIGH HOPE	HOLED OUT
HAVE A FIT	HIGH JUMP	HOLY CITY
HAVE A JOB	HIGH KICK	HOLY FEAR
HAVE A NAP	HIGH LAND	HOLY LAND
HAVE A PEW	HIGH LIFE	HOLY LOCH
HAVE A ROW	HIGH MASS	HOLY WARS
HAVE A RUN	HIGH NECK	HOLY WEEK
HAVE A TRY	HIGH NOON	HOLY WRIT
HAVE DONE	HIGH NOTE	HOME FARM
HAVE LIFE	HIGH RANK	HOME GAME
HAVE PITY	HIGH RATE	HOME HELP
HAY FEVER	HIGH RENT	HOME LIFE
HAZEL NUT	HIGH ROAD	HOME NEWS
HEAD BACK	HIGH SEAS	HOME PARK
HEAD COOK	HIGH SPOT	HOME RULE
HEAD GIRL	HIGH TEAS	HOME RUNS
HEADS OFF	HIGH TIDE	HOME SAFE
HEAD WIND	HIGH TIME	HOME TEAM
HEAR HEAR!	HIGH TONE	HOME TIES
HEAT SPOT	HIGH WAGE	HOME TOWN
HEAT WAVE	HIGH WALL	HOME WINS
HEAVED TO	HIGH WIND	HONEY BEE
HEAVY DAY	HILL FARM	HONEY POT
HEAVY DEW	HILL FOLK	HONG KONG
HEAVY SEA	HIND FOOT	HOOKED IT
HEAVY TAX	HIND LEGS	HOP ABOUT
HEEL OVER	HIP FLASK	HOP ALONG
HELD BACK	HIRED BUS	HOP FIELD
HELD OVER	HIRED CAR	HOT BATHS
HELP DOWN	HIRED MAN	HOT BLOOD

HOT CAKES	IDLE JACK	IN DETAIL
HOT COALS	IDLE RICH	IN DUBLIN
HOT DRINK	IDLE TALK	IN EFFECT
HOT JOINT	ILEX TREE	IN EMBRYO
HOT LUNCH	ILL GRACE	IN EUROPE
HOT MEALS	ILL TASTE	IN EXCESS
HOT MONEY	ILL USAGE	IN FAVOUR
HOT MUSIC	IN ACCORD	IN FLAMES
HOT NIGHT	IN A CROWD	IN FLIGHT
HOT PLATE	IN A CRUSH	IN FLOWER
HOT PUNCH	IN ACTION	INFRA DIG
HOT SCENT	IN A DREAM	IN FRANCE
HOT SPELL	IN A FAINT	INFRA RED
HOT STOVE	IN A FEVER	IN FRENCH
HOT STUFF	IN A FIELD	IN GERMAN
HOTTED UP	IN A FLASH	IN GROUPS
HOT TODDY	IN A FRAME	IN HEAVEN
HOT WATER	IN AFRICA	IN HIDING
HOUR HAND	IN A GROUP	IN HORROR
HOUSE BOY	IN A HURRY	INK SPOTS
HOUSE DOG	IN A JIFFY	INK STAIN
HOUSE FLY	IN AMBUSH	IN LAYERS
HOWL DOWN	IN AND OUT	IN LEAGUE
HOW'S THAT?	IN A PADDY	IN LONDON
HULL CITY	IN A PANIC	IN LUXURY
HULL DOWN	IN ARABIC	IN MADRID
HUMAN CRY	IN ARMOUR	IN MEMORY
HUM AND HA	IN A SENSE	IN MID AIR
HUNT BALL	IN A SLING	IN MOSCOW
HUNT DOWN	IN A SNARE	IN MOTION
HURRY OFF	IN A STATE	IN MY VIEW
HURRY OUT	IN A SWEAT	INNER MAN
HURT LOOK	IN A SWOON	IN NORWAY
HUSHED UP	IN A TRICE	IN NO TIME
HYDE PARK	IN AUGUST	IN NO WISE
HYMN BOOK	IN AUTUMN	INN SIGNS
HYMN TUNE	IN A WHIRL	IN OFFICE
	IN CAMERA	IN OFF RED
I—8	IN CANADA	IN ONE WAY
IAN SMITH	IN CHAINS	IN ORDERS
ICE CREAM	IN CHARGE	IN PENCIL
ICE CUBES	IN CHORUS	IN PENURY
ICED CAKE	IN CHURCH	IN PERSON
ICY BLAST	IN CLOVER	IN PIECES
ICY PATCH	IN COLOUR	IN POCKET
ICY STARE	IN COLUMN	IN POLAND
ICY WASTE	IN COMMON	IN PRISON
ICY WATER	IN CONVOY	IN PUBLIC
IDEAL MAN	IN CREDIT	IN PURDAH
IDEAS MAN	IN DANGER	IN QUIRES
IDÉE FIXE	IN DEMAND	IN QUOTES

IN REASON	IRON BOOT	JUST A FEW
IN RECESS	IRON DUKE	JUST A SEC
IN RELIEF	IRON FIST	JUST GONE
IN REPAIR	IRON GATE	JUST LOSE
IN REPOSE	IRON GRIP	JUST MISS
IN REVOLT	IRON HAND	JUST THEN
IN RUSSIA	IRON HEEL	
IN SAFETY	IRON LUNG	**K—8**
IN SEASON	IRON MASK	KARL MARX
IN SECRET	IRON MINE	KEEL OVER
IN SERIES	IRON RULE	KEEN EDGE
IN SCHOOL	IRON SHOT	KEEN TYPE
IN SHREDS	IRON WILL	KEEN WIND
IN SPASMS	IT'S A CERT	KEEP A CAT
IN SPIRIT	IT'S A FACT	KEEP A DOG
IN SPRING		KEEP A LOG
IN SUMMER	**J—8**	KEEP AT IT
IN SWEDEN	JACK CADE	KEEP AWAY
IN TERROR	JAMMED IN	KEEP BACK
IN THE ACT	JAM PUFFS	KEEP CALM
IN THE AIR	JAM ROLLS	KEEP CAVE
IN THE ARK	JAM TARTS	KEEP COOL
IN THE BAG	JAM TIGHT	KEEP DARK
IN THE BAR	JANE EYRE	KEEP DOWN
IN THE BOX	JAR OF JAM	KEEP FINE
IN THE CUP	JAZZ BAND	KEEP GOAL
IN THE END	JAZZ CLUB	KEEP HOLD
IN THE GYM	JEST BOOK	KEEP IT UP
IN THE NET	JET BLACK	KEEP LEFT
IN THEORY	JET PLANE	KEEP OPEN
IN THE PIT	JEW'S HARP	KEEP PACE
IN THE RAW	JOE LOUIS	KEEP SAFE
IN THE RED	JOG ALONG	KEEPS FIT
IN THE SEA	JOHN ADAM	KEEP SHOP
IN THE SKY	JOHN BULL	KEEPS MUM
IN THE SUN	JOHN DORY	KEEPS OFF
IN THE VAN	JOHN KNOX	KEEPS OUT
IN THE WAR	JOHN NASH	KEEP STEP
IN THE WAY	JOHN PEEL	KEEP TIME
IN THE WET	JOINED IN	KEEP WARM
IN THE ZOO	JOKE BOOK	KEEP WELL
IN TIGHTS	JUMP AT IT	KEMP TOWN
IN UNISON	JUMP BACK	KEPT BACK
IN VENICE	JUMP DOWN	KEPT BUSY
IN VIENNA	JUMP INTO	KEW GREEN
IN WINTER	JUMP OVER	KEY ISSUE
IRISH ELK	JUMP TO IT	KEY MONEY
IRISH JIG	JUMP UPON	KEY MOVES
IRISH SEA	JUNK SHOP	KEY POINT
IRON BAND	JURY LIST	KEY POSTS
IRON BARS	JUST A BIT	KICK BACK

KICK OVER	LARGE RUM	LATIN TAG
KICKS OFF	LARGE SUM	LAUGH OFF
KICKS OUT	LAST BALL	LAW AGENT
KID STUFF	LAST BELL	LAW COURT
KILL PAIN	LAST BOUT	LAW SUITS
KILLS OFF	LAST CALL	LAY ABOUT
KILL TIME	LAST CAST	LAY A FIRE
KIM NOVAK	LAST DAYS	LAY AN EGG
KIND DEED	LAST DROP	LAY ASIDE
KIND FACE	LAST GASP	LAY A TRAP
KIND HOST	LAST HEAT	LAYS BARE
KIND LOOK	LAST HOLE	LAYS DOWN
KIND SOUL	LAST HOME	LAY SIEGE
KIND WORD	LAST HOPE	LAYS OPEN
KING COLE	LAST HOUR	LAY WASTE
KING JOHN	LAST JULY	LEAD MINE
KING KONG	LAST JUNE	LEAD PIPE
KING LEAR	LAST LEGS	LEAD SHOT
KING'S CUP	LAST LINE	LEADS OFF
KING SIZE	LAST LOOK	LEAD UP TO
KISS AWAY	LAST LOVE	LEAK AWAY
KNEE DEEP	LAST MEAL	LEAKS OUT
KNEE GRIP	LAST MOVE	LEAN BACK
KNOCK OFF	LAST NAME	LEAN DIET
KNOCK OUT	LAST OVER	LEAN MEAT
KNOCKS UP	LAST PAGE	LEAN OVER
KNOW BEST	LAST PART	LEAP OVER
KNOW WELL	LAST POST	LEAP YEAR
	LAST RACE	LEAST BIT
L—8	LAST REST	LEAVE OFF
LA BOHÈME	LAST ROSE	LEAVE OUT
LADLE OUT	LAST SEEN	LEEK SOUP
LADY HELP	LAST'S OUT	LEE SHORE
LADY LUCK	LAST TERM	LEFT BACK
LAID FLAT	LAST TEST	LEFT BANK
LAKE COMO	LAST TIME	LEFT FACE
LAKE ERIE	LAST TO GO	LEFT FLAT
LAMB CHOP	LAST WEEK	LEFT FOOT
LAME DOGS	LAST WILL	LEFT HALF
LAME DUCK	LAST WORD	LEFT HAND
LAND AHOY	LAST YEAR	LEFT HOME
LAND A JOB	LAS VEGAS	LEFT HOOK
LAND ARMY	LATE BIRD	LEFT OVER
LAND CRAB	LATE CALL	LEFT SIDE
LAND GIRL	LATE HOUR	LEFT TURN
LAND LINE	LATE MEAL	LEFT WING
LAND'S END	LATE NEWS	LEGAL AGE
LA PALOMA	LATE PASS	LEGAL AID
LARGE EGG	LATE POST	LEG BREAK
LARGE GAP	LATE SHOW	LEG DRIVE
LARGE GIN	LATE WIFE	LEG STUMP

LEMON TEA	LITA ROSA	LONG REST
LEMON PIE	LITTLE ME	LONG RIDE
LEND TONE	LITTLE MO	LONG ROAD
LENT TERM	LIVE A LIE	LONG ROOM
LET ALONE	LIVE BAIT	LONG ROPE
LET BLOOD	LIVE COAL	LONG SHOT
LET DRIVE	LIVED OUT	LONG SLIP
LET IT LIE	LIVE DOWN	LONG STAY
LET IT RIP	LIVE IT UP	LONG STOP
LET LOOSE	LIVE RAIL	LONG SUIT
LET ME SEE	LIVE SHOW	LONG TAIL
LETS DOWN	LIVE UP TO	LONG TERM
LETS FALL	LIVE WELL	LONG TIME
LETS FREE	LIVE WIRE	LONG VIEW
LET SLIDE	LIVING IN	LONG WAIT
LETS PASS	LOAN CLUB	LONG WALK
LETS SLIP	LOCAL INN	LONG WAVE
LEVEL OFF	LOCAL LAD	LONG WORD
LEVEL OUT	LOCAL PUB	LOOK ARCH
LEVELS UP	LOCAL RAG	LOOK AWAY
LEWIS GUN	LOCAL TAX	LOOK BACK
LIAR DICE	LOCH NESS	LOOK BLUE
LIE ABOUT	LOCK AWAY	LOOK COOL
LIE AWAKE	LOCKED IN	LOOK DOWN
LIE CLOSE	LOCKED UP	LOOKED AT
LIE DOGGO	LOG CABIN	LOOKED IN
LIE HEAVY	LOG FIRES	LOOKED ON
LIE IN BED	LOIN CHOP	LOOKED UP
LIES DOWN	LONE HAND	LOOK GLUM
LIES FLAT	LONE WOLF	LOOK GOOD
LIE STILL	LONG ACRE	LOOK GRIM
LIFE PEER	LONG DROP	LOOK HERE
LIFE SPAN	LONG FACE	LOOK INTO
LIFE WORK	LONG GONE	LOOK IT UP
LIGHT ALE	LONG HAIR	LOOK LEFT
LIGHT CAR	LONG HAUL	LOOK LIKE
LIGHT RAY	LONG JUMP	LOOK OVER
LIGHTS UP	LONG LANE	LOOK PALE
LIGHT TEA	LONG LEAD	LOOKS BIG
LIKE A MAN	LONG LEGS	LOOKS FOR
LIKE BEST	LONG LIFE	LOOK SICK
LIKE FURY	LONG LINE	LOOKS OUT
LILY POND	LONG LIST	LOOK SPRY
LILY PONS	LONG LOST	LOOK TRUE
LIMBER UP	LONG NOTE	LOOK UP TO
LINGER ON	LONG ODDS	LOOK WELL
LINKED UP	LONG POEM	LOOM OVER
LION CUBS	LONG PULL	LOOP LINE
LION'S DEN	LONG PUTT	LOOSE BOX
LIP SALVE	LONG RACE	LOOSE END
LISTEN IN	LONG READ	LOOSEN UP

LORD AVON
LORD'S DAY
LOSE A LEG
LOSE FACE
LOSE HOPE
LOSE TIME
LOST BALL
LOST CITY
LOST GAME
LOST LOVE
LOST SOUL
LOST TIME
LOT'S WIFE
LOUD BANG
LOUD BOOM
LOUD PEAL
LOUD RING
LOUIS D'OR
LOVED ONE
LOVE GAME
LOVE NEST
LOVE POEM
LOVE SONG
LOVE SUIT
LOW BIRTH
LOW CARDS
LOW CLASS
LOW DIVES
LOW DUTCH
LOWER JAW
LOWER LIP
LOWER SET
LOW GRADE
LOW HEELS
LOW JOINT
LOW LATIN
LOW MARKS
LOW PITCH
LOW POINT
LOW POWER
LOW PRICE
LOW RATES
LOW RENTS
LOW SCORE
LOW SOUND
LOW SPEED
LOW TIDES
LOW VOICE
LOW WAGES
LOW WATER
LUCKY BOY

LUCKY DAY
LUCKY DIP
LUCKY DOG
LUCKY HIT
LUCKY JIM
LUCKY MAN
LUCKY RUN
LUCKY WIN
LUG ABOUT
LUMP SUMS
LUNCH OUT
LUTON HOO
LYING LOW
LYNCH LAW
LYRE BIRD

M—8
MADE EASY
MADE OVER
MADLY GAY
MAD PARTY
MAGIC BOX
MAGIC EYE
MAIL BOAT
MAIN BODY
MAIN CROP
MAIN DECK
MAIN DISH
MAIN FILM
MAIN HALL
MAIN IDEA
MAIN ITEM
MAIN LINE
MAIN MEAL
MAIN PART
MAIN ROAD
MAIN ROOM
MAJOR KEY
MAJOR WAR
MAKE A BED
MAKE A BET
MAKE A BID
MAKE A BOW
MAKE A HIT
MAKE A PUN
MAKE A ROW
MAKE A VOW
MAKE BOLD
MAKE EYES
MAKE FAST
MAKE FIRM

MAKE FREE
MAKE GOOD
MAKE IT UP
MAKE LAWS
MAKE LOVE
MAKE NEWS
MAKE OVER
MAKE PLAY
MAKE PORT
MAKE PUNS
MAKE REAL
MAKE ROOM
MAKE RUNS
MAKE SAFE
MAKE SAIL
MAKES HAY
MAKES OFF
MAKES OUT
MAKE SURE
MAKES WAY
MAKE TIME
MAKE UP TO
MAL DE MER
MALE HEIR
MAN ALIVE
MAN A SHIP
MAN OF GOD
MAN OF LAW
MAN POWER
MAN'S CLUB
MAN TO MAN
MANX CATS
MANY A ONE
MANY MORE
MARCH OFF
MARCH OUT
MARK DOWN
MARKS OFF
MARKS OUT
MARK TIME
MARK WELL
MARRY OFF
MARSH GAS
MARY RAND
MARY ROSE
MARY WEBB
MATA HARI
MAXIM GUN
MAY QUEEN
MEAN TIME
MEAN WELL

MEAT BALL	MORAL LAW	NEAP TIDE
MEAT DISH	MORE TIME	NEAR BEER
MEAT LOAF	MORT SAAL	NEAR EAST
MEAT PIES	MOSS ROSE	NEAR HERE
MEAT SAFE	MOTH BALL	NEAR HOME
MELT AWAY	MOT JUSTE	NEAR MISS
MELT DOWN	MOTOR OIL	NEAR ONES
MEN OF OLD	MOURN FOR	NEAR SIDE
MENS SANA	MOVE AWAY	NEON LAMP
MEN'S WEAR	MOVE BACK	NEON SIGN
MERE IDEA	MOVED OFF	NEON TUBE
MERE LUCK	MOVED OUT	NEST EGGS
MERRY MEN	MOVE FAST	NET PRICE
MESS BILL	MOVE OVER	NET SALES
MESSED UP	MOVIE FAN	NET VALUE
MESS ROOM	MOVING UP	NEVER END
METAL BOX	MOWN DOWN	NEW ANGLE
METAL CAP	MR. PASTRY	NEW BALLS
MEWS FLAT	MUCH LESS	NEW BIRTH
MILD BEER	MUCH MORE	NEW BLOOD
MILE RACE	MUCH ROOM	NEW BRAND
MILES OUT	MUCH TIME	NEW BREAD
MILK BARS	MUD BATHS	NEW BREED
MILK BILL	MUDDLE ON	NEW BROOM
MILK DIET	MUFFLE UP	NEW CROSS
MILK JUGS	MUG'S GAME	NEW DELHI
MILK LOAF	MUSE UPON	NEW DRESS
MILK MAID	MUSK ROSE	NEW FACES
MILK PAIL	MUTE SWAN	NEW FLINT
MILKY WAY	MY CHOICE	NEW FRANC
MILL GIRL	MY FRIEND	NEW HEART
MILL HILL	MY OLD MAN	NEW HOUSE
MILL POND	MY PUBLIC	NEW IDEAS
MIME SHOW	MYRA HESS	NEW ISSUE
MIND'S EYE	MYRNA LOY	NEW LAMPS
MINE HOST		NEW LIGHT
MING VASE	**N—8**	NEW MODEL
MINK COAT	NAG'S HEAD	NEW MONEY
MINK FARM	NAIL A LIE	NEW NOVEL
MINK WRAP	NAIL DOWN	NEW ORDER
MINOR KEY	NAIL FILE	NEW OWNER
MINUS ONE	NAKED EYE	NEW PENNY
MINUS TWO	NAKED MAN	NEW PUPIL
MISS OTIS	NAME PART	NEW SHOES
MIXED BAG	NATAL DAY	NEW SHOOT
MIXED LOT	NAVAL ARM	NEWS ITEM
MOBY DICK	NAVAL GUN	NEWS ROOM
MODEL HAT	NAVAL MAN	NEW STAGE
MONA LISA	NAVY BLUE	NEW STOCK
MOOT CASE	NAVY LIST	NEW STYLE
MOPPED UP	NAVY WEEK	NEW SUITS

NEW TOWNS	NO MATTER	OFF STUMP
NEW TRAIL	NONE LEFT	OFF TO BED
NEW TRIAL	NO NERVES	OFF TO SEA
NEW TRICK	NO OBJECT	OIL DRUMS
NEW TYRES	NO OPTION	OIL LAMPS
NEW VISTA	NO QUORUM	OIL STOVE
NEW WOMAN	NO REMEDY	OIL WELLS
NEW WORLD	NO RETURN	OLD BIRDS
NEXT BEST	NORTH END	OLD BLUES
NEXT DOOR	NORTH SEA	OLD BONES
NEXT MOVE	NO SECRET	OLD BOOTS
NEXT PAGE	NOSED OUT	OLD CHINA
NEXT RACE	NOTA BENE	OLD CROCK
NEXT STEP	NOT A SOUL	OLD CRONY
NEXT TIME	NOT AS YET	OLD DEBTS
NEXT WEEK	NOT AT ALL	OLD DRESS
NEXT YEAR	NOT A WHIT	OLD DUTCH
NICE MESS	NOTE DOWN	OLD FACES
NICE TIME	NOTE WELL	OLD FLAME
NICE WORK	NO THANKS	OLD FOGEY
NIGHT AIR	NOT LEAST	OLD FOLKS
NIGHT OFF	NOT OFTEN	OLD FRUIT
NIGHT OUT	NOT QUITE	OLD GIRLS
NINE DAYS	NO TRUMPS	OLD GLORY
NINE DEEP	NOT SO BAD	OLD GUARD
NINE ELMS	NOT SO HOT	OLD HABIT
NINE FEET	NOT TODAY	OLD HANDS
NINE QUID	NOT VALID	OLD HARRY
NINTH DAY	NO WAY OUT	OLD HAUNT
NINTH ROW	NOW FOR IT	OLD HEADS
NINTH TEE	NO WONDER	OLD MAIDS
NIP OF GIN	NUT BROWN	OLD MOORE
NO ACCENT	NUT CASES	OLD ORDER
NOAH'S ARK		OLD ROGER
NO ANSWER	**O—8**	OLD SALTS
NO APPEAL	OAK CHEST	OLD SARUM
NO BETTER	OAK TREES	OLD SCORE
NOBLE ART	OCEAN BED	OLD SCREW
NO BOTHER	ODD MONEY	OLD STOCK
NO CHANCE	ODD SIGHT	OLD STORY
NO CHANGE	ODD TRICK	OLD STYLE
NO CHARGE	OF COURSE	OLD SWEAT
NO CHOICE	OFF AND ON	OLD THING
NO COLOUR	OFF BREAK	OLD TIMER
NO DESIRE	OFF DRINK	OLD TIMES
NO EFFECT	OFF DRIVE	OLD TRICK
NO EFFORT	OFF GUARD	OLD TUNES
NO ESCAPE	OFF PITCH	OLD WITCH
NO EXCUSE	OFF SALES	OLD WOMAN
NO FUTURE	OFF SHORE	OLD WORLD
NO LONGER	OFF STAGE	OLIVE OIL

ON A BINGE	ONLY ONCE	OPEN TART
ON A CHAIR	ON MONDAY	OPEN TOWN
ON A LEVEL	ON MY LIFE	OPEN VOTE
ON AND OFF	ON ONE LEG	OPEN WIDE
ON A PLATE	ON PARADE	OPEN WORK
ON A SLOPE	ON PAROLE	OPERA HAT
ON A TABLE	ON PATROL	OPIUM DEN
ON A VISIT	ON RECORD	OPTED OUT
ONCE A DAY	ON REMAND	ORB OF DAY
ONCE MORE	ON SAFARI	ORDER OFF
ONCE ONLY	ON SKATES	ORDER OUT
ONCE OVER	ON STILTS	ORDER TEA
ON COURSE	ON STRIKE	OUT AT SEA
ON CREDIT	ON SUNDAY	OUT FIRST
ON DEMAND	ON TARGET	OUT OF BED
ONE BY ONE	ON THE AIR	OUT OF GAS
ONE DOZEN	ON THE DOT	OUT OF OIL
ONE ENTRY	ON THE EBB	OUT OF USE
ONE FIFTH	ON THE HOB	OUT TO WIN
ONE GROSS	ON THE HOP	OVEN BIRD
ONE HEART	ON THE JOB	OVEN DOOR
ONE IN SIX	ON THE MAP	OVERDO IT
ONE IN TEN	ON THE MAT	OVER HERE
ONE IN TWO	ON THE NOD	OVER MUCH
ONE MATCH	ON THE RUN	OVER SEAS
ONE MONTH	ON THE SEA	OVER WE GO
ONE NINTH	ON THE SET	OWE MONEY
ONE OR TWO	ON THE SLY	OX TONGUE
ONE OUNCE	ON THE TOP	
ONE PENNY	ON THE WAY	P—8
ONE PIECE	ON TIP-TOE	PACK A GUN
ONE POINT	ON VELVET	PACKED UP
ONE POUND	ON WHEELS	PACK IT IN
ONE QUART	OPEN ARMS	PACK IT UP
ONE ROUND	OPEN BOAT	PAGAN GOD
ONE'S DUTY	OPEN BOOK	PAGE FIVE
ONE'S HOST	OPEN CITY	PAGE FOUR
ONE SIXTH	OPEN DOOR	PAGE NINE
ONE SPADE	OPENED UP	PAID BACK
ONE STONE	OPEN EYES	PAID CASH
ONE'S WORD	OPEN FIRE	PAID LESS
ONE TENTH	OPEN GAME	PAID MORE
ONE THIRD	OPEN GATE	PAINT OUT
ONE TRICK	OPEN GOAL	PAINT POT
ONE VERSE	OPEN HAND	PAIRS OFF
ONE VOICE	OPEN LAND	PALE BLUE
ONE WHEEL	OPEN MIND	PALE FACE
ON FRIDAY	OPEN NOTE	PALE PINK
ONLY A FEW	OPEN ROAD	PALL MALL
ONLY HOPE	OPEN SHOP	PALM TREE
ONLY JUST	OPENS OUT	PAPER BAG

PAPER HAT	PER ANNUM	PLAY SAFE
PAPER WAR	PERKED UP	PLAY SNAP
PARDON ME	PETER MAY	PLAYS OFF
PARK LANE	PETER OUT	PLAY SOLO
PART SONG	PETER PAN	PLAY UP TO
PART TIME	PET HOBBY	PLAY WELL
PART WITH	PET NAMES	PLAY WITH
PARTY MAN	PET SHOPS	PLEASE GO
PAR VALUE	PHASE ONE	PLUG AWAY
PASS A LAW	PHASE TWO	PLUM CAKE
PASS AWAY	PHONE BOX	PLUM DUFF
PASS BACK	PIANO KEY	PLUNGE IN
PASS BOOK	PICKED UP	PLUS SIGN
PASS DOWN	PICK IT UP	POINT OUT
PASSED BY	PICKS OFF	POKED FUN
PASSED ON	PICKS OUT	POLE JUMP
PASSED UP	PIG SWILL	POLE STAR
PASS IT ON	PILE ARMS	POLISH UP
PASS OVER	PILE IT ON	POLKA DOT
PAST CURE	PINE AWAY	POLO NECK
PAST HELP	PINE CONE	POLO PONY
PAST HOPE	PINE TREE	PONY CLUB
PAST LIFE	PINK COAT	PONY RACE
PAST TIME	PINK GINS	POOL ROOM
PAST WORK	PINK GLOW	POOLS WIN
PAUL MUNI	PINK SPOT	POOR CAST
PAY A CALL	PIN MONEY	POOR CHAP
PAY A FINE	PINNED IN	POOR CROP
PAY CLAIM	PINNED UP	POOR DEAL
PAY CORPS	PINS DOWN	POOR DEAR
PAY COURT	PINT POTS	POOR FISH
PAY EXTRA	PINT SIZE	POOR FOLK
PAY FOR IT	PIPE DOWN	POOR GAME
PAY PAUSE	PLACE BET	POOR HAND
PAYS BACK	PLAIN BOX	POOR JOHN
PAYS CASH	PLAIN MAN	POOR LAND
PAY SHEET	PLANT OUT	POOR LAWS
PAY WAGES	PLAN WELL	POOR MAKE
PEA GREEN	PLAY AWAY	POOR RATE
PEAK FORM	PLAY BACK	POOR RISK
PEAK HOUR	PLAY BALL	POOR SHOT
PEAR TREE	PLAY DICE	POOR SHOW
PEAT FIRE	PLAY DOWN	POOR SIDE
PEAT MOSS	PLAYED ON	POOR SOIL
PEER GYNT	PLAY FAIR	POOR SOUL
PEGGY LEE	PLAY FLAT	POOR VIEW
PEGS AWAY	PLAY GOLF	POPE JOHN
PEN NAMES	PLAY HARD	POPE PAUL
PENNY BUN	PLAY HIGH	POP MUSIC
PEP PILLS	PLAY HOST	POPPY DAY
PEP TALKS	PLAY POLO	POP SONGS

POP STARS
PORE OVER
PORK CHOP
PORK PIES
PORT ARMS
PORT BEAM
PORT ERIN
PORT SAID
PORT SIDE
PORT WINE
POST FREE
POT HERBS
POT OF JAM
POT OF TEA
POT ROAST
POT SHOTS
POURS OUT
POWER CUT
PRESS BOX
PREY UPON
PRICE CUT
PRICE WAR
PRIME CUT
PRIX FIXE
PRO FORMA
PROUD DAY
PROUD MAN
PUB CRAWL
PUB HOURS
PUFF AWAY
PUFFED UP
PULL AWAY
PULL BACK
PULL DOWN
PULLED IN
PULLED UP
PULL HARD
PULL OVER
PULLS OFF
PULLS OUT
PUMPED UP
PUPPY FAT
PURE GOLD
PURE WOOL
PUSH AWAY
PUSH BACK
PUSH DOWN
PUSH HARD
PUSH OVER
PUSH PAST
PUSSY CAT

PUT ABOUT
PUT ASIDE
PUT FORTH
PUT ON TOP
PUT RIGHT
PUTS AWAY
PUTS BACK
PUTS DOWN
PUTS OVER
PUTS UPON
PUT TO BED
PUT TO SEA
PUT TO USE
PUT-UP JOB

Q—8

QUART POT
QUEEN ANT
QUEEN BEE
QUEEN MAB
QUEUED UP
QUICK EAR
QUICK EYE
QUICK ONE
QUICK WIT
QUIET END
QUILL PEN
QUITE MAD
QUIT RENT
QUIZ GAME
QUIZ KIDS
QUIZ TEAM
QUO VADIS?

R—8

RACE AWAY
RACE CARD
RADIO HAM
RADIO SET
RAG DOLLS
RAG TRADE
RAIN HARD
RAINY DAY
RAKE OVER
RAMS HOME
RANK HIGH
RARA AVIS
RARE BIRD
RARE GIFT
RAT'S TAIL
RATTLE ON

RAW DEALS
RAW EDGES
RAW STEAK
REACH OUT
READ OVER
READ WELL
READY CUT
READY FOR
READY PEN
READY WIT
REAL GOLD
REAL LIFE
REAL SELF
REAL SILK
REAL TEST
REAR RANK
REAR VIEW
RECKON ON
RECKON UP
RED BERET
RED BERRY
RED BIDDY
RED BLOOD
RED BRICK
RED CHINA
RED CROSS
RED FACES
RED LABEL
RED LIGHT
RED MAPLE
RED OCHRE
RED PAINT
RED PERIL
RED PIECE
RED QUEEN
RED ROSES
RED SAILS
RED SHIRT
RED SOCKS
RED SPOTS
RED STAMP
RED SUITS
REEF KNOT
REELS OFF
REG DIXON
RELY UPON
RENT ACTS
RENT BOOK
RENT FREE
RENT ROLL
REST CAMP

REST CURE	ROAD RACE	RUM START
REST HOME	ROAD SHOW	RUN ABOUT
RHUM BABA	ROAD SIGN	RUN AFTER
RICE CROP	ROAD TEST	RUN AHEAD
RICE DISH	ROAST PIG	RUN ALONG
RICH AUNT	ROB A BANK	RUN A MILE
RICH FARE	ROCK CAKE	RUN AMUCK
RICH FOLK	ROD LAVER	RUN A RACE
RICH FOOD	ROLL BACK	RUN A RISK
RICH HAUL	ROLL CALL	RUN FOR IT
RICH JOKE	ROLLED IN	RUN RISKS
RICH LAND	ROLLED UP	RUN ROUND
RICH MILK	ROLL OVER	RUNS AWAY
RICH SEAM	ROMAN GOD	RUNS BACK
RICH SOIL	ROMAN LAW	RUNS DOWN
RICH VEIN	ROMP HOME	RUNS HARD
RICH WIFE	ROOM MATE	RUN SHORT
RIDE AWAY	ROOT CROP	RUNS INTO
RIDE DOWN	ROOTS OUT	RUNS OVER
RIDE HARD	ROPED OFF	RUNS RIOT
RIDE OVER	ROPE'S END	RUNS WILD
RIGHT ARM	ROSE BOWL	RUN THIRD
RIGHT EAR	ROSE BUSH	RUN TO FAT
RIGHT EYE	ROSE PINK	RUSH AWAY
RIGHT LEG	ROSY GLOW	RUSH HOUR
RIGHT MAN	ROUGH MAP	RUSH INTO
RIGHT OFF	ROUGH OUT	RUSH MATS
RIGHT OUT	ROUGH SEA	RYDER CUP
RIGHT SET	ROUND BOX	RYE BREAD
RIGHT WAY	ROUND OFF	
RING ROAD	ROUND ONE	S—8
RINGS OFF	ROUND PEG	SABRE JET
RINGS OUT	ROUND SIX	SACK RACE
RING TRUE	ROUND SUM	SADDLE UP
RINSE OUT	ROUNDS UP	SAD HEART
RIPE CORN	ROUND TEN	SAD SIGHT
RIPE LIPS	ROUND TIN	SAD SONGS
RISE LATE	ROUND TWO	SAD STORY
RISEN SUN	ROW A RACE	SAD TO SAY
RIVER CAM	ROYAL BOX	SAD WORLD
RIVER DAM	ROYAL OAK	SAFE SEAT
RIVER DEE	RUB ALONG	SAFE SIDE
RIVER DON	RUBBED IN	SAIL AWAY
RIVER EXE	RUB NOSES	SAINT DAY
RIVER GOD	RUBS DOWN	SALAD OIL
RIVER TAY	RUBS IT IN	SALE ROOM
RIVER USK	RUBY LIPS	SALES TAX
RIVER WYE	RUBY PORT	SALT AWAY
ROAD FUND	RUDE WORD	SALT BEEF
ROAD HOGS	RULED OUT	SALT LAKE
ROAD MAPS	RUM PUNCH	SALT MINE

SALT PORK	SEE STARS	SHARP EAR
SAM COSTA	SEIZED UP	SHARP END
SAME DATE	SELF HELP	SHARP EYE
SAME KIND	SELL DEAR	SHARP WIT
SAME MIND	SELLS OFF	SHEER OFF
SAME NAME	SELLS OUT	SHELL OUT
SAME TIME	SELL WELL	SHIN BONE
SAME VEIN	SEND AWAY	SHIP AHOY
SAM SMALL	SEND BACK	SHIP OARS
SAND DUNE	SEND DOWN	SHIP'S LOG
SANK DOWN	SEND HELP	SHOE LANE
SAVE FACE	SEND HOME	SHOE SHOP
SAVE TIME	SEND WORD	SHOO AWAY
SAVING UP	SENNA POD	SHOOT LOW
SAXE BLUE	SENNA TEA	SHOOT OUT
SAY GRACE	SERVE ILL	SHOOTS UP
SCALED UP	SERVE OUT	SHOP BELL
SCENE ONE	SET ABOUT	SHOP GIRL
SCENE TWO	SET AFOOT	SHORT CUT
SCENT OUT	SET APART	SHORT LEG
SCOOP OUT	SET ASIDE	SHORT ONE
SCORE OFF	SET A TRAP	SHORT RUN
SCORE OUT	SET BOOKS	SHOT AWAY
SCOT FREE	SET FORTH	SHOT DEAD
SCOUT OUT	SET GOING	SHOT DOWN
SCRAPE UP	SET IDEAS	SHOT SILK
SCRUB OUT	SET LUNCH	SHOUT OUT
SEA COAST	SET MEALS	SHOVE OFF
SEA FEVER	SET PAPER	SHOW A LEG
SEA FLOOR	SET PIECE	SHOW BOAT
SEA GREEN	SET PLANS	SHOW CASE
SEALED UP	SET POINT	SHOW DOWN
SEA LORDS	SET PRICE	SHOWED UP
SEA NYMPH	SET RIGHT	SHOW FEAR
SEA POWER	SET SCENE	SHOW GIRL
SEA SCOUT	SETS DOWN	SHOWN OFF
SEA SPRAY	SETS FOOT	SHOWN OUT
SEA STORY	SETS FREE	SHOW OVER
SEAT BELT	SET SMILE	SHOW PITY
SEA WATER	SETS SAIL	SHOW ROOM
SEA WINDS	SET STARE	SHRUG OFF
SEE ABOUT	SETS UPON	SHUT DOWN
SEE AFTER	SET TERMS	SHUTS OFF
SEE AHEAD	SETTLE IN	SHUTS OUT
SEED CAKE	SETTLE UP	SHY CHILD
SEE IT ALL	SEVEN MEN	SHY SMILE
SEE IT OUT	SEWER RAT	SHY THING
SEEKS OUT	SHAKEN UP	SHY WOMAN
SEEM REAL	SHAKE OFF	SICK JOKE
SEE NO ONE	SHAKE OUT	SICK LIST
SEES LIFE	SHARE OUT	SICK ROOM

SIDE ARMS	SIZE FOUR	SMELL OUT
SIDE BETS	SIZE NINE	SMOG MASK
SIDE DISH	SKIM OVER	SMOKE OUT
SIDE DOOR	SKIN DEEP	SNACK BAR
SIDE DRUM	SKIN GAME	SNAKE PIT
SIDE GATE	SKIP OVER	SNAP VOTE
SIDE LINE	SKY PILOT	SNATCH UP
SIDE ROAD	SLACK OFF	SNEAK OFF
SIDE SHOW	SLAG HEAP	SNEAK OUT
SIDE VIEW	SLAP DOWN	SNEAKS IN
SIDE WIND	SLEEP OFF	SNEAKS UP
SIDE WITH	SLEEP OUT	SNOWED IN
SIEGE CAP	SLEEPS IN	SNOWED UP
SIGN AWAY	SLEEPS ON	SNOW HILL
SIGNED ON	SLING OFF	SNOW LINE
SIGN HERE	SLING OUT	SNUB NOSE
SIGNS OFF	SLINGS IN	SNUFF BOX
SILK GOWN	SLIP AWAY	SNUFF OUT
SILLY ASS	SLIP BACK	SOBER MAN
SING HIGH	SLIP INTO	SOB STORY
SING SING	SLIP KNOT	SOB STUFF
SINGS OUT	SLIP PAST	SOFT BALL
SINK BACK	SLIPS OFF	SOFTEN UP
SINK DOWN	SLIPS OUT	SOFT EYES
SINN FEIN	SLIT OPEN	SOFT HAIR
SIT ABOUT	SLOG AWAY	SOFT ROES
SIT ERECT	SLOPE OFF	SOFT SEAT
SIT IT OUT	SLOPES UP	SOFT SKIN
SITS BACK	SLOP OVER	SOFT SOAP
SITS DOWN	SLOW BALL	SOFT SPOT
SIT STILL	SLOW BOAT	SOFT TOYS
SIT TIGHT	SLOW DOWN	SOFT WORD
SIT UNDER	SLOWED UP	SOHO FAIR
SITZ BATH	SLOW PACE	SOLD A PUP
SIX CLUBS	SLOW TIME	SOLE HEIR
SIX DOZEN	SLUM AREA	SOLO CALL
SIX GROSS	SLY JOKES	SOME GOOD
SIX HOLES	SMALL ADS	SOME MORE
SIX HOURS	SMALL BOY	SONG BIRD
SIX MILES	SMALL CAR	SONG HITS
SIX PARTS	SMALL EGG	SONNY BOY
SIX PINTS	SMALL FRY	SON OF GOD
SIX SCORE	SMALL GIN	SORE EYES
SIXTH DAY	SMALL MAN	SORE FEET
SIXTH ROW	SMALL RUM	SORE HEAD
SIXTH TEE	SMALL SUM	SORE NEED
SIX TIMES	SMALL WAY	SORRY END
SIX TO ONE	SMART LAD	SORTS OUT
SIX WEEKS	SMART MAN	SO SIMPLE
SIX YEARS	SMART SET	SOUND BET
SIZE FIVE	SMASH HIT	SOUND BID

SOUND BOX	STANDS UP	ST. PETER'S
SOUND MAN	STAR PART	STRAW HAT
SOUR LOOK	START OFF	STRAY CAT
SOUR MILK	START OUT	STRAY DOG
SOUTH PAW	STARTS UP	STREAK BY
SOUTH SEA	STAR TURN	STREAK IN
SPACE AGE	STAVE OFF	STREAM BY
SPACE MAN	STAY AWAY	STREAM IN
SPACE OUT	STAY DOWN	STRIKE UP
SPARE BED	STAYED IN	STRING UP
SPARE MAN	STAYED UP	STRIP OFF
SPARK OFF	STAY HERE	STROLL BY
SPEAK FOR	STAY OPEN	STRUCK ON
SPEAK OUT	STAYS PUT	STRUCK UP
SPEAKS UP	ST. BRIDE'S	STRUNG UP
SPEED COP	ST. DAVID'S	STUD BOOK
SPELL OUT	STEAK PIE	STUD FARM
SPILT INK	STEEL BAR	STUDY ART
SPIN A WEB	STEEL NIB	STUDY LAW
SPINS OUT	STEN GUNS	STUMPS UP
SPLIT PIN	STEP BACK	STUNT MAN
SPLITS UP	STEP DOWN	SUCK EGGS
SPONGE ON	STEP INTO	SUGAR RAY
SPOON FED	STEP IT UP	SUMMED UP
SPOT CASH	STEP ON IT	SUMMON UP
SPRING UP	STEP OVER	SUMS IT UP
SPRUCE UP	STEPS OUT	SUM TOTAL
SPUN GOLD	ST. GEORGE	SUNNY DAY
SPUN SILK	ST. GILES'S	SUNNY JIM
SPUN YARN	ST. HELENA	SUN SPOTS
SQUAD CAR	ST. HELEN'S	SUN'S RAYS
SQUARE UP	ST. HELIER	SURE CURE
STAFF CAR	STICK OUT	SURE GAIN
STAGE ONE	STICKS TO	SURE LOSS
STAGE SET	STICKS UP	SURE SHOT
STAG HUNT	STIFF LEG	SWAN LAKE
STAKE OUT	ST. JAMES'S	SWAN SONG
ST. ALBANS	ST. MORITZ	SWAP NEWS
STALE AIR	STOCK CAR	SWEAR OFF
STALE BUN	STONE AGE	SWEARS IN
STALL OFF	STOP AWAY	SWEEP OUT
STAMP ACT	STOP DEAD	SWEEPS UP
STAMP OUT	STOP HERE	SWEET AIR
STAND FOR	STOP HOME	SWEET PEA
STAND OFF	STOP OVER	SWEET SUE
STAND OUT	STOP PLAY	SWEET TEA
STAND PAT	STOPS OFF	SWELL MOB
ST. ANDREW	STOPS OUT	SWELL OUT
STANDS BY	STOP WORK	SWELLS UP
STANDS IN	STOUT MAN	SWIM SUIT
STANDS TO	STOW AWAY	SWING LOW

SWITCH ON	TAKING IN	TENSED UP
SWOP OVER	TALK A LOT	TENTH DAY
	TALK BACK	TENTH MAN
T—8	TALK BOSH	TENTH ROW
TABBY CAT	TALK DOWN	TENTH TEE
TABLE BAY	TALK OVER	TEN TIMES
TAG ALONG	TALKS BIG	TEN TO ONE
TAIL AWAY	TALK SHOP	TEN TO SIX
TAIL COAT	TALL GIRL	TEN TO TEN
TAIL WIND	TALL TALE	TEN TO TWO
TAJ MAHAL	TALL TALK	TEN WEEKS
TAKE A BOW	TALL TREE	TEN YEARS
TAKE A BUS	TANK TRAP	TERM TIME
TAKE A CAB	TAP DANCE	TEST CASE
TAKE A NAP	TAPER OFF	TEST TUBE
TAKE A NIP	TAP WATER	TEXAS TEA
TAKE A PEW	TAUT ROPE	TEXT BOOK
TAKE A TIP	TAWNY OWL	THANK GOD
TAKE A VOW	TAXI FARE	THANK YOU
TAKE AWAY	TAXI RANK	THAT SIDE
TAKE BACK	TEA BREAK	THE ANDES
TAKE BETS	TEA CADDY	THE ANGEL
TAKE CARE	TEACH ART	THE ASHES
TAKE DOWN	TEA DANCE	THE BELLS
TAKE FIRE	TEA IN BED	THE BENCH
TAKE FOOD	TEAMED UP	THE BIBLE
TAKE HEED	TEAM GAME	THE BLIND
TAKE HOLD	TEAM MATE	THE BLITZ
TAKE IT IN	TEAM WORK	THE BLUES
TAKE IT UP	TEA PARTY	THE BRAVE
TAKE LIFE	TEAR DOWN	THE BRIDE
TAKEN ILL	TEAR IT UP	THE BRINY
TAKEN OFF	TEAR OPEN	THE BRONX
TAKE NOTE	TEA ROSES	THE BUFFS
TAKEN OUT	TEARS OFF	THE BYRDS
TAKE ODDS	TEA SHOPS	THE CHAIR
TAKE OVER	TEDDY BOY	THE CHASE
TAKE PART	TED HEATH	THE CLOTH
TAKE PITY	TEE SHOTS	THE CONGO
TAKE ROOT	TELL A FIB	THE COUNT
TAKES AIM	TELL A LIE	THE CREED
TAKE SILK	TELL LIES	THE CROWN
TAKES OFF	TELLS OFF	THE DALES
TAKES OUT	TEN CENTS	THE DERBY
TAKE THAT	TEN DOZEN	THE DEVIL
TAKE THIS	TEN GROSS	THE DOWNS
TAKE TIME	TEN HOURS	THE DRAMA
TAKE TOLL	TEN MARKS	THE DUTCH
TAKE VOWS	TEN MILES	THE EARTH
TAKE WINE	TEN PARTS	THE ÉLITE
TAKE WING	TEN SCORE	THE ENEMY

THE FACTS	THE TWINS	TIED GAME
THE FATES	THE TWIST	TIGER BAY
THE FIELD	THE URALS	TIGER CUB
THE FILMS	THE USUAL	TIGER RAG
THE FIRST	THE VOLGA	TIGHT FIT
THE FLEET	THE WAITS	TILL THEN
THE FLOOD	THE WAY IN	TILT OVER
THE GOODS	THE WEALD	TIME BOMB
THE GOONS	THE WELSH	TIME CARD
THE GRAVE	THE WILDS	TIME FUSE
THE GREAT	THE WOLDS	TIME IS UP
THE GREYS	THE WORLD	TIME TEST
THE GROOM	THE WORKS	TIME TO GO
THE HAGUE	THE WORST	TIMOR SEA
THE HAVES	THICK EAR	TIN LIZZY
THE HOUSE	THICK FOG	TIN MINES
THE IDEAL	THIN COAT	TINY HAND
THE IDIOT	THIN DOWN	TINY MITE
THE IRISH	THIN EDGE	TINY TOTS
THE JOKER	THIN HAIR	TIPPED UP
THE KINKS	THINK BIG	TIP TO TOE
THE KORAN	THINK FIT	TIP TO WIN
THE LIMIT	THINK OUT	TIRED MAN
THE LOCAL	THINKS UP	TIRED OUT
THE LORDS	THIN SKIN	TIRED TIM
THE LOSER	THIN TIME	TO A FAULT
THE MAFIA	THIN WIRE	TO AND FRO
THE MITRE	THIRD ACT	TO BE SURE
THE MOORS	THIRD DAY	TOBY JUGS
THE MUSES	THIRD MAN	TODDLE IN
THE NORTH	THIRD ROW	TODDLE UP
THE NOVEL	THIRD SET	TOE TO TOE
THE PANEL	THIRD TEE	TOLL CALL
THE POINT	THIS IS IT	TOM BROWN
THE POOLS	THIS SIDE	TOM JONES
THE PRESS	THIS TIME	TOMMY GUN
THE RAINS	THIS WEEK	TOMMY ROT
THE RIGHT	THIS YEAR	TOM PINCH
THE ROPES	THREE MEN	TOM THUMB
THE SHAKE	THROWN IN	TOM WALLS
THE SHORE	THROW OFF	TO MY MIND
THE SOMME	THROW OUT	TONE DEAF
THE SOUTH	THUMBS UP	TONE DOWN
THE SPURS	TICK OVER	TONE POEM
THE STAGE	TICKS OFF	TON-UP BOY
THE STAKE	TIDE MARK	TOO EAGER
THE STARS	TIDE OVER	TOO EARLY
THE SUDAN	TIDIED UP	TOO LARGE
THE THING	TIDY MIND	TOO QUICK
THE TIMES	TIE A KNOT	TOO SHARP
THE TOWER	TIED DOWN	TOO SMALL

TOO STEEP	TRIED OUT	TWIN BEDS
TOOTH OUT	TRIM AWAY	TWIN BOYS
TOP BRASS	TRIP OVER	TWO BRACE
TOP FLOOR	TROOP OFF	TWO BY TWO
TOP LAYER	TROOP OUT	TWO CARDS
TOP MARKS	TROTS OFF	TWO CLUBS
TOP NOTCH	TROTS OUT	TWO DOZEN
TOP NOTES	TRUE BILL	TWO GROSS
TOPPED UP	TRUE BLUE	TWO HANDS
TOP PLACE	TRUE COPY	TWO HEADS
TOP PRICE	TRUE HEIR	TWO HOLES
TOP PRIZE	TRUE LOVE	TWO HOURS
TOP RATES	TRUE TIME	TWO IN ONE
TOP SCORE	TRUE WORD	TWO LUMPS
TOP SPEED	TRY AGAIN	TWO MILES
TOP SPOTS	TRY FOR IT	TWO MINDS
TOP STAIR	TRY IT OUT	TWO PAGES
TOP TABLE	TRY TO SAY	TWO PAIRS
TOP TO TOE	TUCK AWAY	TWO PARTS
TORY GAIN	TUCKED IN	TWO PINTS
TORY LOSS	TUCKED UP	TWO PUTTS
TOSS AWAY	TUCK SHOP	TWO RANKS
TOSSED UP	TUG ALONG	TWO SCORE
TOTAL SUM	TUG OF WAR	TWO SIDES
TOTAL WAR	TURN AWAY	TWO STARS
TOTE A GUN	TURN BACK	TWO TO ONE
TOTE ODDS	TURN BLUE	TWO WEEKS
TO THE BAD	TURN COLD	TWO WIVES
TO THE END	TURN DOWN	TWO WORDS
TO THE TOP	TURNED IN	TWO YARDS
TOT OF RUM	TURNED ON	TWO YEARS
TOTTED UP	TURNED UP	TYPE SIZE
TOTTER UP	TURN GREY	
TOUCH OFF	TURN INTO	**U—8**
TOUGH GUY	TURN IT IN	UGLY FACE
TOUGH JOB	TURN IT ON	UGLY LOOK
TOUGH NUT	TURN IT UP	UGLY MOOD
TOW ALONG	TURN LEFT	UGLY SCAR
TOWN HALL	TURN OVER	UNCLE MAC
TOWN LIFE	TURN PALE	UNCLE SAM
TOWN TALK	TURNS OFF	UNCLE TOM
TOY MAKER	TURN SOFT	UNCUT GEM
TOY SHOPS	TURN SOUR	UNDER AGE
TOY TRAIN	TURNS OUT	UNDER PAR
TRADE GAP	TURN TAIL	UNDER WAY
TRAIL OFF	TURN UPON	UNTIL NOW
TRAIN SET	TWICE ONE	UPAS TREE
TRAM STOP	TWICE SHY	UP AT DAWN
TRAP FIVE	TWICE SIX	UP IN ARMS
TRAP FOUR	TWICE TEN	UP ON HIGH
TRIAL RUN	TWICE TWO	UPON OATH

UPPER AIR	VINE LEAF	WATER RAT
UPPER CUT	VIVA VOCE	WAT TYLER
UPPER JAW	VIVID RED	WAVE AWAY
UPPER LIP	VOTE DOWN	WAVY HAIR
UPPER SET	VOTE TORY	WAVY LINE
UPPER TEN	VOUCH FOR	WAVY NAVY
UP STREAM		WAX MATCH
UP TO DATE	**W—8**	WAX MERRY
UP TO FORM	WADE INTO	WAX MODEL
UP TO TIME	WAGE BILL	WAX VESTA
UP TO TOWN	WAGED WAR	WAY AHEAD
USED CARS	WAIT A BIT	WEAK CASE
USED HALF	WAITED ON	WEAK CHIN
USED TO IT	WAIT HERE	WEAK EYES
USE FORCE	WAIT UPON	WEAK HEAD
USHER OUT	WALK AWAY	WEAK LINK
USHERS IN	WALK BACK	WEAK SIDE
USUAL WAY	WALK DOWN	WEAK SPOT
UTTER CAD	WALK INTO	WEAK WILL
	WALK OVER	WEAR AWAY
V—8	WALK PAST	WEAR DOWN
VAIN HOPE	WALKS OFF	WEARS OFF
VAIN SHOW	WALKS OUT	WEARS OUT
VAST SIZE	WALLED UP	WEAR WELL
VEER AWAY	WALL GAME	WEIGHS UP
VEER LEFT	WALTZ OUT	WELL AWAY
VERA CRUZ	WANGLE IT	WELL DONE
VERA LYNN	WAN SMILE	WELL HELD
VERSED IN	WANT A LOT	WELL MADE
VERY BEST	WANT MORE	WELL OVER
VERY COLD	WAR CRIME	WELL PAID
VERY DEAR	WAR DANCE	WELL READ
VERY FAIR	WARDS OFF	WELL SAID
VERY FULL	WAR FEVER	WELL TO DO
VERY GOOD	WAR HOUSE	WELL UP IN
VERY HARD	WAR LORDS	WELL USED
VERY KEEN	WARMED UP	WELL WELL!
VERY KIND	WARM OVEN	WENT AWAY
VERY LATE	WARM WORK	WENT BACK
VERY MANY	WAR PAINT	WENT DOWN
VERY MUCH	WAR PARTY	WENT EAST
VERY NEAR	WAR POEMS	WENT FREE
VERY NICE	WAR SCARE	WENT OVER
VERY POOR	WART HOGS	WENT WELL
VERY RICH	WAR YEARS	WENT WEST
VERY SLOW	WASH AWAY	WEST DOOR
VERY SOFT	WASH DOWN	WEST SIDE
VERY SOON	WASHED UP	WEST WIND
VERY TRUE	WATCH OUT!	WEST WING
VERY WARM	WATER ICE	WET PAINT
VERY WELL	WATER JUG	WET PLATE

WET SHEET
WET SPELL
WHALE OIL
WHAT A FAG
WHAT IS IT?
WHAT NEXT?
WHAT OF IT?
WHAT'S NEW?
WHEEL OFF
WHEEL OUT
WHICH WAY?
WHIP HAND
WHISK OFF
WHITE ANT
WHITE EGG
WHITE HOT
WHITE KEY
WHITE LIE
WHITE MAN
WHITE SEA
WHITE TIE
WHIT WEEK
WHO DUN IT?
WHOLE HOG
WHOLE LOT
WHO'S NEXT?
WHY WORRY?
WIDE BALL
WIDE BOYS
WIDE FAME
WIDE GULF
WIDE OPEN
WIDE ROAD
WIDE VIEW
WILD BIRD
WILD BLOW
WILD BOAR
WILD DUCK
WILD FOWL
WILD GOAT
WILD LIFE
WILD LOOK
WILD OATS
WILD ROSE
WILD TALK
WILD WEST
WILD WIND
WILY BIRD
WIN A GAME
WIN A RACE
WIND SOCK

WINDY DAY
WINE BARS
WINE GUMS
WINE LIST
WINE SHOP
WING HALF
WIN GLORY
WIN MONEY
WINS OVER
WIPE AWAY
WIPED OUT
WIRE MESH
WISE GUYS
WISE HEAD
WISE MOVE
WITH CARE
WITH EASE
WITH LOVE
WITTY MAN
WOLF CALL
WOLF CUBS
WOOD FIRE
WOOD PULP
WORD GAME
WORKED UP
WORK EVIL
WORK HARD
WORK LATE
WORK OVER
WORKS OFF
WORKS OUT
WORKS WELL
WORLD WAR
WORN DOWN
WRAP IT UP
WRING DRY
WRING OUT
WRITE OFF
WRITE OUT
WRITES UP
WRONG DAY
WRONG MAN
WRONG WAY
WRY SMILE
WYCH ELMS

X—8
X-RAY UNIT

Y—8
YALE LOCK

YEAR BOOK
YEARN FOR
YEARS AGO
YES AND NO
YET AGAIN
YOGI BEAR
YOU AND ME
YOUNG BOY
YOUNG MAN
YOUNG ONE
YOUR CALL
YOUR DEAL
YOUR MOVE
YOUR TURN
YULE LOGS

Z—8
ZANE GREY
ZERO HOUR

A—9
AARON'S ROD
A BIT FISHY
A BIT STEEP
A BIT STIFF
A BIT THICK
ABLE TO FLY
ABLE TO PAY
ABOUT FACE
ABOUT TIME
ABOUT TURN
ABOVE ZERO
ACID REPLY
ACKER BILK
ACT AS HOST
ACTED WELL
ACT FAIRLY
ACTING FOR
ACT OF LOVE
ACT WISELY
ACUTE PAIN
ADAM FAITH
ADAM SMITH
ADAM STYLE
ADAM'S WINE
ADD A RIDER
ADD A TOUCH
ADD COLOUR
ADD FRILLS
ADDLED EGG
AD NAUSEAM

A DOG'S LIFE	ALL THE WAY	ART DEALER
AD VALOREM	ALL THUMBS	ART EDITOR
AEGEAN SEA	ALL TIED UP	ARTIE SHAW
AFTER DARK	ALMA COGAN	ART MASTER
AFTER DUSK	ALMA MATER	ART MUSEUM
AFTER TIME	ALMOND OIL	ART SCHOOL
AGILE MIND	ALMOST ALL	ART STUDIO
A GOOD DEAL	ALPHA PLUS	AS A RESULT
A GOOD MANY	ALPHA RAYS	ASCOT MILE
AGREE WITH	AMPLE ROOM	ASCOT WEEK
AHOY THERE	AMPLE TIME	ASH BLONDE
AIMED HIGH	ANDY PANDY	ASIA MINOR
AIM HIGHER	ANGEL CAKE	ASK ADVICE
AIM TO KILL	ANGEL FACE	ASK A PRICE
AIR BATTLE	ANGEL FISH	ASK NICELY
AIR LETTER	ANGORA CAT	ASK PARDON
AIR LOSSES	ANGRY LOOK	ASK THE WAY
AIR POCKET	ANIMAL CRY	AS ORDERED
AIR TRAVEL	ANIMAL FAT	ASPEN LEAF
ALARM BELL	ANIMAL OIL	AS PER PLAN
ALARM CALL	ANITA LOOS	AS PLANNED
ALEC WAUGH	ANKLE DEEP	AS THEY SAY
ALERT MIND	ANNUAL FEE	AT A CANTER
ALFIE BASS	ANY MOMENT	AT A GALLOP
ALICE BAND	ANY OFFERS?	AT A GLANCE
ALIEN CORN	ANY TO COME	AT A LOW EBB
ALIEN RACE	APPIAN WAY	AT AN ANGLE
ALL ABOARD	APPLE A DAY	AT ANY RATE
ALL ACTION	APPLE CART	AT ANY TIME
ALL ADRIFT	APPLE TART	AT A PROFIT
ALL AGREED	APPLE TREE	AT LEISURE
ALL AROUND	APRIL FOOL	AT LIBERTY
ALL ASHORE	ARAB HORSE	AT LOW TIDE
ALL AT ONCE	ARAB STEED	ATOMIC AGE
ALL BEHIND	ARCH ENEMY	ATOMIC WAR
ALL BLACKS	ARCH KNAVE	AT ONE BLOW
ALL BUT ONE	ARCH ROGUE	AT ONE TIME
ALL CHANGE	ARCH SMILE	AT PRESENT
ALL COMERS	AREA STEPS	AT THE BACK
ALL FOR ONE	ARID WASTE	AT THE BANK
ALL IN VAIN	ARMED BAND	AT THE BEST
ALL IS LOST	ARMS DEPOT	AT THE DOGS
ALL IS WELL	ARMS LOWER	AT THE DOOR
ALL ON DECK	ARMS RAISE	AT THE FAIR
ALL ON EDGE	ARMY BOOTS	AT THE HEAD
ALLOW BAIL	ARMY CADET	AT THE HELM
ALL SAINTS	ARMY CORPS	AT THE MAIN
ALL SERENE	ARMY GROUP	AT THE MOST
ALL SQUARE	ARMY ISSUE	AT THE NETS
ALL THE DAY	ARNOLD BAX	AT THE OVAL
ALL THE LOT	ART CRITIC	AT THE PEAK

AT THE POST
AT THE REAR
AT THE SIDE
AT THE TIME
ATTIC SALT
AUGUR WELL
AU NATUREL
AUNT SALLY
AWAY MATCH
AZURE BLUE

B—9
BABY GRAND
BABY LINEN
BACK AGAIN
BACK ALLEY
BACK BACON
BACKED OUT
BACK OUT OF
BACK PEDAL
BACK SLANG
BACK STAGE
BACK TEETH
BACK TOOTH
BACK WATER
BACK WHEEL
BACON RIND
BAD ADVICE
BAD ATTACK
BAD CREDIT
BAD CUSTOM
BAD DRIVER
BAD ENOUGH
BAD EXCUSE
BAD FIGURE
BAD FOR ONE
BAD FRIEND
BAD HABITS
BAD HEALTH
BAD HUMOUR
BAD INTENT
BADLY DONE
BADLY DOWN
BADLY HURT
BAD MARKET
BAD MEMORY
BAD PLAYER
BAD POINTS
BAD POLICY
BAD RECORD
BAD REPORT

BAD REPUTE
BAD RESULT
BAD REVIEW
BAD SAILOR
BAD SCRAPE
BAD SEAMAN
BAD SECOND
BAD SPIRIT
BAD TEMPER
BAD TIMING
BAG OF GOLD
BAG O' NAILS
BAG THE LOT
BAKE A CAKE
BAKE A LOAF
BAKE BREAD
BALANCE UP
BALD FACTS
BALD PATCH
BALD TRUTH
BALLET FAN
BALLOT BOX
BALSA WOOD
BALTIC SEA
BAND WAGON
BANDY LEGS
BANK CLERK
BANK PAPER
BARE FACTS
BARE FISTS
BARE KNEES
BARE TRUTH
BARE WALLS
BARE WORDS
BARGE INTO
BARLEY MOW
BAR MAGNET
BARN DANCE
BAR OF IRON
BAR OF SOAP
BARROW BOY
BAR THE WAY
BASE METAL
BASIC NEED
BASIC PLAN
BASIC WAGE
BAS RELIEF
BASS NOTES
BASS VOICE
BATH BRICK
BATH NIGHT

BATH SALTS
BATH TOWEL
BATH WATER
BATTLE CRY
BAY LEAVES
BAY WINDOW
BEACH SUIT
BEACH WEAR
BE ADVISED
BE A MARTYR
BE AN ANGEL
BEAR FRUIT
BEARING UP
BEAR RIGHT
BE AT A LOSS
BE AT FAULT
BEAT MUSIC
BEAU GESTE
BEAU IDEAL
BEAU MONDE
BE A YES-MAN
BE CAREFUL
BE CERTAIN
BECOME DUE
BECOME ONE
BEDDED OUT
BED OF PAIN
BED SHEETS
BEECH TREE
BEEF CURRY
BEER MONEY
BEER ON TAP
BEER STAIN
BEET SUGAR
BEFORE ALL
BEFORE NOW
BEFORE TEA
BE FRIENDS
BEGGED OFF
BEG IN VAIN
BEGIN WELL
BEGIN WORK
BEG PARDON
BEL ESPRIT
BELL METAL
BELL TOWER
BELOW COST
BELOW ZERO
BELT ALONG
BEN JONSON
BEN LOMOND

BENNY HILL	BITING WIT	BLOOD CLOT
BE ONE'S AGE	BIT OF A JOB	BLOOD FEUD
BE ONESELF	BIT OF A LAD	BLOOD HEAT
BE ON GUARD	BIT OF LUCK	BLOOD TEST
BE PRESENT	BITTER CUP	BLOOD TYPE
BE PRUDENT	BITTER END	BLOW A FUSE
BERTA RUCK	BLACK ARTS	BLOW ALONG
BERYL GREY	BLACK BALL	BLOWING UP
BERYL REID	BLACK BEAR	BLUE ANGEL
BE SERIOUS	BLACK BELT	BLUE BLOOD
BEST CHINA	BLACK BESS	BLUE CHIPS
BEST DRESS	BLACK BOOK	BLUE GRASS
BEST ENTRY	BLACK FLAG	BLUE JEANS
BEST GRADE	BLACK GOLD	BLUE LIGHT
BEST OF ALL	BLACK HAIR	BLUE PAINT
BEST SCORE	BLACK HAND	BLUE PETER
BEST TASTE	BLACK HOLE	BLUE PRINT
BEST THING	BLACK JACK	BLUE RINSE
BEST VALUE	BLACK KING	BLUE SKIES
BE SWEET ON	BLACK LACE	BLUE SOCKS
BÊTE NOIRE	BLACK LEAD	BLUE STAMP
BE THE BEST	BLACK LION	BLUE STEEL
BETTER MAN	BLACK LIST	BLUE STORY
BETTER OFF	BLACK LOOK	BLUE TRAIN
BETTER 'OLE	BLACK MARK	BLUE WATER
BETWEEN US	BLACK MASS	BLUE WHALE
BEVIN BOYS	BLACK MONK	BLUNT EDGE
BEYOND ONE	BLACK MOOD	BOARD A BUS
BIG BERTHA	BLACK NOTE	BOARDED UP
BIG CHANCE	BLACK OPAL	BOARD GAME
BIG CHEESE	BLACK PAWN	BOARD ROOM
BIG DEMAND	BLACK ROOK	BOAR'S HEAD
BIG DIPPER	BLACK RUIN	BOAT DRILL
BIG EFFORT	BLACK SPOT	BOAT TRAIN
BIG FREEZE	BLACK SUIT	BOB SAWYER
BIG HEADED	BLACK SWAN	BODY OF MEN
BIG MARGIN	BLANK FILE	BOIL AN EGG
BIG PROFIT	BLANK LOOK	BOILED EGG
BIG TALKER	BLANK MIND	BOILED HAM
BILL SIKES	BLANK PAGE	BOLD FRONT
BILLY FURY	BLANK WALL	BOLD LINES
BILLY GOAT	BLAZE AWAY	BOLD PRINT
BILLY LIAR	BLIND DATE	BOLSTER UP
BINGO CLUB	BLIND ROAD	BONA FIDES
BINGO HALL	BLIND SIDE	BON CHANCE
BIRCH TREE	BLIND SPOT	BONE CHINA
BIRD BRAIN	BLOCK PERM	BON MARCHÉ
BIRD'S NEST	BLOCK VOTE	BON VIVANT
BIRTH MARK	BLOND HAIR	BON VIVEUR
BIRTH RATE	BLOOD BANK	BON VOYAGE
BITE TO EAT	BLOOD BATH	BOOK A ROOM

BOOK A SEAT
BOOK LOVER
BOOK OF JOB
BOOK SEATS
BOOK STORE
BOOK TITLE
BOOK TOKEN
BORE A HOLE
BORN ACTOR
BORN AGAIN
BORN ALIVE
BORN MIMIC
BORN MIXER
BORN SLAVE
BOTANY BAY
BOTH HANDS
BOTH SIDES
BOTTOM DOG
BOTTOMS UP
BOUGHT OFF
BOUGHT OUT
BOUNCE OUT
BOUND BOOK
BOUND OVER
BOWED DOWN
BOWED HEAD
BOWL ALONG
BOWLED OUT
BOWLER HAT
BOW STREET
BOW TO FATE
BOW WINDOW
BOX AND COX
BOX CAMERA
BOX CLEVER
BOXING DAY
BOX NUMBER
BOX OFFICE
BOX OF FIGS
BOY FRIEND
BOYLE'S LAW
BRAIN WAVE
BRAKE DRUM
BRANCH OFF
BRANCH OUT
BRASS BALL
BRASS BAND
BRASS RING
BRASS TACK
BRAVE DEED
BRAVE FACE

BRAZEN OUT
BRAZIL NUT
BREAD LINE
BREAD ROLL
BREAK A LEG
BREAK AWAY
BREAK BACK
BREAK BAIL
BREAK CAMP
BREAK DOWN
BREAK EVEN
BREAK IT UP
BREAK JAIL
BREAK OPEN
BREAK STEP
BREATHE IN
BRENDA LEE
BRET HARTE
BRIAR PIPE
BRICK WALL
BRIDAL BED
BRIDE TO BE
BRIGHT BOY
BRIGHT LAD
BRIGHT RED
BRING BACK
BRING DOWN
BRING HOME
BRING OVER
BRING WORD
BRISK WALK
BRISTLE UP
BROAD BACK
BROAD BEAM
BROAD BEAN
BROAD GRIN
BROAD HINT
BROAD JOKE
BROAD MIND
BROAD VIEW
BROKEN ARM
BROKEN LEG
BROKEN MAN
BROKEN RIB
BROKEN SET
BROKE OPEN
BRONZE AGE
BROOD MARE
BROODY HEN
BROUGHT UP
BROWN BEAR

BROWN BESS
BROWN COAL
BROWN EYES
BROWN HAIR
BROWN LOAF
BROWN STEW
BROWN SUIT
BRUSH AWAY
BRUSHED UP
BRUSH DOWN
BRUSH OVER
BRUSH PAST
BUBBLE CAR
BUBBLE GUM
BUCK TEETH
BUDGET DAY
BUGLE CALL
BULLY BEEF
BUMBLE BEE
BUMPED OFF
BURKE'S LAW
BURMA ROAD
BURMA STAR
BURN A HOLE
BURN ALIVE
BURNT CORK
BURNT DOWN
BURST-OPEN
BURST PIPE
BURST TYRE
BUS DRIVER
BUSH HOUSE
BUSH SHIRT
BUS STRIKE
BUS TICKET
BUSY PLACE
BUY A HOUSE
BUY A ROUND
BUY ON TICK
BUY SHARES
BUZZ ABOUT
BUZZ ALONG
BY ACCLAIM
BY AIR MAIL
BY AUCTION
BY COMMAND
BY CONSENT
BY DEFAULT
BY DEGREES
BY HEARSAY
BY HERSELF

BY HIMSELF	CARPET BAG	CHEAP LINE
BY NO MEANS	CARRIED ON	CHEAP MILK
BY NUMBERS	CARRY AWAY	CHEAP RATE
BY ONESELF	CARRY OVER	CHEAP TRIP
BY REQUEST	CARRY SAIL	CHEAP WINE
BY STEALTH	CAR TRIALS	CHECK MATE
BY THE ACRE	CAR WINDOW	CHECK OVER
BY THE BOOK	CARY GRANT	CHEERED UP
BY THE HOUR	CASHEW NUT	CHERRY PIE
BY THE NOSE	CASH PRICE	CHESS CLUB
BY THE YARD	CASH PRIZE	CHIEF COOK
BY THUNDER	CASH TERMS	CHIEF HOPE
	CAST ABOUT	CHIEF MEAL
C—9	CAST A LOOK	CHIEF PART
CAB DRIVER	CAST AN EYE	CHIEF PORT
CADDIE CAR	CAST A SHOE	CHIEF WHIP
CAFÉ ROYAL	CAST A SHOW	CHILD CARE
CALF'S HEAD	CAST ASIDE	CHILD STAR
CALL AGAIN	CAST A SLUR	CHILD WIFE
CALL A HALT	CAST A VOTE	CHINA CLAY
CALL A TAXI	CAST DOUBT	CHINA DOLL
CALLED FOR	CAST FORTH	CHINA ROSE
CALLED OFF	CAST LOOSE	CHINA SHOP
CALLED OUT	CASTOR OIL	CHIPPED IN
CALL FORTH	CAT AND DOG	CHOICE BIT
CALL HEADS	CATCH A BUS	CHOKE BACK
CALL IT OFF	CATCH COLD	CHOKE DAMP
CALL TAILS	CATCH FIRE	CHOKE DOWN
CALM CHEEK	CATCH FISH	CHOP HOUSE
CAME APART	CAT FAMILY	CHOPPY SEA
CAME LOOSE	CATTLE PEN	CHOSEN FEW
CAMERA SHY	CAUGHT OUT	CHUMP CHOP
CAMPED OUT	CAUSE LIST	CIRCUS ACT
CANAL BANK	CAUSE PAIN	CITY GATES
CANAL TURN	CEASE FIRE	CITY STATE
CANAL ZONE	CEASE TO BE	CIVIC DUTY
CANCEL OUT	CEASE WORK	CIVIL CASE
CANE CHAIR	CEDAR TREE	CIVIL CODE
CANE SUGAR	CEYLON TEA	CIVIL LIFE
CANNY SCOT	CHA CHA CHA	CIVIL LIST
CAN OF BEER	CHAIN DOWN	CIVIL SUIT
CAPE DUTCH	CHAIN GANG	CLAIM BACK
CAPE WRATH	CHAIN MAIL	CLAMP DOWN
CAP IN HAND	CHALKED UP	CLAP HANDS
CARD INDEX	CHALK FARM	CLARA BUTT
CARD PARTY	CHALK IT UP	CLARET CUP
CARD SENSE	CHANCE HIT	CLASH WITH
CARD TABLE	CHASE AWAY	CLEAN BILL
CARD TRICK	CHEAP FARE	CLEAN BLOW
CARGO SHIP	CHEAP GIFT	CLEAN DOWN
CAROL REED	CHEAP JACK	CLEANED UP

CLEAN LIFE	COIN MONEY	CONJURE UP
CLEAR AWAY	COLD AS ICE	COOL CHEEK
CLEAR CASE	COLD BLOOD	COOL DRINK
CLEARED UP	COLD CREAM	COOLED OFF
CLEAR HEAD	COLD DRINK	COOL WATER
CLEAR LEAD	COLD FRAME	COPIED OUT
CLEAR MIND	COLD FRONT	COPPER AGE
CLEAR NOTE	COLD HANDS	CORAL REEF
CLEAR ROAD	COLD HEART	CORDON OFF
CLEAR SOUP	COLD JOINT	CORNY JOKE
CLEAR VIEW	COLD NIGHT	COSMIC RAY
CLEVER DOG	COLD PLATE	COST PRICE
CLEVER MAN	COLD SCENT	COUGHED UP
CLIMB DOWN	COLD SNACK	COUNT DOWN
CLIMB OVER	COLD SOBER	COUNT UPON
CLIP JOINT	COLD SPELL	COUP D'ÉTAT
CLOCHE HAT	COLD STEEL	COURT CARD
CLOCKED IN	COLD SWEAT	COURT CASE
CLOCK GOLF	COLD WATER	COVERED UP
CLOG DANCE	COLLIE DOG	COVER GIRL
CLOSE CALL	COLOUR BAR	COVER OVER
CLOSE COPY	COLWYN BAY	COWES WEEK
CLOSE CROP	COME ABOUT	CRAB SALAD
CLOSED CAR	COME AFTER	CRACK A NUT
CLOSE DOWN	COME ALIVE	CRACKED UP
CLOSE GAME	COME ALONG	CRACK OPEN
CLOSE LOOK	COME AND GO	CRACK SHOT
CLOSE RACE	COME APART	CRASH DOWN
CLOSE UPON	COME CLEAN	CRAZY GANG
CLOSING IN	COME CLOSE	CREAM CAKE
CLOTH EARS	COME EARLY	CREAM PUFF
CLOTH FAIR	COME FIRST	CREEP AWAY
CLOUD OVER	COME FORTH	CRESTA RUN
CLOUDY SKY	COME LOOSE	CRIED DOWN
CLUB MONEY	COME OF AGE	CRIED WOLF
CLUB NIGHT	COME OFF IT	CRIME WAVE
COACH TOUR	COME RIGHT	CROPPED UP
COACH TRIP	COME ROUND	CROSS FIRE
COAL BLACK	COME THIRD	CROSS KEYS
COAL BOARD	COME UNDER	CROSS OVER
COAL FIELD	COMIC CUTS	CROSS WIND
COAL TRUCK	COMIC MASK	CROUCH END
COAST ROAD	COMIC MUSE	CROUCH LOW
COCKED HAT	COMIC SONG	CROWD WORK
COCK ROBIN	COMING MAN	CROWN CORK
COCOA BEAN	COMING OUT	CROWN LAND
CODE OF LAW	COMMON END	CROW'S FEET
COFFEE BAR	COMMON LAW	CROW'S NEST
COFFEE CUP	COMMON LOT	CRUDE JOKE
COFFEE POT	COMMON MAN	CRUDE SALT
COIN A WORD	CONGER EEL	CRUEL BLOW

CRUEL FATE	DANNY KAYE	DECK GAMES
CRUMPLE UP	DARK BLUES	DECOY DUCK
CRUSH DOWN	DARK BROWN	DEEP GRIEF
CRY FOR JOY	DARK CLOUD	DEEP RIVER
CUBAN HEEL	DARK DEEDS	DEEP SLEEP
CUBE SUGAR	DARK DRESS	DEEP SOUTH
CUBIC FOOT	DARK GREEN	DEEP VOICE
CUBIC INCH	DARK HORSE	DEEP WATER
CUBIC YARD	DARK NIGHT	DEMON KING
CUB MASTER	DARTED OUT	DEN OF VICE
CUFF LINKS	DARTS TEAM	DEPOT ONLY
CUPID'S BOW	DASHED OFF	DEPOT SHIP
CUP OF MILK	DASHED OUT	DE QUINCEY
CURIO SHOP	DATE STAMP	DEREK BOND
CURTAIN UP	DATUM LINE	DEREK HART
CURTIS CUP	DAVY JONES	DE RIGUEUR
CURLY HAIR	DAWN OF DAY	DESERT AIR
CURLY KALE	DAY BEFORE	DESERT RAT
CUT A CAPER	DAY IS DONE	DEVIL'S OWN
CUT ACROSS	DAY OF DOOM	DIANA DORS
CUT ADRIFT	DAY OF REST	DIESEL OIL
CUT AND RUN	DAY SCHOOL	DIET SHEET
CUT A TOOTH	DAYS OF OLD	DIG DEEPLY
CUT CAPERS	DEAD AHEAD	DIME NOVEL
CUT IN HALF	DEAD DRUNK	DIM MEMORY
CUT IT FINE	DEAD FAINT	DINING CAR
CUTTING IN	DEAD LUCKY	DINING OUT
CUTTY SARK	DEADLY SIN	DINNER SET
CUT UP WELL	DEAD MARCH	DIRECT HIT
CYCLE TOUR	DEAD QUIET	DIRECT TAX
	DEAD RIGHT	DIRT CHEAP
D—9	DEAD SLEEP	DIRT TRACK
DAILY HELP	DEAD SOBER	DIRTY DICK
DAILY MAIL	DEAD TIRED	DIRTY LOOK
DAILY WORK	DEAD WATER	DIRTY PLAY
DAIRY FARM	DEAD WRONG	DIRTY WORD
DAIRY HERD	DEAL A BLOW	DIRTY WORK
DAIRY MAID	DEAL TABLE	DISH CLOUT
DAISY BELL	DEAN SWIFT	DISHED OUT
DALAI LAMA	DEAR ENEMY	DISH OF TEA
DAMP PATCH	DEAR HEART	DIXIE LAND
DAMP SQUIB	DEAR MADAM	DO A BAD JOB
DAMSON JAM	DEATH BLOW	DO A FAVOUR
DAN ARCHER	DEATH CELL	DO AS ASKED
DANCE A JIG	DEATH DUTY	DOCK BRIEF
DANCE AWAY	DEATH MASK	DOCK GREEN
DANCE BAND	DEATH RATE	DOCTOR WHO
DANCE HALL	DEATH ROLL	DODGE CITY
DANCE STEP	DEATH TRAP	DOG COLLAR
DANCE TUNE	DEATH WISH	DOG EAT DOG
DANDY DICK	DEBIT SIDE	DOG KENNEL

DOG RACING	DO YOU MIND?	DROPPED IN
DOGS OF WAR	DOZEN EGGS	DROP SHORT
DOG'S TOOTH	DRAIN AWAY	DRUG FIEND
DOING FINE	DRAW A BEAD	DRUG HABIT
DOING GOOD	DRAW A LINE	DRUG STORE
DOING TIME	DRAW APART	DRUM MAJOR
DOING WELL	DRAW A VEIL	DRURY LANE
DO IT AGAIN	DRAW BLANK	DRY AS DUST
DO JUSTICE	DRAW BLOOD	DRY GINGER
DOLLAR GAP	DRAW FORTH	DRY HUMOUR
DOLL'S PRAM	DRAW LEVEL	DRY REMARK
DONE BROWN	DRAW MONEY	DRY SEASON
DONE THING	DRAWN FACE	DRY SHERRY
DO NOTHING	DRAWN GAME	DRY SUMMER
DON'T WORRY	DRAW TEARS	DRY WICKET
DO ONE DOWN	DRAW TIGHT	DUBLIN BAY
DO ONE'S BIT	DRAW WATER	DUD CHEQUE
DOPE FIEND	DRAY HORSE	DUDE RANCH
DO PENANCE	DREAM BOAT	DUE NOTICE
DORA BRYAN	DREAM GIRL	DUE REWARD
DO REPAIRS	DREAM LAND	DULL LIGHT
DORSAL FIN	DRESS COAT	DULL SOUND
DO THE DEED	DRESS DOWN	DU MAURIER
DO THE TOWN	DRESSED UP	DUNCE'S CAP
DO TO DEATH	DRESS RING	DUST STORM
DOUBLE ACT	DRESS SHOW	DUSTY ROAD
DOUBLE BED	DRESS SUIT	DUTCH BARN
DOUBLED UP	DRESS WELL	DUTCH DOLL
DOUBLE GIN	DRIED EGGS	DUTCH OVEN
DOUBLE ONE	DRIED FIGS	DUTCH WIFE
DOUBLE ROW	DRIED MILK	DUTY BOUND
DOUBLE RUM	DRIED PEAS	DUTY CALLS
DOUBLE SIX	DRIFT AWAY	DUTY FIRST
DOUBLE TEN	DRILL HALL	DUTY NURSE
DOUBLE TOP	DRINK DEEP	DWARF BEAN
DOUBLE TWO	DRIVE A BUS	DWELL UPON
DOVER ROAD	DRIVE A CAR	DYING DOWN
DOVER SOLE	DRIVE AWAY	DYING DUCK
DO WITHOUT	DRIVE BACK	DYING RACE
DOWN BELOW	DRIVE HARD	DYING SWAN
DOWN GRADE	DRIVE HOME	DYING TO GO
DOWN IN ONE	DRIVEN MAD	DYING WISH
DOWN IN TWO	DRIVE PAST	DYING YEAR
DOWN QUILT	DR. JOHNSON	
DOWN RIVER	DR. KILDARE	E—9
DOWN SOUTH	DROP A BOMB	EACH OF TWO
DOWN STAGE	DROP A HINT	EACH OTHER
DOWN THERE	DROP A LINE	EARLY BIRD
DOWN TOOLS	DROP A NOTE	EARLY CALL
DOWN TRAIN	DROP OF GIN	EARLY DAYS
DOWN UNDER	DROP OF TEA	EARLY DOOR

EARLY HOUR
EARLY LIFE
EARLY PART
EARLY WORM
EARN A NAME
EARN MONEY
EAR OF CORN
EASILY LED
EAST COAST
EASTER DAY
EASTER EGG
EASTER EVE
EAST INDIA
EAST LYNNE
EAST SHEEN
EASY AS PIE
EASY CATCH
EASY DEATH
EASY FIRST
EASY GOING
EASY MONEY
EASY PITCH
EASY TERMS
EASY THING
EASY TIMES
EASY TO RUN
EASY TO SEE
EATEN AWAY
EATING OUT
EAT NO MEAT
EDGED TOOL
EDGE ROUND
EDGE TOOLS
EIGHT DAYS
EIGHT DEEP
EIGHT FEET
EIGHTH DAY
EIGHTH MAN
EIGHTH ROW
EIGHTH TEE
EIGHT QUID
EITHER WAY
EL ALAMEIN
ELBOW ROOM
ELDER WINE
ELDEST SON
ELEVEN MEN
ELMER RICE
EMBER DAYS
EMILE ZOLA
EMIT WAVES

EMPIRE DAY
EMPTY LIFE
EMPTY ROOM
EMPTY SEAT
EMPTY SHOW
EMPTY TALK
EMPTY TANK
END IN GAOL
END IN VIEW
END OF PLAY
END OF TERM
END OF TIME
ENEMY FIRE
EN FAMILLE
ENJOY LIFE
EN PASSANT
EN PENSION
EN RAPPORT
ENTER INTO
ENTRE NOUS
ENTRY CARD
ENTRY FORM
EPIC VERSE
EQUAL RANK
ERIC SYKES
ERRAND BOY
ESKIMO DOG
ESTATE CAR
ET TU BRUTE
EVA BARTOK
EVEN MONEY
EVEN SCORE
EVEN TENOR
EVER AFTER
EVER SINCE
EVERY HOUR
EVERY INCH
EVERY SIDE
EVERY TIME
EVERY WEEK
EVERY WORD
EVERY YEAR
EXACT COPY
EXACT FARE
EXACT TIME
EXIT OMNES
EX OFFICIO
EXTRA COPY
EXTRA FOOD
EXTRA GOOD
EXTRA HELP

EXTRA ROOM
EXTRA SEAT
EXTRA TIME
EXTRA WORK
EYE APPEAL
EYE LOTION
EYE MAKE-UP
EYES FRONT
EYES RIGHT
EYE STRAIN
EZRA POUND

F—9
FACE ABOUT
FACE CREAM
FACE DEATH
FACE FACTS
FACE IT OUT
FACE NORTH
FACE SOUTH
FACE TOWEL
FACE VALUE
FADING OUT
FAGGED OUT
FAIL TO ACT
FAIL TO SEE
FAIL TO WIN
FAINT HOPE
FAINT LINE
FAIR BREAK
FAIR FIELD
FAIR FIGHT
FAIR JUDGE
FAIRLY NEW
FAIR OFFER
FAIR PRICE
FAIR'S FAIR
FAIR SHARE
FAIR START
FAIR TRADE
FAIR TRIAL
FAIR VALUE
FAIR WORDS
FAIRY CAKE
FAIRY DOLL
FAIRY FOLK
FAIRY KING
FAIRY RING
FAIRY TALE
FAIRY WAND

FAITH CURE	FATAL URGE	FIGURE TWO
FAKE ALIBI	FAT CATTLE	FILE A SUIT
FALL AMONG	FAT CHANCE	FILM ACTOR
FALL APART	FAT PROFIT	FILM EXTRA
FALLEN OUT	FEED A COLD	FILM STILL
FALL FOR IT	FEEL A NEED	FILM STUNT
FALL OF MAN	FEEL ANGRY	FILTER TIP
FALL SHORT	FEEL CHEAP	FINAL BOUT
FALL UNDER	FEEL FAINT	FINAL HEAT
FALSE CARD	FEEL FRESH	FINAL HOPE
FALSE CASE	FEEL FUNNY	FINAL MOVE
FALSE COIN	FEEL GIDDY	FINALS DAY
FALSE GODS	FEEL GREAT	FINAL STEP
FALSE HAIR	FEEL HAPPY	FINAL TEST
FALSE IDEA	FEEL QUEER	FIND A CLUE
FALSE MOVE	FEEL RIGHT	FIND A FLAT
FALSE NAME	FEEL SEEDY	FIND A HOME
FALSE NOSE	FEEL SHAME	FIND A WIFE
FALSE NOTE	FEEL SMALL	FIND FAULT
FALSE OATH	FEEL SORRY	FIND MEANS
FALSE PLEA	FEE SIMPLE	FIND PEACE
FALSE STEP	FEET APART	FIND WORDS
FAMILY CAR	FEET FIRST	FINE BIRDS
FAMILY MAN	FELL APART	FINE BLADE
FAMILY PEW	FELT A FOOL	FINE GRAIN
FAMILY ROW	FELT SILLY	FINE LINEN
FAMOUS MAN	FEMALE SEX	FINE POINT
FANCY CAKE	FEMME SOLE	FINE SPORT
FANCY FREE	FENCED OUT	FINE SPRAY
FANCY WORK	FERRET OUT	FINE TIMES
FAN DANCER	FERRY OVER	FINE TOUCH
FANNED OUT	FEUDAL LAW	FINE VOICE
FANNY HILL	FEUDAL TAX	FINE WOMAN
FAR AFIELD	FEVER HEAT	FINISH OFF
FAR BEHIND	FIELD ARMY	FIRE ALARM
FAR BETTER	FIELD GREY	FIRE A SHOT
FAR BEYOND	FIELD TEST	FIRE AT SEA
FAR CORNER	FIFTH FORM	FIRE DRILL
FAR ENOUGH	FIFTH HOLE	FIRE POWER
FARE STAGE	FIFTH PART	FIRM BASIS
FAR FROM IT	FIFTH RACE	FIRM FAITH
FARMED OUT	FIFTH TEST	FIRM GOING
FARM HORSE	FIFTH TIME	FIRM OFFER
FARTHER UP	FIFTY QUID	FIRM PRICE
FAR TOO FEW	FIGHT BACK	FIRM STAND
FAST TRAIN	FIGHT FAIR	FIRST ARMY
FAST WOMAN	FIGHT WITH	FIRST BALL
FATAL BLOW	FIG LEAVES	FIRST BASE
FATAL DOSE	FIGURE ONE	FIRST BELL
FATAL HOUR	FIGURE OUT	FIRST BLOW
FATAL MOVE	FIGURE TEN	FIRST COAT

FIRST COME	FIT TO DROP	FLYING FOX
FIRST COPY	FIVE CARDS	FLYING LOW
FIRST COST	FIVE CLUBS	FLYING MAN
FIRST CROP	FIVE DOZEN	FLY TO ARMS
FIRST FOOT	FIVE GROSS	FOBBED OFF
FIRST FORM	FIVE HOLES	FOG SIGNAL
FIRST GEAR	FIVE HOURS	FOLK DANCE
FIRST HALF	FIVE LUMPS	FOLK MUSIC
FIRST HAND	FIVE MILES	FOLLOW OUT
FIRST HEAT	FIVE OR SIX	FOOD STORE
FIRST HOLE	FIVE PARTS	FOOD VALUE
FIRST HOME	FIVE PINTS	FOOL ABOUT
FIRST LADY	FIVE SCORE	FOOL'S MATE
FIRST LEAD	FIVE TIMES	FOOT FAULT
FIRST LINE	FIVE TO ONE	FORAGE CAP
FIRST LORD	FIVE TO TEN	FOR A START
FIRST LOVE	FIVE TO TWO	FOR A WHILE
FIRST MATE	FIVE TOWNS	FORCE OPEN
FIRST MEAL	FIVE WEEKS	FOR EFFECT
FIRST MOVE	FIVE YEARS	FOREST LAW
FIRST NAME	FIX A PRICE	FOR EXPORT
FIRST PAGE	FIXED GAZE	FORKED OUT
FIRST PART	FIXED IDEA	FORK LUNCH
FIRST POST	FIXED LOOK	FORM A CORE
FIRST RACE	FIXED ODDS	FORMAL BOW
FIRST RATE	FIXED STAR	FORM A RING
FIRST SHOT	FIXED TIME	FORM FOURS
FIRST SIGN	FIXED TYPE	FOR MY PART
FIRST SLIP	FIXED WAYS	FORTY DAYS
FIRST STEP	FIZZLE OUT	FORTY LOVE
FIRST TEAM	FLAKED OUT	FOR VALOUR
FIRST TERM	FLARE PATH	FOSTER SON
FIRST TEST	FLASH BULB	FOUL CRIME
FIRST TIME	FLAT BROKE	FOUL FIEND
FIRST TO GO	FLAT TO LET	FOUL SMELL
FIRST TURN	FLAY ALIVE	FOUL THROW
FIRST WORD	FLESH PINK	FOUR AWAYS
FIRST YEAR	FLESH TINT	FOUR BY TWO
FISHED OUT	FLICK AWAY	FOUR CARDS
FISH KNIFE	FLING AWAY	FOUR CLUBS
FISH PASTE	FLING DOWN	FOUR DOZEN
FISH SLICE	FLING OPEN	FOUR FIVES
FISH STEAK	FLIRT WITH	FOUR FOURS
FISHY EYED	FLIT ABOUT	FOUR GROSS
FISHY LOOK	FLOAT DOWN	FOUR HOLES
FISHY TALE	FLOOD TIDE	FOUR HOURS
FIT FOR USE	FLOOR PLAN	FOUR IN ONE
FIT OF RAGE	FLOOR SHOW	FOUR JACKS
FIT PERSON	FLOUR MILL	FOUR KINGS
FITTED OUT	FLOW OF WIT	FOUR LUMPS
FIT TO BUST	FLY AT ZERO	FOUR MILES

FOUR NINES	FRESH FOOD	FULL SCORE
FOUR PAIRS	FRESH LOAF	FULL SKIRT
FOUR PARTS	FRESH MEAT	FULL SPEED
FOUR PINTS	FRESH MILK	FULL STEAM
FOUR SCORE	FRESH NEWS	FULL STORY
FOUR SIDES	FRESH PEAS	FULL SWING
FOUR SIXES	FRESH ROLL	FULL TABLE
FOURTH DAY	FRESH WIND	FULL TITLE
FOURTH ROW	FRIAR TUCK	FULL VALUE
FOURTH SET	FRIED FISH	FULLY CLAD
FOURTH TEE	FRIED FOOD	FULLY PAID
FOUR TIMES	FRIED RICE	FULLY RIPE
FOUR TO ONE	FRIGID BOW	FUND OF WIT
FOUR WEEKS	FROCK COAT	FUNNY BONE
FOUR WINDS	FROM BELOW	FUNNY FACE
FOUR YEARS	FROM BIRTH	FUNNY FILM
FRANK MUIR	FROM NOW ON	FUNNY HA-HA
FRANS HALS	FRONT DOOR	FUNNY IDEA
FRED EMNEY	FRONT LINE	FUNNY JOKE
FRED KARNO	FRONT PAGE	FUNNY LIFE
FRED PERRY	FRONT RANK	FUNNY TIME
FREE AGENT	FRONT ROOM	FUN PALACE
FREE AS AIR	FRONT SEAT	FUR COLLAR
FREE BOARD	FRONT STEP	FUR GLOVES
FREE CHINA	FRONT STUD	FUR LINING
FREE DRINK	FRONT VIEW	FUR MARKET
FREE ENTRY	FROWN DOWN	FURTHER ON
FREE FIELD	FROWN UPON	FURTHER UP
FREE FIGHT	FROZEN SEA	FUR TRADER
FREE HOUSE	FRUIT BOWL	
FREE LUNCH	FRUIT CAKE	**G—9**
FREE OFFER	FRUIT TART	GAG WRITER
FREE OF TAX	FRUIT TREE	GAIN POWER
FREE PLACE	FULL BLAST	GALA DRESS
FREE PRESS	FULL BLOOM	GALA NIGHT
FREE RANGE	FULL BOARD	GALE FORCE
FREE SCOPE	FULL COVER	GALLOP OFF
FREE SPACE	FULL DRESS	GALWAY BAY
FREE STATE	FULL GLASS	GAME CHIPS
FREE STYLE	FULL GROWN	GAMES ROOM
FREE TRADE	FULL HEART	GAMING ACT
FREE UNION	FULL HOUSE	GAMMA RAYS
FREE VERSE	FULL MARKS	GANG AGLEY
FREE WHEEL	FULL OF FUN	GARDEN BED
FREE WORLD	FULL OF JOY	GAS ATTACK
FREEZE OUT	FULL OF PEP	GAS COOKER
FRESH BAIT	FULL OF WOE	GAS ENGINE
FRESH EGGS	FULL PITCH	GAS ESCAPE
FRESHEN UP	FULL PURSE	GAS HEATER
FRESH FACE	FULL QUOTA	GAS MANTLE
FRESH FISH	FULL SCOPE	GATE HOUSE

GATE MONEY	GIVEN TIME	GO FLAT OUT
GATHER WAY	GIVE PAUSE	GO FOR A CAB
GAVE CHASE	GIVE PLACE	GO FOR A DIP
GAY REVELS	GIVE TERMS	GO FOR A RUN
GENE AUTRY	GIVE VOICE	GO FOR HELP
GENOA CAKE	GIVING OUT	GO FORWARD
GENTLE SEX	GIVING WAY	GO HALF-WAY
GEORGE FOX	GLANCE OFF	GO HAYWIRE
GET A CHILL	GLASS CASE	GO HUNTING
GET ACROSS	GLASS TUBE	GO INDOORS
GET AROUND	GLASS VASE	GO IN FRONT
GET A START	GLIDE AWAY	GOING AWAY
GET BEHIND	GLOAT OVER	GOING BACK
GET BETTER	GLOBAL WAR	GOING BALD
GET CREDIT	GLOOMY DAY	GOING DOWN
GET KILLED	GLORY HOLE	GOING GREY
GET MOVING	GLOSS OVER	GOING HOME
GET THE PIP	GNAW IN TWO	GOING OVER
GETTING ON	GO AGAINST	GOING SLOW
GETTING UP	GO A-MAYING	GOING WELL
GET TO HEAR	GO AND LOOK	GOING WEST
GET TO KNOW	GOAT'S HAIR	GO IN ORBIT
GET UP LATE	GOAT'S MILK	GO IT ALONE
GET WIND OF	GO BEGGING	GOLD BRAID
GET WITH IT	GO BERSERK	GOLD BRICK
GHOST TOWN	GO BETWEEN	GOLD CHAIN
GIDDY GOAT	GO BOATING	GOLD COAST
GIFTED MAN	GO BY COACH	GOLDEN AGE
GIFT HORSE	GO BY PLANE	GOLDEN BOY
GIFT TOKEN	GO BY TRAIN	GOLDEN EGG
GIN AND PEP	GO BY WATER	GOLDEN KEY
GIN BOTTLE	GO DANCING	GOLDEN ROD
GINGER ALE	GOD FORBID	GOLD FEVER
GINGER CAT	GOD OF FIRE	GOLD INGOT
GINGER POP	GOD OF LOVE	GOLD MEDAL
GINGER TOM	GOD OF WINE	GOLD MINER
GIN PALACE	GOD'S IMAGE	GOLD PAINT
GIPSY LOVE	GOD'S TRUTH	GOLD PLATE
GIPSY MOTH	GOES ABOUT	GOLD TOOTH
GIRL GUIDE	GOES AFTER	GOLD WATCH
GIRLS' HOME	GOES AHEAD	GOLF LINKS
GIVE A HAND	GOES BELOW	GOLF MATCH
GIVE A HINT	GOES IN FOR	GOLF WIDOW
GIVE A LEAD	GOES ROUND	GONE TO BED
GIVE A LIFT	GOES TO BED	GONE TO POT
GIVE A TALK	GOES TO POT	GONE UNDER
GIVE BIRTH	GOES TO SEA	GOOD ACTOR
GIVE CHASE	GOES TO SEE	GOOD ALIBI
GIVE EAR TO	GOES UNDER	GOOD ANGEL
GIVE FORTH	GOES WRONG	GOOD BOOKS
GIVEN NAME	GO FISHING	GOOD CATCH

GOOD CAUSE	GOOD SPEED	GRAND TIME
GOOD CHEER	GOOD SPORT	GRAND TOUR
GOOD CLASS	GOOD START	GRAND VIEW
GOOD DEBTS	GOOD STATE	GRASS PLOT
GOOD DODGE	GOOD STOCK	GRAVEL PIT
GOOD EATER	GOOD STORY	GRAVE NEWS
GOOD FAIRY	GOOD STUFF	GRAVE NOTE
GOOD FAITH	GOOD TABLE	GREAT AUNT
GOOD FAULT	GOOD TASTE	GREAT BEAR
GOOD FIELD	GOOD TERMS	GREAT BLOW
GOOD FIGHT	GOOD THING	GREAT CARE
GOOD GOING	GOOD TIMES	GREAT DANE
GOOD GRACE	GOOD TO EAT	GREAT DEAL
GOOD GRIEF	GOOD TONIC	GREAT DEED
GOOD GUESS	GOOD TO SEE	GREAT DRAW
GOOD GUIDE	GOOD TRADE	GREAT FAME
GOOD HABIT	GOOD USAGE	GREAT FEAT
GOOD HANDS	GOOD VALUE	GREAT FIRE
GOOD HEART	GOOD VOICE	GREAT FOLK
GOOD HOTEL	GOOD WAGES	GREAT GAIN
GOOD HOURS	GOOD WOMAN	GREAT GUNS
GOOD HOUSE	GOOD WORKS	GREAT HALL
GOOD IMAGE	GOOD YIELD	GREAT HELP
GOOD JUDGE	GO OFF DUTY	GREAT IDEA
GOOD LAYER	GO ON A DIET	GREAT LIFE
GOOD LIGHT	GO ON AND ON	GREAT LOSS
GOOD LINES	GO ON BOARD	GREAT MANY
GOOD LIVER	GO ONE'S WAY	GREAT MIND
GOOD LOOKS	GO ON LEAVE	GREAT NAME
GOOD LOSER	GOOSE FAIR	GREAT NEWS
GOOD LUNCH	GO OUTSIDE	GREAT PAIN
GOOD LUNGS	GO QUIETLY	GREAT PITY
GOOD MARKS	GO SAILING	GREAT SCOT
GOOD MATCH	GO SKATING	GREAT SEAL
GOOD MIXER	GO THE PACE	GREAT SHIP
GOOD MONEY	GO THROUGH	GREAT TIME
GOOD MUSIC	GO TO EARTH	GREEDY PIG
GOOD NIGHT	GO TO GLORY	GREEK CITY
GOOD ODOUR	GO TO GRASS	GREEK FIRE
GOOD OFFER	GO TO HADES	GREEK FLAG
GOOD ORDER	GO TO PRESS	GREEK GIFT
GOOD PATCH	GO TO SLEEP	GREEK MYTH
GOOD POINT	GO TOWARDS	GREEK PLAY
GOOD PRICE	GO TO WASTE	GREEN BELT
GOOD REPLY	GO WITHOUT	GREEN EYES
GOOD SCORE	GRACE NOTE	GREEN FEES
GOOD SENSE	GRAND DUKE	GREEN FIGS
GOOD SHAPE	GRAND JURY	GREEN FLAG
GOOD SHAVE	GRAND LAMA	GREEN HILL
GOOD SIGHT	GRAND PRIX	GREEN LINE
GOODS LIFT	GRAND SLAM	GREEN PARK

GREEN PEAS
GREEN ROOM
GRETA GYNT
GREY CLOUD
GREY GOOSE
GREY HAIRS
GREY HORSE
GREY SKIES
GRILL ROOM
GRIM DEATH
GRIM SMILE
GRIM TRUTH
GRIND DOWN
GRIP TIGHT
GROUND NUT
GROW ANGRY
GROW APART
GROW FRUIT
GROWING UP
GROW OLDER
GROW PEARS
GROW STALE
GROW TIRED
GROW WEARY
GUARD DUTY
GUARD ROOM
GUARD'S TIE
GUARD'S VAN
GUESS WHEN
GUEST ROOM
GUEST STAR
GUIDE BOOK
GUILTY ACT
GUILTY MAN
GUINEA HEN
GUM ARABIC
GUN BATTLE
GUN TURRET
GUY FAWKES
GYPSY BAND

H—9
HAIL A TAXI
HAIR CREAM
HAIR SHIRT
HAIR STYLE
HAIR TONIC
HALF A LOAF
HALF AN EYE
HALF A PINT
HALF A QUID

HALF A TICK
HALF AWAKE
HALF A YARD
HALF CROWN
HALF DRUNK
HALF HITCH
HALF LIGHT
HALF PRICE
HALF SHARE
HALF SPEED
HALF TRUTH
HALF WAY UP
HALL CAINE
HALL TABLE
HAM AND EGG
HAM COMMON
HAMMER OUT
HAND BASIN
HAND IT OUT
HAND OF GOD
HAND ROUND
HANDS DOWN
HAND'S TURN
HAND TOWEL
HANDY ANDY
HANG ABOUT
HANG HEAVY
HANGING ON
HANG IT ALL
HANG ROUND
HANSOM CAB
HAPPY DAYS
HAPPY GIRL
HAPPY HOME
HAPPY IDEA
HAPPY LIFE
HAPPY MEAN
HAPPY OMEN
HAPPY PAIR
HAPPY TRIO
HARD APORT
HARD CATCH
HARD CLIMB
HARD COURT
HARD FACTS
HARD FIGHT
HARD FRANC
HARD FROST
HARD FRUIT
HARD GOING
HARD GRIND

HARD HEART
HARD KNOCK
HARD LINES
HARDLY ANY
HARD MONEY
HARD MOUTH
HARD STEEL
HARD TIMES
HARD TO GET
HARD TO SAY
HARD TO SEE
HARD USAGE
HARD VOICE
HARD WATER
HARD WORDS
HARE'S FOOT
HARRY LIME
HARRY TATE
HARSH NOTE
HARSH TONE
HARSH WORD
HAT IN HAND
HAVE A BASH
HAVE A BATH
HAVE A BITE
HAVE A CARE
HAVE A CASE
HAVE A CHAT
HAVE A COLD
HAVE A DATE
HAVE A GAME
HAVE A HOPE
HAVE A LARK
HAVE A LOOK
HAVE A MEAL
HAVE AN EGG
HAVE A PLAN
HAVE A REST
HAVE A SALE
HAVE A SEAT
HAVE A SHOT
HAVE A STAB
HAVE A TRIM
HAVE A WISH
HAVE FAITH
HAVE IT OUT
HAVE LUNCH
HAVE MERCY
HAVE ROOTS
HAVE SENSE
HAVE TASTE

HAVE VIEWS	HIGH FEVER	HOLD UNDER
HAVE WORDS	HIGH GRADE	HOLD WATER
HAVING FUN	HIGH HEELS	HOLE IN ONE
HAZEL EYES	HIGH HOPES	HOLLOW OUT
HEAD FIRST	HIGH HORSE	HOLLY BUSH
HEADS I WIN	HIGH JINKS	HOLY BIBLE
HEAD TO TOE	HIGH LEVEL	HOLY GHOST
HEAP ABUSE	HIGH MARKS	HOLY GRAIL
HEAVE AWAY	HIGH PITCH	HOLY MOSES
HEAVE COAL	HIGH PLANE	HOLY PLACE
HEAVY BLOW	HIGH PRICE	HOLY SMOKE
HEAVY COLD	HIGH SCORE	HOLY WATER
HEAVY COST	HIGH SPEED	HOME AGAIN
HEAVY FALL	HIGH SPOTS	HOME FIRES
HEAVY FINE	HIGH STOOL	HOME FLEET
HEAVY GUNS	HIGH TABLE	HOME FRONT
HEAVY HAND	HIGH TOWER	HOME GROWN
HEAVY LIDS	HIGH VALUE	HOME GUARD
HEAVY LOAD	HIGH VOICE	HOME JAMES
HEAVY LOSS	HIGH WAGES	HOME LOVER
HEAVY MEAL	HIGH WATER	HOMELY WIT
HEAVY MIST	HIGH WORDS	HOME MATCH
HEAVY ODDS	HILL TRIBE	HOME OF MAN
HEAVY POLL	HIRE A MAID	HOME TRADE
HEAVY POST	HIRED HAND	HOME TRUTH
HEAVY RAIN	HIRED HELP	HONEST MAN
HEAVY SEAS	HIRED THUG	HOOT OF JOY
HEAVY SNOW	HIS HONOUR	HOPE CHEST
HEAVY TASK	HIT AND RUN	HOP GARDEN
HEAVY TYPE	HITCH HIKE	HOP PICKER
HEAVY WIND	HIT FOR SIX	HORSE FAIR
HEAVY WORK	HIT NUMBER	HORSE RACE
HELL TO PAY	HIT OR MISS	HORSE SHOW
HELP ALONG	HIT PARADE	HOT AS HELL
HELPED OUT	HIT THE HAY	HOTEL BILL
HEM STITCH	HIT WICKET	HOTEL ROOM
HENRY FORD	HIT WILDLY	HOT NUMBER
HENRY HALL	HOG THE LOT	HOT POTATO
HERE BELOW	HOI POLLOI	HOT SHOWER
HERNE HILL	HOIST SAIL	HOT SPRING
HEROIC AGE	HOLD ALOFT	HOT SUMMER
HEY PRESTO	HOLD ALOOF	HOT TEMPER
HIGH ABOVE	HOLD A SALE	HOUND DOWN
HIGH ALTAR	HOLD AT BAY	HOUSE BOAT
HIGH BIRTH	HOLD CHEAP	HOUSE FULL
HIGH BOOTS	HOLD COURT	HOUSE NAME
HIGH CASTLE	HOLD FORTH	HOUSE RENT
HIGH CHAIR	HOLD HANDS	HOUSE ROOM
HIGH COURT	HOLDING ON	HOW ABSURD!
HIGH DUTCH	HOLD STILL	HOW AND WHY
HIGHER PAY	HOLD TIGHT	HOW ARE YOU?

HOW GOES IT?
HUDSON BAY
HUE AND CRY
HUM AND HAW
HUMAN LIFE
HUMAN RACE
HUMAN SOUL
HUMBLE PIE
HUNGRY MAN
HUNTED AIR
HURL ABUSE
HURRIED UP
HURRY AWAY
HURRY BACK
HURRY DOWN
HURRY HOME
HURRY OVER
HURST PARK
HURT PRIDE
HUSH MONEY

I—9
ICE CORNET
ICED DRINK
ICED WATER
ICE HOCKEY
ICY MANNER
ICY REMARK
IDA LUPINO
IDEAL GIFT
IDEAL HOME
IDEAL TIME
IDEAL TYPE
IDEAL WIFE
IDLE BOAST
IDLE FANCY
IDLE HANDS
IDLE HOURS
IDLE STORY
IDLE TEARS
IFS AND ANS
ILL AT EASE
ILL CHANCE
ILL EFFECT
ILL FAVOUR
ILL HEALTH
ILL HUMOUR
ILL REPORT
ILL REPUTE
IN A BAD WAY
IN A BIG WAY

IN A BUNKER
IN A CANTER
IN A CIRCLE
IN A CLINCH
IN A CORNER
IN A CRISIS
IN ADVANCE
IN A FRENZY
IN A GROOVE
IN A HUDDLE
IN A MINUTE
IN A MOMENT
IN A MUDDLE
IN ANY CASE
IN A PICKLE
IN ARREARS
IN A SCRAPE
IN A SECOND
IN A STUPOR
IN A TANGLE
IN A TEMPER
IN A TRANCE
IN AUSTRIA
IN A VACUUM
IN BAD FORM
IN BAD PART
IN BELGIUM
IN BETWEEN
IN BILLETS
IN BLOSSOM
IN BORSTAL
IN CARDIFF
IN CIRCLES
IN CIVVIES
INCOME TAX
IN COMFORT
IN COMMAND
IN COMPANY
IN CONCERT
IN CONTACT
IN CONTROL
IN COPPERS
IN COSTUME
IN COUNCIL
IN CUSTODY
IN DEFAULT
IN DEFENCE
IN DENMARK
IN DESPAIR
IN DIALECT
INDIAN INK

INDIAN TEA
IN DISGUST
IN DISPUTE
IN DRY DOCK
IN DUE TIME
IN EARNEST
IN ECHELON
IN ENGLAND
IN ENGLISH
INERT MASS
IN FASHION
IN FETTERS
IN FRONT OF
IN FULL CRY
IN GENERAL
IN GERMANY
IN GLASGOW
INGLE NOOK
IN HARBOUR
IN HARMONY
IN HARNESS
IN HOLLAND
IN HUNGARY
IN INFANCY
IN IRELAND
IN ITALIAN
IN ITALICS
IN JANUARY
INK BOTTLE
IN KEEPING
INK ERASER
INLAND SEA
INNER EDGE
INNER ROOM
INNER SELF
INNER TUBE
IN NEUTRAL
IN NEW YORK
IN NO DOUBT
IN OCTOBER
IN ONE MOVE
IN ONE WORD
IN OUTLINE
IN PASSING
IN POVERTY
IN PRIVATE
IN PROFILE
IN PROTEST
IN PURSUIT
IN REALITY
IN RESERVE

IN RESPECT	IN THE MOOD	IRON CROSS
IN RETREAT	IN THE MOON	IRONED OUT
IN REVERSE	IN THE NAVY	IRON FRAME
IN RUMANIA	IN THE NECK	IRON GUARD
IN RUSSIAN	IN THE NEST	IRON HORSE
IN SERVICE	IN THE NEWS	IRON NERVE
IN SESSION	IN THE NUDE	IRON TONIC
INSIDE JOB	IN THE OPEN	IRON WORKS
INSIDE OUT	IN THE OVEN	ISLE OF ELY
IN SILENCE	IN THE PACK	ISLE OF MAN
IN SLAVERY	IN THE PARK	IT'S A CINCH
IN SOCIETY	IN THE PAST	IVORY GATE
IN SOME WAY	IN THE PINK	
IN SPANISH	IN THE POST	J—9
IN SUPPORT	IN THE RAIN	JACK BENNY
IN TATTERS	IN THE REAR	JACK FROST
INTER ALIA	IN THE RING	JACK HOBBS
IN THE ALPS	IN THE ROAD	JACK JONES
IN THE AREA	IN THE SAFE	JACK KETCH
IN THE ARMY	IN THE SNOW	JACK PAYNE
IN THE BAND	IN THE SOUP	JACK SPRAT
IN THE BANK	IN THE SWIM	JACK TRAIN
IN THE BATH	IN THE TEAM	JADE GREEN
IN THE BUSH	IN THE TILL	JAMES BOND
IN THE CART	IN THE TOWN	JAMES DEAN
IN THE CITY	IN THE VEIN	JAMES WATT
IN THE COLD	IN THE WAKE	JAM SPONGE
IN THE DARK	IN THE WARS	JANE WYMAN
IN THE DOCK	IN THE WASH	JAY WALKER
IN THE DUSK	IN THE WEST	JELLY BABY
IN THE EAST	IN THE WIND	JENNY LIND
IN THE FACE	INTO FOCUS	JENNY WREN
IN THE FALL	IN TOP FORM	JERSEY COW
IN THE FILE	IN TOP GEAR	JET ENGINE
IN THE FIRE	IN TORMENT	JET FLIGHT
IN THE FOLD	INTO TOUCH	JEWEL CASE
IN THE FRAY	IN TRAFFIC	JOAN OF ARC
IN THE GODS	IN TRANSIT	JOAN REGAN
IN THE HOLD	IN TRIUMPH	JOB OF WORK
IN THE HOME	IN TROUBLE	JOE MILLER
IN THE KNOW	IN UNIFORM	JO GRIMOND
IN THE LAKE	INVOKE AID	JOHN ADAMS
IN THE LEAD	IN WAITING	JOHN BLUNT
IN THE LIFT	IN WRITING	JOHN BROWN
IN THE LOFT	IONIAN SEA	JOHN CABOT
IN THE MAIL	IPSO FACTO	JOHN KEATS
IN THE MAIN	IRISH BULL	JOHN MILLS
IN THE MASS	IRISH EYES	JOHN SMITH
IN THE MIND	IRISH FLAG	JOHN WAYNE
IN THE MINE	IRISH PEER	JOIN HANDS
IN THE MODE	IRISH STEW	JOIN ISSUE

JOINT HEIR
JOINT WILL
JOLLY GOOD
JOLLY TIME
JOLLY WELL
JOT IT DOWN
JUDAS KISS
JUDAS TREE
JUDGE'S CAP
JUDGE WELL
JUG OF MILK
JUMP ABOUT
JUMP AHEAD
JUMP CLEAR
JUNE BRIDE
JUNGLE LAW
JUST A DROP
JUST CAUSE
JUST CLAIM
JUST FANCY
JUST PRICE
JUST RIGHT
JUST THINK

K—9
KATHIE KAY
KEEN FIGHT
KEEN FROST
KEEN MATCH
KEEN PRICE
KEEN SIGHT
KEEP A DATE
KEEP AHEAD
KEEP ALIVE
KEEP APART
KEEP ASIDE
KEEP AT BAY
KEEP CLEAR
KEEP CLOSE
KEEP COUNT
KEEP FAITH
KEEP FRESH
KEEP GOING
KEEP GUARD
KEEP HOUSE
KEEP ON ICE
KEEP ORDER
KEEP QUIET
KEEP SCORE
KEEP SHORT
KEEP SOBER

KEEP STILL
KEEP STOCK
KEEP UNDER
KEEP VIGIL
KEEP WATCH
KEG BITTER
KELLY'S EYE
KEPT AT BAY
KEPT ON ICE
KEPT WOMAN
KERRY BLUE
KEW BRIDGE
KEW PALACE
KEY MOMENT
KEY WORKER
KICKED OFF
KICKED OUT
KID GLOVES
KIEL CANAL
KIND HEART
KINDLY ACT
KIND WORDS
KING CAROL
KING COBRA
KING DAVID
KING HENRY
KING MIDAS
KING PRIAM
KING'S HEAD
KING'S LYNN
KING'S PAWN
KING'S ROAD
KING'S ROOK
KING STORK
KIRBY GRIP
KISS HANDS
KNEEL DOWN
KNEES BEND
KNOCK COLD
KNOCK DOWN
KNOCKED UP
KNOCK HARD
KNOCK ONCE
KNOCK OVER
KNOW AGAIN
KNOW NO LAW
KOREAN WAR
KUBLA KHAN

L—9
LABOUR DAY

LACK DRIVE
LADIES' BAR
LADIES' DAY
LADIES' MAN
LADY'S MAID
LAG BEHIND
LAGER BEER
LA GUARDIA
LAID WASTE
LAKE GARDA
LAKE HURON
LAKE POETS
LAMB'S WOOL
LAMP SHADE
LAND A BLOW
LAND AGENT
LAND AHEAD
LAND FORCE
LAND OF NOD
LAND ROVER
LAND SPEED
LAP RECORD
LARGE AREA
LARGE ARMY
LARGE BEER
LARGE BILL
LARGE CAST
LARGE CITY
LARGE FLAT
LARGE HEAD
LARGE LOAF
LARGE PORT
LARGE ROOM
LARGE SIZE
LARGE TOWN
LARGE TYPE
LARK ABOUT
LASHED OUT
LAS PALMAS
LAST APRIL
LAST CRUMB
LAST DANCE
LAST DITCH
LAST DREGS
LAST DRINK
LAST EVENT
LAST FLING
LAST HOURS
LAST LAUGH
LAST LIGHT
LAST MAN IN

LAST MARCH	LAW REFORM	LETTER BOX
LAST MATCH	LAW REPORT	LETTING UP
LAST MONTH	LAW SCHOOL	LET US PRAY
LAST NIGHT	LAZY BONES	LEVEL BEST
LAST OF ALL	LEAD OXIDE	LEYDEN JAR
LAST OFFER	LEAF MOULD	LIBEL CASE
LAST OF SIX	LEAN YEARS	LIBEL SUIT
LAST OF TEN	LEASE LEND	LIE ASLEEP
LAST OF TWO	LEAST SAID	LIE AT REST
LAST ORDER	LEAVE A GAP	LIE DIRECT
LAST PENNY	LEAVE A TIP	LIE FALLOW
LAST PLACE	LEAVE HOME	LIE HIDDEN
LAST RITES	LEAVE OPEN	LIE IN WAIT
LAST ROUND	LEAVE OVER	LIFE CLASS
LAST SCENE	LEAVE ROOM	LIFE CYCLE
LAST SHIFT	LEAVE WORD	LIFE FORCE
LAST STAGE	LEAVE WORK	LIFE STORY
LAST STAND	LE BOURGET	LIFE STUDY
LAST STRAW	LED ASTRAY	LIFE'S WORK
LAST THING	LEFT ALONE	LIFT A HAND
LAST THROW	LEFT FLANK	LIGHT BLUE
LAST TRAIN	LEFT TO DIE	LIGHT BULB
LAST TRUMP	LEFT TO ROT	LIGHT DIET
LAST VERSE	LEFT WHEEL	LIGHT MEAL
LAST VISIT	LEGAL CODE	LIGHT RAIN
LAST WALTZ	LEGAL FARE	LIGHT SIDE
LAST WORDS	LEGAL HEIR	LIGHTS OUT
LATE CROPS	LEGAL MIND	LIGHT SUIT
LATE ENTRY	LEGAL TERM	LIGHT TANK
LATE EXTRA	LEGER LINE	LIGHT UPON
LATE FROST	LEG GLANCE	LIGHT WAVE
LATE HOURS	LEG OF LAMB	LIGHT WINE
LATE NIGHT	LEG OF PORK	LIGHT WORK
LATER DATE	LEGS APART	LIGHT YEAR
LATE RISER	LEG THEORY	LIKE A BIRD
LATE SHIFT	LEIGH HUNT	LIKE A BOMB
LATE STAGE	LEMON CURD	LIKE A CORK
LATE START	LEMON PEEL	LIKE A DUCK
LATIN CRIB	LEMON SOLE	LIKE A FOOL
LATIN RACE	LENA HORNE	LIKE A KING
LATTER END	LEND A HAND	LIKE A LAMB
LAUGH AWAY	LEND AN EAR	LIKE A LION
LAUGH DOWN	LEND MONEY	LIKE A MULE
LAUGH LINE	LEN HUTTON	LIKE A SHOT
LAUGH OVER	LESSON ONE	LIKELY LAD
LAUNCH OUT	LESSON SIX	LIKE MAGIC
LAVA BREAD	LESSON TEN	LIKE MUSIC
LAWFUL ACT	LESSON TWO	LIKE SMOKE
LAWFUL AGE	LESS SPEED	LIKE WATER
LAWN MOWER	LET HER RIP	LILAC TIME
LAW OFFICE	LE TOUQUET	LILAC TREE

LIME GREEN	LONG DRIVE	LORD DERBY
LIME GROVE	LONG GRASS	LORD MAYOR
LIME JUICE	LONG HOURS	LOSE A LIMB
LION'S CAGE	LONG LEASE	LOSE AN EYE
LION'S MANE	LONG MARCH	LOSE CASTE
LION'S SKIN	LONG NIGHT	LOSE COUNT
LION'S TAIL	LONG PANTS	LOSE FAITH
LION TAMER	LONG PURSE	LOSE HEART
LIP READER	LONG QUEUE	LOSE MONEY
LIQUID AIR	LONG RANGE	LOSER PAYS
LIQUOR LAW	LONG REACH	LOSE TOUCH
LIST PRICE	LONG REIGN	LOSE TRACK
LITTER BIN	LONG SIEGE	LOSING BET
LITTER BUG	LONG SIGHT	LOSING RUN
LITTLE BIT	LONG SINCE	LOST AT SEA
LITTLE BOY	LONG SKIRT	LOST CAUSE
LITTLE DOG	LONG SLEEP	LOST CHORD
LITTLE MAN	LONG SPELL	LOST COUNT
LITTLE ONE	LONG STAGE	LOST HABIT
LITTLE TOE	LONG STORY	LOST SCENT
LITTLE WAY	LONG TRAIN	LOST SHEEP
LIVE AGAIN	LONG TRIAL	LOST SKILL
LIVE ALONE	LONG VISIT	LOT OF GOOD
LIVE APART	LONG VOWEL	LOTS OF FUN
LIVE ISSUE	LONG WHIST	LOUD KNOCK
LIVE ON AIR	LOOK A FOOL	LOUD LAUGH
LIVE OR DIE	LOOK AFTER	LOUD MUSIC
LIVE ROUGH	LOOK AHEAD	LOUD NOISE
LIVING LIE	LOOK ALIVE	LOUD PEDAL
LOADED GUN	LOOK A MESS	LOUD SOUND
LOAD OF HAY	LOOK BLACK	LOUD VOICE
LOAF SUGAR	LOOK BLANK	LOUNGE BAR
LOATH TO GO	LOOKED FOR	LOVE APPLE
LOCAL CALL	LOOK FRESH	LOVE CHILD
LOCAL NAME	LOOK GRAVE	LOVED ONES
LOCAL NEWS	LOOKING UP	LOVE FORTY
LOCAL TIME	LOOK NIPPY	LOVELY DAY
LOCAL VETO	LOOK RIGHT	LOVE LYRIC
LOCKED OUT	LOOK ROUND	LOVE MATCH
LOFTY AIMS	LOOK SEEDY	LOVE MY DOG
LOG OF WOOD	LOOK SHARP	LOVE OF WAR
LONDON BUS	LOOK SILLY	LOVE STORY
LONDON ZOO	LOOK SMALL	LOVE TOKEN
LONG AFTER	LOOK SMART	LOVING CUP
LONG BEACH	LOOK THERE	LOW BRIDGE
LONG BEARD	LOOM LARGE	LOW CHURCH
LONG CHALK	LOOSE BALL	LOW COMEDY
LONG DELAY	LOOSE CASH	LOW DEGREE
LONG DOZEN	LOOSE TALK	LOWER CASE
LONG DRESS	LOOSE TILE	LOWER DECK
LONG DRINK	LORD BYRON	LOWER DOWN

LOWER FORM
LOWER LIFE
LOWER LIMB
LOWER PART
LOW FELLOW
LOW GERMAN
LOW GROUND
LOW INCOME
LOW IN TONE
LOW NUMBER
LOW PERSON
LOW RELIEF
LOW RESORT
LOW RETURN
LOW SALARY
LOW STAKES
LOW STATUS
LUCID MIND
LUCKY DRAW
LUCKY FIND
LUCKY GIRL
LUCKY MOVE
LUCKY OMEN
LUCKY SHOT
LUCKY STAR
LUMP SUGAR
LUNACY ACT
LUNAR YEAR
LUNCH DATE
LUNCH HOUR
LUNCH TIME
LURID PAST
LYING DOWN
LYME REGIS
LYRIC POEM
LYRIC POET

M—9
MADE OF TIN
MADE READY
MAD HATTER
MAD SCHEME
MAGGIE MAY
MAGIC LAMP
MAGIC RING
MAGIC SIGN
MAGIC WAND
MAGIC WORD
MAIDA VALE
MAIL ORDER
MAIL PLANE

MAIL TRAIN
MAIN FORCE
MAIN ISSUE
MAIN POINT
MAIN THEME
MAIN THING
MAJOR DOMO
MAJOR PART
MAJOR POET
MAJOR ROAD
MAJOR SNAG
MAJOR SUIT
MAJOR WORK
MAKE A BACK
MAKE A BOOK
MAKE A CAKE
MAKE A CALL
MAKE A COPY
MAKE A DATE
MAKE A DEAL
MAKE A FACE
MAKE A FIRE
MAKE A FUSS
MAKE A HOLE
MAKE A JOKE
MAKE A KILL
MAKE A LIST
MAKE A LOSS
MAKE A MESS
MAKE A MOVE
MAKE A NOTE
MAKE A PASS
MAKE A PILE
MAKE A PLAN
MAKE A RING
MAKE A SHOW
MAKE A SIGN
MAKE A SLIP
MAKE A STIR
MAKE A TART
MAKE A WILL
MAKE A WISH
MAKE CLEAR
MAKE FACES
MAKE FUN OF
MAKE HASTE
MAKE KNOWN
MAKE LEGAL
MAKE MERRY
MAKE MONEY
MAKE MUSIC

MAKE NOTES
MAKE OR MAR
MAKE PEACE
MAKE PLAIN
MAKE PLANS
MAKE READY
MAKE SENSE
MAKE TERMS
MAKE TIGHT
MAKE-UP MAN
MAKE-UP SET
MAKE VALID
MAKE WHOLE
MAKE WORSE
MAKING HAY
MALE CHOIR
MALE NURSE
MALE SCREW
MALE VOICE
MAN AND BOY
MAN FRIDAY
MAN OF IRON
MAN OF KENT
MAN OF MARK
MAN OF NOTE
MAN OF RANK
MANOR FARM
MANOR PARK
MANY A SLIP
MANY A TIME
MANY HANDS
MANY TIMES
MANY WORDS
MANY YEARS
MAPLE LEAF
MAPLE TREE
MAP OF ROME
MAPPED OUT
MARCH AWAY
MARCH HARE
MARCH PAST
MARCH WIND
MARCO POLO
MARDI GRAS
MARE'S NEST
MARIA MONK
MARKED MAN
MARKET DAY
MARK TWAIN
MARRY WELL
MASKED MAN

MASS MEDIA
MASTER KEY
MASTER SPY
MATCH PLAY
MATE IN ONE
MATE IN TWO
MATT MONRO
MAX ADRIAN
MAX MILLER
MEANS TEST
MEAN TO SAY
MEANT WELL
MEASLY LOT
MEAT JELLY
MEAT PASTE
MEDAL PLAY
MEDIUM DRY
MEIN KAMPF
MEL FERRER
MEN AT WORK
MEND A FUSE
MENTAL AGE
MERCY SEAT
MERE TRUTH
MERE WORDS
MERRY QUIP
MERRY TUNE
MESS ABOUT
METAL DISC
METAL RING
METAL TUBE
METRIC TON
MID-DAY SUN
MIDDLE AGE
MIDDLE WAY
MIGHTY FEW
MIGHTY MAN
MILD STEEL
MILES AWAY
MILK CHURN
MILK DRINK
MILK FLOAT
MILK PUNCH
MILK ROUND
MILK SHAKE
MILK STOUT
MILK TEETH
MILL ABOUT
MILLS BOMB
MINE SHAFT
MINI SKIRT

MINK STOLE
MINOR PART
MINOR POET
MINOR ROAD
MINOR ROLE
MINOR SUIT
MINT JULEP
MINT SAUCE
MINUS SIGN
MINUTE MAN
MISSED OUT
MISS WORLD
MIX A DRINK
MIXED NUTS
MOCK TRIAL
MODEL FARM
MODEL GIRL
MODERN ART
MONEY DOWN
MONIED MAN
MONKEY NUT
MONT BLANC
MOON ABOUT
MOON RIVER
MOOT POINT
MORAL CODE
MORAL EVIL
MORAL TONE
MORE HASTE
MORE LIGHT
MORE MONEY
MORE SCOPE
MORSE CODE
MORTAL SIN
MOSAIC LAW
MOSS GREEN
MOST NOBLE
MOST OF ALL
MOTHER WIT
MOTOR RACE
MOTOR ROAD
MOTOR SHOW
MOTOR TOUR
MOUNTED UP
MOUNT ETNA
MOUTH WASH
MOVE ABOUT
MOVE ALONG
MOVE APART
MOVE HOUSE
MOVE ROUND

MOVIE STAR
MOWED DOWN
MRS. GRUNDY
MR. SPEAKER
MUCH ALIKE
MUCH LATER
MUCH MOVED
MUCH NOISE
MUCH SPACE
MUCH WORSE
MUFFIN MAN
MUFFLED UP
MUG OF BEER
MUM AND DAD
MUSIC CASE
MUSIC HALL
MUSIC ROOM
MUTINY ACT
MUTTON FAT
MUTUAL AID
MUTUAL AIM
MY DARLING
MY DEAR SIR
MY HUSBAND
MY OPINION

N—9

NAKED CITY
NAKED LADY
NANNY GOAT
NARROW WIN
NASTY BLOW
NASTY MESS
NASTY TYPE
NASTY WORD
NATIVE WIT
NAVAL BASE
NAVAL RANK
NAVAL TYPE
NAZI PARTY
NEARLY ALL
NEAR SIGHT
NEAR THING
NEAT DRINK
NEAT TRICK
NEEDS MUST
NEON LIGHT
NET AMOUNT
NET LOSSES
NET PROFIT

NET RESULT	NIGHT BELL	NO PARKING
NET RETURN	NIGHT CLUB	NO QUARTER
NEVER A ONE	NIGHT DUTY	NO REGRETS
NEVER FEAR	NIGHT LIFE	NORTH CAPE
NEVER MIND	NIGHT SPOT	NORTH POLE
NEVER MORE	NIGHT WORK	NORTH SIDE
NEVER REST	NILE DELTA	NORTH STAR
NEVER SEEN	NILE GREEN	NORTH WIND
NEVER STOP	NINE CARAT	NORTH ZONE
NEVER VARY	NINE DOZEN	NOSMO KING
NEW BARNET	NINE GROSS	NO SMOKING
NEW BONNET	NINE HOLES	NO SPIRITS
NEW CUSTOM	NINE HOURS	NO STRINGS
NEW DEALER	NINE LIVES	NOT AT HOME
NEW ENERGY	NINE MILES	NOT FAR OFF
NEW FOREST	NINE MUSES	NOT GUILTY
NEW FRIEND	NINE OR TEN	NOTHING ON
NEW GROUND	NINE PARTS	NOT HUNGRY
NEW GUINEA	NINE SCORE	NOT IN TIME
NEW JERSEY	NINE TIMES	NOT LATELY
NEW MASTER	NINE TO ONE	NOT LIKELY
NEW MEMBER	NINE WEEKS	NOT PROVEN
NEW METHOD	NINE YEARS	NOTRE DAME
NEW MEXICO	NINTH HOLE	NO TROUBLE
NEW PLANET	NINTH PART	NOT SO GOOD
NEW POLICY	NINTH TIME	NOT STRONG
NEW POTATO	NISSEN HUT	NOT TOO BAD
NEW READER	NOBLE LADY	NOT UP TO IT
NEW RECORD	NOBLE LINE	NOT WANTED
NEW REGIME	NOBLE LORD	NOVEL ITEM
NEW ROMNEY	NOBLE PART	NO WAITING
NEW SCHOOL	NOBLE PILE	NO WARNING
NEW SERIES	NO CHICKEN	NUMBER ONE
NEWS FLASH	NO COMMENT	NUMBER SIX
NEWS SHEET	NOD ASSENT	NUMBER TEN
NEW STREET	NO DEFENCE	NUMBER TWO
NEWS VALUE	NO EFFECTS	NUTS IN MAY
NEW YORKER	NO FISHING	
NEXT APRIL	NO FLOWERS	**O—9**
NEXT ISSUE	NO FOOLING	OAST HOUSE
NEXT MAN IN	NO FURTHER	OBJET D'ART
NEXT MARCH	NO GROUNDS	OCEAN LANE
NEXT MONTH	NO HAWKERS	OCEAN WAVE
NEXT OF KIN	NO INKLING	OCTANE GAS
NEXT STAGE	NOISES OFF	ODD CHOICE
NEXT TRAIN	NO KIDDING	ODD CORNER
NEXT WORLD	NO MANNERS	ODD JOB MAN
NICE POINT	NO MEANING	ODD MAN OUT
NICE SLEEP	NO MISTAKE	ODD MOMENT
NICE TASTE	NO MODESTY	ODD NUMBER
NICE TO SEE	NO ONE ELSE	ODD OR EVEN

ODD PERSON	OLD STREET	ON IMPULSE
OFF CENTRE	OLIVE TREE	ONION SKIN
OFF CHANCE	ON ACCOUNT	ONION SOUP
OFF COLOUR	ON A CHARGE	ONLY CHILD
OFF COURSE	ON A PICNIC	ONLY HUMAN
OFFICE BOY	ON ARRIVAL	ON MY RIGHT
OFFICE CAT	ON A STRING	ONE SIDE
OFF MOMENT	ON A TANDEM	ON ONE'S OWN
OFF SEASON	ON AVERAGE	ON ONE'S WAY
OFF TARGET	ON BALANCE	ON PURPOSE
OFF THE AIR	ONCE AGAIN	ON RATIONS
OFF THE MAP	ONCE A WEEK	ON RUNNERS
OFF THE PEG	ONCE A YEAR	ON SUNDAYS
OFF THE SET	ONCE ROUND	ON THE BALL
OF NO AVAIL	ON DEPOSIT	ON THE BEAM
OF NO WORTH	ON DISPLAY	ON THE BEAT
OF ONE MIND	ON DRAUGHT	ON THE BOIL
OF THAT ILK	ON DRY LAND	ON THE BONE
OIL COOKER	ONE ACROSS	ON THE CHIN
OILED SILK	ONE AND ALL	ON THE DOLE
OIL HEATER	ONE AND ONE	ON THE EDGE
OIL TANKER	ONE AND SIX	ON THE FARM
OIL TYCOON	ONE AND TEN	ON THE FIRE
OLD AND NEW	ONE AND TWO	ON THE FLAT
OLD AS ADAM	ONE BETTER	ON THE HEAD
OLD AS TIME	ONE DEGREE	ON THE HOOF
OLD BAILEY	ONE DOLLAR	ON THE HOUR
OLD BRANDY	ONE EIGHTH	ON THE HUNT
OLD BUFFER	ONE FOR ALL	ON THE JURY
OLD CODGER	ONE FOURTH	ON THE LAKE
OLD COUPLE	ONE GALLON	ON THE LAND
OLD CROCKS	ONE GUINEA	ON THE LEAD
OLD CUSTOM	ONE IN FIVE	ON THE LEFT
OLD EMPIRE	ONE IN FOUR	ON THE LINE
OLDEN DAYS	ONE IN NINE	ON THE LIST
OLD FAGGOT	ONE LENGTH	ON THE MAKE
OLD FAMILY	ONE-MAN DOG	ON THE MARK
OLD FELLOW	ONE MINUTE	ON THE MEND
OLD FOSSIL	ONE MOMENT	ON THE MENU
OLD FRIEND	ONE O'CLOCK	ON THE MOON
OLD MASTER	ONE OCTAVE	ON THE MOVE
OLD METHOD	ONE OF MANY	ON THE NAIL
OLD PEOPLE	ONE SECOND	ON THE NOSE
OLD RECORD	ONE'S EQUAL	ON THE PIER
OLD REEKIE	ONE STRIPE	ON THE RACK
OLD RÉGIME	ONE STROKE	ON THE RISE
OLD ROWLEY	ONE TO COME	ON THE ROAD
OLD SAYING	ONE TOO FEW	ON THE ROOF
OLD SCHOOL	ONE WICKET	ON THE SIDE
OLD SCORES	ON HALF PAY	ON THE SPOT
OLD STAGER	ON HOLIDAY	ON THE TOTE

ON THE TOWN	OUT OF DATE	PANT AFTER
ON THE TROT	OUT OF DEBT	PAPAL BULL
ON THE TURF	OUT OF FORM	PAPER BACK
ON THE TURN	OUT OF GEAR	PAPER BILL
ON THE WALL	OUT OF HAND	PAPER CLIP
ON THE WANE	OUT OF LINE	PAPER DOLL
ON THE WING	OUT OF LOVE	PAPER GAME
ON THIN ICE	OUT OF LUCK	PAPER MILL
ON TUESDAY	OUT OF MIND	PAPER OVER
OPEN A SHOP	OUT OF PAIN	PAPER RACK
OPEN COURT	OUT OF PITY	PAPER WORK
OPEN DRAIN	OUT OF PLAY	PARCEL OUT
OPEN EVENT	OUT OF STEP	PARIAH DOG
OPEN FIELD	OUT OF TIME	PARI PASSU
OPEN GRATE	OUT OF TOWN	PARIS GOWN
OPEN GRAVE	OUT OF TRIM	PARK BENCH
OPEN HEART	OUT OF TRUE	PARKED CAR
OPEN HOUSE	OUT OF TUNE	PARK ROYAL
OPEN MATCH	OUT OF TURN	PARTY GAME
OPEN MOUTH	OUT OF WORK	PARTY LINE
OPEN ORDER	OUT ON BAIL	PARTY MOOD
OPEN PORES	OUT WITH IT	PARTY RULE
OPEN PURSE	OUT YONDER	PARTY WALL
OPEN SHIRT	OVER AGAIN	PARTY WHIP
OPEN SKIES	OVER FORTY	PAS DE DEUX
OPEN SPACE	OVER PROOF	PAS DU TOUT
OPEN TO ALL	OVER THERE	PASS ALONG
OPEN WOUND	OVER TO YOU	PASSED OFF
ORANGE GIN	OWEN NARES	PASSED OUT
ORANGE PIP	OWEN TUDOR	PASSING BY
ORDER ARMS	OWN A HOUSE	PASSING ON
ORDER BOOK	OXFORD DON	PASS ROUND
ORDER FORM	OYSTER BAR	PAST GLORY
ORGAN LOFT	OYSTER BED	PAST SHAME
ORGAN STOP		PAST TENSE
ORLOP DECK	**P—9**	PATCHED UP
ORRIS ROOT	PACKED OUT	PATCH IT UP
OTHER DAYS	PADDED OUT	PATNA RICE
OTHER HALF	PAGE EIGHT	PATROL CAR
OTHER SELF	PAGE PROOF	PAUL JONES
OTHER SIDE	PAGE SEVEN	PAVED ROAD
OUR CHOICE	PAGE THREE	PAVED WALK
OUR FATHER	PAINT OVER	PAWN'S MOVE
OUT AND OUT	PAIRED OFF	PAY A VISIT
OUT AT HEEL	PALE BROWN	PAY DOUBLE
OUTER EDGE	PALE GREEN	PAY HOMAGE
OUTER SKIN	PALE HANDS	PAY IN FULL
OUTER TUBE	PALM BEACH	PAYING OUT
OUT FOR TEA	PALMY DAYS	PAY IN KIND
OUT OF A JOB	PANAMA HAT	PAY OFFICE
OUT OF BOND	PANEL GAME	PAY ON CALL

PAY ONE OUT	PIGEON PIE	PLAYED OUT
PAY PACKET	PIGGY BANK	PLAY FALSE
PAY RANSOM	PIG MARKET	PLAY GAMES
PEACE PACT	PILAU RICE	PLAY HAVOC
PEACH TREE	PILLAR BOX	PLAY POKER
PEAKED CAP	PILOT FISH	PLAY ROUGH
PEARL BUCK	PINE AFTER	PLAY SHARP
PEAR MELBA	PINK ICING	PLAY TO WIN
PEGGED OUT	PINK PEARL	PLAY WHIST
PENAL CODE	PIN-UP GIRL	PLEASE SIR
PENAL LAWS	PIOUS DUTY	PLOD ALONG
PENAL WORK	PIOUS HOPE	PLUGGED IN
PEN AND INK	PIPE DREAM	PLUMP DOWN
PEN FRIEND	PIPE MAJOR	PLUS FOURS
PENNY BANK	PIPE MUSIC	PLY A TRADE
PENNY POST	PIPING HOT	POETIC ART
PENNY WISE	PISTON ROD	POINT DUTY
PEPPER POT	PITCH DARK	POISON GAS
PEP UP PILL	PITCHED IN	POISON IVY
PER CAPITA	PITCH INTO	POISON PEN
PER CENTUM	PITCH UPON	POKE FUN AT
PER CONTRA	PIT PONIES	POKER DICE
PERRY COMO	PIT STALLS	POKER FACE
PETAL SOFT	PIT WORKER	POKER HAND
PETER COOK	PIXIE RING	POLA NEGRI
PETER WEST	PLACE A BET	POLAR BEAR
PETIT FOUR	PLACE KICK	POLE VAULT
PET NOTION	PLACE NAME	POLICE BOX
PETROL CAN	PLAIN CAKE	POLICE CAR
PETROL TAX	PLAIN COOK	POLICE DOG
PET THEORY	PLAIN FACT	POLISH OFF
PETTY CASH	PLAIN FOOD	POLITE ACT
PETTY JURY	PLAIN JANE	POLO MATCH
PEWTER POT	PLAIN WORK	POODLE CUT
PHONE CALL	PLAN AHEAD	POOK'S HILL
PHONEY WAR	PLANE TREE	POOR CATCH
PIANO DUET	PLANT LIFE	POOR CHILD
PIANO LEGS	PLATE RACK	POOR CLASS
PIANO SOLO	PLAY ABOUT	POOR DEVIL
PICK A LOCK	PLAY A CARD	POOR GRADE
PICK A TEAM	PLAY A FISH	POOR GUIDE
PICKED MAN	PLAY A JOKE	POOR HOUSE
PICKED OFF	PLAY AN ACE	POOR JUDGE
PICKED OUT	PLAY A NOTE	POOR LIGHT
PICK FRUIT	PLAY A PART	POOR MARKS
PICK HOLES	PLAY BINGO	POOR MATCH
PICKING UP	PLAY BOWLS	POOR SCORE
PICK OAKUM	PLAY BY EAR	POOR SPORT
PIECE RATE	PLAY CARDS	POOR START
PIED PIPER	PLAY CHESS	POOR STUFF
PIER GLASS	PLAY DARTS	POOR TABLE

POOR TASTE	PROPER WAY	PUT UP BAIL
POOR THING	PROPPED UP	PUT UP WITH
POOR THROW	PROSE POEM	PUZZLE OUT
POOR VALUE	PROUD STEP	
POOR VOICE	PROVE TRUE	**Q—9**
POOR WOMAN	PRUNE AWAY	QUEEN ANNE
POOR YIELD	PUBLIC BAR	QUEEN BESS
POP NUMBER	PUBLIC EYE	QUEEN MARY
POPPED OFF	PUFFED OUT	QUEER BIRD
POP RECORD	PULL A FACE	QUEER CARD
POP SINGER	PULL AHEAD	QUEER COVE
PORT LIGHT	PULL APART	QUEER FISH
PORTO RICO	PULL ASIDE	QUEUE HERE
POST EARLY	PULLED OFF	QUICK FIRE
POT THE RED	PULLED OUT	QUICK SALE
POUND AWAY	PULL FACES	QUICK STEP
POUND NOTE	PULL IT OFF	QUICK TIME
POUR FORTH	PULL IT OUT	QUICK WITS
POWDER KEG	PULL ROUND	QUICK WORK
POWER DIVE	PULL TIGHT	QUIET LIFE
POWER UNIT	PULL WIRES	QUIET READ
PRAY ALOUD	PUNCH BOWL	QUIET TIME
PRESS BACK	PUNCH LINE	QUIET TONE
PRESS CLUB	PUNIC WARS	QUITE A FEW
PRESS DATE	PUPPY LOVE	QUITE FULL
PRESS DOWN	PURE SPITE	QUITE GOOD
PRESSED ON	PURE WATER	QUITE NEAR
PRESS GANG	PURE WHITE	QUITE NICE
PRESS HARD	PURE WOMAN	QUITE SURE
PRESS HOME	PUSH ASIDE	QUITE WELL
PRESS LAWS	PUSHED OFF	
PRESS ROOM	PUSHED OUT	**R—9**
PRESS SEAT	PUT ACROSS	RABBIT PIE
PRESS SHOW	PUT AT EASE	RACE AHEAD
PRETTY BAD	PUT IN GAOL	RACE RIOTS
PRETTY BIG	PUT IN GEAR	RACE TRACK
PRICE LIST	PUT IN HAND	RACING CAR
PRICE RING	PUT IN JAIL	RACING MAN
PRIME BEEF	PUT IN MIND	RACING SET
PRIME COST	PUT IN QUOD	RACING TIP
PRISON VAN	PUT IT DOWN	RACY STYLE
PRIVY SEAL	PUT IT OVER	RADIO MAST
PRIZE BULL	PUT ON AIRS	RADIO PLAY
PRIZE CREW	PUT ON OATH	RADIO STAR
PRIZE LIST	PUT ON SALE	RADIO WAVE
PRIZE POEM	PUT ON SHOW	RAIN BLOWS
PRIZE RING	PUT ON SIDE	RAIN CLOUD
PROOF COPY	PUT ON TAPE	RAIN GAUGE
PRO PATRIA	PUT PAID TO	RAIN WATER
PROPER DAY	PUT TO ROUT	RAISE CAIN
PROPER MAN	PUT TO WORK	RAISE HELL

RALPH LYNN	RED INDIAN	RIGHT NAME
RAPID FIRE	RED LETTER	RIGHT NOTE
RAPID RATE	RED MENACE	RIGHT ROAD
RAREE SHOW	RED MULLET	RIGHT RULE
RARE EVENT	RED PENCIL	RIGHT SIDE
RARE STAMP	RED PEPPER	RIGHT SIZE
RARE STEAK	RED PLANET	RIGHT TIME
RARE TREAT	RED RIBAND	RIGHT TURN
RATE OF PAY	RED RIBBON	RIGHT VIEW
RAT POISON	RED SETTER	RIGHT WING
RATTLE OFF	RED SQUARE	RIGHT WORD
RAVEN HAIR	RED SPIDER	RING A BELL
RAVING MAD	REED ORGAN	RING AGAIN
RAW CARROT	REELED OFF	RING A PEAL
RAW COTTON	REFUSE BIN	RING CRAFT
RAW SPIRIT	RELAY RACE	RING FALSE
RAW TOMATO	RELIEF BUS	RING FENCE
RAY OF HOPE	RELIEF MAP	RING ROUND
REACH HOME	RENT A FLAT	RIN TIN TIN
REACH LAND	REPAIR JOB	RIO GRANDE
READ A BOOK	REPLY PAID	RIOT SQUAD
READ ALOUD	REP PLAYER	RIPE FRUIT
READ IN BED	RESCUE BID	RISE ABOVE
READ MORSE	RHINE WINE	RISE EARLY
READ MUSIC	RIB OF BEEF	RISING AIR
READ VERSE	RICE PAPER	RISING MAN
READY CASH	RICH UNCLE	RISING SUN
READY TO GO	RICH WIDOW	RITUAL ACT
REAL CREAM	RICH WOMAN	RIVAL FIRM
REAL DOUBT	RIDE IT OUT	RIVER AVON
REAL SPORT	RIDE ROUGH	RIVER BANK
REAL THING	RIDING CAP	RIVER BOAT
REAL TONIC	RIDING KIT	RIVER FISH
REAL TRUTH	RIFLE FIRE	RIVER NILE
REAL WORLD	RIFLE SHOT	RIVER STYX
REAR LIGHT	RIGHT AWAY	RIVER TEST
REAR WHEEL	RIGHT BACK	RIVER TRIP
REASON WHY	RIGHT BANK	ROAD AGENT
REBEL ARMY	RIGHT CARD	ROAD BLOCK
RECORD BID	RIGHT DOWN	ROAD BOARD
RECORD RUN	RIGHT FACE!	ROAD DRILL
RECORD SUM	RIGHT FOOT	ROAD METAL
RED CARPET	RIGHT FORM	ROAD SENSE
RED CHEEKS	RIGHT HALF	ROAD TO RIO
RED CHEESE	RIGHT HAND	ROAD WORKS
RED CIRCLE	RIGHT HOOK	ROAST BEEF
RED COTTON	RIGHT IDEA	ROAST DUCK
RED DRAGON	RIGHT LINE	ROAST LAMB
RED DUSTER	RIGHT MIND	ROAST MEAT
RED ENSIGN	RIGHT MOOD	ROAST PORK
RED GROUSE	RIGHT MOVE	ROAST VEAL

ROBIN HOOD	ROUND OATH	RUSH ABOUT
ROCK 'N' ROLL	ROUND POND	RUSH ORDER
ROCK PLANT	ROUND SHOT	RUS IN URBE
ROD OF IRON	ROUND TOUR	RYE WHISKY
ROLL ALONG	ROUND TRIP	
ROLLING UP	ROUTED OUT	S—9
ROLL OF FAT	ROVING EYE	SABLE COAT
ROMAN BATH	ROWAN TREE	SACRED COW
ROMAN CAMP	ROWING MAN	SAD ENDING
ROMAN NOSE	ROYAL ARMS	SAD PLIGHT
ROMAN ORGY	ROYAL BLUE	SAFE CATCH
ROMAN POET	ROYAL DUKE	SAFE HANDS
ROMAN ROAD	ROYAL LINE	SAFE PLACE
ROMAN TYPE	ROYAL MAIL	SAFEST WAY
ROMAN WALL	ROYAL MILE	SAFETY NET
ROMANY RYE	ROYAL MINT	SAGE GREEN
ROOK RIFLE	ROYAL NAVY	SAIL ALONG
ROOK'S MOVE	ROYAL PARK	SAIL FORTH
ROOK'S NEST	ROYAL ROAD	SAILOR BOY
ROOK'S PAWN	ROYAL ROBE	SAILOR HAT
ROOM TO LET	ROYAL SCOT	SAIL ROUND
ROOT CAUSE	ROYAL SEAT	SAINT IVES
ROOTED OUT	ROYAL SHOW	SAINT JOAN
ROPE ONE IN	ROYAL TOUR	SAINT JOHN
ROPE TRICK	ROY CASTLE	SAINT PAUL
ROSE MARIE	ROY ROGERS	SAINT'S DAY
ROSE PETAL	RUBBED OUT	SALAD BOWL
ROSE WATER	RUB GENTLY	SALAD DAYS
ROSS ON WYE	RUDE WORDS	SALE PRICE
ROTTEN EGG	RUE THE DAY	SALES TALK
ROTTEN ROW	RUGBY BALL	SALLY LUNN
ROUGH CAST	RUGBY TEAM	SALOON BAR
ROUGH COAT	RUINED MAN	SALOON CAR
ROUGH COPY	RULE OF LAW	SALT FLATS
ROUGH EDGE	RUM AND PEP	SALT SPOON
ROUGHED IT	RUM BOTTLE	SALT WATER
ROUGH GAME	RUMP STEAK	SAM BROWNE
ROUGH IDEA	RUM RATION	SAME AGAIN
ROUGH LUCK	RUM RUNNER	SAME STAMP
ROUGH PLAN	RUN ACROSS	SAME TO YOU
ROUGH PLAY	RUN A HORSE	SAM WELLER
ROUGH ROAD	RUN AROUND	SANDY SOIL
ROUGH SKIN	RUN ASHORE	SAN MARINO
ROUGH TIME	RUN IT FINE	SANS SOUCI
ROUGH TYPE	RUNNING IN	SANTA CRUZ
ROUGH WORK	RUNNING ON	SARAH GAMP
ROUND FACE	RUN OF LUCK	SAVAGE DOG
ROUND GAME	RUN SECOND	SAVE MONEY
ROUND HAND	RUN TOO FAR	SAVE SPACE
ROUND HEAD	RUN TO SEED	SAVILE ROW
ROUND HOLE	RURAL DEAN	SAW THE AIR

SAX ROHMER	SEE REASON	SHADY TREE
SAY CHEESE	SEE THINGS	SHAGGY DOG
SAY LITTLE	SEIZE UPON	SHAKE A LEG
SAY NO MORE	SELECT FEW	SHAKE DOWN
SAY PLEASE	SELL BADLY	SHAKY HAND
SCALE DOWN	SELL SHORT	SHAM FIGHT
SCAPA FLOW	SELL SPACE	SHAM SLEEP
SCENT GAME	SEND A CHIT	SHANGRI LA
SCHOOL AGE	SEND A WIRE	SHAPE WELL
SCHOOL CAP	SEND FORTH	SHARP BEND
SCHOOL TIE	SENIOR BOY	SHARP BLOW
SCORE A TRY	SENIOR MAN	SHARP EDGE
SCORE CARD	SENNA PODS	SHARP EYES
SCOTCH EGG	SERGE SUIT	SHARP FALL
SCOTCH FIR	SERVE TIME	SHARP NOTE
SCOTS PINE	SERVE WELL	SHARP PAIN
SCRAPE OFF	SET ADRIFT	SHARP RISE
SCRAP IRON	SET ALIGHT	SHARP TURN
SCREAM OUT	SET AT EASE	SHARP WITS
SCREW DOWN	SET AT ODDS	SHARP WORK
SCRUM HALF	SET AT REST	SHED A TEAR
SEA BATTLE	SET A WATCH	SHED BLOOD
SEA BOTTOM	SET COURSE	SHED LIGHT
SEA BREEZE	SET EYES ON	SHEEP FARM
SEALED OFF	SET FIRE TO	SHEER DROP
SEAMY SIDE	SET IN HAND	SHEER FUNK
SEARCH FEE	SET MOVING	SHEER LUCK
SEARCH FOR	SET ON EDGE	SHEER SILK
SEARCH OUT	SET ON FIRE	SHEET IRON
SEA SHANTY	SET ON FOOT	SHELL PEAS
SEA TRAVEL	SET PHRASE	SHIP'S BELL
SEA URCHIN	SET SPEECH	SHIP'S BOAT
SEA VOYAGE	SET SQUARE	SHIP'S GUNS
SECOND ACT	SET THEM UP	SHOCK WAVE
SECOND CUP	SETTING IN	SHOE BRUSH
SECOND DAY	SETTING UP	SHOOT DOWN
SECOND ROW	SETTLED IN	SHOP FLOOR
SECOND SET	SETTLED UP	SHOP FRONT
SECOND TEE	SET TO WORK	SHOP HOURS
SECOND TRY	SET UP SHOP	SHOP TO LET
SECRET ART	SEVEN AGES	SHORN LAMB
SECURE JOB	SEVEN DAYS	SHORT HAIR
SEE A GHOST	SEVEN DEEP	SHORT HEAD
SEE DOUBLE	SEVEN FEET	SHORT HOLE
SEED PEARL	SEVEN QUID	SHORT LIFE
SEEING RED	SEVEN SEAS	SHORT LIST
SEEK A CLUE	SEX APPEAL	SHORT NOTE
SEEK AFTER	SEX SYMBOL	SHORT ODDS
SEEK PEACE	SHADY DEAL	SHORT POEM
SEEK SCOPE	SHADY NOOK	SHORT PUTT
SEE NO EVIL	SHADY SIDE	SHORT READ

SHORT REST	SIMON PURE	SLEEP WELL
SHORT SLIP	SIMPLE SUM	SLEEPY AIR
SHORT SPAN	SIMPLY FAB	SLIDE BACK
SHORT STAY	SING A SONG	SLIDE DOWN
SHORT STEP	SINGLE BED	SLIM WAIST
SHORT TAIL	SINGLE MAN	SLINK AWAY
SHORT TERM	SINGLE OUT	SLINK PAST
SHORT TIME	SING SMALL	SLIPPED IN
SHORT VIEW	SINK A PUTT	SLIPPED UP
SHORT WALK	SINK A WELL	SLIT SKIRT
SHORT WAVE	SIREN SONG	SLOP BASIN
SHORT WORD	SIREN SUIT	SLOPE ARMS
SHORT WORK	SIT AT HOME	SLOPE DOWN
SHORT SOCKS	SITTING UP	SLOPPY JOE
SHOUT DOWN	SIT UP LATE	SLOUCH HAT
SHOVEL HAT	SIX AND ONE	SLOW DEATH
SHOVE PAST	SIX AND SIX	SLOW MARCH
SHOW CAUSE	SIX AND TEN	SLOW MATCH
SHOWED OFF	SIX AND TWO	SLOW MUSIC
SHOWED OUT	SIX A PENNY	SLOW PULSE
SHOW FIGHT	SIX HEARTS	SLOW START
SHOW MERCY	SIX MONTHS	SLOW TEMPO
SHOW ONE IN	SIX O'CLOCK	SLOW TRAIN
SHOW PIECE	SIX OUNCES	SLOW WALTZ
SHOW PLACE	SIX POINTS	SLY AS A FOX
SHOW ROUND	SIX POUNDS	SLY CORNER
SHOW SIGNS	SIX SPADES	SLY HUMOUR
SHOW STYLE	SIXTH FORM	SMALL ARMS
SHRIEK OUT	SIXTH HOLE	SMALL BEER
SHRILL CRY	SIXTH PART	SMALL BORE
SHRIVEL UP	SIXTH RACE	SMALL COAL
SHUT TIGHT	SIXTH TIME	SMALL COIN
SICK LEAVE	SIX TO FOUR	SMALL DEBT
SICKLY HUE	SIX TRICKS	SMALL DOOR
SIDE ISSUE	SIX WHEELS	SMALL FEET
SIGHT GAME	SIZE EIGHT	SMALL FLAT
SIGHT LAND	SIZE SEVEN	SMALL GAME
SIGNAL BOX	SIZE THREE	SMALL HEAD
SIGN A PACT	SKATE OVER	SMALL HOLE
SIGN BELOW	SKETCH MAP	SMALL ITEM
SIGNED OFF	SKETCH OUT	SMALL LOAF
SILK PURSE	SKIM ALONG	SMALL LOAN
SILK SCARF	SKIN DIVER	SMALL MIND
SILK SOCKS	SKIP A MEAL	SMALL PART
SILLY FOOL	SLACK ROPE	SMALL PORT
SILLY TALK	SLACK TIME	SMALL RISK
SILVER CUP	SLANG WORD	SMALL ROOM
SILVER FIR	SLATE CLUB	SMALL SIZE
SILVER FOX	SLAVE AWAY	SMALL SLAM
SILVER SEA	SLAVE CAMP	SMALL SPOT
SILVER URN	SLEEP ON IT	SMALL TALK

SMALL TOWN	SOFT WORDS	SPARE PART
SMALL TWIG	SO IT SEEMS	SPARE ROOM
SMALL TYPE	SOLAR TIME	SPARE TIME
SMART ALEC	SOLAR YEAR	SPARE TYRE
SMARTEN UP	SOLDIER ON	SPARKS FLY
SMART GIRL	SOLE AGENT	SPEAK WELL
SMART PACE	SOLEMN VOW	SPEECH DAY
SMART SUIT	SOLE OWNER	SPEEDED UP
SMART WALK	SO LET IT BE	SPEED IT UP
SMELL A RAT	SOLE TRUST	SPEED KING
SMOKE A LOT	SOLID BALL	SPEND TIME
SMOKE BOMB	SOLID BODY	SPILL OVER
SMOKED EEL	SOLID FOOD	SPILL SALT
SMOKED HAM	SOLID FUEL	SPILT MILK
SMOKE RING	SOLID GOLD	SPIN A COIN
SMOKY CITY	SOLID MASS	SPIN A DISC
SMOKY FIRE	SOLID MEAL	SPIN A YARN
SMOKY ROOM	SOLID TYRE	SPIN DRIER
SMOOTH OUT	SOLID VOTE	SPIN ROUND
SMOOTH SEA	SOLO DANCE	SPIT IT OUT
SMUGGLE IN	SOLO WHIST	SPLIT OPEN
SNAIL PACE	SOME HOPES	SPLIT PEAS
SNAKE BITE	SONG CYCLE	SPLIT VOTE
SNAPPED UP	SONG TITLE	SPONGE BAG
SNEAK AWAY	SON OF A GUN	SPONGE OUT
SNEAK PAST	SOON AFTER	SPORTS CAR
SNOB VALUE	SORE PLACE	SPORTS DAY
SNOW QUEEN	SORE POINT	SPORTS FAN
SNOW SCENE	SORE TRIAL	SPOT CHECK
SNOW STORM	SO TO SPEAK	SPOT DANCE
SNOW WHITE	SOTTO VOCE	SPOT OF INK
SNUGGLE UP	SOUL OF WIT	SPOT PRIZE
SOAP OPERA	SOUND BODY	SPOT TO EAT
SOAR ABOVE	SOUND MIND	SPREAD OUT
SOBER DOWN	SOUND TYPE	SPRING OUT
SOBER FACT	SOUND WAVE	SPUN GLASS
SOB SISTER	SOUP LADLE	SQUARE JAW
SOCIAL WAR	SOUP PLATE	SQUARE LEG
SODA WATER	SOUP SPOON	SQUARE OFF
SOFT DRINK	SOUR CREAM	SQUARE ONE
SOFT FRUIT	SOUR TASTE	SQUARE PEG
SOFT GOING	SOUTH BANK	SQUAT DOWN
SOFT GOODS	SOUTH POLE	SQUEEZE IN
SOFT HEART	SOUTH SEAS	STABLE BOY
SOFT LIGHT	SOUTH WIND	STAFF FUND
SOFT MUSIC	SOUTH ZONE	STAFF ROOM
SOFT PEDAL	SPACE RACE	STAFF WORK
SOFT THING	SPACE SHIP	STAGE DOOR
SOFT TOUCH	SPACE SUIT	STAGE NAME
SOFT VOICE	SPARE CASH	STAGE PLAY
SOFT WATER	SPARE COPY	STAGE SHOW

STAGGER IN	STEEL MILL	STRAW POLL
STAG PARTY	STEEL TAPE	STRAW VOTE
STALE CAKE	STEEP HILL	STRAY AWAY
STALE JOKE	STEP ASIDE	STREAK OUT
STALE LOAF	STEP DANCE	STREAM OUT
STALE NEWS	STEP SHORT	STREET MAP
STAMP DOWN	STICK AT IT	STRETCH UP
STAMP DUTY	STICK 'EM UP	STRIDE OFF
STAND AWAY	STICK FAST	STRIDE OUT
STAND BACK	STICK IT ON	STRIKE OFF
STAND BAIL	STICK TO IT	STRIKE OIL
STAND DOWN	STICKY END	STRIKE OUT
STAND EASY	STIFF GALE	STRIKE PAY
STAND FAST	STIFF NECK	STRING BAG
STAND FIRM	STIFF TEST	STRING OUT
STAND HIGH	STILL LIFE	STRIP BARE
STAND IDLE	STILL MORE	STRIP CLUB
STAND OVER	STILL OPEN	STRONG ALE
ST. ANDREWS	STILL PANCRAS	STRONG ARM
STAND UP TO	STILL ROOM	STRONG BOX
STAR ACTOR	STILL WINE	STRONG MAN
STARE DOWN	STINK BOMB	STRONG TEA
STAR PUPIL	STIRRED UP	STRUCK OFF
STARRY SKY	ST. MATTHEW	STRUCK OUT
STAR SHELL	ST. MICHAEL	STRUNG OUT
START A ROW	STOCK FARM	STUD HORSE
START A WAR	STOCK LIST	STUDIO ONE
START BACK	STOCK PART	STUD POKER
STARTED UP	STOCK PILE	STUDY FORM
START TO GO	STOCK SIZE	STUDY HARD
START WITH	STOKE CITY	SUB JUDICE
START WORK	STOLE AWAY	SUDDEN END
STARVE OUT	STONE COLD	SUDDEN FIT
STATE FAIR	STONE DEAD	SUEZ CANAL
STATE FARM	STONE DEAF	SUGAR BEET
STATUS QUO	STONE WALL	SUGAR CANE
STAY ALIVE	STOOP DOWN	SUGAR PLUM
STAY AWAKE	STOP A BLOW	SUIT AT LAW
STAYED OUT	STOP A LEAK	SULTRY AIR
STAYED PUT	STOP AND GO	SUMMING UP
STAY IN BED	STOP IN BED	SUN BONNET
STAY STILL	STOPPED UP	SUNDAY TEA
ST. BERNARD	STOP PRESS	SUN HELMET
STEAL AWAY	STOP SHORT	SUNK FENCE
STEAL PAST	STOP THIEF!	SUN LOUNGE
STEAL UP ON	STOP VALVE	SUNNY SIDE
STEAM BATH	STORE AWAY	SUN VALLEY
STEAM IRON	STORM CONE	SUN YAT-SEN
STEAM OPEN	STORMY SEA	SUPPOSE SO
STEEL BAND	ST. PANCRAS	SURE THING
STEEL BILL	ST. PATRICK	SURE TO WIN
	STRAP DOWN	

SURVEY MAP	TAKE A NOTE	TALL STORY
SUSAN SHAW	TAKE APART	TALL WOMAN
SWAGGER IN	TAKE A PEEP	TANK CORPS
SWALLOW UP	TAKE A PILL	TAR BARREL
SWARM OVER	TAKE A REST	TASK FORCE
SWEAR BY IT	TAKE A RISK	TASMAN SEA
SWEAR WORD	TAKE A SEAT	TAWNY PORT
SWEEP AWAY	TAKE A SNAP	TAX DEMAND
SWEEP DOWN	TAKE A TAXI	TAX FIDDLE
SWEEP PAST	TAKE A TEST	TAX REBATE
SWEET CORN	TAKE A TOSS	TAX RELIEF
SWEET DISH	TAKE A TRAM	TAY BRIDGE
SWEET NELL	TAKE A TRIP	TEA FOR TWO
SWEET PEAS	TAKE A TURN	TEA GARDEN
SWEET SHOP	TAKE A VIEW	TEA KETTLE
SWEET SONG	TAKE A VOTE	TEA LEAVES
SWEET WINE	TAKE A WALK	TEAR ABOUT
SWELL IDEA	TAKE A WIFE	TEAR ALONG
SWELL TIME	TAKE COVER	TEAR APART
SWEPT AWAY	TAKE DRUGS	TEA RATION
SWING BACK	TAKE HEART	TEAR IN TWO
SWING HIGH	TAKE IN TOW	TED DEXTER
SWISS ALPS	TAKE ISSUE	TEDDY BEAR
SWISS CITY	TAKE LEAVE	TEDDY GIRL
SWISS NAVY	TAKE LUNCH	TELL NO LIE
SWISS ROLL	TAKE MY TIP	TELL NO ONE
SWITCH OFF	TAKEN DOWN	TELL TALES
SWOOP DOWN	TAKE NOTES	TEMPLE BAR
	TAKE ON OIL	TEMPT FATE
T—9	TAKE PAINS	TEN AND ONE
TAB HUNTER	TAKE PLACE	TEN AND SIX
TABLE BIRD	TAKE PRIDE	TEN AND TEN
TABLE FISH	TAKE RISKS	TEN AND TWO
TABLE SALT	TAKE ROOMS	TEN A PENNY
TABLE TALK	TAKE SHAPE	TENDER AGE
TABLE WINE	TAKE SIDES	TEN MONTHS
TAKE ABACK	TAKE SNUFF	TENNIS ACE
TAKE A BATH	TAKE STEPS	TENNIS NET
TAKE A CARD	TAKE STOCK	TEN O'CLOCK
TAKE A CASE	TAKE TURNS	TENOR CLEF
TAKE A COPY	TAKE UP ART	TENOR DRUM
TAKE A CURE	TAKING OFF	TENOR OBOE
TAKE A DROP	TAKING OUT	TEN OUNCES
TAKE A FALL	TALE OF WOE	TEN POINTS
TAKE AFTER	TALK ABOUT	TEN POUNDS
TAKE A HAND	TALKED BIG	TEN ROUNDS
TAKE A HINT	TALKED OUT	TENTH HOLE
TAKE A LOOK	TALK ROUND	TENTH PART
TAKE A MEAL	TALK SENSE	TENTH TIME
TAKE AMISS	TALK TRIPE	TEST MATCH
TAKE AN ELL	TALL ORDER	TEST PAPER

TEST PIECE
TEST PILOT
TEXAS CITY
THAT'S THAT
THE ALBANY
THE ALBION
THE ALLIES
THE AMAZON
THE ARMADA
THE AUTUMN
THE AZORES
THE BALTIC
THE BIG TOP
THE BOARDS
THE BOTTOM
THE BOUNTY
THE BOURSE
THE BOWERY
THE BROADS
THE BUDGET
THE CINEMA
THE CLERGY
THE CREEPS
THE CRIMEA
THE DALEKS
THE DANUBE
THE DELUGE
THE DESERT
THE EMPIRE
THE FALLEN
THE FINISH
THE FLICKS
THE FLOODS
THE FRENCH
THE FUHRER
THE FUTURE
THE GANGES
THE GENTRY
THE GOSPEL
THE GRACES
THE GUARDS
THE HILTON
THE ICE AGE
THE JET AGE
THE JUNGLE
THE KAISER
THE LANCET
THE LATEST
THE LATTER
THE LEVANT
THE LIVING

THE LIZARD
THE LOSERS
THE LOUVRE
THE MAQUIS
THE MASSES
THE MASTER
THE MEDWAY
THEME SONG
THE METHOD
THE MIKADO
THE MINUET
THE MORGUE
THE MOVIES
THE OCCULT
THE OLD VIC
THE OLD WAY
THE ORIENT
THE PAPERS
THE PEOPLE
THE PLAGUE
THE PLOUGH
THE POLICE
THE PUBLIC
THE QUEENS
THE RABBLE
THE RED SEA
THE RINGER
THE RIVALS
THE ROCKET
THE RUBBER
THE SCOTCH
THE SCRIPT
THESE DAYS
THE SENATE
THE SEVERN
THE SHAKES
THE SHIRES
THE SIGHTS
THE SOLENT
THE SPHINX
THE SPLITS
THE SPOILS
THE SPRING
THE SQUIRE
THE STATES
THE STITCH
THE STOCKS
THE STONES
THE STRAND
THE SUMMER
THE TATLER

THE TEMPLE
THE THAMES
THE TICKET
THE TIVOLI
THE UMPIRE
THE UNSEEN
THE WAY OUT
THE WINNER
THE WINTER
THEY'RE OFF!
THICK HAIR
THICK HEAD
THICK MIST
THICK SKIN
THICK SNOW
THICK SOUP
THICK WIRE
THIN BLOOD
THINK BACK
THINK BEST
THINK FAST
THINK HARD
THINK LONG
THINK OVER
THIN ON TOP
THIN SHELL
THIN SLICE
THIN TWINE
THIRD FORM
THIRD GEAR
THIRD HAND
THIRD HEAT
THIRD HOLE
THIRD JUMP
THIRD LINE
THIRD PART
THIRD RACE
THIRD RATE
THIRD TEAM
THIRD TERM
THIRD TEST
THIRD TIME
THIRD WEEK
THIRD YEAR
THIRST FOR
THIRTY ALL
THIS EARTH
THIS MONTH
THIS WAY IN
THIS WAY UP
THORPE BAY

THRASH OUT	TIP AND RUN	TOTEM POLE
THREE ACES	TIPPED OFF	TOTE PRICE
THREE ACTS	TIPSY CAKE	TO THE BONE
THREE DAYS	TIP-UP SEAT	TO THE BRIM
THREE DEEP	TIRED EYES	TO THE EAST
THREE EGGS	TIRING JOB	TO THE FORE
THREE FEET	TIT FOR TAT	TO THE FULL
THREE LAPS	TITHE BARN	TO THE GOOD
THREE ONES	TITIAN RED	TO THE HILT
THREE PIPS	TITLE DEED	TO THE LAST
THREE QUID	TITLE PAGE	TO THE LEFT
THREE SETS	TITLE ROLE	TO THE LIFE
THREE STAR	TITO GOBBI	TO THE MOON
THREE TENS	TO A DEGREE	TO THE WEST
THREE TWOS	TOAST RACK	TO THIS DAY
THROW A FIT	TO BE BRIEF	TOUCH DOWN
THROW AWAY	TODAY WEEK	TOUCHED UP
THROW BACK	TODDLE OFF	TOUCH UPON
THROW DOWN	TOGGED OUT	TOUCH WOOD
THROWN OUT	TOILET SET	TOUGHEN UP
THROW OPEN	TOKEN VOTE	TOUGH LUCK
THROW OVER	TO LEEWARD	TOUGH MEAT
TICKED OFF	TOMMY FARR	TOUGH SKIN
TIC-TAC MAN	TOM PEARSE	TOUGH SPOT
TIDAL FLOW	TOM SAWYER	TOWER HILL
TIDAL RACE	TON OF COAL	TOWER OVER
TIDAL WAVE	TON OF COKE	TOWN CLERK
TIED HOUSE	TON OF LEAD	TOWN CRIER
TIE IN A BOW	TON OF SALT	TOWN HOUSE
TIGER HUNT	TON WEIGHT	TOWN MOUSE
TIGER LILY	TOOK PLACE	TOY POODLE
TIGER MOTH	TOOL CHEST	TRACE BACK
TIGHTEN UP	TOO LITTLE	TRACK DOWN
TIGHT GRIP	TO ONE SIDE	TRACK SUIT
TIGHT HAND	TOO STRONG	TRADE BOOM
TIGHT REIN	TOP DRAWER	TRADE FAIR
TIGHT SPOT	TOP PEOPLE	TRADE MARK
TIME BEING	TOP SECRET	TRADE NAME
TIME CHECK	TOP STOREY	TRADE WIND
TIME FLIES	TOP TO TAIL	TRAIL ARMS
TIME LIMIT	TOP TWENTY	TRAIL BOSS
TIME OF DAY	TOP WEIGHT	TRAIN FARE
TIME OF WAR	TORCH SONG	TRAIN LOAD
TIME STUDY	TORY PARTY	TRAM DEPOT
TIME TAKEN	TOSS ABOUT	TRAMPLE ON
TIME TO EAT	TOSS A COIN	TRAP THREE
TIME TO PAY	TOSS ASIDE	TREAD DOWN
TINDER BOX	TOSS FOR IT	TREE STUMP
TIN HELMET	TOSSING UP	TRIAL GAME
TIN LIZZIE	TOTAL COST	TRIAL JURY
TIN OF SOUP	TOTAL LOSS	TRIAL SPIN

TRIAL TRIP	TURN GREEN	U—9
TRIBAL LAW	TURNING IN	UGLY AS SIN
TRIBAL WAR	TURNING UP	UGLY CROWD
TRICKY BIT	TURN IT OFF	UNCLE TOBY
TRICKY JOB	TURN LOOSE	UNDER A BAN
TRIED HARD	TURN NASTY	UNDER ARMS
TRIED IT ON	TURN RIGHT	UNDER FIRE
TRILBY HAT	TURN ROUND	UNDER OATH
TRIM WAIST	TURN TO ICE	UNDER SAIL
TRIPPED UP	TURN WHITE	UNDER SEAL
TROJAN WAR	TWEED SUIT	UNHEARD OF
TROT ALONG	TWELVE MEN	UNHOLY JOY
TROT IT OUT	TWICE A DAY	UNHOLY ROW
TRUDGE OFF	TWICE FIVE	UNION CARD
TRUE STORY	TWICE FOUR	UNION FLAG
TRUE VALUE	TWICE NINE	UNION JACK
TRUE WORTH	TWICE OVER	UNIT TRUST
TRUMP CARD	TWICE TOLD	UP AGAINST
TRUNK CALL	TWIGGED IT	UP AND AT 'EM
TRUNK LINE	TWIN GIRLS	UP AND AWAY
TRUNK ROAD	TWIN SCREW	UP AND DOWN
TRUSSED UP	TWIN SOULS	UP AND OVER
TRUST DEED	TWO AND ONE	UP COUNTRY
TRUST FUND	TWO AND SIX	UP FOR SALE
TRUTH DRUG	TWO AND TEN	UPPER CASE
TRUTH GAME	TWO AND TWO	UPPER DECK
TRY HARDER	TWO A PENNY	UPPER FORM
TRY IN VAIN	TWO COPIES	UPPER HAND
TRY TO STOP	TWO FIFTHS	UPPER LIMB
TSETSE FLY	TWO FOR ONE	UPPER PART
TUBAL CAIN	TWO FOR TEA	UP THE HILL
TUBE TRAIN	TWO HALVES	UP THE LINE
TUCK ONE IN	TWO HEARTS	UP THE POLE
TUCK ONE UP	TWO LOAVES	UP THE WALL
TUDOR ROSE	TWO MONTHS	UP TO SNUFF
TULIP TREE	TWO NINTHS	URCHIN CUT
TULSE HILL	TWO O'CLOCK	URIAH HEEP
TUMBLE OFF	TWO OUNCES	URSA MAJOR
TUMBLE OUT	TWO POINTS	URSA MINOR
TUMMY ACHE	TWO POUNDS	USE AS A PEG
TUNNY FISH	TWO QUARTS	USUAL TEXT
TUN OF BEER	TWO ROUNDS	UTTER LOSS
TUN OF WINE	TWO SPADES	UTTER RUIN
TURFED OUT	TWO STOOLS	
TURK'S HEAD	TWO STRAWS	V—9
TURN ABOUT	TWO THIRDS	VACANT LOT
TURN AGAIN	TWO TO COME	VADE MECUM
TURN A HAIR	TWO TRICKS	VAGUE HOPE
TURN ASIDE	TWO VERSES	VAGUE IDEA
TURNED OFF	TWO VOICES	VAIN ABUSE
TURNED OUT	TWO WHEELS	VAIN BOAST

VAIN GLORY	WAIT THERE	WATER POLO
VANITY BAG	WAKE EARLY	WATER RATE
VAST FRAME	WAKES WEEK	WATER TANK
VAULT OVER	WALK ABOUT	WAVE ASIDE
VEER RIGHT	WALKED OFF	WAVE A WAND
VEER ROUND	WALKED OUT	WAX CANDLE
VENIAL SIN	WALKER CUP	WAX EFFIGY
VERSE FORM	WALK ON AIR	WAX FIGURE
VERS LIBRE	WALK OUT ON	WAX STRONG
VERY IMAGE	WALTZ HOME	WAY BEHIND
VERY LIGHT	WALTZ KING	WAY OF LIFE
VERY OFTEN	WALTZ TIME	WEAK CHEST
VERY QUICK	WALTZ TUNE	WEAKER SEX
VERY STEEP	WANDER OFF	WEAK HEART
VERY SWEET	WANDER OUT	WEAK POINT
VEX A SAINT	WANTED MAN	WEAK STATE
VICE SQUAD	WAR DAMAGE	WEAK STYLE
VICE VERSA	WAR EFFORT	WEAK THING
VICKI BAUM	WAR GRAVES	WEAK VOICE
VIC OLIVER	WAR HEROES	WEAK WOMAN
VILLA PARK	WAR LEADER	WEALTH TAX
VIN DU PAYS	WARM HEART	WEAR A HALO
VINGT ET UN	WARM NIGHT	WEAR A MASK
VIOLIN BOW	WARM PLACE	WEAR BLACK
VISUAL AID	WARM SPELL	WEAVE A WEB
VITAL PART	WAR MUSEUM	WEB OF LIES
VITAL ROLE	WARM WATER	WEEDED OUT
VIVE LE ROI	WARNED OFF	WEIGH DOWN
VIVID BLUE	WAR OFFICE	WEIGHED IN
VOID SPACE	WAR ON WANT	WELCOME IN
VOLTE FACE	WAR POLICY	WELL AGAIN
VOLUME ONE	WAR RECORD	WELL AHEAD
VOLUME SIX	WAR VICTIM	WELL AIRED
VOLUME TEN	WAR WORKER	WELL BEGUN
VOLUME TWO	WASH CLEAN	WELL BELOW
VOTING AGE	WASHED OUT	WELL OILED
VOTING DAY	WASPS' NEST	WELL SET UP
VOX HUMANA	WASP STING	WELL SPENT
VOX POPULI	WASP WAIST	WELL TAPED
	WASTE AWAY	WELSH BARD
W—9	WASTE FOOD	WELSH HARP
WAGE CLAIM	WASTE LAND	WENT AHEAD
WAGE PAUSE	WASTE TIME	WENT BELOW
WAGES BILL	WATCH OVER	WENT FORTH
WAGE SCALE	WATER BABY	WENT ROUND
WAGE SLAVE	WATER DOWN	WENT TO BED
WAIST HIGH	WATER FOWL	WENT TO POT
WAIT ABOUT	WATER HOLE	WENT TO SEA
WAIT FOR IT!	WATER JUMP	WENT TO WAR
WAIT FOR ME!	WATER LILY	WENT UNDER
WAIT TABLE	WATER MAIN	WENT WRONG

WEST COAST	WIDE FIELD	WORD MAGIC
WEST FRONT	WIDE GUESS	WORK BENCH
WEST POINT	WIDE RANGE	WORKED OUT
WEST WALES	WIDE SCOPE	WORKER BEE
WET SEASON	WIDE SWEEP	WORK IT OUT
WET SPONGE	WIDE WORLD	WORK LOOSE
WET WICKET	WIGAN PIER	WORK OF ART
WHALE MEAT	WILD BEAST	WORK PARTY
WHAT A LARK!	WILD GOOSE	WORKS BAND
WHAT A LIFE!	WILD GRASS	WORK STUDY
WHAT A PITY!	WILD GUESS	WORK TABLE
WHAT'S WHAT	WILD HORSE	WORLD BANK
WHEAT GERM	WILD NIGHT	WORLD FAIR
WHEEL AWAY	WILD PARTY	WORLD'S END
WHERE IS IT?	WILD STATE	WORLD TOUR
WHIP ROUND	WILD THYME	WORSE LUCK
WHISK AWAY	WILL FYFFE	WORST PART
WHITE BEAR	WILL POWER	WORST TEAM
WHITE CITY	WILL TO WIN	WORTH A LOT
WHITE FISH	WIN A FIGHT	WORTH A TRY
WHITE FLAG	WIN A MATCH	WORTHY AIM
WHITE GOLD	WIN A POINT	WRAPPED UP
WHITE HAIR	WIN A PRIZE	WRAP ROUND
WHITE HEAT	WIND GAUGE	WRENCH OUT
WHITE HOPE	WINDING UP	WRITE BACK
WHITE KING	WIND SCALE	WRITE DOWN
WHITE LADY	WINDY SIDE	WRITE HOME
WHITE LEAD	WIN EASILY	WRITE WELL
WHITE LINE	WINE GLASS	WRONG DATE
WHITE LOAF	WINE PARTY	WRONG DOOR
WHITE MARK	WIN FAVOUR	WRONG IDEA
WHITE MEAT	WINGED ANT	WRONG MOVE
WHITE MICE	WINKLE OUT	WRONG NAME
WHITE NILE	WIN OR LOSE	WRONG RATE
WHITE NOTE	WIN RENOWN	WRONG ROAD
WHITE PAWN	WIN THE CUP	WRONG SIDE
WHITE PINE	WIN THE DAY	WRONG STEP
WHITE PORT	WIPE CLEAN	WRONG TIME
WHITE RACE	WIRE FENCE	WRONG TURN
WHITE ROOK	WISE WOMAN	WRONG VIEW
WHITE ROSE	WITCH HUNT	WRONG WORD
WHITE SALE	WITH A BANG	WROUGHT UP
WHITE SPOT	WITH A WILL	WYATT EARP
WHITE STAR	WITH SKILL	WYE VALLEY
WHITE WINE	WITH SUGAR	
WHOLE SKIN	WOMAN'S MAN	Y—9
WICKED LIE	WONDER WHY	YACHT CLUB
WICKED ONE	WOODEN BOX	YACHT RACE
WIDE APART	WOODEN LEG	YARD OF ALE
WIDE AWAKE	WOOD GREEN	YEA AND NAY
WIDE BERTH	WOOD NYMPH	YELLOW DOG

YELLOW SEA
YES PLEASE
YET TO COME
YORKED OUT
YOUNG BIRD
YOUNG GIRL
YOUNG FOLK
YOUNG IDEA
YOUNG LADY
YOUNG LOVE
YOUNG THUG
YOUR FAULT
YOUR GRACE
YOUR SHARE
YOUTH CLUB

Z—9
ZOO INMATE
ZUYDER ZEE

A—10
ABE LINCOLN
A BIT PAST IT
ABJECT FEAR
ABLE FELLOW
ABLE SEAMAN
ABLE TO COPE
ABOARD SHIP
ABOVE BOARD
ABOVE IT ALL
ABOVE PRICE
ABOVE WATER
ABRUPT EXIT
ACE OF CLUBS
ACE SERVICE
ACETIC ACID
ACHING FEET
ACHING VOID
ACID REMARK
ACID TONGUE
ACT AS AGENT
ACT AS COACH
ACT AS GUIDE
ACTIVE LIFE
ACTIVE LIST
ACTIVE MIND
ACTIVE PART
ACT OF FAITH
ACT OF FOLLY
ACT OF GRACE
ACT OF MERCY

ACT OF PIETY
ACT OF UNION
ACT THE FOOL
ACT THE GOAT
ACT THE HERO
ACT THE HOST
ACT THE PART
ACUTE ANGLE
ADAM AND EVE
ADAM'S APPLE
ADD A CLAUSE
ADDIS ABABA
ADELE LEIGH
ADOPTED SON
ADVICE NOTE
ADVISE WELL
AERIAL VIEW
AFRICA STAR
AFTER A TIME
AFTER DEATH
AFTER HOURS
AFTER LUNCH
AFTER TODAY
A GREAT DEAL
A GREAT MANY
AID AND ABET
AIM TOO HIGH
AIR DEFENCE
AIR DISPLAY
AIR FREIGHT
AIR HOSTESS
AIR MARSHAL
AIR SERVICE
AIR WARFARE
ALARM CLOCK
ALBERT HALL
ALF'S BUTTON
ALL BUT A FEW
ALL COLOURS
ALL CORRECT
ALL DAY LONG
ALL FORLORN
ALL FOR LOVE
ALL HALLOWS
ALL HAYWIRE
ALL IN A HEAP
ALL IN ORDER
ALL KEYED UP
ALL MIXED UP
ALL MOD CONS
ALL OF A GLOW

ALL OF A HEAP
ALL OF A KIND
ALL PARTIES
ALL PRESENT
ALL SET TO GO
ALL THE BEST
ALL THE LUCK
ALL THE MORE
ALL THE RAGE
ALL THE REST
ALL THE SAME
ALL THE TIME
ALL THE YEAR
ALL THROUGH
ALL-TIME LOW
ALL TOO SOON
ALL TOO WELL
ALMOND CAKE
ALMOND TREE
ALMOST DEAD
ALMOST FULL
ALMOST OVER
ALPACA COAT
ALPINE CLUB
ALPINE RACE
ALTAR CLOTH
AMBER LIGHT
AMBLE ALONG
AMEN CORNER
AMPLE CAUSE
AMPLE MEANS
AMPLE SCOPE
AMY JOHNSON
AND ALL THAT
AND SO FORTH
AND SO TO BED
AND THE LIKE
AND THE REST
ANGEL CHILD
ANGLED SHOT
ANGORA GOAT
ANGORA WOOL
ANGRY SCENE
ANGRY WORDS
ANILINE DYE
ANIMAL FARM
ANIMAL FOOD
ANIMAL GRAB
ANIMAL LIFE
ANKLE SOCKS
ANNABEL LEE

ANNA NEAGLE	ASTRAL BODY	AXE TO GRIND
ANNE BOLEYN	AT ALL COST	AXLE GREASE
ANNO DOMINI	AT ALL HOURS	
ANNUAL RENT	AT ALL TIMES	**B—10**
ANOTHER DAY	AT ANY PRICE	BABE IN ARMS
ANOTHER WAY	AT A PREMIUM	BABE UNBORN
ANSWER BACK	AT A STRETCH	BABY FARMER
ANY OLD IRON	AT A TANGENT	BABY'S DUMMY
ANY OLD TIME	AT A VENTURE	BABY SITTER
APPLE GREEN	AT DAYBREAK	BACK A HORSE
APPLE SAUCE	AT DAYLIGHT	BACK A LOSER
APPLIED ART	AT FULL TIDE	BACK GARDEN
APRICOT JAM	AT GUN-POINT	BACK IN TIME
APRON STAGE	AT HALF-MAST	BACK MARKER
APT ANALOGY	AT ITS WORST	BACK NUMBER
APT SCHOLAR	AT LONG LAST	BACK RASHER
AQUA FORTIS	ATOMIC BOMB	BACK STAIRS
ARABIAN SEA	ATOMIC PILE	BACK STITCH
ARAB LEAGUE	AT ONE'S BEST	BACK STREET
ARABLE FARM	AT ONE SCOOP	BACK STROKE
ARAB LEGION	AT ONE'S DOOR	BACK TO BACK
ARABLE LAND	AT ONE'S EASE	BACK TO BASE
ARAB STATES	AT ONE'S FEET	BACK TO WORK
ARCHED BACK	AT ONE'S POST	BACON CURER
ARENA STAGE	AT ONE'S SIDE	BAD ACCOUNT
ARMED FORCE	AT SEA LEVEL	BAD ACTRESS
ARMED GUARD	ATTEND MASS	BAD BARGAIN
ARMED TRUCE	AT THE ALTAR	BAD CLIMATE
ARMS AKIMBO	AT THE DERBY	BAD COMPANY
ARM'S LENGTH	AT THE FRONT	BAD CONDUCT
ARMY DOCTOR	AT THE LOCAL	BAD DICTION
ARMY ORDERS	AT THE OPERA	BAD EXAMPLE
ARRIVE LATE	AT THE READY	BAD FORTUNE
ART GALLERY	AT THE SLOPE	BAD GRAMMAR
ARTHUR RANK	AT THE WHEEL	BAD HARVEST
ART STUDENT	AT THE WORST	BAD HUSBAND
ART SUBJECT	AT VARIANCE	BAD LEARNER
ART THEATRE	AT WHAT TIME?	BAD LOOKOUT
AS ARRANGED	AUBURN HAIR	BAD MANAGER
ASCOT HEATH	AULD REEKIE	BAD MANNERS
ASCOT RACES	AU PAIR GIRL	BAD MISTAKE
AS INTENDED	AUTUMN WIND	BAD OUTLOOK
ASK A FAVOUR	AVA GARDNER	BAD QUALITY
ASK FOR HELP	AVANT GARDE	BAD SERVANT
ASK FOR MORE	AVERAGE AGE	BAD SERVICE
ASK FOR TIME	AVERAGE MAN	BAD SOCIETY
ASK TOO MUCH	AVERAGE OUT	BAD TACTICS
AS MAN TO MAN	AVID DESIRE	BAD THEATRE
AS PER USUAL	AWAIT TRIAL	BAD WEATHER
AS PROMISED	AWFUL SIGHT	BAD WRITING
ASTON VILLA	AWKWARD AGE	BAG OF BONES

BAG OF FLOUR
BAG OF NAILS
BAGS OF TIME
BAITED TRAP
BAKED APPLE
BAKED BEANS
BAKER'S SHOP
BALAAM'S ASS
BALANCE DUE
BALLET SHOE
BALL OF FIRE
BALL OF WOOL
BALTIC PORT
BANANA BOAT
BANANA SKIN
BAND LEADER
BAND OF HOPE
BAND OF IRON
BANDY WORDS
BANISH FEAR
BANK RAIDER
BANK ROBBER
BANK TO BANK
BANK VAULTS
BANNED BOOK
BANTAM COCK
BAN THE BOMB
BARBARY APE
BARBED WIRE
BARD OF AVON
BARE BOARDS
BARE CHANCE
BARELY PASS
BARLEY WINE
BAR PARLOUR
BARREN LAND
BASE MOTIVE
BASIC TRUTH
BAT AND BALL
BATH OLIVER
BATTEN DOWN
BATTER DOWN
BATTERY HEN
BEACH GAMES
BEACHY HEAD
BEACON FIRE
BEAK STREET
BEAR GARDEN
BEAR IN MIND
BEAR MALICE
BEAR WITH ME

BEAT HOLLOW
BEAT THE AIR
BEAUTY SHOP
BEAUTY SPOT
BE CHAIRMAN
BECKY SHARP
BECOME LESS
BECOME SANE
BEDDED DOWN
BED OF NAILS
BED OF ROSES
BEEF CATTLE
BEER BARREL
BEER BOTTLE
BEER CELLAR
BEER GARDEN
BEFORE DAWN
BEFORE DUSK
BEFORE LONG
BEFORE NOON
BEFORE TIME
BEG A FAVOUR
BEG FOR MORE
BEG FOR TIME
BEGGAR MAID
BEGIN AGAIN
BEHAVE WELL
BEHIND BARS
BEHIND TIME
BE INFERIOR
BELL THE CAT
BELOW DECKS
BELTED EARL
BE MERCIFUL
BE MISTAKEN
BENDED KNEE
BENEATH ONE
BENT DOUBLE
BEN TRAVERS
BE PREPARED
BERLIN WALL
BE SENSIBLE
BE SOCIABLE
BEST BITTER
BEST CHANCE
BEST EFFORT
BEST FRIEND
BEST OF FIVE
BEST OF PALS
BEST PEOPLE
BEST POLICY

BEST SELLER
BEST SILVER
BEST WAY OUT
BEST WISHES
BE SUPERIOR
BE TOO SMART
BETTE DAVIS
BETTER DAYS
BETTER DEAD
BETTER HALF
BETTER HOLE
BETTER IDEA
BETTER SELF
BETTER SORT
BETTING ACT
BETTING MAN
BEYOND HOPE
BE YOURSELF
BIBLE CLASS
BID AGAINST
BIG BAD WOLF
BIG BROTHER
BIGGER SIZE
BIGGIN HILL
BIG HELPING
BIG SUCCESS
BIG SWINDLE
BIJOU VILLA
BILL AND COO
BILL BENBOW
BILL OF FARE
BILL OF SALE
BING CROSBY
BINGO NIGHT
BIRD IN HAND
BIRD OF PREY
BISCUIT BOX
BISCUIT TIN
BISHOP'S HAT
BITE THE LIP
BITING WIND
BIT OF A MESS
BIT OF FLUFF
BITTER BEER
BITTER BLOW
BITTER PILL
BITTER RICE
BLACK ANGUS
BLACK ARROW
BLACK AS INK
BLACK AS JET

BLACK BEARD	BLOOD SERUM	BOOT POLISH
BLACK BEAST	BLOOD SPORT	BORED STIFF
BLACK BOOKS	BLOODY MARY	BORING WORK
BLACK BOOTS	BLOTTED OUT	BORN LEADER
BLACK BREAD	BLOW BY BLOW	BORN TO RULE
BLACK CLOUD	BLOW ME DOWN	BORSTAL BOY
BLACK DEATH	BLUE AND RED	BOSTON REEL
BLACK DRESS	BLUE CHEESE	BO TO A GOOSE
BLACKED OUT	BLUE DANUBE	BOTTLED ALE
BLACK FRIAR	BLUE DEVILS	BOTTOM GEAR
BLACK HEART	BLUE ENSIGN	BOTTOM RUNG
BLACK HORSE	BLUE GROTTO	BOUGHT OVER
BLACK LACES	BLUE LAGOON	BOULDER DAM
BLACK LOOKS	BLUE MONDAY	BOUNCE BACK
BLACK MAGIC	BLUE MURDER	BOUND TO WIN
BLACK MARIA	BLUE PENCIL	BOWIE KNIFE
BLACK PAINT	BLUE RIBAND	BOWL A BREAK
BLACK PAPER	BLUE RIBBON	BOWLED OVER
BLACK PATCH	BLUE STREAK	BOWL OF RICE
BLACK PIECE	BLUNT WORDS	BOWL OF SOUP
BLACK QUEEN	BOAT RACING	BOW THE KNEE
BLACK SHEEP	BOBBED HAIR	BOX BARRAGE
BLACK SHIRT	BOBBY HOWES	BOXING RING
BLACK SHOES	BODILY HARM	BOX OF DATES
BLACK SOCKS	BODILY PAIN	BOX OF PILLS
BLACK WATCH	BODY SWERVE	BOY AND GIRL
BLACK WIDOW	BOGGED DOWN	BOYS IN BLUE
BLANK PAPER	BOILED BEEF	BRACING AIR
BLANK SHEET	BOILED FISH	BRAIN CHILD
BLANK SPACE	BOILED RICE	BRAIN DRAIN
BLANK STARE	BOILER ROOM	BRAIN FEVER
BLANK VERSE	BOILER SUIT	BRAIN STORM
BLASTED OAK	BOILING HOT	BRANCH LINE
BLAZE A PATH	BOILING OIL	BRASS PLATE
BLAZING SUN	BOLD DESIGN	BRASS TACKS
BLEAK HOUSE	BOLD RELIEF	BRAVE FRONT
BLEED WHITE	BOLD STROKE	BRAVE IT OUT
BLEW THE LOT	BOMBAY DUCK	BREAD FRUIT
BLIND ALLEY	BOMB CRATER	BREAD ROUND
BLIND DRUNK	BOMB DAMAGE	BREAD SAUCE
BLIND FAITH	BONDED DEBT	BREAK A BONE
BLIND GUESS	BOND STREET	BREAK A DATE
BLITZ KRIEG	BONE TO PICK	BREAK A FALL
BLOCK OF ICE	BONUS ISSUE	BREAK AN ARM
BLONDE HAIR	BOOBY PRIZE	BREAK BREAD
BLOOD COUNT	BOOK A TABLE	BREAK COVER
BLOOD DONOR	BOOK CRITIC	BREAK FAITH
BLOOD GROUP	BOOKING FEE	BREAK FORTH
BLOOD HORSE	BOOK OF FATE	BREAK IN TWO
BLOOD MONEY	BOOK REVIEW	BREAK IT OFF
BLOOD ROYAL	BOOK RIGHTS	BREAK LOOSE

BREAK OF DAY	BROWN SHOES	**C—10**
BREAK RANKS	BROWN STONE	CABIN TRUNK
BREAK SHORT	BROWN STUDY	CADET CORPS
BREATHE OUT	BROWN SUGAR	CADET FORCE
BRER RABBIT	BRUSH ASIDE	CADGE A LIFT
BRETT YOUNG	BRUTE FORCE	CAFÉ AU LAIT
BRIDAL GOWN	BUBBLE BATH	CAKE OF SOAP
BRIDAL VEIL	BUBBLE OVER	CALL A TRUCE
BRIDGE A GAP	BUCKET SEAT	CALL BY NAME
BRIDGE CLUB	BUCKET SHOP	CALLED AWAY
BRIDGE HAND	BUCK RABBIT	CALL IT A DAY
BRIDGE OVER	BULK BUYING	CALL OF DUTY
BRIDGE ROLL	BULLET HEAD	CALL SPADES
BRIDLE PATH	BULLET HOLE	CALL TO ARMS
BRIDLE REIN	BULL MARKET	CALL TO MIND
BRIEF VISIT	BUMPER CROP	CALL TRUMPS
BRIGHT BLUE	BUMPING CAR	CAMDEN TOWN
BRIGHT EYES	BUMP SUPPER	CAME IN LAST
BRIGHT IDEA	BURNE JONES	CAME IN VIEW
BRIGHT SIDE	BURNT AMBER	CAMEL CORPS
BRIGHT SPOT	BURNT BLACK	CAMEL'S HUMP
BRIGHT STAR	BURNT TOAST	CAMEL'S MILK
BRING ABOUT	BURST FORTH	CAMEL TRAIN
BRING A CASE	BUSHEY PARK	CAMPING OUT
BRING A SUIT	BUS SHELTER	CANDY FLOSS
BRING FORTH	BUS STATION	CANNED BEER
BRING ROUND	BUSY AS A BEE	CANNED FOOD
BRING TO BAY	BUSY PERSON	CANNEL COAL
BRISK TRADE	BUSY STREET	CANNON BALL
BROAD ACRES	BUSY WORKER	CAP AND GOWN
BROAD ARROW	BUTTER DISH	CAPE COLONY
BROAD BEANS	BUTTONED UP	CAPER SAUCE
BROAD GAUGE	BUY AND SELL	CARBON COPY
BROKEN BACK	BUY BRITISH	CARD PLAYER
BROKEN BONE	BY ACCIDENT	CAREER GIRL
BROKEN DOWN	BY ALL MEANS	CARGO SPACE
BROKEN HOME	BY AND LARGE	CAR LICENCE
BROKEN LINE	BY ANY MEANS	CAROLE CARR
BROKEN NECK	BY CONTRAST	CARRIED OFF
BROKEN NOSE	BY DAYLIGHT	CARRIER BAG
BROKEN REED	BY GASLIGHT	CARRY COALS
BROKEN WORD	BYGONE DAYS	CARRY IT OFF
BROKER'S MAN	BY INSTINCT	CARSON CITY
BROUGHT LOW	BY SNATCHES	CART GREASE
BROWN BOOTS	BY SURPRISE	CASE A JOINT
BROWN BREAD	BY THE CLOCK	CASE OF WINE
BROWNED OFF	BY THE DOZEN	CASE RECORD
BROWN LACES	BY THE RIVER	CASHEW NUTS
BROWN PAINT	BY TRANSFER	CASH IN HAND
BROWN PAPER	BY YOURSELF	CASK OF WINE
BROWN SHIRT		CASPIAN SEA

CAST A CLOUT	CHELSEA SET	CIVIC PRIDE
CAST ANCHOR	CHEQUE BOOK	CIVIL COURT
CAST A SPELL	CHERRY LIPS	CIVIL STATE
CASTING OFF	CHERRY RIPE	CIVIL WRONG
CASUAL WARD	CHERRY TART	CLAP EYES ON
CASUS BELLI	CHERRY TREE	CLAP HOLD OF
CAT BURGLAR	CHESS BOARD	CLAP ON SAIL
CATCH A BALL	CHESS MATCH	CLARK GABLE
CATCH A COLD	CHESS PIECE	CLASP HANDS
CATCH A CRAB	CHEST OF TEA	CLASSY DAME
CATCH A TRAM	CHEVY CHASE	CLAY PIGEON
CATCHY TUNE	CHEWING GUM	CLEAN BREAK
CATHODE RAY	CHEW THE CUD	CLEANED OUT
CATO STREET	CHEW THE FAT	CLEAN FIGHT
CAT'S CRADLE	CHEW THE RAG	CLEAN HABIT
CATTLE FARM	CHEYNE WALK	CLEAN HANDS
CATTLE FOOD	CHICKEN RUN	CLEAN LINEN
CATTLE SHOW	CHIEF CLERK	CLEAN LIVER
CAUGHT COLD	CHIEF POINT	CLEAN SHAVE
CAUGHT FIRE	CHIEF SCOUT	CLEAN SHEET
CAUSE ALARM	CHILD BRIDE	CLEAN SLATE
CAUSE A RIOT	CHILD'S PLAY	CLEAN SWEEP
CAUSE A STIR	CHILLY ROOM	CLEAN TOWEL
CAUSTIC WIT	CHIMNEY TOP	CLEAN WATER
CAXTON HALL	CHINA PLATE	CLEAR AS DAY
CELERY SALT	CHINESE BOX	CLEAR AS MUD
CENTRE HALF	CHIPPING IN	CLEAR FIELD
CERTAIN DAY	CHORUS GIRL	CLEAR IMAGE
CHAIN SMOKE	CHOSEN RACE	CLEAR LIGHT
CHAIN STORE	CHURCH ARMY	CLEAR PRINT
CHAIR COVER	CHURCH DOOR	CLEAR ROUND
CHANCE SHOT	CHURN IT OUT	CLEAR SPACE
CHANGE ENDS	CIDER APPLE	CLEAR STYLE
CHANGE GEAR	CIGAR SMOKE	CLEAR VOICE
CHANGE OVER	CIGAR STORE	CLEAR WATER
CHANGE STEP	CILLA BLACK	CLEFT STICK
CHAPEL FOLK	CINQUE PORT	CLEVER DICK
CHAPTER ONE	CIRCUS RING	CLEVER IDEA
CHAPTER SIX	CITRIC ACID	CLEVER MOVE
CHAPTER TWO	CITY CENTRE	CLEVER SAVE
CHARGE HAND	CITY EDITOR	CLIMB A HILL
CHEAP MONEY	CITY FATHER	CLIMB A TREE
CHEAP PAPER	CITY LIGHTS	CLOCK TOWER
CHEAP SKATE	CITY LIMITS	CLOSED BOOK
CHEAT DEATH	CITY OF BATH	CLOSED DOOR
CHECK POINT	CITY OFFICE	CLOSED MIND
CHEESE DISH	CITY POLICE	CLOSED SHOP
CHEESED OFF	CITY STREET	CLOSE GRIPS
CHEESE RIND	CITY TEMPLE	CLOSE MATCH
CHEESE ROLL	CITY WORKER	CLOSE OF DAY
CHELSEA BUN	CIVIC CROWN	CLOSE ORDER

CLOSE SHAVE
CLOSE STUDY
CLOSE THING
CLOSE WATCH
CLOSING BID
CLOVE HITCH
CLOVEN FOOT
CLOVEN HOOF
CLOVER LEAF
CLUB MEMBER
CLUMSY HAND
COACH PARTY
COAL CELLAR
COARSE FISH
COARSE JOKE
COARSE MIND
COAST ALONG
COAT OF ARMS
COAT OF MAIL
COAT POCKET
COBALT BLUE
COBALT BOMB
COCK A SNOOK
COCONUT OIL
COCONUT SHY
CODDLED EGG
COFFEE BEAN
COFFEE ROOM
COFFIN NAIL
COIL MAGNET
COLD BUFFET
COLD REASON
COLD REGION
COLD SEASON
COLD SHOWER
COLD TONGUE
COLD TURKEY
COLD WINTER
COLE PORTER
COLLEGE BOY
COLLEGE RAG
COLOUR FILM
COLOUR TONE
COME ACROSS
COME ADRIFT
COME AND SEE
COME AROUND
COME ASHORE
COME AT ONCE
COME CLOSER
COMEDY HOUR

COME HITHER
COME IN LAST
COME INSIDE
COME NEARER
COME SECOND
COME TO BITS
COME TO HAND
COME TO HARM
COME TO HEEL
COME TO KNOW
COME TO LIFE
COME TO PASS
COME TO REST
COME TO STAY
COME UNDONE
COMIC OPERA
COMIC PAPER
COMIC STRIP
COMIC VERSE
COMMON BOND
COMMON COLD
COMMON FORM
COMMON FUND
COMMON GOOD
COMMON HERD
COMMON JEST
COMMON LAND
COMMON NAME
COMMON NOUN
COMMON ROOM
COMMON SALT
COMMON SEAL
COMMON SORT
COMMON TALK
COMMON TASK
COMMON TIME
COMMON TYPE
COMPANY LAW
COMPANY TAX
CONAN DOYLE
CONTACT MAN
CONTOUR MAP
COOKED MEAT
COPPER BELT
COPPER COIN
COPPER MINE
COPPER WIRE
COPYING INK
COPY TYPIST
COR ANGLAIS
CORDON BLEU

CORK JACKET
CORNED BEEF
CORNER FLAG
CORNER KICK
CORNER POST
CORNER SEAT
CORNER SHOP
CORNER SITE
CORNET SOLO
COS LETTUCE
COSMIC RAYS
COSTA BRAVA
COSY CORNER
COTTAGE PIE
COTTON MILL
COTTON REEL
COTTON YARN
COUNTED OUT
COUNT HANDS
COUNT HEADS
COUNT ME OUT
COUNTRY INN
COUNTRY PUB
COUNT SHEEP
COUNTY CORK
COUNTY DOWN
COUNTY HALL
COUNTY MAYO
COUNTY TOWN
COUP DE MAIN
COURT DRESS
COURT OF LAW
COURT ORDER
COURT SCENE
COURT USHER
COVER DRIVE
COVERED WAY
COVER POINT
COWBOY SUIT
COW PARSLEY
COX'S ORANGE
CRACK A CRIB
CRACK A JOKE
CRACKED EGG
CRADLE SONG
CRAWL ABOUT
CREDIT CARD
CREDIT NOTE
CREDIT SIDE
CRÊPE PAPER
CRÊPE SOLES

CRICKET BAT
CRICKET CAP
CRIMEAN WAR
CRIME STORY
CROOKED MAN
CROSS IT OFF
CROSS IT OUT
CROSS PATHS
CROSS WORDS
CROUCH DOWN
CROWDED OUT
CROWD ROUND
CROWD SCENE
CROWN AGENT
CROWN DERBY
CROWN GLASS
CROWN LEASE
CROWN PIECE
CRUDE FACTS
CRUDE FORCE
CRUDE METAL
CRUEL SHAME
CRUSTY LOAF
CRUSTY PORT
CRY FOR HELP
CRY OF AGONY
CRY OUT LOUD
CRYSTAL SET
CRY TOO SOON
CUCKOO PINT
CUNARD LINE
CUP AND BALL
CUPID'S DART
CUP OF COCOA
CUP OF WATER
CUP WINNERS
CURATE'S EGG
CURED BACON
CURL THE LIP
CURRANT BUN
CURRENT HIT
CURTAIN OFF
CURTAIN ROD
CURT ANSWER
CURVED LINE
CURZON LINE
CUSTARD PIE
CUT A FIGURE
CUT ASUNDER
CUT A TUNNEL
CUT CORNERS

CUT FLOWERS
CUT FOR DEAL
CUT IT SHORT
CUT THE CAKE
CUT THE COST
CUT THE KNOT
CUT THE TAPE
CUT THROUGH
CUTTING OUT
CUTTLE FISH
CUT UP ROUGH
CYCLE RALLY

D—10

DAB OF PAINT
DAILY BREAD
DAILY DOZEN
DAILY EVENT
DAILY GRIND
DAILY HABIT
DAILY PAPER
DAILY PRESS
DAILY ROUND
DAINTY DISH
DAIRY CREAM
DAIRY FRESH
DAISY CHAIN
DAMASK ROSE
DAMP COURSE
DANCE MUSIC
DANCING MAN
DANGER LINE
DANGER LIST
DANISH BLUE
DARK CLOUDS
DARK COLOUR
DARK CORNER
DARK PURPLE
DARK SECRET
DARTS BOARD
DARTS MATCH
DASH OF SODA
DAS KAPITAL
DATIVE CASE
DAVID FROST
DAVID NIVEN
DAVID NIXON
DAWN ATTACK
DAWN CHORUS
DAWN OF HOPE
DAWN OF LIFE

DAWN OF LOVE
DAWN PATROL
DAY DREAMER
DAY NURSERY
DAY OF GRACE
DAYS GONE BY
DAYS OF YORE
DAYS TO COME
DAY TRIPPER
DEAD CENTRE
DEADEN PAIN
DEAD GROUND
DEAD LETTER
DEADLY BLOW
DEADLY DULL
DEAD MATTER
DEAD ON TIME
DEAD SEASON
DEAD SECRET
DEAD WEIGHT
DEAL GENTLY
DEALT A BLOW
DEAN MARTIN
DEAR BRUTUS
DEAR FRIEND
DEAR READER
DEATH HOUSE
DEATH KNELL
DEATH SCENE
DEATH'S DOOR
DEATH'S HEAD
DEBIT ENTRY
DECENT TYPE
DECK QUOITS
DECK TENNIS
DECLARE OFF
DECLARE WAR
DECREE NISI
DEEP BREATH
DEEPEST DYE
DEEP FREEZE
DEEP IN DEBT
DEEP LITTER
DEEPLY HURT
DEEP PURPLE
DEEP REGRET
DEEP SECRET
DEEP SORROW
DEEP WATERS
DEEP YELLOW
DEER FOREST

DELFT CHINA
DEL SHANNON
DEMAND NOTE
DEMON RUMMY
DEN OF LIONS
DENSE CROWD
DENY ACCESS
DEODAR TREE
DERBY CHINA
DERBY HORSE
DERBY SWEEP
DERNIER CRI
DESERT SONG
DEUCES WILD
DEVIL'S DYKE
DEVIL'S LUCK
DEVIL TO PAY
DICK BARTON
DICK TURPIN
DIE FOR LOVE
DIE OF GRIEF
DIE OF SHOCK
DIEPPE RAID
DIESEL FUEL
DIG A TRENCH
DIG FOR GOLD
DILLY DALLY
DINAH SHORE
DINE AT HOME
DINING CLUB
DINING HALL
DINING ROOM
DINNER BELL
DINNER GONG
DINNER HOUR
DINNER SUIT
DINNER TIME
DIP THE FLAG
DIRECT LINE
DIRTY HABIT
DIRTY LINEN
DIRTY MONEY
DIRTY STORY
DIRTY TRICK
DIRTY WATER
DISC JOCKEY
DISC BRAKES
DISPEL FEAR
DIVINE KING
DIVING BIRD
DIZZY ROUND

DIZZY SPELL
DIZZY WHIRL
DO A BAD TURN
DO A STRETCH
DO AWAY WITH
DO BUSINESS
DOCK LABOUR
DOCK MASTER
DOCTOR FELL
DOCTOR'S FEE
DOG BISCUIT
DOG EATS DOG
DOGGER BANK
DOG LICENCE
DOG'S CHANCE
DOG'S DINNER
DOG TRAINER
DOING RIGHT
DOING WRONG
DO IN THE EYE
DO IT AT ONCE
DO LIKEWISE
DOLLAR AREA
DOLLAR BILL
DOLL'S HOUSE
DONALD DUCK
DON BRADMAN
DONE BY HAND
DONEGAL BAY
DONKEY WORK
DO NOT TOUCH!
DON QUIXOTE
DON'T BE RUDE!
DO ONE PROUD
DO ONE'S BEST
DO ONE'S DUTY
DO ONE'S HAIR
DOOR HANDLE
DOOR TO DOOR
DO OVERTIME
DOPE ADDICT
DOPE PEDLAR
DORIAN GRAY
DOROTHY BAG
DO THE HALLS
DO THE TANGO
DO THE TRICK
DO THE TWIST
DOTTED LINE
DOTTED NOTE
DOUBLE BACK

DOUBLE BASS
DOUBLE BLUE
DOUBLE CHIN
DOUBLE DATE
DOUBLE FIVE
DOUBLE FOUR
DOUBLE LIFE
DOUBLE LOCK
DOUBLE NINE
DOUBLE ROOM
DOUBLE STAR
DOUBLE TAKE
DOUBLE TALK
DOUBLE TIME
DOUBLING UP
DOUBLY SURE
DOUGLAS FIR
DO VIOLENCE
DOWER HOUSE
DOWN AND OUT
DOWN AT HEEL
DOWN THE PIT
D'OYLE CARTE
DRAKE'S DRUM
DRAUGHT ALE
DRAW A BLANK
DRAW A PRIZE
DRAW BREATH
DRAWING INK
DRAW IT FINE
DRAW IT MILD
DRAWN MATCH
DRAWN SWORD
DRAW ONE OUT
DRAW STUMPS
DRAW SWORDS
DR. BARNARDO
DREAM HOUSE
DREAM WORLD
DREAMY EYES
DREAMY LOOK
DRESS SENSE
DRESS SHIRT
DRIED FRUIT
DRIFT ALONG
DRIFT APART
DRINK MONEY
DRINK VODKA
DRINK WATER
DRIVEN SNOW
DROP A BRICK

DROP A CATCH	E—10	EDAM CHEESE
DROP ANCHOR	EACH AND ALL	EDISON BELL
DROP ASTERN	EACH TO EACH	EDMUNDO ROS
DROP BEHIND	EACH-WAY BET	EDWARD LEAR
DROP BY DROP	EAGLE'S NEST	EDWIN DROOD
DROP OF RAIN	EARL'S COURT	EFFECTS MAN
DROPPED OFF	EARLY DOORS	EGG CUSTARD
DROPPED OUT	EARLY HOURS	EGG ON CHIPS
DROP THE HEM	EARLY LUNCH	EGG ON TOAST
DROWNED OUT	EARLY NIGHT	EGG SHAMPOO
DROWNED RAT	EARLY RISER	EIGHT BELLS
DRUG ADDICT	EARLY STAGE	EIGHT DOZEN
DRUMMED OUT	EARLY START	EIGHT DRAWS
DRUMMER BOY	EARLY TO BED	EIGHT GROSS
DRY AS A BONE	EARLY TRAIN	EIGHTH ARMY
DRY BATTERY	EARLY TUDOR	EIGHTH HOLE
DRY CANTEEN	EARLY VISIT	EIGHT HOURS
DRY CLIMATE	EARLY WORKS	EIGHTH PART
DRY MARTINI	EARTHA KITT	EIGHTH RACE
DRY MEASURE	EAR TRUMPET	EIGHTH TIME
DRY ONESELF	EASILY DONE	EIGHT MILES
DRY SHAMPOO	EAST AFRICA	EIGHT PARTS
DRY THE EYES	EAST ANGLIA	EIGHT PINTS
DRY WEATHER	EAST BERLIN	EIGHT SCORE
DUEL OF WITS	EASTER TERM	EIGHTS WEEK
DUE RESPECT	EASTER TIME	EIGHT TIMES
DUFFEL COAT	EASTER WEEK	EIGHT TO ONE
DUKE OF KENT	EAST INDIAN	EIGHT WEEKS
DUKE OF YORK	EAST INDIES	EIGHTY DAYS
DULCE DOMUM	EAST IS EAST	EIGHT YEARS
DULL COLOUR	EAST LONDON	ELEVEN DAYS
DULL MOMENT	EAST OF SUEZ	ELEVEN FEET
DUMB ANIMAL	EAST RIDING	ELEVEN PLUS
DUMB BLONDE	EAST TO WEST	ELEVEN QUID
DUMB CRAMBO	EASY ACCESS	ELINOR GLYN
DUMB WAITER	EASY DOES IT	ELLEN TERRY
DUMMY WHIST	EASY GALLOP	EMERY CLOTH
DUNDEE CAKE	EASY IN MIND	EMERY PAPER
DUSKY BRIDE	EASY MANNER	EMPIRE GOWN
DUSTBIN LID	EASY MARKET	EMPTY BOAST
DUST JACKET	EASY STAGES	EMPTY CHAIR
DUST TO DUST	EASY STREET	EMPTY CURSE
DUTCH BULBS	EASY TARGET	EMPTY GLASS
DUTCH PARTY	EASY TO COPY	EMPTY HOUSE
DUTCH TREAT	EASY VIRTUE	EMPTY PURSE
DUTCH UNCLE	EASY WAY OUT	EMPTY SHELL
DUTY ROSTER	EASY WICKET	EMPTY SOUND
DWARF BEANS	EASY WINNER	EMPTY SPACE
DWARF PLANT	EAT ONE'S HAT	EMPTY TRUCK
DYING CAUSE	EBB AND FLOW	EMPTY WORDS
DYING WORDS	ECCLES CAKE	END IN SMOKE

END PRODUCT
ENEMY AGENT
ENEMY ALIEN
ENEMY FLEET
ENEMY LINES
ENGAGE A CAB
ENGINE ROOM
ENJOY PEACE
ENOCH ARDEN
ENOUGH ROOM
ENOUGH SAID
ENOUGH TIME
ENOUGH TO DO
ENTICE AWAY
ENTRY MONEY
EOLIAN HARP
EPIC POETRY
EPSOM DOWNS
EPSOM RACES
EPSOM SALTS
EQUAL PARTS
EQUAL SHARE
EQUALS SIGN
EQUAL TERMS
EQUAL VALUE
ERIC BARKER
ERIC COATES
ERRING WIFE
ERROL FLYNN
ESCORT DUTY
ESTATE DUTY
ETHEL M. DELL
ETON COLLAR
ETON JACKET
EUSTON ROAD
EVE BOSWELL
EVELYN LAYE
EVEN CHANCE
EVEN NUMBER
EVEN TEMPER
EVEN HIGHER
EVER SO MANY
EVER SO MUCH
EVERY MONTH
EVERY OTHER
EVERY WOMAN
EVIL GENIUS
EVIL INTENT
EVIL SPIRIT
EVIL TEMPER
EXACT IMAGE

EXACT SENSE
EXCESS FARE
EXCISE BILL
EXCISE DUTY
EX DIVIDEND
EXETER CITY
EXIT PERMIT
EXPERT SHOT
EXPORT ONLY
EXPRESS FEE
EXTRA COVER
EXTRA MONEY
EXTRA POWER
EYES OF BLUE
EYE WITNESS

F—10
FACE DANGER
FACE DEFEAT
FACE POWDER
FACE TO FACE
FACE UP TO IT
FACTORY ACT
FADED YOUTH
FAIL TO COME
FAIL TO MEET
FAIL TO MOVE
FAIL TO OBEY
FAINT HEART
FAINT LIGHT
FAINT SOUND
FAIR AMOUNT
FAIR CHANCE
FAIR ENOUGH
FAIR EXCUSE
FAIR INCOME
FAIRLY GOOD
FAIRLY WARM
FAIRLY WELL
FAIR OF FACE
FAIR REPORT
FAIR SAMPLE
FAIR SHARES
FAIR TACKLE
FAIRY QUEEN
FAIRY STORY
FAIRY WORLD
FALL ASLEEP
FALL ASTERN
FALL BEHIND
FALLEN IDOL

FALL FOUL OF
FALLING OFF
FALL IN LINE
FALL IN LOVE
FALL IN WITH
FALL OF SNOW
FALL OF TROY
FALLOW DEER
FALLOW LAND
FALL SILENT
FALL TO BITS
FALSE ALARM
FALSE ALIBI
FALSE BEARD
FALSE CLAIM
FALSE CREED
FALSE FRONT
FALSE HOPES
FALSE IMAGE
FALSE LIGHT
FALSE LOGIC
FALSE PRIDE
FALSE SCENT
FALSE SHAME
FALSE START
FALSE TEETH
FAMILY FEUD
FAMILY FIRM
FAMILY LIFE
FAMILY NAME
FAMILY SEAT
FAMILY TIES
FAMILY TREE
FAMOUS DEED
FAMOUS NAME
FAMOUS WORK
FANCY DRESS
FANCY GOODS
FANCY PRICE
FANCY SOCKS
FANNY ADAMS
FAN THE FIRE
FAR AND AWAY
FAR AND NEAR
FAR AND WIDE
FAR BETWEEN
FAR COUNTRY
FARM ANIMAL
FARM BUTTER
FARMER'S BOY
FARM WORKER

FAR-OFF LAND	FIELD EVENT	FIND FAVOUR
FAR THE BEST	FIELD SPORT	FIND GUILTY
FAR TOO MANY	FIERY CROSS	FIND RELIEF
FAR TOO MUCH	FIERY STEED	FIND THE WAY
FAST ASLEEP	FIESTA TIME	FINE CHANCE
FAST BOWLER	FIFTEEN ALL	FINE FELLOW
FAST COLOUR	FIFTEEN MEN	FINE FETTLE
FAST READER	FIFTH FLOOR	FINE FIGURE
FAST WICKET	FIFTH GREEN	FINE PERSON
FAST WORKER	FIFTH OF MAY	FINE SHOWER
FATAL CAUSE	FIFTH PLACE	FINEST HOUR
FATAL CRASH	FIFTH ROUND	FINE VELLUM
FATAL ERROR	FIFTY MILES	FINE WRITER
FATAL WOUND	FIFTY TIMES	FINGER WAVE
FAT AND LEAN	FIFTY TO ONE	FINISH LAST
FATHER'S DAY	FIFTY YEARS	FINITE VERB
FATHER TIME	FIGHT A DUEL	FIRE A SALVO
FATS WALLER	FIGHT FOR IT	FIRE BUCKET
FATTED CALF	FIGHT IT OUT	FIRE ESCAPE
FAY COMPTON	FIGHT SHY OF	FIRE POLICY
FEARFUL DIN	FILE A CLAIM	FIRE SCREEN
FEATHER BED	FILIAL DUTY	FIRING LINE
FEATHER BOA	FILL IN TIME	FIRM ADVICE
FEAT OF ARMS	FILL THE AIR	FIRM BELIEF
FEEBLE JOKE	FILL THE GAP	FIRM DEMAND
FEEBLE MIND	FILM ADDICT	FIRM DENIAL
FEED THE CAT	FILM CENSOR	FIRM FRIEND
FEED THE DOG	FILM COLONY	FIRM GROUND
FEEL AT EASE	FILM CRITIC	FIRST BATCH
FEEL AT HOME	FILM OF DUST	FIRST BLOOD
FEEL BETTER	FILM REVIEW	FIRST BLUSH
FEEL CHILLY	FILM RIGHTS	FIRST CAUSE
FEEL DEEPLY	FILM STUDIO	FIRST CHILD
FEEL GROGGY	FILTHY TALK	FIRST CLAIM
FEEL HUNGRY	FINAL CAUSE	FIRST CLASS
FEELING ILL	FINAL CLAIM	FIRST DANCE
FEELING SAD	FINAL COUNT	FIRST DRAFT
FEEL NO PITY	FINAL EVENT	FIRST ENTRY
FEEL RELIEF	FINAL FLING	FIRST EVENT
FEEL SECURE	FINAL ISSUE	FIRST FLOOR
FEEL SLEEPY	FINAL OFFER	FIRST FLUSH
FEEL UNWELL	FINAL POINT	FIRST GREEN
FEEL UP TO IT	FINAL PROOF	FIRST HOUSE
FEET OF CLAY	FINAL SCENE	FIRST ISSUE
FELL INTENT	FINAL SCORE	FIRST LIGHT
FENCE ROUND	FINAL STAGE	FIRST MAN IN
FEN COUNTRY	FINAL TERMS	FIRST MATCH
FETTER LANE	FINAL TOUCH	FIRST NIGHT
FEUDAL LORD	FINANCE ACT	FIRST NOVEL
FEVER PITCH	FIND A BASIS	FIRST OF ALL
FIBRE GLASS	FIND A PLACE	FIRST OF MAY

FIRST PLACE	FIVE TO FOUR	FOGGY NIGHT
FIRST PRIZE	FIVE TRICKS	FOG WARNING
FIRST PROOF	FIXED ABODE	FOLDED ARMS
FIRST ROUND	FIXED IDEAS	FOLK DANCER
FIRST SHIFT	FIXED POINT	FOLK SINGER
FIRST SIGHT	FIXED PRICE	FOLLOW SUIT
FIRST STAGE	FIXED SMILE	FOND BELIEF
FIRST STEPS	FIXED STARS	FOND PARENT
FIRST TEETH	FIX THE DATE	FOOD PARCEL
FIRST THING	FIX THE TIME	FOOD SUPPLY
FIRST THROW	FLAG WAVING	FOOD TABLET
FIRST TO ACT	FLAMING RED	FOOL AROUND
FIRST VERSE	FLASH POINT	FOOT BY FOOT
FIRST WATCH	FLAT DENIAL	FOR A CHANGE
FIRST WATER	FLAT GROUND	FOR ALL THAT
FIRST WOMAN	FLAT IN TOWN	FOR ALL TIME
FIRTH OF TAY	FLAT RACING	FOR A SEASON
FISH COURSE	FLAT SEASON	FORCE A DRAW
FISH DINNER	FLATTEN OUT	FORCE APART
FISH FINGER	FLAXEN HAIR	FORCED LOAN
FISHING NET	FLEA CIRCUS	FORCED SALE
FISH KETTLE	FLESH WOUND	FORCE OF LAW
FISH MARKET	FLIGHT DECK	FOR CERTAIN
FISH SUPPER	FLING ABOUT	FOR CHARITY
FISHY STORY	FLING ASIDE	FORE AND AFT
FIT AND WELL	FLINT GLASS	FOREIGN LAW
FIT OF ANGER	FLOAT ABOUT	FOREST FIRE
FIT OF BLUES	FLOAT A LOAN	FOREST HILL
FIT THE BILL	FLOAT ON AIR	FOREST LAND
FIT TO BURST	FLOODED OUT	FOREST TREE
FIT TO PLEAD	FLOOD GATES	FOR EXAMPLE
FIVE AND ONE	FLOOD LEVEL	FORGE AHEAD
FIVE AND SIX	FLOOD WATER	FORGED NOTE
FIVE AND TEN	FLOOR SPACE	FORK SUPPER
FIVE AND TWO	FLOUNCE OUT	FORMAL CALL
FIVE A PENNY	FLOWER SHOW	FORM A QUEUE
FIVE FIFTHS	FLOWER VASE	FORMER DAYS
FIVE HEARTS	FLUID OUNCE	FORMER LAND
FIVE MONTHS	FLY FOR HELP	FORM MASTER
FIVE NINTHS	FLYING BOAT	FOR NOTHING
FIVE O'CLOCK	FLYING BOMB	FOR THE BEST
FIVE OUNCES	FLYING CLUB	FOR TWO PINS
FIVE POINTS	FLYING FISH	FORTY MILES
FIVE POUNDS	FLYING HIGH	FORTY TIMES
FIVE QUARTS	FLYING JUMP	FORTY WINKS
FIVE ROUNDS	FLYING KICK	FORTY YEARS
FIVES COURT	FLYING LEAP	FOSTER HOPE
FIVE SENSES	FLYING SHOT	FOUL MANNER
FIVE SIXTHS	FLY THE FLAG	FOUL MOTIVE
FIVE SPADES	FOAM RUBBER	FOUL STROKE
FIVE STONES	FOCAL POINT	FOUL TEMPER

FOUR-ALE BAR	FREE OF COST	FRUGAL MEAL
FOUR AND ONE	FREE OF DEBT	FRUIT DRINK
FOUR AND SIX	FREE OF DUTY	FRUIT JELLY
FOUR AND TEN	FREE ON RAIL	FRUIT JUICE
FOUR AND TWO	FREE PARDON	FRUIT LOLLY
FOUR A PENNY	FREE SAMPLE	FRUIT SALAD
FOUR BY FOUR	FREE SPEECH	FUEL CRISIS
FOUR EIGHTS	FREE TICKET	FULL BELIEF
FOUR FIFTHS	FREEZE HARD	FULL BOTTLE
FOUR HEARTS	FREEZE ON TO	FULL CHORUS
FOUR IN HAND	FREEZE OVER	FULL CIRCLE
FOUR KNAVES	FRENCH ALPS	FULL EXTENT
FOUR MONTHS	FRENCH BEAN	FULL FIGURE
FOUR NINTHS	FRENCH BRED	FULL GALLOP
FOUR O'CLOCK	FRENCH HORN	FULL GROWTH
FOUR OR FIVE	FRENCH LOAF	FULL IMPORT
FOUR OUNCES	FRENCH PORT	FULL LENGTH
FOUR POINTS	FRENCH ROLL	FULL OF HATE
FOUR POUNDS	FRENCH WINE	FULL OF HOPE
FOUR QUARTS	FRESH BLOOD	FULL OF LIFE
FOUR QUEENS	FRESH BREAD	FULL OF LOVE
FOUR SEVENS	FRESH CREAM	FULL OF NEWS
FOUR SPADES	FRESH FRUIT	FULL OF ZEAL
FOURTH FORM	FRESH HOPES	FULL OF ZEST
FOURTH HAND	FRESH LIGHT	FULL PARDON
FOURTH HOLE	FRESH PAINT	FULL REPORT
FOURTH PART	FRESH SLANT	FULL SISTER
FOURTH RACE	FRESH SPURT	FULL VOLUME
FOUR THREES	FRESH START	FULLY ARMED
FOURTH TEST	FRESH WATER	FULLY AWARE
FOURTH TIME	FRESH WOUND	FULLY WOUND
FOUR TRICKS	FRIED BACON	FUNDED DEBT
FOUR WHEELS	FRIED BREAD	FUNNY STORY
FOX HUNTING	FRIGID TONE	FUNNY THING
FOX TERRIER	FRIGID ZONE	FUSSY STYLE
FRANZ LEHAR	FROM ABROAD	
FRANZ LISZT	FROM BEHIND	
FRAYED EDGE	FROM MEMORY	G—10
FRED ARCHER	FROM THE AIR	GAIETY GIRL
FRED WINTER	FROM THE TOP	GAIN ACCESS
FREE ACCESS	FRONT BENCH	GAIN CREDIT
FREE ACTION	FRONT COVER	GAIN FAVOUR
FREE ADVICE	FRONT TEETH	GAIN GROUND
FREE CHOICE	FRONT TOOTH	GAIN HEIGHT
FREE CHURCH	FRONT WHEEL	GAIN THE DAY
FREE DRINKS	FROZEN FISH	GAIN WEIGHT
FREE FOR ALL	FROZEN FOOD	GALLANT ACT
FREE FRENCH	FROZEN OVER	GALLUP POLL
FREE LABOUR	FROZEN PEAS	GAMBLE AWAY
FREE LIVING	FROZEN SNOW	GAME AND SET
FREE MARKET	FRUGAL DIET	GAME OF DICE

GAME WARDEN	GET EXCITED	GIVE GROUND
GAMING LAWS	GET HITCHED	GIVE IT A TRY
GARAGE HAND	GET IN A MESS	GIVEN A LIFT
GARBAGE MAN	GET IN TOUCH	GIVEN LEAVE
GARDEN CITY	GET MARRIED	GIVE NOTICE
GARDEN FETE	GET NOWHERE	GIVE ORDERS
GARDEN FLAT	GET RATTLED	GIVE PRAISE
GARDEN GATE	GET SPLICED	GIVE RISE TO
GARDEN HOSE	GET STARTED	GIVE THANKS
GARDEN PATH	GET THE BIRD	GIVE THE CUE
GARDEN PEAS	GET THE BOOT	GIVE TONGUE
GARDEN PEST	GET THE FEEL	GIVE UP HOPE
GARDEN SEAT	GET THE HUMP	GIVE UP WORK
GARDEN WALL	GET THE PUSH	GLANCE BACK
GARLIC SALT	GET THE SACK	GLANCE DOWN
GARY COOPER	GET THROUGH	GLANCE OVER
GAS CHAMBER	GETTING HOT	GLASS BEADS
GAS COMPANY	GETTING OFF	GLASS COACH
GAS COUNCIL	GETTING OLD	GLASS OF ALE
GAS LIGHTER	GETTING OUT	GLASS PRISM
GAS ONESELF	GET TO GRIPS	GLASSY LOOK
GAS TURBINE	GET UP EARLY	GLAZED EYES
GAS WARFARE	GET UP STEAM	GLAZED LOOK
GATHER FOOD	GET WEAVING	GLEE SINGER
GATHER WOOL	GHOST STORY	GLIB TONGUE
GATLING GUN	GHOST TRAIN	GLOVE MONEY
GAVE GROUND	GIANT CRANE	GO ALL FUNNY
GAVE NOTICE	GIANT PANDA	GO A LONG WAY
GAVE VENT TO	GIDDY LIMIT	GO BACKWARD
GAY COLOURS	GIDDY SPELL	GO BANKRUPT
GAY COMPANY	GIFT COUPON	GOBI DESERT
GAY GORDONS	GIFT OF LIFE	GO CRACKERS
GEISHA GIRL	GIFT PARCEL	GOD OF MERCY
GENE PITNEY	GILDED CAGE	GO DOWNHILL
GENERAL LEE	GIN AND LIME	GO DOWN WELL
GENERAL RUN	GINGER BEER	GOD WILLING
GENE TUNNEY	GINGER WINE	GO FOR A BLOW
GENIAL HOST	GIPSY DANCE	GO FOR A RIDE
GENTLE BLOW	GIPSY QUEEN	GO FOR A SAIL
GENTLE HEAT	GIRL FRIEND	GO FOR A SPIN
GENTLE PUSH	GIVE A CATCH	GO FOR A SWIM
GEORGE SAND	GIVE ADVICE	GO FOR A TRIP
GERMAN BAND	GIVE A LEG UP	GO FOR A WALK
GERMAN MARK	GIVE AN INCH	GO GINGERLY
GET A LIVING	GIVE A PARTY	GO IN AND OUT
GET A LOOK IN	GIVE A SHOUT	GO IN AND WIN
GET A MOVE ON	GIVE BATTLE	GO IN EASILY
GET A WICKET	GIVE BY WILL	GOING BADLY
GET DRESSED	GIVE COLOUR	GOING CHEAP
GET ELECTED	GIVE CREDIT	GOING FORTH
GET ENGAGED	GIVE FREELY	GOING ROUND

GOING SOUTH	GOOD HEALTH	GO OVERSEAS
GOING UNDER	GOOD HIDING	GO SCOT-FREE
GOLDEN CALF	GOOD HUMOUR	GO SHOOTING
GOLDEN DAYS	GOOD INCOME	GO SHOPPING
GOLDEN DISC	GOOD INTENT	GO SLUMMING
GOLDEN GATE	GOOD JUMPER	GO STRAIGHT
GOLDEN GIRL	GOOD LENGTH	GO SWIMMING
GOLDEN HAIR	GOOD LIVING	GO THE LIMIT
GOLDEN HIND	GOOD MARGIN	GOTHIC ARCH
GOLDEN HORN	GOOD MARKET	GO TO BLAZES!
GOLDEN HOUR	GOOD MEMORY	GO TO CHURCH
GOLDEN MEAN	GOOD MORALS	GO TOGETHER
GOLDEN MILE	GOOD MORROW	GO TO GROUND
GOLDEN RAIN	GOOD NATURE	GO TO HEAVEN
GOLDEN RULE	GOOD NOTICE	GO TO MARKET
GOLD NUGGET	GOOD NUMBER	GO TO PIECES
GOLD SHARES	GOOD PEOPLE	GO TO PRISON
GOLD STRIKE	GOOD PLAYER	GO TO SCHOOL
GOLD THREAD	GOOD POLICY	GO TO THE BAD
GOLF COURSE	GOOD REASON	GO TO THE BAR
GOLF STROKE	GOOD RECORD	GO TO THE TOP
GONE TO SEED	GOOD REPORT	GO TO THE ZOO
GOOD ACCORD	GOOD REPUTE	GOT THE SACK
GOOD ADVICE	GOOD RESULT	GO UPSTAIRS
GOOD AND ALL	GOOD RETURN	GRACE KELLY
GOOD AND BAD	GOOD SAILOR	GRAND CANAL
GOOD AS GOLD	GOOD SEAMAN	GRAND CROSS
GOOD BRAINS	GOOD SECOND	GRAND DUCHY
GOOD CARVER	GOOD SELLER	GRAND HÓTEL
GOOD CELLAR	GOOD SERMON	GRAND LODGE
GOOD CHANCE	GOOD SPEECH	GRAND MARCH
GOOD CINEMA	GOOD STAYER	GRAND OPERA
GOOD DINNER	GOOD STRAIN	GRAND PIANO
GOOD DRIVER	GOODS TRAIN	GRAND SCALE
GOOD EATING	GOOD STROKE	GRAND STAND
GOOD EFFECT	GOOD SUPPLY	GRAND STYLE
GOOD EFFORT	GOODS WAGON	GRAND TOTAL
GOOD ENDING	GOOD TEMPER	GRANNY KNOT
GOOD ENOUGH	GOOD TENANT	GRANT A LOAN
GOOD EXCUSE	GOOD TIMING	GRANT A WISH
GOOD FAMILY	GOOD TIPPER	GRAPE JUICE
GOOD FARMER	GOOD TO HEAR	GRAPHIC ART
GOOD FELLOW	GOOD TO KNOW	GRASS COURT
GOOD FIGURE	GOOD WICKET	GRASS SKIRT
GOOD FOR ONE	GOOD WISHES	GRASS SNAKE
GOOD FOR YOU	GOOD WORKER	GRASS VERGE
GOOD FRIDAY	GO ON A BLIND	GRASS WIDOW
GOOD FRIEND	GO ON A SPREE	GRASSY BANK
GOOD GRACES	GO ON STRIKE	GRAVE DOUBT
GOOD GROUND	GO ON TIPTOE	GRAVE FEARS
GOOD HABITS	GO ON WHEELS	GRAVEL PATH

GRAVELY ILL
GRAVE WORDS
GRAY'S ELEGY
GREASY POLE
GREASY ROAD
GREAT ASSET
GREAT CATCH
GREAT GROSS
GREAT HEART
GREAT HOPES
GREAT JUDGE
GREAT LAKES
GREAT MERIT
GREAT MINDS
GREAT MOGUL
GREAT NIECE
GREAT POWER
GREAT SAINT
GREAT SHOCK
GREAT SPEED
GREAT TREAT
GREAT UNCLE
GREAT VALUE
GREAT WHEEL
GREAT WOMAN
GRECIAN URN
GREEK CROSS
GREEK DRAMA
GREEK VERSE
GREEN BAIZE
GREEN CLOTH
GREEN FIELD
GREEN FLASH
GREEN GRASS
GREEN LIGHT
GREEN PAINT
GREEN SALAD
GREEN STAMP
GREEN STUFF
GREEN TABLE
GRETA GARBO
GREY FRIARS
GREY FUTURE
GREY MATTER
GREY STREAK
GREY TOPPER
GRID SYSTEM
GRILLED HAM
GRIP OF IRON
GROSS ERROR
GROSS VALUE

GROUND ARMS
GROUND BAIT
GROUND CORN
GROUND CREW
GROUND DOWN
GROUND PLAN
GROUND RENT
GROUND RICE
GROUP OF SIX
GROUP OF TEN
GROUSE MOOR
GROW A BEARD
GROW APPLES
GROW BETTER
GROW BIGGER
GROWING BOY
GROWING OLD
GROW LARGER
GROW LONGER
GROWN WOMAN
GROW TALLER
GRUB STREET
GRUFF VOICE
GUESS AGAIN
GUESS RIGHT
GUESS WRONG
GUEST HOUSE
GUEST NIGHT
GUEST TOWEL
GUILTY LOOK
GUILTY MIND
GUINEA FOWL
GUITAR SOLO
GULF OF ADEN
GULF OF SUEZ
GULF STREAM
GUN LICENCE
GUST OF WIND

H—10

HACKNEY CAB
HACK WRITER
HAIR LOTION
HALF A CROWN
HALF A DOZEN
HALF A GLASS
HALF A GROSS
HALF A JIFFY
HALF AN ACRE
HALF AN HOUR
HALF AN INCH

HALF A POUND
HALF A SCORE
HALF A SHAKE
HALF ASLEEP
HALF AS MUCH
HALF BOTTLE
HALF DOLLAR
HALF LENGTH
HALF OF MILD
HALF SHARES
HALF STEWED
HALF VOLLEY
HALF YEARLY
HALL OF FAME
HALL PORTER
HAM AND EGGS
HAMMER AWAY
HAMMER DOWN
HAMMER HOME
HAMMER TOES
HAND IN HAND
HAND IT OVER
HAND LOTION
HAND OF TIME
HAND SIGNAL
HAND TO HAND
HANG AROUND
HANG BEHIND
HAPPY BREED
HAPPY CHILD
HAPPY EVENT
HAPPY KNACK
HAPPY WOMAN
HARBOUR BAR
HARD AS IRON
HARD AS TEAK
HARD ASTERN
HARD AT WORK
HARD CENTRE
HARD CHEESE
HARD GROUND
HARD HITTER
HARD KERNEL
HARD KNOCKS
HARD LABOUR
HARD LESSON
HARD LIQUOR
HARDLY EVER
HARD MASTER
HARD NATURE
HARD PENCIL

HARD RIDING	HEAR NO EVIL	HIGH ESTEEM
HARD SCHOOL	HEART OF OAK	HIGH FAVOUR
HARD TO BEAR	HEART'S EASE	HIGH FIGURE
HARD TO HOLD	HEARTY MEAL	HIGH FLYING
HARD TO TAKE	HEAR VOICES	HIGH GERMAN
HARD WINTER	HEAT STROKE	HIGH GROUND
HARD WORKER	HEAVE A SIGH	HIGH IDEALS
HARPOON GUN	HEAVY CHILL	HIGH INCOME
HARRY WORTH	HEAVY CLOUD	HIGH LIVING
HARSH SOUND	HEAVY FRANC	HIGHLY PAID
HARSH VOICE	HEAVY GOING	HIGH MORALE
HASTY WORDS	HEAVY HEART	HIGH NUMBER
HATCH AN EGG	HEAVY METAL	HIGH OCTANE
HATCH A PLOT	HEAVY NIGHT	HIGH OFFICE
HAVE A CHAIR	HEAVY SLEEP	HIGH PLACES
HAVE A CRACK	HEAVY STORM	HIGH POLISH
HAVE A DRINK	HEAVY STUFF	HIGH PRAISE
HAVE A FIGHT	HEAVY STYLE	HIGH PRIEST
HAVE A FLING	HEAVY SWELL	HIGH REGARD
HAVE A GUESS	HEAVY TOUCH	HIGH RELIEF
HAVE A HEART	HEAVY TREAD	HIGH REPUTE
HAVE A HUNCH	HEAVY WATER	HIGH SALARY
HAVE AN IDEA	HECTIC TIME	HIGH SCHOOL
HAVE A PARTY	HEDY LAMARR	HIGH STAKES
HAVE A SMOKE	HEEL AND TOE	HIGH STATUS
HAVE A SNACK	HELEN WILLS	HIGH STREET
HAVE BRAINS	HELLO DOLLY	HIGH SUMMER
HAVE DINNER	HELL'S BELLS	HILARY TERM
HAVE DOUBTS	HENNA RINSE	HINDER PART
HAVE EFFECT	HENRY FONDA	HIS AND HERS
HAVE FAULTS	HENRY JAMES	HIS MAJESTY
HAVE IN HAND	HENRY MOORE	HIS WORSHIP
HAVE IN MIND	HENRY TUDOR	HIT AND MISS
HAVE IN VIEW	HERB GARDEN	HIT THE MARK
HAVE NO FEAR	HERD OF DEER	HIT THE POST
HAVE NO HOPE	HERE AND NOW	HOBBY HORSE
HAVE NO VOTE	HERE YOU ARE	HOCKEY BALL
HAVE QUALMS	HER MAJESTY	HOCKEY CLUB
HEAD HUNTER	HERMIT CRAB	HOCKEY TEAM
HEAD KEEPER	HEROIC DEED	HOCUS POCUS
HEAD OFFICE	HEROIC POEM	HOLD A PARTY
HEAD OF HAIR	HERR HITLER	HOLD NO HOPE
HEAD TO FOOT	HIDDEN HAND	HOLD OFFICE
HEAD TO TAIL	HIGH AND DRY	HOLD THE KEY
HEAD WAITER	HIGH AND LOW	HOLIDAY PAY
HEAD WARDER	HIGH CHURCH	HOLLOW TREE
HEADY DRINK	HIGH COLLAR	HOLY FATHER
HEALING ART	HIGH COLOUR	HOLY GROUND
HEALTH CURE	HIGH COMEDY	HOLY ISLAND
HEAP OF WORK	HIGH DEGREE	HOLY OFFICE
HEARING AID	HIGHER RANK	HOLY ORDERS

HOLY SPIRIT
HOLY TEMPLE
HOLY TERROR
HOME AND DRY
HOME CIRCLE
HOME COUNTY
HOME FORCES
HOME FOR TEA
HOME GROUND
HOME MARKET
HOME OFFICE
HOME TRUTHS
HOME WATERS
HONEST FACE
HONEST FOLK
HONEST JOHN
HONEST LOOK
HONEST TOIL
HONEST WORK
HONOURS MAN
HOOK AND EYE
HOOKED NOSE
HOPPING MAD
HORNED MOON
HORNED TOAD
HORROR FILM
HORSE LAUGH
HORSE OPERA
HORSE SENSE
HORSE THIEF
HOSTILE ACT
HOT AND COLD
HOT AS HADES
HOT CLIMATE
HOT COCKLES
HOTEL STAFF
HOTEL SUITE
HOT PURSUIT
HOT WEATHER
HOUR BY HOUR
HOUR OF DOOM
HOUR OF NEED
HOURS ON END
HOUSE AGENT
HOUSE GUEST
HOUSE OF GOD
HOUSE ORGAN
HOUSE PARTY
HOUSE RULES
HOUSE TO LET
HOUSING ACT

HOVER ABOUT
HOW DARE YOU!
HOW DO YOU DO?
HOW ON EARTH
HUGE PROFIT
HUG ONESELF
HUG THE LAND
HUMAN BEING
HUMAN CHAIN
HUMAN ERROR
HUMAN FRAME
HUMAN SKILL
HUMAN VOICE
HUMBLE FARE
HUMBLE FOLK
HUMBLE HOME
HUMMING TOP
HUNDRED MEN
HUNGRY LOOK
HUNTING DOG
HUNTING KIT
HUNT THE FOX
HURDLE RACE
HURRY ALONG
HURRY FORTH
HUSKY VOICE
HYBRID RACE
HYMN OF HATE

I—10

ICED COFFEE
ICE SKATING
ICING SUGAR
ICY COLD DAY
ICY SURFACE
IDEAL PLACE
IDEAL WOMAN
IDLE GOSSIP
IDLE MOMENT
IDLE RUMOUR
IDLE THREAT
IF POSSIBLE
ILKLEY MOOR
ILL CONTENT
ILLEGAL ACT
ILL FEELING
ILL FORTUNE
ILL MANNERS
IMPORT DUTY
IMPOSE A BAN
IMPOSE UPON

IN A BAD MOOD
IN ABEYANCE
IN ADDITION
IN A DECLINE
IN A DILEMMA
IN A DRAUGHT
IN A FAIR WAY
IN A FASHION
IN A FERMENT
IN A FLUTTER
IN A GOOD WAY
IN ALLIANCE
IN AN ASYLUM
IN AN UPROAR
IN ANY EVENT
IN A PASSION
IN A TANTRUM
IN AT THE END
IN A TURMOIL
IN A WHISPER
IN BAD ODOUR
IN BAD SHAPE
IN BAD TASTE
IN BARRACKS
IN BOOK FORM
IN BRACKETS
IN BUSINESS
IN CHAMBERS
IN CHANCERY
INCH BY INCH
IN CONFLICT
IN CONTEMPT
IN CONTRAST
IN DARKNESS
IN DARTMOOR
IN DAYLIGHT
IN DECEMBER
IN DEFIANCE
INDEX TABLE
INDIAN ARMY
INDIAN CLUB
INDIAN CORN
INDIAN FILE
INDIAN HEMP
INDIAN MEAL
INDIA PAPER
INDIGO BLUE
IN DISARRAY
IN DISGRACE
IN DISGUISE
IN DISORDER

IN DISTRESS	IN RESPONSE	IN THE ROUND
INDOOR GAME	IN ROTATION	IN THE SCRUM
IN EVERY WAY	INS AND OUTS	IN THE SHADE
IN EVIDENCE	INSANE IDEA	IN THE SLIPS
IN EXCHANGE	IN SCOTLAND	IN THE SLUMS
IN EXTREMIS	IN SEQUENCE	IN THE SOUTH
IN FAVOUR OF	INSIDE EDGE	IN THE STAND
IN FEBRUARY	INSIDE LEFT	IN THE STARS
IN FULL SAIL	INSIDE SEAT	IN THE STUDY
IN FULL VIEW	IN SLOW TIME	IN THE SWING
IN GOOD FORM	IN SOMERSET	IN THE TOWER
IN GOOD PART	IN SOME WAYS	IN THE TRADE
IN GOOD TIME	IN STERLING	IN THE TRAIN
IN GOOD TRIM	IN STITCHES	IN THE VOGUE
IN HOSPITAL	IN SUSPENSE	IN THE WATER
IN HOT BLOOD	IN SYMPATHY	IN THE WILDS
IN HOT WATER	INTENT LOOK	IN THE WINGS
INIGO JONES	IN THE ATTIC	IN THE WOODS
IN JEOPARDY	IN THE BLOOD	IN THE WORLD
INJURY TIME	IN THE CHAIR	IN THE WRONG
INLAND PORT	IN THE CHOIR	INTO BATTLE
INLAND TOWN	IN THE CLEAR	IN TRAINING
INLET VALVE	IN THE DERBY	IN TWO MINDS
IN LONGHAND	IN THE DITCH	IN TWO TICKS
IN LOW WATER	IN THE DOUGH	INVALID OUT
IN MANY WAYS	IN THE DRINK	IN WHISPERS
IN MEMORIAM	IN THE DUMPS	IRISH LINEN
IN MOURNING	IN THE EVENT	IRISH SWEEP
IN NAME ONLY	IN THE FIELD	IRISH TWEED
INNER HOUSE	IN THE FILES	IRON RATION
INNER LIGHT	IN THE FINAL	ISLAND RACE
INNER VOICE	IN THE FLESH	ISLE OF BUTE
IN NOVEMBER	IN THE FRONT	ISLE OF DOGS
IN OFF WHITE	IN THE GRAVE	ISLE OF ELBA
IN ONE PIECE	IN THE HOUSE	ISLE OF MULL
IN ONE'S CUPS	IN THE INDEX	ISLE OF SARK
IN ONE SENSE	IN THE KITTY	ISLE OF SKYE
IN ONE'S HEAD	IN THE LIGHT	ISSUE A WRIT
IN ONE'S MIND	IN THE LOCAL	ISSUE FORTH
IN ONE'S ROOM	IN THE LURCH	ITALIAN CUT
IN PAKISTAN	IN THE MONEY	ITALIC TYPE
IN PARADISE	IN THE NIGHT	IT'S A WANGLE
IN PARALLEL	IN THE NORTH	IVORY BLACK
IN POLITICS	IN THE OCEAN	IVORY COAST
IN PORTUGAL	IN THE PAPER	IVORY PAINT
IN POSITION	IN THE PRESS	IVORY TOWER
IN PRACTICE	IN THE QUEUE	
IN PROGRESS	IN THE RANKS	**J—I0**
IN PROSPECT	IN THE RIGHT	JACK ARCHER
IN QUESTION	IN THE RIVER	JACK HORNER
IN REAL LIFE	IN THE ROUGH	JACK HYLTON

JACK LONDON
JACK SPRATT
JACK WARNER
JAGGED EDGE
JAMAICA INN
JAMAICA RUM
JAMES AGATE
JAMES JOYCE
JAMES MASON
JAM SESSION
JANE AUSTEN
JAR OF HONEY
JOCKEY CLUB
JOCKEY'S CAP
JOE BECKETT
JOHN ARLOTT
JOHN BRIGHT
JOHN BUCHAN
JOHN BUNYAN
JOHN CALVIN
JOHN DRYDEN
JOHN GILPIN
JOHN LENNON
JOHN MILTON
JOHN O'GAUNT
JOHN RUSKIN
JOHN WESLEY
JOIN BATTLE
JOIN FORCES
JOINT OWNER
JOINT STOCK
JOLLY ROGER
JOSE FERRER
JO STAFFORD
JOYS OF LIFE
JUDO EXPERT
JUDO LESSON
JUGGED HARE
JULES VERNE
JUMBLE SALE
JUMP A CLAIM
JUMP FOR JOY
JUMP THE GUN
JUNGLE BOOK
JUNIOR MISS
JURY SYSTEM
JUST AN IDEA
JUST AS WELL
JUST BEFORE
JUST ENOUGH
JUST FOR FUN

JUST FOR NOW
JUST IN CASE
JUST IN TIME
JUST REWARD

K—10
KANSAS CITY
KATHY KIRBY
KAY HAMMOND
KAY KENDALL
KEEN GLANCE
KEEN MEMBER
KEEP A DIARY
KEEP AFLOAT
KEEPING FIT
KEEP IN HAND
KEEP IN MIND
KEEP IN PAWN
KEEP IN PLAY
KEEP IN STEP
KEEP IN TUNE
KEEP IN VIEW
KEEP IT DARK
KEEP MOVING
KEEP POSTED
KEEP SECRET
KEEP SILENT
KEEP STEADY
KEEP TABS ON
KEEP TRYING
KEEP WICKET
KEIR HARDIE
KENNEL CLUB
KENNEL MAID
KENNY BAKER
KENNY LYNCH
KENTISH COB
KENTISH MAN
KETTLE DRUM
KEW GARDENS
KEY WITNESS
KICK UP A ROW
KID BROTHER
KIDNEY BEAN
KID ONESELF
KILL OR CURE
KIND HEARTS
KIND PERSON
KING ALFRED
KING ARTHUR
KING CANUTE

KING EDWARD
KING GEORGE
KING HAROLD
KING OF ARMS
KING'S BENCH
KING'S COURT
KING'S CROSS
KING'S PRIZE
KING'S SCOUT
KING WILLOW
KINKY BOOTS
KISS CANNON
KISS ME KATE
KISS OF LIFE
KISS THE ROD
KITCHEN BOY
KITH AND KIN
KNIFE WOUND
KNOCK ABOUT
KNOCKED OUT
KNOT OF HAIR
KNOW BETTER
KNOW THE LAW
KNOW THE WAY
KU KLUX KLAN

L—10
LABOUR CAMP
LABOUR CLUB
LABOUR POOL
LABOUR VOTE
LACE STITCH
LACK BRAINS
LACK FINISH
LACK OF FOOD
LACK OF FORM
LACK OF NEWS
LACK OF TIME
LACK OF ZEAL
LACK SPIRIT
LADIES' MAID
LADY BE GOOD
LADY DOCKER
LADY DOCTOR
LADY GODIVA
LA GIOCONDA
LAID TO REST
LAKE GENEVA
LAKE LUGANO
LAKE SCHOOL
LAMB CUTLET

LAMB'S TALES	LAST REFUGE	LEAD A TRUMP
LAME EXCUSE	LAST RESORT	LEADED TYPE
LAND AGENCY	LAST RUBBER	LEADEN FEET
LAND AND SEA	LAST SEASON	LEADER PAGE
LAND FORCES	LAST SERIES	LEADING MAN
LAND IN GAOL	LAST SPRING	LEAD PENCIL
LAND IN JAIL	LAST STROKE	LEAD THE WAY
LAND OF SONG	LAST SUMMER	LEAD TRUMPS
LAND REFORM	LAST SUNDAY	LEAD WEIGHT
LAND TENURE	LAST SUPPER	LEAP FOR JOY
LAND TRAVEL	LAST TO COME	LEARNED MAN
LARCENY ACT	LAST VOLUME	LEARN MUSIC
LARGE CROWD	LAST WINTER	LEARN TO FLY
LARGE DRINK	LATE AUTUMN	LEAST OF ALL
LARGE FLEET	LATE DINNER	LEATHER BAG
LARGE HOUSE	LATE FOR TEA	LEAVE ALONE
LARGE ORDER	LATE GOTHIC	LEAVE A MARK
LARGE PARTY	LATE IN LIFE	LEAVE A NOTE
LARGE PIECE	LATENT HEAT	LEAVE A WILL
LARGE POWER	LATE SPRING	LEAVE EARLY
LARGE PRINT	LATEST NEWS	LED TO AGREE
LARGE SCALE	LATEST WORD	LEFT BEHIND
LARGE SPACE	LATE SUMMER	LEFT INSIDE
LARGE STAFF	LATE SUPPER	LEFT WINGER
LARGE STOCK	LATIN PROSE	LEGAL CLAIM
LARGE STONE	LATIN VERSE	LEGAL COSTS
LARGE VODKA	LA TRAVIATA	LEGAL FORCE
LARGE WAIST	LATTER HALF	LEGAL ISSUE
LARRY ADLER	LAUGH IT OFF	LEGAL LIGHT
LAST AUTUMN	LAVISH CARE	LEGAL OWNER
LAST BREATH	LAWFUL WIFE	LEGAL RIGHT
LAST BUT ONE	LAWN TENNIS	LEGAL TITLE
LAST BUT TWO	LAW OFFICER	LEGAL TRIAL
LAST CHANCE	LAW OF LIBEL	LEGS ELEVEN
LAST COURSE	LAW SOCIETY	LEMON DRINK
LAST DEMAND	LAW STUDENT	LEMON JUICE
LAST EASTER	LAWYER'S FEE	LEND COLOUR
LAST FRIDAY	LAY A COURSE	LEND WEIGHT
LAST GLANCE	LAY BROTHER	LENIN'S TOMB
LAST IN LINE	LAY CLAIM TO	LENTIL SOUP
LAST LESSON	LAY HANDS ON	LESSER EVIL
LAST LETTER	LAY IN DRINK	LESSON FIVE
LAST MAN OUT	LAY IN RUINS	LESSON FOUR
LAST MINUTE	LAY IN STOCK	LESSON NINE
LAST MOMENT	LAY SIEGE TO	LETHAL DOSE
LAST MONDAY	LAY THE DUST	LET IT SLIDE
LAST OF FIVE	LAY THE FIRE	LET IT STAND
LAST OF FOUR	LAY THE ODDS	LET ONE KNOW
LAST OF NINE	LAZY PERSON	LET'S FACE IT
LAST ORDERS	LEAD A PARTY	LETTER CARD
LAST PERSON	LEAD ASTRAY	LETTER CASE

LETTER FILE	LIQUID FIRE	LOCAL PAPER
LETTER POST	LIQUID FOOD	LOCAL RATES
LETTER RATE	LIQUID FUEL	LOCAL TRAIN
LETTING OFF	LIQUID MEAL	LOCAL VICAR
LETTING OUT	LIQUOR LAWS	LOCH LOMOND
LEVEL SCORE	LITTER LOUT	LOCK AND KEY
LIE DORMANT	LITTLE BEAR	LOCKED DOOR
LIE IN RUINS	LITTLE BIRD	LOCK OF HAIR
LIE IN STATE	LITTLE DROP	LOCK-UP SHOP
LIFE MEMBER	LITTLE FISH	LONDON AREA
LIFE OF EASE	LITTLE FOLK	LONDON TOWN
LIFE POLICY	LITTLE GAIN	LONDON WALL
LIFE'S BLOOD	LITTLE GIRL	LONELY LIFE
LIFE TO COME	LITTLE GOOD	LONE RANGER
LIGHT A FIRE	LITTLE HOPE	LONG CAREER
LIGHT A PIPE	LITTLE JOHN	LONG CREDIT
LIGHT AS AIR	LITTLE LAMB	LONG CRUISE
LIGHT AS DAY	LITTLE LESS	LONG ENOUGH
LIGHT BLUES	LITTLE MARY	LONGER ODDS
LIGHT BROWN	LITTLE MORE	LONGEST DAY
LIGHT GREEN	LITTLE NELL	LONGEST WAY
LIGHT HEART	LITTLE ROCK	LONG FLIGHT
LIGHT LUNCH	LITTLE ROOM	LONG ISLAND
LIGHT MUSIC	LITTLE SHIP	LONG LADDER
LIGHT OF DAY	LITTLE SLAM	LONG LETTER
LIGHT OPERA	LITTLE TIME	LONG MEMORY
LIGHT SLEEP	LITTLE USED	LONG PERIOD
LIGHT SNACK	LIVE ABROAD	LONG PLAYER
LIGHT TOUCH	LIVE AFLOAT	LONG SPEECH
LIGHT TREAD	LIVE AT EASE	LONG TUNNEL
LIGHT VERSE	LIVE IN DIGS	LONG VISION
LIGHT WOMAN	LIVE IN FEAR	LONG VOYAGE
LIKE A CHARM	LIVE IN HOPE	LONG WINTER
LIKE A FLASH	LIVE IN WANT	LOOK AGHAST
LIKE A THIEF	LIVE IT DOWN	LOOK AROUND
LIKELY SPOT	LIVELY MIND	LOOK AT LIFE
LIKELY TALE	LIVELY TUNE	LOOK A TREAT
LIME STREET	LIVE UP TO IT	LOOK A WRECK
LINDEN TREE	LIVING ROOM	LOOK DOWN ON
LINEN CHEST	LIVING SOUL	LOOK GUILTY
LINE OF DUTY	LIVING WAGE	LOOK INSIDE
LINE OF FIRE	LLOYDS BANK	LOOK INTO IT
LINE OF LIFE	LLOYDS LIST	LOOK IN VAIN
LINE OF TYPE	LOADED DICE	LOOK LIVELY
LINSEED OIL	LOADING BAY	LOOK-OUT MAN
LIONEL BART	LOAD OF COAL	LOOK SLIPPY
LION'S MOUTH	LOAD OF COKE	LOOK YONDER
LION'S SHARE	LOAD OF JUNK	LOOSE COVER
LIP READING	LOBSTER POT	LOOSE LIVER
LIP SERVICE	LOCAL BOARD	LOOSE STATE
LIQUID DIET	LOCAL IDIOM	LOOSE TOOTH

LOOSE WOMAN	LOVELY TIME	LYING KNAVE
LORD ATTLEE	LOVE OF LIFE	LYRIC DRAMA
LORD CURZON	LOVE POTION	LYRIC VERSE
LORD HAW-HAW	LOVERS' KNOT	
LORD HELP US!	LOVERS' LANE	
LORD LISTER	LOVERS' LEAP	**M—10**
LORD NELSON	LOVERS' TIFF	MACHINE AGE
LORD'S TABLE	LOVERS' VOWS	MADE BY HAND
LORD WARDEN	LOVE THIRTY	MADE FAMOUS
LORNA DOONE	LOVING CARE	MADE TO LAST
LOS ANGELES	LOW CEILING	MADE-UP DISH
LOSE A TRICK	LOW COMPANY	MADE USEFUL
LOSE COLOUR	LOW CONTENT	MAD WITH JOY
LOSE CREDIT	LOW CUNNING	MAGIC FLUTE
LOSE FAVOUR	LOW DENSITY	MAGIC POWER
LOSE GROUND	LOWER A FLAG	MAGIC RITES
LOSE HEIGHT	LOWER CLASS	MAGIC SPELL
LOSE NO TIME	LOWER FARES	MAGIC SWORD
LOSE THE DAY	LOWER HOUSE	MAGIC TOUCH
LOSE THE WAY	LOWER LIMIT	MAGIC TRICK
LOSE WEIGHT	LOWER PITCH	MAGIC WORDS
LOSING GAME	LOWER RANKS	MAGIC WORLD
LOSING HAND	LOWER SIXTH	MAGNA CARTA
LOSING SIDE	LOWER WAGES	MAGNUM OPUS
LOSING TEAM	LOWER WORLD	MAIDEN AUNT
LOSING TOSS	LOW IN PRICE	MAIDEN LANE
LOSS OF FACE	LOW OPINION	MAIDEN NAME
LOSS OF HOPE	LOW QUALITY	MAIDEN OVER
LOSS OF LIFE	LOW SPIRITS	MAID MARION
LOSS OF TIME	LOW STATION	MAILED FIST
LOST BATTLE	LOW STATURE	MAIL PACKET
LOST CHANCE	LOW TENSION	MAIN ARTERY
LOST LABOUR	LUCID STYLE	MAIN CHANCE
LOST LEADER	LUCKY BREAK	MAIN CHARGE
LOST TO VIEW	LUCKY CHARM	MAIN CLAUSE
LOST TRIBES	LUCKY GUESS	MAIN COURSE
LOTS OF LUCK	LUCKY PATCH	MAIN OFFICE
LOTS OF ROOM	LUCKY PENNY	MAIN REASON
LOTS OF TIME	LUCKY STARS	MAIN SOURCE
LOUD CHEERS	LUCKY START	MAIN STREAM
LOUD COLOUR	LUGGAGE VAN	MAIN STREET
LOUD OUTCRY	LUMP OF CLAY	MAIN SWITCH
LOUD PRAISE	LUMP OF LEAD	MAJOR CHORD
LOUD REPORT	LUNAR MONTH	MAJOR ISSUE
LOUIS SEIZE	LUNCH BREAK	MAJOR SCALE
LOUNGE SUIT	LUNCH SCORE	MAJOR THIRD
LOVE AFFAIR	LUPINO LANE	MAKE A BREAK
LOVE DEARLY	LURID LIGHT	MAKE A CATCH
LOVE EMBLEM	LURID STYLE	MAKE A CLAIM
LOVE LETTER	LUTINE BELL	MAKE A GUESS
LOVELY GRUB	LUXURY FLAT	MAKE A JOINT

MAKE A MATCH	MARCH TO WAR	MEET THE BUS
MAKE AMENDS	MARCH WINDS	MEET THE EYE
MAKE AN EXIT	MARIA BUENO	MELBA TOAST
MAKE A NOISE	MARIE CURIE	MELTING POT
MAKE A POINT	MARIE LLOYD	MELT THE ICE
MAKE A SCENE	MARIO LANZA	MEMORY LANE
MAKE A STAND	MARK ANTONY	MEMORY TEST
MAKE A START	MARKET HALL	MENIAL WORK
MAKE BETTER	MARKET TOWN	MENTAL CASE
MAKE EYES AT	MARKING INK	MENTAL HOME
MAKE GAME OF	MARK OF CAIN	MENTAL PAIN
MAKE IT A DAY	MARK WYNTER	MENTAL TEST
MAKE NO SIGN	MARRIED MAN	MENTAL WARD
MAKE PASSES	MARRY YOUNG	MERE NOTION
MAKE PUBLIC	MARTIAL LAW	MERE NOVICE
MAKE SPARKS	MARY MARTIN	MERINO WOOL
MAKE THE BED	MARY STUART	MERRY DANCE
MAKE THE TEA	MASKED BALL	MERRY HEART
MAKE TRACKS	MASS APPEAL	MERRY MONTH
MAKE-UP ROOM	MASS ATTACK	MERRY PRANK
MAKE UP TIME	MASS MARKET	MERRY WIDOW
MALE CHORUS	MASS MURDER	MERRY WIVES
MALE DANCER	MASTER MIND	MERSEY BEAT
MALTED MILK	MASTER PLAN	MESS JACKET
MALT LIQUOR	MASTER RACE	METAL PLATE
MAN AND WIFE	MATCH POINT	MEXICO CITY
MAN OF DEEDS	MATCH TRICK	MIAMI BEACH
MAN OF IDEAS	MATINÉE HAT	MICE AND MEN
MAN OF MONEY	MATING CALL	MICKEY FINN
MAN OF MOODS	MATT DILLON	MICK JAGGER
MAN OF PARTS	MATTED HAIR	MIDAS TOUCH
MAN OF PEACE	MATURE MIND	MIDDAY MEAL
MAN OF STEEL	MAXIM GORKY	MIDDLE AGES
MAN OF STRAW	MAY BLOSSOM	MIDDLE DECK
MAN OF TASTE	MAY FLOWERS	MIDDLE EAST
MAN ON TRIAL	MAY MORNING	MIDDLE LIFE
MANOR HOUSE	MEADOW LAND	MIDDLE PART
MAN OR MOUSE?	MEAGRE DIET	MIDDLE ROAD
MAN'S ESTATE	MEAL TICKET	MIDDLE TERM
MAN THE GUNS	MEAN NO HARM	MIDDLE WEST
MAN TO WATCH	MEAN STREAK	MIGHTY ATOM
MANUAL WORK	MEASURE OUT	MIGHTY DEEP
MANY THANKS	MEAT COURSE	MIGHTY FINE
MAO-TSE TUNG	MEAT MARKET	MILD ANSWER
MAPLE SUGAR	MEAT RATION	MILD AS MILK
MAPLE SYRUP	MEDICAL ART	MILD REBUKE
MAP OF SPAIN	MEDICAL MAN	MILD SPOKEN
MAP READING	MEDIUM DONE	MILD WINTER
MARBLE ARCH	MEDIUM RARE	MILES APART
MARCEL WAVE	MEDIUM SIZE	MILK BOTTLE
MARCH FORTH	MEDIUM WAVE	MILL AROUND

MILLED EDGE	MORAL BLAME	MUSICAL EAR
MINCED MEAT	MORAL FIBRE	MUSIC LOVER
MINCED OATH	MORAL ISSUE	MUSIC STAND
MINCE WORDS	MORAL LAPSE	MUSIC STOOL
MINERAL OIL	MORAL POWER	MUSKET FIRE
MINER'S LAMP	MORAL RIGHT	MUSTARD GAS
MINOR CANON	MORAL SENSE	MUSTARD POT
MINOR CHORD	MORAY FIRTH	MUTE APPEAL
MINOR POINT	MORBID FEAR	MUTTON CHOP
MINOR SCALE	MORDANT WIT	MUTUAL LOVE
MINOR THIRD	MORE OR LESS	MY CUP OF TEA
MINUS THREE	MORE TO COME	MY DEAR CHAP
MINUTE BOOK	MORNING SUN	MY FAIR LADY
MINUTE HAND	MORNING TEA	MY GOODNESS!
MIRACLE MAN	MORTAL BLOW	MY HEARTIES
MISERLY PAY	MORTAL COIL	MY OLD DUTCH
MISS A CATCH	MORTAL FEAR	MY OLD WOMAN
MISS A TRICK	MORTAL SPAN	MYSTERY MAN
MISS MUFFET	MOSAIC WORK	
MISS POINTS	MOSS STITCH	**N—10**
MISS THE BUS	MOST LIKELY	NAIL POLISH
MIXED BLOOD	MOST PEOPLE	NAKED FACTS
MIXED BREED	MOTHER LOVE	NAKED FLAME
MIXED BUNCH	MOTHER'S BOY	NAKED LIGHT
MIXED DRINK	MOTHER'S DAY	NAKED STEEL
MIXED GRILL	MOTHER SHIP	NAKED SWORD
MIXED HERBS	MOTOR COACH	NAKED TRUTH
MIXED PARTY	MOTOR RALLY	NAME THE DAY
MIXED TRAIN	MOUNT GUARD	NARROW DOWN
MIXED-UP KID	MOUNT KENYA	NARROW MIND
MOBILE UNIT	MOUNT SINAI	NARROW MISS
MOCK TURTLE	MOUTH ORGAN	NARROW PATH
MODEL DRESS	MOVE ACROSS	NARROW ROAD
MODEL PLANE	MOVE IN A RUT	NARROW VIEW
MODEL TRAIN	MOVE SLOWLY	NASAL ORGAN
MODEL YACHT	MOVE TROOPS	NASAL TWANG
MODE OF LIFE	MOVING BELT	NASTY HABIT
MODERN GIRL	MOVING PART	NASTY KNOCK
MODERN MISS	MOW THE LAWN	NASTY SHOCK
MOIST SUGAR	MR. MICAWBER	NASTY SPILL
MONEYED MAN	MRS. SQUEERS	NASTY TASTE
MONEY ORDER	MR. UNIVERSE	NASTY TRICK
MONEY PRIZE	MUCH BETTER	NATIVE LAND
MONEY TALKS	MUCH SORROW	NATIVE RACE
MONKEY SUIT	MUDDY BOOTS	NATIVE SOIL
MONK'S HABIT	MUDDY WATER	NATURAL GAS
MONTE CARLO	MUFFIN BELL	NATURAL KEY
MONTEGO BAY	MULLED WINE	NATURAL LAW
MONTE VIDEO	MUMBO JUMBO	NATURAL WIT
MOON AROUND	MURDER CASE	NATURE CURE
MOORING FEE	MUSICAL BOX	NAUGHTY BOY

NAUTCH GIRL	NEW RECRUIT	NIP ON AHEAD
NAVAL CADET	NEW RESOLVE	NITRIC ACID
NAVAL CRAFT	NEWS AGENCY	NO APPETITE
NAVAL POWER	NEWS CINEMA	NOBEL PRIZE
NAVAL STORE	NEWS EDITOR	NOBLE BIRTH
NAVY LEAGUE	NEWS LETTER	NOBLE BLOOD
NAZI RÉGIME	NEW SPEAKER	NOBLE HOUSE
NEAR AND FAR	NEWS REPORT	NOBODY ELSE
NEAR AT HAND	NEW UNIFORM	NO DECISION
NEAR ENOUGH	NEW VERSION	NO DISTANCE
NEAR FRIEND	NEW ZEALAND	NOD THE HEAD
NEAR FUTURE	NEXT AUTUMN	NOEL COWARD
NEARLY OVER	NEXT BUT ONE	NO ENTRANCE
NEAR THE END	NEXT BUT TWO	NO FRICTION
NEAR THE SEA	NEXT DOOR TO	NO HARM DONE
NEAR THE TOP	NEXT FRIDAY	NO INTEREST
NEAT AS A PIN	NEXT IN LINE	NO LEFT TURN
NEAT FIGURE	NEXT MONDAY	NO LOVE LOST
NEAT SCOTCH	NEXT PERSON	NO MAN'S LAND
NEAT STROKE	NEXT PLEASE	NOM DE PLUME
NEAT WHISKY	NEXT SEASON	NO MEAN CITY
NECK OF LAMB	NEXT SPRING	NOMINAL FEE
NECK OF LAND	NEXT SUMMER	NOMINAL SUM
NEEDLE'S EYE	NEXT SUNDAY	NONE OF THAT!
NEGRO MUSIC	NEXT TO COME	NO NONSENSE
NELSON EDDY	NEXT VICTIM	NON-STOP RUN
NERVE TONIC	NEXT WINTER	NOODLE SOUP
NERVOUS TIC	NICE ENOUGH	NOONDAY SUN
NESTLE DOWN	NICE PEOPLE	NO PATIENCE
NEVER AGAIN	NICE TO KNOW	NO RESPONSE
NEVER LEARN	NICKEL COIN	NORMAL LIFE
NEVER NEVER	NICK OF TIME	NORMAL LOAD
NEVER WAVER	NIGHT FROST	NORMAL PACE
NEVER WORRY	NIGHT NURSE	NORTH COAST
NEVER WRONG	NIGHT SHIFT	NORTH DEVON
NEVIL SHUTE	NIGHT TRAIN	NORTH DOWNS
NEW ADDRESS	NIGHT WATCH	NORTH WALES
NEW ARRIVAL	NINE AND ONE	NOSE TO TAIL
NEW CHAPTER	NINE AND SIX	NO SHORTAGE
NEW CLOTHES	NINE AND TEN	NO SOLUTION
NEW COINAGE	NINE AND TWO	NO STANDING
NEW COLLEGE	NINE MONTHS	NO STRANGER
NEW CONVERT	NINE O'CLOCK	NO SUCH LUCK
NEW EDITION	NINE OUNCES	NOSY PARKER
NEW ENGLAND	NINE POINTS	NOT A CHANCE
NEW FASHION	NINE POUNDS	NOT CRICKET
NEW HORIZON	NINE TENTHS	NOTE OF HAND
NEW-LAID EGG	NINTH GREEN	NOT FAR AWAY
NEW-MOWN HAY	NINTH OF MAY	NOT FOR SALE
NEW ORLEANS	NINTH PLACE	NO THANK YOU
NEW PROCESS	NINTH ROUND	NOTHING NEW

NOT JUST NOW
NOT LONG AGO
NOT ONE OF US
NOT PRESENT
NOT SO DUSTY
NOT THE SAME
NOT THE TYPE
NOT TO WORRY
NOT VISIBLE
NOT WORKING
NOT WORTH IT
NOVA SCOTIA
NOVEL TITLE
NOW AND THEN
NO WEAKNESS
NOW OR NEVER
NUCLEAR WAR
NUDE FIGURE
NUDIST CAMP
NUDIST CLUB
NUMBER FIVE
NUMBER FOUR
NUMBER NINE
NUT AND BOLT
NUTS AND MAY
NUTTY SLACK

O—10

OBEY ORDERS
OCEAN LINER
OCEAN WAVES
ODD AND EVEN
OEDIPUS REX
OF A PATTERN
OFF BALANCE
OFFER TO PAY
OFFICE DESK
OFFICE GIRL
OFFICE SAFE
OFFICE WORK
OFF LICENCE
OFF ONE'S NUT
OFFSIDE LAW
OFF THE BEAM
OFF THE CUFF
OFF THE CUSH
OFF THE HOOK
OFF THE LAND
OFF THE MARK
OFF THE MENU

OFF THE REEL
OIL COMPANY
OLD AND MILD
OLD AND TRUE
OLD BRIGADE
OLD CLOTHES
OLD COUNTRY
OLD EDITION
OLD ENGLAND
OLD ENGLISH
OLDEN TIMES
OLD ETONIAN
OLD OAK TREE
OLD PALS ACT
OLD ROUTINE
OLD SO-AND-SO
OLD SOLDIER
OLD VERSION
OLD VETERAN
OLD WARRIOR
OLD WINDBAG
OLD YEAR OUT
OLIVE GREEN
OLIVE GROVE
OL' MAN RIVER
ON A CRUSADE
ON ALL FOURS
ON ALL HANDS
ON ALL SIDES
ON APPROVAL
ON BAD TERMS
ON BUSINESS
ONCE A MONTH
ONCE BITTEN
ONCE IN A WAY
ON CRUTCHES
ON DELIVERY
ON EACH SIDE
ONE-ACT PLAY
ONE AND FIVE
ONE AND FOUR
ONE AND NINE
ONE AND ONLY
ONE ANOTHER
ONE AT A TIME
ONE BILLION
ONE DIAMOND
ONE FINE DAY
ONE FURLONG
ONE HUNDRED
ONE IN EIGHT

ONE IN SEVEN
ONE IN THREE
ONE-MAN BAND
ONE MILLION
ONE NO-TRUMP
ONE PER CENT
ONE QUARTER
ONE SEVENTH
ONE'S OWN WAY
ONE SQUARED
ONE SWALLOW
ONE TOO MANY
ONE TWELFTH
ONE WAY ONLY
ON FURLOUGH
ONION SAUCE
ON LOCATION
ONLY CHANCE
ONLY CHOICE
ON MORTGAGE
ON MY HONOUR
ON OCCASION
ON ONE'S BACK
ON ONE'S FEET
ON ONE'S LEGS
ON ONE'S TOES
ON SATURDAY
ON SCHEDULE
ON SENTRY-GO
ON THE ALERT
ON THE BEACH
ON THE BENCH
ON THE BIBLE
ON THE BOARD
ON THE BOOKS
ON THE BOOZE
ON THE BRAIN
ON THE BRINK
ON THE CARDS
ON THE CHEAP
ON THE CLOCK
ON THE CLYDE
ON THE COAST
ON THE CREST
ON THE CROSS
ON THE FENCE
ON THE FILES
ON THE FLANK
ON THE FLOOR
ON THE GREEN
ON THE HALLS

ON THE HOUSE	OPEN MARKET	OUT OF REACH
ON THE LATCH	OPEN PRISON	OUT OF SCALE
ON THE LEVEL	OPEN REVOLT	OUT OF SHAPE
ON THE LINKS	OPEN SEASON	OUT OF SIGHT
ON THE LOOSE	OPEN SECRET	OUT OF SORTS
ON THE MARCH	OPEN SESAME	OUT OF SPITE
ON THE PANEL	OPEN TO VIEW	OUT OF STOCK
ON THE PHONE	OPEN WINDOW	OUT OF TOUCH
ON THE PROWL	OPERA GLASS	OUT OF WATER
ON THE QUIET	OPERA HOUSE	OUT ON A LIMB
ON THE RADIO	OPERA MUSIC	OUT PATIENT
ON THE RAILS	OPIUM EATER	OUTWARD EYE
ON THE RHINE	OPIUM HABIT	OUT WITH HIM!
ON THE RIGHT	OPIUM POPPY	OVER AND OUT
ON THE RIVER	OPTIC NERVE	OVER EXPOSE
ON THE ROCKS	ORANGE PEEL	OVER POLITE
ON THE SANDS	ORANGE TREE	OVER THE AIR
ON THE SCENT	ORANGE WINE	OVER THE BAR
ON THE SHELF	ORDER A MEAL	OVER THE SEA
ON THE SLANT	ORDER PAPER	OVER THE TOP
ON THE SLATE	ORGAN MUSIC	OVER THE WAY
ON THE SOMME	ORIENT LINE	OWE LOYALTY
ON THE SPREE	ORION'S BELT	OWNER'S RISK
ON THE STAFF	OSCAR AWARD	OX-EYE DAISY
ON THE STAGE	OSCAR WILDE	OXFORD BAGS
ON THE STAND	OSTRICH EGG	OXFORD BLUE
ON THE TABLE	OTHER RANKS	OXTAIL SOUP
ON THE TELLY	OTHER WORLD	OXYGEN MASK
ON THE TILES	OUIJA BOARD	OXYGEN TENT
ON THE TRACK	OUR BETTERS	
ON THE TRAIL	OUR VERSION	**P—10**
ON THE VERGE	OUT AND HOME	PACK A PUNCH
ON THE WAGON	OUT AT ELBOW	PACK OF LIES
ON THE WATCH	OUTER COVER	PADDED CELL
ON THE WATER	OUTER SPACE	PAGE ELEVEN
ON THE WAY IN	OUTER WORLD	PAGE TWELVE
ON THE WAY UP	OUT IN FORCE	PAID A VISIT
ON THE WHOLE	OUT IN FRONT	PAIL OF MILK
ON THIS SIDE	OUT OF COURT	PAINED LOOK
ON THURSDAY	OUT OF DOORS	PAIR OF ACES
ON VACATION	OUT OF FOCUS	PAIR OF OARS
OPEN ARREST	OUT OF FUNDS	PAIR OF TENS
OPEN BREACH	OUT OF HOURS	PAIR OF TWOS
OPEN CHEQUE	OUT OF JOINT	PALE AND WAN
OPEN CREDIT	OUT OF MONEY	PALE YELLOW
OPEN DRAWER	OUT OF MY WAY	PALM SUNDAY
OPEN GROUND	OUT OF ORBIT	PANCAKE DAY
OPEN HEARTH	OUT OF ORDER	PAPAL COURT
OPENING BID	OUT OF PLACE	PAPER CHAIN
OPENING DAY	OUT OF PRINT	PAPER MONEY
OPEN LETTER	OUT OF RANGE	PAPER ROUND

PARCEL POST	PEACE TERMS	PIER MASTER
PAR CONTEST	PEACH MELBA	PIGEON POST
PARENT BIRD	PEAK PERIOD	PIG IN A POKE
PARENTS' DAY	PEARL DIVER	PILOT LIGHT
PARENT SHIP	PEARLY KING	PINE FOREST
PARENT TREE	PEAS IN A POD	PINK RIBBON
PARI MUTUEL	PEA-SOUP FOG	PINNED DOWN
PARISH PUMP	PECKHAM RYE	PINT OF BEER
PARK AVENUE	PECK OF DIRT	PINT OF MILD
PARKING BAY	PEDDLE DOPE	PINT OF MILK
PARKING FEE	PEEPING TOM	PIOUS HOPES
PARKING LOT	PEGGED DOWN	PIOUS TRUTH
PART BY PART	PEGGY MOUNT	PIPED MUSIC
PARTED LIPS	PENALTY BOX	PIPES OF PAN
PARTY DRESS	PENCIL CASE	PIRATE FLAG
PARTY FROCK	PENNY BLACK	PIRATE SHIP
PARTY FUNDS	PENNY PIECE	PISTOL SHOT
PARTY PIECE	PENNY PLAIN	PITCH A TENT
PARTY TRICK	PENNY STAMP	PITCH A YARN
PASS FRIEND	PENSION OFF	PITCH BLACK
PASSING FAD	PEPPER MILL	PITH HELMET
PASS MUSTER	PEPYS' DIARY	PLACED LAST
PASS ORDERS	PERFECT FIT	PLACE MONEY
PASS THE CAN	PERIOD PLAY	PLACE ON END
PASS THE HAT	PERRY MASON	PLAGUE SPOT
PAST BELIEF	PERSIAN CAT	PLAIN FACTS
PAST CARING	PERSIAN MAT	PLAIN FOLLY
PAST MASTER	PERSIAN RUG	PLAIN PAPER
PAST RECORD	PETE MURRAY	PLAIN SKIRT
PASTRY CHEF	PETER FINCH	PLAIN SOCKS
PASTRY COOK	PETER PIPER	PLAIN TERMS
PATH OF DUTY	PETER SCOTT	PLAIN TO SEE
PATROL DUTY	PETIT POINT	PLAIN TRUTH
PAUL DOMBEY	PETITS POIS	PLAIN WORDS
PAUL REVERE	PETROL DUMP	PLANE CRASH
PAUL TEMPLE	PETROL PUMP	PLANT A TREE
PAVE THE WAY	PETROL TANK	PLASTIC ART
PAWN TICKET	PETTY CRIME	PLASTIC BAG
PAY A REWARD	PETTY THEFT	PLASTIC MAC
PAY AS YOU GO	PETTY THIEF	PLASTIC TOY
PAY CORKAGE	PHIL ARCHER	PLAT DU JOUR
PAY DAMAGES	PHIL HARRIS	PLATE GLASS
PAYING GAME	PHRASE BOOK	PLAY A CHORD
PAY-OFF LINE	PIANO STOOL	PLAY A SCALE
PAY ONE'S WAY	PIANO TUNER	PLAY AT HOME
PAY ON SIGHT	PICK A FIGHT	PLAY A TRICK
PAY THE BILL	PICK FAULTS	PLAY A WALTZ
PAY THE RENT	PICK STRAWS	PLAY BO-PEEP
PAY TRIBUTE	PICK UP NEWS	PLAY BRIDGE
PEACE OFFER	PICTURE HAT	PLAY HAMLET
PEACE PARTY	PIED-À-TERRE	PLAY HOCKEY

PLAY HOOKEY	POOR SAILOR	PRETTY FAIR
PLAY IT COOL	POOR SECOND	PRETTY GIRL
PLAY POSSUM	POOR SERMON	PRETTY GOOD
PLAY PRANKS	POOR STAYER	PRETTY MESS
PLAY RUGGER	POOR WRETCH	PRETTY PASS
PLAY SCALES	POOR YORICK	PRETTY POLL
PLAY SOCCER	POPLAR TREE	PRETTY SURE
PLAY SQUASH	POPULAR AIR	PRETTY TUNE
PLAY STREET	PORK FILLET	PRETTY WELL
PLAY TENNIS	PORK-PIE HAT	PRICE INDEX
PLAY THE MAN	PORT ARTHUR	PRICE LABEL
PLAY THE WAG	PORT DARWIN	PRICE LEVEL
PLAY TRICKS	PORT ENGINE	PRIMA DONNA
PLAY TRUANT	PORTION OUT	PRIMA FACIE
PLAY TRUMPS	PORT NELSON	PRIME CAUSE
PLENTY MORE	PORT OF CALL	PRIME MOVER
PLENTY TO DO	PORT TALBOT	PRINCE IGOR
PLOT OF LAND	POSTAL RATE	PRINT DRESS
PLOUGH BACK	POST MORTEM	PRIOR CLAIM
PLOVER'S EGG	POST OFFICE	PRISON BARS
PLUCKY CHAP	POTATO PEEL	PRISON CAMP
PLUMB CRAZY	POT HUNTING	PRISON CELL
PLY FOR HIRE	POT OF HONEY	PRISON DIET
POACHED EGG	POT OF MONEY	PRISON FARE
POCKET COMB	POT OF PAINT	PRISON GATE
POETIC VEIN	POTTED MEAT	PRISON YARD
POINT BLANK	POTTER'S BAR	PRIVATE BAR
POINT OF LAW	POT THE BLUE	PRIVATE BUS
POKER PARTY	POT THE PINK	PRIVATE CAR
POLES APART	POUNCE UPON	PRIVATE EYE
POLE TO POLE	POUND OF TEA	PRIVATE LAW
POLICE BALL	POULTRY RUN	PRIVATE WAR
POLICE RAID	POURING WET	PRIVATE WAY
POLICE TRAP	POWDER BLUE	PRIVY PURSE
POLLING DAY	POWDER BOWL	PRIZE COURT
POLO GROUND	POWDER PUFF	PRIZE ENTRY
POLO PLAYER	POWDER ROOM	PRIZE ESSAY
POMPOUS ASS	POWER HOUSE	PRIZE FIGHT
PONDER'S END	POWER PLANT	PRIZE IDIOT
POOR BEGGAR	POWER POINT	PRIZE MONEY
POOR CHANCE	POWER PRESS	PROFITS TAX
POOR CHOICE	PRAIRIE DOG	PROMPT BOOK
POOR EXCUSE	PRAWN CURRY	PROPER CARE
POOR FELLOW	PRAWN SALAD	PROPER MIND
POOR GROUND	PRAYER BOOK	PROPER NAME
POOR HEALTH	PREP. SCHOOL	PROPER NOUN
POOR PEOPLE	PRESENT DAY	PROPER TIME
POOR PLAYER	PRESS AGENT	PROSE WORKS
POOR RELIEF	PRESS AHEAD	PRO TEMPORE
POOR RESULT	PRESS BARON	PROUD BOAST
POOR RETURN	PRETTY FACE	PROUD FLESH

PROUD HEART
PROUD SIGHT
PROVEN FACT
PROWL ABOUT
PRYING EYES
PSYCHIC BID
PUBLIC GOOD
PUBLIC LIFE
PUBLIC PARK
PUBLIC PATH
PUBLIC ROAD
PUBLIC ROOM
PUBLIC SALE
PUBLIC WEAL
PUERTO RICO
PUFF OF WIND
PUFF PASTRY
PULLMAN CAR
PUNCH DRUNK
PUPPET SHOW
PURE ACCENT
PURE CHANCE
PURE COLOUR
PURE REASON
PURE SILVER
PURSED LIPS
PUSH AROUND
PUSH TOO FAR
PUT AND TAKE
PUT AN END TO
PUT A STOP TO
PUT ASUNDER
PUT FORWARD
PUT IN A BOOK
PUT IN A CELL
PUT IN A WORD
PUT IN FRONT
PUT IN IRONS
PUT IN ORDER
PUT IN POWER
PUT IN RHYME
PUT IN VERSE
PUT IN WORDS
PUT ON AN ACT
PUT ON A SHOW
PUT ON BLACK
PUT ON BOARD
PUT ONE OVER
PUT ONE WISE
PUT ON FLESH
PUT ON SPEED

PUT ON TRIAL
PUT THE SHOT
PUT THROUGH
PUTTING OFF
PUTTING OUT
PUT TO DEATH
PUT TO MUSIC
PUT TO SHAME
PUT TO SLEEP
PUTTY MEDAL
PUT UP A SHOW
PUT UP A SIGN
PUZZLED AIR
PUZZLE OVER

Q—10
QUACK, QUACK
QUAI D'ORSAY
QUAINT IDEA
QUAKER GIRL
QUARTER DAY
QUEEN'S HALL
QUEEN'S HEAD
QUEEN'S PAWN
QUEEN'S ROOK
QUEER SOUND
QUICK LUNCH
QUICK MARCH
QUICK TEMPO
QUICK TRICK
QUID PRO QUO
QUIET START
QUITE CLEAR
QUITE CLOSE
QUITE EMPTY
QUITE HAPPY
QUITE RIGHT
QUITE STILL
QUITE WRONG
QUIT OFFICE
QUIZ MASTER

R—10
RABBIT SKIN
RACE HATRED
RACING CARD
RACING FORM
RACING NEWS
RACING TOUT
RADIATE JOY
RADIO DRAMA

RADIO TIMES
RADIUM BOMB
RAGGED EDGE
RAILWAY ACT
RAISE A DUST
RAISE A HAND
RAISE A LOAN
RAISE ALOFT
RAISE MONEY
RAISE STEAM
RAISE TAXES
RALLY ROUND
RANCH HOUSE
RANDOM SHOT
RAPID PULSE
RARE CHANCE
RARING TO GO
RASH BELIEF
RATHER COOL
RATHER FLAT
RATHER GOOD
RATHER LATE
RATION BOOK
RATION CARD
RATTLE AWAY
RAW RECRUIT
RAY CHARLES
RAYNES PARK
RAY OF LIGHT
RAZOR BLADE
RAZOR'S EDGE
RAZOR SHARP
RAZOR STROP
READ A STORY
READ DEEPLY
READY FOR IT
READY MONEY
READY REPLY
READY TO CRY
READY TO DIE
READY TO EAT
REAL DANGER
REAL ESTATE
REAL FRIEND
REALLY MEAN
REAL MADRID
REAL OBJECT
REAL PERSON
REAL SCHOOL
REAL TENNIS
REAR WINDOW

RECENT DATE	RICHARD ROE	RIVER TRENT
RECENT PAST	RICH PEOPLE	RIVER TROUT
RECIPE BOOK	RICH REWARD	RIVER TWEED
RECORD CROP	RICH SOURCE	ROAD SAFETY
RECORD GATE	RICH SUPPLY	ROAD TO FAME
RECORD ROOM	RIDING COAT	ROAD TO HELL
RECORD SALE	RIDING CROP	ROAD TO RUIN
RECORD SHOP	RIDING HIGH	ROAD-UP SIGN
RECORD TIME	RIDING SEAT	ROAST ALIVE
RED ADMIRAL	RIDING WHIP	ROBBER BAND
RED AS A ROSE	RIFLE CORPS	ROBERT ADAM
RED BALLOON	RIFLE RANGE	ROBERT PEEL
RED BIRETTA	RIGHT ABOUT	ROBIN ADAIR
RED CABBAGE	RIGHT AHEAD	ROB THE TILL
RED CURRANT	RIGHT ANGLE	ROCK BOTTOM
RED FLANNEL	RIGHT DRESS	ROCKET BASE
RED HERRING	RIGHT FLANK	ROCKET SITE
RED PIGMENT	RIGHT LINES	ROCK GARDEN
RED, RED ROSE	RIGHT OF WAY	ROCK HUDSON
REFINED OIL	RIGHT ON TOP	ROCK OF AGES
REFORM BILL	RIGHT PLACE	ROCKS AHEAD
REFORM CLUB	RIGHT ROUND	ROCK SALMON
REFUSE BAIL	RIGHT ROYAL	ROCKY COAST
REFUSE DUMP	RIGHT THING	ROD AND LINE
REFUSE TO GO	RIGHT TOTAL	ROGER BACON
RELIEF FUND	RIGHT TRACK	ROLLED GOLD
REMAIN CALM	RIGHT TRAIL	ROLLED OATS
REMAIN DUMB	RIGHT WAY UP	ROLLS OF FAT
REMAND HOME	RIGHT WHEEL	ROMAN EAGLE
REMOTE AGES	RIGHT WOMAN	ROMAN FORUM
REMOVAL MAN	RING FINGER	ROMAN RUINS
REMOVAL VAN	RING MASTER	ROMAN TUNIC
RENEW A BOOK	RINGO STARR	ROMAN VILLA
RENT A HOUSE	RIPEN EARLY	ROMPER SUIT
REPAY A LOAN	RIPE OLD AGE	ROOF GARDEN
REPORT BACK	RIPE TOMATO	ROOM NUMBER
REPORT SICK	RISE HIGHER	ROOM TO MOVE
RESCUE SHIP	RISE IN ARMS	ROOM TO TURN
RESCUE TEAM	RISING COST	ROPE A STEER
RESCUE WORK	RISING TIDE	ROPE LADDER
REST AWHILE	RIVAL CAMPS	ROSE COLOUR
REST CENTRE	RIVAL CAUSE	ROSE GARDEN
REST PERIOD	RIVAL CLAIM	ROSY CHEEKS
RETAIL SHOP	RIVER BASIN	ROTARY CLUB
RETIRED PAY	RIVER CLYDE	ROTTEN HAND
RETIRE HURT	RIVER CRAFT	ROTTEN IDEA
RETURN FARE	RIVER LEVEL	ROTTEN LUCK
RETURN GAME	RIVER MOUTH	ROUGH CIDER
RETURN HALF	RIVER PLATE	ROUGH DRAFT
RETURN HOME	RIVER RHINE	ROUGH GOING
REVIEW COPY	RIVER RHONE	ROUGH GUESS

ROUGH GUIDE	RUDE PERSON	SAFE POLICY
ROUGH HANDS	RUDE REMARK	SAFE REFUGE
ROUGH HOUSE	RUE THE HOUR	SAFETY BELT
ROUGH NIGHT	RUGBY FIELD	SAFETY LAMP
ROUGH STATE	RUGBY MATCH	SAIL A YACHT
ROUGH STONE	RUGBY PITCH	SAILING AID
ROUGH STUFF	RUGBY SCRUM	SAILOR SUIT
ROUGH TRACK	RUGBY TRIAL	SAINT LOUIS
ROUGH USAGE	RUGBY UNION	SAINT PETER
ROUGH WATER	RUGGER BLUE	SALAD CREAM
ROUGH WORDS	RUM AND LIME	SALE OF WORK
ROUND ABOUT	RUN ABREAST	SALES STAFF
ROUND DANCE	RUN AGAINST	SALLY FORTH
ROUND DOZEN	RUN AGROUND	SALMON PINK
ROUND GUESS	RUN A MINUTE	SALT CELLAR
ROUND ROBIN	RUN AT A LOSS	SALTED AWAY
ROUND SCORE	RUN ERRANDS	SALTED BEEF
ROUND TABLE	RUN FOR HELP	SALT OF LIFE
ROUND TERMS	RUN FOR PORT	SAM GOLDWYN
ROUND TOWER	RUN IN PAIRS	SAMPLE BOOK
ROUTE MARCH	RUN LIKE MAD	SAND CASTLE
ROWING BLUE	RUNNER BEAN	SANDIE SHAW
ROWING BOAT	RUNNING OUT	SANDS OF DEE
ROWING CLUB	RUN THE RISK	SANDY BEACH
ROW OF BEANS	RUN THE SHOW	SANE ENOUGH
ROW OF TREES	RUN THROUGH	SANTA CLAUS
ROW UPON ROW	RUN TO EARTH	SANTA LUCIA
ROYAL ASCOT	RUN TO WASTE	SARAH MILES
ROYAL BARGE	RUN UP A BILL	SARDINE TIN
ROYAL BIRTH	RURAL SCENE	SATIN DRESS
ROYAL BLOOD	RUSS CONWAY	SAUCER EYES
ROYAL FLUSH	RUSSIAN EGG	SAVAGE BLOW
ROYAL HOUSE	RUSSIAN TEA	SAVAGE CLUB
ROYAL LODGE	RUSTIC ARCH	SAVAGE RACE
ROYAL SCOTS	RUSTIC SEAT	SAVE A TRICK
ROYAL SUITE	RUSTIC WORK	SAVE LABOUR
ROYAL TRAIN		SAVE THE DAY
ROYAL VISIT	**S—10**	SAVING GAME
ROYAL YACHT	SABBATH DAY	SAVOY HOTEL
ROY EMERSON	SABLE STOLE	SAY A PRAYER
ROY ORBISON	SACK OF COAL	SAY GOOD-BYE
RUB AGAINST	SACK OF COKE	SAY NOTHING
RUBBER BALL	SACK OF CORN	SAY THE WORD
RUBBER BAND	SACK THE LOT	SCALDED CAT
RUBBER HOSE	SACRED BOOK	SCALE MODEL
RUBBER SOLE	SACRED RITE	SCAMPER OFF
RUBBER TUBE	SACRED WRIT	SCARLET HAT
RUBBER TYRE	SAD OUTLOOK	SCARS OF WAR
RUBY MURRAY	SAD TIDINGS	SCENE THREE
RUDE ANSWER	SAFE IN PORT	SCENT SPRAY
RUDE HEALTH	SAFE METHOD	SCHOOL BELL

SCHOOL BOOK	SECOND LINE	SEND FLYING
SCHOOL DAYS	SECOND MATE	SENIOR GIRL
SCHOOL FEES	SECOND NAME	SENSE ORGAN
SCHOOL SONG	SECOND PART	SENT FLYING
SCHOOL TERM	SECOND POST	SENTRY DUTY
SCHOOL YEAR	SECOND RACE	SERENE LOOK
SCORE A BULL	SECOND RANK	SERIOUS AIR
SCORE A DUCK	SECOND SELF	SERVE A MEAL
SCORE A GOAL	SECOND SLIP	SERVE AN ACE
SCOTCH KALE	SECONDS OUT	SERVE A WRIT
SCOTCH MIST	SECOND TEAM	SERVE BADLY
SCOTCH PINE	SECOND TERM	SERVING MAN
SCOTCH REEL	SECOND TEST	SET A COURSE
SCOTS GREYS	SECOND TIME	SET AGAINST
SCOUT ROUND	SECOND WEEK	SET AT LARGE
SCRAPE AWAY	SECOND WIFE	SET FORMULA
SCRAPE HOME	SECOND WIND	SET IN ORDER
SCRAP METAL	SECOND YEAR	SET IN PLACE
SCRAP PAPER	SECRET CODE	SET OF BELLS
SCRATCH MAN	SECRET DOOR	SET OF CHESS
SCRATCH OUT	SECRET FILE	SET OF CLUBS
SCREECH OWL	SECRET PACT	SET OF DARTS
SCREEN IDOL	SECRET SIGN	SET OF EIGHT
SCREEN TEST	SECRET VICE	SET OF RULES
SCREW LOOSE	SECRET VOTE	SET OF SEVEN
SCRIP ISSUE	SEDAN CHAIR	SET OF STUDS
SCUTTLE OFF	SEE ABOUT IT	SET OF TEETH
SEA ANEMONE	SEE A DOCTOR	SET OF THREE
SEA BATHING	SEE A LAWYER	SET OF TOOLS
SEA CAPTAIN	SEE CLEARLY	SET PROBLEM
SEALED BOOK	SEEING LIFE	SET PURPOSE
SEALED LIPS	SEEK ACCORD	SET STORE BY
SEA MONSTER	SEEK ADVICE	SET THE PACE
SEAN O'CASEY	SEEK OFFICE	SETTING OFF
SEA OF FACES	SEEK REFUGE	SETTING OUT
SEA PASSAGE	SEEK SAFETY	SETTING SUN
SEA SERPENT	SEE NOTHING	SETTLE DOWN
SECOND BELL	SEE ONE'S WAY	SET TO MUSIC
SECOND BEST	SEE SERVICE	SET UP HOUSE
SECOND COAT	SEE THE JOKE	SEVEN A SIDE
SECOND COPY	SEE THROUGH	SEVEN CLUBS
SECOND CROP	SEE VISIONS	SEVEN DIALS
SECOND FORM	SEIZE POWER	SEVEN DOZEN
SECOND GEAR	SELECT CLUB	SEVEN GROSS
SECOND HALF	SELL AN IDEA	SEVEN HOURS
SECOND HAND	SELL IN BULK	SEVEN KINGS
SECOND HEAT	SELL SHARES	SEVEN MILES
SECOND HOLE	SELSEY BILL	SEVEN PARTS
SECOND HOME	SEND A CABLE	SEVEN PINTS
SECOND JUMP	SEND BY HAND	SEVEN SCORE
SECOND LEAD	SEND BY POST	SEVEN STARS

SEVENTH DAY	SHOOT A LINE	SICK HUMOUR
SEVENTH ROW	SHOOT FORTH	SICKLY LOOK
SEVENTH TEE	SHOOT IT OUT	SICK OF WORK
SEVEN TIMES	SHOP WINDOW	SICK PARADE
SEVEN TO ONE	SHORE LEAVE	SICK PERSON
SEVEN VEILS	SHORT BURST	SIDE BY SIDE
SEVEN WEEKS	SHORT DRINK	SIDE EFFECT
SEVEN YEARS	SHORT DRIVE	SIDE OF BEEF
SEVERE BLOW	SHORT HAIRS	SIDE POCKET
SEVERE LOOK	SHORT HOURS	SIDE STAKES
SEVERE LOSS	SHORT LEASE	SIDE STREET
SEVERE PAIN	SHORT LEAVE	SIDE TO SIDE
SEVERE TEST	SHORT PANTS	SIDE WINDOW
SEVERN BORE	SHORT PRICE	SIDLE ALONG
SEWAGE FARM	SHORT QUEUE	SIGH DEEPLY
SHABBY DEAL	SHORT RANGE	SIGH NO MORE
SHADY PLACE	SHORT SIGHT	SIGNAL LAMP
SHADY TRICK	SHORT SKIRT	SIGNED COPY
SHAKE HANDS	SHORT SLEEP	SIGNET RING
SHAKE IT OFF	SHORT SPELL	SIGN MANUAL
SHALLOW END	SHORT SPIRIT	SIGN OF LIFE
SHANK'S PONY	SHORT STAGE	SILENT FILM
SHANTY TOWN	SHORT STORY	SILKEN HAIR
SHAPE BADLY	SHORT VISIT	SILKEN HOSE
SHARE A FLAT	SHOT AT DAWN	SILK FABRIC
SHARE A TAXI	SHOVE ASIDE	SILK GLOVES
SHARP FROST	SHOW A LIGHT	SILK SQUARE
SHARP KNIFE	SHOWER BATH	SILLY BILLY
SHARP POINT	SHOW FAVOUR	SILLY DEVIL
SHARP TASTE	SHOW NO PITY	SILLY GOOSE
SHARP TWIST	SHOW NO SIGN	SILLY IDIOT
SHARP VOICE	SHOW SPIRIT	SILLY MID-ON
SHARP WORDS	SHOW TALENT	SILLY POINT
SHED A LIGHT	SHOW THE WAY	SILVER BAND
SHEEP'S EYES	SHOW UP WELL	SILVER COIN
SHEER FLUKE	SHOW VALOUR	SILVER DISC
SHEER FOLLY	SHREWD BLOW	SILVER FOIL
SHEER FORCE	SHREWD FACE	SILVER HAIR
SHEER WASTE	SHREWD IDEA	SILVER MINE
SHEET GLASS	SHREWD MOVE	SILVER RING
SHEET METAL	SHREWD TURN	SILVER STAR
SHEET MUSIC	SHRILL NOTE	SILVER TRAY
SHEET OF ICE	SHRILL TONE	SILVER WIRE
SHIFT ABOUT	SHRINK AWAY	SIMMER DOWN
SHINE FORTH	SHRINK BACK	SIMNEL CAKE
SHIN OF BEEF	SHUFFLE OFF	SIMON PETER
SHIP'S CARGO	SHUFFLE OUT	SIMPLE DIET
SHIRE HORSE	SHUTTING UP	SIMPLE FARE
SHOE A HORSE	SHUT UP SHOP	SIMPLE IDEA
SHOE POLISH	SIAMESE CAT	SIMPLE LIFE
SHOOT AHEAD	SICK AS A DOG	SIMPLE MIND

SIMPLE PAST
SIMPLE SOUL
SINE QUA NON
SING A DIRGE
SING FOR JOY
SING IN TUNE
SINGLE BLOW
SINGLE FARE
SINGLE FILE
SINGLE LIFE
SINGLE LINE
SINGLE MIND
SINGLE NOTE
SINGLE ROOM
SINGLE VOTE
SINK A SHAFT
SINK OR SWIM
SIRE AND DAM
SIR GALAHAD
SIR OR MADAM
SISTER SHIP
SIT AND FUME
SITTING OUT
SIX AND FIVE
SIX AND FOUR
SIX AND NINE
SIX BILLION
SIX COURSES
SIX DEGREES
SIX DOLLARS
SIX FATHOMS
SIX GALLONS
SIX GUINEAS
SIX HUNDRED
SIX MINUTES
SIX OCTAVES
SIX OF CLUBS
SIX OR SEVEN
SIX PER CENT
SIX SQUARED
SIX STROKES
SIXTH FLOOR
SIXTH GREEN
SIXTH OF MAY
SIXTH PLACE
SIXTH ROUND
SIXTH SENSE
SIXTY MILES
SIXTY TIMES
SIXTY YEARS
SIX WICKETS

SIZE ELEVEN
SIZE OF TYPE
SIZE TWELVE
SKETCH BOOK
SKIPPED OFF
SKIPPED OUT
SKIRT ROUND
SKITTLE OUT
SLACKEN OFF
SLACK WATER
SLAP-UP MEAL
SLATE LOOSE
SLAVE DANCE
SLAVE STATE
SLAVE TRADE
SLEEP IT OFF
SLEEP ROUGH
SLEEP TIGHT
SLEIGH RIDE
SLICED LOAF
SLICK CHICK
SLIDE VALVE
SLIGHT BLOW
SLIGHT COLD
SLIM CHANCE
SLIM FIGURE
SLIM VOLUME
SLIP OF A BOY
SLIPPED OFF
SLIPPED OUT
SLOW BOWLER
SLOW GROWTH
SLOW MOTION
SLOW POISON
SLOW WICKET
SMALL BLAME
SMALL BUILD
SMALL CHILD
SMALL CRAFT
SMALL CROWD
SMALL HOPES
SMALL HOURS
SMALL HOUSE
SMALL MEANS
SMALL ORDER
SMALL PIECE
SMALL PRINT
SMALL SCALE
SMALL THING
SMALL VOICE
SMALL WAIST

SMALL WOMAN
SMALL WORLD
SMART HOUSE
SMART WOMAN
SMILE AGAIN
SMITH MINOR
SMOKE A PIPE
SMOKED FISH
SMOKING CAP
SMOKING HOT
SMOOTH AWAY
SMOOTH CHIN
SMOOTH DOWN
SMOOTH FACE
SMOOTH HAIR
SMOOTH OVER
SMOOTH SKIN
SMUGGLE OUT
SNAIL'S PACE
SNAP ANSWER
SNAP INTO IT
SNATCH AWAY
SNEAK ABOUT
SNEAK ROUND
SNEAK THIEF
SNOW AND ICE
SNOW MAIDEN
SNOWY WHITE
SOAKING WET
SOAP BUBBLE
SOAP FLAKES
SOAP POWDER
SOAP RATION
SOAPY WATER
SOBER TRUTH
SOCCER TEAM
SOCIAL CLUB
SOCIAL EVIL
SOCIAL ILLS
SOCIAL LIFE
SOCIAL RANK
SOCIAL RUIN
SOCIAL WORK
SODIUM LAMP
SOFT ANSWER
SOFT AS SILK
SOFT AS SOAP
SOFT CENTRE
SOFT COLLAR
SOFT COLOUR
SOFT GROUND

SOFT NUMBER	SPARE WHEEL	SQUARE MEAL
SOFT PALATE	SPEAK ALOUD	SQUARE MILE
SOFT PENCIL	SPEAK DUTCH	SQUARE ROOT
SOFT TONGUE	SPEAK WELSH	SQUARE SAIL
SOFT WICKET	SPECIAL BUS	SQUARE UP TO
SOHO SQUARE	SPECIAL DAY	SQUARE YARD
SOLAR MONTH	SPEED FIEND	SQUEEZE DRY
SOLEMN FACE	SPEED GAUGE	SQUEEZE OUT
SOLEMN LOOK	SPEED LIMIT	STABLE DOOR
SOLEMN OATH	SPEED TRIAL	STABLE MATE
SOLE RIGHTS	SPELL IT OUT	STACK OF HAY
SOLE TRADER	SPEND MONEY	STAFF NURSE
SOLID BUILD	SPENT FORCE	STAG BEETLE
SOLID FACTS	SPICED WINE	STAGE FEVER
SOLID IVORY	SPICY STORY	STAGGER OFF
SOLID SENSE	SPIDER'S WEB	STAGGER OUT
SOLID WATER	SPIKE JONES	STAKE MONEY
SOLO EFFORT	SPILL BLOOD	STALE BREAD
SOLO FLIGHT	SPINAL CORD	STAMP ALBUM
SON AND HEIR	SPIN BOWLER	STAND ABOUT
SONG OF LOVE	SPIRAL DOWN	STAND ALONE
SONG WRITER	SPIRIT AWAY	STAND ALOOF
SONJA HENIE	SPIRIT LAMP	STAND APART
SONNIE HALE	SPLIT HAIRS	STAND ASIDE
SOON ENOUGH	SPLIT IN TWO	STAND AT BAY
SOOTH TO SAY	SPODE CHINA	STAND CLEAR
SORDID GAIN	SPOKEN WORD	STAND ERECT
SORE THROAT	SPONGE CAKE	STAND FOR IT
SORRY SIGHT	SPONGE DOWN	STAND GUARD
SORRY STATE	SPORTS CLUB	STAND IN AWE
SORRY TO SAY	SPORTS COAT	STANDING BY
SOUND BASIS	SPORTS PAGE	STANDING UP
SOUND RADIO	SPOTTED DOG	STAND ON END
SOUND SENSE	SPREAD FEAR	STAND READY
SOUND SLEEP	SPREAD SAIL	STAND STILL
SOUND TRACK	SPRING AWAY	STAND TO WIN
SOUND VIEWS	SPRING BACK	STAND TREAT
SOUND WAVES	SPRING DOWN	STAND TRIAL
SOUP COURSE	SPRING OPEN	STAND UP FOR
SOUP TICKET	SPRING OVER	STAPLE DIET
SOUR GRAPES	SPRING SALE	STARK NAKED
SOUR NATURE	SPRING SONG	STARLIT SKY
SOUTH COAST	SPRING TIDE	STAR OF HOPE
SOUTH DEVON	SPUN SILVER	STAR PLAYER
SOUTH DOWNS	SQUAD DRILL	START A FIRE
SOUTH WALES	SQUARE CHIN	START AGAIN
SOW THE SEED	SQUARE DEAL	START A RIOT
SPACE PROBE	SQUARE FOOT	START YOUNG
SPANISH FLY	SQUARE GAME	STATE A CASE
SPAN OF LIFE	SQUARE HOLE	STATE COACH
SPARE FRAME	SQUARE INCH	STATED TIME

STATE GRANT	STICKY MESS	STRICT DIET
STATE NURSE	STIFF CLIMB	STRICT TIME
STATE OF WAR	STIFF DRINK	STRIKE BACK
STATE TRIAL	STIFF FENCE	STRIKE CAMP
STATE VISIT	STIFF PRICE	STRIKE DOWN
STATUTE LAW	STILL OWING	STRIKE DUMB
STAY AT HOME	STILL THERE	STRIKE GOLD
STAY BEHIND	STILL WATER	STRIKE HARD
STAY IN A RUT	STIRRUP CUP	STRIKE HOME
STAY INSIDE	STIR THE POT	STRIKE SAIL
STAY UP LATE	STITCHED UP	STRING BAND
ST. DUNSTAN'S	ST. LAWRENCE	STRING TRIO
STEADY BEAM	ST. LUKE'S DAY	STRING VEST
STEADY FLOW	STOCK REPLY	STRIP POKER
STEADY HAND	STOCK STILL	STRIP TEASE
STEADY PACE	STODGY FOOD	STROKE PLAY
STEADY RAIN	STOKE POGES	STRONG BREW
STEADY SALE	STOLE A KISS	STRONG CASE
STEADY WIND	STONE STEPS	STRONG GRIP
STEAK HOUSE	STONE WALLS	STRONG HAND
STEAL A KISS	STONY BROKE	STRONG HEAD
STEAL ALONG	STONY HEART	STRONG LINE
STEALING BY	STONY STARE	STRONG MEAT
STEALING UP	STOOD TRIAL	STRONG MIND
STEAM NAVVY	STOP AT HOME	STRONG PULL
STEAM ORGAN	STOP A TOOTH	STRONG ROOM
STEAM POWER	STOP AT WILL	STRONG SIDE
STEAM RADIO	STOP CRYING	STRONG SUIT
STEAM TRAIN	STOP FOR TEA	STRONG WILL
STEAM YACHT	STOP IN TIME	STRONG WIND
STEEL WORKS	STOPPED ONE	STRUCK DOWN
STEELY LOOK	STOPPED OUT	STRUCK DUMB
STEEP CLIMB	STOP THE BUS	STRUGGLE BY
STEEP PRICE	STOP THE GAP	STRUGGLE ON
STEER CLEAR	STOP THE ROT	ST. STEPHEN'S
STEP ASHORE	STORE OF WIT	STUDIO FLAT
STEP BY STEP	STORK'S NEST	STUDY MUSIC
STEP INSIDE	STORMY LIFE	STUFFED OWL
STEP LIVELY	STOUT HEART	STUFFY ROOM
STEPPED OUT	STOUT WOMAN	STUMP ALONG
STERN CHASE	STRAIGHT BY	STUMPED OUT
STERN TRUTH	STRAIGHT IN	STUMPY TAIL
STERN WORDS	STRAIGHT ON	STURDY LEGS
STEWED BEEF	STRAIGHT UP	SUCH IS LIFE
STEWED EELS	STRANGE MAN	SUCKING PIG
STEWED LAMB	STREAK AWAY	SUDDEN BANG
STEWED MEAT	STREAK PAST	SUDDEN BLOW
STICK IT OUT	STREET ARAB	SUDDEN FEAR
STICK TIGHT	STREET DOOR	SUDDEN HUSH
STICK UP FOR	STREET LAMP	SUDDEN STOP
STICKY BOMB	STRETCH OUT	SUEDE SHOES

SUFFER LOSS	SWING ALONG	TAKE ORDERS
SUFFER PAIN	SWING FOR IT	TAKE PITY ON
SUGAR CANDY	SWING MUSIC	TAKE POISON
SUGAR DADDY	SWING ROUND	TAKE REFUGE
SUMMER CAMP	SWISS GUARD	TAKE THE AIR
SUMMER HEAT	SWISS WATCH	TAKE THE CUP
SUMMER RAIN	SWITCH BACK	TAKE THE RAP
SUMMER SALE	SWITCH OVER	TAKE TO ARMS
SUMMER TERM	SWORD DANCE	TAKE TO TASK
SUMMER TIME	SWORN ENEMY	TAKE UP ARMS
SUM OF MONEY		TAKE UP TIME
SUN AND MOON		TAKING WAYS
SUNDAY BEST	**T—10**	TALENT SHOW
SUNDAY SUIT	TABLE D'HÔTE	TALE OF A TUB
SUN GLASSES	TABLE KNIFE	TALK AWHILE
SUNKEN REEF	TABLE LINEN	TALK IT OVER
SUNNY SMILE	TABLE MONEY	TALK TURKEY
SUNNY SOUTH	TABLE WATER	TALLEST BOY
SUN-RAY LAMP	TAKE A BRIEF	TALLEST MAN
SUNSET GLOW	TAKE A CHAIR	TAME AFFAIR
SUPERB VIEW	TAKE ACTION	TAME ANIMAL
SUPPER TIME	TAKE A DEKKO	TANGLED WEB
SUPPLY BASE	TAKE ADVICE	TAP LIGHTLY
SUPPLY SHIP	TAKE AN OATH	TAP THE LINE
SURE AS FATE	TAKE A PHOTO	TAP THE WIRE
SURE ENOUGH	TAKE A PUNCH	TARGET AREA
SURE GROUND	TAKE A SHARE	TARGET DATE
SURGE AHEAD	TAKE A SNACK	TARGET SHIP
SURPLUS FAT	TAKE AS READ	TARIFF WALL
SWAGGER OUT	TAKE A STAND	TARTAN KILT
SWAN OF AVON	TAKE A TITLE	TART ANSWER
SWEARING IN	TAKE A TRAIN	TASK IN HAND
SWEAT BLOOD	TAKE CHARGE	TASTE BLOOD
SWEAT IT OUT	TAKE CREDIT	TASTY SNACK
SWEEP ALONG	TAKE EFFECT	TATTOO MARK
SWEEP ASIDE	TAKE FLIGHT	TAUT NERVES
SWEEP CLEAN	TAKE FRIGHT	TAX EVASION
SWEET DRINK	TAKE IN HAND	TAXI DRIVER
SWEET HERBS	TAKE IN SAIL	T-BONE STEAK
SWEET MUSIC	TAKE IN VAIN	TEACH CLASS
SWEET SLEEP	TAKE IT BACK	TEACH MUSIC
SWEET SMELL	TAKE IT EASY	TEA CLIPPER
SWEET SMILE	TAKE IT HARD	TEA DRINKER
SWEET SOUND	TAKE KINDLY	TEAM OF FOUR
SWEET SYRUP	TAKE MY HAND	TEAM SPIRIT
SWEET TOOTH	TAKE MY WORD	TEA PLANTER
SWEET VOICE	TAKEN ABACK	TEAR IN HALF
SWEET WORDS	TAKE NO PART	TEAR TO BITS
SWERVE PAST	TAKE NOTICE	TEA SERVICE
SWIM ACROSS	TAKE OFFICE	TEENY WEENY
SWINE FEVER	TAKE ON A JOB	TELL A STORY

TELLING OFF	THE BALKANS	THE MAESTRO
TEN AND FIVE	THE BEATLES	THE MARINES
TEN AND FOUR	THE BEST MAN	THE MAZURKA
TEN AND NINE	THE BIG FIVE	THEME MUSIC
TEN BILLION	THE BOER WAR	THE MENDIPS
TEN DEGREES	THE BRAVEST	THE MESSIAH
TENDER CARE	THE BRONTËS	THE MILITIA
TENDER LOVE	THE CABINET	THE MIXTURE
TENDER MEAT	THE CAPITAL	THE NEEDFUL
TENDER SPOT	THE CHANNEL	THE NEEDLES
TEN DOLLARS	THE COLD WAR	THE NEW LOOK
TEN FATHOMS	THE COMMONS	THE ODYSSEY
TEN GALLONS	THE CRITICS	THE OLD ADAM
TEN GUINEAS	THE CURRAGH	THE OLD FIRM
TEN MILLION	THE CUSTOMS	THE ORKNEYS
TEN MINUTES	THÉ DANSANT	THE PEERAGE
TENNIS BALL	THE DEAD SEA	THE PLANETS
TENNIS CLUB	THE DEEP END	THE PRELUDE
TENNIS STAR	THE DYNASTS	THE PREMIER
TEN OF CLUBS	THE EAST END	THE QUAKERS
TENOR VOICE	THE ENGLISH	THE QUALITY
TEN PAST ONE	THE ETERNAL	THE RED ARMY
TEN PAST SIX	THE EVIL EYE	THE RED FLAG
TEN PAST TWO	THE EVIL ONE	THE REGENCY
TEN PER CENT	THE EXPERTS	THE RENT ACT
TEN SECONDS	THE FAIR SEX	THERE THERE!
TEN SQUARED	THE FAR EAST	THE REVENGE
TENTH GREEN	THE FIDGETS	THE RIOT ACT
TENTH OF MAY	THE FIFTIES	THE RIVIERA
TENTH PLACE	THE FORTIES	THE ROCKERS
TENTH ROUND	THE GALLERY	THE ROCKIES
TEN TO EIGHT	THE GALLOWS	THE SABBATH
TEN TO SEVEN	THE GESTAPO	THE SAME KEY
TEN TO THREE	THE GIGGLES	THE SAPPERS
TEN WICKETS	THE GLAD EYE	THE SEASONS
TEPID WATER	THE GORBALS	THE SEEKERS
TERRA COTTA	THE GUNNERS	THE SHADOWS
TERRA FIRMA	THE HARD WAY	THE SHIVERS
TEST FLIGHT	THE HEIRESS	THE SIXTIES
TEST OF TIME	THE HERMITS	THE SPEAKER
TEST RESULT	THE HOLLIES	THE STARTER
TEST WICKET	THE HORRORS	THE STEPPES
THE ACCUSED	THE JACKPOT	THE ST. LEGER
THE AMAZONS	THE JONESES	THE SUBURBS
THE ANIMALS	THE KNOW-HOW	THE TAIL-END
THE ARCHERS	THE KREMLIN	THE TEMPEST
THE ARSENAL	THE LANCERS	THE THEATRE
THEATRE BAR	THE LAST BUS	THE THINKER
THEATRE FAN	THE LAST LAP	THE THIN MAN
THE BACKING	THE LINCOLN	THE TITANIC
THE BAHAMAS	THE LOW-DOWN	THE TROPICS

THE TWELFTH	THORNY PATH	TIE THE KNOT
THE UNITIES	THREE BALLS	TIGHT DRESS
THE UNKNOWN	THREE BEARS	TIGHT GRASP
THE VATICAN	THREE BRACE	TIGHT PLACE
THE VICTORY	THREE CARDS	TIGHT SKIRT
THE VIKINGS	THREE CLUBS	TILLER GIRL
THE WEATHER	THREE DARTS	TIMBER TREE
THE WEST END	THREE DOZEN	TIME A PUNCH
THE WILLIES	THREE DRAWS	TIME ENOUGH
THICK SKULL	THREE FATES	TIME FACTOR
THICK SLICE	THREE FIVES	TIME FOR BED
THICK TWINE	THREE FOURS	TIME FOR TEA
THIN EXCUSE	THREE GROSS	TIME IN HAND
THING OR TWO	THREE HOLES	TIMELY EXIT
THINK ABOUT	THREE HOURS	TIMELY WORD
THINK AGAIN	THREE IN ONE	TIME OF LIFE
THINK AHEAD	THREE JACKS	TIME OF YEAR
THINK ALIKE	THREE KINGS	TIME, PLEASE
THINK ALOUD	THREE LUMPS	TIME SIGNAL
THINK IT OUT	THREE MILES	TIME TO COME
THINK TWICE	THREE NINES	TIME TO KILL
THINNED OUT	THREE PAIRS	TIME TO LOSE
THIN STRING	THREE PARTS	TIME TO STOP
THIRD CHILD	THREE PINTS	TINKER BELL
THIRD CLASS	THREE PUTTS	TINKER WITH
THIRD FLOOR	THREE SCORE	TINNED CRAB
THIRD GREEN	THREE SIDES	TINNED FISH
THIRD MONTH	THREE SIXES	TINNED FOOD
THIRD OF MAY	THREE STARS	TINNED MEAT
THIRD PARTY	THREE TIMES	TINNED MILK
THIRD PLACE	THREE TO ONE	TINNED SOUP
THIRD POWER	THREE WEEKS	TINNY NOISE
THIRD PRIZE	THREE YEARS	TINNY SOUND
THIRD REICH	THRIFT CLUB	TIN OF BEANS
THIRD ROUND	THROW ABOUT	TIN OF COCOA
THIRD STAGE	THROW A KISS	TIN OF FRUIT
THIRD VERSE	THROW ASIDE	TIN OF PAINT
THIRTY DAYS	THRUST DOWN	TIN SOLDIER
THIRTY LOVE	THRUST HOME	TIN WHISTLE
THIS FRIDAY	THRUST OPEN	TIP A WINNER
THIS MONDAY	THRUST PAST	TIP THE WINK
THIS OR THAT	THUMB A LIFT	TITIAN HAIR
THIS SEASON	THUMB A RIDE	TITLED RANK
THIS SIDE UP	THUMB INDEX	TITLE FIGHT
THIS SPRING	THUMBS DOWN	TITUS OATES
THIS SUMMER	TIDAL BASIN	TOBACCO ROW
THIS SUNDAY	TIDAL RIVER	TODAY'S DATE
THIS WAY OUT	TIDY INCOME	TOE THE LINE
THIS WINTER	TIE IN KNOTS	TOE THE MARK
THOMAS GRAY	TIE-ON LABEL	TOILET SOAP
THOMAS HOOD	TIES OF RACE	TOKEN MONEY

TOLL BRIDGE	TRADE UNION	TRUSS OF HAY
TOMATO SOUP	TRAFFIC COP	TRUSTEE ACT
TOM BOWLING	TRAFFIC JAM	TRUST HOUSE
TONIC SOLFA	TRAGIC MASK	TRY A NEW WAY
TONIC WATER	TRAGIC MUSE	TRYING TIME
TONS OF LOVE	TRAGIC NEWS	TUDOR HOUSE
TONS OF TIME	TRAGIC TALE	TUDOR KINGS
TONY CURTIS	TRAIN CRASH	TUDOR STYLE
TONY WELLER	TRAINED EYE	TUFT OF HAIR
TOO FAR GONE	TRAINED MAN	TUMBLE DOWN
TOOL SETTER	TRAIN FERRY	TUMBLE OVER
TO ONE'S FACE	TRAIN SMASH	TUNING FORK
TOOTING BEC	TRAM DRIVER	TUNNEL INTO
TOP AND TAIL	TRAMPLED ON	TURKEY TROT
TOP BILLING	TRAM TICKET	TURN ADRIFT
TOP HONOURS	TRAPEZE ACT	TURN AROUND
TOPPLE DOWN	TRAVEL BOOK	TURN COLOUR
TOPPLE OVER	TREAD ON AIR	TURN IT DOWN
TOP QUALITY	TREAD WATER	TURN OF DUTY
TOP THE BILL	TREAT BADLY	TURN THE KEY
TORRID ZONE	TREATY PORT	TURN TO DUST
TORY LEADER	TREBLE CLEF	TURN TO GOLD
TOTAL BLANK	TREE DOCTOR	TURN TURTLE
TOTAL WRECK	TREE OF LIFE	TURN YELLOW
TO THE ALTAR	TRENCH COAT	TURTLE DOVE
TO THE NORTH	TRENCH FEET	TURTLE SOUP
TO THE POINT	TRIAL MATCH	TWELFTH DAY
TO THE RIGHT	TRIAL SCENE	TWELFTH MAN
TO THE SOUTH	TRICK OR TWO	TWELFTH ROW
TOUCH AND GO	TRIFLE WITH	TWELVE DAYS
TOUCH JUDGE	TRIGGER OFF	TWELVE FEET
TOUCH LUCKY	TRIM ANKLES	TWELVE QUID
TOUGH BREAK	TRIM FIGURE	TWENTY QUID
TOUGH FIGHT	TRIP ABROAD	TWICE A WEEK
TOUR AROUND	TRIPLE STAR	TWICE A YEAR
TOURING CAR	TRIPLE TIME	TWICE DAILY
TOUR OF DUTY	TRIP TO TOWN	TWICE EIGHT
TO WINDWARD	TROLLEY BUS	TWICE ROUND
TOWN CENTRE	TROOP TRAIN	TWICE SEVEN
TOWN SQUARE	TROTTED OFF	TWICE THREE
TOY SOLDIER	TROTTED OUT	TWINE ROUND
TOY SPANIEL	TROY WEIGHT	TWIN SISTER
TOY TERRIER	TRUDGE PAST	TWIRL ROUND
TRACKER DOG	TRUE CHARGE	TWIST ABOUT
TRACK EVENT	TRUE FRIEND	TWIST MY ARM
TRADE CYCLE	TRUE REPORT	TWIST ROUND
TRADE PAPER	TRUE SAMPLE	TWO AND FIVE
TRADE PRICE	TRUE TO FORM	TWO AND FOUR
TRADER HORN	TRUE TO LIFE	TWO AND NINE
TRADE ROUTE	TRUE TO TYPE	TWO AT A TIME
TRADE TERMS	TRULY RURAL	TWO BILLION

TWO COLOURS	UNPAID BILL	VAL PARNELL
TWO COURSES	UNSOLD BOOK	VAMPIRE BAT
TWO DEGREES	UNTIDY MIND	VANESSA LEE
TWO DOLLARS	UNTIE A KNOT	VANILLA ICE
TWO FATHOMS	UP A GUM TREE	VANITY CASE
TWO GALLONS	UP ALL NIGHT	VANITY FAIR
TWO GUINEAS	UP AND ABOUT	VANTAGE OUT
TWO HUNDRED	UP AND DOING	VAPOUR BATH
TWO LENGTHS	UP AT OXFORD	VARIETY ACT
TWO MASTERS	UP FOR TRIAL	VAST EXTENT
TWO MILLION	UPHILL TASK	VAST PLAINS
TWO MINUTES	UPHILL WALK	VEAL AND HAM
TWO OCTAVES	UPHILL WORK	VEAL CUTLET
TWO OF A KIND	UP IN A PLANE	VENTURE OUT
TWO OF CLUBS	UP IN THE AIR	VERY HUNGRY
TWO OR THREE	UP IN THE SKY	VERY LIKELY
TWO PER CENT	UPON MY SOUL	VERY LITTLE
TWO RASHERS	UPON MY WORD	VERY NEARLY
TWO SECONDS	UPPER BERTH	VERY SELDOM
TWO SQUARED	UPPER CLASS	VETERAN CAR
TWO STRIPES	UPPER CRUST	VICHY WATER
TWO STROKES	UPPER HOUSE	VICIOUS LIE
TWO WICKETS	UPPER LIMIT	VICTOR HUGO
TYBURN TREE	UPPER SIXTH	VICTORY DAY
TYPING POOL	UPPER STORY	VILE BODIES
	UPRIGHT MAN	VILLAGE INN
U—10	UPSIDE DOWN	VINE GROWER
UGLY RUMOUR	UP THE AISLE	VINTAGE CAR
UGLY SISTER	UP THE CREEK	VIOLENT END
UGLY THREAT	UP THE RIVER	VIOLIN CASE
ULTRA VIRES	UP THE SPOUT	VIOLIN SOLO
UNCLE REMUS	UP TO A POINT	VIRGIN CLAY
UNCUT PAGES	UP TO NO GOOD	VIRGIN LAND
UNCUT STONE	UP TO SAMPLE	VIRGIN MARY
UNDER A TREE	UP TO THE HUB	VIRGIN SOIL
UNDER COVER	USE FINESSE	VITAL ERROR
UNDER GLASS	USEFUL HINT	VITAL FLAME
UNDER PROOF	USE THE POST	VITAL FORCE
UNDER STEAM	USUAL THING	VITAL POINT
UNDER TRIAL	UTTERLY BAD	VITAL POWER
UNDER WATER	UTTER TRIPE	VITAL SPARK
UNDUE HASTE		VITAL WOUND
UNION BOARD	**V—10**	VIVID GREEN
UNION CHIEF	VACANT LOOK	VOCAL CORDS
UNION RULES	VACANT POST	VOCAL GROUP
UNIQUE CASE	VACUUM PUMP	VOCAL MUSIC
UNIT OF HEAT	VAIN EFFORT	VOCAL ORGAN
UNIT OF TIME	VAIN PERSON	VOLLEY BALL
UNIT OF WORK	VAIN REGRET	VOTE LABOUR
UNKIND DEED	VALE AND LEA	VOTING LIST
UNKIND WORD	VALID POINT	VOUCH FOR IT

VOWEL SOUND	WATCHED POT	WELSH WALES
VULGAR HERD	WATCH FOR IT	WENT AROUND
	WATER BOARD	WENT DIRECT
W—10	WATER LEVEL	WENT TO TOWN
WADE ACROSS	WATER MELON	WEST AFRICA
WADING BIRD	WATER MUSIC	WEST BERLIN
WAD OF MONEY	WATER NYMPH	WEST INDIAN
WAD OF NOTES	WATER ON TAP	WEST INDIES
WAGE FREEZE	WATER POWER	WEST IS WEST
WAGE PACKET	WATER'S EDGE	WEST LONDON
WAGES CLERK	WATER TOWER	WEST RIDING
WAGES OF SIN	WAVE LENGTH	WESTWARD HO!
WAGON TRAIN	WAX AND WANE	WET BATTERY
WAG THE HEAD	WAXED PAPER	WET BLANKET
WAIT AND SEE	WAXING MOON	WET CANTEEN
WAIT AROUND	WAY IN FRONT	WET CLOTHES
WAIT AWHILE	WAY OFF BEAM	WET SHAMPOO
WALK ACROSS	WAYSIDE INN	WET THROUGH
WALK AROUND	WAY THROUGH	WET WEATHER
WALK BEHIND	WEAK EXCUSE	WHAT AM I BID?
WALK IN FEAR	WEAK STROKE	WHAT A NERVE!
WALK OF LIFE	WEAK WILLED	WHAT A SHAME!
WALK SLOWLY	WEALTHY MAN	WHAT GOES ON?
WALK SOFTLY	WEARY WORLD	WHAT'S YOURS?
WALL OF FIRE	WEATHER EYE	WHEAT FIELD
WALL STREET	WEATHER MAP	WHEEL ABOUT
WALNUT TREE	WEBBED FEET	WHEEL ROUND
WALT DISNEY	WEDDED PAIR	WHELK STALL
WALTZ MUSIC	WEDDED WIFE	WHIFF OF AIR
WALTZ ROUND	WEDDING DAY	WHIPPED OFF
WANDER AWAY	WEED KILLER	WHIRL ROUND
WANING MOON	WEEK BY WEEK	WHIST DRIVE
WANT OF CARE	WEEKLY RENT	WHISTLE FOR
WANT OF LOVE	WEEKLY WAGE	WHITE BREAD
WANT OF ZEAL	WEEP FOR JOY	WHITE CARGO
WARD SISTER	WEEP NO MORE	WHITE CHALK
WAR FOOTING	WEIGH HEAVY	WHITE FRIAR
WAR MEMOIRS	WEIGHING IN	WHITE FROST
WARM FRIEND	WELCOME END	WHITE HORSE
WARMING PAN	WELL BEATEN	WHITE HOUSE
WARNING CRY	WELL BEHIND	WHITE LIGHT
WAR OF WORDS	WELL CAUGHT	WHITE MAGIC
WARPED MIND	WELL ENOUGH	WHITE METAL
WAR SAVINGS	WELL I NEVER!	WHITE MOUSE
WASH AND DRY	WELL IN HAND	WHITE PAINT
WASHING DAY	WELL OF LIFE	WHITE PAPER
WASP'S STING	WELL PLACED	WHITE PIECE
WASTE MONEY	WELL PLAYED	WHITE QUEEN
WASTE PAPER	WELLS FARGO	WHITE SAUCE
WASTE WORDS	WELL VERSED	WHITE SHEET
WATCH CHAIN	WELSH CORGI	WHITE SHIRT

WHITE SLAVE
WHITE SUGAR
WHITE TRASH
WHIT MONDAY
WHIT SUNDAY
WHOLE TRUTH
WHOLE WORLD
WICKED DEED
WICKED WAYS
WIDE APPEAL
WIDE CHOICE
WIDE CIRCLE
WIDELY HELD
WIDE MARGIN
WIDE SCREEN
WIDE VISION
WIDOW'S MITE
WIDOW'S PEAK
WIDOW WOMAN
WIELD POWER
WIFE BEATER
WIG AND GOWN
WILD ANIMAL
WILD CHEERS
WILD CHERRY
WILD FLOWER
WILD HORSES
WILD SCHEME
WILL OF IRON
WILLOW TREE
WILL TO LIVE
WILLY NILLY
WILY PERSON
WIN A RUBBER
WIN BY A GOAL
WIN BY A HEAD
WIN BY A NECK
WINDOW PANE
WINE BIBBER
WINE BOTTLE
WINE CELLAR
WINE TASTER
WINE TAVERN
WINE WAITER
WIN FREEDOM
WIN HONOURS
WINNING BET
WINNING HIT
WINNING RUN
WINNING TRY
WIN ON MERIT

WINTER COAT
WINTER FEED
WINTER SALE
WINTER TIME
WINTER WEAR
WIN THE GAME
WIN THE RACE
WIN THE TOSS
WIN THROUGH
WIRE BASKET
WIRE PUZZLE
WISE CHOICE
WISE OLD OWL
WISH IN VAIN
WISH UNDONE
WITCH HAZEL
WITH A SMILE
WITHER AWAY
WITHIN CALL
WITHIN HAIL
WITHOUT END
WITH REGRET
WITNESS BOX
WIZARD OF OZ
WOMAN HATER
WOMAN'S HOUR
WOMAN'S WORK
WOMEN'S ARMY
WOMEN'S PAGE
WOMEN'S WEAR
WON BY A HEAD
WON BY A NECK
WONDER DRUG
WOODEN CLUB
WOODEN SEAT
WOODEN SHOE
WOOD STREET
WOOLLY HAIR
WORD MAKING
WORD OF A LIE
WORD PUZZLE
WORD SQUARE
WORKING DAY
WORKING MAN
WORK IN HAND
WORK IN VAIN
WORK ON HAND
WORK PERMIT
WORK TO RULE
WORK UNDONE
WORLD ATLAS

WORLD COURT
WORLD POWER
WORLD TITLE
WORLD TRADE
WORRIED MAN
WORST OF ALL
WORST TASTE
WORTH WHILE
WOUNDED MAN
WREAK HAVOC
WRIGGLE OUT
WRITE A BOOK
WRITE ABOUT
WRITE AGAIN
WRITE A NOTE
WRITE A POEM
WRITE A SONG
WRITE BADLY
WRITE BOOKS
WRITE IN INK
WRITE IT OFF
WRITE MUSIC
WRITE NOTES
WRITE PLAYS
WRITE VERSE
WRITING INK
WRITTEN LAW
WRONG LINES
WRONG PLACE
WRONG TOTAL
WRONG TRACK
WRONG WOMAN

X—10
X-RAY CAMERA

Y—10
YARD BY YARD
YEAR BY YEAR
YEARLY RENT
YEAR TO YEAR
YELLOW BOOK
YELLOW FLAG
YELLOW JACK
YELLOW RACE
YELLOW ROSE
YELLOW STAR
YIELD CROPS
YIELD FRUIT
YOUNG BLOOD
YOUNG CHILD

YOUNGER SON
YOUNG IDEAS
YOUNG WOMAN
YOUR CHOICE
YOUR HONOUR
YOURS TRULY
YOU'VE HAD IT
YUL BRYNNER

Z—10
ZIG-ZAG LINE
ZOO ANIMALS

A—11
AARON'S BEARD
ABANDON HOPE
ABANDON SHIP
ABIDE WITH ME
ABLE TO SPEAK
ABODE OF LOVE
ABOVE GROUND
ABOVE NORMAL
ABOVE RUBIES
ABOVE THE LAW
ABSTRACT ART
ACCENT GRAVE
ACCOUNT BOOK
ACCOUNT PAID
ACE OF HEARTS
ACE OF SPADES
ACE OF TRUMPS
ACHING HEART
ACHING TOOTH
ACT AS A BRAKE
ACT IN UNISON
ACTIVE VOICE
ACT OF HOMAGE
ACT ON ADVICE
ACT TOGETHER
ACUTE ACCENT
ACUTE ATTACK
ADD A CODICIL
ADDRESS BOOK
ADDRESS CARD
ADEQUATE SUM
AD INFINITUM
ADMIT BEARER
ADMIT DEFEAT
ADOLF HITLER
ADOPTION ACT
ADRIATIC SEA

ADVANCE BASE
ADVANCE COPY
ADVANCED AGE
ADVANCE DATE
ADVANCE FATE
AEOLIAN HARP
AFFECTED AIR
AFGHAN HOUND
AFRICA HOUSE
AFTER A WHILE
AFTER CHURCH
AFTER DINNER
AFTER SCHOOL
AFTER SUNSET
AFTER SUPPER
AFTER THE WAR
AGAINST TIME
AGE OF WISDOM
AGES AND AGES
AGONY COLUMN
AHEAD OF TIME
AID TO BEAUTY
AID TO MEMORY
AIM STRAIGHT
AIM TO PLEASE
AIR MINISTER
AIR MINISTRY
AIR TERMINAL
AIR TERMINUS
ALAMODE BEEF
ALARM SIGNAL
ALDGATE PUMP
ALFRED MARKS
ALFRED NOYES
ALISTAIR SIM
ALIVE OR DEAD
ALL COCK-EYED
ALL CREATION
ALL FALL DOWN
ALL FOOL'S DAY
ALL FOR MONEY
ALL GOES WELL
ALL HOPE GONE
ALL IN FAVOUR
ALL OF A PIECE
ALL OF A SHAKE
ALL ONE CAN DO
ALLOT SHARES
ALL-OUT DRIVE
ALLOW CREDIT
ALL QUARTERS

ALL SOULS' DAY
ALL STANDING
ALL-STAR CAST
ALL STRAIGHT
ALL THAT JAZZ
ALL THE SIGNS
ALL THE VOGUE
ALL THE WHILE
ALL THE WORLD
ALL TOGETHER
ALL TOGGED UP
ALL TO PIECES
ALL VERY FINE
ALL VERY WELL
ALL WASHED-UP
ALL WEEK LONG
ALMIGHTY GOD
ALMOND PASTE
ALMOST THERE
ALONE I DID IT
ALPINE GUIDE
ALSATIAN DOG
ALTER COURSE
AMATEUR SIDE
AMATEUR TEAM
AMERICAN BAR
AMERICAN WAR
AMERICA'S CUP
AMOS AND ANDY
AMOUR PROPRE
AN APPLE A DAY
ANCIENT CITY
ANCIENT ROME
ANDY STEWART
ANGELIC HOST
ANGELIC LOOK
ANGLING CLUB
ANIMAL TAMER
ANIMAL WORLD
ANISEED BALL
ANITA EKBERG
ANNA LUCASTA
ANNA PAVLOVA
ANNE SHELTON
ANN HATHAWAY
ANNIE BESANT
ANNIE LAURIE
ANNIE OAKLEY
ANN SHERIDAN
ANNUAL EVENT
ANNUAL LEAVE

ANNUAL TREAT
ANN VERONICA
ANOTHER TIME
ANTHONY EDEN
ANTHONY HOPE
ANTIQUE SHOP
ANTI-TANK GUN
ANVIL CHORUS
ANXIOUS TIME
APACHE DANCE
APPEAL COURT
APPEAL JUDGE
APPLE-PIE BED
APRIL SHOWER
ARCTIC OCEAN
ARE YOU READY?
ARMED ATTACK
ARMED BANDIT
ARMED COMBAT
ARMED ESCORT
ARMED FORCES
ARM OF THE LAW
ARM OF THE SEA
ARMOURED CAR
ARMOUR PLATE
ARMS AND LEGS
ARMS COUNCIL
ARMS STRETCH
ARMS TRAFFIC
ARMY BLANKET
ARMY CANTEEN
ARMY OFFICER
ARMY RESERVE
ARMY SURPLUS
AROMATIC GUM
ARRIVE EARLY
ARSENE LUPIN
ART DIRECTOR
ARTEMUS WARD
ARTFUL DODGE
ARTHUR ASKEY
ARTHUR'S SEAT
ARTS COUNCIL
ARTS THEATRE
ASCOT STAKES
AS DRY AS DUST
AS EASY AS PIE
AS GOOD AS NEW
ASK FOR A RISE
ASK FOR MERCY
ASK FOR TERMS

ASK THE PRICE
AS MUCH AGAIN
AS NICE AS PIE
ASSES' BRIDGE
ASSUME A RÔLE
ASSUMED NAME
A STAR IS BORN
ASTRAL PLANE
AS UGLY AS SIN
AS YOU LIKE IT
AT A DISCOUNT
AT A DISTANCE
AT ALL EVENTS
AT ALL POINTS
AT A LOOSE END
AT ATTENTION
AT CAMBRIDGE
AT FIRST HAND
AT FULL SPEED
AT GREAT RISK
AT HALF PRICE
A THING OR TWO
ATHOLE BROSE
AT INTERVALS
ATOMIC CLOCK
ATOMIC POWER
AT ONE'S ELBOW
AT ONE'S HEELS
AT ONE'S PERIL
AT ONE'S WORST
ATTACHÉ CASE
AT THE BOTTOM
AT THE CINEMA
AT THE CIRCUS
AT THE DOUBLE
AT THE FINISH
AT THE MOMENT
AT THE SUMMIT
AT THE TILLER
AT THE WICKET
AT THE ZENITH
AT WHAT PLACE?
AT WHICH TIME?
AUCTION ROOM
AUCTION SALE
AUTHOR'S NOTE
AUTUMN TINTS
AVERAGE HAND
AVERAGE TYPE
AVERAGE WAGE
AVERTED EYES

AVOCADO PEAR
AVOID DEFEAT
AWAY WITH YOU!
AWKWARD TIME
AYES AND NOES

B—II
BABY BUNTING
BABY CLOTHES
BACK A WINNER
BACK HEAVILY
BACK PAYMENT
BACK-ROOM BOY
BACK TO FRONT
BACKWARD BOY
BACON AND EGG
BACON SLICER
BAD BUSINESS
BADEN POWELL
BAD EYESIGHT
BAD FEELINGS
BAD FOR TRADE
BADGE OF RANK
BAD JUDGMENT
BAD LANGUAGE
BAD LIKENESS
BADLY PLACED
BADLY SHAKEN
BADLY WANTED
BAD PRACTICE
BAD TEACHING
BAG OF CRISPS
BAG OF NERVES
BAG OF SWEETS
BAG OF TRICKS
BAGS OF MONEY
BAIT THE TRAP
BAKED POTATO
BAKER'S DOZEN
BAKER STREET
BALCONY SEAT
BALD AS A COOT
BALLOT PAPER
BANANA SPLIT
BANBURY CAKE
BANG THE DOOR
BANK ACCOUNT
BANK BALANCE
BANK CHARGES
BANK DEPOSIT
BANK HOLIDAY

BANK MANAGER	BEAT THE BAND	BEST REGARDS
BANK THE FIRE	BEAT THE BANK	BETTER BY FAR
BARBED ARROW	BEAT THE BOOK	BETTER TERMS
BARBED SHAFT	BEAT THE DRUM	BETTER TIMES
BARBED WORDS	BEAU BRUMMEL	BETTER VALUE
BARBER'S POLE	BEAU SABREUR	BETTER WAGES
BARBER'S SHOP	BEAUTY QUEEN	BETTING SHOP
BARE MIDRIFF	BEAUTY SALON	BETTING SLIP
BARE MINIMUM	BEAUTY SLEEP	BETTY GRABLE
BARGAIN SALE	BEBE DANIELS	BETTY HUTTON
BARKING DOGS	BECK AND CALL	BETTY MARTIN
BARLEY SUGAR	BECOME AWARE	BETWEEN MAID
BARLEY WATER	BECOME SOLID	BEYOND A JOKE
BARNARD'S INN	BED AND BOARD	BEYOND DOUBT
BARON OF BEEF	BE DIFFERENT	BEYOND PRICE
BARON'S COURT	BED OF THE SEA	BICYCLE BELL
BARRACK ROOM	BED OF THORNS	BID DEFIANCE
BARREL ORGAN	BEDSIDE LAMP	BID FAREWELL
BARREN HEATH	BEEF EXTRACT	BIG BUSINESS
BARREN WASTE	BEER SHAMPOO	BIG TURNOVER
BARRIER REEF	BEER TANKARD	BILLIARD CUE
BAR SINISTER	BEES' WEDDING	BILL OF COSTS
BASIC RIGHTS	BEFORE LUNCH	BILLY BUNTER
BASKET CHAIR	BEG FOR MERCY	BILLY COTTON
BAT AN EYELID	BEGGING BOWL	BILLY THE KID
BATED BREATH	BEGIN TO PALL	BILLY WALKER
BATHING POOL	BEG TO DIFFER	BIRD FANCIER
BATTING SIDE	BEHAVE BADLY	BIRD WATCHER
BATTLE ABBEY	BELGIAN PORT	BISHOP'S MOVE
BATTLE ARRAY	BELGIAN TOWN	BISHOP'S PAWN
BATTLE DRESS	BELINDA FAIR	BITE ONE'S LIP
BATTLE ORDER	BELLY DANCER	BITE THE DUST
BATTLE ROYAL	BELOW GROUND	BITTER ALOES
BATTLE SCENE	BELOW STAIRS	BITTER ENEMY
BAY OF BENGAL	BELT OF TREES	BITTER GRIEF
BAY OF BISCAY	BEND FORWARD	BITTER LEMON
BAY OF NAPLES	BEND THE KNEE	BITTER SWEET
BEAM OF LIGHT	BEND THE MIND	BITTER TASTE
BEAR A GRUDGE	BENGAL LIGHT	BITTER TEARS
BEAR BAITING	BENGAL TIGER	BITTER WORDS
BEARDED LADY	BE OF SERVICE	BLACK AND TAN
BEARER BONDS	BE REALISTIC	BLACK AS COAL
BEAR ILL-WILL	BERNARD SHAW	BLACK AS SOOT
BEARING REIN	BERNESE ALPS	BLACK BEAUTY
BEARSKIN RUG	BEST CIRCLES	BLACK BEETLE
BEAR THE COST	BEST CLOTHES	BLACK BISHOP
BEAR THE NAME	BEST EDITION	BLACK BOTTOM
BEAR WITNESS	BEST OF TASTE	BLACK CASTLE
BEAST OF PREY	BEST OF TERMS	BLACK COFFEE
BEAT A TATTOO	BEST OF THREE	BLACK COTTON
BEATEN TRACK	BEST QUALITY	BLACK FRIARS

BLACK FRIDAY
BLACK FOREST
BLACK GRAPES
BLACK KNIGHT
BLACK LETTER
BLACK MARKET
BLACK MONDAY
BLACK PEPPER
BLACK PRINCE
BLACK SQUARE
BLACK TO MOVE
BLACK TO PLAY
BLACK VELVET
BLANK CHEQUE
BLANKET BATH
BLAZE A TRAIL
BLAZING FIRE
BLESS MY SOUL!
BLESS THE DAY
BLIND AS A BAT
BLIND CHANCE
BLIND CORNER
BLIND FLYING
BLOCK LETTER
BLOCK OF WOOD
BLOCK THE WAY
BLOOD ORANGE
BLOOD STREAM
BLOOD VESSEL
BLOODY TOWER
BLOSSOM TIME
BLOW BUBBLES
BLOW FOR BLOW
BLOW ME TIGHT!
BLOW ONE'S TOP
BLOW SKY-HIGH
BLOW THE FIRE
BLOW THE GAFF
BLUE-COAT BOY
BLUE-EYED BOY
BLUE FOR A BOY
BLUE HORIZON
BLUNT REMARK
BLUSH UNSEEN
BOARD SCHOOL
BOATING SONG
BOB CRATCHIT
BODY AND SOUL
BODY POLITIC
BOGNOR REGIS
BOILED BACON

BOILED SHIRT
BOILED SWEET
BOLD AS A LION
BOLD AS BRASS
BOLD ATTEMPT
BOLD OUTLINE
BOLT THE DOOR
BOLT UPRIGHT
BOMBER PILOT
BOMB SHELTER
BOND OF UNION
BONNE BOUCHE
BONNY DUNDEE
BOOKING HALL
BOOK OF VERSE
BOOK OF WORDS
BOOK VOUCHER
BORACIC ACID
BORN ACTRESS
BORN AND BRED
BORROW A BOOK
BORROW MONEY
BOSOM FRIEND
BOSS THE SHOW
BOSTON BEANS
BOTTLED BEER
BOTTLE GREEN
BOTTLE OF GIN
BOTTLE OF INK
BOTTLE OF RUM
BOTTLE PARTY
BOTTOM LAYER
BOTTOM MARKS
BOTTOM TEETH
BOUND TO LOSE
BOW AND ARROW
BOWL A YORKER
BOWL OF FRUIT
BOWL OF PUNCH
BOXING BOOTH
BOXING GLOVE
BOXING MATCH
BOX OF BRICKS
BOX OF CIGARS
BOX OF PAINTS
BOX OF TRICKS
BOY NEXT DOOR
BOYS' BRIGADE
BRACE AND BIT
BRACING WIND
BRAIN DAMAGE

BRAIN INJURY
BRAINS TRUST
BRAISED BEEF
BRAND OF CAIN
BRANDY GLASS
BRASS MONKEY
BRASSY VOICE
BRAVE EFFORT
BRAVE PERSON
BRAZEN IT OUT
BREAD AND JAM
BREAD OF LIFE
BREAD RATION
BREAD STREET
BREAD WINNER
BREAK A HABIT
BREAK BOUNDS
BREAK FOR TEA
BREAK GROUND
BREAK STONES
BREAK THE ICE
BREAK THE LAW
BREATHE FIRE
BREATHE HARD
BREATH OF AIR
BRENNER PASS
BREWER'S DRAY
BRIAN INGLIS
BRIDAL MARCH
BRIDAL PARTY
BRIDAL SUITE
BRIDAL TRAIN
BRIDGE DRIVE
BRIDGE FIEND
BRIDGE PARTY
BRIDGE TABLE
BRIDLE STRAP
BRIEF MOMENT
BRIEF SKETCH
BRIGHT CHILD
BRIGHT GREEN
BRIGHT LIGHT
BRIGHT PUPIL
BRIGHT SPARK
BRING TO BEAR
BRING TO BOOK
BRING TO HEEL
BRING TO LIFE
BRING TO MIND
BRING TO PASS
BRING TO REST

BRING TO RUIN
BRISTOL CITY
BRISTOL MILK
BRITISH ARMY
BRITISH CAMP
BRITISH FLAG
BRITISH LION
BRITISH MADE
BRITISH NAVY
BRITISH RAIL
BRITISH RULE
BRITISH WARM
BRITISH ZONE
BROAD ACCENT
BROAD COMEDY
BROAD SCOTCH
BROADSIDE ON
BROAD STREET
BROGUE SHOES
BROKE GROUND
BROKEN ANKLE
BROKEN BONES
BROKEN GLASS
BROKEN HEART
BRONZED SKIN
BRONZE MEDAL
BROTHER LOVE
BROTH OF A BOY
BROUGHT HOME
BROWN BOMBER
BROWN RIBBON
BROWN SHERRY
BRUNO WALTER
BUDDING POET
BUD FLANAGAN
BUENOS AIRES
BUFFALO BILL
BUFFER STATE
BUILD A HOUSE
BUILT ON SAND
BUILT TO LAST
BUILT-UP AREA
BULGING EYES
BULL AND BUSH
BULL AT A GATE
BULL BAITING
BULLET WOUND
BULL TERRIER
BULLY FOR YOU!
BUMPING RACE
BUNCH OF KEYS

BUNDLE OF FUN
BUNNY RABBIT
BURGLAR BILL
BURIAL AT SEA
BURIAL PLACE
BURIED ALIVE
BURIED AT SEA
BURNING BUSH
BURNT ALMOND
BURNT EFFIGY
BURN TO ASHES
BURNT SIENNA
BURST OF FIRE
BURY ONESELF
BUSHEY HEATH
BUSINESS END
BUSINESS MAN
BUS TERMINUS
BUT ME NO BUTS
BUTTER BEANS
BUYING PRICE
BUYING SPREE
BUY ON CREDIT
BUY OUTRIGHT
BY AUTHORITY
BY FAIR MEANS
BYGONE TIMES
BY LAMPLIGHT
BY MAIN FORCE
BY MESSENGER
BY MISCHANCE
BY MOONLIGHT
BY THAT MEANS
BY THIS TOKEN
BY TRADITION
BY YOUR LEAVE

C—11

CABARET STAR
CABBAGE LEAF
CABBAGE MOTH
CABBAGE ROSE
CABINET SIZE
CABIN WINDOW
CABLE STITCH
CAESAR'S WIFE
CAFÉ DE PARIS
CAFÉ SOCIETY
CAGED ANIMAL
CAIN AND ABEL
CAKE MIXTURE

CAKES AND ALE
CALCUTTA CUP
CALL FOR HELP
CALLING CARD
CALL IT QUITS
CALL ME MADAM
CALLOW YOUTH
CALL THE ROLL
CALL THE TIME
CALL THE TUNE
CALL TO A HALT
CALL TO ORDER
CALM WEATHER
CALYPSO BAND
CAME FORWARD
CAMOMILE TEA
CAMPING SITE
CANADA HOUSE
CANCEL LEAVE
CANDIED PEEL
CANDY KISSES
CANDY STRIPE
CANINE TOOTH
CANNED BEANS
CANNED FRUIT
CANNED GOODS
CANNED MUSIC
CANNING TOWN
CAN OF PETROL
CAP AND BELLS
CAPITAL CITY
CAPITAL FUND
CAPITAL GAIN
CAPITAL IDEA
CAPITAL LEVY
CAPITAL SHIP
CAPTAIN AHAB
CAPTAIN COOK
CAPTAIN HOOK
CAPTAIN KIDD
CAPTAIN WEBB
CARAVAN SITE
CARAWAY SEED
CARBON PAPER
CARDIGAN BAY
CARDINAL RED
CARDINAL SIN
CAREER WOMAN
CARGO VESSEL
CAR INDUSTRY
CARLTON CLUB

CARMEN JONES
CAROL SINGER
CARRION CROW
CARRY ACROSS
CARRY A TORCH
CARRY THE CAN
CARRY THE DAY
CARRY TOO FAR
CARRY WEIGHT
CASE HISTORY
CASE IN POINT
CASH ACCOUNT
CASH A CHEQUE
CASH BETTING
CASH CHEMIST
CASH PAYMENT
CASSIUS CLAY
CAST A GLANCE
CAST AN EYE ON
CAST A SHADOW
CASTILE SOAP
CASTING VOTE
CASTOR SUGAR
CASUAL VISIT
CAT AND MOUSE
CATCH A CHILL
CATCH ALIGHT
CATCH A PLANE
CATCH A THIEF
CATCH A TRAIN
CATCH PHRASE
CATCH THE EYE
CATHODE RAYS
CATS AND DOGS
CATS' CONCERT
CAT'S WHISKER
CATTLE RANCH
CATTLE THIEF
CATTY REMARK
CAUSE DAMAGE
CAUSTIC SODA
CAVALRY UNIT
CAVE DRAWING
CAVE DWELLER
CEASE TO LIVE
CECIL BEATON
CECIL RHODES
CELLAR STEPS
CELLO PLAYER
CELTIC CROSS
CEMENT MIXER

CENTRAL ASIA
CENTRAL HALL
CENTRAL IDEA
CENTRAL LINE
CENTRAL PARK
CENTRE COURT
CENTRE PARTY
CEREAL PLANT
CERTAIN CURE
CERTAIN HOPE
CHAFING DISH
CHAIN LETTER
CHAIN SMOKER
CHAIN STITCH
CHALK CLIFFS
CHALK GARDEN
CHANCERY INN
CHANGE A NOTE
CHANGE BUSES
CHANGE HANDS
CHANGE OF AIR
CHANGE ROUND
CHANGE SEATS
CHANGE SIDES
CHAPEL ROYAL
CHAPTER FIVE
CHAPTER FOUR
CHARGE EXTRA
CHARGE SHEET
CHARIOT RACE
CHARITY BALL
CHARLES LAMB
CHARMED LIFE
CHARM SCHOOL
CHEAP AS DIRT
CHEAP LABOUR
CHEAP REMARK
CHEAP RETURN
CHEAP THRILL
CHEAP TICKET
CHEEK BY JOWL
CHEEKY DEVIL
CHEER LEADER
CHEESE SALAD
CHEESE STRAW
CHEMIN DE FER
CHEMMY PARTY
CHERRY STONE
CHESHIRE CAT
CHESS PLAYER
CHEVAL GLASS

CHICKEN COOP
CHICKEN FARM
CHICKEN FEED
CHICKEN SOUP
CHIEF PRIEST
CHIEF STOKER
CHILD LABOUR
CHILLED BEEF
CHINA ORANGE
CHINESE FOOD
CHINESE JUNK
CHINESE MEAL
CHIT OF A GIRL
CHOICE OF TWO
CHOIR MASTER
CHOOSE A WIFE
CHOOSE SIDES
CHU CHIN CHOW
CHURCH BELLS
CHURCH CHOIR
CHURCH HOUSE
CHURCH LANDS
CHURCH MOUSE
CHURCH MUSIC
CHURCH ORGAN
CHURCH SPIRE
CHURCH TOWER
CINDER TRACK
CINEMA QUEUE
CINEMA USHER
CINEMA WORLD
CINQUE PORTS
CIRCLE ROUND
CIRCULAR SAW
CIRCUS RIDER
CITIZEN KANE
CITRUS FRUIT
CITY COMPANY
CITY COUNCIL
CITY FATHERS
CIVIC CENTRE
CIVIC RIGHTS
CIVIL ACTION
CIVIL ANSWER
CIVIL RIGHTS
CIVIL TONGUE
CIVVY STREET
CLAIM TO FAME
CLAIM TO KNOW
CLAIRE BLOOM
CLAM CHOWDER

CLAP IN IRONS	COARSE GRAIN	COME OUT BEST
CLARET GLASS	COARSE GRASS	COME OUTSIDE
CLARION CALL	COARSE VOICE	COME THIS WAY
CLASH OF ARMS	COASTAL ROAD	COME THROUGH
CLASS HATRED	COAT OF PAINT	COME TO A HALT
CLASSIC RACE	COAT THE PILL	COME TO A HEAD
CLASS SYMBOL	COAXING WAYS	COME TO AN END
CLAUDE DUVAL	COCK AND BULL	COME TO A STOP
CLEAN BOWLED	COCK ONE'S EYE	COME TO BLOWS
CLEAN BREAST	COCK SPARROW	COME TO EARTH
CLEAN COLLAR	COCKTAIL BAR	COME TO GRIEF
CLEAN FORGOT	COCOA BUTTER	COME TO GRIPS
CLEAN RECORD	COCOANUT OIL	COME TO LIGHT
CLEAR A HEDGE	COCONUT PALM	COME TO ORDER
CLEARLY SEEN	CODE MESSAGE	COME TO POWER
CLEAR OF DEBT	COD-LIVER OIL	COME TO TERMS
CLEAR PROFIT	COFFEE BEANS	COME UNSTUCK
CLEAR THE AIR	COFFEE BREAK	COME WHAT MAY
CLEAR THE WAY	COFFEE CREAM	COMIC RELIEF
CLEFT PALATE	COFFEE HOUSE	COMME IL FAUT
CLEVER DODGE	COFFEE SPOON	COMMON CAUSE
CLEVER STUFF	COFFEE STALL	COMMON CHORD
CLEVER TRICK	COFFEE TABLE	COMMON ENEMY
CLINCH A DEAL	COIN A PHRASE	COMMON FAULT
CLOSE ARREST	COLD AS DEATH	COMMON FRONT
CLOSE AT HAND	COLD CLIMATE	COMMON PLEAS
CLOSE BEHIND	COLD COMFORT	COMMON PURSE
CLOSE COMBAT	COLD DRAUGHT	COMMON SENSE
CLOSED DOORS	COLD SHIVERS	COMMON STOCK
CLOSED PURSE	COLD STORAGE	COMMON THIEF
CLOSE FINISH	COLD WEATHER	COMMON TO ALL
CLOSE FRIEND	COLD WELCOME	COMMON TOUCH
CLOSE OF PLAY	COLLECT DUST	COMMON USAGE
CLOSE SEASON	COLLEGE GIRL	COMPLETE ASS
CLOSE SECOND	COLNEY HATCH	COMPLETE SET
CLOSE SECRET	COLOMBO PLAN	COMPOST HEAP
CLOSE THE GAP	COLONIAL WAR	COMPUTER AGE
CLOSING DATE	COLOUR BLIND	CONCERT HALL
CLOSING TIME	COLOUR CHART	CONEY ISLAND
CLOTHES LINE	COLOURED MAN	CONSTANT USE
CLOTH OF GOLD	COLOUR PHOTO	CONTACT LENS
CLOT OF BLOOD	COLOUR PLATE	CONTACT MINE
CLOUD OF DUST	COME A PURLER	CONTOUR LINE
CLUB COLOURS	COME BETWEEN	CONTRACT OUT
CLUB STEWARD	COME FORWARD	CONTROL ROOM
CLUB TO DEATH	COME IN FIRST	CONVERT A TRY
CLUMSY STYLE	COME IN FRONT	COOKERY BOOK
COACHING INN	COME IN HANDY	COOK GENERAL
COAL SCUTTLE	COMELY WENCH	COOL AND CALM
COALS OF FIRE	COME OFF BEST	COOL HUNDRED
COARSE CLOTH	COME OFF WELL	COPPER BEECH

COPPER'S NARK
CORAL ISLAND
CORDON ROUGE
CORFE CASTLE
CORNERED RAT
CORNER HOUSE
CORNER TABLE
CORN IN EGYPT
CORN PLASTER
CORPS D'ÉLITE
CORRECT TIME
COSTUME BALL
COSTUME PLAY
COTTAGE LOAF
COTTON CLOTH
COTTON DRESS
COTTON FIELD
COTTON FROCK
COTTON GOODS
COTTON PLANT
COTTON SOCKS
COTTON WASTE
COUNCIL FLAT
COUNTER HAND
COUNTRY CLUB
COUNTRY CODE
COUNTRY FOLK
COUNTRY LANE
COUNTRY LIFE
COUNTRY SEAT
COUNTRY TOWN
COUNTRY WALK
COUNTY CLARE
COUNTY COURT
COUNTY MATCH
COUP DE GRÂCE
COURT DEFEAT
COURT JESTER
COVER A STORY
COVER CHARGE
COVER GROUND
COWSLIP WINE
CRACK OF DAWN
CRACK OF DOOM
CRACK PLAYER
CRACK TROOPS
CRANE DRIVER
CRASH HELMET
CRAZY NOTION
CRAZY PAVING
CREAM CHEESE

CREAMED RICE
CREATE A NEED
CREATE A RÔLE
CREATE A STIR
CREATE HAVOC
CREDIT ENTRY
CREDIT TERMS
CREDIT TITLE
CRÊPE RUBBER
CRICKET BALL
CRICKET CLUB
CRICKET TEAM
CRIMINAL LAW
CRIMSON LAKE
CRITICAL AGE
CROCK OF GOLD
CROOKED DEAL
CROOKED PATH
CROP FAILURE
CROPPED HAIR
CROQUET BALL
CROQUET CLUB
CROQUET HOOP
CROQUET LAWN
CROSSBOW MAN
CROSS STITCH
CROSS SWORDS
CROSS THE BAR
CROSS THE SEA
CROWDED HOUR
CROWDED ROOM
CROWN A TOOTH
CROWN COLONY
CROWNED HEAD
CROWN JEWELS
CROWN OFFICE
CROWN PRINCE
CRUCIAL TEST
CRUEL TYRANT
CRUMBLE AWAY
CRY FOR MERCY
CRYING SHAME
CRYPTIC CLUE
CRYSTAL BALL
CUB REPORTER
CUCKOO CLOCK
CULINARY ART
CUPID'S ARROW
CUP OF COFFEE
CUP OF POISON
CUP OF SORROW

CUPPED HANDS
CURDLED MILK
CURE OF SOULS
CURLING CLUB
CURLING IRON
CURL OF SMOKE
CURL ONE'S LIP
CURRANT CAKE
CURRANT LOAF
CURRENT DATE
CURRENT NEWS
CURRENT WEEK
CURRENT YEAR
CURRY FAVOUR
CURRY POWDER
CURSE OF CAIN
CURTAIN CALL
CUSTARD TART
CUSTOM HOUSE
CUSTOMS DUTY
CUT A LECTURE
CUT AND DRIED
CUT-AWAY COAT
CUT BOTH WAYS
CUT IN SALARY
CUT OFF SHORT
CUT OF HIS JIB
CUT ONE'S HAIR
CUT THE CARDS
CUT THE GRASS
CUT THE SCENE
CUTTING EDGE
CUTTING WIND
CUT TO PIECES
CYCLE TO WORK
CYCLING CLUB

D—11

DAILY MARKET
DAILY MIRROR
DAILY RECORD
DAILY REPORT
DAILY SKETCH
DAILY WORKER
DAIRY CATTLE
DAME FORTUNE
DAMON RUNYON
DANA ANDREWS
DANCE A TANGO
DANCE A WALTZ
DANCE FOR JOY

DANCING BEAR	DEATH COLUMN	DIE OF HUNGER
DANCING GIRL	DEATHLY HUSH	DIESEL TRAIN
DANGER MONEY	DEATHLY PALE	DIET OF WORMS
DANGER POINT	DEATH NOTICE	DIG AND DELVE
DANIEL DEFOE	DEATH RATTLE	DINNER DANCE
DANISH BACON	DEBORAH KERR	DINNER PARTY
DARK CLOTHES	DEB'S DELIGHT	DINNER WAGON
DARKEST HOUR	DECK OF CARDS	DIRECT ROUTE
DARK GLASSES	DEED OF MERCY	DIRECT STYLE
DARK LANTERN	DEEP BLUE SEA	DIRE STRAITS
DART FORWARD	DEEP CONCERN	DIRK BOGARDE
DARTING PAIN	DEEP FEELING	DISMAL JIMMY
DARTS PLAYER	DEEP IN A BOOK	DISPATCH BOX
DASHED HOPES	DEEP INSIGHT	DISPLAY CARD
DASH FORWARD	DEEP MYSTERY	DISTAFF SIDE
DASH THROUGH	DEEP REMORSE	DISTANT PAST
DATE OF BIRTH	DEEP THINKER	DISTANT VIEW
DATE OF DEATH	DEEP THOUGHT	DISUSED WELL
DAVID JACOBS	DEFENCE WORK	DIVIDE BY SIX
DAWN GODDESS	DEFERRED PAY	DIVIDE BY TEN
DAY AFTER DAY	DEFY THE WHIP	DIVIDE BY TWO
DAY AND NIGHT	DELIVERY MAN	DIVINE BEING
DAY IN, DAY OUT	DELLA ROBBIA	DIVINE GRACE
DAY LABOURER	DE-LUXE MODEL	DIVINE RIGHT
DAY OF PRAYER	DEMON BARBER	DIVINING ROD
DAYS AND DAYS	DEMON BOWLER	DIVISION ONE
DAY'S JOURNEY	DENIS NORDEN	DIVISION SUM
DAYS OF GRACE	DENMARK HILL	DIVISION TWO
DAZZLING WIT	DENNIS NOBLE	DIVORCE CASE
DEAD AGAINST	DENSE FOREST	DIVORCE LAWS
DEAD AND GONE	DENTAL CHAIR	DIVORCE SUIT
DEAD AS A DODO	DE PROFUNDIS	DIZZY HEIGHT
DEAD CERTAIN	DEPTH CHARGE	DO A GOOD TURN
DEAD EARNEST	DERBY COUNTY	DO ALL ONE CAN
DEADEN SOUND	DERBY STAKES	DO A MISCHIEF
DEAD FAILURE	DERBY WINNER	DO A WAR-DANCE
DEAD FLOWERS	DESERT SANDS	DOCTOR OF LAW
DEADLY CRIME	DESERT WASTE	DOFF ONE'S HAT
DEADLY ENEMY	DESERVE WELL	DOING NICELY
DEADLY PERIL	DEVIL OF A JOB	DO IT IN STYLE
DEADLY RIVAL	DEVIL'S ELBOW	DOLEFUL LOOK
DEAD OF NIGHT	DEVOTED WIFE	DOLEFUL TALE
DEAD OR ALIVE	DIAMOND MINE	DOLLY VARDEN
DEAD SILENCE	DIAMOND RING	DO ME A FAVOUR
DEAD TO SHAME	DICK BENTLEY	DOMESTIC PET
DEAF AND DUMB	DICK VAN DYKE	DONALD PEERS
DEAF AS A POST	DO THE TWIST	DONE TO A TURN
DEAF TO MUSIC	DIE BY INCHES	DONE TO DEATH
DEAR BELOVED	DIE FIGHTING	DOOMED TO DIE
DEAR OCTOPUS	DIE LIKE A DOG	DO ONE'S WORST
DEAR OLD PALS	DIE OF FRIGHT	DO REVERENCE

DORIC COLUMN
DORIS ARCHER
DOT AND CARRY
DO THE ROUNDS
DO THE SPLITS
DOUBLE BLANK
DOUBLE CROSS
DOUBLE DOORS
DOUBLE DUMMY
DOUBLE DUTCH
DOUBLE EAGLE
DOUBLE EIGHT
DOUBLE ENTRY
DOUBLE EVENT
DOUBLE FAULT
DOUBLE FIRST
DOUBLE MARCH
DOUBLE SEVEN
DOUBLE SHARE
DOUBLE SHIFT
DOUBLE THREE
DOUBLE TRACK
DOVE OF PEACE
DOVER CASTLE
DOVER PATROL
DOWN AT HEART
DOWN IN PRICE
DOWN PAYMENT
DOWN THE AGES
DOWN THE HILL
DOWN THE LINE
DOWN THE MINE
DOWN THE ROAD
DOWN THE SINK
DOWN THE WELL
DOWN TO EARTH
DOWN YOUR WAY
DRAMA CRITIC
DRAMA SCHOOL
DRAMATIC ART
DRAUGHT BEER
DRAW A CIRCLE
DRAW A SALARY
DRAWING ROOM
DRAW RATIONS
DRAW THE CORK
DRAW THE LINE
DRAW TO AN END
DRAW TO SCALE
DRAW UP A PLAN
DREAM DREAMS

DREAMY MUSIC
DRESS CIRCLE
DRESSED CRAB
DRESS TO KILL
DREYFUS CASE
DRINK ADDICT
DRINK A PINTA
DRINK A TOAST
DRINKING DEN
DRIPPING WET
DRIVE AROUND
DRIVE INSANE
DRIVE ONE MAD
DRIVE SLOWLY
DRIVING RAIN
DRIVING TEST
DROP A CURTSY
DROP A LETTER
DROP AN AITCH
DROP A REMARK
DROP A SITTER
DROP A STITCH
DROP IN PRICE
DROP ME A LINE
DROP OF BLOOD
DROP OF WATER
DROPPED GOAL
DROP THE MASK
DROP TOO MUCH
DROWNING MAN
DRUG TRAFFIC
DRUNKEN ORGY
DRY AS A STICK
DRY CLEANERS
DRY CLEANING
DRY ONE'S EYES
DUAL CONTROL
DUAL PURPOSE
DUCHESSE SET
DUCK-EGG BLUE
DULCET TONES
DULL READING
DULL SCHOLAR
DULL WEATHER
DUMB CHARADE
DUMB DESPAIR
DUMB FRIENDS
DURANCE VILE
DUSTY MILLER
DUTCH CHEESE
DUTCH SCHOOL

DUTCH TULIPS
DUTY OFFICER
DWINDLE AWAY
DYE ONE'S HAIR
DYING BREATH
DYING EMBERS
DYING TO KNOW
DYLAN THOMAS

E—11
EAGER BEAVER
EAR FOR MUSIC
EARL MARSHAL
EARL OF ARRAN
EARLY AUTUMN
EARLY CHURCH
EARLY GOTHIC
EARLY IN LIFE
EARLY RISING
EARLY SPRING
EARLY SUMMER
EARLY TO RISE
EARN A LIVING
EARTH'S CRUST
EARTH TREMOR
EASE THE PAIN
EASILY MOVED
EAST AND WEST
EAST GERMANY
EAST LOTHIAN
EASY PROBLEM
EASY TO GRASP
EASY VICTORY
EAT AND DRINK
EAT AND SLEEP
EATING HOUSE
EAT LIKE A PIG
EAT ONE'S FILL
ECONOMIC AID
ECONOMY SIZE
EDDIE FISHER
EDGE ONE'S WAY
EDGWARE ROAD
EDIBLE FUNGI
EDITH CAVELL
EDMUND BURKE
EDUCATED MAN
EDWARD HEATH
EDWARD MY SON
EGG AND BACON
EGG AND CHIPS

EGG SANDWICH	EMPIRE STYLE	ETERNAL LIFE
EIFFEL TOWER	EMPIRE TRADE	ETERNAL REST
EIGHT AND ONE	EMPTY BOTTLE	ETHEL MERMAN
EIGHT AND SIX	EMPTY LARDER	ETON COLLEGE
EIGHT AND TEN	EMPTY POCKET	EVADE THE LAW
EIGHT AND TWO	EMPTY STREET	EVELYN WAUGH
EIGHTH FLOOR	EMPTY THE BAG	EVENING MEAL
EIGHTH GREEN	EMPTY THREAT	EVENING NEWS
EIGHTH MONTH	EMPTY WALLET	EVENING STAR
EIGHTH OF MAY	ENA SHARPLES	EVER AND A DAY
EIGHTH PLACE	EN CASSEROLE	EVER AND ANON
EIGHTH ROUND	ENDLESS BAND	EVER AND EVER
EIGHT MONTHS	ENDLESS BELT	EVERY EXCUSE
EIGHT NINTHS	ENDLESS TIME	EVERY MINUTE
EIGHT O'CLOCK	END OF THE DAY	EVERY VIRTUE
EIGHT OR NINE	END OF THE WAR	EVIL CONDUCT
EIGHT OUNCES	END ONE'S DAYS	EVIL THOUGHT
EIGHT POINTS	END ONE'S LIFE	EXACT AMOUNT
EIGHT POUNDS	ENEMY ACTION	EXALTED RANK
EIGHT ROUNDS	ENEMY PATROL	EXEUNT OMNES
EIGHTY MILES	ENEMY TROOPS	EXHAUST PIPE
EIGHTY TIMES	ENEMY VESSEL	EXPLAIN AWAY
EIGHTY YEARS	ENGAGED TONE	EXPORT DRIVE
EILEEN JOYCE	ENGINE HOUSE	EXPORT ORDER
ELASTIC BAND	ENGINE POWER	EXPORT TRADE
ELBOW GREASE	ENGLISH HORN	EXPRESS LIFT
ELDERS FIRST	ENGLISH POET	EXPRESS POST
ELDER SISTER	ENGLISH PORT	EXTRA CHARGE
ELDEST CHILD	ENGLISH ROSE	EXTRA STRONG
ELECTION DAY	ENLARGE UPON	EXTREME CASE
ELECTRIC EEL	ENLISTED MAN	EXTREME EDGE
ELECTRIC EYE	ENOCH POWELL	EXTREME PAIN
ELECTRIC FAN	ENTER A PHASE	EYE FOR AN EYE
ELECTRIC RAY	ENTER A STAGE	EYES AND EARS
ELECTRIC VAN	ENTRANCE FEE	
ELEPHANT BOY	EQUAL CHANCE	**F—11**
ELEPHANT GUN	EQUAL HEIGHT	FACE MASSAGE
ELEVEN A SIDE	EQUAL RIGHTS	FACE REALITY
ELEVEN DOZEN	EQUAL SHARES	FACE THE ODDS
ELEVEN GROSS	EQUAL WEIGHT	FACE UPWARDS
ELEVEN HOURS	ERECT FIGURE	FACTORY ACTS
ELEVEN MILES	ERIC PORTMAN	FACTORY BAND
ELEVEN PARTS	ERMINE STOLE	FACTORY HAND
ELEVEN SCORE	ERNEST BEVIN	FACTS OF LIFE
ELEVENTH DAY	ESCAPE DEATH	FADED BEAUTY
ELEVENTH ROW	ESCAPE HATCH	FADING HOPES
ELEVEN TIMES	ESCAPE ROUTE	FADING LIGHT
ELEVEN WEEKS	ESCAPING GAS	FAIL THE TEST
ELLIS ISLAND	ESTATE AGENT	FAIL TO AGREE
EMERALD ISLE	ETERNAL CITY	FAIL TO REPLY
EMERALD RING	ETERNAL HOME	FAIL TO SCORE

FAINT EFFORT	FARM MANAGER	FIELD OF PLAY
FAINTING FIT	FARM PRODUCE	FIELD OF VIEW
FAINT PRAISE	FASHION SHOW	FIELD SPORTS
FAIR COMMENT	FAST BOWLING	FIERCE GLARE
FAIR FORTUNE	FAST COLOURS	FIERY DRAGON
FAIR HEARING	FAST FRIENDS	FIERY ORDEAL
FAIRLY CLOSE	FATAL ATTACK	FIERY SPEECH
FAIR WARNING	FATAL INJURY	FIERY SPIRIT
FAIR WEATHER	FATA MORGANA	FIERY TEMPER
FAIRY CIRCLE	FAT AS BUTTER	FIFTEEN LOVE
FAIRY LIGHTS	FATHER BROWN	FIFTH AVENUE
FAITH HEALER	FATHER IMAGE	FIFTH COLUMN
FALL ASUNDER	FATHERLY EYE	FIFTH LETTER
FALLEN ANGEL	FATIGUE DUTY	FIFTH OF JULY
FALL IN DROPS	FATTY TISSUE	FIFTH OF JUNE
FALLING STAR	FEARFUL BORE	FIFTH STOREY
FALL IN PLACE	FEARFUL ODDS	FIFTH VOLUME
FALL IN PRICE	FEAR OF DEATH	FIGHT FOR AIR
FALL IN RUINS	FEAR TO TREAD	FIGHTING FIT
FALL IN VALUE	FEATURE FILM	FIGHTING MAD
FALL THROUGH	FEEBLE BRAIN	FIGHTING MAN
FALL TO EARTH	FEEBLE GRASP	FIGURE EIGHT
FALSE BOTTOM	FEEDING TIME	FIGURE IT OUT
FALSE CHARGE	FEEL CERTAIN	FIGURE OF FUN
FALSE COLOUR	FEEL NO SHAME	FIJI ISLANDS
FALSE FRIEND	FEEL NOTHING	FILING CLERK
FALSE REPORT	FEEL ONE'S WAY	FILL AN ORDER
FALSE RUMOUR	FEEL PECKISH	FILLET STEAK
FALSE VALUES	FEEL REMORSE	FILL THE BILL
FALSE VANITY	FEEL STRANGE	FILL THE TILL
FAMILY ALBUM	FEEL THE COLD	FILM ACTRESS
FAMILY BIBLE	FEEL THE HEAT	FILM COMPANY
FAMILY CARES	FEEL THE URGE	FILTHY LUCRE
FAMILY CREST	FEEL THE WIND	FINAL ANSWER
FAMILY HOTEL	FELIX AYLMER	FINAL CHOICE
FAMILY MOTTO	FELIX THE CAT	FINAL CLAUSE
FAMILY PARTY	FELL THROUGH	FINAL DEFEAT
FAMILY PRIDE	FEMALE SCREW	FINAL DEMAND
FAMILY TREAT	FEMALE VOICE	FINAL NOTICE
FAMILY VAULT	FEMME FATALE	FINAL REPORT
FAMINE PRICE	FEN DISTRICT	FINAL RESULT
FAMOUS WOMEN	FERTILE LAND	FINAL SPEECH
FAN THE FLAME	FERTILE MIND	FINAL STROKE
FAR-AWAY LOOK	FERTILE SOIL	FINANCE BILL
FAR DISTANCE	FERVENT HOPE	FIND A REFUGE
FARES PLEASE	FESTIVE MOOD	FIND A REMEDY
FAR FROM HERE	FEVERED BROW	FIND A WAY OUT
FAR FROM HOME	FIDDLE ABOUT	FIND FREEDOM
FARMER GILES	FIDEL CASTRO	FIND ONESELF
FARMER'S WIFE	FIELD EVENTS	FIND ONE'S WAY
FARMING TYPE	FIELD OF CORN	FIND SHELTER

FIND THE LADY	FIRST SERVED	FIXED CHARGE
FIND THE TIME	FIRST SINGLE	FIXED INCOME
FINE FLAVOUR	FIRST SKETCH	FIXED SALARY
FINE RAIMENT	FIRST STOREY	FIX THE PRICE
FINE SOLDIER	FIRST STRING	FIX THE TERMS
FINE TEXTURE	FIRST STROKE	FIXTURE LIST
FINE WEATHER	FIRST TO COME	FLAG CAPTAIN
FINE WRITING	FIRST TO LAND	FLAG OFFICER
FINGAL'S CAVE	FIRST TO LAST	FLAG OF TRUCE
FINISH EARLY	FIRST VIOLIN	FLAKY PASTRY
FINISH FIRST	FIRST VOLUME	FLAME COLOUR
FINNISH BATH	FIRST WICKET	FLAMING JUNE
FIRE AND FURY	FISHER OF MEN	FLANK ATTACK
FIRE A SALUTE	FISH FINGERS	FLASH A SMILE
FIRE A VOLLEY	FISHING BIRD	FLASK OF WINE
FIRE BRIGADE	FISHING BOAT	FLAT FOR SALE
FIRE CURTAIN	FISHING LINE	FLAT HUNTING
FIRE SERVICE	FIT FOR A KING	FLAT REFUSAL
FIRE STATION	FIT OF ENERGY	FLAT SURFACE
FIRING PARTY	FIT OF NERVES	FLEET AIR-ARM
FIRING SQUAD	FIT OF TEMPER	FLEET OF CABS
FIRM AS A ROCK	FIT OF TERROR	FLEET OF CARS
FIRM BACKING	FITTING ROOM	FLEET OF FOOT
FIRM CONTROL	FITTING SHOP	FLEET PRISON
FIRM FRIENDS	FITTING TIME	FLEET STREET
FIRM PROMISE	FIT TO BE SEEN	FLESH COLOUR
FIRM RESOLVE	FIVE AND FIVE	FLESH TIGHTS
FIRST CHARGE	FIVE AND FOUR	FLIMSY PAPER
FIRST CHOICE	FIVE AND NINE	FLOATING RIB
FIRST COURSE	FIVE AT A TIME	FLOOD DAMAGE
FIRST COUSIN	FIVE-BAR GATE	FLOOR POLISH
FIRST DEGREE	FIVE COURSES	FLORAL DANCE
FIRST ELEVEN	FIVE-DAY WEEK	FLORA ROBSON
FIRST FIDDLE	FIVE DOLLARS	FLORID STYLE
FIRST FINGER	FIVE EIGHTHS	FLOWING BOWL
FIRST FLIGHT	FIVE FATHOMS	FLOWING HAND
FIRST FRUITS	FIVE FINGERS	FLOWING TIDE
FIRST GLANCE	FIVE GALLONS	FLOW OF WORDS
FIRST IN LINE	FIVE GUINEAS	FLOW THROUGH
FIRST LEADER	FIVE HUNDRED	FLOW TOWARDS
FIRST LEAGUE	FIVE MINUTES	FLUID INTAKE
FIRST LESSON	FIVE OCTAVES	FLUSH OF DAWN
FIRST LETTER	FIVE OF CLUBS	FLUSH OF HOPE
FIRST MAN OUT	FIVE PER CENT	FLUTTER DOWN
FIRST OF JULY	FIVE SQUARED	FLY AWAY PAUL
FIRST OF JUNE	FIVE STROKES	FLYING CORPS
FIRST PERSON	FIVE WICKETS	FLYING FIELD
FIRST REMOVE	FIX BAYONETS	FLYING SPEED
FIRST RUBBER	FIXED AMOUNT	FLYING SQUAD
FIRST SEASON	FIXED ASSETS	FLYING START
FIRST SERIES	FIXED BELIEF	FLYING VISIT

FOLDED HANDS	FORWARD LINE	FREE LIBRARY
FOLK DANCING	FORWARD MOVE	FREE ON BOARD
FOLLOW AFTER	FORWARD PLAY	FREE ONESELF
FOLLOW A PLAN	FOSTER CHILD	FREE PARKING
FOND EMBRACE	FOUL JOURNEY	FREE PASSAGE
FONDEST LOVE	FOUL THE LINE	FREE SERVICE
FOND OF A DRAM	FOUL WEATHER	FREE SPENDER
FOND REGARDS	FOUND A PARTY	FREE THINKER
FOOD COUNTER	FOUNDERS' DAY	FREE THOUGHT
FOOD SUBSIDY	FOUND GUILTY	FREE TO SPEAK
FOOLISH IDEA	FOUNTAIN PEN	FREE TRIBUTE
FOOLISH TALK	FOUR AND FIVE	FRENCH BEANS
FOOL'S ERRAND	FOUR AND FOUR	FRENCH BREAD
FOOLS RUSH IN	FOUR AND NINE	FRENCH CHALK
FOOTBALL FAN	FOUR AT A TIME	FRENCH COAST
FOOT THE BILL	FOUR CORNERS	FRENCH FARCE
FOR ALL TO SEE	FOUR COURSES	FRENCH FRANC
FOR A PURPOSE	FOUR-DAY WEEK	FRENCH FRIED
FORCE A WAY IN	FOUR DEGREES	FRENCH LEAVE
FORCED ENTRY	FOUR DOLLARS	FRENCH MONEY
FORCED LAUGH	FOUR FATHOMS	FRENCH NOVEL
FORCED MARCH	FOUR FIGURES	FRENCH SALON
FORCED SMILE	FOUR GALLONS	FRESH BREEZE
FORCE OF ARMS	FOUR GUINEAS	FRESH BUTTER
FOR DEAR LIFE	FOUR HUNDRED	FRESH FIELDS
FOREIGN BODY	FOUR JUST MEN	FRESH GROUND
FOREIGN COIN	FOUR MINUTES	FRESH SALMON
FOREIGN FILM	FOUR OCTAVES	FRESH TROOPS
FOREIGN LAND	FOUR OF CLUBS	FRET AND FUME
FOREIGN NAME	FOUR PER CENT	FRIDAY NIGHT
FOREIGN NEWS	FOUR SEASONS	FRIED ONIONS
FOREIGN RULE	FOUR SQUARED	FRIENDLY ACT
FOREIGN SOIL	FOUR STROKES	FRIENDLY TIP
FOREIGN TOUR	FOURTH FLOOR	FRIEND OF MAN
FOR INSTANCE	FOURTH GREEN	FRIEND OR FOE
FORLORN HOPE	FOURTH OF MAY	FRIGHTEN OFF
FORMAL DRESS	FOURTH PLACE	FRITTER AWAY
FORMAL OFFER	FOURTH ROUND	FROM SCRATCH
FORMAL VISIT	FOUR WICKETS	FROM THE EAST
FORM AN IMAGE	FOX AND GEESE	FROM THE WEST
FORMER PUPIL	FRAME OF MIND	FROM THE WOOD
FORMER TIMES	FRANK AVOWAL	FROM WITHOUT
FOR PLEASURE	FRANK IFIELD	FRONT GARDEN
FOR SOME TIME	FRANTIC PACE	FRONT LIGHTS
FORSYTE SAGA	FRANTIC RUSH	FRONT WINDOW
FORTH BRIDGE	FRED ASTAIRE	FROSTED LENS
FOR THE NONCE	FREE AND EASY	FROSTY SMILE
FOR THE WORSE	FREE AS A BIRD	FROZEN NORTH
FORT WILLIAM	FREE CITIZEN	FROZEN PIPES
FORTY NIGHTS	FREE COUNTRY	FROZEN SOLID
FORTY THIRTY	FREE ECONOMY	FROZEN STIFF

FROZEN WATER	GAMBLING DEN	GET AN ENCORE
FRUIT MARKET	GAME CHICKEN	GET A RECEIPT
FRUITY VOICE	GAME LICENCE	GET CRACKING
FULL ACCOUNT	GAME OF BOWLS	GET DOWN TO IT
FULL ADDRESS	GAME OF CARDS	GET EVEN WITH
FULL APOLOGY	GAME OF CHESS	GET IN THE WAY
FULL AS AN EGG	GAME OF SKILL	GET INTO A ROW
FULL BROTHER	GAME OF WHIST	GET INTO A RUT
FULL CONSENT	GAME RESERVE	GET INTO DEBT
FULL DETAILS	GAMES MASTER	GET ONE'S GOAT
FULL ENQUIRY	GAMING HOUSE	GET ONE'S WISH
FULL FLAVOUR	GAMING TABLE	GET ON WITH IT
FULL GENERAL	GAMMON STEAK	GET OUT OF BED
FULL MEASURE	GANG ROBBERY	GET SUNBURNT
FULL OF BEANS	GANG WARFARE	GET THE FACTS
FULL OF FIGHT	GARDEN CHAIR	GET THE KNACK
FULL OF GRACE	GARDEN FENCE	GET THE POINT
FULL OF HOLES	GARDEN PARTY	GET THE TASTE
FULL OF IDEAS	GARDEN TOOLS	GETTING WARM
FULL OF MIRTH	GARRICK CLUB	GETTING WELL
FULL OF PRIDE	GATHER ROSES	GET TOGETHER
FULL REGALIA	GATHER ROUND	GET TO THE TOP
FULL SERVICE	GATHER SPEED	GET UNDER WAY
FULL SUPPORT	GAY BACHELOR	GET WELL SOON
FULL-TIME JOB	GAY DECEIVER	GET WISE TO IT
FULLY BOOKED	GAY LOTHARIO	GHASTLY MESS
FULLY RIGGED	GAY NINETIES	GHASTLY PALE
FUN AND GAMES	GENERAL IDEA	GHOST WRITER
FUNERAL HYMN	GENERAL LEVY	GIANT KILLER
FUNERAL PACE	GENERAL POST	GIANT OF A MAN
FUNERAL PILE	GENERAL RATE	GIFT OF MONEY
FUNERAL PYRE	GENERAL VIEW	GIFT VOUCHER
FUNERAL SONG	GENERIC NAME	GILDED YOUTH
FUNNY AFFAIR	GENEROUS ACT	GILD THE LILY
FUNNY PERSON	GENEVA CROSS	GILD THE PILL
FURIOUS PACE	GENTLE BIRTH	GIN AND LEMON
FUTURE HOPES	GENTLE SLOPE	GIN AND TONIC
FUTURE PLANS	GENTLE TOUCH	GINGER GROUP
FUTURE STATE	GENTLE VOICE	GIRLS' SCHOOL
FUTURE TENSE	GENUINE CASE	GIRL STUDENT
	GEORGE BROWN	GIVE AND TAKE
G—11	GEORGE CROSS	GIVE AN ORDER
GAIN CONTROL	GEORGE ELIOT	GIVE A REASON
GAIN IN VALUE	GEORGE MEDAL	GIVE A RULING
GAIN THE LEAD	GEORGE ROBEY	GIVE IT A MISS
GALA EVENING	GERMAN MONEY	GIVE IT A NAME
GALE WARNING	GERM CARRIER	GIVE IT A REST
GALLERY SEAT	GERM WARFARE	GIVE LESSONS
GALLEY PROOF	GET A BAD NAME	GIVEN PERIOD
GALLEY SLAVE	GET A DIVORCE	GIVEN THE TIP
GALLON OF OIL	GET A MENTION	GIVE OFFENCE

GIVE QUARTER	GOLDEN EAGLE	GOOD OFFICES
GIVE SUPPORT	GOLDEN GATES	GOOD OLD DAYS
GIVE THE SACK	GOLDEN GOOSE	GOOD OLD TIME
GIVE THE WORD	GOLDEN SANDS	GOOD OPENING
GIVE TROUBLE	GOLDEN SYRUP	GOOD OPINION
GIVE WARNING	GOLDEN TOUCH	GOOD QUALITY
GLAD TIDINGS	GOLD FILLING	GOOD READING
GLAMOUR GIRL	GOLD RESERVE	GOOD SCHOLAR
GLANCE ASIDE	GO LIKE A BOMB	GOOD SEND OFF
GLANCE TO LEG	GONE FOR EVER	GOOD SERVANT
GLASS HOUSES	GONE FOR GOOD	GOOD SERVICE
GLASS OF BEER	GONE TO EARTH	GOOD SOCIETY
GLASS OF MILK	GONE TO GLORY	GOOD SOLDIER
GLASS OF PORT	GONE TO LUNCH	GOOD SPENDER
GLASS OF WINE	GONE TO WASTE	GOOD SPIRITS
GLASS VESSEL	GOOD ACCOUNT	GOOD SWIMMER
GLASSY STARE	GOOD ACTRESS	GOOD TEMPLAR
GLEAM OF HOPE	GOOD ADDRESS	GOOD THEATRE
GLEEFUL MOOD	GOOD AND EVIL	GOOD TIDINGS
GLEEFUL NEWS	GOOD AS A PLAY	GOOD WEATHER
GLEE SINGERS	GOOD AT HEART	GOOD WORKMAN
GLIB SPEAKER	GOOD BARGAIN	GOOD WRITE-UP
GLIDER PILOT	GOOD BEARING	GO ON A PICNIC
GLYNIS JOHNS	GOOD BEATING	GO ONE BETTER
GLORIOUS DAY	GOOD CITIZEN	GO ON FOR EVER
GLORIOUS FUN	GOOD COMPANY	GO ON HOLIDAY
GLORIOUS ROW	GOOD CONDUCT	GO ON THE DOLE
GLOSSY PAINT	GOOD COUNSEL	GO OUT TO WORK
GNAWING PAIN	GOOD DEFENCE	GO OVER THERE
GO-AHEAD SIGN	GOOD DICTION	GORDIAN KNOT
GO ALL THE WAY	GOOD EVENING	GORDON RIOTS
GO BACKWARDS	GOOD EXAMPLE	GORGON'S HEAD
GO BY DEFAULT	GOOD FEEDING	GOSPEL TRUTH
GO BY THE BOOK	GOOD FEELING	GO THE ROUNDS
GODFREY WINN	GOOD FICTION	GOTHIC STYLE
GOD OF THE SEA	GOOD FORTUNE	GO THROUGH IT
GOG AND MAGOG	GOOD FRIENDS	GO TO BED LATE
GO GREAT GUNS	GOOD GRAMMAR	GO TO HALIFAX
GOING STEADY	GOOD GROUNDS	GO TO JERICHO
GOING STRONG	GOOD HARMONY	GO TO PARTIES
GO IN PURSUIT	GOOD HARVEST	GO TO THE DOGS
GO INTO EXILE	GOOD HEARING	GO TO THE FAIR
GO INTO ORBIT	GOOD HEAVENS	GO TO THE MOON
GOLD BULLION	GOOD HUNTING	GO TO THE WALL
GOLD COINAGE	GOOD HUSBAND	GO TO THE WARS
GOLD DEPOSIT	GOOD INNINGS	GOT UP TO KILL
GOLDEN APPLE	GOOD IN PARTS	GO UP IN SMOKE
GOLDEN ARROW	GOOD MANAGER	GRAIN OF GOLD
GOLDEN BOUGH	GOOD MANNERS	GRAIN OF SALT
GOLDEN BROWN	GOOD MEASURE	GRAIN OF SAND
GOLDEN DREAM	GOOD MORNING	GRAND CANYON

GRAND CIRCLE
GRAND FELLOW
GRAND FINALE
GRAND MANNER
GRAND MASTER
GRAND OLD MAN
GRAND REVIEW
GRAND VIZIER
GRANITE CITY
GRANT ACCESS
GRANT ASYLUM
GRANT A TRUCE
GRAPHIC ARTS
GRAVE ACCENT
GRAVE AFFAIR
GRAVE CHARGE
GRAVE CRISIS
GRAVE DOUBTS
GRAVE MATTER
GRAVEN IMAGE
GRAVE SPEECH
GREASE PAINT
GREAT AMOUNT
GREAT BEAUTY
GREAT BURDEN
GREAT CAESAR
GREAT CHANCE
GREAT CHANGE
GREAT CIRCLE
GREAT DAMAGE
GREAT DANCER
GREAT DANGER
GREAT DARING
GREAT DETAIL
GREAT DIVIDE
GREAT DOINGS
GREAT EFFORT
GREATER GOOD
GREATER PART
GREAT FAVOUR
GREAT FRIEND
GREAT HEALER
GREAT HEIGHT
GREAT HONOUR
GREAT IMPORT
GREAT NEPHEW
GREAT NUMBER
GREAT PLAGUE
GREAT PLAYER
GREAT REGRET
GREAT RELIEF

GREAT SNAKES
GREAT SORROW
GREAT STRAIN
GREAT STRESS
GREAT TALKER
GREAT THINGS
GREAT UNPAID
GREAT WEALTH
GREAT WEIGHT
GRECIAN BEND
GRECIAN KNOT
GRECIAN NOSE
GREEK CHURCH
GREEK COMEDY
GREEK LEGEND
GREEK STATUE
GREEN BOTTLE
GREEN CHEESE
GREEN FIELDS
GREEN GABLES
GREEN GINGER
GREEN PEPPER
GREEN RIBBON
GREER GARSON
GREGORY PECK
GRESHAM'S LAW
GRETNA GREEN
GRILLED CHOP
GRILLED FISH
GRILLED SOLE
GRIM COURAGE
GRIM OUTLOOK
GRIM PASTIME
GRIND TO BITS
GRIP OF STEEL
GRIZZLY BEAR
GROCER'S SHOP
GROSS AMOUNT
GROSS INCOME
GROSS PROFIT
GROSS RETURN
GROSS WEIGHT
GROUND FLOOR
GROUND FROST
GROUND GLASS
GROUND LEVEL
GROUND SPEED
GROUND STAFF
GROUND SWELL
GROUND TO AIR
GROUP OF FIVE

GROUP OF FOUR
GROUP OF NINE
GROUSE MOORS
GROWING GIRL
GROW SHORTER
GROW SMALLER
GROW UPWARDS
GROW YOUNGER
GUAVA CHEESE
GUERILLA WAR
GUEST ARTIST
GUIDING HAND
GUIDING STAR
GUILTY PARTY
GUILTY WOMAN
GULF OF GENOA
GUMMED LABEL
GUSTAV HOLST
GUTTER PRESS

H—11

HACKNEY WICK
HAGGARD LOOK
HAIRPIN BEND
HALCYON DAYS
HALF A BOTTLE
HALF A DOLLAR
HALF A GALLON
HALF A GUINEA
HALF A LEAGUE
HALF A LENGTH
HALF A MINUTE
HALF A MOMENT
HALF AND HALF
HALF AN OUNCE
HALF A SECOND
HALF BROTHER
HALF HOLIDAY
HALF THE TIME
HALTING GAIT
HAMMER IT OUT
HAMMER THROW
HAM OMELETTE
HAMPTON WICK
HAM SANDWICH
HAND AND FOOT
HAND GRENADE
HAND IN GLOVE
HAND OF CARDS
HAND OF DEATH
HANDSOME BOY

HANDSOME MAN	HAVE A HAIR-DO	HEAVE A BRICK
HANDSOME SUM	HAVE A LIKING	HEAVY AS LEAD
HANDSOME TIP	HAVE AND HOLD	HEAVY BOMBER
HANDS ON HIPS	HAVE AN EYE ON	HEAVY BURDEN
HAND TO MOUTH	HAVE AN EYE TO	HEAVY EATING
HANG-DOG LOOK	HAVE ANOTHER	HEAVY FATHER
HANGING BILL	HAVE A PICNIC	HEAVY HUMOUR
HANG ONESELF	HAVE A POLICY	HEAVY OBJECT
HANG THE HEAD	HAVE A SECRET	HEAVY SHOWER
HANG UP TO DRY	HAVE A SHOWER	HEAVY SMOKER
HANKER AFTER	HAVE A SNOOZE	HEAVY WEIGHT
HAPPY AND GAY	HAVE A SQUINT	HECTIC FLUSH
HAPPY CHANCE	HAVE A STROKE	HEDDA GABLER
HAPPY COUPLE	HAVE A THEORY	HELD CAPTIVE
HAPPY DREAMS	HAVE A THIRST	HELD HOSTAGE
HAPPY ENDING	HAVE COMPANY	HELD IN CHECK
HAPPY FAMILY	HAVE COURAGE	HELD IN TRUST
HAPPY MEDIUM	HAVE IN STORE	HELEN JACOBS
HAPPY VALLEY	HAVE NO DOUBT	HELEN OF TROY
HARBOUR A SPY	HAVEN OF REST	HELL ON EARTH
HARBOUR DUES	HAVE NO MERCY	HELPING HAND
HARD AND FAST	HAVE NO VOICE	HENRIK IBSEN
HARD AS NAILS	HAVE ONE'S DAY	HENRY COOPER
HARD AS STEEL	HAVE ONE'S SAY	HENRY COTTON
HARD BARGAIN	HAVE ONE'S WAY	HENRY ESMOND
HARD CONTEST	HAVE REGRETS	HENRY IRVING
HARD DRINKER	HAVE THE URGE	HERALDIC ART
HARD DRIVING	HAVE THE VOTE	HERD OF GOATS
HARD MEASURE	HAVE TROUBLE	HER HIGHNESS
HARD PRESSED	HAYLEY MILLS	HER LADYSHIP
HARD PUT TO IT	HEAD AND TAIL	HEROIC VERSE
HARD SURFACE	HEAD TEACHER	HERO WORSHIP
HARD TO CATCH	HEAD THE LIST	HERRING GULL
HARD TO GRASP	HEALING GIFT	HERRING POND
HARDY ANNUAL	HEAL THE SICK	HIDDEN FIRES
HARICOT BEAN	HEALTHY FEAR	HIDDEN MERIT
HAROLD LLOYD	HEALTHY MIND	HIDDEN PANEL
HARRIS TWEED	HEAPED PLATE	HIDE AND SEEK
HARRY LAUDER	HEAPS OF TIME	HIDING PLACE
HARRY TRUMAN	HEAR NOTHING	HIGH ACCOUNT
HARVEST HOME	HEART ATTACK	HIGH CALLING
HARVEST MOON	HEAR THE CALL	HIGH CEILING
HARVEST TIME	HEART OF GOLD	HIGH CIRCLES
HASTY GLANCE	HEART'S BLOOD	HIGH COMMAND
HASTY TEMPER	HEARTS OF OAK	HIGH CONTENT
HATCHET FACE	HEARTY CHEER	HIGH COURAGE
HATEFUL TASK	HEARTY EATER	HIGH DENSITY
HAUNT OF VICE	HEARTY LAUGH	HIGH DUDGEON
HAVANA CIGAR	HEARTY SMACK	HIGHER CLASS
HAVE A CHOICE	HEAT BARRIER	HIGHER FARES
HAVE A FRIGHT	HEATED WORDS	HIGHER LEVEL

HIGHER POWER
HIGHER WAGES
HIGH FEATHER
HIGH FINANCE
HIGH HOLBORN
HIGH MOTIVES
HIGH OLD TIME
HIGH OPINION
HIGH QUALITY
HIGH RESOLVE
HIGH SHERIFF
HIGH SOCIETY
HIGH SPIRITS
HIGH STATION
HIGH TENSION
HIGH TRAGEDY
HIGH TREASON
HIGH VOLTAGE
HIGHWAY CODE
HIGH-WIRE ACT
HIGH WYCOMBE
HILL AND DALE
HILL COUNTRY
HILTON HOTEL
HINDLE WAKES
HIP AND THIGH
HIPS AND HAWS
HIS EMINENCE
HIS HIGHNESS
HIS LORDSHIP
HISTORY BOOK
HITHER GREEN
HITLER YOUTH
HIT THE TRAIL
H.M.S. PINAFORE
HOARD WEALTH
HOARSE COUGH
HOARSE LAUGH
HOARSE VOICE
HOBBLE SKIRT
HOCKEY MATCH
HOCKEY STICK
HOLD CLASSES
HOLD IN CHECK
HOLD IN LEASH
HOLD IN TRUST
HOLD ONE'S JAW
HOLD ONE'S OWN
HOLD ON TIGHT
HOLD OUT HOPE
HOLD THE BABY

HOLD THE FORT
HOLD THE LEAD
HOLD THE LINE
HOLD THE ROAD
HOLD TO SCORN
HOLIDAY CAMP
HOLIDAY HOME
HOLIDAY MOOD
HOLIDAY SNAP
HOLIDAY TASK
HOLIDAY TIME
HOLIDAY WEAR
HOLLAND PARK
HOLLAND'S GIN
HOLLOW LAUGH
HOLLOW SOUND
HOLLOW TOOTH
HOLLOW TRUCE
HOLLOW TRUTH
HOLLOW VOICE
HOLY TRINITY
HOLY UNCTION
HOLY WEDLOCK
HOME AFFAIRS
HOME AND AWAY
HOME CIRCUIT
HOME COOKING
HOME COUNTRY
HOME FOR GOOD
HOME-MADE JAM
HOME ON LEAVE
HOME SERVICE
HOME STRETCH
HOMO SAPIENS
HONEST DOUBT
HONEST INJUN
HONEST MONEY
HONEST PENNY
HONEST TRUTH
HONEST WOMAN
HONITON LACE
HONOUR A BILL
HONOUR BOUND
HONOURED SIR
HONOURS EASY
HONOURS EVEN
HONOURS LIST
HOPE AND PRAY
HOPE DIAMOND
HOPEFUL SIGN
HORNED VIPER

HORNET'S NEST
HORROR COMIC
HORS D'OEUVRE
HORSE DEALER
HORSE DOCTOR
HORSE GUARDS
HORSE MARINE
HORSE PISTOL
HORSE RACING
HORSE'S MOUTH
HOSPITAL BED
HOSTILE ARMY
HOSTILE VOTE
HOT AS PEPPER
HOT CHESTNUT
HOT-CROSS BUN
HOT-DOG STAND
HOTEL ANNEXE
HOTEL KEEPER
HOTEL LOUNGE
HOTEL PORTER
HOT-WATER TAP
HOUND'S TOOTH
HOURLY VIGIL
HOUR OF TRIAL
HOURS OF WORK
HOUSE ARREST
HOUSE HUNTER
HOUSE MARTIN
HOUSE MASTER
HOUSE MOTHER
HOUSE NUMBER
HOUSE OF CALL
HOUSE OF KEYS
HOUSE OF REST
HOUSE OF YORK
HOUSE ON FIRE
HOVER AROUND
HOWLING WIND
HUDSON RIVER
HUGE EXPENSE
HUGE SUCCESS
HUGHIE GREEN
HUG THE COAST
HUG THE SHORE
HUMAN DYNAMO
HUMAN EFFORT
HUMAN FAMILY
HUMAN NATURE
HUMAN RIGHTS
HUMBLE BIRTH

HUMBLE HEART
HUMBLE STOCK
HUMMING BIRD
HUMS AND HAWS
HUNDRED DAYS
HUNGER MARCH
HUNK OF BREAD
HUNT BIG GAME
HUNTER'S MOON
HUNT FOR A JOB
HUNTING CROP
HUNTING HORN
HUNTING PACK
HUNTING PINK
HUNTING SONG
HUNT IN PAIRS
HUNT THE HARE
HURRIED MEAL
HUSBAND TO BE
HUSHED TONES
HUSH-HUSH JOB

I—II
IAIN MACLEOD
IDEAL SCHEME
IDES OF MARCH
IDLE DISPLAY
IDLE THOUGHT
IF YOU PLEASE
IGNEOUS ROCK
IGNITION KEY
IGNORANT MAN
ILE DE FRANCE
I'LL BE HANGED!
ILLICIT LOVE
IL PENSEROSO
IL TROVATORE
I'M A DUTCHMAN!
IMPOSE A DUTY
IMPROPER USE
IN A BAD STATE
IN A FEW WORDS
IN A FLAT SPIN
IN A GOOD MOOD
IN AGREEMENT
IN A HAYSTACK
IN ALL EVENTS
IN A LOW VOICE
IN A MINORITY
IN AND AROUND
INANE REMARK

IN AN INSTANT
IN A NUTSHELL
IN A QUANDARY
IN A REAL MESS
IN A SMALL WAY
IN AT THE KILL
IN AUSTRALIA
IN AUTHORITY
IN BAD REPAIR
IN CAPTIVITY
IN CHARACTER
IN COLD BLOOD
IN COLLISION
IN COLLUSION
IN COMMITTEE
IN CONDITION
IN CONFUSION
INCUR LOSSES
IN DAYS OF OLD
IN DEEP WATER
IN DETENTION
INDEX FINGER
INDEX NUMBER
INDIAN BRAVE
INDIAN CHIEF
INDIAN CURRY
INDIAN OCEAN
INDIAN SQUAW
INDIAN TRIBE
INDIA OFFICE
INDIA RUBBER
INDIRECT TAX
INDOOR GAMES
IN DREAMLAND
IN DUE COURSE
IN DUE SEASON
IN DUPLICATE
IN DUTY BOUND
IN ECSTASIES
IN EDINBURGH
IN EVERY PORT
IN EXISTENCE
IN FACSIMILE
IN FINE STYLE
IN FOR A PENNY
IN FOR A POUND
IN FOR A STORM
IN FORMATION
INFRA-RED RAY
IN FULL BLAST
IN FULL BLOOM

IN FULL SPATE
IN FULL SWING
IN GOOD FAITH
IN GOOD HANDS
IN GOOD HEART
IN GOOD ODOUR
IN GOOD SHAPE
IN GOOD TASTE
IN GOOD VOICE
IN GRATITUDE
IN GREAT FORM
IN HYSTERICS
IN IGNORANCE
INITIAL MOVE
INJURED BACK
INJURED LOOK
IN LOW RELIEF
IN MINIATURE
INMOST BEING
IN MY OPINION
INNER CIRCLE
INNER MARGIN
INNER TEMPLE
INNOCENT MAN
IN NO RESPECT
INNS OF COURT
IN ONE'S HEART
IN ONE'S POWER
IN ONE'S PRIME
IN ONE'S SHELL
IN ONE'S SLEEP
IN ONE'S TEENS
IN OPEN COURT
IN OPERATION
IN PANTOMIME
IN PRINCIPLE
IN PROFUSION
IN PURGATORY
IN READINESS
IN REBELLION
IN REPERTORY
IN RESIDENCE
IN SAFE HANDS
IN SECLUSION
INSECT WORLD
IN SEPTEMBER
IN SHORTHAND
INSIDE RIGHT
INSIDE STORY
INSIDE TRACK
INSTANT CURE

INTENSE COLD	IN THE VALLEY	JAMES BRIDIE
INTENSE HEAT	IN THE WAKE OF	JAMES CAGNEY
IN THAT PLACE	IN THE WINDOW	JAMESON RAID
IN THE CELLAR	IN THE WINTER	JAM SANDWICH
IN THE CENTRE	IN THE ZENITH	JAM TOMORROW
IN THE CHARTS	IN THIS PLACE	JANE SEYMOUR
IN THE CHORUS	INTO THE BLUE	JAPANESE ART
IN THE CHURCH	INTO THE WIND	JARRING NOTE
IN THE CINEMA	INTO THIN AIR	JAUNTING CAR
IN THE CIRCLE	IN TWO SHAKES	JAWS OF DEATH
IN THE CLOUDS	INVALID DIET	JAZZ SESSION
IN THE CORNER	INVERT SUGAR	JEALOUS WIFE
IN THE CRADLE	IN WHICH CASE	JEAN BOROTRA
IN THE DEPTHS	IONIC COLUMN	JEAN COCTEAU
IN THE DESERT	IRISH BROGUE	JEAN SIMMONS
IN THE FAMILY	IRISH GUARDS	JELLIED EELS
IN THE FIELDS	IRISH SETTER	JET AIRCRAFT
IN THE FINISH	IRISH WHISKY	JINGLE BELLS
IN THE FOREST	IRMA LA DOUCE	JOAN HAMMOND
IN THE FRIDGE	IRON CURTAIN	JOHN GIELGUD
IN THE FUTURE	IRON FILINGS	JOHN GREGSON
IN THE GARAGE	IRON FOUNDRY	JOHN HALIFAX
IN THE GARDEN	IRON PYRITES	JOHN OF GAUNT
IN THE GROOVE	IRON RATIONS	JOHN O'GROATS
IN THE GROUND	IRONY OF FATE	JOHN O'LONDON
IN THE GUARDS	ISAAC NEWTON	JOHN OSBORNE
IN THE GUTTER	ISAAC PITMAN	JOIE DE VIVRE
IN THE JUNGLE	ISLE OF ARRAN	JOINT ACTION
IN THE LOCK-UP	ISLE OF CAPRI	JOINT APPEAL
IN THE MAKING	ISLE OF WIGHT	JOINT EFFORT
IN THE MARGIN	ISSUE SHARES	JOIN THE ARMY
IN THE MARKET	ITALIA CONTI	JOIN THE NAVY
IN THE MIDDLE	ITALIAN ALPS	JOINT OF BEEF
IN THE MIRROR	ITALIAN WINE	JOINT OF LAMB
IN THE MORGUE	ITCHING PALM	JOINT OF PORK
IN THE NAME OF	IT'S A FAIR COP	JOINT OF VEAL
IN THE OFFICE	IT STRIKES ME	JOINT TENANT
IN THE OFFING	IVOR NOVELLO	JOKING APART
IN THE PAPERS	IVORY CASTLE	JOLLY HUNGRY
IN THE PLURAL	IZAAK WALTON	JOSEPH'S COAT
IN THE PULPIT		JOURNEY'S END
IN THE PURPLE	J—11	JUBILEE YEAR
IN THE SADDLE	JACK AND JILL	JUDGMENT DAY
IN THE SEASON	JACK DEMPSEY	JUDY GARLAND
IN THE SECRET	JACK HAWKINS	JUGULAR VEIN
IN THE SPRING	JACK HULBERT	JUKE-BOX JURY
IN THE STALLS	JACKIE TRENT	JULIE ROGERS
IN THE STOCKS	JACK JACKSON	JUMPING BEAN
IN THE STREET	JACK JOHNSON	JUMPING JACK
IN THE STUDIO	JACK OF CLUBS	JUNE WEDDING
IN THE THROES	JAFFA ORANGE	JUNGLE FEVER

JUNGLE GREEN
JUNGLE JUICE
JUNIPER TREE
JURY SERVICE
JUST A CHANCE
JUST A LITTLE
JUST A MINUTE
JUST A MOMENT
JUST A SECOND
JUST DESERTS
JUST FOR ONCE
JUST IMAGINE
JUST MARRIED
JUST PERFECT
JUST THE SAME
JUST THE TIME
JUST VISIBLE
JUST WILLIAM

K—II

KEEN BARGAIN
KEEN CONTEST
KEEN HEARING
KEEN STUDENT
KEEP ABREAST
KEEP AN EYE ON
KEEP A RECORD
KEEP A SECRET
KEEP COMPANY
KEEP COUNSEL
KEEP IN CHECK
KEEP IN SIGHT
KEEP IN STOCK
KEEP IN STORE
KEEP IN TOUCH
KEEP IT GOING
KEEP ONE'S JOB
KEEP OUT OF IT
KEEP RIGHT ON
KEEP SMILING
KEEP THE CASH
KEEP TRACK OF
KEEP WAITING
KELLOGG PACT
KEMPTON PARK
KENNETH MORE
KENSAL GREEN
KENTISH TOWN
KEY INDUSTRY
KEY POSITION
KEY QUESTION

KHAKI SHORTS
KICK AGAINST
KICK UP A DUST
KICK UP A FUSS
KIDNEY BEANS
KILKENNY CAT
KILLER WHALE
KILLING PACE
KILL ONESELF
KIND FRIENDS
KIND GESTURE
KINDRED SOUL
KIND REGARDS
KIND THOUGHT
KIND WELCOME
KING CHARLES
KINGDOM COME
KING EMPEROR
KING OF BIRDS
KING OF CLUBS
KING OF KINGS
KING PENGUIN
KING RICHARD
KING'S BISHOP
KING'S BOUNTY
KING'S COLOUR
KING'S FLIGHT
KING'S KNIGHT
KING SOLOMON
KING'S RANSOM
KING WILLIAM
KIRK DOUGLAS
KISSING GAME
KISSING GATE
KISS ME, HARDY
KISS OF JUDAS
KISS OF PEACE
KISS THE BOOK
KISS THE DUST
KITCHEN FIRE
KITCHEN HAND
KITCHEN MAID
KITCHEN SINK
KITCHEN UNIT
KNIGHT'S MOVE
KNIGHT'S PAWN
KNIT THE BROW
KNITTING BEE
KNOCK AROUND
KNOCK IT BACK
KNOCK ON WOOD

KNOTTY POINT
KNOW A LITTLE
KNOW BY HEART
KNOW BY SIGHT
KNOWING LOOK
KNOW ONE'S JOB
KNOW ONE'S WAY
KNOW THE FORM
KNOW THYSELF
KNOW TOO MUCH
KNUCKLE DOWN
KUALA LUMPUR

L—II

LABOUR FORCE
LABOUR PARTY
LABRADOR DOG
LACK COURAGE
LACK OF DRIVE
LACK OF FAITH
LACK OF FLAIR
LACK OF MONEY
LACK OF POWER
LACK OF SCOPE
LACK OF SENSE
LACK OF SHAPE
LACK OF SLEEP
LACK OF TASTE
LACK SPARKLE
LADIES FIRST
LADIES' NIGHT
LA DOLCE VITA
LADY ALMONER
LADY BARNETT
LADY MACBETH
LADY MACDUFF
LADY TEACHER
LAKE LUCERNE
LAKE ONTARIO
LAKE SUCCESS
LAMBETH WALK
LANDING GEAR
LAND MEASURE
LAND OF ROSES
LANKY FIGURE
LANTERN JAWS
LAPIS LAZULI
LAP OF LUXURY
LAPSE OF TIME
LARGE AMOUNT

LARGE AS LIFE
LARGE BRANDY
LARGE CIRCLE
LARGE FAMILY
LARGE INCOME
LARGE NUMBER
LARGE PROFIT
LARGE SALARY
LARGE SCOTCH
LARGE SCREEN
LARGE SHERRY
LARGE SUPPLY
LARGE VESSEL
LARGE VOLUME
LARGE WHISKY
LASH OF A WHIP
LAST ADDRESS
LAST ARRIVAL
LAST ATTEMPT
LAST BASTION
LAST CENTURY
LAST CHAPTER
LAST EDITION
LAST EVENING
LAST FOR EVER
LAST HONOURS
LAST INNINGS
LAST JANUARY
LAST JOURNEY
LAST OF EIGHT
LAST OF SEVEN
LAST OF THREE
LAST OUTPOST
LAST QUARTER
LAST TO LEAVE
LAST TRIBUTE
LAST TUESDAY
LAST VESTIGE
LATE ARRIVAL
LATE AT NIGHT
LATE EDITION
LATE EVENING
LATE FOR WORK
LATE HARVEST
LATE HUSBAND
LATE STARTER
LATEST CRAZE
LATEST ISSUE
LATEST MODEL
LATEST SCORE
LATEST SHADE

LATEST STYLE
LATEST THING
LATIN CHURCH
LATIN LESSON
LATIN MASTER
LATIN PRIMER
LAUGHING GAS
LAUNDRY BILL
LAUNDRY MAID
LAUREL CROWN
LAW AND ORDER
LAWFUL ORDER
LAW MERCHANT
LAW OF NATURE
LAW OF THE SEA
LAY ABOUT ONE
LAY IN AMBUSH
LAY IN A STOCK
LAY OUT MONEY
LAY PREACHER
LAY THE CLOTH
LAY THE GHOST
LAY THE TABLE
LAZY HOLIDAY
LEADEN HOURS
LEADING CASE
LEADING EDGE
LEADING LADY
LEADING NOTE
LEADING PART
LEADING RÔLE
LEADING WREN
LEAGUE MATCH
LEAN AGAINST
LEAN AS A RAKE
LEAN FORWARD
LEAN TOWARDS
LEARN A HABIT
LEARN A TRADE
LEARN TO HATE
LEARN TO LOVE
LEARN TO PLAY
LEARN TO READ
LEARN TO RIDE
LEARN TO WALK
LEARN WISDOM
LEATHER BELT
LEATHER COAT
LEATHER LANE
LEATHER SOLE
LEAVE A SPACE

LEAVE A TRAIL
LEAVE BEHIND
LEAVE FALLOW
LEAVE IT OPEN
LEAVE IT TO ME
LEAVE NO HOPE
LEAVE SCHOOL
LEAVE UNDONE
LEAVE UNSAID
LECTURE HALL
LECTURE TOUR
LEDGER CLERK
LEFT HANGING
LEFT LUGGAGE
LEFT OUTSIDE
LEGAL ACTION
LEGAL ADVICE
LEGAL BATTLE
LEGAL ENTITY
LEGAL JARGON
LEGAL REMEDY
LEGAL RULING
LEGAL TENDER
LEG OF MUTTON
LEISURE TIME
LEMON BARLEY
LEMON SQUASH
LEMON YELLOW
LEND SUPPORT
LEON TROTSKY
LESLIE CARON
LESS AND LESS
LESSER BREED
LESSON EIGHT
LESSON SEVEN
LESSON THREE
LESS TROUBLE
LET A MAN DOWN
LET IN THE SUN
LET OFF STEAM
LEVEL FLIGHT
LEVEL TEMPER
LIBEL ACTION
LIBERAL ARTS
LIBERAL VIEW
LIBERTY BOAT
LIBERTY HALL
LIBERTY SHIP
LIBRARY BOOK
LIBRARY LIST
LICK OF PAINT

LICK THE DUST
LIE AT ANCHOR
LIE DETECTOR
LIE END TO END
LIE IN AMBUSH
LIE IN PRISON
LIE ON VELVET
LIE PARALLEL
LIFE HISTORY
LIFE OF BLISS
LIFE OF CRIME
LIFE OR DEATH
LIFE PARTNER
LIFE PEERAGE
LIFE SAVINGS
LIFT A FINGER
LIFT THE ROOF
LIFT THE VEIL
LIGHT A MATCH
LIGHT BOMBER
LIGHT BREEZE
LIGHT COLOUR
LIGHT COMEDY
LIGHT DUTIES
LIGHTER FUEL
LIGHTER VEIN
LIGHT OF FOOT
LIGHT RELIEF
LIGHT REMARK
LIGHT THE GAS
LIGHT THE WAY
LIGHT VESSEL
LIGHT WEIGHT
LIGHT YELLOW
LIKE A MASTER
LIKE AN ARROW
LIKE AN IDIOT
LIKE A PARROT
LIKE A STATUE
LIKE A STREAK
LIKE A TROJAN
LIKE FOR LIKE
LIKE IT OR NOT
LIKELY STORY
LIKE THE IDEA
LIKE THE WIND
LILAC DOMINO
LILLI PALMER
LILY LANGTRY
LILY MARLENE
LIMB OF SATAN

LIMITED TIME
LIMPID STYLE
LINCOLN CITY
LINCOLN'S INN
LINE DRAWING
LINEN DRAPER
LINE OF MARCH
LINE OF SIGHT
LION RAMPANT
LISLE THREAD
LIST OF ITEMS
LIST OF NAMES
LITERARY MAN
LITERARY SET
LITMUS PAPER
LITTLE ANGEL
LITTLE DEVIL
LITTLE KNOWN
LITTLE SPACE
LITTLE THING
LITTLE TO SAY
LITTLE WHILE
LITTLE WOMAN
LITTLE WOMEN
LITTLE VALUE
LIVE FOR EVER
LIVE IN DREAD
LIVE IN PEACE
LIVE IN STYLE
LIVELONG DAY
LIVELY DANCE
LIVELY PARTY
LIVELY PITCH
LIVE ON BOARD
LIVE THEATRE
LIVE THROUGH
LIVING BEING
LIVING DEATH
LIVING IMAGE
LIVING PROOF
LIVING SPACE
LIVING THING
LIZARD POINT
LLOYD GEORGE
LOAD OF STRAW
LOAD OF TRIPE
LOAF OF BREAD
LO AND BEHOLD
LOAN OF MONEY
LOCAL BRANCH
LOCAL COLOUR

LOCAL CUSTOM
LOCAL GOSSIP
LOCAL OPTION
LOCAL TALENT
LOCK THE DOOR
LOCUM TENENS
LOGICAL MIND
LOGICAL STEP
LONDON CRIES
LONDON DOCKS
LONDON PRIDE
LONDON STAGE
LONDON STONE
LONG ACCOUNT
LONG CLOTHES
LONG DROUGHT
LONG HOLIDAY
LONG INNINGS
LONG JOURNEY
LONG, LONG AGO
LONG MEASURE
LONG SERVICE
LONG SESSION
LONG STRETCH
LONG STRIDES
LONG TIME AGO
LONG WEEK-END
LOOK A FRIGHT
LOOK ASKANCE
LOOK DAGGERS
LOOK FOOLISH
LOOK FOR DIGS
LOOK FORWARD
LOOK FOR WORK
LOOK GHASTLY
LOOK LIKE NEW
LOOK-OUT POST
LOOK OUTSIDE
LOOK PLEASED
LOOK THE PART
LOOK THROUGH
LOOK VOLUMES
LOOP THE LOOP
LOOSE CHANGE
LOOSE LIVING
LOOSE MORALS
LOOSE THREAD
LORD BALDWIN
LORD BOOTHBY
LORD PROVOST
LORD RUSSELL

LORDS' DEBATE	LOW ALTITUDE	MADEIRA WINE
LORD'S PRAYER	LOW COMEDIAN	MADE OF MONEY
LORD'S SUPPER	LOWER ANIMAL	MADE OF STRAW
LORRY DRIVER	LOWER SCHOOL	MADE TO ORDER
LOSE A CHANCE	LOW ESTIMATE	MADE WELCOME
LOSE CONTROL	LOW FOREHEAD	MADONNA LILY
LOSE COURAGE	LOW LATITUDE	MADRAS CURRY
LOSE FRIENDS	LOW POSITION	MAD SCRAMBLE
LOSE ONE'S ALL	LOW PRESSURE	MAD WITH RAGE
LOSE ONESELF	LOW RAINFALL	MAGIC CARPET
LOSE ONE'S WAY	LOW STANDARD	MAGIC CIRCLE
LOSE SIGHT OF	LOYAL FRIEND	MAGIC MIRROR
LOSE THE GAME	L-SHAPED ROOM	MAGIC MOMENT
LOSE THE LEAD	LUCID MOMENT	MAGIC POTION
LOSE THE RACE	LUCILLE BALL	MAGIC RECIPE
LOSE THE TOSS	LUCKY BEGGAR	MAGIC REMEDY
LOSE THE VOTE	LUCKY CHANCE	MAGIC SQUARE
LOSS OF BLOOD	LUCKY ESCAPE	MAGINOT LINE
LOSS OF FAITH	LUCKY FELLOW	MAGNUM BONUM
LOSS OF MONEY	LUCKY MASCOT	MAILING LIST
LOSS OF NERVE	LUCKY MOMENT	MAIL SERVICE
LOSS OF SIGHT	LUCKY NUMBER	MAIN ELEMENT
LOSS OF SMELL	LUCKY RASCAL	MAIN FEATURE
LOSS OF SOUND	LUCKY STREAK	MAIN MEANING
LOSS OF TOUCH	LUCKY STRIKE	MAIN PROBLEM
LOSS OF VALUE	LUCKY STROKE	MAIN PURPOSE
LOSS OF VOICE	LUCKY WINNER	MAIN STATION
LOST HORIZON	LUDGATE HILL	MAJOR CRISIS
LOST TO SHAME	LUGGAGE RACK	MAJOR PLANET
LOST TO SIGHT	LULL TO SLEEP	MAKE A CHANGE
LOST WEEK-END	LUMP OF SUGAR	MAKE A CHOICE
LOTS AND LOTS	LUNCHEON CAR	MAKE A CORNER
LOTS OF MONEY	LUNDY ISLAND	MAKE A DETOUR
LOUD AND LONG	LUXURY FOODS	MAKE A FOOL OF
LOUD PROTEST	LUXURY GOODS	MAKE A LIVING
LOUD SPEAKER	LUXURY HOTEL	MAKE AND MEND
LOUIS QUINZE	LUXURY PRICE	MAKE AN ENTRY
LOUIS TREIZE	LYRIC POETRY	MAKE AN ERROR
LOUNGE ABOUT		MAKE AN OFFER
LOVE AND HATE	**M—11**	MAKE A PACKET
LOVE FIFTEEN	MACASSAR OIL	MAKE A PROFIT
LOVE IS BLIND	MACHINE HAND	MAKE A RECORD
LOVELY MONEY	MACHINE SHOP	MAKE A REMARK
LOVELY NIGHT	MACHINE TOOL	MAKE A REPORT
LOVELY SIGHT	MACKEREL SKY	MAKE A SEARCH
LOVE OF MONEY	MADE A KNIGHT	MAKE A SIGNAL
LOVE OF ORDER	MADE A MEMBER	MAKE A SPEECH
LOVE OF TRUTH	MADE IN ITALY	MAKE A SPLASH
LOVE OR MONEY	MADE IN JAPAN	MAKE BELIEVE
LOVE PHILTRE	MADE IN SPAIN	MAKE CERTAIN
LOVING WORDS	MADEIRA CAKE	MAKE CHANGES

MAKE CONTACT
MAKE DEMANDS
MAKE ENEMIES
MAKE EXCUSES
MAKE FRIENDS
MAKE HEADWAY
MAKE HISTORY
MAKE INROADS
MAKE IT CLEAR
MAKE IT PLAIN
MAKE IT STICK
MAKE LIGHTER
MAKE LIGHT OF
MAKE MUCH ADO
MAKE NO NOISE
MAKE NO SOUND
MAKE OBVIOUS
MAKE ONE'S BED
MAKE ONE'S BOW
MAKE ONE'S WAY
MAKE OR BREAK
MAKE SMALLER
MAKES NO ODDS
MAKE SPORT OF
MAKE THE FIRE
MAKE THE PACE
MAKE TROUBLE
MAKE WELCOME
MAKE WHOOPEE
MALACCA CANE
MALAY STATES
MALE DESCENT
MALMSEY WINE
MALT VINEGAR
MAN AND WOMAN
MAN AT THE TOP
MAN BITES DOG
MANFRED MANN
MAN FROM MARS
MANICURE SET
MAN IN CHARGE
MAN IN OFFICE
MANLY FIGURE
MANLY SPIRIT
MAN OF ACTION
MAN OF GENIUS
MAN OF HONOUR
MAN OF METTLE
MAN OF MUSCLE
MAN OF PRAYER
MAN OF RENOWN

MAN OF REPUTE
MAN ON THE JOB
MAN PROPOSES
MANSARD ROOF
MAN THE PUMPS
MAN THE WALLS
MAP OF EUROPE
MAP OF FRANCE
MAP OF GREECE
MAP OF LONDON
MAP OF NORWAY
MAP OF SWEDEN
MARBLE HALLS
MARCH IN STEP
MARCH OF TIME
MARIA CALLAS
MARIE STOPES
MARINE CORPS
MARINE STORE
MARITIME LAW
MARKED CARDS
MARKET OVERT
MARKET PLACE
MARKET PRICE
MARKET RASEN
MARKET TREND
MARKET VALUE
MARKET WOMAN
MARK MY WORDS
MARK THE SPOT
MARRIAGE TIE
MARRIED LIFE
MARRIED NAME
MARRON GLACÉ
MARRYING MAN
MARSHAL FOCH
MARSHAL TITO
MARSTON MOOR
MARTIAL RACE
MARTIN'S BANK
MASONIC HALL
MASSED BANDS
MASS EMOTION
MASSIVE ROCK
MASS MEETING
MATE IN THREE
MATERIAL AID
MATINÉE IDOL
MATT SURFACE
MATURE YEARS
MAUNDY MONEY

MAX BEERBOHM
MAX BYGRAVES
MAY THE FIFTH
MAY THE FIRST
MAY THE NINTH
MAY THE SIXTH
MAY THE TENTH
MAY THE THIRD
ME AND MY GIRL
MEANING LOOK
MEAN NOTHING
MEASURE TIME
MEAT EXTRACT
MEDAL RIBBON
MEDICAL BOOK
MEDICAL CARE
MEDICAL CASE
MEDICAL TEST
MEDICAL WARD
MEDICINE HAT
MEDICINE MAN
MEDIUM BUILD
MEEK AND MILD
MEET HALFWAY
MEET ONE'S END
MEET THE BILL
MEGATON BOMB
MELODY MAKER
MELTING MOOD
MELT IN TEARS
MEMBERS ONLY
MEMORIAL DAY
MENAI STRAIT
MEN AND WOMEN
MENDIP HILLS
MENTAL ERROR
MENTAL GRASP
MENTAL IMAGE
MENTAL LAPSE
MENTALLY ILL
MENTAL POWER
MENTAL SHOCK
MENTAL STATE
MERE FEELING
MERE NOTHING
MERLE OBERON
MERRY ANDREW
MERSEY DOCKS
MERSEY SOUND
MERVYN JOHNS
METAL POLISH

MEWS COTTAGE	MOB HYSTERIA	MORTISE LOCK
MICKEY MOUSE	MOB VIOLENCE	MOSAIC FLOOR
MIDDLE CLASS	MOCKING BIRD	MOSELLE WINE
MIDDLE POINT	MOCK MODESTY	MOSQUITO NET
MIDDLE STUMP	MODERN BLOCK	MOTHER CAREY
MIDDLE WATCH	MODERN DANCE	MOTHER EARTH
MIDLAND BANK	MODERN DRESS	MOTHER GOOSE
MIDLAND TOWN	MODERN HOUSE	MOTHER'S HELP
MIDNIGHT OIL	MODERN IDEAS	MOTHER'S MILK
MIDNIGHT SUN	MODERN IDIOM	MOTHER'S RUIN
MIGHT AS WELL	MODERN LATIN	MOTION STUDY
MILD CLIMATE	MODERN MUSIC	MOTIVE FORCE
MILD FLUTTER	MODERN NOVEL	MOTIVE POWER
MILD REPROOF	MODERN STYLE	MOTLEY CROWD
MILD WEATHER	MODERN TIMES	MOTOR LAUNCH
MILE A MINUTE	MODERN TREND	MOTOR RACING
MILE END ROAD	MODERN USAGE	MOTOR TRIALS
MILITARY AID	MODERN YOUTH	MOULIN ROUGE
MILITARY LAW	MODEST HOPES	MOUNT A HORSE
MILITARY MAN	MODEST MEANS	MOUNTAIN AIR
MILKING TIME	MOIRA LISTER	MOUNTAIN ASH
MILK PUDDING	MOLLY MALONE	MOUNTAIN DEW
MINCING LANE	MONDAY NIGHT	MOUNTAIN TOP
MIND THE BABY	MONEY FOR JAM	MOUNT ARARAT
MIND THE STEP	MONEY MARKET	MOUNT VERNON
MINERAL VEIN	MONEY MATTER	MOUTH HONOUR
MINIMUM WAGE	MONEY SPIDER	MOVABLE TYPE
MINOR DETAIL	MONEY'S WORTH	MOVE FORWARD
MINOR INJURY	MONEY TO BURN	MOVE QUICKLY
MINOR MATTER	MONKEY ABOUT	MOVE TO ANGER
MINOR PLANET	MONTE CRISTO	MOVE TO TEARS
MINSTREL BOY	MONTHLY RENT	MOVE TOWARDS
MINT FLAVOUR	MONTH'S LEAVE	MOVING FORCE
MINT OF MONEY	MOON GODDESS	MOVING SCENE
MINUTE STEAK	MOP ONE'S BROW	MOVING STORY
MINUTE WALTZ	MORAL APATHY	MOVING WORDS
MIRACLE DRUG	MORAL DEFECT	MOW THE GRASS
MIRACLE PLAY	MORAL EFFECT	MRS. MALAPROP
MISS A CHANCE	MORAL IMPACT	MUCH MARRIED
MISS A SITTER	MORE AND MORE	MUCH OBLIGED
MISSED CATCH	MORE THAN ONE	MUCH THE SAME
MISS ENGLAND	MORNING CALL	MUCH TROUBLE
MISSING HEIR	MORNING COAT	MUCH WENLOCK
MISSING LINK	MORNING POST	MUFFLED DRUM
MISS NOTHING	MORNING STAR	MUM'S THE WORD
MISS ONE'S WAY	MORRIS DANCE	MURDER TRIAL
MISS THE BOAT	MORTAL AGONY	MURKY DEPTHS
MISS THE MARK	MORTAL ENEMY	MUSCOVY DUCK
MISS THE POST	MORTALLY ILL	MUSEUM PIECE
MISTER RIGHT	MORTAL PERIL	MUSICAL NOTE
MIXED SCHOOL	MORTAL WOUND	MUSICAL SHOW

MUSICAL TRIO
MUSICAL WORK
MUSIC CRITIC
MUSIC LESSON
MUSIC MASTER
MUSTARD BATH
MUSTARD SEED
MUSWELL HILL
MUTTON CURRY
MUTUAL TERMS
MYSTERY BOAT
MYSTERY PLAY
MYSTERY SHIP
MYSTERY TOUR
MYSTERY TRIP
MYSTIC RITES

N—11
NAGGING PAIN
NAGGING WIFE
NAIL VARNISH
NAME NO NAMES
NAOMI JACOBS
NARROW GAUGE
NARROW SHAVE
NARROW TRAIL
NASAL ACCENT
NASTY PEOPLE
NASTY TEMPER
NASTY TUMBLE
NATIVE CHIEF
NATIVE DRESS
NATIVE HEATH
NATIVE STATE
NATIVE TRIBE
NAT KING COLE
NATURAL BENT
NATURAL GIFT
NATURAL LIFE
NATURE LOVER
NATURE STUDY
NAUGHTY GIRL
NAUGHTY WORD
NAVAL BATTLE
NAVAL RATING
NAVAL STORES
NAVEL ORANGE
NAZI GERMANY
NEAR AND DEAR
NEAR FAILURE
NEARLY READY

NEARLY THERE
NEAR ONE'S END
NEAR PERFECT
NEAR THE BONE
NEAR THE EDGE
NEAR THE MARK
NEAR THE WIND
NEAT AND TIDY
NEAT AND TRIM
NECK AND CROP
NECK AND NECK
NEEDLE MATCH
NEEDLE POINT
NEGRO MELODY
NELSON TOUCH
NE PLUS ULTRA
NERVE CENTRE
NETBALL TEAM
NET CURTAINS
NETHER LIMBS
NETHER WORLD
NET PRACTICE
NET RECEIPTS
NEUTRAL TINT
NEUTRAL ZONE
NEVER BEFORE
NEVER ENDING
NEVER FORGET
NEVER ON TIME
NEVER SAY DIE
NEW APPROACH
NEW ATLANTIS
NEW-BORN BABE
NEW-BORN BABY
NEW BRIGHTON
NEWGATE GAOL
NEW HEBRIDES
NEW POTATOES
NEW PROSPECT
NEWS CAPTION
NEWS IN BRIEF
NEWS SUMMARY
NEWTON ABBOT
NEW TO THE JOB
NEW YEAR'S DAY
NEW YEAR'S EVE
NEW YORK CITY
NEXT CENTURY
NEXT CHAPTER
NEXT IN ORDER
NEXT JANUARY

NEXT OCTOBER
NEXT STATION
NEXT TUESDAY
NICE AND EVEN
NICE MANNERS
NICE PICTURE
NIGHT AND DAY
NIGHT ATTIRE
NIGHT CURFEW
NIGHT EDITOR
NIGHT FLIGHT
NIGHT FLYING
NIGHT PATROL
NIGHT PORTER
NIGHT SCHOOL
NIGHT SISTER
NIGHT WORKER
NINE AND FIVE
NINE AND FOUR
NINE AND NINE
NINE DEGREES
NINE DOLLARS
NINE FATHOMS
NINE GALLONS
NINE GUINEAS
NINE HUNDRED
NINE MINUTES
NINE OF CLUBS
NINE PER CENT
NINE SQUARED
NINETY MILES
NINETY TIMES
NINETY YEARS
NINE WICKETS
NINTH LETTER
NINTH OF JULY
NINTH OF JUNE
NINTH STOREY
NINTH VOLUME
NIP IN THE AIR
NIP IN THE BUD
NIP OF BRANDY
NIP OF WHISKY
NO ADMISSION
NO AUTHORITY
NOBBY CLARKE
NOBLE EFFORT
NOBLE FAMILY
NOBLE FIGURE
NOBLE NATURE
NOBLE SAVAGE

NOBLE STRAIN
NOBODY'S FOOL
NO CIRCULARS
NOD ONE'S HEAD
NO EXCEPTION
NO GENTLEMAN
NOGGIN OF ALE
NO GREAT LOSS
NO HOPE AT ALL
NO ILLUSIONS
NOISE ABROAD
NOMADIC RACE
NOM DE GUERRE
NOMINAL HEAD
NOMINAL LIST
NOMINAL RATE
NOMINAL RENT
NONE SO BLIND
NONE THE LESS
NONE TOO WARM
NO, NO, NANETTE
NON-STOP SHOW
NO OBJECTION
NO QUESTIONS
NORFOLK SUIT
NO RIGHT TURN
NORMAL SIGHT
NORMAL STATE
NORMAN STYLE
NORTH AFRICA
NORTH BORNEO
NORTH DAKOTA
NORTH ISLAND
NORTH LONDON
NORTH RIDING
NOSE FOR NEWS
NOSEY PARKER
NOT A BIT OF IT
NOT ALL THERE
NOT A RED CENT
NOT FAR WRONG
NOTHING LEFT
NOTHING LIKE
NOTHING MUCH
NOTHING TO DO
NOTHING TO IT
NOTICE BOARD
NOT MUCH GOOD
NOT-OUT SCORE
NO-TRUMP HAND
NOT SPEAKING

NOT THE THING
NOTTING HILL
NOTTS COUNTY
NOTTS FOREST
NOT UP-TO-DATE
NOT UP TO MUCH
NOT VERY MANY
NOT VERY MUCH
NOT VERY WELL
NOT YOUR TYPE
NO VACANCIES
NOW AND AGAIN
NOWHERE NEAR
NOWHERE TO GO
NUCLEAR BOMB
NULL AND VOID
NUMBER EIGHT
NUMBER PLATE
NUMBER SEVEN
NUMBER THREE
NUPTIAL VOWS
NURSE CAVELL
NURSERY GAME
NURSERY MAID
NURSERY TALE
NURSING HOME

O—11

OAK-APPLE DAY
OBITER DICTA
OBLIQUE LINE
OBTUSE ANGLE
OCEAN TRAVEL
ODDLY ENOUGH
ODDS AGAINST
ODDS AND ENDS
OFFER ADVICE
OFFER A PRICE
OFFER NO HOPE
OFFICE BLOCK
OFFICE CLOCK
OFFICE HOURS
OFFICE PARTY
OFFICE STAFF
OFFICE STOOL
OFFICE SWEEP
OFF ONE'S BEAT
OFF ONE'S FEED
OFF ONE'S FOOD
OFF ONE'S HEAD
OFF-SIDE RULE

OFF THE BOOZE
OFF THE COAST
OFF THE GREEN
OFF THE LEASH
OFF THE POINT
OFF THE RAILS
OFF THE SCENT
OFF THE STAGE
OFF THE TRACK
OF GOOD STOCK
OF ILL REPUTE
OF LATE YEARS
OF NO ACCOUNT
OIL AND WATER
OIL OF CLOVES
OIL PAINTING
OIL REFINERY
OLD AND TRIED
OLD CUSTOMER
OLDER SISTER
OLD FAITHFUL
OLD GREY MARE
OLD KENT ROAD
OLD KING COLE
OLD MAN RIVER
OLD MEMORIES
OLD OAK CHEST
OLD OFFENDER
OLD OLD STORY
OLD POTATOES
OLD TRAFFORD
OLD WAR-HORSE
OLIVE BRANCH
OLIVER LODGE
OLIVER TWIST
OMAR KHAYYAM
OMNIBUS BOOK
ON ALL POINTS
ON AN AVERAGE
ON A PEDESTAL
ON A PITTANCE
ON AUTHORITY
ON BOARD SHIP
ON BOTH SIDES
ONCE OR TWICE
ONCE REMOVED
ONE AND A HALF
ONE AND EIGHT
ONE AND SEVEN
ONE AND THREE
ON EASY TERMS

ONE ELEVENTH	ON THE STAIRS	ORDERLY ROOM
ONE FARTHING	ON THE STOCKS	ORDER TO VIEW
ONE GOOD TURN	ON THE SWINGS	ORDINARY MAN
ONE IN THE EYE	ON THE TARGET	ORDNANCE MAP
ONE IN TWELVE	ON THE THAMES	ORGANIC LIFE
ONE-MAN REVUE	ON THE THRONE	ORIEL WINDOW
ONE MAN'S MEAT	ON THE WAGGON	ORIENTAL ART
ONE MEAT BALL	ON THE WAY OUT	ORIGINAL SIN
ONE'S BETTERS	ON TWO WHEELS	ORNATE STYLE
ONE SHILLING	ONUS OF PROOF	ORPHAN CHILD
ONE'S HOSTESS	ONWARD MARCH	ORSON WELLES
ONE SPOONFUL	ON WEDNESDAY	ORTHODOX JEW
ONE'S VERY OWN	OPAQUE GLASS	OSTRICH FARM
ONE SYLLABLE	OPEN ACCOUNT	OTHER PEOPLE
ONE THOUSAND	OPEN-AIR LIFE	OUT AND ABOUT
ON EVERY SIDE	OPEN-AIR TYPE	OUT COURTING
ON GOOD TERMS	OPEN AND SHUT	OUTDOOR GAME
ON HORSEBACK	OPEN CIRCUIT	OUTDOOR LIFE
ONION SELLER	OPEN COUNTRY	OUTER CIRCLE
ONLY THE BEST	OPENING MOVE	OUTER OFFICE
ON NO ACCOUNT	OPENING TIME	OUTER TEMPLE
ON ONE'S GUARD	OPEN MEETING	OUT FOR A DUCK
ON ONE'S HANDS	OPEN OUTWARD	OUT FOR BLOOD
ON ONE'S KNEES	OPEN QUARREL	OUT FOR KICKS
ON ONE'S PLATE	OPEN RUPTURE	OUT OF ACTION
ON ONE'S RIGHT	OPEN SCANDAL	OUT OF BOUNDS
ON POINT DUTY	OPEN THE BALL	OUT OF BREATH
ON PRINCIPLE	OPEN THE CASE	OUT OF DANGER
ON PROBATION	OPEN THE DOOR	OUT OF FAVOUR
ON THE AGENDA	OPEN THE EYES	OUT OF HUMOUR
ON THE ATTACK	OPEN THE GATE	OUT OF OFFICE
ON THE BOARDS	OPEN THE SAFE	OUT OF PETROL
ON THE BOTTLE	OPEN THIS END	OUT OF POCKET
ON THE BRIDGE	OPEN TO DOUBT	OUT OF REPAIR
ON THE CARPET	OPEN TO ERROR	OUT OF SCHOOL
ON THE COMMON	OPEN TO OFFER	OUT OF SEASON
ON THE CORNER	OPEN VERDICT	OUT OF THE ARK
ON THE COURSE	OPEN WARFARE	OUT OF THE BAG
ON THE DANUBE	OPERA BOUFFE	OUT OF THE CUP
ON THE FIDDLE	OPERA SINGER	OUT OF THE SKY
ON THE FRINGE	OPINION POLL	OUT OF THE SUN
ON THE GROUND	OPIUM ADDICT	OUT OF THE WAY
ON THE INSIDE	OPIUM SMOKER	OUT ON STRIKE
ON THE MARKET	OPPOSITE SEX	OUTRIGHT WIN
ON THE MORROW	OPPOSITE WAY	OUTSIDE EDGE
ON THE PARISH	ORANGE DRINK	OUTSIDE HELP
ON THE RAZZLE	ORANGE GROVE	OUTSIDE LEFT
ON THE RECORD	ORANGE JUICE	OUTSIDE WORK
ON THE SCALES	ORCHID HOUSE	OUTWARD SELF
ON THE SCREEN	ORDER DINNER	OUTWARD SHOW
ON THE SQUARE	ORDERLY DUTY	OVER AGAINST

OVER AND OVER
OVER ANXIOUS
OVERCAST SKY
OVER SHE GOES
OVER THE EDGE
OVER THE HILL
OVER THE LINE
OVER THE MARK
OVER THE MOON
OVER THE ODDS
OVER THE ROAD
OVER THE SIDE
OVER THE WALL
OVERTIME PAY
OWNER DRIVER
OWN FREE WILL
OXFORD COACH
OXFORD GROUP
OXFORD SHOES
OXFORD UNION
OYSTER SHELL

P—11
PABLO CASALS
PACE THE DECK
PACKAGE DEAL
PACKED HOUSE
PACKED LUNCH
PACKET OF TEN
PACK OF CARDS
PACK OF FOOLS
PACK UP AND GO
PAGAN PEOPLE
PAGE HEADING
PAID SERVANT
PAID TRIBUTE
PAIL OF WATER
PAINFUL TASK
PAINTED LADY
PAINTED SHIP
PAINTED VEIL
PAINT IN OILS
PAIR OF BOOTS
PAIR OF CLOGS
PAIR OF CUFFS
PAIR OF DUCKS
PAIR OF FIVES
PAIR OF FOURS
PAIR OF HANDS
PAIR OF HORNS

PAIR OF JACKS
PAIR OF KINGS
PAIR OF LACES
PAIR OF NINES
PAIR OF PANTS
PAIR OF PUMPS
PAIR OF SHOES
PAIR OF SIXES
PAIR OF SOCKS
PAIR OF SPATS
PAIR OF SPURS
PAIR OF STAYS
PAIR OF STEPS
PAIR OF TONGS
PALACE GUARD
PALAIS GLIDE
PALE AS DEATH
PAMPAS GRASS
PANAMA CANAL
PANCAKE RACE
PANDIT NEHRU
PANDORA'S BOX
PANEL DOCTOR
PANE OF GLASS
PAPER PROFIT
PAPIER MÂCHÉ
PARAFFIN OIL
PARISH CLERK
PARISH VICAR
PARLOUR GAME
PARLOUR MAID
PARSNIP WINE
PARSON'S NOSE
PART COMPANY
PART FRIENDS
PARTING GIFT
PARTING SHOT
PART PAYMENT
PART-TIME JOB
PARTY LEADER
PARTY MEMBER
PARTY SLOGAN
PARTY SPIRIT
PARTY SYSTEM
PAS DE CALAIS
PASS A REMARK
PASSING RICH
PASSING SHOW
PASSING WHIM
PASSING WORD
PASSION PLAY

PASSION WEEK
PASSIVE ROLE
PASS THE BALL
PASS THE BUCK
PASS THE PORT
PASS THE SALT
PASS THE TEST
PASS THE TIME
PASS THIS WAY
PASS THROUGH
PAST AND GONE
PASTEL SHADE
PAST HISTORY
PAST THE POST
PATH TO GLORY
PAT KIRKWOOD
PAT OF BUTTER
PATROL PLANE
PATRON OF ART
PATRON SAINT
PATTERN SHOP
PAUL ROBESON
PAX VOBISCUM
PAY A FORFEIT
PAY AND A HALF
PAY A PENALTY
PAY A PREMIUM
PAY BY CHEQUE
PAY CASH DOWN
PAY INCREASE
PAYING GUEST
PAY INTEREST
PAY ON DEMAND
PAY ON THE DOT
PAY THE COSTS
PAY THE DEVIL
PAY THE PIPER
PAY THE PRICE
PAY THE SCORE
PAY THE TABLE
PAY UP OR ELSE!
PEACEFUL END
PEACE OF MIND
PEACE PLEDGE
PEACE SPEECH
PEACE TREATY
PEACH BRANDY
PEACOCK BLUE
PEAL OF BELLS
PEARL BARLEY
PEARL BUTTON

PEARLY GATES	PICK THE LOCK	PLAY FORWARD
PEARLY QUEEN	PICK UP SPEED	PLAYING CARD
PEBBLE BEACH	PICNIC PARTY	PLAY MARBLES
PEBBLY BEACH	PICTURE BOOK	PLAY ON WORDS
PELTING RAIN	PIECE OF CAKE	PLAY PONTOON
PENAL COLONY	PIECE OF LAND	PLAY THE BALL
PENAL REFORM	PIECE OF LUCK	PLAY THE FOOL
PENAL SYSTEM	PIECE OF NEWS	PLAY THE GAME
PENALTY AREA	PIE IN THE SKY	PLAY THE HARP
PENALTY GOAL	PIERCED EARS	PLAY THE HERO
PENALTY KICK	PIGEON'S MILK	PLAY THE HOST
PENALTY LINE	PILE OF CHIPS	PLAY THE LEAD
PENALTY SPOT	PILE OF MONEY	PLEAD GUILTY
PEN AND PAPER	PILLION RIDE	PLEASANT DAY
PENNY POINTS	PILLION SEAT	PLEASURE MAD
PENSION FUND	PILLOW FIGHT	PLENTY TO EAT
PENSIVE MOOD	PILOT ENGINE	PLOT A COURSE
PERFECT CASE	PILOT SCHEME	PLUMB WICKET
PERFECT CURE	PILOT VESSEL	PLUM PUDDING
PERFECT FOOL	PILSEN LAGER	PLUS OR MINUS
PERFECT LADY	PILTDOWN MAN	PLYMOUTH HOE
PERFECT TRIM	PINCH OF SALT	POCKET GUIDE
PERIOD DRESS	PINT MEASURE	POCKET MONEY
PERIOD HOUSE	PINT OF CIDER	POCKET VENUS
PERIOD PIECE	PINT OF STOUT	POETIC STYLE
PERSIAN GULF	PINT TANKARD	POETS' CORNER
PERSIAN LAMB	PIPE CLEANER	POINT A MORAL
PERSONAL LAW	PIPE OF PEACE	POINTED CLUE
PET AVERSION	PIPE ON BOARD	POINT OF TIME
PETER DAWSON	PIPE TOBACCO	POINT OF VIEW
PETER GRIMES	PIRATE RADIO	POINT THE WAY
PETER O'TOOLE	PITHY REMARK	POKER PLAYER
PETER'S PENCE	PITHY SAYING	POKER SCHOOL
PETER WIMSEY	PLACE OF CALL	POKE THE FIRE
PETROL FUMES	PLACE OF REST	POLAR CIRCLE
PETTY TYRANT	PLAIN ANSWER	POLAR LIGHTS
PETULA CLARK	PLAIN FIGURE	POLAR REGION
PEWTER PLATE	PLAIN LIVING	POLE VAULTER
PHANTOM SHIP	PLAIN PEOPLE	POLICE COURT
PHOENIX PARK	PLAIN SPEECH	POLICE FORCE
PHONE NUMBER	PLAIN STUPID	POLICE STATE
PHOTO FINISH	PLASTER CAST	POLO SWEATER
PIANO LESSON	PLASTIC BOMB	PONY AND TRAP
PIANO PLAYER	PLATE ARMOUR	PONY EXPRESS
PICK A WINNER	PLAY AGAINST	POOLS COUPON
PICKET FENCE	PLAY-BOY TYPE	POOR CALIBRE
PICK FLOWERS	PLAY COWBOYS	POOR COMPANY
PICK HOLES IN	PLAY CRICKET	POOR HARVEST
PICK ONE'S WAY	PLAYER PIANO	POOR LOOK-OUT
PICK POCKETS	PLAY FOR LOVE	POOR OLD SOUL
PICK THE BEST	PLAY FOR TIME	POOR OPINION

POOR OUTLOOK
POOR QUALITY
POOR SOLDIER
POOR SWIMMER
POOR VINTAGE
POPULAR HERO
POPULAR NAME
POPULAR PLAY
POPULAR SONG
POPULAR TUNE
POPULAR WILL
PORK BUTCHER
PORTLAND BAY
PORT OF ENTRY
PORT OF SPAIN
PORT THE HELM
POSTAGE FREE
POSTAGE PAID
POST A LETTER
POSTAL ORDER
POSTAL UNION
POSTERN GATE
POTATO CHIPS
POTATO CRISP
POTATO SALAD
POT OF COFFEE
POTS AND PANS
POTS OF MONEY
POTTED PLANT
POTTER ABOUT
POTTER'S CLAY
POT THE BLACK
POTTING SHED
POULTRY FARM
POURING RAIN
POWER OF GOOD
PRACTICE RUN
PRACTISE LAW
PRAED STREET
PRAIRIE FIRE
PRAIRIE WOLF
PRANCE ABOUT
PRAY FOR RAIN
PRECISE TIME
PREMIUM BOND
PRESENT ARMS
PRESENT TIME
PRESS A CLAIM
PRESSED BEEF
PRESS NOTICE
PRESS OFFICE

PRESS ONWARD
PRESS TICKET
PRESTER JOHN
PRETTY AWFUL
PRETTY DANCE
PRETTY PENNY
PRETTY POLLY
PRETTY SCENE
PRETTY SMART
PRE-WAR PRICE
PREY TO FEARS
PRICE OF FAME
PRICE TICKET
PRICKLY HEAT
PRICKLY PEAR
PRIDE AND JOY
PRIDE OF RANK
PRIEST'S HOLE
PRIME FACTOR
PRIME NUMBER
PRIME OF LIFE
PRIMROSE DAY
PRIMUS STOVE
PRINCESS IDA
PRINTED PAGE
PRINTED WORD
PRINTER'S INK
PRINTER'S PIE
PRINTING INK
PRISON BREAK
PRISON GATES
PRISON GUARD
PRISON HOUSE
PRISON WALLS
PRIVATE BANK
PRIVATE BILL
PRIVATE HELL
PRIVATE LIFE
PRIVATE LINE
PRIVATE MASS
PRIVATE PATH
PRIVATE ROAD
PRIVATE ROOM
PRIVATE SALE
PRIVATE TALK
PRIVATE VIEW
PRIVATE WARD
PRIVET HEDGE
PRIZE CATTLE
PROBATE DUTY
PROBE DEEPLY

PROBLEM PLAY
PRODIGAL SON
PROM CONCERT
PROMISE WELL
PROMPT REPLY
PROOF READER
PROOF SPIRIT
PROPER PLACE
PROPER PRIDE
PROPER SENSE
PROPERTY TAX
PROS AND CONS
PROSE POETRY
PROTEIN DIET
PROUD FATHER
PROVE GUILTY
PRUSSIC ACID
PUBLIC ALARM
PUBLIC BATHS
PUBLIC ENEMY
PUBLIC FUNDS
PUBLIC HOUSE
PUBLIC IMAGE
PUBLIC MONEY
PUBLIC PURSE
PUBLIC TASTE
PUBLIC WORKS
PUBLIC WRONG
PUDDING FACE
PUDDING LANE
PUFF AND BLOW
PUFF OF SMOKE
PULL ASUNDER
PULL ONE'S LEG
PULL STRINGS
PULL THROUGH
PULL UP SHORT
PUMICE STONE
PUPPET STATE
PURCHASE TAX
PURE ALCOHOL
PURE ENGLISH
PURE FICTION
PURE IN HEART
PURE MOTIVES
PURE SCIENCE
PURL OR PLAIN
PURPLE HEART
PURPLE PATCH
PURSE OF GOLD
PUSH AND PULL

PUSH FORWARD
PUSH THROUGH
PUSS IN BOOTS
PUT A SPOKE IN
PUT IN A CLAIM
PUT IN CHARGE
PUT IN DANGER
PUT IN LIGHTS
PUT IN MOTION
PUT IN OFFICE
PUT IN PRISON
PUT IN THE WAY
PUT INTO CODE
PUT INTO TYPE
PUT IT MILDLY
PUT ON A SPURT
PUT ON A STUNT
PUT ONE'S CASE
PUT ON PAROLE
PUT ON RECORD
PUT ON THE MAP
PUT ON WEIGHT
PUT OUT TO SEA
PUT STRAIGHT
PUT THE LID ON
PUT TO FLIGHT
PUT TOGETHER
PUT TO RANSOM
PUT TO RIGHTS
PUTT THE SHOT
PUT UP A BLACK
PUT UP A BLUFF
PUT-UP AFFAIR
PUT UP A FIGHT
PUT WISE TO IT
PUZZLE IT OUT
PYJAMA PARTY

Q—11
QUACK DOCTOR
QUACK REMEDY
QUART BOTTLE
QUARTER DECK
QUARTER LEFT
QUARTER MILE
QUART OF BEER
QUARTO PAPER
QUEEN MOTHER
QUEEN SALOTE
QUEEN'S BENCH
QUEEN'S COURT

QUEER PERSON
QUEER STREET
QUICK ANSWER
QUICK FREEZE
QUICK GLANCE
QUICK GROWTH
QUICK PROFIT
QUICK RETURN
QUICK TEMPER
QUICK TONGUE
QUICK WORKER
QUIET DREAMS
QUIETEN DOWN
QUIET PLEASE!
QUITE AT HOME
QUITE ENOUGH
QUITE LIKELY
QUIT THE RING
QUOTED PRICE

R—11
RABBIT PUNCH
RABBIT'S FOOT
RACE HISTORY
RACE MEETING
RACE PROBLEM
RACE SUICIDE
RACIAL PRIDE
RACING EIGHT
RACING MODEL
RACING SLANG
RACING WORLD
RACING YACHT
RACK AND RUIN
RACY FLAVOUR
RADAR SCREEN
RADIANT HEAT
RADIATE LOVE
RADICAL CURE
RADICAL IDEA
RADICAL SIGN
RADIO BEACON
RADIO SIGNAL
RAGGED ROBIN
RAGTIME ARMY
RAGTIME BAND
RAILWAY ARCH
RAILWAY LINE
RAINBOW'S END
RAIN OF BLOWS
RAIN OR SHINE

RAINY SEASON
RAISE A CHEER
RAISE A LAUGH
RAISE A STORM
RAISED VOICE
RAISE MORALE
RAISE ON HIGH
RAISE PRICES
RAISE THE BID
RAISE THE HEM
RAISON D'ÊTRE
RALLY AROUND
RALLYING CRY
RAMBLER ROSE
RANGING SHOT
RANK AND FILE
RANSOM MONEY
RANT AND RAVE
RAPID CHANGE
RAPID EFFECT
RAPID GLANCE
RAPID GROWTH
RAPID MOTION
RAPID SPEECH
RARE EXAMPLE
RARE QUALITY
RASH PROMISE
RATTLE ALONG
RAW MATERIAL
REACH BOTTOM
REACH SAFETY
REACH THE END
REACH THE TOP
READ A SPEECH
READING DESK
READING GAOL
READING LAMP
READING LIST
READING ROOM
READ THE WILL
READ THROUGH
READY ACCESS
READY ANSWER
READY ENOUGH
READY FOR BED
READY FOR USE
READY RETORT
READY TO DROP
READY TO HAND
READY TONGUE
READY TO WEAR

READY WORKER
REAM OF PAPER
REAP A PROFIT
REAPING HOOK
REAR ADMIRAL
REBECCA WEST
REBEL ATTACK
REBEL LEADER
RECEIPT BOOK
RECEIVE NEWS
RECENT ISSUE
RECENT TIMES
RECORD ALBUM
RECORD CROWD
RECORD ENTRY
RECORD SCORE
RECORD TOKEN
RED AND BLACK
RED AND GREEN
RED AND WHITE
RED BURGUNDY
RED-HOT COALS
RED-HOT POKER
RED MAHOGANY
RED, RED ROBIN
RED SQUIRREL
RED TRIANGLE
REDUCED FARE
REDUCED RATE
REDUCE SPEED
REFINED GOLD
REFLEX LIGHT
REFUGEE CAMP
REFUSE A GIFT
REFUSE TO ACT
REFUSE TO MIX
REFUSE TO PAY
REGATTA WEEK
REGENCY BUCK
REGENT'S PARK
REGULAR ARMY
REGULAR HERO
REGULAR LIFE
REGULAR VERB
REGULAR WORK
RELEASE DATE
RELIEF FORCE
RELIEF PARTY
REMAIN ALOOF
REMAIN AWAKE
REMNANT SALE

REMOTE CAUSE
RENEW A LEASE
RENEWED HOPE
RENTAL VALUE
RENT ASUNDER
RENT CONTROL
REPORT STAGE
REQUEST ITEM
REQUEST NOTE
REQUEST STOP
REQUIEM MASS
RESCUE FORCE
RESCUE PARTY
RESCUE SQUAD
RESERVE FUND
RESERVE TEAM
REST ASSURED
REST CONTENT
REST IN PEACE
RETAIL PRICE
RETAIL TRADE
RETIRED LIFE
RETIRED LIST
RETIRE TO BED
RETIRING AGE
RETURN A BLOW
RETURN FIGHT
RETURN MATCH
RETURN VISIT
REVERSE GEAR
REVERSE SIDE
REVISED COPY
REX HARRISON
RHODE ISLAND
RHUBARB TART
RHYMED VERSE
RICE PUDDING
RICH HARVEST
RICH HUSBAND
RICH IN IDEAS
RIDE A TANDEM
RIDING BOOTS
RIDING HABIT
RIGGED TRIAL
RIGHT AMOUNT
RIGHT ANSWER
RIGHT AS RAIN
RIGHT A WRONG
RIGHT INSIDE
RIGHT MOMENT
RIGHT NUMBER

RIGHT PEOPLE
RIGHT SIDE UP
RIGHTS OF MAN
RIGHT TO VOTE
RIGHT WINGER
RIGHT YOU ARE
RIGOR MORTIS
RINGING TONE
RING OF ROSES
RING OF TRUTH
RING THE BELL
RIOT OF SOUND
RISE AGAINST
RISE AND FALL
RISE IN PRICE
RISE TO A PEAK
RISE TO POWER
RISE TO SPEAK
RISING COSTS
RISING SALES
RITUAL DANCE
RIVER DANUBE
RIVER GANGES
RIVER JORDAN
RIVER LAUNCH
RIVER MEDWAY
RIVER MERSEY
RIVER OF LAVA
RIVER PATROL
RIVER POLICE
RIVER SEVERN
RIVER THAMES
RIVER TRAVEL
ROAD HAULAGE
ROAD REPAIRS
ROADSIDE INN
ROAD SURFACE
ROAD SWEEPER
ROAD TRAFFIC
ROARING FIRE
ROAR OF ANGER
ROASTING HOT
ROAST MUTTON
ROAST POTATO
ROAST TURKEY
ROBBER BARON
ROBE OF STATE
ROBERT BRUCE
ROBERT BURNS
ROBERT CLIVE
ROBERT DONAT

ROCK AND ROLL
ROCKET RANGE
ROCK THE BOAT
ROCK TO SLEEP
ROD IN PICKLE
ROES ON TOAST
ROLLER BLIND
ROLLER TOWEL
ROLLING GAIT
ROLLING HOME
ROLLING ROAD
ROLL INTO ONE
ROLL OF DRUMS
ROLL OF PAPER
ROLL THE LAWN
ROLL-TOP DESK
ROMAN CANDLE
ROMAN CHURCH
ROMAN EMPIRE
ROMANTIC ART
ROMNEY MARSH
ROOKERY NOOK
ROOM SERVICE
ROSES ARE RED
ROSY OUTLOOK
ROSY PICTURE
ROTARY PRESS
ROTARY VALVE
ROTTEN APPLE
ROUGE ET NOIR
ROUGH GROUND
ROUGH MANNER
ROUGH SCHEME
ROUGH SKETCH
ROUGH TONGUE
ROUND CHEEKS
ROUND FIGURE
ROUND LETTER
ROUND NUMBER
ROUND OBJECT
ROUND OF BEEF
ROUND OF FIRE
ROUND OF GOLF
ROUSING SONG
ROW OF HOUSES
ROW OF MEDALS
ROWS AND ROWS
ROWTON HOUSE
ROYAL ASSENT
ROYAL CIRCLE
ROYAL FAMILY

ROYAL MARINE
ROYAL OCTAVO
ROYAL PALACE
ROYAL PARDON
ROYAL PURPLE
ROYAL SALUTE
RUBBER GLOVE
RUBBER HEELS
RUBBER PLANT
RUBBER SOLES
RUBBER STAMP
RUBBISH DUMP
RUBBISH HEAP
RUB TOGETHER
RUBY WEDDING
RUDDY CHEEKS
RUDE GESTURE
RUGBY LEAGUE
RUGBY SCHOOL
RUGBY TACKLE
RUGGER FIELD
RUGGER MATCH
RUGGER PITCH
RUGGER SCRUM
RUINED HOUSE
RUIN ONESELF
RULE OF FORCE
RULE OF MIGHT
RULE OF THREE
RULE OF THUMB
RULING CLASS
RULING PARTY
RULING POWER
RULING PRICE
RUM CUSTOMER
RUMMAGE SALE
RUMOUR HAS IT
RUN A MAN DOWN
RUN AN ERRAND
RUN FOR COVER
RUN FOR MAYOR
RUN INTO DEBT
RUN INTO FORM
RUN INTO PORT
RUN MESSAGES
RUNNER BEANS
RUNNING AMOK
RUNNING COLD
RUNNING COST
RUNNING DOWN
RUNNING FIRE

RUNNING JUMP
RUNNING KNOT
RUNNING OVER
RUNNING RIOT
RUNNING WILD
RUN PARALLEL
RUN SMOOTHLY
RUN STRAIGHT
RUN TOGETHER
RUN UP A SCORE
RUSH FORWARD
RUSH THROUGH
RUSSIAN BATH
RUSSIAN EGGS

S—11
SABRINA FAIR
SACK OF FLOUR
SACRED HEART
SACRED MUSIC
SACRED TRUST
SAD FAREWELL
SADLY MISSED
SAD TO RELATE
SAFE AND SURE
SAFE AND WELL
SAFE BREAKER
SAFE COMPANY
SAFE CONDUCT
SAFE CUSTODY
SAFE DEPOSIT
SAFE JOURNEY
SAFE KEEPING
SAFE LANDING
SAFE RETREAT
SAFETY CATCH
SAFETY FIRST
SAFETY MATCH
SAFETY RAZOR
SAFETY STRAP
SAFETY VALVE
SAFFRON CAKE
SAGO PUDDING
SAILING BOAT
SAILING CLUB
SAILING DATE
SAILING SHIP
SAILING TIME
SAILOR'S HOME
SAILOR'S KNOT
SAINT GEORGE

SAINT HELENA	SCOUT AROUND	SEEK A WAY OUT
SAINT HELIER	SCOUT MASTER	SEE NEXT WEEK
SALMON STEAK	SCRAP DEALER	SEE STRAIGHT
SALMON TROUT	SCRAPE ALONG	SEE THE LIGHT
SAL VOLATILE	SCRAPPY MEAL	SEE THE POINT
SAME FOOTING	SCRATCH CREW	SEE THE TRUTH
SAME MEANING	SCRATCH RACE	SEE THE WORLD
SAME OLD GAME	SCRATCH SIDE	SEETHING MOB
SAME PATTERN	SCRATCH TEAM	SELF CONTROL
SAMUEL PEPYS	SCRATCHY PEN	SELF-MADE MAN
SANCHO PANZA	SEA ELEPHANT	SELL AT A LOSS
SANDOWN PARK	SEA FRONTAGE	SELLING LINE
SANDS OF TIME	SEAM BOWLING	SELLING RACE
SANDWICH BAR	SEARCH PARTY	SELL THE PASS
SAPPHIRE SEA	SEASIDE TOWN	SELL TICKETS
SATANIC HOST	SEAT OF KINGS	SENATE HOUSE
SATIN FINISH	SEAT OF POWER	SEND A LETTER
SATIN STITCH	SEAT ONESELF	SEND AN ORDER
SAUCEPAN LID	SECOND CHILD	SEND A SIGNAL
SAUDI ARABIA	SECOND CLASS	SEND FOR A CAB
SAUSAGE MEAT	SECOND EVENT	SEND FOR HELP
SAUSAGE ROLL	SECOND FLOOR	SEND PACKING
SAVAGE BEAST	SECOND FRONT	SEND TO SLEEP
SAVAGE BRUTE	SECOND GRADE	SENILE DECAY
SAVAGE SCENE	SECOND GREEN	SENIOR PUPIL
SAVAGE TRIBE	SECOND HOUSE	SENSE OF DUTY
SAVE NOTHING	SECOND JOINT	SENSE OF LOSS
SAVE ONESELF	SECOND MONTH	SENSE OF PAIN
SAVE THE MARK	SECOND OF MAY	SENSIBLE BOY
SAVING GRACE	SECOND PARTY	SENSIBLE MAN
SAVINGS BANK	SECOND PLACE	SENT HAYWIRE
SAVOIR FAIRE	SECOND PRIZE	SENT PACKING
SAVOURY DISH	SECOND ROUND	SERIAL STORY
SCALDED MILK	SECOND SHIFT	SERIOUS BOOK
SCARED STIFF	SECOND SIGHT	SERIOUS LOOK
SCENT BOTTLE	SECONDS LATE	SERIOUS LOSS
SCENT DANGER	SECOND STAGE	SERIOUS MIND
SCENTED SOAP	SECOND TEETH	SERIOUS MOOD
SCILLY ISLES	SECOND VERSE	SERIOUS PLAY
SCHOOL BADGE	SECOND YOUTH	SERIOUS STEP
SCHOOL BOARD	SECRET AGENT	SERIOUS TALK
SCHOOL HOURS	SECRET ENEMY	SERIOUS VEIN
SCHOOL HOUSE	SECRET HAUNT	SERIOUS VIEW
SCHOOL OF ART	SECRET PLACE	SERVANT GIRL
SCHOOL TREAT	SECURED LOAN	SERVE A FAULT
SCORE A POINT	SECURE GRASP	SERVE NOTICE
SCORE FREELY	SEE A DENTIST	SERVICE FLAT
SCORE SLOWLY	SEE DAYLIGHT	SERVICE ROAD
SCOTCH BROTH	SEED OF DOUBT	SERVICE ROOM
SCOTS ACCENT	SEE EYE TO EYE	SERVING TIME
SCOTS GUARDS	SEE FAIR PLAY	SET AN AMBUSH

SET AND MATCH	SHARP CORNER	SHORT NOTICE
SET A PROBLEM	SHARP LESSON	SHORT OF CASH
SET AT NAUGHT	SHARP REBUFF	SHORT OF FOOD
SET IN MOTION	SHARP TEMPER	SHORT OF TIME
SET MOVEMENT	SHARP TONGUE	SHORT OF WORK
SET OF CHAIRS	SHARP TWINGE	SHORT PERIOD
SET OF STAMPS	SHAVEN CROWN	SHORT SHRIFT
SET ONE RIGHT	SHAVING SOAP	SHORT SPEECH
SET QUESTION	SHEAF OF CORN	SHORT STROLL
SET STANDARD	SHED THE LOAD	SHORT SUPPLY
SET STRAIGHT	SHEEP FARMER	SHORT TEMPER
SET THE ALARM	SHEER LUNACY	SHORT VOYAGE
SET THE FIELD	SHEER MURDER	SHORT WAY OFF
SET THE SCENE	SHEET ANCHOR	SHORT WEIGHT
SETTING FREE	SHEET COPPER	SHOT THROUGH
SETTLING DAY	SHERRY GLASS	SHOUT FOR JOY
SET TO RIGHTS	SHERRY PARTY	SHOUT HURRAH
SET UP A CLAIM	SHIFT WORKER	SHOW A PROFIT
SET UP IN TYPE	SHILLING TIP	SHOW COURAGE
SEVEN AND ONE	SHINING HOUR	SHOW FEELING
SEVEN AND SIX	SHIP OF STATE	SHOW NO FIGHT
SEVEN AND TEN	SHIP'S COURSE	SHOW NO MERCY
SEVEN AND TWO	SHIP'S DOCTOR	SHOW OF FORCE
SEVEN DWARFS	SHIP'S MASTER	SHOW OF HANDS
SEVEN HEARTS	SHIP'S PAPERS	SHOW ONE'S AGE
SEVEN MONTHS	SHIP'S PURSER	SHOW ONESELF
SEVEN NINTHS	SHIP'S STOKER	SHOW PROMISE
SEVEN O'CLOCK	SHOAL OF FISH	SHOW PROWESS
SEVEN OUNCES	SHOCK OF HAIR	SHOW RESPECT
SEVEN POINTS	SHOCK TROOPS	SHOW RESULTS
SEVEN POUNDS	SHODDY GOODS	SHOW THE FLAG
SEVEN SPADES	SHOE LEATHER	SHOW UP AGAIN
SEVEN TENTHS	SHOOTING BOX	SHOW WILLING
SEVENTH HOLE	SHOOTING WAR	SHREWD GUESS
SEVENTH PART	SHOOT TO KILL	SHRILL SOUND
SEVENTH RACE	SHOP COUNTER	SHRILL VOICE
SEVENTH TIME	SHOP DOORWAY	SHUN COMPANY
SEVEN TO FOUR	SHOP FOR SALE	SHUT THE DOOR
SEVERE FROST	SHOPPING BAG	SHUT THE GATE
SEVERE SHOCK	SHOP STEWARD	SIAMESE TWIN
SEVERE STYLE	SHORT AND FAT	SICK AT HEART
SEWING CLASS	SHORT ANSWER	SICK BENEFIT
SEXTON BLAKE	SHORTEN SAIL	SICKLY SMILE
SHABBY TRICK	SHORTEST BOY	SICK TO DEATH
SHAGGY BEARD	SHORTEST DAY	SIDE AGAINST
SHALLOW DISH	SHORTEST MAN	SIDE OF BACON
SHALLOW MIND	SHORTEST WAY	SIDE TURNING
SHAM ILLNESS	SHORT JACKET	SIDNEY JAMES
SHANKS'S PONY	SHORT LESSON	SIEGE OF TROY
SHARP ANSWER	SHORT LETTER	SIERRA LEONE
SHARP ATTACK	SHORT MEMORY	SIGNAL CORPS

SIGNAL LIGHT	SITTING DUCK	SLICE OF MEAT
SIGNS OF WEAR	SITTING ROOM	SLIDING DOOR
SILAS MARNER	SITTING SHOT	SLIDING ROOF
SILENT MIRTH	SIX AND A HALF	SLIDING SEAT
SILENT NIGHT	SIX AND EIGHT	SLIGHT DOUBT
SILLY ANSWER	SIX AND SEVEN	SLIGHT PAUSE
SILLY DONKEY	SIX AND THREE	SLIPPED DISC
SILLY DUFFER	SIX DIAMONDS	SLIPPER BATH
SILLY PERSON	SIX FEET TALL	SLIP OF A GIRL
SILLY REMARK	SIX FURLONGS	SLIP OF PAPER
SILLY SEASON	SIX NO-TRUMPS	SLIP THROUGH
SILVER BIRCH	SIX OF HEARTS	SLOPING DESK
SILVER MEDAL	SIX OF SPADES	SLOPING EDGE
SILVER MONEY	SIX OF TRUMPS	SLOPING FACE
SILVER PAPER	SIXPENNY TIP	SLOPING ROOF
SILVER PLATE	SIX SEVENTHS	SLOPING TYPE
SILVER SPOON	SIXTH LETTER	SLOPPY SMILE
SILVERY MOON	SIXTH OF JULY	SLOT MACHINE
SILVERY TONE	SIXTH OF JUNE	SLOUCH ALONG
SIMNEL BREAD	SIX THOUSAND	SLOW AND SURE
SIMPLE HEART	SIXTH STOREY	SLOW BOWLING
SIMPLE SIMON	SIXTH VOLUME	SLOW BUT SURE
SIMPLE SOUND	SKATING RINK	SLOW DECLINE
SIMPLE STYLE	SKEIN OF WOOL	SLOW DEGREES
SIMPLE TASTE	SKELETON KEY	SLOW FOXTROT
SIMPLE TRUTH	SKETCHY MEAL	SLOW PROCESS
SIMPLON PASS	SKILLED WORK	SLOW STARTER
SIMPLY AWFUL	SKIMMED MILK	SLOW TO ANGER
SINEWS OF WAR	SKIM THROUGH	SLOW TO LEARN
SINGING BIRD	SKIN AND BONE	SLUM DWELLER
SINGING FOOL	SKIN DISEASE	SMALL AMOUNT
SINGLE BERTH	SKIN MASSAGE	SMALL BITTER
SINGLE ENTRY	SKYE TERRIER	SMALL CHANCE
SINGLE HEART	SLAB OF STONE	SMALL CHANGE
SINGLE PIECE	SLACK MARKET	SMALL CHARGE
SINGLE STATE	SLACK SEASON	SMALL CIRCLE
SINGLE TRACK	SLADE SCHOOL	SMALL FAMILY
SINGLE VOICE	SLAM THE DOOR	SMALL FARMER
SINGLE WOMAN	SLATE PENCIL	SMALL INCOME
SINKING FAST	SLAVE LABOUR	SMALL LETTER
SINKING FUND	SLAVE MARKET	SMALL MATTER
SINKING SHIP	SLAVE TO DUTY	SMALL NUMBER
SINK THE BOAT	SLEEP DOUBLE	SMALL PROFIT
SIP OF BRANDY	SLEEPING BAG	SMALL SALARY
SIR JOHN HUNT	SLEEPING CAR	SMALL SCOTCH
SIR LANCELOT	SLEEPING DOG	SMALL SHERRY
SISTER SHIPS	SLEIGH BELLS	SMALL VESSEL
SISTER SUSIE	SLENDER HOPE	SMALL WHISKY
SIT-DOWN MEAL	SLICED BREAD	SMART DEVICE
SITTING BULL	SLICE OF CAKE	SMART PEOPLE
SITTING DOWN	SLICE OF LUCK	SMART PERSON

SMART RETORT
SMART SAYING
SMART TALKER
SMELL DANGER
SMILE PLEASE
SMOKE A CIGAR
SMOKED GLASS
SMOKED TROUT
SMOKE SCREEN
SMOKE SIGNAL
SMOKING ROOM
SMOOTH AS ICE
SMOOTH WATER
SNAKE POISON
SNAKES ALIVE!
SNAP OUT OF IT
SNATCH A KISS
SNOWED UNDER
SNOW LEOPARD
SOB BITTERLY
SOBER COLOUR
SOBER PERSON
SOCCER MATCH
SOCIAL CLASS
SOCIAL GROUP
SOCIAL PARTY
SOCIAL ROUND
SOCIAL SCALE
SOCIAL WHIRL
SOCIETY LADY
SOCIETY NEWS
SOCIETY PAGE
SODA AND MILK
SO FAR, SO GOOD
SOFT AND RIPE
SOFT OUTLINE
SOILED GOODS
SOILED LINEN
SOIL EROSION
SOLAR PLEXUS
SOLAR SYSTEM
SOLD FOR A PUP
SOLDIER KING
SOLDIER'S KIT
SOLDIER'S PAY
SOLE AND HEEL
SOLE COMFORT
SOLEMN MUSIC
SOLEMN TRUTH
SOLE SUPPORT
SOLID FIGURE

SOLID GROUND
SOLID MATTER
SOLID SILVER
SOLITARY MAN
SOLWAY FIRTH
SOMEONE ELSE
SOME TIME AGO
SONG CONTEST
SONG OF SONGS
SONG RECITAL
SONNY LISTON
SOPHIA LOREN
SORDID STORY
SORELY TRIED
SORE PRESSED
SORE SUBJECT
SORRY FIGURE
SORRY PLIGHT
SOUND ADVICE
SOUND ASLEEP
SOUND CREDIT
SOUND IN MIND
SOUND PLAYER
SOUND POLICY
SOUND REASON
SOUP KITCHEN
SOUTH AFRICA
SOUTH BY EAST
SOUTH BY WEST
SOUTH DAKOTA
SOUTH EALING
SOUTH HARROW
SOUTH LONDON
SOUTH MOLTON
SOUTH RIDING
SOVIET UNION
SPACE FLIGHT
SPACE OF TIME
SPACE TRAVEL
SPADE GUINEA
SPANISH GOLD
SPANISH MAIN
SPANISH TOWN
SPANISH WINE
SPARE A PENNY
SPARE THE ROD
SPARK OF LIFE
SPARTAN FARE
SPARTAN LIFE
SPATE OF NEWS
SPEAK FIRMLY

SPEAK FREELY
SPEAK FRENCH
SPEAK GERMAN
SPEAK NO EVIL
SPEAK OPENLY
SPEAK POLISH
SPEAK SLOWLY
SPEAK SOFTLY
SPECIAL CASE
SPECIAL DIET
SPECIAL DUTY
SPECIAL GIFT
SPECIAL JURY
SPECIAL LINE
SPECIAL NOTE
SPECK OF DUST
SPEED MANIAC
SPEED RECORD
SPEED TRIALS
SPELL DANGER
SPELLING BEE
SPELL OF DUTY
SPELL OF WORK
SPEND FREELY
SPICE OF LIFE
SPIKED SHOES
SPINNING TOP
SPIRIT LEVEL
SPLIT SECOND
SPOILS OF WAR
SPOILT CHILD
SPOIL THE FUN
SPORTING DOG
SPORTING GUN
SPORTING MAN
SPORTS ARENA
SPORTS MODEL
SPORTS SHIRT
SPOTTED DICK
SPOT THE BALL
SPREAD GLOOM
SPRING A LEAK
SPRING APART
SPRING A TRAP
SPRING FEVER
SPRING ONION
SPRING VALVE
SPRING WATER
SPROUT WINGS
SQUARE DANCE
SQUARE WORLD

SQUASH COURT	ST. AUGUSTINE	STOCK LETTER
SQUEEZE PLAY	STAY INDOORS	STOCK MARKET
SQUIRE'S LADY	STAY IN SIGHT	STOCK PHRASE
STACK OF COAL	STAY NEUTRAL	STOLE A MARCH
STACK OF WORK	STAY OUTSIDE	STOLEN FRUIT
STAFF OF LIFE	STAY THE PACE	STOLEN GOODS
STAGE EFFECT	STAY TOO LONG	STONE QUARRY
STAGE FRIGHT	ST. DAVID'S DAY	STONE'S THROW
STAGE MAKE-UP	STEADY FLAME	STONY GROUND
STAGE PLAYER	STEADY LIGHT	STOP A BULLET
STAGE STRUCK	STEADY PULSE	STOP BURNING
STAIR CARPET	STEADY TREND	STOP OUTSIDE
STAKE A CLAIM	STEAL A MARCH	STOP PAYMENT
STALK ABROAD	STEAMED FISH	STOP SMOKING
STALKY AND CO.	STEAM ENGINE	STOP TALKING
STAMP DEALER	STEAMING HOT	STOP TEASING
STAND A DRINK	STEAM LAUNCH	STOP THE FLOW
STAND AGHAST	STEEL GIRDER	STOP TO THINK
STANDARD ONE	STEEL HELMET	STOP WORKING
STAND A ROUND	ST. ELMO'S FIRE	STORE OF NUTS
STAND AROUND	STEM THE TIDE	STORM CENTRE
STAND AT EASE	STEM TO STERN	STORM CLOUDS
STAND IN FEAR	STEP FORWARD	STORM SIGNAL
STAND IN LINE	STEP OUTSIDE	STORM TROOPS
STAND IN NEED	STEP THIS WAY	STORMY NIGHT
STAND OR FALL	STERILE LAND	STORMY SCENE
STAND SQUARE	STERN REBUKE	STORY WRITER
STAND TO GAIN	STEWED FRUIT	STOUT CORTEZ
STAND TO LOSE	STEWED PEARS	STOUT EFFORT
STAR CHAMBER	STICK IN A RUT	STOUT FELLOW
STARCHY FOOD	STICK OF ROCK	STRAIGHT BAT
STAR CLUSTER	STICKY LABEL	STRAIGHT HIT
STAR OF DAVID	STICKY PAPER	STRAIGHT MAN
STAR OF INDIA	STICKY STUFF	STRAIGHT OFF
STAR QUALITY	STIFF BREEZE	STRAIGHT OUT
STARRY NIGHT	STIFF COLOUR	STRAIGHT RUN
STAR STUDDED	STIFLE A YAWN	STRAIGHT SET
START A FIGHT	STILL HOPING	STRAIGHT TIP
START AFRESH	STILL TO COME	STRAIGHT WIN
STARTER'S GUN	STILL TONGUE	STRANGE LAND
START SAVING	STILL WATERS	STRAY BULLET
STATE A CLAIM	STILL WITH IT	STRAY REMARK
STATED TERMS	STIR A FINGER	STREAM FORTH
STATELY HOME	STIR ONE'S TEA	STREET CRIES
STATE OF FLUX	STIRRUP PUMP	STREET LEVEL
STATE OF MIND	STIR THE FIRE	STREET OF INK
STATE PRISON	ST. JOHN'S WOOD	STREET SCENE
STATE SCHOOL	ST. MARGARET'S	STRICT ORDER
STATE SECRET	STOCK ANSWER	STRICT TEMPO
STATUTE BOOK	STOCK EXCUSE	STRICT TRUTH
STATUTE MILE	STOCK IN HAND	STRIDE ALONG

STRIKE A BLOW	SUMMIT LEVEL	SWIVEL CHAIR
STRIKE A NOTE	SUMMIT TALKS	SWOLLEN HEAD
STRIKE A POSE	SUM OF THINGS	SWORD IN HAND
STRIKE BLIND	SUNDAY HOURS	SWORD THRUST
STRIKE LUCKY	SUNDAY JOINT	SYDNEY SMITH
STRING ALONG	SUNDAY LUNCH	SYRUP OF FIGS
STRING BEANS	SUNDAY NIGHT	
STRING MUSIC	SUNDAY PAPER	**T—11**
STRIP OF LAND	SUNDAY TIMES	TABLE FOR TWO
STRIVE AFTER	SUNDRY ITEMS	TABLE TENNIS
STRONG DRINK	SUNK IN GLOOM	TACTICAL WAR
STRONG FAITH	SUNNY SIDE UP	TAINTED GOLD
STRONG LIGHT	SUNSET STRIP	TAKE A CENSUS
STRONG POINT	SUPERIOR AIR	TAKE A CHANCE
STRONG PULSE	SUPPER PARTY	TAKE A CORNER
STRONG SMELL	SUPPER TABLE	TAKE A COURSE
STRONG TASTE	SUPPORT LIFE	TAKE A CRUISE
STRONG VIEWS	SUPPLY DEPOT	TAKE A DEGREE
STRONG VOICE	SUPREME GOOD	TAKE A GANDER
STRONG WORDS	SURE FOOTING	TAKE A HEADER
STUB ONE'S TOE	SURFACE AREA	TAKE A LETTER
STUDENT BODY	SURFACE MAIL	TAKE AN OFFER
STUDENT DAYS	SURPLUS CASH	TAKE A NUMBER
STUDENTS' RAG	SURREY HILLS	TAKE A PLEDGE
STUDIO COUCH	SUSSEX DOWNS	TAKE A POWDER
STUFFED BIRD	SWALLOW DIVE	TAKE A STROLL
STUFFED FOWL	SWANEE RIVER	TAKE A TICKET
STUFF IT AWAY	SWANSEA TOWN	TAKE A TUMBLE
STUMBLE OVER	SWARM OF ANTS	TAKE A WICKET
STUMBLE UPON	SWARM OF BEES	TAKE BY FORCE
STUMP ORATOR	SWEAR AN OATH	TAKE BY STORM
STUNT FLYING	SWEAR ON OATH	TAKE CAPTIVE
STURDY FRAME	SWEDISH BATH	TAKE CHANCES
STURDY LIMBS	SWEENEY TODD	TAKE COMFORT
ST. VALENTINE	SWEET AND LOW	TAKE COMMAND
SUAVE MANNER	SWEET AS A NUT	TAKE COUNSEL
SUBLIME LIFE	SWEET DREAMS	TAKE COURAGE
SUCH AND SUCH	SWEET NATURE	TAKE LESSONS
SUDDEN BREAK	SWEET PICKLE	TAKE LIGHTLY
SUDDEN DEATH	SWEET POTATO	TAKE NO RISKS
SUDDEN SHOCK	SWEET SHERRY	TAKE OFFENCE
SUE FOR LIBEL	SWEET TEMPER	TAKE ON BOARD
SUE FOR PEACE	SWEET THINGS	TAKE ONE'S CUE
SUET PUDDING	SWELLED HEAD	TAKE ON TRUST
SUFFER A BLOW	SWIFT GLANCE	TAKE ON WATER
SUFFER A LOSS	SWIFT OF FOOT	TAKE-OVER BID
SUICIDE CLUB	SWISS CANTON	TAKE POT-LUCK
SUICIDE NOTE	SWISS CHALET	TAKE SHELTER
SUICIDE PACT	SWISS CHEESE	TAKE STOCK OF
SUIT OF CARDS	SWISS GUARDS	TAKE THE BAIT
SUMMER DRESS	SWISS RESORT	TAKE THE CAKE

TAKE THE HELM	TEA INTERVAL	TEST CRICKET
TAKE THE HINT	TEAM CAPTAIN	TESTING TIME
TAKE THE LEAD	TEA MERCHANT	TEST OF SKILL
TAKE THE LIFT	TEAM OF MULES	THAMES BASIN
TAKE THE OATH	TEAM SUPPORT	THANK HEAVEN!
TAKE THE VEIL	TEAR ASUNDER	THAT IS TO SAY
TAKE THOUGHT	TEARS OF PITY	THAT'S THE WAY
TAKE TIME OFF	TEARS OF RAGE	THAT'S TORN IT
TAKE TO COURT	TEA STRAINER	THE ALMIGHTY
TAKE TO DRINK	TEA WITH MILK	THE ALPHABET
TAKE TO HEART	TEDIOUS TASK	THE ATLANTIC
TAKE TOO MUCH	TEDIOUS WORK	THEATRE BILL
TAKE TROUBLE	TEEMING RAIN	THEATRE CLUB
TAKE UMBRAGE	TEEN-AGE CLUB	THEATRE LAND
TAKE UP A CASE	TEETH ON EDGE	THEATRE SEAT
TAKE WARNING	TELEGRAM BOY	THEATRE SHOW
TALENT MONEY	TELL AGAINST	THE AVENGERS
TALENT SCOUT	TELL NO TALES	THE BARBICAN
TALKING BIRD	TELL THE TALE	THE BASTILLE
TALKING DOLL	TELL THE TIME	THE BEREAVED
TALK OUT TIME	TEMPLE BELLS	THE BEST PART
TALK RUBBISH	TEMPUS FUGIT	THE BIG HOUSE
TALK TOO MUCH	TEN AND A HALF	THE BISMARCK
TALK TREASON	TEN AND EIGHT	THE BITER BIT
TALK TWADDLE	TEN AND SEVEN	THE BLUE LAMP
TALL AND SLIM	TEN AND THREE	THE BOAT RACE
TALLEST GIRL	TENDER HEART	THE CANARIES
TAMMANY HALL	TENDER MERCY	THE CENOTAPH
TAM O'SHANTER	TENDER STEAK	THE CHAMPION
TANK WARFARE	TENDER YEARS	THE CHEVIOTS
TAPE MACHINE	TEND THE SICK	THE CLASSICS
TAP ONE'S FEET	TENNIS COURT	THE COLONIES
TAP ONE'S FOOT	TENNIS DRESS	THE CONQUEST
TAP THE WIRES	TENNIS ELBOW	THE CREATION
TARRY AWHILE	TENNIS MATCH	THE CRUEL SEA
TARTAN PLAID	TEN OF HEARTS	THE CRUSADES
TARTAN SHIRT	TEN OF SPADES	THE DAY AFTER
TARTAN SKIRT	TEN OF TRUMPS	THE EIGHTIES
TARTAN SOCKS	TEN OR ELEVEN	THE ELEMENTS
TASTY MORSEL	TENSE MOMENT	THE FAITHFUL
TATE GALLERY	TENTH LETTER	THE FINE ARTS
TAX INCREASE	TENTH OF JULY	THE FIRST TWO
TEA AND CAKES	TENTH OF JUNE	THE FUGITIVE
TEA AND TOAST	TEN THOUSAND	THE GAME IS UP
TEA CANISTER	TENTH STOREY	THE GREATEST
TEACHER'S PET	TENTH VOLUME	THE GREAT WAR
TEACH SCHOOL	TERM OF ABUSE	THE GREEN MAN
TEACH TO READ	TERM OF YEARS	THE GOLD RUSH
TEACH TO RIDE	TERRY THOMAS	THE GOOD BOOK
TEACH TO SWIM	TERSE SPEECH	THE HAVE-NOTS
TEA FOR THREE	TESSIE O'SHEA	THE HEBRIDES

THE HIGH SEAS	THE PROPHETS	THIRD STROKE
THE HOLY CITY	THE PYRAMIDS	THIRD VOLUME
THE HOLY LAND	THE PYRENEES	THIRST AFTER
THE HUNT IS UP	THE REVEREND	THIRSTY WORK
THE HUSTINGS	THERMAL UNIT	THIRTY FORTY
THE INFINITE	THE SERVICES	THIRTY MILES
THE INKSPOTS	THE SKIN GAME	THIRTY TIMES
THE INNER MAN	THE SORBONNE	THIRTY YEARS
THE INNOCENT	THESPIAN ART	THIS AND THAT
THE INTERIOR	THE SQUEAKER	THIS CENTURY
THE JUNGFRAU	THE SUPREMES	THIS DAY WEEK
THE KATTEGAT	THE TAJ MAHAL	THIS ENGLAND
THE KING AND I	THE TALISMAN	THIS INSTANT
THE LAST GASP	THE THIRD MAN	THIS MORNING
THE LAST PAGE	THE THIRTIES	THIS TUESDAY
THE LAST POST	THE TWENTIES	THOMAS HARDY
THE LAST WORD	THE TREASURY	THRASH IT OUT
THE LIBERALS	THE UNIVERSE	THREAD BEADS
THE LISTENER	THE VERY FACT	THREAT OF WAR
THE LOVED ONE	THE VERY SAME	THREE AND ONE
THE LOWLANDS	THE VERY SPOT	THREE AND SIX
THE LUCY SHOW	THE WALL GAME	THREE AND TEN
THE LUDDITES	THE WAXWORKS	THREE AND TWO
THE MAJORITY	THE WELL-TO-DO	THREE A PENNY
THE MARATHON	THE WHOLE HOG	THREE CHEERS
THE MIDLANDS	THE WHOLE LOT	THREE COPIES
THE MILKY WAY	THE WILD DUCK	THREE DECKER
THE MIND'S EYE	THE WOOLSACK	THREE EIGHTS
THE MINISTRY	THICK SPEECH	THREE FIFTHS
THE MINORITY	THICK STRING	THREE GRACES
THE MOHICANS	THIEF OF TIME	THREE HEARTS
THE MONUMENT	THIN AS A LATH	THREE KNAVES
THE MOUNTIES	THIN AS A RAKE	THREE MONTHS
THE NAKED EYE	THINKING CAP	THREE O'CLOCK
THE NEAR EAST	THINK IT OVER	THREE OR FOUR
THE NEW WORLD	THINK MUCH OF	THREE OUNCES
THE NINETIES	THINK WELL OF	THREE POINTS
THE OBSERVER	THIN RED LINE	THREE POUNDS
THE OCCIDENT	THIRD CHOICE	THREE QUARTS
THE OLD FOLKS	THIRD COURSE	THREE QUEENS
THE OLD GUARD	THIRD DEGREE	THREE SEVENS
THE OLD WORLD	THIRD ESTATE	THREE SPADES
THE ONCE-OVER	THIRD FINGER	THREE TENTHS
THE OPEN ROAD	THIRD LEAGUE	THREE THREES
THE OTHER DAY	THIRD LESSON	THREE TRICKS
THE OTHER MAN	THIRD LETTER	THREE WHEELS
THE OTHER ONE	THIRD OF JULY	THREE WISHES
THE OTHER WAY	THIRD OF JUNE	THREE VERSES
THE PANTHEON	THIRD PERSON	THRESH ABOUT
THE PENNINES	THIRD SEASON	THROUGH ROAD
THE PENTAGON	THIRD STOREY	THROUGH TRIP

THROW A LIGHT	TOKEN OF LOVE	TOWN DWELLER
THROW A PARTY	TOLL THE BELL	TRADE SECRET
THROW A PUNCH	TOMATO JUICE	TRADING POST
THROW STONES	TOMATO SAUCE	TRAFFIC LANE
THRUST ASIDE	TOMMY ATKINS	TRAGIC EVENT
THUMPING LIE	TOMMY COOPER	TRAGIC IRONY
TICKLED PINK	TOMMY DORSEY	TRAGIC SCENE
TICKLE TROUT	TOMMY STEELE	TRAIL BEHIND
TICKLISH JOB	TOMMY TUCKER	TRAIL BLAZER
TIDAL WATERS	TONE CONTROL	TRAIL DRIVER
TIDE ONE OVER	TONE OF VOICE	TRAIL OF DUST
TIED COTTAGE	TON OF BRICKS	TRAIL OF SAND
TIED IN A KNOT	TO NO PURPOSE	TRAINED BAND
TIES OF BLOOD	TONS AND TONS	TRAMPLE DOWN
TIGHT CORNER	TONS OF MONEY	TRANSFER FEE
TILL THE SOIL	TONY HANCOCK	TRAVEL ABOUT
TIMBER TRADE	TOO FAMILIAR	TRAVEL AGENT
TIME AND TIDE	TOO MUCH ROOM	TRAVEL ALONG
TIME ELEMENT	TOP-BACK ROOM	TRAVEL LIGHT
TIME IS MONEY	TOPICAL NEWS	TREACLE TART
TIME MACHINE	TOP SERGEANT	TREAD SOFTLY
TIME OF NIGHT	TOP TO BOTTOM	TREAD WARILY
TIMES CHANGE	TORCH SINGER	TREE DWELLER
TIMES SQUARE	TORPEDO BOAT	TREE SURGERY
TIME TO GET UP	TORPEDO TUBE	TRENCH FEVER
TIME TO LEAVE	TOSS AND TURN	TRENT BRIDGE
TIME TO SPARE	TOTAL AMOUNT	TRIAL BY JURY
TIME TO START	TOTAL CHANGE	TRIAL FLIGHT
TIME TO THINK	TOTAL DEFEAT	TRIAL PERIOD
TIME TO WASTE	TOTAL NUMBER	TRIAL STAKES
TINKER'S CUSS	TOTAL OUTPUT	TRICK RIDING
TINKER'S DAMN	TO THE BOTTOM	TRIED BY JURY
TINNED BEANS	TO THE LETTER	TRIM THE HAIR
TINNED FRUIT	TO THE MINUTE	TRIM THE LAMP
TINNED GOODS	TO THE RESCUE	TRIM THE WICK
TINNED MUSIC	TO THE TUNE OF	TRINITY HALL
TINNED PEARS	TO THE UTMOST	TRINITY TERM
TIN OF POLISH	TOTTER ABOUT	TRIPLE CROWN
TIN OF SALMON	TOUCH BOTTOM	TRIPLE EVENT
TIN PAN ALLEY	TOUCH GROUND	TRIP LIGHTLY
TIN SOLDIERS	TOUCH TYPING	TRITE REMARK
TIP THE SCALE	TOUCH TYPIST	TRIUMPH OVER
TIRED OF LIFE	TOUGH AS TEAK	TRIVIAL LOSS
TISSUE PAPER	TOUR DE FORCE	TROJAN HORSE
TITLE HOLDER	TOUSLED HAIR	TROPICAL KIT
TOAST MASTER	TOUT DE SUITE	TROPICAL SEA
TOBACCO ROAD	TOUT LE MONDE	TROPICAL SUN
TOBOGGAN RUN	TOWER BRIDGE	TROUBLE FREE
TODDLE ALONG	TOWER OF PISA	TROUBLE SPOT
TOFFEE APPLE	TOWN AND GOWN	TROUT STREAM
TOILET WATER	TOWN COUNCIL	TRUCK DRIVER

TRUDGE ALONG	TWELVE YEARS	UNBROKEN RUN
TRUE ACCOUNT	TWENTY MILES	UNCALLED FOR
TRUE COLOURS	TWENTY TIMES	UNDER A CLOUD
TRUE EQUINOX	TWENTY TO ONE	UNDER A CURSE
TRUE PICTURE	TWENTY WEEKS	UNDER ARREST
TRUE READING	TWICE A MONTH	UNDER A SPELL
TRUE TO SCALE	TWICE AS MUCH	UNDER CANVAS
TRULY SPOKEN	TWICE AS NICE	UNDER DURESS
TRUMPET CALL	TWICE ELEVEN	UNDER NOTICE
TRUNDLE DOWN	TWICE THE MAN	UNDER ORDERS
TRUST TO LUCK	TWICE TWELVE	UNDER PAROLE
TRUSTY STEED	TWICE WEEKLY	UNDER REPAIR
TRUSTY SWORD	TWICE YEARLY	UNDER REVIEW
TRUTH TO TELL	TWIN BROTHER	UNDER STRAIN
TRYING TIMES	TWIN SISTERS	UNDER STRESS
TRY ONE'S BEST	TWIST AROUND	UNDER THE MAT
TRY ONE'S HAND	TWIST THE ARM	UNDER THE SEA
TRY ONE'S LUCK	TWO AND A HALF	UNDER THE SUN
TRY TO BE FAIR	TWO AND EIGHT	UNDER WEIGHT
TRY TO PLEASE	TWO AND SEVEN	UNDYING LOVE
TRY, TRY AGAIN	TWO AND THREE	UNEASY TRUCE
TUBE STATION	TWO DIAMONDS	UNFAIR MEANS
TUDOR PERIOD	TWO EXTREMES	UNFAIR PRICE
TUESDAY WEEK	TWO-FEET TALL	UNFIT FOR USE
TUFT OF GRASS	TWO-FOOT RULE	UNFOLD A TALE
TUITION FEES	TWO FURLONGS	UNHOLY NOISE
TURKISH BATH	TWO HUSBANDS	UNIFORM HEAT
TURN AGAINST	TWO NO-TRUMPS	UNIFORM SIZE
TURN CRIMSON	TWO OF A TRADE	UNION LEADER
TURN HOSTILE	TWO OF SPADES	UNITED FRONT
TURN OF SPEED	TWO OF TRUMPS	UNITED PRESS
TURN OUT WELL	TWO'S COMPANY	UNIT OF SOUND
TURN THE PAGE	TWO SEVENTHS	UNLAWFUL ACT
TURN THE TIDE	TWO THOUSAND	UNLICKED CUB
TURN TO ASHES	TYPE A LETTER	UNLUCKY STAR
TURN TO STONE	TYPICAL CASE	UNSHED TEARS
TURN TRAITOR	TYPING ERROR	UNSOUND MIND
TURN UPWARDS	TYPING SPEED	UNTIMELY END
TWEED JACKET	TYPISTS' POOL	UNUSUAL NAME
TWELFTH HOLE	TYROLEAN HAT	UP AGAINST IT
TWELFTH HOUR		UP AND COMING
TWELFTH PART	**U—11**	UP FOR THE CUP
TWELVE DOZEN	UGLY RUFFIAN	UP FOR THE DAY
TWELVE GROSS	UGLY SISTERS	UPHILL CLIMB
TWELVE HOURS	UGLY THOUGHT	UPHILL FIGHT
TWELVE MILES	UGLY WEATHER	UP ON A CHARGE
TWELVE PARTS	ULTIMATE END	UPPER CIRCLE
TWELVE PENCE	ULTIMA THULE	UPPER SCHOOL
TWELVE SCORE	ULTRA VIOLET	UPPER STOREY
TWELVE TIMES	UMBRELLA MAN	UPRIGHT POST
TWELVE WEEKS	UNABLE TO PAY	UPS AND DOWNS

UP THE REBELS!
UP THE STAIRS
UP THE STREET
UP THE THAMES
UP TO SCRATCH
UP TO THE EARS
UP TO THE EYES
UP TO THE HILT
UP TO THE MARK
UP TO THE NECK
UPWARD TREND
URSULA BLOOM
USELESS WORD
USE ONE'S EARS
USE ONE'S HEAD
USE ONE'S LOAF
USE ONE'S WITS
USE THE KNIFE
USE THE 'PHONE
USE THE PRESS
USE VIOLENCE
USUAL CUSTOM
UTMOST SPEED
UTTER BUNKUM
UTTER COWARD
UTTER DEFEAT
UTTER MISERY

V—11
VACANT HOUSE
VACANT STARE
VACUUM BRAKE
VACUUM FLASK
VAGRANCY ACT
VAIN ATTEMPT
VAL DOONICAN
VALE OF TEARS
VALID REASON
VALLEY FORGE
VANITY TABLE
VAPOUR TRAIL
VARIETY SHOW
VAST ACREAGE
VAST EXPANSE
VAST EXPENSE
VATICAN CITY
VAULTED ROOF
VELVET GLOVE
VELVET TREAD
VENETIAN RED
VENUS DI MILO

VERY PLEASED
VERY SPECIAL
VERY STRANGE
VERY WELL OFF
VERY WORRIED
VESTA TILLEY
V FOR VICTORY
VICAR OF BRAY
VICTORIA DAY
VICTORY ROLL
VICTORY SIGN
VIENNA WOODS
VILLAGE FÉTE
VILLAGE HALL
VILLAGE LIFE
VILLAGE POND
VILLAGE PUMP
VILLAGE SHOP
VILLAGE TALK
VILLAGE TEAM
VINTAGE PORT
VINTAGE WINE
VINTAGE YEAR
VIOLENT BLOW
VIOLENT RAGE
VIRGIN BIRTH
VIRGIN QUEEN
VIRILE STYLE
VISITING DAY
VITAL ENERGY
VITAMIN PILL
VIVID COLOUR
VIVID YELLOW
VIVIEN LEIGH
VOCAL CHORDS
VOCAL EFFORT
VOCAL NUMBER
VOCAL ORGANS
VOCAL TALENT
VOICE OF DOOM
VOID OF SENSE
VOLATILE OIL
VOLATILE WIT
VOLCANIC ASH
VOLUME THREE
VOTE AGAINST
VOTE BY PROXY
VOTE LIBERAL
VOTE TO ORDER
VOTING PAPER

W—11
WADDLE ALONG
WADE THROUGH
WAG ONE'S HEAD
WAGON WHEELS
WAILING WALL
WAIT A MINUTE
WAIT A MOMENT
WAIT A SECOND
WAIT AT TABLE
WAITING GAME
WAITING LIST
WAITING ROOM
WAKE THE DEAD
WAKE UP EARLY
WAKING DREAM
WAKING HOURS
WALK IN FRONT
WALKING PACE
WALKING RACE
WALKING TOUR
WALK OFF WITH
WALK OUT WITH
WALK QUICKLY
WALK TOWARDS
WALK UPRIGHT
WALL OF DEATH
WALL OF FLAME
WALLOW IN MUD
WALTER MITTY
WALTER SCOTT
WALT WHITMAN
WANDER ABOUT
WANDER ALONG
WANING LIGHT
WANT OF FAITH
WAR AND PEACE
WAR CRIMINAL
WARD OF COURT
WARD ORDERLY
WARM AS TOAST
WARM CLIMATE
WARM CLOTHES
WARM COUNTRY
WAR MEASURES
WAR MEMORIAL
WAR MINISTER
WARM WEATHER
WARM WELCOME
WAR NEUROSES
WARNING LOOK

WARNING NOTE
WARNING SHOT
WARNING SIGN
WAR OF NERVES
WARP AND WEFT
WARP AND WOOF
WASHING SOAP
WASHING SODA
WASTE GROUND
WASTE NO TIME
WASTE OF TIME
WATCHFUL EYE
WATCH POCKET
WATCH POINTS
WATER BABIES
WATER COLOUR
WATERED SILK
WATERLOO CUP
WATER OF LIFE
WATER PISTOL
WATER SKIING
WATER SPORTS
WATER SUPPLY
WATER TRAVEL
WATER VAPOUR
WATERY GRAVE
WAVE GOODBYE
WEAK AS WATER
WEAKEST LINK
WEAK LOOKING
WEAK SERVICE
WEAK STOMACH
WEALD OF KENT
WEAR AND TEAR
WEARY WILLIE
WEATHER SHIP
WEATHER SIDE
WEAVE A SPELL
WEAVE SPELLS
WEB OF DECEIT
WEDDED BLISS
WEDDING CAKE
WEDDING CARD
WEDDING HYMN
WEDDING RING
WEDDING VOWS
WEEKLY PAPER
WEEK'S NOTICE
WEIGH ANCHOR
WEIRD SISTER
WELCOME GIFT

WELCOME HOME
WELCOME SIGN
WELFARE WORK
WELL AND GOOD
WELL CONTENT
WELL GROOMED
WELL IN FRONT
WELL MATCHED
WELL OUT OF IT
WELL-READ MAN
WELL-TO-DO MAN
WELL WORTH IT
WELL WRITTEN
WELSH ACCENT
WELSH BORDER
WELSH COLLIE
WELSH GUARDS
WELSH LEGEND
WELSH RABBIT
WELSH WIZARD
WEND ONE'S WAY
WENDY HILLER
WENT FLAT OUT
WEST AFRICAN
WEST BY NORTH
WEST BY SOUTH
WEST CENTRAL
WEST COUNTRY
WESTERN ROLE
WESTERN ROLL
WEST GERMANY
WET ONE'S LIPS
WHACKING LIE
WHAT A RELIEF!
WHAT HAVE YOU
WHAT'S MY LINE?
WHAT YOU WILL
WHEEL OF LIFE
WHEN PIGS FLY
WHIPPING BOY
WHISTLE AWAY
WHISTLE STOP
WHITE AS MILK
WHITE AS SNOW
WHITE BISHOP
WHITE CASTLE
WHITE CIRCLE
WHITE CLIFFS
WHITE COFFEE
WHITE COLLAR
WHITE COTTON

WHITE ENSIGN
WHITE FRIARS
WHITE HORSES
WHITE KNIGHT
WHITE PEPPER
WHITE POWDER
WHITE RABBIT
WHITE RIBBON
WHITE RUSSIA
WHITE SQUARE
WHITE TO MOVE
WHITE TO PLAY
WHITSUN WEEK
WHITTLE AWAY
WHITTLE DOWN
WHO GOES HOME?
WHOLE NUMBER
WICKED FAIRY
WICKED UNCLE
WICKED WITCH
WICKED WORLD
WICKER CHAIR
WIDEN THE GAP
WIDE READING
WIDE VARIETY
WIDOW'S CRUSE
WIDOW'S WEEDS
WIELD THE BAT
WIGHTMAN CUP
WILD COUNTRY
WILD DELIGHT
WILD FLOWERS
WILFUL WASTE
WILLIAM PEAR
WILLIAM PENN
WILLIAM PITT
WILLIAM TELL
WILLING HAND
WILLING HELP
WILL OF ALLAH
WIN A FORTUNE
WINDING ROAD
WIND ONE'S WAY
WINDY CORNER
WINE AND DINE
WINE HARVEST
WINE VINEGAR
WINGED HORSE
WINGED WORDS
WING FORWARD
WING ONE'S WAY

WINK OF SLEEP	WITHOUT PITY	WRINGING WET
WINNING CARD	WITH RESERVE	WRITE A LYRIC
WINNING GAME	WITH RESPECT	WRITE A NOVEL
WINNING GOAL	WITH THE TIDE	WRITE A STORY
WINNING HAND	WITH THE WIND	WRITE IT DOWN
WINNING LEAD	WITTY REMARK	WRITE POETRY
WINNING LINE	WITTY RETORT	WRITING DESK
WINNING MOVE	WITTY SPEECH	WRITING ROOM
WINNING POST	WIZARD PRANG	WRITTEN WORD
WINNING SHOT	WOBURN ABBEY	WRONG ANSWER
WINNING SIDE	WOLF WHISTLE	WRONG CHANGE
WINNING TEAM	WOMAN DOCTOR	WRONG COURSE
WINNING TOSS	WOMAN DRIVER	WRONG MOMENT
WINNING WAYS	WOMAN'S WORLD	WRONG NUMBER
WIN ON POINTS	WOMEN POLICE	WRONG PERSON
WIN OUTRIGHT	WOMEN'S GUILD	WRONG TICKET
WINSOME WAYS	WOOD ALCOHOL	WROUGHT IRON
WINSON GREEN	WOODEN FRAME	
WINTER SLEEP	WOODEN HORSE	Y—11
WINTER WHEAT	WOODEN SPOON	YACHTING CAP
WIN THE FIGHT	WOOL SHEARER	YACHT RACING
WIN THE MATCH	WORD FOR WORD	YARD MEASURE
WIN THE POOLS	WORD OF MOUTH	YEAR AND A DAY
WIN THE TITLE	WORD PERFECT	YEAR OF GRACE
WIN THE TRICK	WORD PICTURE	YEARS GONE BY
WINTRY SMILE	WORDS FAIL ME!	YEARS TO COME
WIPE THE EYES	WORK AGAINST	YELLOW FEVER
WIRELESS SET	WORK AND PLAY	YELLOW METAL
WISDOM TOOTH	WORK AS A TEAM	YELLOW OCHRE
WISE AS AN OWL	WORKING LIFE	YELLOW PAINT
WISE AS SOLON	WORKING WEEK	YELLOW PERIL
WISE COUNSEL	WORKS OUTING	YELLOW PRESS
WISE OLD BIRD	WORK TO DEATH	YELLOW RIVER
WISHING WELL	WORK WONDERS	YELLOW SANDS
WITCH DOCTOR	WORLD BEATER	YELLOW SPOTS
WITCHES' BREW	WORLD CRUISE	YIELD A POINT
WITCH'S SPELL	WORLD EVENTS	YOLK OF AN EGG
WITH ABANDON	WORLDLY WISE	YORK MINSTER
WITH HONOURS	WORLD RECORD	YOU AND YOURS
WITHIN AN ACE	WORLDS APART	YOUNG AND OLD
WITHIN DOORS	WORLD TO COME	YOUNGEST BOY
WITHIN RANGE	WORLD-WAR ONE	YOUNGEST SON
WITHIN REACH	WORLD-WAR TWO	YOUNG MONKEY
WITHIN SIGHT	WORM ONE'S WAY	YOUNG PEOPLE
WITH KNOBS ON	WORRIED LOOK	YOUNG PERSON
WITH MEANING	WORSE TO COME	YOUNG RASCAL
WITHOUT BIAS	WORTH SEEING	YOUR MAJESTY
WITHOUT FAIL	WORTHY CAUSE	YOUR OPINION
WITHOUT HOPE	WRAPPED LOAF	YOURS ALWAYS
WITHOUT LOSS	WRESTLE WITH	YOUR VERSION
WITHOUT PEER	WRETCHED MAN	YOUR VERY OWN

YOUR WORSHIP
YOUTH CENTRE
YOUTH HOSTEL
YOUTH LEADER

A—12
ABBEY THEATRE
ABILITY TO MIX
ABJECT SPIRIT
ABLATIVE CASE
ABOUT AVERAGE
ABOVE AVERAGE
ABOVE THE LINE
ABRUPT MANNER
ABSOLUTE COLD
ABSOLUTE FACT
ABSOLUTE FOOL
ABSOLUTE RULE
ABSOLUTE ZERO
ABSTRACT IDEA
ABSTRACT NOUN
ABSTRACT TERM
ABSURD MANNER
ABUSE THE MIND
ACADEMY AWARD
ACCEPT ADVICE
ACCEPT DEFEAT
ACCEPT IN TOTO
ACCEPT OFFICE
ACCIDENT SPOT
ACE IN THE HOLE
ACHILLES' HEEL
ACROSS THE SKY
ACROSS THE WAY
ACT FOOLISHLY
ACT IN CONCERT
ACTION SCHOOL
ACTIVE MEMBER
ACT LIKE A FOOL
ACT LIKE MAGIC
ACT OF CHARITY
ACT OF COURAGE
ACT OF TREASON
ACT OF WORSHIP
ACT ON IMPULSE
ACTOR MANAGER
ADAGIO DANCER
ADD A FEW WORDS
ADDER'S TONGUE
ADDITION SIGN
ADD TO THE LIST

ADELINA PATTI
ADHESIVE TAPE
ADJUTANT BIRD
ADMIT NOTHING
ADMIT ONE'S AGE
ADMITTED FACT
ADMITTED FREE
ADOLPH HITLER
ADOPTED CHILD
ADVANCED IDEA
ADVANCE GUARD
ADVANCE PARTY
AERATED WATER
AERIAL SURVEY
AESOP'S FABLES
AFFECTED AIRS
A FINE ROMANCE
AFRICAN QUEEN
AFTERNOON NAP
AFTERNOON TEA
AFTER SUNDOWN
AFTER THE BALL
AFTER THE FACT
AFTER THE RAIN
AGE OF CONSENT
AGREED RESULT
AGREE TO TERMS
AIM AT THE MOON
AIR COMMODORE
AIR-FORCE BLUE
AIR OF MYSTERY
AIR OF TRIUMPH
AIR ONE'S VIEWS
AIR PASSENGER
AIR PERSONNEL
AIR-SEA RESCUE
AIR TRANSPORT
AIR TRAVELLER
ALADDIN'S CAVE
ALADDIN'S LAMP
ALAN MELVILLE
ALAS AND ALACK!
ALBERT BRIDGE
ALBERT FINNEY
ALDOUS HUXLEY
ALEC GUINNESS
ALEXANDRA DAY
ALFRESCO MEAL
ALGERIAN WINE
ALICE SPRINGS
ALIEN ELEMENT

ALIGN ONESELF
ALL AND SUNDRY
ALL ATTENTION
ALL BY ONESELF
ALLIED FORCES
ALLIED TROOPS
ALL IN THE GAME
ALL IN THE MIND
ALL IS NOT LOST
ALL MOONSHINE
ALL MY OWN WORK
ALL NIGHT LONG
ALL OF A DITHER
ALL OF A QUIVER
ALL OF A SUDDEN
ALL OF THE TIME
ALL ON ONE SIDE
ALL ON ONE'S OWN
ALL OR NOTHING
ALLOTTED SPAN
ALLOTTED TASK
ALLOW TO STAND
ALL SAINTS' DAY
ALL STEAMED UP
ALL THE BETTER
ALL THE FAMILY
ALL THE OTHERS
ALL TO PLAY FOR
ALL TO THE GOOD
ALMOND TOFFEE
A LONG TIME AGO
ALPACA JACKET
ALPHA TO OMEGA
ALPINE FLOWER
ALPINE GARDEN
ALTER THE CASE
AMATEUR ACTOR
AMATEUR BOXER
AMATEUR STAGE
AMERICAN FILM
AMERICAN FLAG
AMERICAN NAVY
A MILE A MINUTE
AMONG FRIENDS
AMOROUS DITTY
AMUSE ONESELF
ANCHOVY PASTE
ANCHOVY SAUCE
ANCIENT HOUSE
ANCIENT ROMAN
ANCIENT RUINS

ANCIENT TIMES	ARCTIC WINTER	AS SURE AS FATE
ANCIENT WORLD	ARDENT SPIRIT	AS SWEET AS PIE
ANEURIN BEVAN	ARGUE THE CASE	AS UNDERSTOOD
ANGELIC SMILE	ARGUE THE TOSS	AT A LATER DATE
ANGEL OF DEATH	ARMED ROBBERY	AT ALL HAZARDS
ANGEL OF MERCY	ARMISTICE DAY	AT ARM'S LENGTH
ANGELS OF MONS	ARMY CHAPLAIN	AT CLOSE GRIPS
ANGORA RABBIT	ARMY EXERCISE	AT DEATH'S DOOR
ANGRY SILENCE	ARMY GRATUITY	AT FIRST SIGHT
ANIMAL DOCTOR	ARMY PAY CORPS	AT FULL GALLOP
ANNA KARENINA	ARMY QUARTERS	AT FULL LENGTH
ANNE HATHAWAY	ARNOLD WESKER	ATHLETE'S FOOT
ANNE OF CLEVES	ARRANGE A DATE	ATLANTIC CITY
ANNUAL AFFAIR	ARRESTER GEAR	ATOMIC ENERGY
ANNUAL BUDGET	ARRIVE ON TIME	ATOMIC NUMBER
ANNUAL DINNER	ART CRITICISM	ATOMIC THEORY
ANNUAL OUTING	ARTERIAL ROAD	ATOMIC WEIGHT
ANNUAL REPORT	ARTESIAN WELL	AT SECOND-HAND
ANNUAL RETURN	ARTFUL DODGER	AT SOME LENGTH
ANOTHER GUESS	ARTHUR MILLER	ATTAR OF ROSES
ANOTHER STORY	ARTISTIC WORK	ATTEND CHURCH
ANOTHER THING	ARTIST'S MODEL	AT THE LAUNDRY
ANY QUESTIONS	ARTIST'S PROOF	AT THE SEASIDE
ANYTHING GOES	ART OF DEFENCE	AT THE STATION
APOSTLE SPOON	ART OF HEALING	AT THE THEATRE
APPEAL TO ARMS	ART TREASURES	AT THE WEIGH-IN
APPLE BLOSSOM	ASBESTOS SUIT	AT WHICH PLACE
APPLE FRITTER	AS BLACK AS INK	AUCTION ROOMS
APPLE HARVEST	AS BUSY AS A BEE	AULD LANG SYNE
APPLE OF SODOM	ASCENSION DAY	AUSTIN FRIARS
APPLE ORCHARD	AS CLEAR AS DAY	AUTUMN CROCUS
APPLY FOR A JOB	AS CLEAR AS MUD	AUTUMN LEAVES
APPLY FOR BAIL	ASCOT GOLD CUP	AVERAGE CHILD
APPLY ONESELF	AS GOOD AS DEAD	AVERAGE SPEED
APPLY THE MIND	AS GOOD AS EVER	AVERAGE WOMAN
APPROACH ROAD	AS GOOD AS GOLD	AWAIT PAYMENT
APPROACH SHOT	ASHES TO ASHES	AWAKE THE DEAD
APPROVED LIST	ASH WEDNESDAY	AWAY DULL CARE!
APRIL IN PARIS	ASK A QUESTION	AWAY FROM HOME
APRIL SHOWERS	ASK FOR ADVICE	AWFUL SILENCE
APRON STRINGS	ASK FOR CREDIT	AWKWARD SQUAD
APTITUDE TEST	ASK ME ANOTHER	
APT QUOTATION	ASK NO FAVOURS	
AQUATIC PLANT	ASK QUESTIONS	B—12
AQUATIC SPORT	AS LIGHT AS AIR	BABY CARRIAGE
AQUILINE NOSE	AS MUCH AS EVER	BABY SNATCHER
ARCH CRIMINAL	ASSEMBLY HALL	BACHELOR FLAT
ARCH OF HEAVEN	ASSEMBLY LINE	BACHELOR GIRL
ARCH ONE'S BACK	ASSEMBLY ROOM	BACK AND FORTH
ARCTIC CIRCLE	ASSUMED TITLE	BACK AND FRONT
ARCTIC REGION	AS SURE AS EGGS	BACK ENTRANCE

BACK OF BEYOND	BAND OF HEROES	BEATEN HOLLOW
BACK-ROOM BOYS	BAND TOGETHER	BEATING HEART
BACK THE FIELD	BANG IN THE EYE	BEAT THE CLOCK
BACK TO MOTHER	BANG ONE'S HEAD	BEAT THE COUNT
BACK TO NATURE	BANKER'S DRAFT	BEAUTY DOCTOR
BACK TO NORMAL	BANKER'S ORDER	BEAUTY OF MIND
BACKWARD STEP	BANKING HOURS	BECHER'S BROOK
BACON AND EGGS	BANK INTEREST	BECOME PUBLIC
BAD BEGINNING	BARBARA KELLY	BECOME SILENT
BAD BEHAVIOUR	BARBARY COAST	BED OF NETTLES
BAD CHARACTER	BARBARY SHEEP	BED-TIME STORY
BAD CONDUCTOR	BARBER'S CHAIR	BEEF SANDWICH
BAD DIGESTION	BARCLAY'S BANK	BEEF SAUSAGES
BAD ELOCUTION	BARE CUPBOARD	BEFORE CHRIST
BADGE OF MERIT	BAREFACED LIE	BEFORE DINNER
BAD HALFPENNY	BARE MAJORITY	BEFORE SUPPER
BAD HOUSEWIFE	BARE ONE'S HEAD	BEFORE THE WAR
BAD INFLUENCE	BARGAIN PRICE	BEG FOR CRUMBS
BADLY BEHAVED	BARKING CREEK	BEGGAR'S OPERA
BADLY DAMAGED	BARNABY RUDGE	BEHIND THE BAR
BADLY WOUNDED	BARNACLE BILL	BELGIAN CONGO
BAD NEIGHBOUR	BARNES BRIDGE	BELOVED ENEMY
BAD OF ITS KIND	BARNES COMMON	BELOW AVERAGE
BAD QUALITIES	BARNYARD FOWL	BELOW THE BELT
BAD REPORTING	BAROQUE STYLE	BELOW THE KNEE
BAD TREATMENT	BARRED WINDOW	BELOW THE LINE
BAG OF TOFFEES	BARREL OF BEER	BELOW THE MARK
BAILEY BRIDGE	BARS AND BOLTS	BENARES BRASS
BAKED CUSTARD	BASEBALL TEAM	BEND BACKWARD
BAKEWELL TART	BASEMENT FLAT	BEND SINISTER
BAKING POWDER	BASIC ENGLISH	BEND THE ELBOW
BALANCED DIET	BASK IN THE SUN	BENEFIT MATCH
BALANCED MIND	BASS CLARINET	BENEFIT NIGHT
BALANCE SHEET	BATCH OF BREAD	BENIGN MANNER
BALANCE WHEEL	BATHING BEACH	BENNY GOODMAN
BALANCING ACT	BATTERING RAM	BE OFF WITH YOU!
BALCONY SCENE	BATTING ORDER	BEREFT OF LIFE
BALKAN STATES	BATTLE OF LIFE	BERING STRAIT
BALLAD SINGER	BATTLE OF WITS	BERNARD MILES
BALL AND CHAIN	BAY AT THE MOON	BERTRAM MILLS
BALL BEARINGS	BAYONET DRILL	BESETTING SIN
BALLET DANCER	BEACH PYJAMAS	BESIDE THE SEA
BALLET MASTER	BEAMING SMILE	BEST OF THE LOT
BALLET SCHOOL	BEANS ON TOAST	BEST ONE CAN DO
BALL OF STRING	BEARDED WOMAN	BETHNAL GREEN
BALL OF THREAD	BEAR DOWN UPON	BET ON THE SIDE
BALL-POINT PEN	BEARD THE LION	BETRAY A TRUST
BALM OF GILEAD	BEARER CHEQUE	BETTER CHOICE
BALTIC STATES	BEAR THE BLAME	BETTER THINGS
BAMBOO SHOOTS	BEAR THE BRUNT	BETTING HOUSE
BANBURY CROSS	BEAT A RETREAT	BETWEEN MEALS

BETWEEN TIMES	BLACK CLOTHES	BOLT ONE'S FOOD
BEVERLY HILLS	BLACK COUNTRY	BOMB DISPOSAL
BEXHILL ON SEA	BLACK DESPAIR	BONFIRE NIGHT
BEYOND A DOUBT	BLACK LOOK-OUT	BONNY WEE LASS
BEYOND BELIEF	BLACK OR WHITE	BOOK A PASSAGE
BEYOND BOUNDS	BLACK OUTLOOK	BOOK A SLEEPER
BEYOND REASON	BLACK PUDDING	BOOKING CLERK
BEYOND RECALL	BLADE OF GRASS	BOOK LEARNING
BEYOND REPAIR	BLARNEY STONE	BOOK OF PSALMS
BEYOND THE LAW	BLASTED HEATH	BOOK OF STAMPS
BIB AND TUCKER	BLAST FURNACE	BOOK OF WISDOM
BIBLE SOCIETY	BLAZE OF GLORY	BORDER BALLAD
BIBLE THUMPER	BLAZE OF LIGHT	BORED TO DEATH
BICYCLE CHAIN	BLEACHED HAIR	BORED TO TEARS
BICYCLE THIEF	BLEAK LOOK-OUT	BORIS KARLOFF
BIDE ONE'S TIME	BLEAK OUTLOOK	BORN IN A TRUNK
BIG AND LITTLE	BLEED TO DEATH	BORN OPTIMIST
BIG HINDRANCE	BLESSED STATE	BORROW A FIVER
BIG OFFENSIVE	BLIND BARGAIN	BORROW A POUND
BILLIARD BALL	BLIND IMPULSE	BORROWED TIME
BILLIARD HALL	BLITHE SPIRIT	BOSOM FRIENDS
BILLIARD REST	BLOATER PASTE	BOTH ENDS MEET
BILLIARD ROOM	BLOCK LETTERS	BOTH TOGETHER
BILL OF HEALTH	BLOCK OF FLATS	BOTTLED CIDER
BILL OF LADING	BLOCK OF STONE	BOTTLED FRUIT
BILL OF RIGHTS	BLOOD AND IRON	BOTTLE OF BEER
BILLYCOCK HAT	BLOOD AND SAND	BOTTLE OF HOCK
BIRDCAGE WALK	BLOOD BROTHER	BOTTLE OF MILK
BIRD'S-EYE VIEW	BLOOD DISEASE	BOTTLE OF PORT
BIRD WATCHING	BLOOM OF YOUTH	BOTTLE OF WINE
BIRTH CONTROL	BLOSSOM FORTH	BOTTLE OPENER
BIRTHDAY CAKE	BLOW A WHISTLE	BOTTOM DOLLAR
BIRTHDAY CARD	BLOWN SKY-HIGH	BOTTOM DRAWER
BIRTHDAY GIFT	BLOW OFF STEAM	BOTTOM WEIGHT
BIRTHDAY SUIT	BLOW TO PIECES	BOULTER'S LOCK
BISHOP'S APRON	BLUE AS THE SKY	BOUNCING BABY
BISHOP'S MITRE	BLUE-BLACK INK	BOUNDARY LINE
BITE ONE'S LIPS	BLUE STOCKING	BOUND EDITION
BITE THE THUMB	BLUE WITH COLD	BOW AND SCRAPE
BIT OF AN UPSET	BLUFF KING HAL	BOWLING ALLEY
BIT OF SCANDAL	BOARD MEETING	BOWLING GREEN
BIT OF TROUBLE	BOARD OF TRADE	BOXING GLOVES
BITTERLY COLD	BOB MONKHOUSE	BOX OF MATCHES
BITTER MEMORY	BOB UP AND DOWN	BOX ON THE EARS
BITTER ORANGE	BODY OF TROOPS	BOY ARTIFICER
BITTER STRIFE	BODY SNATCHER	BOY MEETS GIRL
BITTER TONGUE	BOHEMIAN GIRL	BRACE OF BIRDS
BLACK AND BLUE	BOILED SWEETS	BRACE ONESELF
BLACK AND TANS	BOILING POINT	BRAIN SURGEON
BLACK AS NIGHT	BOILING WATER	BRAIN SURGERY
BLACK AS PITCH	BOIL WITH RAGE	BRAIN WASHING

BRAISED STEAK
BRAMBLE JELLY
BRANCH MEMBER
BRANCH OFFICER
BRANDED GOODS
BRANDING IRON
BRANDY BOTTLE
BRANDY BUTTER
BRASS SECTION
BRAVE AS A LION
BRAVE ATTEMPT
BRAVE WARRIOR
BREAD AND MILK
BREAD AND WINE
BREAD PUDDING
BREAK A RECORD
BREAK CONTACT
BREAKFAST CUP
BREAK NO BONES
BREAK RECORDS
BREAK SURFACE
BREAK THE BANK
BREAK THE NEWS
BREAK THE RULE
BREAK THE SEAL
BREAK THROUGH
BREAST POCKET
BREAST STROKE
BREATHE AGAIN
BREATH OF LIFE
BREECHES BUOY
BREEZY MANNER
BRICK BY BRICK
BRIDGE LESSON
BRIDGE PLAYER
BRIDGE THE GAP
BRIEF OUTLINE
BRIEF SUMMARY
BRIGADE MAJOR
BRIGHT COLOUR
BRIGHT LIGHTS
BRIGHTON ROCK
BRIGHT PERIOD
BRIGHT PURPLE
BRIGHT YELLOW
BRILLIANT WIT
BRING A CHARGE
BRING COMFORT
BRING FORWARD
BRING THROUGH
BRING TO A HEAD

BRING TO AN END
BRING TO LIGHT
BRING TO TERMS
BRING TO TRIAL
BRISTOL BOARD
BRISTOL CREAM
BRITISH ISLES
BROAD OUTLINE
BROAD OUTLOOK
BROKEN ACCENT
BROKEN GROUND
BROKEN THREAD
BROKEN VOYAGE
BROKEN WINDOW
BROOK NO DELAY
BROUGHT FORTH
BROWN AND MILD
BROWN WINDSOR
BRUCE FORSYTH
BRUIN THE BEAR
BRUSH AGAINST
BRUSH AND COMB
BRUSSELS LACE
BUCKING HORSE
BUDDHIST MONK
BUDDING ACTOR
BUDDING YOUTH
BUDGET SPEECH
BUGLE-CALL RAG
BUILD A BRIDGE
BUILDER'S MATE
BUILDING LAND
BUILDING PLOT
BUILDING SITE
BUILT OF STONE
BUILT ON A ROCK
BULBOUS PLANT
BULLDOG BREED
BULL ELEPHANT
BUNCH OF ROSES
BUNDLE OF RAGS
BUNSEN BURNER
BURGLAR ALARM
BURIAL GROUND
BURMA CHEROOT
BURNHAM SCALE
BURNING FEVER
BURNING GLASS
BURNING SHAME
BURNING TORCH
BURNT ALMONDS

BURNT FINGERS
BURNT TO ASHES
BURN WITH LOVE
BURST OF ANGER
BURST OF SOUND
BURST OF SPEED
BURY ONE'S HEAD
BUS CONDUCTOR
BUSINESS DEAL
BUSINESS LIFE
BUSINESS TRIP
BUSTER KEATON
BUTCHER'S SHOP
BUTTERED ROLL
BUTTERFLY NET
BUYER'S MARKET
BY A LONG CHALK
BY COMPARISON
BY EASY STAGES
BY FAR THE BEST
BY PERSUASION
BY THE SEASIDE
BY THE WAYSIDE
BY WAY OF A JOKE

C—12
CABBAGE PATCH
CABIN CRUISER
CABINET MAKER
CABIN STEWARD
CABLE RAILWAY
CABLE'S LENGTH
CAFÉ CHANTANT
CAIRN TERRIER
CAKED WITH MUD
CALABASH PIPE
CALAMITY JANE
CALENDAR YEAR
CALL A MEETING
CALL FOR ORDER
CALL INTO PLAY
CALL IT SQUARE
CALL OF THE SEA
CALL THE BANNS
CALL TO PRAYER
CALL TO THE BAR
CALYPSO MUSIC
CAMP FOLLOWER
CANARY YELLOW
CANDID CAMERA
CANDID CRITIC

CANDID FRIEND
CANDLE GREASE
CANNON FODDER
CANNON STREET
CANON COLLINS
CANVEY ISLAND
CAPABLE HANDS
CAPE PROVINCE
CAPITAL ASSET
CAPITAL CRIME
CAPITAL GAINS
CAPITAL GOODS
CAPTAIN BLOOD
CAPTAIN SCOTT
CARAFE OF WINE
CARAWAY SEEDS
CARBOLIC ACID
CARBOLIC SOAP
CARDBOARD BOX
CARDINAL'S HAT
CAREFREE MIND
CAREFUL STUDY
CARELESS TALK
CARIBBEAN SEA
CARNEGIE HALL
CARNIVAL TIME
CARNIVAL WEEK
CARPET KNIGHT
CARRIAGE PAID
CARRY A REPORT
CARRY FORWARD
CARRY ONE'S BAT
CARRY THROUGH
CARTE BLANCHE
CARVING KNIFE
CASE OF MURDER
CASE OF SCOTCH
CASE OF WHISKY
CASE THE JOINT
CASE TO ANSWER
CASH AND CARRY
CASH CUSTOMER
CASH ON DEMAND
CASH REGISTER
CAST AWAY FEAR
CAST-IRON CASE
CAST ONE'S VOTE
CAST THE BLAME
CASUAL GLANCE
CASUAL LABOUR
CASUAL MANNER

CASUAL REMARK
CASUALTY LIST
CASUALTY WARD
CASUAL WORKER
CAT AND FIDDLE
CATCH A TARTAR
CATCH BENDING
CATCH NAPPING
CATCH SIGHT OF
CATCH THE POST
CATCH THE TUBE
CAT'S WHISKERS
CATTLE DEALER
CATTLE MARKET
CAUSE CÉLÈBRE
CAUSE OF DELAY
CAUSE OFFENCE
CAUSE TROUBLE
CAUTION MONEY
CAUTIOUS MOVE
CAUTIOUS TYPE
CAVALRY HORSE
CAVALRY TWILL
CAVEAT EMPTOR
CEASE TO EXIST
CEILING PRICE
CEMENT A UNION
CENTURIES OLD
CERTAIN DEATH
CERTAIN ISSUE
CERTAINLY NOT
CERTAIN PLACE
C'EST LA GUERRE
CHAISE LONGUE
CHALLENGE CUP
CHAMBER MUSIC
CHAMPAGNE CUP
CHANCE REMARK
CHANCERY LANE
CHANGE COLOUR
CHANGE COURSE
CHANGE HORSES
CHANGE OF DIET
CHANGE OF FACE
CHANGE OF LUCK
CHANGE OF MIND
CHANGE OF MOOD
CHANGE PLACES
CHANGE TRAINS
CHANGING ROOM
CHAOTIC STATE

CHAPTER HOUSE
CHAPTER THREE
CHARING CROSS
CHARITY MATCH
CHARLES BOYER
CHARLES PEACE
CHARLES READE
CHARLES'S WAIN
CHARLEY'S AUNT
CHARLIE DRAKE
CHARNEL HOUSE
CHARTER PARTY
CHARTER PLANE
CHASE SHADOWS
CHEAP-DAY FARE
CHEAP EDITION
CHEAP SUCCESS
CHEAP TWISTER
CHEAT AT CARDS
CHECK THE TILL
CHEDDAR GORGE
CHEEK TO CHEEK
CHEEKY MONKEY
CHEERFUL FIRE
CHEERFUL MOOD
CHEERY MANNER
CHEESE STRAWS
CHELSEA CHINA
CHEMICAL FUEL
CHEMICAL TEST
CHEMISTRY SET
CHEMIST'S SHOP
CHERISH HOPES
CHERRY BRANDY
CHESS OPENING
CHESS PROBLEM
CHESTNUT TREE
CHEVIOT HILLS
CHICKEN CURRY
CHICKEN LIVER
CHIEF CASHIER
CHIEF JUSTICE
CHIEF MOURNER
CHIEF OFFICER
CHIEF OF STAFF
CHIEF SKIPPER
CHIEF STEWARD
CHIEF SUSPECT
CHIEF WITNESS
CHILDE HAROLD
CHILDISH WAYS

CHILD PRODIGY
CHILDREN'S TOY
CHILD WELFARE
CHILLI PEPPER
CHILLY MANNER
CHIMNEY SWEEP
CHINA CABINET
CHINESE WHITE
CHOCOLATE BAR
CHOCOLATE BOX
CHOCOLATE EGG
CHOICE MORSEL
CHOOSE FREELY
CHOP AND CHIPS
CHOSEN CAREER
CHOSEN PEOPLE
CHRISTIAN ERA
CHRISTMAS BOX
CHRISTMAS DAY
CHRISTMAS EVE
CHROME YELLOW
CHUBBY CHEEKS
CHURCH BAZAAR
CHURCH LIVING
CHURCH MEMBER
CHURCH OF ROME
CHURCH PARADE
CHURCH SCHOOL
CIGARETTE ASH
CIGARETTE END
CIGARETTE TIN
CINEMA SCREEN
CINEMA STUDIO
CIRCLE AROUND
CIRCUIT COURT
CIRCUIT JUDGE
CIRCULAR TOUR
CITY ALDERMAN
CITY BOUNDARY
CITY MERCHANT
CITY OF LONDON
CIVIC WELCOME
CIVIL DEFENCE
CIVILIAN LIFE
CIVILIZED MAN
CIVIL LIBERTY
CIVIL SERVANT
CIVIL SERVICE
CLAIM A REWARD
CLAIM DAMAGES
CLAP THE HANDS

CLASH OF STEEL
CLASH OF VIEWS
CLASPED HANDS
CLASSICAL AGE
CLASSICAL ART
CLASSIC STYLE
CLASS WARFARE
CLEAN LICENCE
CLEAR AS A BELL
CLEAR OUTLINE
CLEAR PASSAGE
CLEAR THE PATH
CLEAR THE ROAD
CLEAR THE ROOM
CLEAR THOUGHT
CLEAR WARNING
CLEAR WEATHER
CLENCHED FIST
CLERICAL GARB
CLERICAL GREY
CLERICAL WORK
CLERK OF WORKS
CLEVER MANNER
CLEVER SPEECH
CLEVER STROKE
CLIFFORD'S INN
CLIFF RAILWAY
CLIFF RICHARD
CLIMB TO POWER
CLINGING VINE
CLING LIKE IVY
CLINK GLASSES
CLIPPED HEDGE
CLIP THE WINGS
CLIVE OF INDIA
CLOCK WATCHER
CLOCKWORK TOY
CLOSE BARGAIN
CLOSE CONTACT
CLOSE CONTEST
CLOSED CIRCLE
CLOSED DRAWER
CLOSE HARMONY
CLOSE TEXTURE
CLOSE THE DOOR
CLOSE THE EYES
CLOSE THE GATE
CLOSE TO DEATH
CLOSING PRICE
CLOSING WORDS
CLOTHES BRUSH

CLOTHES HORSE
CLOTHES SENSE
CLOTHING CLUB
CLOTTED CREAM
CLOUD EFFECTS
CLOUDLESS SKY
CLOUD OF SMOKE
CLOUD OF STEAM
CLUB OFFICIAL
CLUB SANDWICH
CLUB TOGETHER
CLUMP OF TREES
CLUTCH OF EGGS
COACH AND FOUR
COACH AND PAIR
COACHING DAYS
COACH STATION
COAL INDUSTRY
COAL MERCHANT
COAL SHORTAGE
COARSE FABRIC
COARSE MANNER
COASTAL TRADE
COAST TO COAST
COAT AND SKIRT
CODE NAPOLEON
CODE OF HONOUR
COILED SPRING
COLD AS MARBLE
COLD COMPRESS
COLD SHOULDER
COLD-WATER TAP
COLIN COWDREY
COLLAR AND TIE
COLLECT TAXES
COLOGNE WATER
COLONEL BLIMP
COLONEL BOGEY
COLONIAL LIFE
COLOURED BIRD
COLOUR SCHEME
COMBAT TROOPS
COMB ONE'S HAIR
COME A CROPPER
COME AND GET IT
COME DOWN A PEG
COME IN SECOND
COME IN TO LAND
COME INTO LINE
COME INTO PLAY
COME INTO VIEW

COME IN USEFUL	CONCERT GRAND	COULD BE WORSE
COME IT STRONG	CONCERT PARTY	COUNCIL HOUSE
COME OUT ON TOP	CONCERT PITCH	COUNCIL OF WAR
COME OVER HERE	CONCRETE FACT	COUNT DRACULA
COME TO A CLOSE	CONCRETE PATH	COUNTER CLAIM
COME TO A POINT	CONCRETE POST	COUNTRY DANCE
COME TOGETHER	CONDEMNED MAN	COUNTRY HOUSE
COME TO NAUGHT	CONFUSED MIND	COUNTRY MOUSE
COME TO NO GOOD	CONIC SECTION	COUNT THE COST
COME TO NO HARM	CONSOLE TABLE	COUNT THE DAYS
COME TO PIECES	CONTENTED MAN	COUNT THE RISK
COME TO THE END	CONTOUR LINES	COUNT UP TO TEN
COME UP FOR AIR	CONTROL PANEL	COUNTY ANTRIM
COME UPSTAIRS	CONTROL TOWER	COUNTY FAMILY
COME UP TRUMPS	CONVEX MIRROR	COUNTY SCHOOL
COMIC SECTION	CONVEYOR BELT	COUPE JACQUES
COMING EVENTS	CONVICTED MAN	COURSE OF DUTY
COMMANDO RAID	COOKERY CLASS	COURSE OF LIFE
COMMANDO UNIT	COOKING APPLE	COURSE OF LOVE
COMMIT A CRIME	COOK THE BOOKS	COURSE OF TIME
COMMIT BIGAMY	COOK UP A STORY	COURSE OF WORK
COMMIT MURDER	COOL CUSTOMER	COURSE RECORD
COMMITTEE MAN	COOLING AGENT	COURTEOUS ACT
COMMON ACCENT	COOLING PLANT	COURTESY CALL
COMMON AS DIRT	COOL JUDGMENT	COURT MARTIAL
COMMON CENTRE	COOL THOUSAND	COURT OFFICER
COMMON FACTOR	COPIOUS NOTES	COURT PLASTER
COMMON FRIEND	COPPER KETTLE	COURT SUMMONS
COMMON GENDER	COPYRIGHT ACT	COUSIN GERMAN
COMMON GOSSIP	CORDIAL SMILE	COVENT GARDEN
COMMON GROUND	CORNET PLAYER	COVENTRY CITY
COMMON HATRED	CORN EXCHANGE	COVERED COURT
COMMON LAWYER	CORN IN ISRAEL	COVERED DRAIN
COMMON MARKET	CORNISH CREAM	COVERED WAGON
COMMON ORIGIN	CORNISH PASTY	COVER THE COST
COMMON PEOPLE	CORN MERCHANT	COVER THE LOSS
COMMON PERSON	CORN ON THE COB	CRACK A BOTTLE
COMMON PRAYER	CORONER'S JURY	CRACKED VOICE
COMMON PRISON	CORRECT DRESS	CRACKING PACE
COMMON SAYING	CORRECT STYLE	CRACKING SHOW
COMMON SPEECH	CORRECT THING	CRACK-POT IDEA
COMMUNAL FARM	COSSACK DANCE	CRACK THE WHIP
COMPANIES ACT	COST ACCOUNTS	CRAFTY FELLOW
COMPANION WAY	COST OF LIVING	CRAIG DOUGLAS
COMPARE NOTES	COST OF UPKEEP	CRAMPED STYLE
COMPASS POINT	COST THE EARTH	CRASHING BORE
COMPLETE LIST	COSTUME PIECE	CRASH LANDING
COMPOSE MUSIC	COTTAGE PIANO	CRAVEN SPIRIT
COMPOS MENTIS	COTTON GLOVES	CREAM CRACKER
COMPOUND TIME	COTTON THREAD	CREAM SHAMPOO
CONCEITED PUP	COUGH MIXTURE	CREATE A SCENE

CREATIVE MIND
CREATIVE MOOD
CREATIVE URGE
CREATIVE WORK
CREDIT TITLES
CRÊPE DE CHINE
CRÊPE SUZETTE
CRESCENT MOON
CRICKET EXTRA
CRICKET MATCH
CRICKET PITCH
CRICKET SCORE
CRICKET STUMP
CRIMINAL CASE
CRIMINAL CODE
CRIMINAL SUIT
CRIMINAL TYPE
CRIPPLING TAX
CRITICAL TIME
CROMWELL ROAD
CROSSED LINES
CROSSED WIRES
CROSS OF DAVID
CROSS SECTION
CROSS THE LINE
CROSS THE ROAD
CROSSWORD FAN
CROWNED HEADS
CROWN WITNESS
CRUDE MANNERS
CRUDE METHODS
CRUISE AROUND
CRUSHING BLOW
CRUST OF BREAD
CRY LIKE A BABY
CRY OF DESPAIR
CRY ONE'S WARES
CRYPTIC SMILE
CRYSTAL CLEAR
CRYSTAL GLASS
CUBIC CONTENT
CULINARY HERB
CULLODEN MOOR
CUP AND SAUCER
CUPBOARD LOVE
CUP FINALISTS
CURDS AND WHEY
CURIOUS SIGHT
CURIOUS SOUND
CURIOUS THING
CURL OF THE LIP

CURL UP AND DIE
CURRANT BREAD
CURRENCY NOTE
CURRENT CRAZE
CURRENT ISSUE
CURRENT MONTH
CURRENT OF AIR
CURRENT PRICE
CURRENT TIMES
CURRENT TREND
CURRY AND RICE
CURTIS REPORT
CURVE INWARDS
CUSHION COVER
CUSHION OF AIR
CUSTOM DUTIES
CUSTOMS UNION
CUT AND THRUST
CUT FOR TRUMPS
CUT OFF THE GAS
CUT OF ONE'S JIB
CUT ONE'S NAILS
CUT ONE'S TEETH
CUT THE CACKLE
CUTTING TEETH
CUTTING WORDS
CUT TO RIBBONS
CUT TO THE BONE
CYNICAL SMILE
CZAR OF RUSSIA

D—12
DAGGERS DRAWN
DAILY EXPRESS
DAILY ROUTINE
DAILY SERVICE
DAINTY HABITS
DAINTY PALATE
DAIRY FARMING
DAIRY PRODUCE
DALMATIAN DOG
DAMAGED GOODS
DAME MYRA HESS
DANCE HOSTESS
DANCE OF DEATH
DANCE ROUTINE
DANCE SESSION
DANDY DINMONT
DANGEROUS JOB
DANGEROUS MAN
DANGER SIGNAL

DANISH BUTTER
DANISH PASTRY
DANSE MACABRE
DARBY AND JOAN
DARKENED MIND
DARK THOUGHTS
DASH TO PIECES
DAVID GARRICK
DAVID KOSSOFF
DAYLIGHT RAID
DAY OF LEISURE
DAY OF WORSHIP
DEAD AS MUTTON
DEAD LANGUAGE
DEADLY COMBAT
DEADLY POISON
DEADLY SECRET
DEADLY WEAPON
DEAD MAN'S HAND
DEAD-SEA FRUIT
DEAD STRAIGHT
DEAFENING ROW
DEAF TO REASON
DEAL THE CARDS
DEAR DEPARTED
DEAREST HEART
DEAR OLD THING
DEARTH OF FOOD
DEATH CHAMBER
DEATH PENALTY
DEATH WARRANT
DEBATING HALL
DEBIT BALANCE
DEBT OF HONOUR
DECIDING VOTE
DECIMAL POINT
DEEP FEELINGS
DEEP INTEREST
DEEP-LAID PLOT
DEEP MOURNING
DEEP-SEA DIVER
DEEP THOUGHTS
DEFENCE BONDS
DEFENCE MEDAL
DEFINITE TIME
DEJECTED LOOK
DELICATE HINT
DELIVERY DATE
DELIVERY NOTE
DEMAND RANSOM
DEMON FOR WORK

DENIS COMPTON	DIRTY WEATHER	DO THE NEEDFUL
DEN OF THIEVES	DISASTER AREA	DO THE WASHING
DEPUTY LEADER	DISCOVERY BAY	DOUBLE BARREL
DESCENT OF MAN	DISHONEST ACT	DOUBLE BRANDY
DESERT ISLAND	DISPATCH CASE	DOUBLE ELEVEN
DESERVE A RISE	DISPENSE WITH	DOUBLE FLOWER
DESIGN CENTRE	DISTRICT BANK	DOUBLE SCOTCH
DESK CALENDAR	DISTRICT LINE	DOUBLES MATCH
DESPATCH CASE	DIVE FOR COVER	DOUBLE THE BID
DESPERATE BID	DIVIDE BY FIVE	DOUBLE TWELVE
DESPERATE MAN	DIVIDE BY FOUR	DOUBLE TWENTY
DESSERT KNIFE	DIVIDE BY NINE	DOUBLE VISION
DESSERT SPOON	DIVIDED SKIRT	DOUBLE WHISKY
DETACHED MIND	DIVIDING LINE	DOUGHTY DEEDS
DETACHED VIEW	DIVIDING WALL	DOWN PLATFORM
DETAILED PLAN	DIVINE COMEDY	DOWNRIGHT LIE
DEVIL MAY CARE	DIVINE NATURE	DOWN THE AISLE
DEVIL OF A MESS	DIVINE RIGHTS	DOWN THE DRAIN
DEVIL OF A TIME	DIVISION BELL	DOWN THE FIELD
DEVIL'S ISLAND	DIVISION SIGN	DOWN THE HATCH
DEVIL'S TATTOO	DIVORCE COURT	DOWN THE RIVER
DEVIL WORSHIP	DIZZY FEELING	DOWN THE SPOUT
DEVIOUS MEANS	DIZZY HEIGHTS	DOWN THE YEARS
DEVIOUS PATHS	DO A HAND'S TURN	DOWNWARD BEND
DEVOID OF FEAR	DO AS ONE'S TOLD	DOWNWARD PATH
DEVON VIOLETS	DO AS OTHERS DO	DOZEN OYSTERS
DIAGONAL LINE	DO AS ROME DOES	DRAGGING FEET
DIALLING TONE	DOCK LABOURER	DRAG ONE'S FEET
DIAMOND CLASP	DOCTOR FOSTER	DRAGON'S BLOOD
DIAMOND TIARA	DOCTOR JEKYLL	DRAGON'S TEETH
DIANA'S TEMPLE	DOCTOR WATSON	DRAMATIC FORM
DICTATE TERMS	DOG IN A MANGER	DRAMATIC POEM
DIE IN HARNESS	DO IT YOURSELF	DRAMATIC POET
DIE IN ONE'S BED	DOMBEY AND SON	DRAPERY STORE
DIESEL ENGINE	DOMESDAY BOOK	DRAUGHT CIDER
DIFFICULT JOB	DOMESTIC HELP	DRAUGHT HORSE
DIFFICULT SUM	DOMINANT FACT	DRAUGHT STOUT
DIFFUSED HEAT	DONALD WOLFIT	DRAW A MEANING
DIG IN THE RIBS	DONEGAL TWEED	DRAW A PENSION
DIG ONESELF IN	DONKEY ENGINE	DRAW A PICTURE
DIG ONE'S GRAVE	DONKEY'S YEARS	DRAWING PAPER
DIG UP THE PAST	DO NO MAN WRONG	DRAW INTEREST
DING-DONG RACE	DO NOT DISTURB	DRAWN TO SCALE
DINING SALOON	DOOMSDAY BOOK	DRAW THE BLIND
DIN IN THE EARS	DO ONE A FAVOUR	DRAW THE MORAL
DIRECT ACTION	DO ONE'S UTMOST	DRAW THE SWORD
DIRECT COURSE	DORMER WINDOW	DRAW THE TEETH
DIRECT METHOD	DOROTHY TUTIN	DRAW TO A CLOSE
DIRECT OBJECT	DORSET SQUARE	DRAW TOGETHER
DIRECT SPEECH	DOSE OF PHYSIC	DREADFUL BORE
DIRE DISTRESS	DO THE HONOURS	DREADFUL PAIN

DREAD SUMMONS
DREAM OF YOUTH
DRESDEN CHINA
DRESS CLOTHES
DRESSED IN RED
DRESSING CASE
DRESSING DOWN
DRESSING GOWN
DRESSING ROOM
DRESS THE PART
DRESS UNIFORM
DRINK HEAVILY
DRINKING BOUT
DRINKING CLUB
DRINKING ORGY
DRINKING SONG
DRINKING TIME
DRINK OF WATER
DRIVE FORWARD
DRIVE THROUGH
DRIVE TO DRINK
DRIVING FORCE
DROP A CLANGER
DROP A CURTSEY
DROP OF BRANDY
DROP OF SCOTCH
DROP OF WHISKY
DROPPED CATCH
DROP THE PILOT
DROWN ONESELF
DRUNK AS A LORD
DRUNKEN BRAWL
DUCKING STOOL
DUCK ONE'S HEAD
DUCK'S DISEASE
DUE DEFERENCE
DULL MONOTONY
DUMB CHARADES
DUMB CREATURE
DUM-DUM BULLET
DUNMOW FLITCH
DUPLICATE KEY
DURING THE DAY
DURING THE WAR
DUST AND ASHES
DUTCH AUCTION
DUTCH COMFORT
DUTCH COURAGE
DUTCH GUILDER
DYERS' COMPANY
DYNAMIC FORCE

E—12

EALING COMMON
EAR AND THROAT
EARLY CLOSING
EARLY EDITION
EARLY ENGLISH
EARLY MORNING
EARLY WARNING
EARNED INCOME
EARNEST MONEY
EARN ONE'S KEEP
EASE ONE'S MIND
EASILY SOLVED
EAST CHINA SEA
EASTER BONNET
EASTER ISLAND
EASTERLY GALE
EASTER MONDAY
EASTER PARADE
EASTER RISING
EASTER SUNDAY
EASY ON THE EYE
EASY PAYMENTS
EASY SOLUTION
EASY TO PLEASE
EAT HUMBLE-PIE
EATING HABITS
EAT ONE'S WORDS
EAT SPARINGLY
EAU DE COLOGNE
ECONOMY DRIVE
EDGAR WALLACE
EDGE OF BEYOND
EDIBLE FUNGUS
EDITH SITWELL
EDWARD GIBBON
EEL-PIE ISLAND
EFFORT OF WILL
EGGS AND BACON
EGYPTIAN GODS
EIGHT AND FIVE
EIGHT AND FOUR
EIGHT AND NINE
EIGHT DEGREES
EIGHT DOLLARS
EIGHT FATHOMS
EIGHT GALLONS
EIGHT GUINEAS
EIGHTH LETTER
EIGHTH OF JULY
EIGHTH OF JUNE

EIGHTH STOREY
EIGHT HUNDRED
EIGHTH VOLUME
EIGHT MINUTES
EIGHT OF CLUBS
EIGHT PER CENT
EIGHT SQUARED
EIGHT WICKETS
ELBOW ONE'S WAY
ELDER BROTHER
ELDEST SISTER
ELECTION DATE
ELECTION YEAR
ELECTRIC BELL
ELECTRIC BLUE
ELECTRIC BULB
ELECTRIC FIRE
ELECTRIC HARE
ELECTRIC HORN
ELECTRIC IRON
ELECTRIC LAMP
ELECTRIC OVEN
ELECTRIC PLUG
ELECTRIC WIRE
ELEGANT LINES
ELEVEN AND ONE
ELEVEN AND SIX
ELEVEN AND TEN
ELEVEN AND TWO
ELEVEN MONTHS
ELEVEN O'CLOCK
ELEVEN OUNCES
ELEVEN POINTS
ELEVENTH HOLE
ELEVENTH HOUR
ELGIN MARBLES
ELIXIR OF LIFE
ELVIS PRESLEY
ELY CATHEDRAL
EMERALD GREEN
EMPEROR WALTZ
EMPTY FEELING
EMPTY STOMACH
EMPTY VESSELS
END IN FAILURE
ENDLESS CHAIN
ENDLESS WORRY
END OF CHAPTER
END OF THE LINE
END OF THE ROAD
END OF THE WEEK

END OF THE YEAR
ENDURING FAME
ENDURING LOVE
ENFIELD RIFLE
ENGAGED IN WAR
ENGINE DRIVER
ENGLISH MONEY
ENGLISH VERSE
ENJOY ONESELF
ENORMOUS MEAL
ENQUIRE AFTER
ENQUIRY AGENT
ENRICO CARUSO
ENTERIC FEVER
ENTRANCE FREE
ENTRANCE HALL
EPPING FOREST
EQUAL CONTEST
EQUAL THE BEST
ERIC ROBINSON
ERMINE COLLAR
ERUDITE STYLE
ESCAPE CLAUSE
ESCAPE NOTICE
ESCORT VESSEL
ESSAYS OF ELIA
ESSENTIAL OIL
ESTEEM HIGHLY
ETERNAL YOUTH
ETERNITY RING
ETON WALL-GAME
EUGENE O'NEILL
EUROPEAN CITY
EVENING CLASS
EVENING DRESS
EVENING PAPER
EVEN TEMPERED
EVE OF THE POLL
EVER AND AGAIN
EVER-OPEN DOOR
EVER SO LITTLE
EVERY FEW DAYS
EVERY MAN JACK
EVERY MORNING
EVERY QUARTER
EVERY SO OFTEN
EVERY TUESDAY
EVIL SPEAKING
EVIL THOUGHTS
EVOKE THE PAST
EXACT ACCOUNT

EXACTLY RIGHT
EXACT MEANING
EXACT SCIENCE
EXALTED STYLE
EXCEL ONESELF
EXCESS PROFIT
EXCESS WEIGHT
EXCHANGE RATE
EXCITING BOOK
EXCITING NEWS
EXCITING PLAY
EXERCISE BOOK
EXERT ONESELF
EXHAUST VALVE
EXPANSE OF SEA
EXPANSE OF SKY
EXPERT ADVICE
EXPLODED IDEA
EXPORT MARKET
EXPOSED NERVE
EXPRESS GRIEF
EXPRESS SPEED
EXPRESS TRAIN
EX-SERVICE MAN
EXTEND CREDIT
EXTENDED PLAY
EXTERIOR WALL
EXTRA EDITION
EXTRA SPECIAL
EXTREMES MEET
EXTREME VIEWS
EXTREME YOUTH
EYE FOR BEAUTY
EYE FOR COLOUR
EYE OF A NEEDLE
EYES OF THE LAW
EYE ON THE BALL

F—12
FABLED ANIMAL
FABULOUS SIZE
FACE BOTH WAYS
FACE DISGRACE
FACE THE ENEMY
FACE THE FACTS
FACE THE FRONT
FACE THE ISSUE
FACE THE MUSIC
FACE THE TRUTH
FACT AND FANCY
FAERIE QUEENE

FAILING LIGHT
FAILING SIGHT
FAIL IN HEALTH
FAIL TO APPEAR
FAIL TO FINISH
FAINT ATTEMPT
FAIR DECISION
FAIR EXCHANGE
FAIR PROSPECT
FAIR QUESTION
FAIR TO MEDIUM
FAIT ACCOMPLI
FAITHFUL COPY
FALL BACK UPON
FALL BY THE WAY
FALLEN ARCHES
FALL HEADLONG
FALL IN BATTLE
FALLING SALES
FALLING TEARS
FALL IN PRICE
FALL INTO LINE
FALL INTO RUIN
FALL OF FRANCE
FALL TO PIECES
FALSE ACCOUNT
FALSE ADDRESS
FALSE COLOURS
FALSE ECONOMY
FALSE HORIZON
FALSE MODESTY
FALSE PICTURE
FALSE PROPHET
FALSE VERDICT
FALSE WITNESS
FALSE WORSHIP
FAMILIAR FACE
FAMILIAR RING
FAMILY AFFAIR
FAMILY CIRCLE
FAMILY DOCTOR
FAMILY FRIEND
FAMILY JEWELS
FAMILY LAWYER
FAMILY MATTER
FAMINE RELIEF
FANCY ONESELF
FAN THE EMBERS
FAN THE FLAMES
FAR DIFFERENT
FARE THEE WELL

FAREWELL SONG
FARMHOUSE TEA
FARMING STOCK
FARM LABOURER
FAROE ISLANDS
FASCIST PARTY
FASHION HOUSE
FASHION MODEL
FASHION PLATE
FAST AND LOOSE
FAST THINKING
FATAL BLUNDER
FATAL DISEASE
FATAL MISTAKE
FATHER AND SON
FATHER FIGURE
FATHER THAMES
FATIGUE PARTY
FAT LOT OF GOOD
FAT OF THE LAND
FATUOUS SMILE
FAULTY SWITCH
FEAR EXPOSURE
FEAR THE WORST
FEAT OF MEMORY
FEATURE STORY
FEDERAL AGENT
FEDERAL COURT
FEDERAL STATE
FEDERAL UNION
FEEBLE ATTACK
FEEBLE EFFORT
FEEBLE EXCUSE
FEEBLE SPEECH
FEED THE BRUTE
FEEL DOUBTFUL
FEEL GRATEFUL
FEEL HELPLESS
FEEL HOMESICK
FEEL ONE'S FEET
FEEL STRONGLY
FEEL SUPERIOR
FEEL SYMPATHY
FEEL THE PANGS
FEEL THE PINCH
FEET FOREMOST
FELL HEADLONG
FELLOW MEMBER
FERTILE BRAIN
FESTIVAL HALL
FESTIVE BOARD

FEUDAL SYSTEM
FEUDAL TENURE
FEVERISH COLD
FIELDING SIDE
FIELD KITCHEN
FIELD MARSHAL
FIELD OFFICER
FIELD OF STUDY
FIELD OF WHEAT
FIERCE ATTACK
FIERCE HATRED
FIERCE TEMPER
FIERY FURNACE
FIFTEEN FORTY
FIFTEEN MILES
FIFTH CENTURY
FIFTH OF APRIL
FIFTH OF MARCH
FIFTY DOLLARS
FIFTY GUINEAS
FIFTY PER CENT
FIGHT AGAINST
FIGHTER PILOT
FIGHTER PLANE
FIGHTING COCK
FIGHTING TALK
FIGHTING TRIM
FIGHT ONE'S WAY
FIGURE SKATER
FILING SYSTEM
FILL A VACANCY
FILM DIRECTOR
FILM FESTIVAL
FILM INDUSTRY
FILM MAGAZINE
FILM PREMIERE
FILM PRODUCER
FINAL ACCOUNT
FINAL ATTEMPT
FINAL CURTAIN
FINAL EDITION
FINAL EPISODE
FINAL OPINION
FINAL OUTCOME
FINAL PAYMENT
FINAL PROCESS
FINAL VICTORY
FINAL WARNING
FINANCIAL AID
FIND A FORMULA
FIND A HUSBAND

FIND AN OUTLET
FIND NO FAVOUR
FIND ONE'S FEET
FIND ONE'S LEGS
FIND PLEASURE
FIND THE CAUSE
FIND THE MONEY
FIND THE PLACE
FINE AND DANDY
FINE AND LARGE
FINE FEATHERS
FINE FEATURES
FINE GOINGS-ON
FINE PROSPECT
FINER FEELING
FINE SPECIMEN
FINISHED WORK
FINISH SECOND
FINISH THE JOB
FINSBURY PARK
FIRE AND SWORD
FIRE AND WATER
FIRE AT RANDOM
FIREMAN'S LIFT
FIRE OF LONDON
FIRE PRACTICE
FIRESIDE CHAT
FIRESIDE TALK
FIRM DECISION
FIRM FOOTHOLD
FIRMLY ROOTED
FIRM MEASURES
FIRM PRESSURE
FIRM PROPOSAL
FIRST-AID POST
FIRST AND LAST
FIRST ARRIVAL
FIRST ATTEMPT
FIRST CENTURY
FIRST CHAPTER
FIRST EDITION
FIRST FOOTING
FIRST INNINGS
FIRST OF APRIL
FIRST OFFENCE
FIRST OFFICER
FIRST OF MARCH
FIRST PAYMENT
FIRST QUARTER
FIRST READING
FIRST REFUSAL

FIRST RESERVE	FLOATING DEBT	FOOT AND MOUTH
FIRST SEA-LORD	FLOATING DOCK	FOOTBALL CLUB
FIRST SERVICE	FLOATING FUND	FOOTBALL POOL
FIRST SESSION	FLOATING MINE	FOOTBALL TEAM
FIRST THOUGHT	FLOATING VOTE	FOOTPLATE MAN
FIRST TIME OUT	FLOCK OF BIRDS	FOOT REGIMENT
FIRST TO LEAVE	FLOCK OF GEESE	FOR A LIFETIME
FIRST TURNING	FLOCK OF GOATS	FOR AMUSEMENT
FIRST-YEAR MAN	FLOCK OF SHEEP	FOR A RAINY DAY
FIRTH OF CLYDE	FLODDEN FIELD	FORCE AN ENTRY
FIRTH OF FORTH	FLOOD OF TEARS	FORCE AN ISSUE
FISH AND CHIPS	FLOOD OF WATER	FORCED GAIETY
FISH FOR TROUT	FLOOD OF WORDS	FORCED LABOUR
FISHING FLEET	FLOOR SERVICE	FORCE MAJEURE
FISHING SMACK	FLOUNCE ABOUT	FORCE OF HABIT
FISHING SPEAR	FLOWERED SILK	FORCE ONE'S WAY
FIT AND PROPER	FLOWER GARDEN	FORCE THE PACE
FIT AS A FIDDLE	FLOWER MARKET	FOREIGN AGENT
FITFUL BREEZE	FLOWER-POT MEN	FOREIGN LANDS
FIT OF MADNESS	FLOWER SELLER	FOREIGN MONEY
FITTED CARPET	FLOWERY STYLE	FOREIGN PARTS
FIVE AND A HALF	FLOWING LOCKS	FOREIGN STAMP
FIVE AND EIGHT	FLOWING WATER	FOREIGN TRADE
FIVE AND SEVEN	FLUENT FRENCH	FOREST OF DEAN
FIVE AND THREE	FLUID MEASURE	FOREST RANGER
FIVE-DAY MATCH	FLURRY OF SNOW	FOREVER AMBER
FIVE DIAMONDS	FLUSH OF YOUTH	FOR GALLANTRY
FIVE FEET TALL	FLUTED COLUMN	FORGE A CHEQUE
FIVE FURLONGS	FLY AWAY PETER	FORGE ONE'S WAY
FIVE-LINE WHIP	FLYING BEETLE	FORK OUT MONEY
FIVE NO-TRUMPS	FLYING CARPET	FORMAL GARDEN
FIVE OF HEARTS	FLYING CIRCUS	FORMAL SPEECH
FIVE OF SPADES	FLYING COLUMN	FORMER FRIEND
FIVE OF TRUMPS	FLYING DOCTOR	FOR PITY'S SAKE
FIVE SEVENTHS	FLYING GROUND	FOR THE BETTER
FIVE THOUSAND	FLYING SAUCER	FOR THE MOMENT
FIVE-YEAR PLAN	FLYING TACKLE	FOR THE RECORD
FIXED CAPITAL	FLY INTO A RAGE	FORTY FIFTEEN
FIXED PAYMENT	FOAM MATTRESS	FORTY PER CENT
FIXED PURPOSE	FOGGY WEATHER	FORTY THIEVES
FIXED ROUTINE	FOLDING CHAIR	FORWARD DRIVE
FLAGON OF WINE	FOLDING DOORS	FORWARD MARCH
FLAMING HEART	FOLDING STOOL	FORWARD PUPIL
FLASHING EYES	FOLD ONE'S ARMS	FOSTER FATHER
FLASH OF LIGHT	FOLLOW ADVICE	FOSTER MOTHER
FLEECY CLOUDS	FOLLOW MY LEAD	FOSTER PARENT
FLEET OF SHIPS	FOLLOW THE SEA	FOSTER SISTER
FLEET OF TAXIS	FOND OF A GLASS	FOUL LANGUAGE
FLIGHT NUMBER	FOOD AND DRINK	FOUND MISSING
FLIGHT OF TIME	FOOD SHORTAGE	FOUND WANTING
FLIMSY EXCUSE	FOOD SUPPLIES	FOUR AND A HALF

FOUR AND EIGHT
FOUR AND SEVEN
FOUR AND THREE
FOUR DIAMONDS
FOUR FEATHERS
FOUR FEET TALL
FOUR FREEDOMS
FOUR FURLONGS
FOUR HORSEMEN
FOUR NO-TRUMPS
FOUR OF HEARTS
FOUR OF SPADES
FOUR OF TRUMPS
FOURPENNY ONE
FOUR QUARTERS
FOUR SEVENTHS
FOURTEEN DAYS
FOURTH ESTATE
FOURTH FINGER
FOURTH LEAGUE
FOURTH LETTER
FOURTH OF JULY
FOURTH OF JUNE
FOUR THOUSAND
FOURTH SEASON
FOURTH STOREY
FOURTH VOLUME
FOX AND HOUNDS
FRACTURED ARM
FRACTURED LEG
FRAGRANT WEED
FRANCIS BACON
FRANCIS DRAKE
FRANK COUSINS
FRANK SINATRA
FRANTIC HASTE
FRAYED NERVES
FREDDIE MILLS
FREE AS THE AIR
FREE DELIVERY
FREE FROM CARE
FREE FROM DEBT
FREE FROM PAIN
FREE FROM RAIN
FREE FROM VICE
FREE FROM WANT
FREE MOVEMENT
FREE OF CHARGE
FREE QUARTERS
FREE THINKING
FREE TO CHOOSE

FREEZING COLD
FREIGHT TRAIN
FRENCH ACCENT
FRENCH CUSTOM
FRENCH GUINEA
FRENCH LESSON
FRENCH MASTER
FRENCH PASTRY
FRENCH POLISH
FRENCH POODLE
FRENCH WINDOW
FRENZIED RAGE
FRESH ADVANCE
FRESH AS PAINT
FRESH CHAPTER
FRESH COURAGE
FRESH FLOWERS
FRESH HERRING
FRESH OUTLOOK
FRIAR'S BALSAM
FRIDAY'S CHILD
FRIEND INDEED
FRIEND IN NEED
FRIENDLY CHAT
FRIENDLY FACE
FRIENDLY HAND
FRIENDLY WORD
FRIGHTEN AWAY
FROM ALL SIDES
FROM DAY TO DAY
FROM END TO END
FROM THE FIRST
FROM THE NORTH
FROM THE SOUTH
FROM THE START
FROM TOP TO TOE
FRONT AND BACK
FRONTIER ZONE
FRONT PARLOUR
FROSTED GLASS
FROZEN ASSETS
FRUIT MACHINE
FUEL MERCHANT
FULHAM PALACE
FULL CAPACITY
FULL COVERAGE
FULL DAYLIGHT
FULLER'S EARTH
FULL MATURITY
FULL OF ACTION
FULL OF ENERGY

FULL OF HORROR
FULL OF SORROW
FULL OF SPIRIT
FULL PRESSURE
FULLY DRESSED
FULLY ENGAGED
FULLY SECURED
FUME WITH RAGE
FUND OF HUMOUR
FUNERAL MARCH
FUNERAL RITES
FUNNY FEELING
FUN OF THE FAIR
FUR-LINED COAT
FURNITURE VAN
FURNIVAL'S INN
FURTHER DELAY
FURTHER PLANS
FUTILE EFFORT
FUTURE EVENTS

G—12

GAIN A FOOTING
GAIN A HEARING
GAIN A VICTORY
GAIN CURRENCY
GAIN ONE'S ENDS
GAIN PRESTIGE
GAIN STRENGTH
GALA OCCASION
GALLON OF BEER
GALLON OF MILK
GAMBLING DEBT
GAMBLING GAME
GAMBLING HELL
GAME AND MATCH
GAME OF CHANCE
GAME OF TENNIS
GAME PRESERVE
GAMING TABLES
GAMMON RASHER
GARBLED STORY
GARDEN OF EDEN
GARDEN ROLLER
GARDEN SUBURB
GARDEN TROWEL
GARRISON TOWN
GARTER STITCH
GAS POISONING
GATE-LEG TABLE
GENERAL ALARM

GENERAL ALERT	GIPSY CARAVAN	GLOBE THEATRE
GENERAL BOOTH	GIRLS AND BOYS	GLOOMY ASPECT
GENERAL GRANT	GIVE A CONCERT	GLORIOUS MESS
GENERAL ISSUE	GIVE A LECTURE	GLORIOUS TIME
GENERAL SMUTS	GIVE AN ENCORE	GLORIOUS VIEW
GENERAL STAFF	GIVE A PRESENT	GLOWING TERMS
GENERAL STALL	GIVE A RECEIPT	GO AND EAT COKE
GENERAL TERMS	GIVE A SUMMARY	GO BACK IN TIME
GENERAL TREND	GIVE AUDIENCE	GO BACK TO WORK
GENERAL USAGE	GIVE EVIDENCE	GO BY THE BOARD
GENERAL VOICE	GIVE FIRST-AID	GOD BE WITH YOU
GENERAL WOLFE	GIVE HIM SOCKS	GO DOWNSTAIRS
GENITIVE CASE	GIVE IN CHARGE	GO FIFTY-FIFTY
GENTLE BREEZE	GIVE IT A TWIST	GO FOR A BURTON
GENTLEMAN JIM	GIVE IT THE GUN	GO FOR A CRUISE
GENTLE NATURE	GIVE JUDGMENT	GO FOR A STROLL
GENTLE READER	GIVEN A CHANCE	GO FOR A VOYAGE
GENTLE REBUKE	GIVEN A PARDON	GO FOR NOTHING
GENTLY DOES IT!	GIVEN THE BIRD	GO HOT AND COLD
GEORGE BORROW	GIVEN THE BOOT	GOING BEGGING
GEORGE ORWELL	GIVEN THE CANE	GOING CONCERN
GEORGE ROMNEY	GIVEN THE PUSH	GO INTO DETAIL
GERMAN LESSON	GIVEN THE SACK	GO INTO HIDING
GERMAN SCHOOL	GIVEN THE SLIP	GOLD BRACELET
GERMAN SILVER	GIVEN THE VOTE	GOLDEN FLEECE
GERM OF AN IDEA	GIVE ONE A LIFT	GOLDEN GLOVES
GET CLEAN AWAY	GIVE ONE'S BEST	GOLDEN NUMBER
GET CLEAR AWAY	GIVE ONE'S LIFE	GOLDEN REMEDY
GET INTO A MESS	GIVE ONE'S VOTE	GOLDEN SQUARE
GET NO SUPPORT	GIVE ONE'S WORD	GOLDEN SUNSET
GET ONE'S CARDS	GIVE PLEASURE	GOLDERS GREEN
GET ONE'S EYE IN	GIVE SECURITY	GOLDFISH BOWL
GET OUT OF HAND	GIVE THE ALARM	GOLDFISH POND
GET PLASTERED	GIVE THE FACTS	GOLD MERCHANT
GET PROMOTION	GIVE THE ORDER	GOLD RESERVE
GET TECHNICAL	GIVE UP EATING	GOLD STANDARD
GET THE CREDIT	GIVE UP OFFICE	GOLF CHAMPION
GET THE NEEDLE	GIVE UP TRYING	GONE IN A FLASH
GET THE STITCH	GLADSTONE BAG	GONE TO GROUND
GET THE WIND UP	GLADYS COOPER	GOOD AND READY
GET WELL-OILED	GLANCING BLOW	GOOD APPETITE
GIANT DESPAIR	GLARING ERROR	GOOD ARGUMENT
GIANT'S STRIDE	GLASS FACTORY	GOOD BREEDING
GIDDY FEELING	GLASS OF STOUT	GOOD BUSINESS
GIDDY HEIGHTS	GLASS OF WATER	GOOD CLEAN FUN
GIFT OF THE GAB	GLASS SLIPPER	GOOD CROSSING
GIN AND FRENCH	GLASS STOPPER	GOOD DAY'S WORK
GIN AND ORANGE	GLASS TANKARD	GOOD DELIVERY
GINGER BRANDY	GLASS TOO MUCH	GOOD EYESIGHT
GINGER ROGERS	GLASS TUMBLER	GOOD FEATURES
GINGHAM FROCK	GLEAM OF LIGHT	GOOD FOR TRADE

GOOD GRACIOUS	GO TO THE POLLS	GREEK TRAGEDY
GOOD JUDGMENT	GO TO THE RACES	GREEK VERSION
GOOD LIKENESS	GO UP IN FLAMES	GREEN FINGERS
GOOD LINGUIST	GO WITH A SWING	GREEN HOWARDS
GOOD LISTENER	GRACE DARLING	GREEN IN MY EYE
GOOD MATERIAL	GRACEFUL EXIT	GREEN WITH AGE
GOOD OLD TIMES	GRACIE FIELDS	GREY EMINENCE
GOOD PHYSIQUE	GRACIOUS LADY	GREY SQUIRREL
GOOD POSITION	GRAHAM GREENE	GRIEVOUS PAIN
GOOD PRACTICE	GRAIN HARVEST	GRILLED BACON
GOOD PROGRESS	GRAIN OF SENSE	GRILLED STEAK
GOOD QUARTERS	GRAIN OF TRUTH	GRILLED TROUT
GOOD QUESTION	GRAND CENTRAL	GRIM BUSINESS
GOOD RECOVERY	GRAND DUCHESS	GRIM LAUGHTER
GOOD RIDDANCE	GRAND FEELING	GRIND ONE'S AXE
GOOD ROUND SUM	GRAND GUIGNOL	GRIPPING TALE
GOOD SHEPHERD	GRAND LARCENY	GRIT THE TEETH
GOOD SHOOTING	GRAND MISTAKE	GROCERY CHAIN
GOOD SMACKING	GRAND OPENING	GROCERY STORE
GOOD SPANKING	GRAND SEND-OFF	GROPE ONE'S WAY
GOODS STATION	GRAPE HARVEST	GROSS BLUNDER
GOOD TEMPLARS	GRASS WIDOWER	GROSS NEGLECT
GOOD THINKING	GRATED CHEESE	GROSS RETURNS
GOOD THRILLER	GRATING LAUGH	GROSS TONNAGE
GOOD-TIME GIRL	GRATING VOICE	GROUND GINGER
GOOD WATCH-DOG	GRAVE MISTAKE	GROUND TO DUST
GOODWIN SANDS	GRAVE OFFENCE	GROUP CAPTAIN
GOODWOOD PARK	GRAVE SCANDAL	GROUP OF EIGHT
GO ON ALL FOURS	GREAT BRAVERY	GROUP OF SEVEN
GO ON AN ERRAND	GREAT BRITAIN	GROUP OF THREE
GO ON AS BEFORE	GREAT COMFORT	GROUP THERAPY
GO ONE'S OWN WAY	GREAT COMPANY	GROUSE SEASON
GO ON THE SPREE	GREAT EASTERN	GROW ANIMATED
GO ON THE STAGE	GREAT EXPENSE	GROWING CHILD
GOOSE PIMPLES	GREAT FORTUNE	GROWING PAINS
GO OVER THE TOP	GREAT FRIENDS	GROWING THING
GORGEOUS TIME	GREAT MALVERN	GROW POTATOES
GO-SLOW POLICY	GREAT PAINTER	GROW RADISHES
GO-SLOW STRIKE	GREAT RESPECT	GROW TOGETHER
GOSSIP COLUMN	GREAT SECRECY	GRUDGING HAND
GOSSIP WRITER	GREAT SOLDIER	GUARD AGAINST
GO SWIMMINGLY	GREAT SUCCESS	GUARDED REPLY
GO THE SAME WAY	GREAT TRAGEDY	GUERRILLA WAR
GOTHIC SCRIPT	GREAT TRIUMPH	GUESSING GAME
GO TO A WEDDING	GREAT URGENCY	GUIDING LIGHT
GO TO EXTREMES	GREAT VARIETY	GUILT COMPLEX
GO TO HOSPITAL	GREAT VICTORY	GUILTY PERSON
GO TO ONE'S HEAD	GRECIAN STYLE	GUILTY SECRET
GO TO THE DEVIL	GREEK PROFILE	GUITAR PLAYER
GO TO THE FRONT	GREEK SCHOLAR	GUITAR STRING
GO TO THE OPERA	GREEK THEATRE	GULF OF MEXICO

GUNSHOT WOUND	HARD CURRENCY	HEAD FOREMOST
GUY MANNERING	HARD DRINKING	HEAD GARDENER
GUYS AND DOLLS	HARD FEELINGS	HEAD IN THE AIR
GUY'S HOSPITAL	HARD MATTRESS	HEADLINE NEWS
	HARD MEASURES	HEAD MISTRESS
H—12	HARD QUESTION	HEAD OF CATTLE
HABEAS CORPUS	HARD SHOULDER	HEAD OUT TO SEA
HABIT FORMING	HARD STRUGGLE	HEAD SHRINKER
HABITUAL LIAR	HARD SWEARING	HEADS OR TAILS
HACKING COUGH	HARD THINKING	HEAD THE QUEUE
HACK TO PIECES	HARD THOUGHTS	HEADY MIXTURE
HADRIAN'S WALL	HARD TO COME BY	HEADY PERFUME
HAIR MATTRESS	HARD TO FATHOM	HEALING CREAM
HAIR OF THE DOG	HARD TO HANDLE	HEALING POWER
HAIR RESTORER	HARD TO PLEASE	HEALING TOUCH
HAIR'S BREADTH	HARD TRAINING	HEALTH CENTRE
HALF DISTANCE	HARE AND HOUND	HEALTH RESORT
HALF MEASURES	HARICOT BEANS	HEALTHY STATE
HALF MOURNING	HARLEY STREET	HEAP OF STONES
HALF OF BITTER	HARMLESS DRUG	HEAPS OF MONEY
HALF-SEAS OVER	HAROLD PINTER	HEAR A PIN DROP
HALF-WAY HOUSE	HAROLD WILSON	HEAR IN CAMERA
HALLEY'S COMET	HARRY CORBETT	HEART AND HAND
HALL OF MEMORY	HARRY SECOMBE	HEART AND SOUL
HALTING PLACE	HARVEST MOUSE	HEART DISEASE
HAM AND TONGUE	HARVEST QUEEN	HEART FAILURE
HAMBURG STEAK	HASTY PUDDING	HEAR THE TRUTH
HAMPTON COURT	HASTY RETREAT	HEART OF FLINT
HANDEL'S LARGO	HATTON GARDEN	HEART OF STONE
HANDFUL OF MEN	HAUNTED HOUSE	HEART'S DESIRE
HANDICAP RACE	HAUTE COUTURE	HEART SURGERY
HAND OVER FIST	HAVE A FLUTTER	HEART TO HEART
HAND OVER HAND	HAVE A PURPOSE	HEART TROUBLE
HANDS AND FEET	HAVE A RELAPSE	HEARTY ASSENT
HAND'S BREADTH	HAVE A VACANCY	HEATING AGENT
HANGING JUDGE	HAVE FEELINGS	HEAT OF BATTLE
HANGMAN'S ROPE	HAVE NO ANSWER	HEAT OF THE DAY
HANG ONE'S HEAD	HAVE NO CHOICE	HEAT OF THE SUN
HANG TOGETHER	HAVE NO DOUBTS	HEAVE IN SIGHT
HANS ANDERSEN	HAVE NO OPTION	HEAVEN FORBID!
HAPPY AS A KING	HAVE ONE'S WILL	HEAVENLY BODY
HAPPY AS A LARK	HAVE PATIENCE	HEAVENLY CITY
HAPPY HOLIDAY	HAVE PRIORITY	HEAVENLY HOST
HAPPY LANDING	HAVE SCRUPLES	HEAVENS ABOVE!
HAPPY NEW YEAR	HAVE THE FACTS	HEAVY AT HEART
HAPPY OUTCOME	HAVE THE FLOOR	HEAVY BIDDING
HAPPY RELEASE	HAVE THE KNACK	HEAVY BRIGADE
HAPPY RETURNS	HAVE THE LAUGH	HEAVY DRINKER
HAPPY THOUGHT	HAVE THE MEANS	HEAVY PENALTY
HAPPY WARRIOR	HAVE THE POWER	HEAVY SLEEPER
HARBOUR LIGHT	HAZARD A GUESS	HEAVY TRAFFIC

HEAVY VEHICLE
HEAVY WEATHER
HEDGE SPARROW
HEIGHT OF FAME
HEINOUS CRIME
HEIR APPARENT
HELD IN COMMON
HELD TO RANSOM
HELEN SHAPIRO
HELL LET LOOSE
HELL OF A NOISE
HELP YOURSELF
HENRY PURCELL
HERBAL REMEDY
HERD INSTINCT
HERD OF CATTLE
HERD TOGETHER
HERE AND THERE
HEROIC POETRY
HERO OF THE DAY
HERO'S WELCOME
HEWERS OF WOOD
HIDDEN DANGER
HIDDEN DEPTHS
HIDDEN MENACE
HIDDEN TALENT
HIDDEN WEALTH
HIDE ONE'S FACE
HIDE ONE'S HEAD
HIDEOUS CRIME
HIDEOUS NOISE
HIDE THE TRUTH
HIGH ALTITUDE
HIGH BUILDING
HIGH DIVIDEND
HIGHER DEGREE
HIGHER ORDERS
HIGH ESTIMATE
HIGHEST POINT
HIGHEST SCORE
HIGH FIDELITY
HIGHGATE HILL
HIGH INTEREST
HIGH IN THE AIR
HIGHLAND CLAN
HIGHLAND REEL
HIGH LATITUDE
HIGHLY AMUSED
HIGHLY STRUNG
HIGHLY VALUED
HIGH MOUNTAIN

HIGH OFFICIAL
HIGH POSITION
HIGH PRESSURE
HIGH RAINFALL
HIGH STANDARD
HIGH STANDING
HIGH VELOCITY
HILLY COUNTRY
HIP- HIP HURRAH!
HIRED SERVANT
HIRE PURCHASE
HIS REVERENCE
HIT A BOUNDARY
HITCHING POST
HIT ON THE HEAD
HIT THE BOTTLE
HIT THE STUMPS
HIT THE TARGET
HOARY WITH AGE
HOCKEY PLAYER
HOIST THE FLAG
HOIST THE SAIL
HOLD A MEETING
HOLD DOWN A JOB
HOLD IN COMMON
HOLD IN ESTEEM
HOLD IN HORROR
HOLD IN PLEDGE
HOLD ONE'S LEAD
HOLD OUT A HAND
HOLD OUT HOPES
HOLD THE CARDS
HOLD THE FIELD
HOLD THE REINS
HOLD THE STAGE
HOLD TOGETHER
HOLD TO RANSOM
HOLIDAY HAUNT
HOLIDAY MONEY
HOLLAND HOUSE
HOLLOW CHEEKS
HOLLOW SPHERE
HOLLOW SQUARE
HOLLOW THREAT
HOLLOW VESSEL
HOLY ALLIANCE
HOLY MACKEREL
HOLY OF HOLIES
HOME COMFORTS
HOME COUNTIES
HOME FROM HOME

HOME INDUSTRY
HOMELY PERSON
HOME-MADE CAKE
HOME PRODUCTS
HOMING PIGEON
HONEST FELLOW
HONEST LABOUR
HONEST LIVING
HONEYED WORDS
HONORARY RANK
HONOUR BRIGHT
HONOURED NAME
HONOURS OF WAR
HOODED TERROR
HOOKS AND EYES
HOPE DEFERRED
HOPELESS CASE
HOPELESS LOSS
HOPELESS MESS
HOPELESS TASK
HORN OF PLENTY
HORRIBLE BORE
HORS DE COMBAT
HORSE AND CART
HORSE AND TRAP
HORSE BLANKET
HORSE DEALING
HORSE MARINES
HORSE SOLDIER
HORSE TRAINER
HOSPITAL CASE
HOSPITAL SHIP
HOSPITAL WARD
HOSTILE CROWD
HOSTILE FORCE
HOSTILE PRESS
HOT AND STRONG
HOTBED OF VICE
HOT CHESTNUTS
HOT CHOCOLATE
HOT CROSS-BUNS
HOTEL OMNIBUS
HOT FAVOURITE
HOT GOSPELLER
HOT-WATER PIPE
HOUND TO DEATH
HOURLY CHIMES
HOUR OF DANGER
HOUR OF THE DAY
HOUSE AND HOME
HOUSE BREAKER

HOUSE COLOURS
HOUSE FOR SALE
HOUSEHOLD GOD
HOUSE OF CARDS
HOUSE OF LORDS
HOUSE OF PEERS
HOUSE OF TUDOR
HOUSE OF USHER
HOUSE PAINTER
HOUSE SPARROW
HOUSE SURGEON
HOUSE TO HOUSE
HOUSE WARMING
HOUSEY HOUSEY
HOW'S THE ENEMY?
HUMAN AFFAIRS
HUMANE KILLER
HUMAN ELEMENT
HUMAN FAILING
HUMAN FRAILTY
HUMAN REMAINS
HUMAN SPECIES
HUMBLE ORIGIN
HUMBLE PERSON
HUMMING SOUND
HUMOROUS VEIN
HUMPTY DUMPTY
HUNDRED A YEAR
HUNDRED LINES
HUNDRED MILES
HUNDRED TO ONE
HUNDRED YARDS
HUNDRED YEARS
HUNGER STRIKE
HUNK OF CHEESE
HUNTING FIELD
HUNTING LODGE
HUNTING SPEAR
HUNTSMAN'S CRY
HURL DEFIANCE
HURRIED VISIT
HURT FEELINGS
HYDRAULIC RAM
HYDROGEN BOMB
HYMN OF PRAISE

I—12
ICE-CREAM SODA
ICY RECEPTION
IDEAL HUSBAND
IDENTITY CARD

IDENTITY DISC
IDLE THOUGHTS
IF THE CAP FITS
IGNEOUS ROCKS
ILLEGAL ENTRY
ILLICIT GAINS
ILLICIT MEANS
ILLICIT STILL
ILL-TIMED JEST
IMMORTAL FAME
IMMORTAL NAME
IMMORTAL POET
IMMORTAL SOUL
IMPERIAL PINT
IMPERIAL RULE
IMPLIED TRUTH
IMPROPER WORD
IN A BAD TEMPER
IN A COLD SWEAT
IN A DEAD FAINT
IN A GOOD LIGHT
IN ALL HONESTY
IN A LOUD VOICE
IN AN ACCIDENT
IN AN ARMCHAIR
IN APPEARANCE
IN A SHORT TIME
IN ATTENDANCE
IN AT THE DEATH
IN CASE OF NEED
INCHCAPE ROCK
INCHES TALLER
INCOMING TIDE
IN CONCLUSION
IN CONFERENCE
IN CONFIDENCE
INCREASED PAY
IN DEEP WATERS
INDELIBLE INK
INDIAN MILLET
INDIAN MUTINY
INDIAN SUMMER
IN DIFFICULTY
INDIRECT HINT
INDOOR AERIAL
INDOOR SPORTS
IN EMPLOYMENT
INFANT IN ARMS
INFANTRY UNIT
INFANT SCHOOL
INFERIOR RANK

IN FINE FETTLE
INFINITE TIME
INFRA-RED LAMP
INFRA-RED RAYS
IN FULL FLIGHT
IN GOOD HEALTH
IN GOOD REPAIR
IN GOOD SUPPLY
IN HIGH FAVOUR
IN HIGH RELIEF
IN HOLY ORDERS
IN HOT PURSUIT
INITIAL STAGE
INJURED PARTY
INJURED PRIDE
IN LEAGUE WITH
IN LIKE MANNER
IN LOVE AND WAR
IN LOW SPIRITS
IN MODERATION
IN NEED OF HELP
INNER CABINET
INNER COATING
INNER SANCTUM
IN OCCUPATION
IN ONE RESPECT
IN ONE'S FAVOUR
IN ONE'S HEYDAY
IN ONE'S OLD AGE
IN ONE'S SENSES
IN ONE'S STRIDE
IN OPPOSITION
IN OTHER WORDS
IN OUR OPINION
IN PARTICULAR
IN POOR HEALTH
IN POSSESSION
IN PROCESSION
IN PROPORTION
IN QUARANTINE
IN RECORD TIME
IN RETIREMENT
IN RETROSPECT
INSANE ASYLUM
INSECURE HOLD
IN SETTLEMENT
IN SILHOUETTE
IN SINGLE FILE
IN SLOW MOTION
IN SUBJECTION
IN SUCCESSION

INTEGRAL PART
INTEREST FREE
INTEREST RATE
INTERIOR WALL
IN TERMS OF LAW
IN THE BALANCE
IN THE BALCONY
IN THE BEDROOM
IN THE CABINET
IN THE CAPITAL
IN THE COUNTRY
IN THE CRYSTAL
IN THE DAYTIME
IN THE DEEP END
IN THE EVENING
IN THE EXTREME
IN THE FASHION
IN THE GALLERY
IN THE HONOURS
IN THE INTERIM
IN THE KITCHEN
IN THE LIBRARY
IN THE LONG RUN
IN THE MORNING
IN THE NURSERY
IN THE OLD DAYS
IN THE OPEN AIR
IN THE PADDOCK
IN THE PARLOUR
IN THE PEERAGE
IN THE PICTURE
IN THE PRESENT
IN THE RUNNING
IN THE SHADOWS
IN THE SUBURBS
IN THE THEATRE
IN THE TROPICS
IN THE VERY ACT
IN THE VILLAGE
IN THE YEAR ONE
IN TRIPLICATE
IN UNDERTONES
IN UTMOST NEED
INVALID CHAIR
INVERSE ORDER
INVERSE RATIO
INVERTED SNOB
INVERTED TURN
INVISIBLE INK
INVISIBLE MAN
INVOICE CLERK

IN YUGOSLAVIA
IRISH COLLEEN
IRISH TERRIER
IRISH WHISKEY
IRON AND STEEL
IRONING BOARD
IRVING BERLIN
ISLAND OF CUBA
ISLE OF CYPRUS
ISLE OF THANET
ISOLATED CASE
ISSUE A THREAT
ITALIAN MONEY
IT ALL DEPENDS
IT'S AN ILL WIND
IT'S A PLEASURE

J—12

JACKET POTATO
JACKIE COOGAN
JACK IN OFFICE
JACK OF HEARTS
JACK OF SPADES
JACK OF TRUMPS
JACK ROBINSON
JACK SHEPPARD
JACOB'S LADDER
JADE NECKLACE
JAMES BOSWELL
JAMES STEWART
JAMES THURBER
JANETTE SCOTT
JANUARY SALES
JAUNDICED EYE
JAZZ FESTIVAL
JEAN METCALFE
JE NE SAIS QUOI
JERMYN STREET
JIG-SAW PUZZLE
JIMMY DURANTE
JIMMY EDWARDS
JIMMY WHEELER
JIM THE PENMAN
JOAN CRAWFORD
JOG THE MEMORY
JOHN CLEMENTS
JOHNNY MATHIS
JOIN IN THE FUN
JOIN ONE'S SHIP
JOINT ACCOUNT
JOINT CONCERN

JOIN THE CHOIR
JOIN THE DANCE
JOIN THE ENEMY
JOIN THE PARTY
JOIN THE QUEUE
JOIN THE RANKS
JOINT HOLDING
JOIN TOGETHER
JOINT TENANCY
JOINT TRUSTEE
JOKING MATTER
JOLLY JACK TAR
JOLLY SWAGMAN
JONATHAN WILD
JORDAN ALMOND
JOSEPH CONRAD
JOSEPH COTTON
JOSEPH STALIN
JUDGE AND JURY
JUDGMENT SEAT
JULIAN HUXLEY
JULIE ANDREWS
JULIENNE SOUP
JULIUS CAESAR
JULY THE FIFTH
JULY THE FIRST
JULY THE NINTH
JULY THE SIXTH
JULY THE TENTH
JULY THE THIRD
JUMP THE QUEUE
JUMP THE RAILS
JUNE THE FIFTH
JUNE THE FIRST
JUNE THE NINTH
JUNE THE SIXTH
JUNE THE TENTH
JUNE THE THIRD
JUNIOR SCHOOL
JUNIOR TYPIST
JUST AS YOU SAY
JUST FOR SPITE
JUST THE THING
JUST THIS ONCE
JUVENILE LEAD

K—12

KEEN APPETITE
KEEN AS A RAZOR
KEEN INTEREST
KEEN PLEASURE

KEEP ACCOUNTS	KNIFE GRINDER	LADY JANE GREY
KEEP A LOOK-OUT	KNIGHT ERRANT	LADY MARGARET
KEEP A PROMISE	KNIGHTLY DEED	LADY MAYORESS
KEEP CHEERFUL	KNIT A SWEATER	LADY NICOTINE
KEEP-FIT CLASS	KNIT ONE'S BROW	LADY'S BICYCLE
KEEP GOOD TIME	KNIT THE BROWS	LADY SUPERIOR
KEEP GUESSING	KNIT TOGETHER	LAGER AND LIME
KEEP IN PRISON	KNOCK AGAINST	LAISSEZ FAIRE
KEEP IN PURDAH	KNOCK OFF WORK	LAKE DISTRICT
KEEP IN REPAIR	KNOCK-OUT BLOW	LAKE MAGGIORE
KEEP ONE'S FEET	KNOW FOR A FACT	LAKE MICHIGAN
KEEP ONE'S HEAD	KNOW FULL WELL	LAKE SUPERIOR
KEEP ONE'S SEAT	KNOW NO BETTER	LAKE VICTORIA
KEEP ONE'S WORD	KNOW NO BOUNDS	LAKE WINNIPEG
KEEP ON TRYING	KNOW ONE'S DUTY	LAMBENT LIGHT
KEEP PRISONER	KNOW THE DRILL	LAMB SANDWICH
KEEP THE BOOKS	KNOW THE FACTS	LANDED ESTATE
KEEP THE PEACE	KNOW THE ROPES	LANDED GENTRY
KEEP THE SCORE	KNOW THE SCORE	LANDING CRAFT
KEEP TOGETHER	KNOW THE TRUTH	LANDING PARTY
KEEP UP-TO-DATE	KNOW THE WORST	LANDING PLACE
KENNETH HORNE	KNOW WHAT TO DO	LANDING STRIP
KEPT ON A LEASH	KNUCKLE UNDER	LAND OF DREAMS
KETTLE OF FISH	KNUR AND SPELL	LAND OF PLENTY
KEY OF THE DOOR		LAND SURVEYOR
KEY SIGNATURE		LAND TRANSFER
KEYSTONE COPS	**L—12**	LANTERN SLIDE
KEY TO THE SAFE	LABOURED JOKE	LAP OF THE GODS
KHAKI UNIFORM	LABOUR IN VAIN	LARGE ACCOUNT
KILL BY INCHES	LABOUR LEADER	LARGE EXPANSE
KILL OUTRIGHT	LABOUR MARKET	LARGE HELPING
KINDLING WOOD	LABOUR OFFICE	LARGE PORTION
KING AND QUEEN	LABOUR OF LOVE	LARGE SECTION
KING OF BEASTS	LABOUR POLICY	LARGE VARIETY
KING OF FRANCE	LACE CURTAINS	LASH THE WAVES
KING OF HEARTS	LACKING MONEY	LAST BUT THREE
KING OF SPADES	LACKING POINT	LAST DELIVERY
KING OF TRUMPS	LACKING POISE	LAST ELECTION
KING'S COLLEGE	LACKING PROOF	LAST FRONTIER
KING'S COUNSEL	LACKING SENSE	LASTING PEACE
KING'S ENGLISH	LACK INTEREST	LAST JUDGMENT
KING'S HIGHWAY	LACK OF BRAINS	LAST RESOURCE
KING'S PROCTOR	LACK OF FINISH	LAST SATURDAY
KITCHEN CHAIR	LACK OF POLISH	LAST SYLLABLE
KITCHEN RANGE	LACK OF PROFIT	LAST THURSDAY
KITCHEN STOVE	LACK OF REASON	LAST TO ARRIVE
KITCHEN TABLE	LACK OF SPIRIT	LATE IN THE DAY
KNACKER'S YARD	LACK OF WISDOM	LATE LAMENTED
KNAVE OF CLUBS	LACROSSE TEAM	LATE MARRIAGE
KNEE BREECHES	LADDER OF FAME	LATENT ENERGY
KNIFE AND FORK	LADY HAMILTON	LATENT TALENT

LATEST REPORT
LATIN AMERICA
LATIN GRAMMAR
LATIN QUARTER
LATIN TEACHER
LAUGH OUT LOUD
LAUGH TO SCORN
LAUNCHING PAD
LAUREL WREATH
LAVENDER HILL
LAVISH PRAISE
LAW OF ENGLAND
LAW OF GRAVITY
LAW OF THE LAND
LAWS OF MOTION
LAWYER'S BRIEF
LAY A FINGER ON
LAY DOWN A PLAN
LAYER ON LAYER
LAY IT ON THICK
LEAD A GAY LIFE
LEADER WRITER
LEADING ACTOR
LEADING LIGHT
LEAD IN PRAYER
LEAD THE DANCE
LEAD THE FIELD
LEANING TOWER
LEAP IN THE AIR
LEARN A LESSON
LEARN BY HEART
LEARNED JUDGE
LEARN TO DRIVE
LEARN TO RELAX
LEARN TO WRITE
LEATHER GOODS
LEATHER STRAP
LEAVE A LEGACY
LEAVE IT ALONE
LEAVE NO DOUBT
LEAVE NO TRACE
LEAVE NO WISER
LEAVE OFF WORK
LEAVE THE ARMY
LEAVE THE NAVY
LEAVE THE NEST
LEAVE THE ROOM
LED ONE A DANCE
LED TO BELIEVE
LEFT AND RIGHT
LEFT-HAND BEND

LEFT-HAND SIDE
LEFT-HAND TURN
LEFT IN THE AIR
LEFT NO CHOICE
LEFT SHOULDER
LEFT STANDING
LEFT TO CHANCE
LEGAL ADVISER
LEGAL CUSTODY
LEGAL DEFENCE
LEGAL FICTION
LEGAL JOURNAL
LEGAL OPINION
LEGAL PROCESS
LEGAL VERDICT
LEGS TOGETHER
LEG TO STAND ON
LEISURE HOURS
LEMON PUDDING
LENGTH OF TIME
LESSON ELEVEN
LESSON TWELVE
LESS THAN COST
LETHAL WEAPON
LET ONESELF GO
LET OUT ON HIRE
LETTER OPENER
LETTER WRITER
LET THINGS RIP
LET WELL ALONE
LEVEL PEGGING
LEVEL STRETCH
LEWIS CARROLL
LEYTON ORIENT
LIBERAL DONOR
LIBERAL PARTY
LIBERAL SHARE
LIBERTY HORSE
LIBYAN DESERT
LICENSING ACT
LICENSING LAW
LICK ONE'S LIPS
LIE OF THE LAND
LIE PROSTRATE
LIFE AND DEATH
LIFE IMMORTAL
LIFE INSTINCT
LIFE INTEREST
LIFE IN THE RAW
LIFE OF LUXURY
LIFE SENTENCE

LIFT ONE'S HAND
LIFT THE ELBOW
LIGHT A CANDLE
LIGHT AND AIRY
LIGHT AND DARK
LIGHT BRIGADE
LIGHT CAVALRY
LIGHT CRUISER
LIGHT DRAGOON
LIGHTED TORCH
LIGHT FINGERS
LIGHTNING ROD
LIGHT OF HEART
LIGHT RAILWAY
LIGHT READING
LIGHT SLEEPER
LIGHT THE LAMP
LIGHT TRAFFIC
LIGHT VEHICLE
LIKE HOT CAKES
LIKE OLD BOOTS
LIKE SARDINES
LIKE THE DEVIL
LIKE UNTO LIKE
LIKE WILDFIRE
LILY OF LAGUNA
LIMB FROM LIMB
LIMB OF THE LAW
LIMITED MEANS
LIMITED SCOPE
LIMITED SCORE
LIMITED SPACE
LINCOLN GREEN
LINE OF ACTION
LINE OF BATTLE
LINE OF FLIGHT
LINE REGIMENT
LINE UPON LINE
LINGUA FRANCA
LINK TOGETHER
LIQUEUR GLASS
LIQUID ASSETS
LIQUID MAKE-UP
LIST OF VOTERS
LITERAL ERROR
LITERAL TRUTH
LITERARY AIMS
LITERARY CLUB
LITERARY FAME
LITERARY HACK
LITERARY LION

LITERARY PAGE	LONG AND OFTEN	LOSE THE ASHES
LITERARY STAR	LONG CORRIDOR	LOSE THE MATCH
LITERARY WORK	LONG DISTANCE	LOSE THE SCENT
LITTER BASKET	LONG DIVISION	LOSING BATTLE
LITTLE CHANCE	LONG DRAWN-OUT	LOSING HAZARD
LITTLE CHANGE	LONGEST NIGHT	LOSING TICKET
LITTLE DEMAND	LONG EXPECTED	LOSS OF CUSTOM
LITTLE DORRIT	LONG FAREWELL	LOSS OF ENERGY
LITTLE ENOUGH	LONG-FELT WANT	LOSS OF HEALTH
LITTLE FINGER	LONG FOR PEACE	LOSS OF HONOUR
LITTLE HITLER	LONG SENTENCE	LOSS OF MEMORY
LITTLE MONKEY	LONG STANDING	LOSS OF MORALE
LITTLE PEOPLE	LONG-TERM LOAN	LOSS OF PROFIT
LITTLE SISTER	LONG-TERM VIEW	LOSS OF REASON
LITTLE SQUIRT	LONG TROUSERS	LOSS OF SPEECH
LITTLE TERROR	LONG VACATION	LOSS OF VISION
LITTLE THANKS	LONG WAY ROUND	LOSS OF WEIGHT
LITTLE THINGS	LONSDALE BELT	LOST AND FOUND
LITTLE TIN GOD	LOOK BOTH WAYS	LOST ELECTION
LITTLE WONDER	LOOK DOWNCAST	LOST FOR A WORD
LIVE AND LEARN	LOOK DOWN UPON	LOST FOR WORDS
LIVE FOR KICKS	LOOK ONE'S BEST	LOST IN WONDER
LIVE FOR TODAY	LOOK PECULIAR	LOST PROPERTY
LIVE IN A DREAM	LOOK PLEASANT	LOTUS BLOSSOM
LIVE IN CLOVER	LOOK SHEEPISH	LOUD AND CLEAR
LIVE IN LUXURY	LOOK SIDEWAYS	LOUD APPLAUSE
LIVELY DEBATE	LOOK SUPERIOR	LOUD LAUGHTER
LIVE ON CREDIT	LOOSE CLOTHES	LOUIS GOLDING
LIVE ONE'S LIFE	LOOSE CONDUCT	LOUIS PASTEUR
LIVER SAUSAGE	LOOSE GARMENT	LOUNGE LIZARD
LIVERY STABLE	LORD ADVOCATE	LOVE INTEREST
LIVE TOGETHER	LORD ALMIGHTY	LOVELY FIGURE
LIVING MATTER	LORD LEIGHTON	LOVE OF NATURE
LIVING MEMORY	LORD MACAULAY	LOVING COUPLE
LIVING TISSUE	LORD OF APPEAL	LOW CHURCHMAN
LOAD SHEDDING	LORD TENNYSON	LOW CONDITION
LOBSTER PATTY	LORETTA YOUNG	LOW COUNTRIES
LOBSTER SALAD	LOSE BUSINESS	LOW-DOWN TRICK
LOCAL AFFAIRS	LOSE INTEREST	LOWER ANIMALS
LOCAL DIALECT	LOSE MOMENTUM	LOWER BRACKET
LOCAL FEELING	LOSE ONE'S FORM	LOWER CHAMBER
LOCALISED WAR	LOSE ONE'S GRIP	LOWER CLASSES
LOCK-UP GARAGE	LOSE ONE'S HAIR	LOWER ONESELF
LODGING HOUSE	LOSE ONE'S HEAD	LOWER REGIONS
LOGICAL ERROR	LOSE ONE'S LIFE	LOWER THE FLAG
LOGICAL ORDER	LOSE ONE'S SEAT	LOWEST BIDDER
LONDON BRIDGE	LOSE ONE'S WIFE	LOWEST DEPTHS
LONDON EDITOR	LOSE ONE'S WITS	LOW FREQUENCY
LONDON LIGHTS	LOSE PATIENCE	LOW VALUATION
LONDON SEASON	LOSE PRESTIGE	LOW WATER MARK
LONG ANCESTRY	LOSE STRENGTH	LOYAL CITIZEN

LOYAL SUBJECT	MAKE ABSOLUTE	MAN OF DESTINY
LOYAL SUPPORT	MAKE A CENTURY	MAN OF FASHION
LUCIFER MATCH	MAKE A CIRCUIT	MAN OF FORTUNE
LUCKY AT CARDS	MAKE A CURTSEY	MAN OF HIS WORD
LUCKY VENTURE	MAKE A DEAD SET	MAN OF LEISURE
LUGGAGE LABEL	MAKE ADVANCES	MAN OF LETTERS
LULWORTH COVE	MAKE A FAUX PAS	MAN OF MYSTERY
LUMBER JACKET	MAKE A FORTUNE	MAN OF SCIENCE
LUMP TOGETHER	MAKE A GESTURE	MAN OF THE HOUR
LUSH PASTURES	MAKE A GET-AWAY	MAN ON THE MOON
LUST FOR POWER	MAKE A HUNDRED	MAN ON THE SPOT
LUXURIOUS BED	MAKE A LANDING	MAN OVERBOARD
LUXURY CRUISE	MAKE A LONG ARM	MANSION HOUSE
LYRIC THEATRE	MAKE A MISTAKE	MAN THE BREACH
	MAKE AN APPEAL	MAN-TO-MAN TALK
M—12	MAKE AN ARREST	MANUAL LABOUR
MACHINE TOOLS	MAKE AN EFFORT	MANUAL WORKER
MAD AS A HATTER	MAKE AN ESCAPE	MANY A LONG DAY
MADDING CROWD	MAKE A NEW WILL	MANY RESPECTS
MADE IN FRANCE	MAKE A PRESENT	MANY YEARS AGO
MADE IN HEAVEN	MAKE A PROMISE	MAP OF AUSTRIA
MAGIC FORMULA	MAKE A PROTEST	MAP OF BELGIUM
MAGIC LANTERN	MAKE A REQUEST	MAP OF DENMARK
MAGNETIC FISH	MAKE BAD BLOOD	MAP OF ENGLAND
MAGNETIC MINE	MAKE BANKRUPT	MAP OF GERMANY
MAGNETIC POLE	MAKE ENDS MEET	MAP OF HOLLAND
MAGNETIC TAPE	MAKE IT SNAPPY	MAP OF IRELAND
MAIDEN FLIGHT	MAKE MISCHIEF	MARATHON RACE
MAIDEN SPEECH	MAKE NO PROFIT	MARCHING SONG
MAIDEN STAKES	MAKE ONE'S EXIT	MARGINAL LAND
MAIDEN VOYAGE	MAKE ONE SIT UP	MARGINAL NOTE
MAID OF HONOUR	MAKE ONE'S MARK	MARGINAL SEAT
MAIN BUSINESS	MAKE ONE'S PILE	MARIE CELESTE
MAIN DRAINAGE	MAKE ONE'S WILL	MARIE CORELLI
MAIN ENTRANCE	MAKE OUT A CASE	MARIE TEMPEST
MAIN INDUSTRY	MAKE PROGRESS	MARIE THERESA
MAIN QUESTION	MAKE SPEECHES	MARINE ANIMAL
MAIN SEQUENCE	MAKE THE GRADE	MARINE ENGINE
MAÎTRE D'HÔTEL	MAKE-UP ARTIST	MARINE GROWTH
MAJOR BARBARA	MAKE UP LEEWAY	MARINE PARADE
MAJOR EDITION	MALAY STRAITS	MARINE STORES
MAJOR GENERAL	MALTESE CROSS	MARITIME ALPS
MAJORITY RULE	MALVERN HILLS	MARIUS GORING
MAJORITY VOTE	MAN ABOUT TOWN	MARKED MANNER
MAJOR PREMISE	MAN AT THE HELM	MARKET GARDEN
MAJOR PROPHET	MANDERIN DUCK	MARKET SQUARE
MAJOR TRAGEDY	MANGO CHUTNEY	MARKET STREET
MAKE A BARGAIN	MANILLA PAPER	MARKET TRENDS
MAKE A BEE-LINE	MAN IN THE DOCK	MARK OF ESTEEM
MAKE A BEQUEST	MAN IN THE MOON	MARK OF GENIUS
MAKE A BONFIRE	MAN-MADE FIBRE	MARK THE CARDS

MARK THE SCORE
MARLEY'S GHOST
MARLON BRANDO
MARMALADE CAT
MARRIAGE KNOT
MARRIAGE RATE
MARRIAGE TIES
MARRIAGE VOWS
MARRIED BLISS
MARRIED WOMAN
MARRY BY PROXY
MARRY IN HASTE
MARSHALL PLAN
MARTIAL MUSIC
MARTIN LUTHER
MARX BROTHERS
MARY OF ARGYLL
MARY PICKFORD
MASONIC LODGE
MASSED CHOIRS
MASSES OF FOOD
MASS HYSTERIA
MASS MOVEMENT
MASS MURDERER
MASS OF NERVES
MASTER AND MAN
MASTER CUTLER
MASTER GUNNER
MASTER OF ARTS
MASTER SPIRIT
MASTER STROKE
MASTER TAILOR
MATCHING PAIR
MATERIAL GAIN
MATERNAL LOVE
MATING SEASON
MATTER IN HAND
MATTER OF FACT
MAXIMUM PRICE
MAXIMUM SPEED
MAYPOLE DANCE
MAY THE EIGHTH
MAY THE FOURTH
MAY THE SECOND
MEAN BUSINESS
MEAN MISCHIEF
MEANS TO AN END
MEASURED MILE
MEAT AND DRINK
MEAT SANDWICH
MEDICAL BOARD

MEDICAL CHECK
MEDICAL STAFF
MEDICINE BALL
MEDIUM HEIGHT
MEDIUM SHERRY
MEET BY CHANCE
MEETING HOUSE
MEETING PLACE
MEETING POINT
MEET IN SECRET
MEET ONE'S FATE
MEET THE PLANE
MEET THE TRAIN
MELTED BUTTER
MELTED CHEESE
MELTING POINT
MELT THE HEART
MEMORIAL HALL
MEND ONE'S WAYS
MEN OF HARLECH
MENTAL ASYLUM
MENTAL EFFORT
MENTAL ENERGY
MENTAL HEALTH
MENTALLY SICK
MENTAL STRAIN
MENTAL STRESS
MERCHANT BANK
MERCHANT NAVY
MERCHANT SHIP
MERCY KILLING
MERE FLEA-BITE
MERE PITTANCE
MERRY ENGLAND
MERRY MONARCH
MERRY OLD SOUL
MERSEY TUNNEL
MESSENGER BOY
METAL FATIGUE
METEOR SHOWER
METHOD ACTING
METRICAL UNIT
METRIC SYSTEM
MEZZO SOPRANO
MICHAEL ARLEN
MICHAEL MILES
MICKEY ROONEY
MIDDLE AND LEG
MIDDLE COURSE
MIDDLE FINGER
MIDDLE TEMPLE

MIDDLE WICKET
MIDNIGHT BLUE
MIDNIGHT HOUR
MIDNIGHT MASS
MIDNIGHT SWIM
MIDSUMMER DAY
MIGHT AND MAIN
MIGHT IS RIGHT
MIGHTY EFFORT
MIGHTY HUNTER
MILES PER HOUR
MILE UPON MILE
MILFORD HAVEN
MILITARY BAND
MILITARY BASE
MILITARY BODY
MILITARY CAMP
MILITARY DUTY
MILITARY LIFE
MILITARY PACE
MILITARY RANK
MILITARY TYPE
MILITARY UNIT
MILK AND A DASH
MILK AND HONEY
MILK AND SUGAR
MILK AND WATER
MILKING STOOL
MILK SHORTAGE
MILLION YEARS
MINCE MATTERS
MINCING STEPS
MIND HOW YOU GO!
MIND YOUR HEAD!
MIND YOUR STEP!
MINERAL SALTS
MINERAL WATER
MINERAL WORLD
MINIATURE DOG
MINING EXPERT
MINING RIGHTS
MINOR AILMENT
MINORITY RULE
MINORITY VOTE
MINOR PREMISE
MINOR PROPHET
MINOR SET-BACK
MINOR TRAGEDY
MINSTREL SHOW
MISPLACED WIT
MISSED CHANCE

MISSING PIECE
MISS THE PLANE
MISS THE POINT
MISS THE TRAIN
MISS UNIVERSE
MISTAKEN IDEA
MISTRESS FORD
MIXED BATHING
MIXED COMPANY
MIXED DOUBLES
MIXED FARMING
MIXED MOTIVES
MIXED PICKLES
MIX IN SOCIETY
MOATED GRANGE
MOBILE COLUMN
MODEL HUSBAND
MODEL PATIENT
MODEL RAILWAY
MODE OF LIVING
MODERATE RENT
MODERN SCHOOL
MODEST INCOME
MODEST PERSON
MODUS VIVENDI
MOIRA SHEARER
MOLL FLANDERS
MOMENT OF TIME
MONASTIC LIFE
MONASTIC VOWS
MONDAY'S CHILD
MONETARY HELP
MONETARY UNIT
MONEYED CLASS
MONEY MATTERS
MONEY TO SPARE
MONKEY GLANDS
MONKEY JACKET
MONKEY PUZZLE
MONKEY TRICKS
MONTH BY MONTH
MONTHLY VISIT
MONTH'S NOTICE
MOOR OF VENICE
MOOT QUESTION
MORAL CONDUCT
MORAL COURAGE
MORALITY PLAY
MORALLY BOUND
MORAL SCIENCE
MORAL STAMINA

MORAL SUPPORT
MORAL VICTORY
MORE'S THE PITY
MORE THAN EVER
MORE THAN ONCE
MORNING AFTER
MORNING DRESS
MORNING GLORY
MORNING PAPER
MORRIS DANCER
MORTAL COMBAT
MORTAL TERROR
MORTE D'ARTHUR
MORTGAGE DEED
MOSQUITO BITE
MOST EXCITING
MOST GRACIOUS
MOST OF THE DAY
MOST REVEREND
MOTE IN THE EYE
MOTHER AND SON
MOTHER CHURCH
MOTHER GRUNDY
MOTHERLY LOVE
MOTHER NATURE
MOTHER OF MINE
MOTHERS' UNION
MOTHER TONGUE
MOTOR BICYCLE
MOTOR CRUISER
MOTORING CLUB
MOTOR LICENCE
MOTOR SCOOTER
MOTOR VEHICLE
MOUND OF EARTH
MOUNTAIN GOAT
MOUNTAIN LAKE
MOUNTAIN PASS
MOUNTAIN PEAK
MOUNTAIN TARN
MOUNT A LADDER
MOUNT EVEREST
MOUNT OF VENUS
MOUNT OLYMPUS
MOUNT PEGASUS
MOURA LYMPANY
MOUSTACHE CUP
MOUTH TO MOUTH
MOVABLE FEAST
MOVED TO TEARS
MOVE SIDEWAYS

MOVING APPEAL
MOVING FINGER
MOVING SPEECH
MOVING SPIRIT
MOVING TARGET
MUCH IMPROVED
MUCH IN DEMAND
MUCH MISTAKEN
MUD IN YOUR EYE
MUFFLED DRUMS
MUFFLED TONES
MUFFLED VOICE
MUGGY WEATHER
MULBERRY BUSH
MULBERRY TREE
MULTIPLE SHOP
MULTIPLE STAR
MUNICH CRISIS
MUNICIPAL LAW
MURDER CHARGE
MURDER VICTIM
MURDER WEAPON
MURIEL PAVLOW
MUSCATEL WINE
MUSHROOM SOUP
MUSICAL PIECE
MUSICAL SCALE
MUSICAL SCORE
MUSICAL SOUND
MUSICAL VOICE
MUSIC AT NIGHT
MUSIC LICENCE
MUSIC TEACHER
MUTED STRINGS
MUTTON CUTLET
MUTUAL FRIEND
MUTUAL HATRED
MUTUAL PROFIT
MUTUAL REGARD
MY BLUE HEAVEN
MY DEAR FELLOW
MY DEAR WATSON
MY GOOD FRIEND
MYSTERY STORY

N—12

NAIL POLISHER
NAIL SCISSORS
NAKED REALITY
NAME IN LIGHTS
NARROW DEFEAT

NARROW ESCAPE	NEAR RELATION	NICKEL SILVER
NARROW GROOVE	NEAR RELATIVE	NIGEL PATRICK
NARROW MARGIN	NEAR THE COAST	NIGGLING PAIN
NARROW SQUEAK	NEAR THE SHORE	NIGHT CLASSES
NARROW STREET	NEAR THE TRUTH	NIGHT CLOTHES
NARROW THE GAP	NECKING PARTY	NIGHT DRIVING
NARROW TUNNEL	NECK OF MUTTON	NIGHT FIGHTER
NATIONAL BANK	NEEDLESS RISK	NIGHT NURSERY
NATIONAL DEBT	NEGATIVE POLE	NIGHT OF BLISS
NATIONAL DISH	NEGATIVE SIGN	NIGHT PROWLER
NATIONAL FLAG	NEGATIVE VOTE	NINE AND A HALF
NATIONAL GAME	NEON LIGHTING	NINE AND EIGHT
NATIONAL GRID	NERVE ONESELF	NINE AND SEVEN
NATIONAL HERO	NERVOUS STATE	NINE AND THREE
NATIONAL PARK	NERVOUS WRECK	NINE OF HEARTS
NATIONAL POLL	NEST OF TABLES	NINE OF SPADES
NATIONAL ROAD	NEUTER GENDER	NINE OF TRUMPS
NATIONAL STUD	NEUTRAL POWER	NINE OUT OF TEN
NATION IN ARMS	NEUTRAL STATE	NINE THOUSAND
NATIVE CUSTOM	NEVER DESPAIR	NINTH CENTURY
NATIVE TONGUE	NEVER GO WRONG	NINTH OF APRIL
NATIVE TROOPS	NEVER THE SAME	NINTH OF MARCH
NATIVITY PLAY	NEVER TOO LATE	NITROUS OXIDE
NATURAL BREAK	NEVER YOU MIND!	NO ADMITTANCE
NATURAL CHARM	NEW AMSTERDAM	NO BED OF ROSES
NATURAL CHILD	NEW BRUNSWICK	NOBLE BEARING
NATURAL COVER	NEW DEPARTURE	NOBLE DESCENT
NATURAL DEATH	NEW ENGLANDER	NOBLE EDIFICE
NATURAL ENEMY	NEW HAMPSHIRE	NOBLE GESTURE
NATURAL FIBRE	NEW INVENTION	NOBLE MANNERS
NATURAL ORDER	NEW JERUSALEM	NOBODY'S CHILD
NATURAL PRIDE	NEWLY MARRIED	NOBODY'S FAULT
NATURAL SCALE	NEW PARAGRAPH	NO-CLAIM BONUS
NATURAL STATE	NEWS BULLETIN	NO COMPARISON
NAUGHTY CHILD	NEWS OF THE DAY	NO DIFFERENCE
NAUTICAL FLAG	NEW STATESMAN	NO DOUBT AT ALL
NAUTICAL LIFE	NEW TECHNIQUE	NO EARTHLY USE
NAUTICAL MILE	NEW TESTAMENT	NO END OF MONEY
NAUTICAL ROLL	NEW YORK STATE	NO FIXED ABODE
NAVAL ATTACHÉ	NEW ZEALANDER	NO FLIES ON HIM
NAVAL BRIGADE	NEXT ELECTION	NO IMPORTANCE
NAVAL COLLEGE	NEXT QUESTION	NOLENS VOLENS
NAVAL COMMAND	NEXT SATURDAY	NOMINAL POWER
NAVAL OFFICER	NEXT THURSDAY	NOMINAL PRICE
NAVAL RESERVE	NIAGARA FALLS	NOMINAL RULER
NAVAL SERVICE	NICE AND HANDY	NOMINAL VALUE
NAVAL STATION	NICE AND SWEET	NONE THE WISER
NAVAL TACTICS	NICE AND TIGHT	NONE THE WORSE
NAVAL UNIFORM	NICE BUSINESS	NONE WHATEVER
NAVAL WARFARE	NICELY PLACED	NON-STOP REVUE
NEAR DISTANCE	NICE QUESTION	NON-STOP TRAIN

NO PREFERENCE	OCEAN TRAFFIC	OMINOUS CLOUD
NORMAN WISDOM	ODDS AND EVENS	OMISSION MARK
NORTH AMERICA	ODD SENSATION	OMIT NO DETAIL
NORTH BRITAIN	ODDS-ON CHANCE	ON A GOOD THING
NORTH COUNTRY	OF EVIL REPUTE	ON A LEVEL WITH
NORTHERN LINE	OFFER A CHOICE	ON AN EVEN KEEL
NORTH GERMANY	OFFER A REWARD	ON A STRETCHER
NORTH SHIELDS	OFFER FOR SALE	ONCE AND AGAIN
NORTH TO SOUTH	OFFERTORY BOX	ONCE IN A WHILE
NOTABLE POINT	OFF HIS OWN BAT	ONCE TOO OFTEN
NOTARY PUBLIC	OFF HIS ROCKER	ON COMMISSION
NOT A STITCH ON	OFFICER CADET	ONE AND A PENNY
NOTHING AMISS	OFFICERS' MESS	ONE AND ELEVEN
NOTHING AT ALL	OFFICIAL COPY	ONE AND TWENTY
NOTHING DOING	OFFICIAL DUTY	ONE-DAY STRIKE
NOTHING FOR IT	OFFICIAL FORM	ONE FELL SWOOP
NOTHING KNOWN	OFFICIAL LIST	ONE FOR HIS NOB
NOTHING TO ADD	OFFICIAL VIEW	ONE FOR THE POT
NOTHING TO EAT	OFF LIKE A SHOT	ONE-HORSE SHOW
NOTHING TO PAY	OFF ONE'S CHUMP	ONE-HORSE TOWN
NOTHING TO SAY	OFF ONE'S GUARD	ONE JUMP AHEAD
NOTICE TO QUIT	OFF ONE'S HANDS	ONE-LEGGED MAN
NO TIME TO LOSE	OFF THE COURSE	ONE LONG DREAM
NOT IN KEEPING	OFF THE RECORD	ONE MOVE AHEAD
NOT IN THE MOOD	OFF THE SCREEN	ONE OF THE BEST
NOT WORTH A RAP	OF GREAT WORTH	ONE OF THE GANG
NOUVEAU RICHE	OF MICE AND MEN	ONE OF THE LADS
NOVEMBER DAYS	OIL OF JUNIPER	ON EQUAL TERMS
NUDIST COLONY	OIL OF VITRIOL	ONE'S FAIR NAME
NUMBER ELEVEN	OIL THE WHEELS	ONE-SIDED VIEW
NUMBER-ONE MAN	OKLAHOMA CITY	ONE-TRACK MIND
NUMBER, PLEASE	OLD AS HISTORY	ONE-WAY STREET
NUMBER TWELVE	OLD BATTLE-AXE	ON FIRM GROUND
NUMBER TWENTY	OLDER BROTHER	ON FOUR WHEELS
NUMB WITH COLD	OLD FAVOURITE	ONLY DAUGHTER
NURSERY CLASS	OLD FOLKS' HOME	ON ONE'S HONOUR
NURSERY RHYME	OLD FOR HIS AGE	ON ONE'S METTLE
NURSERY STORY	OLD GENTLEMAN	ON ONE'S UPPERS
NURSING STAFF	OLD HARROVIAN	ON REFLECTION
NUT CHOCOLATE	OLD HUNDREDTH	ON SAFE GROUND
NUTMEG GRATER	OLD MAN'S BEARD	ON SENTRY DUTY
NUTS AND BOLTS	OLD MORTALITY	ON SUFFERANCE
	OLD PRETENDER	ON TELEVISION
O—12	OLD SCHOOL TIE	ON THE AVERAGE
OBITER DICTUM	OLD SHOULDERS	ON THE CEILING
OBJECT LESSON	OLD TESTAMENT	ON THE COUNCIL
OBJECT OF PITY	OLD-TIME DANCE	ON THE COUNTER
OBLIQUE ANGLE	OLD-TIME WALTZ	ON THE DECLINE
OBSTACLE RACE	OLD WIVES' TALE	ON THE DEFENCE
OCCULT POWERS	OLYMPIC GAMES	ON THE FAIRWAY
OCEANS OF TIME	OLYMPIC MEDAL	ON THE FAR SIDE

ON THE HORIZON
ON THE LEE-SIDE
ON THE LOOK-OUT
ON THE OFF-SIDE
ON THE ONE HAND
ON THE OUTSIDE
ON THE PAY-ROLL
ON THE QUI VIVE
ON THE RAMPAGE
ON THE REBOUND
ON THE RETREAT
ON THE SURFACE
ON THE TERRACE
ON THE TOP RUNG
ON THE TOW-PATH
ON THE UP-AND-UP
ON THE UPGRADE
ON THE WARPATH
ON THE WAY DOWN
ON WITH THE JOB
OPEN ALL NIGHT
OPEN CARRIAGE
OPEN CHAMPION
OPEN CONFLICT
OPENING NIGHT
OPENING SCENE
OPENING WORDS
OPEN ONE'S EYES
OPEN OUTWARDS
OPEN QUESTION
OPEN SANDWICH
OPEN TO ATTACK
OPEN TO CHANCE
OPEN TO CHOICE
OPERA COMIQUE
OPERA GLASSES
OPERATIC ARIA
OPERATIC STAR
OPIUM TRAFFIC
OPPOSING SIDE
OPPOSING TEAM
OPPOSITE CAMP
OPPOSITE ENDS
OPPOSITE SIDE
OPTICAL GLASS
ORANGE PIPPIN
ORANGE SQUASH
ORDEAL BY FIRE
ORDER IN COURT
ORDER OF MERIT
ORDINARY FARE

ORGAN BUILDER
ORGAN OF SIGHT
ORGAN RECITAL
ORIEL COLLEGE
ORIGINAL COPY
ORIGINAL COST
ORIGINAL IDEA
ORIGINAL PLAN
OSBORNE HOUSE
OTHER EXTREME
OUNCE OF FLESH
OUNCE OF SENSE
OUNCE OF SNUFF
OUR ANCESTORS
OUTDATED WORD
OUTDOOR GAMES
OUTDOOR SPORT
OUTDOOR STAFF
OUTER GARMENT
OUT FOR A SPREE
OUT FOR SCALPS
OUTGOING SHIP
OUTGOING TIDE
OUT IN THE COLD
OUT IN THE OPEN
OUT OF BALANCE
OUT OF COMPANY
OUT OF CONCEIT
OUT OF CONTEXT
OUT OF CONTROL
OUT OF DRAWING
OUT OF EARSHOT
OUT OF FASHION
OUT OF HARMONY
OUT OF HARNESS
OUT OF HEARING
OUT OF KEEPING
OUT OF ONE'S HAT
OUT OF ONE'S WAY
OUT OF SERVICE
OUT OF SPIRITS
OUT OF THE BLUE
OUT OF THE RACE
OUT OF THE ROAD
OUT OF THE ROOM
OUT OF THE WIND
OUT OF THE WOOD
OUT OF TROUBLE
OUT OF UNIFORM
OUTRIGHT GIFT
OUTSIDE COURT

OUTSIDE PRICE
OUTSIDE RIGHT
OUTWARD BOUND
OUTWARD SIGNS
OVER AND ABOVE
OVERDO THINGS
OVERNIGHT BAG
OVER ONE'S HEAD
OVER THE COALS
OVER THE HILLS
OVER THE LIMIT
OVER THE VERGE
OVER THE WATER
OVER THE WAVES
OVER THE WORST
OVER THE YEARS
OWE OBEDIENCE
OXFORD ACCENT
OXFORD CIRCUS
OXFORD STREET

P—12

PABLO PICASSO
PACIFIC OCEAN
PACKET OF PINS
PACK OF HOUNDS
PACK OF WOLVES
PACK ONE'S BAGS
PADDLING POOL
PAGE OF HONOUR
PAID-UP MEMBER
PAINFUL SIGHT
PAINTED IMAGE
PAINTED OCEAN
PAINTED WOMAN
PAINTING BOOK
PAINT THE LILY
PAINT THE WALL
PAIR OF BRACES
PAIR OF EIGHTS
PAIR OF GLOVES
PAIR OF HORSES
PAIR OF KNAVES
PAIR OF PLIERS
PAIR OF QUEENS
PAIR OF SCALES
PAIR OF SEVENS
PAIR OF SHEARS
PAIR OF SHORTS
PAIR OF SKATES
PAIR OF SLACKS

PAIR OF THREES	PASTORAL POEM	PERMIT TO LAND
PAIR OF TIGHTS	PATENT OFFICE	PERSONA GRATA
PAIR OF TRUNKS	PATENT REMEDY	PERSONAL CALL
PAISLEY SCARF	PATENT RIGHTS	PERSONAL GAIN
PAISLEY SHAWL	PATERNAL LOVE	PERSONAL LOAN
PALE AS A GHOST	PATERNAL ROOF	PERSONAL NOTE
PALETTE KNIFE	PATIENT AS JOB	PERSON OF NOTE
PALMERS GREEN	PAT ON THE BACK	PETER AND PAUL
PAPER PATTERN	PAT ON THE HEAD	PETER CUSHING
PAPER THE ROOM	PATROL LEADER	PETER SELLARS
PAPER THE WALL	PATTERN MAKER	PETER USTINOV
PAPER WEDDING	PAUPER'S GRAVE	PET GRIEVANCE
PARADE GROUND	PAW THE GROUND	PETROL ENGINE
PARADISE LOST	PAY A DIVIDEND	PETROL RATION
PARAFFIN LAMP	PAY AS YOU EARN	PETTING PARTY
PARALLEL BARS	PAY AS YOU WEAR	PETTY DETAILS
PARISH CHURCH	PAY ATTENTION	PETTY LARCENY
PARISH PRIEST	PAY DIVIDENDS	PETTY OFFICER
PARISH RELIEF	PAY IN ADVANCE	PETTY TREASON
PARISH SCHOOL	PAYING-IN BOOK	PHARAOH'S TOMB
PARKING METER	PAYING-IN SLIP	PHILIP HARBEN
PARKING PLACE	PAY ONE'S DEBTS	PHONE CHARGES
PARKING SPACE	PAY ONE'S SHARE	PHYSICAL PAIN
PARLOUR TRICK	PAY ON THE NAIL	PIANO RECITAL
PARLOUS STATE	PEACE ON EARTH	PICK A QUARREL
PARMA VIOLETS	PEACH BLOSSOM	PICKED TROOPS
PARQUET FLOOR	PEACOCK'S TAIL	PICKLED ONION
PARSLEY SAUCE	PEAK DISTRICT	PICK OUT A TUNE
PART EXCHANGE	PEANUT BUTTER	PICK TO PIECES
PARTHIAN SHOT	PEARL FISHING	PICNIC BASKET
PARTIAL TRUTH	PEARL HARBOUR	PICNIC HAMPER
PARTING GUEST	PEASE PUDDING	PICTORIAL ART
PARTING WORDS	PEDIGREE HERD	PICTURE FRAME
PART OF SPEECH	PELT WITH RAIN	PICTURE HOUSE
PART OF THE ACT	PEN AND PENCIL	PICTURE PAPER
PART OF THE WAY	PENCIL SKETCH	PICTURE STORY
PART ONE'S HAIR	PENNY FOR THEM	PIECE BY PIECE
PART-TIME WORK	PENNY WHISTLE	PIECE OF BREAD
PARTY IN POWER	PEOPLE'S PARTY	PIECE OF CHALK
PARTY MANNERS	PEPPER'S GHOST	PIECE OF MUSIC
PASSAGE MONEY	PERFECT FIFTH	PIECE OF PAPER
PASSING FANCY	PERFECT IMAGE	PIERCED HEART
PASSING PHASE	PERFECT MATCH	PIERCING LOOK
PASSION FRUIT	PERFECT ORDER	PIERCING NOTE
PASSIVE VOICE	PERFECT PEACE	PIG'S TROTTERS
PASS JUDGMENT	PERFECT SIGHT	PILE UP A SCORE
PASS SENTENCE	PERFECT STYLE	PILLAR-BOX RED
PASS THE CRUET	PERFECT TENSE	PILLAR OF SALT
PASS THE SAUCE	PERFECT WRECK	PILLAR TO POST
PAST MIDNIGHT	PERMANENT JOB	PILLION RIDER
PAST ONE'S BEST	PERMANENT WAY	PILOT OFFICER

PINCH OF SNUFF
PING-PONG BALL
PINK AND WHITE
PINK ELEPHANT
PINK FOR A GIRL
PIN ONE'S FAITH
PIN ONE'S HOPES
PINT OF BITTER
PINT OF WALLOP
PIONEER CORPS
PITCH AND TOSS
PLACE AN ORDER
PLACE BETTING
PLACE IN ORDER
PLACE OF BIRTH
PLACE OF EXILE
PLAIN AND PURL
PLAIN CLOTHES
PLAIN COOKING
PLAIN DEALING
PLAIN ENGLISH
PLAIN SAILING
PLAINTIVE CRY
PLAIN WRAPPER
PLANE SPOTTER
PLAN OF ACTION
PLAN OF ATTACK
PLANT ONESELF
PLASTER SAINT
PLATES OF MEAT
PLATINUM RING
PLATONIC LOVE
PLAY CHARADES
PLAY DOMINOES
PLAY DRAUGHTS
PLAY FOOTBALL
PLAY FOR A DRAW
PLAY FORFEITS
PLAY FOR MONEY
PLAYING CARDS
PLAYING FIELD
PLAY LEAP-FROG
PLAY OLD HARRY
PLAY ONE FALSE
PLAY ONE'S PART
PLAY OPPOSITE
PLAY ROULETTE
PLAY SKITTLES
PLAY THE BANJO
PLAY THE CLOWN
PLAY THE DEUCE

PLAY THE DEVIL
PLAY THE FIELD
PLAY THE HALLS
PLAY THE ORGAN
PLAY THE PIANO
PLAY WITH FIRE
PLEAD POVERTY
PLEA FOR MERCY
PLEA FOR PEACE
PLEA OF GUILTY
PLEASANT NEWS
PLEASANT TIME
PLEASANT TRIP
PLEASANT WEEK
PLEASURE BOAT
PLEASURE TRIP
PLEATED DRESS
PLEATED SKIRT
PLENTY IN HAND
PLENTY OF GUTS
PLENTY OF ROOM
PLENTY OF ROPE
PLENTY OF TIME
PLIGHTED WORD
PLIMSOLL LINE
PLIMSOLL MARK
PLOUGHED LAND
PLOUGH MONDAY
PLUCK A PIGEON
PLUMBER'S MATE
PLUS AND MINUS
PLYMOUTH ROCK
POETIC FRENZY
POET LAUREATE
POINT AT ISSUE
POINT BY POINT
POINT OF ISSUE
POINT OF ORDER
POINTS SYSTEM
POINT TO POINT
POISONED DART
POKE IN THE EYE
POKER SESSION
POLAR REGIONS
POLES ASUNDER
POLICE ACTION
POLICE CORDON
POLICE ESCORT
POLICE MATTER
POLICE PATROL
POLICE PERMIT

POLITE PHRASE
POLITICAL MAP
POLITICAL SET
POLLING BOOTH
POLYTHENE BAG
PONS ASINORUM
POOL OF LABOUR
POOL OF LONDON
POOR ARGUMENT
POOR CREATURE
POOR DELIVERY
POOR FEATURES
POOR IN SPIRIT
POOR LINGUIST
POOR PHYSIQUE
POOR PROSPECT
POOR RELATION
POOR RELATIVE
POOR SPECIMEN
POPULAR BRAND
POPULAR FANCY
POPULAR FRONT
POPULAR MUSIC
POPULAR NOVEL
POPULAR PRESS
POPULAR PRICE
POPULAR SPORT
PORGY AND BESS
PORK AND BEANS
PORK SAUSAGES
PORT ADELAIDE
PORT AND LEMON
PORTER'S LODGE
PORTLAND BILL
PORTLAND BOWL
PORTLAND VASE
PORTLY FIGURE
PORT OF LONDON
PORT SUNLIGHT
POSE A PROBLEM
POSITIVE POLE
POSITIVE SIGN
POSSIBLE NEED
POSTAGE STAMP
POSTED ABROAD
POST MERIDIAN
POST OF HONOUR
POST-WAR WORLD
POTATO CRISPS
POTATO FAMINE
POTTER'S WHEEL

POULTRY HOUSE
POUND FOOLISH
POUND OF FLESH
POUND OF SUGAR
POUND THE BEAT
POUR WITH RAIN
POUTER PIGEON
POWDER MONKEY
POWER OF SIGHT
POWER STATION
POWERS THAT BE
PRACTICE GAME
PRACTISED EYE
PRAY FOR MERCY
PRAY FOR PEACE
PRECIOUS BANE
PRECIOUS LAMB
PREEN ONESELF
PREMIUM BONDS
PREMIUM OFFER
PREPARE A CASE
PREPARE A MEAL
PREPARED TEXT
PRESENT TENSE
PRESS COUNCIL
PRESS CUTTING
PRESSED STEEL
PRESS FORWARD
PRESS GALLERY
PRESS HAND-OUT
PRESSING NEED
PRESS OFFICER
PRESS ONWARDS
PRESS THE BELL
PRESSURE PUMP
PRETTY ACTIVE
PRETTY PICKLE
PRETTY SPEECH
PRETTY USEFUL
PRICE CONTROL
PRICE OF MONEY
PRICKLY PLANT
PRIDE OF LIONS
PRIDE OF PLACE
PRIDE ONESELF
PRIMITIVE ART
PRIMITIVE MAN
PRIMO CARNERA
PRIMROSE HILL
PRIMROSE PATH
PRINCE ALBERT

PRINCE EDWARD
PRINCE GEORGE
PRINCE PHILIP
PRINCE REGENT
PRINCE RUPERT
PRINCESS ANNE
PRINCIPAL BOY
PRINTED SHEET
PRINTER'S COPY
PRISON RECORD
PRISON REFORM
PRISON WARDEN
PRISON WARDER
PRIVATE BEACH
PRIVATE CLASS
PRIVATE FIGHT
PRIVATE HOTEL
PRIVATE HOUSE
PRIVATE LIVES
PRIVATE MEANS
PRIVATE PARTY
PRIVATE TUTOR
PRIVATE VISIT
PRIVATE WORLD
PRIVATE WRONG
PRIVY COUNCIL
PRIZE EDITION
PROBATE COURT
PROBLEM CHILD
PROFIT MARGIN
PROFIT MOTIVE
PROMISED LAND
PROMISE TO PAY
PROMPT ACTION
PROMPT ANSWER
PROMPT CORNER
PROOF OF GUILT
PROPER COURSE
PROPER PERSON
PROPERTY DEAL
PROPHET OF WOE
PROTEST MARCH
PROTOTYPE CAR
PROUD AS PUNCH
PROUD PRESTON
PROVEN GUILTY
PROVE THE RULE
PROVIDE LUNCH
PRUNING KNIFE
PRUSSIAN BLUE
PSYCHIC FORCE

PUBLIC AFFAIR
PUBLIC APATHY
PUBLIC DEMAND
PUBLIC FIGURE
PUBLIC HEALTH
PUBLIC NOTICE
PUBLIC OFFICE
PUBLIC ORATOR
PUBLIC OUTCRY
PUBLIC POLICY
PUBLIC SCHOOL
PUBLIC SPEECH
PUBLIC SPIRIT
PUDDING BASIN
PUFFING BILLY
PUFFIN ISLAND
PULL A FAST ONE
PULLING POWER
PULL THE WIRES
PULL TOGETHER
PULL TO PIECES
PULP MAGAZINE
PUNCH AND JUDY
PUPIL TEACHER
PURE NONSENSE
PURL AND PLAIN
PURSE THE LIPS
PURSUE A THEME
PURSUIT PLANE
PUSH ONE'S LUCK
PUT AN END TO IT
PUT A QUESTION
PUT A SOCK IN IT
PUT A STOP TO IT
PUT IN ITALICS
PUT IN SPLINTS
PUT IN THE DOCK
PUT INTO FORCE
PUT INTO RHYME
PUT INTO SHAPE
PUT INTO WORDS
PUT IN WRITING
PUT IT BLUNTLY
PUTNEY BRIDGE
PUTNEY COMMON
PUT ONE ACROSS
PUT ONE'S OAR IN
PUT ON ONE SIDE
PUT ON THE LIST
PUT ON THE RACK
PUT OUT OF GEAR

PUT THE CAT OUT	RACING DRIVER	RAY ELLINGTON
PUT THE WIND UP	RACING JARGON	RAY OF COMFORT
PUTTING GREEN	RACING SEASON	REACH FORWARD
PUT TO AUCTION	RACING STABLE	REACT AGAINST
PUT TO GOOD USE	RADAR STATION	REACT SHARPLY
PUT TO THE RACK	RADIANT SMILE	READ AND WRITE
PUT TO THE TEST	RADICAL ERROR	READING GLASS
PUT TO THE VOTE	RADIO AMATEUR	READ ONE'S HAND
PUT TO TORTURE	RADIO LICENCE	READ ONE'S PALM
PUT UP FOR SALE	RADIO MESSAGE	READ THE CARDS
	RADIO NETWORK	READ THE SIGNS
Q—I2	RADIO STATION	READ THE STARS
QUARTER FINAL	RAFFLE TICKET	READY CONSENT
QUARTER RIGHT	RAGING TEMPER	READY FOR WEAR
QUARTER TO ONE	RAGLAN SLEEVE	READY TO BURST
QUARTER TO SIX	RAGS AND BONES	READY TO LEARN
QUARTER TO TEN	RAGS TO RICHES	READY TO LEAVE
QUARTER TO TWO	RAIDING PARTY	READY TO START
QUART MEASURE	RAILWAY HOTEL	REALM OF PLUTO
QUEEN CONSORT	RAILWAY LINES	REAL PRESENCE
QUEEN OF CLUBS	RAILWAY TRAIN	REAL PROPERTY
QUEEN OF SHEBA	RAILWAY TRUCK	REAL SECURITY
QUEEN OF TONGA	RAINBOW TROUT	REAR ENTRANCE
QUEEN'S BISHOP	RAINY CLIMATE	REAR ONE'S HEAD
QUEEN'S BOUNTY	RAINY WEATHER	RECALL TO LIFE
QUEEN'S COLOUR	RAISE A FAMILY	RECALL TO MIND
QUEEN'S FLIGHT	RAISED VOICES	RECEIVING END
QUEEN'S GAMBIT	RAISE ONE'S HAT	RECEIVING SET
QUEEN'S KNIGHT	RAISE THE ANTE	RECENT EVENTS
QUEEN'S SPEECH	RAISE THE DEAD	RECITE POETRY
QUEEN TITANIA	RAISE THE DUST	RECORD OFFICE
QUEER FEELING	RAISE THE FARE	RECORD OUTPUT
QUESTION MARK	RAISE THE RENT	RECORD PLAYER
QUESTION TIME	RAISE THE ROOF	RED AND YELLOW
QUEUE JUMPING	RAISE THE WIND	RED CORPUSCLE
QUICK JOURNEY	RAKE TOGETHER	RED FOR DANGER
QUICK RETURNS	RAMBLING ROSE	RED IN THE FACE
QUIET WEDDING	RANDOM EFFORT	RED-LETTER DAY
QUIET WEEK-END	RANDOM SAMPLE	RED STOCKINGS
QUITE CERTAIN	RANK OUTSIDER	REDUCED FARES
QUITE CORRECT	RAPID DECLINE	REDUCED PRICE
QUITE IN ORDER	RAPID SPEAKER	REDUCED SPEED
QUIT ONE'S POST	RAPID STRIDES	REDUCE IN RANK
QUIT THE SCENE	RAPID TRANSIT	REDUCE TO PULP
QUIT THE STAGE	RAPIER THRUST	REDUCE TO SIZE
QUOTE THE ODDS	RASPBERRY JAM	RED WITH ANGER
	RASPING VOICE	REEFER JACKET
R—I2	RATABLE VALUE	REEL OF COTTON
RABBIT WARREN	RATHER LITTLE	REFINED SUGAR
RACE OF GIANTS	RATHER POORLY	REFINED TASTE
RACIAL HATRED	RAVEN TRESSES	REFLEX ACTION

REFORM SCHOOL	RESERVED SEAT	RINGING SOUND
REFUSE CREDIT	RESERVE PRICE	RINGING TONES
REFUSE OFFICE	RESERVE STOCK	RING IN THE NEW
REFUSE TO MEET	RESIDE ABROAD	RINGSIDE SEAT
REFUSE TO MOVE	RESORT TO ARMS	RIO DE JANEIRO
REFUSE TO PLAY	RESTING ACTOR	RIOT OF COLOUR
REFUSE TO SIGN	RESTING PLACE	RIPE TOMATOES
REFUSE TO VOTE	REST OF THE DAY	RIP VAN WINKLE
REFUSE TO WORK	REST ONE'S CASE	RISE AND SHINE
REGAL BEARING	REST ONE'S EYES	RISE IN REVOLT
REGENCY HOUSE	RESTORE ORDER	RISE TO THE FLY
REGENCY STYLE	RETAIL DEALER	RISE TO THE TOP
REGENT'S CANAL	RETAINING FEE	RISING GROUND
REGENT STREET	RETURN A VISIT	RISING PRICES
REGIONAL NEWS	RETURN OF POST	RISK ONE'S LIFE
REGULAR BRICK	RETURN TICKET	RISK ONE'S NECK
REGULAR DEMON	RETURN TO BASE	RIVAL COMPANY
REGULAR HABIT	RETURN TO PORT	RIVER OF BLOOD
REGULAR HOURS	RETURN VOYAGE	RIVER SHANNON
REGULAR MEALS	REVERSE ORDER	RIVER STEAMER
REGULAR ORDER	REVERT TO TYPE	RIVER TRAFFIC
REIGN SUPREME	REVOLVER SHOT	ROAD ACCIDENT
REITH LECTURE	RHESUS MONKEY	ROAD JUNCTION
RELEVANT FACT	RHYMING SLANG	ROADSIDE CAFÉ
RELIEF WORKER	RICHARD CONTE	ROAR FOR MERCY
RELIGIOUS WAR	RICHMOND HILL	ROARING TRADE
REMAIN AT HOME	RICHMOND PARK	ROAR WITH PAIN
REMAIN BEHIND	RICH RELATION	ROAR WITH RAGE
REMAIN SEATED	RICH RELATIVE	ROAST CHICKEN
REMAIN SILENT	RIDE AT ANCHOR	ROASTED ALIVE
REMAIN SINGLE	RIDE BARE-BACK	ROBE OF HONOUR
REMOTE CHANCE	RIDE FOR A FALL	ROBERT BEATTY
REMOTE FUTURE	RIDE FULL TILT	ROBERT GRAVES
REMOTE OBJECT	RIDER HAGGARD	ROBERT MORLEY
REMOVE BODILY	RIDE THE STORM	ROBERT NEWTON
REMOVE ERRORS	RIDE TO HOUNDS	ROBERT TAYLOR
RENDER THANKS	RIDING LESSON	ROBUST HEALTH
REND THE SKIES	RIDING MASTER	ROCKING HORSE
RENÉE HOUSTON	RIDING SCHOOL	ROGATION DAYS
RENT A CARAVAN	RIDING STABLE	ROGATION WEEK
RENT A COTTAGE	RIFLE BRIGADE	ROLLER SKATES
RENT TRIBUNAL	RIGHT AND LEFT	ROLLING STOCK
REPAIR OUTFIT	RIGHTFUL HEIR	ROLLING STONE
REPEAT ACTION	RIGHT-HAND MAN	ROLL OF HONOUR
REPORTED CASE	RIGHT OF ENTRY	ROLL ONE'S EYES
REPTILE HOUSE	RIGHT OR WRONG	ROMAN EMPEROR
REPUTED OWNER	RIGHT OUTSIDE	ROMAN FIGURES
RESCUE WORKER	RIGHT QUALITY	ROMAN HISTORY
RESEARCH TEAM	RIGHT THROUGH	ROMAN HOLIDAY
RESEARCH WORK	RIG THE MARKET	ROMAN LETTERS
RESERVED LIST	RINGING LAUGH	ROMAN NUMBERS

ROMAN REMAINS	ROYAL CHARTER	**S—12**
ROMAN SOLDIER	ROYAL CIRCLES	SACRED NUMBER
ROMANTIC FOOL	ROYAL COMMAND	SACRED PLEDGE
ROMANTIC GIRL	ROYAL CONSENT	SADDLE OF LAMB
ROMANTIC IDEA	ROYAL DYNASTY	SADLER'S WELLS
RONALD COLMAN	ROYAL HUNT CUP	SAD SPECTACLE
RONALD SHINER	ROYAL MARINES	SAFE AND SOUND
RONNIE HILTON	ROYAL SOCIETY	SAFE AS HOUSES
ROOM AT THE TOP	ROYAL WARRANT	SAFE CROSSING
ROOM FOR DOUBT	ROYAL WEDDING	SAFE DISTANCE
ROOM THIRTEEN	ROYAL WELCOME	SAFETY DEVICE
ROOM TO EXPAND	RUBBER CHEQUE	SAFETY FACTOR
ROPE OF ONIONS	RUBBER DINGHY	SAGE AND ONION
ROPE OF PEARLS	RUBBER GLOVES	SAHARA DESERT
ROSE AND CROWN	RUB ONE'S HANDS	SAILING BARGE
ROSE-HIP SYRUP	RUB SHOULDERS	SAINT BERNARD
ROSE OF TRALEE	RUDE REMINDER	SAINT PANCRAS
ROSE TO THE TOP	RUGBY COLOURS	SAINT PATRICK
ROSETTA STONE	RUGGER GROUND	SAINT SWITHIN
ROSY PROSPECT	RUGGER PLAYER	SALE OR RETURN
ROTARY ACTION	RUINED CASTLE	SALES FIGURES
ROTTEN BRANCH	RUINOUS FOLLY	SALES MANAGER
ROUGH COUNTRY	RULE OF TERROR	SALIENT ANGLE
ROUGH DIAMOND	RULE THE ROOST	SALIENT POINT
ROUGH DRAWING	RUMOURS OF WAR	SALOON PRICES
ROUGH JUSTICE	RUN-AWAY HORSE	SALTED ALMOND
ROUGH MANNERS	RUN-AWAY MATCH	SALTED BUTTER
ROUGH PASSAGE	RUN AWAY TO SEA	SALT LAKE CITY
ROUGH PICTURE	RUN-AWAY TRAIN	SALUTING BASE
ROUGH SURFACE	RUN FOR OFFICE	SALVADOR DALI
ROUGH TEXTURE	RUN FOR SAFETY	SALVAGE CORPS
ROUGH WEATHER	RUN LIKE A DEER	SALVAGE MONEY
ROUND BY ROUND	RUN LIKE A HARE	SAMPLE BOTTLE
ROUND FIGURES	RUNNING COSTS	SAMUEL BUTLER
ROUND OF CALLS	RUNNING FIGHT	SAN FRANCISCO
ROUND OF TOAST	RUNNING FLUSH	SAN SEBASTIAN
ROUND THE BACK	RUNNING TITLE	SAPPHIRE RING
ROUND THE BEND	RUNNING TRACK	SARACEN'S HEAD
ROUND THE CAPE	RUNNING WATER	SARDONIC GRIN
ROUND THE EDGE	RUN OF BAD LUCK	SATAN'S PALACE
ROUND THE FIRE	RUN OF THE MILL	SATURDAY CLUB
ROUND THE MOON	RUN ON THE BANK	SAUCE TARTARE
ROUND THE TOWN	RUPERT BROOKE	SAVAGE ATTACK
ROUSE ONESELF	RUSH HEADLONG	SAVAGE TEMPER
ROUSING CHEER	RUSHING WATER	SAVE ONE'S FACE
ROUTINE CHECK	RUSSIAN BOOTS	SAVE ONE'S LIFE
ROVING REPORT	RUSSIAN DANCE	SAVE ONE'S NECK
ROW OF BUTTONS	RUSSIAN NOVEL	SAVE ONE'S SKIN
ROYAL ACADEMY	RUSSIAN SALAD	SAVE OUR SOULS
ROYAL ARSENAL	RUSSIAN VODKA	SAVING CLAUSE
ROYAL BANQUET	RUSTIC BRIDGE	SAVING FACTOR

SAVINGS STAMP
SAVOY CABBAGE
SAY A FEW WORDS
SAY A GOOD WORD
SAY A MOUTHFUL
SAY ONE'S PIECE
SAY SOMETHING
SCALE DRAWING
SCALLOP SHELL
SCARLET FEVER
SCARLET WOMAN
SCENE OF CHAOS
SCENE STEALER
SCENTED PAPER
SCEPTRED ISLE
SCHOLAR GIPSY
SCHOOL BLAZER
SCHOOL FRIEND
SCHOOL MATRON
SCHOOL OUTING
SCHOOL REPORT
SCHOOL SPORTS
SCOOP THE POOL
SCORCHING HOT
SCORE A SINGLE
SCORE THROUGH
SCOTCH BONNET
SCOTCH HUMOUR
SCOTCH WHISKY
SCOTLAND YARD
SCOTTISH PEER
SCOTTISH REEL
SCOUT'S HONOUR
SCRAMBLED EGG
SCRAP OF PAPER
SCRIPT WRITER
SCROLL OF FAME
SCULLERY MAID
SCUTTLE A SHIP
SEAFARING MAN
SEAL A BARGAIN
SEALED ORDERS
SEAL OF OFFICE
SEALSKIN COAT
SEA OF GALILEE
SEA OF MARMORA
SEA OF TROUBLE
SEARCH IN VAIN
SEASONAL WIND
SEASON TICKET
SEAT OF HONOUR

SECLUDED SPOT
SECOND CHANCE
SECOND CHOICE
SECOND COURSE
SECOND COUSIN
SECOND DANIEL
SECOND DEGREE
SECOND ELEVEN
SECOND FIDDLE
SECOND FINGER
SECOND GLANCE
SECOND LEAGUE
SECOND LESSON
SECOND LETTER
SECOND NATURE
SECOND OF JULY
SECOND OF JUNE
SECOND PERSON
SECOND RUBBER
SECOND SEASON
SECOND SERIES
SECOND STOREY
SECOND STRING
SECOND TO NONE
SECOND VIOLIN
SECOND VOLUME
SECRET BALLOT
SECRET DRAWER
SECRET ERRAND
SECRET PAPERS
SECRET POLICE
SECRET TREATY
SECRET WEAPON
SECURE FUTURE
SECURE OLD-AGE
SECURITY LEAK
SECURITY RISK
SEE AT A GLANCE
SEEDED PLAYER
SEED MERCHANT
SEEDS OF DECAY
SEEDS OF DOUBT
SEE IN THE DARK
SEE IT THROUGH
SEEK A FORMULA
SEEK A FORTUNE
SEEK AN EFFECT
SEEK A QUARREL
SEEK GUIDANCE
SEESAW MOTION
SEE THE SIGHTS

SEETHING MASS
SELL FOR A SONG
SELLING PLATE
SELLING PRICE
SELL ON CREDIT
SELL ONE'S SOUL
SELL THE DUMMY
SEND A MESSAGE
SEND TO PRISON
SENIOR BRANCH
SENIOR MASTER
SENIOR MEMBER
SENIOR PURSER
SENIOR SCHOOL
SENSE OF GUILT
SENSE OF SHAME
SENSE OF SIGHT
SENSE OF SMELL
SENSE OF TASTE
SENSE OF TOUCH
SENSE OF WRONG
SENSIBLE GIRL
SENSITIVE EAR
SENT TO BLAZES
SENT TO SCHOOL
SEPARATE WAYS
SERENE NATURE
SERENE TEMPER
SERIAL NUMBER
SERIAL RIGHTS
SERIOUSLY ILL
SERIOUS MUSIC
SERIOUS OFFER
SERIOUS RIVAL
SERIOUS WOUND
SERRIED RANKS
SERVANT CLASS
SERVANTS' HALL
SERVE AT TABLE
SERVE ITS TURN
SERVICE CHIEF
SERVICE DEPOT
SERVICE DRESS
SERVICE OF GOD
SERVICE RIFLE
SERVING HATCH
SET AN EXAMPLE
SET A STANDARD
SET AT LIBERTY
SET BY THE EARS
SET OF LANCERS

SET ONE AT EASE	SHAH OF PERSIA	SHORN OF GLORY
SET ONE'S TEETH	SHAKE THE HEAD	SHORT ACCOUNT
SET PROGRAMME	SHALLOW GRAVE	SHORT CIRCUIT
SETTLE A SCORE	SHALLOW WATER	SHORT COMMONS
SETTLE IN TOWN	SHAMELESS LIE	SHORTER HOURS
SETTLE THE DAY	SHARE CAPITAL	SHORTEST GIRL
SEVEN AND FIVE	SHARE THE LOAD	SHORT EXTRACT
SEVEN AND FOUR	SHARE THE LOOT	SHORT JOURNEY
SEVEN AND NINE	SHARP LOOK-OUT	SHORTLY AFTER
SEVEN COURSES	SHARP OUTLINE	SHORT MEASURE
SEVEN DEGREES	SHARP REPROOF	SHORT OF FUNDS
SEVEN DOLLARS	SHAVING BRUSH	SHORT OF MONEY
SEVEN EIGHTHS	SHAVING STICK	SHORT OF SPACE
SEVEN FATHOMS	SHEEPISH GRIN	SHORT OF STAFF
SEVEN GALLONS	SHEEPISH LOOK	SHORT OF WORDS
SEVEN GUINEAS	SHEEP'S TONGUE	SHORT PASSAGE
SEVEN HUNDRED	SHEER TORTURE	SHORT ROMANCE
SEVEN LEAGUES	SHEET OF FLAME	SHORT SESSION
SEVEN MINUTES	SHEET OF GLASS	SHORT SUMMARY
SEVEN OCTAVES	SHEET OF PAPER	SHORT TENANCY
SEVEN OF CLUBS	SHEET OF WATER	SHORT TIME AGO
SEVEN OR EIGHT	SHEIK OF ARABY	SHORT VERSION
SEVEN PER CENT	SHELLING PEAS	SHOT AND SHELL
SEVEN SISTERS	SHEPHERD'S PIE	SHOT IN THE ARM
SEVEN SQUARED	SHERRY TRIFLE	SHOT ONE'S BOLT
SEVENTH FLOOR	SHETLAND PONY	SHOT TO PIECES
SEVENTH GREEN	SHINING LIGHT	SHOULDER ARMS
SEVENTH OF MAY	SHINING WHITE	SHOUT FOR HELP
SEVENTH PLACE	SHIPPING LANE	SHOUT THE ODDS
SEVENTH ROUND	SHIPPING LINE	SHOVE HA'PENNY
SEVENTY MILES	SHIP'S BISCUIT	SHOW APTITUDE
SEVENTY TIMES	SHIP'S CAPTAIN	SHOW BUSINESS
SEVENTY YEARS	SHIP'S COMPANY	SHOWER OF RAIN
SEVEN VIRTUES	SHIP'S COMPASS	SHOW INTEREST
SEVEN WICKETS	SHIP'S STEWARD	SHOWN THE DOOR
SEVEN WISE MEN	SHIRLEY EATON	SHOW OF REASON
SEVEN WONDERS	SHIRT SLEEVES	SHOW ONE ROUND
SEVERAL TIMES	SHIVERING FIT	SHOW ONE'S FACE
SEVERE ATTACK	SHOCKING COLD	SHOW ONE'S HAND
SEVERE CRITIC	SHOCKING PINK	SHOW PRUDENCE
SEVERE MASTER	SHOCK TACTICS	SHRIMPING NET
SEVERE STRAIN	SHOCK THERAPY	SHUFFLE ALONG
SEVERE WINTER	SHOE REPAIRER	SHUT OFF STEAM
SEVERN BRIDGE	SHOE-SHINE BOY	SHUT ONE'S EYES
SEVERN TUNNEL	SHOOTER'S HILL	SHUT YOUR TRAP!
SEWING CIRCLE	SHOOTING PAIN	SIAMESE TWINS
SEW ON A BUTTON	SHOOTING STAR	SICK AND TIRED
SHADE OF DOUBT	SHOOT ONESELF	SICK OF TRYING
SHADOW BOXING	SHOOT THE MOON	SIDE ENTRANCE
SHADY RETREAT	SHOPPING LIST	SIDE MOVEMENT
SHAFT OF LIGHT	SHORE TO SHORE	SIDE OF MUTTON

SIDNEY STREET	SIXTEEN MILES	SLOW PROGRESS
SIEGE OF PARIS	SIXTH CENTURY	SLOW PUNCTURE
SIERRA NEVADA	SIXTH OF APRIL	SLUM PROPERTY
SIGH OF RELIEF	SIXTH OF MARCH	SMALL ACCOUNT
SIGHTING SHOT	SIXTY MINUTES	SMALL COMFORT
SIGMUND FREUD	SIXTY PER CENT	SMALL FORTUNE
SIGNAL DEFEAT	SIXTY SECONDS	SMALL HELPING
SIGNAL REWARD	SKEIN OF GEESE	SMALL HOLDING
SIGN LANGUAGE	SKELETON CREW	SMALL LETTERS
SIGN OF DANGER	SKIFFLE GROUP	SMALL MEASURE
SIGN ONE'S NAME	SKIN AND BONES	SMALL MERCIES
SILENT LETTER	SKIN GRAFTING	SMALL PORTION
SILENT PRAYER	SKITTLE ALLEY	SMALL PURPOSE
SILK STOCKING	SKYE BOAT-SONG	SMALL SAVINGS
SILLY SUFFOLK	SLACKEN SPEED	SMALL WRITING
SILVER DOLLAR	SLAP IN THE EYE	SMART CLOTHES
SILVER LINING	SLAVE TO DRINK	SMART DEALING
SILVER SALVER	SLAVE TRAFFIC	SMART OFFICER
SILVER SCREEN	SLEEPING DOGS	SMART SERVANT
SILVER STREAK	SLEEPING LION	SMART TURN-OUT
SILVER TEA-POT	SLEEPING PILL	SMASH AND GRAB
SILVER THREAD	SLEEP SOUNDLY	SMASHING BLOW
SIMPLE ANSWER	SLEEP SWEETLY	SMELL SWEETLY
SIMPLE ATTIRE	SLENDER HOPES	SMILE SWEETLY
SIMPLE BEAUTY	SLENDER MEANS	SMOKE A LITTLE
SIMPLE DEVICE	SLENDER PURSE	SMOKED SALMON
SIMPLE EFFORT	SLENDER WAIST	SMOKED TONGUE
SIMPLE MATTER	SLICE OF BREAD	SMOKER'S COUGH
SIMPLE PERSON	SLICE OF LEMON	SMOKER'S HEART
SIMPLE REMEDY	SLICE OF TOAST	SMOKE TOO MUCH
SINGING VOICE	SLICE THE BALL	SMOOTH TEMPER
SING IN UNISON	SLIDING PANEL	SMOOTH THE WAY
SINGLE COMBAT	SLIDING SCALE	SMOOTH TONGUE
SINGLE NUMBER	SLIGHT CHANCE	SNACK COUNTER
SINGLE PERSON	SLIGHT CHANGE	SNAKE CHARMER
SINGLE SCOTCH	SLIGHT DAMAGE	SNAP AND SNARL
SINGLES MATCH	SLIGHT FIGURE	SNAP DECISION
SINGLE TICKET	SLIGHT INJURY	SNAP JUDGMENT
SINGLE WHISKY	SLIGHTLY DEAF	SNOW CRYSTALS
SINISTER MOVE	SLIMMING DIET	SOAP AND WATER
SIR HENRY WOOD	SLIP AND SLIDE	SOBER THOUGHT
SIR JOHN MOORE	SLIP OF A THING	SOCIAL CENTRE
SIR TOBY BELCH	SLIP OF THE PEN	SOCIAL CIRCLE
SIT AT THE BACK	SLIP THE CABLE	SOCIAL CREDIT
SIT IN COUNCIL	SLIP UP ON A JOB	SOCIAL MISFIT
SIX AND A PENNY	SLITHER ALONG	SOCIAL SEASON
SIX AND ELEVEN	SLOANE SQUARE	SOCIAL STATUS
SIX FEET UNDER	SLOANE STREET	SOCIAL SURVEY
SIX OF THE BEST	SLOPING SIDES	SOCIAL UNREST
SIXPENCE EACH	SLOW MOVEMENT	SOCIAL WORKER
SIX SHILLINGS	SLOW OF SPEECH	SOCIETY WOMAN

SOCK IN THE EYE	SPANISH TANGO	SPLIT THE VOTE
SODA FOUNTAIN	SPANKING PACE	SPOILED CHILD
SOFT AS BUTTER	SPARE A COPPER	SPORTING LIFE
SOFT AS VELVET	SPARE BEDROOM	SPORTING NEWS
SOFT CURRENCY	SPARE NO PAINS	SPORT OF KINGS
SOFT HANDLING	SPARE-TIME JOB	SPORT ONE'S OAK
SOFT NOTHINGS	SPARKING PLUG	SPORTS EDITOR
SOLAR ECLIPSE	SPARKLING WIT	SPORTS GROUND
SOLEMN THREAT	SPARTAN BREED	SPORTS JACKET
SOLE SURVIVOR	SPATE OF WORDS	SPORTS MASTER
SOLID CITIZEN	SPEAK CLEARLY	SPORTS REPORT
SOLITARY LIFE	SPEAK ENGLISH	SPORTS TROPHY
SOLITARY WALK	SPEAKING PART	SPOT AND PLAIN
SOLOMON'S SEAL	SPEAKING TUBE	SPOT OF BOTHER
SOMETHING NEW	SPEAK ITALIAN	SPOT OF WHISKY
SOMETHING OLD	SPEAK PLAINLY	SPREAD ABROAD
SOME TIME BACK	SPEAK RAPIDLY	SPREAD CANVAS
SON ET LUMIÈRE	SPEAK RUSSIAN	SPRING BUDGET
SONG AND DANCE	SPEAK SPANISH	SPRING GREENS
SONG OF A SHIRT	SPEAK VOLUMES	SPRING ONIONS
SONG OF PRAISE	SPECIAL AGENT	SPRING SEASON
SONIC BARRIER	SPECIAL CHARM	SPRING TO MIND
SON OF THE SOIL	SPECIAL ISSUE	SPURN AN OFFER
SONS OF BELIAL	SPECIAL NURSE	SQUARE NUMBER
SOPRANO VOICE	SPECIAL OFFER	STACK OF CHIPS
SORE DISTRESS	SPECIAL POINT	STACK OF STRAW
SORRY OUTCOME	SPECIAL PRICE	STACK THE DECK
SOUL OF HONOUR	SPECIAL TERMS	STAFF CAPTAIN
SOUND AND FURY	SPECIAL TRAIN	STAFF COLLEGE
SOUND AS A BELL	SPECIAL TREAT	STAFF OFFICER
SOUND BACKING	SPECIFIC HEAT	STAFF PROBLEM
SOUND BARRIER	SPECIMEN COPY	STAGE A STRIKE
SOUND EFFECTS	SPECIMEN PAGE	STAGE BY STAGE
SOUND OF MUSIC	SPEECH DEFECT	STAGE EFFECTS
SOUND SLEEPER	SPEED OF LIGHT	STAGE MANAGER
SOUND TACTICS	SPEED OF SOUND	STAGE VILLAIN
SOUP OF THE DAY	SPEEDY ANSWER	STAGE WHISPER
SOUTH AFRICAN	SPELLING GAME	STAINED GLASS
SOUTH AMERICA	SPENCER TRACY	STALL FOR TIME
SOUTHEND PIER	SPEND A PACKET	STAMP AUCTION
SOUTHERN AREA	SPICK AND SPAN	STAMP MACHINE
SOUTH PACIFIC	SPIDER AND FLY	STAMP OF TRUTH
SOUTH SHIELDS	SPIKE THE GUNS	STAND ABASHED
SOVIET RUSSIA	SPILL THE MILK	STAND ACCUSED
SPACE FICTION	SPILL THE SALT	STAND A CHANCE
SPACE STATION	SPINAL COLUMN	STAND AGAINST
SPACE TO BUILD	SPIN LIKE A TOP	STAND AND WAIT
SPADE AND FORK	SPIN THE WHEEL	STANDARD LAMP
SPANISH DANCE	SPIRIT OF EVIL	STANDARD RATE
SPANISH MONEY	SPLENDID TIME	STANDARD ROSE
SPANISH ONION	SPLIT THE ATOM	STANDARD SIZE

STANDARD TIME
STANDARD WORK
STAND BETWEEN
STAND IN FRONT
STANDING ARMY
STANDING JOKE
STANDING ONLY
STANDING ROOM
ST. ANDREW'S DAY
STAND THE PACE
STAND THE TEST
STAND-UP FIGHT
STAND UPRIGHT
STAND WAITING
STANLEY BLACK
ST. ANNE'S ON SEA
STARK MADNESS
STARK REALITY
STARLIT NIGHT
STAR MATERIAL
STARRING ROLE
STARTING GATE
STARTING POST
START PACKING
START TALKING
START TO CHEER
START TOO LATE
START TOO SOON
STARVE A FEVER
STATE CONTROL
STATED PERIOD
STATE FUNERAL
STATE LIBRARY
STATE LOTTERY
STATE OF BLISS
STATE OF GRACE
STATE OF PEACE
STATE OF SIEGE
STATE PENSION
STATE SCHOLAR
STATE SUBSIDY
STATION HOTEL
STATION WAGON
STATUE OF EROS
STATUS SYMBOL
STAYING POWER
STAY ONE'S HAND
STAY THE NIGHT
STAY TO DINNER
STAY TO THE END
ST. BERNARD DOG

STEADY DEMAND
STEADY INCOME
STEAK TARTARE
STEAL THE SHOW
STEALTHY STEP
STEAM TURBINE
STEAM WHISTLE
STEERING GEAR
STEP BACKWARD
STEP ON THE GAS
STERLING AREA
STERN REALITY
STEWED APPLES
STEWED PRUNES
ST. GEORGE'S DAY
STICK NO BILLS
STICK OF BOMBS
STICK OF CHALK
STICK OR TWIST
STICK TO PROSE
STICKY TOFFEE
STICKY WICKET
STIFF PENALTY
STILETTO HEEL
STINGING BLOW
STINGING PAIN
STIRLING MOSS
STIRRING GAME
STIRRING NEWS
STIRRING TALE
STIR THE BLOOD
STIR UP STRIFE
STITCH IN TIME
ST. JAMES'S PARK
ST. LOUIS BLUES
ST. MARYLEBONE
STOCK COMPANY
STOCK EXAMPLE
STOCKING FEET
STOCK IN TRADE
STOKE THE FIRE
STOLEN KISSES
STONE OF SCONE
STONE TO DEATH
STOOD THE TEST
STOOGE AROUND
STOP AND START
STOP DRINKING
STOP FIGHTING
STOP-GO POLICY
STOP LAUGHING

STOP ONE'S EARS
STOP SWANKING
STOP THE CLOCK
STOP THE FIGHT
STOP THE NIGHT
STOP WORRYING
STORAGE SPACE
STORM BREWING
STORM OF ABUSE
STORM TROOPER
STORM WARNING
STORMY CAREER
STORMY DEBATE
STORMY PETREL
STORMY TEMPER
STOUT AND MILD
STOUT OF HEART
STOVEPIPE HAT
ST. PETERSBURG
STRAIGHT AWAY
STRAIGHT BACK
STRAIGHT DEAL
STRAIGHT DOWN
STRAIGHT DROP
STRAIGHTEN UP
STRAIGHT FACE
STRAIGHT HAIR
STRAIGHT HOME
STRAIGHT LEFT
STRAIGHT LINE
STRAIGHT NOSE
STRAIGHT PART
STRAIGHT PLAY
STRAIGHT ROAD
STRAIGHT SETS
STRAIGHT SHOT
STRAIGHT TALK
STRAIN A POINT
STRAIT JACKET
STRAND OF HAIR
STRANGE FACES
STRANGE PLACE
STRANGE TO SAY
STRANGE WOMAN
STRAPPING LAD
STREAK OF LUCK
STREAKY BACON
STREAM OF CARS
STREET ARTIST
STREET CORNER
STREET MARKET

STREETS AHEAD
STREET SELLER
STREET SINGER
STREET TRADER
STREET URCHIN
STREET VENDOR
STRETCH NYLON
STRETCH TIGHT
STRICTLY TRUE
STRICT ORDERS
STRIFE AND WOE
STRIKE A CHORD
STRIKE ACTION
STRIKE A LIGHT
STRIKE A MATCH
STRIKE BOTTOM
STRIKE IT RICH
STRIKE ME DEAD!
STRIKE ME PINK!
STRIKE TERROR
STRIKE THE EYE
STRIKE WEAPON
STRING OF LIES
STRIP CARTOON
STRIP OF PAPER
STRIP OF WATER
STRIVE IN VAIN
STROKE OF LUCK
STROKE OF WORK
STROKE THE CAT
STROKE THE DOG
STRONG-ARM MAN
STRONG AS AN OX
STRONG COLOUR
STRONG DEMAND
STRONG DENIAL
STRONG DESIRE
STRONGLY MADE
STRONG NERVES
STRONG THIRST
STRONG WHISKY
STRUGGLE HARD
STUDENT OF LAW
STUDY CLOSELY
STUFFED HEART
STUFFED OLIVE
STUFFED SHIRT
STUFF ONESELF
STUMBLE ALONG
STUMP ORATORY
STUNNING BLOW

STUPID ANSWER
STUPID FELLOW
STYGIAN SHORE
SUBDUED LIGHT
SUBMARINE PEN
SUBTLE CHANGE
SUCCESS STORY
SUCK AN ORANGE
SUDDEN ATTACK
SUDDEN CHANGE
SUDDEN MOTION
SUDDEN STRAIN
SUDDEN TWITCH
SUFFER DEFEAT
SUFFOLK PUNCH
SUGAR CONTENT
SUGAR IS SWEET
SUGAR REFINER
SUGAR THE PILL
SUICIDAL IDEA
SUITE OF ROOMS
SUIT OF ARMOUR
SUIT YOURSELF
SULTAN'S HAREM
SULTAN'S WIVES
SUMMARY COURT
SUMMER MONTHS
SUMMER RESORT
SUMMER SCHOOL
SUMMER SEASON
SUNDAY DINNER
SUNDAY'S CHILD
SUNDAY SCHOOL
SUNKEN CHEEKS
SUNKEN GARDEN
SUNNY WEATHER
SUNSHINE ROOF
SUN-TAN LOTION
SUPERB FIGURE
SUPERB FINISH
SUPERIOR AIRS
SUPERIOR RANK
SUPERIOR TYPE
SUPPORT A WIFE
SUPREME BEING
SUPREME COURT
SUPREME ISSUE
SUPREME POWER
SURE TO PLEASE
SURGE FORWARD
SURGERY HOURS

SURGICAL CASE
SURGICAL WARD
SURPLUS FLESH
SURPLUS GOODS
SURPLUS STOCK
SURPRISE MOVE
SUSAN HAYWARD
SUSAN MAUGHAN
SUSTAIN A LOSS
SWALLOW WHOLE
SWARM OF FLIES
SWARM OF GNATS
SWARM UP A ROPE
SWAY TO AND FRO
SWEAR FALSELY
SWEDISH DRILL
SWEEP THE DECK
SWEEP THROUGH
SWEET ADELINE
SWEET AND SOUR
SWEET AS HONEY
SWEET AS SUGAR
SWEET CONTENT
SWEET MARTINI
SWEET PICKLES
SWEET REVENGE
SWEET SIXTEEN
SWEET SUCCESS
SWEET THOUGHT
SWEET VIOLETS
SWEET WILLIAM
SWIFT CURRENT
SWIFT TO ANGER
SWIMMING BATH
SWIMMING CLUB
SWIMMING GALA
SWIMMING POOL
SWIM UP-STREAM
SWING THE LEAD
SWISS COTTAGE
SWOLLEN RIVER
SWORD OF STATE
SWORN ENEMIES
SYCAMORE TREE
SYDNEY BRIDGE
SYDNEY CARTON

T—12
TABLE A MOTION
TABLE MANNERS
TABLET OF SOAP

TAIL OF THE EYE
TAILORED SUIT
TAILOR'S DUMMY
TAILOR'S GOOSE
TAILS YOU LOSE!
TAINTED GOODS
TAINTED MONEY
TAKE A BEATING
TAKE A HOLIDAY
TAKE A LIBERTY
TAKE A LOOK-SEE
TAKE A PENALTY
TAKE A POT-SHOT
TAKE A PRIDE IN
TAKE A READING
TAKE DELIVERY
TAKE DOWN A PEG
TAKE EXERCISE
TAKE FOR A RIDE
TAKE GOOD CARE
TAKE IT FROM ME
TAKE MEASURES
TAKE MY ADVICE
TAKE NO DENIAL
TAKE NO NOTICE
TAKE ON A PILOT
TAKE ONE'S EASE
TAKE ONE'S HOOK
TAKE ONE'S NAME
TAKE ONE'S PICK
TAKE ONE'S TIME
TAKE ONE'S TURN
TAKE ONE'S WORD
TAKE PLEASURE
TAKE PRISONER
TAKE THE BLAME
TAKE THE CHAIR
TAKE THE COUNT
TAKE THE FIELD
TAKE THE FLOOR
TAKE THE MICKY
TAKE THE POINT
TAKE THE PRIZE
TAKE THE REINS
TAKE THE STAGE
TAKE THE STAND
TAKE THE TRICK
TAKE TO FLIGHT
TAKE TO PIECES
TAKE TO THE AIR
TAKE UP A STAND

TAKE UP OFFICE
TALCUM POWDER
TALE OF A SHIRT
TALK AT LENGTH
TALK AT RANDOM
TALK BUSINESS
TALKING POINT
TALK NONSENSE
TALK OF ANGELS
TALK POLITICS
TALK STRAIGHT
TALK TO NOBODY
TALLEST WOMAN
TALLOW CANDLE
TANGLED SKEIN
TANKARD OF ALE
TANK REGIMENT
TAP AT THE DOOR
TAPE RECORDER
TAP ON THE HEAD
TAP THE BARREL
TARIFF REFORM
TASTE OF HONEY
TASTES DIFFER
TAX COLLECTOR
TAX INSPECTOR
TEACH SKATING
TEAM OF HORSES
TEARING HURRY
TEAR ONE'S HAIR
TEARS OF GRIEF
TEAR TO PIECES
TEAR TO SHREDS
TEA WITH LEMON
TEEM WITH RAIN
TEEN-AGE DREAM
TEEN-AGE YEARS
TELEGRAPH BOY
TELEPHONE BOX
TELL A WHOPPER
TELL EVERYONE
TELL FORTUNES
TELL ME A STORY
TELL-TALE SIGN
TELL THE TRUTH
TELL THE WORLD
TEMPLE OF FAME
TEMPORARY JOB
TEMPT FORTUNE
TEMPTING BAIT
TEN AND A PENNY

TEN AND ELEVEN
TENANT FARMER
TEN-GALLON HAT
TENNIS LESSON
TENNIS PLAYER
TENNIS RACKET
TEN-POUND NOTE
TEN SHILLINGS
TENTH CENTURY
TENTH OF APRIL
TENTH OF MARCH
TERMINAL HOME
TERM OF OFFICE
TERRACED ROOF
TERRIBLE TIME
TEST-TUBE BABY
TEXAS RANGERS
THAMES DITTON
THAMES TUNNEL
THAMES VALLEY
THATCHED ROOF
THE ACROPOLIS
THE ADMIRALTY
THE ALCHEMIST
THE ALL-BLACKS
THE ANTARCTIC
THE ANTIPODES
THE APPLE-CART
THE ARCADIANS
THE ARGENTINE
THE ARGONAUTS
THEATRE OF WAR
THEATRE QUEUE
THEATRE ROYAL
THEATRE USHER
THEATRE WORLD
THE BACHELORS
THE BIG DIPPER
THE BITTER END
THE BLUE ANGEL
THE BOSPHORUS
THE BOY FRIEND
THE CATACOMBS
THE CATECHISM
THE CHILTERNS
THE COMMON MAN
THE CONQUEROR
THE CONTINENT
THE COTSWOLDS
THE CRUSADERS
THE DARK BLUES

THE DAY BEFORE	THE REAL THING	THIS ABOVE ALL
THE DEEP SOUTH	THERE AND BACK	THIS SATURDAY
THE DEFENDERS	THERE AND THEN	THIS THURSDAY
THE DEVIL'S OWN	THE REICHSTAG	THIS VERY ROOM
THE DIE IS CAST	THE REMAINDER	THOMAS ARNOLD
THE DOLOMITES	THERE'S THE RUB	THOMAS EDISON
THE DONE THING	THERMOS FLASK	THOMAS WOLSEY
THE DOVER ROAD	THE SAME THING	THOSE AGAINST
THE FALL OF MAN	THE SEAMY SIDE	THREAD OF LIFE
THE FAVOURITE	THE SEARCHERS	THREAT OF RAIN
THE FIVE TOWNS	THE SEVEN SEAS	THREE-ACT PLAY
THE FOLLOWING	THE SEVENTIES	THREE AND FIVE
THE FOUR WINDS	THE SOUTH-EAST	THREE AND FOUR
THE GENTLE SEX	THE SOUTH-WEST	THREE AND NINE
THE GRAMPIANS	THE SPECTATOR	THREE AT A TIME
THE GUILDHALL	THE STORY GOES	THREE BY THREE
THE HAPPY MEAN	THE THING TO DO	THREE COLOURS
THE HAYMARKET	THE TRUTH GAME	THREE COURSES
THE HEREAFTER	THE UPPER HAND	THREE-DAY WEEK
THE HERMITAGE	THE VERY DEVIL	THREE DEGREES
THE HIGHLANDS	THE VERY IMAGE	THREE DOLLARS
THE HIMALAYAS	THE VERY PLACE	THREE EIGHTHS
THE IMMORTALS	THE VERY THING	THREE FATHOMS
THE IRONSIDES	THE WEAKER SEX	THREE FIGURES
THE IVY LEAGUE	THE WHOLE TIME	THREE GALLONS
THE LAST DITCH	THE WILL TO WIN	THREE GUESSES
THE LAST LAUGH	THE WOMENFOLK	THREE GUINEAS
THE LAST STRAW	THE WORM TURNS	THREE HUNDRED
THE LAST TRUMP	THE WORST OF IT	THREE LENGTHS
THE LIMELIGHT	THE YARDBIRDS	THREE MILLION
THE LISTENERS	THE YOUNG IDEA	THREE MINUTES
THE LOST CHORD	THICK AND FAST	THREE OCTAVES
THE MAD HATTER	THICK AND THIN	THREE OF A KIND
THE MAYFLOWER	THICK GLASSES	THREE OF CLUBS
THE MORSE CODE	THIEVES' SLANG	THREE PER CENT
THE MOUSETRAP	THIN AS A WAFER	THREE-PLY WOOD
THEN AND THERE	THIN DISGUISE	THREE-PLY WOOL
THE NEW FOREST	THINGS CHANGE	THREE RASHERS
THE NORTH-EAST	THINGS TO COME	THREE'S A CROWD
THE NORTH-WEST	THINK ABOUT IT	THREE SISTERS
THE OLD BAILEY	THIN MATERIAL	THREE SQUARED
THE OLD ONE-TWO	THIRD CENTURY	THREE STOOGES
THE OLD SCHOOL	THIRD CHANNEL	THREE STRIPES
THE OTHER SIDE	THIRD CHAPTER	THREE STROKES
THE OUTSKIRTS	THIRD EDITION	THREE UNITIES
THE PALLADIUM	THIRD OF APRIL	THREE WICKETS
THE PARTHENON	THIRD OFFICER	THREE WISE MEN
THE PIPER'S SON	THIRD OF MARCH	THREE WITCHES
THE POLONAISE	THIRD QUARTER	THROATY LAUGH
THE POTTERIES	THIRD READING	THROTTLE DOWN
THE PROVINCES	THIRTEEN DAYS	THROUGH COACH

THROUGH TRAIN
THROW A GLANCE
THROW A SWITCH
THYROID GLAND
TICKET HOLDER
TICKET OFFICE
TICKET POCKET
TIDE OF EVENTS
TIE ONE'S HANDS
TIGHT AS A LORD
TIGHT BANDAGE
TIGHT SQUEEZE
TILL ALL HOURS
TILL DOOMSDAY
TILL NEXT TIME
TILTING MATCH
TIMBERED ROOF
TIME AND AGAIN
TIME AND A HALF
TIME AND MONEY
TIME AND PLACE
TIME AND SPACE
TIME EXPOSURE
TIME FOR LUNCH
TIMELY ADVICE
TIME SCHEDULE
TIME TO FINISH
TIME TO GO HOME
TIME WILL TELL
TINKER'S CURSE
TINNED SALMON
TINTERN ABBEY
TIP THE SCALES
TIP THE WINNER
TIRED OF IT ALL
TIRED TO DEATH
TISSUE OF LIES
TITLED PEOPLE
TITLED PERSON
TITTLE TATTLE
TO ALL INTENTS
TOASTING FORK
TOBACCO JUICE
TOBACCO PLANT
TOBACCO POUCH
TOBACCO SMOKE
TOBACCO STAIN
TO ERR IS HUMAN
TOKEN GESTURE
TOKEN PAYMENT
TOMATO CATSUP

TOM COURTENAY
TOMMY HANDLEY
TOMMY TRINDER
TONGUE OF LAND
TOO HOT TO HOLD
TOOK A DIM VIEW
TOOLS OF TRADE
TOO MANY COOKS
TO ONE'S CREDIT
TOOTH AND CLAW
TOOTH AND NAIL
TOOT ONE'S HORN
TOPLESS DRESS
TOP OF THE BILL
TOP OF THE FORM
TOP OF THE HILL
TOP OF THE MILK
TOP OF THE POLL
TOP OF THE POPS
TOP OF THE TREE
TOREADOR SONG
TORN TO SHREDS
TORY MAJORITY
TORY MINORITY
TOSS A PANCAKE
TOSS FOR SIDES
TOSS ONE'S HEAD
TOSS THE CABER
TOTAL ECLIPSE
TO THE GALLOWS
TO THE LAST MAN
TOTTER AROUND
TOUCH OF FROST
TOUCH ONE'S CAP
TOUCHY PERSON
TOUGH AS NAILS
TOUGH AS STEEL
TOUR DE FRANCE
TOURIST CLASS
TOURIST TRADE
TOUT ENSEMBLE
TOWERING RAGE
TOWER OF BABEL
TOWN PLANNING
TOWN SURVEYOR
TRACER BULLET
TRACING PAPER
TRADE FIGURES
TRADE JOURNAL
TRADE RETURNS
TRADE SURPLUS

TRADING HOUSE
TRADING STAMP
TRAFFIC LIGHT
TRAFFIC RULES
TRAFFORD PARK
TRAGIC ENDING
TRAGIC LOVERS
TRAILING EDGE
TRAINED NURSE
TRAINED VOICE
TRAINING SHIP
TRAIN JOURNEY
TRAIN OF IDEAS
TRAIN ROBBERY
TRAIN SERVICE
TRAIN SPOTTER
TRAIN THE MIND
TRAITOR'S GATE
TRAMP STEAMER
TRANQUIL MIND
TRAPPIST MONK
TRAVEL ABROAD
TRAVEL AGENCY
TRAVEL AROUND
TRAVEL BUREAU
TRAVEL BY LAND
TRAVEL BY TUBE
TREAD LIGHTLY
TREASURE HUNT
TREASURY BILL
TREASURY NOTE
TREAT IN STORE
TREAT LIGHTLY
TREAT ROUGHLY
TREATY OF ROME
TREBLE CHANCE
TRENCHANT WIT
TRENCH MORTAR
TRESPASS UPON
TRESTLE TABLE
TREVOR HOWARD
TRIAL BALANCE
TRIAL IN COURT
TRIBAL CUSTOM
TRIBAL SYSTEM
TRICK CYCLIST
TRIED IN COURT
TRIFLING TALK
TRIGGER HAPPY
TRIM THE SAILS
TRINITY HOUSE

TRIPE DRESSER
TRIVIAL ROUND
TROMBONE SOLO
TROOP CARRIER
TROPHY HUNTER
TROPICAL BIRD
TROPICAL FISH
TROPICAL HEAT
TROPICAL MOON
TROPICAL SUIT
TROPICAL WIND
TROTTING PACE
TROUBLE AHEAD
TROUBLED MIND
TROUSER PRESS
TROUT FISHING
TRUE BELIEVER
TRUE FEELINGS
TRUE TO NATURE
TRUE TO THE END
TRUMPET BLAST
TRUNDLE ALONG
TRUSS OF STRAW
TRUST COMPANY
TRUSTEE STOCK
TRUSTY FRIEND
TRUTH WILL OUT
TRYING PERSON
TRY ONE'S SKILL
TSAR OF RUSSIA
TUBELESS TYRE
TUESDAY NIGHT
TUGBOAT ANNIE
TUNES OF GLORY
TUNNEL OF LOVE
TURKISH TOWEL
TURN A DEAF EAR
TURNED-UP NOSE
TURNHAM GREEN
TURNING POINT
TURN INTO CASH
TURN OF EVENTS
TURN OF PHRASE
TURN OF SPEECH
TURN ONE'S BACK
TURN ONE'S HEAD
TURN ON THE GAS
TURN ON THE TAP
TURN THE PAGES
TURN THE SCALE
TURN THE SCREW

TURN THE TAP ON
TURN UP TRUMPS
TWELFTH GREEN
TWELFTH NIGHT
TWELFTH OF MAY
TWELFTH PLACE
TWELFTH ROUND
TWELVE AND ONE
TWELVE AND SIX
TWELVE AND TEN
TWELVE AND TWO
TWELVE MONTHS
TWELVE O'CLOCK
TWELVE OUNCES
TWELVE POINTS
TWELVE POUNDS
TWELVE TRICKS
TWENTY POINTS
TWENTY POUNDS
TWICE AS HEAVY
TWICE AS QUICK
TWICE MONTHLY
TWICE NIGHTLY
TWICE REMOVED
TWICE THE SIZE
TWIN BROTHERS
TWIN CHILDREN
TWINGE OF PAIN
TWIST AND BUST
TWIST AND TURN
TWIST ONE'S ARM
TWO AND A PENNY
TWO AND ELEVEN
TWO IN THE BUSH
TWO-SEATER CAR
TWO SHILLINGS
TWO SIXPENCES
TWO-SPEED GEAR
TWO SYLLABLES
TWO-WAY STREET
TYPHOID FEVER
TYPING LESSON
TYPIST'S ERROR
TYRE PRESSURE

U—12

UGLY CUSTOMER
UGLY DUCKLING
UMBRELLA BIRD
UMPTEEN TIMES
UNABLE TO COPE

UNABLE TO HELP
UNABLE TO MOVE
UNBROKEN LINE
UNCERTAIN JOY
UNCUT DIAMOND
UNDER A BUSHEL
UNDER A LADDER
UNDER AND OVER
UNDER A STRAIN
UNDER CONTROL
UNDER ENQUIRY
UNDER HATCHES
UNDER LICENCE
UNDER ONE ROOF
UNDER ONE'S HAT
UNDER PROTEST
UNDER SHERIFF
UNDER TENSION
UNDER THE HEEL
UNDER THE LASH
UNDER THE ROSE
UNDER THE SKIN
UNDER THE WING
UNEVEN CHANCE
UNFAIR CHOICE
UNFIT FOR WORK
UNHAPPY TIMES
UNIFORM SPEED
UNION MEETING
UNITED ACTION
UNITED EFFORT
UNITED STATES
UNIT OF ENERGY
UNIT OF LENGTH
UNKINDEST CUT
UNKNOWN THING
UNLUCKY PATCH
UNMARRIED MAN
UNPAID LABOUR
UNPAID WORKER
UNTIE THE KNOT
UNTIMELY JEST
UNTOLD WEALTH
UNUSUAL TWIST
UNWORTHY PART
UNWRITTEN LAW
UP FOR AUCTION
UP IN A BALLOON
UP IN THE HILLS
UP ONE'S SLEEVE
UP ONE'S STREET

UPON MY HONOUR
UPPER CHAMBER
UPPER CIRCLES
UPPER CLASSES
UPPER REGIONS
UPRIGHT GRAND
UPRIGHT PIANO
UPSTAIRS ROOM
UP THE CHIMNEY
UP TO MISCHIEF
UP TO ONE'S EYES
UP TO ONE'S NECK
UP TO STANDARD
UP TO STRENGTH
UP TO THE NINES
UP TO THE WAIST
UPWARD GLANCE
UPWARD MOTION
UPWARD STROKE
UP WITH THE SUN
URGENT DEMAND
URGENT MATTER
USEFUL ADVICE
USE OF KITCHEN
USE ONE'S BRAIN
USE ONE'S HANDS
UTMOST EXTENT
UTTER FAILURE
UTTER POVERTY
UTTER RUBBISH
UTTER SILENCE
UTTER THREATS

V—12
VACANT OFFICE
VALE OF SORROW
VALET SERVICE
VALIANT HEART
VALUED ADVICE
VALUED FRIEND
VANDYKE BEARD
VANTAGE POINT
VARIABLE GEAR
VARIETY HOUSE
VARIETY STAGE
VARIOUS TYPES
VARSITY MATCH
VAST QUANTITY
VEGETABLE DYE
VEGETABLE OIL

VEILED THREAT
VENETIAN LACE
VENI, VIDI, VICI
VENTURE FORTH
VENTURE TO SAY
VERBAL ATTACK
VERNAL SEASON
VERONICA LAKE
VERTICAL LINE
VERY REVEREND
VERY TOUCHING
VESTED RIGHTS
VIALS OF WRATH
VICE-LIKE GRIP
VICTIM OF FATE
VICTORIA LINE
VICTORIAN AGE
VICTORIAN ERA
VICTORIA PLUM
VICTORY AT SEA
VICTORY BONDS
VICTORY MARCH
VICTORY MEDAL
VILLAGE GREEN
VILLAGE IDIOT
VIM AND VIGOUR
VINCENT PRICE
VIN ORDINAIRE
VIOLENT DEATH
VIOLENT STORM
VIOLENT UPSET
VIOLET CARSON
VIOLIN PLAYER
VIOLIN STRING
VIRGIN FOREST
VIRGINIA MAYO
VIRGINIA REEL
VIRULENT TONE
VISIBLE MEANS
VISIT FRIENDS
VISITING CARD
VISITING TEAM
VISITING TIME
VISITORS' BOOK
VISIT THE SICK
VITAL CONCERN
VIVE LA FRANCE
VIVID PICTURE
VOCATIVE CASE
VODKA AND LIME
VOLCANIC ROCK

VOLGA BOATMAN
VOLUME OF FIRE
VOODOO DOCTOR
VOODOO PRIEST
VOTE IN FAVOUR
VOTE OF THANKS
VOW OF SILENCE
VULGAR TASTES

W—12
WAGE INCREASE
WAG OF THE HEAD
WAG THE FINGER
WAITING WOMAN
WAIT ONE'S TURN
WALK GINGERLY
WALKING MATCH
WALK ON STILTS
WALK ON TIPTOE
WALK SIDEWAYS
WALK STRAIGHT
WALK THE EARTH
WALK THE PLANK
WALK TOGETHER
WALK WITH EASE
WALLED GARDEN
WANDERING JEW
WAND OF OFFICE
WANTED PERSON
WARLIKE TRIBE
WARM THE BLOOD
WARM THE HEART
WARNING LIGHT
WARNING SOUND
WARNING VOICE
WAR TO END WARS
WASH AND DRY UP
WASHED ASHORE
WASH ONE'S FACE
WASH ONE'S HAIR
WASTED EFFORT
WASTED LABOUR
WASTE NOTHING
WASTE NO WORDS
WASTE OF MONEY
WASTE PRODUCT
WATCH AND PRAY
WATCH AND WAIT
WATCH CLOSELY
WATCH REPAIRS
WATER BISCUIT

WATER COLOURS	WELL AND TRULY	WILBUR WRIGHT
WATER DIVINER	WELL DESERVED	WILD APPLAUSE
WATER HYDRANT	WELL DISPOSED	WILD CREATURE
WATERING CART	WELL IN POCKET	WILD HYACINTH
WATER SPANIEL	WELL-MADE SUIT	WILD LAUGHTER
WAVE FAREWELL	WELL REPORTED	WILD-WEST SHOW
WAXWORKS SHOW	WELL TAILORED	WILFUL DAMAGE
WAYNE FONTANA	WELL-TIMED ACT	WILFUL MURDER
WAYS AND MEANS	WELSH COSTUME	WILLIAM BLAKE
WAYWARD CHILD	WELSH DRESSER	WILLIAM BOOTH
WEAK APPROACH	WELSH RAREBIT	WILLIAM RUFUS
WEAK ARGUMENT	WEST BROMWICH	WILLING HANDS
WEAKER VESSEL	WEST-END STAGE	WILLING HEART
WEAKEST POINT	WESTERLY WIND	WILLING HORSE
WEAK SOLUTION	WESTERN FRONT	WILLING PARTY
WEALTHY WIDOW	WESTERN ISLES	WILLING SLAVE
WEAPONS OF WAR	WESTERN UNION	WILLING VOTER
WEAR BLINKERS	WESTERN WORLD	WILL OF HEAVEN
WEAR MOURNING	WEST VIRGINIA	WILL O' THE WISP
WEAR THE CLOTH	WET TO THE SKIN	WILTON CARPET
WEAR THE CROWN	WHALE OF A TIME	WIN BY A LENGTH
WEATHER CHART	WHAT'S COOKING?	WINDING TRAIL
WEATHER GAUGE	WHAT'S THE GAME?	WINDMILL GIRL
WEATHER GLASS	WHAT'S THE ODDS?	WIND OF CHANGE
WEB OF CUNNING	WHAT THE DEUCE?	WINDOW SCREEN
WEDDED COUPLE	WHEN AND WHERE?	WINDSOR CHAIR
WEDDING BELLS	WHERE AND WHEN?	WIND THE CLOCK
WEDDING DRESS	WHETHER OR NOT	WINDY WEATHER
WEDDING FEAST	WHET THE KNIFE	WINE AND WOMEN
WEDDING GROUP	WHICH IS WHICH?	WINE IMPORTER
WEDDING GUEST	WHIFF OF SMOKE	WINE MERCHANT
WEDDING MARCH	WHILE YOU WAIT	WINGED INSECT
WEDDING RITES	WHIPPED CREAM	WIN HANDS DOWN
WEDGWOOD BLUE	WHIPPING POST	WIN IN A CANTER
WEEK-END LEAVE	WHIPSNADE ZOO	WINNING HORSE
WEEK-END PARTY	WHISKY GALORE	WINNING SCORE
WEEKLY COLUMN	WHISTLE FOR IT	WINNING SMILE
WEEKLY MARKET	WHITE CABBAGE	WIN ONE'S SPURS
WEEKLY REPORT	WHITE FEATHER	WINSOME SMILE
WEEKLY SALARY	WHITE HEATHER	WINTER ABROAD
WEEP WITH RAGE	WHITE OF AN EGG	WINTER GARDEN
WEIGH HEAVILY	WHITE RUSSIAN	WINTER RESORT
WEIGH ONESELF	WHITE WEDDING	WINTER SEASON
WEIGHT FOR AGE	WHITHER BOUND?	WINTER SPORTS
WEIRD SISTERS	WHO GOES THERE?	WIN THE BATTLE
WELCOME EVENT	WICKED TYRANT	WIN THE RUBBER
WELCOME GUEST	WICKER BASKET	WIPE ONE'S EYES
WELCOME SIGHT	WICKET KEEPER	WIPE ONE'S FEET
WELD TOGETHER	WIDE CURRENCY	WIPE THE FLOOR
WELFARE STATE	WIDELY SPACED	WISE DECISION
WELL ADVANCED	WIDOW TWANKEY	WIT AND WISDOM

WITCHING HOUR
WITCH OF ENDOR
WITH ALL HASTE
WITH ALL SPEED
WITH AN ACCENT
WITH A PURPOSE
WITH IMPUNITY
WITHIN BOUNDS
WITHIN LIMITS
WITHIN RADIUS
WITHIN REASON
WITH INTEREST
WITHIN THE LAW
WITH ONE VOICE
WITH OPEN ARMS
WITH OPEN EYES
WITHOUT A BEAN
WITHOUT A CARE
WITHOUT A CENT
WITHOUT A HOPE
WITHOUT A WORD
WITHOUT CAUSE
WITHOUT DELAY
WITHOUT DOUBT
WITHOUT FAULT
WITHOUT LIMIT
WITHOUT PRICE
WITHOUT STINT
WITHOUT SUGAR
WITH PLEASURE
WITH THIS RING
WOMAN IN WHITE
WOMAN'S HONOUR
WOMAN STUDENT
WOMAN TO WOMAN
WOMEN'S RIGHTS
WON BY A STREET
WON IN A CANTER
WOODEN BUCKET
WOOD SHAVINGS
WOOLLEN SOCKS
WOOL MERCHANT
WORD IN SEASON

WORD IN THE EAR
WORD OF ADVICE
WORD OF HONOUR
WORDS OF CHEER
WORDY WARFARE
WORKABLE PLAN
WORK FOR PEACE
WORKING CLASS
WORKING HOURS
WORKING MODEL
WORKING ORDER
WORKING PARTY
WORKING WIVES
WORKING WOMAN
WORK MIRACLES
WORK OFF STEAM
WORK ONE'S WILL
WORK OVERTIME
WORKS CANTEEN
WORKS COUNCIL
WORKS MANAGER
WORK TOGETHER
WORLDLY GOODS
WORLD OF SPORT
WORLD OF TODAY
WORM'S EYE VIEW
WORRIED FROWN
WORRYING TIME
WORRY TO DEATH
WORSE FOR WEAR
WORTH A PACKET
WORTH NOTHING
WORTHY OF NOTE
WOULD YOU MIND?
WOUNDED PRIDE
WRACK AND RUIN
WRETCHED DIGS
WRITE A CHEQUE
WRITE A LETTER
WRITE AN ESSAY
WRITE A REPORT
WRITE A SONNET
WRITER'S CRAMP

WRITHE IN PAIN
WRITING PAPER
WRITING TABLE
WRITTEN MUSIC
WRITTEN ORDER
WRITTEN REPLY
WRITTEN TERMS
WRONG ADDRESS
WRONG MEANING
WRONG SIDE OUT
WRONG SOCIETY
WRONG TURNING
WRONG VERDICT

Y—12

YACHTING CLUB
YANKEE DOODLE
YARD AND A HALF
YEARLY SALARY
YEARS OF STUDY
YELLOW BASKET
YELLOW COLOUR
YELLOW FLOWER
YELLOW RIBBON
YELLOW STREAK
YELL WITH PAIN
YOUNG AT HEART
YOUNG ENGLAND
YOUNGEST GIRL
YOUNG HOPEFUL
YOUNG IN HEART
YOUNG WOODLEY
YOUR EMINENCE
YOUR HIGHNESS
YOUR LADYSHIP
YOUR LORDSHIP
YOUR OWN FAULT
YOURS IN HASTE

Z—12

ZACHARY SCOTT
ZIGZAG COURSE

A—13
ABERDEEN ANGUS
ABIDE BY THE LAW
ABJECT APOLOGY
ABJECT POVERTY
ABJECT SLAVERY
ABOUT ONE'S EARS
ABOVE ONE'S HEAD
ABOVE REPROACH
ABOVE SEA-LEVEL
ABOVE STRENGTH
ABRAHAM'S BOSOM
ABRUPT DESCENT
ABSENCE OF MIND
ABSENT FRIENDS
ABSOLUTE POWER
ABSOLUTE PROOF
ABSOLUTE RULER
ABSOLUTE TRUST
ABSTRACT TERMS
ABUSIVE SPEECH
ABYSSINIAN CAT
ACADEMIC DRESS
ACADEMIC TITLE
ACCEPT AN OFFER
ACCEPTED TRUTH
ACCEPT PAYMENT
ACCIDENT PRONE
ACCORDION BAND
ACCOUNTS CLERK
ACCUSED PERSON
ACCUSE FALSELY
ACE OF DIAMONDS
ACHES AND PAINS
ACQUIRED SKILL
ACQUIRED TASTE
ACQUIT ONESELF
ACROSS AND DOWN
ACROSS COUNTRY
ACROSS THE ROAD
ACT AS CHAIRMAN
ACT FOR THE BEST
ACTING CAPTAIN
ACTING MANAGER
ACTION PAINTER
ACTION PICTURE
ACTIVE PARTNER
ACTIVE SERVICE
ACTIVE VOLCANO
ACT LIKE A CHARM
ACT LIKE A TONIC

ACT OF COURTESY
ACT OF HUMANITY
ACT OF KINDNESS
ACT OF VIOLENCE
ACUTE DISTRESS
ADAM FIREPLACE
ADDED PLEASURE
ADDED STRENGTH
ADDING MACHINE
ADEQUATE CAUSE
A DEUCE OF A MESS
ADIPOSE TISSUE
ADJUST THE TYPE
ADMIRAL NELSON
ADMIRALTY ARCH
ADMISSION CARD
ADMISSION FREE
ADMITTED GUILT
ADVANCED LEVEL
ADVANCED PUPIL
ADVANCE NOTICE
ADVISE AGAINST
ADVISORY BOARD
AERIAL RAILWAY
AERIAL TORPEDO
AERIAL WARFARE
AFFECTED STYLE
AFFECTED VOICE
AFFORDING HOPE
AFRAID TO SPEAK
AFTER A FASHION
AFTER MIDNIGHT
AFTERNOON POST
AFTERNOON REST
AFTER THE EVENT
AFTER THE STORM
AGAIN AND AGAIN
AGAINST THE LAW
AGE OF CHIVALRY
AGREE TO DIFFER
AIR A GRIEVANCE
AIR-FORCE CROSS
AIR OF APPROVAL
AIR ON A G STRING
AIR OPERATIONS
AIRPORT LOUNGE
AIR-RAID WARDEN
AIRS AND GRACES
ALEXANDER POPE
ALEXANDRA PARK
ALFRED DREYFUS

ALICE BLUE GOWN
ALL CHANGE HERE
ALL-DAY SESSION
ALLEGED MOTIVE
ALLEGED REASON
ALL FOR NOTHING
ALL FOR THE BEST
ALL FOR THE GOOD
ALL HALLOWS' EVE
ALLIED ADVANCE
ALLIED LANDING
ALLIGATOR PEAR
ALLIGATOR SKIN
ALL IN A FLUSTER
ALL IN GOOD TIME
ALL IN ONE PIECE
ALL-IN WRESTLER
ALL OF A TREMBLE
ALL OF A TWITTER
ALL THE ANSWERS
ALL THE WINNERS
ALL-TIME RECORD
ALLUVIAL PLAIN
ALMOND BLOSSOM
ALONG THE COAST
A LONG WAY AFTER
A LONG WAY AHEAD
ALPHA AND OMEGA
ALPINE CLIMBER
ALTER THE RULES
ALTOGETHER BAD
ALWAYS ON THE GO
AMATEUR BOXING
AMATEUR GOLFER
AMATEUR PLAYER
AMATEUR SLEUTH
AMATEUR STATUS
AMATEUR TALENT
AMERICAN CLOTH
AMERICAN EAGLE
AMERICAN NEGRO
AMERICAN ORGAN
AMERICAN SLANG
AMOROUS GLANCE
AMUSEMENT PARK
ANATOLE FRANCE
ANCESTRAL HALL
ANCESTRAL HOME
ANCIENT BRITON
ANCIENT GREECE
ANCIENT GRUDGE

ANCIENT LIGHTS
ANCIENT WISDOM
ANDREW JACKSON
ANGELIC VOICES
ANGEL PAVEMENT
ANGRY YOUNG MAN
ANGUISH OF MIND
ANGULAR FIGURE
ANIMAL KINGDOM
ANIMAL RESERVE
ANIMAL SPIRITS
ANIMAL TRAINER
ANIMATED SMILE
ANNOTATED TEXT
ANNUAL ECLIPSE
ANNUAL FIXTURE
ANNUAL HOLIDAY
ANNUAL MEETING
ANNUAL PAYMENT
ANNUAL PREMIUM
ANOINT WITH OIL
ANONYMOUS GIFT
ANOTHER CHANCE
ANOTHER MATTER
ANOTHER PLEASE
ANSWER THE BELL
ANSWER THE HELM
ANTHONY NEWLEY
ANTHONY QUAYLE
ANTHROPOID APE
ANTIQUE DEALER
ANTONY ADVERSE
ANXIOUS MOMENT
ANYBODY'S GUESS
APPEAL FOR HELP
APPEALING LOOK
APPEAR IN COURT
APPLE DUMPLING
APPLE FRITTERS
APPLE OF THE EYE
APPLE-PIE ORDER
APPLE TURNOVER
APPLY FOR A LOAN
APPLY FOR LEAVE
APPLY PRESSURE
APPLY THE BRAKE
APPLY THE MATCH
APOLLO THEATRE
APOSTLES' CREED
APPOINTED TIME
APRICOT BRANDY

APRIL FOOL'S DAY	ASHDOWN FOREST
APRIL THE FIFTH	AS HEAVY AS LEAD
APRIL THE FIRST	ASK A POLICEMAN
APRIL THE NINTH	ASK FOR NOTHING
APRIL THE SIXTH	ASK FOR TROUBLE
APRIL THE TENTH	ASK PERMISSION
APRIL THE THIRD	AS LARGE AS LIFE
ARABIAN DESERT	AS LIKELY AS NOT
ARABIAN NIGHTS	AS LONG AS MY ARM
ARC DE TRIOMPHE	AS PALE AS DEATH
ARCHIE ANDREWS	ASPARAGUS TIPS
ARCTIC REGIONS	AS RIGHT AS RAIN
ARDENT ADMIRER	ASSEMBLY ROOMS
ARDENT SPIRITS	ASSERT ONESELF
ARGUE THE POINT	ASSUME AN ALIAS
ARMAMENTS RACE	ASSUME COMMAND
ARMED CONFLICT	AS SURE AS CAN BE
ARMS AND THE MAN	AS SWEET AS A NUT
ARMS PROGRAMME	AS THIN AS A LATH
ARMY COMMANDER	A STITCH IN TIME
ARMY ESTIMATES	AS TRUE AS STEEL
ARMY EXERCISES	AS WARM AS TOAST
ARMY PAY-OFFICE	AS WEAK AS WATER
ARNOLD BENNETT	ATALANTA'S RACE
AROUND THE TOWN	AT AN ADVANTAGE
ARRANGE A MATCH	AT A STANDSTILL
ARREARS OF WORK	AT FULL STRETCH
ART COLLECTION	AT GREAT LENGTH
ART DEPARTMENT	ATHLETE'S HEART
ART EXHIBITION	ATHLETIC COACH
ARTHUR ENGLISH	ATLANTIC LINER
ARTICLED CLERK	ATLANTIC OCEAN
ARTICLES OF WAR	AT LOGGERHEADS
ARTIFICIAL ARM	ATOMIC FISSION
ARTIFICIAL FLY	ATOMIC REACTOR
ARTIFICIAL LEG	ATOMIC WARFARE
ARTILLERY FIRE	ATOMIC WARHEAD
ARTISTIC VALUE	AT ONE'S LEISURE
ARTISTS' COLONY	AT ONE'S OWN RISK
ARTISTS' RIFLES	AT ONE'S WITS' END
ARTIST'S STUDIO	AT RIGHT-ANGLES
ART OF SPEAKING	AT SHORT NOTICE
ARTS AND CRAFTS	ATTEND COLLEGE
AS BLIND AS A BAT	AT THE CONTROLS
AS BOLD AS BRASS	AT THE DENTIST'S
AS DARK AS NIGHT	AT THE LAST GASP
AS DARK AS PITCH	AT THE RINGSIDE
AS FAR AS IT GOES	AT THE SAME TIME
AS FULL AS AN EGG	AT THE WAXWORKS
AS GOOD AS A PLAY	ATTORNEY AT LAW
AS HARD AS NAILS	ATTRACT NOTICE

AT YOUR SERVICE
AUCTION BRIDGE
AUDITORY NERVE
AUDREY HEPBURN
AUGEAN STABLES
AUTHENTIC WORK
AUTOMATIC LIFT
AUTOMATIC LOCK
AUTUMN COLOURS
AUXILIARY VERB
AVENGING ANGEL
AVENUE OF TREES
AVERAGE AMOUNT
AVERAGE FIGURE
AVERAGE HEIGHT
AVERAGE PERSON
AVERAGE WEIGHT
AVERT ONE'S EYES
AVOID THE ISSUE
AWAY FROM IT ALL
AWKWARD PERSON

B—13
BABBLING BROOK
BACHELOR OF LAW
BACK-HAND DRIVE
BACK IN HARNESS
BACK IN THE FOLD
BACK OF THE HAND
BACK OF THE HEAD
BACK OF THE NECK
BACK ONE'S FANCY
BACK THE WINNER
BACK TO THE LAND
BACK TO THE WALL
BACKWARD CHILD
BACON SANDWICH
BAD COMPLEXION
BAD CONNECTION
BAD CONSCIENCE
BADGE OF OFFICE
BAD IMPRESSION
BADLY HAMMERED
BADLY REPORTED
BAD MANAGEMENT
BAD REPUTATION
BAD UPBRINGING
BAG AND BAGGAGE
BAGGY TROUSERS
BALANCE IN HAND
BALD ADMISSION

BALD STATEMENT
BALL AND SOCKET
BALLET DANCING
BALLOON ASCENT
BALLY NUISANCE
BAMBOO CURTAIN
BAND OF OUTLAWS
BAND OF ROBBERS
BANG ON THE HEAD
BANKER'S CREDIT
BANK MESSENGER
BANK OF ENGLAND
BANK OF IRELAND
BANK OVERDRAFT
BANKRUPT STOCK
BANKS AND BRAES
BANK STATEMENT
BAPTISMAL NAME
BAPTISM OF FIRE
BAPTIST CHURCH
BARBARA MULLEN
BARBECUE PARTY
BARBER SURGEON
BARCELONA NUTS
BARE-BACK RIDER
BARE EXISTENCE
BARE-FACED LIAR
BARE ONE'S TEETH
BARGAIN HUNTER
BARK AT THE MOON
BARK ONE'S SHINS
BAR OF THE HOUSE
BARRISTER'S WIG
BARTERED BRIDE
BASHFUL MANNER
BASIC INSTINCT
BASQUE COUNTRY
BASSO PROFUNDO
BATHED IN TEARS
BATHING BEAUTY
BATHING TRUNKS
BATTER PUDDING
BATTERSEA PARK
BATTERY OF GUNS
BATTLE CRUISER
BATTLE HONOURS
BATTLE OF WORDS
BAYONET CHARGE
BAYSWATER ROAD
BEANS AND BACON
BEAR THE BURDEN

BEAST OF BELSEN
BEAST OF BURDEN
BEAT ALL-COMERS
BEATLES' RECORD
BEAT ONE HOLLOW
BEAT THE BOUNDS
BEAT THE RECORD
BEAUFORT SCALE
BEAUTIFUL FACE
BEAUTIFUL VIEW
BEAUTY CONTEST
BEAUTY CULTURE
BEAUTY PARLOUR
BECOME A MARTYR
BECOME A MEMBER
BECOME A NEW MAN
BECOME ENGAGED
BECOME EXTINCT
BECOME FRIENDS
BE CONSPICUOUS
BEDSIDE MANNER
BEETLING BROWS
BEFORE THE DAWN
BEFORE THE FACT
BEFORE THE MAST
BEFORE THE WIND
BEG FOR FAVOURS
BEGGING LETTER
BEGINNER'S LUCK
BEGIN TO WEAKEN
BEG PERMISSION
BEHAVE ONESELF
BEHIND THE LINE
BEHIND THE VEIL
BE IN DISFAVOUR
BE IN THE SADDLE
BELATED EFFORT
BELISHA BEACON
BELLES LETTRES
BELONGING TO ME
BELONGING TO US
BELOVED OBJECT
BELOW FREEZING
BELOW SEA-LEVEL
BELOW STANDARD
BELOW STRENGTH
BE MY VALENTINE
BEND BACKWARDS
BEND IN THE ROAD
BENEATH NOTICE
BENEATH THE SUN

BE OF GOOD CHEER
BE OF GOOD HEART
BERNARD BRADEN
BESIDE ONESELF
BESIDE THE MARK
BESSEMER STEEL
BEST BEHAVIOUR
BEST END OF NECK
BESTIR ONESELF
BEST OF A BAD JOB
BEST OF FRIENDS
BEST OF ITS KIND
BEST OF MOTIVES
BEST THING TO DO
BETTER ONESELF
BETTER OR WORSE
BEYOND ALL HELP
BEYOND COMPARE
BEYOND CONTROL
BEYOND DISPUTE
BEYOND MEASURE
BEYOND ONE'S KEN
BEYOND THE PALE
BEYOND THE VEIL
BICYCLE RACING
BID FOR FREEDOM
BIG-GAME HUNTER
BIG WHITE CHIEF
BILLIARD TABLE
BIRD IN THE HAND
BIRD OF ILL OMEN
BIRD OF PASSAGE
BIRD ON THE WING
BIRD SANCTUARY
BIRD'S-NEST SOUP
BIRDS OF THE AIR
BIRTHDAY PARTY
BIRTHDAY TREAT
BISCUIT BARREL
BITE ONE'S NAILS
BITE ONE'S THUMB
BITING SARCASM
BIT OF A MYSTERY
BIT OF NONSENSE
BITS AND PIECES
BITTER DRAUGHT
BITTER FLAVOUR
BITTER QUARREL
BITTER REMORSE
BLACK AND WHITE
BLACK AS A SWEEP

BLACK DIAMONDS
BLACKPOOL ROCK
BLANKET FINISH
BLANKET OF SNOW
BLANKET STITCH
BLAZE OF COLOUR
BLAZE THE TRAIL
BLAZING TEMPER
BLEEDING HEART
BLESS THE BRIDE
BLIGHTED HOPES
BLINDING LIGHT
BLINDING STORM
BLIND IN ONE EYE
BLINDMAN'S BUFF
BLISSFUL STATE
BLOCK CAPITALS
BLOOD BROTHERS
BLOOD PRESSURE
BLOOD RELATION
BLOODSHOT EYES
BLOODY ASSIZES
BLOTTING PAPER
BLOW GREAT GUNS
BLUE IN THE FACE
BLUNT QUESTION
BLUSH FOR SHAME
BLUSHING BRIDE
BOARDING HOUSE
BOARDING PARTY
BOB'S YOUR UNCLE
BODY CORPORATE
BODY OF OPINION
BOHEMIAN GLASS
BOLSHOI BALLET
BOMBER COMMAND
BONY STRUCTURE
BOOKING OFFICE
BOOK OF GENESIS
BOOK OF THE FILM
BOOK OF THE PLAY
BOOK OF THE YEAR
BOOK OF TICKETS
BOOK ONE'S BERTH
BOOMING MARKET
BOON COMPANION
BOOSTER ROCKET
BOOT AND SADDLE
BORDER BALLADS
BORDER COUNTRY
BORN IN WEDLOCK

BORN ORGANISER
BORN YESTERDAY
BORROWED MONEY
BORSTAL SYSTEM
BOSTON TERRIER
BOSTON TWO-STEP
BOTTLED SWEETS
BOTTLE OF SCENT
BOTTLE OF STOUT
BOTTLE OF WATER
BOTTOMLESS PIT
BOUGHT AND SOLD
BOUNDARY FENCE
BOUNDARY STONE
BOUNDLESS DEEP
BOWLER'S WICKET
BOWLING CREASE
BOW TO THE STORM
BOX OF BISCUITS
BOX OF CRACKERS
BOX OF DOMINOES
BOX THE COMPASS
BRACE OF SHAKES
BRANCH LIBRARY
BRANCH MEETING
BRANDY AND PORT
BRANDY AND SODA
BRASS BEDSTEAD
BRASS FARTHING
BRAVE NEW WORLD
BREACH OF FAITH
BREACH OF TRUST
BREAD AND WATER
BREAD POULTICE
BREAD SHORTAGE
BREADTH OF MIND
BREADTH OF VIEW
BREAK A JOURNEY
BREAK A PROMISE
BREAKDOWN GANG
BREAKERS AHEAD
BREAKFAST DISH
BREAKFAST FOOD
BREAKFAST TIME
BREAKING POINT
BREAK INTO A RUN
BREAK INTO SONG
BREAK IT GENTLY
BREAK OFF SHORT
BREAK ONE'S BACK
BREAK ONE'S DUCK

BREAK ONE'S FAST
BREAK ONE'S NECK
BREAK ONE'S WORD
BREAK THE PEACE
BREAK THE RULES
BREAK THE SPELL
BREAK TO PIECES
BREAST THE TAPE
BREATHE FREELY
BREATHING ROOM
BREATHING TUBE
BRED IN THE BONE
BRIDE AND GROOM
BRIDGE BUILDER
BRIDGE OF BOATS
BRIDGE OF SIGHS
BRIDGE PROBLEM
BRIEF INTERVAL
BRIGHTON BEACH
BRIGHTON BELLE
BRIGHTON RACES
BRILLIANT IDEA
BRILLIANT MIND
BRING AN ACTION
BRING INTO LINE
BRING INTO PLAY
BRING TO A CLOSE
BRING TOGETHER
BRING UP TO DATE
BRISKET OF BEEF
BRISK MOVEMENT
BRISTOL ROVERS
BRITISH COLONY
BRITISH CONSUL
BRITISH EMPIRE
BRITISH GUIANA
BRITISH LEGION
BRITISH MUSEUM
BRITISH PUBLIC
BROAD DAYLIGHT
BROKEN ENGLISH
BROKEN PROMISE
BROKEN ROMANCE
BROKEN SILENCE
BROOK NO DENIAL
BROTHERLY LOVE
BROUGHT TO BOOK
BROWN AS A BERRY
BRUSH ONE'S HAIR
BRUSQUE MANNER
BRUTE STRENGTH

BUBONIC PLAGUE
BUCKET OF WATER
BUDDING AUTHOR
BUDDING GENIUS
BUDGET SURPLUS
BUFF ORPINGTON
BUILDING BLOCK
BULLS AND BEARS
BUMPER HARVEST
BUNCH OF GRAPES
BURDEN OF GUILT
BURDEN OF POWER
BURDEN OF PROOF
BURIAL CUSTOMS
BURIAL SERVICE
BURKE'S PEERAGE
BURLESQUE SHOW
BURNING DESIRE
BURNING THIRST
BURN ONE'S BOATS
BURN ONE'S MONEY
BURN TO A CINDER
BURNT OFFERING
BURN WITH ANGER
BURSTING POINT
BURST OF ENERGY
BURST THE BONDS
BURTON ON TRENT
BUSH TELEGRAPH
BUSINESS HOURS
BUSINESS HOUSE
BUSINESS LUNCH
BUSINESS TERMS
BUSINESS WOMAN
BUSINESS WORLD
BUTLER'S PANTRY
BUTTERED TOAST
BUTTERFLY KISS
BUTTON YOUR LIP
BY ALL ACCOUNTS
BY APPOINTMENT
BY ARRANGEMENT
BY CANDLELIGHT
BY INSTALMENTS
BY THE ROADSIDE
BY UNDERGROUND
BY WORD OF MOUTH

C—13
CABINET MEMBER
CALCULATED LIE

CALENDAR MONTH
CALL FOR TRUMPS
CALL INTO BEING
CALL OF THE WILD
CALL ONE'S BLUFF
CALL THE POLICE
CALL TO ACCOUNT
CALL TO WITNESS
CAMBRIDGE BLUE
CAMEL-HAIR COAT
CAMERA OBSCURA
CAMPAIGN MEDAL
CAMPING GROUND
CANARY ISLANDS
CANDID OPINION
CANNIBAL TRIBE
CAPACITY CROWD
CAPACITY HOUSE
CAPE CANAVERAL
CAPITAL CHARGE
CAPITAL FELLOW
CAPITAL LETTER
CAPITAL MURDER
CAP OF DARKNESS
CAPTAIN CUTTLE
CAPTAIN KETTLE
CAPTAIN'S TABLE
CARAFE OF WATER
CARBON DIOXIDE
CARDINAL POINT
CAREER OF CRIME
CAREFUL DRIVER
CARNEGIE TRUST
CARNIVAL QUEEN
CARPET CLEANER
CARPET SWEEPER
CARRIER PIGEON
CARRY THE BLAME
CARRY THE TORCH
CARRY TO EXCESS
CARTRIDGE CASE
CARVE ONE'S NAME
CARVE THE JOINT
CASH IN ADVANCE
CASH IN THE BANK
CASHMERE SHAWL
CASH ON THE NAIL
CASSE NOISETTE
CAST IN ONE'S LOT
CAST-IRON ALIBI
CASTLE IN SPAIN

CASUAL CLOTHES
CASUAL MEETING
CASUAL VISITOR
CAT-AND-DOG LIFE
CATCH A GLIMPSE
CATCH AT STRAWS
CATCH UNAWARES
CATERING CORPS
CATHEDRAL CITY
CATHEDRAL TOWN
CATHERINE PARR
CATHOLIC FAITH
CAT O' NINE TAILS
CATTLE BREEDER
CATTLE FARMING
CAUGHT BENDING
CAUGHT IN A TRAP
CAUGHT NAPPING
CAUSE A FLUTTER
CAUSE FOR ALARM
CAUSE OF INJURY
CAUSTIC REMARK
CAVALRY CHARGE
CAVALRY SCHOOL
CAVALRY TROOPS
CAYENNE PEPPER
CELEBRATED MAN
CELESTIAL BODY
CELESTIAL CITY
CELESTIAL POLE
CEMENT MIXTURE
CENTRAL AFRICA
CENTRAL EUROPE
CENTRAL FIGURE
CENTRAL LONDON
CENTRAL OFFICE
CENTRE FORWARD
CENTRE OF TRADE
CERTAIN EXTENT
CERTAIN PERSON
CERTIFIED MILK
CHAIN OF EVENTS
CHAIN OF OFFICE
CHAIN REACTION
CHALLENGE FATE
CHAMP AT THE BIT
CHAMPION BOXER
CHANCE MEETING
CHANCE ONE'S ARM
CHANGE A CHEQUE
CHANGED PERSON

CHANGE OF FRONT	CHILTERN HILLS
CHANGE OF HEART	CHIMNEY CORNER
CHANGE OF PLACE	CHIMNEY-POT HAT
CHANGE OF SCENE	CHINESE PUZZLE
CHANGE OF VENUE	CHOCOLATE DROP
CHANGING ROOMS	CHOICE OF WORDS
CHANGING VOICE	CHOIR PRACTICE
CHANNEL BRIDGE	CHOP AND CHANGE
CHANNEL TUNNEL	CHOPPING BLOCK
CHARACTER PART	CHORAL CONCERT
CHARGE ACCOUNT	CHORAL SERVICE
CHARGE TOO MUCH	CHORAL SOCIETY
CHARITY BAZAAR	CHORUS OF ABUSE
CHARLES DARWIN	CHRIS CHATAWAY
CHARLES WESLEY	CHRISTIAN NAME
CHARLOT'S REVUE	CHRISTMAS CAKE
CHARM BRACELET	CHRISTMAS CARD
CHARMED CIRCLE	CHRISTMAS FAIR
CHARM OF MANNER	CHRISTMAS GIFT
CHARTER FLIGHT	CHRISTMAS ROSE
CHASE ONE'S TAIL	CHRISTMAS TREE
CHEAP AND NASTY	CHURCHILL TANK
CHECK THE SPEED	CHURCH OFFICER
CHEDDAR CHEESE	CHURCH SERVICE
CHEERFUL GIVER	CHURCH STEEPLE
CHEERFUL SIGHT	CHURCH WEDDING
CHEESE AND WINE	CIGARETTE CARD
CHEESE BISCUIT	CIGARETTE CASE
CHEF DE CUISINE	CIGARETTE GIRL
CHELSEA BRIDGE	CIRCLE OF LIGHT
CHELTENHAM SPA	CIRCUS MANAGER
CHEMICAL AGENT	CITY OF THE DEAD
CHERISH AN IDEA	CIVIL AVIATION
CHERRY BLOSSOM	CIVIL ENGINEER
CHERRY ORCHARD	CIVILIAN DRESS
CHESS CHAMPION	CIVIL MARRIAGE
CHEST EXPANDER	CIVIL QUESTION
CHESTNUT BROWN	CLAIM THE CROWN
CHESTNUT HORSE	CLAPHAM COMMON
CHICKEN FARMER	CLAP OF THUNDER
CHIEF ARMOURER	CLAP ONE'S HANDS
CHIEF ENGINEER	CLAP ON THE BACK
CHIEF OF POLICE	CLARENCE HOUSE
CHILDHOOD DAYS	CLASSIC REMARK
CHILDISH PRANK	CLASS STRUGGLE
CHILD OF NATURE	CLEAN THE SLATE
CHILDREN'S BOOK	CLEARANCE SALE
CHILDREN'S GAME	CLEARING HOUSE
CHILDREN'S HOME	CLEAR SPEAKING
CHILDREN'S HOUR	CLEAR THE COURT
CHILLY WELCOME	CLEAR THE DECKS

CLEAR THE TABLE
CLEAR THINKING
CLEMENT ATTLEE
CLENCHED TEETH
CLERICAL BLACK
CLERICAL DRESS
CLERICAL ERROR
CLERICAL STAFF
CLIFFS OF DOVER
CLIMBING IRONS
CLIMBING PLANT
CLIMBING SHRUB
CLIMB LIKE A CAT
CLINCH THE DEAL
CLING TOGETHER
CLIP ONE'S WINGS
CLIP ONE'S WORDS
CLIPPED SPEECH
CLOSED CHAPTER
CLOSED CIRCUIT
CLOSE FIGHTING
CLOSELY ALLIED
CLOSE ONE'S EYES
CLOSE PRISONER
CLOSE QUARTERS
CLOSE RELATIVE
CLOSE SECURITY
CLOSE THE RANKS
CLOSE TOGETHER
CLOSE TO NATURE
CLOSING SEASON
CLOSING SPEECH
CLOSING STAGES
CLOTHES BASKET
CLOTHING TRADE
CLOUD THE ISSUE
COARSE FISHING
COASTAL RESORT
COASTAL WATERS
COAST DOWNHILL
COBBLED STREET
COCKER SPANIEL
COCKNEY ACCENT
COCK OF THE WALK
COCKTAIL DRESS
COCKTAIL PARTY
COCKTAIL STICK
CODE OF CONDUCT
COFFEE ESSENCE
COFFEE GROUNDS
COFFEE PLANTER

COLD AS CHARITY
COLD COLLATION
COLD IN THE HEAD
COLD RECEPTION
COLD-WATER CURE
COLLECTION BOX
COLLECT STAMPS
COLLEGE OF ARMS
COLONIAL HOUSE
COLONIAL STYLE
COLOURED CHALK
COLOURED SLIDE
COLOURED WATER
COLOUR PROBLEM
COLUMN OF ROUTE
COLUMN OF SMOKE
COMBINED FORCE
COMBINE FORCES
COME ALONGSIDE
COME AWAY EMPTY
COME BACK AGAIN
COME DOWN HEADS
COME DOWN TAILS
COMEDY ACTRESS
COMEDY THEATRE
COME IN CONTACT
COME INTO BEING
COME INTO FORCE
COME INTO MONEY
COME INTO SIGHT
COME OUT EASILY
COME OVER QUEER
COME TO A BAD END
COME TO A CLIMAX
COME TO A CRISIS
COME TO NOTHING
COME TO ONESELF
COME TO THE BALL
COME TO THE FAIR
COME TO THE FORE
COME UNDER FIRE
COME UNINVITED
COME UP FOR MORE
COME UP SMILING
COMING SHORTLY
COMMERCIAL ART
COMMERCIAL LAW
COMMIT A FELONY
COMMIT AN ERROR
COMMIT ONESELF
COMMIT PERJURY

COMMIT SUICIDE
COMMITTEE ROOM
COMMIT TO PAPER
COMMON ASSAULT
COMMON CARRIER
COMMON CONSENT
COMMON FEATURE
COMMON GROUNDS
COMMON HONESTY
COMMON MEASURE
COMMON MISTAKE
COMMON PATTERN
COMMON PURPOSE
COMMON SOLDIER
COMMUNION WINE
COMMUNIST BLOC
COMPANY LAWYER
COMPANY MERGER
COMPANY REPORT
COMPASS NEEDLE
COMPLAINT BOOK
COMPLETE WORKS
COMPLEX SYSTEM
COMPONENT PART
COMPOSING ROOM
COMPRESSED AIR
COMRADE IN ARMS
CONCEDE A POINT
CONCERT ARTIST
CONCRETE MIXER
CONCRETE OFFER
CONDEMNED CELL
CONDENSED FORM
CONDENSED MILK
CONDUCTED TOUR
CONFIDENCE MAN
CONFINED PLACE
CONFINED SPACE
CONFINED TO BED
CONFIRMED CASE
CONFIRMED LIAR
CONGRESS MEDAL
CONGRESS PARTY
CONISTON WATER
CONNECTING ROD
CONNIE FRANCIS
CONSCRIPT ARMY
CONSTANT LOSER
CONSTANT NYMPH
CONSUL GENERAL
CONSUMER GOODS

CONTACT LENSES
CONTENTED MIND
CONTENT TO REST
CONTINUITY MAN
CONTRITE HEART
CONTROL CENTRE
CONTROL PRICES
CONVENT SCHOOL
COOKERY LESSON
COOKING MEDIUM
COOKING SHERRY
COOK ONE'S GOOSE
COOLING BREEZE
COOL ONE'S HEELS
COOL RECEPTION
COPPER COINAGE
CORAL NECKLACE
CORONATION CUP
CORONER'S COURT
CORPORATE BODY
CORPS DE BALLET
CORPUS CHRISTI
CORPUS DELICTI
CORRECT ACCENT
CORRECT ANSWER
CORRECT SPEECH
CORRIDOR TRAIN
COSTLY FAILURE
COSTLY VENTURE
COTSWOLD HILLS
COTSWOLD STONE
COTTAGE CHEESE
COTTON PLANTER
COULD BE BETTER
COULEUR DE ROSE
COUNCIL ESTATE
COUNCIL SCHOOL
COUNTING HOUSE
COUNTRY COUSIN
COUNTRY CUSTOM
COUNTRY SQUIRE
COUNT THE HOURS
COUNTY BOROUGH
COUNTY COUNCIL
COUNTY CRICKET
COURSE BETTING
COURSE OF STUDY
COURT CIRCULAR
COURT DISASTER
COURTESY TITLE
COURT INTRIGUE

COURT OF APPEAL
COURT OF RECORD
COURT REPORTER
COVERED MARKET
COWARD AT HEART
CRABBED OLD AGE
CRACK REGIMENT
CRAFTSMAN'S JOB
CRAVEN COTTAGE
CRAZY BUSINESS
CRAZY PAVEMENT
CREAM OF TARTAR
CREATE A RUMPUS
CREATE A VACUUM
CREATE DISCORD
CREATE TROUBLE
CREDIT ACCOUNT
CREDIT BALANCE
CREDIT COMPANY
CREDIT SQUEEZE
CREEPING JENNY
CRÊME DE MENTHE
CRIBBAGE BOARD
CRICKET ELEVEN
CRICKET GROUND
CRICKET SEASON
CRICKET UMPIRE
CRICK ONE'S NECK
CRIME REPORTER
CRIMINAL CLASS
CRIMINAL COURT
CRIMINAL ERROR
CRIMINAL TRIAL
CRIMINAL WORLD
CRIPPLING BLOW
CRITICAL ANGLE
CRITICALLY ILL
CRITICAL POWER
CRITICAL STAGE
CROCHET NEEDLE
CROIX DE GUERRE
CROQUET MALLET
CROSSED CHEQUE
CROSSED IN LOVE
CROSS ONE'S MIND
CROSS ONE'S PALM
CROSS ONE'S PATH
CROSS PURPOSES
CROSS THE FLOOR
CROSS THE OCEAN
CROWDED CANVAS

CROWDED STREET
CROWD OF PEOPLE
CROWD TOGETHER
CROWN COLONIES
CROWNING GLORY
CROWNING MERCY
CROWN OF THORNS
CROWN PRINCESS
CROWN PROPERTY
CRUCIAL MOMENT
CRUCIAL PERIOD
CRUDE ESTIMATE
CRUISING SPEED
CRUSHING REPLY
CRUSH TO PIECES
CRY BLUE MURDER
CRY FOR NOTHING
CRY FOR THE MOON
CRY LIKE A CHILD
CRY OF DERISION
CRYPTIC REMARK
CRYSTAL GAZING
CRYSTAL PALACE
CUBIC CAPACITY
CUBIC CONTENTS
CUCUMBER FRAME
CUDDLE UP CLOSE
CULTIVATED MAN
CUNNING FELLOW
CUP THAT CHEERS
CURIOSITY SHOP
CURIOUS DESIGN
CURIOUS EFFECT
CURIOUS TO KNOW
CURRENT ASSETS
CURRENT BELIEF
CURRENT EVENTS
CURRENT NUMBER
CURRENT REPORT
CURRENT RUMOUR
CURRENT SERIES
CURSE AND SWEAR
CURSORY GLANCE
CURTAIN OF FIRE
CURTAIN RAISER
CUT DOWN TO SIZE
CUT OFF A CORNER
CUT ONE'S LOSSES
CUT ONE'S THROAT
CUT THE PAINTER
CUTTING REMARK

CUTTING RETORT
CUT TO THE QUICK
CYCLE OF EVENTS
CYCLE OF THE SUN
CYRIL FLETCHER

D—13
DADDY AND MUMMY
DADDY LONG-LEGS
DAILY DELIVERY
DAILY PRACTICE
DAILY PURSUITS
DAME CLARA BUTT
DAME COMMANDER
DAMP THE ARDOUR
DANCE THE POLKA
DANCE THE TANGO
DANCE WITH RAGE
DANCING LESSON
DANCING MASTER
DANCING SCHOOL
DANDELION WINE
DANDIE DINMONT
DANGEROUS BEND
DANGEROUS DRUG
DANGEROUS GAME
DANGEROUS LEAK
DANTE'S INFERNO
DARE-DEVIL TYPE
DARING ATTEMPT
DARK CONTINENT
DARKEST AFRICA
DARNING NEEDLE
DASH ONE'S HOPES
DAUGHTER OF EVE
DAUNTLESS HERO
DAWN OF A NEW ERA
DAY OF JUDGMENT
DAY OF MOURNING
DAYS AND NIGHTS
DAYS OF THE WEEK
DAY TO REMEMBER
DAZZLING SMILE
DEAD AND BURIED
DEAD AS THE DODO
DEAD CERTAINTY
DEADLY SILENCE
DEAD MAN'S CHEST
DEAD MEN'S SHOES
DEAD RECKONING

DEARLY BELOVED
DEATH AND GLORY
DEATH-BED SCENE
DEATH BY INCHES
DEATH REGISTER
DEATH SENTENCE
DEATH STRUGGLE
DEBATING POINT
DEBT COLLECTOR
DEBTORS' PRISON
DECIDE AGAINST
DECIDUOUS TREE
DECIMAL SYSTEM
DECLINE OF LIFE
DECORATIVE ART
DEDICATED LIFE
DEED OF RELEASE
DEEP ANTIPATHY
DEEP BREATHING
DEEP GRATITUDE
DEEP IN THOUGHT
DEEPLY TOUCHED
DEEP-SEA DIVING
DEFEND ONESELF
DEFINITE PROOF
DEFRAY THE COST
DEFY AUTHORITY
DEGREE OF SKILL
DEIGN TO NOTICE
DELAYED ACTION
DELIBERATE LIE
DELICATE CHILD
DELICATE POINT
DELICATE SHADE
DELICATE STAGE
DELICATE TOUCH
DELIGHT THE EAR
DELPHIC ORACLE
DELUDE ONESELF
DE LUXE EDITION
DEMAND JUSTICE
DEMAND PAYMENT
DEMERARA SUGAR
DEMON PATIENCE
DEN OF INIQUITY
DENTAL SURGEON
DENTAL SURGERY
DENTIST'S CHAIR
DENTIST'S DRILL
DENY THE CHARGE
DEPARTED GLORY

DEPRESSED AREA
DEPRIVE OF LIFE
DEPTH OF WINTER
DEPUTY PREMIER
DEPUTY SHERIFF
DESERT WARFARE
DESERVE NOTICE
DESERVING CASE
DESERVING POOR
DESIRED EFFECT
DESIRED OBJECT
DESOLATE SCENE
DESPATCH CLERK
DESPATCH RIDER
DESPERATE MOVE
DESPERATE RUSH
DETACHED HOUSE
DETECTIVE WORK
DEUCE OF HEARTS
DEVILISH FUNNY
DEVIL'S KITCHEN
DEVIL'S OWN LUCK
DEVIOUS MANNER
DEVOID OF SENSE
DEVOID OF TRUTH
DEVOUT ADMIRER
DIAGONAL LINES
DIAL THE POLICE
DIAMOND BROOCH
DIAMOND CUTTER
DIAMOND SCULLS
DIATONIC SCALE
DICE WITH DEATH
DIE AT ONE'S POST
DIE FLEDERMAUS
DIE OF EXPOSURE
DIE OF LAUGHING
DIFFERENT KIND
DIFFERENT TUNE
DIFFERENT VIEW
DIFFICULT CASE
DIFFICULT TASK
DIFFUSED LIGHT
DIGESTIVE PILL
DIG FOR VICTORY
DIG IN ONE'S TOES
DIGNIFIED EXIT
DIG ONE'S TOES IN
DING-DONG FIGHT
DINNER AT EIGHT
DINNER SERVICE

DIONNE WARWICK
DIPLOMATIC BAG
DIRECT CONTACT
DIRECT CURRENT
DIRECT DESCENT
DIRECTION POST
DIRE NECESSITY
DISCOUNT HOUSE
DISMAL FAILURE
DISOBEY ORDERS
DISPATCH RIDER
DISPUTED POINT
DISTANT COUSIN
DISTANT FUTURE
DISTANT OBJECT
DISTRICT COURT
DISTRICT NURSE
DISTURBED MIND
DIVIDE AND RULE
DIVIDE BY EIGHT
DIVIDE BY SEVEN
DIVIDE BY THREE
DIVIDED WE FALL
DIVINE JUSTICE
DIVINE SERVICE
DIVISION LOBBY
DIVISION THREE
DIVORCE DECREE
DO AS YOU PLEASE
DOCTOR FAUSTUS
DOCTOR JOHNSON
DOCTOR KILDARE
DOCTOR OF MUSIC
DOCTOR'S ORDERS
DOCTOR THE WINE
DODGE IN AND OUT
DODGE THE ISSUE
DOLL'S HOSPITAL
DOLPHIN SQUARE
DOME OF ST. PAUL'S
DOMESTIC BLISS
DONE FOR EFFECT
DON'T BELIEVE IT
DON'T FENCE ME IN
DON'T MENTION IT
DO ONESELF WELL
DOOR TO SUCCESS
DORMITORY AREA
DORMITORY TOWN
DOROTHY LAMOUR
DOROTHY SAYERS

DOTING HUSBAND
DOTS AND DASHES
DOUBLE BASSOON
DOUBLE DEALING
DOUBLE FIFTEEN
DOUBLE FIGURES
DOUBLE GLOSTER
DOUBLE HARNESS
DOUBLE HELPING
DOUBLE MEANING
DOUBLE OR QUITS
DOUBLE PORTION
DOUBLE SIXTEEN
DOUBLE TROUBLE
DOUBLE WEDDING
DOUBTFUL POINT
DOUBTFUL REPLY
DOWNING STREET
DOWN ON THE FARM
DOWNRIGHT LIAR
DOWN THE COURSE
DOWN THE STAIRS
DOWN THE STRAND
DOWN THE STREET
DOWN THE THAMES
DOWN TO BEDROCK
DOWNWARD CURVE
DOWNWARD SLOPE
DOWNWARD TREND
DRAB EXISTENCE
DRAGOON GUARDS
DRAINING BOARD
DRAIN THE DREGS
DRAMA FESTIVAL
DRAMATIC SCENE
DRASTIC REMEDY
DRAW A PARALLEL
DRAW ATTENTION
DRAW A VEIL OVER
DRAWING MASTER
DRAWN FROM LIFE
DRAW ONE'S SCREW
DRAW ONE'S SWORD
DRAW THE BLINDS
DREADED MOMENT
DREADFUL SIGHT
DREADFUL STORY
DREADFUL VOICE
DREAM SEQUENCE
DREARY OUTLOOK
DRENCHING RAIN

DRESS DESIGNER
DRESSED TO KILL
DRESSING TABLE
DRESS MATERIAL
DRESS OPTIONAL
DRIBS AND DRABS
DRILL SERGEANT
DRINKING GLASS
DRINKING PARTY
DRINKING STRAW
DRINKING WATER
DRINK ONE'S FILL
DRINK TO EXCESS
DRIVE A BARGAIN
DRIVE HEADLONG
DRIVE-IN CINEMA
DRIVEN TO DRINK
DRIVE WITH CARE
DRIVING LESSON
DRIVING MIRROR
DRIVING SCHOOL
DROP OF QUININE
DROP ONE'S GUARD
DROP ONE'S VOICE
DROPPED STITCH
DRUM-HEAD COURT
DRUNKEN SAILOR
DRUNKEN STUPOR
DRYING MACHINE
DUAL OWNERSHIP
DUBIOUS MANNER
DUCHESS OF KENT
DUELLING SWORD
DUE REFLECTION
DUKE ELLINGTON
DUKE OF BEDFORD
DUKE OF NORFOLK
DUKE OF WINDSOR
DULL AND DREARY
DULLING EFFECT
DUMB INSOLENCE
DUODENAL ULCER
DURING REPAIRS
DUSTING POWDER
DWELLING HOUSE
DYED IN THE WOOL
DYNAMIC ENERGY

E—13
EACH-WAY DOUBLE
EACH-WAY TREBLE

EAGER TO PLEASE
EAMONN ANDREWS
EARL OF WARWICK
EARLY DECISION
EARN A DIVIDEND
EARNEST DESIRE
EARTHLY THINGS
EASE THE BURDEN
EASILY AROUSED
EASILY MANAGED
EASILY PLEASED
EASTERN BAZAAR
EASTERN CHURCH
EAST GRINSTEAD
EAT LIKE A HORSE
EAT WITH RELISH
ECLIPSE STAKES
ECONOMIC VALUE
EDGAR ALLAN POE
EDIFYING STORY
EDINBURGH ROCK
EDITION DE LUXE
EDITORIAL DESK
EDITOR IN CHIEF
EDMUND SPENSER
EDWARDIAN DAYS
EFFACE ONESELF
EGGSHELL CHINA
EGYPTIAN MUMMY
EIGHT AND A HALF
EIGHT AND EIGHT
EIGHT AND SEVEN
EIGHT AND THREE
EIGHT-DAY CLOCK
EIGHTEEN CARAT
EIGHTEEN HOLES
EIGHTEEN MILES
EIGHTEEN PENCE
EIGHT FURLONGS
EIGHTH CENTURY
EIGHTH OF APRIL
EIGHTH OF MARCH
EIGHT OF HEARTS
EIGHT OF SPADES
EIGHT OF TRUMPS
EIGHTSOME REEL
EIGHT THOUSAND
EIGHTY PER CENT
EJECTION ORDER
ELABORATE MEAL
ELECTION AGENT

ELECTION FEVER
ELECTION NIGHT
ELECTORAL ROLL
ELECTRIC CABLE
ELECTRIC CHAIR
ELECTRIC CLOCK
ELECTRIC DRILL
ELECTRIC FENCE
ELECTRIC LIGHT
ELECTRIC METER
ELECTRIC MIXER
ELECTRIC MOTOR
ELECTRIC ORGAN
ELECTRIC PIANO
ELECTRIC POWER
ELECTRIC RAZOR
ELECTRIC SHOCK
ELECTRIC STORM
ELECTRIC STOVE
ELECTRIC TORCH
ELECTRIC TRAIN
ELEMENT OF RISK
ELEPHANT'S TUSK
ELEVEN AND FIVE
ELEVEN AND FOUR
ELEVEN AND NINE
ELEVEN GUINEAS
ELEVEN MINUTES
ELEVEN PER CENT
ELEVENTH GREEN
ELEVENTH OF MAY
ELEVENTH PLACE
ELEVENTH ROUND
ELUSIVE PERSON
ELY CULBERTSON
ELYSIAN FIELDS
EMERGENCY CALL
EMERGENCY EXIT
EMERGENCY STOP
EMERGENCY WARD
EMINENTLY FAIR
EMOTIONAL LIFE
EMPIRE BUILDER
EMPTY PROMISES
EMULSION PAINT
END IN DISASTER
ENDLESS EFFORT
END OF THE MONTH
END OF THE STORY
END OF THE WORLD
END UP IN PRISON

ENDURANCE TEST	EVIL INFLUENCE
ENDURE FOR EVER	EXACT LIKENESS
ENEMY AIRCRAFT	EXALTED PERSON
ENFORCE THE LAW	EXCELLENT SHOT
ENGAGED COUPLE	EXCESS BAGGAGE
ENGAGED SIGNAL	EXCESSIVE ZEAL
ENGAGING SMILE	EXCESS LUGGAGE
ENGINE FAILURE	EXCESS PROFITS
ENGINE TROUBLE	EXCHANGE BLOWS
ENGLISH GARDEN	EXCHANGE CARDS
ENGLISH LESSON	EXCHANGE IDEAS
ENGLISH MASTER	EXCHANGE SHOTS
ENGLISH SETTER	EXCHANGE VALUE
ENJOY IMMUNITY	EXCHANGE VIEWS
ENJOY IMPUNITY	EXCHANGE WORDS
ENLARGED HEART	EXCHEQUER BOND
ENORMOUS SALES	EXCISE OFFICER
ENOUGH'S ENOUGH	EXCITING MATCH
ENQUIRING MIND	EXCITING SCENE
ENTER A PROTEST	EXCLUSIVE CLUB
ENTER THE LISTS	EXCURSION RATE
ENTRANCE MONEY	EXCUSE-ME DANCE
EQUABLE TEMPER	EXCUSE ONESELF
EQUAL DIVISION	EXECUTIVE BODY
EQUAL QUANTITY	EXEMPLI GRATIA
ERECT A BARRIER	EXERCISE A PULL
ERIC LINKLATER	EXERCISE POWER
ERNEST MARPLES	EXERT PRESSURE
ERRAND OF MERCY	EXORBITANT FEE
ESCAPE ME NEVER	EXPECTANT HEIR
ESCORT CARRIER	EXPECTED THING
ESPRIT DE CORPS	EXPECT TOO MUCH
ESSENTIAL PART	EXPENSIVE ITEM
ESTIMATED COST	EXPENSIVE LINE
ESTIMATED TIME	EXPERT OPINION
ETON AND HARROW	EXPERT TUITION
EUCALYPTUS OIL	EXPERT WITNESS
EUSTON STATION	EXPLOSION SHOT
EVADE THE ISSUE	EXPOSED TO VIEW
EVASION OF DUTY	EXPRESS DESIRE
EVASIVE ACTION	EXPRESS LETTER
EVASIVE ANSWER	EXPRESS REGRET
EVENING PRAYER	EXTENSIVE VIEW
EVENING STROLL	EXTERIOR ANGLE
EVEN THINGS OUT	EXTINCT ANIMAL
EVERGREEN TREE	EXTRACT A TOOTH
EVERY FEW HOURS	EXTRACT OF BEEF
EVERY FEW YEARS	EXTREME HATRED
EVERY OTHER DAY	EXTREMELY NICE
EVERY SATURDAY	EXTREME OLD AGE
EVERY THURSDAY	EYEBROW PENCIL

EYELASH CURLER
EYELESS IN GAZA
EYES LIKE A HAWK
EYES LIKE STARS
EYE TO BUSINESS

F—13
FABIAN SOCIETY
FABULOUS BEAST
FABULOUS STORY
FACE DOWNWARDS
FACED WITH RUIN
FACE HEAVY ODDS
FACIAL MASSAGE
FACT OR FICTION
FACTORY HOOTER
FACULTY MEMBER
FACULTY OF ARTS
FAILING HEALTH
FAIL MISERABLY
FAIL TO CONNECT
FAINT WITH FEAR
FAIR AND SQUARE
FAIR APPRAISAL
FAIR CONDITION
FAIRLY CERTAIN
FAIRLY CONTENT
FAIRLY WELL OFF
FAIRLY WRITTEN
FAIR RECEPTION
FAIR TREATMENT
FAIRY PRINCESS
FAKE JEWELLERY
FALL FROM GRACE
FALLING LEAVES
FALLING PRICES
FALLING VALUES
FALL INTO A RAGE
FALL INTO A TRAP
FALL INTO ERROR
FALL INTO PLACE
FALL OF JERICHO
FALL OUT OF LOVE
FALL OVERBOARD
FALL PROSTRATE
FALSE CLAIMANT
FALSE EVIDENCE
FALSE OPTIMISM
FALSE POSITION
FALSE TEACHING
FALSETTO VOICE

FAMILIAR FACES
FAMILIAR SIGHT
FAMILIAR STYLE
FAMILIAR TERMS
FAMILIAR VOICE
FAMILY BUTCHER
FAMILY CONCERN
FAMILY FAILING
FAMILY MATTERS
FAMILY PRAYERS
FAMILY QUARREL
FAMILY REUNION
FAMILY WELFARE
FAR-AWAY PLACES
FAREWELL PARTY
FARM BUILDINGS
FARTHEST POINT
FASCIST REGIME
FASHION PARADE
FATAL ACCIDENT
FATAL CASUALTY
FATAL DECISION
FATHER NEPTUNE
FATHER WILLIAM
FAVOURITE TUNE
FAVOUR ONE SIDE
FEAR OF HEIGHTS
FEAR OF THE DARK
FEAST OF REASON
FEAST ONE'S EYES
FEATHER DUSTER
FEATHER PILLOW
FEATHER STITCH
FEATURE EDITOR
FED AND WATERED
FEDERAL STATES
FED TO THE TEETH
FEEBLE ATTEMPT
FEEBLE GESTURE
FEEDING BOTTLE
FEED THE FLAMES
FEEL EXHAUSTED
FEEL MORTIFIED
FEEL NO EMOTION
FEEL ONE'S PULSE
FEIGN SICKNESS
FELLOW CITIZEN
FELLOW FEELING
FELLOW SOLDIER
FEMALE WARRIOR
FEMININE CHARM

FEMININE LOGIC	FIND A FOOTHOLD
FEMININE WILES	FIND A LOOP-HOLE
FENCING LESSON	FIND A SOLUTION
FENCING MASTER	FIND ONE'S LEVEL
FENCING SCHOOL	FIND ONE'S MATCH
FERTILE GROUND	FIND SALVATION
FERTILE REGION	FIND THE NEEDLE
FERVENT DESIRE	FIND THE REMEDY
FESTIVE SEASON	FINE CHARACTER
FESTIVE SPIRIT	FINE GENTLEMAN
FETCH AND CARRY	FINER FEELINGS
FEVER HOSPITAL	FINE SELECTION
FEVERISH HASTE	FINE SITUATION
FEVERISH STATE	FINE TOOTH-COMB
FICTION WRITER	FINGER OF SCORN
FIDDLERS THREE	FINISHING POST
FIELD DRESSING	FINISH THE RACE
FIELD HOSPITAL	FINNAN HADDOCK
FIELD OF ACTION	FINNEGAN'S WAKE
FIELD OF BATTLE	FIRE A QUESTION
FIELD OF HONOUR	FIRE INSURANCE
FIELD OF VISION	FIREWORK PARTY
FIFTEEN AND SIX	FIRM FAVOURITE
FIFTEEN AND TEN	FIRM HANDSHAKE
FIFTEEN AND TWO	FIRM PRINCIPLE
FIFTEEN ROUNDS	FIRM TREATMENT
FIFTEEN THIRTY	FIRST-AID CLASS
FIFTEENTH HOLE	FIRST BIRTHDAY
FIFTH DIVIDEND	FIRST DELIVERY
FIFTH OF AUGUST	FIRST DIVIDEND
FIFTH SYMPHONY	FIRST DIVISION
FIFTY THOUSAND	FIRST LANGUAGE
FIGHTER PATROL	FIRST OF AUGUST
FIGHTING DRUNK	FIRST OFFENDER
FIGHT PROMOTER	FIRST OF THE FEW
FIGURE OF EIGHT	FIRST QUESTION
FIGURE SKATING	FIRST SYMPHONY
FILING CABINET	FIRST THOUGHTS
FILLET OF STEAK	FIRST TO ARRIVE
FILL ONE'S GLASS	FIRST WORLD WAR
FILM PROJECTOR	FISHING RIGHTS
FILTER THROUGH	FISHING SEASON
FINAL DECISION	FISHING TACKLE
FINAL DIVIDEND	FISHY BUSINESS
FINAL ESTIMATE	FIT FOR NOTHING
FINAL JUDGMENT	FIT FOR THE GODS
FINAL MOVEMENT	FITFUL SLUMBER
FINANCIAL NEWS	FIT LIKE A GLOVE
FINANCIAL PAGE	FIT OF COUGHING
FINANCIAL RUIN	FIT OF LAUGHTER
FINANCIAL YEAR	FIT OF THE BLUES

FIT OF THE SULKS
FITS AND STARTS
FIVE AND A PENNY
FIVE AND ELEVEN
FIVE-O'CLOCK TEA
FIVE-POUND NOTE
FIVE SHILLINGS
FIXED DOMICILE
FIXED INTERVAL
FLANDERS POPPY
FLANK MOVEMENT
FLASHING SMILE
FLASH IN THE PAN
FLASH OF GENIUS
FLAT OF THE HAND
FLEA IN ONE'S EAR
FLEMISH SCHOOL
FLESH AND BLOOD
FLICKER OF HOPE
FLIGHT OF FANCY
FLIGHT OF STEPS
FLITCH OF BACON
FLOAT A COMPANY
FLOATING VOTER
FLOCK TOGETHER
FLOODS OF TEARS
FLORA AND FAUNA
FLORAL PATTERN
FLORAL TRIBUTE
FLOUR AND WATER
FLOWERING TREE
FLOWER OF YOUTH
FLOWERY SPEECH
FLOW LIKE WATER
FLOW OF SPIRITS
FLOW OF TRAFFIC
FLUSHED CHEEKS
FLYING COLOURS
FLYING MACHINE
FLYING OFFICER
FLYING TRAPEZE
FLY THE COUNTRY
FOLD ONE'S HANDS
FOLIES BERGÈRE
FOLLOWING WIND
FOLLOW ROUTINE
FOLLOW THE BAND
FOLLOW THE FLAG
FOLLOW THE HERD
FOLLOW THE HUNT
FOLLOW THE ROAD

FOLLOW THROUGH
FOND OF COMFORT
FOND OF DISPLAY
FOOD AND WARMTH
FOOD FOR FISHES
FOOD OF THE GODS
FOOD POISONING
FOOLISH ACTION
FOOLISH FELLOW
FOOLISH PERSON
FOOLISH VIRGIN
FOOLSCAP PAPER
FOOL'S PARADISE
FOOTBALL FIELD
FOOTBALL MATCH
FOOTBALL PITCH
FOOTBALL POOLS
FOR AND AGAINST
FORBIDDEN GAME
FORBIDDEN TREE
FORCE A PASSAGE
FORCED LANDING
FORCED SAVINGS
FORCE ONE'S HAND
FORCE THE ISSUE
FORCIBLE ENTRY
FOREHAND DRIVE
FOREIGN ACCENT
FOREIGN EDITOR
FOREIGN FIELDS
FOREIGN LEGION
FOREIGN MARKET
FOREIGN OFFICE
FOREIGN ORIGIN
FOREIGN POLICY
FOREIGN SHORES
FOREIGN TONGUE
FOREIGN TRAVEL
FOREST OF ARDEN
FOREST OF MASTS
FORGET ONESELF
FOR GOOD AND ALL
FORK LIGHTNING
FORMAL PROTEST
FORMAL REQUEST
FORM AN OPINION
FOR MERCY'S SAKE
FORMER STUDENT
FORM OF ADDRESS
FORM OF WORSHIP
FOR THE PRESENT

FORTIFIED POST
FORTIFIED TOWN
FORTUNE HUNTER
FORTUNES OF WAR
FORTUNE'S WHEEL
FORTUNE TELLER
FORTY-HOUR WEEK
FORTY THOUSAND
FOSTER BROTHER
FOUNDED ON FACT
FOUNDER MEMBER
FOUNT OF HONOUR
FOUNT OF WISDOM
FOUR AND A PENNY
FOUR AND ELEVEN
FOUR AND TWENTY
FOUR FARTHINGS
FOUR-POSTER BED
FOUR SHILLINGS
FOUR SYLLABLES
FOURTEEN MILES
FOURTH CENTURY
FOURTH OF APRIL
FOURTH OFFICER
FOURTH OF MARCH
FOWLS OF THE AIR
FRAGRANT SMELL
FRAME A PICTURE
FRANKIE HOWERD
FRANTIC APPEAL
FRATERNITY PIN
FREAK OF NATURE
FREE ADMISSION
FREE AS THE WIND
FREE FROM BLAME
FREE FROM ERROR
FREE FROM FAULT
FREE FROM GUILE
FREE FROM GUILT
FREEHOLD HOUSE
FREE RENDERING
FREE TO CONFESS
FREE-TRADE AREA
FREEZE TO DEATH
FREEZING AGENT
FREEZING POINT
FREIGHT CHARGE
FRENCH ACADEMY
FRENCH CRICKET
FRENCH CUISINE
FRENCH GRAMMAR

FRENCH MUSTARD
FRENCH PERFUME
FRENCH TEACHER
FRENCH WINDOWS
FREQUENCY BAND
FRESH-AIR FIEND
FRESH APPROACH
FRESH AS A DAISY
FRESH EVIDENCE
FRESH OUTBREAK
FRICTION MATCH
FRIDAY EVENING
FRIDAY MORNING
FRIED POTATOES
FRIED TOMATOES
FRIEND AT COURT
FRIEND IN COURT
FRIENDLY MATCH
FRIENDLY TERMS
FRIENDLY TOUCH
FRIEND'S FRIEND
FRIGHTFUL TIME
FRINGE BENEFIT
FRITZ KREISLER
FROM A DISTANCE
FROM ONE'S HEART
FROM THE BOTTOM
FROM THE CRADLE
FROM THE OUTSET
FRONTAL ATTACK
FRONT ENTRANCE
FRONTIER GUARD
FRONT-PAGE NEWS
FRONT POSITION
FROSTY WEATHER
FROSTY WELCOME
FROZEN BALANCE
FROZEN TO DEATH
FRUIT AND CREAM
FRUITLESS TASK
FRUIT MERCHANT
FRYING TONIGHT
FULL ASSURANCE
FULL IN THE FACE
FULL OF COURAGE
FULL OF MEANING
FULL OF PROMISE
FULL OF REGRETS
FULL OF THE NEWS
FULL OWNERSHIP
FULL PROGRAMME

FULL TO THE BRIM
FULL TREATMENT
FULLY EQUIPPED
FULLY LICENSED
FULLY OCCUPIED
FULLY RESTORED
FUMBLE THE BALL
FUME WITH ANGER
FUNERAL SERMON
FUNNY BUSINESS
FUNNY PECULIAR
FUR AND FEATHER
FURIOUS TEMPER
FURNISHED FLAT
FURNISHED ROOM
FURTHER NOTICE
FURTHEST POINT
FUSS AND BOTHER
FUTILE ATTEMPT
FUTILE PURSUIT
FUTURE HUSBAND
FUTURE OUTLOOK
FUTURE PERFECT

G—13

GADARENE SWINE
GAGGLE OF GEESE
GAIETY THEATRE
GAIN ADMISSION
GAIN SUPREMACY
GALE-FORCE WIND
GALLANT MEMBER
GAMES MISTRESS
GAME TO THE LAST
GANG OF THIEVES
GANGWAY PLEASE
GARBLED REPORT
GARDENING CLUB
GARDEN OF WEEDS
GARDEN PRODUCE
GARDEN SYRINGE
GARLIC SAUSAGE
GASP FOR BREATH
GATHER FLOWERS
GAY YOUNG THING
GENERAL CUSTER
GENERAL DEALER
GENERAL EXODUS
GENERAL FRANCO
GENERAL GORDON

GENERAL MARKET
GENERAL PARDON
GENERAL PUBLIC
GENERAL READER
GENERAL STORES
GENERAL STRIKE
GENERAL SURVEY
GENEROUS GIVER
GENEROUS OFFER
GENEROUS SHARE
GENEROUS TERMS
GENIUS WILL OUT
GENTLE AS A LAMB
GENTLE BEARING
GENTLE MANNERS
GENTLE REPROOF
GENUINE REGARD
GEORGE GISSING
GEORGE SANDERS
GEORGIAN HOUSE
GERMAN MEASLES
GERMAN SAUSAGE
GET AT THE FACTS
GET AT THE TRUTH
GET AWAY WITH IT
GET IN ON THE ACT
GET IT STRAIGHT
GET OFF LIGHTLY
GET ONE'S HAND IN
GET ONE'S OWN WAY
GET ON TOGETHER
GET OUT OF SIGHT
GET THE GIGGLES
GET THE MESSAGE
GET THERE FIRST
GETTING ON A BIT
GET TO ONE'S FEET
GET TO WINDWARD
GIACONDA SMILE
GIFT OF TONGUES
GIN AND BITTERS
GIN AND ITALIAN
GIPSY'S WARNING
GIRTON COLLEGE
GIUSEPPE VERDI
GIVE A DOG A BONE
GIVE A FIRM DATE
GIVE AN ACCOUNT
GIVE AN EXAMPLE
GIVE AN OPINION
GIVE-AWAY PRICE

GIVE COMMUNION
GIVE IT A CHANCE
GIVEN A NEW LOOK
GIVEN IN CHARGE
GIVE NO QUARTER
GIVE NO TROUBLE
GIVEN THE STRAP
GIVEN THE WORKS
GIVEN TO EXCESS
GIVE ONESELF UP
GIVE ONE THE LIE
GIVE ONE THE PIP
GIVE THE SIGNAL
GIVE UP ALL HOPE
GIVE UP SMOKING
GIVE UP THE IDEA
GIVE UTTERANCE
GLACIAL PERIOD
GLAD OF A CHANCE
GLASS AND CHINA
GLASS MOUNTAIN
GLASS OF SHERRY
GLASS OF WHISKY
GLASS WITH CARE
GLASSY SURFACE
GLEAM OF HUMOUR
GLIMMER OF HOPE
GLOATING SMILE
GLOOMY OUTLOOK
GLOOMY PICTURE
GLORIA SWANSON
GLORIOUS DEVON
GLORIOUS MUSIC
GLORIOUS REIGN
GLORIOUS YEARS
GLOWING CHEEKS
GLOWING EMBERS
GLOWING REPORT
GLOW WITH PRIDE
GNASH THE TEETH
GO AS YOU PLEASE
GODDESS OF LOVE
GOD OF LAUGHTER
GO FOR A JOURNEY
GOING FOR A SONG
GOING STRAIGHT
GO INTO A TRANCE
GO INTO DETAILS
GOLD AND SILVER
GOLDEN HAMSTER
GOLDEN JUBILEE

GOLDEN TRESSES
GOLDEN WEDDING
GOLD MEDALLIST
GO LIKE THE WIND
GONE TO THE DOGS
GOOD ACOUSTICS
GOOD AFTERNOON
GOOD AND PROPER
GOOD AT FIGURES
GOOD BEGINNING
GOOD BEHAVIOUR
GOOD BREAKFAST
GOOD CHARACTER
GOOD CONDITION
GOOD CONDUCTOR
GOOD DIGESTION
GOOD FOR A LAUGH
GOOD GROUNDING
GOOD HOUSEWIFE
GOOD HUSBANDRY
GOOD INFLUENCE
GOOD NEIGHBOUR
GOOD PROSPECTS
GOOD QUEEN BESS
GOOD RECEPTION
GOOD SAMARITAN
GOOD SELECTION
GOOD SPORTSMAN
GOOD TALKING-TO
GOOD THRASHING
GOOD WALLOPING
GOODWOOD RACES
GOODY TWO-SHOES
GO OFF ONE'S HEAD
GO ON THE PARISH
GO THE WHOLE HOG
GO TO THE BOTTOM
GO TO THE CINEMA
GO TO THE CIRCUS
GO TO THE MOVIES
GO TO THE OFFICE
GO TO THE RESCUE
GO UNDERGROUND
GOVERNING BODY
GO WITH THE TIDE
GRADUAL CHANGE
GRAIN OF POWDER
GRAMMAR SCHOOL
GRAND ALLIANCE
GRAND ENTRANCE
GRAND FUNCTION

GRAND JUNCTION
GRAND NATIONAL
GRAND STRATEGY
GRANT A DIVORCE
GRANT A REQUEST
GRANT IMMUNITY
GRAPES OF WRATH
GRAPPLING IRON
GRASP AT A STRAW
GRASP OF DETAIL
GRATEFUL HEART
GRATE ON THE EAR
GRAVE DECISION
GRAVE THOUGHTS
GREASE THE PALM
GREAT DISTANCE
GREATER LONDON
GREAT IN NUMBER
GREAT INTEREST
GREAT KINDNESS
GREATLY MISSED
GREAT MAJORITY
GREAT OCCASION
GREAT PATIENCE
GREAT PLEASURE
GREAT QUANTITY
GREAT SALT LAKE
GREAT STRENGTH
GREAT THOUGHTS
GREAT UNWASHED
GREAT WEST ROAD
GREAT WHITE WAY
GREAT YARMOUTH
GREEK ALPHABET
GREEK LANGUAGE
GREEN FRACTURE
GREEN PASTURES
GREENWICH TIME
GREEN WITH ENVY
GREENWOOD TREE
GREETINGS CARD
GREYHOUND RACE
GRILLED CUTLET
GRIN AND BEAR IT
GRIND INTO DUST
GRIND THE TEETH
GRIND TO POWDER
GRIP LIKE A VICE
GRIPPING STORY
GRIT ONE'S TEETH
GROANING BOARD

GROAN INWARDLY
GROSS RECEIPTS
GROUP ACTIVITY
GROW BEAUTIFUL
GROW DESPERATE
GROW DOWNWARDS
GRUELLING HEAT
GRUELLING PACE
GRUELLING RACE
GRUELLING TIME
GRUYÈRE CHEESE
GUARDED REMARK
GUARDIAN ANGEL
GUARD OF HONOUR
GUARDS' OFFICER
GUERRILLA BAND
GUEST OF HONOUR
GUIDED MISSILE
GUILTY FEELING
GUNNERY SCHOOL
GUNPOWDER PLOT
GUSHING LETTER
GUTTERAL VOICE
GYPSY'S WARNING

H—13
HACKING JACKET
HAILE SELASSIE
HAIL OF BULLETS
HAIR OF THE HEAD
HALE AND HEARTY
HALF A FARTHING
HALF SOVEREIGN
HALF THE BATTLE
HALF THE NUMBER
HALF-TIME SCORE
HALL OF JUSTICE
HALL OF MIRRORS
HALLOWED PLACE
HALTING SPEECH
HALVE THE MATCH
HAMILTON HOUSE
HANDLE ROUGHLY
HAND OF BANANAS
HAND OUT ADVICE
HANDSOME OFFER
HANDSOME STYLE
HANDSOME THING
HANG BY A THREAD
HANGING GARDEN
HANGING MATTER

HANG ONE'S HAT UP	HAVELOCK ELLIS
HANG UP ONE'S HAT	HAVEN OF REFUGE
HANNEN SWAFFER	HAVE NO REGRETS
HANOVER SQUARE	HAVE NO SECRETS
HAPPILY IN LOVE	HAVE NO TROUBLE
HAPPY ACCIDENT	HAVE ONE'S FLING
HAPPY BIRTHDAY	HAVE ONE'S WHACK
HAPPY FAMILIES	HAVE THE ANSWER
HAPPY MARRIAGE	HAVE THE HONOUR
HAPPY MEMORIES	HAVE THE OPTION
HAPPY WANDERER	HAVE THE WIND UP
HARBOUR LIGHTS	HAYLING ISLAND
HARBOUR MASTER	HAYWARDS HEATH
HARD-BOILED EGG	HEADLONG SPEED
HARDEN ONESELF	HEAD OF THE FORM
HARD-LUCK STORY	HEAD OF THE POLL
HARD NECESSITY	HEAD OVER HEELS
HARD OF HEARING	HEADS TOGETHER
HARD TO BELIEVE	HEALING SPIRIT
HARD TO IMAGINE	HEAL THE BREACH
HARD TO SATISFY	HEALTH OFFICER
HARD TO SWALLOW	HEALTH SERVICE
HARDWARE STORE	HEALTH VISITOR
HARE AND HOUNDS	HEALTHY COLOUR
HARMONIC SCALE	HEAPS OF PEOPLE
HARROWING TALE	HEAR BOTH SIDES
HARROWING TIME	HEARD IN CAMERA
HARRY THE HORSE	HEARTH AND HOME
HARSH CONTRAST	HEART OF HEARTS
HARSH DECISION	HEART OF MARBLE
HARSH SENTENCE	HEART'S CONTENT
HARVEST SUNDAY	HEARTY DISLIKE
HARVEST SUPPER	HEARTY WELCOME
HASTEN ONE'S END	HEATED DISPUTE
HASTY DECISION	HEATED QUARREL
HATEFUL OBJECT	HEATH ROBINSON
HATFIELD HOUSE	HEAT TREATMENT
HATTER'S CASTLE	HEAVEN HELP HIM!
HATTIE JACQUES	HEAVENLY CHOIR
HAVE A BAD NIGHT	HEAVENLY TWINS
HAVE A BREATHER	HEAVEN ON EARTH
HAVE A GOOD MIND	HEAVILY LOADED
HAVE A GOOD TALK	HEAVY DOWNPOUR
HAVE A GOOD TIME	HEAVY EXPENSES
HAVE A MANICURE	HEAVY HYDROGEN
HAVE AN ADDRESS	HEAVY INDUSTRY
HAVE A TOOTH OUT	HEAVY MATERIAL
HAVE A WALK-OVER	HEAVY SENTENCE
HAVE DELUSIONS	HEIGHT OF FOLLY
HAVE HALF A MIND	HELD FOR RANSOM
HAVE HYSTERICS	HELL UPON EARTH

HELPFUL ADVICE	HOLD IN BONDAGE
HENLEY REGATTA	HOLD IN RESPECT
HENRY FIELDING	HOLD ONE GUILTY
HENRY THE FIFTH	HOLD ONE'S PEACE
HENRY THE FIRST	HOLD THAT TIGER!
HENRY THE SIXTH	HOLD THE RECORD
HENRY THE THIRD	HOLD THE RUDDER
HERALDIC SWORD	HOLD THE SCALES
HERCULEAN TASK	HOLD THE STAKES
HERCULE POIROT	HOLE AND CORNER
HER EXCELLENCY	HOLE IN THE ROAD
HEROIC COUPLET	HOLIDAY CHALET
HEW OUT A CAREER	HOLIDAY COURSE
HIDDEN MEANING	HOLIDAY RESORT
HIDDEN RESERVE	HOLIDAY SEASON
HIGH AND MIGHTY	HOLIDAY SPIRIT
HIGH BIRTH-RATE	HOLLOW FEELING
HIGH CHARACTER	HOLLOW MOCKERY
HIGH CHURCHMAN	HOLLOW VICTORY
HIGH COLOURING	HOLLYWOOD BOWL
HIGH ENDEAVOUR	HOLY COMMUNION
HIGHER BRACKET	HOLY INNOCENTS
HIGHEST BIDDER	HOLY MATRIMONY
HIGH EXPLOSIVE	HOME ECONOMICS
HIGH FREQUENCY	HOME FOR THE DAY
HIGHLAND CHIEF	HOME INTERESTS
HIGHLAND DANCE	HOME-MADE BREAD
HIGHLAND DRESS	HOME PROGRAMME
HIGHLAND FLING	HOMERIC BATTLE
HIGHLAND GAMES	HOME SECRETARY
HIGHLY PLEASED	HOME SWEET HOME
HIGH VALUATION	HOMEWARD BOUND
HIGH-WATER MARK	HONEST ATTEMPT
HIGHWAY PATROL	HONEST DEALING
HIGHWAY ROBBER	HONEYDEW MELON
HIKING HOLIDAY	HONOR BLACKMAN
HILAIRE BELLOC	HONOURABLE MAN
HINDU RELIGION	HONOUR AND OBEY
HIRED ASSASSIN	HONOURED GUEST
HIS EXCELLENCY	HONOURS DEGREE
HISTORIC SCENE	HOOK OF HOLLAND
HISTORIC TENSE	HOPE AND BELIEF
HISTORY LESSON	HOPELESS STATE
HISTORY MASTER	HORACE WALPOLE
HISTRIONIC ART	HORATIO NELSON
HIT THE JACKPOT	HORRIBLE CRIME
HIT THE UPRIGHT	HORRIBLE NOISE
HOBSON'S CHOICE	HORRIBLE SIGHT
HOLD AN INQUEST	HORSE AND GROOM
HOLD AN INQUIRY	HORSE CHESTNUT
HOLD AN OPINION	HORSESHOE BEND

HOSPITAL NURSE
HOSPITAL TRAIN
HOSTILE ATTACK
HOSTILE CRITIC
HOSTILE MANNER
HOST OF FRIENDS
HOT-HOUSE PLANT
HOT ON THE SCENT
HOT ON THE TRAIL
HOUR AFTER HOUR
HOURLY SERVICE
HOUR OF TRIUMPH
HOURS AND HOURS
HOUSEHOLD GODS
HOUSEHOLD HINT
HOUSEHOLD LOAF
HOUSEHOLD WORD
HOUSE MAGAZINE
HOUSE OF BRICKS
HOUSE OF ORANGE
HOUSE OF PRAYER
HOUSE OF REFUGE
HOUSE ON WHEELS
HOUSE PROPERTY
HOUSING ESTATE
HUB OF INDUSTRY
HUGH GAITSKELL
HUMAN ACTIVITY
HUMAN CREATURE
HUMAN DOCUMENT
HUMANE SOCIETY
HUMAN INTEREST
HUMAN PROGRESS
HUMAN TRIANGLE
HUMAN WEAKNESS
HUMBLE ADMIRER
HUMBLE APOLOGY
HUMBLE OPINION
HUMBLE REQUEST
HUMBLE SERVANT
HUMBLE STATION
HUMPBACK WHALE
HUNDRED AND ONE
HUNDRED POUNDS
HUNGER MARCHER
HUNGRY FORTIES
HUNTING SEASON
HURRICANE LAMP
HURRIED GLANCE
HURRIED SPEECH
HURT ONE'S PRIDE

HYDRAULIC JACK
HYDRAULIC LIFT

I—13
IAN CARMICHAEL
ICE-CREAM WAFER
IDEALLY SUITED
IDENTICAL TWIN
IF YOU DON'T MIND!
ILL MANAGEMENT
IMAGINARY LINE
IMITATION WARE
IMPENDING DOOM
IMPERIAL CROWN
IMPERIAL EAGLE
IMPERIAL GUARD
IMPERIAL TOKAY
IMPLICIT FAITH
IMPORTANT POST
IMPUDENT ROGUE
IN A CLEFT STICK
IN A GENERAL WAY
IN A GOOD TEMPER
IN ALL FAIRNESS
IN ALL RESPECTS
IN ALL WEATHERS
IN AN AMBULANCE
IN AN EMERGENCY
IN AN UNDERTONE
IN A SORRY STATE
IN A STILL VOICE
IN A STRANGE WAY
IN AT THE FINISH
INBORN ABILITY
INCENSE BURNER
IN CIRCULATION
INCLINED PLANE
IN COLD STORAGE
INCOME BRACKET
INCOMES POLICY
INCOME-TAX FORM
IN COMPETITION
IN CONFINEMENT
IN CONSEQUENCE
IN CONVULSIONS
INCREASED WAGE
INCREASE OF PAY
INCUR A PENALTY
IN DEAD EARNEST
INDECENT HASTE
IN DESPERATION

INDIAN CHUTNEY	IN SHORT SUPPLY
INDIRECT ROUTE	INSIDE FORWARD
IN DIRE TROUBLE	IN SIGHT OF LAND
INDOOR SERVANT	IN SO MANY WORDS
IN EVERY DETAIL	IN SOME MEASURE
INFANT BAPTISM	INSPECTION PIT
INFANT PRODIGY	INSPIRED GUESS
INFERIOR GOODS	INSPIRED WORDS
IN FINE FEATHER	INSTANT COFFEE
INFINITE SPACE	INSULAR HABITS
INFLATED IDEAS	INSURANCE CARD
INFLATED PRICE	INSURANCE RISK
IN FOR A STRETCH	INSURED PERSON
INFORM AGAINST	IN SWITZERLAND
INFORMAL DRESS	INTEREST RATES
INFORMAL PARTY	INTERIM PERIOD
IN FORMER TIMES	INTERIM REPORT
IN FULL FEATHER	INTERVAL MUSIC
IN FULL MEASURE	IN THE ABSTRACT
IN FULL RETREAT	IN THE AIR FORCE
IN GREAT DEMAND	IN THE AUDIENCE
INGRID BERGMAN	IN THE BASEMENT
IN HIGH FEATHER	IN THE BUSINESS
IN HONOUR BOUND	IN THE CORRIDOR
IN IMAGINATION	IN THE DARKNESS
INITIAL LETTER	IN THE DAYLIGHT
INITIAL OUTLAY	IN THE DISTANCE
INITIAL STAGES	IN THE DISTRICT
INITIATION FEE	IN THE DOG-HOUSE
INK ERADICATOR	IN THE DOLDRUMS
INLAND REVENUE	IN THE FOUNTAIN
IN LIQUIDATION	IN THE GLOAMING
IN MORTAL PERIL	IN THE INTERIOR
INNATE ABILITY	IN THE INTERVAL
INNER CONFLICT	IN THE LION'S DEN
INNER HEBRIDES	IN THE MAJORITY
INNOCENT PARTY	IN THE MEANTIME
IN ONE'S ELEMENT	IN THE MIND'S EYE
IN ONE SENTENCE	IN THE MINORITY
IN ONE'S OWN NAME	IN THE NEGATIVE
IN PARTNERSHIP	IN THE ORIGINAL
IN PERSPECTIVE	IN THE PAVILION
IN POINT OF FACT	IN THE SAME BOAT
IN PREPARATION	IN THE SAME CAMP
IN QUEER STREET	IN THE SERVICES
INQUIRING MIND	IN THE SINGULAR
INQUIRY OFFICE	IN THE STIRRUPS
IN SAFE KEEPING	IN THE STRAIGHT
IN SCANDINAVIA	IN THE SUNSHINE
IN SELF-DEFENCE	IN THE TREASURY
INSERT A NOTICE	IN THE TRENCHES

IN THE TWILIGHT
IN THE USUAL WAY
IN THE VANGUARD
IN THE VICINITY
IN THE WRONG BOX
INTIMATE REVUE
INTIMATE STYLE
INTIMATE TERMS
IN TIMES OF YORE
INTO THE BREACH
IN TOWN TONIGHT
IN TREPIDATION
IN VARIOUS WAYS
INVERNESS CAPE
INVERTED ORDER
INVERTED PLEAT
IN VINO VERITAS
INVITE TENDERS
INVOLVED STYLE
IRISH BAGPIPES
IRISH LANGUAGE
IRISH REGIMENT
IRREGULAR VERB
ISLE OF SHEPPEY
ISLES OF GREECE
ISOBEL BARNETT
ISOLATION WARD
ISSUE A COMMAND
ISSUE A SUMMONS
ISSUED CAPITAL
ITALIAN LESSON
IT'S NOT CRICKET
IVORY CHESSMAN

J—13
JACK THE RIPPER
JACOBEAN STYLE
JAUNDICED VIEW
JEKYLL AND HYDE
JENNIFER JONES
JET PROPULSION
JEWELLER'S SHOP
JOAN GREENWOOD
JOB'S COMFORTER
JOG ONE'S MEMORY
JOHANN STRAUSS
JOHN CONSTABLE
JOHN MASEFIELD
JOIN THE ANGELS
JOIN THE FORCES
JOINT PARTNERS

JOLLY GOOD CHAP
JONATHAN SWIFT
JORDAN ALMONDS
JOSEPH ADDISON
JOYCE GRENFELL
JUDAS ISCARIOT
JUDGE ADVOCATE
JUDGE JEFFREYS
JUDICIAL COURT
JULIA LOCKWOOD
JULY THE EIGHTH
JULY THE FOURTH
JULY THE SECOND
JUMP AT AN OFFER
JUMPING SEASON
JUMP OVERBOARD
JUMP THE COURSE
JUNE THE EIGHTH
JUNE THE FOURTH
JUNE THE SECOND
JUNGLE WARFARE
JUNIOR COUNSEL
JUNIOR PARTNER
JUNIOR SERVICE
JUST A FEW LINES
JUST AS YOU LIKE
JUST PUBLISHED
JUST-SO STORIES
JUVENILE COURT

K—13
KAISER WILHELM
KEEN AS MUSTARD
KEEP AN ACCOUNT
KEEP GOOD HOURS
KEEP IN CUSTODY
KEEP IN THE DARK
KEEP LATE HOURS
KEEP ONE'S END UP
KEEP ONE'S EYE IN
KEEP ONE'S HAT ON
KEEP ONE'S PLACE
KEEP ON THE BEAM
KEEP OPEN HOUSE
KEEP THE CHANGE
KEEP TO ONESELF
KEEP TO THE LEFT
KEEP UP THE PACE
KEEP YOUR SEATS
KENTUCKY DERBY
KEPT IN RESERVE

KEPT IN THE DARK
KEPT ON THE TROT
KEY TO A MYSTERY
KICK INTO TOUCH
KICK ONE'S HEELS
KICK THE BUCKET
KICK UP A SHINDY
KILL THE RUMOUR
KINDRED SPIRIT
KING OF DENMARK
KING OF ENGLAND
KING'S BIRTHDAY
KING'S CHAMPION
KING'S EVIDENCE
KING'S RHAPSODY
KISS AND CUDDLE
KISS AND MAKE UP
KISS IN THE RING
KISS THE GROUND
KITCHEN GARDEN
KIT INSPECTION
KNAVE OF HEARTS
KNAVE OF SPADES
KNAVE OF TRUMPS
KNAVISH TRICKS
KNEW IN ADVANCE
KNIT ONE'S BROWS
KNOCK-DOWN BLOW
KNOCK-OUT DROPS
KNOCK SIDEWAYS
KNOCK SPOTS OFF
KNOTTY PROBLEM
KNOW BACKWARDS
KNOWING FELLOW
KNOWING PERSON
KNOW ONE'S PLACE
KNOW WHAT'S WHAT

L—13
LA BELLE FRANCE
LABOUR TROUBLE
LABOUR VICTORY
LABURNUM GROVE
LACE INSERTION
LACK OF CANDOUR
LACK OF CAUTION
LACK OF FEELING
LACK OF HARMONY
LACK OF MEANING
LACK OF RESPECT
LACK OF WARNING

LADIES' FINGERS
LADIES' GALLERY
LADS AND LASSES
LADY BOUNTIFUL
LADY COMPANION
LADY IN WAITING
LADY OF LEISURE
LADY OF QUALITY
LADY OF SHALOTT
LADY OF THE LAKE
LADY OF THE LAMP
LADY PRINCIPAL
LAKE CONSTANCE
LAKE ULLSWATER
LAMBETH BRIDGE
LAMBETH PALACE
LAMBING SEASON
LANCE PERCIVAL
LANDING GROUND
LAND IN THE SOUP
LAND-LOCKED SEA
LAND OF PROMISE
LAND OF THE FREE
LAND ON THE MOON
LANE OF TRAFFIC
LAPSE OF MEMORY
LAPSUS LINGUAE
LARGE AND SMALL
LARGE AUDIENCE
LARGE MAJORITY
LARGE MINORITY
LARGE PRACTICE
LARGE QUANTITY
LARGE-SCALE MAP
LAST CHRISTMAS
LAST EXTREMITY
LAST HANDSHAKE
LAST OF THE LINE
LAST WEDNESDAY
LATE AFTERNOON
LATE BREAKFAST
LATE FOR DINNER
LATE FOR SCHOOL
LATE-NIGHT NEWS
LATENT ABILITY
LATEST FASHION
LATIN AMERICAN
LATIN LANGUAGE
LATTICE WINDOW
LAUGH AT DANGER
LAUGHING HYENA

LAUGHING STOCK
LAUGHING WATER
LAUGH OUTRIGHT
LAUNCHING SITE
LAUNDRY BASKET
LAVENDER WATER
LAWFUL WEDLOCK
LAW OF AVERAGES
LAW OF CONTRACT
LAY BY THE HEELS
LAY DOWN THE LAW
LAY IN THE GRAVE
LEAD A DOG'S LIFE
LEAD BY THE HAND
LEAD BY THE NOSE
LEADING DANCER
LEADING SEAMAN
LEADING STOKER
LEAD ONE A DANCE
LEAD ONE ASTRAY
LEAD POISONING
LEAGUE CRICKET
LEAGUE OF PEACE
LEAMINGTON SPA
LEAN BACKWARDS
LEAP IN THE DARK
LEARNED FRIEND
LEARNER DRIVER
LEARN THE ROPES
LEARN THE TRUTH
LEATHER GLOVES
LEATHER JACKET
LEAVE A FORTUNE
LEAVE A MESSAGE
LEAVE HALF-DONE
LEAVE HOSPITAL
LEAVE IN THE AIR
LEAVE NO CHOICE
LEAVE NO OPTION
LEAVE ONE'S CARD
LEAVE STANDING
LEAVE THE STAGE
LEAVE TO APPEAL
LED TO THE ALTAR
LEFT AT THE POST
LEFT-HAND DRIVE
LEFT-HAND SCREW
LEFT TO ONESELF
LEGAL CURRENCY
LEGAL DOCUMENT
LEGAL EVIDENCE

LEGAL GUARDIAN
LEGAL LANGUAGE
LEGAL POSITION
LEGAL SENTENCE
LEMON MERINGUE
LEMON SQUEEZER
LEOPARD'S SPOTS
LES MISERABLES
LESTER PIGGOTT
LET GO THE REINS
LETHAL CHAMBER
LET IN DAYLIGHT
LET OUT A SECRET
LETTER PERFECT
LETTERS OF FIRE
LETTERS OF GOLD
LETTERS PATENT
LET THINGS SLIP
LEVEL CROSSING
LIABLE TO ERROR
LIBERAL LEADER
LIBERAL MINDED
LIBERAL POLICY
LIBRARY TICKET
LICENCE HOLDER
LICENCE TO KILL
LICENSED TRADE
LICENSING LAWS
LICK INTO SHAPE
LICK ONE'S CHOPS
LIE ON ONE'S BACK
LIFE ASSURANCE
LIFEBOAT DRILL
LIFE HEREAFTER
LIFE INSURANCE
LIFELONG ENEMY
LIFELONG HABIT
LIFE OF LEISURE
LIFETIME'S WORK
LIFT ATTENDANT
LIGHT AND SHADE
LIGHT AS A FAIRY
LIGHT COMEDIAN
LIGHT FINGERED
LIGHT INDUSTRY
LIGHT INFANTRY
LIGHTNING MOVE
LIGHT OF MY EYES!
LIGHT OF MY LIFE!
LIGHT OF NATURE
LIGHT SENTENCE

LIGHT THE STOVE
LIGHT TRAINING
LIKE A BAD PENNY
LIKE CLOCKWORK
LIKE GRIM DEATH
LIKE LIGHTNING
LIKE MEETS LIKE
LIKE ONE O'CLOCK
LIMITED AMOUNT
LIMITED APPEAL
LIMITED CHOICE
LIMITED NUMBER
LIMITED PERIOD
LIMITED SEASON
LIMITED SUPPLY
LIMP HANDSHAKE
LINEAR MEASURE
LINE OF ADVANCE
LINE OF CONDUCT
LINE OF COUNTRY
LINE OF DEFENCE
LINE OF RETREAT
LINE OF THOUGHT
LINGERING LOOK
LINGERING NOTE
LIQUEUR BRANDY
LIQUEUR WHISKY
LIQUID MEASURE
LIQUID SHAMPOO
LISTENING POST
LIST OF RUNNERS
LITERARY AGENT
LITERARY STYLE
LITERARY THEFT
LITERARY WORKS
LITERARY WORLD
LITTLE AND GOOD
LITTLE BOY BLUE
LITTLE BUT GOOD
LITTLE COMFORT
LITTLE SIR ECHO
LITTLE THEATRE
LITTLE TO SPARE
LITTLE TROUBLE
LIVE BROADCAST
LIVE CARTRIDGE
LIVE FOR THE DAY
LIVE IN COMFORT
LIVE IN HARMONY
LIVE IN HISTORY
LIVE IN POVERTY

LIVE IN SQUALOR
LIVE IN THE PAST
LIVE LIKE A LORD
LIVEN THINGS UP
LIVE ON NOTHING
LIVE PROGRAMME
LIVER AND BACON
LIVE RECORDING
LIVERY COMPANY
LIVERY SERVANT
LIVID WITH RAGE
LIVING THEATRE
LOAD OF RUBBISH
LOAD OF TROUBLE
LOCAL CURRENCY
LOCAL LANDMARK
LOCAL PREACHER
LODGE AN APPEAL
LOFTY AMBITION
LOFTY CONTEMPT
LOFTY THOUGHTS
LOGICAL ACTION
LOGICAL RESULT
LOMBARD STREET
LONDON AIRPORT
LONDON GAZETTE
LONDON SPECIAL
LONE-STAR STATE
LONG PARAGRAPH
LONG TIME NO SEE!
LONG WAY BEHIND
LONG WAY TO FALL
LONNIE DONEGAN
LOOK DANGEROUS
LOOK DIFFERENT
LOOK IMPORTANT
LOOK IN THE FACE
LOOK OVER THERE
LOOK SURPRISED
LOOK UP AND DOWN
LOOSE THINKING
LORD AND MASTER
LORD KITCHENER
LORDLY GESTURE
LORD MAYOR'S DAY
LORD PRESIDENT
LORD PRIVY SEAL
LORD PROTECTOR
LORDS TEMPORAL
LOSE COHERENCE
LOSE HANDS DOWN

LOSE ONE'S FAITH
LOSE ONE'S HEART
LOSE ONE'S LOOKS
LOSE ONE'S MONEY
LOSE ONE'S NERVE
LOSE ONE'S PLACE
LOSE ONE'S SHIRT
LOSE ONE'S SIGHT
LOSE ONE'S STAKE
LOSE ONE'S VOICE
LOSE THE BATTLE
LOSE THE RUBBER
LOSE THE THREAD
LOSS OF BALANCE
LOSS OF CONTROL
LOSS OF FORTUNE
LOSS OF FREEDOM
LOST IN THOUGHT
LOST IN TRANSIT
LOTS OF FRIENDS
LOTTERY TICKET
LOUD EXPLOSION
LOUIS QUATORZE
LOVE AND KISSES
LOVE OF COUNTRY
LOVE OF THE GAME
LOVE ONE'S ENEMY
LOVE ON THE DOLE
LOVING GESTURE
LOWER AND LOWER
LOWER ONE'S FLAG
LOWER REGISTER
LOWER THE LIGHT
LOWER THE PRICE
LOWLAND SCOTCH
LOW VISIBILITY
LOYAL DEVOTION
LOYALIST CAUSE
LUCID ARGUMENT
LUCID INTERVAL
LUCK OF THE DRAW
LUCK OF THE GAME
LUCKY SIXPENCE
LUCKY TALISMAN
LUCRATIVE DEAL
LUDGATE CIRCUS
LUKEWARM WATER
LUMINOUS PAINT
LUNATIC ASYLUM
LUNATIC FRINGE
LUNCHEON PARTY

LUNCHEON TABLE
LUXURIOUS FOOD
LUXURY HOLIDAY
LYCEUM THEATRE
LYRICAL POETRY
LYRICAL PRAISE

M—13
MACHINE MINDER
MADAME TUSSAUD
MADE IN ENGLAND
MADE IN GERMANY
MADE IN IRELAND
MAD ENTERPRISE
MADE THE WEIGHT
MADE TO MEASURE
MADISON SQUARE
MAGAZINE RIFLE
MAGAZINE STORY
MAGNETIC FIELD
MAGNETIC NORTH
MAGNETIC POLES
MAGNETIC STORM
MAIDEN CENTURY
MAID OF ALL WORK
MAID OF ORLEANS
MAIDS OF HONOUR
MAIMED FOR LIFE
MAIN CHARACTER
MAJOR DISASTER
MAJOR INCIDENT
MAJOR INTERVAL
MAKE A COME-BACK
MAKE A CONQUEST
MAKE A CROSSING
MAKE A DECISION
MAKE A GOOD WIFE
MAKE ALLOWANCE
MAKE A LONG NOSE
MAKE A MESS OF IT
MAKE AN ATTEMPT
MAKE AN OPENING
MAKE A PROPOSAL
MAKE DO AND MEND
MAKE ECONOMIES
MAKE INQUIRIES
MAKE MINCEMEAT
MAKE MINE MUSIC
MAKE NO DEMANDS
MAKE NO MISTAKE
MAKE OBEISANCE

MAKE ONE'S DEBUT
MAKE ONE'S PEACE
MAKE ONE'S POINT
MAKE OVERTURES
MAKE PROVISION
MAKE REDUNDANT
MAKE SHORT WORK
MAKE THE ASCENT
MAKE THE EFFORT
MAKE THE FUR FLY
MAKE THINGS HUM
MALADIE DU PAYS
MALTESE FALCON
MANAGING CLERK
MAN AT THE WHEEL
MAN OF BREEDING
MAN OF BUSINESS
MAN OF DECISION
MAN OF EMINENCE
MAN OF FEW WORDS
MAN OF LEARNING
MAN OF PROPERTY
MAN OF THE WORLD
MANSFIELD PARK
MAP OF SCOTLAND
MAP OF THE WORLD
MARCH OF EVENTS
MARCH THE FIFTH
MARCH THE FIRST
MARCH THE NINTH
MARCH THE SIXTH
MARCH THE TENTH
MARCH THE THIRD
MARGARET SMITH
MARGIN OF ERROR
MARGIN OF PROOF
MARGOT FONTEYN
MARILYN MONROE
MARINE COMPASS
MARINE OFFICER
MARITIME TRADE
MARKET DRAYTON
MARK OF RESPECT
MARRIAGE BANNS
MARRIAGE BELLS
MARRIAGE FEAST
MARRIAGE LINES
MARRIAGE RITES
MARRIED COUPLE
MARRY A FORTUNE
MARTELLO TOWER

MARTIAL SPIRIT
MARY MAGDALENE
MASS EXECUTION
MASS FORMATION
MASTER BUILDER
MASTER MARINER
MASTER'S TICKET
MATCH-BOX LABEL
MATCH ONE'S WITS
MATERIAL ISSUE
MATERIAL POINT
MATERIAL SENSE
MATERNITY WARD
MATINÉE JACKET
MATTHEW ARNOLD
MATURE THOUGHT
MAXIMUM AMOUNT
MAXIMUM CHARGE
MAXIMUM GROWTH
MAXIMUM POINTS
MAY THE SEVENTH
MAY THE TWELFTH
MEALS ON WHEELS
MEANS OF ACCESS
MEANS OF ASCENT
MEANS OF ESCAPE
MEANS OF SAFETY
MEASURED TREAD
MEASURE OF LAND
MEASURE SWORDS
MEAT AND TWO VEG
MECHANICAL AID
MECHANICAL MAN
MEDAL OF HONOUR
MEDICAL ADVICE
MEDICAL SCHOOL
MEDICINAL BATH
MEDICINE CHEST
MEDICINE GLASS
MEDIUM QUALITY
MEET ONE'S MAKER
MEET ONE'S MATCH
MELODY MIXTURE
MELTON MOWBRAY
MEMORIAL STONE
MEND A PUNCTURE
MENTAL BALANCE
MENTAL CALIBRE
MENTAL CRUELTY
MENTAL DISEASE
MENTAL FATIGUE

MENTAL HYGIENE
MENTAL ILLNESS
MENTALLY ALERT
MENTALLY BLIND
MENTALLY SOUND
MENTAL PATIENT
MENTAL PICTURE
MENTAL PROCESS
MENTAL RESERVE
MENTAL THERAPY
MENTAL TORMENT
MENTAL TORTURE
MENTAL TROUBLE
MERCANTILE LAW
MERCENARY ARMY
MERCI BEAUCOUP
MERE BAGATELLE
MERE EXISTENCE
MERMAID TAVERN
MERRIE ENGLAND
MERTHYR TYDFIL
MERTON COLLEGE
MESS OF POTTAGE
MESSY BUSINESS
METALLIC SOUND
METAL MERCHANT
METRIC MEASURE
MICHAELMAS DAY
MICK THE MILLER
MIDDLE-AGED MAN
MIDDLE CLASSES
MIDDLE ENGLISH
MIDLAND ACCENT
MIDLAND COUNTY
MIDSUMMER'S DAY
MILD AND BITTER
MILD EXPLETIVE
MILE AFTER MILE
MILES AND MILES
MILITARY CLOAK
MILITARY CROSS
MILITARY DRESS
MILITARY FORCE
MILITARY MARCH
MILITARY MEDAL
MILITARY MUSIC
MILITARY STAFF
MILITARY STORE
MILK CHOCOLATE
MILLING THRONG
MIND OF ONE'S OWN

MINERAL SPRING
MINIMUM AMOUNT
MINIMUM CHARGE
MINISTER OF WAR
MINOR COUNTIES
MINOR INCIDENT
MINOR INTERVAL
MINT CONDITION
MINUS QUANTITY
MIRACLE WORKER
MISCHIEF AFOOT
MISSING PERSON
MISSPENT YOUTH
MISS PINKERTON
MISS THE TARGET
MIXED BLESSING
MIXED FEELINGS
MIXED FOURSOME
MIXED MARRIAGE
MIXED METAPHOR
MOBILE CANTEEN
MOBILE LIBRARY
MOBILE WARFARE
MODELLING CLAY
MODE OF ADDRESS
MODERATE MEANS
MODERATE PRICE
MODERATE SKILL
MODERATE SPEED
MODERN COSTUME
MODERN ENGLISH
MODERN FASHION
MODERN HISTORY
MODERN METHODS
MODERN OUTLOOK
MODERN PAINTER
MODERN SETTING
MODERN SOCIETY
MODERN WARFARE
MODEST DEMANDS
MODEST FORTUNE
MODEST REQUEST
MODUS OPERANDI
MOMENT OF TRUTH
MONASTIC ORDER
MONDAY EVENING
MONDAY MORNING
MONETARY VALUE
MONEY IN THE BAG
MONEY TROUBLES
MONOTONOUS JOB

MONTHLY REPORT
MONTHLY SALARY
MOONLESS NIGHT
MOONLIGHT FLIT
MORAL CONFLICT
MORAL PRESSURE
MORAL STRENGTH
MORAL TRAINING
MORAL WEAKNESS
MORBID CRAVING
MORE THAN A JOKE
MORNING COFFEE
MORNING PRAYER
MORTALITY RATE
MORTAL REMAINS
MOST DESIRABLE
MOST EXCELLENT
MOTH-BALL FLEET
MOTHER COUNTRY
MOTHER HUBBARD
MOTHER OF PEARL
MOTHER SHIPTON
MOTION PICTURE
MOTOR MECHANIC
MOUNTAIN CHAIN
MOUNTAIN RANGE
MOUNTAIN SHEEP
MOUNTAIN SLOPE
MOUNTAIN TRAIL
MOUNTED POLICE
MOUNTED TROOPS
MOUNTING ANGER
MOUNT OF OLIVES
MOUNT PLEASANT
MOVE IN SOCIETY
MOVE MOUNTAINS
MOVING ACCOUNT
MOVING PICTURE
MOWING MACHINE
MUCH REGRETTED
MUDDLE THROUGH
MULTIPLE STORE
MULTIPLY BY SIX
MULTIPLY BY TEN
MULTIPLY BY TWO
MULTUM IN PARVO
MUMMY AND DADDY
MUNICIPAL BANK
MUNICIPAL PARK
MURAL PAINTING
MURDER MYSTERY

MURDER WILL OUT
MUSE OF DANCING
MUSE OF HISTORY
MUSICAL CHAIRS
MUSICAL COMEDY
MUSICAL STRESS
MUSIC FESTIVAL
MUSIC-HALL JOKE
MUSIC-HALL STAR
MUSIC-HALL TURN
MUSIC MISTRESS
MUSTARD PICKLE
MUSTARD YELLOW
MUTUAL BENEFIT
MUTUAL CONSENT
MUTUAL DISLIKE
MUTUAL FRIENDS
MUTUAL RESPECT
MYSTERY OF LIFE
MYSTERY WRITER
MYTHICAL BEING

N—13
NAGGING TONGUE
NAME ONE'S PRICE
NARRATIVE POEM
NARROW OUTLOOK
NARROW PASSAGE
NARROW VICTORY
NASTY BUSINESS
NATIONAL DANCE
NATIONAL DRESS
NATIONAL DRINK
NATIONAL GUARD
NATIONAL PRIDE
NATIONAL SPORT
NATIONAL TRUST
NATIONAL UNITY
NATIVE COSTUME
NATIVE QUARTER
NATURAL BEAUTY
NATURAL CAUSES
NATURAL COLOUR ,
NATURAL COURSE
NATURAL HAZARD
NATURAL SYSTEM
NATURAL TALENT
NATURAL WEALTH
NATURE RESERVE
NATURE WORSHIP
NAVAL BARRACKS

NAVAL EXPLOITS
NAVAL HOSPITAL
NEAPOLITAN ICE
NEAR NEIGHBOUR
NEAR ONE'S HEART
NEAR THE GROUND
NEAR THE WICKET
NEAT AS A NEW PIN
NECESSARY EVIL
NECK OR NOTHING
NEEDLESS TO SAY
NEGATIVE REPLY
NELLIE WALLACE
NELSON'S COLUMN
NERVE HOSPITAL
NERVES OF STEEL
NERVOUS ENERGY
NERVOUS SYSTEM
NERVOUS TWITCH
NESTING SEASON
NEST OF HORNETS
NETHER REGIONS
NEUTRAL COLOUR
NEUTRAL CORNER
NEUTRAL GROUND
NEVER LOOK BACK
NEVER ON SUNDAY
NEW BOND STREET
NEW EXPERIMENT
NEW FOUNDATION
NEWGATE PRISON
NEW IMPRESSION
NEW REGULATION
NEW RESOLUTION
NEW SOUTH WALES
NEWSPAPER FILE
NEWSPAPER RACK
NEXT BEST THING
NEXT CHRISTMAS
NEXT GENTLEMAN
NEXT ON THE LIST
NEXT TO NOTHING
NEXT WEDNESDAY
NICE AND TENDER
NICKEL COINAGE
NIGHTLY VISITS
NIGHT MUST FALL
NIGHT OF TERROR
NIGHT WATCHMAN
NIMBLE FINGERS
NINE AND A PENNY

NINE AND ELEVEN
NINE SHILLINGS
NINETEEN MILES
NINETY PER CENT
NINTH OF AUGUST
NINTH SYMPHONY
NO ALTERNATIVE
NOBLE AMBITION
NOBODY ON EARTH
NO BONES BROKEN
NO EXPECTATION
NO EXTRA CHARGE
NO GREAT SHAKES
NO HIDING PLACE
NO HOLDS BARRED
NOMINAL CHARGE
NOMINATION DAY
NONSENSE RHYME
NONSENSE VERSE
NON-STOP TALKER
NO OIL PAINTING
NOOK AND CRANNY
NORFOLK BROADS
NORFOLK JACKET
NORMAL SERVICE
NORMAN ENGLISH
NORMAN VAUGHAN
NORTH AMERICAN
NORTH AND SOUTH
NORTH ATLANTIC
NORTH CAROLINA
NORTH-EAST WIND
NOTABLE SPEECH
NOTE OF CENSURE
NOTE OF TRIUMPH
NOTE OF WARNING
NOT GOOD ENOUGH
NOTHING LIKE IT
NOTHING TO COME
NOTHING TO GAIN
NOTHING TO GO ON
NOTHING TO LOSE
NOT IMPOSSIBLE
NOT IN LUCK'S WAY
NOT IN THE LEAST
NOT LONG TO WAIT
NOT MY CUP OF TEA
NOT NEGOTIABLE
NOT ON YOUR LIFE
NUCLEAR ENERGY
NUISANCE VALUE

NUMBER ENGAGED
NUMERICAL LIST
NURSERY GARDEN
NURSERY SCHOOL
NURSERY SLOPES
NURSING SISTER

O—13
OBEY AN IMPULSE
OBJECTIVE CASE
OBJECT OF MIRTH
OBJECT OF PRIDE
OBJECT OF SCORN
OBLIGE A FRIEND
OBSCURE MOTIVE
OBSERVER CORPS
OCCUPY THE MIND
OCEANS OF MONEY
OFF AT A TANGENT
OFFER AN EXCUSE
OFF-HAND MANNER
OFFICE CLEANER
OFFICE MANAGER
OFFICE OF WORKS
OFFICE ROUTINE
OFFICIAL REPLY
OFF ONE'S OWN BAT
OFF ONE'S ROCKER
OFF-SEASON RATE
OFF THE DEEP END
OFF THE FAIRWAY
OFF THE SUBJECT
OF LITTLE WORTH
OIL AND VINEGAR
OLD-AGE PENSION
OLD AS THE HILLS
OLD CAMPAIGNER
OLD-CLOTHES MAN
OLD CROCKS' RACE
OLDER AND WISER
OLDER THAN TIME
OLD FATHER TIME
OLD FOUNDATION
OLD IN THE TOOTH
OLD TRADITIONS
OLD WIVES' TALES
OLYMPIC RECORD
OMNIBUS VOLUME
ON A BROOMSTICK
ON A GRAND SCALE
ON A LARGE SCALE

ON A SHOE-STRING
ON A SMALL SCALE
ON BENDED KNEES
ONCE AND FOR ALL
ONCE UPON A TIME
ONE AND THE SAME
ONE FOR THE ROAD
ONE IN A HUNDRED
ONE IN A MILLION
ONE OF THE CROWD
ONE OR THE OTHER
ONE'S PROSPECTS
ONE'S RELATIVES
ONE-WAY TRAFFIC
ONE WICKET DOWN
ON HER BEAM ENDS
ON ITS LAST LEGS
ONLY EXCEPTION
ON ONE'S OWN FEET
ON PAIN OF DEATH
ON TENTER-HOOKS
ON THE CONTRARY
ON THE DOOR-STEP
ON THE FACE OF IT
ON THE FIRST LAP
ON THE FRONTIER
ON THE HIGH SEAS
ON THE INCREASE
ON THE LEFT SIDE
ON THE LONG SIDE
ON THE NEAR-SIDE
ON THE PAVEMENT
ON THE PLATFORM
ON THE PREMISES
ON THE ROOF-TOPS
ON THE SAFE SIDE
ON THE SCAFFOLD
ON THE SCROUNGE
ON THE SICK LIST
ON THE STRENGTH
ON THE WIRELESS
ON WINGS OF SONG
OPEN A CAMPAIGN
OPEN-AIR MARKET
OPEN AN ACCOUNT
OPEN CONSONANT
OPENED IN ERROR
OPEN HOSTILITY
OPENING GAMBIT
OPENING SPEECH
OPEN ONE'S HEART

OPEN ONE'S MOUTH
OPEN ONE'S PURSE
OPEN REBELLION
OPEN THE DEBATE
OPEN THE DRAWER
OPEN THE WINDOW
OPERATION ROOM
OPERATIVE WORD
OPPOSITE CAMPS
OPPOSITE POLES
OPPOSITE SIDES
OPPOSITE VIEWS
OPTICAL DEVICE
ORANGE BITTERS
ORANGE BLOSSOM
ORANGE FLAVOUR
ORB AND SCEPTRE
ORDEAL BY WATER
ORDER A RETREAT
ORDERLY MANNER
ORDER OF BATTLE
ORDER OF THE DAY
ORDINAL NUMBER
ORDINARY SHARE
ORDINARY STOCK
ORDNANCE CORPS
ORGANIC CHANGE
ORGANIC MATTER
ORGAN OF SPEECH
ORGAN OF VISION
ORIGINAL MODEL
ORKNEY ISLANDS
OSBERT SITWELL
OTHER WAY ROUND
OTTOMAN EMPIRE
OUT AT THE ELBOW
OUTBOARD MOTOR
OUTBREAK OF WAR
OUTDOOR RELIEF
OUTDOOR SPORTS
OUTER DARKNESS
OUTER HEBRIDES
OUT FOR THRILLS
OUT-HEROD HEROD
OUT LIKE A LIGHT
OUT OF BUSINESS
OUT-OF-DATE IDEA
OUT OF HARM'S WAY
OUT OF INTEREST
OUT OF KINDNESS
OUT OF MISCHIEF

OUT OF MOURNING
OUT OF ONE'S HEAD
OUT OF ONE'S MIND
OUT OF PATIENCE
OUT OF POSITION
OUT OF PRACTICE
OUT OF SYMPATHY
OUT OF TRAINING
OUT ON ONE'S FEET
OUTSIDE CHANCE
OUTSIDE THE LAW
OVER-ALL LENGTH
OVERHEAD CABLE
OVERHEAD WIRES
OVERLAND ROUTE
OVERLAND TRAIN
OVERNIGHT CASE
OVERSEAS TRADE
OVER THE BORDER
OVER THE STICKS
OVER THE WICKET
OVER TWENTY-ONE
OWNER OCCUPIER
OXFORD COLLEGE
OXFORD ENGLISH

P—13
PACE UP AND DOWN
PACIFIC ISLAND
PACKET OF SEEDS
PACK OF THIEVES
PAGAN FESTIVAL
PAGAN LOVE SONG
PAID BY THE HOUR
PAIN IN THE NECK
PAINT A PICTURE
PAINT ONE'S FACE
PAIR OF BELLOWS
PAIR OF GARTERS
PAIR OF GLASSES
PAIR OF KIPPERS
PAIR OF PINCERS
PAIR OF PYJAMAS
PAIR OF SANDALS
PALACE THEATRE
PALAIS DE DANSE
PALE AS A CORPSE
PALE IMITATION
PALE WITH ANGER
PAMELA FRANKAU
PANDA CROSSING

PANELLED WALLS	PATHETIC SIGHT
PANEL OF JUDGES	PATIENCE OF JOB
PANG OF REMORSE	PATRIOTIC SONG
PANGS OF HUNGER	PAUL McCARTNEY
PANIC MEASURES	PAVED WITH GOLD
PANTOMIME DAME	PAWN IN THE GAME
PAPER-BACK BOOK	PAX BRITANNICA
PAPER CLIPPING	PAY BY THE PIECE
PAPER CURRENCY	PAY LIP-SERVICE
PAPER SHORTAGE	PAYMENT IN KIND
PAPER THE WALLS	PAYMENT IN LIEU
PARACHUTE JUMP	PAY THE PENALTY
PARAFFIN STOVE	PEACE AND QUIET
PARALLEL LINES	PEACE OFFERING
PAR EXCELLENCE	PEAK OF SUCCESS
PARIS AND HELEN	PEAL OF THUNDER
PARIS CREATION	PEARL NECKLACE
PARIS FASHIONS	PEBBLE GLASSES
PARISH COUNCIL	PECULIAR SMELL
PARK ATTENDANT	PECUNIARY LOSS
PARKINSON'S LAW	PEGGY ASHCROFT
PAR OF EXCHANGE	PENALTY CLAUSE
PARROT FASHION	PENCIL DRAWING
PART AND PARCEL	PENDULUM CLOCK
PARTIAL CHANGE	PENINSULAR WAR
PARTIAL EXCUSE	PENNY DREADFUL
PARTLY COVERED	PENNY FARTHING
PART OF HISTORY	PENSION SCHEME
PART OF THE PLAN	PEOPLE AT LARGE
PART OF THE TIME	PEPPER AND SALT
PARTY OFFICIAL	PERCUSSION CAP
PARTY POLITICS	PERFECT CIRCLE
PASSAGE OF ARMS	PERFECT FOURTH
PASSAGE OF TIME	PERFECT FRIGHT
PASS AND REPASS	PERFECT NUMBER
PASS AN OPINION	PERFECT RHYTHM
PASSENGER LIST	PERFECT SCREAM
PASSENGER SHIP	PERFECT SQUARE
PASSING GLANCE	PERFECT TIMING
PASSING REMARK	PERFECT WICKET
PASSION FLOWER	PERFORM A STUNT
PASSION SUNDAY	PERIOD COSTUME
PASS THE BUTTER	PERISHING COLD
PASS THE PEPPER	PERKIN WARBECK
PASS UNNOTICED	PERMANENT HOME
PAST BEHAVIOUR	PERMANENT PASS
PAST ENDURANCE	PERMANENT POST
PAST ONE'S PRIME	PERMANENT WAVE
PATENT LEATHER	PERSIAN CARPET
PATENT PENDING	PERSIAN GARDEN
PATENT SWINDLE	PERSIAN MARKET

PERSONAL ABUSE
PERSONAL CHARM
PERSONAL CLAIM
PERSONAL GUEST
PERSONAL PRIDE
PERSONAL STYLE
PERSONAL TOUCH
PETER CAVANAGH
PETER THE GREAT
PETIT DÉJEUNER
PETROL LIGHTER
PETROL STATION
PETTICOAT LANE
PETTY OFFICIAL
PETTY SESSIONS
PEWTER TANKARD
PHANTOM FIGURE
PHYSICAL FORCE
PHYSICAL JERKS
PHYSICALLY FIT
PHYSICAL POWER
PHYSICAL WRECK
PHYSICS MASTER
PIANO CONCERTO
PIANO EXERCISE
PICK AND CHOOSE
PICK AND SHOVEL
PICKLED WALNUT
PICK OF THE POPS
PICK ONE'S WORDS
PICK THE WINNER
PICK UP A LIVING
PICTS AND SCOTS
PICTURE PALACE
PIDGIN ENGLISH
PIECE OF ADVICE
PIECE OF STRING
PIECES OF EIGHT
PIECE TOGETHER
PIG AND WHISTLE
PIGEON FANCIER
PILE OF RUBBISH
PILOT'S LICENCE
PILTDOWN SKULL
PING-PONG TABLE
PINK ELEPHANTS
PINKY AND PERKY
PIN-STRIPE SUIT
PIONEER SPIRIT
PIOUS THOUGHTS
PIPE OF TOBACCO

PISTACHIO NUTS
PISTOLS FOR TWO
PITCH DARKNESS
PITCHED BATTLE
PITCH ONE'S TENT
PITH AND MARROW
PLACE END TO END
PLACE IN THE SUN
PLACE OF HONOUR
PLACE OF REFUGE
PLACE ON RECORD
PLAIN ENVELOPE
PLAIN FEATURES
PLAIN LANGUAGE
PLAIN QUESTION
PLAIN SPEAKING
PLAUSIBLE TALE
PLAY A LONE HAND
PLAY FOR SAFETY
PLAY HARD TO GET
PLAYING TRICKS
PLAY ONE'S CARDS
PLAY THE DESPOT
PLAY THE FIDDLE
PLAY THE GUITAR
PLAY THE MARKET
PLAY THE MARTYR
PLAY THE TYRANT
PLAY THE VIOLIN
PLAY THE WANTON
PLAY UPON WORDS
PLEAD FOR MERCY
PLEAD INNOCENT
PLEAD THE CAUSE
PLEA OF ABSENCE
PLEASED TO COME
PLEASE ONESELF
PLEDGE ONESELF
PLENTIFUL FARE
PLENTY OF MONEY
PLENTY TO SPARE
PLOUGH A FURROW
PLOUGHED FIELD
PLOUGH THE LAND
PLUCKED PIGEON
PLUMB NONSENSE
PLYMOUTH SOUND
PNEUMATIC TYRE
POCKET BOROUGH
POCKET EDITION
POETICAL WORKS

POETIC JUSTICE
POETIC LICENCE
POETRY READING
POINTED REMARK
POINTED SAYING
POINT FOR POINT
POINT IN COMMON
POINT IN FAVOUR
POINT OF HONOUR
POINT OF THE JAW
POISONED ARROW
POISON THE MIND
POLAR EXPLORER
POLICEMAN'S LOT
POLICE MESSAGE
POLICE OFFICER
POLICE STATION
POLICE WHISTLE
POLISHED ACTOR
POLISHED STYLE
POLITE FICTION
POLITE FORMULA
POLITE REFUSAL
POLITE SOCIETY
POLITE WELCOME
POLITICAL BLOC
POLITICAL NEWS
POLITICAL UNIT
POLITICAL VIEW
POMERANIAN DOG
PONTIUS PILATE
PONTOON BRIDGE
POOL RESOURCES
POOR BUT HONEST
POOR CONDITION
POOR IN QUALITY
POORLY DRESSED
POOR PERFORMER
POOR PROSPECTS
POOR RECEPTION
POPPING CREASE
POPULAR BALLAD
POPULAR CHOICE
POPULAR DECREE
POPULAR DEMAND
POPULAR ESTEEM
POPULAR FIGURE
POPULAR PEOPLE
POPULAR PRICES
POPULAR RESORT
POPULAR SINGER

POPULATED AREA
PORTABLE RADIO
PORT ELIZABETH
PORTLAND STONE
POSE A QUESTION
POSITIVE PROOF
POSTAL ADDRESS
POSTAL SERVICE
POSTED MISSING
POSTER COLOURS
POSTE RESTANTE
POSTMAN'S KNOCK
POST-OFFICE RED
POST-WAR CREDIT
POTTED SHRIMPS
POULTRY FARMER
POUND OF APPLES
POUND OF BUTTER
POUND STERLING
POUR OUT THE TEA
POWDER AND SHOT
POWDER COMPACT
POWDER SHAMPOO
POWER AND GLORY
POWERFUL VOICE
POWER OF SPEECH
POWER OF THE LAW
POWER POLITICS
PRACTICAL JOKE
PRACTICAL MIND
PRACTICAL TEST
PRACTICE MATCH
PRACTICE ROUND
PRACTISED HAND
PRACTISED LIAR
PRAIRIE OYSTER
PRAWN COCKTAIL
PRAYER MEETING
PRAYING MANTIS
PRECIOUS METAL
PRECIOUS STONE
PRECIOUS WORDS
PRECISE MOMENT
PRECISION TOOL
PREFER A CHARGE
PREPARE A DRINK
PREPARE FOR WAR
PRESENT EVENTS
PRESENT MOMENT
PRESS CAMPAIGN
PRESS CUTTINGS

PRESSED FLOWER

PRESSED TONGUE

PRESS EXCHANGE

PRESS FASTENER

PRESSING CLAIM

PRESS ONE'S SUIT

PRESSURE GAUGE

PRESSURE GROUP

PRETTY PICTURE

PREY ON THE MIND

PRICE INCREASE

PRIM AND PROPER

PRIMARY COLOUR

PRIMARY SCHOOL

PRIME MINISTER

PRIMEVAL CHAOS

PRIMITIVE FORM

PRINCE CHARLES

PRINCE CONSORT

PRINCE OF PEACE

PRINCE OF WALES

PRINCESS DRESS

PRINCESS ROYAL

PRINCE'S STREET

PRINCE WILLIAM

PRINCIPAL FOOD

PRINCIPAL PART

PRINCIPAL TOWN

PRINTED LETTER

PRINTED MATTER

PRINTER'S DEVIL

PRINTER'S ERROR

PRINTING PRESS

PRINTING WORKS

PRISONER OF WAR

PRISONER'S BASE

PRISON VISITOR

PRIVATE AFFAIR

PRIVATE INCOME

PRIVATE LESSON

PRIVATE LETTER

PRIVATE MATTER

PRIVATE MEMBER

PRIVATE OFFICE

PRIVATE PERSON

PRIVATE REASON

PRIVATE SCHOOL

PRIVATE SOURCE

PRIZE SPECIMEN

PROBABLE ERROR

PROCESSED FOOD

PROCESS OF TIME

PRODUCER GOODS

PROFANE PERSON

PROFIT AND LOSS

PROFIT SHARING

PROFOUND SLEEP

PROFUSE THANKS

PROGRESS CHART

PROLONGED NOTE

PROMENADE DECK

PROMISING IDEA

PROMPT PAYMENT

PROMPT SERVICE

PROOF POSITIVE

PROPER CHARLEY

PROPERTY OWNER

PROPOSE A TOAST

PROSAIC PERSON

PROSPEROUS MAN

PROVE ONE'S CASE

PROVIDE AN HEIR

PROVING GROUND

PUBLIC ADDRESS

PUBLIC AFFAIRS

PUBLIC ANALYST

PUBLIC COMMENT

PUBLIC COMPANY

PUBLIC GALLERY

PUBLIC HANGING

PUBLIC HIGHWAY

PUBLIC HOLIDAY

PUBLIC INQUIRY

PUBLIC LECTURE

PUBLIC LIBRARY

PUBLIC MEETING

PUBLIC OPINION

PUBLIC OUTRAGE

PUBLIC PROTEST

PUBLIC RECORDS

PUBLIC SCANDAL

PUBLIC SERVANT

PUBLIC SERVICE

PUBLIC SPEAKER

PUBLIC TRUSTEE

PUBLIC UTILITY

PUBLIC VEHICLE

PUBLIC WARNING

PUBLIC WORSHIP

PUBLISHED WORK

PULITZER PRIZE

PULL A LONG FACE

PULL INTO SHAPE
PULL NO PUNCHES
PUNCTURED TYRE
PUNISHING WORK
PUPPET THEATRE
PURCHASE MONEY
PURCHASE PRICE
PURE AND SIMPLE
PURE IN THOUGHT
PURE MISCHANCE
PURE PREJUDICE
PURPLE AND GOLD
PURPLE EMPEROR
PURPLE HEATHER
PURPLE PASSAGE
PURSE ONE'S LIPS
PURSER'S OFFICE
PUSH-BUTTON WAR
PUSHED FOR TIME
PUSH TO THE WALL
PUT IN FOR A RISE
PUT IN JEOPARDY
PUT IN THE KITTY
PUT IN THE SHADE
PUT IN THE WRONG
PUT ONE'S BACK UP
PUT ONESELF OUT
PUT ONE'S FEET UP
PUT ONE'S HAIR UP
PUT ON PRESSURE
PUT ON THE BRAKE
PUT ON THE LIGHT
PUT ON THE SCREW
PUT ON THE STAGE
PUT OUT A FEELER
PUT OUT FEELERS
PUT OUT OF COURT
PUT OUT OF JOINT
PUT OUT OF SIGHT
PUT OUT TO GRASS
PUT PEN TO PAPER
PUT THE BRAKE ON
PUT THE CAP ON IT
PUT THE LID ON IT
PUT TO THE BLUSH
PUT TO THE PROOF
PUT TO THE SWORD
PUT UP THE BANNS
PUT UP THE MONEY
PUT UP THE PRICE

Q—13
QUADRUPLE TIME
QUALITY STREET
QUANTUM THEORY
QUARTER BOTTLE
QUARTERLY RENT
QUARTER TO FIVE
QUARTER TO FOUR
QUARTER TO NINE
QUEEN CAROLINE
QUEEN OF HEARTS
QUEEN OF SPADES
QUEEN OF THE MAY
QUEEN OF TRUMPS
QUEEN'S COLLEGE
QUEEN'S COUNSEL
QUEEN'S ENGLISH
QUEEN'S HIGHWAY
QUEEN'S PROCTOR
QUEEN VICTORIA
QUEER CUSTOMER
QUEER GOINGS-ON
QUEER THE PITCH
QUICK AS A FLASH
QUICK MOVEMENT
QUICK RECOVERY
QUICK-SET HEDGE
QUICK THINKING
QUICK TURNOVER
QUIET AS A MOUSE
QUITE POSITIVE
QUITE POSSIBLE
QUITE THE THING
QUIZ PROGRAMME
QUOTATION MARK

R—13
RACE PREJUDICE
RACING CIRCUIT
RACING TIPSTER
RACING TRAINER
RACK ONE'S BRAIN
RADIANT ENERGY
RADIATION BELT
RADICAL CHANGE
RADICAL REFORM
RADIO OPERATOR
RADIO RECEIVER
RAG-AND-BONE MAN
RAGING TEMPEST
RAGING TORRENT

RAID THE LARDER	REACT IN FAVOUR
RAILWAY BRIDGE	READER'S DIGEST
RAILWAY ENGINE	READ FOR THE BAR
RAILWAY SHARES	READING MATTER
RAILWAY SIDING	READING PUBLIC
RAILWAY SIGNAL	READ THE FUTURE
RAILWAY SYSTEM	READ THE LESSON
RAILWAY TICKET	READY-MADE SUIT
RAILWAY TUNNEL	READY RECKONER
RAISE A BARRIER	READY RESPONSE
RAISE CHICKENS	READY, STEADY, GO!
RAISED GLASSES	READY TO ATTACK
RAISE ONE'S EYES	READY TO POUNCE
RAISE ONE'S HAND	READY TO SPRING
RAISE THE ALARM	REAL-LIFE STORY
RAISE THE FUNDS	REALMS OF FANCY
RAISE THE MONEY	REAP THE FRUITS
RAISE THE PRICE	REAP THE REWARD
RAISE THE SIEGE	RECEIPT IN FULL
RAISE THE TEMPO	RECEIVE NOTICE
RAISE THE VOICE	RECEIVE ORDERS
RAKE'S PROGRESS	RECENT ARRIVAL
RAKE UP THE PAST	RECEPTION DESK
RALLYING POINT	RECEPTION ROOM
RALPH WIGHTMAN	RECEPTIVE MIND
RANGE OF CHOICE	RECKLESS SPEED
RANGE OF COLOUR	RECKLESS YOUTH
RAPE OF THE LOCK	RECLAIMED LAND
RAPID PROGRESS	RECORD ATTEMPT
RAPID TURNOVER	RECORD BREAKER
RAPT ATTENTION	RECORD COUNTER
RASH BEHAVIOUR	RECORDED MUSIC
RASHER OF BACON	RECORD ROUND-UP
RASH STATEMENT	RECORD SESSION
RASPBERRY CANE	RED AS A LOBSTER
RATEABLE VALUE	RED-CROSS NURSE
RATE COLLECTOR	REDEEM A PLEDGE
RATE FOR THE JOB	RED RAG TO A BULL
RATES AND TAXES	RED RIDING HOOD
RATIONAL DRESS	RED SEALING-WAX
RAVAGES OF TIME	RED SKY AT NIGHT
RAVENOUS BEAST	REDUCE TO ASHES
RAVING LUNATIC	REDUCE TO SCALE
RAYMOND BAXTER	REDUCE TO TEARS
RAYMOND MASSEY	REDUCING AGENT
RAY OF SUNSHINE	REDUCING PILLS
REACH A NEW HIGH	REFERENCE BOOK
REACH A VERDICT	REFER TO DRAWER
REACH MATURITY	REFINED ACCENT
REACH ONE'S GOAL	REFINED PALATE
REACH THE LIMIT	REFUSE A CHANCE

REFUSE AN OFFER
REFUSE PAYMENT
REFUSE THE BAIT
REFUSE TO SPEAK
REGAIN COMMAND
REGAIN CONTROL
REGAIN THE LEAD
REGENCY STRIPE
REGRET THE LOSS
REGULAR FORCES
REGULAR HABITS
REGULAR INCOME
REGULAR PEOPLE
REGULAR READER
REGULAR SALARY
REGULAR STAGES
REGULAR TROOPS
REGULAR VISITS
REHEARSAL ROOM
REIGNING QUEEN
REIGN OF TERROR
REJECTION SLIP
RELATIVE MERIT
RELATIVE PROOF
RELATIVE VALUE
RELATIVE WORTH
RELAXED THROAT
RELEASE ON BAIL
REMAIN AT PEACE
REMAIN HOPEFUL
REMAIN NEUTRAL
REMAIN PASSIVE
REMAIN THE SAME
REMAIN UPRIGHT
REMAIN VISIBLE
REMARKABLE BOY
REMARKABLE MAN
REMITTANCE MAN
REMOTE CONTROL
REMOTE VILLAGE
REMOVE ONE'S HAT
RENEWED ENERGY
RENEW ONE'S VOWS
RENT COLLECTOR
RENT IN ADVANCE
REPEAT A SIGNAL
REPEAT ONESELF
REPEL AN ATTACK
REPETITIVE JOB
REPLY BY RETURN
REPORT FOR DUTY

REPUBLICAN ERA
RESERVED TABLE
RESERVE ELEVEN
RESIGN ONESELF
RESPECT THE LAW
RESTAURANT CAR
RESTIVE NATURE
RESTLESS NIGHT
REST ONE'S BONES
RESTORE TO LIFE
REST SATISFIED
RETAIL TRADING
RETAINING WALL
RETARDED BRAIN
RETARDED CHILD
RETIRED PEOPLE
RETROUSSÉ NOSE
RETURN A FAVOUR
RETURN A PROFIT
RETURN JOURNEY
RETURN SERVICE
RETURN TO EARTH
REVENUE CUTTER
REVERSE MOTION
REVOLT AGAINST
REVOLVING DOOR
REWARD OFFERED
REYNARD THE FOX
RHODES SCHOLAR
RHONDDA VALLEY
RHYMED COUPLET
RIBSTON PIPPIN
RICEYMAN STEPS
RICHARD BURTON
RICHARD HEARNE
RICHARD TAUBER
RICHARD WAGNER
RICH AS CROESUS
RICHMOND GREEN
RICH OFFERINGS
RIDE A TRICYCLE
RIDE POST-HASTE
RIDE ROUGH-SHOD
RIDE THE WINNER
RIFLE PRACTICE
RIFT IN THE LUTE
RIGHT AND WRONG
RIGHT APPROACH
RIGHT AT THE END
RIGHT DECISION
RIGHT-DOWN LIAR

RIGHTFUL OWNER
RIGHTFUL SHARE
RIGHT-HAND BEND
RIGHT-HAND SIDE
RIGHT-HAND TURN
RIGHT OF ACCESS
RIGHT OF APPEAL
RIGHT OF CHOICE
RIGHT OF SEARCH
RIGHT ON THE DOT
RIGHT OPPOSITE
RIGHT REVEREND
RIGHT SHOULDER
RIGHT TO THE END
RIGHT TO THE TOP
RIGHT UP TO DATE
RING OUT THE OLD
RIOT OF EMOTION
RIOTOUS LIVING
RISE IN DISGUST
RISE OF THE TIDE
RISE TO THE BAIT
RISING SPIRITS
RISK ONE'S MONEY
RISKY BUSINESS
RITUAL KILLING
RIVAL BUSINESS
RIVER CROSSING
RIVERSIDE WALK
ROAD DIVERSION
ROAD TO SUCCESS
ROAD TRANSPORT
ROAST CHESTNUT
ROAST POTATOES
ROBBINS REPORT
ROBERT BRIDGES
ROBERT MITCHUM
ROBERTSON HARE
ROBERT SOUTHEY
ROCKET WARFARE
ROCK THE CRADLE
ROGUE ELEPHANT
ROGUES' GALLERY
ROLL AND BUTTER
ROLLED INTO ONE
ROLLER COASTER
ROLLING IN CASH
ROLLING STONES
ROLL IN THE DUST
ROMAN ALPHABET
ROMAN CATHOLIC

ROMAN NUMERALS
ROMANTIC NOVEL
ROMANTIC SCENE
ROMANTIC STORY
ROMNEY MARSHES
RONALD CHESNEY
ROOM TO BREATHE
ROOM WITH A VIEW
ROOT AND BRANCH
ROOTED DISLIKE
ROOT OF ALL EVIL
ROOT VEGETABLE
ROPE AND PULLEY
ROTATE THE CROP
ROTTEN BOROUGH
ROUGH AND READY
ROUGH CROSSING
ROUGH CUSTOMER
ROUGH ESTIMATE
ROUGH EXTERIOR
ROUGH HANDLING
ROUGH QUARTERS
ROULETTE TABLE
ROULETTE WHEEL
ROUND-ABOUT WAY
ROUND AND ABOUT
ROUND AND ROUND
ROUNDLY ABUSED
ROUND OF DRINKS
ROUND OF GAIETY
ROUND OF VISITS
ROUND THE BLOCK
ROUND THE CLOCK
ROUND THE EARTH
ROUND THE HOUSE
ROUND THE TABLE
ROUND THE WAIST
ROUND THE WORLD
ROUSING CHEERS
ROUSING CHORUS
ROUSING SERMON
ROUTINE DUTIES
ROUTINE MATTER
ROYAL AERO CLUB
ROYAL AIR FORCE
ROYAL EXCHANGE
ROYAL FUNCTION
ROYAL HIGHNESS
ROYAL HOSPITAL
ROYAL MARRIAGE
ROYAL OCCASION

ROYAL STANDARD
RUBBER PLANTER
RUB OF THE GREEN
RUDE AWAKENING
RUGBY FOOTBALL
RUGGED COUNTRY
RUINED FOR LIFE
RUINOUS CHARGE
RULE BRITANNIA
RULE OF THE ROAD
RULING CLASSES
RULING PASSION
RUN FOR SHELTER
RUN IN THE BLOOD
RUN INTO DANGER
RUN LIKE BLAZES
RUNNING BATTLE
RUNNING BUFFET
RUNNING STREAM
RUN OF THE GREEN
RUN OF THE HOUSE
RUN ON SMOOTHLY
RUN ON THE ROCKS
RUN OUT OF FUNDS
RUN OUT OF MONEY
RUN OUT OF STEAM
RUN OUT OF WORDS
RUN THINGS FINE
RURAL DISTRICT
RURAL INDUSTRY
RUSHING STREAM
RUSH INTO PRINT
RUSSELL SQUARE
RUSSIAN BALLET
RUSSIAN LESSON

S—13
SACRED EDIFICE
SAFE ANCHORAGE
SAFETY CURTAIN
SAFETY HARNESS
SAFETY MEASURE
SAFFRON WALDEN
SAGE AND ONIONS
SAILING MASTER
SAILING ORDERS
SAILING VESSEL
SAINT AUGUSTUS
SAINT LAWRENCE
SAINT NICHOLAS
SALAD DRESSING

SALARIED CLASS
SALE BY AUCTION
SALMON FISHING
SALT AND PEPPER
SALT-WATER FISH
SALUTE THE FLAG
SALVATION ARMY
SAMUEL JOHNSON
SAND IN THE EYES
SARATOGA TRUNK
SATELLITE TOWN
SATURDAY NIGHT
SAUCE PIQUANTE
SAUTÉ POTATOES
SAVE ONE'S BACON
SAY BO TO A GOOSE
SCALDING TEARS
SCARCITY VALUE
SCARED TO DEATH
SCARLET RUNNER
SCARLETT O'HARA
SCENE OF STRIFE
SCENIC RAILWAY
SCHOOL EDITION
SCHOOL HOLIDAY
SCHOOL OF MUSIC
SCHOOL PREFECT
SCHOOL UNIFORM
SCIENCE MASTER
SCIENCE MUSEUM
SCIENTIFIC AGE
SCILLY ISLANDS
SCORCHED EARTH
SCORE A CENTURY
SCORE A SUCCESS
SCORING STROKE
SCOTCH AND SODA
SCOTCH TERRIER
SCRAMBLED EGGS
SCRAPE A LIVING
SCRAPE THROUGH
SCRAP MERCHANT
SCRATCH PLAYER
SCRATCH RUNNER
SCREEN VERSION
SCRIBBLED NOTE
SCRIPT WRITING
SEALED VERDICT
SEAL OF SECRECY
SEA OF TROUBLES
SEA OPERATIONS

SEARCHING LOOK	SELL BY AUCTION
SEARCH WARRANT	SELLER'S MARKET
SEASIDE RESORT	SEMPER FIDELIS
SEAT OF JUSTICE	SEND A POSTCARD
SECOND ATTEMPT	SEND A REMINDER
SECOND CENTURY	SEND A TELEGRAM
SECOND CHAMBER	SEND TO JERICHO
SECOND CHAPTER	SENIOR PARTNER
SECOND EDITION	SENIOR SERVICE
SECOND FEATURE	SENSELESS TALK
SECOND-HAND CAR	SENSE OF DANGER
SECOND HELPING	SENSE OF HUMOUR
SECOND HUSBAND	SENSE OF INJURY
SECOND INNINGS	SENSE OF RELIEF
SECOND OF APRIL	SENSE OF TIMING
SECOND OFFENCE	SENSE OF VALUES
SECOND OFFICER	SENSIBLE CHILD
SECOND OF MARCH	SENSIBLE WOMAN
SECOND OPINION	SEPARATE COVER
SECOND QUARTER	SEPARATE ROOMS
SECOND READING	SEPTEMBER MORN
SECOND SERVICE	SEPTEMBER TIDE
SECOND TURNING	SERGEANT MAJOR
SECRET ARRIVAL	SERGEANTS' MESS
SECRETARY BIRD	SERIOUS CHARGE
SECRET FORMULA	SERIOUS DAMAGE
SECRET INQUIRY	SERIOUS DANGER
SECRET MEETING	SERIOUS DEFEAT
SECRET PASSAGE	SERIOUS INJURY
SECRET PROCESS	SERIOUS MATTER
SECRET SERVICE	SERIOUS PERSON
SECRET SESSION	SERPENT'S TOOTH
SECRET SOCIETY	SERVE A PURPOSE
SECRET THOUGHT	SERVE AS A MODEL
SECRET WRITING	SERVE ONE RIGHT
SECURE FOOTING	SERVE ONE'S TIME
SECURITY CHECK	SERVE ONE'S TURN
SEDENTARY LIFE	SERVE THE DEVIL
SEE FOR ONESELF	SERVE UP DINNER
SEE HOW THEY RUN	SERVICE CHARGE
SEEK ADVENTURE	SERVIETTE RING
SEEK A SOLUTION	SET A NEW RECORD
SEEMLY CONDUCT	SET AT DEFIANCE
SEE ONE THROUGH	SET AT VARIANCE
SEE THINGS DONE	SET ONE'S SIGHTS
SEIZE THE CROWN	SET THE FASHION
SELECT CIRCLES	SETTING LOTION
SELECT COMPANY	SETTLEMENT DAY
SELECTION LIST	SEVEN AND A HALF
SELFISH MOTIVE	SEVEN AND EIGHT
SELL AT A PROFIT	SEVEN AND SEVEN

SEVEN AND THREE	SHELTERED SPOT
SEVEN DIAMONDS	SHEPHERD'S BUSH
SEVEN FURLONGS	SHEPTON MALLET
SEVEN NO-TRUMPS	SHERATON TABLE
SEVEN OF HEARTS	SHERIFF'S POSSE
SEVEN OF SPADES	SHERRY COBBLER
SEVEN OF TRUMPS	SHETLAND ISLES
SEVEN SLEEPERS	SHIFTING SANDS
SEVENTH HEAVEN	SHIFTING SCENE
SEVENTH LETTER	SHIFT THE BLAME
SEVENTH OF JULY	SHIFT THE SCENE
SEVENTH OF JUNE	SHILLING PIECE
SEVEN THOUSAND	SHILLING STAMP
SEVENTH STOREY	SHINING ARMOUR
SEVENTH VOLUME	SHINING KNIGHT
SEVEN-YEAR ITCH	SHIP IN A BOTTLE
SEVEN YEARS OLD	SHIP OF THE LINE
SEVEN YEARS' WAR	SHIPPING AGENT
SEVERE ILLNESS	SHIPPING CLERK
SEVERE WEATHER	SHIPPING ORDER
SEVILLE ORANGE	SHIP'S CHANDLER
SEWING MACHINE	SHIP'S CORPORAL
SHADES OF NIGHT	SHIP'S REGISTER
SHADOW CABINET	SHIRLEY BASSEY
SHADOW FACTORY	SHIRLEY TEMPLE
SHADOW OF DEATH	SHOCK ABSORBER
SHADOW OF DOUBT	SHOCKING STATE
SHADY BUSINESS	SHOOTING BRAKE
SHAKE ONE'S FIST	SHOOTING MATCH
SHAKE ONE'S HEAD	SHOOTING PAINS
SHAKE WITH COLD	SHOOTING PARTY
SHAKE WITH FEAR	SHOOTING RANGE
SHALLOW STREAM	SHOOT STRAIGHT
SHALLOW VESSEL	SHOOT THE WORKS
SHAME THE DEVIL	SHOP ASSISTANT
SHAMPOO AND SET	SHOP DETECTIVE
SHAPELY FIGURE	SHOPPING SPREE
SHARE EXPENSES	SHORT AND SWEET
SHARE THE BLAME	SHORT DISTANCE
SHARP AS A KNIFE	SHORTEST NIGHT
SHARP AS A RAZOR	SHORTEST ROUTE
SHARP FEATURES	SHORTEST WOMAN
SHARP PRACTICE	SHORTHAND NOTE
SHARP'S THE WORD	SHORTLY BEFORE
SHAVING SALOON	SHORT OF BREATH
SHED LIGHT UPON	SHORT OF CHANGE
SHEEP AND GOATS	SHORT OF SPEECH
SHEEPSKIN COAT	SHORT OF TALENT
SHEER NONSENSE	SHORT SENTENCE
SHELTERED LIFE	SHORT SYNOPSIS
SHELTERED SIDE	SHORT-TERM LOAN

SHORT TROUSERS	SIMPLE PROBLEM
SHORT VACATION	SIMPLE REQUEST
SHOT IN THE BACK	SIMPLY FURIOUS
SHOT IN THE DARK	SIMPLY KILLING
SHOULDER STRAP	SINCERELY FELT
SHOUTING MATCH	SINGING MASTER
SHOW ANIMOSITY	SING IN HARMONY
SHOW DEFERENCE	SINGLE ARTICLE
SHOW FORESIGHT	SINGLE PURPOSE
SHOW NO REMORSE	SINGLE THOUGHT
SHOW NO RESPECT	SINGLETON LEAD
SHOW ONE'S CARDS	SING LIKE A BIRD
SHOW ONE'S PACES	SING LIKE A LARK
SHOW ONE'S TEETH	SING ME TO SLEEP
SHOW RESTRAINT	SING-SONG VOICE
SHREDDED WHEAT	SING THE CHORUS
SHROPSHIRE LAD	SIR DON BRADMAN
SHROVE TUESDAY	SIRLOIN OF BEEF
SHUT YOUR MOUTH	SIR ROBERT PEEL
SICK OF WAITING	SISTER OF MERCY
SICK UNTO DEATH	SISTINE CHAPEL
SIDE ELEVATION	SIT-DOWN STRIKE
SIEGFRIED LINE	SIT IN CONCLAVE
SIGNAL EXAMPLE	SIT IN JUDGMENT
SIGNAL FAILURE	SIT IN THE FRONT
SIGNAL SUCCESS	SIT ON ONE'S TAIL
SIGNAL VICTORY	SIT ON THE FENCE
SIGNATURE TUNE	SIT ON THE FLOOR
SIGNED ARTICLE	SITTING PRETTY
SIGNIFY ASSENT	SITTING TARGET
SIGNIFY LITTLE	SITTING TENANT
SIGN OF EMOTION	SIX O'CLOCK NEWS
SIGN OF FATIGUE	SIX OF DIAMONDS
SIGN OF SUCCESS	SIXPENNY PIECE
SIGN THE PLEDGE	SIXPENNY STAMP
SILENT CONSENT	SIXTEEN AND SIX
SILENT PARTNER	SIXTEEN AND TEN
SILENT PROTEST	SIXTEEN AND TWO
SILENT SERVICE	SIXTEEN OUNCES
SILK STOCKINGS	SIXTEENTH HOLE
SILLY QUESTION	SIXTH OF AUGUST
SILLY SYMPHONY	SIXTH SYMPHONY
SILVER AND GOLD	SIXTY THOUSAND
SILVER COINAGE	SKELETON STAFF
SILVER JUBILEE	SKETCHES BY BOZ
SILVER PLATTER	SKI-ING HOLIDAY
SILVER TANKARD	SKILLED LABOUR
SILVER THIMBLE	SKILLED WORKER
SILVER THREADS	SKINFUL OF WINE
SILVER WEDDING	SKIN TREATMENT
SIMON STYLITES	SKITTLES MATCH

SLANDER ACTION
SLANGING MATCH
SLAP AND TICKLE
SLAP IN THE FACE
SLAP ON THE BACK
SLEEPING PILLS
SLEEP LIKE A LOG
SLEEP LIKE A TOP
SLEIGHT OF HAND
SLENDER CHANCE
SLENDER INCOME
SLICK OPERATOR
SLIGHTLY BUILT
SLIGHT QUARREL
SLING ONE'S HOOK
SLIP INTO PLACE
SLIPPERY SLOPE
SLIP THE COLLAR
SLOPING GROUND
SLOW AND STEADY
SLUM CLEARANCE
SMACK ONE'S LIPS
SMALL ADDITION
SMALL BUSINESS
SMALL CAPITALS
SMALL DIVIDEND
SMALL INVESTOR
SMALL MAJORITY
SMALL OFFERING
SMALL POTATOES
SMALL PRACTICE
SMALL QUANTITY
SMART TROUSERS
SMASH TO PIECES
SMEAR CAMPAIGN
SMELLING SALTS
SMOKED HADDOCK
SMOKED SAUSAGE
SMOKE-FREE ZONE
SMOKELESS FUEL
SMOKELESS ZONE
SMOKER'S THROAT
SMOKING JACKET
SMOOTH AS GLASS
SMOOTHING IRON
SMOOTH JOURNEY
SMOOTH MANNERS
SMOOTH PASSAGE
SMOOTH SAILING
SMOOTH SURFACE
SMOOTH TEXTURE

SMUGGLED GOODS
SNOOKER PLAYER
SNOWBALL FIGHT
SOAP-BOX ORATOR
SOARING PRICES
SOBER AS A JUDGE
SOBER ESTIMATE
SOBER THOUGHTS
SOCIAL CIRCLES
SOCIAL CLIMBER
SOCIAL DEMANDS
SOCIAL EVENING
SOCIAL MACHINE
SOCIAL OUTCAST
SOCIAL PROBLEM
SOCIAL RE-UNION
SOCIAL SCIENCE
SOCIAL SERVICE
SOCIAL SUCCESS
SOCIAL WELFARE
SOCIETY COLUMN
SOCIETY GOSSIP
SOCIETY PEOPLE
SOFTEN THE BLOW
SOFT IN THE HEAD
SOIL ONE'S HANDS
SOLDIERS THREE
SOLDIER'S TUNIC
SOLEMN PROMISE
SOLEMN SILENCE
SOLEMN WARNING
SOLE OWNERSHIP
SOLICIT ORDERS
SOLITAIRE RING
SOLOMON GRUNDY
SOLVE A PROBLEM
SOME OF THE TIME
SOME OTHER TIME
SOMERSET HOUSE
SOMETHING DONE
SOMETHING ELSE
SOMETHING LIKE
SOMETHING NICE
SOMETHING OVER
SOMETHING TO DO
SOME TIME LATER
SOMEWHERE ELSE
SONG OF SOLOMON
SONG OF THE FLEA
SONG OF TRIUMPH
SON OF A SEA COOK

SONS AND LOVERS
SOONER OR LATER
SOONEST MENDED
SOON FORGOTTEN
SOOTHING MUSIC
SOOTHING SYRUP
SOOTHING TOUCH
SOOTHING WORDS
SOP TO CERBERUS
SORRY BUSINESS
SORTING OFFICE
SORT THINGS OUT
SOUND A FANFARE
SOUND ARGUMENT
SOUND CURRENCY
SOUND DETECTOR
SOUND DOCTRINE
SOUNDING BOARD
SOUNDING BRASS
SOUND JUDGMENT
SOUND MATERIAL
SOUND ONE'S HORN
SOUND THE ALARM
SOURCE OF LIGHT
SOURCE OF POWER
SOURCE OF PRIDE
SOUR SUBSTANCE
SOUSED HERRING
SOUTH CAROLINA
SOUTH CHINA SEA
SOUTH-EAST WIND
SOUTHERN CROSS
SOUTHERN STATE
SOUTH OF FRANCE
SPANISH ARMADA
SPANISH GUITAR
SPANISH LESSON
SPANISH ONIONS
SPARE A THOUGHT
SPARE NO EFFORT
SPARKLING WINE
SPARK OF GENIUS
SPARTAN REGIME
SPEAK AT LENGTH
SPEAKER'S NOTES
SPEAKING TERMS
SPEAKING VOICE
SPEAK ONE'S MIND
SPEAK THE TRUTH
SPECIAL BRANCH
SPECIAL FAVOUR

SPECIAL FRIEND
SPECIAL NUMBER
SPECIAL PRAYER
SPECIAL SCHOOL
SPECIFIED DOSE
SPECK OF COLOUR
SPECTACLE CASE
SPEECH THERAPY
SPEED MERCHANT
SPEEDWAY TRACK
SPELL DISASTER
SPEND A FORTUNE
SPENDING MONEY
SPENDING POWER
SPENDING SPREE
SPIKE MILLIGAN
SPIKE ONE'S GUNS
SPILL THE BEANS
SPINNING JENNY
SPINNING WHEEL
SPIN OF THE COIN
SPIRITED REPLY
SPIRIT OF YOUTH
SPIRITUAL LIFE
SPIRITUAL PEER
SPIRITUAL SELF
SPIRITUAL SONG
SPIRIT WRITING
SPIT AND POLISH
SPITEFUL WOMAN
SPITTING IMAGE
SPLINTER GROUP
SPLINTER PARTY
SPLIT DECISION
SPLITTING HEAD
SPOILT DARLING
SPOIL THE CHILD
SPORTING EVENT
SPORTING GOODS
SPORTING OFFER
SPORTING PRESS
SPORTING PRINT
SPORTING RIFLE
SPORTING WORLD
SPORTS EDITION
SPORTS STADIUM
SPOT OF TROUBLE
SPOT THE WINNER
SPRAINED ANKLE
SPREAD A RUMOUR
SPREAD THE LOAD

SPREAD THE NEWS
SPRING BALANCE
SPRING BLOSSOM
SPRING CHICKEN
SPRING FLOWERS
SPRING MADNESS
SPRING MEETING
SPRING THE TRAP
SPRING THROUGH
SPY OUT THE LAND
SQUARE BASHING
SQUARE MEASURE
SQUASH RACKETS
SQUIRE OF DAMES
STAB IN THE BACK
STACK THE CARDS
STAFF ENTRANCE
STAFF OF OFFICE
STAFF PROBLEMS
STAFF SERGEANT
STAGGERING SUM
STAKE ONE'S LIFE
STAMP OF GENIUS
STAND AND FIGHT
STAND AND STARE
STANDARD BREAD
STANDARD GAUGE
STANDARD MODEL
STANDARD PRICE
STANDARD USAGE
STANDING ORDER
STANDING START
STAND IN THE WAY
STAND ON TIPTOE
STAND OPPOSITE
STAND OUT A MILE
STAND PREPARED
STAND TOGETHER
STAND TO REASON
STANLEY LUPINO
STAR AND GARTER
STARBOARD BEAM
STARBOARD SIDE
STAR OF THE SHOW
STAR PERFORMER
START A QUARREL
STARTING POINT
STARTING PRICE
START LAUGHING
STARTLING NEWS
STAR TREATMENT

START THINKING
START TO FINISH
START TOGETHER
STATE BOUNDARY
STATE CARRIAGE
STATE CRIMINAL
STATE FUNCTION
STATE MONOPOLY
STATE OCCASION
STATE OF FRENZY
STATE OF NATURE
STATE OF REASON
STATE OF UNREST
STATE ONE'S CASE
STATE PRISONER
STATE RELIGION
STATIC WARFARE
STATION IN LIFE
STATION MASTER
STATUTORY MILE
STAY INCOGNITO
STAY OVERNIGHT
STAY THE COURSE
STAY UNMARRIED
ST. BARTHOLOMEW
ST. BERNARD PASS
ST. CRISPIN'S DAY
STEADY ADVANCE
STEADY AS A ROCK
STEAK AND CHIPS
STEAL A MARCH ON
STEEL INDUSTRY
STEERAGE CLASS
STEERING WHEEL
STEP OUT OF LINE
STEPTOE AND SON
STERLING WORTH
STERN MEASURES
STEVE DONOGHUE
STICKING POINT
STICK IN THE MUD
STICK LIKE GLUE
STICK OF CELERY
STICK TOGETHER
STICKY PROBLEM
STIFF AND STARK
STIFF AS A BOARD
STIFF AS A POKER
STIFF SENTENCE
STIFF UPPER-LIP
STILETTO HEELS

STILL LEMONADE
STILTON CHEESE
STIR IN THE WIND
STIRRING MUSIC
STIRRING TIMES
STIR THE EMBERS
STIR UP TROUBLE
STOCK EXCHANGE
STOCK QUESTION
STOLEN ARTICLE
STOLE THE TARTS
STOMACH POWDER
STONE THE CROWS!
STOP AT NOTHING
STOP BREATHING
STOPPING PLACE
STOPPING TRAIN
STOP-PRESS NEWS
STORMY MEETING
STORMY PASSAGE
STORMY SESSION
STORMY WEATHER
ST. PATRICK'S DAY
ST. PAUL'S SCHOOL
STRAIGHT ACTOR
STRAIGHT AHEAD
STRAIGHT ANGLE
STRAIGHT DRAMA
STRAIGHT DRIVE
STRAIGHTEN OUT
STRAIGHT FIGHT
STRAIGHT FLUSH
STRAIGHT RIGHT
STRAIN AT A GNAT
STRAIN ONESELF
STRAIN THE EYES
STRAIT OF DOVER
STRANGE DEVICE
STRANGE GROUND
STRANGE MANNER
STRAPPING GIRL
STRAWBERRY BED
STRAWBERRY ICE
STRAWBERRY JAM
STRAWBERRY TEA
STRAW MATTRESS
STRAY CUSTOMER
STRAY FROM HOME
STREAK OF LIGHT
STREAMING COLD
STREAM OF BLOOD

STREAM OF LIGHT
STREAM OF TEARS
STREAM OF WATER
STREET BETTING
STREET CLOTHES
STRESS THE FACT
STRETCH A POINT
STRETCHER CASE
STRETCH OF LAND
STRETCH OF ROAD
STRICT INQUIRY
STRICTLY LEGAL
STRICT PARENTS
STRIKE IT LUCKY
STRIKE THE BALL
STRIKE THE FLAG
STRIKE THE HOUR
STRIKE UP A TUNE
STRIKING CLOCK
STRIKING FORCE
STRING OF BEADS
STRING OF NAMES
STRING OF OATHS
STRING QUARTET
STRIP LIGHTING
STRONG AS A LION
STRONG BACKING
STRONG CURRENT
STRONG DEFENCE
STRONG DISLIKE
STRONG EMOTION
STRONG FEELING
STRONG GROUNDS
STRONG PROTEST
STRONG REQUEST
STRONG STOMACH
STRONG SUPPORT
STRONG SWIMMER
STRUGGLE ALONG
ST. SWITHIN'S DAY
STUDENT PRINCE
STUDY ALL SIDES
STUDY MEDICINE
STUDY THE FACTS
STUDY THE PLANS
STUDY THE STARS
STUFFED MARROW
STUFFED OLIVES
STUFFED TURKEY
STUMBLE ACROSS
STUNG TO ACTION

STUNTED GROWTH
ST. VITUS'S DANCE
SUBJECT MATTER
SUBJECT TO DUTY
SUB-MACHINE GUN
SUBMARINE BASE
SUBMARINE CREW
SUBMIT A REPORT
SUBURBAN HOUSE
SUBURBAN VILLA
SUCCESSFUL MAN
SUCCESS SYMBOL
SUCK ONE'S THUMB
SUDDEN DISLIKE
SUDDEN IMPULSE
SUDDEN THOUGHT
SUE FOR DAMAGES
SUE FOR DIVORCE
SUFFER A STROKE
SUFFER DAMAGES
SUFFERING CATS!
SUFFER TORMENT
SUGAR AND SPICE
SUGARED ALMOND
SUGARLESS DIET
SUGAR REFINERY
SUGGESTION BOX
SUICIDAL MANIA
SUITABLE MATCH
SUIT OF CLOTHES
SULPHURIC ACID
SULTAN'S PALACE
SUMMER HOLIDAY
SUMMER MADNESS
SUMMER SESSION
SUMMER VISITOR
SUMMIT MEETING
SUNBURN LOTION
SUNDAY CLOSING
SUNDAY CLOTHES
SUNDAY EVENING
SUNDAY MORNING
SUNDAY SERVICE
SUN-DRIED BRICK
SUNK IN DESPAIR
SUPERIOR BEING
SUPERIOR COURT
SUPERIOR FORCE
SUPREME SOVIET
SURE OF ONESELF
SURE OF SUCCESS

SURFACE RAIDER
SURGEON'S KNIFE
SURGICAL KNIFE
SURPLUS ENERGY
SURPRISE PARTY
SURPRISE VISIT
SURTAX BRACKET
SUSPECT A TRICK
SUSPENDER BELT
SUSTAINED NOTE
SWANEE WHISTLE
SWAP AND CHANGE
SWAY IN THE WIND
SWEATED LABOUR
SWEEPING CLAIM
SWEEPING GAINS
SWEEP THE BOARD
SWEEP THE FLOOR
SWEET CHESTNUT
SWEET LAVENDER
SWEET NOTHINGS
SWEET SURPRISE
SWEET THOUGHTS
SWEET TO THE EAR
SWELLING SAILS
SWELL THE RANKS
SWELTERING SUN
SWIM LIKE A FISH
SWIMMING MATCH
SWING ONE'S ARMS
SWORN EVIDENCE
SYDNEY HARBOUR
SYMPHONIC POEM

T—13
TABLEAU VIVANT
TABLE DELICACY
TABLE MOUNTAIN
TAKE A BACK SEAT
TAKE A BREATHER
TAKE ADVANTAGE
TAKE A FIRM HOLD
TAKE A HIGH TONE
TAKE A LONG TIME
TAKE AN AVERAGE
TAKE A SHORT CUT
TAKE A SNAPSHOT
TAKE BY THE HAND
TAKE DICTATION
TAKE EXCEPTION
TAKE FOR GOSPEL

TAKE GREAT CARE
TAKE IN BAD PART
TAKE IN LODGERS
TAKE IN WASHING
TAKE IT IN TURNS
TAKE IT TO COURT
TAKE IT TO HEART
TAKE LIBERTIES
TAKEN AT RANDOM
TAKEN DOWN A PEG
TAKEN FOR A RIDE
TAKE NO CHANCES
TAKE NO REFUSAL
TAKEN PRISONER
TAKEN UNAWARES
TAKE OFF WEIGHT
TAKE ONE'S FANCY
TAKE ONE'S LEAVE
TAKE ONE'S PLACE
TAKE ONE'S PULSE
TAKE ONE'S STAND
TAKE OUT TRUMPS
TAKE SANCTUARY
TAKE SERIOUSLY
TAKE SHORTHAND
TAKE SOUNDINGS
TAKE THE CREDIT
TAKE THE DAY OFF
TAKE THE MICKEY
TAKE THE PLEDGE
TAKE THE PLUNGE
TAKE THE SALUTE
TAKE THE STRAIN
TAKE THE TILLER
TAKE THE WATERS
TAKE TO ONE'S BED
TAKE TO THE ROAD
TALENT CONTEST
TALENT SPOTTER
TALK FOR EFFECT
TALK GIBBERISH
TALKING PARROT
TALK IN RIDDLES
TALK LIKE A FOOL
TALK OF THE TOWN
TALK OUT OF TURN
TALK PRIVATELY
TALK TO ONESELF
TANGIBLE ASSET
TANKARD OF BEER
TANKARD OF MILD

TAN THE HIDE OFF
TAPE RECORDING
TAP ONE'S CLARET
TAR AND FEATHER
TASTE FOR MUSIC
TAUGHT A LESSON
TAURUS THE BULL
TAWNY COLOURED
TAXABLE INCOME
TAX CONCESSION
TAX ONE'S MEMORY
TEACHING STAFF
TEACH SWIMMING
TEAM OF EXPERTS
TEA PLANTATION
TEAR OFF A STRIP
TEARS OF SORROW
TEAR TO RIBBONS
TEAR UP THE ROAD
TECHNICAL TERM
TELEGRAPH LINE
TELEGRAPH POLE
TELEGRAPH POST
TELEGRAPH WIRE
TELEPHONE BILL
TELEPHONE BOOK
TELEPHONE CALL
TELEPHONE LINE
TELEPHOTO LENS
TELEVISION FAN
TELEVISION SET
TELL A GOOD TALE
TELL A GOOD YARN
TELL AN UNTRUTH
TELL AT A GLANCE
TELLING EFFECT
TELL ME ANOTHER
TELL ONE'S BEADS
TEMPERATE ZONE
TEMPER THE WIND
TEMPLE OF DIANA
TEMPORAL POWER
TEMPORARY HOME
TEMPORARY LEAD
TEMPORARY LOAN
TEMPORARY RANK
TEMPORARY STOP
TEMPTING OFFER
TEMPT THE DEVIL
TENANT FOR LIFE
TEN CIGARETTES

TENDER FEELING
TENDER MERCIES
TENDER PASSION
TEN-DOLLAR BILL
TENEMENT HOUSE
TEN OF DIAMONDS
TENOR CLARINET
TENPENNY STAMP
TENPIN BOWLING
TENTH OF AUGUST
TEPID RESPONSE
TERMINAL POINT
TERRIBLE CHILD
TERRIBLE HAVOC
TERRIBLE TWINS
TERRIFIC STORM
TERRORIST ARMY
TERRORIST BAND
TEST-BAN TREATY
TEST CRICKETER
THANE OF CAWDOR
THANK GOODNESS!
THANKLESS TASK
THE ABDICATION
THEATRE CRITIC
THEATRE SISTER
THEATRE TICKET
THE BARBARIANS
THE BEST OF LUCK
THE BEST PEOPLE
THE BIG BAD WOLF
THE BLUE DANUBE
THE CHALLENGER
THE CHARLESTON
THE COLLECTION
THE COMMON HERD
THE DEEPEST DYE
THE DEUCE TO PAY
THE DEVIL TO PAY
THE DIRECT ROAD
THE DOLL'S HOUSE
THE EISTEDDFOD
THE EMBANKMENT
THE FIRST TRAIN
THE FIRST WATER
THE FOOTLIGHTS
THE GIDDY LIMIT
THE GOLDEN RULE
THE GONDOLIERS
THE GOVERNMENT
THE GUILLOTINE

THE HONOURABLE
THE INS AND OUTS
THE ISRAELITES
THE JOY STRINGS
THE KERRY DANCE
THE LAST SUPPER
THE LAW IS AN ASS
THE LIBERATION
THE LIGHT BLUES
THE MAGIC FLUTE
THE MAIN CHANCE
THE MATTERHORN
THE MERRY WIDOW
THE METROPOLIS
THE MILLENNIUM
THE MOODY BLUES
THE NOES HAVE IT
THE NORTH DOWNS
THE OLD BRIGADE
THE OLD COUNTRY
THE OPPOSITION
THE OTHER WOMAN
THE OTHER WORLD
THE QUAKER GIRL
THE RESISTANCE
THE ROUNDHEADS
THE SAME ANSWER
THE SCOTS GREYS
THE SECOND-RATE
THE SERPENTINE
THE SHALLOW END
THE SIMPLE LIFE
THE SMALL HOURS
THE SNOW MAIDEN
THE SOUTH DOWNS
THE SPOKEN WORD
THE THREE BEARS
THE TIME IS RIPE
THE UNDERWORLD
THE UNEMPLOYED
THE UNEXPECTED
THE UNFORESEEN
THE VANQUISHED
THE VIGILANTES
THE WATER-WAGON
THE WHITE HOUSE
THE WHOLE TRUTH
THE WHOLE WORLD
THE WILDERNESS
THE WILL TO LIVE
THE WINSLOW BOY

THE WIZARD OF OZ	THREE OF TRUMPS
THICK WITH DUST	THREEPENNY BIT
THIEF OF BAGDAD	THREE QUARTERS
THING OF BEAUTY	THREE SEVENTHS
THINK BETTER OF	THREE THOUSAND
THINK LITTLE OF	THRICE BLESSED
THINK STRAIGHT	THROES OF AGONY
THINK THE WORST	THROUGH A STRAW
THIRD DIVIDEND	THROW A LIGHT ON
THIRD DIVISION	THROW IN THE AIR
THIRD ENGINEER	THUMB ONE'S NOSE
THIRD OF AUGUST	THUMP THE TABLE
THIRD SYMPHONY	THURSDAY NIGHT
THIRTEEN HOURS	TICHBORNE CASE
THIRTEEN MILES	TICKET MACHINE
THIRTEEN TIMES	TICKET OF LEAVE
THIRTEEN WEEKS	TICKETS PLEASE
THIRTEEN YEARS	TIDAL MOVEMENT
THIRTY FIFTEEN	TIDE OF AFFAIRS
THIRTY GUINEAS	TIED UP IN KNOTS
THIRTY MINUTES	TIE WITH STRING
THIRTY-ONE DAYS	TILT AT THE RING
THIRTY PER CENT	TILT THE SCALES
THIRTY SECONDS	TIME AFTER TIME
THIS LITTLE PIG	TIME AND MOTION
THIS WEDNESDAY	TIME FOR DINNER
THOMAS À BECKET	TIME FOR SUPPER
THOMAS BEECHAM	TIMELY RETREAT
THOMAS CARLYLE	TIMELY WARNING
THORNY PROBLEM	TIME MARCHES ON
THORNY SUBJECT	TIME OF ARRIVAL
THOROUGH ROGUE	TIME OUT OF MIND
THOSE IN FAVOUR	TIMES OF STRESS
THOUSAND MILES	TIME TO REFLECT
THOUSAND YEARS	TIMID AS A MOUSE
THREAD A NEEDLE	TIMON OF ATHENS
THREAD ONE'S WAY	TINNED PEACHES
THREE AND A HALF	TIN OF SARDINES
THREE AND EIGHT	TIP-AND-RUN RAID
THREE AND SEVEN	TIP ONE THE WINK
THREE AND THREE	TIPPED THE WINK
THREE BAGS FULL	TIRED OF LIVING
THREE-DAY MATCH	TIRESOME CHORE
THREE DIAMONDS	TITLE OF HONOUR
THREE FEET TALL	TOAD IN THE HOLE
THREE-FOOT RULE	TO A HIGH DEGREE
THREE FURLONGS	TOASTED CHEESE
THREE-LINE WHIP	TO BE CONTINUED
THREE NO-TRUMPS	TO BE OR NOT TO BE
THREE OF HEARTS	TOGETHER AGAIN
THREE OF SPADES	TOKEN OF ESTEEM

TOLL OF THE ROAD	TRADING VESSEL
TOMATO KETCHUP	TRAFFIC ISLAND
TOMORROW NIGHT	TRAFFIC LIGHTS
TOMORROW WE DIE	TRAFFIC SIGNAL
TONGUE IN CHEEK	TRAFFIC WARDEN
TONGUE OF FLAME	TRAIL ONE'S COAT
TONGUE TWISTER	TRAINED SINGER
TONGUE WAGGING	TRAIN OF CAMELS
TOO GOOD BY HALF	TRAIN OF EVENTS
TOO GOOD TO LAST	TRAIN SPOTTING
TOO LITTLE ROOM	TRAIN TERMINUS
TOO MUCH PEPPER	TRAITOR'S DEATH
TOOTING COMMON	TRAM CONDUCTOR
TOO WEAK TO RISE	TRANQUIL SCENE
TOP OF THE CLASS	TRANSISTOR SET
TOP OF THE SCALE	TRANSPORT CAFÉ
TOP OF THE TABLE	TRAPEZE ARTIST
TOP-SECRET FILE	TRAVEL BY TRAIN
TORE OFF A STRIP	TRAVELLER'S JOY
TORRENT OF RAIN	TRAVEL LIGHTLY
TO SOME PURPOSE	TREACLE TOFFEE
TOSTI'S "GOODBYE"	TREAD THE STAGE
TOTAL DARKNESS	TREASURE CHEST
TO THE BACKBONE	TREASURE HOUSE
TOUCHING SCENE	TREASURE TRAIL
TOUCH-OF COLOUR	TREASURE TROVE
TOUCH OF GARLIC	TREASURY BENCH
TOUCH OF GENIUS	TREASURY BILLS
TOUCH OF NATURE	TREASURY BONDS
TOUCH OF THE SUN	TREAT LIKE DIRT
TOUCH ONE'S TOES	TREAT WITH CARE
TOUCH ON THE RAW	TREE OF LIBERTY
TOUCH THE HEART	TREMENDOUS JOB
TOUGH CUSTOMER	TRENCH WARFARE
TOURIST AGENCY	TREND OF EVENTS
TOURIST CENTRE	TRIAL AND ERROR
TOURIST SEASON	TRIAL MARRIAGE
TOURIST TICKET	TRIBAL WARFARE
TOURIST TROPHY	TRICK QUESTION
TOUR OF BRITAIN	TRICKY PROBLEM
TOUT FOR CUSTOM	TRIFLING ERROR
TOWER OF LONDON	TRIGGER FINGER
TOWN AND AROUND	TRILLING SOUND
TOY WITH AN IDEA	TRINITY CHURCH
TRACTOR DRIVER	TRIUMPHAL ARCH
TRADE DISCOUNT	TRIVIAL MATTER
TRADE ENTRANCE	TROPICAL FRUIT
TRADE MAGAZINE	TROPICAL PLANT
TRADE UNIONIST	TROPICAL STORM
TRADING CENTRE	TROTTING RACES
TRADING ESTATE	TROUSER BUTTON

TRUE CRITERION
TRUE STATEMENT
TRUE TO HIS SALT
TRUE TO ONESELF
TRUE TO THE LAST
TRUE UNTO DEATH
TRULY GRATEFUL
TRULY GREAT MAN
TRUMPET PLAYER
TRUST ACCOUNTS
TRUST TO CHANCE
TRUSTY SERVANT
TRYING JOURNEY
TRYSTING PLACE
TRYSTING POINT
TUBE OF MUSTARD
TUESDAY'S CHILD
TUNNEL THROUGH
TURKISH COFFEE
TURN A BLIND EYE
TURN CLOCKWISE
TURN DOWNWARDS
TURNED TO STONE
TURNING WICKET
TURN INSIDE OUT
TURN INTO MONEY
TURN OFF THE GAS
TURN OFF THE TAP
TURN OF THE CARD
TURN OF THE TIDE
TURN ON THE HEAT
TURN THE CORNER
TURN THE HEAT ON
TURN THE TABLES
TURN TO ACCOUNT
TURN TO THE LEFT
TURQUOISE BLUE
TWEED TROUSERS
TWELFTH LETTER
TWELFTH OF JULY
TWELFTH OF JUNE
TWELVE AND FIVE
TWELVE AND FOUR
TWELVE AND NINE
TWELVE DOLLARS
TWELVE GOOD MEN
TWELVE GUINEAS
TWELVE MINUTES
TWELVE PER CENT
TWELVE SQUARED
TWENTY DOLLARS

TWENTY GUINEAS
TWENTY MINUTES
TWENTY-ONE DAYS
TWENTY PER CENT
TWICE-TOLD TALE
TWILIGHT SLEEP
TWINKLING EYES
TWINKLING FEET
TWINKLING STAR
TWIST AND SHAKE
TWIST AND TWIRL
TWISTED NATURE
TWIST THE WORDS
TWO-EDGED SWORD
TWO-LETTER WORD
TWO-MASTED SHIP
TWO OF DIAMONDS
TWOPENNY STAMP
TWOS AND THREES
TWO-TIERED CAKE
TWO-WAY STRETCH
TWO-WAY TRAFFIC

U—13
UGLY SITUATION
ULTERIOR PLANS
ULTIMATE CAUSE
UMBRELLA STAND
UNABLE TO PLEAD
UNANIMOUS VOTE
UNARMED COMBAT
UNATTACHED MAN
UNBOLT THE DOOR
UNBOUNDED LOVE
UNBROKEN FRONT
UNBROKEN HORSE
UNCROWNED KING
UNDATED CHEQUE
UNDECLARED WAR
UNDER CONTRACT
UNDER-COVER MAN
UNDER MILK WOOD
UNDER ONE'S NOSE
UNDER ONE'S SKIN
UNDER ONE'S WING
UNDER PRESSURE
UNDER SENTENCE
UNDER STRENGTH
UNDER THE KNIFE
UNDER THE TABLE
UNDER THE THUMB

UNDER TRAINING
UNDER TWO FLAGS
UNDUE PRESSURE
UNEASY FEELING
UNEVEN CONTEST
UNEVEN SURFACE
UNFAIR PICTURE
UNFAIR VERDICT
UNFRIENDLY ACT
UNFURL THE FLAG
UNGUARDED HOUR
UNHAPPY REMARK
UNIFORM WEIGHT
UNIONIST PARTY
UNION JACK CLUB
UNITED IN DEATH
UNITED KINGDOM
UNITED NATIONS
UNITED WE STAND
UNIT OF CURRENT
UNIVERSAL AUNT
UNIVERSAL BUTT
UNIVERSITY RAG
UNKIND THOUGHT
UNKNOWN ORIGIN
UNKNOWN PERSON
UNLAWFUL ENTRY
UNLOCK THE DOOR
UNLUCKY CHOICE
UNLUCKY COLOUR
UNLUCKY IN LOVE
UNLUCKY NUMBER
UNLUCKY PERSON
UNPAID SERVANT
UNSECURED DEBT
UNSECURED LOAN
UNSEEN DANGERS
UNSKILLED WORK
UNSOLVED CRIME
UNTIMELY DEATH
UNTOLD NUMBERS
UNVEIL A STATUE
UNWANTED CHILD
UNWORTHY CAUSE
UP AT CAMBRIDGE
UP BOYS AND AT 'EM
UP IN THE CLOUDS
UP IN THE SADDLE
UPPER REGISTER
UPRIGHT FELLOW
UPRIGHT FIGURE

UPRIGHT PERSON
UP THE MOUNTAIN
UP TO HIS TRICKS
UP TO SOMETHING
UP TO THE ELBOWS
UP TO THE MINUTE
UPTURNED GLASS
UP WITH THE DAWN
UP WITH THE LARK
URBAN DISTRICT
USEFUL PURPOSE
USEFUL STAND-BY
USE OF BATHROOM
USE ONE'S BRAINS
USUAL CHANNELS
USUAL QUESTION
UTTER CONTEMPT
UTTER DEVOTION
UTTER NONSENSE

V—13
VACUUM CLEANER
VALENTINE CARD
VALENTINE'S DAY
VALE OF EVESHAM
VALIANT EFFORT
VALID ARGUMENT
VALID CONTRACT
VALLEY OF DEATH
VALUE FOR MONEY
VALUE ONE'S LIFE
VALUE RECEIVED
VANTAGE GROUND
VARIABLE WINDS
VARICOSE VEINS
VARIETY ARTIST
VARNISHING DAY
VAUDEVILLE ACT
VAULTING HORSE
VAULT OF HEAVEN
VEAL AND HAM PIE
VEER TO THE LEFT
VEGETABLE DIET
VEGETABLE DISH
VEGETABLE LIFE
VEGETABLE SOUP
VENERABLE BEDE
VENETIAN BLIND
VENETIAN GLASS
VENOMOUS SNAKE
VERBAL QUIBBLE

VERNAL EQUINOX
VERSATILE MIND
VERTICAL PLANE
VERY DIFFERENT
VESSEL OF WRATH
VETERAN TROOPS
VEXED IN SPIRIT
VEXED QUESTION
VICIOUS CIRCLE
VICIOUS GOSSIP
VICTOR HERBERT
VICTORIA CROSS
VICTORIA FALLS
VICTORIAN DAYS
VICTORY PARADE
VIENNESE GLASS
VIENNESE WALTZ
VILLAGE BEAUTY
VILLAGE CHURCH
VILLAGE GOSSIP
VILLAGE SCHOOL
VILLAGE SMITHY
VILLAGE SQUIRE
VILLAGE STREET
VINEGARY SMILE
VIOLATE THE LAW
VIOLENT ATTACK
VIOLENT CHANGE
VIOLENT EFFORT
VIOLENT NATURE
VIOLENT SPEECH
VIOLENT TEMPER
VIOLIN RECITAL
VIRGINIA STOCK
VIRGINIA WATER
VIRGINIA WOOLF
VIRGIN ISLANDS
VIRULENT ABUSE
VISIBLE EFFECT
VISITING HOURS
VISITING TERMS
VITAL QUESTION
VITAMIN TABLET
VOICE OF REASON
VOICE TRAINING
VOID OF FEELING
VOLLEY OF ABUSE
VOLUME CONTROL
VOLUME OF SMOKE
VOLUNTARY ARMY
VOLUNTARY GIFT

VOLUNTARY WORK
VOLUNTEER ARMY
VOTED A FAILURE
VOTE OF CENSURE
VOTES FOR WOMEN
VULGAR DISPLAY

W—13
WAG ONE'S FINGER
WAIT FOR ORDERS
WAIT PATIENTLY
WALK BACKWARDS
WALKING-ON PART
WALK INTO A TRAP
WALK THE BOARDS
WALK UP AND DOWN
WALLOW IN MONEY
WALLS HAVE EARS
WALTER PIDGEON
WALTER RALEIGH
WANDERING MIND
WANTED ON BOARD
WANT OF COURAGE
WANT OF THOUGHT
WAR DEPARTMENT
WARDOUR STREET
WARLIKE HABITS
WARLIKE MANNER
WARLIKE PEOPLE
WARM RECEPTION
WARNING NOTICE
WARNING SIGNAL
WAR TO THE DEATH
WAR TO THE KNIFE
WASHING POWDER
WASH ONE'S HANDS
WASH THE DISHES
WASPISH NATURE
WASTE OF BREATH
WATCH AND CHAIN
WATCH EXPENSES
WATCHING BRIEF
WATCH ONE'S STEP
WATCH THE BIRDY
WATCH THE CLOCK
WATERING PLACE
WATER SHORTAGE
WATER SOFTENER
WATLING STREET
WAVE OF FEELING

WAVE OF THE HAND	WHATEVER YOU DO
WAY OF ALL FLESH	WHIRLING ROUND
WAY OF THE CROSS	WHISKY AND SODA
WAY OF THE WORLD	WHISPER SOFTLY
WAY OF THINKING	WHITE AS A GHOST
WAYSIDE TAVERN	WHITE AS A SHEET
WAY TO THE STARS	WHITE AS MARBLE
WEAK AS A KITTEN	WHITE ELEPHANT
WEAK CHARACTER	WHITE FLANNELS
WEAK IN THE HEAD	WHITE HORSE INN
WEAK ON HIS PINS	WHITE OF THE EYE
WEARING TIGHTS	WHITE SAPPHIRE
WEATHER BUREAU	WHOLE OF THE DAY
WEATHER EXPERT	WHOLESOME FOOD
WEATHER REPORT	WHOOPING COUGH
WEB OF INTRIGUE	WIDE INTERESTS
WEDGWOOD CHINA	WIDE KNOWLEDGE
WEDNESDAY WEEK	WIDE OF THE MARK
WEED THE GARDEN	WIDE PUBLICITY
WEEK AFTER NEXT	WIDOW'S PENSION
WEEK AFTER WEEK	WIELD THE BATON
WEEK IN, WEEK OUT	WILD AND WOOLLY
WEEKLY ACCOUNT	WILD-CAT STRIKE
WEEKLY PAYMENT	WILDEST DREAMS
WEEK OF SUNDAYS	WILFUL SILENCE
WEEKS AND WEEKS	WILLIAM CAXTON
WEEPING WILLOW	WILLIAM COWPER
WEIGH THINGS UP	WILLIAM MORRIS
WEIGHTY MATTER	WILLIAM WALTON
WELCOME RELIEF	WILLING HELPER
WELFARE CENTRE	WILLING WORKER
WELFARE WORKER	WILL OF ONE'S OWN
WELL-AIMED SHOT	WILLOW PATTERN
WELL BROUGHT UP	WILLOWY FIGURE
WELL-KNIT FRAME	WIMPOLE STREET
WELL PRESERVED	WINDING COURSE
WELL-SPENT LIFE	WINDING STAIRS
WELL THOUGHT OF	WINDOW CLEANER
WELL TO THE FORE	WINDOW DRESSER
WELL TURNED OUT	WINDOW SHOPPER
WELSH REGIMENT	WINDSOR CASTLE
WENT LIKE A BOMB	WINED AND DINED
WESTERLY WINDS	WIN FIRST PRIZE
WESTERN CHURCH	WING COMMANDER
WESTERN DESERT	WINGED MONSTER
WESTERN EUROPE	WINGED VICTORY
WESTERN POWERS	WINNIE THE POOH
WEST HAM UNITED	WINNING COUPON
WEST OF ENGLAND	WINNING DOUBLE
WEST SIDE STORY	WINNING HAZARD
WHAT DO YOU KNOW?	WINNING NUMBER

WINNING STREAK
WINNING STROKE
WINNING TICKET
WINNING TREBLE
WINTER GARDENS
WINTER HOLIDAY
WINTER SESSION
WINTER VISITOR
WINTER WEATHER
WIN THE JACKPOT
WINTRY WEATHER
WIPE OFF THE MAP
WIPE ONE'S HANDS
WIRED FOR SOUND
WIRELESS WAVES
WISE AS SOLOMON
WISH OTHERWISE
WITH A BAD GRACE
WITH A FLOURISH
WITH A HIGH HAND
WITH AUTHORITY
WITH BOTH HANDS
WITH CERTAINTY
WITHERING LOOK
WITHIN EARSHOT
WITHIN HEARING
WITHIN MEASURE
WITH ONE ACCORD
WITHOUT A DOUBT
WITHOUT A HITCH
WITHOUT A RIVAL
WITHOUT CHARGE
WITHOUT MALICE
WITHOUT NOTICE
WITHOUT NUMBER
WITHOUT REASON
WITHOUT REGARD
WITHOUT REMARK
WITHOUT WARMTH
WITHOUT WEIGHT
WITH RESTRAINT
WITH THE LID OFF
WITH THE STREAM
WOLF AT THE DOOR
WOLF IN THE FOLD
WONDERFUL NEWS
WOOD ENGRAVING
WOOLLEN GLOVES
WORD IN ONE'S EAR
WORD OF COMFORT
WORD OF COMMAND

WORD OF WARNING
WORDS AND MUSIC
WORDS OF WISDOM
WORD TO THE WISE
WORDY ARGUMENT
WORK LIKE MAGIC
WORKMEN'S TRAIN
WORK OF FICTION
WORK ONE'S WAY UP
WORK THE ORACLE
WORK UP A LATHER
WORK WITH A WILL
WORLD CHAMPION
WORLDLY WISDOM
WORLD OF NATURE
WORLD PREMIÈRE
WORLD-WIDE FAME
WORM ONE'S WAY IN
WORN TO A SHADOW
WORSE AND WORSE
WORSE THAN EVER
WORST POSSIBLE
WORTH A FORTUNE
WORTH A MILLION
WORTHLESS JUNK
WORTH MILLIONS
WORTH ONE'S SALT
WORTH VISITING
WRAPPING PAPER
WRITE AT LENGTH
WRITE IN PENCIL
WRITE ONE'S NAME
WRITHE IN AGONY
WRITTEN ANSWER
WRITTEN MATTER
WRITTEN PERMIT
WRITTEN SPEECH
WRONG APPROACH
WRONG DECISION
WRONG TENDENCY

X—13
X-RAY APPARATUS

Y—13
YARDS AND YARDS
YEAR AFTER YEAR
YEAR IN, YEAR OUT
YEHUDI MENUHIN
YELLOW BUNTING
YELLOW WAGTAIL

YELLOW WITH AGE
YEOMAN SERVICE
YORKSHIRE POST
YOUNG CHILDREN
YOUNGER SISTER
YOUNGEST CHILD
YOUNG HOOLIGAN
YOUR NUMBER'S UP
YOUTH MOVEMENT

Z—13
ZEBRA CROSSING

A—14
A BOOK AT BEDTIME
ABOVE CRITICISM
ABOVE SUSPICION
ABOVE THE GROUND
A BOW AT A VENTURE
ABRAHAM LINCOLN
ABRUPT ENTRANCE
ABSOLUTE DECREE
ABSOLUTE MASTER
ABSOLUTE PIFFLE
ABSTRACT DESIGN
ABSTRACT NUMBER
ABUSE ONE'S POWER
ACADEMIC DEGREE
ACADEMIC MANNER
ACCESSIBLE SPOT
ACCIDENT POLICY
ACCORDING TO LAW
ACCORDION PLEAT
ACCUSATIVE CASE
ACCUSING FINGER
ACHIEVE ONE'S AIM
ACHIEVE VICTORY
ACHILLES' TENDON
ACROSS THE OCEAN
ACROSS THE RIVER
ACT ACCORDINGLY
ACT AS A LANDMARK
ACT AS GUARANTOR
ACT IMMEDIATELY
ACT IN GOOD FAITH
ACTION FOR LIBEL
ACTION PAINTING
ACTION STATIONS
ACTIVE INTEREST
ACTIVE STRENGTH
ACT THE BUSYBODY

ADDRESS THE BALL
ADDRESS UNKNOWN
ADD TO ONE'S GRIEF
ADELPHI TERRACE
ADELPHI THEATRE
ADEQUATE AMOUNT
ADEQUATE INCOME
ADEQUATE REASON
ADJUST THE HANDS
ADMIRALTY CHART
ADMIRALTY HOUSE
ADMIT THE CHARGE
ADOPTION PAPERS
ADVANCE BOOKING
ADVANCING YEARS
ADVENTURE STORY
ADVERSE BALANCE
AESTHETIC SENSE
AESTHETIC TASTE
AFFAIRE DE COEUR
AFFAIR OF HONOUR
AFFAIRS OF STATE
AFFECTED MANNER
AFFECTED SPEECH
AFFILIATED BODY
AFTER BREAKFAST
AFTER CHRISTMAS
AFTER-DINNER NAP
AFTER LIGHTS-OUT
AFTER THE DELUGE
AGAINST ALL ODDS
AGAINST THE ODDS
AGAINST THE TIDE
AGAINST THE WIND
AGATHA CHRISTIE
AGE OF IGNORANCE
AGE OF INNOCENCE
AGREE IN MEANING
AIM AT THE TARGET
AIRBORNE FORCES
AIRBORNE TROOPS
AIRING CUPBOARD
AIR OF GRIEVANCE
AIR ONE'S OPINION
AIR PHOTOGRAPHY
AIR-RAID SHELTER
AIR-RAID WARNING
AIR VICE-MARSHAL
ALBERT EINSTEIN
ALBERT MEMORIAL
ALCOCK AND BROWN

ALCOHOLIC DRINK	APPEAR IN PUBLIC
ALDWYCH THEATRE	APPLE CHARLOTTE
ALEXANDRE DUMAS	APPLE OF DISCORD
ALFRED TENNYSON	APPLE OF ONE'S EYE
ALFRED THE GREAT	APPLES AND PEARS
ALL GUNS BLAZING	APPLIED PHYSICS
ALL HANDS ON DECK	APPLIED SCIENCE
ALLIED LANDINGS	APPLY THE BRAKES
ALL IN A DAY'S WORK	APPROVED SCHOOL
ALL-IN WRESTLING	APRIL THE EIGHTH
ALL KINDS OF WAYS	APRIL THE FOURTH
ALLOTTED SPHERE	APRIL THE SECOND
ALL OVER THE SHOP	ARABIC NUMERALS
ALL-ROUND PLAYER	ARBITER OF TASTE
ALL THE KING'S MEN	ARMCHAIR CRITIC
ALL WELL AND GOOD	ARMS OF MORPHEUS
ALMIGHTY DOLLAR	ARMY CADET FORCE
ALPES MARITIMES	ARMY MANOEUVRES
ALSACE LORRAINE	AROUND THE WORLD
AMATEUR COMPANY	ARRANT NONSENSE
AMERICAN ACCENT	ARROGANT MANNER
AMERICAN INDIAN	ART FOR ART'S SAKE
AMERICAN LEGION	ARTFUL CUSTOMER
AMERICAN PATROL	ARTICLE OF FAITH
AMERICAN SCHOOL	ARTIFICIAL HAND
AMERICAN TROOPS	ARTIFICIAL LAKE
AMMUNITION DUMP	ARTIFICIAL LIMB
AMONGST FRIENDS	ARTIFICIAL POND
ANCIENT BRITAIN	ARTIFICIAL SILK
ANCIENT HISTORY	ARTISTIC EFFECT
ANCIENT LINEAGE	ARTISTIC EFFORT
ANCIENT MARINER	ART OF REASONING
ANDAMAN ISLANDS	AS A GENERAL RULE
ANDREW CARNEGIE	AS BLACK AS NIGHT
ANGINA PECTORIS	AS BRAVE AS A LION
ANGLICAN CHURCH	ASCENDING ORDER
ANIMAL CRACKERS	ASCENDING SCALE
ANNUAL TURNOVER	AS DEAD AS MUTTON
ANNUS MIRABILIS	AS DRUNK AS A LORD
ANONYMOUS DONOR	AS FAST AS YOU CAN
ANOTHER OPINION	AS FIT AS A FIDDLE
ANOTHER VERSION	AS FRESH AS PAINT
ANSWER ONE'S NAME	AS GOOD AS A FEAST
ANTARCTIC OCEAN	AS GREEN AS GRASS
ANY SUGGESTIONS?	AS HARD AS A STONE
ANYTHING TO COME	ASK FORGIVENESS
APARTMENT HOUSE	AS MAD AS A HATTER
APARTMENT TO LET	AS PALE AS A GHOST
APPEAL FOR FUNDS	AS PLAIN AS PLAIN
APPEAL FOR MERCY	AS SAFE AS HOUSES
APPEAL TO REASON	ASSENTING PARTY

AS SMART AS PAINT
ASSOCIATION CUP
AS SOFT AS BUTTER
AS SOFT AS VELVET
AS SOUND AS A BELL
AS SWEET AS SUGAR
AS THE CASE MAY BE
AS THE CROW FLIES
AS TIGHT AS A DRUM
AT DAGGERS DRAWN
ATHLETIC GROUND
ATHLETIC SPORTS
ATLANTIC FLIGHT
ATLANTIC ROLLER
ATLAS MOUNTAINS
AT ONE FELL SWOOP
AT ONE'S DISPOSAL
A TOWN LIKE ALICE
ATTACKING FIELD
ATTACK OF NERVES
ATTEMPT TOO MUCH
AT THE RIGHT TIME
AT THE THRESHOLD
AT THIS JUNCTURE
ATTITUDE OF MIND
AUF WIEDERSEHEN
AUGUST THE FIFTH
AUGUST THE FIRST
AUGUST THE NINTH
AUGUST THE SIXTH
AUGUST THE TENTH
AUGUST THE THIRD
AUGUSTUS CAESAR
AURORA BOREALIS
AUSTRALIA HOUSE
AUSTRALIAN BUSH
AUTOGRAPH ALBUM
AUTOMATIC RIFLE
AUTOMOBILE CLUB
AVERAGE ABILITY
AVIATION SPIRIT
AVOID A DECISION
AVOID BLOODSHED
AWKWARD SILENCE

B—14
BABES IN THE WOOD
BACHELOR OF ARTS
BACK-SEAT DRIVER
BACKS TO THE WALL
BACKWARD GLANCE

BACONIAN THEORY
BAD CIRCULATION
BAD FOR BUSINESS
BAD HANDWRITING
BAD HOUSEKEEPER
BADMINTON COURT
BAD VENTILATION
BAGATELLE TABLE
BALANCED BUDGET
BALANCE OF POWER
BALANCE OF TRADE
BALANCING TRICK
BALL AT ONE'S FEET
BALLET MISTRESS
BALLIOL COLLEGE
BALL OF THE THUMB
BALLOON BARRAGE
BALMORAL CASTLE
BALTIC EXCHANGE
BANANA FRITTERS
BANDED TOGETHER
BAND OF BROTHERS
BAND OF PILGRIMS
BANE OF ONE'S LIFE
BANGERS AND MASH
BANKING ACCOUNT
BANK OF SCOTLAND
BANNER HEADLINE
BANQUETING HALL
BARE-BACK RIDING
BARE ESSENTIALS
BARELY POSSIBLE
BARGAIN COUNTER
BARKIS IS WILLIN'
BAR OF CHOCOLATE
BARRAGE BALLOON
BAR THE ENTRANCE
BASIC SUBSTANCE
BASKET-BALL TEAM
BATHING COSTUME
BATHING MACHINE
BATHROOM SCALES
BATTING AVERAGE
BATTLE OF NASEBY
BATTLE STATIONS
BAYEUX TAPESTRY
BEACH INSPECTOR
BE-ALL AND END-ALL
BEAR ALLEGIANCE
BEAT GENERATION
BEAT ONE'S BRAINS

BEAT ONE'S BREAST
BEAT THE BIG DRUM
BEAT TO A FRAZZLE
BEAUTIFUL VOICE
BEAUTIFUL WOMAN
BECOME A CITIZEN
BECOME AIRBORNE
BECOME A PATIENT
BECOME CHAMPION
BEDROOM SLIPPER
BEDSIDE READING
BED-SITTING ROOM
BEFORE AND AFTER
BEFORE AND SINCE
BEFORE DAYLIGHT
BEFORE MIDNIGHT
BEFORE ONE'S EYES
BEFORE ONE'S TIME
BEFORE THE JUDGE
BEG FORGIVENESS
BEG THE QUESTION
BEHIND ONE'S BACK
BEHIND SCHEDULE
BEHIND THE CLOCK
BEHIND THE TIMES
BEHIND THE WHEEL
BELGRAVE SQUARE
BELIEVE IT OR NOT
BELLE OF NEW YORK
BELLE OF THE BALL
BELOW THE GROUND
BENCH OF BISHOPS
BENEATH ACCOUNT
BENEFIT SOCIETY
BENEVOLENT FUND
BEREFT OF REASON
BERKELEY SQUARE
BERLIN QUESTION
BESEECHING LOOK
BESIDE THE POINT
BEST DRESSED MAN
BEST INTENTIONS
BEST LEG FORWARD
BEST OF THE BUNCH
BETSEY TROTWOOD
BETTER FEELINGS
BETTER THAN EVER
BETTER THAN MOST
BETTER THOUGHTS
BETWEEN FRIENDS
BETWEEN THE EYES

BEWARE OF THE DOG
BEYOND ALL DOUBT
BEYOND HUMAN AID
BEYOND REPROACH
BEYOND THE GRAVE
BEYOND THE LIMIT
BID GOOD MORNING
BIFOCAL GLASSES
BIG-GAME HUNTING
BIGGEST PORTION
BIJOU RESIDENCE
BILLIARD MARKER
BILLIARD PLAYER
BILLIARD SALOON
BILL OF EXCHANGE
BIRD OF PARADISE
BIRTH OF A NATION
BISHOP AUCKLAND
BITE ONE'S TONGUE
BIT OF A COME-DOWN
BIT OF A NUISANCE
BITTER FEELINGS
BITTER MEMORIES
BITTER STRUGGLE
BITTER THOUGHTS
BITUMINOUS COAL
BLACK AS THUNDER
BLACK-EYED SUSIE
BLACK IN THE FACE
BLACKPOOL TOWER
BLACK STOCKINGS
BLANK CARTRIDGE
BLASTING POWDER
BLAZING INFERNO
BLEACHING AGENT
BLENHEIM ORANGE
BLENHEIM PALACE
BLESS THIS HOUSE
BLIND IGNORANCE
BLIND REASONING
BLOCK AND TACKLE
BLOCK OF OFFICES
BLOOD POISONING
BLOUSE AND SKIRT
BLOW EVERYTHING
BLOW HOT AND COLD
BLOWING BUBBLES
BLOW SMOKE-RINGS
BLOW THE EXPENSE
BLOW THE MAN DOWN
BLUE-COAT SCHOOL

BLUE SPECTACLES	BREAKFAST TABLE
BLUNT STATEMENT	BREAKNECK SPEED
BOA CONSTRICTOR	BREAK NEW GROUND
BOARDING SCHOOL	BREAK ONE'S HEART
BOARD OF CONTROL	BREAK THE CORDON
BOARD OF INQUIRY	BREAK THE RECORD
BOARD RESIDENCE	BREAK THE THREAD
BODILY MOVEMENT	BREAST THE WAVES
BODILY STRENGTH	BREATHE HEAVILY
BODILY WEAKNESS	BREATHE REVENGE
BODY OF SOLDIERS	BREATHING SPACE
BOILED POTATOES	BREATH OF SEA AIR
BOLD EXPERIMENT	BREATH OF SPRING
BONNIE SCOTLAND	BREEDING GROUND
BOOK DEPARTMENT	BREWERS' COMPANY
BOOK OF NONSENSE	BRIEF ENCOUNTER
BOOK OF PROVERBS	BRIEF INTERLUDE
BOOK OF THE MONTH	BRIGHT AND EARLY
BOOK PRODUCTION	BRIGHT AS SILVER
BOOMING ECONOMY	BRIGHT PROSPECT
BOON COMPANIONS	BRIGHT'S DISEASE
BORDERLINE CASE	BRIGITTE BARDOT
BORDER MINSTREL	BRIMFUL OF IDEAS
BORDER REGIMENT	BRING GOOD CHEER
BORDER SKIRMISH	BRING IN A PROFIT
BOROUGH COUNCIL	BRING INTO BEING
BORROWED PLUMES	BRING INTO FOCUS
BOSTON CRACKERS	BRING TO ACCOUNT
BOSTON TEA PARTY	BRING TO JUSTICE
BOTTLE OF BRANDY	BRING TO THE BOIL
BOTTLE OF BUBBLY	BRING TO THE FORE
BOTTLE OF CLARET	BRING UP THE REAR
BOTTLE OF SCOTCH	BRISTOL CHANNEL
BOTTLE OF SWEETS	BRISTOL FASHION
BOTTLE OF WHISKY	BRITANNIA METAL
BOTTOM OF THE BAG	BRITISH COUNCIL
BOTTOM OF THE SEA	BRITISH EMBASSY
BOUGHT FOR A SONG	BRITISH SUBJECT
BOUT OF SICKNESS	BRITTLE AS GLASS
BOWLING AVERAGE	BROAD IN THE BEAM
BOWL OF CHERRIES	BROAD SHOULDERS
BOXER REBELLION	BROADWAY MELODY
BOYS WILL BE BOYS	BROKEN CONTRACT
BRACING CLIMATE	BROKEN MARRIAGE
BRADSHAW'S GUIDE	BROKE THE WICKET
BREACH OF ORDERS	BROKE TO THE WIDE
BREAD AND BUTTER	BRONCHIAL TUBES
BREAD AND CHEESE	BROOKLYN BRIDGE
BREAD AND SCRAPE	BROOK NO REFUSAL
BREADFRUIT TREE	BROTHER OFFICER
BREAKFAST IN BED	BROTHERS IN ARMS

BROUGHT TO LIGHT
BRUSH ONE'S TEETH
BRUSSELS CARPET
BUBBLING STREAM
BUCKET AND SPADE
BUILDING BRICKS
BULLDOG COURAGE
BULLET-PROOF CAR
BUMP OF LOCALITY
BUNCH OF BANANAS
BUNCH OF FLOWERS
BUNDLE OF NERVES
BURIED TREASURE
BURN AT THE STAKE
BURNHAM BEECHES
BURNISHED BRASS
BURNT SACRIFICE
BURNT TO A CINDER
BURST INTO FLAME
BURST INTO TEARS
BURST ONE'S BONDS
BURST THE BUBBLE
BURY ONE'S TALENT
BURY THE HATCHET
BUS CONDUCTRESS
BUSINESS CAREER
BUSINESS LETTER
BUSINESS MATTER
BUSINESS ON HAND
BUSINESS TYCOON
BUSMAN'S HOLIDAY
BUTTONS AND BOWS
BUY A PIG IN A POKE
BY A LONG STRETCH
BY PRESCRIPTION
BY THE SAME TOKEN

C—14
CABBAGE LETTUCE
CABINET MEETING
CABINET PUDDING
CAGE ME A PEACOCK
CALAMINE LOTION
CALCIUM CARBIDE
CALCULATED ODDS
CALCULATED RISK
CALF'S-FOOT JELLY
CALLED TO THE BAR
CALL FOR A REPORT
CALLING ALL CARS
CALL IN QUESTION

CALL OFF THE DOGS
CALM REFLECTION
CAMBRIDGE COACH
CAMP COMMANDANT
CAMPHORATED OIL
CAMPING HOLIDAY
CANADIAN POLICE
CANNING FACTORY
CANTERBURY BELL
CANTERBURY LAMB
CAPABLE OF PROOF
CAPE OF GOOD HOPE
CAPITAL OFFENCE
CAPITAL OF ITALY
CAPITAL OF SPAIN
CAPTAIN BOYCOTT
CAPTIVE BALLOON
CARAVAN HOLIDAY
CARBON MONOXIDE
CARDEW ROBINSON
CARDIAC DISEASE
CARDINAL NEWMAN
CARDINAL NUMBER
CARDINAL POINTS
CARDINAL VIRTUE
CARDINAL WOLSEY
CAREFUL THOUGHT
CARMELITE ORDER
CARPET SLIPPERS
CARRY ONE'S POINT
CARTRIDGE PAPER
CASEMENT WINDOW
CASH ON DELIVERY
CAST ASPERSIONS
CAST INTO PRISON
CAST-IRON EXCUSE
CASTLE IN THE AIR
CASTLES IN SPAIN
CAST SHEEP'S EYES
CASUAL LABOURER
CASUAL OBSERVER
CATCH ONE'S DEATH
CATCH RED-HANDED
CATCH THE BREATH
CATHEDRAL CLOSE
CATHERINE BOYLE
CATHERINE WHEEL
CATHODE-RAY TUBE
CAT ON HOT BRICKS
CAT OUT OF THE BAG
CAUGHT IN A STORM

CAUGHT IN THE ACT
CAUGHT ON THE HOP
CAUGHT STEALING
CAUGHT UNAWARES
CAULIFLOWER EAR
CAUSE AND EFFECT
CAUSE A STOPPAGE
CAUSE CONFUSION
CAUSE FOR REGRET
CAUTIONARY TALE
CAVALRY OFFICER
CELESTIAL BLISS
CELESTIAL GLOBE
CENTRAL AMERICA
CENTRAL HEATING
CENTRAL STATION
CERTAIN VICTORY
CHAINED TO A DESK
CHAIN OF COMMAND
CHAIN OF THOUGHT
CHAIR THE WINNER
CHALK AND CHEESE
CHALLENGE ROUND
CHAMPAGNE GLASS
CHAMPAGNE LUNCH
CHAMPION GOLFER
CHAMPION JOCKEY
CHANCERY OFFICE
CHANGE OF BELIEF
CHANGE OF COURSE
CHANGE ONE'S LUCK
CHANGE ONE'S MIND
CHANGE ONE'S NAME
CHANGE ONE'S TUNE
CHANGE ONE'S WAYS
CHANGE PARTNERS
CHANGE THE ORDER
CHANGE THE VENUE
CHANNEL ISLANDS
CHANNEL STEAMER
CHANNEL SWIMMER
CHAPTER HEADING
CHARACTER ACTOR
CHARACTER STUDY
CHARCOAL BURNER
CHARGE THE EARTH
CHARITABLE DEED
CHARITABLE GIFT
CHARITY MEETING
CHARLES CHAPLIN
CHARLES DICKENS

CHARLES GARVICE
CHARLIE CHESTER
CHARLOTTE RUSSE
CHARMING FELLOW
CHARMING MANNER
CHARRED REMAINS
CHASE ME CHARLIE
CHEAP EXCURSION
CHECKING SYSTEM
CHEER TO THE ECHO
CHEESE SANDWICH
CHEMICAL CHANGE
CHEMICAL ENERGY
CHEMISTRY CLASS
CHESHIRE CHEESE
CHESTNUT SUNDAY
CHEST OF DRAWERS
CHEST PROTECTOR
CHEWING TOBACCO
CHICKEN IN ASPIC
CHIEF CONSTABLE
CHIEF EXECUTIVE
CHIEF INSPECTOR
CHILD ALLOWANCE
CHILD OF FORTUNE
CHILDREN'S NURSE
CHILDREN'S PARTY
CHILDREN'S STORY
CHINESE CRACKER
CHINESE LANTERN
CHINESE LAUNDRY
CHINESE TORTURE
CHIPPING BARNET
CHIPPING NORTON
CHOCOLATE CREAM
CHOCOLATE WAFER
CHOPPED PARSLEY
CHRISTMAS BONUS
CHRISTMAS CAROL
CHRISTMAS CHEER
CHRISTMAS DAISY
CHRISTMAS PARTY
CHRISTOPHER FRY
CHROMATIC SCALE
CHRONIC INVALID
CHUCK OVERBOARD
CHUCK UP ONE'S JOB
CHURCH ASSEMBLY
CHURCH DOCTRINE
CHURCH MILITANT
CHURCH PROPERTY

CIGARETTE PAPER
CIRCLE THE EARTH
CIRCULAR COURSE
CIRCULAR LETTER
CIRCULAR TICKET
CITY MAGISTRATE
CIVILIZED WORLD
CIVIL LIBERTIES
CLAIM ATTENTION
CLAIM THE REWARD
CLAP INTO PRISON
CLARENDON PRESS
CLASH OF CYMBALS
CLASS CONSCIOUS
CLASSICAL LATIN
CLASSICAL MUSIC
CLASSICAL TASTE
CLASSIC EXAMPLE
CLASSIC QUALITY
CLASSICS MASTER
CLASS PREJUDICE
CLEAN AS A NEW PIN
CLEAN ONE'S TEETH
CLEANSING CREAM
CLEAN THE SILVER
CLEAR AS CRYSTAL
CLEAR STATEMENT
CLEAR THE GROUND
CLEAR THE THROAT
CLEMENT WEATHER
CLERICAL COLLAR
CLERICAL DUTIES
CLERICAL WORKER
CLICK ONE'S HEELS
CLIMB A MOUNTAIN
CLIMBING PRICES
CLOAK AND DAGGER
CLOCKWORK TRAIN
CLOISTERED LIFE
CLOSE AN ACCOUNT
CLOSE ATTENTION
CLOSELY GUARDED
CLOSE ONE'S MOUTH
CLOSE PROXIMITY
CLOSE THE WINDOW
CLOSE TO THE WIND
CLOTHING COUPON
CLOUD FORMATION
CLOUT ON THE HEAD
CLUB MEMBERSHIP
CLUBS ARE TRUMPS

CLUSTER OF STARS
CLUTCH AT STRAWS
COACH AND HORSES
COALING STATION
COARSE LANGUAGE
COASTAL BATTERY
COASTAL COMMAND
COASTAL EROSION
COCK OF THE NORTH
COCKTAIL SHAKER
COFFEE STRAINER
COHERENT MANNER
COIN OF THE REALM
COLLAR ATTACHED
COLLECTED POEMS
COLLECTIVE FARM
COLLECTIVE NOUN
COLLECT ONESELF
COLLECTOR'S ITEM
COLLEGE PUDDING
COLLEGE STUDENT
COLONIAL OFFICE
COLONIAL SYSTEM
COLORADO BEETLE
COLOUR QUESTION
COLOUR SERGEANT
COMBINED EFFORT
COME BACK TO ERIN
COME DOWNSTAIRS
COMEDY OF ERRORS
COME FACE TO FACE
COME FROM BEHIND
COME FULL CIRCLE
COME-HITHER LOOK
COME INTO FAVOUR
COME ON THE SCENE
COME ROUND AGAIN
COME SECOND BEST
COME TO A DEAD-END
COME TO THE FRONT
COME TO THE POINT
COMFORTABLY OFF
COMIC INTERLUDE
COMING OF ARTHUR
COMING-OUT PARTY
COMMANDING LEAD
COMMAND OF WORDS
COMMAND RESPECT
COMMAND SILENCE
COMMAND SUPPORT
COMMERCIAL ROOM

COMMIT A FAUX PAS
COMMIT FOR TRIAL
COMMIT HARA-KIRI
COMMITTEE STAGE
COMMIT TO MEMORY
COMMIT TO PRISON
COMMON ANCESTOR
COMMON COURTESY
COMMON CURRENCY
COMMON ENTRANCE
COMMON FRONTIER
COMMON HUMANITY
COMMON INFORMER
COMMON INTEREST
COMMON MULTIPLE
COMMON NUISANCE
COMMON OR GARDEN
COMMON PARLANCE
COMMON PRACTICE
COMMON PROPERTY
COMMON SERJEANT
COMMUNION BREAD
COMMUNION TABLE
COMMUNIST PARTY
COMMUNITY CHEST
COMPANION PIECE
COMPANY MANNERS
COMPANY MATTERS
COMPANY MEETING
COMPANY OFFICER
COMPASS BEARING
COMPASS READING
COMPLEAT ANGLER
COMPLETE ANSWER
COMPLETE CHANGE
COMPLETE FIASCO
COMPONENT PARTS
COMPOSED MANNER
COMPOSE ONESELF
COMPULSORY LOAN
COMRADES IN ARMS
CONCEALED DRIVE
CONCERT PIANIST
CONDEMN TO DEATH
CONDUCT A SEARCH
CONFER A BENEFIT
CONFERENCE ROOM
CONFIRMED ENEMY
CONFIRMED HABIT
CONIFEROUS TREE
CONJUGAL RIGHTS

CONJURING TRICK
CONQUERING HERO
CONSIGN TO EARTH
CONSTANT READER
CONSTANT STRAIN
CONSTANT SUPPLY
CONSULTING ROOM
CONSUMER DEMAND
CONTAIN ONESELF
CONTINUITY GIRL
CONTRACT BRIDGE
CONTRARY ADVICE
CONTROLLED RENT
CONTROL ONESELF
CONVERSION LOAN
CONVEY A MEANING
COOKING UTENSIL
COPPER SULPHATE
COPS AND ROBBERS
COPYHOLD ESTATE
CORDIAL WELCOME
CORNFLOWER BLUE
CORNISH RIVIERA
CORPORATION TAX
CORRUGATED IRON
COTTON EXCHANGE
COTTON INDUSTRY
COUNCIL CHAMBER
COUNCIL MEETING
COUNCIL OF STATE
COUNTLESS TIMES
COUNT ONE'S BEADS
COUNT ONE'S MONEY
COUNTRY BUMPKIN
COUNTRY COTTAGE
COUNTRY RETREAT
COUNTY PALATINE
COURSE OF ACTION
COURSE OF EVENTS
COURTING COUPLE
COURT OF INQUIRY
COURT OF JUSTICE
COURT PROCEDURE
COVERED WITH ICE
COVERING LETTER
CRACK OF THE WHIP
CRADLE SNATCHER
CRAMP ONE'S STYLE
CRANBERRY SAUCE
CRASH ONE'S GEARS
CRASS IGNORANCE

CRASS STUPIDITY
CREAM OF SOCIETY
CREATE AN EFFECT
CREATE AN UPROAR
CREATE A SCANDAL
CREATIVE ARTIST
CREATIVE GENIUS
CREATIVE WORKER
CREATIVE WRITER
CREDIT CUSTOMER
CREDIT TRANSFER
CREST OF THE WAVE
CRICKET FIXTURE
CRICKET RESULTS
CRIME DETECTION
CRIME DOESN'T PAY
CRIME OF PASSION
CRIME PASSIONEL
CRIMINAL CHARGE
CRIMINAL LAWYER
CRIMINAL RECORD
CRINOLINE DRESS
CRISS CROSS QUIZ
CRITICAL MOMENT
CRITICAL PERIOD
CROCODILE TEARS
CROOK THE FINGER
CROSSED FINGERS
CROSS ONE'S HEART
CROSS REFERENCE
CROSS THE BORDER
CROSS THE BRIDGE
CROSS THE STREET
CROWN AND ANCHOR
CROWNING STROKE
CROWN OF THE HEAD
CROWN OF THE ROAD
CRUMBLING POWER
CRUMB OF COMFORT
CRUSHING DEFEAT
CRUSHING REMARK
CRUSHING RETORT
CRY ONE'S EYES OUT
CULTIVATED LAND
CULTIVATED MIND
CULTURAL CENTRE
CUP FINAL TICKET
CUP OF HAPPINESS
CURB ONE'S TEMPER
CURDLE THE BLOOD
CURIOUS MIXTURE

CURRANT PUDDING
CURRENT ACCOUNT
CURRENT AFFAIRS
CURRENT EDITION
CURRENT FASHION
CURRENT OPINION
CURRIED CHICKEN
CURTAIN LECTURE
CURTAIN OF SMOKE
CUSTOM AND USAGE
CUSTOMS BARRIER
CUSTOMS OFFICER
CUT A FINE FIGURE
CUT A POOR FIGURE
CUT FOR PARTNERS
CUTLERS' COMPANY
CUT OFF ONE'S NOSE
CUT OFF THE JOINT
CUT-THROAT PRICE
CUT-THROAT RAZOR

D—14
DAILY ENDEAVOUR
DAILY HAPPENING
DAILY NEWSPAPER
DAILY TELEGRAPH
DAILY TRAVELLER
DAMAGING REPORT
DAME EDITH EVANS
DAME ELLEN TERRY
DANCE PROGRAMME
DANCING ACADEMY
DANCING DERVISH
DANCING LICENCE
DANCING PARTNER
DANGEROUSLY ILL
DARING YOUNG MAN
DARK COMPLEXION
DARKEN ONE'S DOOR
DAVID TOMLINSON
DAVID WHITFIELD
DAY IN AND DAY OUT
DAYLIGHT SAVING
DAY OF ATONEMENT
DAY OF RECKONING
DAZZLING BEAUTY
DEAD MAN'S HANDLE
DEAD TO THE WORLD
DEAL A DEATH BLOW
DEAN AND CHAPTER
DEAR AT THE PRICE

DEATH BY BURNING
DEATHLY SILENCE
DEBASED COINAGE
DEBATABLE POINT
DEBIT AND CREDIT
DECEIVE ONESELF
DECENT INTERVAL
DECENTLY HOUSED
DECIDING FACTOR
DECIMAL COINAGE
DECISIVE FACTOR
DECLINE AND FALL
DECLINE IN VALUE
DECLINE TO STAND
DECLINING YEARS
DECREE ABSOLUTE
DEEP DEPRESSION
DEEPLY AFFECTED
DEEPLY OFFENDED
DEEP REFLECTION
DEEP-SEA FISHING
DEFEAT THE ENEMY
DEFENCE COUNSEL
DEFENCE IN DEPTH
DEFENCE MEASURE
DEFENCE WITNESS
DEFERRED SHARES
DEFINITE FIGURE
DEFRAY EXPENSES
DEGREES OF FROST
DELAYING ACTION
DELICATE HEALTH
DELICIOUS TASTE
DELIVER A SERMON
DELIVER A SPEECH
DEMAND A HEARING
DEMAND A RE-COUNT
DEMAND ENTRANCE
DEMAND SECURITY
DENTAL PRACTICE
DEPARTED SPIRIT
DEPART FROM LIFE
DEPARTING GUEST
DEPOSIT ACCOUNT
DEPRESSED CLASS
DEPRESSING NEWS
DEPRIVED PERSON
DEPTH OF FEELING
DEPTHS OF MISERY
DEPUTY CHAIRMAN
DERBY FAVOURITE

DERELICT VESSEL
DEROGATORY TERM
DESERT ONE'S POST
DESIRABLE THING
DESPATCH BY MAIL
DESPERATE STATE
DETACHED MANNER
DETAILED REPORT
DETECTIVE NOVEL
DETECTIVE STORY
DETENTION ORDER
DEVELOP THE MIND
DEVIL INCARNATE
DEVIL OF A TEMPER
DEVIL'S ADVOCATE
DEVIL'S DISCIPLE
DEVOTED ADMIRER
DEVOTED HUSBAND
DEVOTION TO DUTY
DIAMOND JUBILEE
DIAMOND WEDDING
DIARY OF A NOBODY
DICTATE A LETTER
DICTATION SPEED
DICTIONARY WORD
DIE IN ONE'S SHOES
DIEU ET MON DROIT
DIFFERENT ANGLE
DIFFICULT CATCH
DIFFICULT CLIMB
DIG IN ONE'S HEELS
DIGNIFIED STYLE
DIG ONE'S SPURS IN
DIMINUTIVE SIZE
DING-DONG BATTLE
DINNER AND DANCE
DINNER IS SERVED
DIPLOMATIC BODY
DIPLOMATIC MOVE
DIRECT APPROACH
DIRECT EVIDENCE
DIRECT OPPOSITE
DIRECT QUESTION
DIRECT TAXATION
DISABLED PERSON
DISCHARGE A DEBT
DISCORDANT NOTE
DISCOUNT BROKER
DISGUISED VOICE
DISORDERED MIND
DISTILLED WATER

DISTORTED IMAGE
DISTRESSED AREA
DISTRESS SIGNAL
DISTURBED NIGHT
DISTURBED SLEEP
DIVIDE BY ELEVEN
DIVIDE BY TWELVE
DIVIDED LOYALTY
DIVIDE THE HOUSE
DIVISION OF WORK
DIVORCED PERSON
DOCTOR BARNARDO
DOCTORS' COMMONS
DOCTOR'S DILEMMA
DOCTOR'S MANDATE
DODGE THE COLUMN
DOG IN THE MANGER
DOLL'S FURNITURE
DOMESTIC ANIMAL
DOMESTIC DRUDGE
DOMESTIC POLICY
DOMINION STATUS
DONALD CAMPBELL
DONKEY SERENADE
DO ONESELF PROUD
DOROTHY PERKINS
DOSE OF MEDICINE
DOT AND CARRY ONE
DOUBLE EIGHTEEN
DOUBLE ENTENDRE
DOUBLE EXPOSURE
DOUBLE FOURTEEN
DOUBLE NEGATIVE
DOUBLE NINETEEN
DOUBLE STANDARD
DOUBLE STOPPING
DOUBLET AND HOSE
DOUBLE THIRTEEN
DOUBTFUL FUTURE
DOUBTFUL ORIGIN
DOUBTFUL TEMPER
DOUBTING THOMAS
DOUGHTY WARRIOR
DOWAGER DUCHESS
DOWN IN THE DUMPS
DOWN IN THE MOUTH
DOWN IN THE WORLD
DOWN LAMBETH WAY
DOWN MEMORY LANE
DOWN ON ONE'S LUCK
DOWNSTAIRS ROOM

DOWN THE CHIMNEY
DOWNWARD MOTION
DOWNWARD STROKE
DOZENS OF PEOPLE
DRAIN ONE'S GLASS
DRAMATIC CRITIC
DRAMATIC EFFECT
DRAMATIC FINISH
DRAPERS' COMPANY
DRAWERS OF WATER
DRAW FIRST BLOOD
DRAW THE CURTAIN
DRAW THE LONG-BOW
DRAW THE RATIONS
DREAMING SPIRES
DREGS OF SOCIETY
DRESSED IN BLACK
DRESSED OVER ALL
DRESS FOR DINNER
DRESS REHEARSAL
DRINKING HABITS
DRINKING TROUGH
DRINKING VESSEL
DRINK LIKE A FISH
DRIVE CAREFULLY
DRIVE TO DESPAIR
DRIVE TO THE WALL
DRIVING LICENCE
DROP FROM THE SKY
DROP IN THE OCEAN
DROP OFF TO SLEEP
DROP THE SUBJECT
DROWNED IN TEARS
DUBIOUS COMPANY
DUBLIN BAY PRAWN
DUCKS AND DRAKES
DUELLING PISTOL
DUEL TO THE DEATH
DUKE OF BURGUNDY
DUKE OF CLARENCE
DUKE OF CORNWALL
DUPLICATE SHEET
DURATION OF LIFE
DURING THE NIGHT
DUTY-FREE DRINKS
DWELL ON THE PAST
DYING FOR A DRINK

E—14
EACH FOR HIMSELF
EARL OF HAREWOOD

EARLY BREAKFAST
EARLY VICTORIAN
EARN ONE'S LIVING
EARTH SATELLITE
EAR TO THE GROUND
EASE OF HANDLING
EASTER HOLIDAYS
EASTER OFFERING
EASTER VACATION
EASY COME, EASY GO
EASY CONSCIENCE
EASY IN ONE'S MIND
EAT ONE'S HEAD OFF
ECONOMIC CRISIS
ECONOMY OF WORDS
EDITORIAL CHAIR
EDITORIAL STAFF
EDUCATE THE MIND
EDUCATIONAL TOY
EDWARDIAN HOUSE
EFFICIENCY TEST
EIGHT AND A PENNY
EIGHT AND ELEVEN
EIGHTEEN AND SIX
EIGHTEEN AND TEN
EIGHTEEN AND TWO
EIGHTEENTH HOLE
EIGHTH OF AUGUST
EIGHTH SYMPHONY
EIGHT SHILLINGS
EIGHTY THOUSAND
ELABORATE STYLE
ELDERBERRY WINE
ELDER STATESMAN
ELDEST DAUGHTER
ELECTION RESULT
ELECTRICAL UNIT
ELECTRIC CHARGE
ELECTRIC COOKER
ELECTRIC GUITAR
ELECTRIC HEATER
ELECTRICITY CUT
ELECTRIC KETTLE
ELECTRIC SHAVER
ELECTRIC WASHER
ELEMENTARY RULE
ELEMENT OF DOUBT
ELEMENT OF TRUTH
ELEPHANT'S TRUNK
ELEVEN AND A HALF
ELEVEN AND EIGHT

ELEVEN AND SEVEN
ELEVEN AND THREE
ELEVEN OR TWELVE
ELEVENTH LETTER
ELEVENTH OF JULY
ELEVENTH OF JUNE
ELEVEN THOUSAND
ELICIT THE TRUTH
ELIZABETHAN AGE
ELIZABETHAN ERA
ELIZA DOOLITTLE
ELLA FITZGERALD
ELOCUTION CLASS
ELOQUENT TONGUE
EMINENT SOLDIER
EMINENT SPEAKER
EMOTIONAL WRECK
EMPEROR OF JAPAN
EMPHATIC DENIAL
EMPIRE LOYALIST
EMPTY OF MEANING
EMPTY PLEASURES
ENCLOSE A CHEQUE
ENDEARING SMILE
ENDLESS PROBLEM
ENDLESS TROUBLE
END OF ALL THINGS
END OF THE MATTER
END OF THE STREET
ENDS OF THE EARTH
ENDURE TO THE END
ENEMY OF FREEDOM
ENEMY OF MANKIND
ENEMY TERRITORY
ENFANT TERRIBLE
ENGAGED IN TRADE
ENGAGEMENT RING
ENGAGE THE ENEMY
ENGAGING MANNER
ENGLISH BY BIRTH
ENGLISH CHANNEL
ENGLISH GRAMMAR
ENGLISH HISTORY
ENGLISH MUSTARD
ENGLISH TEACHER
ENIGMATIC SMILE
ENJOY ILL HEALTH
ENLARGE THE MIND
ENLIGHTENED AGE
ENORMOUS NUMBER
ENTERTAIN A HOPE

ENTER THE CHURCH
EQUABLE CLIMATE
EQUALLY DIVIDED
EQUAL THE RECORD
ERRATIC CONDUCT
ESCAPED CONVICT
ESPRESSO COFFEE
ETHEREAL BEAUTY
EUCALYPTUS TREE
EVADE DETECTION
EVAPORATED MILK
EVENING CLOTHES
EVENING SERVICE
EVERGREEN PLANT
EVERGREEN SHRUB
EVERY BIT AS MUCH
EVERY INCH A KING
EVERY SECOND DAY
EVERYTHING GOES
EVIDENCE OF OATH
EVIL REPUTATION
EXACTING MASTER
EXCEED THE LIMIT
EXCELLENT MARKS
EXCHANGE OF VOWS
EXCHANGE VISITS
EXCITABLE STATE
EXCURSION TRAIN
EXECUTION BLOCK
EXECUTIVE SUITE
EXERT AUTHORITY
EXHIBIT FEELING
EXPANSIVE SMILE
EXPENSE ACCOUNT
EXPENSIVE PAPER
EXPLAIN ONESELF
EXPLODED BELIEF
EXPORT MERCHANT
EXPOSE TO DANGER
EXPRESS COMMAND
EXPRESS ONESELF
EXPRESS PURPOSE
EXPRESS REGRETS
EXPURGATED BOOK
EXQUISITE TASTE
EXTENDED CREDIT
EXTENSIVE FIELD
EXTENSIVE SALES
EXTINCT VOLCANO
EXTREME DISLIKE
EXTREME PENALTY

EXTREME POVERTY
EXTREME UNCTION
EYE FOR BUSINESS

F—14
FABULOUS WEALTH
FABULOUS WRITER
FACE OF THE GLOBE
FACE UP TO THINGS
FACT AND FICTION
FACTORY CHIMNEY
FACTS OF THE CASE
FAIL IN ONE'S DUTY
FAIL TO INTEREST
FAIR COMPARISON
FAIR COMPLEXION
FAIR TO MIDDLING
FAIR TO MODERATE
FAIRY GODMOTHER
FAITHFUL FRIEND
FAITHFUL REPORT
FAITHFUL SPOUSE
FALL DOWNSTAIRS
FALL INTO DISUSE
FALL ON EVIL DAYS
FALL ON ONE'S FEET
FALSE COLOURING
FALSE EYELASHES
FALSELY ACCUSED
FALSE MOUSTACHE
FALSE PRETENCES
FALSE REASONING
FALSE STATEMENT
FALTERING STEPS
FALTERING VOICE
FAME AND FORTUNE
FAMILIAR MANNER
FAMILIAR SPIRIT
FAMILY BUSINESS
FAMILY HEIRLOOM
FAMILY LIKENESS
FAMILY PORTRAIT
FAMILY RETAINER
FAMILY SKELETON
FANCY-DRESS BALL
FAREWELL SPEECH
FAREWELL TO ARMS
FAR-FLUNG EMPIRE
FARMING SUBSIDY
FAST AND FURIOUS
FATALLY WOUNDED

FATHER SUPERIOR
FAT-STOCK PRICES
FATUOUS ATTEMPT
FAVOURABLE WIND
FAVOURED PERSON
FAVOURITE PIECE
FEARLESS HITTER
FEAST OF STEPHEN
FEAT OF STRENGTH
FEATURE PICTURE
FEATURES EDITOR
FEDERAL COUNCIL
FEEL THE BENEFIT
FEEL THE DRAUGHT
FELLOW COMMONER
FELLOW CREATURE
FEMININE APPEAL
FEMININE GENDER
FEMME DE CHAMBRE
FEND FOR ONESELF
FEVERISH DESIRE
FICTITIOUS NAME
FIELD AMBULANCE
FIELD ARTILLERY
FIELD OF INQUIRY
FIELD TELEGRAPH
FIFTEEN AND FIVE
FIFTEEN AND FOUR
FIFTEEN AND NINE
FIFTEEN PER CENT
FIFTEENTH GREEN
FIFTEENTH OF MAY
FIFTEENTH ROUND
FIFTH COLUMNIST
FIFTH OF JANUARY
FIFTH OF OCTOBER
FIFTY-ONE AND SIX
FIFTY-SIX AND SIX
FIFTY-TWO AND SIX
FIGHTER COMMAND
FIGHTING CHANCE
FIGHTING SPIRIT
FIGHT TO A FINISH
FIGURE OF SPEECH
FILLETED PLAICE
FILLING STATION
FILL THE VACANCY
FILL UP THE RANKS
FILL WITH DISMAY
FILTHY LANGUAGE
FINAL INTENTION

FINAL RECKONING
FINANCIAL TIMES
FINANCIAL WORRY
FIND A PUBLISHER
FINDERS, KEEPERS
FIND THE MEANING
FINGER IN THE PIE
FINGERS AND TOES
FINGER'S BREADTH
FINIAN'S RAINBOW
FINISHING TOUCH
FINISH STRONGLY
FINITE QUANTITY
FIRE A BROADSIDE
FIRE DEPARTMENT
FIREMAN'S HELMET
FIREMAN'S LADDER
FIRE PROTECTION
FIRM CONVICTION
FIRM FOUNDATION
FIRM GOVERNMENT
FIRM IMPRESSION
FIRM MANAGEMENT
FIRM OPPOSITION
FIRST AND SECOND
FIRST-BORN CHILD
FIRST CHRISTMAS
FIRST-CLASS FARE
FIRST-CLASS IDEA
FIRST-CLASS SHOT
FIRST CONDITION
FIRST-FLOOR·FLAT
FIRST INTENTION
FIRST MAGNITUDE
FIRST OF JANUARY
FIRST OF OCTOBER
FIRST ON THE LIST
FIRST PRINCIPLE
FIRST-RATE ACTOR
FIRST SECRETARY
FIRST TIME LUCKY
FIRST TIME ROUND
FIRST VIOLINIST
FISHERMAN'S YARN
FISHING LICENCE
FISHING VILLAGE ,
FISH OUT OF WATER
FIT OF GIDDINESS
FIT THE OCCASION
FIVE-BARRED GATE
FIVE-DOLLAR BILL

FIVE OF DIAMONDS

FIVEPENNY STAMP

FIXED ALLOWANCE

FLAG LIEUTENANT

FLAG OF DISTRESS

FLASHING STREAM

FLAT AS A PANCAKE

FLAT ON ONE'S BACK

FLAT ON ONE'S FACE

FLATTER ONESELF

FLEE THE COUNTRY

FLEETING GLANCE

FLIGHT OF STAIRS

FLIGHT SERGEANT

FLIPPANT SPEECH

FLOATING BRIDGE

FLOATING KIDNEY

FLOATING PALACE

FLOCK OF PIGEONS

FLOG A DEAD HORSE

FLOOD WITH LIGHT

FLOWERING PLANT

FLOWERING SHRUB

FLUSH OF TRIUMPH

FLUSH WITH ANGER

FLUSH WITH MONEY

FLY FOR ONE'S LIFE

FLYING BEDSTEAD

FLYING BUTTRESS

FLYING DUTCHMAN

FLYING FORTRESS

FLYING SCOTSMAN

FLYING SQUIRREL

FLY INTO A TEMPER

FLY TO THE RESCUE

FLY-WEIGHT TITLE

FOAM AT THE MOUTH

FOLD UP ONE'S TENT

FOLLOW A CALLING

FOLLOW A PATTERN

FOLLOW MY LEADER

FOLLOW ONE'S NOSE

FOLLOW THE CROWD

FOLLOW THE SCENT

FOLLOW THE TRAIL

FOOD CONTROLLER

FOOD FOR THE GODS

FOOD FOR THE MIND

FOOD FOR THOUGHT

FOOD PRODUCTION

FOOTBALL COUPON

FOOTBALL GROUND

FOOTBALL LEAGUE

FOOTBALL PLAYER

FOOTBALL SEASON

FOR ALL THE WORLD

FORBIDDEN FRUIT

FORBID THE BANNS

FORCED MARRIAGE

FORCE OF GRAVITY

FORCIBLE DEMAND

FOREIGN AFFAIRS

FOREIGN CAPITAL

FOREIGN COUNTRY

FOREIGN SERVICE

FOREIGN STATION

FOR EVER AND A DAY

FOR EVER AND EVER

FOR HEAVEN'S SAKE!

FOR LOVE OR MONEY

FORMAL APPROACH

FORMAL OCCASION

FORMAL SANCTION

FORM AN ESTIMATE

FORMATIVE YEARS

FORMIDABLE TASK

FOR THE DURATION

FOR THE LAST TIME

FOR THE LIFE OF ME

FOR THE MOST PART

FORTUNATE EVENT

FORTY-ONE AND SIX

FORTY-SIX AND SIX

FORTY-TWO AND SIX

FOR WANT OF A NAIL

FOSTER DAUGHTER

FOUNDERS' SHARES

FOUR-MASTED SHIP

FOUR-MILE RADIUS

FOUR-MINUTE MILE

FOUR OF DIAMONDS

FOURPENNY STAMP

FOURTEEN AND SIX

FOURTEEN AND TEN

FOURTEEN AND TWO

FOURTEEN OUNCES

FOURTEEN POUNDS

FOURTEENTH HOLE

FOURTH DIVIDEND

FOURTH DIVISION

FOURTH OF AUGUST

FOURTH SYMPHONY

FRACTIONAL PART
FRAGRANT MEMORY
FRAIL STRUCTURE
FRANKIE VAUGHAN
FRANK STATEMENT
FREEDOM FROM WAR
FREE ENTERPRISE
FREE FROM DANGER
FREEMASONS' HALL
FREE OF INTEREST
FREEZING MANNER
FRENCH CANADIAN
FRENCH DRESSING
FRENCH LANGUAGE
FRENCH POLISHER
FRENCH VERMOUTH
FRESHWATER FISH
FREUDIAN SCHOOL
FRIENDLY ACTION
FRIENDLY CRITIC
FRIENDLY DEBATE
FRIENDLY NATION
FRIGHTFUL SIGHT
FROM BAD TO WORSE
FROM BANK TO BANK
FROM EAST TO WEST
FROM HAND TO HAND
FROM HEAD TO FOOT
FROM SIDE TO SIDE
FROM THE CONTEXT
FROM TIME TO TIME
FROM WALL TO WALL
FRONT ELEVATION
FRONT-PAGE STORY
FROTH AND BUBBLE
FROZEN SHOULDER
FULFIL A PROMISE
FULHAM BROADWAY
FULL COMPLEMENT
FULL DIRECTIONS
FULL EMPLOYMENT
FULL MEMBERSHIP
FULL OF INTEREST
FULL OF MISCHIEF
FULL OF NONSENSE
FULL OF VITALITY
FULL-SCALE MODEL
FULL SETTLEMENT
FULL SPEED AHEAD
FULL STEAM AHEAD
FULL TO CAPACITY

FULLY CONSCIOUS
FULLY DEVELOPED
FULLY FASHIONED
FULLY FURNISHED
FUNERAL ORATION
FUNERAL PARLOUR
FUNNY PROGRAMME
FUR-LINED GLOVES
FURNISHED HOUSE
FURNISH SUPPORT
FURNITURE STORE
FURTHER DETAILS
FURTHER OUTLOOK

G—14
GAIN ADMITTANCE
GAIN CONFIDENCE
GAIN EXPERIENCE
GAIN POSSESSION
GAINS AND LOSSES
GAIN THE MASTERY
GAIN THE VICTORY
GALLANT COMPANY
GALLANT SOLDIER
GALLOPING MAJOR
GALVANIZED IRON
GAMBLING CHANCE
GAME OF DRAUGHTS
GAME OF SKITTLES
GARBLED VERSION
GARGANTUAN MEAL
GARLAND OF ROSES
GATHERING STORM
GATHER MOMENTUM
GATHER STRENGTH
GATHER TOGETHER
GATWICK AIRPORT
GENERAL AMNESTY
GENERAL BENEFIT
GENERAL CONSENT
GENERAL COUNCIL
GENERAL MANAGER
GENERAL MEETING
GENERAL OFFICER
GENERAL OUTLINE
GENERAL OUTLOOK
GENERAL POVERTY
GENERAL RELEASE
GENERAL ROUTINE
GENERAL SERVANT

GENERAL SERVICE	GIVE ASSURANCES
GENERAL SURGEON	GIVE FULL CREDIT
GENERAL SURGERY	GIVE GENEROUSLY
GENERAL WARRANT	GIVE IN MARRIAGE
GENEROUS AMOUNT	GIVE IT A THOUGHT
GENEROUS NATURE	GIVEN A REPRIEVE
GENEROUS PRAISE	GIVE ONE A ROCKET
GENEROUS SPIRIT	GIVE ONE HIS HEAD
GENIE OF THE LAMP	GIVE ONE'S ASSENT
GENTLE BREEDING	GIVE ONE THE BIRD
GENTLE HANDLING	GIVE ONE THE PUSH
GENTLEMAN CROOK	GIVE ONE THE SLIP
GENTLEMAN'S CODE	GIVE PERMISSION
GENTLEMAN USHER	GIVE THE GLAD EYE
GENTLE REMINDER	GIVE TO THE WORLD
GENUINE ARTICLE	GIVE UP DRINKING
GENUINE EXAMPLE	GIVE UP ONE'S SEAT
GENUINE RESPECT	GIVE UP THE GHOST
GEORGE BRADSHAW	GLAMOROUS NIGHT
GEORGE GERSHWIN	GLARING MISTAKE
GEORGE HARRISON	GLASGOW RANGERS
GEORGE MEREDITH	GLEAMING ARMOUR
GEORGE MITCHELL	GLOBE ARTICHOKE
GEORGE SIMENON	GLOOMY FORECAST
GERMAN LANGUAGE	GLOOMY PROSPECT
GET AN EXTENSION	GLORIOUS MUDDLE
GET INTO TROUBLE	GLORIOUS SUNSET
GET IT IN THE NECK	GLOSSY MAGAZINE
GET OFF SCOT-FREE	GLOWING ACCOUNT
GET ONE'S DESERTS	GLOWING COLOURS
GET ONE'S FEET WET	GLOW WITH HEALTH
GET ONE'S OWN BACK	GLUTTON FOR FOOD
GET OUT OF THE WAY	GLUTTON FOR WORK
GET THE BEST OF IT	GNASH ONE'S TEETH
GET THE BETTER OF	GO DOWN FIGHTING
GET THE BREEZE UP	GOD SAVE THE KING!
GET THE HANG OF IT	GOD'S OWN COUNTRY
GET THE WHIP-HAND	GOING! GOING! GONE!
GHASTLY MISTAKE	GOING GREAT GUNS
GHOST OF A CHANCE	GOING TO THE DOGS
GIANT REFRESHED	GO INTO HOSPITAL
GIANT'S CAUSEWAY	GO INTO MOURNING
GIFTED COMPOSER	GO INTO RAPTURES
GILBERT HARDING	GOLDEN PHEASANT
GIMCRACK STAKES	GOLDEN TREASURY
GINGERBREAD MAN	GOLDSMITHS' HALL
GIRD UP THE LOINS	GOLF TOURNAMENT
GIRL IN A MILLION	GO LIKE HOT CAKES
GIVE A MAN HIS DUE	GONE BY THE BOARD
GIVE AN INSTANCE	GONE FOR A BURTON
GIVE ASSISTANCE	GOOD BACKGROUND

GOOD-BYE MR. CHIPS
GOOD COMPANIONS
GOOD COMPARISON
GOOD COMPLEXION
GOOD CONSCIENCE
GOOD DISCIPLINE
GOOD FELLOWSHIP
GOOD FOR NOTHING
GOOD FOR THE SOUL
GOOD FOUNDATION
GOOD IMPRESSION
GOOD INTENTIONS
GOOD INVESTMENT
GOOD LITERATURE
GOOD MANAGEMENT
GOOD NEIGHBOURS
GOOD REPUTATION
GOOD RESOLUTION
GOODS IN TRANSIT
GOOD TIME-KEEPER
GOOD UPBRINGING
GO OFF LIKE A BOMB
GO OFF THE HANDLE
GOOSEBERRY BUSH
GOOSEBERRY FOOL
GO OUT OF ONE'S WAY
GORDON RICHARDS
GO TO ANY LENGTHS
GO TO CONFESSION
GO TO THE COUNTRY
GO TO THE SEASIDE
GO TO THE THEATRE
GO UP IN THE WORLD
GOVERNMENT LOAN
GOVERNMENT POST
GOVERNMENT WHIP
GO WEST, YOUNG MAN
GO WITH THE TIMES
GRACE AND FAVOUR
GRACIOUS LIVING
GRADUAL DECLINE
GRADUATED SCALE
GRAIN OF COMFORT
GRAIN OF MUSTARD
GRAND COMMITTEE
GRAND CONDITION
GRANDSTAND VIEW
GRAPHIC ACCOUNT
GRAPHIC DRAWING
GRASP THE NETTLE
GRAVE ADMISSION

GRAVE SITUATION
GRAVE STATEMENT
GRAVE SUSPICION
GRAVEYARD COUGH
GREASE ONE'S PALM
GREAT BED OF WARE
GREAT IGNORANCE
GREAT INJUSTICE
GREAT IN STATURE
GREAT NORTH ROAD
GREAT RECEPTION
GREAT SACRIFICE
GREAT SCOUNDREL
GREAT STATESMAN
GREAT VARIATION
GRECIAN PROFILE
GREEN LINE COACH
GREEN VEGETABLE
GRENADIER GUARD
GREYHOUND DERBY
GREYHOUND TRACK
GRIND ONE'S TEETH
GRIST TO THE MILL
GROCER'S COMPANY
GROPE IN THE DARK
GROSS INJUSTICE
GROSVENOR HOUSE
GROUND LANDLORD
GROUNDLESS FEAR
GROUSE SHOOTING
GROWING ANXIETY
GROW UP TOGETHER
GROW VEGETABLES
GRUB STREET HACK
GRUDGING PRAISE
GUERRILLA CHIEF
GUERRILLA FORCE
GUESS THE ANSWER
GUEST CELEBRITY
GUIDED BY REASON
GUILTY OF MURDER
GUN EMPLACEMENT
GURKHA REGIMENT
GUTTURAL ACCENT
GUTTURAL SPEECH

H—14
HACKNEY MARSHES
HALF A SOVEREIGN
HALF-DAY HOLIDAY
HALF-MOON STREET

HALFPENNY STAMP
HALF-SPOKEN WORD
HALLÉ ORCHESTRA
HALLOWEEN PARTY
HALT FOR A MOMENT
HAMMER AND TONGS
HAMPSTEAD HEATH
HAND EMBROIDERY
HANDLE TENDERLY
HANDLE WITH CARE
HAND ON THE TORCH
HANDSOME MARGIN
HANDSOME PROFIT
HANGING GARDENS
HANG OUT A SIGNAL
HANG THE EXPENSE
HAPPILY MARRIED
HAPPY CHILDHOOD
HAPPY CHRISTMAS
HARBOUR REVENGE
HARD DISCIPLINE
HARDENED SINNER
HARDLY ANYTHING
HARDLY CREDIBLE
HARD NUT TO CRACK
HARD TASKMASTER
HARD TO CONVINCE
HARD TO DESCRIBE
HARRY BELAFONTE
HARSH TREATMENT
HAUNTING MELODY
HAVE A GOOD NIGHT
HAVE A SUSPICION
HAVE COMPASSION
HAVE CONFIDENCE
HAVE IT BOTH WAYS
HAVE MISGIVINGS
HAVE NO SCRUPLES
HAVE ONE'S DOUBTS
HAVE ONE'S OWN WAY
HAVE THE COURAGE
HAVE THE KNOW-HOW
HEAD ABOVE WATER
HEADACHE POWDER
HEAD FOR FIGURES
HEAD FOR HEIGHTS
HEADLONG FLIGHT
HEAD OF THE HOUSE
HEAD OF THE RIVER
HEAD OF THE TABLE
HEALTHY OUTLOOK

HEALTHY RESPECT
HEART CONDITION
HEART OF ENGLAND
HEARTY APPETITE
HEARTY APPROVAL
HEARTY LAUGHTER
HEATED ARGUMENT
HEATHER MIXTURE
HEAVEN AND EARTH
HEAVIER THAN AIR
HEAVY ARTILLERY
HEAVY TRANSPORT
HEAVY WITH SLEEP
HEEL OF ACHILLES
HEIGHT OF GENIUS
HEIGHT OF SUMMER
HEIR TO A FORTUNE
HELD IN CONTEMPT
HELL-FIRE CORNER
HELL FOR LEATHER
HELL HATH NO FURY
HELPLESS VICTIM
HELP ONE ANOTHER
HEMEL HEMPSTEAD
HENLEY ON THAMES
HENRY THE EIGHTH
HENRY THE FOURTH
HENRY THE SECOND
HERALDIC COLOUR
HERALDIC DEVICE
HERALDIC SHIELD
HERALD'S COLLEGE
HERBERT SPENCER
HEREFORD CASTLE
HERO AND LEANDER
HIDDEN TREASURE
HIDEOUS PATTERN
HIGH AS A STEEPLE
HIGH CASUALTIES
HIGH CHANCELLOR
HIGH COMMISSION
HIGH COURT JUDGE
HIGH IN THE SCALE
HIGHLAND CATTLE
HIGH-LEVEL TALKS
HIGHLY EDUCATED
HIGHLY ESTEEMED
HIGHLY ORIGINAL
HIGHLY POLISHED
HIGHLY POSSIBLE
HIGHLY SEASONED

HIGH PERCENTAGE
HIGHWAY ROBBERY
HIP MEASUREMENT
HISTORICAL PLAY
HISTORICAL WORK
HISTORIC MOMENT
HISTORY TEACHER
HIT OVER THE HEAD
HIVE OF ACTIVITY
HIVE OF INDUSTRY
HOB-NAILED BOOTS
HOLD AN ARGUMENT
HOLD AN ELECTION
HOLD EVERYTHING
HOLD IN ABEYANCE
HOLD IN CONTEMPT
HOLDING COMPANY
HOLDING QUALITY
HOLD IN SUSPENSE
HOLD ONE'S BREATH
HOLD ONE'S GROUND
HOLD ONE'S HEAD UP
HOLD ONE'S HORSES
HOLD ONE'S TONGUE
HOLD UP ONE'S HEAD
HOLIDAY TRAFFIC
HOLIDAY WITH PAY
HOLIER THAN THOU
HOLLOWAY PRISON
HOLLOW LAUGHTER
HOLLOW PRETENCE
HOME DEPARTMENT
HOMELESS PERSON
HOME ON THE RANGE
HOMES FOR HEROES
HONEYMOON HOTEL
HONORARY DEGREE
HONORARY FELLOW
HONORARY MEMBER
HONORARY STATUS
HONOUR AND GLORY
HOPE AND BELIEVE
HOPE FOR THE BEST
HOPELESS MISFIT
HOP, SKIP AND JUMP
HORIZONTAL BARS
HORIZONTAL LINE
HORSE AND HOUNDS
HORSE ARTILLERY
HORSE OF THE YEAR
HOSPITAL ANNEXE

HOSPITAL MATRON
HOSPITAL SUNDAY
HOSTILE COUNTRY
HOSTILE VERDICT
HOSTILE WITNESS
HOT-AIR MERCHANT
HOT AND BOTHERED
HOTEL DETECTIVE
HOTLY CONTESTED
HOT ON ONE'S HEELS
HOT ON ONE'S TRAIL
HOT-WATER BOTTLE
HOT-WATER SUPPLY
HOT-WATER SYSTEM
HOUSE DECORATOR
HOUSE DETECTIVE
HOUSEHOLD GOODS
HOUSEHOLD LINEN
HOUSEHOLD STAFF
HOUSEMAID'S KNEE
HOUSE OF COMMONS
HOUSE OF HANOVER
HOUSE OF ONE'S OWN
HOUSE OF THE LORD
HOUSE OF WINDSOR
HOUSE OF WORSHIP
HOUSE PHYSICIAN
HOUSING PROBLEM
HOUSING PROJECT
HOWLING DERVISH
HOWLING SUCCESS
HOW THE LAND LIES
HUMAN ENDEAVOUR
HUMAN RELATIONS
HUMAN SACRIFICE
HUMAN SUFFERING
HUMBLE DWELLING
HUMBLE PETITION
HUMPBACK BRIDGE
HUMPHREY BOGART
HUNDRED DOLLARS
HUNDRED GUINEAS
HUNDRED PER CENT
HUNT HIGH AND LOW
HUNT THE SLIPPER
HUNT THE THIMBLE
HURT EXPRESSION
HUSBAND AND WIFE
HYDE PARK CORNER
HYDE PARK ORATOR
HYDRAULIC POWER

HYDRAULIC PRESS
HYPHENATED WORD
HYPNOTIC TRANCE

I—14
ICE-CREAM CORNET
ICE-CREAM SUNDAE
IDEAL COMPANION
IDENTICAL TWINS
IDENTITY PARADE
IGNOMINIOUS END
IGNORANT MASSES
IGNORANT PERSON
ILLEGAL TRAFFIC
ILL-GOTTEN GAINS
ILL-TIMED REMARK
IMAGINARY POINT
IMMEDIATE REPLY
IMMEMORIAL ELMS
IMMINENT DANGER
IMMORAL CONDUCT
IMMOVABLE FEAST
IMPART MOMENTUM
IMPENDING STORM
IMPERATIVE MOOD
IMPERFECT RHYME
IMPERFECT TENSE
IMPERIAL BALLET
IMPERIAL GALLON
IMPERIAL PURPLE
IMPERIAL WEIGHT
IMPLACABLE MOOD
IMPLIED CONSENT
IMPORTANT EVENT
IMPOSING FIGURE
IMPOSSIBLE TASK
IMPROPER PERSON
IMPROVE MATTERS
IMPROVE ONESELF
IMPUDENT CHARGE
IMPUDENT SPEECH
IMPURE THOUGHTS
IN A LITTLE WHILE
IN ALL INNOCENCE
IN A MORTAL HURRY
IN ANCIENT TIMES
IN ANOTHER CLASS
IN ANTICIPATION
IN A STATE OF FLUX
INCENDIARY BOMB
IN CERTAIN CASES

INCLINE ONE'S EAR
INCLUSIVE TERMS
INCOMING TENANT
IN COURSE OF TIME
INCREASED FARES
INCREASED SPEED
IN DEEP MOURNING
INDEFINITE TIME
INDEPENDENT AIR
INDIAN ELEPHANT
INDICATIVE MOOD
IN DIFFICULTIES
INDIRECT EFFECT
INDIRECT METHOD
INDIRECT OBJECT
INDIRECT SPEECH
INDUSTRIAL AREA
INDUSTRAIL ARTS
IN EVERY QUARTER
IN EVERY RESPECT
INEXORABLE FATE
INFERIOR NATURE
INFERIOR STATUS
INFINITE NUMBER
INFORMAL SPEECH
INFRINGE THE LAW
INGRAINED HABIT
INITIAL ATTEMPT
INITIAL EXPENSE
INITIATIVE TEST
INJURED HUSBAND
INLAND WATERWAY
IN LOCO PARENTIS
INMOST THOUGHTS
INNERMOST BEING
INNER SANCTUARY
INNINGS VICTORY
INNOCENT ABROAD
INNOCENT REMARK
INNOCENT VICTIM
INNS OF CHANCERY
IN ONE'S BORN DAYS
IN ONE'S MIND'S EYE
IN ONE'S OWN LIGHT
IN ONE'S OWN RIGHT
IN ORDER OF MERIT
IN RELATIONSHIP
IN ROUND NUMBERS
INSIDE POSITION
IN SOUTH AMERICA
INSPIRE RESPECT

INSTANT DISLIKE
INSULATED CABLE
INSULTING WORDS
INSULT TO INJURY
INSURANCE AGENT
INSURANCE CLAIM
INTENSE DISLIKE
INTENSE FEELING
INTENSE LONGING
INTENSIVE STUDY
INTERESTED LOOK
INTERNAL STRIFE
INTERNMENT CAMP
INTERVAL OF TIME
IN THE AFTERNOON
IN THE AGGREGATE
IN THE ASCENDANT
IN THE BEGINNING
IN THE FIRM'S TIME
IN THE FOREFRONT
IN THE HEADLINES
IN THE LIMELIGHT
IN THE MEANWHILE
IN THE MOONLIGHT
IN THE MOUNTAINS
IN THE NEWSPAPER
IN THE NEXT WORLD
IN THE ORCHESTRA
IN THE PROVINCES
IN THE PUBLIC EYE
IN THE SAME CLASS
IN THE THICK OF IT
INTIMATE CIRCLE
INTIMATE FRIEND
INTO A COCKED HAT
INTO THE BARGAIN
INTRINSIC VALUE
INTRINSIC WORTH
INTRODUCE A BILL
INVARIABLE RULE
INVENT AN EXCUSE
INVERTED COMMAS
INVETERATE LIAR
INVINCIBLE ARMY
INVITE A QUARREL
INVITE RIDICULE
IRISH FREE STATE
IRISH PEASANTRY
IRONS IN THE FIRE
IRREGULAR UNION
ISLAND IN THE SUN

ISLAND PARADISE
IT'S A SMALL WORLD

J—14
JACK OF DIAMONDS
JACOBITE RISING
JAYNE MANSFIELD
JEALOUS HUSBAND
JESSIE MATTHEWS
JIMMINY CRICKET
JOAN SUTHERLAND
JOBS FOR THE BOYS
JOHN BARLEYCORN
JOHN BROWN'S BODY
JOHN DRINKWATER
JOHN GALSWORTHY
JOHN LOGIE BAIRD
JOHN THE BAPTIST
JOIN IN MARRIAGE
JOINT COMMITTEE
JOIN THE COLOURS
JOIN THE RAT-RACE
JOINT LIABILITY
JOINT OWNERSHIP
JOINT-STOCK BANK
JOSHUA REYNOLDS
JUDE THE OBSCURE
JUDICIAL MANNER
JUDICIAL MURDER
JUDICIAL NOTICE
JULIAN CALENDAR
JULY THE SEVENTH
JULY THE TWELFTH
JUMPING CRACKER
JUNE THE SEVENTH
JUNE THE TWELFTH
JUNIOR REPORTER
JUPITER PLUVIUS

K—14
KEEP A GOOD TABLE
KEEP A TIGHT REIN
KEEP EARLY HOURS
KEEP IN SUSPENSE
KEEP IN THE SHADE
KEEP ONE'S CHIN UP
KEEP ONE'S FIGURE
KEEP ONE'S HAIR ON
KEEP ONE'S HAND IN
KEEP ONE'S SENSES
KEEP ONE'S TEMPER

KEEP OUT OF SIGHT
KEEP STRAIGHT ON
KEEP THE COLD OUT
KEEP TO THE RIGHT
KEEP TO THE RULES
KEEP UNDER COVER
KEEP WELL IN HAND
KENSINGTON GORE
KEPT IN HIS PLACE
KEYSTONE COMEDY
KIDNEY AND BACON
KIDNEY POTATOES
KILLED IN ACTION
KINDLY INTEREST
KING AND COUNTRY
KING ARTHUR'S MEN
KING OF DIAMONDS
KING'S MESSENGER
KITCHEN CABINET
KITCHEN DRESSER
KITCHEN UTENSIL
KNIGHT IN ARMOUR
KNIGHTS OF MALTA
KNITTING NEEDLE
KNIVES AND FORKS
KNOCK-ABOUT TURN
KNOCK AT THE DOOR
KNOCK-DOWN PRICE
KNOCK INTO SHAPE
KNOCK ON THE DOOR
KNOCK ON THE HEAD
KNOW A MOVE OR TWO
KNOW BY INSTINCT
KNOW FOR CERTAIN
KNOWLEDGE OF LAW
KNOWN CHARACTER
KNOW ONE'S ONIONS
KNOW WHEN TO STOP

L—14
LABOUR EXCHANGE
LABOUR MAJORITY
LABOUR MINORITY
LABOUR MOVEMENT
LABOUR THE POINT
LACK OF EVIDENCE
LACK OF FRICTION
LACK OF INTEREST
LACK OF JUDGMENT
LACK OF PRACTICE
LACK OF STRENGTH

LACK OF SYMPATHY
LACK OF TRAINING
LACRIMA CHRISTI
LADY CHATTERLEY
LADY OF THE HOUSE
LADY OF THE MANOR
LADY WINDERMERE
LAID BY THE HEELS
LAID ON THE SHELF
LAKE WINDERMERE
LAME CONCLUSION
LANCASTER HOUSE
LAND COMMISSION
LANDED INTEREST
LANDED PROPERTY
LAND OF NO RETURN
LAND ON ONE'S FEET
LANGUAGE MASTER
LANTERN LECTURE
LARGE OVERDRAFT
LARGER THAN LIFE
LASSIES AND LADS
LAST APPEARANCE
LAST CONNECTION
LAST GENERATION
LASTING BENEFIT
LASTING QUALITY
LASTING SUCCESS
LAST INSTALMENT
LAST IN THE QUEUE
LATE NIGHT FINAL
LATEST BULLETIN
LATH AND PLASTER
LATTER-DAY SAINT
LAUGHING MATTER
LAUNCH AN ATTACK
LAUNCHING STAGE
LAUREL AND HARDY
LAURENCE HARVEY
LAURENCE STERNE
LAW ENFORCEMENT
LAWFUL OCCASION
LAW OF THE JUNGLE
LAY DOWN A CELLAR
LAY ON TRANSPORT
LEADING ACTRESS
LEADING ARTICLE
LEADING CITIZEN
LEADING COUNSEL
LEADING STRINGS
LEAD THE FASHION

LEAD TO THE ALTAR
LEAGUE FOOTBALL
LEAPS AND BOUNDS
LEARNED COUNSEL
LEARNED SOCIETY
LEASEHOLD HOUSE
LEAVE A LOOPHOLE
LEAVE DESTITUTE
LEAVE NO ADDRESS
LEAVE OF ABSENCE
LEAVE SENSELESS
LEAVE THE GROUND
LEAVE WELL ALONE
LEDA AND THE SWAN
LEEWARD ISLANDS
LEFT HIGH AND DRY
LEFT IN THE LURCH
LEFT SPEECHLESS
LEFT UNFINISHED
LEGAL AUTHORITY
LEGAL CHICANERY
LEGAL ETIQUETTE
LEGAL FORMALITY
LEGAL LIABILITY
LEGALLY BINDING
LEGAL OWNERSHIP
LEGAL PROCEDURE
LEGION OF HONOUR
LEMONADE POWDER
LEMONADE SHANDY
LENDING LIBRARY
LEND ME YOUR EARS
LESLIE MITCHELL
LET DOWN LIGHTLY
LET DOWN THE SIDE
LET OR HINDRANCE
LETTER OF ADVICE
LETTER OF CREDIT
LETTER OF THE LAW
LET THE SIDE DOWN
LET THINGS SLIDE
LETTRE DE CACHET
LIAISON OFFICER
LIBERAL HELPING
LIBRARY EDITION
LICK ONE'S WOUNDS
LICK THE PLATTER
LIFE EXPECTANCY
LIFELONG FRIEND
LIFE OF PLEASURE
LIFE WITH FATHER

LIFT UP ONE'S HEAD
LIGHT AND BITTER
LIGHT ARTILLERY
LIGHT BREAKFAST
LIGHTEN THE LOAD
LIGHTER THAN AIR
LIGHT FANTASTIC
LIGHTING-UP TIME
LIGHTNING FLASH
LIGHTNING SPEED
LIGHT PROGRAMME
LIGHTS OF LONDON
LIGHT TRANSPORT
LIKE A BOMBSHELL
LIKE A MILLSTONE
LILY-WHITE HANDS
LIMITED COMPANY
LIMITED EDITION
LIMITING FACTOR
LINE OF APPROACH
LINE OF BUSINESS
LINGERING DEATH
LINK IN THE CHAIN
LION OF THE NORTH
LISLE STOCKINGS
LISTEN TO REASON
LIST OF CONTENTS
LITERAL ACCOUNT
LITERAL MEANING
LITERARY CRITIC
LITERARY DIGEST
LITERARY EDITOR
LITERARY OUTPUT
LITTLE AND OFTEN
LITTLE BROWN JUG
LITTLE BY LITTLE
LITTLE CHILDREN
LITTLE CORPORAL
LITTLE DISTANCE
LITTLE IN COMMON
LITTLE INTEREST
LITTLE LEARNING
LITTLE PITCHERS
LITTLE PROGRESS
LITTLE RESPONSE
LITTLE STRANGER
LIVE A CLEAN LIFE
LIVE AMMUNITION
LIVE AND LET LIVE
LIVE ON ONE'S WITS
LIVER AND ONIONS

LIVE TO A HUNDRED
LIVING LANGUAGE
LIVING QUARTERS
LIVING REMINDER
LIVING STANDARD
LLOYD'S REGISTER
LOADED QUESTION
LOAD ON ONE'S MIND
LOAD WITH CHAINS
LOCAL AUTHORITY
LOCAL NEWSPAPER
LOFTY AMBITIONS
LOGICAL CONDUCT
LOGICAL PROCESS
LONDONDERRY AIR
LONDON HOSPITAL
LONDON REGIMENT
LONDON RHAPSODY
LONDON SCOTTISH
LONDON TERMINUS
LONG ENGAGEMENT
LONGHAND WRITER
LONG IN THE TOOTH
LONG JOHN SILVER
LONG-LOST FRIEND
LONG PARLIAMENT
LONG-TERM POLICY
LOOK FOR TROUBLE
LOOK IN THE GLASS
LOOK ON ALL SIDES
LOOK PROSPEROUS
LOOK TO THE FRONT
LOOSE BEHAVIOUR
LOOSE RENDERING
LORD CHANCELLOR
LORD LIEUTENANT
LORD MAYOR'S SHOW
LORD OF CREATION
LORD OF THE ISLES
LORD OF THE MANOR
LORD PALMERSTON
LORDS AND LADIES
LORDS SPIRITUAL
LORD'S TAVERNERS
LOSE CONFIDENCE
LOSE ONE'S MEMORY
LOSE ONE'S REASON
LOSE ONE'S TEMPER
LOSE ONE'S TICKET
LOSE ONE'S TONGUE
LOSS OF APPETITE

LOSS OF INTEREST
LOSS OF PRESTIGE
LOSS OF STRENGTH
LOST TO THE WORLD
LOT TO ANSWER FOR
LOUIS ARMSTRONG
LOVE IN A COTTAGE
LOVE IN IDLENESS
LOVELY TO LOOK AT
LOVE OF PLEASURE
LOVING KINDNESS
LOWER ONE'S VOICE
LOW TEMPERATURE
LOYAL SUPPORTER
LUBRICATING OIL
LUCK OF THE DEVIL
LUCK OF THE IRISH
LUCREZIA BORGIA
LUNATIC AT LARGE
LUNCHEON BASKET
LUNCH-TIME SCORE
LYON KING OF ARMS
LYTTON STRACHEY

M—14
MACARONI CHEESE
MACHINE-GUN POST
MADAM BUTTERFLY
MADAM POMPADOUR
MADE FOR THE PART
MAGNETIC NEEDLE
MAGNOLIA STREET
MAIL-VAN ROBBERY
MAIN ATTRACTION
MAIN INGREDIENT
MAINTENANCE MAN
MAJOR OPERATION
MAKE A BEGINNING
MAKE A BIG SPLASH
MAKE A BOLT FOR IT
MAKE A COMPLAINT
MAKE A DISCOVERY
MAKE A GOOD GUESS
MAKE A GOOD SCORE
MAKE A GOOD START
MAKE ALLOWANCES
MAKE AN ENTRANCE
MAKE AN ESTIMATE
MAKE A NIGHT OF IT
MAKE A REFERENCE
MAKE A STATEMENT

MAKE DELIVERIES
MAKE EXCEPTIONS
MAKE FEW DEMANDS
MAKE FOR THE DOOR
MAKE NO PROGRESS
MAKE PROVISIONS
MAKE REPARATION
MAKE RINGS ROUND
MAKE SACRIFICES
MAKE THE RUNNING
MAKE THINGS EASY
MAKE UP A QUARREL
MAKE UP ONE'S MIND
MALCOLM SARGENT
MALE VOICE CHOIR
MANAGING EDITOR
MAN AND SUPERMAN
MANCHESTER CITY
MANDARIN ORANGE
MAN-EATING SHARK
MAN IN THE STREET
MAN OF CHARACTER
MAN OF INFLUENCE
MAN OF MANY PARTS
MAN OF SUBSTANCE
MAN OF THE MOMENT
MAN OF THE PEOPLE
MAN ON HORSEBACK
MAN'S BEST FRIEND
MAN THE DEFENCES
MANUAL LABOURER
MAPPIN TERRACES
MARATHON RUNNER
MARCHING ORDERS
MARCH THE EIGHTH
MARCH THE FOURTH
MARCH THE SECOND
MARCUS ANTONIUS
MARCUS AURELIUS
MARGIN OF ERROR
MARGIN OF PROFIT
MARGIN OF SAFETY
MARINE ENGINEER
MARITIME NATION
MARKED TENDENCY
MARKET GARDENER
MARKETING BOARD
MARKET RESEARCH
MARK OF APPROVAL
MARK OF THE BEAST
MARK OUT A COURSE

MARRIAGE BROKER
MARRIAGE BUREAU
MARRIAGE MARKET
MARSUPIAL POUCH
MASHED POTATOES
MASS PRODUCTION
MASTERMAN READY
MASTER OF HOUNDS
MATCH FOR ANYONE
MATERIAL WEALTH
MATRON OF HONOUR
MATTER OF CHOICE
MATTER OF COURSE
MATTER OF RECORD
MATTER OF REGRET
MATTERS OF STATE
MAUNDY THURSDAY
MAY THE ELEVENTH
MEANS OF SUPPORT
MECHANISED ARMY
MEDICAL ADVISER
MEDICAL COLLEGE
MEDICAL HISTORY
MEDICAL OFFICER
MEDICAL SCIENCE
MEDICAL STUDENT
MEDICINAL VALUE
MEDICINE BOTTLE
MEERSCHAUM PIPE
MELT IN THE MOUTH
MEMBER OF THE BAR
MEMBERSHIP CARD
MENDICANT ORDER
MENTAL ATTITUDE
MENTAL CAPACITY
MENTAL CONFLICT
MENTAL DISORDER
MENTAL EXERCISE
MENTAL HOSPITAL
MENTAL SICKNESS
MENTAL STIMULUS
MENTAL STRUGGLE
MENTAL WEAKNESS
MERCHANT BANKER
MERCHANT PRINCE
MERCHANT SEAMAN
MERCHANT TAILOR
MERCHANT VESSEL
MERMAID THEATRE
MERRY AND BRIGHT
MERRY CHRISTMAS

METEORIC SHOWER	MONOTONOUS LIFE
MEZZANINE FLOOR	MONROE DOCTRINE
MICHAEL BENTINE	MONSTROUS CRIME
MICHAEL FARADAY	MONTHLY ACCOUNT
MICHAELMAS TERM	MONTHLY PAYMENT
MICHAEL WILDING	MONTH OF SUNDAYS
MIDDLE DISTANCE	MONUMENTAL WORK
MIDDLE OF THE DAY	MOONLIGHT NIGHT
MIDDLE REGISTER	MORAL BLACKMAIL
MIDNIGHT REVELS	MORAL CERTAINTY
MIDSHIPMAN EASY	MORAL CHARACTER
MIDSUMMER NIGHT	MORAL COWARDICE
MILD PUNISHMENT	MORAL IGNORANCE
MILITARY ATTACK	MORAL NECESSITY
MILITARY CAREER	MORAL PRINCIPLE
MILITARY ESCORT	MORAL TURPITUDE
MILITARY GENIUS	MORE THAN A MATCH
MILITARY PARADE	MORE THAN ENOUGH
MILITARY POLICE	MORE TO THE POINT
MILITARY SCHOOL	MORNING SERVICE
MILITARY SPIRIT	MOROCCO LEATHER
MILITARY TATTOO	MOST HONOURABLE
MILK OF MAGNESIA	MOST OF THE NIGHT
MILLION DOLLARS	MOTHER AND CHILD
MILL ON THE FLOSS	MOTHER'S DARLING
MIND OVER MATTER	MOTHERS' MEETING
MINERAL DEPOSIT	MOTHER SUPERIOR
MINERAL KINGDOM	MOTLEY ASSEMBLY
MINESTRONE SOUP	MOTOR AMBULANCE
MINING ENGINEER	MOTOR TRANSPORT
MINISTRY OF FOOD	MOUNTAIN RESORT
MINOR OPERATION	MOUNTING DANGER
MISSIONARY WORK	MOUNT THE THRONE
MISTER MICAWBER	MOVE TO LAUGHTER
MISTLETOE BOUGH	MOVING PAVEMENT
MNEMONIC DEVICE	MUCH IN EVIDENCE
MOBILE FEATURES	MUCH-MARRIED MAN
MOCK TURTLE SOUP	MULTIPLY BY FIVE
MODEL AEROPLANE	MULTIPLY BY FOUR
MODEL BEHAVIOUR	MULTIPLY BY NINE
MODEL HOUSEHOLD	MUNITIONS OF WAR
MODERATE DEGREE	MURDER MOST FOUL
MODERATE HEALTH	MUSCULAR ENERGY
MODERATE HEIGHT	MUSEUM SPECIMEN
MODERATE INCOME	MUSHROOM GROWTH
MODERATE WEIGHT	MUSHROOM SUBURB
MODERN BUILDING	MUSICAL ABILITY
MODERN LANGUAGE	MUSICAL EVENING
MODS AND ROCKERS	MUSICAL GLASSES
MONEY IN THE BANK	MUSICAL MOMENTS
MONKEY BUSINESS	MUSICAL PRODIGY

MUSICAL QUALITY
MUSIC PUBLISHER
MUSTARD PLASTER
MUTE ADMIRATION
MUTUAL GOODWILL
MUTUAL SYMPATHY
MUZZLE VELOCITY
MY LADY NICOTINE

N—14

NAME AND ADDRESS
NAMELESS TERROR
NAME YOUR POISON
NAMING CEREMONY
NAPOLEON BRANDY
NAPOLEONIC CODE
NAPOLEONIC WARS
NARRATIVE VERSE
NARROW INTERVAL
NARROW MAJORITY
NASTY BIT OF WORK
NATIONAL ANTHEM
NATIONAL CREDIT
NATIONAL CRISIS
NATIONAL DEVICE
NATIONAL EMBLEM
NATIONAL FIGURE
NATIONAL HEALTH
NATIONAL INCOME
NATIONAL SPIRIT
NATIONAL STATUS
NATIONAL WEALTH
NATIONAL WINNER
NATION-WIDE HUNT
NATIVE COMPOUND
NATIVE LANGUAGE
NATIVE QUARTERS
NATURAL HARBOUR
NATURAL HISTORY
NATURAL IMPULSE
NATURAL PROCESS
NATURAL SCIENCE
NAVAL ARCHITECT
NAVAL EXERCISES
NAVAL OPERATION
NAVIGABLE RIVER
NEANDERTHAL MAN
NEAR NEIGHBOURS
NEAR THE KNUCKLE
NEAT AS A BANDBOX
NEEDLES AND PINS

NE'ER CAST A CLOUT
NEGATIVE ACTION
NEGATIVE ANSWER
NEGATIVE RESULT
NEGRO SPIRITUAL
NERVOUS TENSION
NETHER GARMENTS
NEUTRAL COUNTRY
NEVER-NEVER LAND
NEVER SATISFIED
NEW CONSIGNMENT
NEW-FANGLED IDEA
NEW LAMPS FOR OLD
NEW LEASE OF LIFE
NEWS OF THE WORLD
NEWSPAPER WORLD
NEXT BEST FRIEND
NEXT GENERATION
NICE DIFFERENCE
NICELY BALANCED
NICE PERCEPTION
NIGGER MINSTREL
NIGHT BLINDNESS
NIGHT-CLUB QUEEN
NIL DESPERANDUM
NINE DAYS' WONDER
NINE MEN'S MORRIS
NINE O'CLOCK NEWS
NINE OF DIAMONDS
NINEPENNY STAMP
NINETEEN AND SIX
NINETEEN AND TEN
NINETEEN AND TWO
NINETEENTH HOLE
NINETEEN TWENTY
NINETY THOUSAND
NINTH OF JANUARY
NINTH OF OCTOBER
NIPPED IN THE BUD
NOBLESSE OBLIGE
NOBODY'S DARLING
NO END OF A FELLOW
NO FIXED ADDRESS
NO HALF MEASURES
NOISE ABATEMENT
NO JOKING MATTER
NOMINAL CAPITAL
NOMINAL DAMAGES
NOMINATIVE CASE
NORMAL SOLUTION
NORMAN CONQUEST

NO ROOM AT THE INN
NO ROOM FOR DOUBT
NORTH AUSTRALIA
NORTHERN ACCENT
NORTHERN LIGHTS
NORTH OF ENGLAND
NORTH OF THE WASH
NORTHWARD BOUND
NOSE OUT OF JOINT
NO STOMACH FOR IT
NOTHING DAUNTED
NOTHING TO OFFER
NOTHING TO SPARE
NOTHING VENTURE
NO THOROUGHFARE
NO TROUBLE AT ALL
NOUN OF ASSEMBLY
NOVEL SITUATION
NO VISIBLE MEANS
NUCLEAR FISSION
NUCLEAR PHYSICS
NUCLEAR REACTOR
NUCLEAR WARFARE
NUMBER THIRTEEN
NUMERICAL ORDER
NURSERY CANNONS
NURSING SERVICE
NUTS AND RAISINS
NYLON STOCKINGS

O—14
OBITUARY NOTICE
OBJECT OF TERROR
OBSCURE PROBLEM
OBSERVATION CAR
OCCASIONAL SHOT
OCCUPYING FORCE
OCEAN GREYHOUND
OCTAVIUS CAESAR
OEDIPUS COMPLEX
OFFER AN OPINION
OFFICE BUILDING
OFFICE OF PROFIT
OFFICER OF STATE
OFFICERS AND MEN
OFFICIAL CENSUS
OFFICIAL NOTICE
OFFICIAL REPORT
OFFICIAL SECRET
OFFICIAL SOURCE
OFFICIAL STRIKE

OFF LIKE A STREAK
OFFSET PRINTING
OFF THE PREMISES
OFF WITH THE HEAD
OF HUMAN BONDAGE
OLD BOYS' REUNION
OLD CLOTHES SHOP
OLD FOLKS AT HOME
OLD MAN OF THE SEA
OLD MOTHER RILEY
OLD PEOPLE'S HOME
OLD-TIME DANCING
OLD-WORLD GARDEN
OLIVER CROMWELL
OMNIBUS EDITION
ON A HEROIC SCALE
ON A HIGHER PLANE
ONE AND A QUARTER
ONE AND SIXPENCE
ONE AND TENPENCE
ONE AND TWOPENCE
ONE-ARMED BANDIT
ONE CLAIM TO FAME
ONE CROWDED HOUR
ONE FINE MORNING
ONE IN A THOUSAND
ONE-MAN BUSINESS
ONE NIGHT OF LOVE
ONE OF THE FAMILY
ONE OF THE PEOPLE
ONE OF THESE DAYS
ONE THAT GOT AWAY
ONLY TOO PLEASED
ON ONE CONDITION
ON ONE'S BEAM-ENDS
ON ONE'S DEATH-BED
ON ONE'S HIND LEGS
ON ONE'S LAST LEGS
ON ONE'S OWN TERMS
ON PLEASURE BENT
ON PUBLIC GROUND
ON SHORT RATIONS
ON SUBSCRIPTION
ON THE BAND-WAGON
ON THE CONTINENT
ON THE DEBIT SIDE
ON THE DEFENSIVE
ON THE DOWNGRADE
ON THE HOME FRONT
ON THE LARGE SIZE
ON THE OFF CHANCE

ON THE OFFENSIVE
ON THE OTHER HAND
ON THE OTHER SIDE
ON THE OUTSKIRTS
ON THE PROMENADE
ON THE RIGHT SIDE
ON THE SHADY SIDE
ON THE SHORT LIST
ON THE SHORT SIDE
ON THE SMALL SIDE
ON THE SUNNY SIDE
ON THE TELEPHONE
ON THE THRESHOLD
ON THE TIGHT SIDE
ON THE TOUCH-LINE
ON THE WRONG FOOT
ON THE WRONG SIDE
ON THE WRONG TRACK
ON TO A GOOD THING
ON WITH THE DANCE
OPEN-AIR CONCERT
OPEN-AIR SERVICE
OPEN-AIR SPEAKER
OPEN-AIR THEATRE
OPEN-CAST MINING
OPEN CONFESSION
OPEN DISCUSSION
OPEN-DOOR POLICY
OPENING BATSMAN
OPEN PARLIAMENT
OPEN THE BIDDING
OPEN THE INNINGS
OPEN THE SLUICES
OPEN TO ARGUMENT
OPEN TO QUESTION
OPEN TOURNAMENT
OPERATING TABLE
OPERATIONS ROOM
OPPOSITE NUMBER
OPPOSITION WHIP
ORCHESTRA STALL
ORDER IN ADVANCE
ORDER IN COUNCIL
ORDERLY CONDUCT
ORDERLY OFFICER
ORDER OF THE BATH
ORDER OF THE BOOT
ORDINARY SEAMAN
ORDINARY SHARES
ORDNANCE SURVEY
ORGANIC DISEASE

ORGANISED GAMES
ORNAMENTAL POND
ORNAMENTAL TREE
ORTHODOX CHURCH
OSTRICH FEATHER
OTHER FISH TO FRY
OUNCE OF TOBACCO
OUT-AND-OUT ROGUE
OUTDOOR MEETING
OUTDOOR SERVANT
OUT FOR THE COUNT
OUTGOING TENANT
OUT OF CHARACTER
OUT OF CONDITION
OUT OF CURIOSITY
OUT OF ONE'S DEPTH
OUT OF ONE'S SHELL
OUT OF THE COMMON
OUT OF THE GUTTER
OUT OF THIS WORLD
OUTSIDE ONE'S KEN
OUTSIDE OPINION
OVERCOME BY FEAR
OVERDUE ACCOUNT
OVER THE COUNTER
OVER THE RAINBOW
OXFORD MOVEMENT
OXYGEN CYLINDER

P—14
PACKET OF CRISPS
PACKET OF TWENTY
PACKING STATION
PACK OF NONSENSE
PACK ONE'S TRUNKS
PAGES OF HISTORY
PAINT AND POWDER
PAINT A PORTRAIT
PAIR OF BREECHES
PAIR OF CALIPERS
PAIR OF CLIPPERS
PAIR OF CRUTCHES
PAIR OF SCISSORS
PAIR OF SLIPPERS
PAIR OF TROUSERS
PAIR OF TWEEZERS
PALM OF ONE'S HAND
PANCAKE LANDING
PANCAKE TUESDAY
PANGS OF REMORSE
PANTOMIME QUEEN

PANZER DIVISION
PARADISE FOR TWO
PARALLEL COURSE
PARCHMENT PAPER
PARISH MAGAZINE
PARISH REGISTER
PARKING PROBLEM
PARLIAMENT HILL
PARMESAN CHEESE
PAROXYSM OF RAGE
PARTIAL CONSENT
PARTIAL ECLIPSE
PARTIAL SUCCESS
PARTING PRESENT
PARTISAN SPIRIT
PARTNER IN CRIME
PARTY MACHINERY
PARTY PROGRAMME
PASS DOWN THE CAR
PASSENGER PLANE
PASSENGER TRAIN
PASSING THOUGHT
PASSIONATE PLEA
PASS THE MUSTARD
PAST AND PRESENT
PAST EXPERIENCE
PASTORAL LETTER
PAST PARTICIPLE
PAST REDEMPTION
PATCHWORK QUILT
PATÉ DE FOIE GRAS
PATENT MEDICINE
PATERNOSTER ROW
PAUSE FOR A WHILE
PAUSE FOR BREATH
PAVEMENT ARTIST
PAVING MATERIAL
PAYABLE AT SIGHT
PAY A COMPLIMENT
PAY NO ATTENTION
PEACE AND PLENTY
PEACEFUL ENDING
PEACE IN OUR TIME
PEAL OF LAUGHTER
PEARLS OF WISDOM
PECULIAR PEOPLE
PECULIAR PERSON
PEDIGREE CATTLE
PEER OF THE REALM
PEG-TOP TROUSERS
PENAL SERVITUDE

PENCIL AND PAPER
PENNY FOR THE GUY
PENNY IN THE SLOT
PENSIONABLE AGE
PEPPERCORN RENT
PERCUSSION BAND
PERFECT DARLING
PERFECT EXAMPLE
PERFECT SETTING
PERFECT SILENCE
PERFORMING BEAR
PERFORMING FLEA
PERFORMING SEAL
PERPETUAL BLISS
PERPETUAL WORRY
PERSONAL APPEAL
PERSONAL COLUMN
PERSONAL ESTATE
PERSONAL ESTEEM
PERSONAL FACTOR
PERSONAL FAVOUR
PERSONAL LETTER
PERSONAL MATTER
PERSONAL REMARK
PERSON IN CHARGE
PERSON OF REPUTE
PERSONS UNKNOWN
PERSON TO PERSON
PERTINENT REPLY
PETER AND GORDON
PETER THE HERMIT
PETROLEUM JELLY
PETROL SHORTAGE
PETTY GRIEVANCE
PHOTOGRAPH WELL
PHRASE AND FABLE
PHYSICAL BEAUTY
PHYSICAL ENERGY
PICCADILLY LINE
PICKLED CABBAGE
PICKLED HERRING
PICK OF THE BUNCH
PICK UP A FEW TIPS
PICK UP STRENGTH
PICKWICK PAPERS
PICTURE GALLERY
PICTURE OF GLOOM
PICTURE WRITING
PIERCE THE HEART
PIERCING GLANCE
PIETRO ANNIGONI

PILE ON THE AGONY
PILGRIM FATHERS
PILLAR OF THE LAW
PILLAR OF WISDOM
PILOTLESS PLANE
PINCER MOVEMENT
PINCH AND SCRAPE
PINEAPPLE JUICE
PINNACLE OF FAME
PINS AND NEEDLES
PITCH OVERBOARD
PLACE IN HISTORY
PLACE OF ONE'S OWN
PLACE OF WORSHIP
PLAGUE OF LONDON
PLAICE AND CHIPS
PLAIN AND SIMPLE
PLAIN CHOCOLATE
PLAIN STATEMENT
PLANETARY ORBIT
PLANNED ECONOMY
PLANNING OFFICE
PLAN OF CAMPAIGN
PLANTATION SONG
PLASTER OF PARIS
PLASTIC SURGEON
PLASTIC SURGERY
PLATFORM ORATOR
PLATFORM TICKET
PLATINUM BLONDE
PLAUSIBLE ROGUE
PLAY AT SOLDIERS
PLAY FOR ENGLAND
PLAY GOOSEBERRY
PLAY THE TRAITOR
PLAY THE VILLAIN
PLAY TO THE CROWD
PLEAD IGNORANCE
PLEAD NOT GUILTY
PLEAD ONE'S CAUSE
PLEASANT DREAMS
PLEASANT MANNER
PLEASANT PEOPLE
PLEASED AS PUNCH
PLEASE TURN OVER
PLEASURE CRUISE
PLEASURE GROUND
PLEASURE LAUNCH
PLEASURE SEEKER
PLEDGE ONE'S WORD
PLOT ONE'S COURSE

M.C.D.—15

PLOUGHING MATCH
PLOUGH THE WAVES
PLUCK UP COURAGE
PLUMB THE DEPTHS
PLUNGED IN GRIEF
PLUNGE INTO DEBT
PNEUMATIC BRAKE
PNEUMATIC DRILL
POCKET AN INSULT
POET AND PEASANT
POETRY IN MOTION
POINT OF CONTACT
POINT OUT THE WAY
POINT WELL TAKEN
POISED TO STRIKE
POISONOUS PLANT
POKE ONE'S NOSE IN
POLARIZED GLASS
POLICEMAN'S BEAT
POLICE SERGEANT
POLISH CORRIDOR
POLISH OFF A MEAL
POLITICAL AGENT
POLITICAL EXILE
POLITICAL PARTY
POLITICAL SPIRIT
POLLING STATION
PONTEFRACT CAKE
POOR MAN'S FRIEND
POOR MAN'S LAWYER
POOR VISIBILITY
POOR VOCABULARY
POPPA PICCOLINO
POP THE QUESTION
POPULAR CONCERT
POPULAR EDITION
POPULAR OPINION
POPULAR REQUEST
POPULAR SCIENCE
POPULAR VERDICT
PORTLAND CEMENT
PORTRAIT ARTIST
POSITIVE ACTION
POSITIVE CHARGE
POSITIVE COLOUR
POSITIVE DEGREE
POSITIVE MENACE
POSSESSIVE CASE
POSSESSIVE LOVE
POSTAL DELIVERY
POSTAL DISTRICT

POSTHUMOUS FAME
POST-WAR CREDITS
POWDER AND PAINT
POWDER MAGAZINE
POWERFUL SPEECH
PRACTICAL JOKER
PRACTISE DECEIT
PRECIOUS LITTLE
PRE-NATAL CLINIC
PREPARE A BUDGET
PREPARED SPEECH
PREPARE ONESELF
PRESCRIBED TEXT
PRESENCE OF MIND
PRESENT A CHEQUE
PRESENT ADDRESS
PRESENT COMPANY
PRESERVED FRUIT
PRESIDENT ELECT
PRESIDING JUDGE
PRESSED FOR TIME
PRESS FOR ACTION
PRESSING DANGER
PRESSING DUTIES
PRESS THE BUTTON
PRESSURE COOKER
PRESSURE OF WORK
PREVAILING WIND
PREY ON ONE'S MIND
PRICE OF SILENCE
PRICE REDUCTION
PRICKLY FEELING
PRIMA BALLERINA
PRIMARY MEANING
PRIME CONDITION
PRIMEVAL FOREST
PRIMITIVE TRIBE
PRIMROSE LEAGUE
PRIMROSE YELLOW
PRINCE CHARMING
PRINCE OF ORANGE
PRINCE OF ROGUES
PRISON CHAPLAIN
PRISON GOVERNOR
PRISON SENTENCE
PRIVATE ADDRESS
PRIVATE CITIZEN
PRIVATE COMPANY
PRIVATE HEARING
PRIVATE OPINION
PRIVATE SOCIETY

PRIVATE SOLDIER
PRIVATE TEACHER
PRIVATE TUITION
PRIZE-GIVING DAY
PROBABLE WINNER
PRO BONO PUBLICO
PRODUCE RESULTS
PRODUCTION LINE
PROFITABLE DEAL
PROFITLESS TASK
PROFOUND EFFECT
PROFOUND SECRET
PROGRAMME MUSIC
PROGRESS OF TIME
PROGRESS REPORT
PROHIBITION ERA
PROLIFIC WRITER
PROMISING PUPIL
PROMISING START
PROMISSORY NOTE
PROMPT DECISION
PROMPT DELIVERY
PROOF OF POSTING
PROPER FRACTION
PROPOSE A MOTION
PROPOSED ACTION
PROSCENIUM ARCH
PROSPEROUS YEAR
PROTECTED STATE
PROTEST AGAINST
PROTEST MEETING
PROTEST TOO MUCH
PROVE EXPENSIVE
PROVEN INNOCENT
PROVE ONE'S POINT
PROVIDE HEATING
PROVOST MARSHAL
PUBLIC APPLAUSE
PUBLIC DISGRACE
PUBLIC ENTRANCE
PUBLIC EXPOSURE
PUBLIC FOOTPATH
PUBLIC INTEREST
PUBLICITY AGENT
PUBLIC NUISANCE
PUBLIC PROPERTY
PUBLIC SPIRITED
PUBLISHER'S NOTE
PULL ONE'S WEIGHT
PULL THE STRINGS
PULL THE TRIGGER

PUMPING STATION
PUNCH ON THE HEAD
PUNCH ON THE NOSE
PUNITIVE ACTION
PURE CONJECTURE
PURSUIT OF POWER
PUSHED FOR MONEY
PUSH OUT THE BOAT
PUSH THE BOAT OUT
PUT IN A BAD LIGHT
PUT IN A GOOD WORD
PUT IN ONE'S PLACE
PUT IN THE MIDDLE
PUT IN THE STOCKS
PUT IT IN WRITING
PUT IT TO THE VOTE
PUT NEW LIFE INTO
PUT OFF THE SCENT
PUT ON A BOLD FACE
PUT ON A PEDESTAL
PUT ONE'S SPOKE IN
PUT ON THE AGENDA
PUT ON THE MARKET
PUT ON THE SCALES
PUT OUT OF ACTION
PUT OUT THE LIGHT
PUT THE CLOCKS ON
PUT THE HELM DOWN
PUT THE KETTLE ON
PUT THE KIBOSH ON
PUT THE QUESTION
PUT THINGS RIGHT
PUT UNDER ARREST
PUT UP A GOOD SHOW
PUT UP A STRUGGLE
PYRRHIC VICTORY

Q—14
QUALITY OF MERCY
QUARTER OF A YARD
QUARTER PAST ONE
QUARTER PAST SIX
QUARTER PAST TEN
QUARTER PAST TWO
QUARTER TO EIGHT
QUARTER TO SEVEN
QUARTER TO THREE
QUEEN ANNE HOUSE
QUEEN ANNE'S GATE
QUEEN ANNE STYLE
QUEEN CHARLOTTE

QUEEN ELIZABETH
QUEEN OF ENGLAND
QUEEN'S BIRTHDAY
QUEEN'S EVIDENCE
QUEEN'S PLEASURE
QUEEN'S SHILLING
QUEEN'S SUBJECTS
QUEER IN THE HEAD
QUEER ONE'S PITCH
QUEER SITUATION
QUESTION MASTER
QUESTION OF TIME
QUICK AS THOUGHT
QUICK-FIRING GUN
QUICK LOOK ROUND
QUICK ON THE DRAW
QUICK VENGEANCE
QUITE A STRANGER
QUITE DIFFERENT
QUIVER AND SHAKE
QUIVER WITH RAGE
QUOTATION MARKS

R—14
RACING CALENDAR
RACKED WITH PAIN
RADICAL OUTLOOK
RADIO ANNOUNCER
RADIO ASTRONOMY
RADIO FREQUENCY
RADIO PROGRAMME
RADIO TELEGRAPH
RADIO TELEPHONE
RADIO TELESCOPE
RADIO THERAPIST
RAGS AND TATTERS
RAILWAY COMPANY
RAILWAY CUTTING
RAILWAY JOURNEY
RAILWAY SLEEPER
RAILWAY STATION
RAILWAY VIADUCT
RAILWAY WARRANT
RAIN IN TORRENTS
RAISE A MEMORIAL
RAISE A QUESTION
RAISED EYEBROWS
RAISED PLATFORM
RAISE ONE'S GLASS
RAISE ONE'S HOPES
RAISE ONE'S VOICE

RAISE THE SIGHTS	REFRESH ONESELF
RAKE IN THE MONEY	REFUGEE PROBLEM
RAKE OUT THE FIRE	REFUSE A HEARING
RANGE OF MEANING	REFUSE DISPOSAL
RAPID PROMOTION	REGAL SPLENDOUR
RAPT EXPRESSION	REGIMENTAL BAND
RARE ATMOSPHERE	REGISTERED MAIL
RARE OCCURRENCE	REGISTERED POST
RASH ASSUMPTION	REGISTRY OFFICE
RATE OF EXCHANGE	REGULAR BEDTIME
RATE OF INTEREST	REGULAR SERVICE
RATE OF PROGRESS	REGULAR SOLDIER
RATTLE THE SABRE	REGULATION SIZE
RAVENOUS HUNGER	REIGNING BEAUTY
REACH A DECISION	REIGNING FAMILY
REACH AGREEMENT	RELATIVE CLAUSE
REACH FOR THE SKY	RELATIVE VALUES
REACH THE DEPTHS	RELIC OF THE PAST
REACH THE ZENITH	RELIEVING FORCE
READING GLASSES	RELIGIOUS FAITH
READ MEN'S HEARTS	RELIGIOUS HOUSE
READ THE MINUTES	RELIGIOUS MANIA
READ THE RIOT ACT	RELIGIOUS ORDER
REALLY AND TRULY	RELIGIOUS RITES
REAPING MACHINE	RELIGIOUS TRACT
REAP THE BENEFIT	REMAINS OF A MEAL
REAP THE HARVEST	REMARKABLE GIRL
REAR-VIEW MIRROR	REMEMBRANCE DAY
REAR-VIEW WINDOW	REMOTE ANCESTOR
REASONABLE TIME	REMOVE FRICTION
RECEIVE A LEGACY	RENDER A SERVICE
RECEIVE A LETTER	RENEW ONE'S YOUTH
RECEIVE QUARTER	RENEW THE ATTACK
RECEIVING ORDER	REPAIRING LEASE
RECEPTION CLERK	REPEATING RIFLE
RECKLESS DRIVER	REPEATING WATCH
RECKLESS GAMBLE	REPORTED SPEECH
RECORDING ANGEL	REPORT PROGRESS
RECORD TURNOVER	REPRESS THE NEWS
RECOVER ONESELF	REPUBLICAN VOTE
RECREATION ROOM	REPULSIVE FORCE
REDUCE IN NUMBER	RESEARCH WORKER
REDUCE TO POWDER	RESERVE ACCOUNT
REED INSTRUMENT	RESIDENT ABROAD
REFECTORY TABLE	RESISTANCE COIL
REFINED SOCIETY	RESISTANCE UNIT
REFLECTED GLORY	RESPECT ONESELF
REFLECTED IMAGE	RESPONSIBLE MAN
REFLECTIVE MOOD	RESTLESS NATURE
REFORMED CHURCH	REST ON ONE'S OARS
REFRESHMENT BAR	RESTORE HARMONY

RESTORE TO POWER
RESTRICTED AREA
RETAILER OF NEWS
RETAINING FORCE
RETROGRADE STEP
RETURN A VERDICT
RETURN TO HEALTH
RETURN TO NORMAL
RETURN TO SENDER
REVENGE IS SWEET
REVENGE ONESELF
REVENUE OFFICER
REVERSIBLE COAT
REVERT TO NORMAL
REVISED EDITION
REVISED VERSION
REVOLVING DOORS
REVOLVING STAGE
RHAPSODY IN BLUE
RHEUMATIC FEVER
RHINOCEROS HIDE
RHODE ISLAND RED
RHYME NOR REASON
RHYMING COUPLET
RICHARD MURDOCH
RICHARD STRAUSS
RICH IN VITAMINS
RICHMOND BRIDGE
RICH VOCABULARY
RIDE A COCK-HORSE
RIDE SIDE-SADDLE
RIDING BREECHES
RIGHT ABOUT FACE
RIGHT ABOUT TURN
RIGHT AND PROPER
RIGHT AS A TRIVET
RIGHT DIRECTION
RIGHT FIRST TIME
RIGHT FROM WRONG
RIGHT-HAND DRIVE
RING IN ONE'S EARS
RING THE CHANGES
RIPE EXPERIENCE
RISE IN THE WORLD
RISE TO ONE'S FEET
RISK EVERYTHING
RITUAL PRACTICE
ROAD TO THE ISLES
ROAD TRAFFIC ACT
ROARING FORTIES
ROARING SUCCESS

ROAR OF LAUGHTER
ROBERT BROWNING
ROBERT CUMMINGS
ROBERT HELPMANN
ROBERT THE BRUCE
ROBIN REDBREAST
ROBINSON CRUSOE
ROCKY MOUNTAINS
RODENT OPERATOR
ROD FOR ONE'S BACK
ROD, POLE OR PERCH
ROGER BANNISTER
ROLL A CIGARETTE
ROLLED UMBRELLA
ROLLING COUNTRY
ROLLING EXPANSE
ROLLING IN MONEY
ROMANTIC AFFAIR
ROMANTIC COMEDY
ROMEO AND JULIET
ROOF OF THE MOUTH
ROOF OF THE WORLD
ROOM FOR DISPUTE
ROSES ALL THE WAY
ROSES OF PICARDY
ROUGH AND TUMBLE
ROUGH TREATMENT
ROUND SHOULDERS
ROUND THE CORNER
ROUND THE HOUSES
ROUND THE WICKET
ROUSE CURIOSITY
ROUTE NATIONALE
ROVING REPORTER
ROW OVER NOTHING
ROYAL ARTILLERY
ROYAL AUTHORITY
ROYAL ENCLOSURE
ROYAL ENGINEERS
ROYAL FUSILIERS
ROYAL HOUSEHOLD
ROYAL RECEPTION
ROYAL RESIDENCE
ROYAL TANK CORPS
RUBBER OF BRIDGE
RUB THE WRONG WAY
RUDYARD KIPLING
RUGGED FEATURES
RUINOUS EXPENSE
RULE ABSOLUTELY
RULE OUT OF ORDER

RULES OF CRICKET
RULES OF THE GAME
RUMP PARLIAMENT
RUNAWAY VICTORY
RUN FOR DEAR LIFE
RUN FOR ONE'S LIFE
RUN INTO TROUBLE
RUN LIKE A RABBIT
RUN LIKE THE WIND
RUNNING ACCOUNT
RUNNING REMARKS
RUNNING REPAIRS
RUN OF THE MARKET
RUN OUT OF PETROL
RUN THE GAUNTLET
RUN UP AN ACCOUNT
RUN WITH THE HARE
RUN WITH THE PACK
RUSH-HOUR TRAVEL
RUSH INTO THINGS
RUSH ONE'S FENCES
RUSSIAN LEATHER
RUSTLE OF SPRING

S—14
SACK OF POTATOES
SACRED PRECINCT
SACRED WRITINGS
SADDER AND WISER
SADDLE OF MUTTON
SAFETY MEASURES
SAGE REFLECTION
SALIENT FEATURE
SALINE SOLUTION
SALISBURY PLAIN
SALT OF THE EARTH
SALUTARY LESSON
SAMUEL PICKWICK
SAMUEL PLIMSOLL
SARAH BERNHARDT
SARTOR RESARTUS
SATANIC MAJESTY
SATELLITE STATE
SATURDAY'S CHILD
SAUSAGE AND MASH
SAVELOY SAUSAGE
SAVE ONE'S BREATH
SAVINGS ACCOUNT
SAY GOOD-MORNING
SAYING AND DOING
SAY ONE'S PRAYERS

SCALE OF CHARGES
SCALP TREATMENT
SCATTER THE SEED
SCENARIO WRITER
SCHEME OF THINGS
SCHOLASTIC POST
SCHOOL BUILDING
SCHOOL GOVERNOR
SCHOOL HOLIDAYS
SCHOOL MAGAZINE
SCHOOL OF WHALES
SCIENCE FICTION
SCIENTIFIC GAME
SCOBIE BREASLEY
SCORE A BULL'S EYE
SCOTCH AND WATER
SCOTCH THE SNAKE
SCOTCH WOODCOCK
SCOTS FUSILIERS
SCOTTISH CHURCH
SCOTTISH LEAGUE
SCOTTISH OFFICE
SCRAPE TOGETHER
SCRATCH A LIVING
SCREAMING FARCE
SCROLL OF HONOUR
SCRUBBING BRUSH
SCRUPULOUS CARE
SCUM OF THE EARTH
SEA-GOING VESSEL
SEALED ENVELOPE
SEAL OF APPROVAL
SEARCH FOR TRUTH
SEASIDE HOLIDAY
SEASONABLE GIFT
SEASONABLE TIME
SEASONED TIMBER
SEAT IN THE LORDS
SEAT OF LEARNING
SEAT ON THE BENCH
SEAT ON THE BOARD
SECLUDED CORNER
SECOND DIVIDEND
SECOND DIVISION
SECOND ENGINEER
SECOND-HAND BOOK
SECOND-HAND SHOP
SECOND INTERVAL
SECOND MARRIAGE
SECOND OF AUGUST
SECOND-RATE MIND

SECOND SYMPHONY
SECOND THOUGHTS
SECOND WORLD WAR
SECRET INTRIGUE
SECURE A VICTORY
SECURE FOOTHOLD
SECURE POSITION
SECURITY POLICE
SEE JUSTICE DONE
SEE WHAT HAPPENS
SEIDLITZ POWDER
SEIZE THE CHANCE
SELECTION BOARD
SELF-SERVICE BAR
SEMI-FINAL MATCH
SEMI-FINAL ROUND
SEND A MESSENGER
SEND IN ONE'S CARD
SEND ONE PACKING
SEND TO THE STAKE
SENIOR REGIMENT
SENIOR WRANGLER
SENSELESS ORDER
SENSE OF BALANCE
SENSE OF DECENCY
SENSE OF HEARING
SENSE OF LOYALTY
SENSE OF PURPOSE
SENSITIVE PAPER
SENSITIVE PLANT
SENTIMENTAL BOY
SENT TO COVENTRY
SEPARATE TABLES
SERENE HIGHNESS
SERIES OF EVENTS
SERIOUS ATTEMPT
SERIOUS ILLNESS
SERIOUS MISTAKE
SERIOUS OFFENCE
SERIOUS STUDENT
SERIOUS SUBJECT
SERIOUS THOUGHT
SERIOUS TROUBLE
SERVANT PROBLEM
SERVE A SENTENCE
SERVES ONE RIGHT
SERVICE STATION
SET A BAD EXAMPLE
SET ARRANGEMENT
SET OF GOLF-CLUBS
SET THINGS RIGHT

SETTLE ACCOUNTS
SETTLE A QUARREL
SETTLED PURPOSE
SETTLED WEATHER
SETTLE ONE'S HASH
SEVEN AGES OF MAN
SEVEN AND A PENNY
SEVEN AND ELEVEN
SEVEN SHILLINGS
SEVENTEEN MILES
SEVENTH CENTURY
SEVENTH OF APRIL
SEVENTH OF MARCH
SEVENTY PER CENT
SEVERE SENTENCE
SHADOW MINISTER
SHADOW OF A DOUBT
SHADY CHARACTER
SHAGGY-DOG STORY
SHAKE LIKE A LEAF
SHAKE OF THE HEAD
SHAKE THE BOTTLE
SHAKE UP AND DOWN
SHALLOW PRETEXT
SHANNON AIRPORT
SHARE THE SPOILS
SHARP AS A NEEDLE
SHARP ENCOUNTER
SHARPEN THE WITS
SHARP REJOINDER
SHARPS AND FLATS
SHATTERING BLOW
SHEEPDOG TRIALS
SHEEP'S CLOTHING
SHEET LIGHTNING
SHEFFIELD PLATE
SHEFFIELD STEEL
SHEPHERD'S CROOK
SHEPHERD'S PURSE
SHERLOCK HOLMES
SHERWOOD FOREST
SHILLING A POUND
SHINING EXAMPLE
SHIP IN DISTRESS
SHIPPING CENTRE
SHIPPING OFFICE
SHIP'S CARPENTER
SHIVER AND SHAKE
SHOCKED SILENCE
SHOCKING TEMPER
SHOCK TREATMENT

SHOOTING RIGHTS	SIMPLY FABULOUS
SHOOTING SEASON	SIMPLY STARVING
SHOOTING TROPHY	SINCERE APOLOGY
SHOOT THE RAPIDS	SINGLE INSTANCE
SHOPPING ARCADE	SINGULAR NUMBER
SHOPPING BASKET	SINKING FEELING
SHOPPING CENTRE	SINK LIKE A STONE
SHORT AND STOCKY	SINK OF INIQUITY
SHORTHAND SPEED	SINS OF OMISSION
SHORT OF CAPITAL	SINS OF THE FLESH
SHORT PARAGRAPH	SIR ADRIAN BOULT
SHORT STATEMENT	SIR EDWARD ELGAR
SHOT-GUN WEDDING	SIR HENRY IRVING
SHOULDER OF LAMB	SIR HUGH WALPOLE
SHOULDER OF VEAL	SIR ISAAC NEWTON
SHOW A BOLD FRONT	SIR ISAAC PITMAN
SHOW COMPASSION	SIR JAMES BARRIE
SHOW MODERATION	SIR JOHN GIELGUD
SHOW OF STRENGTH	SIR WALTER SCOTT
SHOW OF SYMPATHY	SIT ON THE GROUND
SHOW ONE'S TICKET	SIT ON THE THRONE
SHOW ONE THE DOOR	SIX AND SIXPENCE
SHOW RELUCTANCE	SIX AND TENPENCE
SHOW REPENTANCE	SIX AND TWOPENCE
SHREWD OBSERVER	SIXES AND SEVENS
SHRIMP COCKTAIL	SIX FEET OF EARTH
SHUTTLE SERVICE	SIXTEEN AND FIVE
SICKENING SIGHT	SIXTEEN AND FOUR
SIEGE OF LUCKNOW	SIXTEEN AND NINE
SIGH WITH RELIEF	SIXTEEN PER CENT
SIGMUND ROMBERG	SIXTEENTH GREEN
SIGNALS OFFICER	SIXTEENTH OF MAY
SIGN OF GOOD LUCK	SIXTH OF JANUARY
SIGN OF STRENGTH	SIXTH OF OCTOBER
SIGN OF THE CROSS	SIXTY-SIX AND SIX
SIGN OF THE TIMES	SIXTY-TWO AND SIX
SIGN OF WEAKNESS	SIX WICKETS DOWN
SILENCE IN COURT	SKATE ON THIN ICE
SILENCE REIGNED	SKILLED WORKMAN
SILENT REPROACH	SKITTLES PLAYER
SILKS AND SATINS	SLASHING ATTACK
SILVANA MANGANO	SLAVE OF FASHION
SILVER BRACELET	SLAVE OF THE LAMP
SILVER STANDARD	SLAVE TO FASHION
SIMPLE ADDITION	SLEEPING BEAUTY
SIMPLE EQUATION	SLEEPING TABLET
SIMPLE FRACTION	SLEEPLESS NIGHT
SIMPLE FRACTURE	SLEEP LIKE A BABY
SIMPLE INTEREST	SLEEP OF THE JUST
SIMPLE SENTENCE	SLEEPY SICKNESS
SIMPLE SOLUTION	SLIP ONE'S MEMORY

SLOW-MOTION FILM
SLOW PROCESSION
SLUGS AND SNAILS
SLUM POPULATION
SMALL-BORE RIFLE
SMALL OF THE BACK
SMALL REDUCTION
SMALL-TIME CROOK
SMART INVENTION
SMASHING DEFEAT
SMELL OF BURNING
SMILING THROUGH
SMOKE-ROOM STORY
SMOKING CONCERT
SMOOTH AS MARBLE
SMOOTH AS VELVET
SMOOTH CROSSING
SMOOTH ONE'S PATH
SNATCH A VERDICT
SNIP OFF THE ENDS
SOBERLY DRESSED
SOCIAL ACTIVITY
SOCIAL CLIMBING
SOCIAL DEMOCRAT
SOCIAL INFERIOR
SOCIAL PLANNING
SOCIAL POSITION
SOCIAL REGISTER
SOCIAL SECURITY
SOCIAL STANDING
SOCIAL SUPERIOR
SOCIETY ISLANDS
SOCIETY WEDDING
SODIUM CHLORIDE
SOFT FURNISHING
SOFT-SHOE DANCER
SOLDIER'S CHORUS
SOLE BONNE FEMME
SOLED AND HEELED
SOLEMN ENTREATY
SOLEMNLY AFFIRM
SOLEMN OCCASION
SOLE POSSESSION
SOLE PROPRIETOR
SOLID SUBSTANCE
SOLOMON ISLANDS
SOLVE THE RIDDLE
SOME DAY OR OTHER
SOMETHING EXTRA
SOMETHING FISHY
SOMETHING TO SAY

SOMEWHERE ABOUT
SO MUCH THE WORSE
SONG OF THE SHIRT
SONGS OF SOLOMON
SORE AFFLICTION
SOUND CHARACTER
SOUND EDUCATION
SOUND PRINCIPLE
SOUND REASONING
SOUND RECORDING
SOUND THE CHARGE
SOURCE OF DANGER
SOUR EXPRESSION
SOUSED MACKEREL
SOUTH AUSTRALIA
SOUTHERN ACCENT
SOUTHERN ASPECT
SOUTHERN REGION
SOUTHERN STATES
SOUTH OF ENGLAND
SOUTH SEA BUBBLE
SOVEREIGN POWER
SOVEREIGN STATE
SPACE PROGRAMME
SPACE TRAVELLER
SPARE NO EXPENSE
SPARING OF WORDS
SPEAKERS' CORNER
SPEAK ESPERANTO
SPEAK IN EARNEST
SPEAK IN RIDDLES
SPEAK OUT OF TURN
SPEAK THE TONGUE
SPECIAL DAMAGES
SPECIAL EDITION
SPECIAL FEATURE
SPECIAL LICENCE
SPECIAL MENTION
SPECIAL MISSION
SPECIAL REQUEST
SPECIAL SERVICE
SPECIAL TROUBLE
SPECIAL VERDICT
SPECIFIC ANSWER
SPECIFIC OBJECT
SPECIFIC REMEDY
SPEECH TRAINING
SPEED OF THOUGHT
SPEED THE PLOUGH
SPEEDWAY RACING
SPEEDY RECOVERY

SPELLING LESSON
SPENT CARTRIDGE
SPINNING MOTION
SPIRITED ATTACK
SPIRIT OF THE AGE
SPIRIT OF THE LAW
SPIRITS OF SALTS
SPIRITUAL NEEDS
SPIRITUAL POWER
SPLENDID CHANCE
SPLIT ONE'S SIDES
SPOIL FOR A FIGHT
SPOIL THE EFFECT
SPOIL THE MARKET
SPOKEN LANGUAGE
SPOKEN LIKE A MAN
SPORTING CHANCE
SPORTING FINISH
SPORTS PAVILION
SPORTS REPORTER
SPRAY OF FLOWERS
SPREAD MISCHIEF
SPRIG OF HEATHER
SPRINGHEEL JACK
SPRING IN THE AIR
SPRING MATTRESS
SQUADRON LEADER
SQUARE ACCOUNTS
SQUARE BRACKETS
SQUASH RACQUETS
STAGE A COMEBACK
STAGE CARPENTER
STAGE DIRECTION
STAGGERED HOURS
STAGGERING BLOW
STAINLESS STEEL
STAKE ONE'S CLAIM
STAMFORD BRIDGE
STAMP COLLECTOR
STAMPING GROUND
STANDARD WEIGHT
STAND CONDEMNED
STAND CONVICTED
STAND CORRECTED
STANDING CUSTOM
STANDING ORDERS
STAND IN THE DOCK
ST. ANDREW'S CROSS
STANDS TO REASON
STAND THE RACKET
STAND THE STRAIN

STANLEY BALDWIN
STAPLE INDUSTRY
STAR ATTRACTION
STARBOARD WATCH
STARE IN THE FACE
STARTER'S ORDERS
STARTING HANDLE
STARTING PISTOL
START SOMETHING
START TO QUARREL
STARVATION DIET
STARVATION WAGE
STATE DOCUMENTS
STATE OF AFFAIRS
STATE OF DENMARK
STATE OWNERSHIP
STATIONERS' HALL
STAY-AT-HOME TYPE
STAY ON THE SHELF
ST. CLEMENT DANES
STEADY INCREASE
STEADY PROGRESS
STEAK AND KIDNEY
STEAK AND ONIONS
STEEL ENGRAVING
STEEL ONE'S HEART
STEEPED IN CRIME
STEERING COLUMN
STEM THE CURRENT
STEPHEN LEACOCK
STEPHEN SPENDER
STEP ON THE JUICE
STEP UP THE SPEED
STERLING SILVER
STEWART GRANGER
ST. GEORGE'S CROSS
STICK AT NOTHING
STICK OF RHUBARB
STICKS OUT A MILE
STICK UP A NOTICE
STIFF AS A RAMROD
STILL-LIFE STUDY
STINGING NETTLE
STING IN THE TAIL
STIRLING CASTLE
STIR ONE'S STUMPS
STIRRING SPEECH
ST. JAMES'S PALACE
ST. JAMES'S STREET
STOCK-CAR RACING
STOCK CHARACTER

STOCKINGED FEET	STRING TOGETHER
STOCKTON ON TEES	STRIP FOR ACTION
STOKE NEWINGTON	STRIP-TEASE SHOW
STOKE THE BOILER	STRIVE FOR GLORY
STOLEN PROPERTY	STROKE OF GENIUS
STOMACH TROUBLE	STROKE OF THE PEN
STONE-COLD SOBER	STRONG ARGUMENT
STOOP TO CONQUER	STRONG AS A HORSE
STORAGE BATTERY	STRONG FEELINGS
STORE DETECTIVE	STRONG IN THE ARM
STORM IN A TEA-CUP	STRONG LANGUAGE
STORMY EXCHANGE	STRONGLY WORDED
STRADDLE A HORSE	STRONG MEASURES
STRAIGHT ANSWER	STRONG POSITION
STRAIGHT AS A DIE	STRONG RIGHT ARM
STRAIGHT COMEDY	STRONG SOLUTION
STRAIN AT THE BIT	STUBBORN FELLOW
STRAINED MUSCLE	STUDIO AUDIENCE
STRAIN ONE'S EYES	STUDIO PORTRAIT
STRAIN THE TRUTH	STUMBLING BLOCK
STRAITS OF DOVER	STUPID QUESTION
STRAND OF COTTON	STYLISH FASHION
STRANGE BUT TRUE	SUBMERGED TENTH
STRANGE DESTINY	SUBMIT TO DEFEAT
STRANGE FEELING	SUBSTANTIAL SUM
STRANGE REQUEST	SUCCESSFUL PLAY
STRATEGIC SKILL	SUDDEN DOWNPOUR
STRAWBERRY FAIR	SUDDEN MOVEMENT
STRAWBERRY HILL	SUDDEN PROGRESS
STRAWBERRY MARK	SUGAR-PLUM FAIRY
STRAWBERRY ROAN	SUITABLE TENANT
STRAW IN THE WIND	SUMMARY JUSTICE
STREAK OF HUMOUR	SUMMER HOLIDAYS
STREAM-LINED CAR	SUMMER VACATION
STREET FIGHTING	SUMPTUOUS FEAST
STREET LIGHTING	SUNK IN OBLIVION
STREET MUSICIAN	SUPERIOR PERSON
STRENGTH OF MIND	SUPPORT A FAMILY
STRENGTH OF WILL	SUPPORTERS' CLUB
STRETCH OF WATER	SUPPORTING CAST
STRICTLY HONEST	SUPPORTING FILM
STRICT TRAINING	SUPPORTING PART
STRIKE A BALANCE	SUPPORTING ROLE
STRIKE A BARGAIN	SUPREME COMMAND
STRIKE A NEW NOTE	SUPREME CONTROL
STRIKE ONE'S FLAG	SUPREME COUNCIL
STRIKE WITH FEAR	SURFACE TENSION
STRIKING EFFECT	SURGICAL SPIRIT
STRING OF HORSES	SURPRISE ATTACK
STRING OF ONIONS	SURPRISE PACKET
STRING OF PEARLS	SURRENDER VALUE

SUSPEND PAYMENT
SUSPICIOUS MIND
SUZANNE LENGLEN
SWAGGER CLOTHES
SWALLOW THE BAIT
SWALLOW THE PILL
SWARM OF INSECTS
SWARTHY SKINNED
SWEAR TO SECRECY
SWEEPING ACTION
SWEEPING GLANCE
SWEEPING REMARK
SWEEP THE BOARDS
SWEET AND TWENTY
SWEET SEVENTEEN
SWEETS OF OFFICE
SWEET SUBSTANCE
SWEET SURRENDER
SWELL WITH PRIDE
SWELTERING HEAT
SWIFT AS AN ARROW
SWIMMING LESSON
SWIMMING TRUNKS
SWIM THE CHANNEL
SWORD SWALLOWER
SWORN STATEMENT
SWORN TO SECRECY
SYBIL THORNDIKE

T—14
TABLE OF WEIGHTS
TACTICAL WEAPON
TAILOR-MADE SUIT
TAKE AN INTEREST
TAKE A RISE OUT OF
TAKE BY SURPRISE
TAKE FIRST PRIZE
TAKE FOR GRANTED
TAKE IN GOOD PART
TAKE IN MARRIAGE
TAKE IT FROM HERE
TAKE NO INTEREST
TAKE ONE'S CHANCE
TAKE ONE'S CHOICE
TAKE ONESELF OFF
TAKE ONE'S FENCES
TAKE ONE'S HAT OFF
TAKE OUT A PATENT
TAKE OUT A POLICY
TAKE POSSESSION
TAKE PRECEDENCE

TAKE THE BISCUIT
TAKE THE EDGE OFF
TAKE THE GILT OFF
TAKE THE LIBERTY
TAKE THE TROUBLE
TAKE THINGS EASY
TAKE TO THE BOATS
TAKE TO THE HILLS
TAKE TO THE WATER
TAKE TO THE WOODS
TAKE UP AN OPTION
TAKE UP THE SLACK
TALK IN A WHISPER
TALKING PICTURE
TALK OF THE DEVIL
TANGIBLE OBJECT
TANGLED THREADS
TANNED BY THE SUN
TAPIOCA PUDDING
TAP OUT A MESSAGE
TARGET PRACTICE
TARPAULIN SHEET
TARTAN TROUSERS
TASTE OF THE WHIP
TAXED TO THE HILT
TEA AND BISCUITS
TEA AND SYMPATHY
TEAR OFF THE MASK
TECHNICAL HITCH
TECHNICAL SKILL
TEETH OF THE WIND
TELEGRAPH WIRES
TELEPHONE KIOSK
TELEPHONE WIRES
TELESCOPIC LENS
TELESCOPIC VIEW
TELEVISION MAST
TELEVISION PLAY
TELEVISION STAR
TELL A TALL STORY
TELL EVERYTHING
TEMPLE OF APOLLO
TEMPORARY ABODE
TEMPORARY LEASE
TEMPORARY VISIT
TEN AND A QUARTER
TEN AND SIXPENCE
TEN AND TENPENCE
TEN AND TWOPENCE
TENDER FEELINGS
TEN-MINUTE ALIBI

TENSE SITUATION
TENTH OF JANUARY
TENTH OF OCTOBER
TERM OF CONTEMPT
TERMS OF THE WILL
TERRIBLE ORDEAL
TERRIBLE WRENCH
TESTIFY AGAINST
TEST OF STRENGTH
THANKLESS CHILD
THANKS A MILLION
THANKS VERY MUCH
THAT CERTAIN AGE
THAT'S THE TICKET
THEATRICAL STAR
THE AUTHORITIES
THE BEE'S WEDDING
THE BEST CIRCLES
THE BLACK FOREST
THE BLACK PRINCE
THE CESAREWITCH
THE COMMON TOUCH
THE CORINTHIANS
THE CRUCIFIXION
THE DARDANELLES
THE END OF THE DAY
THE ETERNAL CITY
THE EXACT AMOUNT
THE EXTREMITIES
THE FIRST CUCKOO
THE FIRST PERSON
THE FLINTSTONES
THE FORSYTE SAGA
THE FOUR JUST MEN
THE GOLDEN BOUGH
THE GOOD OLD DAYS
THE GRAND MANNER
THE GRAND OLD MAN
THE GREAT DIVIDE
THE HIGHWAY CODE
THE INQUISITION
THEIR MAJESTIES
THE JUNGLE BOOKS
THE LILAC DOMINO
THE LORD'S PRAYER
THE LOTUS-EATERS
THE MINSTREL BOY
THE NELSON TOUCH
THE NETHERLANDS
THE OLD GREY MARE
THE OLD OAK CHEST

THE PHILLIPINES
THE PLANEMAKERS
THE PLANETARIUM
THE POLICE FORCE
THE POLYTECHNIC
THE REFORMATION
THE RENAISSANCE
THE RESTORATION
THE SEVEN DWARFS
THE SHINING HOUR
THE SINGING FOOL
THE STAR CHAMBER
THE TIME MACHINE
THE UNCONSCIOUS
THE UNDERGROUND
THE UNDERSIGNED
THE VICAR OF BRAY
THE WATER BABIES
THE WHEREWITHAL
THE WINTER'S TALE
THE WORST IS OVER
THICK AS THIEVES
THICK OF THE FRAY
THIEVES' KITCHEN
THIEVING MAGPIE
THINK CAREFULLY
THINK OF ANOTHER
THINK OF A NUMBER
THINK OF THE PAST
THINK THINGS OUT
THIRD DIMENSION
THIRD-FLOOR BACK
THIRD OF JANUARY
THIRD OF OCTOBER
THIRD-PARTY RISK
THIRD PROGRAMME
THIRD TIME LUCKY
THIRST FOR BLOOD
THIRTEEN AND SIX
THIRTEEN AND TEN
THIRTEEN AND TWO
THIRTEEN MONTHS
THIRTEEN OUNCES
THIRTEENTH HOLE
THIRTEEN TRICKS
THIRTIETH OF MAY
THIRTY THOUSAND
THIRTY YEARS' WAR
THIS HAPPY BREED
THIS IS YOUR LIFE
THOMAS SHERATON

THORN IN THE SIDE
THOROUGH SEARCH
THOUGHTFUL MOOD
THOUSAND AND ONE
THOUSAND POUNDS
THREADING BEADS
THREAD TOGETHER
THREATEN DANGER
THREE AND A PENNY
THREE AND ELEVEN
THREE BLIND MICE
THREE-BOTTLE MAN
THREE-CARD TRICK
THREE FARTHINGS
THREE MEN IN A TUB
THREE-MILE LIMIT
THREE-PIECE SUIT
THREE SHILLINGS
THREE-SPEED GEAR
THREE SYLLABLES
THRILLER WRITER
THROAT PASTILLE
THROATY CHUCKLE
THROUGH THE AGES
THROUGH THE MILL
THROUGH THE NOSE
THROUGH THE POST
THROUGH THE TOWN
THROW IN ONE'S LOT
THROW LIGHT UPON
THROW OF THE DICE
THROW OVERBOARD
THROW THE HAMMER
THROW TO THE DOGS
THURSDAY ISLAND
THURSDAY'S CHILD
TICKLED TO DEATH
TICKLISH MATTER
TIMBER MERCHANT
TIME FOR THOUGHT
TIME IMMEMORIAL
TIMELY REMINDER
TIME OF ONE'S LIFE
TIME WITHOUT END
TIN OF PILCHARDS
TIP OF THE TONGUE
TIRELESS WORKER
TOAD OF TOAD HALL
TO A GREAT EXTENT
TO A LARGE DEGREE
TO A LARGE EXTENT

TOASTED TEA-CAKE
TOAST OF THE TOWN
TOBACCO AUCTION
TOBACCO LICENCE
TOBACCO PLANTER
TOIL AND TROUBLE
TOKEN OF RESPECT
TOOTH FOR A TOOTH
TOP-HAT AND TAILS
TOPICAL SUBJECT
TOP OF ONE'S VOICE
TOP OF THE CHARTS
TOP OF THE LADDER
TOP OF THE LEAGUE
TORRENTIAL RAIN
TORRENT OF ABUSE
TORTURE CHAMBER
TORTURED BY FEAR
TOTAL ABSTAINER
TOTAL IGNORANCE
TOTAL IMMERSION
TO THE BITTER END
TO THE END OF TIME
TOUCH A SOFT SPOT
TOUGH AS LEATHER
TOURING COMPANY
TOUR THE COUNTRY
TOWN AND COUNTRY
TOWN COUNCILLOR
TRACKED VEHICLE
TRACTION ENGINE
TRADE REFERENCE
TRADING STATION
TRAFFIC CONTROL
TRAFFIC DENSITY
TRAFFIC PROBLEM
TRAINED SOLDIER
TRAINING GROUND
TRAINING SCHOOL
TRAIN OF THOUGHT
TRANSFER BY DEED
TRANSITIVE VERB
TRANSPORT HOUSE
TRANSPORT PLANE
TRAVEL BROCHURE
TRAVELLER'S REST
TRAVELLER'S TALE
TRAVELLING TIME
TRAVEL THE WORLD
TREACLE PUDDING
TREAD THE BOARDS

TREAD UNDERFOOT
TREASURE ISLAND
TREMBLE TO THINK
TREMBLING HANDS
TREMBLING VOICE
TRIANGULAR DUEL
TRICKLE OF BLOOD
TRICKLE OF WATER
TRICK OF FORTUNE
TRICKY BUSINESS
TRICKY QUESTION
TRIED FOR MURDER
TRIFLING AMOUNT
TRIFLING CHARGE
TRIFLING MATTER
TRIFLING REMARK
TRINITY COLLEGE
TRIPE AND ONIONS
TRIPLE ALLIANCE
TRISTRAM SHANDY
TRIUMPHAL CROWN
TROOP MOVEMENTS
TROOP THE COLOUR
TROPIC OF CANCER
TROUBLE BREWING
TROUBLED WATERS
TROUBLE IN STORE
TROUPE OF ACTORS
TROUSERS POCKET
TRUE CONFESSION
TRUMPED-UP STORY
TRUNDLE THEM OUT
TRY AND TRY AGAIN
TRY ONE'S FORTUNE
TRY ONE'S HARDEST
TUESDAY EVENING
TUESDAY MORNING
TUMBLER OF WATER
TUNBRIDGE WELLS
TURF ACCOUNTANT
TURKISH DELIGHT
TURKISH TOBACCO
TURN AT THE WHEEL
TURN DOWN THE BED
TURN DOWN THE GAS
TURN EVERY STONE
TURN OFF THE HEAT
TURN OF THE SCREW
TURN OF THE WHEEL
TURN ON ONE'S HEEL
TURN ON THE LIGHT

TURN OUT TO GRASS
TURN RIGHT ROUND
TURN TOPSYTURVY
TURN TO THE RIGHT
TURN UP ONE'S NOSE
TURN UPSIDE DOWN
TWELFTH CENTURY
TWELFTH OF APRIL
TWELFTH OF MARCH
TWELVE AND A HALF
TWELVE AND EIGHT
TWELVE AND SEVEN
TWELVE AND THREE
TWELVE APOSTLES
TWELVE THOUSAND
TWENTIETH OF MAY
TWENTY THOUSAND
TWICE THE WEIGHT
TWIST OF TOBACCO
TWISTS AND TURNS
TWITTER OF BIRDS
TWO AND A QUARTER
TWO AND SIXPENCE
TWO AND TENPENCE
TWO AND TWOPENCE
TWO-HANDED SWORD
TWO-HEADED EAGLE
TWO WICKETS DOWN
TYPICAL EXAMPLE

U—14
ULTERIOR MOTIVE
ULTERIOR OBJECT
ULTIMATE RESULT
ULTRA-VIOLET RAY
UNABLE TO CHOOSE
UNACCOUNTED FOR
UNBALANCED MIND
UNBOSOM ONESELF
UNBROKEN SPIRIT
UNCIVILIZED MAN
UNCLE TOM'S CABIN
UNDER A HANDICAP
UNDER AN EMBARGO
UNDER CROSS-FIRE
UNDER DETENTION
UNDERGO REPAIRS
UNDER GUARANTEE
UNDER ONE'S THUMB
UNDER RESTRAINT
UNDER SUSPICION

UNDER THE BONNET
UNDER THE CARPET
UNDER THE DOCTOR
UNDER THE GROUND
UNDER THE HAMMER
UNDER THE HARROW
UNDER TREATMENT
UNDER TWENTY-ONE
UNDRESS UNIFORM
UNDUE INFLUENCE
UNEARNED INCOME
UNEASY PROGRESS
UNFAMILIAR WORD
UNIFORM PATTERN
UNINVITED GUEST
UNIQUE OCCASION
UNITED SERVICES
UNIVERSAL AGENT
UNIVERSAL AUNTS
UNIVERSAL JOINT
UNIVERSAL PEACE
UNIVERSITY TERM
UNIVERSITY TOWN
UNIVERSITY VOTE
UNKNOWN COUNTRY
UNKNOWN ELEMENT
UNKNOWN SOLDIER
UNKNOWN WARRIOR
UNLIMITED SCOPE
UNLIMITED SPACE
UNMARRIED WOMAN
UNOCCUPIED FLAT
UNPLEASANT DUTY
UNPLOUGHED LAND
UNREQUITED LOVE
UNSALTED BUTTER
UNSETTLING NEWS
UNSUITABLE TIME
UNTER DEN LINDEN
UNWELCOME GUEST
UPHILL STRUGGLE
UPON REFLECTION
UPRIGHT POSTURE
USUAL SIGNATURE
USURP THE THRONE

V—14
VACATE ONE'S SEAT
VAGRANCY CHARGE
VAGUE SUSPICION
VAIN AS A PEACOCK

VALET DE CHAMBRE
VALID OBJECTION
VALSE DES FLEURS
VANILLA FLAVOUR
VANISHING CREAM
VANISHING POINT
VANISHING TRICK
VARIABLE TEMPER
VARIETY THEATRE
VARIOUS COLOURS
VARIOUS REASONS
VARNISH REMOVER
VARYING SUCCESS
VAST DIFFERENCE
VAST EXPERIENCE
VATICAN COUNCIL
VAUDEVILLE SHOW
VEER TO THE RIGHT
VEGETABLE CURRY
VEGETABLE FIBRE
VEGETABLE SALAD
VEGETABLE WORLD
VEGETARIAN DIET
VEGETARIAN DISH
VEGETARIAN MEAL
VENDING MACHINE
VENERABLE BEARD
VENERABLE RUINS
VENETIAN CARPET
VENETIAN SCHOOL
VENETIAN WINDOW
VENUS AND ADONIS
VERBAL ARGUMENT
VERBAL CONTRACT
VERBAL EVIDENCE
VERBATIM REPORT
VERIFY THE FACTS
VERSATILE ACTOR
VERTICAL FLIGHT
VESTED INTEREST
VETERAN SERVICE
VICTIM OF CHANGE
VICTORIA PALACE
VICTORIA REGINA
VIEW WITH FAVOUR
VIOLENT QUARREL
VIOLENT TEMPEST
VIOLETS ARE BLUE
VIOLIN CONCERTO
VISIBLE EXPORTS
VISIBLE HORIZON

VITAL PRINCIPLE
VOICE AN OPINION
VOLATILE LIQUID
VOLUNTEER CORPS
VOTING STRENGTH
VULGAR FRACTION
VULGAR LANGUAGE
VULGAR PARLANCE
VULNERABLE SPOT

W—14

WAG A FOREFINGER
WAGGING TONGUES
WAIFS AND STRAYS
WAIT TILL THE END
WAKE WITH A START
WALKING HOLIDAY
WALKING LIBRARY
WALK INTO A PUNCH
WALK INTO DANGER
WALLOW IN LUXURY
WALLS OF JERICHO
WALPURGIS NIGHT
WALTER DE LA MARE
WALTZ COTILLION
WANTED BY THE LAW
WANT FOR NOTHING
WANT OF ALACRITY
WANT OF PRACTICE
WANT OF SYMMETRY
WARD IN CHANCERY
WARD OF THE COURT
WARDROBE DEALER
WARM FRIENDSHIP
WARM TO ONE'S WORK
WARNER BROTHERS
WARNING EXAMPLE
WAR OF ATTRITION
WAR OF EXPANSION
WARRANT OFFICER
WARREN HASTINGS
WARSAW CONCERTO
WARS OF THE ROSES
WARWICK DEEPING
WASH AND BRUSH-UP
WASH DIRTY LINEN
WASHING MACHINE
WASHINGTON POST
WASTE ONE'S WORDS
WATCH CAREFULLY
WATCH COMMITTEE

WATCH THE BIRDIE
WATERLOO BRIDGE
WATER ON THE KNEE
WATER THE GARDEN
WATER THE HORSES
WATER THE WICKET
WAVE OF VIOLENCE
WAVERLEY NOVELS
WEAK AT THE KNEES
WE ARE NOT AMUSED
WEARING APPAREL
WEATHER BALLOON
WEATHER OUTLOOK
WEATHER PROPHET
WEATHER STATION
WEDDING MORNING
WEDDING PRESENT
WEDDING SERVICE
WEDNESDAY NIGHT
WEEK-END VISITOR
WEEKLY MAGAZINE
WEEK'S GOOD CAUSE
WEIGH ONE'S WORDS
WEIGHTY PROBLEM
WELFARE OFFICER
WELL ACQUAINTED
WELL-CHOSEN WORD
WELL-EARNED REST
WELLINGTON BOOT
WELL-READ PERSON
WELL-WORN PHRASE
WELL WORTH WHILE
WELSH MOUNTAINS
WEMBLEY STADIUM
WENT WITH A SWING
WESTERN GERMANY
WEST HARTLEPOOL
WET ONE'S WHISTLE
WHAT DO YOU THINK?
WHAT IN THE WORLD?
WHAT OF THE CLOCK?
WHAT OF THE NIGHT?
WHAT'S THE DAMAGE?
WHAT'S THE MATTER?
WHAT THE DICKENS!
WHEELED TRAFFIC
WHEEL OF FORTUNE
WHICH WAY TO TURN
WHIGS AND TORIES
WHITE CHRISTMAS
WHITE CORPUSCLE

WHITE IN THE FACE
WHITE MAN'S GRAVE
WHITER THAN SNOW
WHITSUN HOLIDAY
WHOLE-MEAL BREAD
WHOLESALE PRICE
WIDDICOMBE FAIR
WIDELY BELIEVED
WIDEN THE BREACH
WIDE OF THE TRUTH
WIDE-OPEN SPACES
WIDE VOCABULARY
WIELD THE WILLOW
WIFE IN NAME ONLY
WILD ACCUSATION
WILD ENTHUSIASM
WILD EXCITEMENT
WILD-GOOSE CHASE
WILFRED PICKLES
WILLIAM AND MARY
WILLIAM HOGARTH
WILLING AND ABLE
WIN BY A KNOCK-OUT
WIND INSTRUMENT
WINDOW CURTAINS
WINDOW DRESSING
WINDOW ENVELOPE
WINDOW SHOPPING
WIND UP A COMPANY
WINE BY THE GLASS
WINIFRED ATWELL
WINNER TAKES ALL
WIN SECOND PRIZE
WINTER CLOTHING
WINTER PLANTING
WINTER QUARTERS
WINTER WOOLLIES
WISE AS A SERPENT
WITH A GOOD GRACE
WITH ALL MY HEART
WITH A VENGEANCE
WITHHOLD ASSENT
WITHOUT BLEMISH
WITHOUT CEASING
WITHOUT CONTEXT
WITHOUT MEASURE
WITHOUT PURPOSE
WITHOUT REMORSE
WITHOUT RESERVE
WITHOUT RESPECT
WITHOUT STRINGS

WITHOUT WARNING
WITH PERMISSION
WITH THE COLOURS
WITH THE CURRENT
WOMAN OF FASHION
WOMEN'S LAND ARMY
WOMEN'S QUARTERS
WOMEN'S SUFFRAGE
WONDERFUL SIGHT
WONDERFUL WORLD
WOOLLEN SWEATER
WOOLLY THINKING
WORCESTER SAUCE
WORKING CAPITAL
WORKING CLOTHES
WORKING FOREMAN
WORKING HOLIDAY
WORK IN PROGRESS
WORK LIKE A CHARM
WORK LIKE A HORSE
WORK LIKE A NAVVY
WORK LIKE BLAZES
WORK ONE'S TICKET
WORK TO SCHEDULE
WORLDLY AFFAIRS
WORLD OF FASHION
WORLD OF MEANING
WORLD OF ONE'S OWN
WORLD OF REALITY
WORLD SITUATION
WORMWOOD SCRUBS
WORN TO A FRAZZLE
WORTH A BOB OR TWO
WORTH IMITATING
WORTH ONE'S WHILE
WORTHY CHAMPION
WORTHY OF ESTEEM
WORTHY OF PRAISE
WORTHY OF REMARK
WRAPPED IN GLOOM
WRATH OF THE GODS
WREAK VENGEANCE
WRESTLING MATCH
WRIGHT BROTHERS
WRING ONE'S HANDS
WRITTEN APOLOGY
WRITTEN CONSENT
WRITTEN IN VERSE
WRITTEN MESSAGE
WRONG DIRECTION
WRONGFUL ARREST

Y—14

YACHTING CENTRE
YELLOWISH BROWN
YELLOW JAUNDICE
YELLOW SAPPHIRE
YORKSHIRE DALES
YORKSHIRE MOORS
YOUNG AND TENDER
YOUNGER BROTHER
YOUNGEST SISTER
YOUNG LOCHINVAR
YOUNG MAN'S FANCY
YOUNG PRETENDER
YOUNG SHOULDERS
YOU'RE TELLING ME!
YOUR EXCELLENCY
YOURS SINCERELY
YOU SHOULD WORRY!

A—15

ABANDON ONE'S POST
ABERDEEN TERRIER
ABLAZE WITH LIGHT
ABODE OF WARRIORS
ABOVE EVERYTHING
ABOVE THE AVERAGE
ABOVE THE SURFACE
ABOVE THE WEATHER
ABRIDGED VERSION
ABRUPT DEPARTURE
ABSOLUTE MINIMUM
ABSOLUTE MONARCH
ABSTRACT PAINTER
ABSTRACT SCIENCE
ABUNDANCE OF FOOD
ABUSE OF LANGUAGE
ACADEMIC CIRCLES
ACCEPT A PROPOSAL
ACCEPTED MEANING
ACCEPTED VERSION
ACCIDENTAL DEATH
ACCIDENT OF BIRTH
ACCORDING TO PLAN
ACCOUNT RENDERED
ACCREDITED AGENT
A CHRISTMAS CAROL
ACQUISITIVE MIND
ACROSS THE STREET
ACTIVE SUPPORTER
ACT OF AGGRESSION
ACT OF DEDICATION

ACT OF FRIENDSHIP
ACT OF PARLIAMENT
ACT OF PROVIDENCE
ACT OF SETTLEMENT
ACT THE GIDDY GOAT
ADDED ATTRACTION
ADDISON'S DISEASE
ADD TO ONE'S INCHES
ADHESIVE PLASTER
ADJUTANT GENERAL
ADMIT EVERYTHING
ADOPTION SOCIETY
A DROP IN THE OCEAN
ADVANCED BOOKING
ADVANCED IN YEARS
ADVANCED STUDENT
ADVANCED STUDIES
ADVANCED THINKER
ADVERTISING SITE
AEROPLANE TRIALS
AFFLUENT SOCIETY
AFRAID OF COMPANY
AFTER MY OWN HEART
AFTERNOON SIESTA
AGAINST ONE'S WILL
AGAINST THE CLOCK
AGAINST THE GRAIN
AGAINST THE RULES
AGE OF AUTOMATION
AGE OF DISCRETION
AGING POPULATION
AGREE BEFOREHAND
AGREE ON A VERDICT
AGREE TO DISAGREE
AHEAD OF SCHEDULE
AIDER AND ABETTER
AIMLESS ACTIVITY
AIR CHIEF MARSHAL
AIR CONDITIONING
AIRCRAFT CARRIER
AIREDALE TERRIER
AIR FORCE OFFICER
AIR FORCE RESERVE
AIR MINISTRY ROOF
AIR OF DETACHMENT
ALBERT CHEVALIER
ALDERSHOT TATTOO
ALEXANDRA PALACE
ALFRED HITCHCOCK
ALIMENTARY CANAL
A LITTLE LEARNING

ALIVE AND KICKING
ALL ALONG THE LINE
ALL FOUR QUARTERS
ALL MANNER OF WAYS
ALL-NIGHT SESSION
ALL-NIGHT SITTING
ALLOTMENT HOLDER
ALL OVER THE PLACE
ALL PASSION SPENT
ALL PULL TOGETHER
ALL-ROUND ABILITY
ALL-ROUND ATHLETE
ALL THE TRIMMINGS
ALL THE WORLD OVER
ALL THE YEAR ROUND
ALONE IN THE WORLD
ALTERNATIVE PLAN
ALTERNATIVE VOTE
AMATEUR CHAMPION
AMATEUR FOOTBALL
AMBIGUOUS SAYING
AMBITIOUS SCHEME
AMBULANCE DRIVER
AMERICAN EMBASSY
AMERICAN IN PARIS
AMMUNITION BOOTS
AMUSEMENT ARCADE
ANCIENT LANGUAGE
ANCIENT MONUMENT
ANCIENT PEDIGREE
ANDERSON SHELTER
AND SO SAY ALL OF US
ANGULAR VELOCITY
ANIMAL MAGNETISM
ANIMATED CARTOON
ANIMATED GESTURE
ANNIE GET YOUR GUN
ANNIVERSARY DATE
ANNOUNCE ONESELF
ANONYMOUS LETTER
ANOTHER CUP OF TEA
ANTARCTIC CIRCLE
ANTE-NATAL CLINIC
ANTE POST BETTING
ANTHONY TROLLOPE
ANTI-AIRCRAFT GUN
ANTIQUE MERCHANT
ANXIETY NEUROSIS
ANXIOUS TO PLEASE
ANY PORT IN A STORM
APPEALING GLANCE

APPEALING MANNER
APPLICATION FORM
APPLIED RESEARCH
APPLY THE CLOSURE
APPROACH MANHOOD
APPROXIMATE COST
APRIL THE SEVENTH
APRIL THE TWELFTH
ARMED NEUTRALITY
ARMED TO THE TEETH
AROUND THE CORNER
ARRIVAL PLATFORM
ARTICLES FOR SALE
ARTICLES OF FAITH
ARTIFICIAL FIBRE
ARTIFICIAL LIGHT
ARTIFICIAL SMILE
ARTIFICIAL STONE
ARTIFICIAL TEETH
ART OF MANAGEMENT
AS A MATTER OF FACT
AS AN ALTERNATIVE
ASCEND THE THRONE
ASCENSION ISLAND
AS FAR AS POSSIBLE
AS FAR AS YOU CAN GO
AS FRESH AS A DAISY
AS GENTLE AS A LAMB
AS GOOD AS ONE GETS
AS HARD AS GRANITE
AS KEEN AS MUSTARD
ASK FOR ONE'S CARDS
AS LIKE AS TWO PEAS
AS LONG AS YOU LIKE
AS NEAT AS A NEW PIN
AS OLD AS THE HILLS
AS QUIET AS A MOUSE
AS RICH AS CROESUS
ASSISTANT MASTER
ASSISTED PASSAGE
ASSOCIATED IDEAS
ASSORTED TOFFEES
AS STIFF AS A POKER
ASSUME A DISGUISE
AS THE SAYING GOES
ASTRAL INFLUENCE
ASTRONOMER ROYAL
A STUDY IN SCARLET
AS WHITE AS A SHEET
AT A DISADVANTAGE
AT A LOSS FOR WORDS

AT CLOSE QUARTERS
AT CROSS PURPOSES
ATLANTIC CHARTER
ATOMIC SUBMARINE
ATTEMPTED MURDER
AT THE CROSS-ROADS
AT THE DROP OF A HAT
ATTORNEY GENERAL
AT TRINITY CHURCH
AUGUST THE EIGHTH
AUGUST THE FOURTH
AUGUST THE SECOND
AUSTERITY BUDGET
AUTOGRAPH HUNTER
AUTOMATIC CHANGE
AUTOMATIC PISTOL
AUTUMNAL EQUINOX
AUXILIARY FORCES
AUXILIARY TROOPS
AVERAGE SPECIMEN
AWKWARD CUSTOMER
AWKWARD POSITION
AWKWARD QUESTION

B—15

BABY-FACED NELSON
BACHELOR OF MUSIC
BACHELOR'S BUTTON
BACKGROUND MUSIC
BACK OF THE BEYOND
BACKSTAGE NERVES
BACKWARD PEOPLES
BALACLAVA HELMET
BALANCE THE BOOKS
BALLROOM DANCING
BANKRUPTCY COURT
BANKS OF THE CLYDE
BANNER HEADLINES
BANNS OF MARRIAGE
BARBARA STANWYCK
BARBER OF SEVILLE
BARE POSSIBILITY
BARE SUBSISTENCE
BARGAIN BASEMENT
BARNUM AND BAILEY
BARON MUNCHAUSEN
BARRISTER'S CLERK
BARROW IN FURNESS
BARTHOLOMEW FAIR
BASIC INGREDIENT
BATCH OF RECRUITS

BATS IN THE BELFRY
BATTERSEA BRIDGE
BATTLE OF BRITAIN
BATTLE OF FLOWERS
BATTLE OF JUTLAND
BATTLE OF THE NILE
BAYONET PRACTICE
BEAST OF THE FIELD
BEATEN ON THE POST
BEAUTIFUL FIGURE
BEAUTY TREATMENT
BEAUTY UNADORNED
BECOME ENAMOURED
BECOME INVISIBLE
BED AND BREAKFAST
BEE IN ONE'S BONNET
BEER AND SKITTLES
BEFORE BREAKFAST
BEFORE THE FINISH
BEGINNERS, PLEASE
BEGINNING AND END
BEGIN THE BEGUINE
BEHAVE NATURALLY
BEHIND THE SCENES
BEHIND THE STUMPS
BELLOW LIKE A BULL
BELONG TO THE PAST
BELOW THE AVERAGE
BELOW THE HORIZON
BELOW THE SURFACE
BENEATH CONTEMPT
BENEFIT OF CLERGY
BENITO MUSSOLINI
BENJAMIN BRITTEN
BERNE CONVENTION
BERNESE OBERLAND
BERTRAND RUSSELL
BESSEMER PROCESS
BEST FOOT FORWARD
BEST OF ALL WORLDS
BET ON A CERTAINTY
BETRAY THE SECRET
BETTER AND BETTER
BETTER RELATIONS
BETWEEN THE LINES
BETWEEN TWO FIRES
BETWEEN YOU AND ME
BEVERIDGE REPORT
BEVERLEY NICHOLS
BEVERLEY SISTERS
BEWARE OF THE BULL

BEYOND ALL BOUNDS
BEYOND CRITICISM
BEYOND ONE'S DEPTH
BEYOND ONE'S GRASP
BEYOND ONE'S MEANS
BEYOND ONE'S PRIME
BEYOND ONE'S REACH
BEYOND THE FRINGE
BIGGER AND BETTER
BIGGER AND BIGGER
BILLIARDS PLAYER
BINDING CONTRACT
BIRDS OF A FEATHER
BIRTHDAY HONOURS
BIRTHDAY PRESENT
BIRTH OF THE BLUES
BITE ONE'S HEAD OFF
BLACK AS MIDNIGHT
BLACK AS THE DEVIL
BLACKBURN ROVERS
BLACK-COAT WORKER
BLACKMAIL LETTER
BLACKWALL TUNNEL
BLACKWATER FEVER
BLEACHING POWDER
BLISSFULLY HAPPY
BLOOD AND THUNDER
BLOOMSBURY GROUP
BLOW HOT; BLOW COLD
BLOW TO ONE'S PRIDE
BLUES IN THE NIGHT
BLUNT INSTRUMENT
BLUSHING HONOURS
BOARD AND LODGING
BOARDING OFFICER
BODLEIAN LIBRARY
BODY-LINE BOWLING
BODY OF KNOWLEDGE
BODY TEMPERATURE
BOLD IMAGINATION
BOLTED AND BARRED
BOLT FROM THE BLUE
BONDED WAREHOUSE
BOOKMAKER'S CLERK
BOOK OF REFERENCE
BORN IN THE PURPLE
BORROWING POWERS
BOTANICAL GARDEN
BOTTLE OF PERFUME
BOTTLE OF VINEGAR
BOTTOMLESS PURSE

BOTTOM OF THE FORM
BOTTOM OF THE HILL
BOTTOM OF THE POLL
BOTTOM THE WEAVER
BOWL AT THE STUMPS
BOWLED BY A YORKER
BOWLING ANALYSIS
BOW-STREET RUNNER
BOX OF CHOCOLATES
BRASS INSTRUMENT
BRAVE ALL HAZARDS
BREACH OF PROMISE
BREAD OF IDLENESS
BREAKFAST CEREAL
BREAKING OF BREAD
BREAK ON THE WHEEL
BREAK THE BAD NEWS
BREAK THE SILENCE
BREAST OF CHICKEN
BREATHE ONE'S LAST
BREATHLESS HURRY
BREATH OF SCANDAL
BRICKS AND MORTAR
BRIDES IN THE BATH
BRIDGE OF THE NOSE
BRIGADE OF GUARDS
BRIGADIER GERARD
BRIGHT AND BREEZY
BRIGHT AS A BUTTON.
BRIGHT AS A NEW PIN
BRIGHTON AND HOVE
BRIGHT PROSPECTS
BRIGHT YOUNGSTER
BRILLIANT SUNSET
BRING IN A VERDICT
BRING IN NEW BLOOD
BRING TO FRUITION
BRISTLE WITH RAGE
BRITISH COLUMBIA
BRITISH HONDURAS
BRITISH PASSPORT
BRITISH RAILWAYS
BROAD-BRIMMED HAT
BROADEN ONE'S MIND
BROADLY SPEAKING
BRONZE MEDALLIST
BROTHER JONATHAN
BROTHER OFFICERS
BROWN AS MAHOGANY
BRUSSELS SPROUTS
BUBBLE AND SQUEAK.

BUDDING CHAMPION
BUDGET ESTIMATES
BUILDING SOCIETY
BULLDOG DRUMMOND
BULLET-PROOF VEST
BULL'S-EYE LANTERN
BUMP OF KNOWLEDGE
BURIAL OF THE DEAD
BURLINGTON HOUSE
BURNHAM ON CROUCH
BURNING QUESTION
BURN ONE'S BRIDGES
BURN ONE'S FINGERS
BURNT AT THE STAKE
BURNT TO A FRAZZLE
BURST AT THE SEAMS
BURST INTO FLAMES
BURST INTO FLOWER
BURST OF APPLAUSE
BURST OF LAUGHTER
BUSINESS ADDRESS
BUSINESS AFFAIRS
BUSINESS AS USUAL
BUSINESS CIRCLES
BUSINESS COLLEGE
BUSINESS CONTACT
BUSINESS FOOTING
BUSINESS MANAGER
BUSINESS MEETING
BUSINESS METHODS
BUSINESS ROUTINE
BUSINESS VENTURE
BUTTERFLY COLLAR
BUTTERFLY STROKE
BUTTON MUSHROOMS
BY FITS AND STARTS
BY HOOK OR BY CROOK
BY THE SHORT HAIRS
BYZANTINE EMPIRE
BYZANTINE SCHOOL

C—15
CABINET MINISTER
CALCIUM CHLORIDE
CALCULATING MIND
CALEDONIAN CANAL
CALL AN AMBULANCE
CALL ATTENTION TO
CALL IN THE DOCTOR
CALL IN THE POLICE
CALL NO MAN MASTER

CALL TO SURRENDER
CALM AS A MILL-POND
CAMBERWELL GREEN
CAMBRIDGE CIRCUS
CAMEMBERT CHEESE
CAME TO THE THRONE
CANADIAN PACIFIC
CANDLEWICK COVER
CANTERBURY BELLS
CANTERBURY TALES
CAPABILITY BROWN
CAPITAL GAINS TAX
CAPITAL OF FRANCE
CAPITAL OF NORWAY
CAPITAL OF SWEDEN
CAPITAL SENTENCE
CARDIFF ARMS PARK
CARDINAL NUMBERS
CARDINAL VIRTUES
CARDS ON THE TABLE
CARELESS DRIVING
CARELESS RAPTURE
CARES OF THE WORLD
CARPENTER'S BENCH
CARRIAGE AND PAIR
CARRIAGE FORWARD
CARRY CONVICTION
CARRY OUT ONE'S BAT
CARRY THE CAN BACK
CASH IN ONE'S CHIPS
CASH TRANSACTION
CASTING DIRECTOR
CASTLES IN THE AIR
CASTOR AND POLLUX
CASUAL REFERENCE
CASUALTY STATION
CAT AND THE FIDDLE
CATCH AS CATCH CAN
CATCH BY THE HEELS
CATCH ONE NAPPING
CATCH ONE'S BREATH
CATERING OFFICER
CATHEDRAL SQUARE
CAUGHT AMIDSHIPS
CAUGHT AND BOWLED
CAUGHT RED-HANDED
CAUSE A SENSATION
CAVALRY REGIMENT
CEASELESS ENERGY
CEDARS OF LEBANON
CELESTIAL SPHERE

CELLULOID COLLAR
CELLULOID EMPIRE
CENTRAL POSITION
CENTRE OF GRAVITY
CERTAIN EVIDENCE
CERTAIN QUANTITY
CERTIFIED INSANE
CHAMPAGNE BOTTLE
CHAMPAGNE SUPPER
CHANCE DISCOVERY
CHANCE ENCOUNTER
CHANCE OF SUCCESS
CHANGE DIRECTION
CHANGE OF ADDRESS
CHANGE OF CLIMATE
CHANGE OF CLOTHES
CHANGE OF COSTUME
CHANGE OF FORTUNE
CHANGE OF OPINION
CHANGE OF PURPOSE
CHANGE OF SCENERY
CHANGE OF TACTICS
CHANGE ONE'S IDEAS
CHANNEL CROSSING
CHANTREY BEQUEST
CHAPTER AND VERSE
CHARACTER SKETCH
CHARCOAL DRAWING
CHARGE TOO LITTLE
CHARITABLE CAUSE
CHARLES KINGSLEY
CHARLES LAUGHTON
CHARLES THE FIRST
CHARLOTTE BRONTË
CHATSWORTH HOUSE
CHEAP AT THE PRICE
CHEAP RESTAURANT
CHEAT THE GALLOWS
CHECK ONE'S COURSE
CHECK THE RECORDS
CHEERFUL CONSENT
CHEERFUL OLD SOUL
CHELSEA ARTS BALL
CHELSEA BARRACKS
CHEMICAL FORMULA
CHEMICAL PROCESS
CHEMICAL WARFARE
CHEQUERED CAREER
CHERCHEZ LA FEMME
CHESS TOURNAMENT
CHICKEN MARYLAND

CHICKEN SANDWICH
CHIEF MAGISTRATE
CHILDHOOD FRIEND
CHILDISH ATTEMPT
CHILD PSYCHOLOGY
CHILDREN'S ANNUAL
CHILDREN'S CORNER
CHILLED WITH FEAR
CHILLY RECEPTION
CHIPPED POTATOES
CHOCOLATE ÉCLAIR
CHOCOLATE FINGER
CHOCOLATE SUNDAE
CHOICE OF COLOURS
CHOICE OF WEAPONS
CHOOSE ONE'S WORDS
CHRISTMAS ANNUAL
CHRISTMAS DINNER
CHRISTMAS ISLAND
CHRISTMAS SEASON
CHRISTMAS SPIRIT
CHRISTOPHER WREN
CHRIST'S HOSPITAL
CHURCH OF ENGLAND
CIGARETTE COUPON
CIGARETTE HOLDER
CINDERELLA DANCE
CIRCLE OF FRIENDS
CITY AND SUBURBAN
CITY CORPORATION
CIVILIAN CLOTHES
CLAIMS OF SOCIETY
CLAIM THE VICTORY
CLAPHAM JUNCTION
CLASHING COLOURS
CLASH OF OPINIONS
CLASSICAL BALLET
CLASSICAL WRITER
CLASSIC FEATURES
CLASSICS SCHOLAR
CLEAN AS A WHISTLE
CLEANING UTENSIL
CLEAN THE WINDOWS
CLEAR AS DAYLIGHT
CLEAR CONSCIENCE
CLEAR IN ONE'S MIND
CLEAR ONE'S THROAT
CLEAR REFLECTION
CLENCH ONE'S FISTS
CLENCH ONE'S TEETH
CLERK OF THE COURT

CLERK OF THE HOUSE
CLERK OF THE WORKS
CLEVER DECEPTION
CLIFF MICHELMORE
CLING LIKE THE IVY
CLINICAL LECTURE
CLINICAL SURGERY
CLOAK-ROOM TICKET
CLOSE AS AN OYSTER
CLOSE COMPANIONS
CLOSE FRIENDSHIP
CLOSER AND CLOSER
CLOSE TO THE SHORE
CLOSING-DOWN SALE
CLOTHING COUPONS
CLOUD-CUCKOO LAND
COACHING STATION
COCKPIT OF EUROPE
COCKTAIL CABINET
CODE OF BEHAVIOUR
COLD AS CHRISTMAS
COLD COMFORT FARM
COLDSTREAM GUARD
COLERIDGE TAYLOR
COLLAPSIBLE BOAT
COLLECT EVIDENCE
COLLECTING POINT
COLLECTION PLATE
COLLECT MATERIAL
COLLECT ONE'S WITS
COLLECTOR'S PIECE
COLLIERY MANAGER
COLLISION COURSE
COLORADO SPRINGS
COLOUR BLINDNESS
COLOURFUL BORDER
COLOURING MATTER
COLOURLESS FLUID
COLOUR PREJUDICE
COMBINATION LOCK
COME DOWN TO EARTH
COME HOME TO ROOST
COME IN LIKE A LION
COME INTO CONTACT
COME INTO ONE'S OWN
COME INTO THE OPEN
COME OUT ON STRIKE
COME TO A DEAD STOP
COME TO A DECISION
COME TO A FULL STOP
COME TO ATTENTION

COME TO THE RESCUE
COME TO THINK OF IT
COME UP TO SCRATCH
COMFORTABLE SEAT
COMFORTING WORDS
COMMANDING VOICE
COMMERCIAL HOTEL
COMMERCIAL VALUE
COMMISSION AGENT
COMMIT AN OFFENCE
COMMIT TO WRITING
COMMON AGREEMENT
COMMON COMPLAINT
COMMON KNOWLEDGE
COMMON OWNERSHIP
COMMUNAL FEEDING
COMMUNAL KITCHEN
COMMUNITY CENTRE
COMPANION IN ARMS
COMPANION LADDER
COMPANION VOLUME
COMPANY DIRECTOR
COMPANY PROMOTER
COMPLÉTE ABANDON
COMPLETE CONTROL
COMPLETE DEBACLE
COMPLETE EDITION
COMPLETE FAILURE
COMPLETE SWINDLE
COMPLETE VICTORY
COMPLETE WASH-OUT
COMPLEX SENTENCE
COMPOUND A FELONY
COMPULSORY GAMES
CONCERTED ACTION
CONCERTED EFFORT
CONCERT PLATFORM
CONCLUSIVE PROOF
CONDITIONAL MOOD
CONDITION POWDER
CONFERENCE TABLE
CONFESS THE TRUTH
CONFIDENCE TRICK
CONFUSE THE ISSUE
CONGENITAL IDIOT
CONSCIENCE MONEY
CONSCIOUS HUMOUR
CONSENTING PARTY
CONSIDERABLE SUM
CONSIGNMENT NOTE
CONSOLATION RACE

CONSTANT ANXIETY
CONSTANT CHATTER
CONSULAR SERVICE
CONSUMMATE SKILL
CONTEMPT OF COURT
CONTINENTAL TIME
CONTROLLED PRICE
CONVENIENT PLACE
CONVERSION TABLE
CONVIVIAL PERSON
COOKING UTENSILS
COOK THE ACCOUNTS
COOL AS A CUCUMBER
CORDIAL GREETING
CORNER THE MARKET
CORONATION COACH
CORONATION ROBES
CORONATION STONE
CORONER'S INQUEST
CORONER'S VERDICT
CORRECTED PROOFS
CORRECT ESTIMATE
CORRUGATED PAPER
COTTAGE BY THE SEA
COTTAGE HOSPITAL
COTTAGE INDUSTRY
COUNCIL OF ELDERS
COUNCIL OF EUROPE
COUNSEL'S OPINION
COUNTERFEIT COIN
COUNTER IRRITANT
COUNT FOR NOTHING
COUNT ONE'S CHANGE
COUNTRY OF ORIGIN
COUNT THE MINUTES
COUNT THE TAKINGS
COUNTY CRICKETER
COURT DRESSMAKER
COURT OF JUDGMENT
COVER MUCH GROUND
COVER ONE'S TRACKS
CRADLE OF THE DEEP
CRAMPED QUARTERS
CRAZY MIXED-UP KID
CREAMED POTATOES
CREASE RESISTANT
CREATE AN OPENING
CREATE A NUISANCE
CREATE A STOPPAGE
CREATIVE WRITING
CREATURE COMFORT

CREATURE OF HABIT
CREDULOUS PERSON
CREEPING BARRAGE
CREMORNE GARDENS
CRICKET PAVILION
CRIMINAL AT LARGE
CRIMINAL CLASSES
CRIMINAL LUNATIC
CRIMINAL NEGLECT
CRIMINAL OFFENCE
CRIPPLED FOR LIFE
CRITICAL OPINION
CROOKED SIXPENCE
CROSS-COUNTRY RUN
CROSSING THE LINE
CROSS THE CHANNEL
CROSS THE RUBICON
CROSSWORD PUZZLE
CROWD PSYCHOLOGY
CRUCIAL QUESTION
CRUSADING SPIRIT
CRUSHING VICTORY
CRUX OF THE MATTER
CUCKOO IN THE NEST
CUDGEL ONE'S BRAIN
CULTIVATE A HABIT
CULTIVATED PEARL
CULTIVATED TASTE
CUP OF BITTERNESS
CURRENT EXPENSES
CURSE OF SCOTLAND
CURTAIN MATERIAL
CUSTOMS OFFICIAL
CUT AND COME AGAIN
CUT A SORRY FIGURE
CUT DOWN EXPENSES
CUT ONESELF LOOSE

D—15

DAILY OCCURRENCE
DAME LAURA KNIGHT
DAME NELLIE MELBA
DAMNING EVIDENCE
DAMON AND PYTHIAS
DAMPENED SPIRITS
DANCE ATTENDANCE
DANCE OF THE HOURS
DANCING MISTRESS
DANGEROUS CORNER
DANGEROUS PERSON
DANGEROUS VOYAGE

DANGEROUS WEAPON
DASH TO THE GROUND
DAVID AND GOLIATH
DAVY JONES' LOCKER
DAYLIGHT ROBBERY
DAY OF ABSTINENCE
DAY OF LIBERATION
DEAD AS A DOORNAIL
DEAD ON THE TARGET
DEAFENING CHEERS
DEAF TO ALL ADVICE
DEAL DESTRUCTION
DEAR LITTLE THING
DEATH BY DROWNING
DEATH ON THE ROADS
DEBT OF GRATITUDE
DECEIVED HUSBAND
DECIMAL FRACTION
DECISIVE VICTORY
DECLARED MISSING
DECLARE ONE'S LOVE
DECREE OF NULLITY
DEFECTIVE MEMORY
DEFECTIVE VISION
DEFENCE MINISTER
DEFENSIVE BATTLE
DEFENSIVE WEAPON
DEFERRED PAYMENT
DEFINITE ARTICLE
DELAYED REACTION
DELAYING TACTICS
DELICATE BALANCE
DELIRIUM TREMENS
DELIVERED BY HAND
DELIVER JUDGMENT
DELIVER THE GOODS
DEMAND AND SUPPLY
DEMAND ATTENTION
DEMENTIA PRAECOX
DEMOCRATIC PARTY
DEMOLITION SQUAD
DENIAL OF JUSTICE
DENTAL TREATMENT
DEPARTMENT STORE
DEPARTURE LOUNGE
DEPTHS OF DESPAIR
DESCENDING ORDER
DESCRIBE A CIRCLE
DESERTED VILLAGE
DESIGN FOR LIVING
DESIGNING FEMALE

DESIRABLE OBJECT
DESOLATE COUNTRY
DESPERATE PLIGHT
DESPERATE REMEDY
DETACHED OPINION
DETAILED ACCOUNT
DETENTION CENTRE
DETERRENT EFFECT
DEVALUE THE POUND
DEVELOPMENT AREA
DEVILLED KIDNEYS
DEVIL'S COMPANION
DEVIL'S PUNCH BOWL
DEVONSHIRE CREAM
DEVONSHIRE HOUSE
DIAMOND MERCHANT
DIAMOND NECKLACE
DIAMOND SMUGGLER
DICKIE HENDERSON
DICKIE VALENTINE
DICK WHITTINGTON
DIE IN THE ATTEMPT
DIE WITH LAUGHTER
DIFFERENT TASTES
DIFFICULT CHOICE
DIFFICULT MATTER
DIFFICULT PERSON
DIFFIDENT MANNER
DIG ONE'S OWN GRAVE
DINING-ROOM TABLE
DIPLOMATIC AGENT
DIPLOMATIC CORPS
DIPLOMATIC STAFF
DIRECT INFLUENCE
DIRECTION FINDER
DIRECTOR GENERAL
DIRT-TRACK RACING
DISAPPEARING ACT
DISARMAMENT PLAN
DISCARDED CUSTOM
DISCHARGE PAPERS
DISGUISE ONESELF
DISLOCATED ELBOW
DISORDERED BRAIN
DISORDERLY HOUSE
DISPENSE CHARITY
DISPENSE JUSTICE
DISPLACED PERSON
DISPOSABLE GOODS
DISPUTE THE FACTS
DISTANT LIKENESS

DISTANT PROSPECT
DISTANT RELATIVE
DISTINCTIVE NOTE
DISTORT THE TRUTH
DISTRESSING NEWS
DISTRESS WARRANT
DISTRICT OFFICER
DISTRICT RAILWAY
DISTRICT VISITOR
DISTURB THE PEACE
DIVIDEND WARRANT
DIVINE MESSENGER
DIVINITY STUDENT
DO A ROARING TRADE
DO AS THE ROMANS DO
DOCTOR OF SCIENCE
DOCUMENTARY FILM
DOG WITH TWO TAILS
DO-IT-YOURSELF FAN
DO-IT-YOURSELF KIT
DOLLAR RESOURCES
DOLLARS AND CENTS
DOMESTIC AFFAIRS
DOMESTIC ECONOMY
DOMESTIC OFFICES
DOMESTIC PROBLEM
DOMESTIC SCIENCE
DOMESTIC SERVANT
DOMESTIC SERVICE
DONE IN COLD BLOOD
DO ONE'S LEVEL BEST
DORA COPPERFIELD
DORCHESTER HOTEL
DORMITORY SUBURB
DO THE CHARLESTON
DO THE CIVIL THING
DO THE IMPOSSIBLE
DO THE RIGHT THING
DO THE WRONG THING
DO THINGS IN STYLE
DOUBLE ADVANTAGE
DOUBLE INDEMNITY
DOUBLE OR NOTHING
DOUBLE-QUICK TIME
DOUBLE SEVENTEEN
DOUBLE THE STAKES
DOUBLE WHITE LINE
DOUBLE YOUR MONEY
DOUBTFUL STARTER
DOWN IN THE DEPTHS
DOWN IN THE VALLEY

DOWN THE MOUNTAIN
DOWN THE STRAIGHT
DOWN TO THE GROUND
DOZENS AND DOZENS
DRAIN TO THE DREGS
DRAMATIC GESTURE
DRAMATIC SETTING
DRAMATIC SOCIETY
DRASTIC MEASURES
DRAW A COMPARISON
DRAW A DEEP BREATH
DRAW AN INFERENCE
DRAW A RED HERRING
DRAW CONCLUSIONS
DRAW IN ONE'S HORNS
DRAW INSPIRATION
DRAW ONE'S PENSION
DRAW THE CURTAINS
DREAMER OF DREAMS
DRESSING STATION
DRILLING MACHINE
DRILL INSTRUCTOR
DRINK ONE'S HEALTH
DRINK ON THE HOUSE
DRIVEN TO THE WALL
DRIVE RECKLESSLY
DROOPING SPIRITS
DROP IN THE BUCKET
DROP OF GOOD STUFF
DROP OVER THE SIDE
DRUG ON THE MARKET
DRUM AND FIFE BAND
DRUMHEAD SERVICE
DUAL CARRIAGE-WAY
DUAL PERSONALITY
DUBIOUS BLESSING
DUBLIN BAY PRAWNS
DUCHY OF CORNWALL
DUELLING PISTOLS
DUKE OF EDINBURGH
DUKE OF LANCASTER

E—15

EAGER FOR THE FRAY
EARLY-CLOSING DAY
EARLY-MORNING TEA
EARNING CAPACITY
EARTHLY PARADISE
EASTERN COUNTIES
EASTERN QUESTION
EASY-PACED WICKET

EAT ONE'S HEART OUT
EBENEZER SCROOGE
ECLIPSE OF THE SUN
ECONOMIC WARFARE
EDINBURGH CASTLE
EDITORIAL COLUMN
EDITOR'S DECISION
EDMUND HOCKRIDGE
EDWARD THE FOURTH
EDWARD THE SECOND
EGG-AND-SPOON RACE
EIGHTEEN AND FIVE
EIGHTEEN AND FOUR
EIGHTEEN AND NINE
EIGHTEEN HUNDRED
EIGHTEEN PER CENT
EIGHTEENTH GREEN
EIGHTEENTH OF MAY
EIGHTH OF JANUARY
EIGHTH OF OCTOBER
EIGHT O'CLOCK NEWS
EIGHT OF DIAMONDS
EIGHTPENNY STAMP
EIGHTY-ONE AND SIX
EIGHTY-SIX AND SIX
EIGHTY-TWO AND SIX
ELABORATE DESIGN
ELABORATE DETAIL
ELECTION ADDRESS
ELECTION RESULTS
ELECTORAL DEFEAT
ELECTORAL SYSTEM
ELECTRICAL FAULT
ELECTRIC BATTERY
ELECTRIC BLANKET
ELECTRIC CIRCUIT
ELECTRIC CURRENT
ELECTRIC FURNACE
ELECTRICITY BILL
ELECTRIC MACHINE
ELECTRIC RAILWAY
ELECTRIC TOASTER
ELECTRONIC BRAIN
ELEVATED RAILWAY
ELEVEN AND A PENNY
ELEVEN AND ELEVEN
ELEVEN SHILLINGS
ELEVENTH CENTURY
ELEVENTH OF APRIL
ELEVENTH OF MARCH
ELIZABETH TAYLOR

ELOCUTION LESSON
EMANUEL SHINWELL
EMERALD BRACELET
EMERALD NECKLACE
EMERGENCY POWERS
EMERGENCY RATION
EMOTIONAL RELIEF
ENCASED IN ARMOUR
ENDEAVOUR TO HELP
ENDLESS ARGUMENT
ENDLESS ATTEMPTS
END OF ONE'S TETHER
END OF THE CENTURY
END OF THE CHAPTER
END OF THE JOURNEY
ENDOWMENT POLICY
ENEMY OF PROGRESS
ENERGETIC PERSON
ENGAGEMENT DIARY
ENGINEER A STRIKE
ENGLAND AND WALES
ENGLISH LANGUAGE
ENGLISHMAN'S HOME
ENJOY GOOD HEALTH
ENJOY POOR HEALTH
ENTENTE CORDIALE
ENTER PARLIAMENT
EPICUREAN TASTES
EPSOM RACECOURSE
EQUESTRIAN SKILL
ERNEST HEMINGWAY
ERRONEOUS BELIEF
ERROR OF JUDGMENT
ERROR OF OMISSION
ESCAPED PRISONER
ESCAPE MECHANISM
ESPOUSE THE CAUSE
ESSENTIAL CLAUSE
ESTABLISH A CLAIM
ETERNAL TRIANGLE
ETON BOATING-SONG
EVENING STANDARD
EVEN MONEY CHANCE
EVERLASTING FAME
EVERY MOTHER'S SON
EVERY NOW AND THEN
EVERYONE'S FRIEND
EVIDENCE IN COURT
EXAGGERATED IDEA
EXALTED POSITION
EXAMINATION HALL

EXCELLENT CHANCE
EXCELLENT REASON
EXCELLENT RESULT
EXCEPTIONAL WORD
EXCESSIVE CHARGE
EXCESSIVE WEIGHT
EXCHANGE AND MART
EXCHANGE CONTROL
EXCHANGE GLANCES
EXCHANGE LETTERS
EXCHANGE OF VIEWS
EXCHANGE SIGNALS
EXCLAMATION MARK
EXCLUSIVE REPORT
EXCLUSIVE RIGHTS
EXCURSION TICKET
EXERCISE CONTROL
EXERCISE THE MIND
EXERCISE THE VETO
EXHAUSTION POINT
EXORBITANT PRICE
EXPANDING BULLET
EXPECT OTHERWISE
EXPENSE NO OBJECT
EXPENSIVE TASTES
EXPERT KNOWLEDGE
EXPLODE WITH RAGE
EXPLOSIVE CHARGE
EXPLOSIVE DEVICE
EXPORT AND IMPORT
EXPOSED POSITION
EXPOSED TO DANGER
EXPRESS CONTEMPT
EXPRESS DELIVERY
EXPRESSIVE SMILE
EXQUISITE CHOICE
EXTENSION OF TIME
EXTORTIONATE FEE
EXTREME KINDNESS
EXTREME MEASURES
EXTREME PATIENCE
EYEBROW TWEEZERS

F—15

FACE LIKE A FIDDLE
FACE THE OTHER WAY
FACE THE PROSPECT
FACT OF THE MATTER
FACTS AND FIGURES
FADED REPUTATION
FAIR MAID OF PERTH

FAIR MEANS OR FOUL
FAIR WEAR AND TEAR
FAITHFUL ACCOUNT
FAITHFUL PROMISE
FAITHFUL SERVANT
FALKLAND ISLANDS
FALL ON HARD TIMES
FALL TO THE GROUND
FALSE ACCUSATION
FALSE APPEARANCE
FALSE CONCEPTION
FALSE IMPRESSION
FALSE REPUTATION
FAMILY ALLOWANCE
FAMILY GATHERING
FAMILY LOYALTIES
FAMILY SOLICITOR
FAMOUS LAST WORDS
FANCY-DRESS DANCE
FANNY BY GASLIGHT
FAN-TAILED PIGEON
FAREWELL ADDRESS
FAR FROM THE TRUTH
FARMING ACCOUNTS
FARTHING DAMAGES
FASHIONABLE AREA
FASTER THAN SOUND
FATAL ATTRACTION
FATHER AND MOTHER
FATHER CHRISTMAS
FATHER CONFESSOR
FATHERLESS CHILD
FAVOURABLE ISSUE
FAVOURABLE REPLY
FAVOURABLE START
FAVOURABLE TERMS
FEAR FOR ONE'S LIFE
FEAST FOR THE GODS
FEATHERED FRIEND
FEATHER ONE'S NEST
FEDERAL REPUBLIC
FEEBLE IMITATION
FEEL COMFORTABLE
FEEL IN ONE'S BONES
FEET ON THE GROUND
FELLOWSHIP HOUSE
FELLOW TRAVELLER
FEMININE PRONOUN
FENCED ENCLOSURE
FENCHURCH STREET
FESTIVAL GARDENS

FESTIVE OCCASION	FIRST WICKET DOWN
FIELD OF ACTIVITY	FISH AND CHIP SHOP
FIELD PUNISHMENT	FISHING INDUSTRY
FIFTEEN AND A HALF	FISHMONGERS' HALL
FIFTEEN AND EIGHT	FIT OF GENEROSITY
FIFTEEN AND SEVEN	FIT OF THE VAPOURS
FIFTEEN AND THREE	FIVE AND A QUARTER
FIFTEENTH LETTER	FIVE AND SIXPENCE
FIFTEENTH OF JULY	FIVE AND TENPENCE
FIFTEENTH OF JUNE	FIVE AND TWOPENCE
FIFTEEN THOUSAND	FIVE WICKETS DOWN
FIFTH OF DECEMBER	FIXED IMPRESSION
FIFTH OF FEBRUARY	FLAGGING SPIRITS
FIFTH OF NOVEMBER	FLAMBOROUGH HEAD
FIFTY-FIVE AND SIX	FLAMING NUISANCE
FIFTY-NINE AND SIX	FLANNEL TROUSERS
FIGHT FOR FREEDOM	FLAWLESS DIAMOND
FIGHT LIKE DEVILS	FLAWLESS MANNERS
FIGHT TO THE DEATH	FLEETING GLIMPSE
FIGURATIVE SENSE	FLEET OPERATIONS
FILL IN THE CRACKS	FLEMISH LANGUAGE
FILTH AND SQUALOR	FLICK OF THE WRIST
FINANCE MINISTER	FLING INTO PRISON
FINANCIAL CRISIS	FLIRT WITH THE LAW
FINANCIAL WIZARD	FLOATING CAPITAL
FINDING'S KEEPING	FLOOR OF THE HOUSE
FINE OPPORTUNITY	FLOURISHING TIME
FINISHED PRODUCT	FLOWER OF THE ARMY
FINISHING SCHOOL	FLY INTO A PASSION
FINISHING STROKE	FLY OFF THE HANDLE
FIREWORK DISPLAY	FOLLOW PRECEDENT
FIRST-AID STATION	FOLLOW THE HOUNDS
FIRST APPEARANCE	FOLLOW THE PLOUGH
FIRST BEGINNINGS	FOND OF THE BOTTLE
FIRST-CLASS HOTEL	FOOL OF THE FAMILY
FIRST-CLASS MATCH	FOOTBALL RESULTS
FIRST-FLOOR FRONT	FOOT OF THE LADDER
FIRST IMPORTANCE	FOR ALL ONE'S WORTH
FIRST IMPRESSION	FOR A YEAR AND A DAY
FIRST INSTALMENT	FORBIDDEN GROUND
FIRST INTENTIONS	FORCE AN ENTRANCE
FIRST IN THE FIELD	FORCE THE BIDDING
FIRST IN THE QUEUE	FORCIBLE FEEDING
FIRST LIEUTENANT	FOREIGN CURRENCY
FIRST OCCURRENCE	FOREIGN EXCHANGE
FIRST OF DECEMBER	FOREIGN LANGUAGE
FIRST OF FEBRUARY	FOREIGN MINISTER
FIRST OF NOVEMBER	FORENSIC CHEMIST
FIRST PORT OF CALL	FORFEIT ONE'S BAIL
FIRST PRINCIPLES	FORGED SIGNATURE
FIRST-RATE ACTING	FORGET ONE'S PIECE

FORGIVING NATURE
FOR GOODNESS' SAKE!
FORGOTTEN CUSTOM
FORKED LIGHTNING
FORM A GOVERNMENT
FORMAL AGREEMENT
FORMAL COMPLAINT
FORMAL STATEMENT
FOR MANY A LONG DAY
FOR OLD TIMES' SAKE
FOR THE FIRST TIME
FOR THE THIRD TIME
FOR THE TIME BEING
FORTY-EIGHT HOURS
FORTY-FIVE AND SIX
FORTY-FOUR AND SIX
FORTY-NINE AND SIX
FORTY-NINTH STATE
FORWARDING AGENT
FORWARD MOVEMENT
FOR WHAT IT'S WORTH
FOSTER AN OPINION
FOUNDATION CREAM
FOUNDATION STONE
FOUNTAIN OF YOUTH
FOUR AND A QUARTER
FOUR AND-SIXPENCE
FOUR AND TWOPENCE
FOURTEEN AND FIVE
FOURTEEN AND FOUR
FOURTEEN AND NINE
FOURTEEN PER CENT
FOURTEENTH GREEN
FOURTEENTH OF MAY
FOURTH DIMENSION
FOURTH OF JANUARY
FOURTH OF OCTOBER
FOUR WICKETS DOWN
FRAGRANT PERFUME
FRANCIS OF ASSISI
FRANCO-GERMAN WAR
FRANKLY SPEAKING
FREDERICK DELIUS
FREE ASSOCIATION
FREEDOM FROM FEAR
FREEDOM FROM WANT
FREEDOM OF ACCESS
FREEDOM OF ACTION
FREEDOM OF CHOICE
FREEDOM OF SPEECH
FREEDOM OF THE AIR

FREE FROM SLAVERY
FREEHAND DRAWING
FREELANCE WRITER
FREE OF INCOME-TAX
FREE TRANSLATION
FREEZE ONE'S BLOOD
FREEZING MIXTURE
FRENCH BREAKFAST
FRENCH DICTATION
FRENCH GRAND PRIX
FRENCH PEASANTRY
FRENCH SUBTITLES
FRENZIED EFFORTS
FREQUENT VISITOR
FRESH COMPLEXION
FRICASSEE OF VEAL
FRICTIONAL FORCE
FRIDAY AFTERNOON
FRIENDLY FEELING
FRIENDLY FOOTING
FRIENDLY GESTURE
FRIENDLY ISLANDS
FRIENDLY RIVALRY
FRIENDLY SOCIETY
FRIGHTENED CHILD
FROG IN THE THROAT
FROM ALL QUARTERS
FROM FIRST TO LAST
FROM HAND TO MOUTH
FROM LEFT TO RIGHT
FROM OBSERVATION
FROM STEM TO STERN
FROM THE ROOF-TOPS
FROM TOP TO BOTTOM
FRONT-LINE TROOPS
FROTH AT THE MOUTH
FRUITFUL SESSION
FRUITLESS SEARCH
FRUITS OF VICTORY
FUEL TO THE FLAMES
FULL-BOTTOMED WIG
FULL-DRESS DEBATE
FULL EXPLANATION
FULL OF INCIDENTS
FULL OF SURPRISES
FULL SPEED ASTERN
FULLY GUARANTEED
FUND OF KNOWLEDGE
FUNERAL CEREMONY
FUNERAL DIRECTOR
FURNISH EVIDENCE

FURNITURE POLISH
FUTURE EXISTENCE
FUTURE REFERENCE

G—15
GAIN A REPUTATION
GAIN INFORMATION
GAIN ONE'S FREEDOM
GALA PERFORMANCE
GALL AND WORMWOOD
GAME FOR ANYTHING
GAME, SET AND MATCH
GARDEN OF ENGLAND
GARGANTUAN FEAST
GATE-LEGGED TABLE
GATHERING CLOUDS
GATHERING STICKS
GENERAL ASSEMBLY
GENERAL DE GAULLE
GENERAL DELIVERY
GENERAL ELECTION
GENERAL FACTOTUM
GENERAL HOSPITAL
GENERAL INTEREST
GENERAL LAUGHTER
GENERAL OVERHAUL
GENERAL PRACTICE
GENERATING PLANT
GENEROUS GESTURE
GENEROUS HELPING
GENEROUS MEASURE
GENTLEMAN FARMER
GEOFFREY CHAUCER
GEOGRAPHY LESSON
GEORGE THE FOURTH
GET CONFIDENTIAL
GET DOWN TO THE JOB
GET INTO HOT WATER
GET INTO MISCHIEF
GET ONE'S MONKEY UP
GET ON ONE'S NERVES
GET ON SWIMMINGLY
GET ON WITH THE JOB
GET OUT OF THE ROAD
GET OUT OF TROUBLE
GET THE ADVANTAGE
GET THE UPPER HAND
GET THE WORST OF IT
GET UP TO MISCHIEF
GET YOUR SKATES ON
GHOSTS OF THE PAST

GIFT FROM THE GODS
GIN AND ANGOSTURA
GIRD UP ONE'S LOINS
GIRLISH LAUGHTER
GIST OF THE MATTER
GIVE A LEATHERING
GIVE FULL DETAILS
GIVE IN THE MIDDLE
GIVE ONE A BAD TIME
GIVE ONE'S CONSENT
GIVE ONESELF AIRS
GIVE ONESELF AWAY
GIVE ONE THE WORKS
GIVE PARTICULARS
GIVE THE ALL-CLEAR
GIVE THE GAME AWAY
GIVE THE PASSWORD
GIVE THE SHOW AWAY
GIVE UP THE SPONGE
GLITTERING PRIZE
GLOBE ARTICHOKES
GLOOMY COMPANION
GLORIOUS HOLIDAY
GLORIOUSLY DRUNK
GLORIOUS TWELFTH
GLORIOUS VICTORY
GLUT ON THE MARKET
GO A LONG WAY ROUND
GO BY UNDERGROUND
GODDESS OF WISDOM
GOD-FORSAKEN HOLE
GOD SAVE THE QUEEN
GO IN FOR LUXURIES
GO INTO ECSTASIES
GOLDEN HANDSHAKE
GOLDEN RETRIEVER
GOLDEN SOVEREIGN
GONE WITH THE WIND
GOOD CIRCULATION
GOOD CITIZENSHIP
GOOD CONNECTIONS
GOOD DAY'S JOURNEY
GOOD ENOUGH TO EAT
GOOD HANDWRITING
GOOD HOUSEKEEPER
GOODNESS OF HEART
GOOD RESOLUTIONS
GOOD VENTILATION
GO OFF AT A TANGENT
GO OFF THE DEEP END
GO OUT OF BUSINESS

GO OVER THE GROUND
GORGEOUS WEATHER
GO THE LONGEST WAY
GO THROUGH WITH IT
GO TO MUCH TROUBLE
GO TO THE SCAFFOLD
GOVERNMENT GRANT
GOVERNMENT HOUSE
GOVERNOR GENERAL
GO WITHOUT SAYING
GO WITH THE STREAM
GRACE BEFORE MEAT
GRACEFUL GESTURE
GRADUAL PROGRESS
GRAMOPHONE MUSIC
GRAND INQUISITOR
GRANDIOSE MANNER
GRAND UNION CANAL
GRANT ABSOLUTION
GRANULATED SUGAR
GRAPEFRUIT JUICE
GRAVE MISGIVINGS
GREASE THE WHEELS
GREAT ASSISTANCE
GREATEST RESPECT
GREAT EXCITEMENT
GREAT EXHIBITION
GREAT IMPORTANCE
GREATLY ESTEEMED
GREATLY INDEBTED
GREATLY SUPERIOR
GREAT MISFORTUNE
GREAT POPULARITY
GREEK MEETS GREEK
GREEK RESTAURANT
GREEN CHARTREUSE
GREENHOUSE PLANT
GRENADIER GUARDS
GREYHOUND RACING
GRIEVOUS MISTAKE
GRILLED SAUSAGES
GRILLED TOMATOES
GRIST FOR THE MILL
GROCERY BUSINESS
GROSS NEGLIGENCE
GROSVENOR SQUARE
GROUND-FLOOR FLAT
GROUND-NUT SCHEME
GROW INDIFFERENT
GUARDED LANGUAGE
GUESS ONE'S WEIGHT

GUILTY BEHAVIOUR
GUILTY BUT INSANE
GUNNER'S DAUGHTER
GUNNERY PRACTICE
GUY DE MAUPASSANT

H—15
HACKNEY CARRIAGE
HACKNEYED PHRASE
HACKNEYED SAYING
HAGUE CONVENTION
HAIL AND FAREWELL
HAILING DISTANCE
HALF AS MUCH AGAIN
HALF-TERM HOLIDAY
HALF THE DISTANCE
HALIBUT-LIVER OIL
HAMMER AND SICKLE
HANDFUL OF SILVER
HANDSOME APOLOGY
HANDSOME FORTUNE
HANDSOME PRESENT
HAND-TO-HAND FIGHT
HANGED BY THE NECK
HANGING ORNAMENT
HANG OUT THE FLAGS
HANG UP A STOCKING
HANSEL AND GRETEL
HAPPY AS A SANDBOY
HAPPY IN ONE'S WORK
HARBOUR FEELINGS
HARBOUR OF REFUGE
HARD AND FAST RULE
HARDEN ONE'S HEART
HARDNESS OF HEART
HARE AND TORTOISE
HARMLESS LUNATIC
HAROLD MACMILLAN
HARP ON ONE STRING
HARROW ON THE HILL
HARVEST FESTIVAL
HAUL DOWN THE FLAG
HAUNCH OF VENISON
HAUNTING REFRAIN
HAVE A BONE TO PICK
HAVE AN INTERVIEW
HAVE A SWEET TOOTH
HAVE ONE'S REVENGE
HAVE THE BEST OF IT
HAVE THE LAST WORD

HAVE THE PLEASURE
HAVE THE WHIP-HAND
HAVE WHAT IT TAKES
HAZARD AN OPINION
HEAD IN THE CLOUDS
HEAD OF THE FAMILY
HEAD OF THE SCHOOL
HEAD-ON COLLISION
HEALING OINTMENT
HEALTH AND WEALTH
HEALTH INSURANCE
HEALTHY APPETITE
HEALTHY EXERCISE
HEAP COALS OF FIRE
HEARSAY EVIDENCE
HEARTBREAK HOUSE
HEARTLESS MANNER
HEARTS ARE TRUMPS
HEARTY BREAKFAST
HEARTY GREETINGS
HEAT OF THE MOMENT
HEAVEN BE PRAISED
HEAVY CASUALTIES
HEAVY PUNISHMENT
HEIGHT OF FASHION
HEIR PRESUMPTIVE
HEIR TO THE THRONE
HENRY THE SEVENTH
HERBACEOUS PLANT
HERBERT MORRISON
HEREDITARY TITLE
HEREWARD THE WAKE
HERMIONE GINGOLD
HEROIC QUALITIES
HERRING INDUSTRY
HESITATION WALTZ
HIDE UNDERGROUND
HIGHER AND HIGHER
HIGHER CRITICISM
HIGHER EDUCATION
HIGHLAND COSTUME
HIGHLY COMMENDED
HIGHLY CONNECTED
HIGHLY DANGEROUS
HIGHLY DELIGHTED
HIGHLY EFFICIENT
HIGHLY QUALIFIED
HIGH TEMPERATURE
HIPPOCRATIC OATH
HIS MASTER'S VOICE
HISTORICAL NOVEL

HISTORIC PRESENT
HIT BELOW THE BELT
HIT THE HEADLINES
HIT THE HIGH SPOTS
HOLD ONE TO RANSOM
HOLD OUT ONE'S HAND
HOLD THE BEST HAND
HOLD UP YOUR HANDS
HOLE IN THE CORNER
HOLE IN THE GROUND
HOLES AND CORNERS
HOLIDAY BY THE SEA
HOLY ROMAN EMPIRE
HOME CONSUMPTION
HOMERIC LAUGHTER
HOMEWARD JOURNEY
HOME WITH THE MILK
HOMICIDAL MANIAC
HONEYMOON COUPLE
HONEYSUCKLE ROSE
HONOURS OF BATTLE
HOPE AGAINST HOPE
HOPELESS FAILURE
HORIZONTAL PLANE
HORNS OF A DILEMMA
HORRIBLE WEATHER
HORSE-SHOE MAGNET
HOSPITAL ALMONER
HOSPITAL GROUNDS
HOSPITAL SURGEON
HOSTILE EVIDENCE
HOTEL PROPRIETOR
HOT FROM THE PRESS
HOURS OF BUSINESS
HOURS OF IDLENESS
HOUSEHOLD CHORES
HOUSEHOLD DRUDGE
HOUSEHOLD TROOPS
HOUSING MINISTER
HOUSING SHORTAGE
HOVER ON THE BRINK
HOW GOES THE ENEMY?
HUCKLEBERRY FINN
HUDDLED TOGETHER
HUMAN EXPERIENCE
HUMANLY POSSIBLE
HUMANLY SPEAKING
HUMID ATMOSPHERE
HUNDRED THOUSAND
HUNDRED YEARS WAR
HUNGER AND THIRST

HUNGRY AS A HUNTER
HUSH-HUSH SUBJECT

I—15
ICE-CREAM PARLOUR
ICE-CREAM SELLERS
ICE HOCKEY PLAYER
IDEAL SUGGESTION
IDLEWILD AIRPORT
ILLUSTRATED WORK
ILLUSTRIOUS PAST
IMITATION PEARLS
IMMACULATE STYLE
IMMEDIATE ACTION
IMMERSED IN STUDY
IMMERSION HEATER
IMMORTAL DREAMER
IMMOVABLE OBJECT
IMPENDING DANGER
IMPERIAL COLLEGE
IMPERIAL MEASURE
IMPLORING GLANCE
IMPORTANT MATTER
IMPORTANT PERSON
IMPOSSIBLE STORY
IMPRESSIVE SCENE
IMPROBABLE STORY
IMPROVED VERSION
IMPROVE IN HEALTH
IMPROVE ON NATURE
IMPULSIVE NATURE
IN A LESSER DEGREE
IN ALL CONSCIENCE
IN ALL DIRECTIONS
IN ALL LIKELIHOOD
INANIMATE MATTER
IN APPLE-PIE ORDER
IN A STRAIGHT LINE
INAUGURAL SPEECH
IN BLACK AND WHITE
INCIDENTAL MUSIC
INCLINE ONE'S HEAD
INCLUSIVE CHARGE
INCOME-TAX DEMAND
INCOME-TAX REBATE
INCOME-TAX RELIEF
INCOME-TAX RETURN
IN CONSIDERATION
INCREASED DEMAND
INDELIBLE PENCIL
INDEPENDENCE DAY

INDIAN ROPE-TRICK
INDIA-RUBBER BALL
INDIA-RUBBER BAND
INDIRECT CURRENT
INDIVIDUAL STYLE
INDOOR FIREWORKS
INDULGENT PARENT
INDUSTRIAL PLANT
IN EXTREME DANGER
INFAMOUS CONDUCT
INFANT MORTALITY
INFANTRY SOLDIER
INFERIOR ARTICLE
INFERIOR NUMBERS
INFERIOR QUALITY
INFERIOR VERSION
INFERNAL MACHINE
INFERNAL REGIONS
INFIRM OF PURPOSE
INFORMATION DESK
INFORMATION ROOM
INFORMED OPINION
IN FULL AGREEMENT
INGENIOUS DEVICE
INGENIOUS EXCUSE
INIQUITOUS PRICE
INITIAL EXPENSES
INJURED INNOCENT
IN JUXTAPOSITION
INNINGS DECLARED
INNOCENTS ABROAD
IN ONE'S RIGHT MIND
INORDINATE PRIDE
INORGANIC MATTER
IN SEARCH OF TRUTH
INSECURE FOOTING
IN SHARP CONTRAST
INSPECTOR FRENCH
INSTANT RESPONSE
INSTRUMENT BOARD
INSTRUMENT PANEL
INSUPERABLE ODDS
INSURANCE BROKER
INSURANCE OFFICE
INSURANCE POLICY
INTELLIGENT FOLK
INTELLIGENT TALK
INTERESTED PARTY
INTERIM DIVIDEND
INTERNAL AFFAIRS
IN THE ACCUSATIVE

IN THE ALTOGETHER
IN THE BACKGROUND
IN THE FIRST PLACE
IN THE FOREGROUND
IN THE LABORATORY
IN THE LAST RESORT
IN THE LIGHT OF DAY
IN THE LION'S MOUTH
IN THE MANNER BORN
IN THE MELTING-POT
IN THE MIDDLE EAST
IN THE NEAR FUTURE
IN THE NICK OF TIME
IN THE RIGHT PLACE
IN THE SAME BREATH
IN THE SHOP-WINDOW
IN THE SMALL HOURS
IN THE VERNACULAR
IN THE WILDERNESS
IN THE WITNESS-BOX
IN THE WRONG PLACE
INVALID CARRIAGE
INVENTIVE GENIUS
INVESTMENT TRUST
INVEST WITH POWER
INVISIBLE EXPORT
INVISIBLE IMPORT
INVITATION WALTZ
INVITED AUDIENCE
IRISH SWEEPSTAKE
IRREGULAR TROOPS
IRREPARABLE HARM
IRREPARABLE LOSS
ISLAND CONTINENT
ISSUE A CHALLENGE
ITALIAN VERMOUTH
IT'S THAT MAN AGAIN
IVAN THE TERRIBLE

J—15
JACK OF ALL TRADES
JANUARY THE FIFTH
JANUARY THE FIRST
JANUARY THE NINTH
JANUARY THE SIXTH
JANUARY THE TENTH
JANUARY THE THIRD
JERRY-BUILT HOUSE
JEWEL AND WARRISS
JOBBING GARDENER
JOCKEY FOR PLACES

JOIN IN THE CHORUS
JOINT GOVERNMENT
JOIN THE MAJORITY
JOINT OPERATIONS
JOINT POSSESSION
JOLLY GOOD FELLOW
JUDGE FOR ONESELF
JUDGMENT OF PARIS
JUDGMENT SUMMONS
JUICE OF THE GRAPE
JULY THE ELEVENTH
JUMPING-OFF PLACE
JUNE THE ELEVENTH
JUNIOR BARRISTER
JUPITER SYMPHONY
JUST ABOUT ENOUGH

K—15
KATHLEEN FERRIER
KEEN COMPETITION
KEENLY CONTESTED
KEEP AT A DISTANCE
KEEPER OF THE KEYS
KEEP IN CAPTIVITY
KEEP IN IGNORANCE
KEEP NOTHING BACK
KEEP OFF THE GRASS
KEEP ONE GUESSING
KEEP ONE'S BALANCE
KEEP ONE'S COUNSEL
KEEP ONE'S PROMISE
KEEP ONE'S SHIRT ON
KEEP ON THE COURSE
KEEP OUT OF THE WAY
KEEP THE DOOR OPEN
KEEP THINGS GOING
KEEP TO THE MIDDLE
KEEP UNDER ARREST
KENNETH MCKELLAR
KERB-SIDE PARKING
KEY TO THE MYSTERY
KICK UP ONE'S HEELS
KID-GLOVE METHODS
KIDNEYS AND BACON
KINDLE OF KITTENS
KINDNESS OF HEART
KINGDOM OF HEAVEN
KING OF THE BEASTS
KING OF THE CASTLE
KING OF THE FOREST
KING OF THE JUNGLE

KITTEN ON THE KEYS
KNAVE OF DIAMONDS
KNIGHT COMMANDER
KNIGHT OF THE BATH
KNIGHT OF THE ROAD
KNIGHTS TEMPLARS
KNITTING MACHINE
KNITTING PATTERN
KNOW A THING OR TWO
KNOW ONE'S OWN MIND

L—15

LABOUR CANDIDATE
LABOUR RELATIONS
LABOUR SUPPORTER
LACK OF EDUCATION
LACK OF KNOWLEDGE
LACK OF WILL POWER
LADDER OF SUCCESS
LADIES' COMPANION
LADIES IN WAITING
LAND OF MY FATHERS
LAND OF THE LIVING
LANDSCAPE ARTIST
LANGUAGE BARRIER
LANGUAGE PROBLEM
LANGUAGE TEACHER
LARGE PERCENTAGE
LARGE POPULATION
LAST BUT NOT LEAST
LASTING MONUMENT
LAST PERFORMANCE
LATEST INVENTION
LATEST QUOTATION
LAUGH AND GROW FAT
LAUGHING JACKASS
LAUGH LIKE A DRAIN
LAUGH LIKE A HYENA
LAUGH OUT OF COURT
LAUGHTER IN COURT
LAURENCE OLIVIER
LAVENDER HILL MOB
LAY DOWN ONE'S ARMS
LAY DOWN ONE'S LIFE
LEAD A DOUBLE LIFE
LEAD A MERRY DANCE
LEADER OF FASHION
LEADER OF SOCIETY
LEADER OF THE BAND
LEADING BUSINESS
LEADING NOVELIST

LEADING QUESTION
LEADING THE FIELD
LEAGUE OF NATIONS
LEAP OVER THE MOON
LEARN ONE'S LESSON
LEATHER INDUSTRY
LEAVE FOOTPRINTS
LEAVE IN SUSPENSE
LEAVE IN THE LURCH
LEAVE IT TO CHANCE
LEAVE NOTHING OUT
LEAVE THE COUNTRY
LEAVE UNFINISHED
LEGAL DEPARTMENT
LEGAL PROFESSION
LEGAL SEPARATION
LEGAL SETTLEMENT
LEG BEFORE WICKET
LEGISLATIVE BODY
LEGITIMATE CLAIM
LEGITIMATE DRAMA
LEGITIMATE STAGE
LEGUMINOUS PLANT
LEICESTER SQUARE
LEIGHTON BUZZARD
LEISURED CLASSES
LEMON CHEESE-CAKE
LENGTH OF SERVICE
LENGTHY ARGUMENT
LENGTHY BUSINESS
LENIENT SENTENCE
LEONARDO DA VINCI
LESSEN THE STRAIN
LESS THAN THE DUST
LET DOWN ONE'S HAIR
LET ONE'S HAIR DOWN
LETTER OF REQUEST
LET THERE BE LIGHT!
LETTRES DE CACHET
LIBERAL MAJORITY
LIBERAL MINORITY
LICENCE ENDORSED
LICK AND A PROMISE
LICK ONE'S FINGERS
LIE IN ONE'S THROAT
LIE LIKE A TROOPER
LIFE-BOAT STATION
LIFT THE RECEIVER
LIFT UP ONE'S VOICE
LIFT UP YOUR HEART
LIGHT AS A FEATHER

LIGHT LITERATURE
LIGHT MACHINE-GUN
LIGHTNING SKETCH
LIGHTNING STRIKE
LIGHT OF THE WORLD
LIGHT PUNISHMENT
LIKE A DROWNED RAT
LIKE A DUTCH UNCLE
LIKE A HOUSE AFIRE
LIKE QUICKSILVER
LILY OF THE VALLEY
LINCOLN HANDICAP
LINCOLN MEMORIAL
LINE OF DIRECTION
LINE ONE'S POCKETS
LINK WITH THE PAST
LIQUID RESOURCES
LIST TO STARBOARD
LITERARY CIRCLES
LITERARY FORGERY
LITERARY OUTLINE
LITERARY SUBJECT
LITTLE ENGLANDER
LITTLE GENTLEMAN
LITTLE KNOWLEDGE
LITTLE MISS FIX-IT
LITTLE OR NOTHING
LITTLE WOODEN HUT
LIVE DANGEROUSLY
LIVE IN A SMALL WAY
LIVE IN SECLUSION
LIVE LIKE A PAUPER
LIVERPOOL STREET
LIVING TESTIMONY
LOADED WITH MONEY
LOAD OFF ONE'S MIND
LOAVES AND FISHES
LOCAL GOVERNMENT
LOCAL INHABITANT
LOCH NESS MONSTER
LOCKED AND BOLTED
LODGE A COMPLAINT
LOGICAL ARGUMENT
LOGICAL SEQUENCE
LONDON ALLOWANCE
LONDON TRANSPORT
LONG ARM OF THE LAW
LONGEST WAY ROUND
LONG LIVE THE KING!
LONG-TERM SOLDIER
LONG-WINDED STORY

LOOK BACK IN ANGER
LOOK FOR A WELCOME
LOOK FOR SYMPATHY
LOOK THE OTHER WAY
LOOK TO THE FUTURE
LORD CHAMBERLAIN
LORD HIGH ADMIRAL
LORD HIGH STEWARD
LORD MAYOR'S COACH
LORDS AND COMMONS
LORDS OF CREATION
LOSE COUNTENANCE
LOSE ONE'S BALANCE
LOSE ONE'S FOOTING
LOSE ONE'S HUSBAND
LOSE ONE'S STRIPES
LOSE ON THE SWINGS
LOSE THE ELECTION
LOST OPPORTUNITY
LOVE ME, LOVE MY DOG
LOVE OF ADVENTURE
LOVER AND HIS LASS
LOWER ONE'S SIGHTS
LOW SUBSCRIPTION
LUKEWARM SUPPORT
LUMP IN THE THROAT
LUNCHEON SAUSAGE
LUNCHEON VOUCHER
LUTON GIRLS' CHOIR
LUXURIANT GROWTH

M—15

MAD AS A MARCH HARE
MAGAZINE ARTICLE
MAGAZINE SECTION
MAGIC INSTRUMENT
MAGNETIC COMPASS
MAGNIFYING GLASS
MAGNIFYING POWER
MAIN CLAIM TO FAME
MAIN LINE STATION
MAJESTY OF THE LAW
MAJORITY VERDICT
MAKE A COLLECTION
MAKE A CONFESSION
MAKE A FRESH START
MAKE ALTERATIONS
MAKE AN ASSERTION
MAKE AN EXCEPTION
MAKE APPLICATION
MAKE A PREDICTION

MAKE A RESOLUTION
MAKE A SUGGESTION
MAKE COMPARISONS
MAKE CONCESSIONS
MAKE CORRECTIONS
MAKE ONE'S FORTUNE
MAKE REPARATIONS
MAKE RESTITUTION
MAKE SHORT WORK OF
MAKE THE BEST OF IT
MAKE THE MOST OF IT
MAKE THINGS CLEAR
MAKE THINGS WORSE
MALE SUPERIORITY
MALIGNANT GROWTH
MALIGN INFLUENCE
MALVERN FESTIVAL
MANIC DEPRESSION
MANILLA ENVELOPE
MAN IN POSSESSION
MANNEQUIN PARADE
MAN OF EXPERIENCE
MANY-HEADED BEAST
MARCH OF PROGRESS
MARCH THE SEVENTH
MARCH THE TWELFTH
MARGINAL COMMENT
MARIE ANTOINETTE
MARINE INSURANCE
MARINER'S COMPASS
MARK OF AUTHORITY
MARK THE OCCASION
MARLENE DIETRICH
MARRIAGEABLE AGE
MARRIAGE ADVISER
MARRIAGE BY PROXY
MARRIAGE LICENCE
MARRIAGE PARTNER
MARRIAGE PORTION
MARRIAGE SERVICE
MARRIED QUARTERS
MARSHALLING YARD
MARY'S LITTLE LAMB
MASCULINE GENDER
MASQUERADE DRESS
MASS INFORMATION
MASS OBSERVATION
MASTER CARPENTER
MASTER CRAFTSMAN
MASTER OF SCIENCE
MATERIAL BENEFIT

MATERIAL SUCCESS
MATERIAL WITNESS
MATERNAL FEELING
MATTER OF OPINION
MAXIMUM PRESSURE
MAY THE FIFTEENTH
MAY THE SIXTEENTH
MAY THE THIRTIETH
MAY THE TWENTIETH
MEANS OF APPROACH
MEAN WHAT ONE SAYS
MEASURE OF LENGTH
MECHANICAL MEANS
MECHANICAL POWER
MEMBER OF SOCIETY
MEMBER OF THE CAST
MEMORIAL SERVICE
MENTAL AGITATION
MENTAL BREAKDOWN
MENTAL DEFECTIVE
MENTAL FACULTIES
MENTAL TELEPATHY
MENTAL TREATMENT
MERCENARY TROOPS
MERCHANT SERVICE
MERE COINCIDENCE
MERRY AS A CRICKET
MERRY MONTH OF MAY
MESSAGE RECEIVED
METHOD OF WORKING
MEXICAN HAIRLESS
MICHAEL FLANDERS
MICHAEL HOLLIDAY
MICHAELMAS DAISY
MICHAELMAS GOOSE
MICHAEL REDGRAVE
MIDDLE-AGE SPREAD
MIDDLE OF THE ROAD
MIDDLE OF THE ROOM
MIDLAND COUNTIES
MIDNIGHT MATINEE
MILITARY ACADEMY
MILITARY BEARING
MILITARY COLLEGE
MILITARY COLOURS
MILITARY FUNERAL
MILITARY HISTORY
MILITARY HONOURS
MILITARY MISSION
MILITARY SERVICE
MILITARY STATION

MILITARY TACTICS
MILITARY TRIBUNE
MILITARY TWO-STEP
MILITATE AGAINST
MILLICENT MARTIN
MILLIONAIRE'S ROW
MIND ONE'S MANNERS
MIND THE WET PAINT
MINIATURE POODLE
MINISTER OF POWER
MINISTER OF STATE
MINISTER OF WORKS
MINISTRY OF POWER
MINISTRY OF STATE
MINISTRY OF WORKS
MIRROR OF FASHION
MISERABLE SINNER
MISS ONE'S FOOTING
MISTRESS QUICKLY
MIXTURE AS BEFORE
MODEL OF INDUSTRY
MODE OF BEHAVIOUR
MODERATE DEMANDS
MODERATE DRINKER
MODERATE SUCCESS
MODEST BEHAVIOUR
MOLOTOV COCKTAIL
MOMENT OF MADNESS
MONASTERY GARDEN
MONDAY AFTERNOON
MONEY FOR NOTHING
MONEY FOR OLD ROPE
MONEY MAKES MONEY
MONTE CARLO RALLY
MONTH AFTER MONTH
MONTHLY MAGAZINE
MONTHLY PAYMENTS
MONTHS AND MONTHS
MONTHS OF THE YEAR
MONUMENTAL MASON
MOON AND SIXPENCE
MOONLIGHT SONATA
MORAL INJUNCTION
MORAL OBLIGATION
MORAL PHILOSOPHY
MORAL REARMAMENT
MORAL STANDPOINT
MORBID CURIOSITY
MORE THAN WELCOME
MORRISON SHELTER
MOST INTERESTING

MOST RESPECTABLE
MOTHER AND FATHER
MOTHERING SUNDAY
MOTHERLESS CHILD
MOTIVATING FORCE
MOTLEY GATHERING
MOTORING OFFENCE
MOUNTAIN OF FLESH
MOUNTAINOUS AREA
MOUNTAIN RAILWAY
MOUNTAIN TORRENT
MOUTH OF THE RIVER
MOVING SPECTACLE
MOVING STAIRCASE
MUCH OF A MUCHNESS
MUCH SOUGHT AFTER
MULBERRY HARBOUR
MULTIPLY BY EIGHT
MULTIPLY BY SEVEN
MULTIPLY BY THREE
MUNICH AGREEMENT
MURAL DECORATION
MURDEROUS WEAPON
MUSICAL DIRECTOR
MUSICAL FESTIVAL
MUSICAL INTERVAL
MUSIC-HALL ARTIST
MUSIC HATH CHARMS
MUSTARD AND CRESS
MUSTER UP COURAGE
MUTUAL AFFECTION
MUTUAL AGREEMENT
MUTUAL HOSTILITY
MUTUAL INSURANCE
MUTUAL SUSPICION
MY LEARNED FRIEND
MYTHOLOGICAL AGE

N—15

NATIONAL COLOURS
NATIONAL COSTUME
NATIONAL DEFENCE
NATIONAL GALLERY
NATIONAL HOLIDAY
NATIONAL LIBERAL
NATIONAL LIBRARY
NATIONAL LOTTERY
NATIONAL SAVINGS
NATIONAL SERVICE
NATIONAL SOCIETY
NATIONAL THEATRE

NATURAL APTITUDE
NATURAL CAPACITY
NATURAL INSTINCT
NAUGHTY NINETIES
NAVAL ENGAGEMENT
NAVAL OPERATIONS
NAVAL TOURNAMENT
NAVIGATION LIGHT
NEARER AND NEARER
NEAREST RELATIVE
NEAT AS NINEPENCE
NEAT BUT NOT GAUDY
NEAT HANDWRITING
NEAT PIECE OF WORK
NECK-AND-NECK RACE
NECTAR OF THE GODS
NEEDLE AND COTTON
NEEDLE AND THREAD
NEGATIVE REQUEST
NEGLECT ONE'S DUTY
NEGOTIABLE BONDS
NERVOUS DISORDER
NEVER A CROSS WORD
NEVER-ENDING TASK
NEW ACQUAINTANCE
NEWCASTLE ON TYNE
NEWCASTLE UNITED
NEW ENGLISH BIBLE
NEWFOUNDLAND DOG
NEWGATE CALENDAR
NEWS COMMENTATOR
NEW SCOTLAND YARD
NEWS FROM NOWHERE
NEWSPAPER REPORT
NEWSPAPER SELLER
NIBBLE AT THE BAIT
NICE DISTINCTION
NICE LITTLE THING
NIGGER MINSTRELS
NIGHT AFTER NIGHT
NIGHT ON THE TILES
NIGHT STARVATION
NINE AND A QUARTER
NINE AND SIXPENCE
NINE AND TENPENCE
NINE AND TWOPENCE
NINETEEN AND FIVE
NINETEEN AND FOUR
NINETEEN AND NINE
NINETEEN PER CENT
NINETEENTH OF MAY

NINETY-ONE AND SIX
NINE WICKETS DOWN
NINTH OF DECEMBER
NINTH OF FEBRUARY
NINTH OF NOVEMBER
NOBEL PEACE PRIZE
NOBLE SENTIMENTS
NOBODY'S BUSINESS
NO CONCERN OF MINE
NO DISTANCE AT ALL
NOISY NEIGHBOURS
NOMINATION PAPER
NON COMPOS MENTIS
NONE BUT THE BRAVE
NORFOLK DUMPLING
NORMAL BEHAVIOUR
NORMAL PROCEDURE
NORTHERN IRELAND
NORTH OF THE RIVER
NORTH OF THE TWEED
NO STONE UNTURNED
NOT A LIVING THING
NOTHING IN COMMON
NOT IN THE RUNNING
NOT OUT OF THE WOOD
NOT STRONG ENOUGH
NOTTING HILL GATE
NOVEL EXPERIENCE
NUCLEAR REACTION
NUFFIELD COLLEGE
NUREMBERG TRIALS
NURSE A GRIEVANCE
NURSE AN AMBITION
NURSERY HANDICAP
NUTCRACKER SUITE

O—15
OBEDIENT SERVANT
OBEY REGULATIONS
OBJECT OF CHARITY
OBJECT OF DISLIKE
OBJECT OF WORSHIP
OBLIQUE QUESTION
OBSERVATION POST
OCCASIONAL TABLE
OCCUPYING TENANT
OCTOBER THE FIFTH
OCTOBER THE FIRST
OCTOBER THE NINTH
OCTOBER THE SIXTH
OCTOBER THE TENTH

OCTOBER THE THIRD
ODDS-ON FAVOURITE
ODOUR OF SANCTITY
OFFENSIVE MANNER
OFFENSIVE REMARK
OFFENSIVE WEAPON
OFFER IN EXCHANGE
OFFICER IN CHARGE
OFFICER MATERIAL
OFFICER OF THE DAY
OFFICIAL INQUIRY
OFFICIAL JOURNAL
OFFICIOUS PERSON
OFF TO A FINE START
OFF TO A GOOD START
OF THE FIRST WATER
OLD ACQUAINTANCE
OLD-AGE PENSIONER
OLD AS METHUSELAH
OLD CONTEMPTIBLE
OLDER GENERATION
OLD FATHER THAMES
OLIVER GOLDSMITH
OMNIA VINCIT AMOR
ON ACTIVE SERVICE
ONCE IN A BLUE MOON
ONCE IN A LIFETIME
ONE AFTER ANOTHER
ONE AND FIVEPENCE
ONE AND FOURPENCE
ONE AND NINEPENCE
ONE MAN WENT TO MOW
ONE OF THE COMPANY
ONE OVER THE EIGHT
ONE STAGE AT A TIME
ONE THING AT A TIME
ONE WAY OR ANOTHER
ON HANDS AND KNEES
ON ONE'S HIGH HORSE
ON SPEAKING TERMS
ON THE BORDERLINE
ON THE BRADEN BEAT
ON THE BRIGHT SIDE
ON THE CREDIT SIDE
ON THE DOTTED LINE
ON THE RIGHT LINES
ON THE RIGHT SCENT
ON THE RIGHT TRACK
ON THE ROAD TO RUIN
ON THE WATER-WAGON
ON THE WRONG LINES

ON THE WRONG SCENT
ON THE WRONG TRACK
ON TOP OF THE WORLD
ON VISITING TERMS
ON WITH THE MOTLEY
OPEN-AND-SHUT CASE
OPEN COMPETITION
OPEN HOSTILITIES
OPENING CEREMONY
OPENING SENTENCE
OPEN SCHOLARSHIP
OPEN THE QUESTION
OPEN THE THROTTLE
OPEN TO CRITICISM
OPEN TO OBJECTION
OPEN TO SUSPICION
OPEN TO THE PUBLIC
OPPORTUNE MOMENT
OPPORTUNE REMARK
OPPOSING COUNSEL
OPPOSITE EXTREME
OPPOSITE MEANING
OPPOSITE PARTIES
OPPOSITION BENCH
OPPOSITION PARTY
OPTICAL ILLUSION
ORAL EXAMINATION
ORANGE FREE STATE
ORANGE MARMALADE
ORCHESTRAL MUSIC
ORCHESTRA STALLS
ORDERLY CORPORAL
ORDERLY SERGEANT
ORDNANCE OFFICER
ORGANISED LABOUR
ORIENTAL SCHOLAR
ORIGINAL MEANING
ORIGIN OF SPECIES
ORNAMENTAL PLANT
OUNCE OF PRACTICE
OUR MUTUAL FRIEND
OUTDOOR CLOTHING
OUTDOOR EXERCISE
OUT OF COMMISSION
OUT OF EMPLOYMENT
OUT OF HIS ELEMENT
OUT OF ONE'S SENSES
OUT OF PROPORTION
OUT OF THE COUNTRY
OUT OF THE PICTURE
OUT OF THE RUNNING

OUT-OF-THE-WAY SPOT
OUTRIGHT SCANDAL
OUTSIDE INTEREST
OUTSTANDING DEBT
OVER AND DONE WITH
OVERCOME BY GRIEF
OVERFLOW MEETING
OVERHEAD CHARGES
OVERHEAD RAILWAY
OVERSTEP THE MARK
OVER THE BASE-LINE

P—15
PADDINGTON GREEN
PAINT THE TOWN RED
PAIR OF CALLIPERS
PAIR OF COMPASSES
PAIR OF DUMB-BELLS
PAIR OF STOCKINGS
PALACE OF SOVIETS
PALAEOLITHIC AGE
PARACHUTE TROOPS
PARAGON OF VIRTUE
PARENTAL CONSENT
PARENTAL CONTROL
PARKHURST PRISON
PARTIAL LIKENESS
PARTNERS IN CRIME
PARTY CONFERENCE
PASS ALONG PLEASE
PASS A RESOLUTION
PASS AWAY THE TIME
PASSIVE INTEREST
PASSIVE RESISTER
PASS ROUND THE HAT
PASS THE HAT ROUND
PASS WITH HONOURS
PASTEURIZED MILK
PATCH UP A QUARREL
PATENTLY OBVIOUS
PATERNAL FEELING
PATRICK CAMPBELL
PATRON OF THE ARTS
PATTERN OF VIRTUE
PAUSE FOR A MOMENT
PAWNBROKER'S SIGN
PAYABLE ON DEMAND
PAY COMPENSATION
PAY OFF OLD SCORES
PAY ONE'S RESPECTS
PEACE AT ANY PRICE

PEACE CONFERENCE
PEACE WITH HONOUR
PEACHES AND CREAM
PECULIAR FLAVOUR
PENAL SETTLEMENT
PENCIL SHARPENER
PENNY IN THE POUND
PEOPLE IN GENERAL
PEOPLE OF FASHION
PEOPLE OF QUALITY
PER ARDUA AD ASTRA
PERCENTAGE BASIS
PEREGRINE FALCON
PERFECT CREATURE
PERFECT INTERVAL
PERFECT LIKENESS
PERFECTLY HONEST
PERFECT NONSENSE
PERFECT NUISANCE
PERFECT STRANGER
PERFECT TREASURE
PERFORMING FLEAS
PERILOUS VENTURE
PERIOD FURNITURE
PERISHABLE GOODS
PERMANENT RECORD
PERPETUAL MOTION
PERSONAL ACCOUNT
PERSONAL AFFRONT
PERSONAL BENEFIT
PERSONAL EFFECTS
PERSONALITY CULT
PERSONAL OPINION
PERSONAL PRONOUN
PERSONAL REASONS
PERSONAL SERVICE
PERSONA NON GRATA
PERTINENT REMARK
PESTLE AND MORTAR
PETER AND THE WOLF
PETER THE PAINTER
PETITION OF RIGHT
PETRIFIED FOREST
PETROL RATIONING
PHOTOGRAPH ALBUM
PHYSICAL CRAVING
PHYSICAL CULTURE
PHYSICAL FATIGUE
PHYSICAL SCIENCE
PICK UP THE PIECES
PICK UP THE THREAD

PICTURE OF HEALTH
PICTURE OF MISERY
PICTURE POSTCARD
PIECE OF EVIDENCE
PIECE OF GOOD NEWS
PIECE OF NONSENSE
PIECE OF ONE'S MIND
PILLAR OF SOCIETY
PINCHED WITH COLD
PINK OF CONDITION
PIOUS SENTIMENTS
PIPPED AT THE POST
PIT OF THE STOMACH
PLACE OF BUSINESS
PLAGUE OF LOCUSTS
PLAIN-CLOTHES MAN
PLANETARY SYSTEM
PLANNING OFFICER
PLAY A DOUBLE GAME
PLAY A LOSING GAME
PLAY CAT AND MOUSE
PLAYERS' ENTRANCE
PLAY FIRST FIDDLE
PLAY HIDE-AND-SEEK
PLAY ONE'S OWN HAND
PLAY THE BAGPIPES
PLAY THE INFORMER
PLAY THE PARASITE
PLAYTHING OF FATE
PLAY TIDDLYWINKS
PLEASANT EVENING
PLEASANT FLAVOUR
PLEASURE GARDENS
PLEASURE GROUNDS
PLEASURE STEAMER
PLIGHT ONE'S TROTH
PLOUGH THE FIELDS
PLUM IN ONE'S MOUTH
PLYMOUTH BROTHER
PLYMOUTH HARBOUR
POCKET ONE'S PRIDE
POETICAL JUSTICE
POINT-BLANK RANGE
POINTED REMINDER
POINTLESS REMARK
POINT OF NO RETURN
POLAR EXPEDITION
POLICE CONSTABLE
POLICE INSPECTOR
POLISHED MANNERS
POLITICAL ASYLUM

POLITICAL CAREER
POLITICAL EVENTS
POLITICAL OFFICE
POLITICAL RIGHTS
POLITICAL SPEECH
POLITICAL THEORY
POLITICAL WEAPON
POLITICAL WRITER
POMP AND CEREMONY
POOR CIRCULATION
POOR CONSOLATION
POOR VENTILATION
POPEYE THE SAILOR
POPULAR LANGUAGE
PORTMANTEAU WORD
PORTRAIT GALLERY
PORTRAIT OF A LADY
PORTRAIT PAINTER
POSITION OF POWER
POSITION OF TRUST
POSITIVE ELEMENT
POST-DATED CHEQUE
POST-OFFICE GUIDE
POTENTIAL DANGER
POTENTIAL ENERGY
POWER OF ATTORNEY
POWER OF JUDGMENT
POWER OF RECOVERY
POWER OF THE PRESS
PRACTICAL RESULT
PRACTISE SORCERY
PRAIRIE SCHOONER
PRAYER FOR THE DAY
PREACH THE GOSPEL
PREACH TO THE WISE
PRECARIOUS STATE
PREFECT OF POLICE
PREFERENCE SHARE
PREFERRED SHARES
PRELIMINARY HEAT
PRELIMINARY STEP
PREMEDITATED ACT
PRE-PAID TELEGRAM
PREPARED TO FIGHT
PRESERVED GINGER
PRESERVING SUGAR
PRESIDENT NASSER
PRESS CONFERENCE
PRESSED FOR FUNDS
PRESSED FOR MONEY
PRESSED FOR SPACE

PRESS FOR PAYMENT
PRESS THE TRIGGER
PRESTON NORTH END
PRETTY MUCH ALIKE
PREVAILING TASTE
PREVAILING WINDS
PREVIOUS OFFENCE
PRICE ON ONE'S HEAD
PRICE REGULATION
PRICK ONE'S EARS UP
PRICK UP ONE'S EARS
PRIMARY ELECTION
PRIMITIVE COLOUR
PRINCE OF DENMARK
PRINCIPAL CLAUSE
PRINCIPAL PERSON
PRIOR CONDITIONS
PRIOR ENGAGEMENT
PRISONER OF STATE
PRISONER OF ZENDA
PRISONER'S FRIEND
PRIVATE CARRIAGE
PRIVATE CHANNELS
PRIVATE DEVOTION
PRIVATE HOSPITAL
PRIVATE LANGUAGE
PRIVATE PRACTICE
PRIVATE PROPERTY
PRIVATE QUARTERS
PRIVATE TEACHING
PRIVILEGED CLASS
PRIVY COUNCILLOR
PROBABLE STARTER
PROCESSED CHEESE
PRODIGAL'S RETURN
PROFESSED BELIEF
PROFESSIONAL AIR
PROFESSIONAL FEE
PROFESSIONAL MAN
PROFOUND THINKER
PROFOUND THOUGHT
PROGRAMME PARADE
PROGRAMME SELLER
PROHIBITION DAYS
PROHIBITION ZONE
PROLONG THE AGONY
PRONOUNCE GUILTY
PROOF OF PURCHASE
PROPERLY DRESSED
PROPER TREATMENT
PROPOSE MARRIAGE

PROSPECTIVE WIFE
PROUD AS A PEACOCK
PROVE ACCEPTABLE
PROVIDE THE MEANS
PROVINCIAL PAPER
PRUNES AND PRISMS
PUBLIC CHARACTER
PUBLIC DECEPTION
PUBLIC EDUCATION
PUBLIC ENCLOSURE
PUBLIC EXECUTION
PUBLIC KNOWLEDGE
PUBLIC MANIFESTO
PUBLIC OWNERSHIP
PUBLIC RELATIONS
PUBLIC-SCHOOL BOY
PUBLIC TRANSPORT
PUBLISH THE BANNS
PULL FOR THE SHORE
PULL ONE'S PUNCHES
PULL OUT THE STOPS
PULL-UP FOR CARMEN
PULL UP ONE'S SOCKS
PUNCTUATION MARK
PURCHASING POWER
PURE COINCIDENCE
PURELY AND SIMPLY
PURE MATHEMATICS
PURR WITH CONTENT
PURSUE AN INQUIRY
PURSUE THE MATTER
PUSS IN THE CORNER
PUT AN END TO IT ALL
PUT BACK THE CLOCK
PUT IN A WORD OR TWO
PUT IN POSSESSION
PUT IN QUARANTINE
PUT IN THE PICTURE
PUT INTO PRACTICE
PUT IT ANOTHER WAY
PUT IT ON THE SHELF
PUT ONE'S FOOT DOWN
PUT ONE'S FOOT IN IT
PUT ONE'S NAME DOWN
PUT ON ONE'S ARMOUR
PUT THE CLOCK BACK
PUTTING IT MILDLY
PUT UP A GOOD FIGHT
PUT UP FOR AUCTION

Q—15

QUALIFIED PERSON
QUARTERLY REVIEW
QUARTER OF AN HOUR
QUARTER OF A POUND
QUARTER PAST FIVE
QUARTER PAST FOUR
QUARTER PAST NINE
QUARTER SESSIONS
QUARTER TO ELEVEN
QUARTER TO TWELVE
QUEEN OF DIAMONDS
QUEEN OF THE SOUTH
QUEEN'S MESSENGER
QUICKEN THE PULSE
QUICK OFF THE MARK
QUICK SUCCESSION
QUIET AS THE GRAVE
QUIET RESENTMENT
QUITE A CHARACTER
QUITE DELIGHTFUL
QUITE THE REVERSE
QUOTE FROM MEMORY

R—15

RACE AGAINST TIME
RACIAL TOLERANCE
RACING CERTAINTY
RACKING HEADACHE
RADIO-ACTIVE ZONE
RADIO ASTRONOMER
RADIO JOURNALISM
RAILWAY ACCIDENT
RAILWAY CARRIAGE
RAILWAY JUNCTION
RAILWAY TERMINUS
RAIN CATS AND DOGS
RAIN STOPPED PLAY
RAISE A HUE AND CRY
RAISE OBJECTIONS
RAISE ONE'S SIGHTS
RAISE THE CURTAIN
RAISE THE SUBJECT
RAISE VEGETABLES
RALPH RICHARDSON
RAMSAY MACDONALD
RAPID SUCCESSION
RATTLING SUCCESS
RAZE TO THE GROUND
REACH FOR THE MOON
REACH PERFECTION

REACH ROCK-BOTTOM
READY AND WILLING
READY-BUILT HOUSE
READY FOR THE FRAY
READY-MADE EXCUSE
REARGUARD ACTION
REASONABLE DOUBT
REASONABLE OFFER
REASONABLE TERMS
RECENT DISCOVERY
RECEPTION CENTRE
RECKLESS EXPENSE
RECKLESS SPENDER
RECORDING STUDIO
RECOVER LOST TIME
RECOVER ONE'S MIND
RECOVER THE ASHES
RECRUITING DRIVE
RED-CURRANT JELLY
REDUCE TO NOTHING
REDUCE TO POVERTY
REDUCE TO SILENCE
RED, WHITE AND BLUE
REFILL ONE'S GLASS
REFLECTED VISION
REFRESHER COURSE
REFRESHMENT ROOM
REFRESHMENT TENT
REFUSE COLLECTOR
REGIMENTAL BADGE
REGIMENTAL MARCH
REGIMENTAL STAFF
REGIMENT OF WOMEN
REGISTRATION FEE
REGULAR CUSTOMER
REGULAR EXERCISE
REGULAR FEATURES
REGULAR PRACTICE
REGULATION DRESS
REGULATION SPEED
REIGNING MONARCH
RELATIVE DENSITY
RELATIVELY QUIET
RELATIVE PRONOUN
RELAXING CLIMATE
RELEASE ONE'S HOLD
RELIABLE QUALITY
RELIABLE SERVICE
RELIGIOUS BELIEF
RELIGIOUS MANIAC
REMARKABLE CHILD

REMARKABLE SIGHT
REMARKABLE VOICE
REMARKABLE WOMAN
REMEMBER NOTHING
REMOVE ALL TRACES
REMOVE MOUNTAINS
REMOVE THE TRACES
RENDER AN ACCOUNT
RENDER NECESSARY
RENT RESTRICTION
RE-OPEN OLD WOUNDS
REPAIRING CLAUSE
REPAIR THE DAMAGE
REPENT AT LEISURE
REPUBLICAN PARTY
REPULSE AN ATTACK
RESEARCH CHEMIST
RESERVE OF ENERGY
RESERVE STRENGTH
RESIDENTIAL AREA
RESIDENT SURGEON
RESTORATION FUND
RESTORATION PLAY
RESTORE TO HEALTH
RESTORE TO REASON
RESTORE TO SANITY
RESTRAINING HAND
RESTRICT IMPORTS
RESURRECTION DAY
RETORT COURTEOUS
RETURN IN TRIUMPH
RETURN TO SERVICE
RETURN TO THE PAST
REVERSION TO TYPE
RICHARD DIMBLEBY
RICHARD THE THIRD
RICHLY FURNISHED
RIDE A BROOMSTICK
RIDE A HOBBY-HORSE
RIDE OUT THE STORM
RIGHT DOWN THE CAR
RIGHT HONOURABLE
RIGHT OFF THE REEL
RIGHT OF PURCHASE
RIGHTS AND WRONGS
RIGHT TO THE POINT
RIGHT WAVELENGTH
RIGID DISCIPLINE
RINGING APPLAUSE
RIPE FOR MISCHIEF
RISE FROM THE DEAD

RISE WITH THE LARK
RITUAL FIRE-DANCE
ROARING TWENTIES
ROARS OF LAUGHTER
ROBBED OF FREEDOM
ROBIN GOODFELLOW
ROB WITH VIOLENCE
ROCK-BOTTOM PRICE
ROCK OF GIBRALTAR
ROGER DE COVERLEY
ROGET'S THESAURUS
ROLL OF WALLPAPER
ROLY-POLY PUDDING
ROMULUS AND REMUS
ROOM TEMPERATURE
ROOM TO SWING A CAT
ROOTED OBJECTION
ROOTED TO THE SPOT
ROOT OF THE MATTER
ROSS AND CROMARTY
ROTATION OF CROPS
ROTTEN AT THE CORE
ROTTEN TO THE CORE
ROUGHLY SPEAKING
ROUNDABOUT ROUTE
ROUND OF APPLAUSE
ROUND OF PLEASURE
ROYAL ALBERT HALL
ROYAL AND ANCIENT
ROYAL COMMISSION
ROYAL OPERA HOUSE
ROYAL TOURNAMENT
RUBBER TRUNCHEON
RUDDY COMPLEXION
RUDE FOREFATHERS
RUFFLED FEATHERS
RUFFLED FEELINGS
RUIN ONE'S CHANCES
RULES OF FOOTBALL
RUN A TEMPERATURE
RUN-AWAY MARRIAGE
RUN FOR ONE'S MONEY
RUN FOR PRESIDENT
RUN LIKE WILD-FIRE
RURAL POPULATION
RUSSIAN LANGUAGE
RUSSIAN ROULETTE

S—15
SAFETY IN NUMBERS
SAIL INTO THE WIND

SAIL NEAR THE WIND	SECONDARY COLOUR
SAILOR'S HORNPIPE	SECONDARY MATTER
SAINT GEORGE'S DAY	SECONDARY MODERN
SAINT MARYLEBONE	SECONDARY SCHOOL
SALES RESISTANCE	SECOND-BEST THING
SALLY IN OUR ALLEY	SECOND CHILDHOOD
SALMON AND SHRIMP	SECOND FAVOURITE
SAMSON AGONISTES	SECOND-HAND GOODS
SANDWICH ISLANDS	SECOND IN COMMAND
SARATOGA SPRINGS	SECOND INTENTION
SARDINE SANDWICH	SECOND OF JANUARY
SARDINES ON TOAST	SECOND OF OCTOBER
SATURATION POINT	SECOND-RATE HOTEL
SATURDAY EVENING	SECOND TIME ROUND
SATURDAY MORNING	SECRET ANIMOSITY
SAUSAGE AND CHIPS	SECRET COURTSHIP
SAUSAGES AND MASH	SECRET INFLUENCE
SAVAGE CRITICISM	SECRET STAIRCASE
SAVE APPEARANCES	SECURITY COUNCIL
SAVINGS MOVEMENT	SECURITY MEASURE
SAVOURY OMELETTE	SECURITY OFFICER
SAY THE MAGIC WORD	SEEDS OF MISTRUST
SAY WITH EMPHASIS	SEEK A COMPROMISE
SCALENE TRIANGLE	SEEK INFORMATION
SCALES OF JUSTICE	SEEK ONE'S FORTUNE
SCALE THE HEIGHTS	SEE NAPLES AND DIE
SCENE OF THE CRIME	SEE ONE'S WAY CLEAR
SCHEDULED FLIGHT	SEE THE FUNNY SIDE
SCHNEIDER TROPHY	SEE WHAT YOU CAN DO
SCHOLASTIC AGENT	SELECT COMMITTEE
SCHOOLBOY HOWLER	SELF-EDUCATED MAN
SCHOOL INSPECTOR	SELF-IMPOSED TASK
SCHOOL OF DANCING	SELF-SERVICE SHOP
SCHOOL OF THOUGHT	SELL INTO SLAVERY
SCIENTIFIC BOXER	SELL ONE'S COUNTRY
SCIENTIFIC WORLD	SEMOLINA PUDDING
SCOTTISH TERRIER	SEND AN ULTIMATUM
SCOTTISH THISTLE	SEND ROUND THE HAT
SCRAPE THE BARREL	SEND THE CAP ROUND
SCRATCH OF THE PEN	SEND TO THE BOTTOM
SCRATCH ONE'S HEAD	SENIOR BARRISTER
SCRIBBLING BLOCK	SENIORES PRIORES
SCRIMP AND SCRAPE	SENSATIONAL NEWS
SCRIPTURE LESSON	SENSATION MONGER
SCRUFF OF THE NECK	SENSE OF DISTANCE
SEA ISLAND COTTON	SENSE OF PLEASURE
SEARCHING GLANCE	SENSE OF SECURITY
SEARCH ONE'S HEART	SENSITIVE MARKET
SEASIDE LANDLADY	SENSITIVE NATURE
SEATING CAPACITY	SENSUAL PLEASURE
SEAWORTHY VESSEL	SENTENCE OF DEATH

SENTENCE TO DEATH
SENTIMENTAL GIRL
SEPARATION ORDER
SERIOUS ACCIDENT
SERIOUS LANGUAGE
SERIOUS QUESTION
SERMONS IN STONES
SERVANT QUESTION
SERVED WITH A WRIT
SERVE TWO MASTERS
SERVICE INCLUDED
SERVICE REVOLVER
SESAME AND LILIES
SET A GOOD EXAMPLE
SET A LOW STANDARD
SET OF FALSE TEETH
SET OF QUADRILLES
SETTLE AN ACCOUNT
SETTLE OLD SCORES
SETTLE THE MATTER
SET UP IN BUSINESS
SEVEN DEADLY SINS
SEVEN OF DIAMONDS
SEVENPENNY STAMP
SEVENTEEN AND SIX
SEVENTEEN AND TWO
SEVENTEENTH HOLE
SEVENTH OF AUGUST
SEVENTH SYMPHONY
SEVEN TIMES SEVEN
SEVENTY THOUSAND
SEVERE THRASHING
SHABBY GENTILITY
SHABBY TREATMENT
SHADY REPUTATION
SHAKE LIKE A JELLY
SHAKEN TO THE CORE
SHALLOW ARGUMENT
SHARPEN ONE'S WITS
SHARP IMPRESSION
SHEATHE THE SWORD
SHEEPSKIN JACKET
SHEER PERFECTION
SHEFFIELD UNITED
SHEPHERD'S MARKET
SHETLAND ISLANDS
SHIFT FOR ONESELF
SHIFT ONE'S GROUND
SHIP OF THE DESERT
SHIPPING COMPANY
SHIPPING MAGNATE

SHIP'S COMPLEMENT
SHIVER ME TIMBERS
SHOCKING SCANDAL
SHOCKING WEATHER
SHOOTING GALLERY
SHORTHAND TYPIST
SHORTHAND WRITER
SHORT OF PRACTICE
SHORT-TERM POLICY
SHOTGUN MARRIAGE
SHOT IN THE LOCKER
SHOUT OF LAUGHTER
SHOW DISCOURTESY
SHOW FAVOURITISM
SHOW INGRATITUDE
SHOW ONE'S COLOURS
SHOW TO ADVANTAGE
SHRED OF EVIDENCE
SHRINKING VIOLET
SHUFFLE THE CARDS
SICKNESS BENEFIT
SIEGE OF MAFEKING
SIGHT FOR THE GODS
SIGHT-SEEING TOUR
SIGN OF THE ZODIAC
SIGN THE REGISTER
SILENCE IS GOLDEN
SILENT AS THE TOMB
SILVER MEDALLIST
SIMPLE PLEASURES
SIMPLY AND SOLELY
SINCE THE YEAR DOT
SING ANOTHER SONG
SING ANOTHER TUNE
SINK ONE'S CAPITAL
SINK TO ONE'S KNEES
SINK TO THE BOTTOM
SIN OF COMMISSION
SIR EDWARD GERMAN
SIR FRANCIS DRAKE
SIR JOHN FALSTAFF
SISTER OF CHARITY
SITUATION VACANT
SITUATION WANTED
SIX AND FIVEPENCE
SIX AND FOURPENCE
SIX AND NINEPENCE
SIXTEEN AND A HALF
SIXTEEN AND EIGHT
SIXTEEN AND SEVEN
SIXTEEN AND THREE

SIXTEENTH LETTER	SOLICITOR'S CLERK
SIXTEENTH OF JULY	SOLID FOUNDATION
SIXTEENTH OF JUNE	SOLO PERFORMANCE
SIXTEEN THOUSAND	SOMEBODY OR OTHER
SIXTH OF DECEMBER	SOME CONSOLATION
SIXTH OF FEBRUARY	SOMERSET MAUGHAM
SIXTH OF NOVEMBER	SOMETHING IN HAND
SIXTY-FIVE AND SIX	SOMETHING ROTTEN
SIXTY-FOUR AND SIX	SOMETHING TO COME
SKELETON SERVICE	SOMETHING TO GO ON
SKIM THE ROOF-TOPS	SOME TIME OR OTHER
SKIN OF ONE'S TEETH	SOMEWHERE AROUND
SKIP OUT OF THE WAY	SO MUCH THE BETTER
SLAB OF CHOCOLATE	SORRY FOR ONESELF
SLACKEN ONE'S PACE	SOUND EXPRESSION
SLAKE ONE'S THIRST	SOUND INVESTMENT
SLANG EXPRESSION	SOUND OF BOW BELLS
SLAPSTICK COMEDY	SOUND THE KEYNOTE
SLEEPING DRAUGHT	SOUND THE RETREAT
SLEEPING PARTNER	SOURCE OF TROUBLE
SLEEVELESS DRESS	SOUTH AFRICAN WAR
SLIGHT VARIATION	SOUTHERN RAILWAY
SLINGS AND ARROWS	SOUTH KENSINGTON
SLIP OF THE TONGUE	SOUTH OF THE RIVER
SLIPPERY AS AN EEL	SOUTH OF THE TWEED
SLIPPERY SURFACE	SOUTH SEA ISLANDS
SLOUGH OF DESPOND	SOVEREIGN REMEDY
SLOW BOAT TO CHINA	SOW ONE'S WILD OATS
SLOW IN THE UPTAKE	SPADES ARE TRUMPS
SLOWLY AND SURELY	SPANISH BURGUNDY
SLOWLY BUT SURELY	SPANISH CHESTNUT
SMALL PERCENTAGE	SPANISH LANGUAGE
SMELTING FURNACE	SPARRING PARTNER
SMOKE A CIGARETTE	SPEAK FOR ONESELF
SMOKY ATMOSPHERE	SPEAK IN A WHISPER
SNAKE IN THE GRASS	SPEAK OF THE DEVIL
SNAP ONE'S FINGERS	SPECIAL DELIVERY
SNAP ONE'S NOSE OFF	SPECIAL OCCASION
SOAKED TO THE SKIN	SPECIAL PLEADING
SOARING AMBITION	SPECIFIC GRAVITY
SOARING THOUGHTS	SPEED-BOAT RACING
SOBERING THOUGHT	SPEEDY VENGEANCE
SOB ONE'S HEART OUT	SPELLING MISTAKE
SOCIAL GATHERING	SPINAL COMPLAINT
SOCIAL INSURANCE	SPIRAL STAIRCASE
SOCIAL OSTRACISM	SPIRITED DISPLAY
SODA-WATER SYPHON	SPLASH ONE'S MONEY
SODIUM CARBONATE	SPLENDID VICTORY
SOFT-NOSED BULLET	SPLENDID WEATHER
SOFT-SHOE SHUFFLE	SPLIT INFINITIVE
SOLD INTO SLAVERY	SPOIL EVERYTHING

SPOIL ONE'S RECORD
SPOILS OF VICTORY
SPORTING CONDUCT
SPORTING FIXTURE
SPORTING GESTURE
SPORTS ANNOUNCER
SPORTS EQUIPMENT
SPOT ADVERTISING
SPOTLESSLY CLEAN
SPRAY OF DIAMONDS
SPREAD ONE'S WINGS
SPREAD THE GOSPEL
SPRING A SURPRISE
SPRINGER SPANIEL
SPUR OF THE MOMENT
SQUARE THE CIRCLE
SQUATTER'S RIGHTS
SQUATTING RIGHTS
SQUEEZED TO DEATH
STABLE COMPANION
STAGE DIRECTIONS
STAGE-DOOR JOHNNY
STAKE EVERYTHING
STAMP COLLECTING
STAMP COLLECTION
STAMP OF APPROVAL
STAND AND DELIVER
STANDARD EDITION
STANDARD ENGLISH
STANDARD PRODUCT
STAND BARE-HEADED
STAND IN FULL VIEW
STANDING OVATION
STAND IN THE LIGHT
STAND IN THE QUEUE
STAND NO NONSENSE
STAND ON CEREMONY
STAND ONE'S GROUND
STAND ON ONE'S HEAD
STAND ON ONE'S TOES
STAND STOCK-STILL
STANLEY HOLLOWAY
STANLEY MATTHEWS
STARK, STARING MAD
STAR OF BETHLEHEM
STARS AND STRIPES
START AN ARGUMENT
STARVED WITH COLD
STATE APARTMENTS
STATE ASSISTANCE
STATE DEPARTMENT

STATE ENTERPRISE
STATELESS PERSON
STATEMENT OF FACT
STATEMENT ON OATH
STATE OF COLLAPSE
STATE OF CONFLICT
STATE OF DISORDER
STATE OF EQUALITY
STATE OF SOBRIETY
STATION APPROACH
STATUE OF LIBERTY
STAY OF EXECUTION
STAY UNDERGROUND
STAY WHERE YOU ARE
STEALER OF HEARTS
STEAL THE THUNDER
STENTORIAN VOICE
STICKING PLASTER
STICK LIKE A LEECH
STICK OF DYNAMITE
STICKS AND STONES
STICK THE SPURS IN
STICK TO ONE'S GUNS
STICK TO ONE'S LAST
STICK TO THE FACTS
STICK TO THE POINT
STICK TO THE RULES
STICK TO THE TRUTH
STICKY SITUATION
STILL AS THE GRAVE
STILL OF THE NIGHT
STILL, SMALL VOICE
STIR THE PORRIDGE
STIR UP THE EMBERS
ST. MARTIN'S SUMMER
ST. MICHAEL'S MOUNT
STOCKS AND SHARES
STOCKTAKING SALE
STOMACH DISORDER
STOOD UP STRAIGHT
STOP ME AND BUY ONE!
STOPPED THE FIGHT
STOP THE BLEEDING
STOP WHERE YOU ARE
STORM OF APPLAUSE
STRAIGHT ACTRESS
STRAIGHT BOURBON
STRAIGHT DEALING
STRAIGHT IN FRONT
STRAIGHT STRETCH
STRAIN ONE'S LUNGS

STRAIN THE NERVES
STRANGE GOINGS-ON
STRANGE TO RELATE
STRAPPING FELLOW
STRATFORD ON AVON
STRAWS IN THE WIND
STREAM OF THOUGHT
STREAM OF TRAFFIC
STREET DIRECTORY
STRENUOUS EFFORT
STRESS AND STRAIN
STRETCHER BEARER
STRETCH ONE'S LEGS
STRICKEN IN YEARS
STRICTLY NEUTRAL
STRICTLY PRIVATE
STRIKE A BAD PATCH
STRIKE AN AVERAGE
STRIKE A RICH VEIN
STRIKE UP THE BAND
STRIKING SUCCESS
STRING ORCHESTRA
STRING QUARTETTE
STRINGS ATTACHED
STRIVE FOR EFFECT
STROLLING PLAYER
STRONG INFLUENCE
STRONG OBJECTION
STRONG, SILENT MAN
STRONG SITUATION
STRONG WILL POWER
STRUGGLE FOR LIFE
STRUGGLE THROUGH
STUBBORN AS A MULE
STUNT ONE'S GROWTH
ST. VALENTINE'S DAY
STYGIAN DARKNESS
SUBJUNCTIVE MOOD
SUBMARINE CHASER
SUBMIT A QUESTION
SUBSTANTIAL MEAL
SUBURBAN STATION
SUCCESS ALL ROUND
SUCH SWEET SORROW
SUDDEN DEPARTURE
SUFFER IN SILENCE
SUGAR PLANTATION
SUITABLE PARTNER
SUITED TO THE PART
SUIT THE OCCASION
SUM AND SUBSTANCE

SUMMER LIGHTNING
SUMMER RESIDENCE
SUMMON UP COURAGE
SUNDAY AFTERNOON
SUNDAY NEWSPAPER
SUNDAY TELEGRAPH
SUN, MOON AND STARS
SUPERIOR NUMBERS
SUPERIOR OFFICER
SUPERIOR QUALITY
SUPERSONIC SPEED
SUPPLY AND DEMAND
SUPREME CONTEMPT
SURE OF ONE'S FACTS
SURPRISE IN STORE
SURPRISE VISITOR
SURPRISING THING
SUSPECTED PERSON
SUSPECT FOUL PLAY
SUSPEND SENTENCE
SUSPENSE ACCOUNT
SUSTAINED ACTION
SUSTAINED EFFORT
SUSTAIN INJURIES
SWALLOW AN INSULT
SWALLOW-TAIL COAT
SWEAR ALLEGIANCE
SWEAR ON THE BIBLE
SWEAT OF ONE'S BROW
SWEEPING CHANGES
SWEEPING REFORMS
SWEEPING SUCCESS
SWEEPING VICTORY
SWEEP THE CHIMNEY
SWEET FANNY ADAMS
SWEET SIMPLICITY
SWEET TO THE TASTE
SWIM FOR THE SHORE
SWIMMING COSTUME
SWIM WITH THE TIDE
SWORD OF DAMOCLES
SYDNEY WOODERSON
SYLVIA PANKHURST
SYMBOL OF JUSTICE
SYMPHONY CONCERT
SYNTHETIC RUBBER
SYSTEMATIC STUDY

T—15
TABLEAUX VIVANTS
TABLE DECORATION

TABLE OF CONTENTS	TEN AND FIVEPENCE
TABLES AND CHAIRS	TEN AND FOURPENCE
TAILOR AND CUTTER	TEN AND NINEPENCE
TAKE A COLLECTION	TEN COMMANDMENTS
TAKE A DEEP BREATH	TENSE ATMOSPHERE
TAKE A FLYING LEAP	TEN-SHILLING NOTE
TAKE A PHOTOGRAPH	TENTH OF DECEMBER
TAKE A RESOLUTION	TENTH OF FEBRUARY
TAKE A SECOND LOOK	TENTH OF NOVEMBER
TAKE A STRONG LINE	TERENCE RATTIGAN
TAKE FRENCH LEAVE	TERM OF REFERENCE
TAKE INTO ACCOUNT	TERRIBLE TRAGEDY
TAKE INTO CUSTODY	TERRIBLE WEATHER
TAKE IT LYING DOWN	TERRIFIC SERVICE
TAKE IT ON THE CHIN	TERRITORIAL ARMY
TAKE IT OR LEAVE IT	TEST OF ENDURANCE
TAKEN AT THE FLOOD	THANKSGIVING DAY
TAKE ONE'S COAT OFF	THATCHED COTTAGE
TAKE ONE'S MEASURE	THE AMOROUS PRAWN
TAKE PRECAUTIONS	THE ANCIENT WORLD
TAKE THE BLOOM OFF	THE ARTFUL DODGER
TAKE THE CHILL OFF	THE BACK OF BEYOND
TAKE THE LONG VIEW	THE BARON KNIGHTS
TAKE THE SEA ROUTE	THE BEGGAR'S OPERA
TAKE THE SHILLING	THE BLACK COUNTRY
TAKE TO ONE'S HEELS	THE BOHEMIAN GIRL
TAKE TO THE BOTTLE	THE CAT AND FIDDLE
TAKE UP THE THREAD	THE COAST IS CLEAR
TALE OF TWO CITIES	THE COMMON MARKET
TALES OF HOFFMANN	THE COMMON PEOPLE
TANGERINE ORANGE	THE COMMONWEALTH
TANKARD OF BITTER	THE COST OF LIVING
TAPERED TROUSERS	THE DANCING YEARS
TASTE OF THE STRAP	THE DEMON ALCOHOL
TATTENHAM CORNER	THE DESCENT OF MAN
TATTERED AND TORN	THE DEVIL YOU KNOW
TEAR ONE'S CLOTHES	THE ELEVENTH HOUR
TEAR ONESELF AWAY	THE EMPEROR JONES
TEARS OF LAUGHTER	THE END OF THE ROAD
TECHNICAL SCHOOL	THE FIRST SWALLOW
TELEGRAPH OFFICE	THE FOUR FEATHERS
TELEPHONE NUMBER	THE FOURTH ESTATE
TELEPHONE SYSTEM	THE FOURTH OF JULY
TELESCOPIC SIGHT	THE GARDEN OF EDEN
TELEVISION TABLE	THE GOLDEN FLEECE
TELL IT NOT IN GATH	THE HAPPY WARRIOR
TELL ONE'S FORTUNE	THE HOUSE OF USHER
TEMPERANCE HOTEL	THE INVISIBLE MAN
TEMPORARY RELIEF	THE KING'S ENGLISH
TEMPT PROVIDENCE	THE LAP OF THE GODS
TENACIOUS MEMORY	THE LAST MINSTREL

THE LATE-LAMENTED
THE LONDON SEASON
THE LONG VACATION
THE LOW COUNTRIES
THE MAN IN THE MOON
THE MARSEILLAISE
THE MERRY MONARCH
THE MORNING AFTER
THE NAME'S THE SAME
THE OLD PRETENDER
THE PLOT THICKENS
THE POTTER'S WHEEL
THE POWERS THAT BE
THE PRETTY THINGS
THE PRIMROSE PATH
THE PROMISED LAND
THE QUEEN OF SHEBA
THE ROYAL SOCIETY
THE SHOW MUST GO ON
THE SKY'S THE LIMIT
THE SOUND OF MUSIC
THE SUBCONSCIOUS
THE SUN NEVER SETS
THE SUPERNATURAL
THE THANKSGIVING
THE THREE ESTATES
THE TIME WILL COME
THE UNTOUCHABLES
THE VERY REVEREND
THE WOMAN IN WHITE
THE WORLD AT LARGE
THE WORSE FOR WEAR
THIEF IN THE NIGHT
THINK BETTER OF IT
THINK THINGS OVER
THINLY SCATTERED
THIN ON THE GROUND
THIRD OF DECEMBER
THIRD OF FEBRUARY
THIRD OF NOVEMBER
THIRTEEN AND FIVE
THIRTEEN AND FOUR
THIRTEEN AND NINE
THIRTEEN AT TABLE
THIRTEEN MINUTES
THIRTEEN OF A SUIT
THIRTEEN PER CENT
THIRTEENTH GREEN
THIRTEENTH OF MAY
THIRTIETH OF JULY
THIRTIETH OF JUNE

THIRTY-NINE STEPS
THIRTY-ONE AND SIX
THIRTY-SIX AND SIX
THIRTY-TWO AND SIX
THIS YEAR OF GRACE
THORN IN ONE'S SIDE
THORN IN THE FLESH
THOUSAND GUINEAS
THREATENING LOOK
THREE BRASS BALLS
THREE-LEGGED RACE
THREE-LETTER WORD
THREE LITTLE PIGS
THREE-MASTED SHIP
THREE MEN IN A BOAT
THREE MUSKETEERS
THREE OF DIAMONDS
THREEPENNY OPERA
THREEPENNY PIECE
THREEPENNY STAMP
THREE-PIECE SUITE
THREE-TIERED CAKE
THREE TIMES THREE
THRILLED WITH JOY
THRILLING CLIMAX
THROUGH CARRIAGE
THROUGH THE NIGHT
THROUGH THE YEARS
THROW IN ONE'S HAND
THROW IN THE TOWEL
THROW OFF THE YOKE
THROW OUT A FEELER
THROW TO THE WINDS
THUMBNAIL SKETCH
THURSDAY EVENING
THURSDAY MORNING
TICKET COLLECTOR
TICKET INSPECTOR
TICKLE ONE'S FANCY
TICKLE THE PALATE
TICKLISH PROBLEM
TIED HAND AND FOOT
TIES OF AFFECTION
TIGHTEN ONE'S BELT
TIGHTEN ONE'S GRIP
TIGHT-ROPE WALKER
TILLER OF THE SOIL
TILL WE MEET AGAIN
TIME OF DEPARTURE
TIME ON ONE'S HANDS
TIP OF ONE'S TONGUE

TIPPED CIGARETTE
TITANIC STRENGTH
TITUS ANDRONICUS
TO HAVE AND TO HOLD
TO LITTLE PURPOSE
TOMATOES ON TOAST
TOM, DICK AND HARRY
TOMORROW EVENING
TOMORROW MORNING
TOM, THE PIPER'S SON
TONSORIAL ARTIST
TOO CLEVER BY HALF
TOO FULL FOR WORDS
TOO GOOD TO BE TRUE
TOOK THE LONG VIEW
TOOLS OF THE TRADE
TOOTHSOME MORSEL
TOPICAL ALLUSION
TOPICAL INTEREST
TOP-LEVEL MEETING
TOP OF THE MORNING
TOSSING THE CABER
TOTAL ABSTINENCE
TOTAL CASUALTIES
TO THE FULL EXTENT
TO THE MANNER BORN
TOUCH ROCK-BOTTOM
TOUGH ASSIGNMENT
TOUGH NUT TO CRACK
TOURIST INDUSTRY
TOWERING PASSION
TOWER OF STRENGTH
TRADE COMMISSION
TRADE DELEGATION
TRADE SUPPLEMENT
TRADITIONAL FARE
TRADITIONAL JAZZ
TRAFALGAR SQUARE
TRAFFIC MOVEMENT
TRAIN CONNECTION
TRAINING COLLEGE
TRAIN OF THOUGHTS
TRANSFER A PLAYER
TRANSPORT SYSTEM
TRAVEL INCOGNITO
TRAVEL IN COMFORT
TRAVELLER'S TALES
TRAVELLING CLOCK
TRAVELLING CRANE
TREASURED MEMORY
TREATED LIKE DIRT

TREATY OF LOCARNO
TREE OF KNOWLEDGE
TREMBLE WITH FEAR
TREMBLING POPLAR
TREND OF THE TIMES
TRESPASS AGAINST
TRIAL OF STRENGTH
TRICK OF THE TRADE
TRICKY SITUATION
TRIUMPHANT SMILE
TROOP OF SOLDIERS
TROUBLE-FREE MIND
TRUE TO THE LETTER
TRUMPED-UP CHARGE
TRY ANYTHING ONCE
TRY ONE'S PATIENCE
TRY ONE'S STRENGTH
TURN A SOMERSAULT
TURN A WILLING EAR
TURN FOR THE WORSE
TURN IN ONE'S GRAVE
TURN OFF THE LIGHT
TURN OUT A FAILURE
TURN OUT THE GUARD
TURN OUT THE LIGHT
TURN THE LIGHT OFF
TURN UP THE VOLUME
TWELFTH OF AUGUST
TWELVE AND A PENNY
TWELVE AND ELEVEN
TWELVE DISCIPLES
TWELVE-MILE LIMIT
TWELVE SHILLINGS
TWENTIETH LETTER
TWENTIETH OF JULY
TWENTIETH OF JUNE
TWENTY-FOUR HOURS
TWENTY-ONE AND SIX
TWENTY QUESTIONS
TWENTY SHILLINGS
TWENTY-SIX AND SIX
TWENTY-TWO AND SIX
TWIST OF THE WRIST
TWO AND FIVEPENCE
TWO AND FOURPENCE
TWO AND NINEPENCE
TWO-FISTED ATTACK
TWO OF EVERYTHING
TWO-STROKE ENGINE

U—15
ULTRA-VIOLET RAYS
UMPIRE'S DECISION
UNANIMOUS CHOICE
UNBRIDLED TONGUE
UNCIVILIZED RACE
UNDENIABLE TRUTH
UNDER A FALSE NAME
UNDERARM BOWLING
UNDER CLOSE GUARD
UNDER COMPLEMENT
UNDER COMPULSION
UNDER CORRECTION
UNDER-COVER AGENT
UNDER DISCIPLINE
UNDER DISCUSSION
UNDER LOCK AND KEY
UNDER OBLIGATION
UNDER ONE'S BREATH
UNDER-SEA WARFARE
UNDER THE COUNTER
UNDER THE SURFACE
UNDER THE WEATHER
UNDERWATER CRAFT
UNDESERVING CASE
UNEMPLOYMENT PAY
UNEQUAL STRUGGLE
UNEXPECTED EVENT
UNEXPECTED VISIT
UNFAIR ADVANTAGE
UNFAIR TREATMENT
UNFEELING PERSON
UNFINISHED STATE
UNFOUNDED REPORT
UNFROCKED PRIEST
UNFURNISHED FLAT
UNFURNISHED ROOM
UNGUARDED MINUTE
UNGUARDED MOMENT
UNGUARDED REMARK
UNHAPPY MEMORIES
UNION IS STRENGTH
UNITED PROVINCES
UNIVERSAL REMEDY
UNIVERSITY GRANT
UNKIND CRITICISM
UNKNOWN QUANTITY
UNLEAVENED BREAD
UNLUCKY THIRTEEN
UNMARRIED MOTHER
UNPAID SECRETARY

UNPUBLISHED WORK
UNSKILLED LABOUR
UNSOLVED MYSTERY
UNTOUCHED BY HAND
UNTROUBLED SLEEP
UNTRUE STATEMENT
UNVARNISHED TALE
UP BEFORE THE BEAK
UP GUARDS AND AT 'EM!
UPRIGHT CARRIAGE
UPRIGHT POSITION
UP THE GARDEN PATH
UP TO THE EYEBROWS
URBAN POPULATION
UTTER A FALSEHOOD
UTTER STARVATION

V—15
VACCINATION MARK
VAIN EXPECTATION
VANCOUVER ISLAND
VANILLA ICE-CREAM
VARSITY BOAT-RACE
VAST IMPROVEMENT
VAUGHAN WILLIAMS
VAUXHALL GARDENS
VEGETABLE GARDEN
VEGETABLE MARKET
VEGETABLE MARROW
VENERABLE PRIEST
VENGEANCE IS MINE
VERBAL AGREEMENT
VERBAL CRITICISM
VETO THE PROPOSAL
VICHY GOVERNMENT
VICTORIA STATION
VICTORY IN THE AIR
VIOLATE THE TERMS
VIOLENT CONTRAST
VIOLENT EXERCISE
VIOLENT OUTBURST
VIOLENT REACTION
VIOLENT STRUGGLE
VIRGINIA CREEPER
VIRGINIA TOBACCO
VIRGIN TERRITORY
VISIBLE DISTANCE
VISION OF DELIGHT
VITAL STATISTICS
VOICE PRODUCTION
VOLLEY OF THUNDER

VOLUNTARY SCHOOL
VULNERABLE POINT

W—15
WADDLE LIKE A DUCK
WAISTCOAT POCKET
WAITING FOR GODOT
WALKING DISTANCE
WALK INTO TROUBLE
WALL OF MOUNTAINS
WALRUS MOUSTACHE
WALTZING MATILDA
WANDERING WILLIE
WANTED FOR MURDER
WAR PREPARATIONS
WASHED OVERBOARD
WASTE NOT, WANT NOT
WASTE ONE'S BREATH
WATCH ON THE RHINE
WATCH WITH MOTHER
WATERLOO STATION
WATER ON THE BRAIN
WATERTIGHT ALIBI
WEALTH OF NATIONS
WEAR THE BREECHES
WEAR THE TROUSERS
WEATHER FORECAST
WEATHER THE STORM
WEDDING CEREMONY
WEDNESDAY'S CHILD
WEEK-END SHOPPING
WEEKLY NEWSPAPER
WEIGHING MACHINE
WEIGHT OF NUMBERS
WEIGHT OF OPINION
WEIGHTY ARGUMENT
WELCOME STRANGER
WELLINGTON BOOTS
WELL-MEANING TYPE
WELL REPRESENTED
WENT LIKE THE WIND
WESTERN ALLIANCE
WESTMINSTER BANK
WESTMINSTER HALL
WET THE BABY'S HEAD
WHATEVER HAPPENS
WHAT'S THE VERDICT?
WHERE THERE'S LIFE
WHET THE APPETITE
WHIFF OF FRESH AIR
WHILE THERE'S LIFE

WHIRLING DERVISH
WHISPER TOGETHER
WHISTLE-STOP TOUR
WHISTLING KETTLE
WHITED SEPULCHRE
WHITEHALL PALACE
WHITE MAN'S BURDEN
WHITER THAN WHITE
WHITES OF THE EYES
WHITSUN VACATION
WHOLESALE DEALER
WHOLESALE MURDER
WHOM THE GODS LOVE
WIELD THE SCEPTRE
WIENER SCHNITZEL
WIFE AND CHILDREN
WILD IMAGINATION
WILL AND BEQUEATH
WILLIAM CONGREVE
WILLIAM OF ORANGE
WILLIAM THE FIRST
WILLIAM THE THIRD
WILLING TO PLEASE
WILL SHAKESPEARE
WIMBLEDON COMMON
WIN BY A SHORT HEAD
WINCHESTER RIFLE
WINDMILL THEATRE
WINDSCREEN WIPER
WINDWARD ISLANDS
WINE BY THE BARREL
WINES AND SPIRITS
WINNING POSITION
WINNING SEQUENCE
WINTER SPORTSMAN
WIN THE LAST ROUND
WIRELESS LICENCE
WIRELESS MESSAGE
WIRELESS STATION
WISDOM OF SOLOMON
WISE MEN OF GOTHAM
WISHFUL THINKING
WISH YOU WERE HERE
WITCHES' CAULDRON
WITH A DIFFERENCE
WITH A LITTLE LUCK
WITH COMPLIMENTS
WITHERING GLANCE
WITHHOLD PAYMENT
WITHIN EASY REACH
WITHIN ONE'S GRASP

WITHOUT AN EFFORT
WITHOUT A PURPOSE
WITHOUT A SCRATCH
WITHOUT CEREMONY
WITHOUT INCIDENT
WITHOUT INTEREST
WITHOUT PARALLEL
WITHOUT THINKING
WOMAN OF FEW WORDS
WOMAN OF THE WORLD
WOMAN'S INTUITION
WOMAN'S PRIVILEGE
WOMEN'S INSTITUTE
WOODCUTTERS' BALL
WOODEN PARTITION
WOOLLEN INDUSTRY
WOOLWICH ARSENAL
WORK AGAINST TIME
WORKERS' PLAYTIME
WORKING MAJORITY
WORKING-MAN'S CLUB
WORK LIKE A NIGGER
WORK LIKE A TROJAN
WORK OF REFERENCE
WORK ONE'S PASSAGE
WORK UNDERGROUND
WORLD GOVERNMENT
WORLD OF COMMERCE
WORLD OF LEARNING
WORLD WITHOUT END
WORTHY ADVERSARY

WOUNDED FEELINGS
WRESTLING SCHOOL
WRETCHED WEATHER
WRINKLED WITH AGE
WRITING MATERIAL
WRITTEN CONTRACT
WRITTEN EVIDENCE
WRITTEN LANGUAGE
WRONG ASSUMPTION
WRONG IMPRESSION
WRONG WAVE-LENGTH
WROUGHT-IRON GATE

X—15
XMAS DECORATIONS

Y—15
YELLOWSTONE PARK
YELL WITH DELIGHT
YEOMEN OF ENGLAND
YESTERDAY'S PAPER
YIELD GRACEFULLY
YIELD TO PRESSURE
YORKSHIRE RELISH
YOU NEVER CAN TELL
YOUNG AND HEALTHY
YOUNGER DAUGHTER
YOUNGEST BROTHER
YOURS FAITHFULLY
YOURS OBEDIENTLY
YOUTH-CLUB LEADER

WORDS

A—3	AXE	CAP	DOT	FED
ABC	AYE	CAR	DRY	FEE
ACE		CAT	DUB	FEN
ACT	**B—3**	CAW	DUD	FEW
ADD	BAA	CID	DUE	FEY
ADO	BAD	COB	DUG	FEZ
AFT	BAG	COD	DUN	FIB
AGA	BAH	COG	DUO	FIE
AGE	BAN	COL	DYE	FIG
AGO	BAR	CON		FIN
AHA	BAT	COO	**E—3**	FIR
AID	BAY	COP	EAR	FIT
AIL	BBC	COS	EAT	FIX
AIM	BED	COT	EAU	FLU
AIN	BEE	COW	EBB	FLY
AIR	BEG	COX	EEL	FOB
AIT	BEN	COY	E'EN	FOE
ALB	BET	CRY	E'ER	FOG
ALE	BEY	CUB	EFT	FOP
ALL	BIB	CUD	EGG	FOR
ALP	BID	CUE	EGO	FOX
ALT	BIG	CUP	EKE	FRO
AMP	BIN	CUR	ELF	FRY
ANA	BIS	CUT	ELK	FUG
AND	BIT	CWT	ELL	FUN
ANN	BOA		ELM	FUR
ANT	BOB	**D—3**	EMU	
ANY	BOG	DAB	END	**G—3**
APE	BOO	DAD	EON	GAB
APT	BOW	DAM	ERA	GAD
ARC	BOX	DAN	ERE	GAG
ARE	BOY	DAW	ERG	GAL
ARK	BOZ	DAY	ERR	GAP
ARM	BUD	DEB	ESS	GAR
ART	BUG	DEE	ETC	GAS
ASH	BUM	DEN	EVE	GAT
ASK	BUN	DEW	EWE	GAY
ASP	BUS	DIB	EYE	GEE
ASS	BUT	DID		GEM
ATE	BUY	DIE	**F—3**	GEN
AUK	BYE	DIG	FAD	GET
AVA		DIM	FAG	GIB
AVE	**C—3**	DIN	FAN	GIE
AWA	CAB	DIP	FAR	GIG
AWE	CAD	DOE	FAT	GIN
AWL	CAM	DOG	FAY	GNU
AWN	CAN	DON	FEB	GOB

GOD	IMP	LAY	MUG	ORC
GOG	INK	LBW	MUM	ORE
GOT	INN	LEA		ORT
GUM	ION	LED	**N—3**	OUR
GUN	I.O.U.	LEE	NAB	OUT
GUT	IRE	LEG	NAG	OVA
GUY	IRK	LEI	NAP	OWE
GYM	ISM	LEO	NAY	OWL
GYP	ITS	LET	N.C.O.	OWN
	IVY	LEW	NEB	
H—3		LEX	NEE	**P—3**
HAD		LIB	NEO	PAD
HAG	**J—3**	LID	NET	PAH
HAH	JAB	LIE	NEW	PAL
HAM	JAG	LIP	NIB	PAM
HAP	JAM	LIT	NIL	PAN
HAS	JAP	LOB	NIP	PAP
HAT	JAR	LOG	NIT	PAR
HAW	JAW	LOO	NIX	PAS
HAY	JAY	LOP	NOB	PAT
HEM	JET	LOT	NOD	PAW
HEN	JEW	LOW	NOG	PAX
HEP	JIB	LSD	NOR	PAY
HER	JIG	LUD	NOT	PEA
HEW	JOB	LUG	NOW	PEG
HEY	JOE	LYE	NUB	PEN
HID	JOG		NUN	PEP
HIE	JOT	**M—3**	NUT	PER
HIM	JOY	MAB	NYE	PET
HIP	JUG	MAC		PEW
HIS	JUT	MAD	**O—3**	PIE
HIT		MAN	OAF	PIG
HOB	**K—3**	MAP	OAK	PIN
HOD	KAY	MAR	OAR	PIP
HOE	KEG	MAT	OAT	PIT
HOG	KEN	MAW	OBI	PLY
HOP	KEY	MAY	OCH	POD
HOT	KID	MEN	ODD	POE
HOW	KIM	MET	ODE	POM
HUB	KIN	MEW	O'ER	POP
HUE	KIP	MID	OFF	POT
HUG	KIT	MIX	OFT	POW
HUM		MOA	OHM	PRO
HUN	**L—3**	MOB	OHO	PRY
HUT	LAC	MOO	OIL	PUB
	LAD	MOP	OLD	PUG
	LAG	MOT	ONE	PUN
I—3	LAM	MOW	OOF	PUP
ICE	LAP	MRS	OPE	PUS
ICY	LAR	MUD	OPT	PUT
ILK	LAW		ORB	PYX
ILL	LAX			

R—3	SEC	TED	VIZ	A—4
RAG	SEE	TEE	VOW	ABBE
RAJ	SEN	TEG		ABED
RAM	SET	TEN	W—3	ABET
RAN	SEW	THE	WAD	ABLE
RAP	SEX	THO'	WAG	ABLY
RAS	SHE	THY	WAN	ABUT
RAT	SHY	TIC	WAR	ACER
RAW	SIC	TIE	WAS	ACHE
RAY	SIN	TIN	WAT	ACID
RED	SIP	TIP	WAX	ACME
REF	SIR	TIS	WAY	ACNE
REP	SIS	TIT	WEB	ACRE
RET	SIT	TOD	WED	ADAM
REV	SIX	TOE	WEE	ADIT
REX	SKI	TOG	WEN	ADZE
RIB	SKY	TOM	WET	AFAR
RID	SLY	TON	WHO	AGED
RIG	SOB	TOO	WHY	AGOG
RIM	SOD	TOP	WIG	AGUE
RIO	SOL	TOR	WIN	AHEM
RIP	SON	TOT	WIT	AHOY
ROB	SOP	TOW	WOE	AIDE
ROC	SOS	TOY	WON	AIRY
ROD	SOT	TRY	WOO	AJAR
ROE	SOU	TUB	WOT	AKIN
ROM	SOW	TUG	WOW	ALAR
RON	SOX	TUN	WRY	ALAS
ROT	SOY	TUP	WYE	ALEE
ROW	SPA	TUT		ALGA
ROY	SPY	TWA	Y—3	ALLY
RUB	STY	TWO	YAH	ALMA
RUE	SUB		YAK	ALMS
RUG	SUE	U—3	YAM	ALOE
RUM	SUM	UGH	YAP	ALPS
RUN	SUN	ULT	YAW	ALSO
RUT	SUP	UNA	YEA	ALTO
RYE		UNO	YEN	ALUM
	T—3	URE	YEP	AMBO
S—3	TAB	URN	YES	AMEN
SAC	TAG	USE	YET	AMID
SAD	TAJ		YEW	AMMO
SAG	TAN	V—3	YON	AMOK
SAL	TAP	V.A.D.	YOU	AMYL
SAM	TAR	VAN		ANEW
SAP	TAT	VAT	Z—3	ANIL
SAT	TAU	VET	ZED	ANNA
SAW	TAW	VEX	ZIP	ANON
SAX	TAX	VIA	ZOO	ANTE
SAY	TEA	VIE		APED
SEA	TEC	VIM		APEX

APSE	BANG	BIRD	BRER	CASH
AQUA	BANK	BITE	BREW	CASK
ARAB	BANT	BLAB	BRIE	CAST
ARCH	BARB	BLED	BRIG	CAVE
AREA	BARD	BLEW	BRIM	CAVY
ARIA	BARE	BLOB	BRIO	CEDE
ARID	BARK	BLOC	BROW	CELL
ARIL	BARM	BLOT	BUCK	CELT
ARMS	BARN	BLOW	BUDE	CENT
ARMY	BART	BLUB	BUFF	CERE
ARTS	BASE	BLUE	BUHL	CERT
ARTY	BASH	BLUR	BULB	CHAP
ARUM	BASK	BOAR	BULK	CHAR
ASHY	BASS	BOAT	BULL	CHAT
ASIA	BAST	BODE	BUMP	CHEF
ATOM	BATH	BODY	BUNG	CHEW
ATOP	BAWD	BOER	BUNK	CHIC
AUNT	BAWL	BOGY	BUOY	CHIN
AURA	BAYS	BOIL	BURN	CHIP
AUTO	BEAD	BOKO	BURR	CHIT
AVER	BEAK	BOLD	BURY	CHOP
AVID	BEAM	BOLE	BUSH	CHOW
AVON	BEAN	BOLL	BUSS	CHUB
AVOW	BEAR	BOLT	BUST	CHUG
AWAY	BEAT	BOMB	BUSY	CHUM
AWED	BEAU	BOND	BUTT	CITE
AWRY	BECK	BONE	BUZZ	CITY
AXED	BEDE	BONY	BYRE	CLAD
AXIL	BEEF	BOOB		CLAM
AXIS	BEEN	BOOK	**C—4**	CLAN
AXLE	BEER	BOOM	CADE	CLAP
AYAH	BEET	BOON	CADI	CLAW
	BELL	BOOR	CAFÉ	CLAY
B—4	BELT	BOOT	CAGE	CLEF
BAAL	BEND	BORE	CAIN	CLIO
BAAS	BENT	BORN	CAKE	CLIP
BABA	BERG	BOSH	CAKY	CLOD
BABE	BEST	BOSS	CALF	CLOG
BABU	BETA	BOTH	CALL	CLOT
BABY	BEVY	BOUT	CALM	CLOY
BACK	BIAS	BOWL	CAME	CLUB
BADE	BIDE	BOWS	CAMP	CLUE
BAIL	BIER	BRAD	CANE	COAL
BAIT	BIFF	BRAE	CANT	COAT
BAKE	BIKE	BRAG	CAPE	COAX
BALD	BILE	BRAN	CARD	COCA
BALE	BILK	BRAT	CARE	COCK
BALL	BILL	BRAW	CARL	COCO
BALM	BIND	BRAY	CARP	CODA
BAND	BINE	BRED	CART	CODE
BANE	BING	BREN	CASE	COIF

COIL	CURL	DESK	DRAM	EDAM
COIN	CURT	DEWY	DRAT	EDDA
COIR	CUSP	DHOW	DRAW	EDDY
COKE	CUTE	DIAL	DRAY	EDEN
COLD	CYST	DICE	DREE	EDGE
COLE	CZAR	DICK	DREY	EDGY
COLT		DIDO	DREW	EDIT
COMA	**D—4**	DIED	DRIP	EGAD
COMB	DACE	DIET	DROP	EIRE
COME	DADO	DIGS	DRUB	ELAN
CONE	DAFT	DIKE	DRUG	ELIA
CONK	DAGO	DILL	DRUM	ELMO
CONS	DAIL	DIME	DUAL	ELSE
COOK	DAIS	DINE	DUCE	ELUL
COOL	DALE	DING	DUCK	EMIR
COON	DALI	DINT	DUCT	EMIT
COOP	DAME	DIRE	DUDE	ENOW
COOT	DAMN	DIRK	DUDS	ENSA
COPE	DAMP	DIRT	DUEL	ENVY
COPT	DANE	DISC	DUET	EPEE
COPY	DANK	DISH	DUFF	EPIC
CORD	DARE	DISK	DUKE	ERGO
CORE	DARK	DISS	DUKW	ERIC
CORK	DARN	DIVA	DULL	ERIN
CORM	DART	DIVE	DULY	ERNE
CORN	DASH	DOCK	DUMA	EROS
COSH	DATA	DODO	DUMB	ERSE
COST	DATE	DOER	DUMP	ERST
COSY	DAUB	DOFF	DUNE	ESPY
COTE	DAVY	DOGE	DUNG	ETCH
COUP	DAWN	DOLE	DUNK	ETNA
COVE	DAZE	DOLL	DUPE	ETON
COWL	D-DAY	DOLT	DUSE	ETUI
CRAB	DEAD	DOME	DUSK	EVEN
CRAG	DEAF	DONE	DUST	EVER
CRAM	DEAL	DOOM	DUTY	EVIL
CRAN	DEAN	DOOR	DYAK	EWER
CRAW	DEAR	DOPE	DYED	EXAM
CREW	DEBT	DORA	DYER	EXIT
CRIB	DECK	DORY	DYKE	EXON
CROP	DEED	DOSE		EYED
CROW	DEEM	DOSS	**E—4**	EYOT
CRUX	DEEP	DOTE	EACH	EYRE
CUBE	DEER	DOTH	EARL	EYRY
CUFF	DEFT	DOUR	EARN	
CULL	DEFY	DOVE	EASE	**F—4**
CULM	DELL	DOWN	EAST	FACE
CULT	DEMY	DOZE	EASY	FACT
CURB	DENE	DOZY	EBON	FADE
CURD	DENT	DRAB	ECHO	FAIL
CURE	DENY	DRAG	ECRU	FAIN

FAIR	FLEX	GAIT	GOLF	HARM
FAKE	FLIP	GALA	GONE	HARP
FALL	FLIT	GALE	GONG	HART
FAME	FLOE	GALL	GOOD	HASH
FANG	FLOG	GAME	GOOF	HASP
FARE	FLOP	GAMP	GORE	HATE
FARM	FLOW	GANG	GORY	HATH
FARO	FLUE	GAOL	GOSH	HAUL
FASH	FLUX	GAPE	GOTH	HAVE
FAST	FOAL	GARB	GOUT	HAWK
FATE	FOAM	GASH	GOWN	HAZE
FAUN	FOIL	GASP	GRAB	HAZY
FAWN	FOLD	GATE	GRAF	HEAD
FEAR	FOLK	GAUD	GRAM	HEAL
FEAT	FOND	GAUL	GRAY	HEAP
FEED	FONT	GAVE	GREW	HEAR
FEEL	FOOD	GAWK	GREY	HEAT
FEET	FOOL	GAZE	GRID	HEBE
FELL	FOOT	GEAR	GRIM	HEED
FELT	FORD	GENT	GRIN	HEEL
FEND	FORE	GERM	GRIP	HEIR
FERN	FORK	GEUM	GRIT	HELD
FETE	FORM	GIBE	GROG	HELL
FEUD	FORT	GIFT	GROW	HELM
FIAT	FOUL	GILD	GRUB	HELP
FIFE	FOUR	GILL	GULF	HEMP
FILE	FOWL	GILT	GULL	HERB
FILL	FOXY	GIMP	GULP	HERD
FILM	FRAU	GIRD	GUSH	HERE
FIND	FRAY	GIRL	GUST	HERN
FINE	FREE	GIRT	GYVE	HERO
FINN	FRET	GIST		HERR
FIRE	FROG	GIVE	**H—4**	HERS
FIRM	FROM	GLAD	HACK	HEWN
FISH	FUEL	GLEE	HAFT	HICK
FIST	FULL	GLEN	HA-HA	HIDE
FIVE	FUME	GLIB	HAIL	HIED
FIZZ	FUMY	GLIM	HAIR	HIGH
FLAG	FUND	GLOW	HAKE	HIKE
FLAK	FUNK	GLUE	HALE	HILL
FLAM	FURL	GLUM	HALF	HILT
FLAN	FURY	GLUT	HALL	HIND
FLAP	FUSE	G-MAN	HALO	HINT
FLAT	FUSS	GNAT	HALT	HIRE
FLAW	FUZZ	GNAW	HAME	HISS
FLAX		GOAD	HAND	HIST
FLAY	**G—4**	GOAL	HANG	HIVE
FLEA	GAEL	GOAT	HANK	HOAR
FLED	GAFF	GOBY	HARD	HOAX
FLEE	GAGE	GODS	HARE	HOBO
FLEW	GAIN	GOLD	HARK	HOCK

HOED	IMPI	**K—4**	LAME	LIFT
HOLD	INCA	KALE	LAMP	LIKE
HOLE	INCH	KEEL	LANA	LILT
HOLM	INKY	KEEN	LAND	LILY
HOLT	INTO	KEEP	LANE	LIMB
HOLY	IOTA	KELP	LANK	LIME
HOME	IRAN	KEMP	LAPP	LIMN
HOMY	IRIS	KENT	LARD	LIMP
HONE	IRON	KEPI	LARK	LIMY
HONK	ISIS	KEPT	LASH	LINE
HOOD	ISLE	KERB	LASS	LING
HOOF	ITCH	KHAN	LAST	LINK
HOOK	ITEM	KICK	LATE	LINO
HOOP		KILL	LATH	LINT
HOOT		KILN	LAUD	LION
HOPE	**J—4**	KILO	LAVA	LIRA
HOPS	JACK	KILT	LAVE	LIRE
HORN	JADE	KIND	LAWN	LISP
HOSE	JAIL	KINE	LAZE	LIST
HOST	JAMB	KING	LAZY	LIVE
HOUR	JANE	KINK	LEAD	LOAD
HOVE	JAPE	KIRK	LEAF	LOAF
HOWL	JAZZ	KISS	LEAK	LOAM
HUED	JEAN	KITE	LEAL	LOAN
HUFF	JEEP	KITH	LEAN	LOBE
HUGE	JEER	KIWI	LEAP	LOCH
HULK	JEHU	KNAP	LEAR	LOCK
HULL	JERK	KNEE	LEDA	LODE
HUMP	JEST	KNEW	LEEK	LOFT
HUNG	JIFF	KNIT	LEER	LOIN
HUNK	JILL	KNOB	LEES	LOLL
HUNT	JILT	KNOT	LEET	LONE
HURL	JINX	KNOW	LEFT	LONG
HURT	JOCK	KNUR	LEND	LOOK
HUSH	JOEY	KRIS	LENO	LOOM
HUSK	JOHN	KUDU	LENS	LOON
HYMN	JOKE	KURD	LENT	LOOP
HYPO	JOLT	KYLE	LESS	LOOS
	JOSS		LEST	LOOT
	JOVE	**L—4**	LETT	LOPE
	JOWL	LACE	LEVY	LORD
I—4	JUDO	LACK	LEWD	LORE
IBEX	JUDY	LADE	LIAR	LORN
IBIS	JU-JU	LADY	LICE	LORY
ICED	JUMP	LAIC	LICK	LOSE
ICON	JUNE	LAID	LIDO	LOSS
IDEA	JUNK	LAIN	LIED	LOST
IDES	JUNO	LAIR	LIEF	LOTH
IDLE	JURY	LAKE	LIEN	LOUD
IDLY	JUST	LAMA	LIEU	LOUR
IDOL		LAMB	LIFE	LOUT
IMAM				

LOVE	MEEK	MOTE	NOEL	OUSE
LUCK	MEET	MOTH	NOLL	OUST
LUDO	MELT	MOUE	NONE	OVAL
LUFF	MEMO	MOVE	NOOK	OVEN
LUGE	MEND	MOWN	NOON	OVER
LULL	MENU	MUCH	NORM	OVUM
LUMP	MERE	MUCK	NOSE	OWED
LUNG	MESH	MUFF	NOSY	OXEN
LURE	MESS	MULE	NOTE	OYES
LURK	METE	MULL	NOUN	OYEZ
LUSH	MEWS	MURK	NOUS	
LUST	MICA	MUSE	NOVA	**P—4**
LUTE	MICE	MUSH	NOWT	PACE
LYNX	MIEN	MUSK	NUDE	PACK
LYON	MIKE	MUST	NULL	PACT
LYRE	MILD	MUTE	NUMB	PAGE
	MILE	MUTT		PAID
M—4	MILK	MYTH	**O—4**	PAIL
MACE	MILL		OAKS	PAIN
MADE	MIME	**N—4**	OAST	PAIR
MAGI	MIND	NAIL	OATH	PALE
MAID	MINE	NAME	OBEY	PALI
MAIL	MING	NAPE	OBIT	PALL
MAIM	MINK	NARD	OBOE	PALM
MAIN	MINT	NARK	ODDS	PANE
MAKE	MINX	NAVE	ODIN	PANG
MALE	MIRE	NAVY	OGEE	PANT
MALL	MIRY	NAZE	OGLE	PAPA
MALT	MISS	NAZI	OGPU	PARA
MAMA	MIST	NEAP	OGRE	PARD
MANE	MITE	NEAR	OILY	PARE
MANX	MITT	NEAT	OKAY	PARK
MANY	MOAN	NECK	OLIO	PARR
MARE	MOAT	NEED	OMAR	PART
MARK	MOCK	NEEP	OMEN	PASS
MARL	MODE	NE'ER	OMIT	PAST
MARS	MODS	NEON	ONCE	PATE
MART	MOKE	NERO	ONER	PATH
MASH	MOLE	NESS	ONLY	PAUL
MASK	MOLL	NEST	ONUS	PAVE
MASS	MONK	NETT	ONYX	PAWL
MAST	MOOD	NEWS	OOZE	PAWN
MATE	MOON	NEWT	OPAL	PAYE
MAUD	MOOR	NEXT	OPEN	PEAK
MAUL	MOOT	NIBS	OPUS	PEAL
MAZE	MOPE	NICE	ORAL	PEAR
MEAD	MOPS	NICK	ORFE	PEAT
MEAL	MORE	NIGH	ORGY	PECK
MEAN	MORN	NINE	OTIC	PEEK
MEAT	MOSS	NISI	OUCH	PEEL
MEED	MOST	NODE	OURS	PEEP

PEER	PONY	QUIN	RIFE	RUMP
PEKE	POOH	QUIP	RIFF	RUNE
PELF	POOL	QUIT	RIFT	RUNG
PELT	POOP	QUIZ	RIGA	RUNT
PENT	POOR	QUOD	RILE	RUSE
PEON	POPE		RILL	RUSH
PERI	PORE	**R—4**	RIME	RUSK
PERK	PORK	RACE	RIND	RUSS
PERM	PORT	RACK	RING	RUST
PERT	POSE	RACY	RINK	RUTH
PESO	POSH	RAFT	RIOT	RYOT
PEST	POST	RAGE	RIPE	
PHEW	POSY	RAID	RISE	**S—4**
PHIZ	POUR	RAIL	RISK	SACK
PHUT	POUT	RAIN	RITE	SAFE
PICA	PRAM	RAKE	RIVE	SAGA
PICE	PRAY	RALE	ROAD	SAGE
PICK	PREP	RAMP	ROAM	SAGO
PICT	PREY	RAND	ROAN	SAID
PIED	PRIG	RANI	ROAR	SAIL
PIER	PRIM	RANK	ROBE	SAKE
PIKE	PROA	RANT	ROCK	SAKI
PILE	PROD	RAPE	RODE	SALE
PILL	PROM	RAPT	ROLE	SALT
PINE	PROP	RARE	ROLL	SAME
PING	PROS	RASH	ROME	SAND
PINK	PROW	RASP	ROMP	SANE
PINT	PROX	RATE	ROOD	SANG
PIPE	PUCE	RAVE	ROOF	SANK
PISH	PUCK	RAZE	ROOK	SANS
PITH	PUFF	READ	ROOM	SARD
PITY	PULL	REAL	ROOT	SARI
PLAN	PULP	REAM	ROPE	SARK
PLAY	PUMA	REAP	ROPY	SASH
PLEA	PUMP	REAR	ROSE	SATE
PLOD	PUNK	REDE	ROSS	SAUL
PLOP	PUNT	REED	ROSY	SAVE
PLOT	PUNY	REEF	ROTA	SAWN
PLOY	PUPA	REEK	ROTE	SAXE
PLUG	PURE	REEL	ROUE	SCAB
PLUM	PURL	REIN	ROUP	SCAN
PLUS	PURR	REIS	ROUT	SCAR
POEM	PUSH	RELY	ROVE	SCOT
POET	PUSS	REND	RUBY	SCOW
POKE	PUTT	RENT	RUCK	SCUD
POKY	PYRE	REST	RUDD	SCUM
POLE		RHEA	RUDE	SCUT
POLL	**Q—4**	RICE	RUED	SEAL
POLO	QUAD	RICH	RUFF	SEAM
POMP	QUAY	RICK	RUIN	SEAN
POND	QUID	RIDE	RULE	SEAR

SEAT	SIZE	SOIL	SUDS	TAXI
SECT	SKEP	SOKE	SUED	TEAK
SEED	SKEW	SOLA	SUET	TEAL
SEEK	SKID	SOLD	SUEZ	TEAM
SEEM	SKIM	SOLE	SUIT	TEAR
SEEN	SKIN	SOLO	SULK	TEAT
SEEP	SKIP	SOME	SUMP	TEED
SEER	SKIT	SONG	SUNG	TEEM
SELF	SKUA	SOON	SUNK	TELL
SELL	SKYE	SOOT	SURE	TEND
SEMI	SLAB	SORE	SURF	TENT
SEND	SLAG	SORT	SWAB	TERM
SENT	SLAM	SO-SO	SWAG	TERN
SEPT	SLAP	SOUL	SWAM	TEST
SERB	SLAT	SOUP	SWAN	THAN
SERE	SLAV	SOUR	SWAP	THAT
SERF	SLAY	SOWN	SWAT	THAW
SETT	SLED	SOYA	SWAY	THEE
SEWN	SLEW	SPAM	SWIG	THEM
SHAD	SLID	SPAN	SWIM	THEN
SHAG	SLIM	SPAR	SWOP	THEW
SHAH	SLIP	SPAT	SWOT	THEY
SHAW	SLIT	SPEC	SWUM	THIN
SHED	SLOE	SPED	SYCE	THIS
SHEW	SLOG	SPIN		THOR
SHIM	SLOP	SPIT	T—4	THOU
SHIN	SLOT	SPIV	TACK	THRO
SHIP	SLOW	SPOT	TACT	THUD
SHOD	SLUG	SPRY	TAEL	THUG
SHOE	SLUM	SPUD	TAFT	THUS
SHOO	SLUR	SPUN	TAIL	TICK
SHOP	SLUT	SPUR	TAKE	TIDE
SHOT	SMEE	STAB	TALC	TIDY
SHOW	SMEW	STAG	TALE	TIED
SHUN	SMUG	STAR	TALK	TIER
SHUT	SMUT	STAY	TALL	TIFF
SICK	SNAG	STEM	TAME	TIKE
SIDE	SNAP	STEN	TAMP	TILE
SIFT	SNIP	STEP	TANG	TILL
SIGH	SNOB	STET	TANK	TILT
SIGN	SNOW	STEW	TAPE	TIME
SIKH	SNUB	STIR	TARA	TINE
SILK	SNUG	STOP	TARE	TING
SILL	SOAK	STOW	TARN	TINT
SILO	SOAP	STUB	TARO	TINY
SILT	SOAR	STUD	TART	TIRE
SINE	SOCK	STUN	TASK	TOAD
SING	SODA	STYE	TASS	TOBY
SINK	SOFA	STYX	TA-TA	TO-DO
SIRE	SOFT	SUCH	TATE	TOED
SITE	SOHO	SUCK	TAUT	TOFF

TOGA	'TWAS	VISA	WEND	WOVE
TOGS	TWIG	VIVA	WENT	WRAP
TOIL	TWIN	VIVE	WEPT	WREN
TOLD	TWIT	VOCE	WERE	WRIT
TOLL	TYKE	VOID	WERT	
TOMB	TYNE	VOLE	WEST	**X—4**
TOME	TYPE	VOLT	WHAT	XMAS
TONE	TYRE	VOTE	WHEN	X-RAY
TONY	TYRO		WHET	
TOOK			WHEW	**Y—4**
TOOL	**U—4**	**W—4**	WHEY	YANK
TOOT	UGLY	WADE	WHIG	YARD
TOPE	ULNA	WADI	WHIM	YARN
TORE	UNCO	WAFT	WHIN	YAWL
TORN	UNDO	WAGE	WHIP	YAWN
TORT	UNIT	WAIF	WHIT	YAWS
TORY	UNTO	WAIL	WHOA	YEAH
TOSH	UPAS	WAIN	WHOM	YEAR
TOSS	UPON	WAIT	WICK	YELL
TOTE	URDU	WAKE	WIDE	YELP
TOUR	URGE	WALE	WIFE	YOGA
TOUT	URSA	WALK	WILD	YOGI
TOWN	USED	WALL	WILE	YO-HO
TRAM	USER	WALT	WILL	YOKE
TRAP		WAND	WILT	YOLK
TRAY	**V—4**	WANE	WILY	YORE
TREE	VAIN	WANT	WIND	YOUR
TREK	VALE	WARD	WINE	YOWL
TRET	VAMP	WARE	WING	YO-YO
TREY	VANE	WARM	WINK	YULE
TRIM	VARY	WARN	WIPE	
TRIO	VASE	WARP	WIRE	**Z—4**
TRIP	VAST	WART	WIRY	ZANY
TROD	VEAL	WARY	WISE	ZEAL
TROT	VEER	WASH	WISH	ZEBU
TROY	VEIL	WASP	WISP	ZEPP
TRUE	VEIN	WATT	WITH	ZERO
TRUG	VEND	WAVE	WOAD	ZEST
TSAR	VENT	WAVY	WOLD	ZETA
TUBA	VERB	WAXY	WOLF	ZEUS
TUBE	VERT	WEAK	WOMB	ZINC
TUCK	VERY	WEAL	WONT	ZING
TUFT	VEST	WEAN	WOOD	ZION
TUNA	VETO	WEAR	WOOF	ZONE
TUNE	VICE	WEED	WOOL	ZOOM
TURF	VIDE	WEEK	WORD	ZULU
TURK	VIED	WEEP	WORE	
TURN	VIEW	WEFT	WORK	**A—5**
TUSH	VILE	WEIR	WORM	ABACK
TUSK	VINE	WELD	WORN	ABAFT
TUTU	VIOL	WELL	WORT	ABASE
		WELT		ABASH

ABATE	AGLOW	AMPLE	ASDIC	BACON
ABBEY	AGONE	AMPLY	ASHEN	BADGE
ABBOT	AGONY	AMUCK	ASHES	BADLY
ABEAM	AGREE	AMUSE	ASHET	BAGGY
ABELE	AHEAD	ANENT	ASIAN	BAIRN
ABHOR	AHEAP	ANGEL	ASIDE	BAIZE
ABIDE	AIDED	ANGER	ASKED	BAKED
ABIES	AILED	ANGLE	ASKEW	BAKER
ABLER	AIMED	ANGRY	ASPEN	BALED
ABODE	AIRED	ANISE	ASPIC	BALER
ABOIL	AISLE	ANKLE	ASSAY	BALMY
ABOUT	AITCH	ANNEX	ASSES	BALSA
ABOVE	ALACK	ANNOY	ASSET	BAMBI
ABUSE	ALARM	ANNUL	ASTER	BANAL
ABYSS	ALBUM	ANODE	ASTIR	BANDY
ACHED	ALDER	ANONA	ASTON	BANJO
ACORN	ALERT	ANTIC	ATILT	BANNS
ACRID	ALGAE	ANVIL	ATLAS	BANTU
ACTED	ALIAS	ANZAC	ATOLL	BARED
ACTON	ALIBI	AORTA	ATONE	BARGE
ACTOR	ALIEN	APACE	ATTAR	BARMY
ACUTE	ALIGN	APART	ATTIC	BARON
ADAGE	ALIKE	APHIS	AUDIT	BARRY
ADAPT	ALIVE	APING	AUGER	BASAL
ADDED	ALLAH	APISH	AUGHT	BASED
ADDER	ALLAY	APORT	AUGUR	BASIC
ADDLE	ALLEY	APPAL	AUNTY	BASIL
ADEPT	ALL-IN	APPLE	AURAL	BASIN
ADIEU	ALLOT	APPLY	AVAIL	BASIS
ADMIT	ALLOW	APRIL	AVAST	BASSO
ADMIX	ALLOY	APRON	AVENS	BASTE
ADOBE	ALOES	APTLY	AVERT	BATCH
ADOPT	ALOFT	ARABY	AVIAN	BATED
ADORE	ALONE	ARECA	AVION	BATHE
ADORN	ALONG	ARENA	AVOID	BATON
ADSUM	ALOOF	ARGON	AWAIT	BATTY
ADULT	ALOUD	ARGOT	AWAKE	BAULK
AEGIS	ALPHA	ARGUE	AWARD	BAYED
AERIE	ALTAR	ARGUS	AWARE	BEACH
AESOP	ALTER	ARIEL	AWASH	BEADS
AFFIX	AMASS	ARIES	AWFUL	BEADY
AFIRE	AMAZE	ARISE	AWING	BE-ALL
AFOOT	AMBER	ARMED	AWOKE	BEANO
AFTER	AMBIT	AROMA	AXIAL	BEARD
AGAIN	AMBLE	AROSE	AXIOM	BEAST
AGAPE	AMEER	ARRAS	AZTEC	BEAUX
AGATE	AMEND	ARRAY	AZURE	BEDEW
AGAVE	AMISS	ARROW		BEECH
AGENT	AMITY	ARSON	B—5	BEEFY
AGILE	AMONG	ARYAN	BABEL	BEERY
AGLEY	AMOUR	ASCOT	BACCY	BEFIT

BEFOG	BLAST	BORAX	BROIL	CABLE
BEGAD	BLAZE	BORED	BROKE	CACAO
BEGAN	BLEAK	BORER	BRONX	CACHE
BEGAT	BLEAR	BORNE	BROOD	CADDY
BEGET	BLEAT	BORON	BROOK	CADET
BEGIN	BLEED	BOSOM	BROOM	CADGE
BEGOT	BLEND	BOSSY	BROSE	CADRE
BEGUM	BLESS	BOTCH	BROTH	CAGED
BEGUN	BLEST	BOTHY	BROWN	CAGEY
BEIGE	BLIMP	BOUGH	BRUIN	CAIRN
BEING	BLIND	BOUND	BRUNT	CAKED
BELAY	BLINK	BOWED	BRUSH	CAMEL
BELCH	BLISS	BOWEL	BRUTE	CAMEO
BELGA	BLOCK	BOWER	BUDDY	CANAL
BELIE	BLOKE	BOWIE	BUDGE	CANDY
BELLE	BLOND	BOWLS	BUFFS	CANED
BELOW	BLOOD	BOXED	BUGGY	CANNA
BENCH	BLOOM	BOXER	BUGLE	CANNY
BERET	BLOWN	BOYER	BUILD	CANOE
BERRY	BLOWY	BRACE	BUILT	CANON
BERTH	BLUED	BRACT	BULGE	CANTO
BERYL	BLUER	BRAID	BULGY	CAPER
BESET	BLUES	BRAIN	BULKY	CAPON
BESOM	BLUEY	BRAKE	BULLY	CARAT
BESOT	BLUFF	BRAND	BUMPY	CARED
BETEL	BLUNT	BRASH	BUNCE	CARET
BETTY	BLURB	BRASS	BUNCH	CARGO
BEVEL	BLURT	BRAVE	BUNNY	CARIB
BHANG	BLUSH	BRAVO	BUNTY	CAROB
BIBLE	BOARD	BRAWL	BURGH	CAROL
BIDDY	BOAST	BRAWN	BURKE	CARRY
BIGHT	BOBBY	BRAZE	BURLY	CARTE
BIGOT	BOCHE	BREAD	BURNT	CARVE
BIJOU	BODED	BREAK	BURRO	CASED
BILGE	BODGE	BREAM	BURST	CASTE
BILLY	BOGEY	BREED	BUSBY	CATCH
BINGE	BOGGY	BREVE	BUSES	CATER
BINGO	BOGIE	BRIAR	BUSHY	CATTY
BIPED	BOGUS	BRIBE	BUTTS	CAULK
BIRCH	BOHEA	BRICK	BUTTY	CAUSE
BIRTH	BOLAS	BRIDE	BUXOM	CAVIL
BISON	BONED	BRIEF	BUYER	CAWED
BITCH	BONES	BRIER	BWANA	CEASE
BITER	BONNE	BRILL	BY-LAW	CEDAR
BLACK	BONUS	BRINE	BY-WAY	CEDED
BLADE	BOOBY	BRING		CELLO
BLAME	BOOED	BRINK	C—5	CERES
BLAND	BOOST	BRINY	CABAL	CHAFE
BLANK	BOOTH	BRISK	CABBY	CHAFF
BLARE	BOOTS	BROAD	CABER	CHAIN
BLASE	BOOTY	BROCK	CABIN	CHAIR

CHALK	CITED	COMET	CRAZY	CURRY
CHAMP	CIVET	COMIC	CREAK	CURSE
CHANT	CIVIC	COMMA	CREAM	CURVE
CHAOS	CIVIL	COMPO	CREDO	CUSHY
CHAPS	CIVVY	CONCH	CREED	CUTER
CHARD	CLACK	CONEY	CREEK	CUTTY
CHARM	CLAIM	CONGE	CREEL	CYCLE
CHART	CLAMP	CONGO	CREEP	CYDER
CHARY	CLAMS	CONIC	CREPE	CYNIC
CHASE	CLANG	COOED	CREPT	CZECH
CHASM	CLANK	COOEE	CRESS	
CHEAP	CLARE	COOMB	CREST	**D—5**
CHEAT	CLASH	CO-OPT	CREWE	DADDY
CHECK	CLASP	COPAL	CRICK	DAILY
CHEEK	CLASS	COPED	CRIED	DAIRY
CHEEP	CLEAN	COPER	CRIER	DAISY
CHEER	CLEAR	COPRA	CRIES	DALAI
CHESS	CLEAT	COPSE	CRIME	DALLY
CHEST	CLEEK	CORAL	CRIMP	DAMON
CHICK	CLEFT	CORGI	CRISP	DANCE
CHIDE	CLERK	CORNY	CROAK	DANDY
CHIEF	CLICK	CORPS	CROCK	DARBY
CHILD	CLIFF	COSTS	CROFT	DARED
CHILI	CLIMB	COUGH	CRONE	DATED
CHILL	CLIME	COULD	CRONY	DATUM
CHIME	CLING	COUNT	CROOK	DAUNT
CHINA	CLINK	COUPE	CROON	DAVIT
CHINE	CLOAK	COURT	CRORE	DAZED
CHINK	CLOCK	COVER	CROSS	DEALT
CHIPS	CLOSE	COVET	CROUP	DEATH
CHIRP	CLOTH	COVEY	CROWD	DEBAR
CHIVE	CLOUD	COWED	CROWN	DEBIT
CHOCK	CLOUT	COWER	CRUDE	DEBUT
CHOIR	CLOVE	COWRY	CRUEL	DECAY
CHOKE	CLOWN	COYLY	CRUET	DECOR
CHOPS	CLUCK	COYPU	CRUMB	DECOY
CHORD	CLUMP	COZEN	CRUMP	DECRY
CHORE	CLUNG	CRACK	CRUSE	DEFER
CHOSE	CLUNK	CRAFT	CRUSH	DEIFY
CHUCK	CLUNY	CRAIG	CRUST	DEIGN
CHUMP	COACH	CRAKE	CRYPT	DEITY
CHUNK	COAST	CRAMP	CUBAN	DEKKO
CHURL	COATI	CRANE	CUBED	DELAY
CHURN	COBRA	CRANK	CUBIC	DELFT
CHUTE	COCKY	CRAPE	CUBIT	DELTA
CIDER	COCOA	CRASH	CUPID	DELVE
CIGAR	CODED	CRASS	CURED	DEMOB
CINCH	CODEX	CRATE	CURER	DEMON
CIRCA	COLIC	CRAVE	CURIE	DEMUR
CIRCE	COLIN	CRAWL	CURIO	DENIM
CISSY	COLON	CRAZE	CURLY	DENSE

DEPOT	DOSED	DUCAL	ELFIN	EVENT
DEPTH	DOTED	DUCAT	ELGIN	EVERT
DERBY	DOTTY	DUCHY	ELIDE	EVERY
DETER	DOUBT	DULLY	ELITE	EVICT
DEUCE	DOUGH	DUMMY	ELOPE	EVOKE
DEVIL	DOUSE	DUMPS	ELUDE	EXACT
DHOBI	DOVER	DUMPY	ELVER	EXALT
DHOTI	DOWDY	DUNCE	EMBED	EXCEL
DIANA	DOWEL	DUPED	EMBER	EXEAT
DIARY	DOWER	DUSKY	EMEER	EXERT
DICED	DOWNY	DUSTY	EMEND	EXILE
DICKY	DOWRY	DUTCH	EMERY	EXIST
DICTA	DOYEN	DWARF	EMMET	EXPEL
DIGIT	DOZED	DWELL	EMPTY	EXTOL
DIMLY	DOZEN	DWELT	ENACT	EXTRA
DINAR	DRAFT	DYING	ENDED	EXUDE
DINED	DRAIN		END-ON	EXULT
DINER	DRAKE		ENDOR	EYING
DINGO	DRAMA	**E—5**	ENDOW	EYRIE
DINGY	DRANK	EAGER	ENEMY	
DINKY	DRAPE	EAGLE	ENJOY	
DIODE	DRAWL	EAGRE	ENNUI	**F—5**
DIRGE	DRAWN	EARED	ENROL	FABLE
DIRTY	DREAD	EARLY	ENSUE	FACED
DITCH	DREAM	EARTH	ENTER	FACET
DITTO	DREAR	EASED	ENTRY	FADDY
DITTY	DREGS	EASEL	ENVOI	FAGIN
DIVAN	DRESS	EATEN	ENVOY	FAINT
DIVED	DRIED	EAVES	EPHOD	FAIRY
DIVER	DRIER	EBBED	EPOCH	FAITH
DIVES	DRIFT	EBONY	EPSOM	FAKED
DIVOT	DRILL	ECLAT	EQUAL	FAKIR
DIXIE	DRILY	EDGED	EQUIP	FALSE
DODGE	DRINK	EDICT	ERASE	FAMED
DODGY	DRIVE	EDIFY	ERATO	FANCY
DOGGO	DROIT	EDUCE	ERECT	FARAD
DOGGY	DROLL	EERIE	ERICA	FARED
DOGMA	DROME	EGGED	ERODE	FARCE
DOILY	DRONE	EGRET	ERRED	FATAL
DOING	DROOL	EIDER	ERROR	FATED
DOLCE	DROOP	EIGHT	ERUPT	FATES
DOLED	DROPS	EJECT	ESSAY	FATLY
DOLLY	DROSS	EKING	ESTER	FATTY
DOMED	DROVE	ELAND	ESTOP	FAULT
DONAH	DROWN	ELATE	ETHER	FAUNA
DONAT	DRUID	ELBOW	ETHIC	FAUST
DONNA	DRUNK	ELDER	ETHOS	FEAST
DONOR	DRUPE	ELECT	ETHYL	FED-UP
DOPED	DRYAD	ELEGY	ETUDE	FEIGN
DORIC	DRYER	ELEMI	EVADE	FEINT
DORMY	DRYLY	ELEVE	EVENS	FELIX

FELON	FLIER	FREAK	GAUZE	GOLLY
FEMUR	FLIES	FREED	GAUZY	GONER
FENCE	FLING	FREER	GAVEL	GOODS
FERNY	FLINT	FRESH	GAWKY	GOODY
FERRY	FLIRT	FRIAR	GAYER	GOOSE
FETCH	FLOAT	FRIED	GAZED	GORED
FETED	FLOCK	FRILL	GECKO	GORGE
FEVER	FLONG	FRISK	GEESE	GORSE
FEWER	FLOOD	FRITZ	GELID	GOUDA
FIBRE	FLOOR	FRIZZ	GENET	GOUGE
FICHU	FLORA	FROCK	GENIE	GOURD
FIELD	FLOSS	FROND	GENOA	GOUTY
FIEND	FLOUR	FRONT	GENRE	GRACE
FIERY	FLOUT	FROST	GENUS	GRADE
FIFTH	FLOWN	FROTH	GET-UP	GRAFT
FIFTY	FLUFF	FROWN	GHOST	GRAIL
FIGHT	FLUID	FROZE	GHOUL	GRAIN
FILCH	FLUKE	FRUIT	GIANT	GRAND
FILED	FLUKY	FRUMP	GIBED	GRANT
FILLY	FLUNG	FRYER	GIBUS	GRAPE
FILMY	FLUSH	FUDGE	GIDDY	GRAPH
FILTH	FLUTE	FUGUE	GIGOT	GRASP
FINAL	FLYER	FULLY	GIPSY	GRASS
FINCH	FOAMY	FUNGI	GIRTH	GRATE
FINED	FOCAL	FUNKY	GIVEN	GRAVE
FINER	FOCUS	FUNNY	GIVER	GRAVY
FINIS	FOGEY	FURRY	GIVES	GRAZE
FIORD	FOGGY	FURZE	GLACE	GREAT
FIRED	FOIST	FUSED	GLADE	GREBE
FIRST	FOLIO	FUSEE	GLAND	GREED
FIRTH	FOLLY	FUSIL	GLARE	GREEK
FISHY	FORAY	FUSSY	GLASS	GREEN
FITCH	FORBY	FUSTY	GLAZE	GREET
FITLY	FORCE	FUZZY	GLEAM	GREYS
FIVER	FORGE		GLEAN	GRIEF
FIVES	FORGO	G—5	GLEBE	GRILL
FIXED	FORME	GABLE	GLIDE	GRIME
FJORD	FORTE	GAFFE	GLINT	GRIMY
FLAIL	FORTH	GAILY	GLOAT	GRIND
FLAIR	FORTY	GALOP	GLOBE	GRIPE
FLAKE	FORUM	GAMED	GLOOM	GRIST
FLAKY	FOSSE	GAMIN	GLORY	GRITS
FLAME	FOUND	GAMMA	GLOSS	GROAN
FLANK	FOUNT	GAMUT	GLOVE	GROAT
FLARE	FOXED	GAPED	GLUED	GROCK
FLASH	FOYER	GARTH	GLUEY	GROIN
FLASK	FRAIL	GASSY	GNARL	GROOM
FLECK	FRAME	GATED	GNASH	GROPE
FLEET	FRANC	GAUDY	GNOME	GROSS
FLESH	FRANK	GAUGE	GODLY	GROUP
FLICK	FRAUD	GAUNT	GOING	GROUT

GROVE	HAVEN	HORDE	IMPLY	JETTY
GROWL	HAVER	HORNY	INANE	JEWEL
GROWN	HAVOC	HORSE	INAPT	JEWRY
GRUEL	HAWSE	HORSY	INCOG	JIBED
GRUFF	HAZEL	HOTEL	INCUR	JIFFY
GRUNT	HEADS	HOTLY	INDEX	JIMMY
GUANO	HEADY	HOUND	INEPT	JINGO
GUARD	HEARD	HOURI	INERT	JINKS
GUAVA	HEART	HOUSE	INFER	JOINT
GUESS	HEATH	HOVEL	INFIX	JOIST
GUEST	HEDGE	HOVER	INGLE	JOKED
GUIDE	HEFTY	HOWDY	INGOT	JOKER
GUILD	HEIGH	HUBBY	INKED	JOLLY
GUILE	HELIX	HUFFY	IN-LAW	JONAH
GUISE	HELLO	HULLO	INLAY	JOUST
GULCH	HELOT	HUMAN	INLET	JUDAS
GULES	HE-MAN	HUMID	INNER	JUDGE
GULLY	HENCE	HUMPH	INPUT	JUICE
GUNNY	HENNA	HUMUS	INSET	JUICY
GUSTO	HENRY	HUNCH	INTER	JULEP
GUSTY	HEROD	HUNKS	INURE	JUMBO
GUTTA	HERON	HURRY	IONIC	JUMPY
GUTTY	HEWED	HUSKY	IRAQI	JUNTA
GUYED	HEWER	HUSSY	IRATE	JUROR
GYPSY	HIKED	HUTCH	IRENE	
GYVES	HIKER	HYDRA	IRISH	**K—5**
	HILLY	HYDRO	IRKED	KAPOK
	HINDI	HYENA	IRONS	KAYAK
H—5	HINDU	HYRAX	IRONY	KEDGE
HABIT	HINGE	HYTHE	ISLAM	KEEPS
HADES	HINNY		ISLET	KETCH
HADJI	HIPPO	**I—5**	ISSUE	KEYED
HAIRY	HIRED	ICENI	ITCHY	KHAKI
HALLO	HIRER	ICHOR	IVIED	KIDDY
HALMA	HITCH	ICIER	IVORY	KINGS
HALVE	HIVED	ICILY	IXION	KINKY
HANDY	HIVES	ICING		KIOSK
HANKY	HOARD	IDEAL	**J—5**	KITTY
HAPLY	HOARY	IDIOM	JABOT	KLOOF
HAPPY	HOBBY	IDIOT	JADED	KNACK
HARDY	HOCUS	IDLED	JAMES	KNARL
HARED	HODGE	IDLER	JAMMY	KNAVE
HAREM	HOIST	IDRIS	JAPAN	KNEAD
HARPY	HOLLY	IDYLL	JAUNT	KNEED
HARRY	HOMER	IGLOO	JAWED	KNEEL
HARSH	HONED	ILIAD	JEANS	KNELL
HASTE	HONEY	ILIUM	JELLY	KNELT
HASTY	HOOCH	IMAGE	JEMMY	KNIFE
HATCH	HOOEY	IMAGO	JENNY	KNOCK
HATED	HOPED	IMBUE	JERKY	KNOLL
HAULM	HOPPY	IMPEL	JERRY	KNOUT

KNOWN	LEASH	LOCAL	MADGE	MECCA
KNURL	LEAST	LOCUM	MADLY	MEDAL
KOALA	LEAVE	LODGE	MAFIA	MEDIA
KOPJE	LEDGE	LOFTY	MAGIC	MEDOC
KORAN	LEECH	LOGAN	MAGOG	MELEE
KRAAL	LEERY	LOGIC	MAHDI	MELON
KRAIT	LEGAL	LOLLY	MAIZE	MERCY
KRONE	LEGER	LOOFA	MAJOR	MERGE
KUDOS	LEGGY	LOONY	MAKER	MERIT
KUKRI	LEMON	LOOPY	MALAY	MERLE
KULAK	LEMUR	LOOSE	MALTY	MERRY
KVASS	LENTO	LOPED	MAMBA	MESSY
	LEPER	LORDS	MAMMA	METAL
L—5	LETHE	LORIS	MAMMY	METED
LABEL	LET-UP	LORRY	MANED	METER
LACED	LEVEE	LOSER	MANET	METRE
LADEN	LEVEL	LOTTO	MANGE	MEWED
LADLE	LEVER	LOTUS	MANGO	MEZZO
LAGER	LEWIS	LOUGH	MANGY	MIAOW
LAIRD	LIANA	LOUIS	MANIA	MICKY
LAITY	LIBEL	LOUSE	MANLY	MIDAS
LAKER	LIBRA	LOUSY	MANNA	MIDDY
LAMED	LICIT	LOVAT	MANOR	MIDGE
LANCE	LIEGE	LOVED	MANSE	MID-ON
LANKY	LIFER	LOVER	MAORI	MIDST
LAPEL	LIGHT	LOWER	MAPLE	MIGHT
LAPSE	LIKED	LOWLY	MARCH	MILCH
LARCH	LIKEN	LOYAL	MARGE	MILER
LARDY	LILAC	LUCID	MARRY	MILKY
LARGE	LIMBO	LUCKY	MARSH	MIMED
LARGO	LIMIT	LUCRE	MASAI	MIMIC
LARRY	LINED	LUGER	MASHY	MINCE
LARVA	LINEN	LUMPY	MASON	MINED
LASSO	LINER	LUNAR	MASSA	MINER
LATCH	LINGO	LUNCH	MASSE	MINIM
LATER	LINKS	LUNGE	MATCH	MINOR
LATEX	LISLE	LUPIN	MATED	MINUS
LATHE	LISTS	LURCH	MATER	MIRTH
LATIN	LITHE	LURED	MATEY	MISER
LAUGH	LITHO	LURID	MATIN	MISSY
LAURA	LITRE	LUSTY	MAUVE	MISTY
LAVED	LIVED	LYCEE	MAVIS	MITRE
LAXLY	LIVEN	LYING	MAWKY	MIXED
LAY-BY	LIVER	LYMPH	MAXIM	MIXER
LAYER	LIVID	LYNCH	MAYBE	MIX-UP
LAZED	LLAMA	LYRIC	MAYOR	MOCHA
LEACH	LLANO		MEALY	MODEL
LEAFY	LOACH	**M—5**	MEANS	MODUS
LEANT	LOAMY	MACAW	MEANT	MOGUL
LEARN	LOATH	MACON	MEATH	MOIRE
LEASE	LOBBY	MADAM	MEATY	MOIST

MOLAR	MUSTY	NIZAM	OKAPI	OXLIP
MOLLY	MUTED	NOBBY	OLDEN	OZONE
MOLTO	MUZZY	NOBEL	OLDER	
MONDE	MYOPE	NOBLE	OLEIC	**P—5**
MONEY	MYRRH	NOBLY	OLIVE	PACED
MONTE		NODAL	OMAHA	PACER
MONTH	**N—5**	NODDY	OMBRE	PADDY
MOOCH	NABOB	NOHOW	OMEGA	PADRE
MOODY	NACRE	NOISE	ONION	PAEAN
MOOED	NADIR	NOISY	ONSET	PAGAN
MOONY	NAIAD	NOMAD	OOMPH	PAGED
MOOSE	NAIVE	NONCE	OOZED	PAINT
MOPED	NAKED	NONET	OPERA	PALED
MORAL	NAMED	NOOSE	OPINE	PALMY
MORAY	NANNY	NORMA	OPIUM	PALSY
MORON	NAPOO	NORSE	OPTED	PANDA
MORSE	NAPPY	NORTH	OPTIC	PANED
MOSES	NASAL	NOSED	ORANG	PANEL
MOSSY	NASTY	NOSEY	ORATE	PANIC
MOTET	NATAL	NOTCH	ORBED	PANSY
MOTHY	NATTY	NOTED	ORBIT	PANTS
MOTIF	NAVAL	NOVEL	ORDER	PAPAL
MOTOR	NAVEL	NOYAU	OREAD	PAPAW
MOTTO	NAVVY	NUDGE	ORGAN	PAPER
MOULD	NAWAB	NURSE	ORIEL	PAPPY
MOULT	NAZIS	NUTTY	ORION	PARCH
MOUND	NEATH	NYLON	ORLON	PARED
MOUNT	NEDDY		ORLOP	PARKY
MOURN	NEEDS	**O—5**	ORMER	PARRY
MOUSE	NEEDY	OAKEN	ORRIS	PARSE
MOUSY	NEGRO	OAKUM	OSIER	PARTS
MOUTH	NEGUS	OARED	OTHER	PARTY
MOVED	NEIGH	OASIS	OTTER	PASHA
MOVER	NERVE	OATEN	OUGHT	PASSE
MOWED	NERVY	OBEAH	OUIJA	PASTE
MOWER	NEVER	OBESE	OUNCE	PASTY
MUCKY	NEWEL	OCCUR	OUSEL	PATCH
MUCUS	NEWLY	OCEAN	OUTDO	PATEN
MUDDY	NEWSY	OCHRE	OUTER	PATER
MUFTI	NICER	OCTET	OUTRE	PATIO
MUGGY	NICHE	ODDLY	OVATE	PATLY
MULCH	NIECE	ODEON	OVERT	PATTY
MULCT	NIFTY	ODEUM	OVINE	PAUSE
MUMMY	NIGHT	ODIUM	OVOID	PAVAN
MUMPS	NIHIL	ODOUR	OVULE	PAVED
MUNCH	NINNY	OFFAL	OWING	PAWED
MURAL	NINON	OFFER	OWLET	PAWKY
MURKY	NINTH	OFLAG	OWNED	PAYEE
MUSED	NIOBE	OFTEN	OWNER	PAYER
MUSHY	NIPPY	OGLED	OX-EYE	PEACE
MUSIC	NITRE	OILED	OXIDE	PEACH

PEAKY	PLAIN	PRIDE	QUAIL	RASED
PEARL	PLAIT	PRIED	QUAKE	RATED
PEASE	PLANE	PRIMA	QUAKY	RATEL
PEATY	PLANK	PRIME	QUALM	RATIO
PECAN	PLANT	PRIMO	QUANT	RATTY
PEDAL	PLATE	PRINK	QUART	RAVED
PEGGY	PLATO	PRINT	QUASH	RAVEL
PEKOE	PLAZA	PRIOR	QUASI	RAVEN
PENAL	PLEAD	PRISE	QUEEN	RAWLY
PENCE	PLEAT	PRISM	QUEER	RAYON
PENNY	PLEBS	PRIVY	QUELL	RAZED
PEONY	PLIED	PRIZE	QUERY	RAZOR
PERCH	PLUCK	PROBE	QUEST	REACH
PERDU	PLUMB	PROEM	QUEUE	REACT
PERIL	PLUME	PRONE	QUICK	READY
PERKY	PLUMP	PRONG	QUIET	REALM
PERRY	PLUSH	PROOF	QUIFF	RE-ARM
PESKY	POACH	PROPS	QUILL	REBEL
PETAL	PODGE	PROSE	QUILT	REBID
PETER	PODGY	PROSY	QUINS	REBUS
PETIT	POESY	PROUD	QUIRE	REBUT
PEWIT	POILU	PROVE	QUIRK	RECCE
PHASE	POINT	PROWL	QUITE	RECTO
PHIAL	POISE	PROXY	QUITS	RECUR
PHLOX	POKED	PRUDE	QUOIN	REDAN
PHONE	POKER	PRUNE	QUOIT	REDLY
PHOTO	POLAR	PSALM	QUOTA	RE-DYE
PIANO	POLIO	PSHAW	QUOTE	REEDY
PICOT	POLKA	PUFFY	QUOTH	REEVE
PIECE	POLLY	PUKKA		REFER
PIETY	POPPY	PULED	**R—5**	REFIT
PIGMY	PORCH	PULPY	RABBI	REFIX
PILAU	PORED	PULSE	RACED	REGAL
PILAW	PORKY	PUNCH	RACER	REICH
PILED	POSED	PUNIC	RADAR	REIGN
PILOT	POSER	PUPIL	RADII	REINS
PINED	POSSE	PUPPY	RADIO	RELAX
PINKY	POTTO	PUREE	RADIX	RELAY
PINNY	POTTY	PURER	RAGED	RELET
PIN-UP	POUCH	PURGE	RAINY	RELIC
PIOUS	POULT	PURSE	RAISE	RELIT
PIPED	POUND	PUSSY	RAJAH	REMIT
PIPER	POWER	PUT-UP	RAKED	RENAL
PIPIT	PRANG	PYGMY	RALLY	RENEW
PIQUE	PRANK	PYLON	RALPH	RENTE
PITCH	PRATE	PYRUS	RANCH	REPAY
PITHY	PRAWN		RANEE	REPEL
PIVOT	PREEN	**Q—5**	RANGE	REPLY
PIXIE	PRESS	QUACK	RANGY	REPOT
PLACE	PRICE	QUADS	RAPID	RESET
PLAID	PRICK	QUAFF	RARER	RESIN

RESOW	ROUSE	SAPID	SCRUB	SHEET
RETCH	ROUTE	SAPOR	SCRUM	SHEIK
RETRY	ROVED	SAPPY	SCUFF	SHELF
REVEL	ROVER	SARUM	SCULL	SHELL
REVUE	ROWAN	SATAN	SCURF	SHEWN
RHEUM	ROWDY	SATED	SEAMY	SHIED
RHINE	ROWED	SATIN	SEDAN	SHIFT
RHINO	ROWEL	SATYR	SEDGE	SHINE
RHOMB	ROWER	SAUCE	SEEDY	SHINY
RHYME	ROYAL	SAUCY	SEINE	SHIRE
RIANT	RUCHE	SAUTE	SEIZE	SHIRK
RIBES	RUDDY	SAVED	SENNA	SHIRT
RIDER	RUDER	SAVER	SENSE	SHOAL
RIDGE	RUGBY	SAVOY	SEPAL	SHOCK
RIFLE	RUING	SAVVY	SEPIA	SHONE
RIGHT	RULED	SAWED	SEPOY	SHOOK
RIGID	RULER	SAXON	SERAI	SHOOT
RIGOR	RUMBA	SAY-SO	SERGE	SHORE
RILED	RUMMY	SCALA	SERIF	SHORN
RIMED	RUNIC	SCALD	SERUM	SHORT
RINSE	RUN-IN	SCALE	SERVE	SHOUT
RIPEN	RUNNY	SCALP	SETAE	SHOVE
RIPER	RUPEE	SCALY	SET-TO	SHOWN
RIPON	RURAL	SCAMP	SET-UP	SHOWY
RISEN	RUSTY	SCANT	SEVEN	SHRED
RISER	RUTTY	SCARE	SEVER	SHREW
RISKY		SCARF	SEWER	SHRUB
RIVAL	S—5	SCARP	SHACK	SHRUG
RIVEN	SABLE	SCENA	SHADE	SHUCK
RIVER	SABOT	SCENE	SHADY	SHUNT
RIVET	SABRE	SCENT	SHAFT	SHYLY
ROACH	SADLY	SCION	SHAKE	SIBYL
ROAST	SAFER	SCOFF	SHAKO	SIDED
ROBED	SAGAN	SCOLD	SHAKY	SIDLE
ROBIN	SAHIB	SCONE	SHALE	SIEGE
ROBOT	SAINT	SCOOP	SHALL	SIEVE
ROCKY	SAITH	SCOOT	SHALT	SIGHT
RODEO	SALAD	SCOPE	SHAME	SIGMA
ROGER	SALIC	SCORE	SHANK	SILKY
ROGUE	SALIX	SCORN	SHAPE	SILLY
ROMAN	SALLY	SCOTS	SHARD	SINCE
ROMEO	SALMI	SCOUR	SHARE	SINEW
RONDO	SALON	SCOUT	SHARK	SINGE
ROOMY	SALTS	SCOWL	SHARP	SINUS
ROOST	SALTY	SCRAG	SHAVE	SIOUX
ROPED	SALVE	SCRAM	SHAWL	SIRED
ROSIN	SALVO	SCRAP	SHEAF	SIREN
ROTOR	SAMBO	SCREE	SHEAR	SISAL
ROUGE	SAMMY	SCREW	SHEEN	SISSY
ROUGH	SANDY	SCRIM	SHEEP	SIXTH
ROUND	SANER	SCRIP	SHEER	SIXTY

SIZED	SMELT	SOUPY	SPRAY	STOCK
SKATE	SMILE	SOUSE	SPREE	STOEP
SKEAN	SMIRK	SOUTH	SPRIG	STOIC
SKEIN	SMITE	SOWAR	SPRIT	STOKE
SKIED	SMITH	SOWED	SPUME	STOLE
SKIER	SMOCK	SOWER	SPURN	STOMA
SKIFF	SMOKE	SPACE	SPURT	STONE
SKILL	SMOKY	SPADE	SQUAB	STONY
SKIMP	SMOTE	SPAHI	SQUAD	STOOD
SKINK	SNACK	SPAKE	SQUAT	STOOK
SKIRL	SNAIL	SPANK	SQUAW	STOOL
SKIRT	SNAKE	SPARE	SQUIB	STOOP
SKULK	SNAKY	SPARK	SQUID	STORE
SKULL	SNARE	SPASM	STACK	STORK
SKUNK	SNARL	SPATE	STAFF	STORM
SLACK	SNATH	SPAWN	STAGE	STORY
SLADE	SNEAD	SPEAK	STAGY	STOUP
SLAIN	SNEAK	SPEAR	STAID	STOUR
SLAKE	SNEER	SPECK	STAIN	STOUT
SLANG	SNICK	SPECS	STAIR	STOVE
SLANT	SNIDE	SPEED	STAKE	STRAD
SLASH	SNIFF	SPELL	STALE	STRAP
SLATE	SNIPE	SPELT	STALK	STRAW
SLATY	SNOEK	SPEND	STALL	STRAY
SLAVE	SNOOD	SPERM	STAMP	STREW
SLEEK	SNOOP	SPICE	STAND	STRIP
SLEEP	SNORE	SPICK	STANK	STROP
SLEET	SNORT	SPICY	STARE	STRUM
SLEPT	SNOUT	SPIED	STARK	STRUT
SLICE	SNOWY	SPIKE	START	STUCK
SLICK	SNUFF	SPIKY	STATE	STUDY
SLIDE	SOAPY	SPILL	STAVE	STUFF
SLIME	SOBER	SPILT	STEAD	STUMP
SLIMY	SOGGY	SPINE	STEAK	STUNG
SLING	SOLAR	SPINY	STEAL	STUNK
SLINK	SOLDO	SPIRE	STEAM	STUNT
SLOOP	SOLED	SPITE	STEED	STYLE
SLOPE	SOL-FA	SPLAY	STEEL	STYLO
SLOSH	SOLID	SPLIT	STEEP	SUAVE
SLOTH	SOLUS	SPODE	STEER	SUEDE
SLUMP	SOLVE	SPOIL	STERN	SUETY
SLUNG	SONIC	SPOKE	STEVE	SUGAR
SLUNK	SONNY	SPOOF	STICK	SUING
SLUSH	SOOTH	SPOOK	STIFF	SUITE
SLYLY	SOOTY	SPOOL	STILE	SULKS
SMACK	SOPPY	SPOON	STILL	SULKY
SMALL	SORBO	SPOOR	STILT	SULLY
SMART	SORER	SPORE	STING	SUNNY
SMASH	SORRY	SPORT	STINK	SUN-UP
SMEAR	SOUGH	SPOUT	STINT	SUPER
SMELL	SOUND	SPRAT	STOAT	SURER

SURGE	TAMIL	THING	TOPER	TRUMP
SURLY	TAMMY	THINK	TOPIC	TRUNK
SWAIN	TANGO	THIRD	TOQUE	TRUSS
SWALE	TANGY	THOLE	TORCH	TRUST
SWAMP	TANSY	THONG	TORSO	TRUTH
SWANK	TAPED	THORN	TOTAL	TRY-ON
SWARD	TAPER	THOSE	TOTEM	TRYST
SWARF	TAPIR	THREE	TOTED	TUBBY
SWARM	TARDY	THREW	TOUCH	TUBED
SWATS	TARRY	THROB	TOUGH	TUBER
SWEAR	TASTE	THROE	TOWED	TUDOR
SWEAT	TASTY	THROW	TOWEL	TULIP
SWEDE	TATTY	THUMB	TOWER	TULLE
SWEEP	TAUNT	THUMP	TOWNY	TUNED
SWEET	TAWNY	THYME	TOXIC	TUNER
SWELL	TAXED	TIARA	TOXIN	TUNIC
SWEPT	TEACH	TIBET	TOYED	TUNNY
SWIFT	TEASE	TIBIA	TRACE	TURFY
SWILL	TEDDY	TIDAL	TRACK	TURPS
SWINE	TEENS	TIDED	TRACT	TUTOR
SWING	TEENY	TIGER	TRADE	TUTTI
SWIPE	TEETH	TIGHT	TRAIL	TWAIN
SWIRL	TEHEE	TILED	TRAIN	TWANG
SWISH	TEMPO	TILER	TRAMP	TWEAK
SWISS	TEMPT	TILTH	TRASH	TWEED
SWOON	TENCH	TIMED	TRAWL	TWEEN
SWOOP	TENET	TIMID	TREAD	TWERP
SWORD	TENON	TIMON	TREAT	TWICE
SWORE	TENOR	TINED	TREED	TWILL
SWORN	TENSE	TINGE	TREND	TWINE
SWUNG	TENTH	TINNY	TRESS	TWIRL
SYLPH	TEPEE	TIPSY	TREWS	TWIST
SYNOD	TEPID	TIRED	TRIAL	TWITE
SYRUP	TEPOR	TITAN	TRIBE	TWIXT
	TERRA	TITHE	TRICE	TYING
	TERRY	TITLE	TRICK	TYPED
T—5	TERSE	TIZZY	TRIED	
TABBY	TESTY	TOADY	TRIER	U—5
TABLE	THANE	TOAST	TRILL	U-BOAT
TABOO	THANK	TO-DAY	TRIPE	UDDER
TACIT	THEFT	TODDY	TRITE	UHLAN
TACKY	THEIR	TOKAY	TROLL	UKASE
TAFFY	THEME	TOKEN	TRONC	ULCER
TAILS	THERE	TOMMY	TROOP	ULNAR
TAINT	THERM	TONAL	TROTH	ULTRA
TAKEN	THESE	TONED	TROUT	UMBEL
TAKER	THETA	TONGA	TROVE	UMBER
TALES	THICK	TONIC	TRUCE	UMBRA
TALLY	THIEF	TOOTH	TRUCK	UNAPT
TALON	THIGH	TOPAZ	TRUER	UNARM
TAMED	THINE	TOPEE	TRULY	UNBAR
TAMER				

UNBID	VAPID	VYING	WHICH	WORTH
UNCLE	VASTY		WHIFF	WOULD
UNCUT	VAULT	**W—5**	WHILE	WOUND
UNDER	VAUNT	WADED	WHINE	WOVEN
UNDID	VELDT	WADER	WHIRL	WRACK
UNDUE	VENAL	WAFER	WHISK	WRATH
UNFED	VENOM	WAGED	WHIST	WREAK
UNFIT	VENUE	WAGER	WHITE	WRECK
UNFIX	VENUS	WAGES	WHIZZ	WREST
UNIFY	VERGE	WAGON	WHOLE	WRING
UNION	VERSE	WAIST	WHOOP	WRIST
UNITE	VERSO	WAITS	WHORL	WRITE
UNITY	VERST	WAIVE	WHOSE	WRONG
UNLED	VERVE	WAKEN	WHOSO	WROTE
UNLET	VESPA	WALTZ	WIDEN	WRUNG
UNMAN	VESTA	WANED	WIDER	WRYLY
UNPEG	VETCH	WANLY	WIDOW	
UNPEN	VEXED	WARES	WIDTH	**X—5**
UNPIN	VIAND	WASHY	WIELD	XEBEC
UNSET	VICAR	WASTE	WIGHT	X-RAYS
UNTIE	VIGIL	WATCH	WILLY	
UNTIL	VILER	WATER	WINCE	**Y—5**
UNWED	VILLA	WAVED	WINCH	YACHT
UP-END	VIOLA	WAVER	WINDY	YAHOO
UPPER	VIPER	WAXED	WINED	YAWED
UPSET	VIRGO	WAXEN	WIPED	YEARN
URBAN	VIRTU	WEALD	WIPER	YEAST
URGED	VIRUS	WEARY	WIRED	YIELD
URIAL	VISIT	WEAVE	WISER	YODEL
USAGE	VISOR	WEDGE	WISPY	YOKED
USHER	VISTA	WEEDS	WITCH	YOKEL
USING	VITAL	WEEDY	WITHY	YOUNG
USUAL	VIVAT	WEEPY	WITTY	YOURS
USURP	VIVID	WEIGH	WIVES	YOUTH
USURY	VIZOR	WEIRD	WODEN	YUCCA
UTTER	VOCAL	WELSH	WOMAN	
UVULA	VODKA	WENCH	WOMEN	**Z—5**
	VOGUE	WHACK	WOODY	ZEBRA
V—5	VOICE	WHALE	WOOED	ZEBUS
VAGUE	VOILE	WHANG	WOOER	ZINCO
VALET	VOMIT	WHARF	WORDY	ZONAL
VALID	VOTED	WHEAT	WORLD	ZONED
VALSE	VOTER	WHEEL	WORMY	
VALUE	VOUCH	WHELK	WORRY	
VALVE	VOWED	WHELP	WORSE	
VANED	VOWEL	WHERE	WORST	

A—6	ADMIRE	ALLIED	APLOMB
ABACUS	ADONIS	ALLIES	APPEAL
ABASED	ADORED	ALL-OUT	APPEAR
ABATED	ADRIFT	ALLUDE	APPEND
ABBESS	ADROIT	ALLURE	ARABIC
ABDUCT	ADVENT	ALMOND	ARABIS
ABIDED	ADVERT	ALMOST	ARABLE
ABJECT	ADVICE	ALPACA	ARBOUR
ABJURE	ADVISE	ALPINE	ARCADE
ABLAZE	AENEID	ALPINI	ARCADY
ABLEST	AERATE	ALUMNA	ARCHED
ABLOOM	AERIAL	ALUMNI	ARCHER
ABOARD	AFFAIR	ALWAYS	ARCHLY
ABOUND	AFFECT	AMAZED	ARCING
ABRADE	AFFIRM	AMAZON	ARCTIC
ABROAD	AFFORD	AMBLED	ARDENT
ABRUPT	AFFRAY	AMBLER	ARDOUR
ABSENT	AFGHAN	AMBUSH	ARGALI
ABSORB	AFLAME	AMOEBA	ARGENT
ABSURD	AFLOAT	AMORAL	ARGOSY
ABUSED	AFRAID	AMOUNT	ARGUED
ACACIA	AFRESH	AMPERE	ARIGHT
ACCEDE	AGARIC	AMPLER	ARISEN
ACCENT	AGEING	AMULET	ARMADA
ACCEPT	AGENCY	AMUSED	ARMIES
ACCESS	AGENDA	ANCHOR	ARMING
ACCORD	AGHAST	ANCONA	ARMLET
ACCOST	AGNATE	ANGINA	ARMOUR
ACCRUE	AGOING	ANGLED	ARMPIT
ACCUSE	AGOUTI	ANGLER	ARNICA
ACETIC	AGREED	ANGOLA	AROUND
ACHING	AIDING	ANGORA	AROUSE
ACIDIC	AILING	ANIMAL	ARRACK
ACK-ACK	AIMING	ANIMUS	ARRANT
ACQUIT	AIR-BED	ANKLET	ARREAR
ACROSS	AIR-GUN	ANNALS	ARREST
ACTING	AIRILY	ANNEAL	ARRIVE
ACTION	AIRING	ANNEXE	ARTERY
ACTIVE	AIRMAN	ANNUAL	ARTFUL
ACTUAL	AIR-SAC	ANOINT	ARTIST
ACUITY	AIRWAY	ANONYM	ASCEND
ACUMEN	AKIMBO	ANSWER	ASCENT
ADAGIO	ALARUM	ANTHEM	ASHAKE
ADDICT	ALBEIT	ANTHER	ASHLAR
ADDING	ALBERT	ANTLER	ASHORE
ADDLED	ALBINO	ANYHOW	ASH-PAN
ADDUCE	ALBION	ANYWAY	ASH-PIT
ADHERE	ALCOVE	APACHE	ASKANT
ADJOIN	ALIGHT	APATHY	ASKARI
ADJURE	ALKALI	APIARY	ASKING
ADJUST	ALLEGE	APIECE	ASLANT

ASLEEP	AWAKEN	BANYAN	BAYARD
ASPECT	AWEIGH	BANZAI	BAYEUX
ASPIRE	AWHEEL	BAOBAB	BAYING
ASSAIL	AWHILE	BARBED	BAZAAR
ASSENT	AWNING	BARBEL	BEACHY
ASSERT	AYE-AYE	BARBER	BEACON
ASSESS	AZALEA	BARDIC	BEADED
ASSIGN		BARELY	BEADLE
ASSIST	**B—6**	BAREST	BEAGLE
ASSIZE	BAAING	BARGED	BEAKER
ASSORT	BABBLE	BARGEE	BEAMED
ASSUME	BABOON	BARING	BEARER
ASSURE	BACKED	BARIUM	BEATEN
ASTERN	BACKER	BARKED	BEATER
ASTHMA	BADGER	BARKER	BEAUNE
ASTRAL	BAFFLE	BARKIS	BEAUTY
ASTRAY	BAGFUL	BARLEY	BEAVER
ASTUTE	BAGGED	BARMAN	BECALM
ASYLUM	BAGMAN	BARNEY	BECAME
ATHENE	BAGNIO	BARONY	BECKET
AT-HOME	BAILED	BARQUE	BECKON
ATKINS	BAILEY	BARRED	BECOME
ATOMIC	BAILIE	BARREL	BEDAUB
ATONED	BAITED	BARREN	BED-BUG
ATTACH	BAKERY	BARROW	BEDDED
ATTACK	BAKING	BARSAC	BEDDER
ATTAIN	BALAAM	BARTER	BEDECK
ATTEND	BALDER	BARTON	BEDLAM
ATTEST	BALDLY	BASALT	BEETLE
ATTIRE	BALEEN	BASELY	BEFALL
ATTUNE	BALING	BASHED	BEFORE
AUBURN	BALKAN	BASING	BEFOUL
AUGURY	BALKED	BASKED	BEGGAR
AUGUST	BALLAD	BASKET	BEGGED
AUNTIE	BALLET	BASQUE	BEGONE
AURIST	BALLOT	BASSET	BEHALF
AURORA	BALSAM	BASTED	BEHAVE
AUSSIE	BALTIC	BATEAU	BEHEAD
AUSTER	BAMBOO	BATHED	BEHELD
AUSTIN	BANANA	BATHER	BEHEST
AUTHOR	BANDED	BATHOS	BEHIND
AUTUMN	BANDIT	BATMAN	BEHOLD
AVAUNT	BANGED	BATTED	BELDAM
AVENGE	BANGLE	BATTEN	BELFRY
AVENUE	BANISH	BATTER	BELIAL
AVERSE	BANKED	BATTLE	BELIED
AVIARY	BANKER	BAUBLE	BELIEF
AVIDLY	BANNED	BAWBEE	BELLOW
AVOCET	BANNER	BAWLED	BELONG
AVOWAL	BANTAM	BAWLEY	BELTED
AVOWED	BANTER	BAXTER	BEMOAN

BEMUSE	BITING	BOOING	BREACH
BENDER	BITTEN	BOOKED	BREAST
BENGAL	BITTER	BOOKIE	BREATH
BENIGN	BLAMED	BOOMED	BREECH
BENNET	BLANCH	BOOTED	BREEKS
BENUMB	BLARED	BOOTEE	BREEZE
BENZOL	BLAZED	BO-PEEP	BREEZY
BERATE	BLEACH	BORAGE	BRETON
BERBER	BLEARY	BORDER	BREVET
BEREFT	BLENNY	BOREAS	BREWED
BERLIN	BLIGHT	BORING	BREWER
BERTHA	BLITHE	BORROW	BRIBED
BESIDE	BLONDE	BORZOI	BRIDAL
BESTED	BLOODY	BOSCHE	BRIDGE
BESTIR	BLOTCH	BOSSED	BRIDLE
BESTOW	BLOTTO	BOSTON	BRIGHT
BETAKE	BLOUSE	BOTANY	BRITON
BETHEL	BLOWED	BOTHER	BROACH
BETIDE	BLOWER	BOTHIE	BROADS
BETONY	BLOWZY	BOTTLE	BROGAN
BETRAY	BLUEST	BOTTOM	BROGUE
BETTED	BLUING	BOUFFE	BROKEN
BETTER	BLUISH	BOUGHT	BROKER
BETTOR	BOATER	BOUNCE	BROLLY
BEWAIL	BOBBED	BOUNTY	BRONCO
BEWARE	BOBBIN	BOURSE	BRONZE
BEYOND	BOBBLE	BOVINE	BROOCH
BIASED	BODEGA	BOWERY	BROODY
BIBBER	BODGER	BOWING	BROUGH
BICEPS	BODICE	BOWLED	BROWSE
BICKER	BODILY	BOWLER	BRUISE
BIDDER	BODING	BOWMAN	BRUTAL
BIDING	BODKIN	BOW-SAW	BRUTUS
BIFFED	BOFFIN	BOW-TIE	BRYONY
BIGAMY	BOGGLE	BOW-WOW	BUBBLE
BIG-END	BOG-OAK	BOXING	BUBBLY
BIGGER	BOILED	BOYISH	BUCKED
BIG-WIG	BOILER	BRACED	BUCKET
BIKING	BOLDER	BRACER	BUCKLE
BILKED	BOLDLY	BRAHMA	BUDDED
BILKER	BOLERO	BRAINY	BUDDHA
BILLED	BOLTED	BRAISE	BUDGET
BILLET	BOMBED	BRAKED	BUFFED
BILLIE	BON-BON	BRANCH	BUFFER
BILLOW	BONDED	BRANDY	BUFFET
BINDER	BONING	BRASSY	BUGLER
BIRDIE	BONNET	BRAVED	BULGAR
BISECT	BONNIE	BRAVER	BULGED
BISHOP	BONZER	BRAWNY	BULKED
BISLEY	BOODLE	BRAZED	BULLET
BISTRO	BOOHOO	BRAZEN	BUMPED

BUMPER	CABMAN	CANUCK	CAVERN
BUNDLE	CACHED	CANVAS	CAVIAR
BUNGED	CACHET	CANYON	CAVIES
BUNGLE	CACHOU	CAPFUL	CAVING
BUNION	CACKLE	CAPPED	CAVITY
BUNKED	CACTUS	CAPTOR	CAVORT
BUNKER	CADDIE	CARAFE	CAXTON
BUNKUM	CADDIS	CARBON	CAYMAN
BUNSEN	CADGED	CARBOY	CAYUSE
BUNTER	CADGER	CARDED	CEASED
BUOYED	CAESAR	CAREEN	CEDING
BURBLE	CAGING	CAREER	CELERY
BURDEN	CAHOOT	CARESS	CELLAR
BUREAU	CAIMAN	CARFAX	CELTIC
BURGEE	CAIQUE	CARIES	CEMENT
BURGLE	CAJOLE	CARMAN	CENSER
BURIAL	CAKING	CARMEN	CENSOR
BURIED	CALICO	CARNAL	CENSUS
BURMAN	CALIPH	CARNET	CENTRE
BURNED	CALLED	CARPED	CEREAL
BURNER	CALLER	CARPEL	CERISE
BURNET	CALLOW	CARPET	CHAFED
BURRED	CALMED	CARROT	CHAFER
BURROW	CALMLY	CARTED	CHAISE
BURSAR	CALVED	CARTEL	CHALET
BURTON	CAMBER	CARTER	CHALKY
BUSHEL	CAMERA	CARTON	CHANCE
BUSIED	CAMLET	CARVED	CHANCY
BUSILY	CAMPED	CARVER	CHANGE
BUSKER	CAMPER	CASHED	CHANTY
BUSMEN	CAMPUS	CASHEW	CHAPEL
BUSTED	CANAPE	CASING	CHAPPY
BUSTER	CANARD	CASINO	CHARGE
BUSTLE	CANARY	CASKET	CHARON
BUTANE	CANCAN	CASQUE	CHASED
BUTLER	CANCEL	CASSIA	CHASER
BUTTED	CANCER	CASTLE	CHASSE
BUTTER	CANDID	CASTOR	CHASTE
BUTTON	CANDLE	CASUAL	CHATTY
BUYING	CANINE	CATCHY	CHEEKY
BUZZED	CANING	CATGUT	CHEERY
BUZZER	CANKER	CATHAY	CHEESE
BYE-BYE	CANNED	CATKIN	CHEESY
BYGONE	CANNON	CATNIP	CHEQUE
BY-PASS	CANNOT	CATSUP	CHERRY
BY-PLAY	CANOPY	CATTLE	CHERUB
BY-ROAD	CANTAB	CAUCUS	CHESTY
BY-WORD	CANTED	CAUDAL	CHEVAL
	CANTER	CAUGHT	CHEWED
C—6	CANTON	CAUSED	CHILDE
CABLED	CANTOR	CAVEAT	CHILLI

CHILLY	CLICHE	COLDER	COQUET
CHIMED	CLIENT	COLDLY	CORBEL
CHINTZ	CLIMAX	COLLIE	CORDED
CHIPPY	CLINCH	COLLOP	CORDON
CHIRPY	CLINIC	COLONY	CORKED
CHISEL	CLIQUE	COLOUR	CORKER
CHITTY	CLOCHE	COLUMN	CORNEA
CHOICE	CLOSED	COMBAT	CORNED
CHOKED	CLOSER	COMBED	CORNER
CHOKER	CLOSET	COMBER	CORNET
CHOLER	CLOTHE	COMEDY	CORONA
CHOOSE	CLOUDY	COMELY	CORPSE
CHOOSY	CLOVEN	COMFIT	CORPUS
CHOPIN	CLOVER	COMING	CORRAL
CHOPPY	CLOYED	COMMIT	CORSET
CHORAL	CLUMSY	COMMON	CORTES
CHORUS	CLUTCH	COMPEL	COSHED
CHOSEN	COARSE	COMPLY	COSIER
CHOUGH	COATED	CONCHY	COSILY
CHROME	COATEE	CONCUR	COSINE
CHUBBY	COAXED	CONNED	COSMIC
CHUKKA	COAXER	CONDOR	COSMOS
CHUMMY	COBALT	CONFAB	COSSET
CHURCH	COBBLE	CONFER	COSTER
CICADA	COBNUT	CONGEE	COSTLY
CICELY	COBURG	CONGER	COTTAR
CICERO	COBWEB	CONKED	COTTER
CINDER	COCKED	CONKER	COTTON
CINEMA	COCKER	CONSUL	COUGAR
CINQUE	COCKLE	CONTRA	COUPLE
CIPHER	COCOON	CONVEX	COUPON
CIRCLE	CODDED	CONVEY	COURSE
CIRCUS	CODDLE	CONVOY	COUSIN
CIRRUS	CODGER	COOEED	COVERT
CITING	CODIFY	COOING	COWARD
CITRIC	CODING	COOKED	COW-BOY
CITRON	CODLIN	COOKER	COWING
CITRUS	COERCE	COOKIE	COWLED
CIVICS	COEVAL	COOLED	COW-MAN
CLAMMY	COFFEE	COOLER	COWRIE
CLARET	COFFER	COOLIE	COYOTE
CLASSY	COFFIN	COOLLY	CRABBY
CLAUSE	COGENT	COOPED	CRADLE
CLAWED	COGNAC	COOPER	CRAFTY
CLAYEY	CO-HEIR	COPECK	CRAGGY
CLEAVE	COHERE	COPIED	CRAMBO
CLENCH	COHORT	COPIER	CRANED
CLERGY	COILED	COPING	CRANKY
CLERIC	COINED	COPPED	CRANNY
CLEVER	COINER	COPPER	CRATED
CLEVIS	COKING	COPTIC	CRATER

CRAVAT	CURLEW	DARKER	DEFECT
CRAVED	CURSED	DARKLY	DEFEND
CRAVEN	CURTLY	DARNED	DEFIED
CRAYON	CURTSY	DARNEL	DEFILE
CRAZED	CURVED	DARNER	DEFINE
CREAMY	CUSTOM	DARTED	DEFORM
CREASE	CUTEST	DASHED	DEFRAY
CREATE	CUTLER	DATING	DEFTLY
CRECHE	CUTLET	DATIVE	DEGREE
CREDIT	CUT-OFF	DAUBED	DE-ICER
CREEPY	CUT-OUT	DAVITS	DEJECT
CREOLE	CUTTER	DAWDLE	DELETE
CRESTA	CUTTLE	DAWNED	DELUDE
CRETIN	CYCLED	DAY-BED	DELUGE
CREWEL	CYGNET	DAY-FLY	DELVED
CRIKEY	CYMBAL	DAZING	DEMAND
CRINGE	CYMRIC	DAZZLE	DEMEAN
CRISES	CYPHER	DEACON	DEMISE
CRISIS	CYPRUS	DEADEN	DEMODE
CRISPY		DEADLY	DEMURE
CRITIC	D—6	DEAFEN	DENIAL
CROCUS	DABBED	DEAFLY	DENIED
CROTCH	DABBLE	DEALER	DENIER
CROUCH	DACOIT	DEARER	DENOTE
CROWED	DAFTLY	DEARIE	DENSER
CRUDER	DAGGER	DEARLY	DENTAL
CRUISE	DAHLIA	DEARTH	DENTED
CRUMBY	DAINTY	DEBASE	DENUDE
CRUNCH	DAMAGE	DEBATE	DEODAR
CRUSTY	DAMASK	DEBRIS	DEPART
CRUTCH	DAMMED	DEBTOR	DEPEND
CRYING	DAMNED	DEBUNK	DEPICT
CUBISM	DAMPED	DECADE	DEPLOY
CUBIST	DAMPEN	DECAMP	DEPORT
CUCKOO	DAMPER	DECANT	DEPOSE
CUDDLE	DAMPLY	DECEIT	DEPUTE
CUDGEL	DAMSEL	DECENT	DEPUTY
CULLED	DAMSON	DECIDE	DERAIL
CUPFUL	DANCED	DECKED	DERATE
CUPOLA	DANCER	DECKLE	DERIDE
CUPPED	DANDER	DECODE	DERIVE
CUP-TIE	DANDLE	DECREE	DERMAL
CURACY	DANGER	DEDUCE	DERMIS
CURARE	DANGLE	DEDUCT	DESCRY
CURATE	DANIEL	DEEMED	DESERT
CURBED	DANISH	DEEPEN	DESIGN
CURDLE	DAPHNE	DEEPER	DESIRE
CURFEW	DAPPER	DEEPLY	DESIST
CURING	DAPPLE	DEFACE	DESPOT
CURLED	DARING	DEFAME	DETACH
CURLER	DARKEN	DEFEAT	DETAIL

DETAIN	DISBAR	DOTARD	DULLED
DETECT	DISBUD	DOTING	DULLER
DETEST	DISCUS	DOTTED	DUMBLY
DETOUR	DISHED	DOTTLE	DUMDUM
DETUNE	DISMAL	DOUANE	DUMPED
DEUCED	DISMAY	DOUBLE	DUNLIN
DEVICE	DISOWN	DOUCHE	DUNNED
DEVISE	DISPEL	DOUGHY	DUPING
DEVOID	DISTIL	DOURLY	DURBAR
DEVOTE	DISUSE	DOUSED	DURESS
DEVOUR	DITHER	DOWNED	DURHAM
DEVOUT	DIVERS	DOWSED	DURING
DEWLAP	DIVERT	DOWSER	DUSTER
DEXTER	DIVEST	DOYLEY	DUYKER
DIADEM	DIVIDE	DOZING	DYEING
DIAPER	DIVINE	DRACHM	DYNAMO
DIATOM	DIVING	DRAGON	DYNAST
DIBBED	DOBBIN	DRAPED	
DIBBER	DOCILE	DRAPER	E—6
DIBBLE	DOCKED	DRAWER	EAGLET
DICING	DOCKER	DREAMT	EAR-CAP
DICKER	DOCKET	DREAMY	EARFUL
DICKEY	DOCTOR	DREARY	EARNED
DICTUM	DODDER	DREDGE	EARTHY
DIDDLE	DODGED	DRENCH	EARWIG
DIESEL	DODGER	DRESSY	EASIER
DIETED	DOFFED	DRIEST	EASILY
DIFFER	DOGATE	DRIVEL	EASING
DIGEST	DOG-FOX	DRIVEN	EASTER
DIGGER	DOGGED	DRIVER	EATING
DIK-DIK	DOINGS	DRONED	EBBING
DIKING	DOLING	DROPSY	ECARTE
DILATE	DOLLAR	DROVER	ECHOED
DILUTE	DOLLED	DROWSY	ECLAIR
DIMITY	DOLLOP	DRUDGE	ECZEMA
DIMMED	DOLMEN	DRY-BOB	EDDIED
DIMMER	DOLOUR	DRY-FLY	EDGING
DIMPLE	DOMAIN	DRYING	EDIBLE
DIMPLY	DOMINO	DRYISH	EDITED
DINGHY	DONATE	DRY-ROT	EDITOR
DINGLE	DONJON	DUBBED	EDUCED
DINING	DONKEY	DUBBIN	EERILY
DINKUM	DOODLE	DUCKED	EFFACE
DINNED	DOOMED	DUENNA	EFFECT
DINNER	DOPING	DUFFEL	EFFETE
DIPOLE	DORCAS	DUFFER	EFFIGY
DIPPED	DORIAN	DUFFLE	EFFLUX
DIPPER	DORMER	DUGONG	EFFORT
DIRECT	DORSAL	DUGOUT	EGG-CUP
DIREST	DOSAGE	DUIKER	EGGING
DISARM	DOTAGE	DULCET	EGG-NOG

EGOISM	ENMESH	ETHNIC	FACILE
EGOIST	ENMITY	EUCHRE	FACING
EGRESS	ENNEAD	EUCLID	FACTOR
EIFFEL	ENOUGH	EULOGY	FADING
EIGHTH	ENRAGE	EUNUCH	FAERIE
EIGHTY	ENRICH	EUREKA	FAG-END
EITHER	ENROBE	EUSTON	FAGGED
ELAINE	ENSIGN	EVADED	FAGGOT
ELAPSE	ENSUED	EVENER	FAILED
ELATED	ENSURE	EVENLY	FAIRER
ELDEST	ENTAIL	EVILLY	FAIRLY
ELEVEN	ENTICE	EVINCE	FAKING
ELFISH	ENTIRE	EVOKED	FALCON
ELICIT	ENTITY	EVOLVE	FALLAL
ELIXIR	ENTOMB	EXCEED	FALLEN
ELOPED	ENTRAP	EXCEPT	FALLOW
ELUDED	ENTREE	EXCESS	FALSER
ELVISH	ENVIED	EXCISE	FALTER
ELYSEE	ENWRAP	EXCITE	FAMILY
EMBALM	ENZYME	EXCUSE	FAMINE
EMBARK	EOCENE	EXEMPT	FAMISH
EMBLEM	EOLITH	EXEUNT	FAMOUS
EMBODY	EQUATE	EXHALE	FANGED
EMBOSS	EQUINE	EXHORT	FANNED
EMBRYO	EQUITY	EXHUME	FAN-TAN
EMERGE	ERASED	EXILED	FARINA
EMETIC	ERASER	EXODUS	FARING
EMIGRE	EREBUS	EXOTIC	FARMED
EMPIRE	ERENOW	EXPAND	FARMER
EMPLOY	ERMINE	EXPECT	FARROW
ENABLE	ERODED	EXPEND	FASCIA
ENAMEL	EROTIC	EXPERT	FASTED
ENCAGE	ERRAND	EXPIRE	FASTEN
ENCAMP	ERRANT	EXPIRY	FASTER
ENCASE	ERRATA	EXPORT	FATHER
ENCASH	ERRING	EXPOSE	FATHOM
ENCORE	ERSATZ	EXTANT	FATTED
END-ALL	ESCAPE	EXTEND	FATTEN
ENDEAR	ESCHEW	EXTENT	FATTER
ENDING	ESCORT	EXTORT	FAUCET
ENDIVE	ESCUDO	EXUDED	FAULTY
ENDURE	ESKIMO	EYEING	FAVOUR
ENERGY	ESPIAL	EYELET	FAWNED
ENFOLD	ESPIED	EYELID	FEALTY
ENGAGE	ESPRIT		FEARED
ENGINE	ESSENE	**F—6**	FEDORA
ENGULF	ESTATE	FABIAN	FEEBLE
ENIGMA	ESTEEM	FABLED	FEEBLY
ENJOIN	ETCHED	FABRIC	FEEDER
ENLACE	ETCHER	FACADE	FEELER
ENLIST	ETHICS	FACIAL	FELINE

FELLAH	FINGER	FLOPPY	FORKED
FELLED	FINIAL	FLORAL	FORMAL
FELLER	FINING	FLORET	FORMAT
FELLOE	FINISH	FLORID	FORMED
FELLOW	FINITE	FLORIN	FORMER
FELONY	FINNAN	FLOSSY	FORMIC
FELTED	FINNED	FLOURY	FOSSIL
FEMALE	FIRING	FLOWER	FOSTER
FENCED	FIRKIN	FLUENT	FOUGHT
FENCER	FIRMED	FLUFFY	FOULED
FENDED	FIRMLY	FLUKED	FOULLY
FENDER	FISCAL	FLUNKY	FOURTH
FENIAN	FISHED	FLURRY	FOWLER
FENNEL	FISHER	FLUTED	FOXILY
FERRER	FISHES	FLUXED	FOXING
FERRET	FISTED	FLYING	FRACAS
FERVID	FISTIC	FLY-NET	FRAMED
FESCUE	FITFUL	FOALED	FRAPPE
FESTAL	FITTED	FOAMED	FRAYED
FESTER	FITTER	FOBBED	FREELY
FETISH	FIXING	FO'C'SLE	FREEZE
FETTER	FIXITY	FODDER	FRENCH
FETTLE	FIZZED	FOEMAN	FRENZY
FEUDAL	FIZZER	FOETID	FRESCO
FEWEST	FIZZLE	FOGGED	FRIARY
FIACRE	FLABBY	FOIBLE	FRIDAY
FIANCE	FLAGON	FOILED	FRIDGE
FIASCO	FLAKED	FOKKER	FRIEND
FIBBED	FLAMED	FOLDED	FRIEZE
FIBBER	FLANGE	FOLDER	FRIGHT
FIBULA	FLANKS	FOLLOW	FRIGID
FICKLE	FLARED	FOMENT	FRINGE
FIDDLE	FLASHY	FONDER	FRISKY
FIDGET	FLATLY	FONDLE	FROGGY
FIERCE	FLATTY	FONDLY	FROLIC
FIGARO	FLAUNT	FOOLED	FROSTY
FIGURE	FLAVIN	FOOTED	FROTHY
FILIAL	FLAXEN	FOOTER	FROWSY
FILING	FLAYED	FOOTLE	FROZEN
FILLED	FLEDGE	FOOZLE	FRUGAL
FILLER	FLEECE	FORAGE	FRUITY
FILLET	FLEECY	FORBID	FRUMPY
FILLIP	FLESHY	FORBYE	FUDDLE
FILMED	FLEXED	FORCED	FUDGED
FILTER	FLEXOR	FORDED	FULFIL
FILTHY	FLICKS	FOREGO	FULHAM
FINALE	FLIGHT	FOREST	FULLER
FINDER	FLIMSY	FORGED	FULMAR
FINELY	FLINCH	FORGER	FUMBLE
FINERY	FLINTY	FORGET	FUNDED
FINEST	FLITCH	FORGOT	FUNGUS

FUNKED	GARCON	GIFTED	GOLFER
FUNNEL	GARDEN	GIGGLE	GONGED
FURIES	GARGLE	GIGOLO	GOODLY
FURLED	GARISH	GILDED	GOOGLY
FURORE	GARLIC	GILDER	GOPHER
FURROW	GARNER	GILLIE	GORGED
FUSING	GARNET	GILPIN	GORGET
FUSION	GARRET	GIMBAL	GORGIO
FUSSED	GARTER	GIMLET	GORGON
FUTILE	GAS-BAG	GINGER	GORING
FUTURE	GASCON	GIRDED	GOSHEN
	GASHED	GIRDER	GOSPEL
G—6	GASKET	GIRDLE	GOSSIP
GABBLE	GAS-MAN	GITANA	GOTHIC
GABLED	GASPED	GIVING	GOUGED
GADDED	GASPER	GLADLY	GOVERN
GADFLY	GASSED	GLANCE	GOWNED
GADGET	GATEAU	GLARED	GRACED
GAELIC	GATHER	GLASSY	GRACES
GAFFED	GATING	GLAZED	GRADED
GAFFER	GAUCHE	GLAZER	GRAINS
GAGGED	GAUCHO	GLIBLY	GRAMME
GAGGLE	GAUGED	GLIDED	GRANGE
GAIETY	GAYEST	GLIDER	GRANNY
GAINED	GAZEBO	GLOBAL	GRASSY
GAITER	GAZING	GLOOMY	GRATER
GALAXY	GEARED	GLORIA	GRATIS
GALLEY	GEEZER	GLOSSY	GRAVEL
GALLIC	GEIGER	GLOVED	GRAVEN
GALLON	GEISHA	GLOVER	GRAVER
GALLOP	GEMINI	GLOWED	GRAVES
GALLUP	GENDER	GLOWER	GRAZED
GALOOT	GENERA	GLUING	GREASE
GALORE	GENEVA	GLUMLY	GREASY
GALOSH	GENIAL	GNAWED	GREATS
GAMBIT	GENIUS	GNOMON	GREECE
GAMBLE	GENTLE	GOADED	GREEDY
GAMBOL	GENTLY	GOATEE	GREENS
GAMELY	GENTRY	GO-BANG	GRETNA
GAMING	GEORGE	GOBBET	GRIEVE
GAMMER	GERMAN	GOBBLE	GRILLE
GAMMON	GERUND	GOBLET	GRILSE
GANDER	GEW-GAW	GOBLIN	GRIMED
GANGER	GEYSER	GO-CART	GRIMLY
GANNET	GHARRY	GO-DOWN	GRINGO
GANTRY	GHETTO	GODSON	GRIPED
GAOLED	GIBBER	GODWIT	GRIPPE
GAOLER	GIBBET	GOFFER	GRISLY
GAPING	GIBBON	GOGGLE	GRITTY
GARAGE	GIBING	GOITRE	GROATS
GARBLE	GIBLET	GOLDEN	GROCER

GROGGY	HALLOO	HEADER	HICCUP
GROOVE	HALLOW	HEALED	HIDDEN
GROPED	HALOED	HEALER	HIDING
GROTTO	HALTED	HEALTH	HIEING
GROUND	HALTER	HEAPED	HIGHER
GROUSE	HALVED	HEARER	HIGHLY
GROVEL	HAMLET	HEARSE	HIKING
GROWER	HAMMAM	HEARTH	HILARY
GROWTH	HAMMER	HEARTY	HINDER
GROYNE	HAMPER	HEATED	HINDOO
GRUBBY	HANDED	HEATER	HINGED
GRUDGE	HANDLE	HEAVED	HINTED
GRUMPY	HANGAR	HEAVEN	HIPPED
GRUNDY	HANGED	HEBREW	HIRING
GUFFAW	HANKER	HECATE	HISSED
GUIDED	HANSEL	HECKLE	HITHER
GUIDER	HANSOM	HECTIC	HITTER
GUIDON	HAPPEN	HECTOR	HOARSE
GUILTY	HARASS	HEDGED	HOAXED
GUINEA	HARDEN	HEEDED	HOAXER
GUITAR	HARDER	HEE-HAW	HOBBLE
GULLED	HARDLY	HEELED	HOBNOB
GULLET	HARD-UP	HEIFER	HOCKEY
GULLEY	HARING	HEIGHT	HOEING
GULPED	HARKED	HELIUM	HOGGET
GUMMED	HARKEN	HELMET	HOLDER
GUN-MAN	HARLOT	HELPED	HOLD-UP
GUN-MEN	HARMED	HELPER	HOLIER
GUNNEL	HARPED	HEMMED	HOLILY
GUNNER	HARRIS	HEMPEN	HOLLOW
GUN-SHY	HARROW	HERALD	HOMAGE
GURGLE	HASTEN	HERBAL	HOMELY
GURKHA	HAT-BOX	HERDED	HOMILY
GURNET	HATING	HEREAT	HOMING
GUSHED	HAT-PEG	HEREBY	HONEST
GUSHER	HAT-PIN	HEREIN	HONING
GUSSET	HATRED	HEREOF	HONKED
GUTTED	HATTED	HEREON	HONOUR
GUTTER	HATTER	HERESY	HOODED
GUZZLE	HAULED	HERETO	HOODIE
GYBING	HAUNCH	HERMES	HOODOO
GYPSUM	HAVANA	HERMIT	HOOFED
GYRATE	HAVING	HERNIA	HOOKAH
	HAWHAW	HEROIC	HOOKED
H—6	HAWKED	HEROIN	HOOKER
HACKED	HAWKER	HERPES	HOOPED
HACKLE	HAWSER	HERREN	HOOPER
HAGGIS	HAY-BOX	HETMAN	HOOP-LA
HAGGLE	HAZARD	HEWING	HOOPOE
HAILED	HAZILY	HEYDAY	HOOTED
HALLOA	HEADED	HIATUS	HOOTER

HOPING	**I—6**	INDUCT	INWARD
HOPPED	IAMBIC	INFAMY	IODINE
HOPPER	IAMBUS	INFANT	IONIAN
HORNED	IBERIA	INFECT	IRKING
HORNER	IBIDEM	INFEST	IRONED
HORNET	ICARUS	INFIRM	IRONER
HORRID	ICE-AGE	INFLOW	IRONIC
HORROR	ICE-AXE	INFLUX	ISABEL
HOSIER	ICE-CAP	INFORM	ISLAND
HOSTEL	ICE-MAN	INFUSE	ISOBAR
HOT-BED	ICE-SAW	INHALE	ISRAEL
HOT-DOG	ICICLE	INHERE	ISSUED
HOT-POT	ICIEST	INJECT	ISSUER
HOTTER	IDIOCY	INJURE	ITALIC
HOURLY	IDLING	INJURY	ITCHED
HOUSED	IGNITE	INK-BAG	ITSELF
HOWDAH	IGNORE	INKING	
HOWLED	IGUANA	INK-POT	**J—6**
HOWLER	ILLUME	INK-SAC	JABBED
HOYDEN	IMBIBE	INLAID	JABBER
HUBBUB	IMBUED	INLAND	JACKAL
HUDDLE	IMMUNE	INMATE	JACKED
HUFFED	IMMURE	INMOST	JACKET
HUGELY	IMPACT	INNATE	JAGGED
HUMANE	IMPAIR	INROAD	JAGUAR
HUMBLE	IMPALA	INRUSH	JAILED
HUMBLY	IMPALE	INSANE	JAILER
HUMBUG	IMPART	INSECT	JAMMED
HUMMED	IMPEDE	INSERT	JANGLE
HUMOUR	IMPEND	INSIDE	JARGON
HUMPED	IMPISH	INSIST	JARRED
HUNGER	IMPORT	INSOLE	JASPER
HUNGRY	IMPOSE	INSPAN	JAUNTY
HUNTED	IMPOST	INSTAL	JAWING
HUNTER	IMPUGN	INSTEP	JAZZED
HURDLE	IMPURE	INSTIL	JEERED
HURLED	IMPUTE	INSULT	JENNET
HURRAH	INBORN	INSURE	JERBOA
HURTLE	INBRED	INTACT	JERKED
HUSHED	INCHED	INTAKE	JERKIN
HUSKED	INCISE	INTEND	JERSEY
HUSSAR	INCITE	INTENT	JESTED
HUSSIF	INCOME	INTERN	JESTER
HUSTLE	INDEED	INTONE	JESUIT
HUTTED	INDENT	INURED	JETSAM
HYBRID	INDIAN	INVADE	JEWESS
HYMNAL	INDICT	INVENT	JEWISH
HYPHEN	INDIGO	INVERT	JIBBED
HYSSOP	INDITE	INVEST	JIGGED
	INDOOR	INVITE	JIGGLE
	INDUCE	INVOKE	JIG-SAW

JILTED	KENNEL	LACTIC	LAXITY
JINGLE	KERNEL	LADDER	LAYING
JOBBER	KERSEY	LADDIE	LAYMAN
JOB-LOT	KETTLE	LADING	LAY-OUT
JOCKEY	KEY-MEN	LADLED	LAZIER
JOCOSE	KIBOSH	LAGGED	LAZILY
JOCUND	KICKED	LAGOON	LAZING
JOGGED	KICKER	LAID-UP	LAZULI
JOHNNY	KIDDED	LAMBED	LEADED
JOINED	KIDDER	LAMELY	LEADEN
JOINER	KIDNAP	LAMENT	LEADER
JOKING	KIDNEY	LAMINA	LEAD-IN
JOLTED	KILLED	LAMING	LEAFED
JORDAN	KILLER	LAMMAS	LEAGUE
JOSEPH	KILTED	LAMMED	LEAKED
JOSSER	KILTIE	LANCED	LEANED
JOSTLE	KIMONO	LANCER	LEANER
JOTTED	KINDER	LANCET	LEAN-TO
JOVIAL	KINDLE	LANDAU	LEAPED
JOYFUL	KINDLY	LANDED	LEASED
JOYOUS	KINEMA	LAPDOG	LEAVEN
JUDAIC	KINGLY	LAPFUL	LEAVER
JUDGED	KINKED	LAPPED	LEDGER
JUGFUL	KIPPER	LAPSED	LEERED
JUGGED	KIRSCH	LARDED	LEEWAY
JUGGLE	KIRTLE	LARDER	LEGACY
JUJUBE	KISMET	LARGER	LEGATE
JULIAN	KISSED	LARIAT	LEGATO
JUMBLE	KISSER	LARRUP	LEG-BYE
JUMPED	KIT-BAG	LARVAE	LEGEND
JUMPER	KITTEN	LARVAL	LEGGED
JUNGLE	KLAXON	LARYNX	LEGION
JUNIOR	KNIFED	LASCAR	LEGIST
JUNIUS	KNIGHT	LASHED	LEGUME
JUNKER	KNOBBY	LASSIE	LENDER
JUNKET	KNOTTY	LASTED	LENGTH
JURIST	KOODOO	LASTLY	LENTEN
JUSTER	KOREAN	LATEEN	LENTIL
JUSTLY	KOSHER	LATELY	LESION
JUTTED	KOW-TOW	LATENT	LESSEE
	KULTUR	LATEST	LESSEN
	KUMMEL	LATHER	LESSER
K—6		LATTER	LESSON
KAFFIR		LAUDED	LESSOR
KAISER		LAUDER	LETHAL
KANAKA	L—6	LAUNCH	LET-OFF
KAOLIN	LAAGER	LAUREL	LETTER
KEELED	LABIAL	LAVING	LEVANT
KEENED	LABOUR	LAVISH	LEVITE
KEENER	LACING	LAWFUL	LEVITY
KEENLY	LACKED	LAWYER	LEWDLY
KEEPER	LACKEY		

LEYDEN	LOAFED	LUGGER	MANFUL
LIABLE	LOAFER	LULLED	MANGER
LIAISE	LOANED	LUMBAR	MANGLE
LIBYAN	LOATHE	LUMBER	MANIAC
LICHEN	LOBATE	LUMPED	MANIOC
LICKED	LOBBED	LUNACY	MANNED
LIDDED	LOCALE	LUNATE	MANNER
LIEDER	LOCATE	LUNGED	MANTEL
LIFTED	LOCKED	LUPINE	MANTIS
LIFTER	LOCKER	LURING	MANTLE
LIGNUM	LOCKET	LURKED	MANTUA
LIKELY	LOCK-UP	LUSTED	MANUAL
LIKING	LOCUST	LUSTRE	MANURE
LIMBED	LODGED	LUTINE	MAPPED
LIMBER	LODGER	LUXURY	MAQUIS
LIMING	LOFTED	LYCEUM	MARAUD
LIMPED	LOGGED		MARBLE
LIMPET	LOGGIA	M—6	MARBLY
LIMPID	LOG-HUT	MACRON	MARCEL
LINAGE	LOGMAN	MADCAP	MARGIN
LINDEN	LOITER	MADDEN	MARIAN
LINEAL	LOLLED	MADDER	MARINE
LINEAR	LOLLOP	MADMAN	MARKED
LINE-UP	LONELY	MADRAS	MARKER
LINGER	LONGER	MAENAD	MARKET
LINING	LOOFAH	MAGGOT	MARMOT
LINKED	LOOKED	MAGNET	MAROON
LINNET	LOOKER	MAGNUM	MARQUE
LINTEL	LOOMED	MAGPIE	MARRED
LIONEL	LOOPED	MAGYAR	MARRON
LIPPED	LOOPER	MAHOUT	MARROW
LIQUID	LOOSEN	MAIDEN	MARSHY
LIQUOR	LOOTED	MAIGRE	MARTEN
LISBON	LOOTER	MAILED	MARTIN
LISPED	LOPING	MAIMED	MARTYR
LISSOM	LOPPED	MAINLY	MARVEL
LISTED	LORDED	MAKE-UP	MASCOT
LISTEN	LORDLY	MAKING	MASHED
LISTER	LOSING	MALADY	MASHER
LITANY	LOTION	MALAGA	MASHIE
LITCHI	LOUDER	MALICE	MASKED
LITMUS	LOUDLY	MALIGN	MASKER
LITTER	LOUNGE	MALLET	MASQUE
LITTLE	LOUVRE	MALLOW	MASSED
LIVELY	LOVELY	MALTED	MASSIF
LIVERY	LOVING	MAMMAL	MASTED
LIVING	LOWEST	MAMMON	MASTER
LIZARD	LOWING	MANAGE	MASTIC
LLOYD'S	LUBBER	MANANA	MATING
LOADED	LUFFED	MANCHU	MATINS
LOADER	LUGGED	MANEGE	MATRIX

MATRON	MERLIN	MINOAN	MONODY
MATTED	MERMAN	MINTED	MOOING
MATTER	MESHED	MINUET	MOONED
MATURE	MESSED	MINUTE	MOONER
MAULED	METEOR	MIRAGE	MOOTED
MAUNDY	METHOD	MIRING	MOOTER
MAUSER	METHYL	MIRROR	MOPING
MAY-BUG	METIER	MISCUE	MOPISH
MAY-DAY	METING	MISERE	MOPPED
MAY-FLY	METRIC	MISERY	MOPPET
MAYHAP	METTLE	MISFIT	MORALE
MAYHEM	MEWING	MISHAP	MORASS
MEADOW	MIASMA	MISLAY	MORBID
MEAGRE	MICKLE	MISLED	MORGUE
MEALIE	MICRON	MISSAL	MORMON
MEANLY	MID-AIR	MISSED	MOROSE
MEASLY	MIDDAY	MISSEL	MORRIS
MEDDLE	MIDDEN	MISSIS	MORROW
MEDIAL	MIDDLE	MISTER	MORSEL
MEDIAN	MIDGET	MISUSE	MORTAL
MEDICO	MID-OFF	MITRAL	MORTAR
MEDIUM	MID-RIB	MITRED	MOSAIC
MEDLAR	MIDWAY	MITTEN	MOSLEM
MEDLEY	MIGHTY	MIXING	MOSQUE
MEDUSA	MIGNON	MIZZEN	MOSTLY
MEEKER	MIKADO	MOANED	MOTHER
MEEKLY	MILADY	MOATED	MOTION
MEETLY	MILDEN	MOBBED	MOTIVE
MEGILP	MILDER	MOBCAP	MOTLEY
MEGOHM	MILDEW	MOBILE	MOTTLE
MEGRIM	MILDLY	MOB-LAW	MOULDY
MELLOW	MILIEU	MOCKED	MOUNTY
MELODY	MILKED	MOCKER	MOUSER
MELTED	MILKEN	MODENA	MOUSSE
MELTER	MILKER	MODERN	MOUTHY
MELTON	MILLED	MODEST	MOVIES
MEMBER	MILLER	MODIFY	MOVING
MEMOIR	MILLET	MODISH	MOWING
MEMORY	MILORD	MODULE	MUCKED
MENACE	MIMING	MOHAIR	MUCKER
MENAGE	MIMOSA	MOHAWK	MUCKLE
MENDED	MINCED	MOIETY	MUCOUS
MENDER	MINCER	MOLOCH	MUDDLE
MENIAL	MINDED	MOLEST	MUD-PIE
MENTAL	MINDER	MOLTEN	MUFFED
MENTOR	MINGLE	MOMENT	MUFFIN
MERCER	MINIFY	MONDAY	MUFFLE
MERELY	MINING	MONGOL	MUGGED
MERGED	MINION	MONIED	MULISH
MERGER	MINNIE	MONIES	MULLED
MERINO	MINNOW	MONKEY	MULLET

MUMBLE	NEARER	NODDLE	OARAGE
MUMMER	NEARLY	NODOSE	OARING
MURDER	NEATLY	NODULE	OBELUS
MURMUR	NEBULA	NOGGIN	OBERON
MURPHY	NECKED	NONAGE	OBEYED
MUSCAT	NECTAR	NONARY	OBEYER
MUSCLE	NEED-BE	NON-COM	OBITER
MUSEUM	NEEDED	NON-EGO	OBJECT
MUSING	NEEDER	NOODLE	OBLATE
MUSKET	NEEDLE	NOOSED	OBLIGE
MUSLIM	NEEDLY	NORDIC	OBLONG
MUSLIN	NEGATE	NORMAL	OBOIST
MUSSED	NEPHEW	NORMAN	OBSESS
MUSSEL	NEREID	NORROY	OBTAIN
MUSTER	NERVED	NO-SIDE	OBTUSE
MUTATE	NESTED	NOSING	OBVERT
MUTELY	NESTLE	NOTARY	OCCULT
MUTING	NESTOR	NOTICE	OCCUPY
MUTINY	NETHER	NOTIFY	OCELOT
MUTISM	NETTED	NOTING	O'CLOCK
MUTTER	NETTLE	NOTION	OCTANE
MUTTON	NEUTER	NOUGAT	OCTANT
MUTUAL	NEWISH	NOUGHT	OCTAVE
MUZZLE	NIBBED	NOVENA	OCTAVO
MYOPIA	NIBBLE	NOVICE	OCULAR
MYOPIC	NICELY	NOWAYS	ODDITY
MYRIAD	NICENE	NOWISE	ODIOUS
MYRTLE	NICEST	NOZZLE	OEDEMA
MYSELF	NICETY	NUANCE	OFFEND
MYSTIC	NICHED	NUBIAN	OFFICE
	NICKED	NUBILE	OFFING
N—6	NICKEL	NUCLEI	OFFISH
NAGGED	NICKER	NUDELY	OFFSET
NAGGER	NIGGER	NUDGED	OGLING
NAILED	NIGGLE	NUDISM	OGRESS
NAILER	NIMBLE	NUDIST	OIL-CAN
NAMELY	NIMBLY	NUDITY	OIL-GAS
NAMING	NIMBUS	NUGGET	OILING
NAPERY	NIMROD	NUMBED	OIL-MAN
NAPKIN	NINETY	NUMBER	OIL-NUT
NAPPED	NIPPED	NUNCIO	OLDEST
NARROW	NIPPER	NURSED	OLDISH
NATANT	NIPPLE	NURSER	OLIVER
NATION	NITRIC	NUTANT	OLIVET
NATIVE	NITWIT	NUTMEG	OMELET
NATTER	NO-BALL	NUT-OIL	OMENED
NATURE	NOBBLE	NUTRIA	OMNIUM
NAUGHT	NOBLER	NUZZLE	ONAGER
NAUSEA	NOBODY		ONCOST
NEAPED	NODDED	**O—6**	ONE-MAN
NEARBY	NODDER	OAFISH	ONE-WAY

ONFLOW	OUTFIT	PALTRY	PATCHY
ONIONY	OUTFLY	PAMPAS	PATENT
ONRUSH	OUTING	PAMPER	PATHIC
ONWARD	OUTLAW	PANADA	PATHOS
OODLES	OUTLAY	PANAMA	PATINA
OOLITE	OUTLET	PANDER	PATOIS
OOZING	OUTPUT	PANDIT	PATROL
OPAQUE	OUTRUN	PANFUL	PATRON
OPENED	OUTSET	PANNED	PATTED
OPENER	OUTWIT	PANTED	PATTEN
OPENLY	OVALLY	PANTER	PATTER
OPIATE	OVERDO	PANTRY	PAUNCH
OPINED	OWLERY	PANZER	PAUPER
OPPOSE	OWLISH	PAPACY	PAUSED
OPPUGN	OWNING	PAPERY	PAUSER
OPTICS	OXALIC	PAPISH	PAVAGE
OPTIME	OX-EYED	PAPISM	PAVANE
OPTING	OXFORD	PAPIST	PAVING
OPTION	OXLIKE	PAPUAN	PAWING
ORACLE	OXTAIL	PARADE	PAWNED
ORALLY	OXYGEN	PARCEL	PAWNEE
ORANGE	OYSTER	PARDON	PAWNER
ORATED		PAREIL	PAWPAW
ORATOR	P—6	PARENT	PAY-DAY
ORCHID	PACIFY	PARGET	PAYING
ORDAIN	PACING	PARIAH	PAY-OFF
ORDEAL	PACKED	PARING	PEACHY
ORDURE	PACKER	PARISH	PEAHEN
ORGASM	PACKET	PARITY	PEAKED
ORGIES	PADDED	PARKED	PEALED
ORIENT	PADDER	PARKER	PEA-NUT
ORIGAN	PADDLE	PARKIN	PEA-POD
ORIGIN	PADUAN	PARLEY	PEARLY
ORIOLE	PAGING	PARODY	PEBBLE
ORISON	PAGODA	PAROLE	PEBBLY
ORMULU	PAINED	PARROT	PECKED
ORNATE	PAIRED	PARSED	PECKER
ORPHAN	PALACE	PARSEE	PECTEN
ORPHIC	PALATE	PARSON	PECTIC
OSIRIS	PALELY	PARTED	PECTIN
OSMIUM	PALING	PARTER	PEDANT
OSPREY	PALISH	PARTLY	PEDATE
OSSIFY	PALLAS	PASSED	PEDDLE
OSTEND	PALLED	PASSEE	PEDLAR
OSTLER	PALLET	PASSER	PEELED
OTIOSE	PALLID	PASSIM	PEELER
OUSTED	PALLOR	PASTED	PEEPED
OUSTER	PALMAR	PASTEL	PEEPER
OUTBID	PALMED	PASTIL	PEERER
OUTCRY	PALMER	PASTOR	PEEVED
OUTDID	PALTER	PASTRY	PEEWIT

PEGGED	PICKLE	PLACER	POISON
PEG-LEG	PICK-UP	PLACET	POKING
PEG-TOP	PICNIC	PLACID	POLICE
PELLET	PICRIC	PLAGUE	POLICY
PELMET	PIDGIN	PLAGUY	POLING
PELOTA	PIECED	PLAICE	POLISH
PELVIC	PIECER	PLAINT	POLITE
PELVIS	PIEDOG	PLANED	POLITY
PENCIL	PIEMAN	PLANER	POLLED
PENMAN	PIERCE	PLANET	POLLEN
PENNED	PIFFLE	PLAQUE	POLLUX
PENNON	PIGEON	PLASHY	POLONY
PENTAD	PIGNUT	PLASMA	POMACE
PENT-UP	PIG-STY	PLATAN	POMADE
PENULT	PILAFF	PLATED	POMMEL
PENURY	PILFER	PLATEN	POMONA
PEOPLE	PILING	PLATER	POM-POM
PEPPER	PILLAR	PLAYED	POMPON
PEPSIN	PILLAU	PLAYER	PONDER
PEPTIC	PILLED	PLEACH	POODLE
PERIOD	PILLOW	PLEASE	POOLED
PERISH	PILULE	PLEDGE	POOPED
PERKED	PIMPLE	PLEIAD	POORER
PERMIT	PIMPLY	PLENTY	POORLY
PERSON	PINDAR	PLENUM	POPERY
PERTLY	PINEAL	PLEURA	POPGUN
PERUKE	PINGED	PLEXUS	POPISH
PERUSE	PINING	PLIANT	POPLAR
PESETA	PINION	PLIERS	POPLIN
PESTER	PINKED	PLIGHT	POPPED
PESTLE	PINNED	PLINTH	POPPER
PETARD	PINNER	PLOUGH	POPPET
PETITE	PIPING	PLOVER	PORING
PETREL	PIPKIN	PLUCKY	PORKER
PETROL	PIPPED	PLUG-IN	PORKET
PETTED	PIPPIN	PLUMED	POROUS
PEWTER	PIQUED	PLUMPY	PORTAL
PHAROS	PIQUET	PLUNGE	PORTER
PHENOL	PIRACY	PLURAL	PORTLY
PHLEGM	PIRATE	PLUSHY	POSEUR
PHOBIA	PISCES	PLYERS	POSING
PHOEBE	PISTIL	PLYING	POSSET
PHONED	PISTOL	POCKED	POSSUM
PHONEY	PISTON	POCKET	POSTAL
PHONIC	PITCHY	PODDED	POSTED
PHRASE	PITIED	PODIUM	POSTER
PHYSIC	PITIER	POETIC	POTASH
PIAZZA	PITMAN	POETRY	POTATO
PICKED	PITSAW	POGROM	POTBOY
PICKER	PITTED	POISED	POTEEN
PICKET	PLACED	POISER	POTENT

POTHER	PROPEL	PURITY	RABBLE
POTION	PROPER	PURLED	RABIES
POT-LID	PROSED	PURLER	RACIAL
POTMAN	PROSER	PURPLE	RACILY
POTTED	PROSIT	PURRED	RACING
POTTER	PROTON	PURSED	RACKED
POUDRE	PROVED	PURSER	RACKER
POUFFE	PROVEN	PURSUE	RACKET
POUNCE	PROVER	PURVEY	RACOON
POURED	PRUNED	PUSHED	RADIAL
POURER	PRYING	PUSHER	RADIAN
POUTED	PSEUDO	PUTRID	RADISH
POUTER	PSYCHE	PUTSCH	RADIUM
POWDER	PUBLIC	PUTTED	RADIUS
POW-POW	PUCKER	PUTTEE	RAFFIA
PRAISE	PUDDLE	PUTTER	RAFFLE
PRANCE	PUFFED	PUZZLE	RAFTER
PRATED	PUFFIN	PYEDOG	RAGGED
PRATER	PUG-DOG	PYEMIA	RAGING
PRAYED	PUISNE	PYEMIC	RAGLAN
PRAYER	PUKKHA	PYOSIS	RAGMAN
PREACH	PULING	PYRENE	RAGOUT
PRECIS	PULLED	PYRITE	RAG-TAG
PREFAB	PULLER	PYTHON	RAIDED
PREFER	PULLET		RAIDER
PREFIX	PULLEY	**Q—6**	RAILED
PREPAY	PULPED	QUAGGA	RAILER
PRESTO	PULPIT	QUAGGY	RAINED
PRETOR	PULQUE	QUAINT	RAISED
PRETTY	PULSED	QUAKED	RAISER
PRE-WAR	PUMICE	QUAKER	RAISIN
PREYED	PUMMEL	QUARRY	RAJPUT
PREYER	PUMPED	QUARTO	RAKERY
PRICED	PUMPER	QUARTZ	RAKING
PRIDED	PUNCHY	QUAVER	RAKISH
PRIEST	PUNDIT	QUAYED	RAMBLE
PRIMAL	PUNIER	QUEASY	RAMIFY
PRIMER	PUNISH	QUENCH	RAMMED
PRIMLY	PUNNET	QUEUED	RAMMER
PRIMUS	PUNTED	QUINCE	RAMPED
PRINCE	PUNTER	QUINSY	RAMROD
PRIORY	PUPPED	QUINZE	RANCHO
PRISED	PUPPET	QUIRED	RANCID
PRISMY	PURDAH	QUIRKY	RANDOM
PRISON	PURELY	QUIVER	RANGED
PRIVET	PUREST	QUORUM	RANGER
PRIZED	PURGED	QUOTED	RANKER
PROFIT	PURGER		RANKLE
PROLIX	PURIFY	**R—6**	RANKLY
PROMPT	PURISM	RABBIN	RANSOM
PRONTO	PURIST	RABBIT	RANTED

RANTER	REBURY	REGAIN	RENTES
RAPHIA	RECALL	REGALE	RE-OPEN
RAPIER	RECANT	REGARD	REPACK
RAPINE	RECAST	REGENT	REPAID
RAPING	RECEDE	REGILD	REPAIR
RAPPED	RECENT	REGIME	REPASS
RAPPER	RECESS	REGINA	REPAST
RAREFY	RECIPE	REGION	REPEAL
RARELY	RECITE	REGIUS	REPEAT
RAREST	RECKED	REGIVE	REPENT
RARITY	RECKON	REGLOW	REPINE
RASCAL	RECOAL	REGNAL	REPORT
RASHER	RECOCT	REGNUM	REPOSE
RASHLY	RECOIL	REGRET	REPPED
RASING	RECOIN	REHANG	REPUGN
RASPED	RECORD	REHASH	REPUTE
RASPER	RECOUP	REHEAR	REREAD
RASURE	RECTOR	REHEAT	RESAIL
RATHER	RECUSE	REINED	RESALE
RATIFY	REDACT	REJECT	RESCUE
RATING	REDCAP	REJOIN	RESEAT
RATION	REDDEN	RELAID	RESECT
RATTAN	REDEEM	RELATE	RESELL
RAT-TAT	RED-EYE	RELENT	RESEND
RATTED	RED-GUM	RELICT	RESENT
RATTER	RED-HOT	RELIED	RESHIP
RATTLE	RED-OAK	RELIEF	RESIDE
RAVAGE	REDRAW	RELIER	RESIGN
RAVINE	REDUCE	RELISH	RESINY
RAVING	REDUIT	RELIVE	RESIST
RAVISH	RE-DYED	RELOAD	RESOLD
RAWISH	RE-ECHO	RELUME	RESORB
RAZING	REEDED	REMADE	RESORT
READER	REEFED	REMAIN	RESOWN
REALLY	REEFER	REMAKE	RESTED
REALTY	REEKED	REMAND	RESULT
REAMED	REELED	REMARK	RESUME
REAMER	REELER	REMAST	RETAIL
REAPED	REFILL	REMEDY	RETAIN
REAPER	REFINE	REMIND	RETAKE
REARED	REFLEX	REMISE	RETARD
REARER	REFLOW	REMISS	RETINA
REASON	REFLUX	REMOTE	RETIRE
REAVOW	REFOLD	REMOVE	RETOLD
REBATE	REFOOT	RENAME	RETOOK
REBECK	REFORM	RENDER	RETORT
REBIND	REFUEL	RENNET	RETOSS
REBOIL	REFUGE	RENOWN	RETRIM
REBORN	REFUND	RENTAL	RETYRE
REBUFF	REFUSE	RENTED	REUTER
REBUKE	REFUTE	RENTER	REVAMP

REVEAL	RIPEST	ROSIER	RUSHER
REVERE	RIPPED	ROSILY	RUSSET
REVERS	RIPPER	ROSINY	RUSSIA
REVERT	RIPPLE	ROSTER	RUSTED
REVIEW	RIPPLY	ROTARY	RUSTIC
REVILE	RIPSAW	ROTATE	RUSTLE
REVIVE	RISING	ROT-GUT	RUTTED
REVOKE	RISKED	ROTTED	
REVOLT	RISKER	ROTTEN	S—6
REVVED	RISQUE	ROTTER	SABLED
REWARD	RITUAL	ROTUND	SACHET
REWOOD	RIVAGE	ROUBLE	SACKED
REWORD	RIVING	ROUGED	SACKER
RHESUS	ROAMED	ROUMAN	SACRED
RHEUMY	ROAMER	ROUSED	SADDEN
RHYMED	ROARED	ROUSER	SADDLE
RHYMER	ROARER	ROUTED	SADISM
RHYTHM	ROBBED	ROUTER	SAFARI
RIALTO	ROBBER	ROVING	SAFELY
RIBALD	ROBING	ROWING	SAFEST
RIBAND	ROBUST	RUBATO	SAFETY
RIBBED	ROCKED	RUBBED	SAGELY
RIBBON	ROCKER	RUBBER	SAGEST
RICHER	ROCKET	RUBBLE	SAGGED
RICHES	ROCOCO	RUBBLY	SAHARA
RICHLY	RODENT	RUBIED	SAILED
RICKED	ROILED	RUBRIC	SAILER
RIDDEN	ROLAND	RUCKLE	SAILOR
RIDDLE	ROLLED	RUDDER	SALAAM
RIDGED	ROLLER	RUDELY	SALAME
RIDING	ROMAIC	RUDEST	SALARY
RIFFLE	ROMANY	RUEFUL	SALINE
RIFLED	ROMIST	RUFFED	SALIVA
RIFLER	ROMPED	RUFFLE	SALLOW
RIFTED	ROMPER	RUFOUS	SALMON
RIGGED	RONDEL	RUGATE	SALOON
RIGGER	ROOFED	RUGGED	SALTED
RIGOUR	ROOFER	RUGGER	SALTER
RIG-OUT	ROOKED	RUGOSE	SALTLY
RILING	ROOKER	RUINED	SALUKI
RILLED	ROOKIE	RUINER	SALUTE
RILLET	ROOMED	RULING	SALVED
RIMMED	ROOMER	RUMBLE	SALVER
RIMMER	ROOTED	RUMOUR	SALVIA
RINDED	ROOTER	RUMPLE	SAMELY
RINGER	ROOTLE	RUMPUS	SAMIAN
RINSED	ROPERY	RUNLET	SAMITE
RINSER	ROPING	RUNNEL	SAMLET
RIOTED	ROSARY	RUNNER	SAMOAN
RIOTER	ROSERY	RUNWAY	SAMPAN
RIPELY	ROSIED	RUSHED	SAMPLE

SANCHO	SCORER	SEEING	SEWING
SANDAL	SCOTCH	SEEKER	SEXTAN
SANDED	SCOTIA	SEEMED	SEXTET
SANELY	SCRAPE	SEEMER	SEXTON
SANEST	SCRAWL	SEEMLY	SEXUAL
SANIFY	SCREAM	SEEPED	SHABBY
SANITY	SCREED	SEE-SAW	SHADED
SAPPED	SCREEN	SEETHE	SHADOW
SAPPER	SCREWY	SEISED	SHAGGY
SAPPHO	SCRIBE	SEISIN	SHAKEN
SARONG	SCRIMP	SEIZED	SHAKER
SASHES	SCRIPT	SEIZIN	SHAMED
SATEEN	SCROLL	SEIZOR	SHANTY
SATING	SCRUFF	SELDOM	SHAPED
SATINY	SCULPT	SELECT	SHAPER
SATIRE	SCUMMY	SELENE	SHARED
SATRAP	SCURFY	SELLER	SHARER
SATURN	SCURRY	SELVES	SHAVED
SAUCED	SCURVY	SENATE	SHAVER
SAUCER	SCUTUM	SENDER	SHEARS
SAVAGE	SCYLLA	SENILE	SHEATH
SAVANT	SCYTHE	SENIOR	SHEIKH
SAVING	SEA-COB	SENORA	SHEKEL
SAVORY	SEA-COW	SENSED	SHELLY
SAVOUR	SEA-DOG	SENTRY	SHELVE
SAVVEY	SEA-FOX	SEPSIS	SHELVY
SAW-FLY	SEA-GOD	SEPTET	SHERRY
SAWING	SEA-HOG	SEPTIC	SHIELD
SAW-PIT	SEALED	SEPTUM	SHIFTY
SAW-SET	SEALER	SEQUEL	SHIMMY
SAWYER	SEAMAN	SEQUIN	SHINDY
SAXONY	SEAMED	SERAPH	SHINER
SAYING	SEAMER	SEREIN	SHINTO
SCABBY	SEA-MEW	SERENE	SHIRES
SCALED	SEANCE	SERIAL	SHIRTY
SCALER	SEARCH	SERIES	SHIVER
SCALES	SEARED	SERMON	SHOALY
SCANTY	SEASON	SEROUS	SHODDY
SCARAB	SEATED	SERVED	SHOOED
SCARCE	SEA-WAY	SERVER	SHOPPY
SCARED	SECANT	SESAME	SHORED
SCATHE	SECEDE	SESTET	SHORER
SCATTY	SECOND	SET-OFF	SHORTS
SCENIC	SECRET	SETOSE	SHOULD
SCHEME	SECTOR	SET-OUT	SHOVED
SCHISM	SECUND	SETTEE	SHOVEL
SCHOOL	SECURE	SETTER	SHOVER
SCILLA	SEDATE	SETTLE	SHOWER
SCONCE	SEDUCE	SEVERE	SHRANK
SCORCH	SEEDED	SEVRES	SHREWD
SCORED	SEEDER	SEWAGE	SHRIEK

SHRIFT	SINGLE	SLITHY	SNOBBY
SHRIKE	SINGLY	SLIVER	SNOOZE
SHRILL	SINKER	SLOGAN	SNORED
SHRIMP	SINNER	SLOPED	SNORER
SHRINE	SIPHON	SLOPPY	SNOTTY
SHRINK	SIPPED	SLOUCH	SNOUTY
SHRIVE	SIPPER	SLOUGH	SNOWED
SHROUD	SIPPET	SLOVAK	SNUBBY
SHROVE	SIRDAR	SLOVEN	SNUDGE
SHRUNK	SIRING	SLOWER	SNUFFY
SHUCKS	SIRIUS	SLOWLY	SNUGLY
SHYING	SIRRAH	SLUDGE	SOAKED
SICKER	SIRUPY	SLUDGY	SOAKER
SICKEN	SISTER	SLUICE	SOAPED
SICKLE	SITTER	SLUING	SOARED
SICKLY	SIZING	SLUMPY	SOBBED
SIDING	SIZZLE	SLURRY	SOCAGE
SIDLED	SKATED	SLUSHY	SOCCER
SIENNA	SKATER	SLYEST	SOCIAL
SIERRA	SKERRY	SMALLS	SOCKED
SIESTA	SKETCH	SMARMY	SOCKET
SIFTED	SKEWER	SMARTY	SODDEN
SIFTER	SKILLY	SMEARY	SODIUM
SIGHED	SKIMPY	SMELLY	SO-EVER
SIGHER	SKINNY	SMILAX	SOFISM
SIGNAL	SKYISH	SMILED	SOFTEN
SIGNED	SLABBY	SMILER	SOFTER
SIGNER	SLAKED	SMIRCH	SOFTLY
SIGNET	SLANGY	SMITER	SOILED
SIGNOR	SLAP-UP	SMITHY	SOIREE
SILAGE	SLATED	SMOKED	SOLACE
SILENT	SLATER	SMOKER	SOLDER
SILICA	SLAVED	SMOOTH	SOLELY
SILKEN	SLAVER	SMOUCH	SOLEMN
SILLER	SLAVEY	SMUDGE	SO-LONG
SILTED	SLAVIC	SMUDGY	SOLVED
SILVAN	SLAYER	SMUGLY	SOLVER
SILVER	SLEAZY	SMUTCH	SOMBRE
SIMIAL	SLEDGE	SMUTTY	SONANT
SIMIAN	SLEEPY	SNAGGY	SONATA
SIMILE	SLEETY	SNAKED	SONNET
SIMMER	SLEEVE	SNAPPY	SOONER
SIMNEL	SLEIGH	SNARED	SOOTHE
SIMONY	SLEUTH	SNARER	SOPPED
SIMPER	SLEWED	SNATCH	SOPPER
SIMPLE	SLICED	SNEEZE	SORBET
SIMPLY	SLICER	SNIFFY	SORDID
SINEWY	SLIDER	SNIPER	SORELY
SINFUL	SLIGHT	SNIPPY	SOREST
SINGED	SLINKY	SNITCH	SORREL
SINGER	SLIPPY	SNIVEL	SORROW

SORTED	SPOUSE	STATUE	STRESS
SORTER	SPRAIN	STATUS	STREWN
SORTIE	SPRANG	STAVED	STRIAE
SOUGHT	SPRAWL	STAVES	STRIDE
SOURCE	SPREAD	STAYED	STRIFE
SOURER	SPRENT	STAYER	STRIKE
SOURLY	SPRING	STAY-IN	STRING
SOUSED	SPRINT	STEADY	STRIPE
SOVIET	SPRITE	STEAMY	STRIPY
SOWING	SPROUT	STEELY	STRIVE
SOZZLE	SPRUCE	STENCH	STRODE
SPACED	SPRUNG	STEPPE	STROKE
SPACER	SPRYER	STEREO	STROLL
SPADED	SPUNKY	STEWED	STRONG
SPADIX	SPURGE	STICKY	STROVE
SPARED	SPURRY	STIFLE	STRUCK
SPARER	SPYING	STIGMA	STRUNG
SPARES	SPYISM	STILLY	STUBBY
SPARKS	SQUALL	STINGO	STUCCO
SPARRY	SQUARE	STINGY	STUDIO
SPARSE	SQUASH	STITCH	STUFFY
SPAVIN	SQUAWK	STOCKY	STUMER
SPECIE	SQUEAK	STODGE	STUMPS
SPECKY	SQUEAL	STODGY	STUMPY
SPEECH	SQUILL	STOKED	STUPID
SPEEDY	SQUINT	STOKER	STUPOR
SPENCE	SQUIRE	STOLEN	STURDY
SPHERE	SQUIRM	STOLID	STYLAR
SPHINX	SQUIRT	STONED	STYLED
SPICED	STABLE	STONER	STYLET
SPIDER	STABLY	STOOGE	STYLUS
SPIGOT	STAGED	STORED	STYMIE
SPIKED	STAGER	STORER	STYRAX
SPINAL	STAGEY	STORES	SUABLE
SPINED	STAKED	STOREY	SUBDUE
SPINET	STALAG	STORMY	SUBITO
SPINNY	STALER	STOVED	SUBLET
SPIRAL	STALKY	STOVER	SUBMIT
SPIRED	STAMEN	STOWED	SUBORN
SPIRIT	STANCE	STOWER	SUBTIL
SPITED	STANCH	STRAFE	SUBTLE
SPLASH	STANZA	STRAIN	SUBTLY
SPLEEN	STAPLE	STRAIT	SUBURB
SPLICE	STARCH	STRAKE	SUBWAY
SPLINE	STARED	STRAND	SUCKED
SPOKEN	STARER	STRASS	SUCKER
SPONGE	STARRY	STRATA	SUCKLE
SPONGY	STARVE	STRAWY	SUDDEN
SPOOKY	STATED	STREAK	SUEING
SPOONY	STATER	STREAM	SUFFER
SPOTTY	STATIC	STREET	SUFFIX

SUGARY	SWERVE	TANGLE	TEASER
SUITED	SWINGE	TANGLY	TEA-SET
SUITOR	SWIPED	TANKED	TEA-URN
SUIVEZ	SWIPES	TANKER	TEDIUM
SULKED	SWITCH	TANNED	TEEING
SULLEN	SWIVEL	TANNER	TEEMED
SULTAN	SYLVAN	TANNIC	TEETER
SULTRY	SYMBOL	TANNIN	TEETHE
SUMMED	SYNDIC	TANNOY	TELLER
SUMMER	SYNTAX	TAOISM	TEMPER
SUMMIT	SYPHON	TAOIST	TEMPLE
SUMMON	SYRIAC	TAPING	TENACE
SUNBOW	SYRIAN	TAPPED	TENANT
SUNDAE	SYRINX	TAPPER	TENDED
SUNDAY	SYRUPY	TAPPET	TENDER
SUNDER	SYSTEM	TARGET	TENDON
SUN-DEW		TARIFF	TENNER
SUN-DOG		TARMAC	TENNIS
SUNDRY	T—6	TARPON	TENSED
SUN-GOD	TABARD	TARSAL	TENSER
SUN-HAT	TABBED	TARSIA	TENTED
SUNKEN	TABLED	TARSUS	TENTER
SUNLIT	TABLET	TARTAN	TENURE
SUNNED	TABOUR	TARTAR	TENUTO
SUNSET	TACKED	TARTLY	TEPEFY
SUN-TAN	TACKER	TASKED	TERCET
SUPERB	TACKLE	TASKER	TERMED
SUPINE	TACTIC	TASSEL	TERMLY
SUPPED	TAGGED	TASTED	TERROR
SUPPER	TAGGER	TASTER	TESTED
SUPPLE	TAG-RAG	TATLER	TESTER
SUPPLY	TAILED	TATTED	TETCHY
SURELY	TAILOR	TATTER	TETHER
SUREST	TAKE-IN	TATTLE	TETRAD
SURETY	TAKING	TATTOO	TEUTON
SURGED	TALBOT	TAUGHT	THALER
SURREY	TALCKY	TAURUS	THALIA
SURTAX	TALENT	TAUTEN	THANKS
SURVEY	TALKED	TAUTER	THATCH
SUTLER	TALKER	TAVERN	THAWED
SUTTEE	TALLER	TAWDRY	THEBAN
SUTURE	TALLOW	TAWING	THEIRS
SVELTE	TALMUD	TAXIED	THEISM
SWAMPY	TAMELY	TAXING	THEIST
SWANKY	TAMEST	TCHICK	THENAR
SWARDY	TAMPED	TEA-CUP	THENCE
SWARMY	TAMPER	TEAMED	THEORY
SWATCH	TAMPON	TEA-POT	THESIS
SWATHE	TAM-TAM	TEARER	THETIS
SWAYED	TANDEM	TEASED	THEWED
SWEATY	TANGED	TEASEL	THIEVE

THINLY	TIMELY	TONGUE	TRASHY
THIRST	TIMING	TONING	TRAUMA
THIRTY	TIMIST	TONISH	TRAVEL
THORNY	TINDER	TONSIL	TREATY
THORPE	TINGED	TOOLED	TREBLE
THOUGH	TINGLE	TOOTED	TREBLY
THRALL	TINIER	TOOTER	TREMOR
THRASH	TINKER	TOOTHY	TRENCH
THREAD	TINKLE	TOOTLE	TREPAN
THREAT	TINMAN	TOO-TOO	TREPID
THRESH	TINNED	TOP-DOG	TRIBAL
THRICE	TINNER	TOP-HAT	TRICAR
THRIFT	TIN-POT	TOPMAN	TRICKY
THRILL	TINSEL	TOPPED	TRICOT
THRIVE	TINTED	TOPPER	TRIFID
THROAT	TINTER	TOPPLE	TRIFLE
THRONE	TIP-CAT	TORERO	TRILBY
THRONG	TIP-OFF	TORPID	TRIMLY
THROVE	TIPPED	TORPOR	TRINAL
THROWN	TIPPET	TORQUE	TRIODE
THRUSH	TIPPLE	TORRID	TRIPLE
THRUST	TIP-TOE	TOSSED	TRIPLY
THWACK	TIP-TOP	TOSSER	TRIPOD
THWART	TIRADE	TOSS-UP	TRIPOS
THYMOL	TIRING	TOTING	TRISTE
THYMUS	TISANE	TOTTED	TRITON
TIBIAL	TISSUE	TOTTER	TRIUNE
TICKED	TIT-BIT	TOUCAN	TRIVET
TICKER	TITHED	TOUCHY	TROIKA
TICKET	TITLED	TOUPEE	TROJAN
TICKLE	TITTER	TOURED	TROLLY
TICKLY	TITTUP	TOUSLE	TROPHY
TIC-TAC	TOCSIN	TOUTED	TROPIC
TIDIED	TODDLE	TOUTER	TROPPO
TIDIER	TOE-CAP	TOWAGE	TROUGH
TIDILY	TOEING	TOWARD	TROUPE
TIEING	TOFFEE	TOWERY	TROWEL
TIE-PIN	TOGGED	TOWING	TRUANT
TIERCE	TOGGLE	TOWSER	TRUDGE
TIE-WIG	TOILED	TOY-BOX	TRUEST
TIFFIN	TOILER	TOYING	TRUISM
TIGHTS	TOILET	TOYISH	TRUSTY
TILERY	TOLEDO	TOY-MAN	TRYING
TILING	TOLLED	TRACED	TRY-OUT
TILLED	TOLLER	TRACER	TSETSE
TILLER	TOMATO	TRADED	TUBAGE
TILTED	TOMBED	TRADER	TUBBED
TILTER	TOMBOY	TRAGIC	TUBING
TIMBAL	TOM-CAT	TRANCE	TUCKED
TIMBER	TOM-TIT	TRAPES	TUCKER
TIMBRE	TOMTOM	TRAPPY	TUFFET

TUFTED	TYRIAN	UNGIRT	UNSEAT
TUGGED		UNGLUE	UNSEEN
TUGGER	**U—6**	UNGOWN	UNSENT
TUMBLE	UBIETY	UNGUAL	UNSEWN
TUMOUR	UGLIER	UNHAND	UNSHED
TUMULI	UGLIFY	UNHANG	UNSHOD
TUMULT	UGLILY	UNHASP	UNSHOT
TUNDRA	ULLAGE	UNHEWN	UNSHUT
TUNE-IN	ULSTER	UNHOLY	UNSOLD
TUNING	ULTIMO	UNHOOK	UNSOWN
TUNNED	UMBRAL	UNHUNG	UNSPIN
TUNNEL	UMLAUT	UNHURT	UNSTOP
TUPPED	UMPIRE	UNIPED	UNSUNG
TURBAN	UNABLE	UNIQUE	UNSURE
TURBID	UNAWED	UNISON	UNTACK
TURBOT	UNBEND	UNITED	UNTAME
TUREEN	UNBENT	UNITER	UNTIDY
TURFED	UNBIND	UNJUST	UNTIED
TURGID	UNBOLT	UNKEPT	UNTOLD
TURKEY	UNBORN	UNKIND	UNTORN
TURNED	UNBRED	UNKNOT	UNTROD
TURNER	UNCAGE	UNLACE	UNTRUE
TURNIP	UNCASE	UNLAID	UNTUCK
TURN-UP	UNCATE	UNLASH	UNTUNE
TURRET	UNCIAL	UNLENT	UNUSED
TURTLE	UNCLAD	UNLESS	UNVEIL
TUSCAN	UNCLOG	UNLIKE	UNWARY
TUSKED	UNCOIL	UNLOAD	UNWELL
TUSKER	UNCORD	UNLOCK	UNWEPT
TUSSLE	UNCORK	UNMADE	UNWIND
TU-WHIT	UNCURL	UNMAKE	UNWIRE
TU-WHOO	UNDATE	UNMASK	UNWISE
TUXEDO	UNDIES	UNOWED	UNWORN
TWEENY	UNDINE	UNPACK	UNWRAP
TWELVE	UNDOCK	UNPAID	UNYOKE
TWENTY	UNDOER	UNPICK	UPBEAR
TWIGGY	UNDONE	UNPROP	UPCAST
TWINED	UNDULY	UNREAD	UPHILL
TWINER	UNEASE	UNREAL	UPHOLD
TWINGE	UNEASY	UNREST	UPKEEP
TWITCH	UNEVEN	UNRIPE	UPLAND
TWO-PLY	UNFAIR	UNROBE	UPLEAN
T'WOULD	UNFEED	UNROLL	UPLIFT
TWO-WAY	UNFELT	UNROOF	UP-LINE
TYBURN	UNFOLD	UNROOT	UPMOST
TYCOON	UNFREE	UNROPE	UPPING
TYPHUS	UNFURL	UNRULY	UPPISH
TYPIFY	UNGEAR	UNSAFE	UPRISE
TYPING	UNGILD	UNSAID	UPROAR
TYPIST	UNGILT	UNSEAL	UPROOT
TYRANT	UNGIRD	UNSEAM	UPRUSH

UPSHOT	VECTOR	VINERY	WAITED
UPSIDE	VEERED	VINOUS	WAITER
UPTAKE	VEILED	VINTED	WAIVED
UPTURN	VEINED	VINTRY	WAIVER
UPWARD	VELLUM	VIOLET	WAKING
URAEUS	VELOCE	VIOLIN	WALKED
URANIA	VELOUR	VIRAGO	WALKER
URANIC	VELVET	VIRGIN	WALLAH
URANUS	VENDED	VIRILE	WALLED
URBANE	VENDEE	VIROUS	WALLER
URCHIN	VENDER	VIRTUE	WALLET
URGENT	VENDOR	VISAGE	WALLOP
URGING	VENDUE	VISCID	WALLOW
URSINE	VENEER	VISHNU	WALNUT
USABLE	VENERY	VIZIER	WALRUS
USANCE	VENIAL	VISION	WAMBLE
USEFUL	VENITE	VISUAL	WAMPUM
USURER	VENTED	VITALS	WANDER
UTMOST	VERBAL	VIVACE	WANGLE
UTOPIA	VERGED	VIVIFY	WANING
UVULAR	VERGER	VIZARD	WANTED
	VERIFY	VOICED	WANTER
V—6	VERILY	VOIDED	WANTON
VACANT	VERITY	VOIDER	WARBLE
VACATE	VERMIN	VOLANT	WAR-CRY
VACUUM	VERNAL	VOLLEY	WARDED
VAGARY	VERSED	VOLUME	WARDEN
VAGUER	VERSER	VOODOO	WARDER
VAINER	VERSUS	VORTEX	WARIER
VAINLY	VERTEX	VOTARY	WARILY
VALISE	VERVET	VOTING	WARMER
VALLEY	VESPER	VOTIVE	WARMLY
VALLUM	VESSEL	VOWING	WARMTH
VALOUR	VESTAL	VOYAGE	WARNED
VALUED	VESTED	VULCAN	WARPED
VALUER	VESTRY	VULGAR	WARREN
VALVED	VETOED		WASHED
VAMPED	VETTED	W—6	WASHER
VAMPER	VEXING	WADDED	WASH-UP
VANDAL	VIABLE	WADDLE	WASTED
VANISH	VIANDS	WADING	WASTER
VANITY	VICTIM	WAFERY	WATERY
VAN-MAN	VICTOR	WAFFLE	WATTLE
VAPOUR	VICUNA	WAFTED	WAVING
VARIED	VIEWED	WAFTER	WAX-END
VARIER	VIEWER	WAGGED	WAXIER
VARLET	VIGOUR	WAGGLE	WAXING
VASSAL	VIKING	WAGGON	WAYLAY
VASTER	VILELY	WAGING	WEAKEN
VASTLY	VILEST	WAILED	WEAKER
VAULTY	VILIFY	WAILER	WEAKLY

WEALTH	WIDELY	WOMBAT	YOICKS
WEANED	WIDEST	WONDER	YOKING
WEAPON	WIELDY	WONTED	YOLKED
WEARER	WIFELY	WOODED	YONDER
WEASEL	WIGEON	WOODEN	YORKER
WEAVER	WIGGED	WOOING	YOWLED
WEAZEN	WIGGLE	WOOLLY	
WEBBED	WIGWAM	WORDED	**Z—6**
WEB-EYE	WILDER	WORKED	ZEALOT
WEDDED	WILDLY	WORKER	ZENANA
WEDGED	WILFUL	WORMED	ZENITH
WEEDED	WILIER	WORSEN	ZEPHYR
WEEDER	WILILY	WORTHY	ZIG-ZAG
WEEKLY	WILLED	WOUNDY	ZILLAH
WEEPER	WILLER	WRAITH	ZINNIA
WEEVER	WILLOW	WREATH	ZIPPED
WEEVIL	WILTED	WRENCH	ZIRCON
WEIGHT	WIMPLE	WRETCH	ZITHER
WELDED	WINCED	WRIGHT	ZODIAC
WELDER	WINCER	WRITER	ZONATE
WELKIN	WINCEY	WRITHE	
WELLED	WINDED	WYVERN	**A—7**
WELTED	WINDER		ABANDON
WELTER	WINDLE	**X—6**	ABASHED
WENDED	WINDOW	XANADU	ABASING
WET-BOB	WIND-UP	XERXES	ABATING
WETHER	WINGED	X-RAYED	ABDOMEN
WETTER	WINGER		ABETTED
WHALER	WINKED	**Y—6**	ABETTER
WHEEZE	WINKER	YAMMER	ABIDING
WHEEZY	WINKLE	YANKED	ABIGAIL
WHENCE	WINNER	YANKEE	ABILITY
WHERRY	WINNOW	YAPPED	ABJURED
WHILED	WINTRY	YAPPER	ABJURER
WHILES	WIPING	YARNED	ABOLISH
WHILOM	WIRING	YARROW	ABRADED
WHILST	WIZARD	YAWING	ABREAST
WHIMSY	WISDOM	YAWLED	ABRIDGE
WHINED	WISELY	YAWNED	ABROACH
WHINER	WISEST	YCLEPT	ABSCESS
WHINNY	WISHED	YEANED	ABSCOND
WHIPPY	WISHER	YEARLY	ABSENCE
WHISKY	WISTLY	YEASTY	ABSINTH
WHITEN	WITHAL	YELLED	ABSOLVE
WHITER	WITHER	YELLOW	ABSTAIN
WHITES	WITHIN	YELPED	ABUSING
WHOLLY	WITTED	YELPER	ABUSIVE
WHOMSO	WOBBLE	YEOMAN	ABUTTAL
WICKED	WOBBLY	YES-MAN	ABUTTED
WICKER	WOEFUL	YESTER	ABYSMAL
WICKET	WOLVES	YOGISM	ABYSSAL

ACADEMY	ADORNED	A-LA-MORT	AMMETER
ACCEDED	ADRENAL	ALARMED	AMMONAL
ACCLAIM	ADULATE	ALASKAN	AMMONIA
ACCOUNT	ADVANCE	ALBUMEN	AMNESIA
ACCRETE	ADVERSE	ALCALDE	AMNESTY
ACCRUED	ADVISED	ALCHEMY	AMONGST
ACCUSED	ADVISOR	ALCOHOL	AMORIST
ACCUSER	AEOLIAN	ALEMBIC	AMOROUS
ACETATE	AERATED	ALENGTH	AMPHORA
ACETIFY	AERATOR	ALERTLY	AMPLEST
ACETONE	AEROBUS	ALFALFA	AMPLIFY
ACHATES	AFFABLE	ALGEBRA	AMPOULE
ACHERON	AFFABLY	ALIDADE	AMPULLA
ACHIEVE	AFFINED	ALIGNED	AMUSING
ACIDIFY	AFFIXED	ALIMENT	AMUSIVE
ACIDITY	AFFLICT	ALIMONY	AMYLOID
ACK-EMMA	AFFRONT	ALIQUOT	ANAEMIA
ACOLYTE	AFRICAN	ALLAYED	ANAEMIC
ACONITE	AGAINST	ALLEGED	ANAGRAM
ACQUIRE	AGELESS	ALLEGRO	ANALOGY
ACREAGE	AGELONG	ALLERGY	ANALYSE
ACROBAT	AGENDUM	ALLOWED	ANALYST
ACTABLE	AGGRESS	ALLOYED	ANARCHY
ACTRESS	AGILELY	ALLUDED	ANATOMY
ACTUARY	AGILITY	ALLURED	ANCHOVY
ACTUATE	AGITATE	ALLUVIA	ANCIENT
ACUSHLA	AGITATO	ALLYING	ANDANTE
ACUTELY	AGNOMEN	ALMANAC	ANDIRON
ADAMANT	AGONIZE	ALMONER	ANEMONE
ADAPTED	AGROUND	ALMONRY	ANEROID
ADAPTER	AIDLESS	ALMSMAN	ANGELIC
ADDENDA	AILERON	ALREADY	ANGELUS
ADDRESS	AILMENT	ALSATIA	ANGERED
ADDUCED	AIMLESS	ALTERED	ANGEVIN
ADDUCER	AIR-BASE	ALTHAEA	ANGLICE
ADELPHI	AIR-BATH	ALUMNUS	ANGLING
ADENOID	AIR-CELL	ALYSSUM	ANGRILY
ADHERED	AIR-HOLE	AMALGAM	ANGUINE
ADHERER	AIRLESS	AMASSED	ANGUISH
ADIPOSE	AIRLIFT	AMATEUR	ANGULAR
ADJOURN	AIR-LINE	AMATIVE	ANILINE
ADJUDGE	AIR-LOCK	AMATORY	ANILITY
ADJUNCT	AIR-MAIL	AMAZING	ANIMATE
ADJURED	AIR-PORT	AMBAGES	ANIMISM
ADJURER	AIR-PUMP	AMBIENT	ANIMIST
ADMIRAL	AIR-RAID	AMBLING	ANISEED
ADMIRED	AIR-SHIP	AMENDED	ANNATES
ADMIRER	AIR-TRAP	AMENITY	ANNEXED
ADONAIS	AIR-WAYS	AMERCED	ANNOYED
ADOPTED	ALADDIN	AMIABLE	ANNOYER
ADORING	A-LA-MODE	AMIABLY	ANNUITY

ANNULAR	ARBUTUS	ASSAGAI	AVARICE
ANNULET	ARCADED	ASSAULT	AVENGED
ANODYNE	ARCADIA	ASSAYED	AVENGER
ANOMALY	ARCANUM	ASSAYER	AVERAGE
ANOSMIA	ARCHAIC	ASSEGAI	AVERRED
ANOTHER	ARCHERY	ASSUAGE	AVERTED
ANTACID	ARCHING	ASSUMED	AVIATOR
ANT-BEAR	ARCHWAY	ASSURED	AVIDITY
ANTENNA	ARC-LAMP	ASSURER	AVOCADO
ANT-HILL	ARDENCY	ASTATIC	AVOIDED
ANTHONY	ARDUOUS	ASTOUND	AVOWING
ANTHRAX	ARENOSE	ASTRIDE	AWAITED
ANTIQUE	ARIDITY	ASUNDER	AWAKING
ANTI-RED	ARIGHTS	ATAVISM	AWARDED
ANTI-LIKE	ARIPPLE	ATELIER	AWESOME
ANT-LION	ARISING	ATHEISM	AWFULLY
ANTONYM	ARMHOLE	ATHEIST	AWKWARD
ANXIETY	ARMIGER	ATHIRST	AWNLESS
ANXIOUS	ARMLESS	ATHLETE	AXIALLY
ANYBODY	ARMOIRE	ATHWART	AXLE-BOX
ANYWISE	ARMOURY	ATOMIST	AXLE-PIN
APANAGE	AROUSAL	ATOMIZE	AXOLOTL
APELIKE	AROUSED	ATONING	
APHASIA	ARRAIGN	ATROPHY	B—7
APHONIA	ARRANGE	ATTABOY	BABBLED
APISHLY	ARRAYED	ATTACHE	BABBLER
APOCOPE	ARRIVAL	ATTEMPT	BABYISH
APOGEAN	ARSENAL	ATTIRED	BABYISM
APOLOGY	ARSENIC	ATTRACT	BABYLON
APOSTLE	ARTICLE	ATTUNED	BACCHIC
APPAREL	ARTISAN	AUBERGE	BACCHUS
APPEASE	ARTISTE	AUCTION	BACILLI
APPLAUD	ARTLESS	AUDIBLE	BACKEND
APPLIED	ASCETIC	AUDIBLY	BACKING
APPOINT	ASCRIBE	AUDITED	BACK-LOG
APPRISE	ASEPSIS	AUDITOR	BADNESS
APPRIZE	ASEPTIC	AUGMENT	BAFFLED
APPROVE	ASEXUAL	AUGURED	BAFFLER
APRICOT	ASHAMED	AURALLY	BAGGAGE
APRONED	ASHIVER	AUREATE	BAGGING
APROPOS	ASH-TRAY	AUREOLA	BAGPIPE
APSIDAL	ASIATIC	AUREOLE	BAILAGE
APTNESS	ASININE	AURICLE	BAILIFF
AQUARIA	ASKANCE	AUROCHS	BAILING
AQUATIC	ASPERSE	AUSTERE	BAITING
AQUEOUS	ASPHALT	AUSTRAL	BALANCE
ARABIAN	ASPIRED	AUTOBUS	BALCONY
ARABIST	ASPIRIN	AUTOCAR	BALDEST
ARACHIS	ASPRAWL	AUTONYM	BALDISH
ARAMAIC	ASPROUT	AUTOPSY	BALDRIC
ARBITER	ASQUINT	AVAILED	BALEFUL

BALKING	BATH-BUN	BEGONIA	BESPEAK
BALLAST	BATHING	BEGORED	BESPOKE
BALL-BOY	BATSMAN	BEGRIME	BESTIAL
BALLOON	BATTELS	BEGUILE	BESTILL
BALMILY	BATTERY	BEHAVED	BESTING
BALMING	BATTING	BEHOVED	BEST-MAN
BAMBINO	BATTLED	BEJEWEL	BESTREW
BANBURY	BATTLER	BEKNOWN	BETAKEN
BANDAGE	BAULKED	BELACED	BETHINK
BANDANA	BAUXITE	BELATED	BETHUMB
BANDBOX	BAWDILY	BELAYED	BETHUMP
BANDEAU	BAWLING	BELCHED	BETIDED
BANDIED	BAYONET	BELCHER	BETIMES
BANDING	BAY-TREE	BELGIAN	BETITLE
BAND-SAW	BAYWOOD	BELIEVE	BETOKEN
BANEFUL	BEACHED	BELL-HOP	BETROTH
BANGING	BEADING	BELLIED	BETTING
BANKING	BEAMING	BELLING	BETWEEN
BANNING	BEARDED	BELL-MAN	BETWIXT
BANNOCK	BEARING	BELLOWS	BEWITCH
BANQUET	BEARISH	BELOVED	BEZIQUE
BANSHEE	BEAR-PIT	BELTING	BIASING
BANTING	BEASTLY	BELYING	BIAXIAL
BAPTISM	BEATIFY	BEMAZED	BICYCLE
BAPTIST	BEATING	BEMIRED	BIDDING
BAPTIZE	BECAUSE	BEMUSED	BIFOCAL
BARBARY	BECLOUD	BENCHED	BIGGEST
BARBATE	BEDDING	BENCHER	BIGGISH
BARDISM	BEDEVIL	BENDING	BIGOTED
BARGAIN	BEDEWED	BENEATH	BIGOTRY
BARGING	BED-GOWN	BENEFIT	BILGING
BARKING	BED-MATE	BENGALI	BILIOUS
BARMAID	BEDOUIN	BENISON	BILKING
BARMIER	BED-POST	BENZENE	BILLING
BARNABY	BED-REST	BENZOIN	BILLION
BARN-OWL	BED-ROCK	BEPAINT	BILLOWY
BARONET	BEDROOM	BEQUEST	BILTONG
BAROQUE	BEDSIDE	BERATED	BINDING
BARRACK	BED-SORE	BEREAVE	BIOLOGY
BARRAGE	BED-TICK	BERHYME	BIOTICS
BARRIER	BEDTIME	BERRIED	BIPEDAL
BARRING	BEDWARF	BERSERK	BIPLANE
BASENJI	BEEF-TEA	BERTHED	BIRCHED
BASHFUL	BEE-HIVE	BESEECH	BIRDMAN
BASHING	BEE-LINE	BESHAME	BIRETTA
BASILIC	BEE-MOTH	BESHONE	BISCUIT
BASKING	BEESWAX	BESHREW	BISMUTH
BASSOON	BEETLED	BESIDES	BITTERN
BASTARD	BEGGARY	BESIEGE	BITUMEN
BASTING	BEGGING	BESMEAR	BIVALVE
BASTION	BEGLOOM	BESMOKE	BIVOUAC

BIZARRE	BLUCHER	BOOKLET	BRAMBLY
BLABBED	BLUE-CAP	BOOKMAN	BRANCHY
BLABBER	BLUEING	BOOMING	BRANDED
BLACKED	BLUFFED	BOORISH	BRASSIE
BLACKEN	BLUFFER	BOOSTED	BRAVADO
BLACKER	BLUFFLY	BOOSTER	BRAVELY
BLACKLY	BLUNDER	BOOT-LEG	BRAVERY
BLADDER	BLUNGER	BOOZING	BRAVEST
BLAMING	BLUNTED	BORACIC	BRAVING
BLANDLY	BLUNTER	BOREDOM	BRAVURA
BLANKET	BLUNTLY	BOROUGH	BRAWLED
BLANKLY	BLURRED	BORSTAL	BRAWLER
BLARING	BLURTED	BOSOMED	BRAYING
BLARNEY	BLUSHED	BOSSING	BRAZIER
BLASTED	BLUSTER	BOSWELL	BRAZING
BLASTER	BOARDED	BOTANIC	BREADTH
BLATANT	BOARDER	BOTCHED	BREAKER
BLATHER	BOARISH	BOTCHER	BREATHE
BLATTER	BOASTED	BOTTLED	BREEDER
BLAZING	BOASTER	BOTTLER	BREVITY
BLEAKER	BOAT-CAR	BOUDOIR	BREWERY
BLEAKLY	BOAT-FLY	BOULDER	BREWING
BLEATED	BOATFUL	BOULTER	BRIBERY
BLEMISH	BOATING	BOUNCED	BRIBING
BLENDED	BOATMAN	BOUNCER	BRICKED
BLENDER	BOBADIL	BOUNDED	BRIDGED
BLESSED	BOBBING	BOUNDEN	BRIDLED
BLETHER	BOBBISH	BOUNDER	BRIDLER
BLIGHTY	BOB-SLED	BOUQUET	BRIEFED
BLINDED	BOB-STAY	BOURBON	BRIEFER
BLINDER	BOBTAIL	BOWLESS	BRIEFLY
BLINDLY	BODEFUL	BOWLINE	BRIGADE
BLINKED	BOGGLED	BOWLING	BRIGAND
BLISTER	BOILING	BOW-SHOT	BRIMFUL
BLOATED	BOLDEST	BOX-CALF	BRIMMED
BLOATER	BOLLARD	BOX-COAT	BRIMMER
BLOCKED	BOLLING	BOX-IRON	BRINDLE
BLONDIN	BOLOGNA	BOX-KITE	BRINISH
BLOODED	BOLSTER	BOX-WOOD	BRIOCHE
BLOOMED	BOLTING	BOYCOTT	BRISKER
BLOOMER	BOMBARD	BOYHOOD	BRISKET
BLOSSOM	BOMBAST	BRACING	BRISKLY
BLOTCHY	BOMBING	BRACKEN	BRISTLE
BLOTTED	BONANZA	BRACKET	BRISTLY
BLOTTER	BONDAGE	BRAGGED	BRISTOL
BLOWFLY	BONDING	BRAIDED	BRITISH
BLOW-GUN	BONDMAN	BRAILLE	BRITTLE
BLOWING	BONFIRE	BRAINED	BROADEN
BLOW-OUT	BONNILY	BRAISED	BROADER
BLOWZED	BOOKING	BRAKING	BROADLY
BLUBBER	BOOKISH	BRAMBLE	BROCADE

BROILED	BULRUSH	BUZZARD	CALYPSO
BROILER	BULWARK	BUZZING	CAMBIUM
BROKAGE	BUMMALO	BUZZ-SAW	CAMBRIC
BROKING	BUMPING	BY-AND-BY	CAMELOT
BROMIDE	BUMPKIN	BYRONIC	CAMORRA
BRONZED	BUNCHED		CAMPHOR
BROODED	BUNDLED		CAMPING
BROOKED	BUNGLED	C—7	CAMPION
BROTHER	BUNGLER	CABARET	CANDIED
BROUGHT	BUNKING	CABBAGE	CANDOUR
BROWNED	BUNTING	CABBALA	CANASTA
BROWNER	BUOYAGE	CAB-FARE	CANNERY
BROWNIE	BUOYANT	CABINED	CANNING
BROWSED	BUOYING	CABINET	CANTATA
BRUISED	BURDOCK	CABLING	CANTEEN
BRUISER	BURETTE	CABOOSE	CANTING
BRUMOUS	BURGEON	CAB-RANK	CANVASS
BRUSHED	BURGESS	CA'CANNY	CAPABLE
BRUSQUE	BURGHAL	CACKLED	CAPABLY
BRUTIFY	BURGHER	CACKLER	CAP-A-PIE
BRUTISH	BURGLAR	CADDISH	CAPELIN
BRUTISM	BURGLED	CADENCE	CAPERED
BUBBLED	BURLIER	CADENCY	CAPERER
BUBONIC	BURLING	CADENZA	CAPITAL
BUCKING	BURMESE	CADGING	CAPITAN
BUCKISH	BURNING	CAESURA	CAPITOL
BUCKISM	BURNISH	CAFFEIN	CAPORAL
BUCKLED	BURNOUS	CAITIFF	CAPPING
BUCKLER	BURRING	CAJOLED	CAPRICE
BUCKRAM	BURSARY	CAJOLER	CAPRINE
BUCKSAW	BURTHEN	CALCIFY	CAPROIC
BUCOLIC	BURYING	CALCINE	CAPSIZE
BU'DDING	BUSH-CAT	CALCIUM	CAPSTAN
BUDGING	BUSHIDO	CALDRON	CAPSULE
BUDLESS	BUSHMAN	CALENDS	CAPTAIN
BUFFALO	BUSKING	CALIBAN	CAPTION
BUFFING	BUS-STOP	CALIBRE	CAPTIVE
BUFFOON	BUSTARD	CALIPER	CAPTURE
BUGBEAR	BUSTLED	CALKING	CAPULET
BUILT-UP	BUSTLER	CALL-BOY	CARAMEL
BULBOUS	BUSYING	CALLING	CARAVAN
BULGING	BUTCHER	CALLOUS	CARAVEL
BULKIER	BUTLERY	CALMING	CARAWAY
BULKING	BUTMENT	CALOMEL	CARBIDE
BULLACE	BUTT-END	CALORIC	CARBINE
BULL-DOG	BUTTERY	CALORIE	CARCASE
BULLIED	BUTTING	CALTROP	CARDIAC
BULLING	BUTTOCK	CALUMET	CARDING
BULLION	BUTTONS	CALUMNY	CARDOON
BULLOCK	BUXOMLY	CALVARY	CAREFUL
BULL-PUP	BUYABLE	CALVING	CARIBOU

CARIOUS	CAVE-MAN	CHARING	CHILLED
CARKING	CAVIARE	CHARIOT	CHILLER
CARLINE	CAYENNE	CHARITY	CHIMNEY
CARMINE	CEASING	CHARLEY	CHINDIT
CARNAGE	CEDARED	CHARMED	CHINESE
CAROTID	CEDILLA	CHARMER	CHINKED
CAROUSE	CEILING	CHARNEL	CHIP-HAT
CARPING	CELLIST	CHARRED	CHIPPED
CARRIED	CENSING	CHARTED	CHIPPER
CARRIER	CENSURE	CHARTER	CHIRPED
CARRION	CENTAUR	CHASING	CHIRPER
CARROTY	CENTAVO	CHASSIS	CHIRRED
CARTAGE	CENTIME	CHASTEN	CHIRRUP
CARTING	CENTRAL	CHATEAU	CHITTER
CARTOON	CENTRED	CHATTED	CHLORAL
CARVING	CENTURY	CHATTEL	CHLORIC
CASCADE	CERAMIC	CHATTER	CHOIRED
CASCARA	CERTAIN	CHEAPEN	CHOKING
CASE-LAW	CERTIFY	CHEAPER	CHOLERA
CASEMAN	CESSION	CHEAPLY	CHOOSER
CASHIER	CESS-PIT	CHEATED	CHOPPED
CASHING	CHABLIS	CHEATER	CHOPPER
CASSAVA	CHAFFED	CHECKED	CHORALE
CASSOCK	CHAFFER	CHECKER	CHORTLE
CASTING	CHAFING	CHEDDAR	CHOWDER
CASTLED	CHAGRIN	CHEEKED	CHRONIC
CAST-OFF	CHAINED	CHEEPED	CHUCKED
CASUIST	CHAIRED	CHEERED	CHUCKLE
CATALAN	CHALDEE	CHEERIO	CHUMMED
CATARRH	CHALICE	CHEETAH	CHURCHY
CAT-CALL	CHALKED	CHELSEA	CHURNED
CATCHER	CHAMBER	CHEMISE	CHURRED
CATCHUP	CHAMOIS	CHEMIST	CINDERY
CATERAN	CHAMPED	CHEQUER	CIRCEAN
CATERED	CHANCED	CHERISH	CIRCLED
CATERER	CHANCEL	CHEROOT	CIRCLET
CAT-EYED	CHANGED	CHERVIL	CIRCUIT
CAT-FISH	CHANGER	CHESTED	CISTERN
CATHEAD	CHANNEL	CHEVIOT	CITABLE
CATHODE	CHANTED	CHEVRON	CITADEL
CAT-LIKE	CHANTER	CHEWING	CITIZEN
CAT-MINT	CHANTRY	CHIANTI	CITRATE
CAT'S-EYE	CHAOTIC	CHICANE	CITRINE
CAT'S-PAW	CHAPLET	CHICKEN	CIVILLY
CATTISH	CHAPMAN	CHICORY	CIVVIES
CAUDATE	CHAPPED	CHIDING	CLACKED
CAULKED	CHAPTER	CHIEFLY	CLAIMED
CAUSING	CHARADE	CHIFFON	CLAIMER
CAUSTIC	CHARGED	CHIGNON	CLAMANT
CAUTION	CHARGER	CHILEAN	CLAMBER
CAVALRY	CHARILY	CHILIAD	CLAMMED

CLAMOUR	CLOSING	CODFISH	COMPLEX
CLAMPED	CLOSURE	CODICIL	COMPORT
CLAMPER	CLOTHED	CODLING	COMPOSE
CLANGED	CLOTTED	COERCED	COMPOST
CLANKED	CLOUDED	COEXIST	COMPOTE
CLAP-NET	CLOUTED	COGENCY	COMPUTE
CLAPPED	CLOWNED	COGNATE	COMRADE
CLAPPER	CLUBBED	COHABIT	CONCAVE
CLARIFY	CLUBBER	COHERED	CONCEAL
CLARION	CLUB-LAW	COHERER	CONCEDE
CLARITY	CLUB-MAN	COIFFED	CONCEIT
CLASHED	CLUCKED	COILING	CONCEPT
CLASPED	CLUMBER	COINAGE	CONCERN
CLASPER	CLUMPED	COINING	CONCERT
CLASSED	CLUSTER	COJUROR	CONCISE
CLASSIC	CLUTTER	COLDEST	CONCOCT
CLATTER	COACHED	COLDISH	CONCORD
CLAVIER	COACTED	COLICKY	CONCUSS
CLAWING	COAGENT	COLITIS	CONDEMN
CLAYING	COAL-BED	COLLATE	CONDIGN
CLAYISH	COAL-BOX	COLLECT	CONDOLE
CLAY-PIT	COAL-GAS	COLLEEN	CONDONE
CLEANED	COALING	COLLEGE	CONDUCE
CLEANER	COALMAN	COLLIDE	CONDUCT
CLEANLY	COAL-PIT	COLLIER	CONDUIT
CLEANSE	COAL-TAR	COLLOID	CONFECT
CLEAN-UP	COAL-TIT	COLLUDE	CONFESS
CLEARED	COARSEN	COLONEL	CONFEST
CLEARER	COARSER	COLOURS	CONFIDE
CLEARLY	COASTAL	COLTISH	CONFINE
CLEAVED	COASTED	COMBINE	CONFIRM
CLEAVER	COASTER	COMBING	CONFLUX
CLEMENT	COATING	COMFORT	CONFORM
CLEMMED	CO-AXIAL	COMICAL	CONFUSE
CLICKED	COAXING	COMMAND	CONFUTE
CLIMATE	COBBING	COMMEND	CONGEAL
CLIMBED	COBBLED	COMMENT	CONGEST
CLIMBER	COBBLER	COMMERE	CONICAL
CLINKED	COCAINE	COMMODE	CONIFER
CLIPPED	COCKADE	COMMONS	CONJOIN
CLIPPER	COCKEYE	COMMUNE	CONJURE
CLIPPIE	COCKING	COMMUTE	CONJURY
CLOAKED	COCKLED	COMPACT	CONNATE
CLOBBER	COCKLER	COMPANY	CONNECT
CLOCKED	COCKNEY	COMPARE	CONNING
CLOCKER	COCKPIT	COMPART	CONNIVE
CLOGGED	COCO-NUT	COMPASS	CONNOTE
CLOGGER	COCOTTE	COMPEER	CONQUER
CLOSELY	CODDING	COMPERE	CONSENT
CLOSEST	CODDLED	COMPETE	CONSIGN
CLOSE-UP	CODEINE	COMPILE	CONSIST

CONSOLE	COROLLA	COWLING	CRINGED
CONSOLS	CORONER	COWSLIP	CRINGER
CONSORT	CORONET	COXCOMB	CRINKLE
CONSULT	CORRECT	COYNESS	CRINOID
CONSUME	CORRODE	COZENED	CRIPPLE
CONTACT	CORRUPT	COZENER	CRISPED
CONTAIN	CORSAGE	CRABBED	CRISPER
CONTEMN	CORSAIR	CRACKED	CRISPIN
CONTEND	CORSLET	CRACKER	CRISPLY
CONTENT	CORTEGE	CRACKLE	CROAKED
CONTEST	CORVINE	CRADLED	CROAKER
CONTEXT	COSHING	CRAGGED	CROCHET
CONTORT	COSIEST	CRAKING	CROCKED
CONTOUR	COSSACK	CRAMMED	CROCKET
CONTROL	COSTARD	CRAMMER	CROESUS
CONTUSE	COSTING	CRAMPED	CROFTER
CONVENE	COSTIVE	CRAMPON	CROODLE
CONVENT	COSTUME	CRANAGE	CROOKED
CONVERT	COTERIE	CRANIAL	CROONED
CONVICT	COTTAGE	CRANING	CROONER
CONVOKE	COTTONY	CRANIUM	CROPFUL
COOKERY	COUCHED	CRANKED	CROPPED
COOKING	COUGHED	CRANKLE	CROPPER
COOLEST	COULDST	CRASHED	CROQUET
COOLING	COUNCIL	CRASHER	CROSSED
COOLISH	COUNSEL	CRATING	CROSSLY
COOPING	COUNTED	CRAUNCH	CROWBAR
CO-OPTED	COUNTER	CRAVING	CROWDED
CO-PILOT	COUNTRY	CRAWLED	CROWING
COPIOUS	COUPLED	CRAWLER	CROWNED
COPPERY	COUPLER	CRAZIER	CRUCIAL
COPPICE	COUPLET	CRAZILY	CRUCIFY
COPPING	COURAGE	CRAZING	CRUDELY
COPYING	COURANT	CREAKED	CRUDEST
COPYIST	COURIER	CREAMED	CRUDITY
CORACLE	COURSED	CREASED	CRUELTY
CORBEAU	COURSER	CREATED	CRUISED
CORBEIL	COURTED	CREATOR	CRUISER
CORDAGE	COURTER	CREEPER	CRUMBED
CORDATE	COURTLY	CREMATE	CRUMBLE
CORDIAL	COUTEAU	CREMONA	CRUMBLY
CORDING	COUVADE	CRENATE	CRUMPED
CORDITE	COVERED	CREOSOL	CRUMPET
CORINTH	COVETED	CRESSET	CRUMPLE
CORKAGE	COW-BANE	CRESTED	CRUPPER
CORKING	COW-CALF	CREVICE	CRUSADE
CORK-LEG	COWERED	CRIBBED	CRUSADO
CORN-COB	COWHERD	CRICKED	CRUSHED
CORNEAL	COWHIDE	CRICKET	CRUSHER
CORNICE	COWLICK	CRIMPED	CRUSTED
CORNISH	COWLIKE	CRIMSON	CRY-BABY

CRYPTIC	CUSTODY	DASTARD	DECRIAL
CRYSTAL	CUSTOMS	DATABLE	DECRIED
CUBBING	CUT-AWAY	DAUBING	DECRIER
CUBBISH	CUTICLE	DAUNTED	DECROWN
CUBICAL	CUTLASS	DAUPHIN	DEDUCED
CUBICLE	CUTLERY	DAWDLED	DEEDING
CUBITAL	CUTTING	DAWDLER	DEEMING
CUBITED	CUT-WORM	DAWNING	DEEPEST
CUCKOLD	CYCLING	DAY-BOOK	DEEP-SEA
CUDDLED	CYCLIST	DAY-STAR	DEFACED
CUE-BALL	CYCLONE	DAY-TIME	DEFACER
CUFFING	CYCLOPS	DAY-WORK	DEFAMED
CUIRASS	CYNICAL	DAZZLED	DEFAMER
CUISINE	CYPRESS	DEAD-END	DEFAULT
CULLING	CYPRIAN	DEAD-EYE	DEFENCE
CULPRIT	CYPRIOT	DEADISH	DEFIANT
CULTURE	CZARISM	DEAD-SET	DEFICIT
CULVERT		DEALING	DEFILED
CUMULUS	**D—7**	DEANERY	DEFILER
CUNEATE	DABBING	DEAREST	DEFINED
CUNNING	DABBLED	DEATHLY	DEFINER
CUPPING	DABBLER	DEBACLE	DEFLATE
CUPRITE	DABSTER	DEBASED	DEFLECT
CURABLE	DAFTEST	DEBASER	DEFRAUD
CURACAO	DAGGLED	DEBATED	DEFUNCT
CURATOR	DAISIED	DEBATER	DEFYING
CURBING	DALLIED	DEBAUCH	DEGLAZE
CURDING	DALLIER	DEBITED	DEGRADE
CURDLED	DAMAGED	DEBOUCH	DE-ICING
CURE-ALL	DAMMING	DECADAL	DEIFIED
CURETTE	DAMNIFY	DECAGON	DEIFORM
CURIOUS	DAMNING	DECANAL	DEIGNED
CURLING	DAMOSEL	DECAPOD	DEISTIC
CURRANT	DAMPING	DECAYED	DELAYED
CURRENT	DAMPISH	DECAYER	DELAYER
CURRIED	DANCING	DECEASE	DELETED
CURRIER	DANDIFY	DECEIVE	DELIGHT
CURRISH	DANDLED	DECENCY	DELILAH
CURSING	DANELAW	DECIBEL	DELIMIT
CURSIVE	DANGLED	DECIDED	DELIVER
CURSORY	DANGLER	DECIDER	DELOUSE
CURTAIL	DANKISH	DECIMAL	DELPHIC
CURTAIN	DANTEAN	DECKING	DELTAIC
CURTANA	DAPPLED	DECKLED	DELUDED
CURTEST	DARKEST	DECLAIM	DELUDER
CURTSEY	DARKISH	DECLARE	DELUGED
CURVATE	DARLING	DECLINE	DELVING
CURVING	DARNING	DECODED	DEMERIT
CUSHION	DARTING	DECORUM	DEMESNE
CUSSING	DASHING	DECOYED	DEMIGOD
CUSTARD	DASH-POT	DECREED	DEMISED

DEMODED	DEVALUE	DINNING	DISUSED
DEMONIC	DEVELOP	DIOCESE	DITCHED
DEMONRY	DEVIATE	DIORAMA	DITCHER
DENIZEN	DEVILRY	DIOXIDE	DITHERY
DENOTED	DEVIOUS	DIPLOMA	DIURNAL
DENSELY	DEVISED	DIPOLAR	DIVERGE
DENSEST	DEVISEE	DIPPING	DIVERSE
DENSITY	DEVISER	DIPTERA	DIVIDED
DENTING	DEVISOR	DIREFUL	DIVIDER
DENTIST	DEVOLVE	DIRTIED	DIVINER
DENTOID	DEVOTED	DIRTIER	DIVISOR
DENTURE	DEVOTEE	DIRTILY	DIVORCE
DENUDED	DEW-DROP	DISABLE	DIVULGE
DENYING	DEW-FALL	DISAVOW	DIZZIED
DEPLETE	DEWLESS	DISBAND	DIZZIER
DEPLORE	DEXTRAL	DISCARD	DIZZILY
DEPLUME	DIABOLO	DISCERN	DOCKAGE
DEPOSAL	DIAGRAM	DISCOID	DOCKING
DEPOSED	DIALECT	DISCORD	DODGERY
DEPOSIT	DIALLED	DISCOUS	DODGING
DEPRAVE	DIAMOND	DISCUSS	DOESKIN
DEPRESS	DIARCHY	DISDAIN	DOFFING
DEPRIVE	DIARIST	DISEASE	DOG-BANE
DEPUTED	DIBBLED	DISEUSE	DOG-CART
DERANGE	DICE-BOX	DISGUST	DOG-DAYS
DERATED	DICKENS	DISHFUL	DOG-FISH
DERIDED	DICTATE	DISHING	DOGGING
DERIDER	DICTION	DISJOIN	DOGGISH
DERIVED	DIDDLED	DISLIKE	DOGHEAD
DERRICK	DIDDLER	DISMAST	DOG-HOLE
DERVISH	DIE-HARD	DISMISS	DOGLIKE
DESCANT	DIETARY	DISOBEY	DOG-NAIL
DESCEND	DIETING	DISPARK	DOG-ROSE
DESCENT	DIFFUSE	DISPART	DOG'S-EAR
DESERVE	DIGGING	DISPLAY	DOG-STAR
DESIRED	DIGITAL	DISPONE	DOLEFUL
DESIRER	DIGNIFY	DISPORT	DOLLIED
DESPAIR	DIGNITY	DISPOSE	DOLPHIN
DESPISE	DIGRESS	DISPUTE	DOLTISH
DESPITE	DILATED	DISRATE	DOMINIE
DESPOIL	DILATER	DISROBE	DONATOR
DESPOND	DILEMMA	DISROOT	DONNING
DESSERT	DILUENT	DISRUPT	DONNISH
DESTINE	DILUTED	DISSECT	DONSHIP
DESTINY	DILUTER	DISSENT	DOOMING
DESTROY	DIMETER	DISTAFF	DOORMAT
DETERGE	DIMMING	DISTANT	DOORWAY
DETINUE	DIMMISH	DISTEND	DORMANT
DETRACT	DIMNESS	DISTICH	DORMICE
DETRAIN	DIMPLED	DISTORT	DOSSIER
DETRUDE	DINGING	DISTURB	DOTTIER

DOTTING	DRIBLET	DUENESS	EARTHED
DOUBLED	DRIFTED	DUFFING	EARTHEN
DOUBLET	DRIFTER	DUKEDOM	EARTHLY
DOUBTED	DRILLED	DULCIFY	EASEFUL
DOUBTER	DRINKER	DULLARD	EASIEST
DOUCEUR	DRIPPED	DULLEST	EAST-END
DOUCHED	DRIVING	DULLING	EASTERN
DOUGHTY	DRIZZLE	DULLISH	EASTING
DOUREST	DRIZZLY	DUMPING	EATABLE
DOUSING	DROLLED	DUMPISH	EBB-TIDE
DOUTING	DRONING	DUNCIAD	EBONISE
DOVECOT	DRONISH	DUNGEON	EBONITE
DOWABLE	DROOLED	DUNNAGE	EBRIOUS
DOWAGER	DROOPED	DUNNING	ECHELON
DOWDILY	DROPLET	DUNNISH	ECHOING
DOWERED	DROP-NET	DUNNOCK	ECLIPSE
DOWNING	DROPPED	DUPABLE	ECLOGUE
DOWSING	DROPPER	DURABLE	ECOLOGY
DRABBER	DROUGHT	DURABLY	ECONOMY
DRACHMA	DROWNED	DURANCE	ECSTASY
DRACULA	DROWNER	DUSKIER	EDDYING
DRAFTED	DROWSED	DUSKILY	EDENTAL
DRAGGED	DRUBBED	DUSKISH	EDIFICE
DRAGGLE	DRUBBER	DUST-BIN	EDIFIED
DRAG-MAN	DRUDGED	DUSTIER	EDIFIER
DRAG-NET	DRUDGER	DUSTING	EDITING
DRAGOON	DRUGGED	DUSTMAN	EDITION
DRAINED	DRUGGER	DUST-PAN	EDUCATE
DRAINER	DRUGGET	DUTEOUS	EDUCING
DRAPERY	DRUIDIC	DUTIFUL	EFFACED
DRAPING	DRUMMED	DWARFED	EFFECTS
DRAPPIE	DRUMMER	DWELLED	EFFENDI
DRASTIC	DRUNKEN	DWELLER	EGALITY
DRATTED	DRY-DOCK	DWINDLE	EGG-COSY
DRAUGHT	DRY-EYED	DYNAMIC	EGG-FLIP
DRAWBAR	DRY-FOOT	DYNASTY	EGOTISE
DRAWING	DRYNESS		EGOTISM
DRAWLED	DRY-SHOD	**E—7**	EGOTIST
DRAWLER	DUALISM	EAGERLY	EJECTED
DRAW-NET	DUALIST	EAR-ACHE	EJECTOR
DRAYAGE	DUALITY	EAR-DROP	ELAPSED
DRAYMAN	DUBBING	EAR-DRUM	ELASTIC
DREADED	DUBIETY	EAR-HOLE	ELATING
DREAMED	DUBIOUS	EARLDOM	ELATION
DREAMER	DUCALLY	EARLESS	ELBOWED
DREDGED	DUCHESS	EARLIER	ELDERLY
DREDGER	DUCKING	EARMARK	ELECTED
DRESDEN	DUCTILE	EARNEST	ELECTOR
DRESSED	DUDGEON	EARNING	ELECTRO
DRESSER	DUELLED	EARRING	ELEGANT
DRIBBLE	DUELLER	EARSHOT	ELEGIAC

ELEGISE	ENCLASP	ENTERIC	ERUPTED
ELEGIST	ENCLAVE	ENTHRAL	ESCAPED
ELEMENT	ENCLOSE	ENTHUSE	ESCAPER
ELEVATE	ENCLOUD	ENTICED	ESCHEAT
ELEVENS	ENCORED	ENTICER	ESKIMOS
ELF-LOCK	ENCRUST	ENTITLE	ESPARTO
ELIDING	ENDEMIC	ENTRAIN	ESPOUSE
ELISION	ENDIRON	ENTRANT	ESPYING
ELLIPSE	ENDLESS	ENTREAT	ESQUIRE
ELOPING	ENDLONG	ENTRUST	ESSAYED
ELUDING	ENDMOST	ENTWINE	ESSENCE
ELUSION	ENDORSE	ENTWIST	ESTUARY
ELUSIVE	ENDOWED	ENURING	ETCHING
ELUSORY	ENDOWER	ENVELOP	ETERNAL
ELYSIAN	ENDUING	ENVENOM	ETHICAL
ELYSIUM	ENDURED	ENVIOUS	ETONIAN
EMANATE	ENDURER	ENVIRON	EUGENIC
EMBARGO	ENDWAYS	ENVYING	EUPHONY
EMBASSY	ENDWISE	EPAULET	EUTERPE
EMBLAZE	ENERGIC	EPERGNE	EVACUEE
EMBOSOM	ENFORCE	EPICARP	EVADING
EMBOWER	ENFRAME	EPICURE	EVANGEL
EMBOXED	ENGAGED	EPIGRAM	EVASION
EMBRACE	ENGAGER	EPISODE	EVASIVE
EMBROIL	ENGINED	EPISTLE	EVENING
EMBROWN	ENGLISH	EPITAPH	EVERTED
EMENDED	ENGORGE	EPITHET	EVICTED
EMERALD	ENGRAFT	EPITOME	EVICTOR
EMERGED	ENGRAIN	EPOCHAL	EVIDENT
EMINENT	ENGRAVE	EQUABLE	EVIL-EYE
EMITTED	ENGROSS	EQUABLY	EVINCED
EMOTION	ENGUARD	EQUALLY	EVOKING
EMOTIVE	ENHANCE	EQUATED	EVOLVED
EMPALED	ENJOYED	EQUATOR	EWE-LAMB
EMPANEL	ENLACED	EQUERRY	EXACTED
EMPEROR	ENLARGE	EQUINOX	EXACTER
EMPIRIC	ENLIVEN	ERASING	EXACTLY
EMPLANE	ENNOBLE	ERASURE	EXACTOR
EMPOWER	ENOUNCE	ERECTED	EXALTED
EMPRESS	ENQUIRE	ERECTER	EXAMINE
EMPTIED	ENQUIRY	ERECTLY	EXAMPLE
EMPTIER	ENRAGED	ERELONG	EXCERPT
EMULATE	ENROBED	EREMITE	EXCISED
EMULOUS	ENSLAVE	ERMINED	EXCITED
ENABLED	ENSNARE	ERODENT	EXCITER
ENACTED	ENSTAMP	ERODING	EXCLAIM
ENCAGED	ENSUING	EROSION	EXCLUDE
ENCASED	ENSURED	EROSIVE	EXCUSED
ENCAVED	ENTAMED	ERRATIC	EXECUTE
ENCHAIN	ENTENTE	ERRATUM	EXERTED
ENCHANT	ENTERED	ERUDITE	EXHALED

EXHAUST	FAIREST	FEBRILE	FIG-LEAF
EXHIBIT	FAIRING	FEDERAL	FIGMENT
EXHUMED	FAIRISH	FEEDING	FIG-TREE
EXIGENT	FAIR-WAY	FEELING	FIGURAL
EXILING	FALLACY	FEE-TAIL	FIGURED
EXISTED	FALLING	FEIGNED	FIGWORT
EXPANSE	FALSELY	FEINTED	FILBERT
EX-PARTE	FALSEST	FELLING	FILCHED
EXPENSE	FALSIFY	FELONRY	FILCHER
EXPIATE	FALSITY	FELSPAR	FILINGS
EXPIRED	FANATIC	FELTING	FILLING
EXPLAIN	FANCIED	FELUCCA	FILM-FAN
EXPLODE	FANFARE	FEMORAL	FILMING
EXPLOIT	FAN-MAIL	FENCING	FINABLE
EXPLORE	FANNING	FENDING	FINALLY
EXPOSED	FANTAIL	FEOFFEE	FINANCE
EXPOSER	FANTAST	FERMENT	FINDING
EXPOUND	FANTASY	FERNERY	FINESSE
EXPRESS	FAR-AWAY	FERN-OWL	FINICAL
EXPUNGE	FARCEUR	FERRATE	FINICKY
EXTINCT	FARCING	FERRIED	FINLESS
EXTRACT	FARMERY	FERROUS	FINNISH
EXTREME	FARMING	FERRULE	FIRE-ARM
EXTRUDE	FARMOST	FERTILE	FIRE-BAR
EXUDING	FARRAGO	FERVENT	FIRE-BOX
EXULTED	FARRIER	FERVOUR	FIREDOG
EYE-BALL	FARTHER	FESTIVE	FIREFLY
EYE-BOLT	FASCISM	FESTOON	FIREMAN
EYE-BROW	FASCIST	FETCHED	FIREPAN
EYE-HOLE	FASHING	FETLOCK	FIRSTLY
EYE-LASH	FASHION	FEVERED	FISHERY
EYELESS	FAST-DAY	FEWNESS	FISHILY
EYE-SHOT	FASTEST	FIANCEE	FISHING
EYE-WASH	FASTING	FIBBING	FISH-OIL
	FATALLY	FIBROID	FISSILE
F—7	FATEFUL	FIBROUS	FISSION
FACETED	FAT-HEAD	FIBSTER	FISSURE
FACTION	FATIGUE	FIBULAR	FITMENT
FACTORY	FATNESS	FICTILE	FITNESS
FACTUAL	FATTEST	FICTION	FITTING
FACULTY	FATTISH	FICTIVE	FIXABLE
FADDISH	FATUITY	FIDDLED	FIXEDLY
FADDIST	FATUOUS	FIDDLER	FIXTURE
FADE-OUT	FAULTED	FIDGETY	FIZZING
FAGGING	FAWNING	FIELDED	FIZZLED
FAIENCE	FEARFUL	FIELDER	FLACCID
FAILING	FEARING	FIERCER	FLAG-DAY
FAILURE	FEASTED	FIERILY	FLAGGED
FAINTED	FEASTER	FIFTEEN	FLAKING
FAINTER	FEATHER	FIFTHLY	FLAMING
FAINTLY	FEATURE	FIGHTER	FLANEUR

FLANGED	FLORIST	FOOLING	FOUNDED
FLANKED	FLOTAGE	FOOLISH	FOUNDER
FLANKER	FLOTANT	FOOTBOY	FOUNDRY
FLANNEL	FLOTSAM	FOOTING	FOWLING
FLAPPED	FLOUNCE	FOOTLED	FOX-HUNT
FLAPPER	FLOURED	FOOTMAN	FOXLIKE
FLARING	FLOUTED	FOOTPAD	FOX-TAIL
FLASHED	FLOUTER	FOOT-ROT	FOX-TROT
FLASHER	FLOWERY	FOOTWAY	FRAGILE
FLATLET	FLOWING	FOPPERY	FRAILLY
FLATTEN	FLUENCY	FOPPISH	FRAILTY
FLATTER	FLUFFED	FORAGED	FRAME-UP
FLAVOUR	FLUKILY	FORAGER	FRAMING
FLAWING	FLUKING	FORAYED	FRANKED
FLAYING	FLUMMOX	FORBADE	FRANKLY
FLECKED	FLUNKEY	FORBEAR	FRANTIC
FLECKER	FLUSHED	FORBORE	FRAUGHT
FLEDGED	FLUSTER	FORCEPS	FRAYING
FLEECED	FLUTING	FORCING	FRAZZLE
FLEECER	FLUTIST	FORDING	FREAKED
FLEEING	FLUTTER	FORDONE	FRECKLE
FLEETED	FLUVIAL	FOREARM	FRECKLY
FLEETER	FLY-AWAY	FOREIGN	FREEDOM
FLEETLY	FLY-BOOK	FORELEG	FREEING
FLEMING	FLY-FLAP	FOREMAN	FREEMAN
FLEMISH	FLY-HALF	FORERAN	FREESIA
FLESHED	FLY-LEAF	FORERUN	FREEZER
FLESHER	FLY-OVER	FORESAW	FREIGHT
FLESHLY	FLY-PAST	FORESEE	FRESHEN
FLEURET	FLY-TRAP	FORETOP	FRESHER
FLEXILE	FOALING	FOREVER	FRESHET
FLEXING	FOAMING	FORFEIT	FRESHLY
FLEXION	FOBBING	FORFEND	FRETFUL
FLEXURE	FOCUSED	FORGAVE	FRET-SAW
FLICKED	FOE-LIKE	FORGERY	FRETTED
FLICKER	FOG-BANK	FORGING	FRIABLE
FLIGHTY	FOGGIER	FORGIVE	FRIEZED
FLIPPED	FOGGILY	FORGONE	FRIGATE
FLIPPER	FOGGING	FORKING	FRILLED
FLIRTED	FOG-HORN	FORLORN	FRINGED
FLITTED	FOILING	FORMATE	FRISIAN
FLITTER	FOISTED	FORMING	FRISKED
FLIVVER	FOLDING	FORMULA	FRISKER
FLOATED	FOLIAGE	FORSAKE	FRITTED
FLOATER	FOLIATE	FORSOOK	FRITTER
FLOCKED	FOLLIES	FORTIFY	FRIZZED
FLOGGED	FONDANT	FORTUNE	FRIZZLE
FLOODED	FONDEST	FORWARD	FROCKED
FLOORED	FONDLED	FORWENT	FROGGED
FLOORER	FONDLER	FOULARD	FROG-MAN
FLOPPED	FOOLERY	FOULING	FRONDED

FRONTAL	G—7	GAS-OVEN	GIGGLER
FRONTED	GABBING	GASPING	GILDING
FROSTED	GABBLED	GAS-PIPE	GIMBALS
FROTHED	GABBLER	GAS-RING	GIN-FIZZ
FROWARD	GADDING	GASSING	GINGERY
FROWNED	GADDISH	GASTRIC	GINGHAM
FRUITED	GAEKWAR	GATEMAN	GIN-SHOP
FRUITER	GAFFING	GATEWAY	GIRAFFE
FUCHSIA	GAGGING	GATLING	GIRDING
FUDDLED	GAINFUL	GAUDERY	GIRDLED
FUDDLER	GAINING	GAUDILY	GIRDLER
FUDGING	GAINSAY	GAUGING	GIRLISH
FUEHRER	GALATEA	GAULISH	GIRTHED
FUELLED	GALILEE	GAUNTLY	GIZZARD
FULCRUM	GALILEO	GAUNTRY	GLACIAL
FULGENT	GALLANT	GAVOTTE	GLACIER
FULLEST	GALLEON	GAYNESS	GLADDEN
FULL-PAY	GALLERY	GAYSOME	GLADDER
FULSOME	GALLING	GAZELLE	GLAD-EYE
FUMBLED	GALLOWS	GAZETTE	GLAMOUR
FUMBLER	GALUMPH	GEARING	GLANCED
FUNDING	GAMBIST	GELDING	GLARING
FUNERAL	GAMBLED	GELIDLY	GLASSES
FUNGOID	GAMBLER	GEMMING	GLAZIER
FUNGOUS	GAMBOGE	GENERAL	GLAZING
FUNKING	GAMEFUL	GENERIC	GLEAMED
FUNNILY	GAME-LEG	GENESIS	GLEANED
FUNNING	GANGING	GENETIC	GLEANER
FURBISH	GANGLIA	GENITAL	GLEEFUL
FURCATE	GANGWAY	GENOESE	GLIDING
FURIOSO	GAPPING	GENTEEL	GLIMMER
FURIOUS	GARAGED	GENTIAN	GLIMPSE
FURLING	GARBAGE	GENTILE	GLINTED
FURLONG	GARBLED	GENTLER	GLISTEN
FURNACE	GARFISH	GENUINE	GLISTER
FURNISH	GARGLED	GEOLOGY	GLITTER
FURRIER	GARLAND	GEORDIE	GLOATED
FURRING	GARMENT	GERMANE	GLOBATE
FURTHER	GARNISH	GESTAPO	GLOBING
FURTIVE	GAROTTE	GESTURE	GLOBOID
FUSIBLE	GARPIKE	GETABLE	GLOBOSE
FUSSIER	GAS-BUOY	GET-AWAY	GLOBULE
FUSSILY	GAS-COAL	GETTING	GLOOMED
FUSSING	GAS-COKE	GHASTLY	GLORIED
FUSS-POT	GASEITY	GHERKIN	GLORIFY
FUSTIAN	GASEOUS	GHILLIE	GLOSSED
FUSTIER	GAS-FIRE	GHOSTLY	GLOSSER
FUZZIER	GASHING	GIBLETS	GLOTTIC
FUZZLED	GAS-LIME	GIDDILY	GLOTTIS
	GAS-MAIN	GIFTING	GLOWING
	GAS-MASK	GIGGLED	GLUCOSE

GLUE-POT	GRABBER	GREENLY	GRUNTER
GLUMMER	GRABBLE	GREETED	GRUYERE
GLUTTED	GRACING	GREMLIN	GUARDED
GLUTTON	GRADATE	GRENADE	GUDGEON
GNARLED	GRADELY	GREY-HEN	GUELDER
GNARRED	GRADING	GREYISH	GUERDON
GNASHED	GRADUAL	GREYLAG	GUESSED
GNAWING	GRAFTED	GRIDDED	GUESSER
GNOSTIC	GRAFTER	GRIDDLE	GUICHET
GOADING	GRAINED	GRIEVED	GUIDAGE
GO-AHEAD	GRAINER	GRIFFIN	GUIDING
GOATISH	GRAMMAR	GRIFFON	GUILDER
GOBBLED	GRAMPUS	GRILLED	GUILDRY
GOBBLER	GRANARY	GRIMACE	GUIPURE
GOBELIN	GRANDAD	GRIMING	GULLERY
GODDESS	GRANDAM	GRIMMER	GULLIED
GODETIA	GRANDEE	GRINDER	GULLING
GODHEAD	GRANDER	GRINNED	GUM-BOIL
GODHOOD	GRANDLY	GRIPING	GUM-BOOT
GODLESS	GRANDMA	GRIPPED	GUMDROP
GODLIER	GRANGER	GRIPPER	GUMMING
GODLIKE	GRANITE	GRISTLE	GUM-TREE
GODLILY	GRANTED	GRISTLY	GUNBOAT
GODSEND	GRANTEE	GRITTED	GUN-DECK
GODSHIP	GRANTER	GRIZZLE	GUN-FIRE
GODWARD	GRANTOR	GRIZZLY	GUNNERY
GOGGLED	GRANULE	GROANED	GUNNING
GOGGLES	GRAPERY	GROCERY	GUN-ROOM
GOITRED	GRAPHIC	GROOMED	GUNSHOT
GOLFING	GRAPNEL	GROOVED	GUN-SITE
GOLIATH	GRAPPLE	GROPING	GUNWALE
GONDOLA	GRASPED	GROSSER	GURGLED
GONGING	GRASPER	GROSSLY	GURNARD
GOOD-BYE	GRASSED	GROUNDS	GUSHING
GOOD-DAY	GRATIFY	GROUPED	GUSTILY
GOODISH	GRATING	GROUPER	GUTTING
GOODMAN	GRAVELY	GROUSED	GUZZLED
GOOSERY	GRAVEST	GROUSER	GUZZLER
GORDIAN	GRAVIED	GROUTED	GYMNAST
GORGING	GRAVITY	GROWING	GYRATED
GORILLA	GRAVURE	GROWLED	
GORMAND	GRAZIER	GROWLER	H—7
GORSEDD	GRAZING	GROWN-UP	HABITAT
GOSLING	GREASED	GRUBBED	HABITED
GOSSIPY	GREASER	GRUBBER	HABITUE
GOUACHE	GREATER	GRUDGED	HACKBUT
GOUGING	GREATLY	GRUDGER	HACKING
GOULASH	GRECIAN	GRUFFER	HACKLED
GOURMET	GRECISM	GRUFFLY	HACKNEY
GOUTILY	GRECIZE	GRUMBLE	HACK-SAW
GRABBED	GREENER	GRUNTED	HADDOCK

HAFTING	HARKING	HEALTHY	HERITOR
HAGGARD	HARMFUL	HEAPING	HEROINE
HAGGISH	HARMING	HEARING	HEROISM
HAGGLED	HARMONY	HEARKEN	HEROIZE
HAGGLER	HARNESS	HEARSAY	HERONRY
HAILING	HARPING	HEARTED	HERRING
HAIR-CUT	HARPIST	HEARTEN	HERSELF
HAIR-OIL	HARPOON	HEATHEN	HESSIAN
HAIRPIN	HARRIED	HEATING	HEXAGON
HALBERD	HARRIER	HEAVE-TO	HEXAPOD
HALCYON	HARSHER	HEAVIER	HICKORY
HALF-PAY	HARSHLY	HEAVILY	HIDALGO
HALFWAY	HARVEST	HEAVING	HIDEOUS
HALF-WIT	HASHING	HEBRAIC	HIDE-OUT
HALIBUT	HASHISH	HECKLED	HIGGLED
HALOGEN	HASSOCK	HECKLER	HIGGLER
HALTING	HASTIER	HECTARE	HIGHDAY
HALVING	HASTILY	HEDGING	HIGHEST
HALYARD	HASTING	HEDONIC	HIGH-HAT
HAMBURG	HATABLE	HEEDFUL	HIGHWAY
HAMMOCK	HATCHER	HEEDING	HILLIER
HAMSTER	HATCHET	HEELING	HILLMAN
HAMULAR	HATEFUL	HEEL-TAP	HILLOCK
HANDBAG	HATLESS	HEFTIER	HILLTOP
HANDFUL	HAT-RACK	HEFTILY	HIMSELF
HANDIER	HAUBERK	HEIGH-HO	HINNIED
HANDILY	HAUGHTY	HEINOUS	HINTING
HANDING	HAULAGE	HEIRDOM	HIPPING
HANDLED	HAULIER	HEIRESS	HIRABLE
HANDLER	HAULING	HELICAL	HIRCINE
HANDSAW	HAUNTED	HELICON	HIRSUTE
HANG-DOG	HAUNTER	HELL-CAT	HISSING
HANGING	HAUTBOY	HELLENE	HISTORY
HANGMAN	HAUTEUR	HELLISH	HITCHED
HANG-NET	HAWKBIT	HELPFUL	HITTING
HANSARD	HAWKING	HELPING	HITTITE
HAPLESS	HAWK-OWL	HEMLOCK	HOARDED
HAP'ORTH	HAY-BAND	HEMMING	HOARDER
HAPPIER	HAYCOCK	HENBANE	HOAXING
HAPPILY	HAYFORK	HEN-COOP	HOBBLED
HARBOUR	HAY-LOFT	HENNAED	HOBNAIL
HARDEST	HAYRICK	HENNERY	HOGGING
HARDIER	HAYSEED	HENPECK	HOGGISH
HARDILY	HAY-WARD	HENWIFE	HOGWASH
HARDISH	HAYWIRE	HEPATIC	HOGSWEED
HARD-PAN	HAZIEST	HERBAGE	HOISTED
HARDSET	HEADILY	HERBARY	HOISTER
HARD-WON	HEADING	HERBIST	HOLDALL
HAREING	HEADMAN	HERBOUS	HOLDING
HARE-LIP	HEADWAY	HERDING	HOLIDAY
HARICOT	HEALING	HERETIC	HOLIEST

HOLLAND	HUFFILY	IDYLLIC	INANITY
HOLM-OAK	HUFFING	IGNEOUS	INAPTLY
HOLSTER	HUFFISH	IGNITED	INBEING
HOMERIC	HUGGING	IGNITER	INBOARD
HONESTY	HULKING	IGNOBLE	INBOUND
HONEYED	HULLING	IGNOBLY	INBREAK
HONITON	HUMANLY	IGNORED	INBREED
HONKING	HUMBLED	ILL-BRED	INCENSE
HOODING	HUMBLER	ILLEGAL	INCHING
HOODLUM	HUMDRUM	ILL-FAME	INCISED
HOOFING	HUMERUS	ILLICIT	INCISOR
HOOKING	HUMIDLY	ILLNESS	INCITED
HOOPING	HUMMING	ILL-TIME	INCITER
HOOTING	HUMMOCK	ILLUMED	INCLINE
HOPEFUL	HUMULUS	ILL-USED	INCLUDE
HOPKILN	HUNCHED	ILL-WILL	INCOMER
HOPLITE	HUNDRED	IMAGERY	INCUBUS
HOPPING	HUNTING	IMAGINE	INCURVE
HOP-POLE	HURDLED	IMAGING	INDEXED
HOP-VINE	HURDLER	IMBIBED	INDITED
HORIZON	HURLING	IMBIBER	INDOORS
HORMONE	HURRIED	IMBRUED	INDRAWN
HORNBAR	HURRIER	IMBUING	INDUCED
HORNING	HURTFUL	IMITATE	INDULGE
HORNISH	HURTLED	IMMENSE	INEPTLY
HORN-OWL	HUSBAND	IMMERSE	INERTIA
HORRIFY	HUSHABY	IMMORAL	INERTLY
HOSANNA	HUSHING	IMMURED	INEXACT
HOSIERY	HUSKING	IMPALED	INFANCY
HOSPICE	HUSTLED	IMPASSE	INFANTA
HOSTAGE	HUSTLER	IMPEACH	INFANTE
HOSTESS	HUTMENT	IMPEDED	INFERNO
HOSTILE	HYDRANT	IMPERIL	INFIDEL
HOSTLER	HYDRATE	IMPETUS	INFIELD
HOT-FOOT	HYGIENE	IMPIETY	INFIXED
HOTNESS	HYMNIST	IMPINGE	INFLAME
HOTSPUR	HYMNODY	IMPIOUS	INFLATE
HOTTEST		IMPLANT	INFLECT
HOT-WALL		IMPLIED	INFLICT
HOUNDED	I—7	IMPLORE	INFUSED
HOUSAGE	IBERIAN	IMPOSED	INFUSER
HOUSING	ICEBERG	IMPOSER	INGENUE
HOVERED	ICEBOAT	IMPOUND	INGOING
HOVERER	ICE-FLOE	IMPRESS	INGRESS
HOWBEIT	ICEPACK	IMPREST	INHABIT
HOWDY-DO	ICE-RINK	IMPRINT	INHALED
HOWEVER	ICHABOD	IMPROVE	INHALER
HOWLING	ICINESS	IMPULSE	INHERED
HUDDLED	IDEALLY	IMPUTED	INHERIT
HUDDLER	IDIOTIC	IMPUTER	INHIBIT
HUELESS	IDOLISE	INANELY	INHUMAN

INITIAL	IRIDIUM	JEZEBEL	JUMBLED
INJURED	IRKSOME	JIBBING	JUMBLER
INJURER	IRONING	JIB-BOOM	JUMPING
INKHORN	ISHMAEL	JIGGING	JUNIPER
INKLING	ISLAMIC	JIGGLED	JUNKMAN
INKWELL	ISOLATE	JILTING	JUPITER
INLACED	ISOTOPE	JIM-CROW	JURY-BOX
INLAYER	ISSUING	JINGLED	JURY-MAN
INNINGS	ISTHMUS	JITTERS	JUSSIVE
INQUEST	ITALIAN	JITTERY	JUSTICE
INQUIRE	ITALICS	JOBBERY	JUSTIFY
INQUIRY	ITCHING	JOBBING	JUTTING
INSHORE	ITEMISE	JOBLESS	JUVENAL
INSIDER	ITERATE	JOCULAR	
INSIGHT	IVORIED	JOGGING	K—7
INSIPID	IVY-BUSH	JOGGLED	KAMERAD
INSPECT		JOG-TROT	KATYDID
INSPIRE		JOINDER	KEENEST
INSTALL	J—7	JOINERY	KEENING
INSTANT	JABBING	JOINING	KEEPING
INSTEAD	JACINTH	JOINTED	KENTISH
INSULAR	JACKASS	JOINTER	KESTREL
INSULIN	JACKDAW	JOINTLY	KETCHUP
INSURED	JACKING	JOISTED	KEYBOLT
INSURER	JACKPOT	JOLLIER	KEYED-UP
INTEGER	JACK-TAR	JOLLIFY	KEYHOLE
INTENSE	JACOBIN	JOLLILY	KEY-NOTE
INTERIM	JADEDLY	JOLLITY	KEY-RING
INTONED	JAGGING	JOLTING	KHAMSIN
INTRUDE	JAILING	JONQUIL	KHEDIVE
INTRUST	JAMMING	JOSTLED	KICKING
INTWINE	JANGLED	JOTTING	KICK-OFF
INURING	JANITOR	JOUNCED	KIDDING
INVADED	JANUARY	JOURNAL	KILLING
INVADER	JARRING	JOURNEY	KILL-JOY
INVALID	JASMINE	JOUSTED	KILN-DRY
INVEIGH	JAVELIN	JOYLESS	KINDEST
INVERSE	JAWBONE	JOY-RIDE	KINDLED
INVIOUS	JAZZING	JUBILEE	KINDRED
INVITED	JEALOUS	JUDAISM	KINETIC
INVITER	JEERING	JUDAIST	KINGCUP
INVOICE	JEHOVAH	JUDAISE	KINGDOM
INVOKED	JELLIED	JUDGING	KING-PIN
INVOKER	JELLIFY	JUGGING	KINKING
INVOLVE	JERICHO	JUGGINS	KINLESS
INWARDS	JERKING	JUGGLED	KINSHIP
INWOVEN	JESTFUL	JUGGLER	KINSMAN
IODISED	JESTING	JUGULAR	KIRTLED
IONISED	JETTIED	JUICIER	KISSING
IRACUND	JETTING	JU-JITSU	KITCHEN
IRANIAN	JEWELRY	JUKE-BOX	KNACKER

KNAPPED	LAND-TAX	LEAGUER	LEXICAL
KNAPPER	LANGUID	LEAKAGE	LEXICON
KNARLED	LANGUOR	LEAKING	LIAISON
KNAVERY	LANKIER	LEANDER	LIBERAL
KNAVISH	LANOLIN	LEANEST	LIBERTY
KNEADED	LANTERN	LEANING	LIBRARY
KNEE-CAP	LANYARD	LEAPING	LICENCE
KNEE-PAN	LAPPING	LEARNED	LICENSE
KNIFING	LAPPISH	LEARNER	LICITLY
KNITTED	LAPSING	LEASHED	LICKING
KNITTER	LAPWING	LEASING	LIDLESS
KNOBBED	LARCENY	LEATHER	LIE-ABED
KNOBBLY	LARDING	LEAVING	LIFTING
KNOCKED	LARGELY	LECTERN	LIGATED
KNOCKER	LARGEST	LECTION	LIGHTED
KNOCK-ON	LARGISH	LECTURE	LIGHTEN
KNOTTED	LARKING	LEEMOST	LIGHTER
KNOUTED	LASHING	LEERILY	LIGHTLY
KNOW-ALL	LASHKAR	LEERING	LIGNIFY
KNOWING	LASSOED	LEE-SIDE	LIGNITE
KNUCKLE	LASTING	LEE-TIDE	LIGNOSE
KNURLED	LATAKIA	LEEWARD	LIKABLE
KOUMISS	LATCHED	LEGALLY	LIKENED
KREMLIN	LATCHET	LEGATEE	LILY-PAD
KRISHNA	LATENCY	LEGGING	LIMBATE
KURSAAL	LATERAL	LEGHORN	LIMBING
	LATERAN	LEGIBLE	LIME-PIT
L—7	LATHING	LEGIBLY	LIMINAL
LABIATE	LATTICE	LEG-IRON	LIMITED
LACKING	LATVIAN	LEGLESS	LIMITER
LACONIC	LAUDING	LEG-PULL	LIMNING
LACQUER	LAUGHED	LEISURE	LIMPING
LACTATE	LAUGHTER	LEMMING	LINCTUS
LACTOSE	LAUNDER	LENDING	LINEAGE
LADLING	LAUNDRY	LENGTHY	LINEATE
LADY-DAY	LAW-BOOK	LENIENT	LINEMAN
LAGGARD	LAWLESS	LENTOID	LINGUAL
LAGGING	LAW-LORD	LEONINE	LINKAGE
LAKELET	LAW-SUIT	LEOPARD	LINKBOY
LAMBENT	LAXNESS	LEPROSY	LINKING
LAMBING	LAYERED	LEPROUS	LINSEED
LAMBKIN	LAYETTE	LESBIAN	LION-CUB
LAMINAR	LAYLAND	LET-DOWN	LIONESS
LAMMING	LAZIEST	LETTING	LIONISM
LAMP-LIT	LAZY-BED	LETTISH	LIONISE
LAMPOON	LEACHED	LETTUCE	LIPPING
LAMPREY	LEADING	LEUCOMA	LIQUATE
LANCERS	LEAFAGE	LEVELLY	LIQUEFY
LANCING	LEAFING	LEVERED	LIQUEUR
LANDING	LEAFLET	LEVERET	LISPING
LANDTAG	LEAGUED	LEVYING	LISSOME

LISTING	LONG-RUN	LUMPIER	MALAISE
LITERAL	LOOKING	LUMPING	MALARIA
LITHELY	LOOKOUT	LUMPISH	MALAYAN
LITHIUM	LOOMING	LUNATIC	MALISON
LITHOID	LOOPING	LUNCHED	MALLARD
LITOTES	LOOSELY	LUNETTE	MALLING
LITURGY	LOOSING	LUNGING	MALMSEY
LIVABLE	LOOTING	LURCHED	MALTESE
LIVENED	LOPPING	LURCHER	MALTING
LIVE-OAK	LORDING	LURKING	MALTMAN
LIVERED	LORELEI	LUSHING	MAMMARY
LOADING	LORINER	LUSTFUL	MAMMOTH
LOAFING	LOSABLE	LUSTIER	MANACLE
LOAMING	LOTTERY	LUSTILY	MANAGED
LOANING	LOTTING	LUSTING	MANAGER
LOATHED	LOUDEST	LYCHNIS	MANAKIN
LOATHER	LOUNGED	LYDDITE	MANATEE
LOATHLY	LOUNGER	LYING-IN	MANCHET
LOBBIED	LOURING	LYINGLY	MANDATE
LOBBING	LOUSILY	LYNCHED	MANDREL
LOBELIA	LOUTISH	LYRICAL	MANDRIL
LOBSTER	LOVABLE		MANGLED
LOBULAR	LOW-BORN	**M—7**	MANGLER
LOCALLY	LOW-BRED	MACABRE	MANGOLD
LOCATED	LOWDOWN	MACADAM	MANHOLE
LOCKAGE	LOWERED	MACAQUE	MANHOOD
LOCKING	LOW-GEAR	MACHETE	MAN-HOUR
LOCK-JAW	LOWLAND	MACHINE	MAN-HUNT
LOCK-OUT	LOW-LIFE	MADDEST	MANIKIN
LODGING	LOWLILY	MADDING	MANILLA
LOFTIER	LOWNESS	MADEIRA	MANITOU
LOFTILY	LOW-TIDE	MADNESS	MANKIND
LOFTING	LOYALLY	MADONNA	MANLESS
LOG-BOOK	LOYALTY	MAESTRO	MANLIKE
LOGGING	LOZENGE	MAGENTA	MAN-MADE
LOGICAL	LUCENCY	MAGGOTY	MANNING
LOGLINE	LUCERNE	MAGICAL	MANNISH
LOG-REEL	LUCIDLY	MAGINOT	MAN-ROPE
LOG-ROLL	LUCIFER	MAGNATE	MANSARD
LOG-SHIP	LUCKIER	MAGNETO	MANSION
LOGWOOD	LUCKILY	MAGNIFY	MANTLED
LOLLARD	LUFFING	MAHATMA	MANTLET
LOLLING	LUGGAGE	MAHJONG	MAN-TRAP
LOMBARD	LUGGING	MAIL-BAG	MANURED
LONG-AGO	LUGMARK	MAILING	MANX-CAT
LONGBOW	LUGSAIL	MAIL-VAN	MAPPING
LONGEST	LUGWORM	MAIMING	MAPPIST
LONG-HOP	LULLABY	MAINOUR	MARABOU
LONGING	LULLING	MAINTOP	MARBLED
LONGISH	LUMBAGO	MAJESTY	MARCHED
LONG-LEG	LUMINAL	MALACCA	MARCHER

MARCONI	MAY-POLE	MICROHM	MISDEEM
MARINER	MAY-TIME	MIDLAND	MISDOER
MARITAL	MAY-WEED	MID-LIFE	MISDONE
MARKING	MAZURKA	MIDMOST	MISERLY
MARLINE	MEADOWY	MIDRIFF	MISFALL
MARLING	MEANDER	MIDWIFE	MISFIRE
MARLPIT	MEANEST	MIGRANT	MISFORM
MARQUEE	MEANING	MIGRATE	MISGAVE
MARQUIS	MEASLED	MILDEST	MISGIVE
MARRIED	MEASLES	MILDEWY	MISHEAR
MARRING	MEASURE	MILEAGE	MISJOIN
MARROWY	MEAT-TEA	MILFOIL	MISLAID
MARSALA	MECHLIN	MILIARY	MISLEAD
MARSHAL	MEDDLED	MILITIA	MISLIKE
MARTIAL	MEDDLER	MILKILY	MISNAME
MARTINI	MEDIATE	MILKING	MISRATE
MARTLET	MEDICAL	MILKMAN	MISREAD
MARXIAN	MEETING	MILKSOP	MISRULE
MARXISM	MEISSEN	MILL-DAM	MISSAID
MARXIST	MELANGE	MILLIER	MISSEEM
MASHING	MELODIC	MILLING	MISSEND
MASH-TUB	MELTING	MILLION	MISSENT
MASKING	MEMENTO	MIMESIS	MISSILE
MASONIC	MENACED	MIMETIC	MISSING
MASONRY	MENACER	MIMICAL	MISSION
MASSAGE	MENDING	MIMICRY	MISSIVE
MASSEUR	MEN-FOLK	MINARET	MISTAKE
MASSING	MENTHOL	MINCING	MISTELL
MASSIVE	MENTION	MINDFUL	MISTERM
MASTERY	MERCERY	MINDING	MISTFUL
MASTIFF	MERCURY	MINERAL	MISTILY
MASTING	MERGING	MINERVA	MISTIME
MASTOID	MERITED	MINGLED	MISTRAL
MATADOR	MERLING	MINGLER	MISTUNE
MATCHED	MERMAID	MINIBUS	MISUSED
MATCHET	MERRIER	MINIKIN	MITHRAS
MATELOT	MERRILY	MINIMAL	MIXABLE
MATINEE	MESEEMS	MINIMUM	MIXEDLY
MATTING	MESHING	MINIMUS	MIXTURE
MATTOCK	MESSAGE	MINSTER	MIZZLED
MATURED	MESSIAH	MINTING	MOANFUL
MAUDLIN	MESSING	MINUTED	MOANING
MAULING	METHANE	MIOCENE	MOBBING
MAUNDER	METONIC	MIRACLE	MOBBISH
MAWKISH	METTLED	MISCALL	MOBSMAN
MAXIMAL	MEWLING	MISCAST	MOCKERY
MAXIMUM	MEXICAN	MISCITE	MOCKING
MAYFAIR	MIASMAL	MISCUED	MOCK-SUN
MAY-LILY	MIAUING	MISDATE	MODALLY
MAY-MORN	MIAULED	MISDEAL	MODESTY
MAYORAL	MICROBE	MISDEED	MODICUM

MODISTE	MOUTHER	MUTABLY	NEIGHED
MODULUS	MOVABLE	MUTANDA	NEITHER
MOHICAN	MOVABLY	MUTTONY	NEMESIS
MOIDORE	MUCKING	MUZZILY	NEOLOGY
MOILING	MUD-BATH	MUZZLED	NEPOTIC
MOISTEN	MUD-CART	MYNHEER	NEPTUNE
MOLE-RAT	MUDDIED	MYSTERY	NERVING
MOLLIFY	MUDDIER	MYSTIFY	NERVOUS
MOLLUSC	MUDDILY		NEST-EGG
MONARCH	MUDDING	**N—7**	NESTING
MONEYED	MUDDLED	NABBING	NESTLED
MONGREL	MUD-FISH	NAGGING	NESTLER
MONIKER	MUD-FLAT	NAILERY	NET-BALL
MONITOR	MUD-HOLE	NAILING	NET-CORD
MONKISH	MUD-LARK	NAIVELY	NETTING
MONOCLE	MUEZZIN	NAIVETE	NETTLED
MONSOON	MUFFING	NAKEDLY	NETTLER
MONSTER	MUFFLED	NAMABLE	NETWORK
MONTHLY	MUFFLER	NANKEEN	NEURINE
MOOCHED	MUGGING	NAPHTHA	NEUROSE
MOODILY	MUGGINS	NAPLESS	NEUTRAL
MOONING	MUGGISH	NAPPING	NEUTRON
MOONISH	MUGWUMP	NARRATE	NEW-BORN
MOONLIT	MULATTO	NARWHAL	NEWGATE
MOORAGE	MULCHED	NASALLY	NEW-MADE
MOOR-HEN	MULCTED	NASCENT	NEWNESS
MOORING	MULLING	NASTIER	NEWSBOY
MOORISH	MULLION	NASTILY	NEWSMAN
MOOTING	MUMBLED	NATTIER	NIAGARA
MOPPING	MUMBLER	NATTILY	NIBBLED
MORALLY	MUMMERY	NATURAL	NIBBLER
MORDANT	MUMMIED	NATURED	NIBLICK
MORELLO	MUMMIFY	NAUGHTY	NICKING
MORNING	MUMMING	NAZI-ISM	NIGELLA
MOROCCO	MUMPING	NEAREST	NIGGARD
MORPHIA	MUMPISH	NEATEST	NIGGLED
MORTISE	MUNCHED	NEBULAE	NIGGLER
MORTIFY	MUNCHER	NEBULAR	NIGHTIE
MOSELLE	MUNDANE	NECKING	NIGHTLY
MOTORED	MURKIER	NECKLET	NIMBLER
MOTTLED	MURKILY	NECKTIE	NINE-PIN
MOULDED	MURRAIN	NEEDFUL	NINTHLY
MOULDER	MUSCLED	NEEDIER	NIPPERS
MOULTED	MUSETTE	NEEDILY	NIPPIER
MOUNDED	MUSHING	NEEDING	NIPPIES
MOUNTED	MUSICAL	NEEDLED	NIPPING
MOUNTER	MUSK-RAT	NEGATED	NIRVANA
MOURNED	MUSTANG	NEGLECT	NITRATE
MOURNER	MUSTARD	NEGLIGE	NITROUS
MOUSING	MUSTILY	NEGRESS	NOBBLED
MOUTHED	MUTABLE	NEGROID	NOBBLER

NOBLEST	NUTTING	OFFHAND	ORDINAL
NO-CLAIM	NUT-TREE	OFFICER	ORDINEE
NODATED	NUZZLED	OFFSIDE	OREADES
NODDING		OGREISH	ORGANIC
NODULAR	**O—7**	OIL-CAKE	ORIFICE
NODULED	OAFLIKE	OIL-SHOP	ORLEANS
NOGGING	OAK-LEAF	OIL-SKIN	OROLOGY
NOISILY	OAKLING	OIL-WELL	ORPHEAN
NOISING	OARFISH	OLDNESS	ORPHEUS
NOISOME	OARLOCK	OLDSTER	ORTOLAN
NOMADIC	OARSMAN	OLD-TIME	OSCULAR
NOMINAL	OAT-CAKE	OLYMPIA	OSMANLI
NOMINEE	OAT-MEAL	OLYMPIC	OSTEOID
NON-ACID	OBELISK	OLYMPUS	OSTRICH
NONAGON	OBESITY	OMINOUS	OTTOMAN
NONPLUS	OBEYING	OMITTED	OURSELF
NONSTOP	OBLIGED	OMNIBUS	OUSTING
NONSUCH	OBLIGEE	OMNIFIC	OUT-BACK
NON-SUIT	OBLIGER	ONE-EYED	OUTBRAG
NOONDAY	OBLIGOR	ONEFOLD	OUTCAST
NORFOLK	OBLIQUE	ONENESS	OUTCOME
NORWICH	OBLOQUY	ONERARY	OUTCROP
NOSE-BAG	OBSCENE	ONEROUS	OUTDARE
NOSEGAY	OBSCURE	ONESELF	OUTDONE
NOSTRIL	OBSERVE	ONE-STEP	OUTDOOR
NOSTRUM	OBTRUDE	ONGOING	OUTFACE
NOTABLE	OBVERSE	ONWARDS	OUTFALL
NOTABLY	OBVIATE	OPACITY	OUTFLOW
NOTANDA	OBVIOUS	OPALINE	OUTGOER
NOTCHED	OCARINA	OPALISE	OUTGROW
NOTEDLY	OCCIPUT	OPEN-AIR	OUTHAUL
NOTHING	OCCLUDE	OPENING	OUTLAND
NOTICED	OCEANIA	OPERATE	OUTLAST
NOURISH	OCEANIC	OPINING	OUTLEAP
NOVELTY	OCTAGON	OPINION	OUTLIER
NOWHERE	OCTAVUS	OPOSSUM	OUTLINE
NOXIOUS	OCTETTE	OPPIDAN	OUTLIVE
NUCLEAR	OCTOBER	OPPOSED	OUTLOOK
NUCLEUS	OCTOPOD	OPPOSER	OUTMOST
NUDGING	OCTOPUS	OPPRESS	OUTMOVE
NULLIFY	OCTUPLE	OPTICAL	OUTPACE
NULLITY	OCULIST	OPTIMUM	OUTPLAY
NUMBERS	ODDMENT	OPULENT	OUTPOST
NUMBING	ODDNESS	ORATING	OUTPOUR
NUMERAL	ODORANT	ORATION	OUTRAGE
NUNNERY	ODOROUS	ORATORY	OUTRIDE
NUNNISH	ODYSSEY	ORBITAL	OUTRODE
NUPTIAL	OEDIPUS	ORCHARD	OUTSAIL
NURSERY	OFFENCE	ORDERED	OUTSELL
NURSING	OFFERED	ORDERER	OUTSIDE
NURTURE	OFFERER	ORDERLY	OUTSIZE

OUTSOLD	PACKING	PAPRIKA	PAUSING
OUTSPAN	PACKMAN	PAPULAR	PAWNING
OUTSTAY	PADDING	PAPYRUS	PAYABLE
OUTTALK	PADDLED	PARABLE	PAY-BILL
OUTVOTE	PADDLER	PARADED	PAY-BOOK
OUTWALK	PADDOCK	PARADOX	PAY-DIRT
OUTWARD	PADLOCK	PARAGON	PAY-LIST
OUTWEAR	PADRONE	PARAPET	PAY-LOAD
OUTWORK	PAGEANT	PARASOL	PAYMENT
OUTWORN	PAILFUL	PARBOIL	PAY-ROLL
OVARIAN	PAINFUL	PARCHED	PEACHED
OVATION	PAINING	PARESIS	PEACHER
OVERACT	PAINTED	PARETIC	PEACOCK
OVERALL	PAINTER	PARKING	PEA-FOWL
OVER-ATE	PAIRING	PARLOUR	PEAKING
OVERAWE	PALADIN	PARLOUS	PEAKISH
OVERBID	PALATAL	PARODIC	PEALING
OVERBUY	PALAVER	PARQUET	PEARLED
OVERDID	PALETOT	PARRIED	PEASANT
OVERDUE	PALETTE	PARSING	PEA-SOUP
OVEREAT	PALFREY	PARSLEY	PEAT-BOG
OVERFAR	PALLING	PARSNIP	PEAT-HAG
OVERJOY	PALMARY	PARTAKE	PEBBLED
OVERLAP	PALMATE	PARTIAL	PECCANT
OVERLAY	PALMERY	PARTING	PECCAVI
OVERLIE	PALMING	PARTNER	PECKING
OVERMAN	PALMIST	PARVENU	PECKISH
OVERPAY	PALM-OIL	PASCHAL	PECTATE
OVERPLY	PALPATE	PASSAGE	PECTINE
OVERRAN	PALSIED	PASSING	PEDDLED
OVERRUN	PANACEA	PASSION	PEDDLER
OVERSEA	PANACHE	PASSIVE	PEDICEL
OVERSEE	PANCAKE	PASS-KEY	PEDICLE
OVERSET	PANDEAN	PASSMAN	PEELING
OVERSEW	PANDORA	PASTERN	PEEPING
OVERTAX	PANICKY	PASTIME	PEERAGE
OVERTLY	PANNAGE	PASTING	PEERESS
OVERTOP	PANNIER	PASTURE	PEERING
OVIDIAN	PANNING	PATBALL	PEEVISH
OVOIDAL	PANOPLY	PATCHED	PEGASUS
OVOLOGY	PAN-PIPE	PATCHER	PEGGING
OWL-LIKE	PANSIED	PATELLA	PELAGIC
OXIDATE	PANTHER	PATHWAY	PELICAN
OXIDISE	PANTIES	PATIENT	PELISSE
OXONIAN	PANTILE	PATNESS	PELTING
	PANTING	PATRIOT	PENALLY
	PAPALLY	PATTERN	PENALTY
P—7	PAPERED	PATTING	PENANCE
PACIFIC	PAPERER	PAUCITY	PENATES
PACKAGE	PAPILLA	PAULINE	PENDANT
PACK-ICE	PAPOOSE	PAUNCHY	PENDENT

PENGUIN	PETRIFY	PIG-WASH	PITYING
PEN-NAME	PETROUS	PIKELET	PIVOTAL
PENNANT	PETTILY	PIKEMAN	PIVOTED
PENNIED	PETTING	PILEATE	PLACARD
PENNING	PETTISH	PILGRIM	PLACATE
PENSION	PETUNIA	PILLAGE	PLACEBO
PENSIVE	PEW-RENT	PILL-BOX	PLACING
PENTODE	PFENNIG	PILLING	PLACKET
PEOPLED	PHAETON	PILLION	PLAFOND
PEPPERY	PHALANX	PILLORY	PLAGUED
PEPSINE	PHANTOM	PILLOWY	PLAGUER
PEPTICS	PHARAOH	PILOTED	PLAINER
PEPTONE	PHARYNX	PIMENTO	PLAINLY
PERCEPT	PHILTRE	PIMPLED	PLAITED
PERCHED	PHINEAS	PINCERS	PLAITER
PERCHER	PHOEBUS	PINCHED	PLANARY
PERCUSS	PHOENIX	PINCHER	PLANING
PERDURE	PHONATE	PINFOLD	PLANISH
PERFECT	PHONICS	PINGING	PLANKED
PERFIDY	PHOTISM	PINGUID	PLANNED
PERFORM	PHRASED	PINGUIN	PLANNER
PERFUME	PHRENIC	PINHOLE	PLANTAR
PERFUSE	PHYSICS	PINK-EYE	PLANTED
PERGOLA	PIANIST	PINKING	PLANTER
PERHAPS	PIANOLA	PINKISH	PLASHED
PERIAPT	PIASTRE	PINNACE	PLASTER
PERIDOT	PIBROCH	PINNATE	PLASTIC
PERIQUE	PICADOR	PINNING	PLATEAU
PERIWIG	PICCOLO	PINT-POT	PLATING
PERJURE	PICKAXE	PIONEER	PLATOON
PERJURY	PICKING	PIOUSLY	PLATTED
PERKIER	PICKLED	PIP-EMMA	PLATTER
PERKILY	PICQUET	PIPERIC	PLAUDIT
PERKING	PICTISH	PIPETTE	PLAY-BOX
PERMUTE	PICTURE	PIPLESS	PLAY-BOY
PERPLEX	PIEBALD	PIPPING	PLAY-DAY
PERRIER	PIECING	PIQUANT	PLAYFUL
PERSEUS	PIERAGE	PIQUING	PLAYING
PERSIAN	PIERCED	PIRATED	PLEADED
PERSIST	PIERCER	PIROGUE	PLEADER
PERSONA	PIERROT	PISCARY	PLEASED
PERSPEX	PIFFLED	PITAPAT	PLEASER
PERTAIN	PIG-EYED	PITCHED	PLEATED
PERTURB	PIGGERY	PITCHER	PLEDGED
PERUSAL	PIGGING	PITCOAL	PLEDGEE
PERUSED	PIGGISH	PITEOUS	PLEDGER
PERUSER	PIG-IRON	PITFALL	PLENARY
PERVADE	PIG-LEAD	PIT-HEAD	PLENISH
PERVERT	PIGMENT	PITHILY	PLENIST
PESTLED	PIGSKIN	PITIFUL	PLEROMA
PETERED	PIGTAIL	PITTING	PLEURAL

PLEXURE	POMMARD	POUNCED	PREVAIL
PLIABLE	POMPOUS	POUNDED	PREVENT
PLIABLY	PONIARD	POUNDER	PREVIEW
PLIANCY	PONTIFF	POURING	PREYING
PLIMSOL	PONTOON	POUTING	PRICING
PLODDED	POOH-BAH	POVERTY	PRICKED
PLODDER	POOLING	POWDERY	PRICKER
PLOPPED	POOPING	POWERED	PRICKLE
PLOTTED	POOREST	PRAETOR	PRICKLY
PLOTTER	POOR-LAW	PRAIRIE	PRIDIAN
PLUCKED	POPCORN	PRAISED	PRIDING
PLUCKER	POPEDOM	PRAISER	PRIMACY
PLUGGED	POP-EYED	PRALINE	PRIMAGE
PLUGGER	POPPIED	PRANCED	PRIMARY
PLUMAGE	POPPING	PRANGED	PRIMATE
PLUMBED	POPPLED	PRANKED	PRIMELY
PLUMBER	POP-SHOP	PRATIES	PRIMING
PLUMING	POPULAR	PRATING	PRIMULA
PLUMMET	PORCINE	PRATTLE	PRINKED
PLUMPED	PORK-PIE	PRAYING	PRINTED
PLUMPER	PORT-BAR	PREACHY	PRINTER
PLUMPLY	PORTEND	PREBEND	PRISING
PLUNDER	PORTENT	PRECEDE	PRITHEE
PLUNGED	PORTICO	PRECEPT	PRIVACY
PLUNGER	PORTIFY	PRECISE	PRIVATE
PLUVIAL	PORTING	PREDATE	PRIVILY
PLUVIUS	PORTION	PREDICT	PRIVITY
PLY-WOOD	PORTRAY	PREDOOM	PRIZING
POACHED	POSSESS	PREEMPT	PROBANG
POACHER	POSTAGE	PREENED	PROBATE
POETESS	POST-BAG	PREFACE	PROBING
POINTED	POST-BOY	PREFECT	PROBITY
POINTER	POST-DAY	PRELACY	PROBLEM
POISING	POSTERN	PRELATE	PROCEED
POLE-AXE	POSTING	PRELECT	PROCESS
POLE-CAT	POSTMAN	PRELUDE	PROCTOR
POLEMIC	POSTURE	PREMIER	PROCURE
POLENTA	POST-WAR	PREMISE	PRODDED
POLICED	POTABLE	PREMISS	PRODDER
POLITER	POTENCY	PREMIUM	PRODIGY
POLITIC	POT-HERB	PREPAID	PRODUCE
POLLACK	POT-HOLE	PREPARE	PRODUCT
POLLARD	POT-HOOK	PRESAGE	PROFANE
POLL-AXE	POT-LUCK	PRESENT	PROFESS
POLLING	POT-SHOT	PRESIDE	PROFFER
POLL-MAN	POTTAGE	PRESSED	PROFILE
POLL-TAX	POTTERY	PRESSER	PROFUSE
POLLUTE	POTTING	PRESUME	PROGENY
POLYGON	POUCHED	PRETEND	PROGRAM
POLYPUS	POULARD	PRETEXT	PROJECT
POMFRET	POULTRY	PRETZEL	PROLATE

PROLONG	PUFFING	PYROSIS	QUININE
PROMISE	PUFFIER	PYROTIC	QUINTET
PROMOTE	PUFFILY	PYRRHIC	QUIPPED
PRONELY	PUGMILL	PYTHIAD	QUITTAL
PRONGED	PUG-NOSE	PYTHIAN	QUITTED
PRONOUN	PULLING		QUITTER
PROOFED	PULLMAN	**Q—7**	QUI-VIVE
PROPHET	PULL-OUT	QUACKED	QUIXOTE
PROPOSE	PULPING	QUAFFED	QUIZZED
PROPPED	PULPOUS	QUAFFER	QUIZZER
PROSAIC	PULSATE	QUAILED	QUONDAM
PROSIFY	PULSING	QUAKING	QUOTING
PROSILY	PUMPAGE	QUALIFY	
PROSING	PUMPING	QUALITY	**R—7**
PROSODY	PUMPKIN	QUANTIC	RABIDLY
PROSPER	PUNCHED	QUANTUM	RACCOON
PROTEAN	PUNCHER	QUARREL	RACKETY
PROTECT	PUNCTUM	QUARTAN	RACKING
PROTEGE	PUNGENT	QUARTER	RACQUET
PROTEIN	PUNNING	QUARTET	RADDLED
PROTEST	PUNSTER	QUASHED	RADIANT
PROTEUS	PUNTING	QUASSIA	RADIATE
PROUDER	PURGING	QUAVERY	RADICAL
PROUDLY	PURITAN	QUEENED	RADICLE
PROVERB	PURLIEU	QUEENLY	RADIOED
PROVIDE	PURLING	QUEERER	RAFFISH
PROVINE	PURLOIN	QUEERLY	RAFFLED
PROVING	PURPLED	QUELLED	RAFFLER
PROVISO	PURPORT	QUELLER	RAGEFUL
PROVOKE	PURPOSE	QUEROUS	RAG-FAIR
PROVOST	PURRING	QUERIED	RAGGING
PROWESS	PURSING	QUERIST	RAGTIME
PROWLED	PURSUED	QUESTED	RAG-WEED
PROWLER	PURSUER	QUESTER	RAGWORT
PROXIMO	PURSUIT	QUESTOR	RAIDING
PRUDENT	PURVIEW	QUIBBLE	RAIL-CAR
PRUDERY	PUSHFUL	QUICKEN	RAILING
PRUDISH	PUSHING	QUICKER	RAILWAY
PRUNING	PUSTULE	QUICKIE	RAIMENT
PRUSSIC	PUTREFY	QUICKLY	RAINBOW
PRYTHEE	PUTTIED	QUIESCE	RAINING
PSALTER	PUTTING	QUIETED	RAISING
PSYCHIC	PUZZLED	QUIETEN	RAKE-OFF
PUBERTY	PUZZLER	QUIETER	RALLIED
PUBLISH	PYGMEAN	QUIETLY	RAMADAN
PUCKISH	PYJAMAS	QUIETUS	RAMBLED
PUDDING	PYRAMID	QUILLED	RAMBLER
PUDDLED	PYRETIC	QUILTED	RAMEKIN
PUDDLER	PYREXIA	QUILTER	RAMEOUS
PUDDOCK	PYRITES	QUINARY	RAMLINE
PUERILE	PYRITIC	QUINATE	RAMMING

RAMPAGE	REALISM	REDOUBT	REGULUS
RAMPANT	REALIST	REDOUND	REHOUSE
RAMPART	REALITY	REDPOLL	REIGNED
RAMPING	REALLOT	REDRAFT	REINING
RAMPION	REALTOR	REDRAWN	REINTER
RANCHED	RE-ANNEX	REDRESS	REISSUE
RANCHER	REAPING	REDSKIN	REJOICE
RANCOUR	REAPPLY	RED-TAPE	REJOINT
RANGERS	REARGUE	REDUCED	REJUDGE
RANGING	REARING	REDUCER	RELABEL
RANKEST	REARISE	REDWING	RELAPSE
RANKING	REARMED	REDWOOD	RELATED
RANKLED	RE-AROSE	REEKING	RELATER
RANSACK	REAWAKE	RE-ELECT	RELATOR
RANTING	REBATED	REELING	RELAXED
RAPHAEL	REBIRTH	RE-ENACT	RELAYED
RAPIDLY	REBLOOM	RE-ENDOW	RELEASE
RAPPING	REBORED	RE-ENJOY	RELIANT
RAPPORT	REBOUND	RE-ENTER	RELIEVE
RAPTURE	REBUILD	RE-ENTRY	RELIGHT
RAREBIT	REBUILT	RE-EQUIP	RELIVED
RASHEST	REBUKED	RE-ERECT	RELUMED
RASPING	REBUKER	REEVING	RELYING
RATABLE	RECEDED	REFEREE	REMAINS
RATAFIA	RECEIPT	REFINED	REMARRY
RATATAT	RECE'VE	REFINER	REMNANT
RATCHED	RECHEAT	REFLECT	REMODEL
RATCHET	RECITAL	REFLOAT	REMORSE
RATTING	RECITED	REFORGE	REMOTER
RATTLED	RECITER	RE-FOUND	REMOULD
RATTLER	RECKING	REFRACT	REMOUNT
RAT-TRAP	RECLAIM	REFRAIN	REMOVAL
RAUCOUS	RECLAME	REFRAME	REMOVED
RAVAGED	RECLASP	REFRESH	REMOVER
RAVINED	RECLINE	REFUGEE	RENAMED
RAWHIDE	RECLOSE	REFUSAL	RENDING
RAWNESS	RECLUSE	REFUSED	RENEWAL
RAYLESS	RECOUNT	REFUSER	RENEWED
REACHED	RECOVER	REFUTED	RENEWER
REACHER	RECROSS	REFUTER	RENT-DAY
REACTED	RECRUIT	REGALED	RENTIER
REACTOR	RECTIFY	REGALIA	RENTING
READIED	RECTORY	REGALLY	REORDER
READIER	RECURVE	REGATTA	REPAINT
READILY	RED-COAT	REGENCY	REPAPER
READING	REDDEST	REGIMEN	REPINED
READMIT	REDDISH	REGNANT	REPINER
READOPT	RED-EYED	REGORGE	REPLACE
READORN	RED-FISH	REGREET	REPLANT
REAGENT	RED-HEAD	REGRESS	REPLETE
REALISE	REDNESS	REGULAR	REPLEVY

REPLICA	RETAKEN	RICKETY	ROGUERY
REPLIED	RETINUE	RIDDING	ROGUISH
REPLIER	RETIRAL	RIDDLED	ROILING
REPOINT	RETIRED	RIDDLER	ROISTER
REPOSAL	RETOUCH	RIFLING	ROLLICK
REPOSED	RETRACE	RIFTING	ROLLING
REPOSER	RETRACT	RIGGING	ROMANCE
REPRESS	RETREAD	RIGHTED	ROMANIC
REPRINT	RETREAT	RIGHTEN	ROMAUNT
REPRISE	RETRIAL	RIGHTER	ROMPERS
REPROOF	RETRIED	RIGHTLY	ROMPING
REPROVE	RETYPED	RIGIDLY	ROMPISH
REPRUNE	REUNIFY	RIMLESS	RONDEAU
REPTILE	REUNION	RIMMING	ROOFING
REPULSE	REUNITE	RINDING	ROOKERY
REPUTED	REURGED	RINGING	ROOKING
REQUEST	REVALUE	RINGLET	ROOMAGE
REQUIEM	REVELRY	RINSING	ROOMFUL
REQUIRE	REVENGE	RIOTING	ROOMIER
REQUITE	REVENUE	RIOTOUS	ROOMILY
REREDOS	REVERED	RIPCORD	ROOMING
RESCIND	REVERIE	RIPOSTE	ROOSTED
RE-SCORE	REVERSE	RIPPING	ROOSTER
RESCUED	REVERSI	RIPPLED	ROOTING
RESCUER	REVILED	RISIBLE	ROPEWAY
RESEIZE	REVILER	RISIBLY	ROSEATE
RESERVE	REVISAL	RISKIER	ROSE-BAY
RESHAPE	REVISED	RISKING	ROSE-BOX
RESIDED	REVISER	RISOTTO	ROSE-BUD
RESIDER	REVISIT	RISSOLE	ROSETTE
RESIDUE	REVIVAL	RIVALRY	ROSIEST
RESOLVE	REVIVED	RIVETED	ROSTRUM
RESOUND	REVIVER	RIVETER	ROTATED
RESPECT	REVOKED	RIVIERA	ROTATOR
RE-SPELL	REVOLVE	RIVULET	ROTTING
RE-SPELT	REVVING	ROAD-HOG	ROTUNDA
RESPIRE	REWRITE	ROADMAN	ROUGHED
RESPITE	REWROTE	ROAD-MAP	ROUGHEN
RESPLIT	REYNARD	ROADWAY	ROUGHER
RE-SPOKE	RHEMISH	ROAMING	ROUGHLY
RESPOND	RHENISH	ROARING	ROULADE
RESTAMP	RHODIAN	ROASTED	ROULEAU
RESTATE	RHOMBUS	ROASTER	ROUNDED
REST-DAY	RHUBARB	ROBBERY	ROUNDEL
RESTFUL	RHYMING	ROBBING	ROUNDER
RESTING	RHYMIST	ROCKERY	ROUNDLY
RESTIVE	RIBBING	ROCKIER	ROUND-UP
RESTOCK	RIBLESS	ROCKILY	ROUSING
RESTORE	RIBSTON	ROCKING	ROUTINE
RESUMED	RICHEST	RODLIKE	ROUTING
RESURGE	RICKETS	ROE-BUCK	ROWDIER

ROWDILY	SADNESS	SAUCIER	SCHERZO
ROWLOCK	SAFFRON	SAUCILY	SCHOLAR
ROYALLY	SAGGING	SAUCING	SCHOLIA
ROYALTY	SAILING	SAUNTER	SCIATIC
RUB-A-DUB	SAINTED	SAURIAN	SCIENCE
RUBBING	SAINTLY	SAUROID	SCISSOR
RUBBISH	SALIENT	SAUSAGE	SCOFFED
RUB-DOWN	SALLIED	SAVAGED	SCOFFER
RUBICON	SALLOWY	SAVANNA	SCOLDED
RUCHING	SALSIFY	SAVE-ALL	SCOLDER
RUCKING	SALT-BOX	SAVELOY	SCOLLOP
RUCKLED	SALTIER	SAVINGS	SCOOPED
RUCTION	SALTING	SAVIOUR	SCOOPER
RUDDIER	SALTIRE	SAVOURY	SCOOTED
RUDDILY	SALTISH	SAWDUST	SCOOTER
RUFFIAN	SALT-PAN	SAW-FISH	SCORIFY
RUFFING	SALT-PIT	SAW-MILL	SCORING
RUFFLED	SALUTED	SAW-WORT	SCORNED
RUINING	SALVAGE	SAXHORN	SCORNER
RUINOUS	SALVING	SCABIES	SCORPIO
RUMBLED	SAMOVAR	SCABRID	SCOURED
RUMBLER	SAMOYED	SCALDED	SCOURER
RUMMAGE	SAMPLED	SCALENE	SCOURGE
RUMNESS	SAMPLER	SCALING	SCOWLED
RUMPLED	SAMURAI	SCALLOP	SCRAGGY
RUNAWAY	SANCTUM	SCALPED	SCRAPED
RUNNING	SANCTUS	SCALPEL	SCRAPER
RUPTURE	SANDBAG	SCALPER	SCRAPPY
RURALLY	SAND-BOX	SCAMPED	SCRATCH
RUSHING	SAND-BOY	SCAMPER	SCRAWLY
RUSH-MAT	SAND-EEL	SCANDAL	SCRAWNY
RUSSETY	SAND-FLY	SCANNED	SCREECH
RUSSIAN	SAND-PIT	SCANTLE	SCREEVE
RUSTIER	SAPHEAD	SCANTLY	SCREWED
RUSTILY	SAPIENT	SCAPULA	SCREWER
RUSTING	SAPLESS	SCARCER	SCRIBAL
RUSTLED	SAPLING	SCARFED	SCRIBED
RUSTLER	SAPPHIC	SCARIFY	SCRIBER
	SAPPING	SCARING	SCROOGE
S—7	SAP-WOOD	SCARLET	SCRUBBY
SABBATH	SARACEN	SCARPED	SCRUFFY
SACKAGE	SARCASM	SCARRED	SCRUNCH
SACKBUT	SARCOMA	SCATHED	SCRUPLE
SACKFUL	SARDINE	SCATTER	SCUDDED
SACKING	SATANIC	SCAUPER	SCUFFLE
SACRIST	SATCHEL	SCENERY	SCULLED
SADDEST	SATIATE	SCENTED	SCULLER
SADDLED	SATIETY	SCEPTIC	SCUPPER
SADDLER	SATINET	SCEPTRE	SCUTATE
SAD-EYED	SATIRIC	SCHEMED	SCUTTLE
SADIRON	SATISFY	SCHEMER	SCYTHED

SEA-BANK	SEA-WING	SERFAGE	SHATTER
SEA-BEAR	SEA-WOLF	SERFDOM	SHAVIAN
SEA-BEET	SEA-WORM	SERIATE	SHAVING
SEA-BIRD	SECEDED	SERINGA	SHEAFED
SEA-BOAT	SECEDER	SERIOUS	SHEARER
SEA-CALF	SECLUDE	SERPENT	SHEATHE
SEA-CARD	SECONDO	SERRATE	SHEAVED
SEA-COAL	SECRECY	SERRIED	SHEBEEN
SEA-COCK	SECRETE	SERVANT	SHEDDER
SEA-COOK	SECTILE	SERVIAN	SHEERED
SEA-CROW	SECTION	SERVICE	SHEETED
SEA-DACE	SECULAR	SERVILE	SHELLAC
SEA-FIRE	SECURED	SERVING	SHELLED
SEA-FISH	SECURER	SESSION	SHELLER
SEA-FOAM	SEDUCED	SET-BACK	SHELTER
SEA-FOLK	SEDUCER	SET-DOWN	SHELTIE
SEA-FOWL	SEEABLE	SETTING	SHELVED
SEA-GATE	SEEDBED	SETTLED	SHERBET
SEA-GIRT	SEEDILY	SETTLER	SHERIFF
SEA-GULL	SEEDING	SEVENTH	SHEWING
SEA-HARE	SEED-LAC	SEVENTY	SHIFTED
SEA-HAWK	SEED-OIL	SEVERAL	SHIFTER
SEAKALE	SEEKING	SEVERED	SHIKARI
SEA-KING	SEEMING	SEVERER	SHIMMER
SEA-LARK	SEEPAGE	SEXLESS	SHINGLE
SEA-LEGS	SEETHED	SEXTAIN	SHINGLY
SEALERY	SEGMENT	SEXTANT	SHINING
SEA-LIKE	SEIZING	SEXTILE	SHINNED
SEA-LILY	SEIZURE	SHACKLE	SHIP-BOY
SEA-LINE	SELF-FED	SHADIER	SHIPFUL
SEALING	SELFISH	SHADILY	SHIP-MAN
SEA-LION	SELLING	SHADING	SHIPPED
SEA-MARK	SELTZER	SHADOWY	SHIPPER
SEA-MILE	SELVAGE	SHAFTED	SHIP-WAY
SEAMING	SEMATIC	SHAGGED	SHIRKED
SEA-MOSS	SEMI-GOD	SHAKILY	SHIRKER
SEA-PIKE	SEMINAL	SHAKING	SHIRRED
SEA-PORT	SEMIPED	SHALLOP	SHIVERY
SEARING	SEMITIC	SHALLOT	SHOALED
SEA-RISK	SENATOR	SHALLOW	SHOCKED
SEA-ROOM	SENDING	SHAMBLE	SHOCKER
SEA-SALT	SEND-OFF	SHAMING	SHOEING
SEASICK	SENEGAL	SHAMMED	SHOE-TIE
SEASIDE	SENSING	SHAMMER	SHOOING
SEA-SLUG	SENSORY	SHAMPOO	SHOOTER
SEATING	SENSUAL	SHAPELY	SHOP-BOY
SEA-VIEW	SEPTATE	SHAPING	SHOPMAN
SEA-WALL	SEQUENT	SHARING	SHOPPED
SEAWARD	SEQUOIA	SHARPEN	SHOPPER
SEAWEED	SERBIAN	SHARPER	SHORING
SEA-WIFE	SERENER	SHARPLY	SHORTED

...TEN	SILENUS	SKIPPED	SLINGER
SHORTER	SILESIA	SKIPPER	SLIPPED
SHOTGUN	SILICIC	SKIPPET	SLIPPER
SHOTTED	SILICON	SKIRLED	SLIPWAY
SHOUTED	SILK-HAT	SKIRTED	SLITHER
SHOUTER	SILKIER	SKIRTER	SLITTED
SHOVING	SILKILY	SKITTER	SLITTER
SHOW-BOX	SILK-MAN	SKITTLE	SLOBBER
SHOWERY	SILLIER	SKIVING	SLOE-GIN
SHOWILY	SILLILY	SKULKED	SLOGGED
SHOWING	SILTING	SKY-BLUE	SLOGGER
SHOWMAN	SILVERN	SKY-HIGH	SLOPING
SHREDDY	SILVERY	SKYLARK	SLOPPED
SHRILLY	SIMILAR	SKYLINE	SLOTTED
SHRINED	SIMPLER	SKYSAIL	SLOUCHY
SHRIVEL	SINCERE	SKYWARD	SLOWEST
SHRIVEN	SINEWED	SLABBED	SLOWING
SHROUDS	SINGING	SLABBER	SLUBBER
SHRUBBY	SINGLED	SLACKED	SLUDGER
SHUDDER	SINGLET	SLACKEN	SLUGGED
SHUFFLE	SINKING	SLACKER	SLUICED
SHUNNED	SINLESS	SLACKLY	SLUMBER
SHUNNER	SINNING	SLAKING	SLUMMER
SHUNTED	SINUATE	SLAMMED	SLUMPED
SHUNTER	SINUOUS	SLANDER	SLURRED
SHUT-EYE	SIPPING	SLANGED	SLYNESS
SHUTTER	SIRGANG	SLANTED	SMACKED
SHUTTLE	SIRLOIN	SLANTLY	SMACKER
SHYLOCK	SIROCCO	SLAPPED	SMARTED
SHYNESS	SISTINE	SLASHED	SMARTEN
SHYSTER	SITTING	SLASHER	SMARTER
SIAMESE	SITUATE	SLATING	SMARTLY
SIBLING	SIXFOLD	SLAVERY	SMASHED
SICK-BAY	SIXTEEN	SLAVING	SMASHER
SICK-BED	SIXTHLY	SLAVISH	SMASH-UP
SICKEST	SIZABLE	SLAYING	SMATTER
SICKISH	SIZZLED	SLEDDED	SMEARED
SIDEARM	SKATING	SLEDGED	SMELLED
SIDECAR	SKEPFUL	SLEEKED	SMELLER
SIDLING	SKEPTIC	SLEEKER	SMELTED
SIFFLED	SKETCHY	SLEEKLY	SMELTER
SIFTING	SKIDDED	SLEEPER	SMICKER
SIGHING	SKILFUL	SLEETED	SMILING
SIGHTED	SKILLED	SLEIGHT	SMIRKED
SIGHTER	SKILLET	SLENDER	SMITING
SIGHTLY	SKIMMED	SLICING	SMITTEN
SIGNIFY	SKIMMER	SLICKER	SMOKIER
SIGNING	SKIMPED	SLIDDER	SMOKILY
SIGNORA	SKINFUL	SLIDING	SMOKING
SIGNORY	SKINNED	SLIMILY	SMOOTHE
SILENCE	SKINNER	SLIMMER	SMOTHER

SMUDGED	SO-AND-SO	SOUREST	SPHERED
SMUDGER	SOAPBOX	SOURING	SPHERIC
SMUGGLE	SOAPING	SOURISH	SPICERY
SNAFFLE	SOARING	SOUSING	SPICILY
SNAGGED	SOBBING	SOUTANE	SPICING
SNAGGER	SOBERED	SOUTHER	SPIDERY
SNAKING	SOBERLY	SOU'WEST	SPIKING
SNAKISH	SOCIETY	SOZZLED	SPILLED
SNAPPED	SOCKEYE	SPACIAL	SPILLER
SNAPPER	SOCKING	SPACING	SPINACH
SNARING	SOFTEST	SPANGLE	SPINATE
SNARLED	SOFTISH	SPANGLY	SPINDLE
SNARLER	SOIGNEE	SPANIEL	SPINDLY
SNATCHY	SOILING	SPANISH	SPINNER
SNEAKED	SOJOURN	SPANKED	SPINNEY
SNEAKER	SOLACED	SPANKER	SPIRANT
SNEERED	SOLDIER	SPANNED	SPIRING
SNEERER	SOLICIT	SPANNER	SPIRTED
SNEEZED	SOLIDLY	SPARELY	SPITING
SNICKED	SOLIDUS	SPARING	SPITTED
SNICKER	SOLOIST	SPARKED	SPITTER
SNIFFED	SOLOMON	SPARKLE	SPITTLE
SNIFFLE	SOLUBLE	SPARRED	SPLASHY
SNIFTED	SOLVENT	SPARROW	SPLAYED
SNIFTER	SOLVING	SPARTAN	SPLEENY
SNIGGER	SOMATIC	SPASTIC	SPLENIC
SNIGGLE	SOMEHOW	SPATIAL	SPLICED
SNIPING	SOMEONE	SPATTER	SPLODGE
SNIPPED	SONGFUL	SPATULA	SPLODGY
SNIPPER	SONSHIP	SPAWNED	SPLOTCH
SNIPPET	SOOTHED	SPAWNER	SPOILED
SNOOKER	SOOTHER	SPEAKER	SPOILER
SNOOPED	SOOTING	SPEARED	SPONDEE
SNOOPER	SOPHISM	SPEARER	SPONGED
SNOOZED	SOPHIST	SPECIAL	SPONGER
SNOOZER	SOPPING	SPECIES	SPONSAL
SNORING	SOPRANO	SPECIFY	SPONSON
SNORTED	SORCERY	SPECKED	SPONSOR
SNORTER	SORDINE	SPECKLE	SPOOFED
SNOUTED	SORITES	SPECTRA	SPOOLED
SNOW-ICE	SORORAL	SPECTRE	SPOONED
SNOWILY	SOROSIS	SPEEDED	SPORRAN
SNOW-MAN	SORRILY	SPEEDER	SPORTED
SNUBBED	SORTING	SPEED-UP	SPORTER
SNUBBER	SOTTISH	SPELLED	SPOTTED
SNUFFED	SOUFFLE	SPELLER	SPOTTER
SNUFFER	SOULFUL	SPELTER	SPOUSAL
SNUFFLE	SOUNDLY	SPENCER	SPOUTED
SNUGGLE	SOUNDED	SPENDER	SPOUTER
SOAKAGE	SOUNDER	SPEWING	SPRAYED
SOAKING	SOUPCON	SPHERAL	SPRAYEY

SPRIGGY	STAMPED	STERILE	STOWING
SPRIGHT	STAMPER	STERNAL	STRANGE
SPRINGE	STAND-BY	STERNER	STRATUM
SPRINGY	STANDER	STERNLY	STRATUS
SPRUCED	STAND-TO	STERNUM	STRAYED
SPUMING	STAND-UP	STETSON	STRAYER
SPUN-OUT	STAPLED	STEWARD	STREAKY
SPURNED	STAPLER	STEWING	STREAMY
SPURNER	STARCHY	STEWPAN	STRETCH
SPURRED	STARDOM	STEWPOT	STREWED
SPURRER	STARING	STICKER	STRIATE
SPURREY	STARKLY	STICKLE	STRIKER
SPURTED	STARLIT	STIFFEN	STRINGY
SPURTLE	STARRED	STIFFER	STRIPED
SPUR-WAY	STARTED	STIFFLY	STRIVEN
SPUTTER	STARTER	STIFLED	STRIVER
SPY-BOAT	STARTLE	STILLED	STROKED
SPY-HOLE	STARVED	STILLER	STROKER
SQUABBY	STATANT	STILTED	STROPHE
SQUALID	STATELY	STILTON	STUBBED
SQUALLY	STATICS	STIMULI	STUBBLE
SQUALOR	STATING	STINGER	STUBBLY
SQUARED	STATION	STINKER	STUCK-UP
SQUASHY	STATIST	STINTED	STUDDED
SQUATTY	STATUED	STINTER	STUDENT
SQUEEZE	STATURE	STIPEND	STUDIED
SQUELCH	STATUTE	STIPPLE	STUFFED
SQUIFFY	STAUNCH	STIRRED	STUFFER
SQUIRED	STAVING	STIRRER	STUMBLE
STABBED	STAYING	STIRRUP	STUMPED
STABBER	STEALER	STOCKED	STUMPER
STABLED	STEALTH	STOICAL	STUNNED
STACKED	STEAMED	STOKING	STUNNER
STACKER	STEAMER	STOMACH	STUNTED
STADIUM	STEELED	STONILY	STUPEFY
STAFFED	STEEPED	STONING	STUTTER
STAGERY	STEEPEN	STOOGED	STYGIAN
STAGGER	STEEPER	STOOKED	STYLING
STAGING	STEEPLE	STOOPED	STYLISE
STAIDLY	STEEPLY	STOOPER	STYLISH
STAINED	STEERED	STOP-GAP	STYLIST
STAINER	STEERER	STOPPED	STYLITE
STAITHE	STELLAR	STOPPER	STYLOID
STAKING	STEMLET	STORAGE	STYMIED
STATELY	STEMMED	STORIED	SUASION
STALEST	STENCIL	STORING	SUASIVE
STALKED	STENTOR	STORMED	SUASORY
STALKER	STEPNEY	STORMER	SUAVELY
STALLED	STEPPED	STOUTER	SUAVITY
STAMINA	STEPPER	STOUTLY	SUBACID
STAMMER	STEP-SON	STOWAGE	SUBBING

SUBDEAN	SUMMARY	SWAGMAN	SYMPTOM
SUBDUAL	SUMMERY	SWAHILI	SYNAXIS
SUBDUCT	SUMMING	SWALING	SYNCOPE
SUBDUED	SUMMONS	SWALLOW	SYNESIS
SUBDUER	SUMPTER	SWAMPED	SYNODAL
SUBEDIT	SUN-BATH	SWANKED	SYNONYM
SUBFUSC	SUNBEAM	SWAPPED	SYRINGA
SUB-HEAD	SUN-BEAT	SWARDED	SYRINGE
SUBJECT	SUN-BIRD	SWARMED	
SUBJOIN	SUNBURN	SWARTHY	T—7
SUBLATE	SUN-DIAL	SWASHED	TABINET
SUBLIME	SUNDOWN	SWASHER	TABLEAU
SUBRENT	SUN-FISH	SWATTED	TABLING
SUBSALT	SUNLESS	SWATTER	TABLOID
SUBSIDE	SUNNING	SWAYING	TABOOED
SUBSIDY	SUNRISE	SWEALED	TABULAR
SUBSIGN	SUNSPOT	SWEARER	TACITLY
SUBSIST	SUNWARD	SWEATED	TACKING
SUBSOIL	SUNWISE	SWEATER	TACKLED
SUBSUME	SUPPING	SWEDISH	TACTFUL
SUBTEND	SUPPLED	SWEEPER	TACTICS
SUBTILE	SUPPORT	SWEETEN	TACTILE
SUBTLER	SUPPOSE	SWEETER	TACTION
SUBTYPE	SUPREME	SWEETLY	TACTUAL
SUBURBS	SURCOAT	SWELLED	TADPOLE
SUBVENE	SURDITY	SWELTER	TAFFETA
SUBVERT	SURFACE	SWELTRY	TAGGING
SUCCEED	SURFEIT	SWERVED	TAIL-END
SUCCESS	SURGENT	SWERVER	TAILING
SUCCOUR	SURGEON	SWIFTER	TAINTED
SUCCUMB	SURGERY	SWIFTLY	TAKE-OFF
SUCKING	SURGING	SWIGGED	TAKINGS
SUCKLED	SURLIER	SWILLED	TALIPED
SUCKLER	SURLILY	SWILLER	TALIPES
SUCROSE	SURLOIN	SWIMMER	TALKIES
SUCTION	SURMISE	SWINDLE	TALKING
SUFFICE	SURNAME	SWINERY	TALLBOY
SUFFUSE	SURPASS	SWINGED	TALLEST
SUGARED	SURPLUS	SWINGER	TALLIED
SUGGEST	SURTOUT	SWINISH	TALLIER
SUICIDE	SURVIVE	SWIPING	TALLISH
SUITING	SUSPECT	SWIRLED	TALLOWY
SULKIER	SUSPEND	SWISHED	TÁLLY-HO
SULKILY	SUSPIRE	SWISHER	TALONED
SULKING	SUSTAIN	SWIZZLE	TAMABLE
SULLAGE	SUTURAL	SWOLLEN	TAMBOUR
SULLENS	SUTURED	SWOONED	TANGENT
SULLIED	SWABBED	SWOOPED	TANGLED
SULPHUR	SWABBER	SWOPPED	TANGOED
SULTANA	SWADDLE	SWOTTED	TANKAGE
SUMLESS	SWAGGER	SYLPHID	TANKARD

TANNAGE	TEEMING	THAWING	TIDE-WAY
TANNATE	TEENAGE	THEATRE	TIDIEST
TANNERY	TELERGY	THEOREM	TIDINGS
TANNING	TELLING	THERAPY	TIE-BEAM
TANTRUM	TEMPERA	THEREAT	TIERCEL
TAPERED	TEMPEST	THEREBY	TIGHTEN
TAPIOCA	TEMPLAR	THEREIN	TIGHTER
TAPPING	TEMPLED	THEREOF	TIGHTLY
TAPROOM	TEMPLET	THEREON	TIGRESS
TAPROOT	TEMPTED	THERETO	TIGRISH
TAPSTER	TEMPTER	THERMAL	TILBURY
TARDIER	TENABLE	THERMOS	TILLAGE
TARDILY	TENANCY	THESEUS	TILLING
TARNISH	TENDING	THICKEN	TILTING
TARRIED	TENDRIL	THICKER	TIMBREL
TARRIER	TENFOLD	THICKET	TIME-LAG
TARRING	TENSELY	THICKLY	TIMEOUS
TARTISH	TENSEST	THIEVED	TIMIDLY
TARTLET	TENSILE	THIMBLE	TIMOTHY
TASKING	TENSION	THINKER	TIMPANI
TASTIER	TENSITY	THINNED	TIMPANO
TASTILY	TENTHLY	THINNER	TINDERY
TASTING	TENT-PEG	THIRDLY	TINFOIL
TATTERY	TENUITY	THIRSTY	TINGING
TATTING	TENUOUS	THISTLE	TINGLED
TATTLED	TERMING	THISTLY	TINIEST
TATTLER	TERMINI	THITHER	TINKING
TAUNTED	TERMITE	THOLING	TINKLED
TAUNTER	TERNARY	THOUGHT	TINKLER
TAURINE	TERNATE	THREADY	TIN-MINE
TAUTEST	TERRACE	THRIFTY	TINNING
TAXABLE	TERRAIN	THRIVED	TIN-TACK
TAX-FREE	TERRENE	THRIVEN	TINTAGE
TAXI-CAB	TERRIER	THRIVER	TINTING
TAXYING	TERRIFY	THROATY	TINTYPE
TEA-CAKE	TERRINE	THRONAL	TINWARE
TEACHER	TERSELY	THRONED	TIP-CART
TEA-COSY	TERTIAN	THROUGH	TIPPING
TEA-GOWN	TESTACY	THROWER	TIPPLED
TEA-LEAF	TESTATE	THUMBED	TIPPLER
TEAMING	TESTIER	THUMPED	TIPSILY
TEARFUL	TESTIFY	THUMPER	TIPSTER
TEARING	TESTILY	THUNDER	TIPTOED
TEA-ROSE	TESTING	THYROID	TISSUED
TEASING	TETANUS	THYSELF	TITANIA
TEA-TIME	TEXTILE	TIARAED	TITANIC
TEA-TREE	TEXTUAL	TIBETAN	TITHING
TECHNIC	TEXTURE	TICKING	TITLARK
TEDDING	THALIAN	TICKLED	TITLING
TEDIOUS	THANAGE	TICKLER	TITMICE
TEEMFUL	THANKED	TIDDLER	TITULAR

TOADIED	TORTURE	TRAMWAY	TRINITY
TOASTED	TORYISM	TRANCED	TRINKET
TOASTER	TOSSILY	TRANSIT	TRINKLE
TOBACCO	TOSSING	TRANSOM	TRIOLET
TOBYMAN	TOSSPOT	TRANTER	TRIPLED
TOCCATA	TOTALLY	TRAPEZE	TRIPLET
TODDLED	TOTTERY	TRAPPED	TRIPOLI
TODDLER	TOTTING	TRAPPER	TRIPPED
TOE-NAIL	TOUCHED	TRASHED	TRIPPER
TOGGERY	TOUCHER	TRAVAIL	TRIREME
TOILFUL	TOUGHEN	TRAWLED	TRISECT
TOILING	TOUGHLY	TRAWLER	TRITELY
TOLLAGE	TOURING	TREACLE	TRIUMPH
TOLL-BAR	TOURISM	TREACLY	TRIVIAL
TOLLING	TOURIST	TREADER	TROCHEE
TOLLMAN	TOURNEY	TREADLE	TRODDEN
TOMBOLA	TOUSING	TREASON	TROLLED
TOMFOOL	TOUSLED	TREATED	TROLLER
TOMPION	TOUTING	TREATER	TROLLEY
TONGUED	TOWARDS	TREBLED	TROLLOP
TONIGHT	TOWBOAT	TREEING	TROOPED
TONNAGE	TOWERED	TREFOIL	TROOPER
TONNEAU	TOWLINE	TREKKED	TROPICS
TONSURE	TOWNISH	TREKKER	TROTTED
TONTINE	TOW-PATH	TRELLIS	TROTTER
TOOLING	TOW-ROPE	TREMBLE	TROUBLE
TOOTHED	TOYSHOP	TREMBLY	TROUNCE
TOOTING	TOYSOME	TREMOLO	TROUPER
TOOTLED	TRACERY	TRESTLE	TROWING
TOPARCH	TRACHEA	TRIABLE	TRUANCY
TOP-BOOT	TRACING	TRIBUNE	TRUCKED
TOPCOAT	TRACKED	TRIBUTE	TRUCKER
TOP-HOLE	TRACKER	TRICEPS	TRUCKLE
TOPIARY	TRACTOR	TRICKED	TRUDGED
TOPICAL	TRADING	TRICKER	TRUFFLE
TOP-KNOT	TRADUCE	TRICKLE	TRUMPED
TOPLESS	TRAFFIC	TRICKLY	TRUMPET
TOP-MAST	TRAGEDY	TRICKSY	TRUNCAL
TOP-MOST	TRAILED	TRICORN	TRUNDLE
TOPPING	TRAILER	TRIDENT	TRUSSED
TOPPLED	TRAINED	TRIFLED	TRUSTED
TOPSAIL	TRAINEE	TRIFLER	TRUSTEE
TOP-SIDE	TRAINER	TRIFORM	TRUSTER
TOPSMAN	TRAIPSE	TRIGAMY	TRY-SAIL
TOP-SOIL	TRAITOR	TRIGGER	TRYSTED
TORCHON	TRAJECT	TRILLED	TSARINA
TORMENT	TRAM-CAR	TRILOGY	TSARIST
TORNADO	TRAMMEL	TRIMMED	T-SQUARE
TORPEDO	TRAMPED	TRIMMER	TUBBING
TORRENT	TRAMPER	TRINARY	TUBBISH
TORSION	TRAMPLE	TRINGLE	TUBULAR

TUCKING	TWISTER	UNCIVIL	UNICITY
TUCK-OUT	TWITTED	UNCLASP	UNICORN
TUESDAY	TWITTER	UNCLEAN	UNIDEAL
TUFTING	TWOFOLD	UNCLEAR	UNIFIED
TUG-BOAT	TWONESS	UNCLOAK	UNIFIER
TUGGING	TWOSOME	UNCLOSE	UNIFORM
TUITION	TWO-STEP	UNCLOUD	UNITARY
TUMBLED	TYNWALD	UNCOUTH	UNITING
TUMBLER	TYPHOID	UNCOVER	UNJOINT
TUMBREL	TYPHOON	UNCROSS	UNKEMPT
TUMIDLY	TYPHOUS	UNCROWN	UNKNOWN
TUMULAR	TYPICAL	UNCTION	UNLACED
TUMULUS	TYRANNY	UNDATED	UNLADEN
TUNABLE	TZARINA	UNDEIFY	UNLATCH
TUNABLY		UNDERDO	UNLEARN
TUNEFUL	**U—7**	UNDERGO	UNLEASH
TUNNAGE	UKULELE	UNDIGHT	UNLIMED
TUNNERY	ULULATE	UNDOING	UNLINED
TURBINE	ULYSSES	UNDRAPE	UNLIVED
TURFING	UMBERED	UNDRAWN	UNLOOSE
TURGENT	UMBROSE	UNDRESS	UNLOVED
TURGITE	UMPIRED	UNDRIED	UNLUCKY
TURKISH	UMPTEEN	UNEARTH	UNMANLY
TURMOIL	UNACTED	UNEATEN	UNMARRY
TURNCAP	UNAGING	UNEQUAL	UNMEANT
TURNERY	UNAIDED	UNEXACT	UNMEWED
TURNING	UNAIRED	UNFADED	UNMIXED
TURNKEY	UNAPTLY	UNFAITH	UNMOIST
TURN-OUT	UNARMED	UNFILED	UNMORAL
TUSSLED	UNASKED	UNFITLY	UNMOULD
TUSSOCK	UNAWARE	UNFIXED	UNMOVED
TUSSORE	UNBAKED	UNFOUND	UNNAMED
TUTELAR	UNBEGUN	UNFROCK	UNNERVE
TUTORED	UNBLIND	UNFUSED	UNNOTED
TWADDLE	UNBLOCK	UNGIVEN	UNOILED
TWANGED	UNBLOWN	UNGLUED	UNOWNED
TWANGLE	UNBOSOM	UNGODLY	UNPAVED
TWANKED	UNBOUND	UNGUENT	UNPERCH
TWEAKED	UNBOWED	UNHANDY	UNPLAIT
TWEEDLE	UNBRACE	UNHAPPY	UNPLUMB
TWEENIE	UNBRAID	UNHARDY	UNQUIET
TWELFTH	UNBUILT	UNHASTY	UNRAKED
TWIDDLE	UNBURNT	UNHEARD	UNRAVEL
TWIGGED	UNCAGED	UNHEEDY	UNREADY
TWINGED	UNCANNY	UNHINGE	UNREEVE
TWINING	UNCARED	UNHIRED	UNRIVET
TWINKLE	UNCASED	UNHITCH	UNROBED
TWINNED	UNCEDED	UNHIVED	UNROYAL
TWIRLED	UNCHAIN	UNHOPED	UNRULED
TWIRLER	UNCHARY	UNHORSE	UNSATED
TWISTED	UNCINAL	UNHOUSE	UNSCREW

UNSEXED	UPBORNE	VAMPING	VERONAL
UNSHORN	UPBRAID	VAMPIRE	VERSIFY
UNSHOWN	UPENDED	VANDYKE	VERSING
UNSIZED	UPGRADE	VANESSA	VERSION
UNSLING	UPHEAVE	VANILLA	VERTIGO
UNSLUNG	UPLYING	VANNING	VERVAIN
UNSOLID	UPRAISE	VANTAGE	VESICLE
UNSOUND	UPRIGHT	VANWARD	VESTIGE
UNSPELL	UPRISEN	VAPIDLY	VESTING
UNSPENT	UPSTAGE	VAPOURS	VESTRAL
UNSPIED	UPSTART	VAPOURY	VETERAN
UNSPIKE	UPSURGE	VARIANT	VETOING
UNSPILT	UPSWEEP	VARIATE	VIADUCT
UNSPLIT	UP-TRAIN	VARIETY	VIBRANT
UNSPOIL	UPWARDS	VARIOUS	VIBRATE
UNSTACK	URALITE	VARMINT	VIBRATO
UNSTAID	URANITE	VARNISH	VICEROY
UNSTEEL	URANIUM	VARSITY	VICIOUS
UNSTICK	URGENCY	VARYING	VICTORY
UNSTUCK	USELESS	VASTEST	VICTUAL
UNSWEET	USHERED	VATICAN	VIEWING
UNSWEPT	USUALLY	VAULTED	VILLAGE
UNSWORN	USURPED	VAULTER	VILLAIN
UNTAKEN	USURPER	VAUNTED	VILLEIN
UNTAMED	UTENSIL	VEERING	VINEGAR
UNTAXED	UTILISE	VEHICLE	VINTAGE
UNTHINK	UTILITY	VEILING	VINTNER
UNTILED	UTOPIAN	VEINING	VIOLATE
UNTIRED	UTTERED	VEINOUS	VIOLENT
UNTRIED	UTTERER	VELLUMY	VIOLIST
UNTRULY	UTTERLY	VELOURS	VIRGATE
UNTRUSS	UXORIAL	VELVETY	VIRTUAL
UNTRUTH		VENALLY	VISAGED
UNTUNED	**V—7**	VENDING	VIS-A-VIS
UNTWINE	VACANCY	VENISON	VISCOUS
UNTWIST	VACATED	VENOMED	VISIBLE
UNTYING	VACATOR	VENTAGE	VISIBLY
UNURGED	VACCINE	VENTAIL	VISITED
UNUSUAL	VACUITY	VENTING	VISITOR
UNVEXED	VACUOLE	VENT-PEG	VISORED
UNVOWED	VACUOUS	VENTRAL	VITALLY
UNWAGED	VAGRANT	VENTURE	VITAMIN
UNWEARY	VAGUELY	VERANDA	VITIATE
UNWEAVE	VAGUEST	VERBENA	VITRIFY
UNWIRED	VAINEST	VERSIFY	VITRINE
UNWOOED	VALANCE	VERBOSE	VITRIOL
UNWOUND	VALIANT	VERDANT	VIVIDLY
UNWOVEN	VALIDLY	VERDICT	VIXENLY
UNWRUNG	VALUING	VERDURE	VOCABLE
UNYOKED	VALVATE	VERGING	VOCALLY
UNZONED	VAMOOSE	VERIEST	VOICING

VOIDING	WAREFUL	WEAKEST	WHARFED
VOLCANO	WARFARE	WEALDEN	WHARVES
VOLTAGE	WARHOOP	WEALTHY	WHATNOT
VOLTAIC	WARIEST	WEANING	WHEATEN
VOLUBLE	WARLIKE	WEARIED	WHEEDLE
VOLUBLY	WARLOCK	WEARIER	WHEELED
VOLUTED	WAR-LORD	WEARILY	WHEELER
VOTABLE	WARMEST	WEARING	WHEEZED
VOUCHED	WARMING	WEARISH	WHELPED
VOUCHEE	WARNING	WEATHER	WHEREAS
VOUCHER	WARPATH	WEAVING	WHEREAT
VOYAGED	WARPING	WEBBING	WHEREBY
VOYAGER	WARRANT	WEB-FOOT	WHEREIN
VULGATE	WARRING	WEBSTER	WHEREOF
VULPINE	WARRIOR	WEB-TOED	WHEREON
VULTURE	WARSHIP	WEDDING	WHERESO
	WAR-SONG	WEDGING	WHERETO
W—7	WART-HOG	WEDLOCK	WHETHER
WADDING	WAR-WORN	WEEDING	WHETTED
WADDLED	WASHING	WEEKDAY	WHETTER
WADDLER	WASH-OUT	WEEK-END	WHIFFED
WAFERED	WASH-POT	WEENING	WHIFFLE
WAFTING	WASH-TUB	WEEPING	WHILING
WAGERED	WASP-FLY	WEFTAGE	WHIMPER
WAGGERY	WASPISH	WEIGHED	WHIMSEY
WAGGING	WASSAIL	WEIGHER	WHINING
WAGGISH	WASTAGE	WEIGHTY	WHIPPED
WAGGLED	WASTING	WEIRDER	WHIPPER
WAGONER	WASTREL	WEIRDLY	WHIPPET
WAGTAIL	WATCHED	WELCOME	WHIP-SAW
WAILING	WATCHER	WELDING	WHIP-TOP
WAISTED	WATCHET	WELFARE	WHIRLED
WAITING	WATERED	WELLING	WHIRRED
WAIVING	WATERER	WELL-MET	WHIRLER
WAKEFUL	WATTLED	WELL-OFF	WHISKER
WAKENED	WAVELET	WELL-SET	WHISKEY
WAKENER	WAVERED	WELL-WON	WHISPER
WALKING	WAVERER	WELSHED	WHISTLE
WALLABY	WAX-BILL	WELSHER	WHITELY
WALL-EYE	WAX-DOLL	WELTING	WHITEST
WALLING	WAX-MOTH	WENDING	WHITHER
WALLOON	WAX-PALM	WESTERN	WHITING
WALTZED	WAX-TREE	WESTING	WHITISH
WALTZER	WAX-WING	WET-DOCK	WHITLOW
WANGLED	WAXWORK	WETNESS	WHITSUN
WANNESS	WAY-BILL	WETTEST	WHITTLE
WANNISH	WAY-MARK	WETTING	WHIZZED
WANTAGE	WAYSIDE	WETTISH	WHIZZER
WARBLED	WAYWARD	WHACKED	WHOEVER
WARBLER	WAYWISE	WHACKER	WHOOPEE
WARDING	WAYWORN	WHALING	WHOOPED

WHOOPER	WIZENED	WRIGGLY	ZONALLY
WHOPPED	WOBBLED	WRINGER	ZONULAR
WHOPPER	WOBBLER	WRINKLE	ZOOIDAL
WHORLED	WOESOME	WRINKLY	ZOOLITE
WIDENED	WOLF-CUB	WRITHED	ZOOLOGY
WIDENER	WOLF-DOG	WRITING	ZOOMING
WIDGEON	WOLFISH	WRITTEN	
WIDOWED	WOLF-NET	WRONGED	**A—8**
WIDOWER	WOLFRAM	WRONGER	ABASHING
WIELDED	WOMANLY	WRONGLY	ABATABLE
WIELDER	WOOD-ANT	WROUGHT	ABATTOIR
WIGGERY	WOODCUT	WRYNECK	ABDICANT
WIGGING	WOODMAN	WRYNESS	ABDICATE
WIGGLED	WOOLLEN	WYCH-ELM	ABDUCTED
WIGGLER	WOOLMAN		ABDUCTOR
WIGLESS	WOOMERA	**X—7**	ABERDEEN
WILD-CAT	WORDILY	X-RAYING	ABERRANT
WILDEST	WORDING		ABERRATE
WILDING	WORDISH	**Y—7**	ABETMENT
WILDISH	WORK-BAG	YANKING	ABETTING
WILIEST	WORK-BOX	YAPPING	ABEYANCE
WILLING	WORK-DAY	YARDAGE	ABHORRED
WILLOWY	WORKING	YARD-ARM	ABHORRER
WILTING	WORKMAN	YARDING	ABJECTLY
WIMPLED	WORK-SHY	YARD-MAN	ABJURING
WINCHED	WORLDLY	YARNING	ABLATION
WINDAGE	WORMING	YASHMAK	ABLATIVE
WIND-BAG	WORN-OUT	YAWNING	ABLENESS
WINDIER	WORRIED	YEARNED	ABLUTION
WINDILY	WORRIER	YELLING	ABNEGATE
WINDING	WORSHIP	YELLOWY	ABNORMAL
WINDROW	WORSTED	YELPING	ABORTING
WINDSOR	WOTTING	YEW-TREE	ABORTION
WINE-BAG	WOULD-BE	YIDDISH	ABORTIVE
WINGING	WOULDST	YIELDED	ABRADING
WINGLET	WOUNDED	YORKIST	ABRASION
WINKING	WOUNDER	YOUNGER	ABRASIVE
WINNING	WRANGLE	YOWLING	ABRIDGED
WINSOME	WRAPPED	YULE-LOG	ABROGATE
WIRE-MAN	WRAPPER		ABSENTED
WIRE-WAY	WREAKED	**Z—7**	ABSENTEE
WISHFUL	WREAKER	ZANYISM	ABSENTLY
WISTFUL	WREATHE	ZEALFUL	ABSINTHE
WITCHED	WREATHY	ZEALOUS	ABSOLUTE
WITHERS	WRECKED	ZEOLITE	ABSOLVED
WITHOUT	WRECKER	ZESTFUL	ABSOLVER
WITLESS	WRESTED	ZESTING	ABSONANT
WITLING	WRESTER	ZINCOID	ABSORBED
WITNESS	WRESTLE	ZIONISM	ABSTRACT
WITTIER	WRICKED	ZIONIST	ABSTRUSE
WITTILY	WRIGGLE	ZIPPING	ABSURDLY

ABUNDANT	ADENOIDS	AFFORDED	ALIENISM
ABUSABLE	ADEPTION	AFFOREST	ALIENIST
ABUTMENT	ADEQUACY	AFFRIGHT	ALIGHTED
ABUTTING	ADEQUATE	AGAR-AGAR	ALIGNING
ACADEMIC	ADHERENT	AGEDNESS	ALKALINE
ACANTHUS	ADHERING	AGGRIEVE	ALKALOID
ACCEDING	ADHESION	AGITATED	ALLAYING
ACCENTED	ADHESIVE	AGITATOR	ALL-CLEAR
ACCEPTED	ADJACENT	AGLIMMER	ALLEGING
ACCEPTER	ADJOINED	AGNATION	ALLEGORY
ACCEPTOR	ADJUDGED	AGNOSTIC	ALLELUIA
ACCIDENT	ADJURING	AGONISED	ALLERGIC
ACCOLADE	ADJUSTER	AGRARIAN	ALLEYWAY
ACCORDED	ADJUTANT	AGREEING	ALL-FIRED
ACCOSTED	ADMIRING	AGRIMONY	ALL-FOURS
ACCOUTRE	ADMITTED	AGRONOMY	ALLIANCE
ACCREDIT	ADMIXING	AIGRETTE	ALLOCATE
ACCRUING	ADMONISH	AIRBORNE	ALLOTTED
ACCURACY	ADOPTING	AIR-BRAKE	ALLOWING
ACCURATE	ADOPTION	AIR-BRICK	ALLOYING
ACCURSED	ADOPTIVE	AIRCRAFT	ALLSPICE
ACCUSANT	ADORABLE	AIREDALE	ALLUDING
ACCUSING	ADORABLY	AIRFIELD	ALLURING
ACCUSTOM	ADORNING	AIR-GRAPH	ALLUSION
ACERBATE	ADROITLY	AIRINESS	ALLUSIVE
ACERBITY	ADSCRIPT	AIR-LINER	ALLUSORY
ACESCENT	ADULATED	AIR-PILOT	ALLUVIAL
ACHIEVED	ADULATOR	AIRPLANE	ALLUVION
ACIDNESS	ADVANCED	AIR-POWER	ALLUVIUM
ACIDOSIS	ADVERTED	AIR-SCREW	ALMIGHTY
ACONITIC	ADVISING	AIR-SHAFT	ALPHABET
ACORN-CUP	ADVISORY	AIR-SPACE	ALPINIST
ACOUSTIC	ADVOCACY	AIR-STRIP	ALSATIAN
ACQUAINT	ADVOCATE	AIRTIGHT	ALTERING
ACQUIRED	ADVOWSON	ALACRITY	ALTHOUGH
ACRIDITY	AERATING	ALARM-GUN	ALTITUDE
ACRIMONY	AERATION	ALARMING	ALTRUISM
ACROSTIC	AERIALLY	ALARMIST	ALTRUIST
ACTINISM	AERIFIED	ALBACORE	AMARANTH
ACTIVATE	AERIFORM	ALBANIAN	AMASSING
ACTIVELY	AERONAUT	ALBINISM	AMAZEDLY
ACTIVITY	AEROSTAT	ALDEHYDE	AMBITION
ACTUALLY	AESTHETE	ALDERMAN	AMBROSIA
ACTUATED	AFFECTED	ALEATORY	AMBULANT
ADAPTING	AFFIANCE	ALEHOUSE	AMBULATE
ADAPTIVE	AFFINITY	ALFRESCO	AMBUSHED
ADDENDUM	AFFIRMED	ALGERIAN	AMENABLE
ADDICTED	AFFIRMER	ALGORISM	AMENABLY
ADDITION	AFFIXING	ALHAMBRA	AMENDING
ADDUCING	AFFLATUS	ALICANTE	AMERICAN
ADDUCTOR	AFFLUENT	ALIENATE	AMETHYST

AMICABLE	ANTEDATE	APPROVER	ASCENDED
AMICABLY	ANTELOPE	APTEROUS	ASCIDIUM
AMMONIAC	ANTENNAE	APTITUDE	ASCORBIC
AMMONITE	ANTENNAL	AQUARIUM	ASCRIBED
AMORTISE	ANTERIOR	AQUARIUS	ASH-STAND
AMOUNTED	ANTEROOM	AQUATINT	ASPERITY
AMPHIBIA	ANTIBODY	AQUEDUCT	ASPERSED
AMPUTATE	ANTIDOTE	AQUIFORM	ASPHODEL
AMUSABLE	ANTIMONY	AQUILINE	ASPHYXIA
ANABASIS	ANTI-NAZI	ARACHNID	ASPIRANT
ANACONDA	ANTIPHON	ARBITRAL	ASPIRATE
ANAGLYPH	ANTIPOLE	ARBOREAL	ASPIRING
ANALYSED	ANTIPOPE	ARBOURED	ASSAILED
ANALYSER	ANTI-TANK	ARCADIAN	ASSASSIN
ANALYSIS	ANTITYPE	ARCHAISM	ASSAYING
ANALYTIC	ANTLERED	ARCHDUKE	ASSEMBLE
ANARCHIC	ANYTHING	ARCHIVES	ASSENTED
ANATHEMA	ANYWHERE	ARCHNESS	ASSERTED
ANATOMIC	APERIENT	ARCTURUS	ASSESSED
ANCESTOR	APERITIF	ARDENTLY	ASSESSOR
ANCESTRY	APERTURE	ARGONAUT	ASSIGNED
ANCHORED	APHIDIAN	ARGUABLE	ASSIGNEE
ANCHORET	APHORISM	ARGUFIED	ASSIGNOR
ANDERSON	APHORIST	ARGUMENT	ASSISTED
ANECDOTE	APIARIST	ARIDNESS	ASSONANT
ANEURISM	APICALLY	ARMAMENT	ASSORTED
ANEURYSM	APOLLYON	ARMATURE	ASSUAGED
ANGELICA	APOLOGIA	ARMCHAIR	ASSUMING
ANGERING	APOPLEXY	ARMENIAN	ASSURING
ANGLICAN	APOSTASY	ARMORIAL	ASSYRIAN
ANGRIEST	APOSTATE	ARMOURED	ASTERISK
ANIMATED	APPALLED	ARMOURER	ASTEROID
ANIMATOR	APPARENT	AROMATIC	ASTONISH
ANISETTE	APPEALED	AROUSING	ASTRAGAL
ANNALIST	APPEARED	ARPEGGIO	ASTUTELY
ANNAMITE	APPEASED	ARQUEBUS	ATABRINE
ANNEALED	APPEASER	ARRANGED	ATHELING
ANNELIDA	APPENDED	ARRANTLY	ATHENIAN
ANNEXING	APPENDIX	ARRAYING	ATHLETIC
ANNOTATE	APPETITE	ARRESTED	ATLANTIC
ANNOUNCE	APPLAUSE	ARRIVING	ATLANTIS
ANNOYING	APPLE-PIE	ARROGANT	ATOMISED
ANNUALLY	APPLIQUE	ARROGATE	ATOMISER
ANNULATE	APPLYING	ARTERIAL	ATONABLE
ANNULLED	APPOSITE	ARTESIAN	ATREMBLE
ANODISED	APPRAISE	ARTFULLY	ATROCITY
ANOINTED	APPRISED	ARTICLED	ATROPINE
ANSERINE	APPRIZED	ARTIFICE	ATTACHED
ANSWERED	APPROACH	ARTISTIC	ATTACKED
ANT-EATER	APPROVAL	ARTISTRY	ATTACKER
ANTECEDE	APPROVED	ASBESTOS	ATTAINED

ATTENDED
ATTESTED
ATTICISM
ATTIRING
ATTITUDE
ATTORNEY
ATTUNING
AUDACITY
AUDIENCE
AUDITING
AUDITION
AUDITORY
AUGURING
AUGUSTAN
AUGUSTLY
AURICULA
AURIFORM
AUSTRIAN
AUTARCHY
AUTOCRAT
AUTO-DA-FE
AUTO-DYNE
AUTOGYRO
AUTOMATA
AUTONOMY
AUTUMNAL
AVAILING
AVENGING
AVERAGED
AVERRING
AVERSELY
AVERSION
AVIATION
AVIFAUNA
AVOIDING
AVOWABLE
AVOWABLY
AVOWEDLY
AWAITING
AWAKENED
AWARDING
AXLE-TREE

B—8
BABBLING
BABY-FACE
BABY-FARM
BABYHOOD
BACCARAT
BACCHANT
BACHELOR

BACKBITE
BACK-BONE
BACK-CHAT
BACK-DOOR
BACK-DROP
BACKFIRE
BACK-HAND
BACK-LASH
BACK-ROOM
BACKSIDE
BACK-STEP
BACKWARD
BACKWASH
BACONIAN
BACTERIA
BACTRIAN
BADGERED
BADINAGE
BAFFLING
BAGUETTE
BAKELITE
BALANCED
BALANCER
BALDNESS
BALL-COCK
BALLISTA
BALLOTED
BALLROOM
BALLYHOO
BALLYRAG
BALMORAL
BALUSTER
BANALITY
BANDAGED
BANDANNA
BANDEAUX
BANDITTI
BANDSMAN
BANDYING
BANISHED
BANISTER
BANJOIST
BANK-BILL
BANK-BOOK
BANK-NOTE
BANK-RATE
BANKRUPT
BANNERET
BANNEROL
BANTERED
BANTERER

BANTLING
BAPTISED
BARATHEA
BARBARIC
BARBECUE
BARBERRY
BARBETTE
BARBICAN
BARDLING
BAREBACK
BAREFOOT
BARGEMAN
BARITONE
BARNABAS
BARNACLE
BARN-DOOR
BARNYARD
BAROLOGY
BARONAGE
BARONESS
BARONIAL
BAROUCHE
BARRACKS
BARRATOR
BARRATRY
BARRENLY
BARTERED
BARTERER
BARYTONE
BASALTIC
BASEBALL
BASELESS
BASE-LINE
BASEMENT
BASENESS
BASILICA
BASILISK
BASKETRY
BASS-DRUM
BASS-HORN
BASSINET
BASS-TUBA
BASS-VIOL
BASTARDY
BASTILLE
BATAVIAN
BATHROOM
BATSWING
BATTENED
BATTERED
BATTLING

BAULKING
BAVARIAN
BEACHING
BEAD-WORK
BEAMLESS
BEARABLE
BEARABLY
BEARDING
BEARINGS
BEARLIKE
BEARSKIN
BEATIFIC
BEAUTIFY
BEAVERED
BECALMED
BECHAMEL
BECHANCE
BECKONED
BECOMING
BEDAUBED
BED-CHAIR
BEDECKED
BEDEWING
BEDIMMED
BED-LINEN
BEDMAKER
BEDPLATE
BED-QUILT
BED-STAFF
BEDSTEAD
BEDSTRAW
BED-TABLE
BEE-BREAD
BEE-EATER
BEEFIEST
BEER-PUMP
BEERSHOP
BEE'S-WING
BEETLING
BEETROOT
BEFITTED
BEFLOWER
BEFOGGED
BEFOOLED
BEFOULED
BEFRIEND
BEGGARED
BEGGARLY
BEGINNER
BEGOTTEN
BEGRIMED

BEGRUDGE	BESTREWN	BIRD'S-EYE	BLITZING
BEGUILED	BESTRIDE	BIRD-SONG	BLIZZARD
BEHAVING	BESTRODE	BIRTHDAY	BLOATING
BEHEADED	BETAKING	BIRTHDOM	BLOCKADE
BEHEMOTH	BETA-RAYS	BISECTED	BLOCKING
BEHOLDEN	BETEL-NUT	BISECTOR	BLOOD-HOT
BEHOLDER	BETIDING	BISEXUAL	BLOODIED
BEHOVING	BETRAYAL	BITINGLY	BLOODILY
BELABOUR	BETRAYED	BITTERLY	BLOODING
BELAYING	BETRAYER	BI-WEEKLY	BLOOD-RED
BELCHING	BETTERED	BLABBING	BLOOMERS
BELIEVED	BEVELLED	BLACKCAP	BLOOMING
BELIEVER	BEVERAGE	BLACK-FLY	BLOSSOMY
BELITTLE	BEWAILED	BLACK-GUM	BLOTCHED
BELLBIND	BEWARING	BLACKING	BLOTTING
BELL-BIRD	BEWIGGED	BLACKISH	BLOWBALL
BELL-BUOY	BEWILDER	BLACKLEG	BLOW-HOLE
BELLOWED	BIBLICAL	BLACKOUT	BLOW-PIPE
BELL-PULL	BIBULOUS	BLAMABLE	BLUDGEON
BELL-ROPE	BICAUDAL	BLAMABLY	BLUE-BACK
BELL-TENT	BICKERED	BLAMEFUL	BLUEBELL
BELLWORT	BICOLOUR	BLANCHED	BLUEBIRD
BELLYFUL	BICYCLED	BLANDEST	BLUEBOOK
BELLYING	BIDDABLE	BLANDISH	BLUECOAT
BELONGED	BIENNIAL	BLANKEST	BLUE-EYED
BEMOANED	BIGAMIST	BLANKING	BLUEFISH
BENCHING	BIGAMOUS	BLASTING	BLUENESS
BENDABLE	BIG-BONED	BLATANCY	BLUENOSE
BENEDICK	BIGNONIA	BLAZONED	BLUFFEST
BENEDICT	BILBERRY	BLEACHED	BLUFFING
BENEFICE	BILL-BOOK	BLEAKEST	BLUISHLY
BENIGNLY	BILLETED	BLEAKISH	BLUNTING
BENJAMIN	BILL-HEAD	BLEATING	BLUNTISH
BENUMBED	BILLHOOK	BLEEDING	BLURRING
BEQUEATH	BILLIARD	BLENCHED	BLURTING
BERATING	BILLOWED	BLENDING	BLUSHFUL
BERBERRY	BILLY-BOY	BLENHEIM	BLUSHING
BEREAVED	BILLY-CAN	BLESSING	BLUSTERY
BERGAMOT	BINDWEED	BLIGHTED	BOARDING
BERI-BERI	BINNACLE	BLIGHTER	BOASTFUL
BERRYING	BINOMIAL	BLIMPERY	BOASTING
BESIEGED	BIOGRAPH	BLINDAGE	BOAT-HOOK
BESIEGER	BIOMETRY	BLINDEST	BOATRACE
BESMIRCH	BIOSCOPE	BLINDING	BOBBINET
BESOTTED	BIRCHING	BLINDMAN	BOBOLINK
BESOUGHT	BIRDBATH	BLINKERS	BODLEIAN
BESPOKEN	BIRD-CAGE	BLINKING	BODY-LINE
BESSEMER	BIRDCALL	BLISSFUL	BOG-BERRY
BESTIARY	BIRDLIKE	BLISTERY	BOG-EARTH
BESTOWAL	BIRD-LIME	BLITHELY	BOGEYISM
BESTOWED	BIRD-SEED	BLITHEST	BOGEYMAN

BOGGLING	BOUILLON	BRIDLING	BULL-CALF
BOG-WHORT	BOUNCING	BRIEFING	BULLDOZE
BOHEMIAN	BOUNDARY	BRIGHTEN	BULLETIN
BOLDNESS	BOUNDING	BRIGHTLY	BULLFROG
BOLTHOLE	BOWINGLY	BRIMLESS	BULL-HEAD
BOLT-ROPE	BOWSPRIT	BRIMMING	BULL-RING
BOMB-FREE	BOX-PLEAT	BRINDLED	BULL'S-EYE
BONA-FIDE	BOYISHLY	BRINE-PAN	BULLYING
BONDMAID	BRACELET	BRINE-PIT	BULLYRAG
BONDSMAN	BRACKISH	BRINGING	BUMMAREE
BONE-IDLE	BRADBURY	BRISLING	BUNCHING
BONELESS	BRADSHAW	BRISTLED	BUNDLING
BONHOMIE	BRAGGART	BROACHED	BUNGALOW
BONIFACE	BRAGGING	BROADEST	BUNG-HOLE
BONNETED	BRAIDING	BROADISH	BUNGLING
BONSPIEL	BRAIN-FAG	BROCADED	BUNKERED
BOOBYISH	BRAINING	BROCCOLI	BUOYANCY
BOOBYISM	BRAIN-PAN	BROCHURE	BURBERRY
BOOHOOED	BRAISING	BROILING	BURDENED
BOOKCASE	BRAKEMAN	BROKENLY	BURGLARY
BOOK-CLUB	BRAKE-VAN	BROODING	BURGLING
BOOK-DEBT	BRAMBLED	BROOKING	BURGUNDY
BOOKLAND	BRANCHED	BROOKLET	BURROWED
BOOKLESS	BRANDIED	BROUGHAM	BURSTING
BOOK-MARK	BRANDING	BROWBEAT	BUSH-BABY
BOOK-NAME	BRANDISH	BROWLESS	BUSH-BUCK
BOOK-POST	BRAND-NEW	BROWNING	BUSHVELD
BOOKSHOP	BRASSARD	BROWNISH	BUSINESS
BOOKWORM	BRASS-HAT	BROWSING	BUSYBODY
BOOSTING	BRASSICA	BRUISING	BUSYNESS
BOOT-HOOK	BRAWLING	BRUNETTE	BUTCHERY
BOOT-JACK	BRAZENED	BRUSHING	BUTTERED
BOOT-LACE	BRAZENLY	BRUSSELS	BUTTONED
BOOT-LAST	BREACHED	BRUTALITY	BUTTRESS
BOOTLESS	BREAKAGE	BRYOLOGY	BY-PASSED
BOOT-TREE	BREAKING	BUBBLING	BYRONISM
BORDEAUX	BREASTED	BUCKBEAN	BY-STREET
BORDERED	BREATHED	BUCKETED	
BORDERER	BREATHER	BUCKHORN	C—8
BORECOLE	BREECHED	BUCKJUMP	CABIN-BOY
BORROWED	BREECHES	BUCKLING	CABOODLE
BORROWER	BREEDING	BUCKSHEE	CABOTAGE
BOTANIST	BRETHREN	BUCK-SHOT	CABRIOLE
BOTCHERY	BREVIARY	BUCKSKIN	CABSTAND
BOTCHING	BREWSTER	BUDDHISM	CACHALOT
BOTHERED	BRIBABLE	BUDDHIST	CACKLING
BOTTLING	BRICKBAT	BUDGETED	CADENCED
BOTTOMED	BRICKING	BUFFETED	CADILLAC
BOTTOMRY	BRICK-RED	BUILDING	CAERLEON
BOTULISM	BRICK-TEA	BULKHEAD	CAFFEINE
BOUFFANT	BRIDGING	BULKIEST	CAJOLERY

CAJOLING	CAPSICUM	CATCHFLY	CHADBAND
CAKESHOP	CAPSULAR	CATCHING	CHAFFING
CAKE-WALK	CAPTIOUS	CATEGORY	CHAINING
CALABASH	CAPTURED	CATERING	CHAIR-BED
CALAMINE	CAPUCHIN	CATHEDRA	CHAIRING
CALAMITY	CAPYBARA	CATHOLIC	CHAIRMAN
CALCINED	CARAPACE	CATILINE	CHALDRON
CALCULUS	CARBOLIC	CATONIAN	CHALICED
CALENDAR	CARBONIC	CAT'S-FOOT	CHALKING
CALENDER	CARBURET	CAT'S-MEAT	CHALK-PIT
CALF-LOVE	CARDAMOM	CAT'S-TAIL	CHAMPING
CALFSKIN	CARD-CASE	CAULDRON	CHAMPION
CALIBRED	CARDIGAN	CAULKING	CHANCERY
CALIPASH	CARDINAL	CAUSALLY	CHANCING
CALIPERS	CAREENED	CAUSERIE	CHANDLER
CALL-BIRD	CAREERED	CAUSEUSE	CHANGING
CALLIOPE	CAREFREE	CAUSEWAY	CHANTING
CALL-NOTE	CARELESS	CAUTIOUS	CHAPBOOK
CALL-OVER	CARESSED	CAVALIER	CHAPELRY
CALMNESS	CAREWORN	CAVATINA	CHAPERON
CAMBERED	CARILLON	CAVE-BEAR	CHAPITER
CAMBRIAN	CARINATE	CAVERNED	CHAPLAIN
CAMELLIA	CARNIVAL	CAVILLED	CHAPPING
CAMISOLE	CAROLINE	CAVORTED	CHARCOAL
CAMOMILE	CAROLLED	CELERIAC	CHARGING
CAMPAIGN	CAROUSAL	CELERITY	CHARLOCK
CAMP-FIRE	CAROUSED	CELIBACY	CHARMING
CAM-SHAFT	CARPETED	CELIBATE	CHARRING
CAM-WHEEL	CARRIAGE	CELLARER	CHARTING
CANADIAN	CARRIOLE	CELLARET	CHARTISM
CANAILLE	CARRYING	CELLULAR	CHARTIST
CANALISE	CART-LOAD	CEMENTED	CHASSEUR
CANASTER	CARYATID	CEMETERY	CHASTELY
CANDIDLY	CASCADED	CENOTAPH	CHASTISE
CANDYING	CASE-BOOK	CENSORED	CHASTITY
CANE-MILL	CASEMATE	CENSURED	CHASUBLE
CANISTER	CASEMENT	CENTAURY	CHATTELS
CANKERED	CASE-SHOT	CENTRING	CHATTING
CANNIBAL	CASHMERE	CEPHALIC	CHAUFFER
CANNONED	CASKETED	CERAMICS	CHEATING
CANOEIST	CASTANET	CERASTES	CHECKERS
CANONISE	CASTAWAY	CERBERUS	CHECKING
CANOODLE	CAST-IRON	CEREBRAL	CHEEKING
CANOPIED	CASTLING	CEREBRUM	CHEEPING
CANTERED	CASTRATE	CEREMENT	CHEERFUL
CANTICLE	CASUALLY	CEREMONY	CHEERILY
CAPACITY	CASUALTY	CERULEAN	CHEERING
CAPERING	CATACOMB	CERVICAL	CHEMICAL
CAPITANO	CATALYST	CESAREAN	CHENILLE
CAPITATE	CATAPULT	CESSPOOL	CHERUBIC
CAPRIOLE	CATARACT	CETACEAN	CHERUBIM

CHESHIRE	CINCHONA	CLIMATIC	COARSELY
CHESSMAN	CINNABAR	CLIMBING	COARSEST
CHESTING	CINNAMON	CLINCHED	COASTING
CHESTNUT	CIPHERED	CLINGING	COBBLING
CHEVYING	CIRCLING	CLINICAL	COBWEBBY
CHIASMUS	CIRCULAR	CLINKING	COCKADED
CHICANED	CITATION	CLIPPERS	COCKATOO
CHICK-PEA	CITY-BRED	CLIPPING	COCK-CROW
CHILDBED	CIVET-CAT	CLIQUISH	COCKEREL
CHILDISH	CIVILIAN	CLOAKING	COCK-EYED
CHILDREN	CIVILITY	CLOCKING	COCKLING
CHILIASM	CIVILISE	CLODDISH	COCKSPUR
CHILIAST	CLACKING	CLOGGING	COCKSURE
CHILLIER	CLAIMANT	CLOISTER	COCKTAIL
CHILLING	CLAIMING	CLOSE-CUT	CODDLING
CHILTERN	CLAM-BAKE	CLOSETED	CODIFIED
CHIMAERA	CLAMPING	CLOTHIER	CO-EDITOR
CHIMERIC	CLANGING	CLOTHING	COERCING
CHINAMAN	CLANGOUR	CLOTTING	COERCION
CHIN-CHIN	CLANKING	CLOUDILY	COERCIVE
CHINKING	CLANNISH	CLOUDING	COFFERED
CHIPMUNK	CLANSHIP	CLOUDLET	COFFINED
CHIPPING	CLANSMAN	CLOUTING	COGENTLY
CHIRPING	CLAPPING	CLOWNERY	COGITATE
CHIRRING	CLAPTRAP	CLOWNING	COGNOMEN
CHIT-CHAT	CLARENCE	CLOWNISH	COG-WHEEL
CHIVALRY	CLARINET	CLUBBING	COHERENT
CHLORATE	CLASHING	CLUBBISH	COHERING
CHLORIDE	CLASPING	CLUB-FOOT	COHESION
CHLORINE	CLASSIER	CLUB-LAND	COHESIVE
CHLOROUS	CLASSIFY	CLUB-MOSS	COIFFEUR
CHOICELY	CLASSING	CLUB-ROOM	COIFFING
CHOIR-BOY	CLASSMAN	CLUB-ROOT	COIFFURE
CHOLERIC	CLASS-WAR	CLUB-RUSH	COINCIDE
CHOOSING	CLAVICLE	CLUCKING	COINLESS
CHOPPING	CLAYMORE	CLUELESS	COLANDER
CHOP-SUEY	CLEANING	CLUMPING	COLDNESS
CHORALLY	CLEANSED	CLUMSIER	COLE-SLAW
CHORTLED	CLEANSER	CLUMSILY	COLEWORT
CHORUSED	CLEAR-CUT	CLUTCHED	COLISEUM
CHOW-CHOW	CLEAREST	COACH-BOX	COLLAPSE
CHRISTEN	CLEARING	COACHDOG	COLLARED
CHROMIUM	CLEAVAGE	COACHFUL	COLLARET
CHUCKING	CLEAVING	COACHING	COLLATED
CHUCKLED	CLEMATIS	COACHMAN	COLLATOR
CHUMP-END	CLEMENCY	COACTIVE	COLLEGER
CHURLISH	CLENCHED	CO-AGENCY	COLLIDED
CHURNING	CLERICAL	COALESCE	COLLIERY
CICATRIX	CLEVERER	COAL-HOLE	COLLOQUY
CICERONE	CLEVERLY	COAL-MINE	COLLUDED
CIDER-CUP	CLICKING	COAL-SHIP	COLONIAL

COLONISE	CONFUSED	COPULATE	CRABBING
COLONIST	CONFUTED	COPY-BOOK	CRACKING
COLOSSAL	CONGRESS	COPYHOLD	CRACK-JAW
COLOSSUS	CONGREVE	COQUETRY	CRACKLED
COLOURED	CONJOINT	COQUETTE	CRACKNEL
COLUMNAR	CONJUGAL	CORDUROY	CRACK-POT
COLUMNED	CONJUNCT	CORDWAIN	CRADLING
COMATOSE	CONJURED	CORN-BEEF	CRAFTIER
COMBINED	CONJURER	CORNEOUS	CRAFTILY
COME-BACK	CONJUROR	CORNERED	CRAMMING
COMEDIAN	CONNIVED	CORPORAL	CRAMPING
COMMANDO	CONNOTED	CORRIDOR	CRANE-FLY
COMMENCE	CONQUEST	CORRODED	CRANKING
COMMERCE	CONSERVE	CORSELET	CRANNIED
COMMONER	CONSIDER	CORSICAN	CRASHING
COMMONLY	CONSOLED	CORUNDUM	CRAVENLY
COMMUNAL	CONSOMME	CORVETTE	CRAWFISH
COMMUNED	CONSPIRE	COSINESS	CRAWLING
COMMUTED	CONSTANT	COSMETIC	CRAYFISH
COMPARED	CONSTRUE	COSSETED	CRAYONED
COMPETED	CONSULAR	COSTLIER	CRAZIEST
COMPILED	CONSUMED	COST-PLUS	CREAKING
COMPILER	CONSUMER	COSTUMED	CREAMERY
COMPLAIN	CONTANGO	CO-TENANT	CREAMING
COMPLETE	CONTEMPT	COTSWOLD	CREASING
COMPLIED	CONTENTS	COTTAGER	CREATING
COMPOSED	CONTINUE	COTTONED	CREATION
COMPOSER	CONTRACT	COUCHANT	CREATIVE
COMPOUND	CONTRARY	COUCHING	CREATURE
COMPRESS	CONTRAST	COUGHING	CREDENCE
COMPRISE	CONTRITE	COUNTESS	CREDIBLE
COMPUTED	CONTRIVE	COUNTING	CREDIBLY
COMPUTER	CONTUSED	COUPLING	CREDITED
CONCEDED	CONVENED	COURSING	CREDITOR
CONCEIVE	CONVENER	COURTESY	CREEPING
CONCERTO	CONVERGE	COURTIER	CREMATED
CONCLAVE	CONVERSE	COURTING	CREOSOTE
CONCLUDE	CONVEXLY	COUSINLY	CRESCENT
CONCOURS	CONVEYED	COVENANT	CRESTING
CONCRETE	CONVEYOR	COVENTRY	CRETONNE
CONDENSE	CONVINCE	COVERAGE	CREVASSE
CONDOLED	CONVOKED	COVERING	CRIBBAGE
CONDONED	CONVOYED	COVERLET	CRIBBING
CONDUCED	CONVULSE	COVERTLY	CRIMINAL
CONFETTI	COOEEING	COVETING	CRIMPING
CONFIDED	COOK-SHOP	COVETOUS	CRINGING
CONFINED	COOLNESS	COWARDLY	CRINKLED
CONFLICT	COOPERED	COWERING	CRIPPLED
CONFOUND	CO-OPTING	COWHOUSE	CRITERIA
CONFRERE	CO-OPTION	CO-WORKER	CRITICAL
CONFRONT	COPPERED	COXSWAIN	CRITIQUE

CROAKING	CURTNESS	DATE-PLUM	DECODING
CROCKERY	CURTSIED	DAUGHTER	DECORATE
CROCKING	CUSPIDOR	DAUNTING	DECOROUS
CROMLECH	CUSTOMER	DAUPHINE	DECOYING
CROOKING	CUT-GLASS	DAWDLING	DECREASE
CROONING	CUTHBERT	DAYBREAK	DECREPIT
CROPPING	CUTPURSE	DAYDREAM	DECRYING
CROSS-BAR	CUT-WATER	DAYLIGHT	DEDICATE
CROSSBOW	CYCLAMEN	DAY-TO-DAY	DEDUCING
CROSSCUT	CYCLE-CAR	DAZZLING	DEDUCTED
CROSSING	CYCLICAL	DEAD-BEAT	DEEDPOLL
CROTCHED	CYCLONIC	DEADENED	DEEMSTER
CROTCHET	CYLINDER	DEAD-HEAD	DEEPENED
CROUCHED	CYNICISM	DEAD-HEAT	DEEP-LAID
CROUPIER	CYNOSURE	DEADLIER	DEERSKIN
CROWDING	CZARITZA	DEAD-LINE	DEFACING
CROWFOOT		DEADLOCK	DEFAMING
CROWNING		DEADNESS	DEFEATED
CRUCIBLE	**D—8**	DEAD-WOOD	DEFENDED
CRUCIFIX	DABBLING	DEAFENED	DEFENDER
CRUISING	DAB-CHICK	DEAFNESS	DEFERRED
CRUMBLED	DAEDALUS	DEANSHIP	DEFIANCE
CRUMPLED	DAFFODIL	DEARNESS	DEFILING
CRUNCHED	DAFTNESS	DEATH-BED	DEFINING
CRUSADED	DAINTILY	DEBARRED	DEFINITE
CRUSADER	DAIRYING	DEBASING	DEFLATED
CRUSHING	DAIRYMAN	DEBATING	DEFOREST
CRUSTILY	DALES-MAN	DEBILITY	DEFORMED
CRUTCHED	DALLYING	DEBITING	DEFRAYAL
CUBIFORM	DALMATIA	DEBONAIR	DEFRAYED
CUCUMBER	DAMAGING	DEBUNKED	DEFTNESS
CUDDLING	DAMNABLE	DEBUTANT	DEGRADED
CUL-DE-SAC	DAMOCLES	DECADENT	DEIFYING
CULINARY	DAMPENED	DECAMPED	DEIGNING
CULPABLE	DAMPNESS	DECANTED	DEJECTED
CULPABLY	DANDIEST	DECANTER	DEJEUNER
CULTURED	DANDLING	DECAYING	DELAYING
CULVERIN	DANDRUFF	DECEASED	DELECTUS
CUMBRIAN	DANDYISH	DECEIVED	DELEGACY
CUPBOARD	DANDYISM	DECEIVER	DELEGATE
CUPIDITY	DANGLING	DECEMBER	DELETING
CUPREOUS	DANSEUSE	DECENTLY	DELETION
CURATIVE	DAPPLING	DECIDING	DELICACY
CURATORY	DARINGLY	DECIMATE	DELICATE
CURBLESS	DARKENED	DECIPHER	DELIRIUM
CURDLING	DARKLING	DECISION	DELIVERY
CURELESS	DARKNESS	DECISIVE	DELOUSED
CURRENCY	DARK-ROOM	DECK-HAND	DELPHIAN
CURRICLE	DATELESS	DECLARED	DELUDING
CURRYING	DATE-LINE	DECLASSE	DELUGING
CURSEDLY	DATE-PALM	DECLINED	DELUSION

DELUSIVE	DESERTED	DIASTOLE	DISCOUNT
DEMAGOGY	DESERTER	DIATOMIC	DISCOVER
DEMANDED	DESERVED	DIATONIC	DISCREET
DEMARCHE	DESIGNED	DIATRIBE	DISEASED
DEMEANED	DESIGNER	DIBBLING	DISGORGE
DEMENTED	DESIRING	DICKERED	DISGRACE
DEMENTIA	DESIROUS	DICTATED	DISGUISE
DEMERARA	DESISTED	DICTATOR	DISHEVEL
DEMIJOHN	DESOLATE	DIDACTIC	DISINTER
DEMISING	DESPATCH	DIDDLING	DISJOINT
DEMOBBED	DESPISED	DIETETIC	DISLIKED
DEMOCRAT	DESPOTIC	DIFFERED	DISLODGE
DEMOLISH	DESTINED	DIFFRACT	DISLOYAL
DEMONIAC	DETACHED	DIFFUSED	DISMALLY
DEMONISM	DETAILED	DIGESTED	DISMAYED
DEMPSTER	DETAINED	DIGGINGS	DISMOUNT
DEMURELY	DETECTED	DIGITATE	DISORDER
DEMURRED	DETECTOR	DIHEDRAL	DISOWNED
DENARIUS	DETERRED	DILATING	DISPATCH
DENATURE	DETESTED	DILATION	DISPENSE
DENIABLE	DETHRONE	DILATORY	DISPERSE
DENOTING	DETONATE	DILIGENT	DISPIRIT
DENOUNCE	DETRITUS	DILUTING	DISPLACE
DENUDING	DEUCEDLY	DILUTION	DISPOSAL
DEPARTED	DEVALUED	DILUVIAL	DISPOSED
DEFENDED	DEVIATED	DIMINISH	DISPROOF
DEPICTED	DEVILISH	DIMPLING	DISPROVE
DEPILATE	DEVILISM	DINER-OUT	DISPUTED
DEPLETED	DEVILLED	DING-DONG	DISQUIET
DEPLORED	DEVISING	DINGIEST	DISROBED
DEPLOYED	DEVOLVED	DINORNIS	DISSOLVE
DEPONENT	DEVONIAN	DINOSAUR	DISSUADE
DEPORTED	DEVOTING	DIOCESAN	DISTANCE
DEPORTEE	DEVOTION	DIORAMIC	DISTASTE
DEPOSING	DEVOURED	DIPLOMAT	DISTINCT
DEPRAVED	DEVOUTLY	DIRECTED	DISTRACT
DEPRIVED	DEWBERRY	DIRECTLY	DISTRAIN
DEPUTING	DEWINESS	DIRECTOR	DISTRAIT
DEPUTISE	DEXTROSE	DIRTIEST	DISTRESS
DERAILED	DEXTROUS	DIRTYING	DISTRICT
DERANGED	DIABETES	DISABLED	DISTRUST
DERATING	DIABETIC	DISABUSE	DISUNION
DERELICT	DIABOLIC	DISAGREE	DISUNITE
DERIDING	DIAGNOSE	DISALLOW	DISUNITY
DERISION	DIAGONAL	DISARMED	DITCHING
DERISIVE	DIALLING	DISARRAY	DITHERED
DERISORY	DIALOGUE	DISASTER	DITTY-BAG
DERIVING	DIAMETER	DISBURSE	DITTY-BOX
DEROGATE	DIANTHUS	DISCIPLE	DIVE-BOMB
DESCRIBE	DIAPASON	DISCLAIM	DIVERGED
DESCRIED	DIASTASE	DISCLOSE	DIVERTED

DIVESTED	DOORLESS	DRAWABLE	DRY-GOODS
DIVIDEND	DOOR-NAIL	DRAWBACK	DRY-NURSE
DIVIDING	DOOR-POST	DRAWBOLT	DRY-PLATE
DIVINELY	DOOR-STEP	DRAW-GEAR	DRY-POINT
DIVINITY	DORMANCY	DRAWLING	DRY-STONE
DIVISION	DORMOUSE	DRAW-LINK	DUCHESSE
DIVORCED	DORSALLY	DRAW-WELL	DUCKBILL
DIVORCEE	DOTARDLY	DREADFUL	DUCK-HAWK
DIVULGED	DOTINGLY	DREADING	DUCKLING
DIZZYING	DOTTEREL	DREAMFUL	DUCK-MOLE
DOCILITY	DOUBLETS	DREAMILY	DUCK'S-EGG
DOCKYARD	DOUBLING	DREAMING	DUCK-SHOT
DOCTORED	DOUBLOON	DREARILY	DUCK-WEED
DOCTRINE	DOUBTFUL	DREDGING	DUELLING
DOCUMENT	DOUBTING	DRENCHED	DUELLIST
DODDERED	DOUCHING	DRESSING	DUETTING
DODDERER	DOUGHBOY	DRIBBLING	DUETTIST
DOGBERRY	DOUGHNUT	DRIBBLED	DUKELING
DOG-EARED	DOUM-PALM	DRIBBLET	DUKERIES
DOGESHIP	DOURNESS	DRIFT-ICE	DUKESHIP
DOG-FACED	DOVECOTE	DRIFTING	DULCIMER
DOGGEDLY	DOVE-EYED	DRIFT-NET	DULL-EYED
DOGGEREL	DOVELIKE	DRIFT-WAY	DULLNESS
DOG-HOUSE	DOVETAIL	DRILLING	DUMB-BELL
DOG-LATIN	DOWDYISH	DRINKING	DUMBNESS
DOGMATIC	DOWDYISM	DRIPPING	DUMB-SHOW
DOG'S-BODY	DOWELLED	DRIVABLE	DUMPLING
DOG'S-MEAT	DOWEL-PIN	DRIZZLED	DUNGAREE
DOG'S-NOSE	DOWERING	DROLLERY	DUNG-CART
DOG-TIRED	DOWNCAST	DROOLING	DUNG-FORK
DOGTOOTH	DOWNCOME	DROOPING	DUNG-HILL
DOG-WATCH	DOWNFALL	DROP-GOAL	DUODENAL
DOLDRUMS	DOWNHILL	DROPPING	DUODENUM
DOLLED-UP	DOWNLAND	DROPSIED	DUOLOGUE
DOLOMITE	DOWN-LINE	DROPWORT	DURATION
DOLOROSO	DOWNPOUR	DROUGHTY	DUST-CART
DOLOROUS	DOWNWARD	DROWNING	DUST-COAT
DOMELIKE	DOXOLOGY	DROWSILY	DUST-HOLE
DOMESDAY	DOZINESS	DROWSING	DUTCHMAN
DOMESTIC	DRAFTING	DRUBBING	DUTIABLE
DOMICILE	DRAGGING	DRUDGERY	DUTY-FREE
DOMINANT	DRAGGLED	DRUDGING	DUTY-PAID
DOMINATE	DRAG-HOOK	DRUGGING	DWARFING
DOMINEER	DRAG-HUNT	DRUGGIST	DWARFISH
DOMINION	DRAGOMAN	DRUIDISM	DWELLING
DOMINOES	DRAINAGE	DRUMFIRE	DWINDLED
DONATING	DRAINING	DRUMFISH	DYE-HOUSE
DONATION	DRAMATIC	DRUMHEAD	DYE-STUFF
DOOMSDAY	DRAM-SHOP	DRUMMING	DYNAMICS
DOOR-BELL	DRAUGHTS	DRUNKARD	DYNAMISM
DOOR-KNOB	DRAUGHTY	DRY-CLEAN	DYNAMIST

DYNAMITE	EGYPTIAN	EMENDING	ENFILADE
DYNASTIC	EIGHTEEN	EMERGENT	ENFOLDED
	EIGHTHLY	EMERGING	ENFORCED
E—8	EJECTING	EMERITUS	ENGAGING
EAGLE-OWL	EJECTION	EMERSION	ENGENDER
EARPHONE	EJECTIVE	EMIGRANT	ENGINEER
EARTHING	ELAPSING	EMIGRATE	ENGRAVED
EARTH-NUT	ELATEDLY	EMINENCE	ENGRAVER
EASEMENT	ELBOWING	EMISSARY	ENGULFED
EASINESS	ELDORADO	EMISSION	ENHANCED
EASTERLY	ELDRITCH	EMISSIVE	ENJOINED
EASTWARD	ELECTING	EMITTING	ENJOYING
EAU-DE-VIE	ELECTION	EMPHASIS	ENLACING
EBENEZER	ELECTIVE	EMPHATIC	ENLARGED
EBONISED	ELECTRIC	EMPLANED	ENLARGER
ECLECTIC	ELECTRON	EMPLOYED	ENLISTED
ECLIPSED	ELEGANCE	EMPLOYEE	ENMESHED
ECLIPTIC	ELEGANCY	EMPLOYER	ENNOBLED
ECONOMIC	ELEGIAST	EMPORIUM	ENORMITY
ECSTATIC	ELEGISED	EMPTYING	ENORMOUS
EDENTATA	ELEPHANT	EMPURPLE	ENOUNCED
EDENTATE	ELEVATED	EMPYREAN	ENQUIRED
EDGE-TOOL	ELEVATOR	EMULATED	ENQUIRER
EDGEWAYS	ELEVENTH	EMULATOR	ENRAGING
EDGEWISE	ELF-CHILD	EMULSIFY	ENRICHED
EDGINESS	ELICITED	EMULSINE	ENROLLED
EDIFYING	ELIGIBLE	EMULSION	ENSCONCE
EDITRESS	ELIGIBLY	EMULSIVE	ENSHRINE
EDUCABLE	ELLIPSIS	ENABLING	ENSHROUD
EDUCATED	ELLIPTIC	ENACTING	ENSLAVED
EDUCATOR	ELONGATE	ENACTION	ENSNARED
EDUCIBLE	ELOQUENT	ENACTIVE	ENSURING
EDUCTION	ELSEWISE	ENCAMPED	ENTAILED
EEL-GRASS	ELVISHLY	ENCASHED	ENTANGLE
EEL-SPEAR	EMACIATE	ENCASING	ENTERING
EERINESS	EMANATED	ENCIRCLE	ENTHRONE
EFFACING	EMBALMED	ENCLOSED	ENTHUSED
EFFECTED	EMBALMER	ENCOMIUM	ENTICING
EFFICACY	EMBANKED	ENCORING	ENTIRELY
EFFLUENT	EMBARKED	ENCROACH	ENTIRETY
EFFLUVIA	EMBATTLE	ENCUMBER	ENTITLED
EFFUSING	EMBEDDED	ENCYCLIC	ENTOMBED
EFFUSION	EMBEZZLE	ENDANGER	ENTR'ACTE
EFFUSIVE	EMBITTER	ENDEARED	ENTRAILS
EGG-PLANT	EMBLAZON	ENDORSED	ENTRANCE
EGG-SHELL	EMBODIED	ENDOWING	ENTREATY
EGG-SLICE	EMBOLDEN	ENDURING	ENTRENCH
EGG-SPOON	EMBOLISM	ENERGISE	ENTWINED
EGG-TOOTH	EMBOSSED	ENERVATE	ENVELOPE
EGG-WHISK	EMBRACED	ENFACING	ENVIABLE
EGOISTIC	EMBUSSED	ENFEEBLE	ENVIABLY

ENVIRONS	ETRUSCAN	EXHUMING	FAINTEST
ENVISAGE	EUGENICS	EXIGENCY	FAINTING
EOLITHIC	EULOGISE	EXISTENT	FAINTISH
EPHEMERA	EULOGIST	EXISTING	FAIRNESS
EPICERIE	EUPHONIC	EX-LIBRIS	FAITHFUL
EPICYCLE	EURASIAN	EXORCISE	FALCONER
EPIDEMIC	EUROPEAN	EXORCISM	FALCONET
EPIGRAPH	EVACUATE	EXPANDED	FALCONRY
EPILEPSY	EVADABLE	EXPECTED	FALDERAL
EPILOGUE	EVENNESS	EXPEDITE	FALLIBLE
EPIPHANY	EVENSONG	EXPENDED	FALLOWED
EPISODIC	EVENTFUL	EXPERTLY	FALSETTO
EQUALISE	EVENTIDE	EXPIATED	FALTERED
EQUALITY	EVENTUAL	EXPIRING	FAMILIAR
EQUALLED	EVERMORE	EXPLICIT	FAMISHED
EQUATING	EVERSION	EXPLODED	FAMOUSLY
EQUATION	EVERTING	EXPLORED	FANCIFUL
EQUIPAGE	EVERYDAY	EXPLORER	FANCYING
EQUIPPED	EVERYONE	EXPONENT	FANDANGO
ERASABLE	EVICTING	EXPORTED	FANGLESS
ERECTING	EVICTION	EXPORTER	FANLIGHT
ERECTION	EVIDENCE	EXPOSING	FANTASIA
EREWHILE	EVILDOER	EXPOSURE	FARCICAL
ERUPTING	EVINCING	EXPUNGED	FAREWELL
ERUPTION	EVOLVING	EXTENDED	FAR-FLUNG
ERUPTIVE	EXACTING	EXTENSOR	FARINOSE
ESCALADE	EXACTION	EXTERIOR	FARMYARD
ESCALLOP	EXALTING	EXTERNAL	FARRIERY
ESCAPADE	EXAMINED	EXTOLLED	FARROWED
ESCAPING	EXAMINEE	EXTORTED	FARTHEST
ESCAPISM	EXAMINER	EXTRUDED	FARTHING
ESCAPIST	EXCAVATE	EXULTANT	FASCISTA
ESCHEWED	EXCEEDED	EXULTING	FASCISTI
ESCORTED	EXCEPTED	EYEGLASS	FASTENED
ESCULENT	EXCHANGE	EYE-PIECE	FASTNESS
ESOTERIC	EXCISING	EYE-TEETH	FATALISM
ESPALIER	EXCISION	EYE-TOOTH	FATALIST
ESPECIAL	EXCITING	EYE-WATER	FATALITY
ESPOUSAL	EXCLUDED		FATHERED
ESPOUSED	EXCUSING		FATHERLY
ESSAYING	EXECRATE	F—8	FATHOMED
ESSAYISH	EXECUTED	FABULOUS	FATIGUED
ESSAYIST	EXECUTOR	FACE-ACHE	FATTENED
ESTEEMED	EXEMPLAR	FACELESS	FAUBOURG
ESTIMATE	EXEMPTED	FACIALLY	FAULTILY
ESTRANGE	EXEQUIES	FACILELY	FAULTING
ESURIENT	EXERCISE	FACILITY	FAUTEUIL
ETCETERA	EXERTING	FACTIOUS	FAVOURED
ETERNITY	EXERTION	FACTOTUM	FEARLESS
ETHEREAL	EXHALING	FADELESS	FEARSOME
ETHNICAL	EXHORTED	FADINGLY	FEASIBLE

FEASIBLY	FILCHING	FLAGGING	FLOODLIT
FEASTING	FILIALLY	FLAGRANT	FLOORING
FEATHERY	FILIGREE	FLAG-SHIP	FLOPPILY
FEATURED	FILLETED	FLAMBEAU	FLOPPING
FEBRUARY	FILMGOER	FLAMINGO	FLORALLY
FECKLESS	FILM-STAR	FLANKING	FLORENCE
FEDERATE	FILTERED	FLAP-JACK	FLORIDLY
FEEBLISH	FILTHIER	FLAPPING	FLOTILLA
FEED-PIPE	FILTHILY	FLASHILY	FLOUNCED
FEIGNING	FILTRATE	FLASHING	FLOUNDER
FEINTING	FINALIST	FLATFISH	FLOURING
FELICITY	FINALITY	FLATFOOT	FLOURISH
FELLSIDE	FINANCED	FLAT-IRON	FLOUTING
FELO-DE-SE	FINDABLE	FLATNESS	FLOWERED
FEMININE	FINENESS	FLAT-RACE	FLOWERET
FEMINISE	FINE-SPUN	FLATTERY	FLUENTLY
FEMINISM	FINESSED	FLATTEST	FLUFFING
FEMINIST	FINGERED	FLATTISH	FLUIDITY
FENCIBLE	FINISHED	FLAT-WORM	FLUMMERY
FEROCITY	FINISHER	FLAUNTED	FLUORIDE
FERRETED	FIRE-BACK	FLAUTIST	FLUORINE
FERRYING	FIRE-BALL	FLAWLESS	FLURRIED
FERRYMAN	FIRE-BOMB	FLAX-LILY	FLUSHING
FERVENCY	FIRECLAY	FLAX-SEED	FLUSTERY
FERVIDLY	FIREDAMP	FLEA-BANE	FLYBLOWN
FESTALLY	FIRE-HOSE	FLEA-BITE	FLY-MAKER
FESTERED	FIRELOCK	FLECKING	FLY-PAPER
FESTIVAL	FIRE-PLUG	FLEECING	FLY-SHEET
FETCHING	FIRESHIP	FLEETEST	FLYWHEEL
FETTERED	FIRESIDE	FLEETING	FOAMLESS
FEUDALLY	FIRE-STEP	FLETCHER	FOCUSING
FEVERFEW	FIREWOOD	FLEXIBLE	FOG-BOUND
FEVERING	FIRMNESS	FLEXIBLY	FOGGIEST
FEVERISH	FISHABLE	FLICKING	FOLDEROL
FEVEROUS	FISH-BALL	FLIGHTED	FOLDLESS
FIBROSIS	FISH-CAKE	FLIM-FLAM	FOLIAGED
FIDDLING	FISH-GLUE	FLIMSIES	FOLIATED
FIDELITY	FISH-HAWK	FLIMSILY	FOLKLAND
FIDGETED	FISH-HOOK	FLINCHED	FOLKLORE
FIELD-DAY	FISH-MEAL	FLINGING	FOLK-SONG
FIELD-GUN	FISH-POND	FLIP-FLAP	FOLK-TALE
FIELDING	FISH-SKIN	FLIP-FLOP	FOLLICLE
FIENDISH	FISH-TAIL	FLIPPANT	FOLLOWED
FIERCELY	FISHWIFE	FLIPPING	FOLLOWER
FIERCEST	FISSURED	FLIRTING	FOMENTED
FIFTIETH	FITFULLY	FLITTING	FONDLING
FIGHTING	FIVEFOLD	FLOATING	FONDNESS
FIGURANT	FIXATION	FLOCK-BED	FOODLESS
FIGURINE	FIXATIVE	FLOCKING	FOOLSCAP
FIGURING	FIZZLING	FLOGGING	FOOTBALL
FILAMENT	FLABBILY	FLOODING	FOOT-BATH

FOOTFALL	FORESTRY	FREENESS	FUNCTION
FOOTGEAR	FORETELL	FREE-PORT	FUNDABLE
FOOTHILL	FORETOLD	FREE-SHOT	FUNDLESS
FOOTHOLD	FOREWARN	FREE-WILL	FUNEREAL
FOOTLESS	FOREWORD	FREEZING	FUNK-HOLE
FOOTLING	FORGIVEN	FRENZIED	FURBELOW
FOOTMARK	FORGOING	FREQUENT	FURLOUGH
FOOTNOTE	FORMALIN	FRETTING	FURROWED
FOOTPATH	FORMALLY	FRETWORK	FURTHEST
FOOT-RACE	FORMERLY	FREUDIAN	FUSELAGE
FOOT-ROPE	FORMLESS	FRICTION	FUSILIER
FOOTRULE	FORMULAE	FRIENDLY	FUTILELY
FOOTSLOG	FORSAKEN	FRIESIAN	FUTILITY
FOOTSORE	FORSOOTH	FRIGHTEN	FUTURISM
FOOTSTEP	FORSWEAR	FRIGIDLY	FUTURIST
FOOTWEAR	FORSWORE	FRILLING	FUTURITY
FOOTWORN	FORSWORN	FRINGING	
FOOZLING	FORTIETH	FRIPPERY	**G—8**
FORAGING	FORTRESS	FRISKILY	GABBLING
FORAYING	FORTUITY	FRISKING	GABLE-END
FORBORNE	FORWARDS	FRIZZLED	GADABOUT
FORCEDLY	FOSTERED	FROCKING	GADZOOKS
FORCEFUL	FOUGASSE	FRONTAGE	GAINSAID
FORCIBLY	FOULNESS	FRONTIER	GAITERED
FORDABLE	FOUL-PLAY	FRONTING	GALACTIC
FOREBEAR	FOUNDING	FROSTILY	GALILEAN
FOREBODE	FOUNTAIN	FROSTING	GALLIPOT
FORECAST	FOURFOLD	FROTHILY	GALLOPED
FOREDECK	FOURSOME	FROTHING	GALLOWAY
FOREDONE	FOURTEEN	FROU-FROU	GALVANIC
FOREDOOM	FOURTHLY	FROWNING	GAMBLING
FOREFOOT	FOXGLOVE	FRUCTIFY	GAMECOCK
FOREGONE	FOXHOUND	FRUGALLY	GAME-LAWS
FOREHAND	FOXINESS	FRUIT-BUD	GAMENESS
FOREHEAD	FRACTION	FRUIT-FLY	GAMESTER
FORELAND	FRACTURE	FRUITFUL	GANGLION
FORELOCK	FRAGMENT	FRUITING	GANGRENE
FOREMAST	FRAGRANT	FRUITION	GANGSTER
FOREMOST	FRAILISH	FRUITLET	GANYMEDE
FORENAME	FRAME-SAW	FRUMPISH	GAOLBIRD
FORENOON	FRANKING	FUDDLING	GAPINGLY
FORENSIC	FRANKISH	FUELLING	GARBLING
FOREPART	FRANKLIN	FUGITIVE	GARDENED
FOREPEAK	FRAULEIN	FULL-BACK	GARDENER
FORESAID	FREAKISH	FULL-FACE	GARDENIA
FORESAIL	FRECKLED	FULLNESS	GARE-FOWL
FORESEEN	FREEBORN	FULL-STOP	GARGANEY
FORESHIP	FREED-MAN	FUMBLING	GARGLING
FORESHOW	FREEHAND	FUMELESS	GARGOYLE
FORESTAY	FREEHOLD	FUMIGANT	GARISHLY
FORESTER	FREE-LOVE	FUMIGATE	GARNERED

GARRETED	GLASSILY	GOODLIER	GRIMACED
GARRISON	GLAUCOMA	GOODNESS	GRIMALDI
GARROTTE	GLAUCOUS	GOODWIFE	GRIMMEST
GARTERED	GLEAMING	GOODWILL	GRIMNESS
GASIFIED	GLEANING	GOOGLIES	GRINDING
GAS-LIGHT	GLIBNESS	GOOSE-EGG	GRINNING
GAS-METER	GLIMPSED	GORGEOUS	GRIPPING
GAS-MOTOR	GLINTING	GOSSAMER	GRISELDA
GASOLINE	GLISSADE	GOSSIPED	GRITTING
GAS-STOVE	GLOAMING	GOURMAND	GRIZZLED
GAS-TIGHT	GLOATING	GOVERNED	GROANING
GATELESS	GLOBULAR	GOVERNOR	GROG-SHOP
GATE-POST	GLOBULIN	GOWNSMAN	GROOMING
GATHERED	GLOOMILY	GRABBING	GROOVING
GAUNTLET	GLORIOUS	GRACEFUL	GROSBEAK
GAZETTED	GLORYING	GRACIOUS	GROUNDED
GEAR-CASE	GLOSSARY	GRADATED	GROUNDER
GELATINE	GLOSSILY	GRADIENT	GROUPING
GENDARME	GLOSSING	GRADUATE	GROUSING
GENERATE	GLOWERED	GRAFTING	GROUTING
GENEROUS	GLOW-WORM	GRAINING	GROWABLE
GENETICS	GLOXINIA	GRANDDAD	GROWLING
GENIALLY	GLUMMEST	GRANDEST	GRUBBIER
GENITIVE	GLUMNESS	GRANDEUR	GRUBBING
GENOCIDE	GLUTTING	GRANDSON	GRUDGING
GEOMETRY	GLUTTONY	GRANTING	GRUESOME
GEORGIAN	GNASHING	GRANULAR	GRUMBLED
GERANIUM	GOAL-LINE	GRAPHITE	GRUMBLER
GERMANIC	GOATHERD	GRAPPLED	GUARDIAN
GESTURED	GOAT-MOTH	GRASPING	GUARDING
GHOULISH	GOATSKIN	GRASSING	GUERILLA
GIANTESS	GOAT'S-RUE	GRATEFUL	GUERNSEY
GIBBERED	GOBBLING	GRATUITY	GUIDABLE
GIBINGLY	GODCHILD	GRAVAMEN	GUIDANCE
GIDDIEST	GOD-SPEED	GRAVELLY	GUILEFUL
GIGANTIC	GOFFERED	GRAYLING	GUILTILY
GIGGLING	GOGGLING	GREASILY	GULF-WEED
GIG-LAMPS	GOINGS-ON	GREASING	GULLIBLE
GILT-EDGE	GOLD-DUST	GREATEST	GULLIVER
GIMCRACK	GOLDENLY	GREEDILY	GUMPTION
GINGERLY	GOLDFISH	GREENERY	GUM-RESIN
GIN-SLING	GOLD-FOIL	GREEN-FLY	GUN-LAYER
GIRDLING	GOLD-LACE	GREENING	GUNMETAL
GIRLHOOD	GOLD-LEAF	GREENISH	GUNSMITH
GIVE-AWAY	GOLDLESS	GREEN-TEA	GUNSTOCK
GLADDEST	GOLD-MINE	GREETING	GURGLING
GLADIOLI	GOLD-SIZE	GREYNESS	GUTTERED
GLADNESS	GOLF-CLUB	GRID-BIAS	GUTTURAL
GLADSOME	GOLGOTHA	GRIDIRON	GUZZLING
GLANCING	GOLLYWOG	GRIEVOUS	GYMKHANA
GLASSFUL	GONENESS	GRILLING	GYRATING

GYRATION	HANGER-ON	HEADLAND	HERITAGE
GYRATORY	HANGNAIL	HEADLESS	HERMETIC
	HANG-OVER	HEADLINE	HESITANT
H—8	HANKERED	HEADLONG	HESITATE
HABITUAL	HAPPENED	HEAD-REST	HESPERUS
HACIENDA	HAPPIEST	HEADSHIP	HIAWATHA
HAGGLING	HARA-KIRI	HEAD-WIND	HIBERNIA
HAIRLESS	HARANGUE	HEAD-WORK	HIBISCUS
HAIRLINE	HARASSED	HEARABLE	HICCOUGH
HALF-BACK	HARDBAKE	HEARTILY	HICCUPED
HALF-BOOT	HARDENED	HEATHERY	HIGH-BALL
HALF-BRED	HARDIEST	HEAT-SPOT	HIGHBORN
HALF-COCK	HARDNESS	HEAT-WAVE	HIGHBRED
HALF-DEAD	HARDSHIP	HEAVENLY	HIGHBROW
HALF-DONE	HARDTACK	HEAVIEST	HIGHLAND
HALF-FACE	HARDWARE	HECKLING	HIGH-LIFE
HALF-MAST	HARDWOOD	HECTORED	HIGHNESS
HALF-MOON	HAREBELL	HEDGEHOG	HIGH-ROAD
HALF-NOTE	HARMLESS	HEDGE-HOP	HIGH-SPOT
HALF-PAST	HARMONIC	HEDGEROW	HIGH-TIDE
HALF-SEAS	HARRIDAN	HEEDLESS	HI-JACKED
HALF-TIME	HARROWED	HEELBALL	HI-JACKER
HALF-TINT	HARRYING	HEFTIEST	HILARITY
HALF-TONE	HASTENED	HEIGHTEN	HILL-FOLK
HALL-MARK	HASTINGS	HEIRLESS	HILL-FORT
HALLOOED	HATBRUSH	HEIRLOOM	HILLOCKY
HALLOWED	HATCHERY	HELLENIC	HILLSIDE
HALTERED	HATCHING	HELL-FIRE	HINDERED
HAMMERED	HATCHWAY	HELMETED	HINDMOST
HAMPERED	HATSTAND	HELMLESS	HINDUISM
HANDBALL	HAT-TRICK	HELMSMAN	HIP-JOINT
HANDBELL	HAUNTING	HELPLESS	HIRELING
HANDBILL	HAUSFRAU	HELPMATE	HISTORIC
HANDBOOK	HAWAIIAN	HELPMEET	HITCHING
HANDCART	HAWFINCH	HELVETIA	HITHERTO
HANDCUFF	HAWK-EYED	HEMP-SEED	HOARDING
HANDGRIP	HAWK-MOTH	HENCHMAN	HOARSELY
HANDHOLD	HAWTHORN	HEN-HOUSE	HOBBLING
HANDICAP	HAY-FEVER	HEN-ROOST	HOCK-TIDE
HAND-LINE	HAY-FIELD	HEPTAGON	HOGMANAY
HANDLING	HAY-MAKER	HEPTARCH	HOGSHEAD
HANDLOOM	HAY-STACK	HERALDED	HOISTING
HAND-MADE	HAZARDED	HERALDIC	HOLDFAST
HANDMAID	HAZEL-NUT	HERALDRY	HOLINESS
HANDMILL	HAZINESS	HERCULES	HOLLANDS
HAND-PICK	HEADACHE	HERD-BOOK	HOLLOWED
HAND-POST	HEADACHY	HERDSMAN	HOLLOWLY
HANDRAIL	HEAD-BAND	HEREDITY	HOLYROOD
HANDSOME	HEAD-BOOM	HERE-UNTO	HOMEBORN
HAND-WORK	HEADGEAR	HERE-UPON	HOMEBRED
HANDYMAN	HEADIEST	HEREWITH	HOME-FARM

HOMELAND	HOVERING	IDEALISE	IMPERIAL
HOMELESS	HOWITZER	IDEALISM	IMPETIGO
HOMELIKE	HUCKSTER	IDEALIST	IMPINGED
HOME-MADE	HUDDLING	IDEALITY	IMPISHLY
HOMESICK	HUDIBRAS	IDENTIFY	IMPLICIT
HOMESPUN	HUGENESS	IDENTITY	IMPLORED
HOMEWARD	HUGUENOT	IDEOLOGY	IMPLYING
HOMICIDE	HUMANELY	IDLENESS	IMPOLITE
HONESTLY	HUMANISE	IDOLATER	IMPORTED
HONEY-BEE	HUMANISM	IDOLATRY	IMPORTER
HONEYDEW	HUMANIST	IDOLISED	IMPOSING
HONEY-POT	HUMANITY	IGNITING	IMPOSTOR
HONORARY	HUMBLING	IGNITION	IMPOTENT
HONOURED	HUMIDIFY	IGNOMINY	IMPRISON
HOODWINK	HUMIDITY	IGNORANT	IMPROPER
HOOFLESS	HUMILITY	IGNORING	IMPROVED
HOOF-MARK	HUMMOCKY	ILL-BLOOD	IMPROVER
HOOK-WORM	HUMORIST	ILL-FATED	IMPUDENT
HOOLIGAN	HUMOROUS	ILL-TIMED	IMPUGNED
HOOP-IRON	HUMOURED	ILL-TREAT	IMPUNITY
HOPELESS	HUMPBACK	ILLUDING	IMPURELY
HOPINGLY	HUNGERED	ILLUMINE	IMPURITY
HORNBEAM	HUNGRILY	ILLUSION	IMPUTING
HORNBILL	HUNTRESS	ILLUSIVE	INACTION
HORNLESS	HUNTSMAN	ILLUSORY	INACTIVE
HORNPIPE	HURDLING	IMAGINED	INASMUCH
HOROLOGY	HURRYING	IMBECILE	INCENSED
HORRIBLE	HURTLING	IMBIBING	INCEPTOR
HORRIBLY	HUSHED-UP	IMITABLE	INCHOATE
HORRIDLY	HUSH-HUSH	IMITATED	INCIDENT
HORRIFIC	HUSKIEST	IMITATOR	INCISELY
HORSE-BOX	HUSTINGS	IMMANENT	INCISING
HORSE-BOY	HUSTLING	IMMATURE	INCISION
HORSE-CAR	HYACINTH	IMMERSED	INCISIVE
HORSE-FLY	HYDRATED	IMMINENT	INCISORY
HORSEMAN	HYDROGEN	IMMINGLE	INCITING
HOSE-PIPE	HYGIENIC	IMMOBILE	INCLINED
HOSE-REEL	HYMN-BOOK	IMMODEST	INCLUDED
HOSPITAL	HYPERION	IMMOLATE	INCOMING
HOSTELRY	HYPHENED	IMMORTAL	INCREASE
HOTCHPOT	HYPNOSIS	IMMUNISE	INCUBATE
HOTELIER	HYPNOTIC	IMMUNITY	INCURRED
HOTHOUSE		IMPACTED	INCURVED
HOT-PLATE	I—8	IMPAIRED	INDEBTED
HOT-PRESS	ICE-BOUND	IMPALING	INDECENT
HOUNDING	ICE-CREAM	IMPARITY	INDENTED
HOUR-HAND	ICE-FIELD	IMPARTED	INDEXING
HOUSE-BOY	ICE-HOUSE	IMPEDING	INDIAMAN
HOUSE-DOG	ICE-PLANT	IMPELLED	INDICATE
HOUSE-FLY	ICE-WATER	IMPELLER	INDICTED
HOUSE-TAX	ICE-YACHT	IMPENDED	INDIGENT

INDIRECT	INQUIRER	INVITING	JEALOUSY
INDITING	INSANELY	INVOICED	JEANETTE
INDOLENT	INSANITY	INVOKING	JEJUNELY
INDUCING	INSCRIBE	INVOLVED	JELLYBAG
INDUCTED	INSECURE	INWARDLY	JEOPARDY
INDULGED	INSERTED	IODISING	JEREMIAD
INDUSTRY	INSIGNIA	IOLANTHE	JEREMIAH
INEDIBLE	INSISTED	IREFULLY	JEROBOAM
INEQUITY	INSOLENT	IRISHISM	JERRICAN
INEXPERT	INSOMNIA	IRONBARK	JEST-BOOK
INFAMOUS	INSOMUCH	IRONCLAD	JET-BLACK
INFANTRY	INSPIRED	IRON-GREY	JET-PLANE
INFECTED	INSPIRER	IRONICAL	JETTISON
INFERIOR	INSPIRIT	IRONSIDE	JEWELLED
INFERNAL	INSTANCE	IRONWARE	JEWELLER
INFERRED	INSTINCT	IRONWOOD	JEWISHLY
INFESTED	INSTRUCT	IRONWORK	JEW'S-HARP
INFINITE	INSULATE	IRRIGATE	JIGGERED
INFINITY	INSULTED	IRRITANT	JIGGLING
INFIRMLY	INSURING	IRRITATE	JIGMAKER
INFLAMED	INTAGLIO	ISABELLE	JINGLING
INFLATED	INTEGRAL	ISLAMISM	JINGOISM
INFLATOR	INTENDED	ISLAMITE	JOCKEYED
INFORMAL	INTENTLY	ISLANDED	JOCOSELY
INFORMED	INTERACT	ISLANDER	JOCOSITY
INFORMER	INTER-COM	ISOBARIC	JOCUNDLY
INFRA-RED	INTEREST	ISOLATED	JODHPURS
INFRINGE	INTERIOR	ISOTHERM	JOGGLING
INFUSING	INTERLAY	ISSUABLE	JOHANNES
INFUSION	INTERMIX	ISTHMIAN	JOINTING
INFUSIVE	INTERNAL	ITERATED	JOINTURE
INHALANT	INTERNED		JOKINGLY
INHALING	INTERNEE	**J—8**	JOLLIEST
INHERENT	INTERRED	JABBERED	JONATHAN
INHERING	INTERVAL	JACKAROO	JONGLEUR
INHESION	INTIMACY	JACKETED	JOSTLING
INIMICAL	INTIMATE	JACOBEAN	JOUNCING
INIQUITY	INTONING	JACOBITE	JOUSTING
INITIATE	INTREPID	JACQUARD	JOVIALLY
INJECTED	INTRIGUE	JAGGEDLY	JOYFULLY
INJECTOR	INTRUDED	JAILBIRD	JOYOUSLY
INJURING	INTRUDER	JAMBOREE	JOY-STICK
INKINESS	INUNDATE	JANGLING	JUBILANT
INK-MAKER	INVADING	JAPANESE	JUDGMENT
INK-STAND	INVASION	JAPANNED	JUDICIAL
INLAYING	INVASIVE	JAPONICA	JUGGLERY
INNATELY	INVEIGLE	JAUNDICE	JUGGLING
INNOCENT	INVENTED	JAUNTIER	JUGO-SLAV
INNOVATE	INVENTOR	JAUNTILY	JULIENNE
INNUENDO	INVESTED	JAUNTING	JUMBLING
INQUIRED	INVESTOR	JAVANESE	JUNCTION

JUNCTURE	KNUCKLED	LARKSPUR	LEE-SHORE
JUNKETED	KOHINOOR	LARRIKIN	LEFT-HAND
JUSTNESS	KOHLRABI	LARRUPED	LEFTWARD
JUVENILE	KOTOWING	LASSOING	LEFT-WING
		LATCH-KEY	LEGALISE
K—8	**L—8**	LATENESS	LEGALISM
KANGAROO	LABELLED	LATENTLY	LEGALIST
KEDGEREE	LABOURED	LATHERED	LEGALITY
KEEL-HAUL	LABOURER	LATHWORK	LEGATION
KEENNESS	LABURNUM	LATINISE	LEG-BREAK
KEEPSAKE	LACERATE	LATINISM	LEMONADE
KERCHIEF	LACE-WING	LATINIST	LENGTHEN
KEROSENE	LACK-A-DAY	LATINITY	LENIENCE
KEYBOARD	LACKEYED	LATITUDE	LENIENCY
KEY-MONEY	LACROSSE	LATTERLY	LENT-LILY
KEYSTONE	LADDERED	LATTICED	LESSENED
KICKABLE	LADLEFUL	LAUDABLE	LETHARGY
KICKSHAW	LADYBIRD	LAUDABLY	LETTERED
KID-GLOVE	LADYLIKE	LAUDANUM	LEVELLED
KILOGRAM	LADY-LOVE	LAUGHING	LEVELLER
KILOWATT	LADYSHIP	LAUGHTER	LEVERAGE
KINDLIER	LAKE-LAND	LAUNCHED	LEVERING
KINDLING	LAMBENCY	LAUREATE	LEVIABLE
KINDNESS	LAMB-LIKE	LAVA-LIKE	LEVITATE
KING-CRAB	LAMBSKIN	LAVATORY	LEWDNESS
KINGLIKE	LAMENESS	LAVENDER	LEWISITE
KINGPOST	LAMENTED	LAVISHED	LIBATION
KINGSHIP	LAMINATE	LAVISHLY	LIBELLED
KINKAJOU	LAMPLESS	LAWFULLY	LIBERATE
KINSFOLK	LAMP-POST	LAWGIVER	LIBERIAN
KIPPERED	LAND-CRAB	LAW-MAKER	LIBRETTO
KISS-CURL	LANDFALL	LAWYERLY	LICENSED
KNAPPING	LAND-GIRL	LAXATIVE	LICENSEE
KNAPSACK	LANDLADY	LAYERING	LIEGEMAN
KNAPWEED	LANDLESS	LAZINESS	LIFE-BELT
KNEADING	LANDLORD	LEACHING	LIFEBOAT
KNEE-DEEP	LANDMARK	LEADSMAN	LIFEBUOY
KNEE-HIGH	LANDRAIL	LEAFLESS	LIFELESS
KNEELING	LANDSLIP	LEANNESS	LIFELIKE
KNICKERS	LANDSMAN	LEAP-FROG	LIFE-LINE
KNIGHTED	LANDWARD	LEAP-YEAR	LIFELONG
KNIGHTLY	LANDWEHR	LEARNING	LIFE-PEER
KNITTING	LAND-WIND	LEASABLE	LIFE-RAFT
KNITWEAR	LANGUAGE	LEASHING	LIFE-SIZE
KNOCKING	LANGUISH	LEATHERY	LIFE-TIME
KNOCK-OUT	LANKIEST	LEAVENED	LIFE-WORK
KNOTLESS	LAPELLED	LEAVINGS	LIFTABLE
KNOTTIER	LAPIDARY	LEBANESE	LIGAMENT
KNOTTING	LAP-JOINT	LECTURED	LIGATURE
KNOUTING	LARBOARD	LECTURER	LIGHTING
KNOWABLE	LARGESSE	LEE-BOARD	LIGHTISH

LIKEABLE	LOBBYIST	LOVELOCK	MAIL-BOAT
LIKENESS	LOCALISE	LOVELORN	MAIL-CART
LIKENING	LOCALISM	LOVE-NEST	MAIL-CLAD
LIKEWISE	LOCALITY	LOVESICK	MAIN-DECK
LILLIPUT	LOCATING	LOVESOME	MAINLAND
LIME-FREE	LOCATION	LOVINGLY	MAINMAST
LIME-KILN	LOCK-GATE	LOWERING	MAINSAIL
LIMERICK	LOCKSMAN	LOYALIST	MAINSTAY
LIME-TREE	LOCUTION	LUBBERLY	MAINTAIN
LIME-WASH	LODESTAR	LUCIDITY	MAINYARD
LIMITING	LODGINGS	LUCKIEST	MAJESTIC
LINCHPIN	LODGMENT	LUCKLESS	MAJOLICA
LINEALLY	LOG-CABIN	LUCKY-DIP	MAJORITY
LINEARLY	LOG-CANOE	LUKEWARM	MALAPROP
LINESMAN	LOITERED	LUMBERED	MALARIAL
LINGERED	LOITERER	LUMINARY	MAL-DE-MER
LINGERIE	LOLLIPOP	LUMINOUS	MALIGNED
LINGUIST	LOLLOPED	LUMPFISH	MALINGER
LINIMENT	LONDONER	LUNCHEON	MALODOUR
LINNAEUS	LONESOME	LUNCHING	MALT-KILN
LINOLEUM	LONGBOAT	LUNG-FISH	MALT-MILL
LINOTYPE	LONGHAND	LURCHING	MALTREAT
LIONISED	LONG-LEGS	LUSCIOUS	MALTSTER
LIP-STICK	LONG-SHIP	LUSTIEST	MALT-WORM
LIQUIDLY	LONG-SLIP	LUSTROUS	MANACLED
LIQUORED	LONG-STOP	LUTHERAN	MAN-CHILD
LISTENED	LONG-TERM	LYCH-GATE	MAN-EATER
LISTENER	LONGWAYS	LYNCHING	MAN-HATER
LISTEN-IN	LONGWISE	LYNCH-LAW	MAN-HOURS
LISTLESS	LONICERA	LYNX-EYED	MAN-OF-WAR
LITERACY	LOOKER-ON	LYRE-BIRD	MAN-POWER
LITERARY	LOOP-HOLE	LYRICISM	MANDAMUS
LITERATE	LOOP-LINE		MANDARIN
LITERATI	LOOSE-BOX	M—8	MANDATOR
LITIGANT	LOOSENED	MACARONI	MANDIBLE
LITIGATE	LOP-SIDED	MACAROON	MANDOLIN
LITTERED	LORD-LIKE	MACERATE	MANDRAKE
LITTLE-GO	LORDLING	MACHINED	MANDRILL
LITTORAL	LORD'S-DAY	MACKEREL	MANELESS
LIVE-AXLE	LORDSHIP	MADDENED	MANFULLY
LIVE-BAIT	LORIKEET	MADELINE	MANGLING
LIVELONG	LOSINGLY	MADHOUSE	MANGROVE
LIVENING	LOTHARIO	MADRIGAL	MANIACAL
LIVE-RAIL	LOUDNESS	MAGAZINE	MANICURE
LIVERIED	LOUNGING	MAGICIAN	MANIFEST
LIVERISH	LOVEBIRD	MAGNESIA	MANIFOLD
LIVE-WIRE	LOVE-KNOT	MAGNETIC	MANNERLY
LOAD-LINE	LOVELACE	MAGNOLIA	MANORIAL
LOANABLE	LOVELESS	MAHARAJA	MANTILLA
LOATHING	LOVE-LIFE	MAHOGANY	MANTLING
LOBBYING	LOVELILY	MAIDENLY	MANUALLY

MANURING	MAYORESS	METRICAL	MISGUIDE
MARATHON	MAZINESS	MIDDLING	MISHEARD
MARAUDER	MEAGRELY	MIDNIGHT	MISHMASH
MARBLING	MEAL-TIME	MIDSHIPS	MISJUDGE
MARCHING	MEAL-WORM	MIGHTILY	MISNAMED
MARGINAL	MEANNESS	MIGRAINE	MISNOMER
MARGRAVE	MEANTIME	MIGRATED	MISOGAMY
MARIGOLD	MEASURED	MIGRATOR	MISOGYNY
MARINADE	MEAT-SAFE	MILANESE	MISPLACE
MARINATE	MECHANIC	MILDEWED	MISPRINT
MARITIME	MEDDLING	MILDNESS	MISQUOTE
MARJORAM	MEDIATED	MILE-POST	MISRULED
MARKEDLY	MEDIATOR	MILITANT	MISSHAPE
MARKETED	MEDICATE	MILITARY	MISSPELL
MARKSMAN	MEDICINE	MILK-MAID	MISSPELT
MARMOSET	MEDIEVAL	MILK-WEED	MISSPEND
MAROCAIN	MEDIOCRE	MILL-HAND	MISSPENT
MAROONED	MEDITATE	MILLIARD	MISSTATE
MARQUESS	MEEKNESS	MILLIBAR	MISTAKEN
MARQUISE	MEETNESS	MILLINER	MISTEACH
MARRIAGE	MEGALITH	MILLPOND	MISTIMED
MARRYING	MELLOWED	MILLRACE	MISTITLE
MARSH-GAS	MELLOWLY	MILTONIC	MISTRESS
MARSH-HEN	MELODEON	MIMICKED	MISTRIAL
MARSH-TIT	MELODISE	MINATORY	MISTRUST
MARTELLO	MELODIST	MINCE-PIE	MISTUNED
MARTINET	MEMBERED	MINDLESS	MISUSAGE
MARTYRED	MEMBRANE	MINGLING	MISUSING
MARZIPAN	MEMORIAL	MINIMISE	MITIGATE
MASSAGRE	MEMORISE	MINISTER	MITTENED
MASSAGED	MEM-SAHIB	MINISTRY	MIZZLING
MASSEUSE	MENACING	MINORITY	MNEMONIC
MASTERED	MENDABLE	MINOTAUR	MOBILITY
MASTERLY	MENTALLY	MINSTREL	MOBILIZE
MAST-HEAD	MERCHANT	MINUTELY	MOCCASIN
MASTLESS	MERCIFUL	MINUTEST	MOCKABLE
MASTODON	MERICARP	MINUTIAE	MODELLED
MATCH-BOX	MERIDIAN	MINUTING	MODELLER
MATCHING	MERINGUE	MIRRORED	MODERATE
MATERIAL	MERITING	MIRTHFUL	MODERATO
MATERIEL	MERRIEST	MISAPPLY	MODESTLY
MATERNAL	MESSMATE	MISCARRY	MODIFIED
MATHILDA	MESS-ROOM	MISCHIEF	MODIFIER
MATRONLY	MESSUAGE	MISCOUNT	MODISHLY
MATTERED	METALLED	MISCUING	MODULATE
MATTRESS	METALLIC	MISDATED	MOISTURE
MATURELY	METAPHOR	MISDEALT	MOLASSES
MATURING	METEORIC	MISDOING	MOLE-CAST
MATURITY	METERAGE	MISDRAWN	MOLE-HILL
MAVERICK	METHINKS	MISERERE	MOLE-SKIN
MAY-QUEEN	METHODIC	MISFIRED	MOLECULE

MOLESTED	MORTARED	MUNITION	NATATORY
MOLLUSCA	MORTGAGE	MURALLED	NATIONAL
MOMENTUM	MORTISED	MURDERED	NATIVELY
MONARCHY	MORTUARY	MURDERER	NATIVITY
MONASTIC	MOSQUITO	MURIATED	NATTERED
MONDAINE	MOSS-CLAD	MURMURED	NATTIEST
MONETARY	MOSS-ROSE	MUSCATEL	NATURISM
MONEYBOX	MOTHERED	MUSCULAR	NATURIST
MONGOOSE	MOTHERLY	MUSHROOM	NAUSEATE
MONITORY	MOTIONED	MUSICIAN	NAUSEOUS
MONKEYED	MOTIVATE	MUSINGLY	NAUTICAL
MONKFISH	MOTOR-BUS	MUSK-BALL	NAUTILUS
MONKHOOD	MOTOR-CAR	MUSK-DEER	NAVIGATE
MONOCLED	MOTORING	MUSK-PEAR	NAVY-BLUE
MONOGAMY	MOTORIST	MUSK-PLUM	NAZARENE
MONOGRAM	MOTORMAN	MUSK-ROSE	NAZARITE
MONOLITH	MOTTLING	MUSKETRY	NAZIFIED
MONOPOLY	MOUFFLON	MUSQUASH	NEARNESS
MONORAIL	MOULDING	MUSTERED	NEATHERD
MONOTONE	MOULTING	MUTATION	NEATNESS
MONOTONY	MOUNDING	MUTENESS	NEBULOUS
MONOTYPE	MOUNTAIN	MUTILATE	NECKBAND
MONOXIDE	MOUNTIES	MUTINEER	NECKBEEF
MONSIEUR	MOUNTING	MUTINIED	NECKLACE
MONUMENT	MOURNFUL	MUTINOUS	NEEDLESS
MOOCHING	MOURNING	MUTTERED	NEEDLING
MOONBEAM	MOUSE-EAR	MUTUALLY	NEGATING
MOONCALF	MOUTHFUL	MUZZLING	NEGATION
MOONFACE	MOUTHING	MYCELIUM	NEGATIVE
MOONFISH	MOVELESS	MYCOLOGY	NEGLIGEE
MOONLESS	MOVEMENT	MYOSOTIS	NEGROISM
MOORCOCK	MOVINGLY	MYRMIDON	NEIGHING
MOORFOWL	MUCHNESS	MYSTICAL	NEO-LATIN
MOORLAND	MUCILAGE	MYTHICAL	NEOPHYTE
MOOT-HALL	MUCK-HEAP		NEPALESE
MOOTABLE	MUCK-RAKE	**N—8**	NEPOTISM
MOQUETTE	MUDDLING	NACREOUS	NESTLING
MORALIST	MUDDYING	NAIL-FILE	NETTLING
MORALITY	MUDGUARD	NAMELESS	NEURITIS
MORALIZE	MUFFLING	NAMESAKE	NEUROSIS
MORATORY	MULBERRY	NAPOLEON	NEUROTIC
MORAVIAN	MULCHING	NARCISSI	NEW-COMER
MORBIDLY	MULCTING	NARCOSIS	NEWS-HAWK
MOREOVER	MULE-DEER	NARCOTIC	NEWS-REEL
MORIBUND	MULETEER	NARGHILE	NEWS-ROOM
MOROCCAN	MULISHLY	NARRATED	NIBBLING
MOROSELY	MULTIPLE	NARRATOR	NIBELUNG
MORPHEAN	MULTIPLY	NARROWED	NICENESS
MORPHEUS	MUMBLING	NARROWER	NICKNAME
MORPHINE	MUNCHING	NARROWLY	NICOTINE
MORTALLY	MUNIMENT	NATATION	NIGGLING

NIGHT-CAP	NOWADAYS	OCCUPANT	OPEN-EYED
NIGHT-JAR	NUDENESS	OCCUPIED	OPEN-WORK
NIGHT-MAN	NUGATORY	OCCUPIER	OPENCAST
NIGHT-OWL	NUISANCE	OCCURRED	OPENNESS
NIHILISM	NUMBERED	OCHREOUS	OPERA-HAT
NIHILIST	NUMBNESS	OCTOROON	OPERATED
NIHILITY	NUMERARY	OCTUPLET	OPERATIC
NINEFOLD	NUMERATE	OCULARLY	OPERATOR
NINEPINS	NUMEROUS	ODIOUSLY	OPERETTA
NINETEEN	NUMSKULL	ODOMETER	OPIUM-DEN
NITRATED	NUPTIALS	OERLIKON	OPPONENT
NITROGEN	NURSLING	OFF-BREAK	OPPOSING
NOBBLING	NURTURED	OFF-PRINT	OPPOSITE
NOBILITY	NUT-BROWN	OFF-SHOOT	OPTICIAN
NOBLEMAN	NUT-HATCH	OFF-SHORE	OPTIMISM
NOBLESSE	NUTMEGGY	OFF-STAGE	OPTIMIST
NOCTURNE	NUTRIENT	OFFENDED	OPTIONAL
NOISETTE	NUTSHELL	OFFENDER	OPULENCE
NOMADISM	NUZZLING	OFFERING	ORACULAR
NOMINATE		OFFICIAL	ORANGERY
NON-CLAIM	**O—8**	OFFSPRING	ORATORIO
NON-ELECT	OAK-APPLE	OFTTIMES	ORCADIAN
NON-JUROR	OBDURACY	OHMMETER	ORDAINED
NON-MORAL	OBDURATE	OILCLOTH	ORDERING
NON-PARTY	OBEDIENT	OIL-FIELD	ORDINARY
NON-RIGID	OBEISANT	OIL-GLAND	ORDNANCE
NON-TOXIC	OBITUARY	OIL-PAPER	ORGANDIE
NON-UNION	OBJECTED	OIL-PRESS	ORGANISM
NONESUCH	OBJECTOR	OIL-SKINS	ORGANIST
NONSENSE	OBLATION	OILINESS	ORGANISE
NOONTIDE	OBLATORY	OILSTONE	ORIENTAL
NORMALCY	OBLIGANT	OINTMENT	ORIENTED
NORMALLY	OBLIGATE	OLD-TIMER	ORIGINAL
NORSEMAN	OBLIGATO	OLD-WORLD	ORNAMENT
NORTHERN	OBLIGING	OLEANDER	ORNATELY
NORTHING	OBLIVION	OLEASTER	ORPHANED
NORTHMAN	OBSCURED	OLIPHANT	ORTHODOX
NOSE-DIVE	OBSERVED	OLIVE-OIL	OSCULANT
NOSE-RING	OBSERVER	OLYMPIAD	OSCULATE
NOSEBAND	OBSESSED	OLYMPIAN	OSSIFIED
NOSELESS	OBSOLETE	OLYMPICS	OTOSCOPE
NOTANDUM	OBSTACLE	OMELETTE	OUTBOARD
NOTATION	OBSTRUCT	OMISSION	OUTBOUND
NOTCHING	OBTAINED	OMISSIVE	OUTBREAK
NOTEBOOK	OBTRUDED	OMITTING	OUTBURST
NOTELESS	OBTUSELY	ONCE-OVER	OUTCLASS
NOTICING	OBVIATED	ONCOMING	OUTDOING
NOTIFIED	OCCASION	ONE-HORSE	OUTDOORS
NOTIONAL	OCCIDENT	ONE-SIDED	OUTFACED
NOVELIST	OCCLUDED	ONLOOKER	OUTFIELD
NOVEMBER	OCCULTLY	OOLOGIST	OUTFLANK

OUTFLASH	OVERCAST	OVERSHOE	PAMPERED
OUTFLING	OVERCOAT	OVERSHOT	PAMPHLET
OUTFLOWN	OVERCOLD	OVERSIDE	PANCAKED
OUTFLUSH	OVERCOME	OVERSIZE	PANCREAS
OUTGOING	OVERDONE	OVERSLIP	PANDERED
OUTGROWN	OVERDOSE	OVERSOLD	PANELLED
OUTHOUSE	OVERDRAW	OVERSTAY	PANGOLIN
OUTLAWED	OVERDREW	OVERSTEP	PANICKED
OUTLAWRY	OVERFAST	OVERTAKE	PANORAMA
OUTLEAPT	OVERFEED	OVERTASK	PANTHEON
OUTLEARN	OVERFILL	OVERTIME	PAPERING
OUTLINED	OVERFISH	OVERTONE	PARABOLA
OUTLIVED	OVERFLOW	OVERTURE	PARABOLE
OUTLYING	OVERFOLD	OVERTURN	PARADING
OUTMARCH	OVERFOND	OVERWASH	PARADISE
OUTPACED	OVERFULL	OVERWEAR	PARAFFIN
OUTPOWER	OVERGIVE	OVERWIND	PARAKEET
OUTRAGED	OVERGROW	OVERWORK	PARALLAX
OUTRANGE	OVERHAND	OVERWORN	PARALLEL
OUTREACH	OVERHANG	OXIDIZED	PARALYSE
OUTRIDER	OVERHAUL	OX-PECKER	PARAMOUR
OUTRIGHT	OVERHEAD	OX-TONGUE	PARANOIA
OUTSHINE	OVERHEAR		PARASITE
OUTSHONE	OVERHEAT	**P—8**	PARAVANE
OUTSIDER	OVERJUMP	PACIFIED	PARCHING
OUTSLEEP	OVERKIND	PACIFIER	PARDONED
OUTSLEPT	OVERLAID	PACIFISM	PARENTAL
OUTSLIDE	OVERLAIN	PACIFIST	PARGETED
OUTSMART	OVERLAND	PACK-LOAD	PARGETER
OUTSPEAK	OVERLEAF	PACK-MULE	PARISIAN
OUTSPENT	OVERLEAP	PACKETED	PARLANCE
OUTSPOKE	OVERLOAD	PADDLING	PARLEYED
OUTSTAND	OVERLOCK	PAGANISE	PARMESAN
OUTSTARE	OVERLONG	PAGANISH	PARODIED
OUTSTOOD	OVERLOOK	PAGANISM	PARODIST
OUTSTRIP	OVERLORD	PAGINATE	PAROXYSM
OUTSWEAR	OVERMUCH	PAINLESS	PARRYING
OUTVALUE	OVERNEAT	PAINTING	PARTAKEN
OUTVENOM	OVERNICE	PAKISTAN	PARTERRE
OUTVOTED	OVERPAID	PALATIAL	PARTHIAN
OUTWARDS	OVERPASS	PALATINE	PARTICLE
OUTWEIGH	OVERRAKE	PALE-EYED	PARTISAN
OVEN-BIRD	OVERRATE	PALE-FACE	PART-SONG
OVERALLS	OVERRIDE	PALENESS	PASSABLE
OVERARCH	OVERRIPE	PALISADE	PASSABLY
OVERAWED	OVERRULE	PALL-MALL	PASS-BOOK
OVERBEAR	OVERSEAS	PALLIATE	PASSER-BY
OVERBOIL	OVERSEEN	PALLIDLY	PASSOVER
OVERBOLD	OVERSEER	PALM-TREE	PASSPORT
OVERBUSY	OVERSELL	PALPABLE	PASSWORD
OVERCAME	OVERSEWN	PALPABLY	PASTICHE

PASTILLE	PENKNIFE	PHTHISIS	PITIABLY
PASTORAL	PENN'ORTH	PHYSICAL	PITILESS
PASTURED	PENOLOGY	PHYSIQUE	PITTANCE
PATCHING	PENT-ROOF	PIANETTE	PIVOT-MAN
PATENTED	PENTAGON	PICAROON	PIVOTING
PATENTEE	PEN-WIPER	PICKETED	PIXY-RING
PATENTOR	PENWOMAN	PICKLING	PLACATED
PATERNAL	PEOPLING	PICKLOCK	PLACEMAN
PATHETIC	PEPPERED	PICK-ME-UP	PLACIDLY
PATHLESS	PERCEIVE	PICKWICK	PLAGIARY
PATIENCE	PERCHING	PICTURED	PLAGUILY
PATTERED	PERFORCE	PIERCING	PLAGUING
PATTY-PAN	PERFUMED	PIFFLING	PLAITING
PAVEMENT	PERIANTH	PIG-FACED	PLANGENT
PAVILION	PERICARP	PIKEHEAD	PLANKING
PAWNSHOP	PERILOUS	PILASTER	PLANKTON
PAY-CLERK	PERIODIC	PILCHARD	PLANLESS
PAY-SHEET	PERISHED	PILFERED	PLANNING
PEACEFUL	PERJURED	PILLAGED	PLANTAIN
PEACHING	PERMEATE	PILLARED	PLANTING
PEA-GREEN	PERMUTED	PILLOWED	PLANTLET
PEARMAIN	PERORATE	PILOTAGE	PLASHING
PEASECOD	PEROXIDE	PILOTING	PLATEFUL
PEAT-MOOR	PERSONAL	PIN-WHEEL	PLATFORM
PEAT-MOSS	PERSPIRE	PINAFORE	PLATINIC
PECTORAL	PERSUADE	PINCE-NEZ	PLATINUM
PECULIAR	PERTNESS	PINCHERS	PLATONIC
PEDAGOGY	PERUSING	PINCHING	PLATTING
PEDALLED	PERUVIAN	PINE-CLAD	PLATYPUS
PEDANTIC	PERVADED	PINE-CONE	PLAYABLE
PEDANTRY	PERVERSE	PINE-WOOD	PLAYBILL
PEDDLERY	PESTERED	PING-PONG	PLAYBOOK
PEDDLING	PESTLING	PININGLY	PLAYGOER
PEDESTAL	PETERING	PINIONED	PLAYMATE
PEDICURE	PETERMAN	PINK-EYED	PLAYSOME
PEDIGREE	PETITION	PIN-MAKER	PLAYTIME
PEDIMENT	PETRONEL	PIN-MONEY	PLEACHED
PEEP-HOLE	PETULANT	PINNACLE	PLEADING
PEEP-SHOW	PHALANGE	PINPOINT	PLEASANT
PEERLESS	PHANTASM	PIPE-CASE	PLEASING
PEIGNOIR	PHANTASY	PIPE-CLAY	PLEASURE
PEKINESE	PHARISEE	PIPE-FISH	PLEATING
PELLAGRA	PHARMACY	PIPE-LINE	PLEBEIAN
PELL-MELL	PHEASANT	PIPE-RACK	PLECTRUM
PELLUCID	PHILOMEL	PIPE-WORK	PLEDGING
PEMMICAN	PHONE-BOX	PIQUANCY	PLEIADES
PENALISE	PHONETIC	PIRATING	PLETHORA
PENCHANT	PHOSGENE	PISCATOR	PLEURISY
PENDULUM	PHOSPHOR	PISTOLET	PLIANTLY
PENELOPE	PHRASING	PITCHING	PLIGHTED
PENITENT	PHRYGIAN	PITIABLE	PLIOCENE

PLODDING	POND-WEED	POULTICE	PRETTILY
PLOPPING	PONTIFEX	POUNCING	PREVIOUS
PLOTTING	PONTIFIC	POUNDAGE	PRICKING
PLOUGHED	PONY-SKIN	POUNDING	PRICKLED
PLUCKILY	POOH-POOH	POWDERED	PRIDEFUL
PLUCKING	POOL-ROOM	POWERFUL	PRIESTLY
PLUGGING	POOR-LAWS	POW-WOWED	PRIGGERY
PLUG-UGLY	POORNESS	PRACTICE	PRIGGISH
PLUMBAGO	POOR-RATE	PRACTISE	PRIMATES
PLUMB-BOB	POPELING	PRAISING	PRIMEVAL
PLUMBING	POPINJAY	PRANCING	PRIMNESS
PLUM-CAKE	POPISHLY	PRANDIAL	PRIMROSE
PLUM-DUFF	POPULACE	PRANGING	PRINCELY
PLUMELET	POPULATE	PRATTLED	PRINCEPS
PLUMPEST	POPULOUS	PREACHED	PRINCESS
PLUMPING	POROSITY	PREACHER	PRINTING
PLUNGING	PORPHYRY	PREAMBLE	PRIORESS
PLURALLY	PORPOISE	PRECEDED	PRIORITY
PLUTARCH	PORRIDGE	PRECINCT	PRISONER
PLUTONIC	PORTABLE	PRECIOUS	PRISTINE
PLUVIOUS	PORTHOLE	PRECLUDE	PRIZEMAN
POACHING	PORTIERE	PREDATED	PROBABLE
POCHETTE	PORTLAND	PRE-ELECT	PROBABLY
POCKETED	PORTRAIT	PREENING	PROCEEDS
POCKMARK	POSEIDON	PRE-ENTRY	PROCLAIM
POETICAL	POSINGLY	PRE-EXIST	PROCURED
POETIZED	POSITION	PREFACED	PRODDING
POIGNANT	POSITIVE	PREFIXED	PRODIGAL
POIGNARD	POSSIBLE	PREGNANT	PRODUCED
POINTING	POSSIBLY	PREJUDGE	PRODUCER
POISONED	POSTABLE	PRELUDED	PROFANED
POISONER	POST-CARD	PREMIERE	PROFILED
POLARITY	POST-DATE	PREMISED	PROFITED
POLARIZE	POST-FREE	PREMISES	PROFOUND
POLE-JUMP	POST-HORN	PRENATAL	PROGRESS
POLE-STAR	POSTICHE	PRENTICE	PROHIBIT
POLEMICS	POSTMARK	PREPARED	PROLAPSE
POLICING	POST-PAID	PRESAGED	PROLIFIC
POLISHED	POSTPONE	PRESCIND	PROLIXLY
POLITELY	POST-TIME	PRESENCE	PROLOGUE
POLITICS	POSTURED	PRESERVE	PROMISED
POLLUTED	POTATION	PRESIDED	PROMOTED
POLONIUM	POTENTLY	PRESS-BOX	PROMOTER
POLTROON	POTHERED	PRESSING	PROMPTED
POLYGAMY	POT-HOUSE	PRESSMAN	PROMPTER
POLYGLOT	POT-PLANT	PRESSURE	PROMPTLY
POLYGRAM	POTSHERD	PRESTIGE	PRONG-HOE
POMANDER	POT-STICK	PRE-STUDY	PROOFING
POMPEIAN	POT-STILL	PRESUMED	PROPERLY
PONDERED	POTTERED	PRETENCE	PROPERTY
POND-LILY	POUCHING	PRETTIFY	PROPHECY

PROPHESY	PUPATION	QUEASILY	RAFTSMAN
PROPOSAL	PUPPETRY	QUEEN-BEE	RAG-PAPER
PROPOSED	PUPPYISH	QUEENING	RAG-WHEEL
PROPOSER	PUPPYISM	QUEEREST	RAGGEDLY
PROPOUND	PURBLIND	QUEERING	RAGINGLY
PROPPING	PURCHASE	QUEERISH	RAGSTONE
PROROGUE	PURENESS	QUELLING	RAILHEAD
PROSEMAN	PURIFIED	QUENCHED	RAILLERY
PROSPECT	PURPLING	QUENCHER	RAILROAD
PROTEGEE	PURPLISH	QUERYING	RAINBAND
PROTOCOL	PURPOSED	QUESTFUL	RAINBIRD
PROTOZOA	PURSEFUL	QUESTING	RAINCOAT
PROTRACT	PURSE-NET	QUESTION	RAINDROP
PROTRUDE	PURSLANE	QUEUEING	RAINFALL
PROVABLE	PURSUANT	QUIBBLED	RAINLESS
PROVABLY	PURSUING	QUICKEST	RAKEHELL
PROVIDED	PURVEYED	QUICKSET	RAKISHLY
PROVINCE	PURVEYOR	QUIDNUNC	RALLYING
PROVOKED	PUSHBALL	QUIETEST	RAMADHAN
PROWLING	PUSHBIKE	QUIETUDE	RAMBLING
PRUDENCE	PUSS-MOTH	QUILLING	RAMIFIED
PRUNELLA	PUSS-TAIL	QUILL-PEN	RAMPAGED
PRUSSIAN	PUSSY-CAT	QUILTING	RAMPANCY
PRYINGLY	PUTTYING	QUIPPING	RAM'S-HORN
PSALMIST	PUZZLING	QUIRKING	RANCHERO
PSALMODY	PYRIFORM	QUISLING	RANCHING
PSALTERY	PYROXENE	QUIT-RENT	RANCHMAN
PTOMAINE		QUITTING	RANCIDLY
PUBLICAN	Q—8	QUIXOTIC	RANDOMLY
PUBLICLY	QUACKERY	QUIXOTRY	RANKLING
PUCKERED	QUACKING	QUIZZERY	RANKNESS
PUDDLING	QUACKISH	QUIZZING	RANSOMED
PUFF-BALL	QUADRANT	QUOTABLE	RAPACITY
PUFF-PUFF	QUADRATE	QUOTIENT	RAPE-SEED
PUG-FACED	QUADRIGA		RAPIDITY
PUGILISM	QUADROON	R—8	RAREFIED
PUGILIST	QUAFFING	RABBETED	RARENESS
PUISSANT	QUAGMIRE	RABELAIS	RASCALLY
PULINGLY	QUAILING	RABIDITY	RASHNESS
PULLOVER	QUAINTER	RACE-CARD	RATAPLAN
PULSATOR	QUAINTLY	RACE-GOER	RATEABLE
PUMP-ROOM	QUAKERLY	RACINESS	RATE-BOOK
PUNCHEON	QUANDARY	RACK-RENT	RATIFIED
PUNCHING	QUANTITY	RACKETED	RATIONAL
PUNCTUAL	QUARRIED	RADIALLY	RATIONED
PUNCTURE	QUARTERN	RADIANCE	RAT'S-BANE
PUNGENCY	QUARTERS	RADIATED	RAT'S-TAIL
PUNINESS	QUASHING	RADIATOR	RATTLING
PUNISHED	QUATORZE	RADIOING	RAVAGING
PUNITIVE	QUATRAIN	RAFFLING	RAVELLED
PUNITORY	QUAVERED	RAFTERED	RAVENING

RAVENOUS	RECLOTHE	REFUSING	RELIGION
RAVINGLY	RECOILED	REFUTING	RELISHED
RAVISHED	RECOINED	REGAINED	RE-LIVING
RAW-BONED	RE-COLOUR	REGALING	RE-LOADED
RE-ABSORB	RE-COMMIT	REGALITY	REMAINED
RE-ACCUSE	RE-CONVEY	REGARDED	REMAKING
REACHING	RECORDED	RE-GATHER	REMANENT
REACTION	RECORDER	REGICIDE	RE-MANNED
REACTIVE	RECOUPED	REGILDED	REMARKED
READABLE	RECOURSE	REGIMENT	REMARQUE
READABLY	RECOVERY	REGIONAL	REMEDIAL
RE-ADJUST	RECREANT	REGISTER	REMEDIED
RE-AFFIRM	RECREATE	REGISTRY	REMEMBER
REALIZED	RECURRED	REGNANCY	REMINDED
REALNESS	RECURVED	RE-GROUND	REMINDER
RE-APPEAR	RED-FACED	REGROWTH	REMISSLY
REAR-RANK	RED-SHIRT	REGULATE	REMITTAL
RE-ARMING	REDDENED	RE-HANDLE	REMITTED
REARMOST	REDEEMED	REHASHED	RE-MODIFY
REARWARD	REDEEMER	REHEARSE	REMOTELY
RE-ASCEND	REDIRECT	RE-HEATED	REMOVING
RE-ASCENT	RE-DIVIDE	RE-HOUSED	RENAMING
REASONED	RED-NOSED	REIGNING	RENDERED
RE-ASSERT	REDOLENT	RE-IGNITE	RENEGADE
RE-ASSESS	REDOUBLE	RE-IMPORT	RENEWING
RE-ASSIGN	REDSHANK	REIMPOSE	RENOUNCE
REASSURE	REDUCING	REINDEER	RENOVATE
RE-ATTACH	RE-DYEING	RE-INFECT	RENOWNED
RE-ATTAIN	RE-ECHOED	RE-INFUSE	RENTABLE
REBATING	REED-MACE	RE-INSERT	RENT-FREE
REBELLED	REED-STOP	RE-INSURE	RENT-ROLL
RE-BOILED	REEF-KNOT	RE-INVEST	RE-NUMBER
REBUFFED	REELABLE	REISSUED	RE-OBTAIN
REBUKING	RE-EMBARK	REJECTED	RE-OCCUPY
REBURIED	RE-EMBODY	REJOICED	RE-OPENED
REBUTTAL	RE-EMERGE	REJOINER	RE-OPPOSE
REBUTTED	RE-ENFORCE	RE-JUDGED	RE-ORDAIN
RECALLED	RE-ENLIST	REKINDLE	REPAIRED
RECANTED	RE-EXPORT	RELANDED	REPAIRER
RECEDING	REFASTEN	RELAPSED	REPARTEE
RECEIVED	REFERRED	RELATING	REPASSED
RECEIVER	REFILLED	RELATION	REPAYING
RECENTLY	REFINERY	RELAXING	REPEALED
RECESSED	REFINING	RELAYING	REPEATED
RECHARGE	REFITTED	RELEASED	REPEATER
RECISION	REFLEXED	RELEGATE	REPELLED
RECITING	REFORGED	RELEVANT	REPENTED
RECKLESS	REFORMED	RELIABLE	REPINING
RECKONED	REFORMER	RELIABLY	REPLACED
RECLINED	REFRAMED	RELIANCE	RE-PLEDGE
RECLOSED	REFUNDED	RELIEVED	REPLYING

RE-POLISH	RE-STRIKE	RHOMBOID	ROLY-POLY
REPORTED	RESULTED	RHYTHMIC	ROMANCED
REPORTER	RESUMING	RIBALDRY	ROMANCER
REPOSING	RE-SUMMON	RIBBONED	ROMANISE
RE-POTTED	RETAILED	RICHNESS	ROMANISH
REPRIEVE	RETAILER	RICKSHAW	ROMANIST
REPRISAL	RETAINED	RICOCHET	ROMANTIC
REPROACH	RETAINER	RIDDANCE	ROOD-BEAM
REPROVAL	RETAKING	RIDDLING	ROOD-LOFT
REPROVED	RETARDED	RIDEABLE	ROOD-TREE
RE-PRUNED	RETICENT	RIDICULE	ROOFLESS
REPTILIA	RETICULE	RIFENESS	ROOF-TREE
REPUBLIC	RETIRING	RIFF-RAFF	ROOSTING
REPUGNED	RETORTED	RIFLEMAN	ROOT-BEER
REPULSED	RE-TOSSED	RIGADOON	ROOT-CROP
RE-PURIFY	RETRACED	RIGHTFUL	ROOT-HAIR
REPUTING	RETRENCH	RIGHTING	ROOTLESS
REQUIRED	RETRIEVE	RIGIDITY	ROPE-WALK
REQUITAL	RETROACT	RIGOROUS	ROPE-YARN
REQUITED	RE-TRYING	RING-BARK	ROPINESS
RE-ROOFED	RETURNED	RING-BOLT	ROSARIAN
RE-SCORED	RE-UNITED	RINGBONE	ROSARIUM
RESCRIPT	REVALUED	RING-DOVE	ROSE-BUSH
RESCUING	REVAMPED	RINGWORM	ROSE-GALL
RESEARCH	REVEALED	RIPARIAN	ROSE-HUED
RESEATED	REVEILLE	RIPENESS	ROSE-KNOT
RESEMBLE	REVELLED	RIPPLING	ROSEMARY
RESENTED	REVELLER	RISKIEST	ROSE-PINK
RESERVED	REVENGED	RITUALLY	ROSE-ROOT
RESETTLE	REVEREND	RIVALLED	ROSE-TREE
RESIDENT	REVERENT	RIVER-BED	ROSETTED
RESIDUAL	REVERING	RIVER-GOD	ROSE-WOOD
RESIDUUM	REVERSAL	RIVER-HOG	ROSE-WORM
RESIGNED	REVERSED	RIVER-MAN	ROSINESS
RESISTED	RE-VETTED	RIVETING	ROSINING
RE-SOLDER	REVIEWED	ROAD-BOOK	ROSIN-OIL
RESOLUTE	REVIEWER	ROADLESS	ROTARIAN
RESOLVED	REVILING	ROADSIDE	ROTATING
RESONANT	REVISING	ROADSTER	ROTATION
RE-SORTED	REVISION	ROASTING	ROTATIVE
RESOURCE	REVIVIFY	ROBUSTLY	ROTATORY
RESOWING	REVIVING	ROCK-ALUM	ROT-GRASS
RESPIRED	REVOKING	ROCK-CAKE	ROTIFERA
RESPONSE	REVOLTED	ROCK-DOVE	ROTTENLY
RE-STATED	REVOLVED	ROCKETED	ROUGHAGE
REST-CURE	REVOLVER	ROCKLESS	ROUGH-DRY
RESTLESS	REWARDED	ROCK-ROSE	ROUGH-HEW
RESTORED	RE-WORDED	ROCK-SALT	ROUGHING
RESTORER	RHAPSODY	ROCK-WORK	ROUGHISH
RESTRAIN	RHEOSTAT	ROGATION	ROULETTE
RESTRICT	RHETORIC	ROLL-CALL	ROUND-ARM

ROUNDERS	SADDENED	SAND-BIRD	SAW-FRAME
ROUNDING	SADDLERY	SAND-CRAB	SAW-GRASS
ROUNDISH	SADDLING	SAND-DUNE	SAW-HORSE
ROUNDLET	SADDUCEE	SAND-FISH	SAW-TABLE
ROUND-TOP	SADFACED	SAND-FLEA	SCABBARD
ROUTEING	SAGACITY	SAND-HILL	SCABIOSA
ROVINGLY	SAGAMORE	SAND-IRON	SCABIOUS
ROWDYISH	SAGENESS	SAND-REED	SCABROUS
ROWDYISM	SAGO-PALM	SAND-REEL	SCAFFOLD
ROWELLED	SAILABLE	SAND-ROLL	SCALABLE
ROYALISM	SAIL-BOAT	SAND-SHOT	SCALDING
ROYALIST	SAILLESS	SAND-STAR	SCALPING
RUBBISHY	SAIL-LOFT	SAND-TRAP	SCAMPING
RUBICUND	SAIL-PLAN	SAND-WASP	SCAMPISH
RUCKSACK	SAIL-ROOM	SANDWICH	SCANNING
RUDENESS	SAIL-YARD	SAND-WORM	SCANSION
RUDIMENT	SAINFOIN	SAND-WORT	SCANTIES
RUEFULLY	SALACITY	SANENESS	SCANTILY
RUFFLING	SALAD-OIL	SANGUINE	SCAPULAR
RUGGEDLY	SALADING	SANITARY	SCARCELY
RUINABLE	SALARIED	SANSKRIT	SCARCITY
RUINATED	SALEABLE	SAPIDITY	SCARFING
RULELESS	SALEABLY	SAPIENCE	SCARF-PIN
RULINGLY	SALE-ROOM	SAPPHIRE	SCARLESS
RUMANIAN	SALESMAN	SARABAND	SCARRING
RUMBLING	SALE-WORK	SARATOGA	SCATHING
RUMINANT	SALIENCE	SARDONIC	SCAVENGE
RUMINATE	SALIFIED	SARDONYX	SCENARIO
RUMMAGED	SALINITY	SARGASSO	SCENE-MAN
RUMOURED	SALLYING	SARSENET	SCENT-BAG
RUMPLING	SALMONET	SASH-CORD	SCENT-BOX
RUNABOUT	SALOPIAN	SATANISM	SCEPTRED
RUNAGATE	SALT-BUSH	SATANITY	SCHEDULE
RUNNER-UP	SALTLESS	SATIABLE	SCHEMING
RURALISE	SALT-LICK	SATIATED	SCHILLER
RURALISM	SALT-MINE	SATIRIST	SCHNAPPS
RURALIST	SALTNESS	SATIRIZE	SCHOOLED
RURALITY	SALT-WELL	SATURATE	SCHOONER
RUSHLIKE	SALT-WORT	SATURDAY	SCIATICA
RUSTLESS	SALUTARY	SAUCEBOX	SCIMITAR
RUSTLING	SALUTING	SAUCEPAN	SCISSORS
RUTHLESS	SALVABLE	SAUTERNE	SCOFFING
RYE-GRASS	SALVAGED	SAVAGELY	SCOLDING
	SAMENESS	SAVAGERY	SCOOP-NET
S—8	SAMPHIRE	SAVAGING	SCOOPING
SABOTAGE	SAMPLING	SAVANNAH	SCOOTING
SABOTEUR	SANCTIFY	SAVEABLE	SCORCHED
SACKLESS	SANCTION	SAVINGLY	SCORCHER
SACK-RACE	SANCTITY	SAVOURED	SCORNFUL
SACREDLY	SAND-BANK	SAVOYARD	SCORNING
SACRISTY	SAND-BATH	SAWBONES	SCORPION

SCOTCHED	SEACOAST	SEDIMENT	SENTIENT
SCOT-FREE	SEA-CRAFT	SEDITION	SENTINEL
SCOTSMAN	SEA-DEVIL	SEDUCING	SENTRY-GO
SCOTTISH	SEA-EAGLE	SEDULITY	SEPARATE
SCOURGED	SEAFARER	SEDULOUS	SEPTETTE
SCOURING	SEA-FIGHT	SEED-CAKE	SEPTUPLE
SCOUTING	SEA-FRONT	SEED-COAT	SEQUENCE
SCOWLING	SEA-FROTH	SEED-CORN	SERAGLIO
SCRABBLE	SEAGOING	SEED-GALL	SERAPHIC
SCRAGGED	SEA-GREEN	SEED-LEAF	SERAPHIM
SCRAGGLY	SEA-HEATH	SEEDLESS	SERENADE
SCRAMBLE	SEA-HOLLY	SEEDLING	SERENATA
SCRAPING	SEA-HORSE	SEED-PLOT	SERENELY
SCRAPPED	SEA-HOUND	SEEDSMAN	SERENEST
SCRATCHY	SEA-LEVEL	SEEDTIME	SERENITY
SCRAWLED	SEAL-SKIN	SEESAWED	SERGEANT
SCREAMED	SEAMANLY	SEETHING	SERIALLY
SCREAMER	SEAMIEST	SEIDLITZ	SERIATIM
SCREECHY	SEAMLESS	SEIGNEUR	SERJEANT
SCREENED	SEAMSTER	SEIGNIOR	SERRATED
SCREEVER	SEA-NYMPH	SEIZABLE	SERVITOR
SCREWING	SEA-PERCH	SELECTED	SET-PIECE
SCRIBBLE	SEA-PLANE	SELECTOR	SETTLING
SCRIBING	SEA-PLANT	SELF-HEAL	SEVERELY
SCRIMPED	SEA-PURSE	SELF-HELP	SEVERING
SCRIMPLY	SEARCHED	SELFLESS	SEVERITY
SCROFULA	SEARCHER	SELF-LIKE	SEWERAGE
SCROUNGE	SEA-ROVER	SELF-LOVE	SEWER-GAS
SCRUB-OAK	SEASCAPE	SELF-MADE	SEXTETTE
SCRUBBED	SEA-SHELL	SELF-PITY	SEXTUPLE
SCRUBBER	SEA-SHORE	SELFSAME	SEXUALLY
SCRUPLED	SEA-SHRUB	SELF-WILL	SFORZATO
SCRUTINY	SEA-SNAIL	SELLABLE	SHABBIER
SCUDDING	SEA-SNAKE	SELVEDGE	SHABBILY
SCUFFLED	SEASONED	SEMANTIC	SHACKING
SCULLERY	SEA-TROUT	SEMESTER	SHACKLED
SCULLING	SEA-WATER	SEMI-NUDE	SHADDOCK
SCULLION	SEA-WOMAN	SEMINARY	SHADIEST
SCULPTOR	SEA-WRACK	SEMINOLE	SHADOWED
SCUMBLED	SECATEUR	SEMITISM	SHAFTING
SCURRIED	SECEDING	SEMITONE	SHAGREEN
SCURRIES	SECLUDED	SEMOLINA	SHAMBLES
SCURVILY	SECONDED	SEMPSTER	SHAMEFUL
SCUTTLED	SECONDLY	SENILITY	SHAMMING
SCYTHIAN	SECRETED	SENNIGHT	SHAMROCK
SEA-ACORN	SECRETLY	SENORITA	SHANGHAI
SEA-ADDER	SECURELY	SENSEFUL	SHANKING
SEA-BEAST	SECURING	SENSIBLE	SHARP-CUT
SEABOARD	SECURITY	SENSIBLY	SHARPING
SEABORNE	SEDATELY	SENSUOUS	SHARP-SET
SEA-BREAM	SEDATIVE	SENTENCE	SHEARING

SHEATHED	SHOT-HOLE	SIDE-STEP	SKEWBALD
SHEAVING	SHOT-SILK	SIDE-VIEW	SKEWERED
SHEDDING	SHOULDER	SIDEWAYS	SKIDDING
SHEEP-DIP	SHOUTING	SIFFLEUR	SKIM-MILK
SHEEPDOG	SHOW-BILL	SIFFLING	SKIMMING
SHEEPFLY	SHOW-CARD	SIGHTING	SKIMPING
SHEEPISH	SHOW-CASE	SIGNABLE	SKIN-DEEP
SHEEP-PEN	SHOW-DOWN	SIGNALLY	SKINLESS
SHEEP-RUN	SHOWERED	SIGNIEUR	SKINNING
SHEERING	SHOW-ROOM	SIGNLESS	SKIP-JACK
SHEER-LEG	SHOW-YARD	SIGN-POST	SKIPPING
SHEETING	SHRAPNEL	SILENCED	SKIRLING
SHELDUCK	SHREDDED	SILENCER	SKIRMISH
SHELLING	SHREWDLY	SILENTLY	SKIRTING
SHELVING	SHREWISH	SILICATE	SKITTISH
SHEPHERD	SHRIEKED	SILK-WORM	SKITTLES
SHERATON	SHRILLED	SILLABUB	SKULKING
SHIELDED	SHRIMPED	SILURIAN	SKULL-CAP
SHIFTILY	SHRIMPER	SILVANUS	SKUNKISH
SHIFTING	SHRINKER	SIMMERED	SKYLIGHT
SHILLING	SHROUDED	SIMPERED	SKY-PILOT
SHIMMING	SHRUGGED	SIMPLIFY	SKYSCAPE
SHIN-BONE	SHUCKING	SIMULANT	SLABBING
SHINGLED	SHUFFLED	SIMULATE	SLACKING
SHINGLES	SHUNNING	SINCIPUT	SLAMMING
SHINNING	SHUNTING	SINECURE	SLANGILY
SHIPLESS	SHUT-DOWN	SINFULLY	SLANGING
SHIPLOAD	SHUTTING	SINGABLE	SLANTING
SHIPMATE	SIBERIAN	SINGEING	SLAP-BANG
SHIPMENT	SIBILANT	SINGLING	SLAP-DASH
SHIPPING	SIBILATE	SING-SING	SLAPJACK
SHIP-WORM	SICILIAN	SING-SONG	SLAPPING
SHIPYARD	SICKENED	SINGULAR	SLASHING
SHIREMAN	SICKLILY	SINISTER	SLATE-AXE
SHIRKING	SICK-LIST	SINK-HOLE	SLATTERN
SHIRTING	SICKNESS	SIPHONAL	SLAVERED
SHIVERED	SICK-ROOM	SIPHONIC	SLAVONIC
SHOCKING	SIDE-ARMS	SIPHONED	SLEDGING
SHOEBILL	SIDE-BEAM	SISTERLY	SLEEPILY
SHOEHORN	SIDE-COMB	SISYPHUS	SLEEPING
SHOELACE	SIDE-DISH	SITUATED	SLEETING
SHOELESS	SIDE-DRUM	SIXPENCE	SLIDABLE
SHOOTING	SIDE-LINE	SIXPENNY	SLIGHTLY
SHOP-BELL	SIDELING	SIXTIETH	SLIMMING
SHOP-GIRL	SIDE-LOCK	SIZEABLE	SLIMNESS
SHOPPING	SIDELONG	SIZINESS	SLINGING
SHOPWORN	SIDE-NOTE	SIZZLING	SLINKING
SHORTAGE	SIDEREAL	SKEAN-DHU	SLIP-KNOT
SHORT-CUT	SIDE-SHOW	SKELETAL	SLIPPERY
SHORT-LEG	SIDE-SLIP	SKELETON	SLIPPING
SHORT-RIB	SIDESMAN	SKETCHED	SLIPSHOD

SLITHERY	SNAPPING	SOCIALLY	SOREHEAD
SLITTING	SNAPPISH	SOCKETED	SORENESS
SLIVERED	SNAPSHOT	SOCKLESS	SORORITY
SLOGGING	SNARLING	SOCRATES	SORROWED
SLOP-BOWL	SNATCHED	SODDENED	SORTABLE
SLOP-PAIL	SNATCHER	SOFTENED	SOUCHONG
SLOPPING	SNEAKING	SOFT-EYED	SOUGHING
SLOTHFUL	SNEERING	SOFTLING	SOULLESS
SLOTTING	SNEEZING	SOFTNESS	SOUNDING
SLOUCHED	SNICKING	SOFT-SOAP	SOUR-EYED
SLOUGHED	SNIFFING	SOFT-WOOD	SOURNESS
SLOVENLY	SNIPPETY	SOILLESS	SOUR-PUSS
SLOWNESS	SNIPPING	SOIL-PIPE	SOUTHERN
SLOW-WORM	SNIP-SNAP	SOLACING	SOUVENIR
SLUGGARD	SNIVELLY	SOLARIUM	SOZZLING
SLUGGING	SNOBBERY	SOLATIUM	SPACIOUS
SLUGGISH	SNOBBISH	SOLDERED	SPADILLE
SLUICING	SNOOPING	SOLDIERY	SPALPEEN
SLUMMING	SNOOZING	SOLECISE	SPANDREL
SLUMPING	SNORTING	SOLECISM	SPANGLED
SLURRING	SNOWBALL	SOLECIST	SPANIARD
SLUTTISH	SNOWBIRD	SOLEMNLY	SPANKING
SLY-BOOTS	SNOWBOOT	SOLENESS	SPANLESS
SMACKING	SNOWDROP	SOLENOID	SPANNING
SMALL-ALE	SNOWFALL	SOLIDIFY	SPAN-ROOF
SMALLEST	SNOWLESS	SOLIDITY	SPARERIB
SMALLISH	SNOWLIKE	SOLITARY	SPARKING
SMALLPOX	SNOWLINE	SOLITUDE	SPARKLER
SMARTING	SNOW-SLED	SOLSTICE	SPARKLET
SMASHING	SNOWSHOE	SOLUTION	SPARRING
SMEARING	SNUBBING	SOLVABLE	SPARSELY
SMELLING	SNUBBISH	SOLVENCY	SPAVINED
SMELTING	SNUB-NOSE	SOMBRERO	SPAWNING
SMIRCHED	SNUFFBOX	SOMEBODY	SPEAKING
SMIRKING	SNUFFERS	SOMERSET	SPEARING
SMOCKING	SNUFFLED	SOMESUCH	SPEARMAN
SMOKABLE	SNUGGERY	SOMETIME	SPECIFIC
SMOKE-BOX	SNUGGING	SOMEWHAT	SPECIMEN
SMOKE-DRY	SNUGGLED	SOMNIFIC	SPECIOUS
SMOOTHED	SNUGNESS	SONATINA	SPECKING
SMOOTHLY	SOAPBALL	SONG-BIRD	SPECKLED
SMORZATO	SOAPSUDS	SONG-BOOK	SPECTRAL
SMOTHERY	SOAP-TEST	SONGLESS	SPECTRUM
SMOULDER	SOAP-TREE	SONGSTER	SPEEDIER
SMUDGING	SOAPWORT	SON-IN-LAW	SPEEDILY
SMUGGLED	SOB-STUFF	SONORITY	SPEEDING
SMUGGLER	SOBRANJE	SONOROUS	SPEEDWAY
SMUGNESS	SOBRIETY	SOOTHING	SPELLING
SNACK-BAR	SO-CALLED	SORBONNE	SPEND-ALL
SNAFFLED	SOCIABLE	SORCERER	SPENDING
SNAGGING	SOCIABLY	SORDIDLY	SPERM-OIL

SPHAGNUM	SPRINKLE	STAGNATE	STELLATE
SPHERICS	SPRINTED	STAINING	STEMLESS
SPHEROID	SPRINTER	STAIR-ROD	STEMMING
SPHERULE	SPROCKET	STAIRWAY	STEPPING
SPICCATO	SPRUCELY	STALKING	STERLING
SPICE-BOX	SPRUCIFY	STALL-FED	STERNWAY
SPIFFING	SPRUCING	STALLING	STICKING
SPIKELET	SPUN-YARN	STALLION	STICKLER
SPILLING	SPUR-GALL	STALWART	STIFFISH
SPILLWAY	SPUR-GEAR	STAMENED	STIFLING
SPINDLED	SPURIOUS	STAMPEDE	STIGMATA
SPINNING	SPURLESS	STAMPING	STILETTO
SPINSTER	SPURNING	STANDARD	STILLING
SPIRACLE	SPURRING	STANDING	STIMULUS
SPIRALLY	SPURTING	STANDISH	STINGILY
SPIRITED	SPY-GLASS	STAND-OFF	STINGING
SPITEFUL	SPY-MONEY	STAND-PAT	STING-RAY
SPITFIRE	SQUABBLE	STANHOPE	STINKPOT
SPITTING	SQUADRON	STAPLING	STINTING
SPITTOON	SQUALLED	STARCHED	STIPPLED
SPLASHED	SQUANDER	STAR-DUST	STIRRING
SPLATTER	SQUARELY	STAR-FISH	STITCHED
SPLAYING	SQUARING	STAR-GAZE	STOCKADE
SPLENDID	SQUARISH	STARLESS	STOCKIER
SPLICING	SQUASHED	STAR-LIKE	STOCKILY
SPLINTER	SQUATTED	STARLING	STOCKING
SPLITTER	SQUATTER	STARRING	STOCKIST
SPLOTCHY	SQUAWKED	STARTING	STOCKMAN
SPLUTTER	SQUAWMAN	STARTLED	STOCKPOT
SPOILING	SQUEAKED	STARVING	STOICISM
SPOLIATE	SQUEAKER	STARWEED	STOLIDLY
SPONGING	SQUEALED	STARWORT	STONE-PIT
SPOOFING	SQUEEGEE	STATUARY	STOOKING
SPOOKISH	SQUEEZED	STATURED	STOOPING
SPOONFUL	SQUEEZER	STAY-BOLT	STOP-COCK
SPOONILY	SQUIBBED	STAY-LACE	STOPPAGE
SPOONING	SQUIGGLE	STAYSAIL	STOPPING
SPORADIC	SQUINTED	STEADIED	STORABLE
SPORTFUL	SQUIREEN	STEADILY	STORMING
SPORTING	SQUIRING	STEADING	STOWAWAY
SPORTIVE	SQUIRMED	STEALING	STRADDLE
SPOTLESS	SQUIRREL	STEALTHY	STRAGGLE
SPOTTING	SQUIRTED	STEAMING	STRAIGHT
SPOUTING	STABBING	STEAM-TUG	STRAINED
SPRAGGED	STABLING	STEELING	STRAINER
SPRAINED	STACCATO	STEEL-PEN	STRAITEN
SPRAWLED	STACKING	STEEPING	STRANDED
SPRAYING	STAFFING	STEEPLED	STRANGER
SPREADER	STAGGERS	STEERAGE	STRANGLE
SPRIGGED	STAGHORN	STEERING	STRAPPED
SPRINGER	STAGNANT	STEINBOK	STRATEGY

STRATIFY	SUB-GRADE	SUPERMAN	SWERVING
STRAYING	SUB-GROUP	SUPER-TAX	SWIFTEST
STREAKED	SUB-HUMAN	SUPINELY	SWIGGING
STREAMED	SUB-LEASE	SUPPLANT	SWILLING
STREAMER	SUBMERGE	SUPPLIED	SWIMMING
STRENGTH	SUB-ORDER	SUPPLIER	SWINDLED
STRESSED	SUBORNED	SUPPOSED	SWINDLER
STRETCHY	SUBPOENA	SUPPRESS	SWINGING
STREWING	SUB-POLAR	SURCEASE	SWIRLING
STRICKEN	SUBSERVE	SURENESS	SWISHING
STRICTLY	SUBSIDED	SURETIES	SWITCHED
STRIDENT	SUBTITLE	SURF-BOAT	SWOONING
STRIDING	SUBTLETY	SURFACED	SWOOPING
STRIKING	SUBTRACT	SURGICAL	SWOPPING
STRINGED	SUBURBAN	SURMISED	SWORD-ARM
STRIPING	SUBURBIA	SURMOUNT	SWORD-CUT
STRIPPED	SUCCINCT	SURNAMED	SWOTTING
STRIPPER	SUCHLIKE	SURPLICE	SYBARITE
STROKING	SUCKLING	SURPRISE	SYCAMORE
STROLLED	SUDDENLY	SURROUND	SYLLABIC
STROLLER	SUFFERED	SURVEYED	SYLLABLE
STRONGLY	SUFFERER	SURVEYOR	SYLLABUS
STROPPED	SUFFICED	SURVIVAL	SYMBOLIC
STRUGGLE	SUFFIXED	SURVIVED	SYMMETRY
STRUMMED	SUFFRAGE	SURVIVOR	SYMPATHY
STRUMPET	SUFFUSED	SUSPENSE	SYMPHONY
STRUTTED	SUGARING	SWABBING	SYNDROME
STRUTTER	SUICIDAL	SWADDLED	SYNOPSIS
STUBBING	SUITABLE	SWAMPING	SYSTEMIC
STUBBLED	SUITABLY	SWAMP-OAK	
STUBBORN	SUITCASE	SWAN-LIKE	T—8
STUCCOED	SULLENLY	SWAN-NECK	TABBY-CAT
STUD-BOLT	SULLYING	SWANNERY	TABLEAUX
STUD-BOOK	SULPHATE	SWANKING	TABLEFUL
STUDDING	SULPHIDE	SWAPPING	TABOOING
STUD-FARM	SULPHITE	SWARMING	TABULATE
STUDIOUS	SULPHURY	SWASTIKA	TACITURN
STUDWORK	SUMMONED	SWATHING	TACKLING
STUDYING	SUNBURNT	SWATTING	TACTICAL
STUFFING	SUNBURST	SWEARING	TACTLESS
STULTIFY	SUNDERED	SWEATILY	TAFFRAIL
STUMBLED	SUN-DRIED	SWEATING	TAIL-BOOM
STUMPING	SUNDRIES	SWEEPING	TAILLESS
STUNNING	SUNLIGHT	SWEEP-NET	TAILORED
STUNTING	SUN-PROOF	SWEET-BAY	TAIL-RACE
STUPIDLY	SUNSHADE	SWEETING	TAIL-ROPE
STURDILY	SUNSHINE	SWEETISH	TAINTING
STURGEON	SUNSHINY	SWEET-OIL	TAKINGLY
SUB-AGENT	SUPERBLY	SWEET-PEA	TALENTED
SUBDUING	SUPERHET	SWEET-SOP	TALISMAN
SUB-GENUS	SUPERIOR	SWELLING	TALKABLE

TALLNESS	TEETOTUM	THICKSET	TIDEMILL
TALLOWED	TEHEEING	THIEVERY	TIDES-MAN
TALLYING	TELEGRAM	THIEVING	TIDINESS
TALLYMAN	TELEVISE	THIEVISH	TIGER-CAT
TAMARIND	TELLTALE	THINGAMY	TIGERISH
TAMARISK	TEMERITY	THINKING	TIGHT-WAD
TAMEABLE	TEMPERED	THINNESS	TILLABLE
TAMELESS	TEMPLATE	THINNEST	TILT-YARD
TAMENESS	TEMPORAL	THINNING	TIMBERED
TAMPERED	TEMPTING	THINNISH	TIME-BALL
TANGIBLE	TENACITY	THIRSTED	TIME-BILL
TANGIBLY	TENANTED	THIRTEEN	TIME-BOOK
TANGLING	TENANTRY	THOLE-PIN	TIME-CARD
TANNABLE	TENDENCY	THORACIC	TIME-FUSE
TANTALUS	TENDERED	THOROUGH	TIMELESS
TAPERING	TENDERLY	THOUSAND	TIME-WORK
TAPESTRY	TENEMENT	THRALDOM	TIMEWORN
TAPEWORM	TENON-SAW	THRASHED	TIMIDITY
TARBOOSH	TENTACLE	THREADED	TIMOROUS
TARRAGON	TERMINAL	THREATEN	TINCTURE
TARRYING	TERMINUS	THREE-PLY	TINGLING
TARTARIC	TERMLESS	THRESHED	TINKERED
TARTNESS	TERRACED	THRESHER	TINKLING
TASTABLE	TERRAPIN	THRILLED	TINPLATE
TASTE-BUD	TERRIBLE	THRILLER	TINSELLY
TASTEFUL	TERRIBLY	THRIVING	TINSMITH
TATTERED	TERRIFIC	THROBBED	TINSTONE
TATTLING	TERTIARY	THRONGED	TINTLESS
TATTOOED	TESTABLE	THROSTLE	TIPPLING
TAUNTING	TESTATOR	THROTTLE	TIPSTAFF
TAUTENED	TEST-CASE	THROWING	TIRELESS
TAUTNESS	TEST-TUBE	THRUMMED	TIRESOME
TAVERNER	TETCHILY	THUDDING	TITANIUM
TAWDRILY	TETHERED	THUGGERY	TITIVATE
TAXATION	TETRAGON	THUMBING	TITMOUSE
TEA-CADDY	TETRARCH	THUMB-POT	TITTERED
TEA-CHEST	TEUTONIC	THUMPING	TITULARY
TEACHING	TEXT-BOOK	THUNDERY	TOAD-FLAX
TEA-CLOTH	THAILAND	THURSDAY	TOADYING
TEA-HOUSE	THALLIUM	THWACKED	TOADYISH
TEAMSTER	THANKFUL	THWARTED	TOADYISM
TEAMWORK	THANKING	TICK-BEAN	TOBOGGAN
TEA-PARTY	THATCHED	TICKETED	TODDLING
TEA-PLANT	THATCHER	TICKLING	TOGETHER
TEA-SPOON	THEMATIC	TICKLISH	TOILSOME
TEA-TABLE	THEOLOGY	TICK-TICK	TOILWORN
TEARDROP	THEORISE	TICK-TOCK	TOLBOOTH
TEAR-DUCT	THEORIST	TIDEGATE	TOLERANT
TEARLESS	THESPIAN	TIDELESS	TOLERATE
TEETHING	THICKEST	TIDE-LOCK	TOLL-GATE
TEETOTAL	THICKISH	TIDEMARK	TOM-NODDY

TOMAHAWK	TRAGICAL	TRIAXIAL	TRYSTING
TOMBLESS	TRAILING	TRIBUNAL	TSARITSA
TOMMY-BAR	TRAIL-NET	TRICKERY	TUBERCLE
TOMMY-GUN	TRAINING	TRICKILY	TUBEROSE
TOMMY-ROT	TRAIN-OIL	TRICKING	TUBEROUS
TOMORROW	TRAIPSED	TRICKLED	TUCKSHOP
TONALITY	TRAMPING	TRICOLOR	TUG-OF-WAR
TONELESS	TRAMPLED	TRICYCLE	TUMBLING
TONSURED	TRAMROAD	TRIFLING	TUNELESS
TOOTHFUL	TRANCING	TRILLING	TUNGSTEN
TOOTLING	TRANQUIL	TRILLION	TUNING-IN
TOP-DRESS	TRANSACT	TRIMMING	TUNISIAN
TOP-HEAVY	TRANSEPT	TRIMNESS	TURBANED
TOP-NOTCH	TRANSFER	TRIPLANE	TURBIDLY
TOPPLING	TRANSFIX	TRIPLING	TURF-CLAD
TOREADOR	TRANSHIP	TRIPPING	TURGIDLY
TORPIDLY	TRANSMIT	TRIPTYCH	TURKOMAN
TORTILLA	TRAP-BALL	TRIUMVIR	TURMERIC
TORTOISE	TRAP-DOOR	TRIVALVE	TURNCOAT
TORTUOUS	TRAPPING	TROLLING	TURNCOCK
TORTURED	TRAPPIST	TROLLOPY	TURNDOWN
TORTURER	TRASHILY	TROMBONE	TURNOVER
TOTALISE	TRAVERSE	TROOPING	TURNPIKE
TOTALITY	TRAVESTY	TROPHIES	TURNSPIT
TOTTERED	TRAWLING	TROPICAL	TURRETED
TOUCHILY	TREACLED	TROTTING	TUSSOCKY
TOUCHING	TREADING	TROUBLED	TUTELAGE
TOUGHEST	TREADLED	TROUNCED	TUTELARY
TOUGHISH	TREASURE	TROUSERS	TUTORAGE
TOUSLING	TREASURY	TROUTLET	TUTORIAL
TOWERING	TREATING	TRUANTLY	TUTORING
TOWN-HALL	TREATISE	TRUCKAGE	TWANGING
TOWNLESS	TREBLING	TRUCKING	TWEAKING
TOWNSHIP	TRECENTO	TRUCKLED	TWEEZERS
TOWNSMAN	TREE-CRAB	TRUDGEON	TWIDDLED
TOWN-TALK	TREE-DOVE	TRUDGING	TWIDDLER
TOXAEMIA	TREE-FERN	TRUE-BLUE	TWIGGING
TOXICANT	TREE-FROG	TRUE-BORN	TWILIGHT
TOXICITY	TREELESS	TRUE-BRED	TWILLING
TOYISHLY	TREE-NAIL	TRUE-LOVE	TWIN-BORN
TRACHEAL	TREKKING	TRUENESS	TWINKLED
TRACHEAN	TREMBLED	TRUMPERY	TWIRLING
TRACKAGE	TREMBLER	TRUMPING	TWISTING
TRACKING	TRENCHED	TRUNCATE	TWITCHED
TRACKMAN	TRENCHER	TRUNDLED	TWITTING
TRACKWAY	TRENDING	TRUNKFUL	TWO-EDGED
TRACTILE	TRESPASS	TRUNNION	TWO-FACED
TRACTION	TRIALITY	TRUSSING	TWO-PENCE
TRACTIVE	TRIANGLE	TRUSTFUL	TWOPENNY
TRACTORY	TRIARCHY	TRUSTILY	TWO-SIDED
TRADUCED	TRIASSIC	TRUSTING	TWO-SPEED

TYMPANIC	UNCAPPED	UNEARNED	UNITEDLY
TYMPANUM	UNCASING	UNEASILY	UNIVALVE
TYPE-HIGH	UNCAUGHT	UNENDING	UNIVERSE
TYPIFIED	UNCHASTE	UNERRING	UNIVOCAL
TYROLEAN	UNCHEWED	UNEVENLY	UNJOINED
TYROLESE	UNCLENCH	UNFADING	UNJOYFUL
TYRRANIC	UNCLOSED	UNFAIRLY	UNJOYOUS
	UNCLOTHE	UNFASTEN	UNJUDGED
U—8	UNCLOUDY	UNFENCED	UNJUSTLY
UBIQUITY	UNCOATED	UNFILLED	UNKINDLY
UDOMETER	UNCOCKED	UNFIXING	UNKINGLY
UGLINESS	UNCOILED	UNFOLDED	UNLACING
ULTERIOR	UNCOINED	UNFORCED	UNLARDED
ULTIMATA	UNCOMBED	UNFORMED	UNLASHED
ULTIMATE	UNCOMELY	UNFOUGHT	UNLAWFUL
ULULATED	UNCOMMON	UNFRAMED	UNLEARNT
UMBRELLA	UNCOOKED	UNFROZEN	UNLIKELY
UNABASED	UNCORKED	UNFURLED	UNLOADED
UNABATED	UNCOSTLY	UNGAINLY	UNLOCKED
UNAFRAID	UNCOUPLE	UNGENTLE	UNLOOSED
UNAMAZED	UNCTUOUS	UNGENTLY	UNLOVELY
UNAMUSED	UNCURBED	UNGIFTED	UNLOVING
UNATONED	UNCURLED	UNGILDED	UNMAKING
UNAVOWED	UNDAMPED	UNGIRDED	UNMANNED
UNAWARES	UNDEFIED	UNGIVING	UNMAPPED
UNBACKED	UNDENTED	UNGLAZED	UNMARKED
UNBARBED	UNDERACT	UNGLOVED	UNMARRED
UNBARRED	UNDERAGE	UNGLUING	UNMASKED
UNBATHED	UNDERARM	UNGROUND	UNMELTED
UNBEATEN	UNDERBID	UNGUIDED	UNMILKED
UNBELIEF	UNDERCUT	UNGULATA	UNMILLED
UNBIASED	UNDER-DOG	UNGULATE	UNMOCKED
UNBIDDEN	UNDERFED	UNGUMMED	UNMODISH
UNBLAMED	UNDERLAY	UNHANDED	UNMOORED
UNBLOODY	UNDERLET	UNHANGED	UNMOVING
UNBOILED	UNDERLIE	UNHARMED	UNNERVED
UNBOLTED	UNDER-LIP	UNHASPED	UNOPENED
UNBOOTED	UNDERPAY	UNHEATED	UNPACKED
UNBOUGHT	UNDERPIN	UNHEDGED	UNPAIRED
UNBRACED	UNDERTOW	UNHEEDED	UNPEELED
UNBRIDLE	UNDEVOUT	UNHEROIC	UNPEGGED
UNBROKEN	UNDIMMED	UNHINGED	UNPENNED
UNBUCKLE	UNDIPPED	UNHOOKED	UNPICKED
UNBUDDED	UNDIVINE	UNHORSED	UNPINNED
UNBUOYED	UNDOCKED	UNHOUSED	UNPLACED
UNBURDEN	UNDOUBLE	UNICYCLE	UNPOISED
UNBURIED	UNDRAPED	UNIFYING	UNPOSTED
UNBURNED	UNDREAMT	UNIMBUED	UNPRETTY
UNBUTTON	UNDULANT	UNIONISM	UNPRICED
UNCAGING	UNDULATE	UNIONIST	UNPROVED
UNCALLED	UNDULOUS	UNIQUELY	UNPRUNED

UNRAISED	UNTHAWED	USURPING	VENTURED
UNREASON	UNTHREAD	UTILIZED	VERACITY
UNREELED	UNTHROWN	UTTERING	VERANDAH
UNROBING	UNTIDILY	UXORIOUS	VERBALLY
UNROLLED	UNTILLED		VERBATIM
UNROOFED	UNTIMELY	**V—8**	VERBIAGE
UNROUTED	UNTINGED	VACATING	VERDANCY
UNRUFFLE	UNTIRING	VACATION	VERDERER
UNSADDLE	UNTOWARD	VAGABOND	VERIFIED
UNSAFELY	UNTRACED	VAGRANCY	VERMOUTH
UNSALTED	UNTUCKED	VAINNESS	VERONESE
UNSEALED	UNTURFED	VALANCED	VERONICA
UNSEATED	UNTURNED	VALENCIA	VERTEBRA
UNSEEDED	UNTWINED	VALERIAN	VERTICAL
UNSEEING	UNVALUED	VALETING	VESTMENT
UNSEEMLY	UNVARIED	VALHALLA	VESUVIAN
UNSETTLE	UNVEILED	VALIDATE	VEXATION
UNSHADED	UNVENTED	VALIDITY	VEXINGLY
UNSHAKEN	UNVERSED	VALOROUS	VIBRATED
UNSHAVED	UNVOICED	VALUABLE	VIBRATOR
UNSHAVEN	UNWARILY	VAMOOSED	VIBURNUM
UNSLAKED	UNWARMED	VANADIUM	VICARAGE
UNSMOKED	UNWARNED	VANGUARD	VICINITY
UNSOCIAL	UNWASHED	VANISHED	VICTORIA
UNSOILED	UNWEDDED	VANQUISH	VICTUALS
UNSOLDER	UNWEEDED	VAPIDITY	VIEWABLE
UNSOLVED	UNWIELDY	VAPORIZE	VIEWLESS
UNSORTED	UNWISDOM	VAPOROUS	VIGILANT
UNSOUGHT	UNWISELY	VARIABLE	VIGNETTE
UNSPARED	UNWONTED	VARIABLY	VIGOROSO
UNSPEEDY	UNWORTHY	VARIANCE	VIGOROUS
UNSPIKED	UNYOKING	VARICOSE	VILENESS
UNSPOILT	UPHEAVAL	VASCULAR	VILIFIED
UNSPOKEN	UPLIFTED	VASELINE	VILLAGER
UNSTABLE	UPRAISED	VASTNESS	VILLAINY
UNSTATED	UPRISING	VAULTING	VINE-CLAD
UNSTEADY	UPROOTED	VAUNTING	VINE-GALL
UNSTITCH	UPSTAIRS	VEGETATE	VINEGARY
UNSTRUNG	UPSTREAM	VEHEMENT	VINEYARD
UNSUITED	UPSTROKE	VELOCITY	VIOLABLE
UNSURELY	UPTHRUST	VENALITY	VIOLATOR
UNSWAYED	UPTURNED	VENDETTA	VIOLENCE
UNTACKED	UPWARDLY	VENDIBLE	VIPERINE
UNTANGLE	URBANITY	VENDIBLY	VIPERISH
UNTANNED	URBANISE	VENEERED	VIPEROUS
UNTAPPED	URGENTLY	VENERATE	VIRGINAL
UNTASTED	URSIFORM	VENETIAN	VIRGINIA
UNTAUGHT	URSULINE	VENGEFUL	VIRILITY
UNTENDED	USEFULLY	VENOMOUS	VIRTUOSO
UNTESTED	USHERING	VENT-HOLE	VIRTUOUS
UNTETHER	USURIOUS	VENT-PLUG	VIRULENT

VISCERAL	WALTZING	WAYLEAVE	WHIPCORD
VISCOUNT	WANDERED	WEAKENED	WHIPHAND
VISIGOTH	WANDERER	WEAK-EYED	WHIPLASH
VISITANT	WANGLING	WEAKLING	WHIPPING
VISITING	WANTONLY	WEAKNESS	WHIRLING
VITALITY	WARBLING	WEARABLE	WHIRRING
VITALISE	WAR-DANCE	WEARYING	WHISKING
VITIATED	WARDMOTE	WEED-HOOK	WHISTLED
VITREOUS	WARDROBE	WEEDLESS	WHITE-HOT
VIVACITY	WARD-ROOM	WEIGHING	WHITENED
VIVARIUM	WARDSHIP	WEIGHTED	WHITTLED
VIVA-VOCE	WAR-HORSE	WELCOMED	WHIZZING
VIVIFIED	WARINESS	WELDABLE	WHODUNIT
VIVISECT	WARMNESS	WELL-BORN	WHOOPING
VIXENISH	WARPAINT	WELL-BRED	WHOPPING
VOCALIST	WAR-PLANE	WELLDOER	WICKEDLY
VOCALITY	WARRANTY	WELL-HEAD	WIDE-EYED
VOCALIZE	WAR-WEARY	WELL-HOLE	WIDENESS
VOCATION	WAR-WHOOP	WELL-KNIT	WIDENING
VOCATIVE	WASHABLE	WELLNIGH	WIDOWING
VOIDABLE	WASHAWAY	WELL-READ	WIELDING
VOLATILE	WASHBALL	WELLSIAN	WIFEHOOD
VOLCANIC	WASHBOWL	WELL-TO-DO	WIFELESS
VOLITION	WASP-BITE	WELL-WORN	WIFELIKE
VOLLEYED	WASTEFUL	WELSHING	WIGGLING
VOLPLANE	WATCHDOG	WELSHMAN	WIGMAKER
VOMITING	WATCHFUL	WEREWOLF	WILD-FIRE
VORACITY	WATCHING	WESLEYAN	WILD-FOWL
VOTARESS	WATCH-KEY	WESTERLY	WILDNESS
VOUCHING	WATCHMAN	WESTWARD	WILFULLY
VOYAGEUR	WATER-HEN	WET-NURSE	WILINESS
VULGARLY	WATER-ICE	WHACKING	WILLOWED
	WATERING	WHALEMAN	WINCHMAN
W—8	WATERMAN	WHALE-OIL	WINDFALL
WADDLING	WATER-RAM	WHANGHEE	WINDLASS
WAFERING	WATER-RAT	WHANGING	WINDLESS
WAGELESS	WATER-TAP	WHARFAGE	WINDMILL
WAGERING	WATERWAY	WHARFING	WINDOWED
WAGGLING	WATT-HOUR	WHATEVER	WINDPIPE
WAGGONER	WATTLING	WHEATEAR	WIND-PUMP
WAGONFUL	WAVELESS	WHEEDLED	WINDWARD
WAGON-LIT	WAVELIKE	WHEELING	WINE-CASK
WAINSCOT	WAVERING	WHEEZILY	WINELESS
WAITRESS	WAVINESS	WHEEZING	WINESKIN
WAKENING	WAXCLOTH	WHELPING	WING-CASE
WALKABLE	WAXLIGHT	WHENEVER	WINGLESS
WALK-OVER	WAX-PAPER	WHEREVER	WINNOWED
WALLAROO	WAXWORKS	WHETTING	WINTERED
WALL-EYED	WAYFARER	WHIMBREL	WINTERLY
WALLOPED	WAYGOOSE	WHINCHAT	WIRELESS
WALLOWED		WHINNIED	WIRE-WORM

WIRINESS	WOUNDING	ABATEMENT	ACTUALITY
WISEACRE	WRACKING	ABDICATED	ACTUARIAL
WISHBONE	WRANGLED	ABDOMINAL	ACTUATION
WISTARIA	WRANGLER	ABDUCTING	ACUTENESS
WITHDRAW	WRAPPING	ABDUCTION	ADAPTABLE
WITHDREW	WRATHFUL	ABHORRENT	ADDICTING
WITHERED	WREAKING	ABHORRING	ADDICTION
WITHHELD	WREATHED	ABIDINGLY	ADDRESSED
WITHHOLD	WRECKAGE	ABJECTION	ADDRESSEE
WIZARDLY	WRECKING	ABNEGATED	ADDUCIBLE
WIZARDRY	WRENCHED	ABOLITION	ADDUCTION
WOEFULLY	WRESTING	ABOMINATE	ADDUCTIVE
WOLF-FISH	WRESTLED	ABOUNDING	ADENOIDAL
WOLF-SKIN	WRESTLER	ABRIDGING	ADENOTOMY
WOMANISH	WRETCHED	ABROGATED	ADHERENCE
WONDERED	WRIGGLED	ABSCINDED	ADJACENCY
WONDROUS	WRINGING	ABSCONDED	ADJECTIVE
WOOD-ACID	WRINKLED	ABSENTING	ADJOINING
WOODBINE	WRISTLET	ABSOLVING	ADJOURNED
WOODCOCK	WRITHING	ABSORBENT	ADJUDGING
WOODLAND	WRONGFUL	ABSORBING	ADJUNCTLY
WOODLARK	WRONGING	ABSTAINER	ADJUSTING
WOODLESS		ABSTINENT	ADMIRABLE
WOOD-LICE	**X—8**	ABSURDITY	ADMIRABLY
WOODMOTE	XYLONITE	ABUNDANCE	ADMIRALTY
WOOD-PULP		ABUSIVELY	ADMISSION
WOOD-SHED	**Y—8**	ACCENTING	ADMISSIVE
WOODSMAN	YACHTING	ACCEPTING	ADMISSORY
WOOD-VINE	YEAR-BOOK	ACCESSION	ADMITTING
WOODWORK	YEARLING	ACCESSORY	ADMIXTURE
WOOD-WORM	YEARNING	ACCLIVITY	ADOPTABLE
WOOD-WREN	YELLOWED	ACCOMPANY	ADOPTEDLY
WOOINGLY	YEOMANLY	ACCORDING	ADORATION
WOOLSACK	YEOMANRY	ACCORDION	ADORNMENT
WOOLWORK	YIELDING	ACCOUNTED	ADRENALIN
WORD-BOOK	YODELLED	ACCRETION	ADULATING
WORDLESS	YOKELESS	ACCRETIVE	ADULATION
WORKABLE	YOUNGEST	ACCUSABLE	ADULATORY
WORKADAY	YOUNGISH	ACETYLENE	ADULTERER
WORKGIRL	YOURSELF	ACHIEVING	ADULTNESS
WORKROOM	YOUTHFUL	ACIDIFIED	ADUMBRATE
WORKSHOP	YUGO-SLAV	ACIDIFIER	ADVANCING
WORMCAST	YULETIDE	ACIDULATE	ADVANTAGE
WORMGEAR		ACIDULOUS	ADVENTIST
WORM-HOLE	**Z—8**	ACOUSTICS	ADVENTURE
WORMLIKE	ZEPPELIN	ACQUIESCE	ADVERBIAL
WORMWOOD		ACQUIRING	ADVERSARY
WORRYING	**A—9**	ACQUITTAL	ADVERSELY
WORSENED	ABANDONED	ACQUITTED	ADVERSITY
WORSTING	ABASEMENT	ACRIDNESS	ADVERTENT
WORTHILY	ABASHMENT	ACROPOLIS	ADVERTING

ADVERTISE	AIR-VESSEL	AMAZINGLY	ANGLICISM
ADVISABLE	AIR-WORTHY	AMAZONIAN	ANGLIFIED
ADVISABLY	AITCH-BONE	AMBERGRIS	ANGOSTURA
ADVOCATED	ALABASTER	AMBIGUITY	ANGRINESS
AERODROME	ALARM-BELL	AMBIGUOUS	ANGUISHED
AEROMOTOR	ALARM-POST	AMBITIOUS	ANGULARLY
AEROPLANE	ALBATROSS	AMBLINGLY	ANGULATED
AESTHETIC	ALCHEMIST	AMBROSIAL	ANIMALISE
AESTIVATE	ALCOHOLIC	AMBROSIAN	ANIMALISM
AETIOLOGY	ALECONNER	AMBULANCE	ANIMATING
AFFECTING	ALERTNESS	AMBULATED	ANIMATION
AFFECTION	ALETASTER	AMBUSCADE	ANIMOSITY
AFFECTIVE	ALGEBRAIC	AMBUSHING	ANNEALING
AFFIANCED	ALIENABLE	AMENDABLE	ANNOTATED
AFFIDAVIT	ALIENATED	AMENDMENT	ANNOTATOR
AFFILIATE	ALIGHTING	AMIDSHIPS	ANNOUNCED
AFFIRMING	ALIGNMENT	AMOROUSLY	ANNOUNCER
AFFLATION	ALIMENTAL	AMORPHISM	ANNOYANCE
AFFLICTED	ALIMENTED	AMORPHOUS	ANNUITANT
AFFLUENCE	ALINEMENT	AMORTIZED	ANNULARLY
AFFORDING	ALKALISED	AMOUNTING	ANNULATED
AFFRONTED	ALLAYMENT	AMPERSAND	ANNULLING
AFOREHAND	ALLELUIAH	AMPHIBIAN	ANNULMENT
AFORESAID	ALLEMANDE	AMPHIBOLE	ANOINTING
AFORETIME	ALLEVIATE	AMPLENESS	ANOMALISM
AFRICAANS	ALLIGATED	AMPLIFIED	ANOMALOUS
AFTER-CARE	ALLIGATOR	AMPLIFIER	ANONYMOUS
AFTERGLOW	ALLITERAL	AMPLITUDE	ANOPHELES
AFTER-LIFE	ALLOCATED	AMPUTATED	ANSWERING
AFTERMATH	ALLOTTING	AMPUTATOR	ANTARCTIC
AFTERNOON	ALLOWABLE	AMUSEMENT	ANTECEDED
AFTER-PART	ALLOWABLY	AMUSINGLY	ANTEDATED
AFTERWARD	ALLOWANCE	ANALGESIA	ANTENATAL
AGGRAVATE	ALLOWEDLY	ANALOGISE	ANTHELION
AGGREGATE	ALMOND-OIL	ANALOGIST	ANTHOLOGY
AGGRESSOR	ALMSHOUSE	ANALOGOUS	ANTIPATHY
AGGRIEVED	ALOES-WOOD	ANALYSING	ANTIPHONY
AGITATION	ALONGSIDE	ANARCHISM	ANTIPODAL
AGONISING	ALOOFNESS	ANARCHIST	ANTIPODES
AGONISTIC	ALPENHORN	ANATOMISE	ANTIQUARY
AGREEABLE	ALTAR-TOMB	ANATOMIST	ANTIQUATE
AGREEABLY	ALTERABLE	ANCESTRAL	ANTIQUELY
AGREEMENT	ALTERABLY	ANCHORAGE	ANTIQUITY
AGRONOMIC	ALTERCATE	ANCHORING	ANTITOXIC
AIMLESSLY	ALTERNATE	ANCHORITE	ANTITOXIN
AIR-ENGINE	ALTIMETER	ANCIENTLY	ANXIOUSLY
AIR-FILTER	ALTO-VIOLA	ANCILLARY	APARTMENT
AIR-FUNNEL	ALUMINIUM	ANECDOTAL	APATHETIC
AIR-INTAKE	AMARYLLIS	ANGEL-FISH	APARTNESS
AIR-JACKET	AMASSABLE	ANGELICAL	APERITIVE
AIR-POCKET	AMAZEMENT	ANGLICISE	APHORISED

APISHNESS	ARM'S-REACH	ASSURABLE	AUTONOMIC
APOCRYPHA	ARRAIGNED	ASSURANCE	AUXILIARY
APOLOGISE	ARRANGING	ASSUREDLY	AVAILABLE
APOLOGIST	ARRESTING	ASTHMATIC	AVAILABLY
APOSTOLIC	ARROGANCE	ASTOUNDED	AVALANCHE
APPALLING	ARROW-HEAD	ASTRADDLE	AVERAGELY
APPARATUS	ARROWROOT	ASTRAKHAN	AVERAGING
APPEALING	ARSENICAL	ASTROLABE	AVERTEDLY
APPEARING	ARSENIOUS	ASTROLOGY	AVOCATION
APPEASING	ARTEMISIA	ASTRONOMY	AVOCATIVE
APPELLANT	ARTHRITIC	ASYMMETRY	AVOIDABLE
APPELLATE	ARTHRITIS	ATAVISTIC	AVOIDANCE
APPENDAGE	ARTICHOKE	ATHANASIA	AVUNCULAR
APPENDANT	ARTICLING	ATHEISTIC	AWAKENING
APPENDING	ARTICULAR	ATHENAEUM	AWARDABLE
APPERTAIN	ARTIFICER	ATHLETICS	AWESTRUCK
APPETISER	ARTILLERY	ATLANTEAN	AWFULNESS
APPLAUDED	ARTLESSLY	ATOMISING	AWKWARDLY
APPLE-JACK	ASCENDANT	ATONEMENT	AXIOMATIC
APPLE-JOHN	ASCENDENT	ATROCIOUS	
APPLIANCE	ASCENDING	ATROPHIED	B—9
APPLICANT	ASCENSION	ATTACHING	BABYLONIC
APPLICATE	ASCERTAIN	ATTACKING	BACCHANAL
APPOINTED	ASCRIBING	ATTAINDER	BACCHANTE
APPORTION	ASHAMEDLY	ATTAINING	BACILLARY
APPRAISAL	ASPARAGUS	ATTAINTED	BACKBOARD
APPRAISED	ASPERATED	ATTEMPTED	BACKPIECE
APPREHEND	ASPERSING	ATTENDANT	BACKSIGHT
APPRISING	ASPERSION	ATTENDING	BACK-SLANG
APPROBATE	ASPHALTIC	ATTENTION	BACK-SLIDE
APPROVING	ASPIRATED	ATTENTIVE	BACKSTAFF
AQUILEGIA	ASSAILANT	ATTENUATE	BACKWARDS
ARABESQUE	ASSAILING	ATTESTING	BACKWATER
ARACHNOID	ASSAULTED	ATTICISED	BACKWOODS
ARBITRARY	ASSAYABLE	ATTRACTED	BADGERING
ARBITRATE	ASSEMBLED	ATTRIBUTE	BADMINTON
ARBORETUM	ASSENTING	ATTRITION	BAGATELLE
ARCHANGEL	ASSERTING	AUBERGINE	BAILIWICK
ARCH-DRUID	ASSERTION	AUDACIOUS	BAKEHOUSE
ARCHDUCAL	ASSERTIVE	AUGMENTED	BAKESTONE
ARCHDUCHY	ASSESSING	AUSTERELY	BAKSHEESH
ARCH-ENEMY	ASSIDUITY	AUSTERITY	BALALAIKA
ARCHETYPE	ASSIDUOUS	AUSTRALIA	BALANCING
ARCH-FIEND	ASSIGNING	AUTHENTIC	BALCONIED
ARCHITECT	ASSISTANT	AUTHORESS	BALD-PATED
ARCHIVIST	ASSISTING	AUTHORISE	BALEFULLY
ARDUOUSLY	ASSOCIATE	AUTHORITY	BALKINGLY
ARGENTINE	ASSOILING	AUTOCRACY	BALLASTED
ARGUFYING	ASSONANCE	AUTOGRAPH	BALLERINA
ARMADILLO	ASSORTING	AUTOMATIC	BALLISTIC
ARMISTICE	ASSUAGING	AUTOMATON	BALLOT-BOX

BALLOTING	BEAN-STALK	BENGALESE	BISHOPRIC
BALL-POINT	BEARDLESS	BENIGHTED	BITTERISH
BAMBOOZLE	BEATIFIED	BENIGNANT	BLABBERED
BANDAGING	BEATITUDE	BENIGNITY	BLACKBALL
BANDEROLE	BEAU-IDEAL	BENZOLINE	BLACKBIRD
BANDICOOT	BEAU-MONDE	BEREAVING	BLACKCOCK
BANDOLIER	BEAUTEOUS	BERYLLIUM	BLACKENED
BANEFULLY	BEAUTIFUL	BESEECHED	BLACKHEAD
BANISHING	BECALMING	BESETTING	BLACK-JACK
BANQUETED	BECKONING	BESIEGING	BLACK-LEAD
BANQUETTE	BEDAZZLED	BESMEARED	BLACK-LIST
BAPTISING	BEDECKING	BESOTTING	BLACKMAIL
BAPTISMAL	BEDFELLOW	BESPATTER	BLACKNESS
BARBARIAN	BEDLAMITE	BESTIALLY	BLADEBONE
BARBARISM	BEDRAGGLE	BESTIRRED	BLAEBERRY
BARBARITY	BEDRIDDEN	BESTOWING	BLAMELESS
BARBAROUS	BEDSPREAD	BETHOUGHT	BLANCHING
BARBECUED	BEECHMAST	BETHUMBED	BLANDNESS
BARBERING	BEEFEATER	BETOKENED	BLANKETED
BAREBONED	BEEFLOWER	BETRAYING	BLANKNESS
BAREFACED	BEEFSTEAK	BETROTHAL	BLASPHEME
BARGAINED	BEELZEBUB	BETROTHED	BLASPHEMY
BARLEY-MOW	BEER-MONEY	BETTERING	BLATHERED
BARMECIDE	BEFALLING	BEVELLING	BLAZONING
BAROGRAPH	BEFITTING	BEWAILING	BLEACHING
BAROMETER	BEFOGGING	BEWITCHED	BLEAR-EYED
BARONETCY	BEFOOLING	BICKERING	BLEMISHED
BARRELLED	BEFOULING	BICYCLING	BLENCHING
BARRICADE	BEGETTING	BICYCLIST	BLESSEDLY
BARRISTER	BEGGARING	BIFURCATE	BLETHERED
BAR-TENDER	BEGINNING	BIGOTEDLY	BLIGHTING
BARTERING	BEGRIMING	BILATERAL	BLINDFOLD
BASHFULLY	BEGRUDGED	BILINGUAL	BLINDNESS
BASILICAN	BEGUILING	BILLABONG	BLINDWORM
BASILICON	BEHAVIOUR	BILLETING	BLISTERED
BASKETFUL	BEHEADING	BILLIARDS	BLOCKADED
BAS-RELIEF	BEHOLDING	BILLOWING	BLOCKHEAD
BASTINADO	BELEAGUER	BILLY-COCK	BLOOD HEAT
BASTIONED	BELIEVING	BILLY-GOAT	BLOODLESS
BATH-BRICK	BELITTLED	BIMONTHLY	BLOOD-SHED
BATH-CHAIR	BELL-GLASS	BINDINGLY	BLOODSHOT
BATH-METAL	BELLICOSE	BINOCULAR	BLOODWORM
BATTALION	BELL-METAL	BINOMINAL	BLOODYING
BATTENING	BELLOWING	BIOGRAPHY	BLOSSOMED
BATTERING	BELL-PUNCH	BIOLOGIST	BLOTCHING
BATTLE-AXE	BELLYBAND	BIONOMICS	BLUBBERED
BATTLE-CRY	BELLY-ROLL	BIPARTITE	BLUEBEARD
BAWDINESS	BELONGING	BIRTHMARK	BLUE-BERRY
BAYONETED	BELVEDERE	BIRTHRATE	BLUE-BLACK
BAY-WINDOW	BEMOANING	BISECTING	BLUE-BLOOD
BEAN-FEAST	BENEFITED	BISECTION	BLUESTONE

BLUFFNESS	BOUNDLESS	BRILLIANT	BUMBLE-BEE
BLUNDERED	BOUNTEOUS	BRIMSTONE	BUMBLEDOM
BLUNTNESS	BOUNTIFUL	BRIQUETTE	BUMPINESS
BLUSTERED	BOURGEOIS	BRISKNESS	BUMPTIOUS
BLUSTERER	BOWER-BIRD	BRISTLING	BUOYANTLY
BOANERGES	BOW-LEGGED	BRITANNIC	BURDENING
BOARDABLE	BOW-STRING	BRITTLELY	BURGEONED
BOARHOUND	BOW-STRUNG	BRITTLING	BURLESQUE
BOAR-SPEAR	BOW-WINDOW	BROACHING	BURLINESS
BOASTLESS	BOXING-DAY	BROADBEAN	BURNISHED
BOAT-HOUSE	BOX-OFFICE	BROADBILL	BURROWING
BOATSWAIN	BOYCOTTED	BROADBRIM	BUSHINESS
BOB-SLEIGH	BRACKETED	BROADCAST	BUTCHERED
BOBTAILED	BRACTLESS	BROADENED	BUTTERCUP
BODYGUARD	BRAINLESS	BROADNESS	BUTTERFLY
BOG-MYRTLE	BRAINWAVE	BROADSIDE	BUTTERING
BOLD-FACED	BRAKELESS	BROADWAYS	BUTTONING
BOLOGNESE	BRAKES-MAN	BROADWISE	BUXOMNESS
BOLSHEVIK	BRAMBLING	BROCADING	BUZZINGLY
BOLSTERED	BRANCHING	BROKERAGE	BY-PASSAGE
BOMB-AIMER	BRANCHLET	BRONCHIAL	BY-PRODUCT
BOMBARDED	BRASS-BAND	BROOD-MARE	BYSTANDER
BOMBARDON	BRAZENING	BROOKWEED	BYZANTINE
BOMBASTIC	BRAZILIAN	BROTHERLY	
BOMBAZINE	BRAZIL-NUT	BROWNNESS	C—9
BOMB-PROOF	BREACHING	BRUMMAGEM	CABALLERO
BOMBSHELL	BREADLESS	BRUSH-WOOD	CABLEGRAM
BOMBSIGHT	BREAD-ROOM	BRUTALISE	CABRIOLET
BONDSLAVE	BREAKABLE	BRUTALITY	CACOPHONY
BONDWOMAN	BREAKDOWN	BRUTISHLY	CADDIS-FLY
BONIFACE	BREAKFAST	BRYTHONIC	CADETSHIP
BONNETING	BREAKNECK	BUCCANEER	CAESARIAN
BONNINESS	BREASTPIN	BUCKBOARD	CAFETERIA
BON-VIVANT	BREATHING	BUCKETFUL	CAIRNGORM
BOOBY-TRAP	BREECHING	BUCKETING	CALABOOSE
BOOHOOING	BREWHOUSE	BUCKHOUND	CALCIFIED
BOOKISHLY	BRIAR-ROOT	BUCK'S-HORN	CALCINING
BOOKMAKER	BRIDELESS	BUCKTHORN	CALCULATE
BOOK-PLATE	BRIC-A-BRAC	BUCKTOOTH	CALENDULA
BOOKSTALL	BRICK-CLAY	BUCKWAGON	CALIBRATE
BOOKSTAND	BRICKDUST	BUCK-WHEAT	CALIPHATE
BOOKSTORE	BRICK-KILN	BUDGETING	CALLA-LILY
BOOMERANG	BRICKWORK	BUFFETING	CALLIPERS
BOORISHLY	BRICKYARD	BUGLE-CALL	CALLOSITY
BORDERING	BRIDECAKE	BULGARIAN	CALLOUSLY
BORROWING	BRIDESMAN	BULGINESS	CALORIFIC
BOSPHORUS	BRIDEWELL	BULKINESS	CALVINISM
BOTANICAL	BRIDLE-WAY	BULL-FIGHT	CALVINIST
BOTHERING	BRIEFLESS	BULLFINCH	CAMBERING
BOTTOMING	BRIEFNESS	BULLY-BEEF	CAMPANILE
BOULEVARD	BRIGADIER	BULWARKED	CAMPANULA

CAMP-FEVER	CARNIVORA	CAUTERISE	CHAR-A-BANC
CAMPSTOOL	CAROLLING	CAUTIONED	CHARACTER
CANALISED	CAROUSING	CAVALCADE	CHARINESS
CANCELLED	CARPENTER	CAVENDISH	CHARIVARI
CANCEROUS	CARPENTRY	CAVERNOUS	CHARLATAN
CANDIDACY	CARPETING	CAVILLING	CHARLOTTE
CANDIDATE	CARPINGLY	CAVORTING	CHARTERED
CANDIFIED	CARRIABLE	CEASELESS	CHARTLESS
CANDLEMAS	CARTESIAN	CEE-SPRING	CHASEABLE
CANDYTUFT	CARTHORSE	CEILINGED	CHASTENED
CANE-SUGAR	CARTILAGE	CELANDINE	CHASTISED
CANE-CHAIR	CARTOUCHE	CELEBRANT	CHATTERED
CANKER-FLY	CARTRIDGE	CELEBRATE	CHAUFFEUR
CANKERING	CARTWHEEL	CELEBRITY	CHEAPENED
CANKEROUS	CASHEWNUT	CELESTIAL	CHEAPNESS
CANNON-BIT	CASHIERED	CELESTINE	CHEATABLE
CANNONADE	CASSEROLE	CELLARAGE	CHECKMATE
CANNONING	CASSOWARY	CELLARMAN	CHECK-REIN
CANONICAL	CASTIGATE	CELLULOID	CHEEK-BONE
CANONISED	CASTILIAN	CELLULOSE	CHEERLESS
CANOODLED	CASTOR-OIL	CEMENTING	CHEESEFLY
CANOPYING	CASTRATED	CENSORIAL	CHEESEVAT
CANTABILE	CAST-STEEL	CENSORING	CHEMISTRY
CANTALOUP	CASUISTIC	CENSURING	CHEQUERED
CANTERING	CASUISTRY	CENTENARY	CHERISHED
CANTINGLY	CATACLYSM	CENTIGRAM	CHEVALIER
CANVASSED	CATALEPSY	CENTIPEDE	CHICANERY
CANVASSER	CATALOGUE	CENTRALLY	CHICANING
CAPACIOUS	CATALYSER	CENTRE-BIT	CHICKADEE
CAPARISON	CATALYSIS	CENTURION	CHICKLING
CAPILLARY	CATALYTIC	CEREBRATE	CHICKWEED
CAPITALLY	CATAMARAN	CERTAINLY	CHIDINGLY
CAPITULAR	CATAMOUNT	CERTAINTY	CHIEFLESS
CAPRICCIO	CATARRHAL	CERTIFIED	CHIEFTAIN
CAPRICORN	CATCHABLE	CERTITUDE	CHILBLAIN
CAPSIZING	CATCH-CROP	CESSATION	CHILDHOOD
CAPTAINCY	CATCHMENT	CETACEOUS	CHILDLESS
CAPTIVATE	CATCHPOLE	CHAFFERED	CHILDLIKE
CAPTIVITY	CATCHWEED	CHAFFINCH	CHILLNESS
CAPTURING	CATCHWORD	CHAFFLESS	CHINA-CLAY
CARBONATE	CATECHISE	CHAGRINED	CHINA-ROSE
CARBONISE	CATECHISM	CHAIN-GANG	CHINASHOP
CARBUNCLE	CATECHIST	CHAINLESS	CHINATOWN
CARDBOARD	CATERWAUL	CHAIN-MAIL	CHINAWARE
CAREENING	CATHEADED	CHAINWORK	CHIROPODY
CAREERING	CATHEDRAL	CHALLENGE	CHISELLED
CAREFULLY	CAUCASIAN	CHAMFERED	CHITTERED
CARESSING	CAUSALITY	CHAMPAGNE	CHOCK-FULL
CARMELITE	CAUSATION	CHANDLERY	CHOCOLATE
CARNALITY	CAUSATIVE	CHANGEFUL	CHOP-HOUSE
CARNATION	CAUSELESS	CHAPTERED	CHORISTER

CHORTLING
CHORUSING
CHRISTIAN
CHRISTMAS
CHROMATIC
CHROMATIN
CHRYSALIS
CHUCKLING
CHURCHILL
CHURCHING
CHURCHMAN
CICATRICE
CICATRISE
CIGARETTE
CINERARIA
CINGALESE
CIPHERING
CIPHER-KEY
CIRCUITED
CIRCULATE
CIRRHOSIS
CIVILISED
CLAIMABLE
CLAMBERED
CLAMOROUS
CLAMOURED
CLAPBOARD
CLARENDON
CLARET-CUP
CLARIFIED
CLARIONET
CLASSIBLE
CLASSICAL
CLATTERED
CLEANLILY
CLEANNESS
CLEANSING
CLEARANCE
CLEAR-EYED
CLEARNESS
CLEAVABLE
CLEMENTLY
CLENCHING
CLERGYMAN
CLERK-LIKE
CLERKSHIP
CLIENTELE
CLIMACTIC
CLIMBABLE
CLINCHING
CLOAKROOM

CLOCK-GOLF
CLOCKWISE
CLOCKWORK
CLOG-DANCE
CLOISONNE
CLOISTERS
CLOSENESS
CLOSETING
CLOTH-HALL
CLOTHYARD
CLOUDLESS
CLOUDLINE
CLOUT-NAIL
CLOVE-PINK
CLUBBABLE
CLUBHOUSE
CLUSTERED
CLUTCHING
CLUTTERED
COACH-WORK
COAGULANT
COAGULATE
COAL-BLACK
COALESCED
COALFIELD
COAL-HOUSE
COALITION
COAL-MINER
COARSENED
COASTLINE
COASTWISE
COATFROCK
COAXINGLY
COBDENISM
COBDENITE
COBWEBBED
COCHINEAL
COCK-A-HOOP
COCKFIGHT
COCKHORSE
COCKINESS
COCKROACH
COCKSCOMB
COCK'S-FOOT
COCK'S-HEAD
COCOA-BEAN
COCOA-PLUM
COCO-DE-MER
CODIFYING
COEQUALLY
COERCIBLE

COETERNAL
COEXISTED
COFFEE-BUG
COFFEE-CUP
COFFEE-POT
COFFERDAM
COGITABLE
COGITATED
COGNATION
COGNISANT
COGNITION
COGNITIVE
COHABITED
COHEIRESS
COHERENCE
COHERENCY
COHERITOR
COINCIDED
COLCHICUM
COLD-CREAM
COLLAPSED
COLLARING
COLLATING
COLLATION
COLLEAGUE
COLLECTED
COLLECTOR
COLLEGIAN
COLLIDING
COLLIMATE
COLLISION
COLLOCATE
COLLODION
COLLOIDAL
COLLOTYPE
COLLUSION
COLLUSIVE
COLLUSORY
COLONELCY
COLONISED
COLONNADE
COLORIFIC
COLOSSEUM
COLOUR-BOX
COLOURING
COLOURIST
COLOURMAN
COLTSFOOT
COLUMBIAN
COLUMBINE
COMBATANT

COMBATIVE
COMBINING
COMFORTED
COMFORTER
COMICALLY
COMINFORM
COMINTERN
COMMANDED
COMMANDER
COMMENCED
COMMENDED
COMMENSAL
COMMENTED
COMMINGLE
COMMISSAR
COMMITTAL
COMMITTED
COMMITTEE
COMMODITY
COMMONAGE
COMMOTION
COMMOVING
COMMUNING
COMMUNION
COMMUNISE
COMMUNISM
COMMUNIST
COMMUNITY
COMMUTING
COMPACTED
COMPACTLY
COMPANION
COMPARING
COMPASSED
COMPASSES
COMPELLED
COMPELLING
COMPETENT
COMPETING
COMPLAINT
COMPLETED
COMPLEXLY
COMPLIANT
COMPLYING
COMPONENT
COMPORTED
COMPOSING
COMPOSITE
COMPOSTED
COMPOSURE
COMPRISED

COMPUTING	CONGRUOUS	CONTUMELY	CORPORATE
CONCAVELY	CONICALLY	CONTUSING	CORPOREAL
CONCAVITY	CONJOINED	CONTUSION	CORPOSANT
CONCEALED	CONJUGATE	CONUNDRUM	CORPULENT
CONCEDING	CONJURING	CONVENING	CORPUSCLE
CONCEITED	CONNECTED	CONVERGED	CORRECTED
CONCEIVED	CONNECTOR	CONVERSED	CORRECTLY
CONCERNED	CONNEXION	CONVERTED	CORRECTOR
CONCERTED	CONNIVING	CONVEXITY	CORRELATE
CONCIERGE	CONNOTING	CONVEYING	CORRODING
CONCISELY	CONNUBIAL	CONVICTED	CORROSION
CONCLUDED	CO-NOMINEE	CONVINCED	CORROSIVE
CONCOCTED	CONQUERED	CONVIVIAL	CORRUGATE
CONCORDAT	CONQUEROR	CONVOKING	CORRUPTED
CONCOURSE	CONSCIOUS	CONVOLUTE	CORTICATE
CONCRETED	CONSCRIBE	CONVOYING	CORTISONE
CONCUBINE	CONSCRIPT	CONVULSED	CORUSCATE
CONCURRED	CONSENSUS	COOK-HOUSE	COSMOGONY
CONCUSSED	CONSENTED	COOPERAGE	COSMOLOGY
CONDEMNED	CONSERVED	CO-OPERATE	COSSETING
CONDENSED	CONSIGNED	COOPERING	COSTUMIER
CONDENSER	CONSIGNEE	COPARTNER	COTANGENT
CONDIGNLY	CONSIGNOR	CO-PATRIOT	COTILLION
CONDIMENT	CONSISTED	COPESTONE	COTTER-PIN
CONDITION	CONSOLING	COPIOUSLY	COTTON-GIN
CONDOLING	CONSONANT	COPPERING	COTTONING
CONDONING	CONSORTED	COPPERISH	COTYLEDON
CONDUCING	CONSPIRED	COPSE-WOOD	COUNTABLE
CONDUCIVE	CONSTABLE	COPYRIGHT	COUNTERED
CONDUCTED	CONSTANCY	COQUETTED	COUNTLESS
CONDUCTOR	CONSTRAIN	CORALLINE	COUNTRIFY
CONFERRED	CONSTRICT	CORALLITE	COURT-CARD
CONFESSED	CONSTRUCT	CORALLOID	COURTEOUS
CONFESSOR	CONSTRUED	CORAL-REEF	COURTESAN
CONFIDANT	CONSULATE	CORBELLED	COURTLIKE
CONFIDENT	CONSULTED	CORDELIER	COURTSHIP
CONFIDING	CONSUMING	CORDIALLY	COURT-YARD
CONFIGURE	CONTAGION	COREOPSIS	COVERTURE
CONFINING	CONTAINED	CORIANDER	COWARDICE
CONFIRMED	CONTAINER	CORKSCREW	COXCOMBRY
CONFLUENT	CONTENTED	CORMORANT	CRAB-APPLE
CONFORMED	CONTESTED	CORN-BREAD	CRABBEDLY
CONFUCIAN	CONTINENT	CORNCRAKE	CRACKLING
CONFUSING	CONTINUAL	CORNELIAN	CRAFTSMAN
CONFUSION	CONTINUED	CORNERING	CRAMP-IRON
CONFUTING	CONTINUUM	CORNFLOUR	CRANBERRY
CONGEALED	CONTORTED	CORN-POPPY	CRANKCASE
CONGENIAL	CONTOURED	CORN-SALAD	CRAPULENT
CONGESTED	CONTRALTO	CORNSTALK	CRAPULOUS
CONGRUENT	CONTRIVED	COROLLARY	CRASSNESS
CONGRUITY	CONTUMACY	CORONETED	CRAYONING

CRAZINESS	CRUSADING	DAISY-BUSH	DECANTING
CREAM-LIKE	CRUSTACEA	DALLIANCE	DECEITFUL
CREAM-LAID	CRYPTOGAM	DALMATIAN	DECEIVING
CREAM-WOVE	CUBICALLY	DAMASCENE	DECENNIAL
CREDITING	CUCKOLDED	DAMOCLEAN	DECENNIUM
CREDULITY	CUDGELLED	DAMPENING	DECEPTION
CREDULOUS	CULMINATE	DAMPISHLY	DECEPTIVE
CREMATING	CULTIVATE	DANDELION	DECIDABLE
CREMATION	CULTURING	DANDIFIED	DECIDEDLY
CRENATURE	CULTURIST	DANGEROUS	DECIDUOUS
CREPITANT	CUMBERING	DANNEBROG	DECILLION
CREPITATE	CUNEIFORM	DANTESQUE	DECIMALLY
CRESCENDO	CUNNINGLY	DAREDEVIL	DECIMATED
CRETINISM	CUP-BEARER	DARKENING	DECIMETRE
CREVICING	CUPRESSUS	DARTINGLY	DECK-CHAIR
CRIMELESS	CURBSTONE	DARWINIAN	DECK-HOUSE
CRIMSONED	CURIOSITY	DARWINISM	DECLAIMED
CRINKLING	CURIOUSLY	DASH-BOARD	DECLARANT
CRINOLINE	CURLINESS	DASTARDLY	DECLARING
CRIPPLING	CURLINGLY	DATUM-LINE	DECLINING
CRISPNESS	CURRENTLY	DAUNTLESS	DECLIVITY
CRITERION	CURRISHLY	DAVENPORT	DECOCTION
CRITICISE	CURRYCOMB	DAY-LABOUR	DECOLLETE
CRITICISM	CURSORIAL	DAY-SCHOOL	DECOMPLEX
CROCHETED	CURSORILY	DAY-SPRING	DECOMPOSE
CROCODILE	CURTAILED	DEACONESS	DECONTROL
CROOKBACK	CURTAINED	DEAD-ALIVE	DECORATED
CROOKEDLY	CURTILAGE	DEADENING	DECORATOR
CROQUETTE	CURTSYING	DEAFENING	DECOY-DUCK
CROSSBEAM	CURVATURE	DEATH-BLOW	DECREASED
CROSSBILL	CURVETTED	DEATHLESS	DECREEING
CROSS-EYED	CUSHIONED	DEATHLIKE	DECREMENT
CROSS-FIRE	CUSTODIAN	DEATH-MASK	DECUMBENT
CROSS-HEAD	CUSTOMARY	DEATH-RATE	DECUSSATE
CROSSNESS	CUTANEOUS	DEATH-ROLL	DEDICATED
CROSSROAD	CUTICULAR	DEATH-TRAP	DEDUCIBLE
CROSS-WIND	CUTTER-BAR	DEATH-WARD	DEDUCTING
CROSSWISE	CUT-THROAT	DEBARRING	DEDUCTION
CROSS-WORD	CUTTINGLY	DEBATABLE	DEDUCTIVE
CROTCHETY	CYCLOPEAN	DEBAUCHED	DEEPENING
CROUCHING	CYCLORAMA	DEBENTURE	DEEP-TONED
CROWBERRY	CYNICALLY	DEBOUCHED	DEFALCATE
CROW'S-FEET	CYTOPLASM	DEBUTANTE	DEFAULTED
CROW'S-FOOT		DECADENCE	DEFAULTER
CROW'S-NEST		DECAGONAL	DEFEATING
CROW-STONE		DECALCIFY	DEFEATISM
CRUCIFIED	**D—9**	DECALITRE	DEFECTION
CRUCIFORM	DACHSHUND	DECALOGUE	DEFECTIVE
CRUMBLING	DAEDALIAN	DECAMERON	DEFENDANT
CRUMPLING	DAIRY-FARM	DECAMETRE	DEFENDING
CRUNCHING	DAIRY-MAID	DECAMPING	DEFENSIVE

DEFERENCE	DEPARTURE	DESPERATE	DIAGNOSED
DEFERRING	DEPASTURE	DESPISING	DIAGNOSIS
DEFIANTLY	DEPENDANT	DESPOILED	DIALECTAL
DEFICIENT	DEPENDENT	DESPONDED	DIALECTIC
DEFINABLE	DEPENDING	DESPOTISM	DIAL-PLATE
DEFINABLY	DEPICTING	DESTINING	DIAPERING
DEFLATING	DEPILATED	DESTITUTE	DIAPHRAGM
DEFLATION	DEPLENISH	DESTROYED	DIARRHOEA
DEFLECTED	DEPLETING	DESTROYER	DICHOTOMY
DEFLECTOR	DEPLETION	DESUETUDE	DICHROMIC
DEFLEXION	DEPLETIVE	DESULTORY	DICKERING
DEFOLIATE	DEPLETORY	DETACHING	DICTATING
DEFORMING	DEPLORING	DETAILING	DICTATION
DEFORMITY	DEPLOYING	DETAINING	DICTATORY
DEFRAUDED	DEPLUMING	DETECTING	DIDACTICS
DEFRAYING	DEPORTING	DETECTION	DIESINKER
DEISTICAL	DEPOSITED	DETECTIVE	DIETETICS
DEJECTING	DEPOSITOR	DETENTION	DIETITIAN
DEJECTION	DEPRAVING	DETERRING	DIFFERENT
DELEGATED	DEPRAVITY	DETERGENT	DIFFERING
DELICIOUS	DEPRECATE	DETERMINE	DIFFICILE
DELIGHTED	DEPRESSED	DETERRENT	DIFFICULT
DELIMITED	DEPRIVING	DETERRING	DIFFIDENT
DELINEATE	DEPTHLESS	DETESTING	DIFFLUENT
DELIRIOUS	DEPUTISED	DETHRONED	DIFFUSING
DELIVERED	DERAILING	DETONATED	DIFFUSION
DELIVERER	DERANGING	DETONATOR	DIFFUSELY
DEMAGOGIC	DERIVABLE	DETRACTED	DIFFUSIVE
DEMAGOGUE	DERIVABLY	DETRACTOR	DIGESTING
DEMANDANT	DERMATOID	DETRAINED	DIGESTION
DEMANDING	DEROGATED	DETRIMENT	DIGESTIVE
DEMARCATE	DERRING-DO	DETRITION	DIGITALIN
DEMEANING	DERRINGER	DEVASTATE	DIGITALIS
DEMEANOUR	DESCANTED	DEVELOPED	DIGNIFIED
DEMI-MONDE	DESCENDED	DEVELOPER	DIGNITARY
DEMISSION	DESCRIBED	DEVIATION	DIGRESSED
DEMITTING	DESCRYING	DEVIL-FISH	DILATABLE
DEMOCRACY	DESECRATE	DEVILLING	DILIGENCE
DEMULCENT	DESERTING	DEVILMENT	DILUTEDLY
DEMURRAGE	DESERTION	DEVIOUSLY	DIMENSION
DEMURRANT	DESERVING	DEVISABLE	DIMORPHIC
DEMURRING	DESICCANT	DEVITRIFY	DINGINESS
DENIGRATE	DESICCATE	DEVOLUTED	DINING-CAR
DENOUNCED	DESIGNATE	DEVOLVING	DIPHTHONG
DENSENESS	DESIGNING	DEVONPORT	DIPLOMACY
DENTATION	DESIRABLE	DEVOURING	DIPTEROUS
DENTISTRY	DESIRABLY	DEWLAPPED	DIRECTING
DENTITION	DESISTING	DEXTERITY	DIRECTION
DEODORANT	DESOLATED	DEXTEROUS	DIRECTIVE
DEODORISE	DESPAIRED	DIABOLISM	DIRECTORY
DEPARTING	DESPERADO	DIAERESIS	DIREFULLY

DIRIGIBLE	DISLOCATE	DISTILLER	DOWERLESS
DIRTINESS	DISLODGED	DISTORTED	DOWN-GRADE
DIRT-TRACK	DISMANTLE	DISTRAINT	DOWNINESS
DISABLING	DISMASTED	DISTURBED	DOWNRIGHT
DISABUSED	DISMAYING	DISUNITED	DOWN-WARDS
DISACCORD	DISMEMBER	DITHERING	DRABBLING
DISAFFECT	DISMISSAL	DITHYRAMB	DRACONIAN
DISAFFIRM	DISMISSED	DIURNALLY	DRAFTSMAN
DISAGREED	DISOBEYED	DIVAGATED	DRAGGLING
DISAPPEAR	DISOBLIGE	DIVERGENT	DRAGON-FLY
DISARMING	DISOWNING	DIVERGING	DRAINABLE
DISAVOWAL	DISPARAGE	DIVERSELY	DRAINPIPE
DISAVOWED	DISPARATE	DIVERSIFY	DRAMATISE
DISBANDED	DISPARITY	DIVERSION	DRAMATIST
DISBARRED	DISPELLED	DIVERSITY	DRAWN-WORK
DISBELIEF	DISPENSED	DIVERTING	DRAY-HORSE
DISBRANCH	DISPENSER	DIVESTING	DREAM-LAND
DISBUDDED	DISPERSAL	DIVIDABLE	DREAM-LESS
DISBURDEN	DISPERSED	DIVIDEDLY	DREAM-LIKE
DISBURSED	DISPLACED	DIVISIBLE	DRENCHING
DISCARDED	DISPLAYED	DIVISIBLY	DRIBBLING
DISCERNED	DISPLEASE	DIVORCING	DRIFT-LESS
DISCHARGE	DISPORTED	DIVULGING	DRIFT-WOOD
DISCLOSED	DISPOSING	DIZZINESS	DRINKABLE
DISCOLOUR	DISPRAISE	DOCK-CRESS	DRINKLESS
DISCOMFIT	DISPROVED	DOCTORATE	DRIPSTONE
DISCOURSE	DISPUTANT	DOCTORING	DRIVELLED
DISCOVERY	DISPUTING	DOCTRINAL	DRIZZLING
DISCREDIT	DISRATING	DODDERING	DROMEDARY
DISCUSSED	DISREGARD	DODECAGON	DROP-SCENE
DISDAINED	DISRELISH	DOGGINESS	DROPSICAL
DISEMBARK	DISREPAIR	DOGMATISE	DRUM-MAJOR
DISEMBODY	DISREPUTE	DOGMATISM	DRUM-STICK
DISENGAGE	DISROBING	DOGMATIST	DRUNKENLY
DISENTAIL	DISROOTED	DOG'S-TOOTH	DRYASDUST
DISENTOMB	DISRUPTED	DOG-VIOLET	DRYSALTER
DISFAVOUR	DISSECTED	DOLEFULLY	DUALISTIC
DISFIGURE	DISSEMBLE	DOLTISHLY	DUBIOUSLY
DISGORGED	DISSENTED	DOMICILED	DUBITABLE
DISGRACED	DISSENTER	DOMINANCE	DUBITABLY
DISGUISED	DISSERVED	DOMINATED	DUCK-BOARD
DISGUSTED	DISSIPATE	DOMINICAL	DUCK'S-FOOT
DISH-CLOTH	DISSOLUTE	DO-NOTHING	DUCTILELY
DISH-CLOUT	DISSOLVED	DOOR-PLATE	DUCTILITY
DISH-COVER	DISSONANT	DOOR-STONE	DUMB-BELLS
DISHONEST	DISSUADED	DORMITORY	DUMBFOUND
DISHONOUR	DISTANCED	DOUBTLESS	DUMPINESS
DISHWATER	DISTANTLY	DOUGHTILY	DUMPISHLY
DISINFECT	DISTEMPER	DOVE'S-FOOT	DUNGEONED
DISJOINED	DISTENDED	DOWDINESS	DUODECIMO
DISLIKING	DISTILLED	DOWELLING	DUODENARY

DUPLICATE	EJACULATE	EMOTIONAL	ENJOYMENT
DWINDLING	EJECTMENT	EMPHASISE	ENLARGING
DYNAMICAL	ELABORATE	EMPIRICAL	ENLIGHTEN
DYNAMITED	ELBOW-ROOM	EMPLOYING	ENLISTING
DYSENTERY	ELDERSHIP	EMPOWERED	ENLIVENED
DYSPEPSIA	ELDER-WINE	EMPTINESS	ENMESHING
DYSPEPTIC	ELECTORAL	EMULATING	ENOUNCING
DYSTROPHY	ELECTRESS	EMULATION	ENQUIRING
	ELECTRIFY	EMULATIVE	ENRAPTURE
E—9	ELECTRODE	ENACTMENT	ENRICHING
EAGERNESS	ELEGANTLY	ENAMELLED	ENROLLING
EAGLE-EYED	ELEMENTAL	ENAMOURED	ENROLMENT
EARLINESS	ELEVATING	ENCASHING	ENSCONCED
EARMARKED	ELEVATION	ENCAUSTIC	ENSHRINED
EARNESTLY	ELEVATORY	ENCHANTED	ENSLAVING
EARTHWARD	ELICITING	ENCIRCLED	ENSNARING
EARTHWORK	ELIMINATE	ENCLASPED	ENTAILING
EARTHWORM	ELLIPSOID	ENCLOSING	ENTANGLED
EASEFULLY	ELOCUTION	ENCLOSURE	ENTERTAIN
EASY-CHAIR	ELONGATED	ENCOMPASS	ENTHRONED
EASY-GOING	ELOPEMENT	ENCOUNTER	ENTHUSING
EAVESDROP	ELOQUENCE	ENCOURAGE	ENTITLING
EBONISING	ELSEWHERE	ENCRUSTED	ENTOURAGE
EBULLIENT	ELUCIDATE	ENDEARING	EN-TOUT-CAS
ECCENTRIC	EMACIATED	ENDEAVOUR	ENTRANCED
ECLIPSING	EMANATING	ENDLESSLY	ENTREATED
ECONOMICS	EMANATION	ENDOCRINE	ENTRECHAT
ECONOMISE	EMBALMING	ENDORSING	ENTREMETS
ECONOMIST	EMBANKING	ENDOSPERM	ENTRUSTED
ECTOPLASM	EMBARGOED	ENDOWMENT	ENTWINING
EDELWEISS	EMBARKING	ENDURABLE	ENUMERATE
EDITORIAL	EMBARRASS	ENDURABLY	ENUNCIATE
EDUCATING	EMBATTLED	ENDURANCE	ENVELOPED
EDUCATION	EMBEDDING	ENERGETIC	ENVENOMED
EFFECTING	EMBELLISH	ENERGISER	ENVIOUSLY
EFFECTIVE	EMBEZZLED	ENERVATED	ENVISAGED
EFFECTUAL	EMBEZZLER	ENFEEBLED	ENVOYSHIP
EFFICIENT	EMBODYING	ENFILADED	ENWRAPPED
EFFLUENCE	EMBOSSING	ENFOLDING	EPAULETTE
EFFLUVIUM	EMBOWERED	ENFORCING	EPHEMERAL
EFFLUXION	EMBRACING	ENGINE-MAN	EPICENTRE
EFFULGENT	EMBRASURE	ENGIRDING	EPICUREAN
EGLANTINE	EMBROIDER	ENGIRDLED	EPICURISM
EGREGIOUS	EMBROILED	ENGRAVING	EPICYCLIC
EGRESSION	EMBRYONIC	ENGROSSED	EPIDERMAL
EIDER-DOWN	EMENDATOR	ENGULFING	EPIDERMIC
EIDOGRAPH	EMERGENCE	ENHANCING	EPIDERMIS
EIGHTFOLD	EMERGENCY	ENIGMATIC	EPIGRAPHY
EIGHTIETH	EMINENTLY	ENJOINING	EPILEPTIC
EIGHTSOME	EMOLLIENT	ENJOYABLE	EPISCOPAL
EIRENICON	EMOLUMENT	ENJOYABLY	EPISTOLIC

EPITOMISE	EVANESCED	EXECUTIVE	EXTENDING
EQUALISED	EVANGELIC	EXECUTORY	EXTENSILE
EQUALISER	EVAPORATE	EXECUTRIX	ENTENSION
EQUALLING	EVASIVELY	EXEMPLARY	EXTENSIVE
EQUIPMENT	EVENTUATE	EXEMPLIFY	EXTENUATE
EQUIPOISE	EVERGLADE	EXEMPTION	EXTOLLING
EQUIPPING	EVERGREEN	EXEMPTIVE	EXTORTING
EQUITABLE	EVERYBODY	EXERCISED	EXTORTION
EQUIVOCAL	EVIDENTLY	EXFOLIATE	EXTRACTED
ERADICATE	EVOCATION	EXHALABLE	EXTRACTOR
ERECTNESS	EVOLUTION	EXHAUSTED	EXTRADITE
ERRAND-BOY	EXACTABLE	EXHIBITED	EXTREMELY
ERRONEOUS	EXACTNESS	EXHIBITOR	EXTREMISM
ERSTWHILE	EXAMINING	EXHORTING	EXTREMIST
ERUDITELY	EXCALIBUR	EXISTENCE	EXTREMITY
ERUDITION	EXCAVATED	EX-OFFICIO	EXTRICATE
ESCALADED	EXCAVATOR	EXOGAMOUS	EXTRINSIC
ESCALATOR	EXCEEDING	EXOGENOUS	EXTRUDING
ESCHEATED	EXCELLENT	EXONERATE	EXTRUSION
ESCORTING	EXCELSIOR	EXORCISED	EXUBERANT
ESPERANTO	EXCEPTING	EXPANDING	EXUBERATE
ESPIONAGE	EXCEPTION	EXPANSILE	EXUDATION
ESPLANADE	EXCEPTIVE	EXPANSION	EXULTANCY
ESPOUSING	EXCESSING	EXPANSIVE	EYE-BRIGHT
ESQUIRING	EXCESSIVE	EXPATIATE	EYE-OPENER
ESSENTIAL	EXCHANGED	EXPECTANT	
ESTABLISH	EXCHANGER	EXPECTING	F—9
ESTAMINET	EXCHEQUER	EXPEDIENT	FABRICATE
ESTEEMING	EXCISABLE	EXPEDITED	FACE-CLOTH
ESTIMABLE	EXCISEMAN	EXPENDING	FACE-GUARD
ESTIMABLY	EXCITABLE	EXPENSIVE	FACSIMILE
ESTIMATOR	EXCLAIMED	EXPIATING	FACTITIVE
ESTOPPING	EXCLUDING	EXPIATION	FACTORIAL
ESTRANGED	EXCLUSION	EXPIATORY	FACTORISE
ESTREATED	EXCLUSIVE	EXPLAINED	FADDINESS
ESTUARINE	EXCORIATE	EXPLETIVE	FAGGOTING
ETERNALLY	EXCREMENT	EXPLICATE	FAILINGLY
ETHICALLY	EXCRETION	EXPLOITED	FAINTNESS
ETHIOPIAN	EXCRETIVE	EXPLORING	FAIRY-LAMP
ETHNOLOGY	EXCRETORY	EXPLOSION	FAIRYLAND
ETIOLATED	EXCULPATE	EXPLOSIVE	FAIRY-LIKE
ETIQUETTE	EXCURSION	EXPORTING	FAIRY-TALE
ETYMOLOGY	EXCURSIVE	EXPOUNDED	FALDSTOOL
EUCHARIST	EXCUSABLE	EXPRESSED	FALERNIAN
EUCLIDEAN	EXCUSABLY	EXPRESSLY	FALLOPIAN
EULOGIZED	EXECRABLE	EXPULSION	FALLOWING
EUPHEMISE	EXECRABLY	EXPULSIVE	FALSEHOOD
EUPHEMISM	EXECRATED	EXPUNGING	FALSENESS
EUPHONIUM	EXECUTANT	EXPURGATE	FALSIFIED
EVACUATED	EXECUTING	EXQUISITE	FALTERING
EVALUATED	EXECUTION	EXTEMPORE	FAMISHING

FANATICAL	FEUDALISE	FISH-SPEAR	FLUTTERED
FANCY-FREE	FEUDALISM	FISSILITY	FLUXIONAL
FANTAILED	FEUDALITY	FISTULOUS	FLY-BITTEN
FANTASTIC	FEUDATORY	FITTINGLY	FLYING-FOX
FARMHOUSE	FIBRELESS	FITTING-UP	FLYING-JIB
FARMSTEAD	FIBRIFORM	FIXEDNESS	FLY-POWDER
FARROWING	FICTIONAL	FLACCIDLY	FOAMINGLY
FASCIATED	FIDDLE-BOW	FLAGELLUM	FODDERING
FASCINATE	FIDGETING	FLAGEOLET	FOGGINESS
FASHIONED	FIDUCIARY	FLAGRANCY	FOG-SIGNAL
FASTENING	FIELDFARE	FLAG-STAFF	FOLIATION
FATEFULLY	FIELDSMAN	FLAG-STONE	FOLK-DANCE
FATHERING	FIERINESS	FLAMBEAUX	FOLLOWING
FATHOMING	FIFE-MAJOR	FLAMELESS	FOMENTING
FATIGUING	FIFTEENTH	FLAMINGLY	FOOLHARDY
FATTENING	FILIATION	FLANNELLY	FOOLISHLY
FATTINESS	FILIGREED	FLARINGLY	FOOLPROOF
FAULTLESS	FILLETING	FLATTENED	FOOTBOARD
FAVOURING	FILLIPING	FLATTERED	FOOT-FAULT
FAVOURITE	FILMINESS	FLATTERER	FOOTPLATE
FAWNINGLY	FILTERING	FLAUNTING	FOOT-POUND
FEARFULLY	FILTRATED	FLAVOROUS	FOOTPRINT
FEATHERED	FINANCIAL	FLAVOURED	FOOTSTALK
FEATURING	FINANCIER	FLEETNESS	FOOTSTOOL
FEBRIFUGE	FINANCING	FLESHLESS	FOPPISHLY
FECUNDITY	FINEDRAWN	FLICKERED	FORAGE-CAP
FEDERATED	FINESSING	FLIGHTILY	FORASMUCH
FEELINGLY	FINGERING	FLINCHING	FORBIDDEN
FEE-SIMPLE	FINICALLY	FLINT-LOCK	FORCELESS
FEIGNEDLY	FINICKING	FLIPPANCY	FORCEMEAT
FELONIOUS	FINISHING	FLITTERED	FORCE-PUMP
FEMINISED	FIRE-ALARM	FLOATABLE	FOREARMED
FENCELESS	FIREBRAND	FLOOD-GATE	FOREBODED
FENESTRAL	FIREBRICK	FLOOD-MARK	FORE-CABIN
FENLANDER	FIRECREST	FLOOD-TIDE	FORECLOSE
FERMENTED	FIRE-EATER	FLOORLESS	FORECOURT
FEROCIOUS	FIRE-GUARD	FLORIDITY	FOREDATED
FERRETING	FIRE-IRONS	FLOTATION	FOREFRONT
FERROTYPE	FIRE-LIGHT	FLOUNCING	FOREGOING
FERRYBOAT	FIREPLACE	FLOWERING	FOREIGNER
FERTILELY	FIREPROOF	FLOWERPOT	FORE-JUDGE
FERTILISE	FIREWATER	FLOWINGLY	FORESHEET
FERTILITY	FIRMAMENT	FLUCTUATE	FORESHORE
FERVENTLY	FIRSTBORN	FLUIDNESS	FORESHOWN
FESTERING	FIRST-FOOT	FLUKINESS	FORE-SIGHT
FESTIVELY	FIRST-HAND	FLUMMOXED	FORESTALL
FESTIVITY	FIRST-RATE	FLUOR-SPAR	FORETASTE
FESTOONED	FISH-CURER	FLURRYING	FORETOKEN
FETIDNESS	FISHERMAN	FLUSHNESS	FOREWOMAN
FETISHISM	FISHINESS	FLUSTERED	FORFEITED
FETTERING	FISH-KNIFE	FLUTE-LIKE	FORGATHER

FORGETFUL	FRECKLING	FULSOMELY	GARNISHED
FORGIVING	FREEBOARD	FUMIGATED	GARNISHEE
FORLORNLY	FREELIVER	FUNGICIDE	GARNISHER
FORMALISE	FREEMASON	FUNICULAR	GARNITURE
FORMALISM	FREESTONE	FUNNELLED	GARRETEER
FORMALIST	FREE-WHEEL	FUNNINESS	GARROTTED
FORMALITY	FREIGHTED	FURBISHED	GARROTTER
FORMATION	FREIGHTER	FURIOUSLY	GARRULITY
FORMATIVE	FRENCHIFY	FURNISHED	GARRULOUS
FORMULARY	FRENCHMAN	FURNISHER	GARTERING
FORMULATE	FREQUENCY	FURNITURE	GAS-BURNER
FORMULISM	FRESHENED	FURROWING	GAS-CARBON
FORMULIST	FRESHNESS	FURTHERED	GASCONADE
FORSAKING	FRETFULLY	FURTHERER	GAS-COOKER
FORTHWITH	FRIBBLING	FURTIVELY	GAS-ENGINE
FORTIFIED	FRICASSEE	FUSILLADE	GASEOUSLY
FORTITUDE	FRICATIVE	FUSSINESS	GAS-FITTER
FORTNIGHT	FRIGHTFUL	FUSTIGATE	GAS-HOLDER
FORTUNATE	FRIGIDITY	FUSTINESS	GASIFYING
FORTY-FIVE	FRITTERED		GAS-MANTLE
FORWARDED	FRIVOLITY	**G—9**	GASOMETER
FORWARDLY	FRIVOLOUS	GABARDINE	GASPINGLY
FOSSILISE	FRIZZLING	GABERDINE	GAS-RETORT
FOSSORIAL	FROCK-COAT	GADDINGLY	GASTRITIS
FOSTERAGE	FROG-MARCH	GAINFULLY	GASTROPOD
FOSTERING	FROGMOUTH	GAINSAYER	GATE-HOUSE
FOSTER-SON	FROG-SPAWN	GAITERING	GATE-MONEY
FOUNDERED	FROLICKED	GALACTOSE	GATHERING
FOUNDLING	FRONTAGER	GALANTINE	GAUCHERIE
FOUNDRESS	FRONTWARD	GALINGALE	GAUDINESS
FOUR-HORSE	FROSTBITE	GALLANTRY	GAUNTNESS
FOURPENCE	FROSTLESS	GALLERIED	GAVELKIND
FOURPENNY	FROWARDLY	GALLICISE	GAZETTEER
FOUR-SCORE	FRUCTUOUS	GALLICISM	GAZETTING
FOXHUNTER	FRUGALITY	GALLINULE	GEAR-WHEEL
FOXTAILED	FRUIT-CAKE	GALLIVANT	GELIGNITE
FRACTIOUS	FRUIT-TREE	GALLOPING	GEMMATION
FRACTURED	FRUSTRATE	GALLOPADE	GENEALOGY
FRAGILELY	FRUTICOSE	GALL-STONE	GENERALLY
FRAGILITY	FRYING-PAN	GALVANISE	GENERATED
FRAGRANCE	FUGACIOUS	GALVANISM	GENERATOR
FRAGRANCY	FULFILLED	GALVANIST	GENIALITY
FRAILNESS	FULGURITE	GAMBOLLED	GENTEELLY
FRAMEWORK	FULL-BLOWN	GAMMA-RAYS	GENTILITY
FRANCHISE	FULL-DRESS	GAMMONING	GENTLEMAN
FRANCISCA	FULL-FACED	GANG-BOARD	GENUFLECT
FRANGIBLE	FULL-GROWN	GANGRENED	GENUINELY
FRANKNESS	FULL-PITCH	GARDENING	GEOGRAPHY
FRANTICALLY	FULL-SWING	GARIBALDI	GEOLOGISE
FRATERNAL	FULMINANT	GARLANDED	GEOLOGIST
FRAUDLESS	FULMINATE	GARNERING	GEOMETRIC

GERFALCON	GLITTERED	GRAND-AUNT	GRIZZLING
GERMANDER	GLOBE-FISH	GRAND-DUKE	GROOMSMAN
GERMANISM	GLOBOSITY	GRANDIOSE	GROPINGLY
GERMANIUM	GLORIFIED	GRAND-JURY	GROSSNESS
GERMICIDE	GLOWERING	GRANDNESS	GROTESQUE
GERMINANT	GLOWINGLY	GRANDSIRE	GROUNDAGE
GERMINATE	GLUCOSIDE	GRAND-SLAM	GROUND-ASH
GERUNDIAL	GLUEYNESS	GRANULATE	GROUNDING
GERUNDIVE	GLUTINOUS	GRANULOUS	GROUND-IVY
GESTATION	GLYCERIDE	GRAPESHOT	GROUNDNUT
GESTATORY	GLYCERINE	GRAPEVINE	GROUND-OAK
GESTURING	GNAWINGLY	GRAPPLING	GROUNDSEL
GET-AT-ABLE	GOATISHLY	GRASPABLE	GROVELLED
GHOSTLIKE	GO-BETWEEN	GRASS-LAND	GRUELLING
GHOST-MOTH	GODFATHER	GRASSLESS	GRUFFNESS
GIANTLIKE	GODLESSLY	GRASS-PLOT	GRUMBLING
GIBBERING	GODLINESS	GRATIFIED	GRUNDYISM
GIBBERISH	GODMOTHER	GRATINGLY	GUARANTEE
GIDDINESS	GODPARENT	GRATITUDE	GUARANTOR
GIFT-HORSE	GOFFERING	GRAVELESS	GUARD-BOAT
GILL-COVER	GOLDCLOTH	GRAVELLED	GUARDEDLY
GILT-EDGED	GOLDCREST	GRAVEL-PIT	GUARDLESS
GIMLETING	GOLDEN-ROD	GRAVENESS	GUARD-ROOM
GIN-PALACE	GOLDFINCH	GRAVEYARD	GUARDSHIP
GINGERADE	GOLDSMITH	GRAVITATE	GUARDSMAN
GINGER-ALE	GOLF-LINKS	GREATCOAT	GUERRILLA
GINGER-POP	GONDOLIER	GREATNESS	GUESSABLE
GINGLYMUS	GOODNIGHT	GREENBACK	GUESSWORK
GIRANDOLE	GOOSANDER	GREEN-EYED	GUEST-WISE
GIRL-GUIDE	GOOSEFOOT	GREENGAGE	GUIDE-BOOK
GIRLISHLY	GOOSENECK	GREENHORN	GUIDELESS
GIRONDIST	GOOSE-STEP	GREENNESS	GUIDE-POST
GLACIATED	GOOSEWING	GREENROOM	GUIDE-RAIL
GLADDENED	GORGONIAN	GREENSAND	GUIDE-ROPE
GLADIATOR	GOSPELLER	GREENWICH	GUILDHALL
GLADIOLUS	GOSSAMERY	GREENWOOD	GUILELESS
GLADSTONE	GOSSIPING	GREGORIAN	GUILLEMOT
GLAIREOUS	GOTHAMITE	GRENADIER	GUILLOCHE
GLAMOURED	GOUTINESS	GRENADINE	GUILTLESS
GLANDULAR	GOVERNESS	GREYBEARD	GUINEA-PIG
GLARINGLY	GOVERNING	GREYHOUND	GUMMINESS
GLASSLIKE	GRABBLING	GREYSTONE	GUN-BARREL
GLASSWARE	GRACE-NOTE	GRIEVANCE	GUNCOTTON
GLASS-WORK	GRACILITY	GRILL-ROOM	GUNPOWDER
GLASSWORT	GRADATING	GRIMACING	GUNRUNNER
GLENGARRY	GRADATION	GRIMALKIN	GUSHINGLY
GLIDINGLY	GRADATORY	GRIMINESS	GUSTATORY
GLIMMERED	GRADGRIND	GRIPINGLY	GUTTERING
GLIMPSING	GRADUALLY	GRISAILLE	GYMNASIUM
GLISSADED	GRADUATED	GRIST-MILL	GYROSCOPE
GLISTENED	GRADUATOR	GRITSTONE	

H—9	HARDFACED	HEART-WOOD	HIGH BLOWN
HABITABLE	HARDIHOOD	HEATH-CLAD	HIGH-FLIER
HABITABLY	HARDINESS	HEATH-COCK	HIGHFLOWN
HABITUATE	HARDSHELL	HEAVINESS	HIGH-FLYER
HACKNEYED	HARLEQUIN	HEBRIDEAN	HIGH-TONED
HAGGARDLY	HARMFULLY	HECTOGRAM	HIGH-WATER
HAGGISHLY	HARMONICA	HECTORING	HILARIOUS
HAGIOLOGY	HARMONICS	HEDGELESS	HILLINESS
HAG-RIDDEN	HARMONISE	HEEDFULLY	HINDERING
HAILSTONE	HARMONIST	HEEL-PIECE	HINDRANCE
HAILSTORM	HARMONIUM	HEFTINESS	HINDSIGHT
HAIRBROOM	HARNESSED	HEINOUSLY	HINTINGLY
HAIR-BRUSH	HARROVIAN	HEIR-AT-LAW	HIPPOCRAS
HAIR-CLOTH	HARROWING	HELIOGRAM	HISSINGLY
HAIRINESS	HARSHNESS	HELLEBORE	HISTOLOGY
HALF-BLOOD	HARTSHORN	HELLENIAN	HISTORIAN
HALF-BOUND	HARVESTED	HELLENISE	HOAR-FROST
HALF-BREED	HARVESTER	HELLENISM	HOARINESS
HALF-CASTE	HASTINESS	HELLENIST	HOAR-STONE
HALFCROWN	HATCHMENT	HELLBOUND	HOBGOBLIN
HALFPENNY	HATEFULLY	HELLISHLY	HOBNOBBED
HALF-PRICE	HAUGHTILY	HEMICYCLE	HOCUSSING
HALF-ROUND	HAVERSACK	HEMSTITCH	HODOMETER
HALF-SHAFT	HAWK-EAGLE	HENPECKED	HOGBACKED
HALF-TIMER	HAWK-NOSED	HEPATITIS	HOGGISHLY
HALLOWEEN	HAWKSBILL	HEPTARCHY	HOLLANDER
HALTERING	HAWSE-HOLE	HERALDING	HOLLOWING
HALTINGLY	HAYMAKING	HERBALIST	HOLLYHOCK
HAMADRYAD	HAZARDING	HERBARIUM	HOLOCAUST
HAMPERING	HAZARDOUS	HERBIVORE	HOLOGRAPH
HAMSTRING	HEAD-DRESS	HERCULEAN	HOLSTERED
HAMSTRUNG	HEADFRAME	HEREABOUT	HOLYSTONE
HANDBRACE	HEADLINES	HEREAFTER	HOMEBOUND
HANDCUFFS	HEADLIGHT	HERETICAL	HOMESTEAD
HANDGLASS	HEADMONEY	HERITABLE	HOMICIDAL
HANDINESS	HEADPHONE	HERITABLY	HOMOLOGUE
HANDIWORK	HEADPIECE	HERMITAGE	HOMONYMIC
HANDPRESS	HEADSTALL	HERONSHAW	HOMOPHONE
HANDSCREW	HEADSTOCK	HESITANCY	HOMOPHONY
HANDSPIKE	HEADSTONE	HESITATED	HOMOPTERA
HANKERING	HEALINGLY	HETERODOX	HONEY-BEAR
HANSEATIC	HEALTHFUL	HEXACHORD	HONEYCOMB
HAPHAZARD	HEALTHILY	HEXAGONAL	HONEYLESS
HAPPENING	HEARKENED	HEXAMETER	HONEYMOON
HAPPINESS	HEARTACHE	HEXASTYLE	HONEYWORT
HARANGUED	HEARTBURN	HEXATEUCH	HONORIFIC
HARBINGER	HEARTENED	HIBERNATE	HONOURING
HARBOURED	HEARTFELT	HIBERNIAN	HOOKNOSED
HARDBOARD	HEARTHRUG	HIDEBOUND	HOPEFULLY
HARD-BOUND	HEARTLESS	HIDEOUSLY	HOPGARDEN
HARDENING	HEART-SICK	HIERARCHY	HOP-PICKER

HOP-PILLOW	HURTFULLY	IMAGELESS	IMPORTING
HOP-POCKET	HUSBANDED	IMAGINARY	IMPORTUNE
HOP-SCOTCH	HUSBANDRY	IMAGINING	IMPOSABLE
HOREHOUND	HUSHMONEY	IMBROGLIO	IMPOSTURE
HOROSCOPE	HUSKINESS	IMITATING	IMPOTENCE
HOROSCOPY	HYBRIDISE	IMITATION	IMPOTENCY
HORRIFIED	HYBRIDISM	IMITATIVE	IMPOUNDED
HORSEBACK	HYBRIDITY	IMMANENCE	IMPRECATE
HORSE-BEAN	HYDRANGEA	IMMANENCY	IMPRESSED
HORSEHAIR	HYDRAULIC	IMMEDIACY	IMPRINTED
HORSELESS	HYDROLOGY	IMMEDIATE	IMPROMPTU
HORSEMEAT	HYDROSTAT	IMMENSELY	IMPROVING
HORSEPLAY	HYDROXIDE	IMMENSITY	IMPROVISE
HORSEPOND	HYMNOLOGY	IMMERSING	IMPRUDENT
HORSERACE	HYPERBOLA	IMMERSION	IMPUGNING
HORSESHOE	HYPERBOLE	IMMIGRANT	IMPULSION
HORSETAIL	HYPERICUM	IMMIGRATE	IMPULSIVE
HORSEWHIP	HYPHENING	IMMINENCE	IMPUTABLE
HOSTELLER	HYPNOLOGY	IMMODESTY	INABILITY
HOSTILELY	HYPNOTISM	IMMORALLY	INAMORATO
HOSTILITY	HYPNOTIST	IMMOVABLE	INANIMATE
HOT-HEADED	HYPOCAUST	IMMOVABLY	INANITION
HOTTENTOT	HYPOCRISY	IMMUNISED	INAPTNESS
HOUR-GLASS	HYPOCRITE	IMMUTABLE	INARCHING
HOUSE-BOAT	HYSTERICS	IMMUTABLY	INAUDIBLE
HOUSEHOLD		IMPACTING	INAUDIBLY
HOUSE-LEEK		IMPACTION	INAUGURAL
HOUSELESS	I—9	IMPAIRING	INAURATED
HOUSEMAID	ICELANDER	IMPARTIAL	INCAPABLE
HOUSEROOM	ICELANDIC	IMPARTING	INCAPABLY
HOUSEWIFE	ICHNEUMON	IMPASSION	INCARNATE
HOUSEWORK	ICHTHYOID	IMPASSIVE	INCENSING
HOWSOEVER	ICONOLOGY	IMPATIENS	INCENSORY
HUCKABACK	IDEALISED	IMPATIENT	INCENTIVE
HUFFINESS	IDENTICAL	IMPEACHED	INCEPTION
HUFFISHLY	IDEOGRAPH	IMPEDANCE	INCEPTIVE
HUMANISED	IDIOMATIC	IMPELLENT	INCESSANT
HUMANKIND	IGNORAMUS	IMPELLING	INCIDENCE
HUMANNESS	IGNORANCE	IMPENDENT	INCIPIENT
HUMBLE-BEE	IGUANODON	IMPENDING	INCLEMENT
HUMBLE-PIE	ILLEGALLY	IMPERFECT	INCLINING
HUMBUGGED	ILLEGIBLE	IMPERIOUS	INCLUDING
HUMILIATE	ILLEGIBLY	IMPETUOUS	INCLUSION
HUMMOCKED	ILL-HUMOUR	IMPINGING	INCLUSIVE
HUMOURING	ILLIBERAL	IMPIOUSLY	INCOGNITO
HUNCHBACK	ILLICITLY	IMPLANTED	INCOMMODE
HUNDREDTH	ILL-JUDGED	IMPLEMENT	INCORRECT
HUNGARIAN	ILL-NATURE	IMPLICATE	INCORRUPT
HUNGERING	ILLOGICAL	IMPLORING	INCREASED
HURRICANE	ILL-TIMING	IMPOLITIC	INCREMENT
HURRIEDLY	ILLUMINED	IMPORTANT	INCUBATED

INCUBATOR	INFECTION	INNOVATOR	INTERCEPT
INCULCATE	INFECTIVE	INOCULATE	INTERDICT
INCULPATE	INFERENCE	INODORATE	INTERFERE
INCUMBENT	INFERRING	INODOROUS	INTERFOLD
INCURABLE	INFERTILE	INORGANIC	INTERFUSE
INCURABLY	INFESTING	INQUIRING	INTERJECT
INCURIOUS	INFIRMARY	INSATIATE	INTERLACE
INCURRING	INFIRMITY	INSCRIBED	INTERLAID
INCURSION	INFLAMING	INSENSATE	INTERLARD
INCURSIVE	INFLATING	INSERTING	INTERLEAF
INCURVING	INFLATION	INSERTION	INTERLINE
INDECENCY	INFLECTED	INSETTING	INTERLOCK
INDECORUM	INFLEXION	INSIDIOUS	INTERLOPE
INDELIBLE	INFLICTED	INSINCERE	INTERLUDE
INDELIBLY	INFLOWING	INSINUATE	INTERMENT
INDEMNIFY	INFLUENCE	INSIPIDLY	INTERNING
INDEMNITY	INFLUENZA	INSISTENT	INTERNODE
INDENTING	INFOLDING	INSISTING	INTERPLAY
INDENTION	INFORMANT	INSOLENCE	INTERPOSE
INDENTURE	INFORMING	INSOLUBLE	INTERPRET
INDICATED	INFRINGED	INSOLVENT	INTERRING
INDICATOR	INFURIATE	INSPANNED	INTERRUPT
INDICTING	INFUSIBLE	INSPECTED	INTERSECT
INDIGENCE	INFUSORIA	INSPECTOR	INTERVENE
INDIGNANT	INGENIOUS	INSPIRING	INTERVIEW
INDIGNITY	INGENUITY	INSTALLED	INTERWOVE
INDISPOSE	INGENUOUS	INSTANCED	INTESTACY
INDOLENCE	INGESTION	INSTANTLY	INTESTATE
INDRAUGHT	INGLENOOK	INSTIGATE	INTESTINE
INDUCTING	INGRAINED	INSTILLED	INTIMATED
INDUCTION	INGROWING	INSTITUTE	INTONATED
INDUCTIVE	INHABITED	INSULARLY	INTRICACY
INDULGING	INHERENCE	INSULATED	INTRICATE
INDULGENT	INHERITED	INSULATOR	INTRIGUED
INDURATED	INHERITOR	INSULTING	INTRINSIC
INDWELLED	INHABITED	INSURABLE	INTRODUCE
INEBRIATE	INHUMANLY	INSURANCE	INTROVERT
INEBRIETY	INITIALLY	INSURGENT	INTRUDING
INEFFABLE	INITIATED	INTEGRANT	INTRUSION
INEFFABLY	INJECTING	INTEGRATE	INTRUSIVE
INELASTIC	INJECTION	INTEGRITY	INTUITION
INELEGANT	INJURIOUS	INTELLECT	INTUITIVE
INEPTNESS	INJUSTICE	INTENDANT	INUNCTION
INERRABLE	INKBOTTLE	INTENSELY	INUNDATED
INERRABLY	INKHOLDER	INTENSIFY	INUREMENT
INERRANCY	INNERMOST	INTENSION	INUTILITY
INERTNESS	INNERVATE	INTENSITY	INVALIDED
INFANTILE	INNKEEPER	INTENSIVE	INVECTIVE
INFANTINE	INNOCENCE	INTENTION	INVEIGHED
INFATUATE	INNOCUOUS	INTERBRED	INVEIGLED
INFECTING	INNOVATED	INTERCEDE	INVENTING

INVENTION
INVENTIVE
INVENTORY
INVERSELY
INVERSION
INVERTING
INVESTING
INVIDIOUS
INVIOLATE
INVISIBLE
INVISIBLY
INVOICING
INVOLUCRE
INVOLVING
INWROUGHT
IRASCIBLE
IRASCIBLY
IRKSOMELY
IRONBOUND
IRONMOULD
IRONSMITH
IRONSTONE
IRRADIANT
IRRADIATE
IRREGULAR
IRRIGATED
IRRITABLE
IRRITABLY
IRRITANCY
IRRITATED
IRRUPTION
ISINGLASS
ISLAMITIC
ISOLATING
ISOLATION
ISOMETRIC
ISOSCELES
ISRAELITE
ITALICISE
ITERATING
ITERATION
ITERATIVE
ITINERANT
ITINERARY
ITINERATE

J—9
JACARANDA
JACK-KNIFE
JACK-PLANE

JACK-SNIPE
JACK-STRAW
JACK-TOWEL
JACQUERIE
JANISSARY
JANSENISM
JANSENIST
JARRINGLY
JAY-WALKER
JEALOUSLY
JEERINGLY
JELLYFISH
JENNETING
JESSAMINE
JESTINGLY
JEWELLERY
JEWEL-LIKE
JOBMASTER
JOCULARLY
JOINTEDLY
JOINT-HEIR
JOINTRESS
JOLLINESS
JOLLYBOAT
JOLTINGLY
JOSS-HOUSE
JOSS-STICK
JOURNEYED
JOVIALITY
JOYLESSLY
JOCUNDITY
JUDAS-TREE
JUDGEMENT
JUDGESHIP
JUDICIARY
JUDICIOUS
JUICELESS
JUICINESS
JUMPINESS
JUNIORITY
JURIDICAL
JUSTICIAR
JUSTIFIED
JUTTINGLY
JUVENILIA
JUXTAPOSE

K—9
KENNELLED
KENTLEDGE
KERBSTONE

KERNELLED
KIDNAPPED
KIDNAPPER
KILDERKIN
KILN-DRIED
KILOLITRE
KILOMETRE
KINGCRAFT
KINSWOMAN
KIPPERING
KITCHENER
KITTENISH
KITTIWAKE
KNAVISHLY
KNEADABLE
KNEE-PIECE
KNIFE-EDGE
KNIFE-REST
KNIGHTAGE
KNIGHTING
KNITTABLE
KNOCKDOWN
KNOTGRASS
KNOWINGLY
KNOWLEDGE
KNUCKLING
KYMOGRAPH

L—9
LABELLING
LABORIOUS
LABOURING
LABYRINTH
LACE-CORAL
LACE-FRAME
LACERATED
LACHRYMAL
LACTATION
LAGGINGLY
LAIRDSHIP
LAMB'S-WOOL
LAMELLATE
LAMENTING
LAMINATED
LAMPBLACK
LAMPLIGHT
LAMPOONED
LANCEWOOD
LAND-AGENT
LANDAULET
LAND-FORCE

LANDGRAVE
LANDOWNER
LANDSCAPE
LAND-SHARK
LANDSLIDE
LANGUIDLY
LANKINESS
LANTHANUM
LAODICEAN
LARCENOUS
LARGENESS
LARGHETTO
LASSITUDE
LASTINGLY
LATERALLY
LATHERING
LATTICING
LAUDATION
LAUDATORY
LAUGHABLE
LAUGHABLY
LAUNCHING
LAUNDERER
LAUNDRESS
LAURELLED
LAVISHING
LAWGIVING
LAWLESSLY
LAWMAKING
LAWMONGER
LAWNMOWER
LAY-FIGURE
LAZARETTO
LEADINGLY
LEAFINESS
LEAF-METAL
LEAF-MOULD
LEAFSTALK
LEAKINESS
LEAN-FACED
LEAPINGLY
LEARNABLE
LEARNEDLY
LEASEHOLD
LEASTWAYS
LEASTWISE
LEAVENING
LECHERING
LECHEROUS
LECTURING
LEERINGLY

LEGALISED	LIMOUSINE	LONG-DOZEN	MAELSTROM
LEGENDARY	LIMPIDITY	LONGEVITY	MAFFICKED
LEGER-LINE	LIMPINGLY	LONG-FIELD	MAGICALLY
LEGIONARY	LINCRUSTA	LONGINGLY	MAGNESIAN
LEGISLATE	LINEALITY	LONGITUDE	MAGNESIUM
LEISURELY	LINEAMENT	LOOSENESS	MAGNETISE
LEIT-MOTIF	LINEATION	LOQUACITY	MAGNETISM
LENGTHILY	LINGERING	LORGNETTE	MAGNETITE
LENIENTLY	LION-HEART	LOUSINESS	MAGNIFICO
LEPROUSLY	LIONISING	LOUTISHLY	MAGNIFIED
LESSENING	LIQUATING	LOVE-APPLE	MAGNITUDE
LETHARGIC	LIQUATION	LOVE-CHILD	MAHARANEE
LETTER-BOX	LIQUEFIED	LOVE-FEAST	MAHOMEDAN
LETTERING	LIQUIDATE	LOWERMOST	MAILCOACH
LEUCOCYTE	LIQUIDITY	LOWLANDER	MAIL-GUARD
LEVANTINE	LIQUORICE	LOWLINESS	MAIL-TRAIN
LEVANTING	LIQUORISH	LOW-MINDED	MAIN-BRACE
LEVELLING	LISPINGLY	LOW-NECKED	MAINSHEET
LEVELNESS	LISTENING	LUBRICANT	MAJORDOMO
LEVIATHAN	LITERALLY	LUBRICATE	MAJORSHIP
LEVITICUS	LITERATIM	LUBRICITY	MAKE-PEACE
LIABILITY	LITHENESS	LUBRICOUS	MAKESHIFT
LIBELLING	LITHESOME	LUCIDNESS	MALACHITE
LIBELLOUS	LITHOLOGY	LUCK-PENNY	MALADROIT
LIBERALLY	LITHOTINT	LUCRATIVE	MALARIOUS
LIBERATED	LITHOTYPE	LUCUBRATE	MALFORMED
LIBERATOR	LITIGABLE	LUCULLIAN	MALICIOUS
LIBERTINE	LITIGATED	LUDICROUS	MALIGNING
LIBRARIAN	LITIGIOUS	LUMBERMAN	MALIGNANT
LIBRATION	LITTERING	LUMBRICAL	MALIGNITY
LICENSING	LITURGIST	LUMPISHLY	MALLEABLE
LICHENOUS	LIVERWORT	LUNISOLAR	MALLEOLUS
LIFEBLOOD	LIVERYMAN	LUSTFULLY	MALMAISON
LIFEGUARD	LIVIDNESS	LUSTINESS	MAMMALIAN
LIGHTABLE	LOADSTONE	LUXURIANT	MAMMALOGY
LIGHTENED	LOAF-SUGAR	LUXURIATE	MANNIFORM
LIGHTLESS	LOATHSOME	LUXURIOUS	MANACLING
LIGHTNESS	LOBSCOUSE	LYMPHATIC	MAN-AT-ARMS
LIGHTNING	LOCKSMITH		MANCUNIAN
LIGHTSHIP	LOCOMOTOR	M—9	MANDATORY
LIGHTSTONE	LODESTONE	MACCABEAN	MANDOLINE
LIGHT-YEAR	LODGEABLE	MACCABEES	MANDUCATE
LILACEOUS	LOFTINESS	MACEDOINE	MANGANESE
LIME-JUICE	LOGARITHM	MACERATED	MANGINESS
LIMELIGHT	LOGICALLY	MACHINATE	MAN-HANDLE
LIMESTONE	LOGISTICS	MACHINERY	MANIFESTO
LIME-WATER	LOGOGRIPH	MACHINING	MANLINESS
LIMITABLE	LOGOMACHY	MACHINIST	MANNEQUIN
LIMITEDLY	LOLLOPING	MACROCOSM	MANNERISM
LIMITLESS	LOITERING	MADDENING	MANNISHLY
LIMNOLOGY	LONGCLOTH	MADREPORE	MANOEUVRE

MANOMETER	MEALINESS	MESMERISE	MILLEPEDE
MANY-SIDED	MEANDERED	MESMERISM	MILLIGRAM
MARAUDING	MEANINGLY	MESSENGER	MILLINERY
MARCASITE	MEANWHILE	MESSIANIC	MILLIONTH
MARCHPANE	MEASURING	MESSINESS	MILLIPEDE
MARESCHAL	MEATINESS	METABOLIC	MILLSTONE
MARGARINE	MECHANICS	METALLING	MILL WHEEL
MARGINING	MECHANISE	METALLISE	MIMICKING
MARINATED	MECHANIST	METALLIST	MINCEMEAT
MARITALLY	MEDALLION	METALLOID	MINCINGLY
MARKET-DAY	MEDALLIST	METAMERIC	MINEFIELD
MARKETING	MEDIAEVAL	METAPLASM	MINELAYER
MARMALADE	MEDIATING	METEOROID	MINIATURE
MARMOREAL	MEDIATION	METHODISM	MINIMISED
MAROONING	MEDIATORY	METHODIST	MINT-JULEP
MARQUETRY	MEDICABLE	METHOUGHT	MINT-SAUCE
MARROWFAT	MEDICALLY	METHYLATE	MINUTE-GUN
MARROWISH	MEDICATED	METHYLENE	MIRRORING
MARSHLAND	MEDICINAL	METROLOGY	MIRTHLESS
MARSUPIAL	MEDITATED	METRONOME	MISALLIED
MARTIALLY	MEDULLARY	MEZZANINE	MISATTEND
MARTINMAS	MEGAPHONE	MEZZOTINT	MISBECAME
MARTYRING	MEGASCOPE	MICACEOUS	MISBECOME
MARTYRDOM	MELANOSIS	MICROBIAL	MISBEHAVE
MARVELLED	MELIORISM	MICROCOSM	MISBELIEF
MASCULINE	MELLOWING	MICROFILM	MISCALLED
MASSACRED	MELODIOUS	MICROTOME	MISCHANCE
MASSAGING	MELODRAMA	MICROVOLT	MISCREANT
MASSIVELY	MELPOMENE	MIDDLEMAN	MISDATING
MASTERDOM	MELTINGLY	MIDDLINGS	MISDIRECT
MASTERFUL	MEMORABLE	MIDINETTE	MISEMPLOY
MASTERING	MEMORABLY	MID-STREAM	MISERABLE
MASTICATE	MEMORANDA	MID-SUMMER	MISERABLY
MATCHLESS	MEMORISED	MIDWIFERY	MISFORMED
MATCHLOCK	MENAGERIE	MIDWINTER	MISGIVING
MATCHWOOD	MENDACITY	MIGRATING	MISGOTTEN
MATERNITY	MENDELIAN	MIGRATION	MISGOVERN
MATRIARCH	MENDELISM	MIGRATORY	MISGUIDED
MATRICIDE	MENDICITY	MILDEWING	MISHANDLE
MATRIMONY	MENNONITE	MILESTONE	MISINFORM
MATRONAGE	MENSHEVIK	MILITANCY	MISJOINED
MATTERING	MENTALITY	MILITATED	MISJUDGED
MAULSTICK	MENTIONED	MILK-FEVER	MISLAYING
MAUNDERED	MERCENARY	MILK-FLOAT	MIS-MANAGE
MAUSOLEUM	MERCILESS	MILKINESS	MISMARKED
MAWKISHLY	MERCURIAL	MILK-PUNCH	MISNAMING
MAXILLARY	MERCUROUS	MILK-TOOTH	MISPLACED
MAXIMISED	MERCY-SEAT	MILK-VETCH	MISQUOTED
MAYFLOWER	MERGANSER	MILL-BOARD	MISRATING
MAYORALTY	MERRIMENT	MILLENARY	MISREPORT
MEADOW-RUE	MERRINESS	MILLENIAL	MISRULING

MISSHAPED	MONOCHORD	MUDDINESS	NASEBERRY
MISSHAPEN	MONOCOQUE	MULLIONED	NASTINESS
MISSIONER	MONOCULAR	MULTIFORM	NATURALLY
MISSTATED	MONODRAMA	MULTITUDE	NAUGHTILY
MISTAKING	MONOGRAPH	MUMCHANCE	NAUSEATED
MISTAUGHT	MONOLOGUE	MUMMIFIED	NAVELWORT
MISTIMING	MONOMANIA	MUMMIFORM	NAVICULAR
MISTINESS	MONOMETER	MUNDANELY	NAVIGABLE
MISTITLED	MONOPLANE	MUNICIPAL	NAVIGATED
MISTLETOE	MONOTONIC	MUNITIONS	NAVIGATOR
MISTUNING	MONOTREME	MURDERING	NECESSARY
MITHRAISM	MONSIGNOR	MURDERESS	NECESSITY
MITIGATED	MONSTROUS	MURDEROUS	NECK-CLOTH
MNEMONICS	MOODINESS	MURKINESS	NECKLACED
MNEMOSYNE	MOON-DAISY	MURMURING	NECK-PIECE
MOANFULLY	MOONLIGHT	MURMUROUS	NECTARINE
MOBILISED	MOONRAKER	MUSCADINE	NEEDFULLY
MOCKINGLY	MOONSHINE	MUSCOVITE	NEEDINESS
MODELLING	MOONSHINY	MUSEFULLY	NEEDLEFUL
MODERATED	MOONSTONE	MUSHINESS	NEEDLE-GUN
MODERATOR	MORALISED	MUSICALLY	NEFARIOUS
MODERNISE	MORBIDITY	MUSIC-BOOK	NEGATIVED
MODERNISM	MORDACITY	MUSIC-HALL	NEGLECTED
MODERNIST	MORDANTLY	MUSK-APPLE	NEGLIGENT
MODERNITY	MORMONISM	MUSKETEER	NEGOTIATE
MODIFYING	MORTALITY	MUSKINESS	NEGROHEAD
MODULATED	MORTGAGED	MUSK-MELON	NEIGHBOUR
MODULATOR	MORTGAGEE	MUSK-SHREW	NEOLITHIC
MOISTENED	MORTGAGOR	MUSSULMAN	NEPENTHES
MOISTNESS	MORTIFIED	MUSTACHIO	NEPTUNIAN
MOLECULAR	MORTISING	MUSTERING	NERVELESS
MOLE-SHREW	MOSCHATEL	MUSTINESS	NERVOUSLY
MOLESTING	MOSS-GROWN	MUTILATED	NEURALGIA
MOLETRACK	MOSSINESS	MUTINYING	NEURALGIC
MOLLIFIED	MOTHERING	MUTUALITY	NEURATION
MOLLUSCAN	MOTIONING	MUZZINESS	NEUROLOGY
MOMENTARY	MOTOR-BOAT	MYSTICISM	NEUROPATH
MOMENTOUS	MOULDABLE	MYSTIFIED	NEUROTOMY
MONARCHAL	MOULDERED	MYTHICISE	NEUTRALLY
MONARCHIC	MOULD-LOFT	MYTHOLOGY	NEVERMORE
MONASTERY	MOULD-WARP		NEWSPAPER
MONDAYISH	MOUND-BIRD	**N—9**	NEWTONIAN
MONETISED	MOUNTABLE	NAILBRUSH	NICKNAMED
MONEYLESS	MOUSE-HOLE	NAKEDNESS	NICTITATE
MONEYWORT	MOUSE-HUNT	NAMEPLATE	NIGGARDLY
MONGERING	MOUSE-TAIL	NARCISSUS	NIGHT-CLUB
MONGOLIAN	MOUSE-TRAP	NARRATING	NIGHT-FALL
MONKEYING	MOUSTACHE	NARRATION	NIGHT-GOWN
MONKEY-NUT	MOUTHLESS	NARRATIVE	NIGHT-HAWK
MONKSHOOD	MUCKINESS	NARROWING	NIGHT-LESS
MONOBASIC	MUCK-SWEAT	NASALISED	NIGHT-LINE

NIGHTMARE	O—9	ODDFELLOW	ORDAINING
NIGHT-SOIL	OAST-HOUSE	ODOROUSLY	ORDINANCE
NINETIETH	OBBLIGATO	ODOURLESS	ORGANZINE
NIPPINGLY	OBEDIENCE	OENOTHERA	ORGIASTIC
NITRIFIED	OBEISANCE	OFFENSIVE	ORIENTATE
NOBLENESS	OBESENESS	OFFERABLE	ORIFLAMME
NOCTURNAL	OBEYINGLY	OFFERTORY	ORIGINATE
NOISELESS	OBFUSCATE	OFFHANDED	ORPHANAGE
NOISINESS	OBJECTIFY	OFFICERED	ORTHODOXY
NOISOMELY	OBJECTION	OFFICIANT	OSCILLATE
NOMINALLY	OBJECTIVE	OFFICIATE	OSCULATED
NOMINATED	OBJURGATE	OFFICINAL	OSSIFYING
NOMINATOR	OBLIGATED	OFFICIOUS	OSTEOLOGY
NONENTITY	OBLIQUELY	OFFSPRING	OSTEOPATH
NONILLION	OBLIQUITY	OFTENNESS	OSTRACISE
NONPAREIL	OBLIVIOUS	OIL-COLOUR	OTHERNESS
NON-SEXUAL	OBLONGISH	OIL-ENGINE	OTHERWISE
NONSUITED	OBNOXIOUS	OLEOGRAPH	OUT-AND-OUT
NORMALISE	OBSCENELY	OLEOMETER	OUTBRAVED
NORMALITY	OBSCENITY	OLEORESIN	OUTERMOST
NORTH-EAST	OBSCURANT	OLFACTORY	OUTFACING
NORTHERLY	OBSCURELY	OLIGARCHY	OUTGROWTH
NORTHWARD	OBSCURING	OLIGOCENE	OUT-JOCKEY
NORTH-WEST	OBSCURITY	OLIVE-YARD	OUTLANDER
NORWEGIAN	OBSEQUIAL	OMINOUSLY	OUTLASTED
NOSEPIECE	OBSERVANT	OMISSIBLE	OUTLAWING
NOSTALGIA	OBSERVING	ON-LICENCE	OUTLEAPED
NOSTALGIC	OBSESSION	ONSETTING	OUTLINING
NOTEPAPER	OBSTETRIC	ONSLAUGHT	OUTLIVING
NOTIFYING	OBSTINACY	OPALESCED	OUTMANNED
NOTORIETY	OBSTINATE	OPALISING	OUTNUMBER
NOTORIOUS	OBTAINING	OPERATING	OUT-OF-DOOR
NOURISHED	OBTRUDING	OPERATION	OUTPACING
NOVELETTE	OBTRUSION	OPERATISE	OUTPLAYED
NOVICIATE	OBTRUSIVE	OPERATIVE	OUTRAGING
NOVITIATE	OBVERSION	OPPORTUNE	OUTRANGED
NOXIOUSLY	OBVERSELY	OPPOSABLE	OUTRIDDEN
NULLIFIED	OBVERTING	OPPRESSED	OUTRIDING
NUMBERING	OBVIATING	OPPRESSOR	OUTRIGGED
NUMERABLE	OBVIOUSLY	OPTOMETER	OUTRIGGER
NUMERALLY	OCCIPITAL	OPTOPHONE	OUTSAILED
NUMERATED	OCCLUDING	OPULENTLY	OUTSPOKEN
NUMERATOR	OCCLUSION	OPUSCULUM	OUTSPREAD
NUMERICAL	OCCULTISM	ORANGEADE	OUTSTARED
NURSEMAID	OCCUPANCY	ORANGE-MAN	OUT-TALKED
NURTURING	OCCUPYING	ORANGE-MEN	OUTVALUED
NUTRIMENT	OCCURRING	ORANGE-PIP	OUTVOTING
NUTRITION	OCTAGONAL	ORATORIAL	OUTWARDLY
NUTRITIVE	OCTENNIAL	ORBICULAR	OUTWITTED
NUTTINESS	OCTILLION	ORCHESTRA	OUTWORKED
NYSTAGMUS	ODALISQUE	ORCHIDIST	OVERACTED

OVERAWING	PAGEANTRY	PAROCHIAL	PEDALLING
OVERBLOWN	PAINFULLY	PARODYING	PEDICULAR
OVERBOARD	PALANQUIN	PAROTITIS	PEDOMETER
OVERBUILD	PALATABLE	PARQUETRY	PEEVISHLY
OVERCLOUD	PALAVERED	PARRICIDE	PEKINGESE
OVERCROWD	PALE-FACED	PARSIMONY	PELLITORY
OVERDOING	PALISADED	PARSONAGE	PENALISED
OVERDOSED	PALLADIAN	PARTAKING	PEN-AND-INK
OVERDRAFT	PALLADIUM	PARTHENON	PENCILLED
OVERDRIVE	PALLIASSE	PARTIALLY	PENDRAGON
OVERHASTY	PALLIATED	PARTITION	PENDULOUS
OVERJOYED	PALM-HOUSE	PARTITIVE	PENETRATE
OVERLADEN	PALMISTRY	PARTNERED	PENHOLDER
OVERLEAPT	PALPITATE	PARTRIDGE	PENINSULA
OVERLYING	PAMPERING	PASSENGER	PENITENCE
OVERNIGHT	PANCAKING	PASSERINE	PENNIFORM
OVERPOWER	PANDERING	PASSIVELY	PENNILESS
OVERPROOF	PANEGYRIC	PASSIVITY	PENNYWISE
OVERRATED	PANELLING	PASTORALE	PENNYWORT
OVERREACH	PANHANDLE	PASTURAGE	PENSIONED
OVERRULED	PANOPLIED	PASTURING	PENSIONER
OVERSHOOT	PANORAMIC	PATCHOULI	PENSIVELY
OVERSIGHT	PANSLAVIC	PATCHWORK	PENTAGRAM
OVERSLEEP	PANTALOON	PATENTING	PENTECOST
OVERSPEND	PANTHEISM	PATERNITY	PENTHOUSE
OVERSTATE	PANTHEIST	PATHOLOGY	PENURIOUS
OVERSTOCK	PANTINGLY	PATIENTLY	PEPPERBOX
OVERTAKEN	PANTOMIME	PATRIARCH	PEPPERING
OVERTHROW	PAPER-MILL	PATRICIAN	PERCEIVED
OVERTRUMP	PAPILLARY	PATRICIDE	PERCHANCE
OVERVALUE	PARABOLIC	PATRIMONY	PERCHERON
OVERWEIGHT	PARACHUTE	PATRIOTIC	PERCOLATE
OVERWHELM	PARACLETE	PATRISTIC	PERCUSSED
OVERWOUND	PARAGRAPH	PATROLLED	PERDITION
OVIPAROUS	PARALYSED	PATRONAGE	PEREGRINE
OWNERSHIP	PARALYSIS	PATRONESS	PERENNIAL
OXIDATION	PARALYTIC	PATRONISE	PERFECTED
OXIDISING	PARAMOUNT	PATTERING	PERFECTLY
OXYGENATE	PARASITIC	PATTERNED	PERFERVID
OXYGENIZE	PARATAXIS	PAUPERISE	PERFORATE
OXYGENOUS	PARBOILED	PAUSINGLY	PERFORMED
OYSTER-BED	PARBUCKLE	PAYMASTER	PERFORMER
	PARCELLED	PEACEABLE	PERFUMERY
P—9	PARCHMENT	PEACEABLY	PERFUMING
PACEMAKER	PARDONING	PEA-JACKET	PERIMETER
PACHYDERM	PAREGORIC	PEARL-WORT	PERIPHERY
PACIFYING	PARENTAGE	PEASANTRY	PERISCOPE
PACKETING	PARGETING	PECULATED	PERISHING
PACKHORSE	PARHELION	PECUNIARY	PERISTYLE
PADLOCKED	PARLEYING	PEDAGOGIC	PERJURING
PAGANISED	PARLEYVOO	PEDAGOGUE	PERMANENT

PERMEABLE	PHOSPHATE	PLACARDED	PLUTONIUM
PERMEABLY	PHOSPHINE	PLACATING	PNEUMATIC
PERMEATED	PHOSPHITE	PLACE-KICK	PNEUMONIA
PERMITTED	PHOTO-PLAY	PLACIDITY	PNEUMONIC
PERMUTING	PHOTO-STAT	PLAINNESS	POCKETING
PERORATED	PHRENETIC	PLAIN-SONG	POETASTER
PERPENDED	PHYSICIAN	PLAINTIFF	POIGNANCY
PERPETUAL	PHYSICIST	PLAINTIVE	POINTEDLY
PERPLEXED	PHYSICKED	PLANE-IRON	POINTLESS
PERSECUTE	PICKABACK	PLANETARY	POINTSMAN
PERSEVERE	PICKETING	PLANETOID	POISONOUS
PERSIMMON	PICTORIAL	PLANTABLE	POKERWORK
PERSISTED	PICTURING	PLASTERED	POLARIZED
PERSONAGE	PIECEMEAL	PLASTERER	POLEMICAL
PERSONATE	PIECE-WORK	PLATEMARK	POLE-VAULT
PERSONIFY	PIER-GLASS	PLATE-RACK	POLICEMAN
PERSONNEL	PIETISTIC	PLATINISE	POLISHING
PERSPIRED	PIGHEADED	PLATITUDE	POLITESSE
PERSUADED	PIGMENTAL	PLATONISE	POLITICAL
PERTAINED	PIGNORATE	PLATONISM	POLLINATE
PERTINENT	PIKESTAFF	PLATONIST	POLLUTING
PERTURBED	PILFERING	PLAUSIBLE	POLLUTION
PERVADING	PILLAR-BOX	PLAUSIBLY	POLONAISE
PERVASION	PILLORIED	PLAY-ACTOR	POLYANDRY
PERVASIVE	PILLOWING	PLAYFULLY	POLYGONAL
PERVERTED	PILOT-BOAT	PLAYGOING	POLYSTYLE
PESSIMISM	PILOTFISH	PLAYHOUSE	POMMELLED
PESSIMIST	PIMPERNEL	PLAYTHING	POMPADOUR
PESTERING	PINCHBECK	PLEACHING	POMPOSITY
PESTILENT	PINEAPPLE	PLEASANCE	POMPOUSLY
PESTOLOGY	PINIONING	PLENARILY	PONDERING
PETERSHAM	PINNACLED	PLENITUDE	PONDEROUS
PETRIFIED	PIONEERED	PLENTEOUS	POOR-HOUSE
PETROLEUM	PIPESTONE	PLENTIFUL	POPPY-COCK
PETTICOAT	PIPISTREL	PLEURITIC	POPULARLY
PETTINESS	PIQUANTLY	PLIGHTING	POPULATED
PETTISHLY	PIRATICAL	PLINTHITE	PORBEAGLE
PETULANCE	PIROUETTE	PLOUGHBOY	PORCELAIN
PHAGOCYTE	PISCATORY	PLOUGHING	PORCUPINE
PHALANGER	PISCIFORM	PLOUGHMAN	PORRINGER
PHALAROPE	PISTACHIO	PLUMBLINE	PORTATIVE
PHARISAIC	PITCHFORK	PLUMB-RULE	PORTENDED
PHENOMENA	PITCH-PINE	PLUMELESS	PORTERAGE
PHILANDER	PITCHPIPE	PLUMPNESS	PORTERESS
PHILATELY	PITEOUSLY	PLUNDERED	PORTFOLIO
PHILIPPIC	PITHECOID	PLURALISE	PORTRAYAL
PHILOLOGY	PITHINESS	PLURALISM	PORTRAYED
PHLEBITIS	PITIFULLY	PLURALIST	POSSESSED
PHONETICS	PITUITARY	PLURALITY	POSSESSOR
PHONOGRAM	PITYINGLY	PLUS-FOURS	POST-DATED
PHONOLOGY	PIZZICATO	PLUTOCRAT	POST-ENTRY

POSTERIOR	PREDICTED	PRIESTESS	PRONENESS
POSTERITY	PREDOOMED	PRIMARILY	PRONOUNCE
POST-HASTE	PRE-ENGAGE	PRIMATIAL	PROOFLESS
POST-NATAL	PREFACING	PRIMITIVE	PROPAGATE
POSTPONED	PREFATORY	PRINCEDOM	PROPELLED
POSTULANT	PREFERRED	PRINCIPAL	PROPELLER
POSTULATE	PREFIGURE	PRINCIPIA	PROPHETIC
POSTURING	PREFIXING	PRINCIPLE	PROPONENT
POTASSIUM	PREFORMED	PRINTLESS	PROPOSING
POTBOILER	PREGNANCY	PRINTSHOP	PROPRIETY
POTENTATE	PREJUDGED	PRISMATIC	PROROGUED
POTENTIAL	PREJUDICE	PRIVATEER	PROSCRIBE
POT-POURRI	PRELATURE	PRIVATELY	PROSECUTE
POTTERING	PRELUDING	PRIVATION	PROSELYTE
POULTERER	PRELUSIVE	PRIVILEGE	PROSINESS
POULTICED	PREMATURE	PROBATION	PROSODIST
POUNCE-BOX	PREMISING	PROBATIVE	PROSPERED
POURBOIRE	PREMOTION	PROBOSCIS	PROSTRATE
POURPOINT	PREOCCUPY	PROCEDURE	PROTECTED
POWDER-BOX	PREOPTION	PROCEEDED	PROTECTOR
POWDERING	PREORDIAN	PROCESSED	PROTESTED
POWERLESS	PREPACKED	PROCLITIC	PROTHESIS
POWER-LOOM	PREPARING	PRO-CONSUL	PROTOTYPE
POW-WOWING	PREPAYING	PROCREANT	PROTOZOAN
PRACTICAL	PRESAGING	PROCREATE	PROTOZOIC
PRACTISED	PRESBYTER	PROCURING	PROTRUDED
PRAGMATIC	PRESCIENT	PRODUCING	PROUDNESS
PRATINGLY	PRESCRIBE	PROFANELY	PROVENDER
PRATTLING	PRESCRIPT	PROFANING	PROVIDENT
PRAYERFUL	PRESENTED	PROFANITY	PROVIDING
PRAYINGLY	PRESENTLY	PROFESSED	PROVISION
PREACHIFY	PRESERVED	PROFESSOR	PROVISORY
PREACHING	PRESERVER	PROFFERED	PROVOKING
PREAMBLED	PRESIDENT	PROFILING	PROXIMATE
PREBENDAL	PRESIDING	PROFITEER	PROXIMITY
PRECEDENT	PRESSGANG	PROFITING	PRUDENTLY
PRECEDING	PRESSMARK	PROFUSELY	PRUDISHLY
PRECENTOR	PRESS-ROOM	PROFUSION	PRURIENCE
PRECEPTOR	PRESSWORK	PROGNOSIS	PRURIENCY
PRECIPICE	PRESUMING	PROGRAMME	PSALMODIC
PRECISELY	PRETENDED	PROJECTED	PSEUDONYM
PRECISIAN	PRETENDER	PROJECTOR	PSORIASIS
PRECISION	PRETERITE	PROLIXITY	PSYCHICAL
PRECLUDED	PRETTYISH	PROLOGUED	PSYCHOSIS
PRECOCITY	PREVAILED	PROLONGED	PTARMIGAN
PRECURSOR	PREVALENT	PROMENADE	PTOLEMAIC
PREDATING	PREVENTED	PROMINENT	PUBESCENT
PREDATORY	PREVISION	PROMISING	PUBLICISE
PREDESIGN	PRICELESS	PROMOTING	PUBLICIST
PREDICANT	PRICKLING	PROMOTION	PUBLICITY
PREDICATE	PRIDELESS	PROMPTING	PUBLISHED

PUBLISHER	PYRAMIDAL	QUOTATION	RAVELLING
PUCKERING	PYROGENIC	QUOTELESS	RAVISHING
PUERILELY	PYROLATRY		RAZORBACK
PUERILITY	PYROMANCY	**R—9**	RAZORBILL
PUERPERAL	PYROMANIA	RABBETING	RAZOREDGE
PUFF-ADDER	PYROMETER	RABBINATE	RAZORFISH
PUFFINESS	PYROXYLIC	RABBINISM	REACHABLE
PUFFINGLY	PYROXYLIN	RABBINIST	REACTANCE
PUGNACITY		RABBITING	READDRESS
PUISSANCE	**Q—9**	RABIDNESS	READINESS
PULLULATE	QUADRATIC	RACEHORSE	READJOURN
PULMONARY	QUADRATED	RACIALISM	READOPTED
PULMONATE	QUADRILLE	RACKETING	READORNED
PULPINESS	QUADRUPED	RACONTEUR	READY-MADE
PULSATING	QUADRUPLE	RADIALITY	REALISING
PULSATILE	QUAKERISH	RADIANTLY	REALISTIC
PULSATION	QUAKERISM	RADIATING	REALLEGED
PULSATIVE	QUAKINGLY	RADIATION	REANIMATE
PULSATORY	QUALIFIED	RADIATIVE	REANNEXED
PULSELESS	QUARRYING	RADICALLY	REAPPLIED
PULVERISE	QUARRYMAN	RADIOLOGY	REAPPOINT
PUNCHBOWL	QUARTERED	RAFTERING	REAR-GUARD
PUNCTILIO	QUARTERLY	RAG-PICKER	REARRANGE
PUNCTUATE	QUARTETTE	RAIL-FENCE	REASONING
PUNCTURED	QUARTZITE	RAILINGLY	REASSURED
PUNGENTLY	QUASIMODO	RAIN-GAUGE	REAVOWING
PUNISHING	QUAVERING	RAININESS	REBAPTISE
PUPILLARY	QUEEN-POST	RAINPROOF	REBELLING
PUPPYHOOD	QUEERNESS	RAIN-WATER	REBELLION
PURCHASED	QUENCHING	RAJAHSHIP	REBINDING
PURCHASER	QUERULOUS	RAMIFYING	REBLOOMED
PURGATION	QUIBBLING	RAMPAGING	REBOILING
PURGATIVE	QUICKENED	RAMPANTLY	REBOUNDED
PURGATORY	QUICKLIME	RAMPARTED	REBUFFING
PURIFYING	QUICKNESS	RANCIDITY	REBURYING
PURITANIC	QUICKSAND	RANCOROUS	REBUTTING
PURLOINED	QUICKSTEP	RANSACKED	RECALLING
PURPORTED	QUICK-TIME	RANSOMING	RECANTING
PURPOSELY	QUIESCENT	RANTINGLY	RECAPTURE
PURPOSING	QUIESCING	RAPACIOUS	RECASTING
PURPOSIVE	QUIETENED	RAPIDNESS	RECEIPTED
PURSUANCE	QUIETNESS	RAPTORIAL	RECEIVING
PURULENCE	QUINQUINA	RAPTUROUS	RECENSION
PURVEYING	QUINTETTE	RAREE-SHOW	RECEPTION
PUSHINGLY	QUINTUPLE	RAREFYING	RECEPTIVE
PUSTULATE	QUIT-CLAIM	RASCALITY	RECESSING
PUTREFIED	QUITTABLE	RASPATORY	RECESSION
PUTRIDITY	QUITTANCE	RASPBERRY	RECESSIVE
PUZZLEDOM	QUIVERING	RATEPAYER	RECHARGED
PYORRHOEA	QUIXOTISM	RATIONALE	RECHERCHE
PYRACANTH	QUIZZICAL	RATIONING	RECIPIENT

RECKONING	REDOLENCE	REGARDING	RELOADING
RECLAIMED	REDOUBLED	REGICIDAL	RELUCTANT
RECLINATE	REDOUBTED	REGILDING	REMAINDER
RECLINING	REDOUNDED	REGISTRAR	REMAINING
RECLOSING	REDRAFTED	REGORGING	REMANDING
RECLOTHED	REDRAWING	REGRANTED	REMANNING
RECOALING	REDRESSED	REGRADING	REMARKING
RECOASTED	REDUCIBLE	REGRETFUL	REMARRIED
RECOGNISE	REDUCTION	REGRETTED	REMEDYING
RECOILING	REDUNDANT	REGULARLY	REMINDFUL
RECOINING	RE-ECHOING	REGULATED	REMINDING
RECOLLECT	RE-ELECTED	REGULATOR	REMISSION
RECOMBINE	RE-EMERGED	REHANDLED	REMISSIVE
RECOMMEND	RE-ENACTED	REHANGING	REMITTING
RECOMPILE	RE-ENFORCE	REHASHING	REMOULDED
RECOMPOSE	RE-ENTERED	REHEARING	REMOUNTED
RECONCILE	RE-ENTRANT	REHEARSAL	REMOVABLE
RECONDITE	RE-EXAMINE	REHEARSED	RENASCENT
RECONFIRM	REFASHION	RE-HEATING	RENDERING
RECONQUER	REFECTION	REHOUSING	RENDITION
RECONVENE	REFECTORY	REICHSTAG	RENEWABLE
RECONVERT	REFERENCE	RE-IGNITED	RENOVATED
RECORDING	REFERRING	REIMBURSE	RENOVATOR
RECOUNTED	REFILLING	REINFORCE	REOPENING
RECOUPING	REFINEDLY	REINSTALL	REORDERED
RECOVERED	REFITMENT	REINSTATE	REPACKING
RECREANCY	REFITTING	REINSURED	REPAINTED
RECREATED	REFLECTED	REISSUING	REPAIRING
RECREMENT	REFLOATED	REITERATE	REPARABLE
RECROSSED	REFLOWING	REJECTING	REPARABLY
RECRUITED	REFOLDING	REJECTION	REPASSING
RECTANGLE	REFORGING	REJECTIVE	REPASTING
RECTIFIED	REFORMING	REJOICING	REPAYABLE
RECTIFIER	REFORMIST	REJOINDER	REPAYMENT
RECTITUDE	REFORTIFY	REJOINING	REPEALING
RECTORATE	RE-FOUNDED	REJOINTED	REPEATING
RECTORIAL	REFRACTED	REJUDGING	REPELLENT
RECUMBENT	REFRACTOR	REKINDLED	REPELLING
RECURRENT	REFRAINED	RELANDING	REPENTANT
RECURRING	REFRAMING	RELAPSING	REPENTING
RECURVATE	REFRESHED	RELAXABLE	REPERTORY
RECURVING	REFRESHER	RELEASING	REPLACING
REDACTING	REFULGENT	RELEGATED	REPLAITED
REDACTION	REFUNDING	RELENTING	REPLANTED
REDBREAST	REFURBISH	RELETTING	REPLEDGED
REDDENING	REFURNISH	RELEVANCE	REPLENISH
REDEEMING	REFUSABLE	RELEVANCY	REPLETION
REDELIVER	REFUTABLE	RELIEVING	REPLY-PAID
RED-HANDED	REGAINING	RELIGIOUS	REPOINTED
REDINGOTE	REGARDANT	RELIQUARY	REPORTAGE
RED-LETTER	REGARDFUL	RELISHING	REPORTING

REPOSEFUL	RESONANCE	RETROVERT	RIVALLING
REPOSSESS	RESONATED	RETURNING	RIVERSIDE
REPOTTING	RESONATOR	REUNIFIED	ROAD-HOUSE
REPREHEND	RESORBENT	REUNITING	ROADSTEAD
REPRESENT	RESORBING	REVALUING	ROARINGLY
REPRESSED	RESORTING	REVAMPING	ROCK-BASIN
REPRIEVED	RESOUNDED	REVEALING	ROCK-BOUND
REPRIMAND	RESPECTED	REVELLING	ROCK-CRESS
REPRINTED	RESPECTER	REVENGING	ROCKETING
REPROBATE	RE-SPELLED	REVERENCE	ROCKINESS
REPRODUCE	RESPIRING	REVERSELY	ROGUISHLY
REPROVING	RESPONDED	REVERSING	ROISTERED
REPRUNING	RESTAMPED	REVERSION	ROISTERER
REPTILIAN	RESTATING	REVERTING	ROLLICKED
REPUBLISH	RESTEMMED	REVETMENT	ROMANCING
REPUDIATE	RESTFULLY	REVETTING	ROMANISED
REPUGNANT	REST-HOUSE	REVICTUAL	ROMPISHLY
REPULSING	RESTIVELY	REVIEWING	ROOMINESS
REPULSION	RESTOCKED	REVISITED	ROOTSTOCK
REPULSIVE	RESTORING	REVIVABLE	ROPEMAKER
REPUTABLE	RESTRAINT	REVOCABLE	ROQUEFORT
REPUTABLY	RESULTANT	REVOCABLY	ROSACEOUS
REPUTEDLY	RESULTING	REVOLTING	ROSE-APPLE
REQUESTED	RESURGENT	REVOLVING	ROSE-NOBLE
REQUIRING	RESURRECT	REVULSION	ROSE-WATER
REQUISITE	RETAILING	REVULSIVE	ROSINANTE
REQUITING	RETAINING	REWARDING	ROTOGRAPH
RE-READING	RETALIATE	REWORDING	ROTUNDITY
RESCINDED	RETARDING	REWRITING	ROUGH-CAST
RE-SCORING	RETENTION	REWRITTEN	ROUGHENED
RESEATING	RETENTIVE	RHAPSODIC	ROUGH-HEWN
RESECTION	RETEXTURE	RHEUMATIC	ROUGHNESS
RESELLING	RETICENCE	RHINOLOGY	ROUGH-SHOD
RESEMBLED	RETICULAR	RHUMB-LINE	ROUNDED-UP
RESENDING	RETICULUM	RHYMELESS	ROUNDELAY
RESENTFUL	RETORTING	RHYMESTER	ROUNDHEAD
RESERVING	RETORTION	RICE-PAPER	ROUNDNESS
RESERVIST	RETORTIVE	RIDERLESS	ROUNDSMAN
RESETTING	RETOSSING	RIDGE-POLE	ROUSINGLY
RESETTLED	RETOUCHED	RIDICULED	ROWDINESS
RESHIPPED	RETRACING	RIGHTEOUS	ROWELLING
RESIDENCE	RETRACTED	RIGHT-HAND	RUDDINESS
RESIDENCY	RETRACTOR	RIGHTNESS	RUFFIANLY
RESIDUARY	RETREATED	RIGMAROLE	RUINATION
RESIGNING	RETRIEVED	RING-FENCE	RUINOUSLY
RESILIENT	RETRIEVER	RINGLETED	RUMINATED
RESISTANT	RETRIMMED	RING-OUZEL	RUMMAGING
RESISTING	RETROCEDE	RING-STAND	RUMOURING
RESOLUBLE	RETRODDEN	RIOTOUSLY	RUPTURING
RESOLVENT	RETROFLEX	RITUALISM	RUSSOPHIL
RESOLVING	RETROUSSE	RITUALIST	RUSTICATE

RUSTICITY	SANDPAPER	SCHOOLBOY	SEAFARING
RUSTINESS	SANDPIPER	SCHOOLING	SEA-LAWYER
RUTHENIUM	SANDSTONE	SCHOOLMAN	SEA-LETTER
	SANGFROID	SCIENTIAL	SEA-NETTLE
S—9	SANHEDRIN	SCIENTIST	SEARCHING
SACCHARIC	SAPIDNESS	SCINTILLA	SEA-ROBBER
SACCHARIN	SAPIENTLY	SCISSORED	SEA-ROCKET
SACKCLOTH	SAPPINESS	SCLEROSIS	SEASONING
SACRAMENT	SARCASTIC	SCLEROTIC	SEA-SQUIRT
SACRARIUM	SARTORIAL	SCORBUTIC	SEA-URCHIN
SACRIFICE	SASSAFRAS	SCORCHING	SEAWORTHY
SACRILEGE	SASSENACH	SCORIFIED	SEBACEOUS
SACRISTAN	SATELLITE	SCOTCHING	SECESSION
SADDENING	SATIATING	SCOTCHMAN	SECLUDING
SADDLE-BAG	SATIATION	SCOUNDREL	SECLUSION
SADDLEBOW	SATINWOOD	SCRAGGILY	SECLUSIVE
SAFEGUARD	SATIRICAL	SCRAGGING	SECONDARY
SAFETY-PIN	SATIRISED	SCRAMBLED	SECONDING
SAFFLOWER	SATISFIED	SCRAMBLER	SECRETARY
SAFFRONED	SATURATED	SCRAPPING	SECRETING
SAGACIOUS	SATURNIAN	SCRAPBOOK	SECRETION
SAGE-BRUSH	SATURNINE	SCRAP-HEAP	SECRETIVE
SAGITTATE	SAUCEBOAT	SCRATCHED	SECRETORY
SAILCLOTH	SAUCINESS	SCRAWLING	SECTARIAL
SAILMAKER	SAUNTERER	SCREAMING	SECTARIAN
SAIL-PLANE	SAVOURING	SCREECHED	SECTIONAL
SAINT-LIKE	SAVOURILY	SCREENING	SECULARLY
SALACIOUS	SAXIFRAGE	SCREWBALL	SEDENTARY
SALE-PRICE	SAXOPHONE	SCRIBBLED	SEDITIOUS
SALICYLIC	SCALELESS	SCRIBBLER	SEDUCTION
SALIENTLY	SCALINESS	SCRIMMAGE	SEDUCTIVE
SALIFYING	SCALLOPED	SCRIMPING	SEED-GRAIN
SALIVATED	SCALLYWAG	SCRIMSHAW	SEEDINESS
SALLOWISH	SCANTLING	SCRIPTURE	SEED-PEARL
SALLYPORT	SCANTNESS	SCRIVENER	SEEMINGLY
SALTATION	SCAPEGOAT	SCROUNGED	SEE-SAWING
SALTATORY	SCAPEMENT	SCROUNGER	SEGMENTAL
SALTISHLY	SCAPULARY	SCRUBBING	SEGMENTED
SALT-MARSH	SCARECROW	SCRUM-HALF	SEGREGATE
SALTPETRE	SCARF-RING	SCRUMMAGE	SEIGNIORY
SALT-WATER	SCARIFIER	SCRUPLING	SELECTING
SALUBRITY	SCATTERED	SCRUTATOR	SELECTION
SALVARSAN	SCAVENGER	SCUFFLING	SELECTIVE
SALVATION	SCENTLESS	SCULPTURE	SELFISHLY
SAMARITAN	SCEPTICAL	SCUMBLING	SELVEDGED
SANCTUARY	SCHEDULED	SCURRYING	SEMANTICS
SANDALLED	SCHEMATIC	SCUTCHEON	SEMAPHORE
SAND-BLAST	SCHILLING	SCUTTLING	SEMBLANCE
SAND-BLIND	SCHNORKEL	SEA-ANCHOR	SEMIBREVE
SANDGLASS	SCHOLARLY	SEA-BREACH	SEMICOLON
SANDINESS	SCHOLIAST	SEA-BREEZE	SEMI-FLUID

SEMILUNAR	SHAKINESS	SHOWINESS	SINGLETON
SEMINATED	SHALLOWLY	SHOW-PLACE	SINISTRAL
SEMIVOCAL	SHAMBLING	SHREW-MOLE	SINLESSLY
SEMIVOWEL	SHAMELESS	SHRIEKING	SINUOSITY
SENESCENT	SHAMPOOED	SHRILLING	SINUOUSLY
SENESCHAL	SHAPELESS	SHRIMPING	SIPHONAGE
SENIORITY	SHARPENED	SHRIMP-NET	SIPHONING
SENSATION	SHARPNESS	SHRINKAGE	SISYPHEAN
SENSELESS	SHATTERED	SHRINKING	SITUATION
SENSITISE	SHEAR-LEGS	SHROUDING	SIXFOOTER
SENSITIVE	SHEATHING	SHRUBBERY	SIXTEENTH
SENSORIAL	SHEEPCOTE	SHRUBLESS	SKEDADDLE
SENSORIUM	SHEEPFOLD	SHRUGGING	SKETCHILY
SENSUALLY	SHEEP-HOOK	SHUDDERED	SKETCHING
SENTENCED	SHEEPSKIN	SHUFFLING	SKEW-WHIFF
SENTIMENT	SHEEPWALK	SIBILANCE	SKILFULLY
SENTRY-BOX	SHEER-HULK	SIBILANCY	SKINFLINT
SEPARABLE	SHELDRAKE	SIBYLLINE	SKYROCKET
SEPARABLY	SHELLBACK	SICCATIVE	SLABSTONE
SEPARATED	SHELL-FISH	SICKENING	SLACKENED
SEPARATOR	SHIELDING	SIDEBOARD	SLACKNESS
SEPTEMBER	SHIFTLESS	SIDE-LIGHT	SLANDERED
SEPTENARY	SHINGLING	SIDE-TABLE	SLANTWISE
SEPULCHRE	SHINTOISM	SIDETRACK	SLAPSTICK
SEQUACITY	SHIPMONEY	SIGHINGLY	SLATINESS
SEQUESTER	SHIPOWNER	SIGHTLESS	SLAUGHTER
SERENADED	SHIPSHAPE	SIGHTSEER	SLAVE-LIKE
SERMONISE	SHIPWRECK	SIGNAL-BOX	SLAVERING
SERRATION	SHIRTLESS	SIGNAL-GUN	SLAVISHLY
SERVIETTE	SHIVERING	SIGNALIZE	SLAVONIAN
SERVILELY	SHOEBLACK	SIGNALLED	SLEEPLESS
SERVILITY	SHOEBRUSH	SIGNALMAN	SLEIGHING
SERVITUDE	SHOEMAKER	SIGNATORY	SLENDERLY
SESSIONAL	SHOPWOMAN	SIGNATURE	SLIDE-RULE
SETACEOUS	SHORELESS	SIGN-BOARD	SLIGHTING
SET-SQUARE	SHOREWARD	SIGNIFIED	SLIMINESS
SEVEN-FOLD	SHORTCAKE	SIGNORINA	SLIP-COACH
SEVENTEEN	SHORTENED	SILENCING	SLIPPERED
SEVENTHLY	SHORTFALL	SILICATED	SLITHERED
SEVERABLE	SHORTHAND	SILICEOUS	SLIVERING
SEVERALLY	SHORT-HOSE	SILKINESS	SLOBBERED
SEVERALTY	SHORTNESS	SILLINESS	SLOP-BASIN
SEVERANCE	SHORT-SLIP	SILVER-FOX	SLOPINGLY
SEXENNIAL	SHOTPROOF	SILVERING	SLOUCH-HAT
SEXUALITY	SHOULDERS	SIMILARLY	SLOUCHING
SFORZANDO	SHOVELLED	SIMMERING	SLOUGHING
SHACKLING	SHOVELFUL	SIMPLETON	SLOWCOACH
SHADINESS	SHOVEL-HAT	SIMULATED	SLOW-MATCH
SHADOWING	SHOVELLER	SINCERELY	SLUMBERED
SHAFTLESS	SHOWBREAD	SINCERITY	SMALL-ARMS
SHAKEDOWN	SHOWERING	SINGINGLY	SMALL-BEER

SMALLNESS	SOLARISED	SPEARMINT	SPRINGING
SMARTENED	SOLDERING	SPECIALLY	SPRINGBOK
SMARTNESS	SOLDIERLY	SPECIALTY	SPRING-GUN
SMILELESS	SOLEMNISE	SPECIFIED	SPRINKLED
SMILINGLY	SOLEMNITY	SPECKLESS	SPRINKLER
SMIRCHING	SOLICITED	SPECKLING	SPRINTING
SMOCKLESS	SOLICITOR	SPECTACLE	SPROUTING
SMOKE-BOMB	SOLIDNESS	SPECTATOR	SPUR-ROYAL
SMOKELESS	SOLILOQUY	SPECULATE	SPUR-WHEEL
SMOKINESS	SOLITAIRE	SPEECH-DAY	SPUTTERED
SMOOTHING	SOMETHING	SPEECHFUL	SQUABBLED
SMOTHERED	SOMETIMES	SPEECHIFY	SQUALIDLY
SMUG-FACED	SOMEWHERE	SPELLABLE	SQUALLING
SMUGGLING	SOMNOLENT	SPERMATIC	SQUASHING
SMUTCHING	SONNETEER	SPHERICAL	SQUATTING
SNAFFLING	SOOTINESS	SPHINCTER	SQUAWKING
SNAIL-LIKE	SOPHISTRY	SPICINESS	SQUEAKING
SNAKE-BIRD	SOPHOMORE	SPIKENARD	SQUEALING
SNAKE-ROOT	SOPORIFIC	SPILLIKIN	SQUEAMISH
SNAKEWEED	SORCERESS	SPINDLING	SQUEEZING
SNAKE-WOOD	SORRINESS	SPINDRIFT	SQUELCHED
SNATCHING	SORROWFUL	SPINELESS	SQUIGGLED
SNICKERED	SORROWING	SPINNAKER	SQUINTING
SNIFFLING	SORTILEGE	SPINNERET	SQUIRMING
SNIGGERED	SOSTENUTO	SPIRALITY	SQUIRTING
SNIVELLED	SOTTISHLY	SPIRITING	STABILISE
SNOWBERRY	SOTTO-VOCE	SPIRITUAL	STABILITY
SNOWBLIND	SOUBRETTE	SPLASHING	STABLEBOY
SNOW-BOUND	SOULFULLY	SPLAY-FOOT	STABLEMAN
SNOWDRIFT	SOUNDLESS	SPLENDOUR	STACKYARD
SNOWFIELD	SOUNDNESS	SPLENETIC	STAGE-PLAY
SNOWFLAKE	SOUP-PLATE	SPLINTERY	STAGGERED
SNOW-GOOSE	SOUTHDOWN	SPLINTING	STAGHOUND
SNOWSTORM	SOUTH-EAST	SPLIT-RING	STAGINESS
SNUB-NOSED	SOUTHERLY	SPOKESMAN	STAGNANCY
SNUFFLING	SOUTHWARD	SPOLIATED	STAGNATED
SNUGGLING	SOUTH-WEST	SPONSORED	STAIDNESS
SOAPINESS	SOU'-WESTER	SPOON-BAIT	STAINLESS
SOAPSTONE	SOVEREIGN	SPOONBILL	STAIRCASE
SOARINGLY	SPADE-WORK	SPOON-FEED	STAIR-HEAD
SOBERNESS	SPAGHETTI	SPORE-CASE	STAKE-BOAT
SOBRIQUET	SPANGLING	SPORTLESS	STALACTIC
SOCIALISE	SPARENESS	SPORTSMAN	STALEMATE
SOCIALISM	SPARINGLY	SPOUT-HOLE	STALENESS
SOCIALIST	SPARKLING	SPOUTLESS	STALKLESS
SOCIALITE	SPASMODIC	SPRAGGING	STAMMERED
SOCIALITY	SPATTERED	SPRAINING	STAMMERER
SOCIOLOGY	SPATULATE	SPRAWLING	STAMP-DUTY
SODA-WATER	SPEAKABLE	SPREADING	STAMPEDED
SOFTENING	SPEAK-EASY	SPRIGGING	STANCHING
SOJOURNED	SPEARHEAD	SPRIGHTLY	STANCHION

STARBOARD	STIPULATE	STRATAGEM	SUBMERGED
STARCHING	STIRABOUT	STRATEGIC	SUBMITTED
STARGAZER	STITCHERY	STREAKING	SUBNORMAL
STARINGLY	STITCHING	STREAMING	SUB-ORDER
STARLIGHT	STOCKADED	STREAMLET	SUBORNING
STAR-SHELL	STOCK-DOVE	STRENUOUS	SUBSCRIBE
STARTLING	STOCK-FISH	STRESSING	SUBSCRIPT
STATELESS	STOCKINET	STRETCHED	SUBSERVED
STATEMENT	STOCKLESS	STRETCHER	SUBSIDING
STATE-ROOM	STOCKWHIP	STRIATION	SUBSIDISE
STATESMAN	STOCKYARD	STRICTURE	SUBSISTED
STATIONED	STOICALLY	STRINGENT	SUBSTANCE
STATIONER	STOKEHOLD	STRINGING	SUBTENANT
STATISTIC	STOKEHOLE	STRIPLING	SUBTENDED
STATUETTE	STOLIDITY	STRIPPING	SUBVERTED
STATUTORY	STOMACHAL	STROLLING	SUCCEEDED
STAUNCHED	STOMACHER	STROMATIC	SUCCENTOR
STAYMAKER	STOMACHIC	STRONG-BOX	SUCCESSOR
STEADFAST	STONECHAT	STRONTIUM	SUCCOTASH
STEADYING	STONE-COLD	STROPPING	SUCCOURED
STEAMBOAT	STONECROP	STRUCTIVE	SUCCULENT
STEAMPIPE	STONE-DEAD	STRUGGLED	SUCCUMBED
STEAMSHIP	STONE-DEAF	STRUMMING	SUCKERING
STEEL-CLAD	STONELESS	STRUTTING	SUDORIFIC
STEELYARD	STONE-PINE	STRYCHNIC	SUFFERING
STEEPENED	STONEWALL	STUCCOING	SUFFICING
STEEPNESS	STONINESS	STUD-GROOM	SUFFIXING
STEERABLE	STOOL-BALL	STUD-HORSE	SUFFOCATE
STEERSMAN	STOPPERED	STUDIEDLY	SUFFRAGAN
STELLATED	STOP-PRESS	STUMBLING	SUFFUSING
STERILISE	STOP-WATCH	STUPEFIED	SUFFUSION
STERILITY	STOREROOM	STUPIDITY	SUGAR-BEET
STERNMOST	STORESHIP	STUTTERER	SUGAR-CANE
STERNNESS	STORMCOCK	STYLISHLY	SUGARLESS
STERNPOST	STORM-CONE	STYLOBATE	SUGAR-LOAF
STEVEDORE	STORMSAIL	SUB-AGENCY	SUGAR-MILL
STEWARDLY	STORTHING	SUBALTERN	SUGAR-MITE
STEWARTRY	STORYBOOK	SUBCOSTAL	SUGAR-PINE
STIFFENED	STOUTNESS	SUBDEACON	SUGARPLUM
STIFFENER	STOVEPIPE	SUBDIVIDE	SUGGESTED
STIFFNESS	STRADDLED	SUB-EDITOR	SULKINESS
STIGMATIC	STRAGGLED	SUBFAMILY	SULPHURIC
STILL-BORN	STRAGGLER	SUBJACENT	SUMMARILY
STILL-LIFE	STRAINING	SUBJECTED	SUMMARISE
STILLNESS	STRANDING	SUBJOINED	SUMMATION
STILL-ROOM	STRANGELY	SUBJUGATE	SUMMING-UP
STIMULANT	STRANGLED	SUBLIMATE	SUMMONING
STIMULATE	STRANGLER	SUBLIMELY	SUMPTUARY
STINGLESS	STRAPPADO	SUBLIMITY	SUMPTUOUS
STINKBOMB	STRAPPING	SUBLUNARY	SUNBONNET
STIPPLING	STRAPWORK	SUBMARINE	SUNFLOWER

SUNSTROKE	SWINISHLY	TAILORESS	TENANTING
SUPERFINE	SWITCHING	TAILORING	TENDERING
SUPERHEAT	SWITCHMAN	TAILPIECE	TENSENESS
SUPERPOSE	SWIVEL-EYE	TALBOTYPE	TENTATIVE
SUPERSEDE	SWIVELLED	TALKATIVE	TEPEFYING
SUPERVENE	SWORDBELT	TALLOWING	TEPIDNESS
SUPERVISE	SWORDBILL	TALLY-CARD	TEREBINTH
SUPPLIANT	SWORD-CANE	TALLYSHOP	TERMAGANT
SUPPLYING	SWORDFISH	TALMUDIST	TERMINATE
SUPPORTED	SWORDHILT	TAMPERING	TERRACING
SUPPORTER	SWORD-LILY	TANGERINE	TERRIFIED
SUPPOSING	SWORDSMAN	TANTALIZE	TERRITORY
SUPPURATE	SYBARITIC	TARANTULA	TERRORISE
SUPREMACY	SYCOPHANT	TARAXACUM	TERRORISM
SUPREMELY	SYLLABARY	TARDINESS	TERRORIST
SURCHARGE	SYLLABIFY	TARNISHED	TERSENESS
SURCINGLE	SYLLABLED	TARPAULIN	TESTAMENT
SURFACING	SYLLEPSIS	TARTAREAN	TESTATRIX
SURLINESS	SYLLOGISE	TASSELLED	TESTIFIED
SURMISING	SYLLOGISM	TASTELESS	TESTIMONY
SURNAMING	SYLPH-LIKE	TATTERING	TESTINESS
SURPASSED	SYMBIOSIS	TATTOOING	TETHERING
SURPRISED	SYMBIOTIC	TAUTENING	TETRALOGY
SURRENDER	SYMBOLISE	TAUTOLOGY	TETRARCHY
SURROGATE	SYMBOLISM	TAWNINESS	TEXTUALLY
SURVEYING	SYMBOLIST	TAXIDERMY	THANKLESS
SURVIVING	SYMMETRIC	TAXIMETER	THATCHING
SUSPECTED	SYMPHONIC	TEACHABLE	THEOCRACY
SUSPENDED	SYMPHYSIS	TEASELLED	THEOCRASY
SUSPENDER	SYMPOSIUM	TECHNICAL	THEOMACHY
SUSPICION	SYNAGOGUE	TECHNIQUE	THEOMANCY
SUSTAINED	SYNCOPATE	TEDIOUSLY	THEORISED
SWADDLING	SYNDICATE	TELEGRAPH	THEOSOPHY
SWAGGERED	SYNODICAL	TELEMETER	THEREFORE
SWALLOWED	SYNONYMIC	TELEOLOGY	THEREFROM
SWAN'S-DOWN	SYNOPTIST	TELEPATHY	THEREINTO
SWARTHILY	SYNOVITIS	TELEPHONE	THEREUNTO
SWEET-CORN	SYNTHESIS	TELEPHONY	THEREUPON
SWEETENED	SYNTHETIC	TELEPHOTO	THEREWITH
SWEETMEAT	SYRINGING	TELEPRINT	THERMIDOR
SWEETNESS	SYSTEMISE	TELESCOPE	THESAURUS
SWEET-SHOP		TELLINGLY	THICKENED
SWELTERED	**T—9**	TELLURIUM	THICKNESS
SWIFTNESS	TABLATURE	TELLUROUS	THICK-KNEE
SWIMMERET	TABLELAND	TEMPERATE	THICK-SKIN
SWINDLING	TABLE-TALK	TEMPERING	THIGH-BONE
SWINEHERD	TABULARLY	TEMPORARY	THINKABLE
SWING-BOAT	TABULATED	TEMPORISE	THIRSTILY
SWING-DOOR	TACTICIAN	TEMPTRESS	THIRSTING
SWINGEING	TACTILITY	TENACIOUS	THIRTIETH
SWINGLING	TAILBOARD	TENACULUM	THORNBACK

THORNBUSH	TOAD-STONE	TRAITRESS	TRI-WEEKLY
THORNLESS	TOAD-STOOL	TRAMPLING	TROOPSHIP
THRASHING	TOAST-RACK	TRANSCEND	TROUBLING
THREADING	TOLERABLE	TRANSFORM	TROUBLOUS
THREEFOLD	TOLERABLY	TRANSFUSE	TROUNCING
THRESHING	TOLERANCE	TRANSIENT	TROUSERED
THRESHOLD	TOLERATED	TRANSLATE	TROUSSEAU
THRIFTILY	TOLL-BOOTH	TRANSMUTE	TROWELLED
THRILLING	TOMBSTONE	TRANSPIRE	TRUCKLING
THROBBING	TONSORIAL	TRANSPORT	TRUCULENT
THRONGING	TOOTHACHE	TRANSPOSE	TRUMPETED
THROTTLED	TOOTH-LESS	TRAPEZIUM	TRUMPETER
THROWSTER	TOOTH-PICK	TRAPEZOID	TRUNCATED
THRUMMING	TOOTHSOME	TRAUMATIC	TRUNDLING
THRUSTING	TOPICALLY	TRAVELLED	TRUNK-HOSE
THUMB-MARK	TORMENTED	TRAVELLER	TUGGINGLY
THUMB-NAIL	TORMENTIL	TRAVERSED	TUMESCENT
THUMB-RACK	TORMENTOR	TREACHERY	TUNEFULLY
THUNDERED	TORPEDOED	TREADMILL	TUNNELLED
THUNDERER	TORPIDITY	TREASURED	TURBINATE
THWACKING	TORPIFIED	TREASURER	TURBULENT
THWARTING	TORREFIED	TREATMENT	TURFINESS
TICKETING	TORSIONAL	TREE-PIPIT	TURF-SPADE
TIDEGAUGE	TORTURING	TRELLISED	TURGIDITY
TIDE-TABLE	TORTUROUS	TREMBLING	TURNIP-FLY
TIDE-WATER	TOTTERING	TREMULOUS	TURNSTONE
TIGER-LILY	TOUCHABLE	TRENCHANT	TURNTABLE
TIGER-MOTH	TOUCH-HOLE	TRENCHING	TURPITUDE
TIGER-WOOD	TOUCH-WOOD	TREPANNED	TURQUOISE
TIGHTENED	TOUGHENED	TRIATOMIC	TUTORSHIP
TIGHTNESS	TOUGHNESS	TRIBALISM	TWADDLING
TIGHT-ROPE	TOWELLING	TRIBESMAN	TWENTIETH
TIMBERMAN	TOWN-CLERK	TRIBUNATE	TWIDDLING
TIMEPIECE	TOWN-CRIER	TRIBUTARY	TWINKLING
TIME-TABLE	TOWN-HOUSE	TRICKLING	TWISTABLE
TIMIDNESS	TOWN-MAJOR	TRICKSTER	TWITCHING
TIMOCRACY	TOWNSFOLK	TRICOLOUR	TWITTERED
TINCTURED	TRACEABLE	TRICUSPID	TWO-HANDED
TINDERBOX	TRACKLESS	TRIENNIAL	TWO-MASTED
TINKERING	TRACTABLE	TRIHEDRAL	TYPEMETAL
TINSELLED	TRACTABLY	TRIHEDRON	TYPICALLY
TIPSINESS	TRADEMARK	TRILINEAR	TYPIFYING
TIPSY-CAKE	TRADESMAN	TRILITHON	TYRANNISE
TIREDNESS	TRADE-WIND	TRILOBATE	TYRANNOUS
TITILLATE	TRADITION	TRILOBITE	
TITIVATED	TRADUCING	TRINOMIAL	**U—9**
TITRATION	TRAGEDIAN	TRISECTED	UGLIFYING
TITTERING	TRAINABLE	TRITENESS	ULCERATED
TITTLE-BAT	TRAINBAND	TRIUMPHAL	ULTIMATUM
TITULARLY	TRAIN-MILE	TRIUMPHED	ULULATING
TOADEATER	TRAIPSING	TRIVIALLY	ULULATION

UMBELLATE
UMBILICAL
UMBILICUS
UNABASHED
UNACCUSED
UNACTABLE
UNADAPTED
UNADOPTED
UNADORNED
UNADVISED
UNALLOYED
UNALTERED
UNAMENDED
UNAMIABLE
UNAMUSING
UNANIMITY
UNANIMOUS
UNASHAMED
UNASSURED
UNBARRING
UNBEKNOWN
UNBENDING
UNBINDING
UNBLOCKED
UNBLUNTED
UNBOLTING
UNBOSOMED
UNBOUNDED
UNBRACING
UNBRIDLED
UNBRUISED
UNBUCKLED
UNBUCKLES
UNCANNILY
UNCAPPING
UNCEASING
UNCERTAIN
UNCHANGED
UNCHARGED
UNCHARTED
UNCHECKED
UNCLAIMED
UNCLEARED
UNCLIPPED
UNCLOGGED
UNCLOSING
UNCLOTHED
UNCLOUDED
UNCOILING
UNCONCERN
UNCORKING

UNCOUNTED
UNCOUTHLY
UNCOVERED
UNCROPPED
UNCROSSED
UNCROWDED
UNCROWNED
UNCURLING
UNDAMAGED
UNDAUNTED
UNDECEIVE
UNDECIDED
UNDEFILED
UNDEFINED
UNDERDONE
UNDERFEED
UNDERFOOT
UNDERGONE
UNDERHAND
UNDERHUNG
UNDERLAID
UNDERLAIN
UNDERLINE
UNDERLING
UNDERMINE
UNDERMOST
UNDERPAID
UNDERPART
UNDERPLOT
UNDERRATE
UNDERSELL
UNDERSHOT
UNDERSIGN
UNDERSOLD
UNDERTAKE
UNDERTONE
UNDERTOOK
UNDERVEST
UNDERWEAR
UNDERWENT
UNDERWOOD
UNDERWORK
UNDESIRED
UNDILUTED
UNDIVIDED
UNDOUBTED
UNDRAINED
UNDREAMED
UNDRESSED
UNDULATED
UNDUTIFUL

UNEARTHED
UNEARTHLY
UNEATABLE
UNELECTED
UNENGAGED
UN-ENGLISH
UNENVIOUS
UNEQUABLE
UNEQUALLY
UNEXCITED
UNEXERTED
UNEXPIRED
UNEXPOSED
UNFAILING
UNFEELING
UNFEIGNED
UNFITNESS
UNFITTING
UNFLEDGED
UNFOLDING
UNFOUNDED
UNFROCKED
UNFURLING
UNGALLANT
UNGIRDING
UNGRANTED
UNGRUDGED
UNGUARDED
UNGUMMING
UNHANDILY
UNHANDLED
UNHAPPILY
UNHARMFUL
UNHATCHED
UNHEALTHY
UNHEEDFUL
UNHEEDING
UNHELPFUL
UNHINGING
UNHITCHED
UNHOOKING
UNHOPEFUL
UNHORSING
UNHURTFUL
UNIFORMLY
UNIMPEDED
UNIMPLIED
UNINDUCED
UNINJURED
UNINSURED
UNINVITED

UNINVOKED
UNIPAROUS
UNISEXUAL
UNITARIAN
UNIVALENT
UNIVERSAL
UNJOINTED
UNKNOTTED
UNKNOWING
UNLASHING
UNLATCHED
UNLEARNED
UNLEASHED
UNLIGHTED
UNLIMITED
UNLOADING
UNLOCATED
UNLOCKING
UNLOOSING
UNLOVABLE
UNLUCKILY
UNMANNING
UNMANURED
UNMARRIED
UNMASKING
UNMATCHED
UNMERITED
UNMINDFUL
UNMOORING
UNMOULDED
UNMOUNTED
UNMOURNED
UNMUFFLED
UNMUSICAL
UNMUZZLED
UNNAMABLE
UNNATURAL
UNNERVING
UNNOTICED
UNOBVIOUS
UNOFFERED
UNOPPOSED
UNORDERED
UNORDERLY
UNPACKING
UNPAINFUL
UNPAINTED
UNPEGGING
UNPENNING
UNPERUSED
UNPICKING

UNPIERCED	UNSHAPELY	UNWITTILY	VASSALAGE
UNPINNING	UNSHEATHE	UNWOMANLY	VEERINGLY
UNPITYING	UNSHIPPED	UNWORLDLY	VEGETABLE
UNPLAITED	UNSHRIVEN	UNWORRIED	VEHEMENCE
UNPLANTED	UNSIGHTLY	UNWOUNDED	VEHICULAR
UNPLEADED	UNSINKING	UNWRAPPED	VELVETEEN
UNPLEASED	UNSKILFUL	UNWREATHE	VENEERING
UNPLEDGED	UNSKILLED	UNWRECKED	VENERABLE
UNPLUGGED	UNSOUNDLY	UNWRITTEN	VENERABLY
UNPLUMBED	UNSPARING	UNWROUGHT	VENERATED
UNPOINTED	UNSPOILED	UPANISHAD	VENGEANCE
UNPOPULAR	UNSPOTTED	UPBRAIDED	VENIALITY
UNPOTABLE	UNSTAINED	UPHEAVING	VENTILATE
UNPRAISED	UNSTAMPED	UPHOLDING	VENTRALLY
UNPRESSED	UNSTINTED	UPHOLSTER	VENTRICLE
UNPRINTED	UNSTOPPED	UPLIFTING	VENTURING
UNQUIETLY	UNSTRIPED	UPPER-HAND	VERACIOUS
UNREALITY	UNSTUDIED	UPPERMOST	VERBALISE
UNREBUKED	UNSULLIED	UPRIGHTLY	VERBASCUM
UNREFINED	UNTACKING	UPROOTING	VERBOSELY
UNREFUTED	UNTAINTED	UPSETTING	VERBOSITY
UNRELATED	UNTAMABLE	UPTURNING	VERDANTLY
UNRENEWED	UNTANGLED	USELESSLY	VERDIGRIS
UNRESCUED	UNTEMPTED	USHERETTE	VERDUROUS
UNRESTFUL	UNTENABLE	USUALNESS	VERIDICAL
UNRESTING	UNTHANKED	UTILISING	VERIFYING
UNREVISED	UNTIRABLE	UTTERANCE	VERITABLE
UNREVIVED	UNTOUCHED	UTTERMOST	VERITABLY
UNREVOKED	UNTRAINED		VERMICIDE
UNRIDDLED	UNTRIMMED	V—9	VERMICULE
UNRIGGING	UNTRODDEN	VACCINATE	VERMIFORM
UNRIPENED	UNTUCKING	VACILLATE	VERMIFUGE
UNRIPPING	UNTUTORED	VADE-MECUM	VERMILION
UNROLLING	UNTWINING	VAGUENESS	VERMINOUS
UNROASTED	UNTWISTED	VAINGLORY	VERRUCOSE
UNROUNDED	UNUSUALLY	VALANCING	VERSATILE
UNRUFFLED	UNVACATED	VALENTINE	VERSIFIER
UNRUMPLED	UNVARYING	VALIANTLY	VERSIFORM
UNSADDLED	UNVEILING	VALIDATED	VERTEBRAL
UNSALABLE	UNVISITED	VALUATION	VESICULAR
UNSAVOURY	UNWAKENED	VALUELESS	VESTIBULE
UNSCANNED	UNWARLIKE	VAMOOSING	VESTIGIAL
UNSCATHED	UNWATCHED	VAMPIRISM	VESTRYMAN
UNSCOURED	UNWATERED	VANDALISM	VEXATIOUS
UNSCREWED	UNWEARIED	VANISHING	VIABILITY
UNSEALING	UNWEAVING	VAPORISED	VIBRATING
UNSEATING	UNWEIGHED	VAPOURING	VIBRATION
UNSELFISH	UNWELCOME	VARIATION	VICARIATE
UNSETTLED	UNWILLING	VARIEGATE	VICARIOUS
UNSEVERED	UNWINDING	VARIOUSLY	VICENNIAL
UNSHACKLE	UNWINKING	VARNISHED	VICEREGAL

VICIOUSLY	VULGARISM	WATER-FLAG	WHALEBOAT
VICTIMISE	VULGARITY	WATERFLEA	WHALEBONE
VICTORIAN	VULNERARY	WATERFOWL	WHATSOE'ER
VICTORINE	VULTURINE	WATER-GALL	WHEEDLING
VIEW-POINT	VULTURISH	WATER-HOLE	WHEEL-BASE
VIGILANCE	VULTURISM	WATERLESS	WHEREFORE
VINACEOUS	VULTUROUS	WATERLINE	WHEREINTO
VINDICATE		WATERMARK	WHEREUNTO
VINOMETER	W—9	WATERMILL	WHEREUPON
VIOLATING	WAGGISHLY	WATER-POLO	WHEREWITH
VIOLATION	WAGNERIAN	WATER-RAIL	WHETSTONE
VIOLENTLY	WAGONETTE	WATER-RATE	WHICHEVER
VIOLINIST	WAILINGLY	WATERSHED	WHIFFLING
VIRGILIAN	WAISTBAND	WATERSIDE	WHIMPERED
VIRGINIAN	WAISTBELT	WATER-TANK	WHIMSICAL
VIRGINITY	WAISTCOAT	WATER-VOLE	WHININGLY
VIRTUALLY	WAIST-DEEP	WATERWEED	WHINNYING
VIRULENCE	WAITINGLY	WATERWORN	WHINSTONE
VISCIDITY	WAKEFULLY	WATTMETER	WHIPGRAFT
VISCOSITY	WAKE-ROBIN	WAVEMETER	WHIPPER-IN
VISCOUNTY	WALL-FRUIT	WAXWORKER	WHIPSNAKE
VISIONARY	WALLOPING	WAYFARING	WHIPSTOCK
VISITABLE	WALLOWING	WAYWARDLY	WHIRLIGIG
VISUALIZE	WALLPAPER	WAYZGOOSE	WHIRLPOOL
VITALISED	WALL-PLATE	WEAKENING	WHIRLWIND
VITIATING	WALL-SIDED	WEAK-KNEED	WHISKERED
VITIATION	WALPURGIS	WEALTHILY	WHISPERED
VITRIFIED	WANDERING	WEARILESS	WHISPERER
VITRIOLIC	WAREHOUSE	WEARINESS	WHISTLING
VIVACIOUS	WARNINGLY	WEARISOME	WHITEBAIT
VIVIDNESS	WARRANTED	WEATHERED	WHITEBEAM
VIVIFYING	WARRANTEE	WEATHERLY	WHITEFISH
VIZIERATE	WARRANTOR	WEB-FOOTED	WHITEHEAD
VOCALISED	WASHBOARD	WEDGEWISE	WHITE-HEAT
VOICELESS	WASHERMAN	WEDNESDAY	WHITE-IRON
VOL-AU-VENT	WASH-HOUSE	WEED-GROWN	WHITENESS
VOLLEYING	WASHINESS	WEEPINGLY	WHITENING
VOLPLANED	WASHSTAND	WEEVILLED	WHITETAIL
VOLTE-FACE	WASPISHLY	WEIGHABLE	WHITEWASH
VOLTMETER	WASSAILED	WEIGHTILY	WHITEWING
VOLUNTARY	WASTELESS	WEIGHTING	WHITEWOOD
VOLUNTEER	WASTE-PIPE	WEIRDNESS	WHITTLING
VOODOOISM	WATCHCASE	WELCOMING	WHIZZBANG
VORACIOUS	WATCHFIRE	WELCOMELY	WHOLENESS
VOUCHSAFE	WATCHWORD	WELLBEING	WHOLESALE
VULCANISE	WATERBIRD	WELL-HOUSE	WHOLESOME
VULCANISM	WATERBUCK	WELL-TIMED	WHOSOEVER
VULCANIST	WATERBUTT	WELL-WATER	WIDEAWAKE
VULCANITE	WATERCART	WESTERING	WIDOWHOOD
VULGARIAN	WATERFALL	WESTERNER	WIELDABLE
VULGARISE	WATER-FERN	WESTWARDS	WILLINGLY

WILLOWISH	WITTINESS	WORKHOUSE	**X—9**
WILSONITE	WITTINGLY	WORKMANLY	XANTHIPPE
WINDHOVER	WOEBEGONE	WORK-TABLE	XYLOPHONE
WINDINESS	WOLFISHLY	WORKWOMAN	
WINDINGLY	WOLF-HOUND	WORLDLING	**Y—9**
WINDOW-BOX	WOLF'S-BANE	WORLDWIDE	YACHTSMAN
WINEGLASS	WOLF'S-CLAW	WORMEATEN	YANKEEISM
WINE-PRESS	WOLVERINE	WORM-WHEEL	YARDSTICK
WINE-STONE	WOMANHOOD	WORRIMENT	YAWNINGLY
WINKINGLY	WOMANKIND	WORSENING	YELLOWING
WINNINGLY	WOMAN-LIKE	WORTHLESS	YELLOWISH
WINNOWING	WOMENFOLK	WOUNDLESS	YESTERDAY
WINSOMELY	WOMENKIND	WOUND-WORT	YGGDRASIL
WINTERING	WONDERING	WRANGLING	YORKSHIRE
WIREDRAWN	WONDERFUL	WREATHING	YOUNGLING
WIRE-GAUZE	WOOD-ASHES	WRENCHING	YOUNGSTER
WISTFULLY	WOODBLOCK	WRESTLING	
WITCH-HUNT	WOODCHUCK	WRIGGLING	**Z—9**
WITHDRAWN	WOODCRAFT	WRINKLING	ZEALOUSLY
WITHERING	WOOD-HOUSE	WRISTBAND	ZIGZAGGED
WITHSTAND	WOODINESS	WRONGDOER	ZIRCONIUM
WITHSTOOD	WOODLAYER	WRY-NECKED	ZOOGRAPHY
WITLESSLY	WOODLOUSE	WYCH-HAZEL	ZOOLOGIST
WITNESSED	WOOD-NYMPH		ZOOPHYTIC
WITTICISM	WORDINESS		

Puzzle Books

MATHEMATICAL GAMES
C. Lukács and E. Tarján   25p

Here is a book that proves mathematics *can* be fun!

'This is a book for the whole family, with games which can provide endless hours of amusement for any number of players' – HULL DAILY MAIL

'Nothing seems to have been left out . . . those who like to spend their surplus intellectual energy on mathematical games and problems will not find a page wasted' – THE ACCOUNTANT

MAZES
Vladimir Koziakin,   40p

How bright are you? Flex your mental muscles with the most challenging game of the year. Ideal for parties, commuters, night owls, lighthouse keepers and solitary puzzlers.